THE ANNALS
OF
AMERICA

THE ANNALS OF AMERICA

Volume 22

1987 - 2001

A New World Order

ENCYCLOPÆDIA BRITANNICA, INC.

Chicago London New Delhi Paris Sydney Taipei Tokyo Seoul

The editors wish to express their gratitude for permission to reprint
material from the following sources:

Ref 973 An v.22
The Annals of America.

7583546

AFL-CIO for Selection 10. Reprinted by permission.

American Enterprise Institute for Public Policy Research for Selection 95. Reprinted by permission of
The American Enterprise, June 2000.

Roy Beck for Selection 50. Reprinted by permission.

William J. Bennett for Selection 57. Reprinted by permission.

Myles Brand for Selection 105. Reprinted by permission.

Business Week for Selection 67B. Reprinted from April
1, 1996, issue of *Business Week* by special permission,
Copyright © 1996 by The McGraw-Hill Companies,
Inc.

The Chicago Tribune for Selection 102. Reprinted by
permission.

City News Publishing Co., for Selection 5. Reprinted by
permission of *Vital Speeches of the Day,* Nov. 1, 1987, p.
57. Also for Selection 6. Reprinted by permission of
Vital Speeches of the Day, Jan. 1, 1988, p.173. Also for Selection 10. Reprinted by permission of *Vital Speeches of
the Day,* April 1, 1988, p. 373. Also for Selection 11B.
Reprinted by permission of *Vital Speeches of the Day,*
Aug. 1, 1988, p.616. Also for Selection 12. Reprinted by
permission of *Vital Speeches of the Day,* June 1, 1988, p.
510. Also for Selection 14. Reprinted by permission of
Vital Speeches of the Day, Aug. 15, 1988, p. 647. Also for
Selection 28. Reprinted by permission of *Vital Speeches
of the Day,* April 1, 1991, p. 357. Also for Selection 33.

Reprinted by permission of *Vital Speeches of the Day,* May
15, 1991, p. 460. Also for Selection 35. Reprinted by
permission of *Vital Speeches of the Day,* Aug. 15, 1992, p.
652. Also for Selection 36. Reprinted by permission of
Vital Speeches of the Day, Sep. 15, 1992, p. 712. Also for
Selection 42. Reprinted by permission of *Vital Speeches
of the Day,* Sept. 15, 1993, p. 709. Also for Selection 44.
Reprinted by permission of *Vital Speeches of the Day,* July
15, 1993, p. 580. Also for Selection 56. Reprinted by
permission of *Vital Speeches of the Day,* April 1, 1995, p.
354. Also for Selection 74. Reprinted by permission of
Vital Speeches of the Day, Nov. 15, 1997, p. 78. Also for Selection 77. Reprinted by permission of *Vital Speeches of
the Day,* May 1, 1998, p. 418. Also for Selection 80.
Reprinted by permission of *Vital Speeches of the Day,* Oct.
1, 1998, p. 738. Also for Selection 85. Reprinted by permission of *Vital Speeches of the Day,* Oct. 15, 1999, p. 24.
Also for Selection 87. Reprinted by permission of *Vital
Speeches of the Day,* Jan. 1, 2000, p. 170. Also for Selection 90. Reprinted by permission of *Vital Speeches of the
Day,* Jan. 1, 1999, p. 189. Also for Selection 92.
Reprinted by permission of *Vital Speeches of the Day,*
April 15, 2000, p. 412. Also for Selection 103.
Reprinted by permission of *Vital Speeches of the Day,* Jan.
1, 2001, p. 162. Also for Selection 105. Reprinted by
permission of *Vital Speeches of the Day,* April 1, 2001, p.
367.

Commonweal Foundation for Selection 70. © 1997
Commonweal Foundation, reprinted with permission.

Congressional Quarterly Weekly Report for Selection

Contents

Introduction, xvii–xix

Chronology, 1987–2001, xx–xlvii

SELECTIONS

1987

1. *Tower Commission Report on Iran-Contra*, 1

2. RONALD REAGAN: *Remarks at the Brandenburg Gate in West Berlin*, 6

3. WILLIAM J. BRENNAN, JR.: Edwards *v.* Aguillard, 9

4. DAVID BRAND: *Tough Times for Televangelism*, 12

5. ELIZABETH M. WHELAN: *Real Public Health Issues*, 15

6. FELICE N. SCHWARTZ: *Women in Corporate America*, 21

7. WILLIAM F. BUCKLEY, JR.: *Politics and Supreme Court Nominees*, 25

8. OLIVER STONE: *"Greed Is Good,"* Wall Street, 27

9. ALLAN BLOOM: The Closing of the American Mind, 28

1988

10. JOHN J. SWEENEY: *Organized Labor and the Economic Future*, 38

11. SHELBY STEELE and JOHN E. JACOB: *The State of Black America*
    A. STEELE: *Class Division Among African Americans*, 42
    B. JACOB: *A Doomed Generation?*, 49

12. JAMES R. KINCAID: *Mythmaking Among Education Critics*, 55

13. PAUL MONETTE: *Living with AIDS,* 59

14. ANN RICHARDS: *Democrats for Michael Dukakis,* 60

15. PAT ROBERTSON: *Republicans for George Bush,* 64

1989

16. RONALD REAGAN: *Farewell Address to the Nation,* 69

17. GEORGE BUSH: *Inaugural Address,* 72

18. WILLIAM REHNQUIST: Webster *v.* Reproductive Health Services, 77

19. AMY TAN: The Joy Luck Club, 83

20. MICHAEL KINSLEY: *The Collapse of Communism,* 84

21. GEORGE BUSH: *Operation Just Cause,* 87

1990

22. MITCHELL KAPOR and JOHN PERRY BARLOW: *The Information Age and Open Societies,* 89

23. *The* Exxon Valdez *Oil Spill in Alaska,* 92

24. BARBARA BUSH: *Wellesley College Commencement Speech,* 99

25. *The Americans with Disabilities Act,* 102

26. DANA ROHRABACHER, SIDNEY R. YATES, DICK ARMEY, and MAJOR R. OWENS: *Debate on Funding the NEA,* 108

27. HOWELL HEFLIN: *The Keating Five of the S&L Scandal,* 115

28. RICHARD NIXON: *The Post-Cold War World,* 119

1991

29. GEORGE BUSH: *Operation Desert Storm,* 128

30. H. NORMAN SCHWARZKOPF: *The Persian Gulf War,* 131

31. CLARENCE THOMAS: *Supreme Court Confirmation,* 136

32. JOHN MAGINNIS: *The Uneasy Appeal of David Duke,* 140

33. BILL BRADLEY: *Support for the Free Trade Agreement,* 144

1992

34. DAVID GERGEN: *The Los Angeles Riots,* 149

35. JESSE JACKSON, JR.: *Speech to the Democratic National Convention,* 151

36. PAT BUCHANAN: *Speech to the Republican National Convention,* 156

37. JANE O'REILLY: *Year of the Woman,* 161

38. AL GORE: Earth in the Balance, 163

39. NEIL HOWE and WILLIAM STRAUSS: *The New Generation Gap,* 165

1993

40. BILL CLINTON: *First Inaugural Address,* 175

41. *The Waco Crisis,* 179

42. CAROL RIGOLOT: *Books in an Era of Television,* 181

43. GEORGE F. WILL: *Speech Codes on Campus,* 186

44. HILLARY CLINTON: *Attempts at Health Care Reform,* 189

45. LEWIS H. LAPHAM: *Presidential Candidate Perot,* 197

46. BILL CLINTON: *Remarks in Memphis on Urban Renewal,* 202

47. *Street Gangs in California,* 206

48. DARCY FREY: *Escaping Poverty Through Basketball,* 210

49. JAMES HOWARD KUNSTLER: The Geography of Nowhere, 219

1994

50. ROY BECK: *Small Towns, New Immigrants,* 224

51. RICHARD BROOKHISER: *The Whitewater Scandal,* 231

52. *CIA Turncoat Aldrich Ames,* 235

53. *Contract with America,* 251

54. RALPH NADER: *The Flip Side of Free Trade*
    A. *Drop the GATT,* 254
    B. *GATT Hypocrisy,* 256

1995

55. BILL CLINTON: *State of the Union,* 258

56. MADELEINE K. ALBRIGHT: *The United States in the United Nations,* 262

57. WILLIAM J. BENNETT: *Immigration in California,* 267

58. BILL CLINTON: *The Oklahoma City Bombing,* 271

59. JOYCE CAROL OATES: *Where Timothy McVeigh Went,* 273

60. TED KACZYNSKI: *The Unabomber Manifesto,* 275

61. GERTRUDE HIMMELFARB: *The Pitfalls of Postmodernism,* 277

62. HENRY LOUIS GATES, JR.: *The Trial of O. J. Simpson,* 283

63. CHARLES MCGRATH: *The Prime-Time Novel,* 292

64. BRUCE SPRINGSTEEN: "Youngstown," 300

1996

65. *Overview of the Telecommunications Act,* 302

66. BOB DOLE: *Acceptance Speech,* 310

67. GEOFFREY BIBLE, LINDA HIMELSTEIN, DAVID GREISING, and LORI BONGIORNO: *The Case Against Big Tobacco*
    A. BIBLE: *Philip Morris Memo,* 319
    B. HIMELSTEIN, GREISING, BONGIORNO: *Liggett Group Settlement,* 320

68. *The Child Pornography Prevention Act,* 322

69. MAX GITTER: *The Olympic Bombing and Press Leaks,* 324

1997

70. DENNIS O'BRIEN: *The High Cost of Higher Education,* 327

71. DEB PRICE: *Ellen DeGeneres Comes Out on Television,* 330

72. FRANK DEFORD: *The Best Golfer in the World,* 332

73. BORIS GULKO: *Chess: Man Versus Machine,* 335

74. KURT L. SCHMOKE: *Welfare Reform,* 339

75. MARGARET WARNER, RON UNZ, and JAMES LYONS: *Debating Bilingual Education,* 343

76. *Makah Indians Allowed to Hunt Whales,* 347

1998

77. ALAN GREENSPAN: *The Role of Free Markets,* 350

78. *School Voucher Program in Wisconsin,* 357

79. KENNETH W. STARR: *The Starr Report,* 362

80. JOSEPH LIEBERMAN: *Reaction to the Clinton-Lewinsky Affair,* 366

81. *The Digital Millennium Copyright Act,* 372

82. HELENE GOLDBERG: *Radio Therapy,* 378

83. *The Rise of Hip-Hop*
    A. "Don't Believe the Hype," 381
    B. "Tennessee," 382
    C. "Everything Is Everything," 383

1999

84. JAMES K. GLASSMAN and KEVIN A. HASSETT: *Why Stocks Are a Good Buy,* 384

85. CANDACE CORLETT: *Marketing to Older Women on the Internet,* 388

86. *Native American Tribal Gambling,* 393

87. ARTURO VARGAS: *Latino Voters,* 403

88. ANDREW SULLIVAN: *Hate Crimes,* 407

89. Brooklyn Museum *v.* City of New York and Rudolph Giuliani, 412

90. D. STANLEY EITZEN: *American Sport at the End of the Twentieth Century,* 419

2000

91. DANIEL P. JORDAN: *The Thomas Jefferson and Sally Hemings Paternity Debate,* 425

92. GEORGE MAROTTA: *The Stock Market Bubble,* 427

93. *The Vermont Civil Union Act,* 432

94. *The Columbine High School Murders,* 435

95. BOB COSTAS: *The Traditions of Baseball,* 438

96. BARRY R. MCCAFFREY: *Do Not Legalize Drugs,* 441

97. E. J. DIONNE, JR.: *Suburban Politics,* 446

98. ROBERT D. PUTNAM: *Reviving the American Community,* 448

99. CLOTAIRE RAPAILLE: *How Americans Think,* 452

100. LEON JAMES and DIANE NAHL: Road Rage, 454

101. JOHN MCCAIN: *Ban the Soft Money,* 458

102. NAFTALI BENDAVID and BOB KEMPER: *The Disputed Election of 2000,* 463

103. AL GORE: *Concession Speech,* 466

104. ERIC SCHLOSSER: Fast Food Nation, 469

2001

105. MYLES BRAND: *Reforming College Athletics,* 475

106. PAUL WELLSTONE: *The Downside of Standardized Tests,* 480

107. *Club Drugs,* 483

108. *Approval of Stem Cell Research,* 485

109. James L. Watson: *Globalization and Culture,* 488

110. George W. Bush: *Declaration of War on Terrorism,* 494

111. Lucas Miller, Kate Zernike, and Jere Longman: *Air Travel After September 11*
    A. Miller: *In-Flight Security,* 499
    B. Zernike: *Fear of Flying,* 501
    C. Longman: *Airport Delays,* 502

112. Evan Thomas: *The American Taliban,* 505

113. Robert G. Kaiser: *America and the Aftermath of September 11,* 511

Index, 517

Appendix: Contents of The Annals of America, 529

Summary Index of Authors and Sources in The Annals of America, 607

A NEW WORLD ORDER

In Pictures

Culture 53–54

Culture Wars, the political battle over art, culture, and curricula, was central to American life in the period covered in this volume. Beyond the battle lines, *Cats* became the longest-running show on Broadway, jazz found common ground with classical music, and skateboarding became a way of life.

Television and Film 97–98

The entertainment industry was bigger than ever, and television and film went in interesting new directions, marked by the retirement of talk show host Johnny Carson, the emergence of "reality television," the development of actor Tom Hanks as an American icon, and the runaway success of computer animation.

War 147–148

During the Administration of President George Bush, U.S. troops went to Panama, led an international coalition in expelling Iraqi forces from Kuwait in the Persian Gulf War, and were sent to Somalia; under Bill Clinton American troops were committed in the Balkans; and George W. Bush dispatched the U.S. military to Afghanistan to topple the regime that had sheltered the terrorists responsible for attacks on the U.S. on September 11, 2001.

Science, Medicine, and Technology 195–196

By the century's close, AIDS had claimed more than twenty million victims worldwide, while medical science explored methods for stanching the disease; scientists also cultivated human stem cells that offered hope for curing a variety of illnesses and disabilities but raised moral controversy. Meanwhile, new technologies such as cellular phones and palm-held computers made it easier than ever to stay in touch.

Society 249–250

Race-related issues continued to divide Americans as witnessed by the riots in Los Angeles in 1992 and the Million Man March and reaction to the murder trial of O. J. Simpson in 1995. The country was also shocked by a rash of school shootings.

Business and Law 317–318

Before reaching unprecedented highs in the 1990s on the wings of the "new economy," Wall Street was rocked by scandal; the period also saw the tobacco industry and Microsoft taken to court, while fast-food chains took synergistic marketing to new levels with toy premiums tied to major film releases.

Politics 355–356

Scandal and controversy colored the American political landscape from the Iran-Contra Affair to the Bill Clinton-Monica Lewinsky scandal to the disputed presidential election of 2000, yet hope came in many forms for many people, from the Rainbow Coalition to the Contract with America.

Sports 401–402

The world of sports produced many larger-than-life personalities, including tennis' Williams sisters, baseball's "Iron Man" Cal Ripken and record-setting sluggers Mark McGwire and Sammy Sosa, and cycling's Lance Armstrong, but no one loomed larger than basketball's Michael Jordan, who led the world in endorsements and the Chicago Bulls to six NBA championships.

Terrorism 461–462

Long common in much of the world, terrorism afflicted Americans at home and abroad with increasing frequency and severity in the 1990s, culminating in the deadliest terrorist attack to date on September 11, 2001.

Introduction

The United States, and the world, changed fundamentally between New Year's Day 1987 and New Year's Eve 2001. Perhaps most significantly, as the extraordinary twentieth century drew to a close, so too did the "war" that had dominated the United States politically, economically, and culturally for almost fifty years—the Cold War. After President Ronald Reagan and Soviet leader Mikhail Gorbachev met to reduce nuclear arms and Gorbachev promised new openness and economic restructuring, the "evil empire" (as Reagan had once characterized the Soviet Union) seemed less a menace to American democracy than an investment opportunity. The nation found itself, as the first President George Bush noted, part of a "new world order," and for a moment, at least, Americans felt safe and secure in this post-Cold War age. Yet even without the threat of global nuclear war, the world remained a scary place. As communist dictators across Europe fell from power, the United States, now the lone superpower, had to deal with new and unfamiliar crises that seldom lent themselves to the simplistic "good vs. evil" paradigm of the Cold War. In the Persian Gulf War in 1991, the United States led a successful United Nations effort to free Kuwait from Iraqi occupation but stopped short of ousting Iraqi leader Saddam Hussein. The decision bedeviled Bush's successors as Hussein thwarted UN weapons inspections into the next century. There were also U.S. military operations in Somalia, Bosnia and Herzegovina, and Kosovo, but they did little to solve the problems sparking violence in these areas. Prior to the demise of the Soviet Union, the United States had faced one powerful rival that challenged fundamental American values of personal liberty, democracy, and economic freedom. In the post-Cold War world, these same values were less easy to define and defend.

The political landscape was also new and confusing. George Bush's astronomical approval ratings in the immediate aftermath of the Gulf War did little to help his 1992 reelection effort as the nation slid into economic recession. He was also the victim of political challenges from both the right and the left, as voters searched for new voices and bucked the status quo. Conservative journalist Pat Buchanan ran for the Republican presidential nomination in 1992 and 1996 and as the Reform Party nominee in 2000. Texas billionaire H. Ross Perot played upon widespread economic and political discontent to launch independent bids in the 1992 and 1996 presidential elections, both won by Democrat Bill Clinton. For the Green Party, consumer advocate Ralph Nader led quixotic efforts in 1996 and 2000. The end result of these challenges to the two-party system was a series of three presidential elections in which the victor failed to garner a majority of popular votes. In 2000 George W. Bush lost the popular vote by a margin of 500,000 to Al Gore, but the election remained undecided for more than a month until the Supreme Court settled the dispute and Bush took the oath of office.

On the social front, there were challenges to affirmative action by individual states, and the U.S. Supreme Court suggested that the nation's commitment to racial equality had its limits. Race riots in Los Angeles, Miami, and other cities indicated the hostility that lurked beneath boarded-up inner cities, and demands to restrict immigration from Latin America and Asia came to the surface in 1996 when California voters decided to ban state funding for some services to illegal immigrants. In 1992, the "Year of the Woman," an unprecedented number of women were elected to office, and with the election of Bill Clinton that year feminists found a role model in First Lady Hillary Clinton. Family rights were addressed in the Family and Medical Leave Act, passed in 1993, and abortion remained a contentious issue, as federal and state governments flirted with restricting it several times in the 1980s and '90s.

A seemingly continuous series of scandals involving perjury, bribery, influence-peddling, and corruption plagued both the White House and Congress, beginning with the Iran-Contra Affair in 1986–87 and extending to the impeachment and trial of Bill Clinton in 1998–99. As congressional approval ratings declined and anti-incumbency sentiment increased, both conservative and liberal activists favored more direct action both large and small. Antiabortion protestors blocked clinics around the nation, antigovernment militia wrestled with federal agents, and environmental and labor activists joined forces to protest the nascent World Trade Organization. The National Mall in Washington, D.C., became the scene for large demonstrations, promoting everything from handgun safety to reproductive rights to family responsibility. Meanwhile, new technology transformed communication and access to information as e-mail and the Internet became household words and business fixtures. Though the much-heralded "new economy" and accompanying Internet "revolution" did not meet all the early expectations, the Internet did provide alternative space for entrepreneurship and self-expression. By the end of the century, political action frequently took place in on-line chat rooms.

On the cultural front, America blazed new trails while debating age-old questions, such as what is art and what role should government play in either supporting or suppressing it. American sports came to the fore in spectacular fashion. Soccer star Mia Hamm and her teammates shocked the world with their dramatic victory at the 1999 Women's World Cup. Tiger Woods and Venus and Serena Williams broke new ground for minorities in golf and tennis, respectively. And professional baseball returned as "America's pastime" in the summer of 1998 as Mark McGwire and Sammy Sosa thrilled the nation with their chase after Roger Maris' thirty-seven-year-old single-season home-run record. Barry Bonds then broke McGwire's record of seventy home runs by hitting seventy-three home runs in 2001. Meanwhile, with such movies as *The Little Mermaid* (1989) and *Toy Story* (1995), Hollywood resuscitated a moribund genre—the blockbuster, feature-length animated film.

Economically, the country reached staggering new heights. The stock market topped 10,000, the national deficit disappeared, unemployment hit thirty-year lows, charitable giving rose, and unprecedented corporate profits offered a seemingly sure return to small investors and holders of 401(k)s. This success, however, proved fleeting. Not everyone shared in the economic boom, as the gap between the richest and poorest Americans continued to grow and more citizens worried about retaining good jobs and paying for health care. Gigantic mergers in the communications and technology sectors and the corporate and accounting scandals that first surfaced in late 2001 reinforced the popular perception that economic expansion had benefited primarily the wealthy. The boom ended in mid-2000, and the vision of endless growth and government surplus vanished.

Several shootings in public schools and horrific acts of terrorism further shook American exuberance, confidence, and security. In February 1993, Arab terrorists exploded a bomb in the World Trade Center in New York City; in April 1995 American Timothy McVeigh bombed a federal building in Oklahoma City, Oklahoma; in July 1996 another bombing occurred at the Summer Olympic Games in Atlanta, Georgia; that year Ted Kaczynski, the "Unabomber," was arrested after a seventeen-year mail-bomb terror campaign; in 1999, twelve students and a teacher were fatally shot in their suburban Denver, Colorado, high school; and in 2000, the USS *Cole* was attacked by terrorists in the Yemeni port of Aden. But the most devastating blow to American self-assurance came on September 11, 2001, when radical Islamic terrorists hijacked four jetliners and suicidally crashed two of them into the World Trade Center towers and another into the Pentagon. The outpouring of emotion rallied the nation. Military operations in Afghanistan overturned the ruling Taliban regime and dispersed al-Qaeda, the terrorist group responsible for the September 11 attacks, but they failed to capture its leader, Osama bin Laden. At home, a series of anthrax-laced letters distributed through the mail and continual rumors of nuclear and biological terrorism made Americans feel insecure, whether at home or at work. At the dawn of the twenty-first century, the sole remaining superpower seemed resilient but vulnerable, as it faced a volatile new world.

Chronology: 1987 – 2001

1987

January 5. President Ronald Reagan submits $1.024 trillion federal budget for fiscal year 1988 to Congress. He projects $107.8 billion budget deficit.

January 8. Dow Jones Industrial Average sets new record at 2002.25, surpassing the 2000 mark for the first time, a milestone once thought unattainable.

January 9. U.S. Department of Labor announces unemployment rate for 1986 was 7.0 percent.

January 13. In a 6 to 3 decision, U.S. Supreme Court upholds a California law requiring employers to grant up to four months unpaid maternity leave in *California Federal Savings and Loan Association* v. *Guerra.*

January 15. Negotiators from U.S. and U.S.S.R. resume arms control talks in Geneva.

January 25. New York Giants beat Denver Broncos 39–20 in Super Bowl XXI.

February 10. Appearing before a House subcommittee, Surgeon General C. Everett Koop advocates using television advertisements to promote condom use and slow the spread of HIV and AIDS.

February 12. A federal court in Mobile, Ala., finds United Klans of America responsible for the murder and subsequent hanging of an African American by two of its members, and awards plaintiffs $7 million.

February 26. A review board, chaired by former Senator John Tower, releases highly critical report on the Iran-Contra Affair. The report criticizes President Reagan's lack of engagement but blames senior White House staff for illegal activities.

March 4. In a national television address, President Reagan accepts full responsibility for his administration's actions in the Iran-Contra Affair but denies knowledge of illegal activities.

March 19. Popular televangelist Jim Bakker resigns his ministry following allegations of an extramarital affair, blackmail, and misuse of funds.

March 31. In a ruling that came amid a national debate over the use of surrogates during pregnancy, a New Jersey judge awards custody of "Baby M" to her biological father and denies all parental rights to the biological mother, who had signed a contract to carry the child.

April 2. IBM introduces new Personal System/2, vastly expanding the operating capabilities of personal computers. The new system makes software easier to use and expands the market for home computers.

April 17. In response to a growing trade

deficit with Japan and allegations of unfair trade practices, President Reagan imposes a 100 percent tariff on Japanese electronic goods.

May 8. Former Senator Gary Hart halts his campaign for the Democratic Presidential nomination after *The Miami Herald* reports evidence of an affair with actress and model Donna Rice. Hart reenters the race on December 15.

May 17. Iraqi fighter planes hit U.S. frigate *Stark* in Persian Gulf, killing 37 American sailors. Iraqi President Saddam Hussein apologizes for the accident.

May 19. In response to Kuwaiti requests, U.S. announces it will escort Kuwaiti oil tankers that had been repeatedly attacked by Iranian forces. Tensions in Persian Gulf continue to mount.

June 16. New York jury acquits "subway vigilante" Bernhard Goetz of charges stemming from his shooting of four African Americans in a city subway. Goetz claimed he had acted in self-defense.

July 7. Lieutenant Colonel Oliver North testifies at televised congressional committee hearings investigating the sale of arms to Iran. Contradicting President Reagan's own statement, North says he believed Reagan was fully aware that funds from the sales were diverted to the Nicaraguan Contras.

August 24. Marine Sergeant Clayton Lonetree is found guilty of 13 counts of espionage committed while serving at U.S. embassy in Moscow and receives a 30-year prison sentence.

September 16. To combat global warming, representatives of 24 countries, meeting in Montreal, agree to restrict chemicals believed to deplete ozone layer.

September 21. U.S. armed forces seize an Iranian ship laying mines in an area of the Persian Gulf frequented by U.S. vessels.

October 19. On what became known as "Black Monday," Dow Jones Industrial Average falls 508.32 points—the largest one-day drop in history—raising questions about the strength of U.S. economy.

U.S. naval forces attack three Iranian oil platforms in Persian Gulf in retaliation for Iranian attacks on U.S. ships.

October 23. Senate votes 58 to 42 to reject President Reagan's nomination of Robert Bork to U.S. Supreme Court after a bitter fight over his conservative ideology.

October 25. Minnesota Twins defeat St. Louis Cardinals 4 games to 3 to win World Series.

November 18. Senate and House committees release final report on Iran-Contra Affair, finding no evidence directly linking President Reagan to the diversion of funds to the Contras.

December 8. President Reagan and Soviet leader Mikhail Gorbachev sign Intermediate-Range Nuclear Forces Treaty to eliminate medium-range nuclear missiles. The agreement provides for unprecedented mutual inspection of missile bases.

December 11. *Wall Street*, directed by Oliver Stone, is released. Depicting the rise of an ambitious stockbroker in the world of corporate raiders, the movie reflects growing discomfort of Americans with the high-stakes business climate of the 1980s.

December 18. Tom Wolfe's *The Bonfire of the Vanities*, which depicts disparities of wealth in modern America, appears on *Publishers Weekly*'s best-seller list.

1988

January 2. President Reagan and Canadian Prime Minister Brian Mulroney sign trade agreement making the U.S. and Canada the world's largest free-trade zone. Movement for free trade in the Western Hemisphere continues throughout decade.

January 31. Washington Redskins defeat Denver Broncos 42–10 in Super Bowl XXII.

February 5. Federal grand juries in Florida indict Panamanian strongman and former CIA operative Manuel Noriega for money laundering and drug trafficking.

February 24. In *Hustler Magazine* v. *Jerry Falwell*, U.S. Supreme Court overturns $200,000 award to evangelist Jerry Falwell, who had sued *Hustler* and its head, Larry Flynt, for publishing an obscene "parody" of him.

March 2. Signaling a hard line against the U.S.S.R., representatives of NATO meet in Brussels and affirm need to maintain adequate nuclear and conventional forces in Europe.

March 16. Federal grand jury indicts Oliver North on charges of conspiring to defraud the government for his role in the Iran-Contra Affair. Widely viewed as the Reagan Administration's fall guy, North becomes a hero to American conservatives.

March 18. Panamanian government declares a "state of urgency" in face of an attempted coup and financial instability. American efforts to remove Manuel Noriega continue.

March 23. Persian Gulf continues to worry U.S. officials as evidence surfaces that Iraq is using chemical weapons, including cyanide and mustard gas, in its long war with Iran.

March 29. Six Justice Department officials resign, citing the disruption caused by the ongoing ethics investigation of Attorney General Edwin Meese. **July 5.** Meese resigns, though special prosecutor finds insufficient evidence for criminal charges.

April 8. UN announces Soviet withdrawal of

troops from Afghanistan, ending almost a decade of occupation and civil war; move signals Gorbachev's commitment to focus on domestic issues and to improve relations with the West.

April 14. U.S. frigate is damaged after hitting an Iranian mine in Persian Gulf. U.S. responds by destroying two Iranian oil platforms, triggering a series of confrontations between U.S. and Iranian ships.

April 20. Senate votes 69 to 27 to apologize for internment of Japanese Americans during World War II and appropriates $20,000 for each living internee.

April 26. Vice President George Bush wins Pennsylvania Republican primary, clinching the Republican nomination for President.

May 29. President Reagan arrives in Moscow for summit meeting with Gorbachev. **May 31.** Reagan and Gorbachev sign agreements on nuclear testing and other issues.

June 28. U.S.S.R. leader Gorbachev calls for radical restructuring of the Soviet political and economic system to address growing economic and social problems.

July 3. USS *Vincennes* shoots down Iranian airbus killing all 290 on board after mistaking it for a fighter jet. Defense Department begins an investigation of the incident, ultimately vindicating the ship's captain.

July 21. Massachusetts Governor Michael Dukakis, calling for "a new era of greatness," accepts Democratic nomination for president at national convention in Atlanta, Ga.

August 18. In New Orleans, La., Vice President Bush formally accepts Republican nomination for president and names Indiana Senator Dan Quayle as his running mate.

August 23. President Reagan signs comprehensive trade bill that includes (for the first time) consideration of currency surpluses and debt in the less-developed world. As U.S.S.R. begins to soften stance toward West, U.S. policy in the developing world increasingly focuses on economic development rather than strategic significance.

Large demonstrations in Latvia, Estonia, and Lithuania openly challenge Soviet rule and call for full independence, foreshadowing eventual breakup of U.S.S.R.

World Health Organization (WHO) estimates from 5 to 10 million people worldwide are infected with HIV and that there are 200,000 to 250,000 active AIDS cases.

September 27. White House and congressional representatives reach agreement on first major welfare-reform bill in over 50 years. Bill includes provisions for education and work requirements.

October 12. Sundstrand Corp. pleads guilty to fraud charges for overcharging the Defense Department millions of dollars between 1980 and 1986. Company fined $115 million.

October 20. Los Angeles Dodgers upset Oakland A's to win World Series 4 games to 1.

October 21. A federal grand jury indicts former Philippine President Ferdinand Marcos and his wife, Imelda, on charges of embezzling $100 million to purchase three New York City buildings.

October 22. Struggling to cope with a drug epidemic, Congress passes comprehensive bill establishing educational and treatment programs for addicts and approving the death penalty for drug-related murders.

November 8. Vice President Bush elected president, receiving 54 percent of the popular vote and 426 electoral votes. He becomes first sitting Vice President to win election since Martin Van Buren in 1836.

Democrats retain control of both houses of Congress.

November 22. Defense Department unveils B-2 stealth bomber, designed to infiltrate Soviet airspace undetected.

December 7. Soviet leader Gorbachev announces major reductions in Soviet military and withdrawal of some forces from Europe. The move signals increasing economic inability to maintain military dominance in Eastern Europe.

December 14. Secretary of State George Schultz announces U.S. will begin negotiations with Palestinian Liberation Organization (PLO) after Chairman Yāsir 'Arafāt announces at a press conference at the UN in Geneva that PLO formally renounces terrorism and affirms Israel's right to exist.

December 21. A bomb aboard Pan Am flight 103 from London to New York explodes over Lockerbie, Scot., killing all 259 aboard. U.S. offers $500,000 for information on those responsible.

Drexel Burnham Lambert Inc., a major investment company, pleads guilty to six counts of securities fraud and agrees to pay $650 million in fines. The penalty is one of largest ever levied against a corporation for fraud.

December 23. U.S. threatens 100 percent tariff on imports from the European Community (EC) if it bans imports of U.S. meat from animals treated with controversial growth hormones.

1989

January 4. U.S. fighter jets shoot down two Libyan jets over the Mediterranean Sea; incident increases tension between U.S. and Arab states.

January 6. Federal grand jury indicts Teledyne Industries on conspiracy and bribery charges after two-year investigation into procurement of military weapons contracts. Defense Department reputation continues to suffer amid evidence of corruption.

January 16. Miami police officer shoots unarmed African American man fleeing police. Incident sets off three days of rioting.

January 22. San Francisco 49ers defeat Cincinnati Bengals 20–16 in Super Bowl XXIII.

January 23. In a 6 to 3 ruling in *City of Richmond* v. *J. A. Croson Company*, U.S. Supreme Court declares unconstitutional a Richmond, Va., requirement that 30 percent of city public works funds be awarded to minority-owned construction companies. Ruling marks beginning of withdrawal of federal support for affirmative action.

February 7. Facing public outrage over automatic pay increases, Congress rejects a 51 percent pay raise for itself and other federal employees.

March 9. John Tower's nomination as Secretary of Defense is rejected by the Senate (53 to 47) after questions of conflict of interest and allegations of drinking and sexual affairs arise.

March 24. In largest oil tanker disaster in U.S. history, *Exxon Valdez* spills nearly 11 million gallons of crude oil in Prince William Sound off the coast of Alaska.

April 13. Despite inquiries into Reagan Administration's funneling of funds illegally to Nicaraguan Contras, Congress appropriates nearly $50 million in humanitarian aid to Contras.

May 4. Oliver North convicted on 3 of 12 charges stemming from his participation in the Iran-Contra Affair, including destruction of documents and obstruction of Congress. **July 6.** North receives three-year suspended sentence and $150,000 fine.

May 25. President Bush accuses Brazil, India, and Japan of unfair trade practices and threatens to impose heavy import tariffs on their products unless they relax restrictions on U.S. goods.

May 31. House Speaker Jim Wright of Texas announces his resignation after charges that he violated House ethics rules. **June 6.** Representative Tom Foley, of Washington, is elected Speaker.

June 4. Chinese troops crush student-led pro-democracy protest in Beijing's Tiananmen Square, killing thousands. U.S. and other democracies condemn the action, and incident hampers progress in trade relations between China and U.S.

June 10. Federal investigators reveal massive fraud and influence peddling in Department of Housing and Urban Development. Independent contractors accused of embezzling millions of dollars from the government.

June 21. U.S. Supreme Court rules Constitution's First Amendment protection of free speech extends to burning of American flag. The 5 to 4 decision in *Texas* v. *Johnson* prompts national movement for a constitutional amendment to protect the flag.

July 3. In *Webster* v. *Reproductive Health Services*, Supreme Court narrowly upholds (5 to 4) Missouri restrictions on abortion. Ruling buoys pro-life groups and once again thrusts abortion rights to the center of political debate.

August 9. President Bush signs bill providing $300 billion bailout to savings and loan institutions, the largest federal rescue in history.

August 24. U.S. space probe *Voyager 2* exits solar system after sending astonishing photographs of the outer planets back to Earth and greatly expanding astronomers' understanding of solar system.

September 1. In effort to ease tension between their two countries, Japanese Prime Minister Kaifu Toshiki visits White House to discuss trade policy with President Bush.

September 29. In largest drug seizure in U.S. history, Drug Enforcement Agency (DEA) agents uncover 20-ton cache of cocaine and $10 million in cash in a California warehouse. Federal policy toward illegal drugs becomes more strict.

October 17. An earthquake measuring 7.1 on the Richter scale hits San Francisco Bay area. More than 60 people die—most after a double-decker section of Interstate 880 collapses—and more than 3,500 are injured.

October 28. Oakland A's complete 4-game sweep of San Francisco Giants in World Series.

October 31. Congress and President Bush reach agreement on minimum-wage legislation, boosting it to $3.80 per hour effective April 1, 1990. The hike was opposed by most Republicans and business leaders.

November 7. L. Douglas Wilder is elected Governor of Virginia and becomes the first African American elected to serve as state governor in the U.S. Wilder uses the position to launch an abortive presidential bid.

East German government resigns after public demonstrations. **November 9.** Section of Berlin Wall torn down, leading to mass celebrations and to hundreds of thousands of East Germans entering West Berlin freely.

November 10. Bulgarian Communist President Todor Zhivkov resigns, the first hardline ally of the Soviets in the Balkans to give up power.

November 24. Soviet grip on Eastern Europe continues to crumble as Czechoslovak Communist party leaders resign.

November 26. Hungary holds first free elections since 1947, signaling return of democracy to former Soviet satellite states.

December 9. President Bush sends high-ranking White House officials to Beijing, triggering Congressional protest over Chinese action in Tiananmen Square. Economic and political relations with China continue to be contested political issue for years.

December 20. U.S. troops invade Panama and depose de facto ruler Manuel Noriega, who takes sanctuary at the Vatican nunciature in Panama City. He is later handed over to the U.S. to face trial on drug and racketeering charges.

December 22. Romanian President Nicolae Ceausescu is overthrown after bloody fighting. **December 25.** Ceausescu and his wife are executed.

1990

January 3. Manuel Noriega leaves the Vatican nunciature in Panama City and surrenders to U.S. forces. The following day he is arraigned on drug charges in a Florida federal court.

January 28. San Francisco 49ers defeat Denver Broncos 55–10 in Super Bowl XXIV.

February 15. President Bush meets with Latin American presidents in Colombia to discuss efforts to combat drug trafficking.

February 21. Czechoslovakian President Václav Havel addresses Congress and urges U.S. support for the U.S.S.R.'s transition to democracy.

March 3. President Bush meets with Japanese Prime Minister Kaifu Toshiki to discuss contentious Japanese-U.S. trade relations.

March 11. Lithuania declares independence from the U.S.S.R., deepening the Soviet political crisis; other republics and ethnic groups increase agitation for greater autonomy.

April 7. Former National Security Advisor John Poindexter is convicted of five felony counts stemming from the Iran-Contra Affair. **June 11.** Poindexter receives six-month prison sentence.

April 22. A crowd of 750,000 gathers in New York City's Central Park to celebrate Earth Day and promote environmental causes.

April 25. Hubble Space Telescope is launched from the space shuttle *Discovery*. **June 27.** The telescope is found to have a flawed mirror, resulting in distorted images.

May 23. Secretary of the Treasury Nicholas F. Brady tells Congress that the savings and loan bailout could cost U.S. $300 billion over 10 years.

May 24. President Bush, citing China's advances in human rights, recommends renewal of most-favored-nation trade status.

June 11. In *United States* v. *Eichman*, the U.S. Supreme Court strikes down (5 to 4) the federal Flag Protection Act outlawing desecration of American flag. The ruling sparks renewed debate over the limits of free speech and spurs conservatives to seek a constitutional amendment to protect the flag.

June 28. U.S. and Japan sign Strategic Impediments Initiative to reduce U.S. trade deficit. The agreement eases growing anti-Japanese sentiment in U.S.

July 17. Iraq threatens Kuwait and United Arab Emirates (UAE) with force if the two countries continue exceeding Organization of Petroleum Exporting Countries (OPEC) quotas and driving oil prices down.

August 2. Iraq invades Kuwait. President Bush freezes Iraqi assets and imposes economic sanctions. UN condemns attack and orders Iraq to withdraw.

August 3. Professional Golfers' Association (PGA) announces it will not hold tournaments in private clubs that exclude members based on race or sex.

August 6. In what is called Operation Desert Shield, President Bush orders U.S. troops to Saudi Arabia to deter a potential Iraqi assault. UN authorizes trade and financial embargo against Iraq.

September 9. Meeting with Soviet President Gorbachev in Helskini, Fin., President Bush invites him to assume greater diplomatic role in Middle East, a departure from long-standing U.S. policy.

September 17. Philippine President Corazon Aquino demands withdrawal of U.S. forces from six bases. U.S. had granted the Philippines independence in 1946 but retained military bases.

October 3. East and West Germany reunite. The new country has Europe's largest economy.

October 5. Director of Contemporary Arts Center in Cincinnati, Ohio, is acquitted of obscenity charges for displaying homoerotic photographs by artist Robert Mapplethorpe.

October 20. Cincinnati Reds upset Oakland A's to win World Series, sweeping championship in 4 games.

October 27. Congress passes the budget after President Bush, breaking his "no new taxes" campaign pledge, agrees to $164.4 billion tax increase over five years.

November 6. Midterm elections increase Democratic majority in Congress, despite widespread resentment of incumbents and general dissatisfaction with government.

November 15. President Bush signs Clean

Air Act aimed at reducing automobile and utility emissions and ending the use of ozone-depleting chlorofluorocarbons (CFCs).

November 17. In response to economic and political turmoil, Soviet President Gorbachev assumes vast emergency powers. Russian President Boris Yeltsin promises to reject any encroachment on Russian authority.

November 21. Representatives of 34 countries from Europe and North America sign Charter of Paris, formally ending the Cold War. The agreement establishes consultative bodies to encourage cooperation among the former adversaries.

"Junk-bond king" Michael Milken of Drexel Burnham Lambert Inc., receives a 10-year prison sentence for illegal stock-trading activities.

November 29. UN Security Council authorizes force to expel Iraqi forces from Kuwait.

December 6. Iraq announces the release of foreign hostages detained since the invasion of Kuwait. One week later the last Americans depart with U.S. ambassador to Kuwait.

December 18. Attempting to prevent recession, the Federal Reserve Board votes to lower the discount rate for first time since 1986.

December 22. Solidarity leader Lech Walesa becomes the first democratically elected president of Poland since World War II, replacing Wojciech Jaruzelski, the last hardline Communist leader in Eastern Europe.

1991

January 4. Iraq agrees to U.S. proposal for talks in Geneva to end Iraqi occupation of Kuwait. Meeting between U.S. Secretary of State James Baker and Iraqi Foreign Minister Tariq Aziz ends five days later in stalemate.

January 12. In a joint resolution, the House of Representatives (250 to 183) and Senate (52 to 47) vote to authorize President Bush to use force to expel Iraq from Kuwait.

January 16. U.S.-led coalition forces from 28 countries begin air and missile attacks on Iraq and occupied Kuwait in Operation Desert Storm.

January 27. In the closest NFL championship game to date, New York Giants defeat Buffalo Bills 20–19 in Super Bowl XXV.

February 4. National Baseball Hall of Fame directors vote to bar all-time hit leader Pete Rose for betting on games while manager of Cincinnati Reds.

February 27. Senate Ethics Committee finds "credible evidence" of misconduct by Senator Alan Cranston in aiding Lincoln Savings and Loan owner Charles Keating in exchange for campaign contributions. Four other senators—dubbed collectively with Cranston as the "Keating Five"—receive reprimands.

After four-day ground war, U.S.-led forces liberate Kuwait. President Bush announces suspension of operations after Iraq agrees to cease-fire.

March 3. Los Angeles police are videotaped beating African American Rodney King. **March 14.** Based on Los Angeles Police Department and FBI investigations, several officers are indicted.

April 5. Labor Department announces unemployment rate is 6.8 percent—the highest in four years. U.S. economy continues in recession.

May 4. During his University of Michigan commencement address, President Bush denounces trend toward "political correctness" on U.S. college campuses.

May 23. In *Rust* v. *Sullivan*, a divided U.S. Supreme Court upholds (5 to 4) federal ban on abortion counseling in federally funded clinics.

June 12. Calling for economic and political reform, Boris Yeltsin is elected the President of Russia. He becomes the first non-Communist to lead Russia since 1917 and its first ever elected President.

Chicago Bulls win NBA championship, their first of six in 1990s.

June 25. Furthering the post-Cold War disintegration of Eastern Europe, Slovenia and Croatia declare independence from Yugoslavia.

July 15. Members of Operation Rescue, a radical pro-life group, force closure of three abortion clinics in Wichita, Kan. **July 29.** A U.S. district judge orders U.S. marshals to enforce restraining order against group.

July 31. President Bush and Soviet President Gorbachev meet in Moscow and sign Strategic Arms Reduction Treaty (START), vastly reducing long-range nuclear missiles.

August 12. BankAmerica and Security Pacific announce merger—the largest in U.S. history. The combined company becomes the country's second largest bank.

August 18. Soviet hard-liners attempt a coup against President Gorbachev, taking him prisoner. **August 21.** After two days of demonstrations by hundreds of thousands of protesters led by Russian President Boris Yeltsin, Gorbachev is released, and the coup collapses. **August 24.** Gorbachev resigns as leader of Communist Party. **August 29.** The Supreme Soviet suspends all activity of Communist Party, ending 74 years of control.

September 27. Declaring U.S.S.R. no longer a threat to U.S. and Western Europe, President Bush announces unilateral reduction of U.S. nuclear weapons.

October 11. Senate Judiciary Committee holds dramatic televised hearings on nomi-

nation of Clarence Thomas to U.S. Supreme Court after former aide Anita Hill makes public charges of sexual harassment. Thomas, an African American, accuses Senate Democrats of engineering a "high-tech lynching." **October 15.** Senate confirms Thomas 52 to 48.

October 27. Minnesota Twins defeat Atlanta Braves 4 games to 3 to win World Series.

October 29. President Bush and President Gorbachev meet in Madrid to discuss U.S. economic aid to U.S.S.R. Bush refuses further aid without greater economic cooperation among Soviet republics.

November 7. Los Angeles Lakers star Earvin "Magic" Johnson discloses he has tested positive for HIV and is retiring from basketball.

November 14. Justice Department indicts two Libyan military officers for bombing of Pan Am Flight 103 in 1988. Bush Administration alleges the plot was approved by Libyan leader Colonel Muammar Qaddafi.

November 21. President Bush signs Civil Rights Act of 1991. The law eases restrictions on employee lawsuits for racial and sexual discrimination.

December 4. Charles Keating, former chairman of Lincoln Savings and Loan, is convicted on 17 counts of securities fraud.

December 10. Conservative columnist Pat Buchanan announces he will challenge President Bush for the Republican Presidential nomination.

December 18. Anticipating a loss of $7 billion in 1991, General Motors announces it will lay off 74,000 employees and close 21 factories.

December 20. Federal Reserve lowers prime rate to 6.5 percent—the lowest rate in 14 years—in an attempt to curtail growing recession.

December 25. After the Russian Republic seizes the Kremlin and central bank, President Gorbachev resigns and the Soviet Union formally disbands.

1992

January 9. Fish and Wildlife Service recommends restricted logging in nearly 7 million acres of Pacific Northwest to protect Northern Spotted Owl, setting off a clash between logging companies and environmentalists.

Cornell University astronomer Alexander Wolszczan announces the discovery of the first planets outside the solar system, 1,300 light-years from Earth.

January 10. Labor Department reports 7.1 percent unemployment rate—the highest level in five years.

January 17. Centers for Disease Control release a study of first and second 100,000 AIDS cases in U.S. The 200,000 mark had been surpassed in November 1991.

January 26. Washington Redskins defeat Buffalo Bills 37–24 in Super Bowl XXVI.

February 6. In response to public anxiety over rising health care costs, President Bush announces plan to provide affordable health care for most Americans. Democrats previously had released more ambitious plans.

February 18. Pat Buchanan wins 37 percent of vote in New Hampshire Republican primary, indicating strong conservative revolt in party. Former Massachusetts Senator Paul Tsongas wins Democratic primary. Following allegations of a 12-year extramarital affair, Arkansas Governor Bill Clinton finishes second and declares himself the "Comeback Kid."

February 20. Texas billionaire Ross Perot announces on *Larry King Live* television

program that he will run for President if volunteers can get enough signatures to place him on the ballot in all 50 states.

February 24. General Motors posts a record $4.45 billion loss for 1991 and announces plans to lay off an additional 16,000 workers and close 12 more plants.

April 1. House Ethics Committee announces the names of members who had overdrawn House bank accounts for tens of thousands of dollars without interest or penalty.

April 5. Pro-choice rally sponsored by National Organization for Women (NOW) and other groups attracts estimated 500,000 outside White House.

April 8. Tennis great Arthur Ashe announces he contracted HIV from blood transfusion.

April 29. California jury acquits police officers of 1991 beating of African American motorist Rodney King. Riots erupt in Los Angeles, resulting in the deaths of 58 and causing nearly $1 billion in damage.

May 18. U.S. archivist Don Wilson certifies ratification of Twenty-Seventh Amendment to Constitution. First proposed in 1789 and authored by James Madison, the amendment prevents members of Congress from receiving a midterm pay raise.

May 19. In speech extolling family values, Vice President Dan Quayle criticizes television character Murphy Brown for becoming a single parent. Quayle also blames Los Angeles riots on the demise of families and personal responsibility.

June 2. After victories in six state primaries, Arkansas Governor Bill Clinton clinches Democratic nomination for President.

June 3–14. UN "Earth Summit" in Rio de Janeiro adopts agreements on global warming, biodiversity, deforestation, and aid to developing countries. U.S. is criticized for its lack of support for environmental causes.

June 16. President Bush and Russian President Yeltsin agree to dramatic long-term reductions in long-range nuclear missiles.

Former Defense Secretary Caspar W. Weinberger is indicted on five counts of lying to Congress and obstructing congressional inquiry into Iran-Contra Affair.

June 29. In *Planned Parenthood* v. *Casey*, U.S. Supreme Court upholds (5 to 4) Pennsylvania law imposing waiting period for women seeking abortion; the ruling also affirms fundamental right to abortion.

July 2. Federal Reserve Board lowers short-term interest rate to 3 percent—lowest level in 29 years.

July 16. Stating that the Democratic Party had "revitalized" itself, Ross Perot announces he will not run for President despite successful efforts to place his name on ballots in at least 24 states.

August 6. President Bush announces support for use of UN troops to protect the delivery of humanitarian relief to Sarajevo, Bosnia and Herzegovina, under siege by Serb forces engaged in civil war. **August 13.** UN Security Council authorizes troop deployment.

August 12. Representatives from Canada, U.S., and Mexico reach agreement on North American Free Trade Agreement (NAFTA), which eliminates tariffs and restrictions and creates world's largest free-trade zone.

August 24–26. Hurricane Andrew batters south Florida and Louisiana, killing 14 people and forcing evacuation of 2.2 million.

September 14. UN troops arrive in Somalia to ensure distribution of food and relief supplies.

September 22. President Bush vetoes Family and Medical Leave Act, which would have guaranteed workers up to 90 days unpaid leave for family emergencies. **September 30.** House votes to sustain Bush's veto after Senate (68 to 31) votes to override veto.

September 29. NASA announces that the ozone hole above South Pole has grown to a record 8.9 million square miles.

October 1. Ross Perot reenters the Presidential race as an independent, emphasizing the need to end gridlock in Washington and balance the federal budget.

October 24. Toronto Blue Jays defeat Atlanta Braves in World Series 4 games to 2 to become first non-American team to win the championship.

October 30. Federal prosecutor Lawrence E. Walsh releases notes taken by former Secretary of Defense Caspar Weinberger indicating that then-Vice President Bush knew of and approved arms-for-hostages deal with Iran.

November 3. Democrat Bill Clinton is elected President, capturing 43 percent of the vote in a three-way race with Republican George Bush (38 percent) and independent Ross Perot (19 percent). Democrats also retain control of Congress.

November 22. Bob Packwood, Republican Senator from Oregon, is accused by 10 women, mostly former employees, of sexual harassment.

November 26. President Bush offers to send 30,000 troops to aid famine-relief effort in Somalia. **December 3.** UN Security Council approves large-scale U.S.-led force in Somalia.

December 24. President Bush issues blanket pardons for six former Reagan Administration officials in Iran-Contra Affair, including Caspar Weinberger.

1993

January 3. President Bush and Russian President Yeltsin sign second Strategic Arms Reduction Treaty (START II) in Moscow. The treaty calls for elimination of land-based, multiple-warhead missiles and reductions in long-range nuclear missiles.

January 22. Two days after inauguration, President Clinton rescinds federal gag rule on abortion counseling at federally funded clinics.

January 27. Faced with opposition from military officials and Congress, President Clinton announces delay in reversing the government ban on homosexuals in military. **July 19.** Clinton adopts compromise "don't ask, don't tell" policy.

January 31. Dallas Cowboys defeat Buffalo Bills 52–17 in Super Bowl XXVII.

February 11. President Clinton nominates Florida prosecutor Janet Reno as Attorney General after two earlier nominees withdrew over allegations they employed illegal aliens. **March 11.** Reno is confirmed by the Senate and becomes the first woman to head the Justice Department.

February 26. Bomb explodes at World Trade Center in New York City, killing five people. On March 4 and 10, FBI arrests two Arab immigrants for plotting the bombing of the Trade Center and other targets in New York City.

February 28. U.S. planes begin airlifting food and supplies to Muslims under siege by Serb forces in Bosnia and Herzegovina.

March 5. World Meteorological Organization reports ozone levels above Northern Europe are 20 percent below normal, adding more evidence to claims that CFCs deplete the ozone layer.

March 10. Dr. David Gunn is murdered by an antiabortion protestor outside his clinic in Pensacola, Fla., raising concerns over the safety of abortion providers.

April 15. In the most extensive sexual behavior survey since Kinsey Report in 1948, Battelle Human Affairs Research Center reports the percentage of male homosexuals at 1 percent, instead of the widely accepted 10 percent.

April 17. A federal jury convicts two Los Angeles police officers of civil rights violations stemming from the 1991 beating of African American motorist Rodney King. Two other officers are acquitted.

April 19. After 51-day standoff, federal agents attack Waco, Texas, compound of Branch Davidians. Some 80 members of the religious group, including their leader David Koresh, are killed, with many committing suicide as the compound burned to the ground. A report in 2000 ultimately absolved the U.S. government of wrongdoing.

June 21. U.S. Supreme Court rules immigration officials may turn back boats of Haitian refugees without hearings, ending the flight of tens of thousands of Haitians trying to reach U.S.

July 2. Immigration and Naturalization Service (INS) agents detain Egyptian Muslim cleric Sheikh 'Umar 'Abd al-Raḥmān for deportation as FBI examines evidence linking him to the World Trade Center bombing. He is indicted on August 25.

August 10. Ruth Bader Ginsburg is sworn in as the second woman justice on U.S. Supreme Court. President Clinton's first court appointment, she is approved by Senate 96 to 3.

August 12. President Clinton signs $6.2 billion relief bill for areas affected by floods in the Midwest. Heavy rains between June and August had left tens of thousands homeless from North Dakota to Missouri and destroyed crops.

August 25. U.S. imposes trade sanctions on China and Pakistan after announcing Pakistan received missile components from China in the late 1980s.

September 13. Meeting in Washington, D.C., Israeli Prime Minister Yitzhak Rabin and Palestinian leader Yāsir 'Arafāt sign agreement to end violence in Israeli-occupied territories and establish Palestinian self-rule.

October 3–4. Eighteen U.S. soldiers are killed and 75 wounded during confrontation with Somali guerrilla fighters. **October 7.** President Clinton announces withdrawal of all U.S. troops by March 31, 1994.

October 23. Toronto Blue Jays win second straight World Series, defeating Philadelphia Phillies 4 games to 2.

October 26–November 4. Wildfires rage in southern California, destroying more than 1,000 homes and causing $500 million in damage.

October 27. President Clinton presents a national health care reform plan to Congress. The plan is drafted by a commission led by First Lady Hillary Clinton.

November 11. Women's War Memorial is dedicated in Washington, D.C., honoring 11,500 women who served during the Vietnam War.

November 14. By a narrow margin (48.4 percent to 46.2 percent), voters in Puerto Rico reject statehood and opt to remain a U.S. commonwealth. Only 4.4 percent of voters favor complete independence.

November 17. House of Representatives passes (234 to 200) legislation committing U.S. to NAFTA, despite fierce opposition by many House Democrats. **November 20.** Senate passes measure 61 to 38.

November 30. President Clinton signs Brady Handgun Violence Prevention Act, establishing five-day waiting period and background checks for handgun purchasers.

December 4–13. U.S. astronauts repair Hubble Space Telescope. Within weeks, the telescope begins transmitting groundbreaking images of deep space.

December 14. U.S. and European negotiators reach compromise on General Agreement on Tariffs and Trade (GATT) to reduce tariffs and set new regulations.

December 15. Secretary of Defense Les Aspin resigns after heavy criticism of his handling of the Somalia relief mission and stormy relationship with armed forces.

1994

January 14. U.S., Russia, and Ukraine sign agreement to turn over Ukraine's Soviet-era nuclear weapons to Russia in exchange for fuel and security guarantees.

January 17. Earthquake measuring 6.8 on the Richter scale hits Los Angeles, destroying highway overpasses and buildings and killing 61 people. Hundreds of thousands of residents lose electricity and water.

January 30. In Super Bowl rematch, Dallas Cowboys defeat Buffalo Bills 30–13 in Super Bowl XXVIII.

February 3. President Clinton ends trade embargo of Vietnam. Diplomatic relations are not officially restored, but each country opens a liaison office in the other's capital.

February 12. U.S. Olympic Committee allows figure skater Tonya Harding to participate in the games at Lillehammer, Nor., despite the involvement of her associates in an attack on fellow U.S. skater Nancy Kerrigan.

February 22. Federal agents arrest former CIA official Aldrich Ames on charges of passing information about U.S. agents to U.S.S.R. and Russia. The incident raises serious questions about CIA management. **December 28.** CIA director R. James Woolsey, Jr., resigns.

March 4. Federal jury in New York convicts four Arab immigrants of bombing the World Trade Center in February 1993 and of plotting to destroy other New York landmarks.

March 25. Last U.S. troops withdraw from Somalia relief mission. The operation has eased famine, but political instability hinders further humanitarian efforts.

April 22. Former President Richard M. Nixon dies from a stroke in a New York City hospital. President Clinton and the four surviving former Presidents attend the funeral in Yorba Linda, Calif., five days later.

April 28. International Brotherhood of Teamsters ends longest strike in its history. The strike began April 6, provoked by trucking companies' use of low-wage, part-time, nonunion drivers to cut costs.

May 6. In the first-ever civil suit against a sitting President, former Arkansas state employee Paula Jones files a sexual harassment suit against President Clinton, alleging improper sexual advances while he was governor.

May 25. Images sent by Hubble Space Telescope indicate the presence of black holes in space, proving Albert Einstein's theory of relativity. Scientists long assumed the existence of black holes but without evidence.

May 26. President Clinton extends China's most-favored-nation trade status for one year despite lack of progress in human rights and announces that future human rights questions would not affect trade status.

June 17. Los Angeles police charge former football player O. J. Simpson with two counts of first degree murder. Before turning himself in, Simpson leads authorities on a slow-speed chase that is watched by nearly 100 million Americans live on television.

July 26. Congressional hearings begin on Whitewater affair, investigating the involvement of President Clinton and his wife, Hillary, in financial and real-estate dealings in Arkansas in 1980s.

August 12. Federal jury in Anchorage awards Alaskan fishermen nearly $300 million for damages suffered as a result of the 1989 *Exxon Valdez* oil spill in Prince William Sound. The money goes to Alaskan fishermen claiming losses from environmental disaster. **September 16.** Exxon is fined $5 billion in punitive damages.

August 19. In order to head off mass exodus, President Clinton announces Cuban refugees will no longer be granted automatic asylum in U.S.

September 9. U.S. and Cuba reach agreement on refugee policy. U.S. will accept 20,000 Cubans a year, and Cuba will take steps to halt illegal immigrants.

September 14. For the first time since 1904, the World Series is canceled after players' strike ends 1994 baseball season.

September 26. In a major defeat for President Clinton, Senate Majority Leader George Mitchell announces that Congress will not pass any national health care plan in the current session.

September 29. Pan American Health Organization announces the eradication of polio in the Western Hemisphere, although an average of 120,000 cases occur annually in developing countries elsewhere.

October 4. U.S. and China agree on stricter prohibition of the sale of missile technology. U.S. lifts ban on high-tech sales to China imposed after alleged sale of missile parts to Pakistan.

October 7. Responding to a large buildup of Iraqi forces near Kuwaiti border, President Clinton dispatches additional ships, planes, and troops to Persian Gulf. **October 11.** Iraqi forces begin withdrawal.

October 19. *The Bell Curve: Intelligence and Class Structure in American Life,* by Harvard professor Richard Herrnstein and social scientist Charles Murray, is published, sparking angry national debate over alleged correlation between race and intelligence.

October 21. U.S. and North Korea sign agreement to dismantle North Korea's nuclear program. In exchange, U.S. agrees to supply oil and oversee the construction of some light-water nuclear power plants.

November 8. In a stunning upset, Republicans win control of both houses of Congress for the first time in 40 years and claim 11 governorships. The victory was orchestrated by minority whip Newt Gingrich, who authored the campaign's manifesto "Contract with America."

December 8. President Clinton signs Uruguay Round of GATT, a 125-nation treaty establishing World Trade Organization (WTO) to regulate international trade, approved by U.S. negotiators eight months earlier.

December 11. Leaders from 34 Western-Hemisphere countries in meeting in Miami, Fla., approve formation of Free Trade Area of the Americas by 2005. NAFTA is to be incorporated into the trade zone.

December 17. North Korea shoots down a U.S. reconnaissance helicopter that strays into its airspace during training exercises, killing one soldier and capturing one other. **December 22.** After initially refusing to discuss the situation, North Korean officials turn over the remains of the soldier killed. **December 30.** North Korea releases the captured soldier.

December 20. Former President Jimmy Carter announces cease-fire in Bosnia and Herzegovina. The agreement allows UN peacekeepers and relief workers to remain.

1995

January 3. WHO announces that there are more than one million AIDS cases worldwide. U.S. cases account for 9 percent of total.

January 13. Under a provision of the Endangered Species Act, eight gray wolves are released into Yellowstone National Park, despite widespread opposition from ranchers.

January 29. San Francisco 49ers defeat San Diego Chargers 49–26 to win Super Bowl XXIX.

February 3. President Clinton proposes raising national minimum wage to $5.15 over two years. Republicans and business leaders vigorously oppose the measure.

February 4. U.S. trade representative announces 100 percent tariff on all Chinese imports unless Chinese government takes action to end pirating of U.S. publications, software, and recordings. **February 15.** China complies with U.S. demand.

February 17. Citing stagnant economies in Europe and Japan, Commerce Department announces U.S. trade deficit has increased 42 percent from 1993 to $108.1 billion.

February 24. Russian officials refuse to back out of $1 billion deal to build four nuclear reactors in Iran despite threats from members of Congress to end economic aid to Russia.

March 14. Norman Thagard becomes first U.S. astronaut to fly into space on a Russian or Soviet rocket. The joint U.S.-Russia mission ends nearly 40 years of competition for dominance in space.

March 22. President Clinton signs a law prohibiting the federal government from requiring states to enforce high-cost laws or regulations without providing necessary funds. The law effectively ends use of "unfunded mandates."

April 19. A homemade bomb explodes outside Alfred P. Murrah Federal Building in Oklahoma City, Okla., killing 168, including 19 children in the building's day-care center. **August 10.** Federal grand jury indicts antigovernment militants Timothy McVeigh and Terry Nichols.

May 8. President Clinton suspends all U.S. trade with Iran in response to evidence that Iran supports international terrorism and is trying to acquire nuclear weapons.

May 11. Representatives of 174 countries agree to extend indefinitely Nuclear Non-proliferation Treaty, prohibiting nonnuclear states from developing nuclear weapons.

May 22. In *U.S. Term Limits Inc.* v. *Thornton,* U.S. Supreme Court strikes down (5 to 4) Arkansas' state-imposed term limits for members of Congress. The ruling effectively voids term-limit laws in 23 states.

June 12. U.S. Supreme Court rules (5 to 4) in *Adarand Constructors* v. *Pena* that federal programs cannot classify people by race when implementing programs or hiring contractors. The ruling curtails use of affirmative action.

June 29. In *Miller* v. *Johnson,* U.S. Supreme Court rules void (5 to 4) Georgia electoral district drawn to create a majority-black district, declaring race cannot be used as "predominant factor" in creating electoral districts.

July 11. U.S. reestablishes full diplomatic relations with Vietnam. Veterans groups oppose the move, as do many conservative Republicans in Congress.

July 20. University of California Board of Regents votes to end use of affirmative action policies in admission of students.

July 31. Walt Disney announces merger with Capital Cities/ABC television, sparking fears of media concentration in only a few companies.

August 11. Former presidential candidate Ross Perot hosts convention in Dallas, Texas, attended by major politicians of both parties and 3,000 members of United We Stand America, his nascent third party.

August 17. A federal grand jury indicts James and Susan McDougal and Arkansas Governor Jim Guy Tucker on fraud and conspiracy charges. McDougals had been partners with President and Hillary Clinton in Whitewater Development Corp.

August 18. Shannon Faulkner, first female cadet at the Citadel in Charleston, S.C., withdraws five days after enrolling. Faulkner had fought two-year legal battle to join public, all-male military academy.

August 24. Software giant Microsoft releases Windows 95, a new operating system. Despite difficulty interfacing with older systems, the program sells between 18 and 20 million copies by the end of year.

September 1. Rock and Roll Hall of Fame, designed by architect I. M. Pei, opens in Cleveland, Ohio, with exhibits on more than 120 performers.

September 7. After a 33-month investigation into charges of sexual harassment, influence peddling, and obstructing justice, Oregon Senator Bob Packwood resigns rather than face an expulsion vote.

September 22. Time Warner announces a merger with Turner Broadcasting System, creating the largest mass media company in the world. The merger intensifies concern over concentrated ownership of media.

October 1. Sheikh ʿUmar ʿAbd al-Raḥmān and nine others are convicted in New York federal court of bombing World Trade Center and other conspiracy charges.

October 16. Hundreds of thousands of African American men participate in the "Million Man March" in Washington, D.C. The rally, which promoted family and community responsibility, was organized by controversial Nation of Islam leader Louis Farrakhan.

October 28. Atlanta Braves win World Series, defeating Cleveland Indians 4 games to 2.

November 4. Israeli Prime Minister Rabin is assassinated by Israeli extremist opposed to his peace efforts with Arabs. The hardline Likud party comes to power less than a year later.

November 13. Two explosions outside a military training center in Riyadh kill seven, including five Americans. The bombings were likely carried out by Islamic radicals opposed to U.S. presence in Saudi Arabia.

December 1. Massive defense bill becomes law without President Clinton's signature. Clinton initially threatened to veto the $243.3 billion appropriation but wanted congressional funding for deployment of U.S. troops to Bosnia and Herzegovina.

December 14. Bosnian civil war ends with Paris Peace Agreement. The accord's provisions include a contingent of 20,000 U.S. troops as part of a NATO peacekeeping force.

December 31. Republican and Democratic negotiators fail to reach a budget agreement, resulting in the shutdown of U.S. agencies for second time since November.

1996

January 6. Compromise between President Clinton and Congress ends the budget stalemate, and government employees return to work. Clinton agrees to balance the budget with smaller tax cuts.

January 26. Senate approves START II with a vote of 87 to 4. The agreement commits U.S. and Russia to reducing nuclear weapons stockpiles dramatically.

January 28. Dallas Cowboys win Super Bowl XXX, defeating Pittsburgh Steelers 27–17.

February 8. President Clinton signs Telecommunications Act. The law bans the transmission of "indecent" material over computer networks and requires that a "v-chip" be installed in new U.S.-manufactured televisions to screen objectionable programs.

February 20. Conservative columnist Pat Buchanan wins the New Hampshire Republican primary, defeating front-runner Senator Bob Dole.

February 25. In the worst bombing in 20 years, radical Palestinian group Hamas bombs an Israeli bus in West Jerusalem, killing 26 civilians. Suicide bombings continue sporadically over the next five years.

March 7. Japanese court convicts three U.S. soldiers stationed in Okinawa of the rape of a 12-year-old girl in 1995. The event increases pressure from Japanese civilians for U.S. military withdrawal.

March 12. In retaliation for Cuba's February 24 downing of two unarmed planes owned by a Cuban exile group, President Clinton signs legislation tightening the U.S. embargo. The European Union, Canada, and Mexico protest the embargo.

March 22. United Auto Workers vote to end the strike against General Motors (GM). The union had protested outsourcing of machine work to foreign companies. Though outsourcing issue remains unsettled, GM agrees to reduce required overtime and pay each worker $1,700.

April 3. Ted Kaczynski is arrested for "Unabomber" killings, ending the 17-year string of bombings. Authorities were led to Kaczynski after his brother recognized the antitechnology screed published by *The Washington Post.*

April 10. President Clinton vetoes so-called "partial-birth abortion" ban, drawing criticism from conservatives and pro-life groups. Clinton defends the position noting the procedure was performed only in instances of serious medical problems.

May 28. President Clinton's former partners James and Susan McDougal and Arkansas Governor Jim Guy Tucker are convicted of fraud and conspiracy on charges stemming from Whitewater affair.

May 29. Capitalizing on fear generated by recent bombings, Benjamin Netanyahu narrowly defeats Israeli Prime Minister Shimon Peres on a platform of public security and slowing negotiations with Palestinians.

June 5. It is revealed that White House employees requested security files on leading Republicans from the FBI in efforts to uncover potentially incriminating information for the fall campaigns.

June 18. Senate committee investigating Whitewater issues two final reports, one by Democrats exonerating President Clinton, another by Republicans accusing Clinton of abuse of power.

June 20. U.S. Census Bureau reports that gap between the richest 20 percent and rest of U.S. population has reached highest point since end of World War II.

June 25. Truck bomb explodes outside U.S. military complex in Saudi Arabia, killing 19 U.S. soldiers and injuring hundreds of others.

June 26. Supreme Court rules 7 to 1 that state-supported Virginia Military Institute's refusal to enroll female students violates equal-protection clause of 14th Amendment.

July 19. Food and Drug Administration (FDA) panel recommends approval of controversial "abortion pill," RU-486.

July 27. Pipe bomb explodes on the grounds of the Olympic Games in Atlanta, Ga., killing one person and injuring 111 others. The media report security guard Richard Jewell, who had found the bomb, as the chief suspect, but he is later exonerated.

August 9. In an unprecedented decision, a Florida jury finds tobacco company Brown & Williamson Tobacco liable for a smoker who developed lung cancer and orders $750,000 payment in damages.

August 15. Former Senator Robert Dole accepts the Republican presidential nomination in San Diego, Calif. Former Secretary of Housing and Urban Development Jack Kemp is selected as his running mate.

August 22. President Clinton signs bill overhauling welfare system. The legislation establishes work requirements and replaces direct federal payments to individuals with grants to states.

August 27. California Governor Pete Wilson signs an executive order banning state agencies from providing certain benefits to illegal aliens. Illegal aliens are still able to attend primary and secondary schools and receive emergency medical treatment.

August 29. President Clinton and Vice President Al Gore are renominated by the Democratic National Convention in Chicago.

September 21. President Clinton reluctantly signs Defense of Marriage Act, prohibiting federal recognition and federal benefits to partners in same-sex marriages. Congress passed the legislation in anticipation of legalization of same-sex marriage in Hawaii.

1997

October 12. Tens of thousands of Latinos rally at Latino and Immigrants' Rights March in Washington, D.C., in protest of immigration restrictions and discrimination against illegal immigrants.

October 18. Democratic National Committee suspends its chief financial officer for allegedly soliciting illegal campaign contributions from foreign nationals. The party returns $250,000 gift from a South Korean company.

October 26. New York Yankees defeat Atlanta Braves 4 games to 2 to win World Series.

November 5. President Clinton wins reelection over former Senator Bob Dole and Reform Party candidate Ross Perot, capturing 49.2 percent of popular vote and 379 electoral votes. Republicans retain control of both houses of Congress.

November 7. U.S. Army officials announce widespread investigation of alleged sexual assault and harassment at military bases.

November 15. Texaco settles discrimination lawsuit brought by 1,400 African American employees in 1994 for $176.1 million after incriminating audiotape surfaces of company executives discussing destruction of evidence.

November 19. U.S. vetoes second term for UN Secretary-General Boutros Boutros-Ghali, citing his lack of leadership and slow pace of reform.

December 15. U.S. aerospace giant Boeing announces purchase of military aircraft manufacturer McDonnell Douglas, creating largest airplane manufacturing company in world.

December 27. Dow Jones Industrial Average closes at record 6560.91. On average for the year, the Dow gained 26 percent over the previous year, continuing recent stock market boom.

January 21. House of Representatives reprimands Speaker Newt Gingrich for ethics violations and imposes a fine of $300,000.

January 23. Former UN Ambassador Madeleine Albright is sworn in as Secretary of State, becoming the first woman to hold the most senior cabinet post.

January 26. Green Bay Packers win Super Bowl XXXI, defeating New England Patriots 35–21.

February 5. Investment bank Morgan Stanley and brokerage firm Dean Witter announce merger, forming $24 billion company.

February 6. Following a pledge made during his February 4 state of the union address, President Clinton submits a 1998 budget that balances federal budget by 2002.

February 12. Proposed constitutional amendment establishing term limits for members of Congress dies in House of Representatives. Supreme Court previously voided state laws setting term limits.

February 20. U.S. National Institutes of Health panel reports medical benefits of marijuana for seriously ill patients. The announcement fuels movement to legalize medicinal use of marijuana.

March 3. In response to Scottish scientists' cloning of a sheep, President Clinton bans federal funding for human cloning research.

March 11. Senate approves wide investigation into alleged campaign fund-raising irregularities by White House and congressional Democrats.

March 20. President Clinton meets with Russian President Yeltsin in Helsinki to discuss expansion of NATO to incorporate Eastern European countries.

April 7. Classical and jazz performer and composer Wynton Marsalis' opera *Blood on the Fields* wins Pulitzer Prize for music, becoming first jazz composition to win a Pulitzer.

April 19. Widespread flooding along Red River begins, causing damage in upper plains states and central Canada.

April 21. In *Blessing* v. *Freestone,* U.S. Supreme Court rules unanimously that a group of Arizona women could not sue the state for not adequately enforcing federal child-support laws. The ruling sets a precedent by exempting states from enforcing federal laws.

April 24. Senate approves Chemical Weapons Convention, prohibiting the use of poison gas as weapon. The treaty goes into effect five days later.

May 2. Franklin D. Roosevelt Memorial opens in Washington, D.C., after controversy over whether the paralyzed president should be depicted in wheelchair.

May 11. Chess champion Garry Kasparov loses a match to IBM computer program Deep Blue.

May 16. President Clinton formally apologizes to group of African Americans used without their knowledge as test subjects in government research on syphilis in Tuskegee, Ala., between 1932 and 1972.

June 2. Timothy McVeigh is convicted on murder charges for the Oklahoma City bombing. **August 14.** McVeigh is sentenced to death. **December 23.** Codefendant Terry Nichols is convicted of involuntary manslaughter and conspiracy.

June 26. Declaring them in violation of First Amendment protections of free speech, U.S. Supreme Court unanimously overturns portions of Communications Decency Act that banned Internet pornography. The ruling is the first related to free-speech issues and Internet.

July 4. Unmanned U.S. spacecraft *Pathfinder* lands on Mars on mission to record atmospheric data and send images of the red planet back to Earth.

July 8. NATO invites former Soviet satellites Poland, Hungary, and the Czech Republic to join. Russia had resisted such efforts but relented after negotiations in May.

Senate hearings into Democratic fund-raising efforts open to investigate alleged violations by President Clinton and Vice President Gore. **October 31.** Hearings end after no evidence is uncovered.

July 30. Dow Jones Industrial Average hits record 8254.89, fueled by low interest rates and low unemployment.

August 5. Congress and President Clinton implement plan to balance federal budget by 2002. The plan includes cuts in entitlements and discretionary spending.

August 30. Houston Comets defeat New York Liberty 65–51 in first championship game of the Women's National Basketball Association.

September 17. Representatives of 100 countries meeting in Oslo, Nor., adopt a preliminary treaty outlawing the production and use of land mines. **December 3.** The formal signing begins, though without U.S. support.

September 29. FDA approves Combivir, an AIDS medication combining drugs AZT and 3TC.

October 4. Promise Keepers, an evangelical Christian men's organization, attracts hundreds of thousands of participants at rally on National Mall in Washington, D.C.

October 26. Florida Marlins defeat Cleveland Indians in World Series, 4 games to 3.

November 10. Worldcom acquires MCI for $36.5 billion, creating the world's second largest communications company.

December 1. UN meeting on global warming begins in Kyoto, Japan. Delegates adopt first treaty imposing limits on greenhouse gases.

December 11. In response to antitrust charges, a federal judge orders Microsoft to sell its operating system and Internet browser software separately.

1998

January 17. President Clinton is deposed by lawyers representing Paula Jones in a sexual harassment suit, becoming first-ever President to be defendant in civil suit while in office. **November 13.** Clinton agrees to $850,000 settlement.

January 25. Denver Broncos upset Green Bay Packers 31–24 to win Super Bowl XXXII.

January 26. In national television address, President Clinton denies ever having sexual relations with White House intern Monica Lewinsky. Lawyers for Paula Jones had raised the question when deposing the president.

January 28. Justice Department begins handing down indictments in its investigation of 1996 Democratic campaign finance irregularities. Fourteen people are eventually indicted, though Attorney General Janet Reno refuses to appoint independent counsel to investigate President Clinton or Vice President Gore.

February 22. UN announces agreement brokered by Secretary-General Kofi Annan to permit weapons inspectors to return to Iraq.

March 19. Major League Baseball owners approve Australian media baron Rupert Murdoch's purchase of Los Angeles Dodgers for $311 million.

March 24. Police in Jonesboro, Ark., arrest two boys for opening fire on students and teachers during fire alarm. Four people are killed and 11 wounded.

March 27. FDA approves Viagra, a prescription anti-impotency drug manufactured by Pfizer. The drug quickly becomes best-seller.

April 6. Citicorp Bank and Travelers Group Insurance announce a $70 billion merger.

April 27. U.S. Surgeon General David Satcher announces a report on tobacco use among minority groups with evidence that Native Americans are unusually vulnerable to nicotine.

May 11. SBC Communications announces the planned purchase of Ameritech to create the largest local telephone provider in U.S.

May 18. Alleging unfair competition, Justice Department files antitrust lawsuits against Microsoft.

June 8. Norwest bank, based in Minneapolis, Minn., and San Francisco-based Wells Fargo announce merger. The new company will have $191 billion in assets.

June 10. In major victory for school voucher programs, the Wisconsin Supreme Court rules the city of Milwaukee may use tax revenue to support students at private schools. The ruling boosts advocates for government sponsorship of private education.

June 25. In *Clinton* v. *City of New York*, U.S. Supreme Court strikes down (6 to 3) Line Item Veto Act. The law had allowed the President to veto only parts of appropriation and entitlement bills.

July 1. NBA officials lock out players during labor dispute. Eventually, the first two months of the season are canceled.

July 24. Gunman opens fire in U.S. Capitol, killing two security officers before being shot to death.

July 25. Independent counsel Kenneth Starr issues subpoena to President Clinton to testify before a federal grand jury about his relationship with White House intern Monica Lewinsky.

August 7. Two bombs explode simultaneously outside U.S. embassies in Tanzania and Kenya, killing hundreds. U.S. charges Muslim fundamentalist Osama bin Laden and his al-Qaeda terrorist network with the attacks. **August 20.** In retaliation for the bombings, President Clinton orders strikes against terrorist training camps in Afghanistan and The Sudan.

August 17. Eleven days after Monica Lewinsky admits sexual relationship with President Clinton, Clinton tells a national television audience that he "misled" investigators about affair.

August 27. Russian financial problems shock world markets and cause the Dow Jones Industrial Average to drop almost 20 percent.

September 9. Kenneth Starr releases massive report on Whitewater investigation. **September 11.** The Starr Report, which includes grounds for impeachment, is made public and becomes best-seller because of salacious detail.

September 30. For the first time in 29 years, buoyed by the booming economy, the federal government ends fiscal year with a budget surplus.

October 8. Congress votes to hold hearings on impeachment proceedings against President Clinton. **November 19.** Hearings begin.

October 21. New York Yankees complete 4-game sweep of San Diego Padres to win World Series.

November 3. Democrats gain seats in House of Representatives, but Republicans maintain a slim majority. **November 6.** Speaker Newt Gingrich resigns because of his party's losses.

November 6. U.S. scientists report they have isolated and produced human embryonic stem cells for cancer research. The report creates controversy over use of embryonic cells for research.

November 15. Hours before air and missile strikes are scheduled to begin, Iraqi President Saddam Hussein agrees to cooperate with UN weapons inspectors.

November 20. Tobacco companies sign settlement projected to exceed $200 billion with 46 states suing to recover medical expenses for smoking-related illnesses.

December 1. In the largest business merger, Exxon and Mobil agree to $80 billion coupling.

December 16. U.S. and U.K. launch air attacks against Iraq after Saddam Hussein refuses to comply with UN demands for weapons inspections.

December 19. House of Representatives impeaches President Clinton on charges of perjury and obstructing justice for denying under oath an extramarital affair with White House intern Monica Lewinsky.

1999

January 6. Dennis Hastert, Republican representative from Illinois, is elected Speaker of House of Representatives.

January 19. Defense lawyers for President Clinton forcefully deny charges that he committed perjury or obstructed justice in the Whitewater investigation.

January 31. Denver Broncos win second straight title, defeating Atlanta Falcons 34–19 in Super Bowl XXXIII.

February 12. In near party-line vote, the Senate acquits President Clinton of perjury and obstruction charges stemming from the Monica Lewinsky sex scandal.

February 13. President Clinton announces the participation of 4,000 U.S. troops in the NATO peacekeeping force in Kosovo.

March 12. Former Soviet allies Poland, Hungary, and the Czech Republic join NATO.

March 24. NATO forces begin a bombing campaign against Yugoslavia, ending Yugoslav efforts to drive ethnic Albanians from the Serbian province of Kosovo. **June 3.** NATO and Yugoslavia agree to peace terms.

March 29. Dow Jones Industrial Average breaks 10,000 for first time.

March 31. Four New York City police officers are indicted on murder charges for shooting unarmed black immigrant Amadou Diallo. The officers, who had fired 41 shots, claimed they believed Diallo had a gun.

April 5. UN ends sanctions against Libya after two defendants in Pan Am Flight 103 bombing arrive at international court in The Netherlands.

April 20. In the worst-ever school shooting, two students open fire on classmates and teachers at Columbine High School in Colorado, killing 13 and wounding 21 more.

April 22. Largest U.S. telecommunications company AT&T announces plans to purchase cable television giant MediaOne Group.

May 12. Treasury Secretary Robert Rubin announces his resignation. **July 1.** Senate confirms deputy secretary Lawrence H. Summers as Rubin's replacement.

May 21. Yah Lin "Charlie" Trie pleads guilty to illegal fund-raising efforts on behalf of President Clinton and other Democrats. Trie's activities spur a movement for campaign finance reform.

June 23. In three 5-to-4 decisions, the U.S. Supreme Court limits the ability of citizens to sue states for noncompliance with federal laws. The rulings are latest in ongoing battle over states' rights.

June 30. Facing public frustration at overzealous and partisan prosecutors, Congress allows Independent Counsel Act to expire. Appointment of special prosecutors reverts to Justice Department.

July 10. U.S. soccer team defeats China to win Women's World Cup.

August 11. Kansas Board of Education eliminates all references to theory of evolution from state science curriculum.

August 17. Closely following previously successful disarmament talks, U.S. and Russia begin discussion of another strategic arms limitation treaty (START III).

September 4. Center on Budget and Policy releases a study indicating the income gap between rich and poor in U.S. is at greatest level since 1977.

September 7. In the largest media merger in history, Viacom announces plans to purchase CBS for $36 billion.

September 14. House of Representatives passes major campaign finance reform bill. **October 19.** Conservative opposition kills the bill in the Senate.

September 17. After North Korea agrees to end ballistic missile tests, U.S. reduces economic sanctions.

October 5. In largest of a string of recent media mergers, telecommunications giants MCI Worldcom and Sprint announce $115 billion merger.

October 13. Senate rejects (51–48) ratification of Comprehensive Nuclear Test Ban Treaty, which prohibits all nuclear weapons testing.

October 27. New York Yankees sweep Atlanta Braves to win World Series.

November 5. Federal judge rules that software company Microsoft has used its monopoly power to hinder competition.

November 12. President Clinton signs the Financial Services Modernization Act, eliminating barriers between the banking and securities industries. The act repeals the Glass-Steagall Act, which was passed during the Great Depression to prevent bank failures in the wake of the stock market crash.

November 14. UN imposes economic sanctions on Afghanistan after its fundamentalist Islamic Taliban government refuses to hand over suspect Osama bin Laden, wanted in connection with bombings in Africa.

President Clinton and Congress reach agreement to pay U.S. back dues to UN with the understanding that no U.S. funds will go to organizations supporting abortion rights.

November 30. Tens of thousands of activists protest WTO meeting in Seattle, Wash. Demonstrations display the growing alliance between labor and environmentalist groups.

December 10. Los Alamos nuclear scientist Wen Ho Lee is indicted on 59 counts of misuse of classified information as part of an investigation into alleged Chinese espionage. Wen is later exonerated of all but one charge.

December 20. Vermont Supreme Court orders legislature to grant homosexual couples same benefits held by married couples.

December 31. Honoring terms of 1977 treaty, U.S. turns over full control of the Panama Canal to Panama.

2000

January 1. Fears of widespread systems failures because of Y2K computer glitch prove unfounded as the new year arrives without major disruptions.

January 5. INS orders return of 6-year-old Cuban refugee orphan Elian Gonzalez. **April 22.** Agents seize Gonzalez from his Miami relatives.

January 10. Internet services provider America Online announces $165 billion acquisition of Time Warner, forming fourth largest company in the world.

January 30. St. Louis Rams defeat Tennessee Titans 23–16 to win Super Bowl XXXIV.

January 31. After numerous death-row exonerations and questions over racial disparity, Illinois Governor George Ryan orders moratorium on state executions.

February 1. In surprise defeat for Texas Governor George W. Bush, Arizona Senator John McCain wins New Hampshire Republican presidential primary.

February 6. First Lady Hillary Clinton announces candidacy for U.S. Senate seat being vacated by New York's Daniel Patrick Moynihan.

March 2. Federal jury convicts Democratic fund-raiser Maria Hsia of violating federal laws during 1996 campaign, including disguising donations above the limit for individuals.

March 7. Voters in California approve a

measure banning same-sex marriages. More than 30 states already have such laws.

March 16. Independent counsel Robert Ray announces no evidence of wrongdoing against Clinton White House's use of FBI files of Republican officials. **September 20.** Ray ends Whitewater investigation.

April 26. Vermont governor Howard Dean signs first state law recognizing same-sex "civil unions." The law provides homosexual couples with the same basic rights enjoyed by married couples.

May 4. Two hundred protestors are arrested on Puerto Rican island of Vieques, ending a year-long demonstration against naval bombing range.

May 14. Hundreds of thousands of women gather in Washington, D.C., for "Million Mom March," promoting gun-control legislation.

June 7. Washington, D.C., federal judge Thomas P. Jackson orders Microsoft split into two separate companies after finding it violated antitrust laws. Jackson sets October 7 as deadline for separation.

June 12. Columbia University study questions application of death penalty in U.S., reporting that two-thirds of death-row appeals between 1973 and 1995 resulted in not-guilty verdicts or reduced sentences.

June 25. Consumer activist and 1996 presidential candidate Ralph Nader accepts Green Party nomination for President, angering Democrats who fear Nader will throw close election to Bush.

June 28. In *Boy Scouts of America* v. *Dale,* U.S. Supreme Court rules (5 to 4) that Boy Scouts may ban homosexual troop leaders, reversing New Jersey Supreme Court decision. Gay advocacy groups argue that ruling will allow similar organizations to discriminate.

July 8. Leaders of Evangelical Lutheran Church in America and Episcopal Church approve alliance between two denominations, recognizing each other's sacraments and clergy.

July 14. In a class-action lawsuit, a Florida jury assesses $144.8 billion judgment against five tobacco companies found to have knowingly marketed harmful products.

July 25. Governor George Bush announces selection of former Defense Secretary Dick Cheney as running mate. **August 3.** Bush formally accepts Republican presidential nomination at convention in Philadelphia.

August 9. Bridgestone/Firestone, Inc., announce recall of 6.5 million tires used on sport-utility vehicles and trucks; tires are blamed for accidents resulting in 88 deaths.

August 12. Reform Party convention ends in disputed nomination. **September 12.** Federal Election Commission declares conservative columnist Pat Buchanan the Reform Party's official nominee.

August 16. Montana Governor Marc Racicot declares the entire state a disaster area as wildfires burn during the unusually hot and dry summer.

August 17. Vice President Al Gore accepts Democratic presidential nomination in Los Angeles. He selects as running mate Senator Joseph Lieberman, who becomes the first Jewish candidate on a major party presidential ticket.

September 13. Chase Manhattan, the country's third largest bank, announces purchase of J. P. Morgan, the fifth largest bank, creating single financial entity worth $660 billion.

September 28. FDA announces approval of prescription abortion drug RU-486 with strict regulation of its use.

October 10. President Clinton signs legislation permanently establishing normal trade relations with China, despite continued criticism of human rights violations.

October 12. Terrorists bomb USS *Cole* harbored in Yemen port of Aden, killing 17 sailors and injuring 39. Although no group claims credit, attack is widely blamed on radical Islamic terrorists.

October 26. New York Yankees win third straight World Series, defeating New York Mets 4 games to 1 in "Subway Series."

November 7. Television networks announce Republican candidate George W. Bush the winner of the Presidential election, then declare race too close to call. Both Bush and Democrat Al Gore need Florida's 25 electoral votes to be elected. Because the totals are so close and because of charges of voter irregularity and legal challenges by both candidates, there is no clear winner for five weeks.

November 7. Republicans maintain slim majority in House of Representatives, but Senate is evenly split 50–50. First Lady Hillary Clinton becomes first-ever presidential spouse to be elected to public office.

December 12. U.S. Supreme Court halts Florida recount (ordered by the Florida Supreme Court), effectively electing Governor Bush. Although Bush wins the electoral vote, Gore wins the popular vote, the first time since 1888 that a president has entered office without at least a plurality of votes.

December 28. President Clinton announces projected budget surplus of $4.996 trillion for decade beginning fiscal year 2002.

December 29. In the first yearly decline since 1990, the Dow Jones Industrial Average drops 6 percent, closing at 10786.85. The slide reinforces the perception that the economy is headed into recession.

2001

January 17. California Governor Gray Davis declares a state of emergency when a power shortage forces the state to implement rolling blackouts. The crisis ends the state's deregulation of energy industry.

January 19. President Clinton agrees to admit that he lied under oath about his relationship with Monica Lewinsky. In exchange, independent counsel Robert Ray drops perjury and obstruction charges.

January 28. Baltimore Ravens defeat New York Giants 34–7 to win Super Bowl XXXV.

February 9. U.S. submarine *Greenville* collides with Japanese fishing vessel near Hawaii, killing nine passengers. It is later revealed that a number of nonmilitary passengers were at the submarine's controls when ships collided.

February 14. U.S. attorneys begin investigation of pardons granted by President Clinton on his last day in office. Clinton granted clemency to fugitive billionaire Marc Rich allegedly in exchange for campaign contributions from his ex-wife.

February 28. Earthquake measuring 6.8 on Richter scale hits the Pacific Northwest, causing billions of dollars in damage.

March 18. President Bush announces his administration will not regulate carbon dioxide emissions from U.S. power plants, angering environmental groups.

March 20. Environmental Protection Agency (EPA) announces an end to the Clinton Administration's reductions in the permissible level of arsenic in drinking water. **October 31.** EPA reverses the decision and agrees to implement the Clinton Administration's levels.

April 1. U.S. spy plane collides with a Chinese fighter jet over South China Sea; Chinese authorities detain crew for 11 days.

April 2. Senate passes McCain-Feingold campaign finance reform bill, which dies in the House of Representatives July 12 when Republican leaders refuse to bring it to a vote.

May 4. U.S. economy continues to worsen as Labor Department announces 223,000 jobs were lost in April.

May 10. FBI announces discovery of Oklahoma City bombing evidence never turned over to Timothy McVeigh's defense attorneys. McVeigh's execution is delayed by Attorney General John Ashcroft for one month. **June 11.** McVeigh is executed, becoming first federal prisoner executed since 1963.

May 17. Bush Administration releases plan to deal with energy crisis, calling for additional oil exploration, renewed nuclear power production, and conservation. Report becomes controversial when Vice President Cheney refuses to release the names of those who helped draft the policy.

June 5. Democrats regain control of Senate by one vote when Vermont Senator James Jeffords leaves the Republican Party. Senator Tom Daschle of South Dakota becomes majority leader.

June 7. President Bush signs $1.35 trillion tax cut that includes gradual elimination of estate tax. Democrats charge that the cut overwhelmingly favors only the wealthiest Americans.

June 20. Accounting firm Arthur Andersen settles fraud suit brought by Securities and Exchange Commission for $7 million (the largest-ever fine against an accounting firm) in relation to its audits of Waste Management.

June 28. U.S. Court of Appeals reverses lower court ruling that split Microsoft into two companies. **November 2.** Justice Department and Microsoft reach settlement.

July 6. In another blow to U.S. intelligence agencies, FBI agent Robert Hanssen pleads guilty to 15 counts of espionage on behalf of U.S.S.R. and Russia.

July 23. Representatives from 178 countries agree to accept Kyoto Protocol limiting production of greenhouse gasses. U.S. angers signatories by announcing its withdrawal from the treaty.

August 9. In a live television address, President Bush announces he will allow federal money to be used for continued research with embryonic stem cells, but he limits research to those cells already in existence.

August 22. Furthering concern over U.S. economy, the Bush Administration announces the budget surplus will evaporate over coming years.

September 11. In worst act of terrorism in U.S. history, two hijacked commercial jetliners destroy World Trade Center in New York City, another damages the Pentagon outside Washington, D.C., and a fourth crashes in Pennsylvania. More than 3,000 people are killed. **September 12.** Federal authorities link attacks to Islamic extremist Osama bin Laden and al-Qaeda terrorist network. **September 20.** President Bush pledges before Congress to attack Afghanistan unless the Taliban regime turns over bin Laden.

September 21. Congress passes legislation to aid the airline industry after the September 11 attacks and to establish a fund for victims of attacks.

October 5. Florida editor dies of anthrax, the first of five anthrax-induced deaths. Anthrax-laden letters arrive at NBC and CBS news offices in New York City and at Capitol Hill offices. The scare recedes in December, but FBI officials make little progress in investigation.

October 7. U.S. and British forces launch assault on Afghanistan to topple Taliban regime and capture Osama bin Laden.

November 13. Afghan Northern Alliance troops and allies capture Kabul.

October 26. President Bush signs antiterrorism bill expanding power of government to investigate suspected terrorists. **November 19.** Bush signs bill federalizing airport security.

November 4. Arizona Diamondbacks upset heavily favored New York Yankees to win World Series 4 games to 3.

November 28. President Bush announces the federal government in 2002 will run first budget deficit in five years, furthering concern over the economy.

December 1–2. Palestinian suicide bombings kill 25 Israelis. Prime Minister Ariel Sharon breaks off relations with Palestinian leader Yāsir ʿArafāt.

December 2. Enron, world's largest energy trader, files the largest-ever U.S. bankruptcy. Subsequent investigation reveals illegal accounting practices enriched executives at expense of stockholders and employees.

John Walker Lindh, an American expatriate fighting with Taliban forces in Afghanistan, is taken into U.S. custody.

December 12. Federal grand jury indicts French national Zacarias Moussaoui, the alleged "20th Hijacker," on charges of participating in the planning of the September 11 attacks.

December 13. President Bush announces U.S. will withdraw from 1972 Antiballistic Missile Treaty with Russia in order to pursue construction of an antimissile defense shield.

1987

1.

Tower Commission Report on Iran-Contra

The Iran-Contra political scandal that unfolded in late 1986 and 1987 hinged on the U.S. government's sale of weapons to Iran in an attempt to secure the release of American hostages held by Shīʿite terrorists in Lebanon and on the use of the profits from those sales to support the war against the Sandinista government in Nicaragua waged by the so-called Contras, whom President Ronald Reagan characterized as "the moral equivalent of the founding fathers." The first action contravened American neutrality in the Iran-Iraq War and the government's stated policy of refusing to deal with terrorists; the second violated the Boland Amendment, a law passed by Congress in 1984 that banned direct or indirect military aid to the Contras. The question of the administration's (and the President's) awareness of these activities was at the center of joint House-Senate hearings before a nationwide television audience that revealed that a staff member of the National Security Council (NSC), Lieutenant Colonel Oliver North, and his associates had orchestrated the money transfers and raised private funds to support the Contras, then attempted to cover up their efforts. In December 1986, Reagan named respected former Senators John Tower and Edmund Muskie, along with Brent Scowcroft, a longtime adviser on national security, to a Special Review Board (the Tower Commission) to investigate the affair. Their report, released on February 26, 1987, and excerpted below, was far from the indictment of executive complicity proclaimed in some left-liberal publications, but it did both confirm the NSC's arms-for-hostages policy and castigate the Reagan administration for its "management style."

Source: *Report of the President's Special Review Board*, February 26, 1987.

THE ARMS TRANSFERS to Iran and the activities of the NSC staff in support of the Contras are case studies in the perils of policy pursued outside the constraints of orderly process.

The Iran initiative ran directly counter to the Administration's own policies on terrorism, the Iran/Iraq war, and military support to Iran. This inconsistency was never resolved, nor were the consequences of this inconsistency fully considered and provided for. The result taken as a whole was a U.S. policy that worked against itself.

The Board believes that failure to deal adequately with these contradictions resulted in large part from the flaws in the manner in which decisions were made. Established procedures for making national security decisions were ignored. Reviews of the initiative by all the NSC principals were too infrequent. The initiatives were not adequately vetted below the cabinet level. Intelligence resources were underutilized. Applicable legal constraints were not adequately addressed. The whole matter was handled too informally, without adequate written records of what had been considered, discussed, and decided.

This pattern persisted in the implementation of the Iran initiative. The NSC staff assumed direct operational control. The initiative fell within the traditional jurisdictions of the Departments of State, Defense, and CIA. Yet these agencies were largely ignored. Great reliance was placed on a network of private operators and intermediaries. How the initiative was to be carried out never received adequate attention from the NSC principals or a tough working-level review. No periodic evaluation of the progress of the initiative was ever conducted. The result was an unprofessional and, in substantial part, unsatisfactory operation.

In all of this process, Congress was never notified. . . .

FAILURE OF RESPONSIBILITY

The NSC system will not work unless the President makes it work. After all, this system was created to serve the President of the United States in ways of his choosing. By his actions, by his leadership, the President therefore determines the quality of its performance.

By his own account, as evidenced in his diary notes, and as conveyed to the Board by his principal advisors, President Reagan was deeply committed to securing the release of the hostages. It was this intense compassion for the hostages that appeared to motivate his steadfast support of the Iran initiative, even in the face of opposition from his Secretaries of State and Defense.

In his obvious commitment, the President appears to have proceeded with a concept of the initiative that was not accurately reflected in the reality of the operation. The President did not seem to be aware of the way in which the operation was implemented and the full consequences of U.S. participation.

The President's expressed concern for the safety of both the hostages and the Iranians who could have been at risk may have been conveyed in a manner so as to inhibit the full functioning of the system.

The President's management style is to put the principal responsibility for policy review and implementation on the shoulders of his advisors. Nevertheless, with such a complex, high-risk operation and so much at stake, the President should have ensured that the NSC system did not fail him. He did not force his policy to undergo the most critical review of which the NSC participants and the process were capable. At no time did he insist upon accountability and performance review. Had the President chosen to drive the NSC system, the outcome could well have been different. As it was, the most powerful features of the NSC system—providing comprehensive analysis, alternatives and follow-up—were not utilized.

The Board found a strong consensus among NSC participants that the President's priority in the Iran initiative was the release of U.S. hostages. But setting priorities is not enough when it comes to sensitive and risky initiatives that directly affect U.S. national security. He must ensure that the content and tactics of an initiative match his priorities and objectives. He must insist upon accountability. For it is the President who must take responsibility for the NSC system and deal with the consequences.

Beyond the President, the other NSC principals and the National Security Advisor must share in the responsibility for the NSC system.

President Reagan's personal management style places an especially heavy responsibility on his key advisors. Knowing his style, they should have been particularly mindful of the need for special attention to the manner in which this arms sale initiative developed and proceeded. On this score, neither the National Security Advisor nor the other NSC principals deserve high marks.

It is their obligation as members and advisors to the Council to ensure that the President is adequately served. The principal subordinates to the President must not be deterred from urging the President not to proceed on a highly questionable course of action even in the face of his strong conviction to the contrary.

In the case of the Iran initiative, the NSC process did not fail, it simply was largely ignored. The National Security Advisor and the NSC principals all had a duty to raise this issue and insist that orderly process be imposed. None of them did so.

All had the opportunity. While the National Security Advisor had the responsibility to see that an orderly process was observed, his failure to do so does not excuse the other NSC principals. It does not appear that any of the NSC principals called for more frequent consideration of the Iran initiative by the NSC principals in the presence of the President. None of the principals called for a serious vetting of the initiative by even a restricted group of disinterested individuals. The intelligence questions do not appear to have been raised, and legal considerations, while raised, were not pressed. No one seemed to have complained about the informality of the process. No one called for a thorough reexamination once the initiative did not meet expectations or the manner of execution changed. While one or another of the NSC principals suspected that something was amiss, none vigorously pursued the issue.

Mr. Regan also shares in this responsibility. More than almost any Chief of Staff of recent memory, he asserted personal control over the White House staff and sought to extend this control to the National Security Advisor. He was personally active in national security affairs and attended almost all of the relevant meetings regarding the Iran initiative. He, as much as anyone, should have insisted that an orderly process be observed. In addition, he especially should have ensured that plans were made for handling any public disclosure of the initiative. He must bear primary responsibility for the chaos that descended upon the White House when such disclosure did occur.

Mr. McFarlane appeared caught between a President who supported the initiative and the cabinet officers who strongly opposed it. While he made efforts to keep these cabinet officers informed, the Board heard complaints from some that he was not always successful. VADM [Vice Admiral] Poindexter on several occasions apparently sought to exclude NSC principals other than the President from knowledge of the initiative. Indeed, on one or more occasions Secretary Shultz may have been actively misled by VADM Poindexter.

VADM Poindexter also failed grievously on the matter of Contra diversion.

Evidence indicates that VADM Poindexter knew that a diversion occurred, yet he did not take the steps that were required given the gravity of that prospect. He apparently failed to appreciate or ignored the serious legal and political risks presented. His clear obligation was either to investigate the matter or take it to the President—or both. He did neither. Director Casey shared a similar responsibility. Evidence suggests that he received information about the possible diversion of funds to the Contras almost a month before the story broke. He, too, did not move promptly to raise the matter with the President. Yet his responsibility to do so was clear.

The NSC principals other than the President may be somewhat excused by the insufficient attention on the part of the National Security Advisor to the need to keep all the principals fully informed. Given the importance of the issue and the sharp policy divergences involved, however, Secretary Shultz and Secretary Weinberger in particular distanced themselves from the march of events. Secretary Shultz specifically requested to be informed only as necessary to perform his job. Secretary Weinberger had access through intelligence to details about the operation. Their obligation was to give the President their full support and continued advice with respect to the program or, if they could not in conscience do that, to so inform the President. Instead, they simply distanced themselves from the program. They protected the record as to their own positions on this issue. They were not energetic in attempting to protect the President from the consequences of his personal commitment to freeing the hostages.

Director Casey appears to have been informed in considerable detail about the specifics of the Iranian operation. He appears to have acquiesced in and to have encouraged North's exercise of direct operational control over the operation. Because of the NSC staff's proximity to and close identification with the President, this increased the risks to the President if the initiative became public or the operation failed.

There is no evidence, however, that Director Casey explained this risk to the President or made clear to the President that LtCol North, rather than the CIA, was running the operation. The President does not recall ever being informed of this fact. Indeed, Director Casey should have gone further and pressed for operational responsibility to be transferred to the CIA.

Director Casey should have taken the lead in vetting the assumptions presented by the Israelis on which the program was based and in pressing for an early examination of the reliance upon Mr. Ghorbanifar and the second channel as intermediaries. He should also have assumed responsibility for checking out the other intermediaries involved in the operation. Finally, because Congressional restrictions on covert actions are both largely directed at and familiar to the CIA, Director Casey should have taken the lead in keeping the question of Congressional notification active.

Finally, Director Casey, and, to a lesser extent, Secretary Weinberger, should have taken it upon themselves to assess the effect of the transfer of arms and intelligence to Iran on the Iran/Iraq military balance, and to transmit that information to the President. . . .

AFTERMATH—THE EFFORTS TO TELL THE STORY

The Board found evidence that immediately following the public disclosure, the President wanted to avoid providing too much specificity or detail out of concern for the hostages still held in Lebanon and those Iranians who had supported the initiative. In doing so, he did not, we believe, intend to mislead the American public or cover-up unlawful conduct. By at least November 20, the President took steps to ensure that all the facts would come out. From the President's request to Mr. Meese to look into the history of the initiative, to his appointment of this Board, to his request for an Independent Counsel, to his willingness to discuss this matter fully and to review his personal notes with us, the Board is convinced that the President does indeed want the full story to be told.

Those who prepared the President's supporting documentation did not appear, at least initially, to share in the President's ultimate wishes. Mr. McFarlane described for the Board the process used by the NSC staff to create a chronology that obscured essential facts. Mr. McFarlane contributed to the creation of this chronology which did not, he said, present "a full and completely accurate account" of the events and left ambiguous the President's role. This was, according to Mr. McFarlane, done to distance the President from the timing and nature of the President's authorization. He told the Board that he wrote a memorandum on November 18, which tried to, in his own words, "gild the President's motives." This version was incorporated into the chronology. Mr. McFarlane told the Board that he knew the account was "misleading, at least, and wrong, at worst." Mr. McFarlane told the Board that he did provide the Attorney General an accurate account of the President's role.

The Board found considerable reason to question the actions of LtCol North in the aftermath of the disclosure. The Board has no evidence to either confirm or refute that LtCol North destroyed documents on the initiative in an effort to conceal facts from threatened investigations. The Board found indications that LtCol North was involved in an effort, over time, to conceal or withhold important information. The files of LtCol North contained much of the historical documentation that the Board used to construct its narrative. Moreover, LtCol North was the primary U.S. government official involved in the details of the operation. The chronology he produced has many inaccuracies. These "histories" were to be the basis of the "full" story of the Iran initiative. These inaccuracies lend some evidence to the proposition that LtCol North, either on his own or at the behest of others, actively sought to conceal important information.

Out of concern for the protection of classified material, Director Casey and VADM Poindexter were to brief only the Congressional intelligence committees on the "full" story; the DCI [Director of Central Intelligence] before the Committees and VADM Poindexter in private sessions with the chairmen and vice-chairmen. The DCI and VADM Poindexter undertook to do this on November 21, 1986. It appears from the copy of the DCI's testimony and notes of VADM Poindexter's meetings, that they did not fully relate the nature of events as they had occurred. The result is an understandable perception that they were not forthcoming.

The Board is also concerned about various notes that appear to be missing. VADM Poindexter was the official note taker in some key meetings, yet no notes for the meetings can be found. The reason for the lack of such notes remains unknown to the Board. If they were written, they may contain very important information. We have no way of knowing if they exist.

2.

Ronald Reagan: Remarks at the Brandenburg Gate in West Berlin

In the early 1980s relations between the United States and the Soviet Union had deteriorated to a level of hostility not seen since the Cuban Missile Crisis of 1962. By the summer of 1987, however, the Cold War rivalry between the United States and Soviet Union had begun to thaw again. The détente between the two superpowers had come with startling speed, largely as a result of the emergence of Mikhail Gorbachev as Soviet Premier in 1985. A liberal-minded reformer, Gorbachev launched an unprecedented public relations campaign with the explicit goal of defusing Cold War tensions. Meanwhile, he inaugurated sweeping internal reforms in the Soviet Union—known as glasnost *("openness") and* perestroika *("restructuring")—including a substantial reduction in the level of state repression. Nevertheless, despite the welcome reduction in Cold War tensions, the Soviet Union still maintained uncompromising control over Eastern Europe. In June 1987 President Ronald Reagan traveled to West Germany to visit the city of Berlin, which, divided by the Berlin Wall, symbolically represented the division of Europe between East and West. Reagan called on Gorbachev to pull down the Berlin Wall and to end Soviet domination of Eastern Europe. Two years later, in November 1989, the Berlin Wall did fall. Excerpts of Reagan's speech are reprinted here.*

Source: *Public Papers of the Presidents of the United States,* June 12, 1987.

THANK YOU very much. Chancellor Kohl, Governing Mayor Diepgen, ladies and gentlemen: Twenty four years ago, President John F. Kennedy visited Berlin, speaking to the people of this city and the world at the city hall. Well, since then two other presidents have come, each in his turn, to Berlin. And today, I, myself, make my second visit to your city.

We come to Berlin, we American Presidents, because it's our duty to speak, in this place, of freedom. But I must confess, we're drawn here by other things as well: by the feeling of history in this city, more than 500 years older than our own nation; by the beauty of the Grunewald and the Tiergarten; most of all, by your courage and determination. Perhaps the composer, Paul Lincke, understood something about American Presidents. You see, like so many Presidents before me, I come here today because wherever I go, whatever I do: "*Ich hab noch einen koffer in Berlin.*" [I still have a suitcase in Berlin.]

Our gathering today is being broadcast throughout Western Europe and North America. I understand that it is being seen and heard as well in the East. To those listening throughout Eastern Europe, I extend my warmest greetings and the good will of the American people. To those listening in East Berlin, a special word: Although I cannot be with you, I address my remarks to you just as surely as to those standing here before me. For I join you, as I join your fellow countrymen in the West, in this firm, this unalterable belief: *Es gibt nur ein Berlin.* [There is only one Berlin.]

Behind me stands a wall that encircles the free sectors of this city, part of a vast system of barriers that divides the entire continent of Europe. From the Baltic, south, those barriers cut across Germany in a gash of barbed wire, concrete, dog runs, and guardtowers. Farther south, there may be no visible, no obvious wall. But there remain armed guards and checkpoints all the same—still a restriction on the right to travel, still an instrument to impose upon ordinary men and women the will of a totalitarian state. Yet it is here in Berlin where the wall emerges most clearly; here, cutting across your city, where the news photo and the television screen have imprinted this brutal division of a continent upon the mind of the world. Standing before the Brandenburg Gate, every man is a German, separated from his fellow men. Every man is a Berliner, forced to look upon a scar. . . .

We hear much from Moscow about a new policy of reform and openness. Some political prisoners have been released. Certain foreign news broadcasts are no longer being jammed. Some economic enterprises have been permitted to operate with greater freedom from state control. Are these the beginnings of profound changes in the Soviet state? Or are they token gestures, intended to raise false hopes in the West, or to strengthen the Soviet system without changing it? We welcome change and openness; for we believe that freedom and security go together, that the advance of human liberty can only strengthen the cause of world peace.

There is one sign the Soviets can make

Wally McNamee/Corbis

President Ronald Reagan speaks at the Brandenburg Gate in West Berlin, West Germany, on June 12, 1987.

that would be unmistakable, that would advance dramatically the cause of freedom and peace. General Secretary Gorbachev, if you seek peace, if you seek prosperity for the Soviet Union and Eastern Europe, if you seek liberalization: Come here to this gate! Mr. Gorbachev, open this gate! Mr. Gorbachev, tear down this wall!. . .

In Europe, only one nation and those it controls refuse to join the community of freedom. Yet in this age of redoubled economic growth, of information and innovation, the Soviet Union faces a choice: It must make fundamental changes, or it will become obsolete. Today thus represents a moment of hope. We in the West stand ready to cooperate with the East to promote true openness, to break down barriers that separate people, to create a safer, freer world.

And surely there is no better place than Berlin, the meeting place of East and West, to make a start. Free people of Berlin: Today, as in the past, the United States stands for the strict observance and full implementation of all parts of the Four Power Agreement of 1971. Let us use this occasion, the 750th anniversary of this city, to usher in a new era, to seek a still fuller, richer life for the Berlin of the future. Together, let us maintain and develop the ties between the Federal Republic and the Western sectors of Berlin, which is permitted by the 1971 agreement.

And I invite Mr. Gorbachev: Let us work to bring the Eastern and Western parts of the city closer together, so that all the inhabitants of all Berlin can enjoy the benefits that come with life in one of the great cities of the world. To open Berlin still further to all Europe, East and West, let us expand the vital air access to this city, finding ways of making commercial air service to Berlin more convenient, more comfortable, and more economical. We look to the day when West Berlin can become one of the chief aviation hubs in all central Europe. . . .

In these four decades, as I have said, you Berliners have built a great city. You've done so in spite of threats—the Soviet attempts to impose the East-mark, the blockade. Today the city thrives in spite of the challenges implicit in the very presence of this wall. What keeps you here? Certainly there's a great deal to be said for your fortitude, for your defiant courage. But I believe there's something deeper, something that involves Berlin's whole look and feel and way of life—not mere sentiment. No one could live long in Berlin without being completely disabused of illusions. Something

instead, that has seen the difficulties of life in Berlin but chose to accept them, that continues to build this good and proud city in contrast to a surrounding totalitarian presence that refuses to release human energies or aspirations. Something that speaks with a powerful voice of affirmation, that says yes to this city, yes to the future, yes to freedom. In a word, I would submit that what keeps you in Berlin is love—love both profound and abiding.

Perhaps this gets to the root of the matter, to the most fundamental distinction of all between East and West. The totalitarian world produces backwardness because it does such violence to the spirit, thwarting the human impulse to create, to enjoy, to worship. The totalitarian world finds even symbols of love and of worship an affront. Years ago, before the East Germans began rebuilding their churches, they erected a secular structure: the television tower at Alexander Platz. Virtually ever since, the authorities have been working to correct what they view as the tower's one major flaw, treating the glass sphere at the top with paints and chemicals of every kind. Yet even today when the Sun strikes that sphere— that sphere that towers over all Berlin— the light makes the sign of the cross. There in Berlin, like the city itself, symbols of love, symbols of worship, cannot be suppressed.

As I looked out a moment ago from the Reichstag, that embodiment of German unity, I noticed words crudely spray-painted upon the wall, perhaps by a young Berliner, "This wall will fall. Beliefs become reality." Yes, across Europe, this wall will fall. For it cannot withstand faith; it cannot withstand truth. The wall cannot withstand freedom.

3.

WILLIAM J. BRENNAN, JR.: *Edwards v. Aguillard*

The Constitutional separation of church and state was reexamined and refined many times in the twentieth century, notably in court decisions related to the teaching of creationism versus evolution. In the most prominent such case, the Scopes Trial of 1925, in Dayton, Tennessee, attorneys William Jennings Bryan and Clarence Darrow argued the legality of teaching evolutionary science in a high school curriculum. More than 60 years later, in Edwards v. Aguillard, *the U.S. Supreme Court considered whether the Creationism Act in Louisiana violated the "establishment clause" of the First Amendment, which, along with the "free exercise clause," prevents Congress from making laws "respecting an establishment of religion, or prohibiting the free exercise thereof." The Louisiana act stipulated that evolution could be taught only in tandem with creation science. In a seven-to-two decision, the Court found this act unconstitutional, because it sought to advance religion rather than to achieve a greater academic and secular purpose. The Court also ruled that it set unnecessary restrictions on teachers. William J. Brennan, Jr., wrote the majority opinion for the Court in June 1987, and it is excerpted below.*

Source: *Edwin W. Edwards*, etc., et al. *Appellants* v. *Don Aguillard* et al. June 19, 1987.

THE QUESTION FOR DECISION is whether Louisiana's "Balanced Treatment for Creation-Science and Evolution-Science in Public School Instruction" Act (Creationism Act) is facially invalid as violative of the Establishment Clause of the First Amendment. . . .

The Establishment Clause forbids the enactment of any law "respecting an establishment of religion." The Court has applied a three-pronged test to determine whether legislation comports with the Establishment Clause. First, the legislature must have adopted the law with a secular purpose. Second, the statute's principal or primary effect must be one that neither advances nor inhibits religion. Third, the statute must not result in an excessive entanglement of government with religion. *Lemon* v. *Kurtzman*, 403 U.S. 602, 612–613 (1971). State action violates the Establishment Clause if it fails to satisfy any of these prongs. . . .

Lemon's first prong focuses on the purpose that animated adoption of the Act. "The purpose prong of the *Lemon* test asks whether government's actual purpose is to endorse or disapprove of religion." *Lynch* v. *Donnelly*, 465 U.S. 668, 690 (1984) (O'Connor, J., concurring). A governmental intention to promote religion is clear when the State enacts a law to serve a religious purpose. This intention may be evidenced by promotion of religion in general, see *Wallace* v. *Jaffree* (Establishment Clause protects individual freedom of conscience "to select any religious faith or none at all"), or by advancement of a particular religious belief, *e.g.*, *Stone* v. *Graham* (invalidating requirement to post Ten Commandments, which are "undeniably a sacred text in the Jewish and Christian faiths") (footnote omitted); *Epperson* v. *Arkansas* (holding that banning the teaching of evolution in public schools violates the First Amendment since "teaching and learning" must not "be tailored to the principles or prohibitions of any religious sect or dogma"). If the law was enacted for the purpose of endorsing religion, "no consideration of the second or third criteria [of *Lemon*] is necessary." *Wallace* v. *Jaffree*. In this case, the petitioners have identified no clear secular purpose for the Louisiana Act.

True, the Act's stated purpose is to protect academic freedom. This phrase might, in common parlance, be understood as referring to enhancing the freedom of teachers to teach what they will. The Court of Appeals, however, correctly concluded that the Act was not designed to further that goal. We find no merit in the State's argument that the "legislature may not [have] use[d] the terms 'academic freedom' in the correct legal sense. They might have [had] in mind, instead, a basic concept of fairness; teaching all of the evidence." Even if "academic freedom" is read to mean "teaching all of the evidence" with respect to the origin of human beings, the Act does not further this purpose. The goal of providing a more comprehensive science curriculum is not furthered either by outlawing the teaching of evolution or by requiring the teaching of creation science. . . .

Furthermore, the goal of basic "fairness" is hardly furthered by the Act's discriminatory preference for the teaching of creation science and against the teaching of evolution. While requiring that curriculum guides be developed for creation science, the Act says nothing of comparable guides for evolution. Similarly, research services are supplied for creation science but not for evolution. Only "creation scientists" can serve on the panel that supplies the resource services. The Act forbids school boards to discriminate against anyone who "chooses to be a creation-scientist" or to teach "creationism," but fails to protect those who choose to teach evolution or any other non-creation science theory, or who refuse to teach creation science.

If the Louisiana legislature's purpose was solely to maximize the comprehensiveness and effectiveness of science instruction, it would have encouraged the teaching of all scientific theories about the origins of humankind. But under the Act's requirements, teachers who were once free to teach any and all facets of this subject are now unable to do so. Moreover, the Act fails even to ensure that creation science will be taught, but instead requires the teaching of this theory only when the theory of evolution is taught. Thus we agree with the Court of Appeals' conclusion that the Act does not serve to protect academic freedom, but has the distinctly different purpose of discrediting "evolution by counterbalancing its teaching at every turn with the teaching of creation science. . . ."

In this case, the purpose of the Creationism Act was to restructure the science curriculum to conform with a particular religious viewpoint. Out of many possible science subjects taught in the public schools, the legislature chose to affect the teaching of the one scientific theory that historically has been opposed by certain religious sects. As in *Epperson*, the legislature passed the Act to give preference to those religious groups which have as one of their tenets the creation of humankind by a divine creator. The "overriding fact" that confronted the Court in *Epperson* was "that Arkansas' law selects from the body of knowledge a particular segment which it proscribes for the sole reason that it is deemed to conflict with . . . a particular interpretation of the Book of Genesis by a particular religious group." Similarly, the Creationism Act is designed *either* to promote the theory of creation science which embodies a particular religious tenet by requiring that creation science be taught whenever evolution is taught *or* to prohibit the teaching of a scientific theory disfavored by certain religious sects by forbidding the teaching of evolution when creation science is not also taught. The Establishment Clause, however, "forbids *alike* the preference of a religious doctrine *or* the prohibition of theory which is deemed antagonistic to a particular dogma." Because the primary purpose of the Creationism Act is to advance a particular religious belief, the Act endorses religion in violation of the First Amendment. . . .

The Louisiana Creationism Act advances a religious doctrine by requiring either the banishment of the theory of evolution from public school classrooms or the presentation of a religious viewpoint that rejects evolution in its entirety. The Act violates the Establishment Clause of the First Amendment because it seeks to employ the symbolic and financial support of government to achieve a religious purpose. The judgment of the Court of Appeals therefore is *Affirmed.*

———————◆———————

There is no more reason to believe that man descended from some inferior animal than there is to believe that a stately mansion has descended from a small cottage.
WILLIAM JENNINGS BRYAN, The Scopes Trial, July 28, 1925

4.

DAVID BRAND: Tough Times for Televangelism

In the twentieth century, three conservative movements took hold within the American Protestant Church—Pentecostalism, Fundamentalism, and Evangelicalism—which emphasized the preaching of the gospel, the primacy of scripture, the experience of conversion, and active recruitment into the faith. Cults of personality formed around some of the leading preachers, who attracted large followings and, after bridging their ministries onto television, became known as televangelists, winning even greater audiences. By the mid-1980s, following a path blazed by evangelist Billy Graham, the best-known religious broadcasters were Oral Roberts of the United Methodist Church; Jerry Falwell, the Fundamentalist founder of the Liberty Federation (formerly Moral Majority); Jim Bakker and Jimmy Swaggart of the Assemblies of God; and Pat Robertson, a Southern Baptist who temporarily left his seat as host of The 700 Club *in order to run for president. The resulting multimillion-dollar industry, which relied on the donations of its television viewers, was shaken by controversy in March 1987 when Bakker resigned his PTL (Praise the Lord) ministry in the wake of a scandal-tinged bankruptcy and extramarital affair. Swaggart was blamed for publicizing the scandal, and Falwell was left to pick up the pieces as the new PTL head. Meanwhile, Roberts made headlines of his own by claiming that God would end his life if he didn't receive $4.5 million in donations by the end of March. Still, it was Bakker and his wife, Tammy Faye, who became public faces for the embattled faith-based broadcasters. Two years later, Bakker was convicted of financial fraudulence and served five years in jail. This article on the televangelism troubles, written for* Time *magazine by David Brand and others, is reprinted below in its entirety.*

Source: *Time,* August 3, 1987, "God and Money."

BY TURNS ANGRY, bewildered and curious, an anxious crowd descended on the Jefferson Square Theater in Columbia, S.C., last week. Their aim: to play a role in the next installment of a long-running American serial of sex, cash and power—a show resembling some lurid made-for-TV mini-series that might be called *God and Money.* For six hours, harassed officials of the embattled PTL (for Praise the Lord or People That Love) ministry were confronted at a public bankruptcy hearing by members of the flock that had sup-ported the $203 million religious empire created by its ousted leaders, Jim and Tammy Bakker. The officials struggled to assure PTL donors that the foundering television-and-theme-park ministry, now about $68 million in debt, might soon turn a profit. Asserted the new PTL chief operating officer, Harry Hargrave: "We will be able to pay our debts. We are very confident of that."

Someone apparently less confident, though, was Televangelist Jerry Falwell. The Lynchburg, Va., preacher, who took control of PTL after Jim Bakker's March 19 resignation, looked grim as he faced studio cameras later in the week on PTL's regular morning television show. Falwell told viewers that donations had taken a nosedive since PTL formally filed for bankruptcy on June 12. If $1.75 million is not raised by July 31, he announced, PTL might be forced to stop broadcasting on some of the 161 stations that, for a fee, carry the ministry's born-again message. Said Falwell: "There's no more postponing. We've come down to D-day."

But as Falwell spoke, the PTL scandal continued to cast a pall across the entire secretive big business of televangelism. As never before, "skeptics have fuel for their fires," said David Hubbard, president of Fuller Theological Seminary in Pasadena, Calif. "They may see this as reflecting on the excesses of the whole evangelical movement."

Aside from his cash flow, one urgent problem facing Falwell is what to do about the claims of 120,000 PTL "Lifetime Partners" who each gave at least $1,000 to the organization, with the promise of free lodging for three nights a year at the ministry's theme-park hotel. The organization, though, has little hope of fulfilling those pledges because the number of donors exceeds the number of hotel rooms available by 5 to 1. Falwell noted last week that if the court declares those donations, which total $180 million, as debt, PTL will have to close down.

Days of reckoning have seemed to come and go with nightmarish frequency for PTL since Jim Bakker's admission that he had had a sexual tryst with Jessica Hahn, a church secretary from Long Island, N.Y., and had paid out $265,000 in hush money. Last week Hahn's lawyer announced that she would cash in further on the incident by telling her story in *Playboy* for an undisclosed sum.

As last week's bankruptcy hearing wore on—in anticipation of PTL's corporate-reorganization plan due in October—no fewer than 18 investigators from the Justice Department, the U.S. Postal Service and the Internal Revenue Service pored over mountains of the ministry's financial records at its headquarters in Fort Mill, S.C. The officials were readying material for a federal grand jury hearing, scheduled to begin in Charlotte, N.C., on Aug. 17. The focus, according to sources close to the investigation: the possibility of criminal tax fraud, wire fraud and mail fraud by Jim Bakker and other PTL leaders who have left the ministry since Falwell took over.

The House Ways and Means oversight subcommittee has also launched an investigation into the tax-exempt status not only of PTL but also of ten other major televangelist organizations. The committee has asked PTL representatives, among others, to appear at a hearing, probably in September. Texas Democrat J.J. Pickle, a member of the committee, last week met with the eleven religious broadcasters involved in the probe, including Falwell and Preacher Jimmy Swaggart of Baton Rouge, La., to question them closely about TV ministries' finances.

Increasingly, a growing number of Americans are focusing on the doings of the huge, semisecret gospel business empires like PTL that have sprung up in little more than a decade of fervent television preaching. Many are not happy with what they see. A Gallup poll survey this spring showed that since 1980 there has been a sharp decline in American public esteem for four of the country's most important TV preachers: Oklahoma-based Oral Roberts (whose approval rating dropped from 66% to 28%), Swaggart (76% to 44%), Virginia's Pat Robertson (65% to 50%) and California's Robert Schuller (78% to 61%).

The televangelists are also suffering

where it hurts the most—among viewers. Arbitron, which measures the size of local- and cable-television audiences, says most TV ministries have suffered a significant fall in viewership. Concurs Fred Vierra, president of United Cable, the nation's eighth largest operator: "We do not see their audiences growing. They're staying relatively flat." One evangelist cracks, "I was in West Irian on the island of New Guinea, and even some of the Stone Age people are familiar with the PTL scandal. That's how far it has gone."

It may go further. Within weeks of losing his grip on power at the Fort Mill ministry, Bakker began denouncing Falwell as a usurper. A solid core of Bakker loyalists at PTL apparently believes him. One complicating issue is that Falwell is a Fundamentalist, a group that rejects the faith healing and speaking in tongues practiced by the Pentecostal PTL faithful. Amid last week's emergency pitch for donations, Falwell disclosed an apparent plot by dissident PTL members to sabotage his fund-raising efforts. During the funding telethon, PTL lines were jammed by crank and obscene calls. Falwell eventually announced that no pledges would be accepted over the telephone and urged donors to send checks by mail.

One reason the struggle for control at PTL continues is that the stakes, even in bankruptcy, are considerable. For all its financial woes, PTL remains a glittering prize, with its daily TV show, its all-day religious cable service transmitted to 13 million homes, and the splashy, 2,300-acre Heritage USA theme park, the ministry's entertainment centerpiece. PTL's Hargrave denied at the bankruptcy meeting that Falwell had usurped PTL's 518,000-donor mailing list and that checks made out to PTL had gone to the Lynchburg ministry. Bakker loyalists remain unconvinced. Said Robert Zanesky, the lawyer for a group of PTL contributors intent on removing Falwell: "His credibility stinks." Says Ryan Hovis, a bankruptcy lawyer representing Bakker: "No stockholder in Chrysler would sit still if Lee Iacocca were chairman of the board for Ford."

The two central protagonists of the PTL turmoil, meanwhile, continued to parade their opulent life-styles. The couple breezed into San Francisco on July 11 as guests of their flamboyant tort lawyer, Melvin Belli, who is now laying the legal groundwork in his effort to have Bakker reinstated at PTL. During their week-long stay, the Bakkers were billeted on Belli's 105-ft. ocean-going yacht, *The Adequate Reward,* and were taken to parties, dinners and exclusive stores by Belli's wife Lia. Tammy enjoyed a makeover at Lia's favorite hair salon, 77 Maiden Lane.

A week earlier Jim and Tammy Bakker had been supervising $300,000 worth of renovations to their Gatlinburg, Tenn., home, which they bought for $148,000. Hammer in hand, Bakker greeted two TIME correspondents at the house, high above the resort town in the Great Smoky Mountains. Both Jim and Tammy vowed either to return to Fort Mill or to begin their own ministry, perhaps in California. For an hour Bakker defended himself as a "visionary" who had a "dream to build something very special for God's people." He asked, "Even if Jim and Tammy did everything we're accused of, does that give Jerry Falwell the right to steal my dream, my life, my home, my everything and my reputation from me?" Amid the growing investigative ferment surrounding the wounded ministry, it appeared that a host of interested parties would soon be trying to answer that question.

5.

Elizabeth M. Whelan: Real Public Health Issues

Beginning in the 1960s a spate of scientific studies warned of the abundance of toxins in the atmosphere and in the soil, such as pesticides and other chemicals found to be carcinogenic. The reports specified the dangers of environmental pollutants to public health and called for new government regulations. Meanwhile, two major accidents at nuclear power plants further heightened public alarm: an accidental release of nuclear radiation from the Three Mile Island power station in Pennsylvania in 1979 and a meltdown at a nuclear reactor in Chernobyl, Ukraine, in 1986. As growing numbers of Americans began to doubt the safety of nuclear energy, they also saw the need for a sweeping ban of the use of pesticides in agriculture and lawn care. Critics decried these views as alarmist and believed some of the research overstated the dangers posed by chemical toxins in the environment. Others contended that ordinary causes of premature death posed a far greater risk to public health, particularly cigarette smoking, alcohol and drug abuse, and careless driving. Elizabeth Whelan, the executive director (and later president) of the American Council on Science and Health (ACSH), sought to reframe the discussion of public health problems by warning of those that posed the greatest statistical threat and disregarding those with little statistical impact. She ranks public health risks in a speech before the New York Academy of Sciences in September 1987, excerpts of which are reprinted below.

Source: *Vital Speeches of the Day*, November 1, 1987.

My topic today is our nation's apparent bewilderment about the difference between real and hypothetical health risks, bewilderment which is quite understandable given the confusing and conflicting health messages we get from the media. Take just this month for instance: HBO in September is airing a half-hour documentary telling us about the carcinogens, toxins and other nasty stuff in our food and water. Supermarkets have started their annual campaign to alert us that their apples were grown without that maligned agricultural chemical Alar; the Environmental Protection Agency announced its intention to ban the widely used pesticides chlordane and hep-

tachlor because they were carcinogens. Environmentalists introduced legislation in many states claiming lawn-care chemicals were imminent hazards and must be more closely regulated. The New York Giants began their own carcinogen hunt trying to track down a cluster of unexplained diseases. The message is clear: we are surrounded by carcinogens. Ah, but R.J. Reynolds announced it has a new, improved product, not a safer cigarette, mind you, since the ones available now are presumably "safe," but a "cleaner" one, with less tobacco and more of something else which is a trade secret, has not been tested but inhale it anyway. And Mobil Oil placed an ad in national publications defending the right of cigarette manufacturers to advertise, noting that cigarettes were no different from butter, meat, cars and boats, all of which can be misused and cause death. I went into a health food store the other day and asked them what they had to offer over regular food. They told me that pesticides and food additives caused cancer, and that their eggs were organic and laid by happy hens. On the way out, I noticed they were selling natural herbal cough drops for smokers' cough.

I saw a bumper sticker this weekend that said life causes cancer. And I sympathize with people's resignation and bewilderment. I wish to share with you my thoughts on how our public health priorities in the United States are inverted and confused, how we as a nation in pursuit of good health are squishing ants while the elephants run wild, and why this may be one of the most critical domestic issues facing the U.S. today, with both our high standard of living and our unprecedented state of good health in imminent jeopardy.

Gaul may have been divided into three parts but my brief comments today are divided into four parts:

1. a profile of the problem
2. possible explanations for why the problem exists
3. how we as scientists might contribute to the solution, and
4. what the consequences may be if we don't.

1. THE PROBLEM

In defining my concern about inverted health priorities, I start with some assumptions, among them that those of us who work in public health accept that those people who daily protect their health and those who regularly assume

risks have exactly the same mortality rate: 100 percent. The difference is in the timing. Our goal in public health is to provide individuals with the type of information which will allow them to die young at a very old age. In other words, we want to offer folks a shot at avoiding premature mortality.

We obviously have limited resources with which to reach this goal, so we want to put our efforts in preventive medicine on efforts that pay off. We must never lose sight of the reality that the legitimate purpose of any public health regulation—whether it restricts lifestyle factors, bans a chemical, evacuates a population or anything else—is to prevent premature disease and death, and only that. It is not the role of public health personnel to harass industry, to remove from the market useful products and terrify people about hypothetical risks. Nor is it their role to take action in the name of public health when there is no scientific evidence that such activity will promote the public's health.

So, in speaking of preventive premature death—which arbitrarily is defined in ACSH materials as death prior to age 80. I am sure all of us could quibble about these estimates, but we feel they reflect mainstream, ball-park figures on the causes of premature death in the United States today.

Note that in total some two million Americans die each year from all causes. We estimate that fully half of these two million deaths are premature. What are the main causes of premature death?

CIGARETTE SMOKING

The latest peer-reviewed literature indicates that nearly 500,000 premature deaths can be linked with tobacco use, almost exclusively cigarette smoking. That works out to one in four U.S.

deaths each year linked to smoking, smokers being at extraordinarily increased risk of heart and lung disease, cancers of many sites, including lung, bladder, pancreas, esophageal and cervical—and other maladies as well. A thoracic surgeon on my Board refers to his operating room as "Marlboro Country."

For purposes of perspective, it is important to keep in mind how *new* are cigarettes—and their health devastation. Just to pick one widely known individual: the day that [the] President of the U.S. was born, cigarettes were not commercially available. Obviously tobacco has been in use since before Columbus' time, but before cigarettes were introduced tobacco was used in a relatively harmless way.

ALCOHOL ABUSE

ACSH estimates about 100,000 annual deaths due to alcohol abuse, including alcohol's role in auto fatalities, suicide, homicide, liver disease, cancer and other conditions. A distinction, of course, can be drawn between alcohol and cigarettes, in that a) cigarettes are hazardous when used as intended, while alcohol can be consumed by most people without assumption of health risks; and b) while there is no known health benefit associated with tobacco inhalation, there is a growing literature on the protective effect of alcohol (when consumed in moderation) on cardiovascular health and extended longevity.

USE OF OTHER ADDICTIVE SUBSTANCES

Our rough estimate is that there are some 35,000 premature annual deaths from other forms of drug abuse, including AIDS as acquired through shared needles.

NEGLECT OF PREVENTIVE CARE/POOR TREATMENT

Some 275,000 deaths attributable here, including a hefty portion due to individuals not taking advantage of screening techniques to detect diseases that can be treated.

HAZARDOUS LIFESTYLES

We include here reckless driving, promiscuous sexual practices, lack of working smoke detectors, and other causes, totaling about 45,000 annual premature deaths. The number of AIDS deaths will increase dramatically in the next few years, accounting for perhaps as many as 65,000 deaths in the year 1991 alone.

These, then, are the real public health risks we face today.

But what are American consumers focusing on? Well, if you take as your measure of concern the areas reported in the nation's media, and the activities of our local, state and federal regulatory agencies, the concerns, among others, are those listed in Table II. We could add to that list, urea formaldehyde foam, asbestos in hair dryers, hair dyes, irradiated foods, sugar, and more.

Table II: Selected Much Publicized Hypothetical Causes of Death

Trace Levels of:	Estimate Number of Deaths*
Dioxin	0
PCBs	0
EDB	0
Chloradane, heptachlor, DDT (and all other pesticides)	0
Ionizing radiation from U.S. nuclear power plants	0
Lead in air and water	0
Food additives (saccharin, BHA, nitrites, etc.)	0

Best estimate is close to zero.

The best estimate we have on premature mortality due to these alleged causes is approximately zero. With specific regard to cancer mortality, Doll and Peto in their classic publication "The Causes of Cancer" suggest an upper limit of 2 percent of cancers due to outdoor environmental pollution. Regarding food additives, specifically antioxidants, they suggested a negative effect on cancer, in the sense that those compounds may protect against, rather than contribute to the disease.

And we could note, under hypothetical risks, some much-publicized events as well as specific chemicals: The so-called disasters at Three Mile Island and Love Canal. TMI killed or injured no one. The radiation exposure to those near the plant was risk equivalent to inhaling four puffs of a cigarette in a lifetime or crossing the street five times. As for the "tragedy" at Love Canal, a blue ribbon panel appointed by Governor [Mario] Cuomo found no evidence of acute health effects linked to chemical exposure. Yet, you may recall that President [Jimmy] Carter ordered 700 Love Canal families evacuated at a cost to taxpayers of millions of dollars after an EPA report alleged the residents were victims of chromosomal damage. . . .

2.

Item 2 on my list of 4. Why is the most educated, health-conscious society in the world inverting health priorities? Why do we seem so willing to dismantle our technological society in what we believe to be the pursuit of good health? Why is this insistence a "zero risk at any cost" approach applied to regulations about PCBs and dioxin, but not to cigarettes?

I do not have time to go into depth here. But I think the problem can be traced to some widespread but inaccurate premises.

First, there is the prevailing idea that

Model T health is better than today's turbo-charged machines. It is just our bad luck to be living in an age of pesticides, lawn-care chemicals, radiation from nuclear power plants and a legion of "unnatural" substances.

If we could motor back to a more simple, pristine time, we're told, life and health would be so much better. This, of course, is nostalgic nonsense. Early in this century the life expectancy at birth was about 46 years, 35 if you were non-white. Infectious diseases such as typhoid, TB, diphtheria, pneumonia and whooping cough were all common. A spectrum of life-saving pharmaceuticals and medical technology, control of communicable/infectious disease, an improved understanding of nutrition, have contributed to good health, not detracted from it, and created a society where the life expectancy is in the mid-70s and still rising.

Though the popular wisdom is otherwise, the cancer death rate has not increased substantially during the past few decades, but the notion that cancer is more prevalent and a by-product of industrial society seems to feed on itself. Recall W.C. Field's famous remark, "always carry a flagon of whiskey in case of a snakebite . . . and furthermore, always carry a small snake." But conventional wisdom here is not fact. There is no cancer epidemic in the United States. Except for the dramatic rise in lung cancer, rates of other sites have stabilized or declined in recent decades.

Second, despite our advanced educational system, science and technology pose somewhat of a mystery to many Americans. And it is always easier to fear the unknown and the unfamiliar. Cigarettes are known and familiar: dioxin and nuclear power plants are not. Consider a comparison between a nuclear power plant and a swimming pool. Can you imagine a TV camera zooming in on a pool with a grim voice over telling us "there is enough water in this pool to drown 10,000 people?" Related to this is the peculiar human tendency to avoid, at all costs, being introspective. How much more comforting it is to blame the corporation and big government for our ills than it is to examine critically our own personal lifestyles and the primary role our actions may play in determining our fate. How willing we seem to tolerate enormous risks which lie within our control, while protesting the hypothetical risks perceived as outside our control.

Third, Americans are likely to focus on "chemicals" as a cause of disease because there *have* been some legitimate horror stories. Occupational exposures—asbestos, vinyl chloride, beta naphthalmine immediately come to mind—have caused preventable deaths. There have been cases of loss of life involving man-made chemicals—from carelessness, accidents and downright greed. We know that. We must recognize that prudent and constant vigilance is necessary to prevent health-threatening exposure to potentially hazardous substances. There is no debate about this. But many Americans, however, are unable to distinguish between proper chemical regulation and monitoring versus banning or purging of useful, non-health-threatening chemicals and compounds. And the most critical of toxicological adages seems lost on them: "Only the dose makes the poison."

Fourth, we must acknowledge the prevailing view that natural is good and safe and synthetic is evil—a view strongly reinforced by today's food products that boast of "no artificial anything." Associated with this view is a) that only synthetic chemicals cause cancer in man or animals and b) animal testing is an infallible means of extrapolation to man, thus the media's frequent use of the word car-

cinogen—or cancer-causing agent as if synonymous for animal and man.

The reality here, of course, is that nature abounds in toxins and carcinogens; and that animal tests, particularly at high doses, have not been validated as accurate predictors for human cancer and other diseases.

Fifth, in attempting to understand the willingness to eliminate any chemical that causes cancer in animals, many consumers—and regulators—have accepted uncritically the assumption that there are no risks to banning—or not approving—a technology. This is clearly naive. Consider, for example, the risks of not using pesticides: we compete with insects for food.

The ultimate health threat, then, at least in less developed countries is starvation. But then there is the intermediary risk of eating food infested by insects penetrating the grain kernels and introducing microbial and fungal contamination. But we did not hear of the risks of not taking risks when, for example, four years ago EDB was banned. And are there no risks to not approving drugs? Ask the relatives of heart attack victims denied the clot-dissolver TPA, a currently unapproved drug.

Sixth, many corporations are now reinforcing public fears of synthetic chemicals and food processing. Sure "natural organic" is scientific nonsense and there is contradictory evidence about fiber and colon cancer; let's claim it anyway. A major baby food company is advertising that it does not use the agricultural chemical Alar. As mentioned, large supermarket chains are boasting that their produce is grown without benefit of pesticides . . . and the message is reinforced that the way to good health is to avoid "chemicals."

Seventh and finally, the fear of chemicals, in food, air, water. The media focuses on these and other hypothetical risks, and consumer goods must be understood in the context of the reality that the manufacturer of the leading cause of death—cigarettes—has substantial clout in editorial policy, particularly in U.S. magazines and newspapers. With nearly a three billion dollar annual advertising and promotional budget, it is no wonder that cigarette companies have been rewarded with editorial silence in American publications. You have seen the cover of *Newsweek* or *Time* featuring sugar as a hazard to health, or highlighting illicit drugs as a cause of disease, or front page features on the poisoning of America, but you have never seen an in-depth story on the hazards of smoking. A few courageous editors print the truth about cigarettes even though their publications run cigarette ads, but by and large we at the American Council have been unable to find any significant articles on the hazards of smoking in magazines which take cigarette ads, which is almost all of them. When you cannot write about the number one cause of environmentally related death, you have lots of pages to fill with hypothetical causes.

3.

And to point #3 on my list of 4: what can we as scientists do about this? I think you can gather from what I have said so far that we have an exciting opportunity to make significant advances against premature death and disease in this country. But the primary killers in our society aren't hidden away in some toxic dump. They are not lingering in the atmo-

sphere outside a nuclear power plant. They are not lurking in your muffin mix. We know them. They are assailable. And for most of them, miracle drugs are not needed.

We can—today—prevent the major causes of disease and death in this country by altering our lifestyles. But more progress requires focus and direction. Unfortunately, we are like the airline pilot that radios "I have some good news and bad news. The good news is that I am making excellent time. The bad news is that I am lost." At a time when we should be rejoicing about our unprecedented state of good health—and the exciting opportunity to become even healthier—we are living in a fog of despair and nosophobia, literally defined as the morbid fear of illness. And we are blaming our sophisticated society for problems that simply do not exist. As I mentioned, part of the problem can be laid at the doorstep of corporate America which seems all too willing to abandon science in favor of short-term sales.

On the other hand, our representatives—the ones which allocate taxpayer money for disease prevention—carry much of the responsibility for our mixed-up priorities. The Environmental Protection Agency receives *twice* as much money to mitigate hypothetical dangers than does the National Cancer Institute to fight the leading cause of death, cigarette smoking. Congress is allocating 14 billion dollars for Superfund when, as noted in a recent study by the Cato Institute, there is no evidence of any significant health risks associated with chemicals within that law's regulatory domain.

6.

FELICE N. SCHWARTZ: Women in Corporate America

In the 1970s and 1980s American business took on a new look with the rise and success of women managers. Prior to the 1970s, men dominated corporate management positions, monopolizing not only the top executive positions but also the ranks of middle management. Women who attempted to break into management were often greeted with ridicule, as well as outright opposition. Initially, the postwar women's movement focused on issues of reproductive choice, divorce law reform, and expanded educational opportunities. By the 1980s, however, it expanded its focus to combat male chauvinism and gender discrimination in the business world. Though the success of female entrepreneurs and corporate executives garnered increasing attention in the national media, many women still faced a hostile workplace, especially on the highest rungs of the corporate ladder. In an address at the Wharton School of the University of Pennsylvania in Philadelphia in October 1987, Felice Schwartz, founder of Catalyst, an advocacy group for women in business, outlined the major issues facing corporate women. Excerpts of her address are reprinted below.

Source: *Vital Speeches of the Day*, January 1, 1988.

I'M EXTRAORDINARILY PLEASED to be here. You are the people I'd most like to address and with whom I most want to interact. Catalyst's ultimate objective is enabling women to pursue whatever career and family goals they choose. Our strategy for achieving that objective is to raise corporate awareness that women are a critical business resource. As business reporters whose words are read and respected by business leaders, you are probably the most effective bearers of that message to the corporate community. But this isn't a one-way street. I believe that Catalyst's perspective on and experience with companies and individual women can help you construct an accurate picture of those issues created by the massive entry of women into the workforce.

In all honesty I must say that I think much of what appears in the press on the subject of women and the corporation is misleading. Too often we read reports based on the experience of 17 touted as a trend. We hear about difficulties in adjusting to new realities and new beliefs, difficulties which are equated with failure. We hear detailed reports of setback after setback. The setbacks are real, but they are often mistakenly presented as a denial of the essentially steady progress that has already been made. . . .

The presence of women in the management ranks of corporations is a reality. We've grown accustomed to seeing this working woman hanging from the subway strap during commuting hours. We may refer disparagingly to her tailored suit and little tie but we no longer visualize her in a house dress with her hair uncombed. The woman who leaves her children to go to work in the morning is no longer a pariah in her community or her family. Her pay check is more than pin money; it buys essential family staples and often supports the entire family. . . .

Yet the prevailing message from the media on the subject of women and business is one filled with pessimism. We hear about women leaving their employers in the lurch when they go on maternity leave. Or we hear the flip side, that women are overly committed to their careers and neglectful of their families. And in fact, it is true that problems arising from women's new workforce role do exist, side by side with the benefits. . . .

We are in the midst of a difficult period of transition. Why else would *Fortune* run a cover story about child care called "Executive Guilt?" There are some who wish we might turn back the clocks to a previous era when men were at work and women at home, when the responsibilities of each sex seemed simpler. When men produced goods and supported the family, and women produced and reared children, managed the home and supported their husbands' careers.

The reality, however, is that the clocks cannot be turned back. The movement toward a society where men and women have equal opportunities to pursue whatever career and family goals they choose is, I believe, inevitable. Moreover, I believe that the change required to make the transition is less costly—more profitable—than it is to maintain the status quo. Looking ahead I would go far beyond that and say that unless we accelerate the pace and recognize the urgent necessity to assimilate women at every level of management, our country's competitive position in the world economy will be placed in jeopardy. . . .

Now, in closing, I want to take another look at several of the popular news stories I referred to earlier—the ones with a gloomy view of corporate women's prospects for success.

The first story I hear a lot concerns women's supposed lack of job commitment. It is said that because they are the childbearers, women cannot make a sustained commitment to their careers. But today a number of things tell us this just isn't true, as it might have been when most women married, had children and remained at home until their children went to college. Today 23 percent of women are unmarried and 20 percent of married women are childless. Since 1972 the first birth rate for women in their early thirties more than doubled; for women 35–39 the rate rose 83 percent. Moreover, women are having children later and having fewer children. Women have an average of 1.79 children, fewer among the more educated. This combination of figures suggests a longer stretch of time and therefore increased opportunities for women to settle in a field, gain experience, begin to move up the career ladder before committing time and energies to raising a family. Women's employers also benefit from having more time to evaluate their performance, to spot those with leadership potential and to take steps to develop their talents and encourage their job commitment. The decrease in numbers of children for most women also makes a big difference in terms of what emphasis women can give to their careers. A child represents a significant distraction or interruption for a finite period, actually a negligible one when viewed in the context of a lifetime of employment. And I feel confident in predicting that when there is flexibility even those few women who are currently dropping out entirely or for extended periods will cease to do so—that it will soon be possible for women with children to make the same commitment to their careers as men.

The second story concerns pessimism about the wage gap between men and women. It is said that discrimination will perpetuate the 30 or more percent gap that now exists. But this anxiety is unnecessary, I believe. Because occupational segregation, not discrimination, has created the wage gap and perpetrates it, the gap will gradually close. Here's why.

Until now, the tremendous gap between the salaries of women and men meant that married women were beholden by economic pressure to leave their jobs to relocate when the opportunity beckoned for their husbands. This set in motion a vicious cycle, whereby women's careers were disrupted and their career growth stunted. Nor could most women accept a career-expanding relocation offer, practically speaking, since their husbands' income constituted the major portion of the family income. Also, since the woman was not the primary breadwinner, the tendency was for her time to be perceived as more expendable, more available for household chores, caring for the children and aging parents. It's difficult to move up beyond the middle of the pyramid if you are forced to change jobs frequently, are not able to accept relocation opportunities or if you must be home by 5:30 or 6 every day to do the household chores and tend to the children.

Today we are beginning to see a new, more positive cycle replace the old one. It begins with the fact that in 18 percent of all two-income households today, women bring home a fatter paycheck than their husbands. Astounding, isn't it? To me, that percentage suggests the tip of the iceberg of this new trend towards men's and women's income equality. Because if 18 percent of women earn more than their husbands, surely a proportion-

ate number earn as much or nearly the same amount. It follows that when the woman's income is greater, she is more able to take advantage of job opportunities that come her way. Her career has greater value, it demands more respect. If she is married, her husband is more apt to share responsibility for childcare and household chores, even if that means leaving his job on time when his wife works late. As women prepare themselves for business, enter traditionally male fields and move from staff to line positions, the gap in pay will continue to narrow. . . .

The third popular story I hear in the press concerns the flight of women from the corporation. Well, most items about this supposed trend have been riddled with oversights and misperceptions. For starters, one notion is that women who are dropping out of the corporation are leaving in droves to start small businesses of their own. Yes, many are. But the number of these women forming their own businesses is proportional to the total increase in the number of women who have entered the workforce.

A related notion is that those women who leave are lured by the promise of flexibility, flexibility that the corporate sector can't provide. The corporation's an unworkable environment for women, says this logic. True, women who want to combine career and family need flexibility, and so far, the small business owner has been able to gain flexibility— through sacrificing the challenge and financial rewards of a corporate career. Will women continue to make these sacrifices? I doubt it. We are now at the threshold of greater flexibility in the corporation—flexibility deliberately provided in response to the diversity of today's workforce and the escalating need for talent. Rather than jumping on the bandwagon they read about, women would be well advised to hang in. These three stories, I think, reflect some of your anxieties about the resolution of the problems that still face us.

But perhaps the biggest problem—and one that is not often acknowledged—is that we do not recognize that the needs of women and corporations are synergistic. That fact wasn't apparent 15 years ago when women were floundering, unprepared and ambivalent, and when there was an abundant supply of men who could manage and lead. Today we can consider it a real boon that women want to pursue careers and that there are those who have the talent and commitment to lead when the pool of male leaders has been so drastically reduced. It's also a boon that not all able women are ready to go give their all and want to move to the top because the need for able people at the middle is also great, and talented women who want a life outside the corporation can upgrade every level.

Yes, problems exist for business and for women, problems that require resolution. Women's exodus from the home created a vacuum that will take careful planning, a vast investment of funds and a partnership of the family and community, of the private and public sectors to fill. To overcome these problems, vast changes are required in our behaviors and values, in the way we live and in the way work is done, and in the guidelines we use to evaluate performance.

But the motivation of corporate leaders to address these problems has already begun to shift from what is right to what is necessary, from charity to good business. As it becomes increasingly apparent that the issue of women in management is an economic issue, the strategies and solutions will emerge. The cost of failing to develop the leadership capabilities of women will be too great to tolerate. As a result, the workplace will continue to change to benefit women, men and business.

A strong woman is a woman determined
To do something that others are determined not to be done.
MARGE PIERCY, *For a Strong Woman*

7.

WILLIAM F. BUCKLEY, JR.: Politics and Supreme Court Nominees

When Supreme Court Associate Justice Lewis Powell retired in 1987, President Ronald Reagan nominated as his replacement Robert Bork. A Federal Court of Appeals judge and a former Yale Law School professor, Bork was considered among the foremost legal minds in the country. He was also one of the nation's most conservative legal scholars. Traditionally Senate confirmation hearings focused on the competence, rather than the ideology, of the nominee, but a contentious partisan debate broke out during Bork's hearings. Democrats accused Bork of being a right-wing extremist, particularly on the issues of abortion and civil rights. They believed that if Bork were confirmed he would alter the balance of power on the Court in favor of conservatives and that a conservative-controlled Supreme Court would rule unconstitutional major civil rights legislation and strike down the 1973 Roe v. Wade *ruling that protects abortion rights. Republicans, in contrast, accused Democrats of playing politics with the Supreme Court, complaining that the Democrats had turned the nominating process into a political circus. Since Democrats held the majority in the Senate, Republican efforts to save Bork's nomination failed, and the Senate ultimately rejected the nomination. With Bork out of the running, Reagan selected Anthony Kennedy, a Federal Court of Appeals judge and a moderate conservative. The Senate confirmed Kennedy's nomination in 1988. The author of the essay printed below, William F. Buckley, Jr., is the founder of* National Review *magazine and one of the country's leading conservative intellectuals.*

Source: *National Review*, October 23, 1987, "Nice Try."

IT IS A FALLACY to say that because John did A, therefore it is right, and to be expected, that Jim should do A. And the bearing of this is of course Fortas-Bork.

The argument of the liberals is neat, not to say facile. In 1968, President Johnson nominated Abe Fortas to succeed Earl Warren as Chief Justice of the Supreme Court. This was a maneuver. Its background: Earl Warren hated Richard Nixon above all other men alive, and caucused with LBJ to avoid a Chief Justice named by Nixon, who looked like a certainty to win the next election. Deal: Earl Warren would resign before he had intended to do so, giving LBJ first crack at naming a successor. The deal was opposed by leading Republican senators, including Howard Baker and Strom Thurmond. They spoke of the need to inquire into the philosophy of anyone named to the Court. FLASH! Therefore, why shouldn't the Democrats inquire into the philosophy of Robert Bork?

The central contention is over what kind of a Supreme Court we should have. Ever since President Eisenhower appointed Earl Warren, we had a Supreme

Court that, in the course of a generation, affected social and economic policy in America more substantially than Congress did. In respect of religion, we had a Court that overthrew a century and a half's understanding of what public schools were free to do without violating the separation-of-church-and-state amendment. In respect of states' rights, the Supreme Court reached in and said the states had no rights to draw their own electoral boundaries. The equilibrium between individual rights and collective rights against crime was shattered by a string of decisions that resulted in known criminals becoming scofflaws, courtesy of the Supreme Court. In education, local school boards discovered that they no longer had a right to decide basic policy: federal courts would decide which buses should take which children to which schools.

The conservative position throughout the judicial revolution was that the Constitution had not appointed the Supreme Court to make decisions basically legislative in nature. When, therefore, the great historic moment came—the prospective resignation of Earl Warren—legislators who had taken an oath to defend the Constitution asked the only questions truly relevant. These weren't such questions as, Do you believe in abortion? Do you believe in school prayer? Do you believe in busing? Do you believe in the right of the prosecutor to introduce evidence accidentally retrieved? The questions Senator Baker and Senator Thurmond and the successful minority that filibustered against Abe Fortas wanted to ask were roughly translatable as: Do you, Mr. Fortas, believe that the Supreme Court should be the principal agent of social legislation?

Thurmond said at the time, "A man's philosophy, both his philosophy of life and his philosophy of judicial interpretation, are extremely relevant." And Howard Baker said that the Senate must "consider . . . their social, economic, and legal philosophies; and the wisdom and desirability of the appointments at this particular time." He meant by that that if Fortas believed he was being appointed Chief Justice of the Supreme Court in order to press on with the Warren Revolution, then he ought not to be approved. And surely nothing is more relevant than the question of Senator Thurmond: What is the candidate's philosophy of judicial interpretation?

The liberals took a different position, and their hypocrisy now becomes incandescent. Think back to the Detroit nomination of Ronald Reagan, and the plank in the platform stipulating that anyone named to a federal judgeship should be a judicial moderate. There was noisy opposition to the sentence, "We will work for the appointment of judges at all levels of the judiciary who respect traditional family values and the sanctity of innocent human life." That was read as a political party's belief that judges should not arrogate authority over school prayer, the choice of schools, and abortion. The liberals took the position that any probe going beyond the character and competence of a proposed judge was a violation of judicial integrity. But the party and its candidate swept on to victory.

What the opponents of Robert Bork are saying comes down to this: 1) We believe in an activist court that does not hesitate to write social policy. 2) But that social policy must be what we favor; for which reason, 3) Bork, the legal scholar, the veteran teacher, administrator, and judge, is not fit to serve.

8.

Oliver Stone: "Greed Is Good," *Wall Street*

The motion picture Wall Street *was released around the time of the U.S. stock market crash of 1987. Directed by Oliver Stone and cowritten by Stone and Stanley Weiser, the popular film seemed to encapsulate the excesses of the freewheeling financial world of the mid-1980s. It was the time when real-life figures such as stock market speculator Ivan Boesky and junk-bond broker Michael Milken took advantage of laissez-faire policies to make billions of dollars before being indicted for insider trading and other fraudulent practices. A morality play set in contemporary New York City, the movie follows Gordon Gekko, a successful and ruthless corporate raider who takes on a young protégé, Bud Fox. Gekko, who encourages Fox to trample business ethics in order to reap the windfalls of capitalism, symbolizes greed, to which he pledges his allegiance in the speech below. The following lines, often repeated, were delivered by actor Michael Douglas, who won an Academy Award for his portrayal of Gekko in the film. Stone said the lines echoed those of Boesky, who proclaimed "greed is healthy" in a 1985 commencement speech.*

Source: *Wall Street,* 20th Century Fox, 1987.

The point is, ladies and gentlemen, that greed—for lack of a better word—is good. Greed is right. Greed works. Greed terrifies, cuts through and captures the essence of the evolutionary spirit. Greed, in all of its forms—greed for life, for money, for love, knowledge, has marked an upward surge in mankind. And greed—you mark my words—will not only save Teldar Paper, but that other malfunctioning corporation called the USA. Thank you very much.

9.

ALLAN BLOOM: *The Closing of the American Mind*

During the 1960s college campuses erupted in internal upheaval as issues such as the Vietnam War, the Civil Rights Movement, and the sexual revolution divided students along racial, cultural, and ideological lines. Calling for broad institutional change, leftist students challenged what they perceived as the repressive nature of university faculties and administrators. Although conservatives made a resurgence in national politics by the 1980s, college and university campuses continued to turn sharply to the left. The dichotomy of the nation's increasingly conservative political culture and its liberal campus culture attracted the attention of commentators in the 1980s. Liberals viewed universities as an oasis of progressivism in a sea of repression, whereas conservatives complained that universities indoctrinated their students in leftist political activism instead of teaching them the fundamentals of Western culture. The debate intensified when many major schools dropped American history and Western literature as requirements for graduation, replacing them with mandatory courses on multiculturalism and non-Western thought. In 1987 Allan Bloom, a professor of philosophy at the University of Chicago, stoked the debate with his book The Closing of the American Mind: How Higher Education Has Failed Democracy and Impoverished the Souls of Today's Students. *Condemning the growing emphasis on multiculturalism, he called on universities to return to teaching the classics of Western civilization. Bloom's book became a national best-seller and sparked widespread debate. Excerpts from Bloom's book are reprinted below.*

Source: *The Closing of the American Mind*, New York, 1987.

LIBERAL EDUCATION

What image does a first-rank college or university present today to a teen-ager leaving home for the first time, off to the adventure of a liberal education? He has four years of freedom to discover himself—a space between the intellectual wasteland he has left behind and the inevitable dreary professional training that awaits him after the baccalaureate. In this short time he must learn that there is a great world beyond the little one he knows, experience the exhilaration of it and digest enough of it to sustain himself in the intellectual deserts he is destined to traverse. He must do this, that is, if he is to have any hope of a higher life. These are the charmed years when he can, if he so chooses, become anything he wishes and when he has the opportunity to survey his alternatives, not merely those current in his time or provided by careers, but those available to him as a human being. The importance of these years for an American cannot be overestimated. They are civilization's only chance to get to him.

In looking at him we are forced to reflect on what he should learn if he is to be called educated; we must speculate on what the human potential to be fulfilled is. In the specialties we can avoid such speculation, and the avoidance of them is one of specialization's charms. But here it is a simple duty. What are we to teach this person? The answer may not be evident, but to attempt to answer the question is already to philosophize and to begin to educate. Such a concern in itself poses the question of the unity of man and the unity of the sciences. It is childishness to say, as some do, that everyone must be allowed to develop freely, that it is authoritarian to impose a point of view on the student. In that case, why have a university? If the response is "to provide an atmosphere for learning," we come back to our original questions at the second remove. Which atmosphere? Choices and reflection on the reasons for those choices are unavoidable. The university has to stand for something. The practical effects of unwillingness to think positively about the contents of a liberal education are, on the one hand, to ensure that all the vulgarities of the world outside the university will flourish within it, and, on the other, to impose a much harsher and more illiberal necessity on the student—the one given by the imperial and imperious demands of the specialized disciplines unfiltered by unifying thought.

The university now offers no distinctive visage to the young person. He finds a democracy of the disciplines—which are there either because they are autochthonous or because they wandered in recently to perform some job that was demanded of the university. This democracy is really an anarchy, because there are no recognized rules for citizenship and no legitimate titles to rule. In short there is no vision, nor is there a set of competing visions, of what an educated human being is. The question has disappeared, for to pose it would be a threat to the peace. There is no organization of the sciences, no tree of knowledge. Out of chaos emerges dispiritedness, because it is impossible to make a reasonable choice. Better to give up on liberal education and get on with a specialty in which there is at least a prescribed curriculum and a prospective career. On the way the student can pick up in elective courses a little of whatever is thought to make one cultured. The student gets no intimation that great mysteries might be revealed to him, that new and higher motives of action might be discovered within him, that a different and more human way of life can be harmoniously constructed by what he is going to learn.

Simply, the university is not distinctive. Equality for us seems to culminate in the unwillingness and incapacity to make claims of superiority, particularly in the domains in which such claims have always been made—art, religion and philosophy. When Weber found that he could not choose between certain high opposites—reason vs. revelation, Buddha vs. Jesus—he did not conclude that all things are equally good, that the distinction between high and low disappears. As a matter of fact he intended to revitalize the consideration of these great alternatives in showing the gravity and danger involved in choosing among them; they were to be heightened in contrast to the trivial considerations of modern life that threatened to overgrow and render indistinguishable the profound problems the confrontation with which makes the bow of the soul taut. The serious intellectual life was for him the battleground of the great decisions, all of which are spiritual or "value" choices. One can no longer present this or that particular view of the educated or civilized man as authoritative; therefore one must say that education consists in knowing, really knowing, the small number of such views in their integrity. This distinction between profound and superficial—which takes the place of good and bad, true and false—provided a focus for serious study, but it hardly held out against the naturally relaxed democratic tendency to say, "Oh, what's the use?" The first university disruptions at Berkeley were explicitly directed against the multiversity smorgasbord and, I must confess, momentarily and partially engaged my sympathies. It may have even been the case that there was some small element of longing for an education in the motivation of those students. But nothing was done to guide or inform their energy, and the result was merely to add multilife-styles to multidisciplines, the diversity of perversity to the diversity of specialization. What we see so often happening in general happened here too; the insistent demand for greater community ended in greater isolation. Old agreements, old habits, old traditions were not so easily replaced.

Thus, when a student arrives at the university, he finds a bewildering variety of departments and a bewildering variety of courses. And there is no official guidance, no university-wide agreement, about what he *should* study. Nor does he usually find readily available examples, either among students or professors, of a unified use of the university's resources. It is easiest simply to make a career choice and go about getting prepared for that career. The programs designed for those having made such a choice render their students immune to charms that might lead them out of the conventionally respectable. The sirens sing *sotto voce* these days, and the young already have enough wax in their ears to pass them by without danger. These specialties can provide enough courses to take

up most of their time for four years in preparation for the inevitable graduate study. With the few remaining courses they can do what they please, taking a bit of this and a bit of that. No public career these days—not doctor nor lawyer nor politician nor journalist nor businessman nor entertainer—has much to do with humane learning. An education, other than purely professional or technical, can even seem to be an impediment. That is why a countervailing atmosphere in the university would be necessary for the students to gain a taste for intellectual pleasures and learn that they are viable.

The real problem is those students who come hoping to find out what career they want to have, or are simply looking for an adventure with themselves. There are plenty of things for them to do—courses and disciplines enough to spend many a lifetime on. Each department or great division of the university makes a pitch for itself, and each offers a course of study that will make the student an initiate. But how to choose among them? How do they relate to one another? The fact is they do not address one another. They are competing and contradictory, without being aware of it. The problem of the whole is urgently indicated by the very existence of the specialties, but it is never systematically posed. The net effect of the student's encounter with the college catalogue is bewilderment and very often demoralization. It is just a matter of chance whether he finds one or two professors who can give him an insight into one of the great visions of education that have been the distinguishing part of every civilized nation. Most professors are specialists, concerned only with their own fields, interested in the advancement of those fields in their own terms, or in their own personal advancement in a world where all the rewards are on the side of professional distinction. They have been entirely emancipated from the old structure of the university, which at least helped to indicate that they are incomplete, only parts of an unexamined and undiscovered whole. So the student must navigate among a collection of carnival barkers, each trying to lure him into a particular sideshow. This undecided student is an embarrassment to most universities, because he seems to be saying, "I am a whole human being. Help me to form myself in my wholeness and let me develop my real potential," and he is the one to whom they have nothing to say.

Cornell was, as in so many other things, in advance of its time on this issue. The six-year Ph.D. program, richly supported by the Ford Foundation, was directed specifically to high school students who had already made "a firm career choice" and was intended to rush them through to the start of those careers. A sop was given to desolate humanists in the form of money to fund seminars that these young careerists could take on their way through the College of Arts and Sciences. For the rest, the educators could devote their energies to arranging and packaging the program without having to provide it with any substance. That kept them busy enough to avoid thinking about the nothingness of their endeavor. This has been the preferred mode of not looking the Beast in the Jungle in the face—structure, not content. The Cornell plan for dealing with the problem of liberal education was to suppress the students' longing for liberal education by encouraging their professionalism and their avarice, providing money and all the prestige the university had available to make careerism the centerpiece of the university.

The Cornell plan dared not state the radical truth, a well-kept secret: the colleges do not have enough to teach their students, not enough to justify keeping them four years, probably not even three years. If the focus is careers, there is hardly one specialty, outside the hardest of the hard natural sciences, which requires more than two years of preparatory training prior to graduate studies. The rest is just wasted time, or a period of ripening until the students are old enough for graduate studies. For many graduate careers, even less is really necessary. It is amazing how many undergraduates are poking around for courses to take, without any plan or question to ask, just filling up their college years. In fact, with rare exceptions, the courses are parts of specialties and not designed for general cultivation, or to investigate questions important for human beings as such. The so-called knowledge explosion and increasing specialization have not filled up the college years but emptied them. Those years are impediments; one wants to get beyond them. And in general the persons one finds in the professions need not have gone to college, if one is to judge by their tastes, their fund of learning or their interests. They might as well have spent their college years in the Peace Corps or the like. These great universities—which can split the atom, find cures for the most terrible diseases, conduct surveys of whole populations and produce massive dictionaries of lost languages—cannot generate a modest program of general education for undergraduate students. This is a parable for our times.

There are attempts to fill the vacuum painlessly with various kinds of fancy packaging of what is already there—study abroad options, individualized majors, etc. Then there are Black Studies and Women's or Gender Studies, along with Learn Another Culture. Peace Studies are on their way to a similar prevalence. All this is designed to show that the university is with it and has something in addition to its traditional specialties. The latest item is computer literacy, the full cheapness of which is evident only to those who think a bit about what literacy might mean. It would make some sense to promote literacy literacy, inasmuch as most high school graduates nowadays have difficulty reading and writing. And some institutions are quietly undertaking this worthwhile task. But they do not trumpet the fact, because this is merely a high school function that our current sad state of educational affairs has thrust upon them, about which they are not inclined to boast.

Now that the distractions of the sixties are over, and undergraduate education has become more important again (because the graduate departments, aside from the professional schools, are in trouble due to the shortage of academic jobs), university officials have had somehow to deal with the undeniable fact that the students who enter are uncivilized, and that the universities have some responsibility for civilizing them. If one were to give a base interpretation of the schools' motives, one could allege that their concern stems from shame and self-interest. It is becoming all too evident that liberal education—which is what the small band of prestigious institutions are supposed to provide, in contrast to the big state schools, which are thought simply to prepare specialists to meet the practical demands of a complex society—has no content, that a certain kind of fraud is being perpetrated. For a time the great moral consciousness alleged to have been fostered in students by the great universities, especially their vocation as gladiators who fight war and racism, seemed to fulfill the demands of the collective university conscience. They were doing something other than offer-

ing preliminary training for doctors and lawyers. Concern and compassion were thought to be the indefinable X that pervaded all the parts of the Arts and Sciences campus. But when that evanescent mist dissipated during the seventies, and the faculties found themselves face to face with ill-educated young people with no intellectual tastes—unaware that there even are such things, obsessed with getting on with their careers before having looked at life—and the universities offered no counterpoise, no alternative goals, a reaction set in.

Liberal education—since it has for so long been ill-defined, has none of the crisp clarity or institutionalized prestige of the professions, but nevertheless perseveres and has money and respectability connected with it—has always been a battleground for those who are somewhat eccentric in relation to the specialties. It is in something like the condition of churches as opposed to, say, hospitals. Nobody is quite certain of what the religious institutions are supposed to do anymore, but they do have some kind of role either responding to a real human need or as the vestige of what was once a need, and they invite the exploitation of quacks, adventurers, cranks and fanatics. But they also solicit the warmest and most valiant efforts of persons of peculiar gravity and depth. In liberal education, too, the worst and the best fight it out, fakers vs. authentics, sophists vs. philosophers, for the favor of public opinion and for control over the study of man in our times. The most conspicuous participants in the struggle are administrators who are formally responsible for presenting some kind of public image of the education their colleges offer, persons with a political agenda or vulgarizers of what the specialties know, and real teachers of the humane disciplines who actually see their relation to the whole and urgently wish to preserve the awareness of it in their students' consciousness.

So, just as in the sixties universities were devoted to removing requirements, in the eighties they are busy with attempts to put them back in, a much more difficult task. The word of the day is "core." It is generally agreed that "we went a bit far in the sixties," and that a little fine-tuning has now become clearly necessary.

There are two typical responses to the problem. The easiest and most administratively satisfying solution is to make use of what is already there in the autonomous departments and simply force the students to cover the fields, i.e., take one or more courses in each of the general divisions of the university: natural science, social science and the humanities. The reigning ideology here is *breadth,* as was *openness* in the age of laxity. The courses are almost always the already existing introductory courses, which are of least interest to the major professors and merely assume the worth and reality of that which is to be studied. It is general education, in the sense in which a jack-of-all-trades is a generalist. He knows a bit of everything and is inferior to the specialist in each area. Students may wish to sample a variety of fields, and it may be good to encourage them to look around and see if there is something that attracts them in one of which they have no experience. But this is not a liberal education and does not satisfy any longing they have for one. It just teaches that there is no high-level generalism, and that what they are doing is preliminary to the real stuff and part of the childhood they are leaving behind. Thus they desire to get it over with and get on with what their professors do seriously. Without recognition of important questions of common concern, there cannot be serious liberal education, and attempts to establish it will be but failed gestures.

It is more or less precise awareness of the inadequacy of this approach to core curricula that motivates the second approach, which consists of what one might call composite courses. These are constructions developed especially for general-education purposes and usually require collaboration of professors drawn from several departments. These courses have titles like "Man in Nature," "War and Moral Responsibility," "The Arts and Creativity," "Culture and the Individual." Everything, of course, depends upon who plans them and who teaches them. They have the clear advantage of requiring some reflection on the general needs of students and force specialized professors to broaden their perspectives, at least for a moment. The dangers are trendiness, mere popularization and lack of substantive rigor. In general, the natural scientists do not collaborate in such endeavors, and hence these courses tend to be unbalanced. In short, they do not point beyond themselves and do not provide the student with independent means to pursue permanent questions independently, as, for example, the study of Aristotle or Kant as wholes once did. They tend to be bits of this and that. Liberal education should give the student the sense that learning must and can be both synoptic and precise. For this, a very small, detailed problem can be the best way, if it is framed so as to open out on the whole. Unless the course has the specific intention to lead to the permanent questions, to make the student aware of them and give him some competence in the important works that treat of them, it tends to be a pleasant diversion and a dead end—because it has nothing to do with any program of further study he can imagine. If such programs engage the best energies of the best people in the university, they can be beneficial and provide some of the missing intellectual excitement for both professors and students. But they rarely do, and they are too cut off from the top, from what the various faculties see as their real business. Where the power is determines the life of the whole body. And the intellectual problems unresolved at the top cannot be resolved administratively below. The problem is the lack of any unity of the sciences and the loss of will or the means even to discuss the issue. The illness above is the cause of the illness below, to which all the good-willed efforts of honest liberal educationists can at best be palliatives.

Of course, the only serious solution is the one that is almost universally rejected: the good old Great Books approach, in which a liberal education means reading certain generally recognized classic texts, just reading them, letting them dictate what the questions are and the method of approaching them—not forcing them into categories we make up, not treating them as historical products, but trying to read them as their authors wished them to be read. I am perfectly well aware of, and actually agree with, the objections to the Great Books cult. It is amateurish; it encourages an autodidact's self-assurance without competence; one cannot read all of the Great Books carefully; if one only reads Great Books, one can never know what a great, as opposed to an ordinary, book is; there is no way of determining who is to decide what a Great Book or what the canon is; books are made the ends and not the means; the whole movement has a certain coarse evangelistic tone that is the opposite of good taste; it engenders a spurious intimacy with greatness; and so forth. But one thing is certain: wherever the Great Books make up a central part of the curriculum, the students are excited and satisfied, feel they are doing something that is independent and fulfilling, getting some-

thing from the university they cannot get elsewhere. The very fact of this special experience, which leads nowhere beyond itself, provides them with a new alternative and a respect for study itself. The advantage they get is an awareness of the classic—particularly important for our innocents; an acquaintance with what big questions were when there were still big questions; models, at the very least, of how to go about answering them; and, perhaps most important of all, a fund of shared experiences and thoughts on which to ground their friendships with one another. Programs based upon judicious use of great texts provide the royal road to students' hearts. Their gratitude at learning of Achilles or the categorical imperative is boundless. Alexandre Koyré, the late historian of science, told me that his appreciation for America was great when—in the first course he taught at the University of Chicago, in 1940 at the beginning of his exile—a student spoke in his paper of Mr. Aristotle, unaware that he was not a contemporary. Koyré said that only an American could have the naive profundity to take Aristotle as living thought, unthinkable for most scholars. A good program of liberal education feeds the student's love of truth and passion to live a good life. It is the easiest thing in the world to devise courses of study, adapted to the particular conditions of each university, which thrill those who take them. The difficulty is in getting them accepted by the faculty.

None of the three great parts of the contemporary university is enthusiastic about the Great Books approach to education. The natural scientists are benevolent toward other fields and toward liberal education, if it does not steal away their students and does not take too much time from their preparatory studies. But they themselves are interested primarily in the solution of the questions now important in their disciplines and are not particularly concerned with discussions of their foundations, inasmuch as they are so evidently successful. They are indifferent to Newton's conception of time or his disputes with Leibniz about calculus; Aristotle's teleology is an absurdity beneath consideration. Scientific progress, they believe, no longer depends on the kind of comprehensive reflection given to the nature of science by men like Bacon, Descartes, Hume, Kant and Marx. This is merely historical study, and for a long time now, even the greatest scientists have given up thinking about Galileo and Newton. Progress is undoubted. The difficulties about the truth of science raised by positivism, and those about the goodness of science raised by Rousseau and Nietzsche, have not really penetrated to the center of scientific consciousness. Hence, no Great Books, but incremental progress, is the theme for them.

Social scientists are in general hostile, because the classic texts tend to deal with the human things the social sciences deal with, and they are very proud of having freed themselves from the shackles of such earlier thought to become truly scientific. And, unlike the natural scientists, they are insecure enough about their achievement to feel threatened by the works of earlier thinkers, perhaps a bit afraid that students will be seduced and fall back into the bad old ways. Moreover, with the possible exception of Weber and Freud, there are no social science books that can be said to be classic. This may be interpreted favorably to the social sciences by comparing them to the natural sciences, which can be said to be a living organism developing by the addition of little cells, a veritable body of knowledge proving itself to be such by the very fact of this almost unconscious growth, with thousands of parts oblivious to the whole,

nevertheless contributing to it. This is in opposition to a work of imagination or of philosophy, where a single creator makes and surveys an artificial whole. But whether one interprets the absence of the classic in the social sciences in ways flattering or unflattering to them, the fact causes social scientists discomfort. I remember the professor who taught the introductory graduate courses in social science methodology, a famous historian, responding scornfully and angrily to a question I naively put to him about Thucydides with "Thucydides was a fool!"

More difficult to explain is the tepid reaction of humanists to Great Books education, inasmuch as these books now belong almost exclusively to what are called the humanities. One would think that high esteem for the classic would reinforce the spiritual power of the humanities, at a time when their temporal power is at its lowest. And it is true that the most active proponents of liberal education and the study of classic texts are indeed usually humanists. But there is division among them. Some humanities disciplines are just crusty specialties that, although they depend on the status of classic books for their existence, are not really interested in them in their natural state—much philology, for example, is concerned with the languages but not what is said in them—and will and can do nothing to support their own infrastructure. Some humanities disciplines are eager to join the real sciences and transcend their roots in the now overcome mythic past. Some humanists make the legitimate complaints about lack of competence in the teaching and learning of Great Books, although their criticism is frequently undermined by the fact that they are only defending recent scholarly interpretation of the classics rather than a vital, authentic understanding. In their reaction there is a strong element of specialist's jealousy and narrowness. Finally, a large part of the story is just the general debilitation of the humanities, which is both symptom and cause of our present condition.

To repeat, the crisis of liberal education is a reflection of a crisis at the peaks of learning, an incoherence and incompatibility among the first principles with which we interpret the world, an intellectual crisis of the greatest magnitude, which constitutes the crisis of our civilization. But perhaps it would be true to say that the crisis consists not so much in this incoherence but in our incapacity to discuss or even recognize it. Liberal education flourished when it prepared the way for the discussion of a unified view of nature and man's place in it, which the best minds debated on the highest level. It decayed when what lay beyond it were only specialties, the premises of which do not lead to any such vision. The highest is the partial intellect; there is no synopsis. . . .

CONCLUSION

These are the shadows cast by the peaks of the university over the entering undergraduate. Together they represent what the university has to say about man and his education, and they do not project a coherent image. The differences and the indifferences are too great. It is difficult to imagine that there is either the wherewithal or the energy within the university to constitute or reconstitute the idea of an educated human being and establish a liberal education again.

However, the contemplation of this scene is in itself a proper philosophic activity. The university's evident lack of wholeness in an enterprise that clearly demands it cannot help troubling some of its members. The questions are all there. They only need to be addressed continuously and seriously for liberal learning to exist; for it does not consist so much in answers as in the permanent dialogue. It is in such perplexed professors that at least the idea might persevere and help to guide some of the needy young persons at our doorstep. The matter is still present in the university; it is the form that has vanished. One cannot and should not hope for a general reform. The hope is that the embers do not die out.

Men may live more truly and fully in reading Plato and Shakespeare than at any other time, because then they are participating in essential being and are forgetting their accidental lives. The fact that this kind of humanity exists or existed, and that we can somehow still touch it with the tips of our outstretched fingers, makes our imperfect humanity, which we can no longer bear, tolerable. The books in their objective beauty are still there, and we must help protect and cultivate the delicate tendrils reaching out toward them through the unfriendly soil of students' souls. Human nature, it seems, remains the same in our very altered circumstances because we still face the same problems, if in different guises, and have the distinctively human need to solve them, even though our awareness and forces have become enfeebled.

After a reading of the *Symposium* a serious student came with deep melancholy and said it was impossible to imagine that magic Athenian atmosphere reproduced, in which friendly men, educated, lively, on a footing of equality, civilized but natural, came together and told wonderful stories about the meaning of their longing. But such experiences are always accessible. Actually, this playful discussion took place in the midst of a terrible war that Athens was destined to lose, and Aristophanes and Socrates at least could foresee that this meant the decline of Greek civilization. But they were not given to culture despair, and in these terrible political circumstances, their abandon to the joy of nature proved the viability of what is best in man, independent of accidents, of circumstance. We feel ourselves too dependent on history and culture. This student did not have Socrates, but he had Plato's book about him, which might even be better; he had brains, friends and a country happily free enough to let them gather and speak as they will. What is essential about that dialogue, or any of the Platonic dialogues, is reproducible in almost all times and places. He and his friends can think together. It requires much thought to learn that this thinking might be what it is all for. That's where we are beginning to fail. But it is right under our noses, improbable but always present.

Throughout this book I have referred to Plato's *Republic,* which is for me *the* book on education, because it really explains to me what I experience as a man and a teacher, and I have almost always used it to point out what we should not hope for, as a teaching of moderation and resignation. But all its impossibilities act as a filter to leave the residue of the highest and non-illusory possibility. The real community of man, in the midst of all the self-contradictory simulacra of community, is the community of those who seek the truth, of the potential knowers, that is, in principle, of all men to the extent they desire to know. But in fact this includes only a few, the true friends, as Plato was to Aristotle at the very moment they were disagreeing about the nature of the good. Their common concern for the good linked them; their disagreement about it proved they needed one another to understand it. They were absolutely one soul as they looked at the problem. This, according to Plato, is the only real friendship, the only real common good. It is here that

the contact people so desperately seek is to be found. The other kinds of relatedness are only imperfect reflections of this one trying to be self-subsisting, gaining their only justification from their ultimate relation to this one. This is the meaning of the riddle of the improbable philosopher-kings. They have a true community that is exemplary for all other communities.

This is a radical teaching but perhaps one appropriate to our own radical time, in which proximate attachments have become so questionable and we know of no others. This age is not utterly insalubrious for philosophy. Our problems are so great and their sources so deep that to understand them we need philosophy more than ever, if we do not despair of it, and it faces the challenges on which it flourishes. I still believe that universities, rightly understood, are where community and friendship can exist in our times. Our thought and our politics have become inextricably bound up with the universities, and they have served us well, human things being what they are. But for all that, and even though they deserve our strenuous efforts, one should never forget that Socrates was not a professor, that he was put to death, and that the love of wisdom survived, partly because of his *individual* example. This is what really counts, and we must remember it in order to know how to defend the university.

This is the American moment in world history, the one for which we shall forever be judged. Just as in politics the responsibility for the fate of freedom in the world has devolved upon our regime, so the fate of philosophy in the world has devolved upon our universities, and the two are related as they have never been before. The gravity of our given task is great, and it is very much in doubt how the future will judge our stewardship.

1988

10.

JOHN J. SWEENEY: Organized Labor and the Economic Future

In the mid-twentieth century labor unions reached the zenith of their power in American politics. During the 1930s organized labor emerged as a core constituency of the Democratic Party, and New Deal legislation extended government protection to the rights of labor unions. By the 1950s organized labor constituted one-fourth of the nation's workforce and exerted disproportionately large influence on national political and economic life. Throughout the 1960s and 1970s, however, the power of organized labor began to wane, particularly when evidence emerged of its ties to organized crime. In 1981 the administration of President Ronald Reagan delivered a resounding blow to unionism by breaking the strike of the air-traffic controllers. Throughout the 1980s the Reagan administration attempted to freeze the minimum wage and pursue free trade negotiations that threatened the jobs of many American labor union members. John Sweeney, president of the Service Employees International Union, rallied labor opposition to these policies. In an address at the City Club of Cleveland, Ohio, in January 1988, Sweeney urged his audience to support Congressional legislation that would protect worker rights and benefits. Excerpts are reprinted below.

Source: *Vital Speeches of the Day*, April 1, 1988.

THE DECADE OF THE 1980s, the Reagan years, have been tough ones for organized labor.

They began with the firing of the PATCO members, the air traffic controllers, a clear signal to employers that it was open season on labor unions.

They intensified with the stacking of the National Labor Relations Board, which then effectively suspended the Federal laws which protect the rights of workers and their unions.

They crested as the administration all but ceased enforcement actions of the agencies working people depend upon— the Department of Labor, the Occupational Health and Safety Administration, the Environmental Protection Agency, the Equal Employment Opportunity Commission and the Civil Rights Division of the Justice Department.

But now the Reagan years are coming to a close.

He'll soon be gone.

But organized labor will remain.

And not only have we survived, we're already making a comeback.

This year, organized labor will make a political comeback by playing a key role in nominating and electing the next President of the United States.

And next year, as we begin to restore some balance to the playing field, organized labor will continue and intensify a resurgence in organizing and bargaining.

One reason for our comeback is that organized labor, which had grown too comfortable and lost its edge, has undergone several years of intensive soul-searching and we've made a lot of progress in correcting some of our deficiencies.

Our union, the Service Employees Union, is now the fifth-largest and fastest-growing union in the AFL-CIO.

And I know many of you know of the progress we've made because of our local unions here in Cleveland.

But the biggest reason labor is enjoying a comeback is that working people in this country are finding they need unions as never before.

For as long as most of us can remember, "mom and apple pie" have been joined as national code words by "growth" and "opportunity."

You knew that having a job and working hard meant you could support a family and you could live a little better than your parents did.

That's all out the window now.

For the first time in fifty years, for the first time since the great depression, U.S. standards of living are down—the victim of the shortsightedness of American business as well as the myopia of government.

According to the joint economic committee of Congress, a thirty year old man today earns 10 percent less than his father did at the same age.

Despite six years of economic recovery, most American families are living on less today than they did fourteen years ago.

And despite the rise in dual wage earner families, average family income is down about one percent from its 1973 level.

In this same period, American worker's hourly wages dropped six percent and weekly wages dropped 14 percent.

Today, more than half of all Americans earn less than $12,500 a year and thirty-two million Americans are living below the poverty level.

The poverty rate is up 23 percent and the size of the middle class is shrinking as the rich get richer and the poor get poorer.

No small part of the blame for this disastrous slide in the U.S. standard of living belongs to Ronald Reagan and his disastrous economic policies.

And one important underlying cause of the decline has been the shift of our economy from an industrial base, with generally high-paying jobs, to a service base with lower paying jobs.

But, in my opinion, the major cause has been the course steered by American business.

Looking back, the crossroads probably occurred in the mid-1970s.

Driven by the need to compete in a new, more integrated world economy, U.S. businesses faced a choice.

They could compete by improving product quality and productivity through investment in workforce training as well as innovation, while looking to public policy to manage trade.

Or they could seek short-term profits by reversing U.S. job standards, cheapening the workforce and shopping for production sites in other countries.

For the most part, corporate managers chose the latter course . . . and government leaders tagged along.

The consequences have been awful.

With plant shutdowns and moves offshore, over two-million high-paying manufacturing jobs have been permanently lost since 1979.

At the same time, the new service sector jobs being created pay poorly, lack basic benefits and offer little in terms of advancement opportunities.

And employers have used a wide range of tactics to whack away even further at employee salaries and benefits.

One tactic has been to fill openings with part-time and temporary workers, at lower pay rates and with substandard or no benefits. . . .

What's clearly needed is a new social contract between business, labor and government, one that properly recognizes the role of each partner in the economic progress of our nation and encourages cooperation between the three.

It must be a contract that recognizes the fact that a free and vigorous labor movement is essential in a democratic society and then restores the rights of American workers to join and participate in the labor union of their choice.

We could start right here in Cleveland where our District 925 is negotiating with the Cleveland Public Library.

To the library board, I say, "We are both progressive institutions vital to this community—let's work with each other."

The new social contract must also include new initiatives on the part of American business to restore long-term productivity and profitability through investment in employees as well as in plants and equipment and research and development.

And it must be a contract that returns government to its proper role of providing solutions to problems that workers or businesses themselves cannot solve.

This year, the U.S. Congress is considering many such solutions and I want to comment briefly on three of them because they are high on the agenda of the Service Employees International Union.

The first is the minimum wage.

The minimum wage assures that employers don't victimize workers.

But, equally important, it provides a floor that keeps wages at the bottom of the scale from being abnormally depressed.

Since 1981, the minimum wage has been stuck at $3.35 an hour while the cost of living has jumped 27 percent.

And this indeed means that wages have become abnormally depressed.

Abnormally low wages mean workers can't enjoy even a minimal standard of living.

But they also mean the taxpayers end up subsidizing business because the workers require various forms of public assistance just to survive.

Abnormally low wages are also bad economics: people can't spend money if they don't have any, and consumer spending is what makes a capitalistic economy percolate.

Support an increase in the minimum wage—it's good for workers and it's good for business.

The second item on our legislative agenda is called the Family and Medical Leave Act and it will require all employers to provide minimum parental leave to employees.

The U.S. is the only industrialized country in the world without a parental leave policy, although we have one of the highest rates of working women.

Expanded parental and child leave policies cost very little, but they have big payoffs in morale, productivity and reduced employee turnover.

Support the Family and Medical Leave Act—it's good for workers and it's good for business.

The third big item on our agenda is minimum mandated employer health insurance, specifically the Kennedy Bill which will require employers to provide basic health insurance to anyone who works more than 17.5 hours a week.

There are nearly 40 million people in this country who have no health insurance and three-fourths of them are workers and their families.

Employer insurance plans now cover only 66 percent of our population and that percentage is shrinking.

People with no insurance either go without medical care or they have to depend upon public health care.

That undeniably means that individual taxpayers again end up subsidizing business.

And in this case, it also means employers who provide health insurance end up, through the taxes they pay, subsidizing employers who do not provide insurance!

Support minimum mandated health care—it's good for workers and it's good for business.

Again, thank you for inviting me here today.

———◆———

Labor is not fighting for a larger slice of the national pie. Labor is fighting for a larger pie.

WALTER REUTHER, 1945

11.

Shelby Steele and John E. Jacob: The State of Black America

The Civil Rights Movement of the 1950s and 1960s represented the apogee of African American political unity. The effort to defeat Jim Crow segregation and to promote federal legislation on behalf of civil rights and racial equality enjoyed wide support among African Americans of all classes and regions. In part because of such unity, the movement culminated in the passage of the 1964 Civil Rights and 1965 Voting Rights acts, the two most sweeping pieces of civil rights legislation since Reconstruction. Encouragingly, the consequences of the Civil Rights Movement went beyond the political arena. In the movement's wake, the black middle class grew rapidly as African Americans seized upon new and expanding economic opportunities. Nevertheless, two decades later, as the Civil Rights Movement lost steam, a large minority of African Americans remained trapped in urban poverty and despair. In the 1970s and '80s sociologists, other academic observers, and civil rights leaders began to pay closer attention to class divisions within African American communities, often arriving at different conclusions. The first document reprinted below, an essay by author Shelby Steele, explores the intersection of race and class in the lives of middle-class African Americans. The second, a speech delivered by John Jacob, the president and chief executive officer of the National Urban League, before members of Congress in March 1988, addresses the question of how to extend greater opportunities to poor blacks.

Sources: *Commentary,* January 1988, "On Being Black and Middle Class."

Vital Speeches of the Day, August 1, 1988.

A. SHELBY STEELE

CLASS DIVISION AMONG AFRICAN AMERICANS

Not long ago a friend of mine, black like myself, said to me that the term "black middle class" was actually a contradiction in terms. Race, he insisted, blurred class distinctions among blacks. If you were black, you were just black and that was that. When I argued, he let his eyes roll at my naiveté. Then he went on. For us, as black professionals, it was an exercise in self-flattery, a pathetic pretension, to give meaning to such a distinction. Worse, the very idea of class threatened the unity that was vital to the black community as a whole. After all, since when had white America taken note of anything but color when it came to blacks? He then reminded me of an old Malcolm X line that had been popular in the 60's. Question: What is a black man with a Ph.D.? Answer: A nigger.

For many years I had been on my friend's side of this argument. Much of my conscious thinking on the old conundrum of race and class was shaped during my high-school and college years in the race-charged 60's, when the fact of my race took on an almost religious significance. Progressively, from the mid-60's on, more and more aspects of my life found their explanation, their justification, and their motivation in race. My youthful concerns about career, romance, money, values, and even styles of dress became subject to consultation with various oracular sources of racial wisdom. And these ranged from a figure as ennobling as Martin Luther King, Jr. to the underworld elegance of dress I found in jazz clubs on the South Side of Chicago. Everywhere there were signals, and in those days I considered myself so blessed with clarity and direction that I pitied my white classmates who found more embarrassment than guidance in the fact of *their* race. In 1968, inflated by my new power, I took a mischievous delight in calling them culturally disadvantaged.

But now, hearing my friend's comment was like hearing a priest from a church I'd grown disenchanted with. I understood him, but my faith was weak. What had sustained me in the 60's sounded monotonous and off-the-mark in the 80's. For me, race had lost much of its juju, its singular capacity to conjure meaning. And today, when I honestly look at my life and the lives of many other middle-class blacks I know, I can see that race never fully explained our situation in American society. Black though I may be, it is impossible for me to sit in my single-family house with two cars in the driveway and a swing set in the back yard and *not* see the role class has played in my life. And how can my friend, similarly raised and similarly situated, not see it?

Yet despite my certainty I felt a sharp tug of guilt as I tried to explain myself over my friend's skepticism. He is a man of many comedic facial expressions and, as I spoke, his brow lifted in extreme moral alarm as if I were uttering the un-

speakable. His clear implication was that I was being elitist and possibly (dare he suggest?) anti-black—crimes for which there might well be no redemption. He pretended to fear for me. I chuckled along with him, but inwardly I did wonder at myself. Though I never doubted the validity of what I was saying, I felt guilty saying it. Why?

After he left (to retrieve his daughter from a dance lesson) I realized that the trap I felt myself in had a tiresome familiarity and, in a sort of slow-motion epiphany, I began to see its outline. It was like the suddenly sharp vision one has at the end of a burdensome marriage when all the long-repressed incompatibilities come undeniably to light.

What became clear to me is that people like myself, my friend, and middle-class blacks generally are caught in a very specific double bind that keeps two equally powerful elements of our identity at odds with each other. The middle-class values by which we were raised—the work ethic, the importance of education, the value of property ownership, of respectability, of "getting ahead," of stable family life, of initiative, of self-reliance, etc.—are, in themselves, raceless and even assimilationist. They urge us toward participation in the American mainstream, toward integration, toward a strong identification with the society— and toward the entire constellation of qualities that are implied in the word individualism. These values are almost rules for how to prosper in a democratic, free-enterprise society that admires and rewards individual effort. They tell us to work hard for ourselves and our families and to seek our opportunities whenever they appear, inside or outside the confines of whatever ethnic group we may belong to.

But the particular pattern of racial identification that emerged in the 60's and that still prevails today urges middle-class blacks (and all blacks) in the opposite direction. This pattern asks us to see ourselves as an embattled minority, and it urges an adversarial stance toward the mainstream, an emphasis on ethnic consciousness over individualism. It is organized around an implied separatism.

The opposing thrust of these two parts of our identity results in the double bind of middle-class blacks. There is no forward movement on either plane that does not constitute backward movement on the other. This was the familiar trap I felt myself in while talking with my friend. As I spoke about class, his eyes reminded me that I was betraying race. Clearly, the two indispensable parts of my identity were a threat to one another.

Of course when you think about it, class and race are both similar in some ways and also naturally opposed. They are two forms of collective identity with boundaries that intersect. But whether they clash or peacefully coexist has much to do with how they are defined. Being both black and middle-class becomes a double bind when class and race are defined in sharply antagonistic terms, so that one must be repressed to appease the other.

But what is the "substance" of these two identities, and how does each establish itself in an individual's overall identity? It seems to me that when we identify with any collective we are basically identifying with images that tell us what it means to be a member of that collective. Identity is not the same thing as the fact of membership in a collective; it is, rather, a form of self-definition, facilitated by images of what we wish our membership in the collective to mean. In this sense, the images we identify with may reflect the aspirations of the collective more than they reflect reality, and their content can vary with shifts in those aspirations.

But the process of identification is usually dialectical. It is just as necessary to say what we are *not* as it is to say what we are—so that finally identification comes about by embracing a polarity of positive and negative images. To identify as middle-class, for example, I must have both positive and negative images of what being middle-class entails; then I will know what I should and should not be doing in order to be middle-class. The same goes for racial identity.

In the racially turbulent 60's the polarity of images that came to define racial identification was very antagonistic to the polarity that defined middle-class identification. One might say that the positive images of one lined up with the negative images of the other, so that to identify with both required either a contortionist's flexibility or a dangerous splitting of the self. The double bind of the black middle class was in place.

The black middle class has always defined its class identity by means of positive images gleaned from middle-and upper-class white society, and by means of negative images of lower-class blacks. This habit goes back to the institution of slavery itself, when "house" slaves both mimicked the whites they served and held themselves above the "field" slaves. But in the 60's the old bourgeois impulse to dissociate from the lower classes (the "we-they" distinction) backfired when racial identity suddenly called for the celebration of this same black lower class. One of the qualities of a double bind is that one feels it more than sees it, and I distinctly remember the tension and strange sense of dishonesty I felt in those days as I moved back and forth like a bigamist between the demands of class and race.

Though my father was born poor, he achieved middle-class standing through much hard work and sacrifice (one of his favorite words) and by identifying fully with solid middle-class values—mainly hard work, family life, property ownership, and education for his children (all four of whom have advanced degrees). In his mind these were not so much values as laws of nature. People who embodied them made up the positive images in his class polarity. The negative images came largely from the blacks he had left behind because they were "going nowhere."

No one in my family remembers how it happened, but as time went on, the negative images congealed into an imaginary character named Sam who, from the extensive service we put him to, quickly grew to mythic proportions. In our family lore he was sometimes a trickster, sometimes a boob, but always possessed of a catalogue of sly faults that gave up graphic images of everything we should not be. On sacrifice: "Sam never thinks about tomorrow. He wants it now or he doesn't care about it." On work: "Sam doesn't favor it too much." On children: "Sam likes to have them but not to raise them." On money: "Sam drinks it up and pisses it out." On fidelity: "Sam has to have two or three women." On clothes: "Sam features loud clothes. He likes to see and be seen." And so on. Sam's persona amounted to a negative instruction manual in class identity.

I don't think that any of us believed Sam's faults were accurate representations of lower-class black life. He was an instrument of self-definition, not of sociological accuracy. It never occurred to us that he looked very much like the white racist stereotype of blacks, or that he might have been a manifestation of our own racial self-hatred. He simply gave us a counterpoint against which to express our aspirations. If self-hatred was a factor, it was not, for us, a matter of hating lower-class blacks but of hating what we did not want to be.

Still, hate or love aside, it is fundamentally true that my middle-class identity involved a dissociation from images of lower-class black life and a corresponding identification with values and patterns of responsibility that are common to the middle class everywhere. These values sent me a clear message: be both an individual and a responsible citizen, understand that the quality of your life will approximately reflect the quality of effort you put into it, know that individual responsibility is the basis of freedom and that the limitations imposed by fate (whether fair or unfair) are no excuse for passivity.

Whether I live up to these values or not, I know that my acceptance of them is the result of lifelong conditioning. I know also that I share this conditioning with middle-class people of all races and that I can no more easily be free of it than I can be free of my race. Whether all this got started because the black middle class modeled itself on the white middle class is no longer relevant. For the middle-class black, conditioned by these values from birth, the sense of meaning they provide is as immutable as the color of his skin.

I started the 60's in high school feeling that my class-conditioning was the surest way to overcome racial barriers. My racial identity was pretty much taken for granted. After all, it was obvious to the world that I was black. Yet I ended the 60's in graduate school a little embarrassed by my class background and with an almost desperate need to be "black." The tables had turned. I knew very clearly (though I struggled to repress it) that my aspirations and my sense of how to operate in the world came from my class background, yet "being black" required certain attitudes and stances that made me feel secretly a little duplicitous. The inner compatibility of class and race I had known in 1960 was gone.

For blacks, the decade between 1960 and 1969 saw racial identification undergo the same sort of transformation that national identity undergoes in times of war. It became more self-conscious, more narrowly focused, more prescribed, less tolerant of opposition. It spawned an implicit party line, which tended to disallow competing forms of identity. Race-as-identity was lifted from the relative slumber it knew in the 50's and pressed into service in a social and political war against oppression. It was redefined along sharp adversarial lines and directed toward the goal of mobilizing the great mass of black Americans in this warlike effort. It was imbued with a strong moral authority, useful for denouncing those who opposed it and for celebrating those who honored it as a positive achievement rather than a mere birthright.

The form of racial identification that quickly evolved to meet this challenge presented blacks as a racial monolith, a singular people with a common experience of oppression. Differences within the race, no matter how ineradicable, had to be minimized. Class distinctions were one of the first such differences to be sacrificed, since they not only threatened racial unity but also seemed to stand in contradiction to the principle of equality which was the announced goal of the movement for racial progress. The discomfort I felt in 1969, the vague but relentless sense of duplicity, was the result of a historical necessity that put my race and class at odds, that was asking me to cast aside the distinction of my class and identify with a monolithic view of my race.

If the form of this racial identity was the monolith, its substance was victimization. The civil-rights movement and the more radical splinter groups of the late 60's were all dedicated to ending racial victimization, and the form of black identity that emerged to facilitate this goal made blackness and victimization virtually synonymous. Since it was our victimization more than any other variable that identified and unified us, moreover, it followed logically that the purest black was the poor black. It was images of him that clustered around the positive pole of the race polarity; all other blacks were, in effect, required to identify with him in order to confirm their own blackness.

Certainly there were more dimensions to the black experience than victimization, but no other had the same capacity to fire the indignation needed for war. So, again out of historical necessity, victimization became the overriding focus of racial identity. But this only deepened the double bind for middle-class blacks like me. When it came to class we were accustomed to defining ourselves against lower-class blacks and identifying with at least the values of middle-class whites; when it came to race we were now being asked to identify with images of lower-class blacks and to see whites, middle-class or otherwise, as victimizers. Negative lining up with positive, we were called upon to reject what we had previously embraced and to embrace what we had previously rejected. To put it still more personally, the Sam figure I had been raised to define myself against had now become the "real" black I was expected to identify with.

The fact that the poor black's new status was only passively earned by the condition of his victimization, not by assertive, positive action, made little difference. Status was status apart from the means by which it was achieved, and along with it came a certain power—the power to define the terms of access to that status, to say who was black and who was not. If a lower-class black said you were not really "black"—a sell-out, an Uncle Tom—the judgment was all the more devastating because it carried the authority of his status. And this judgment soon enough came to be accepted by many whites as well.

In graduate school I was once told by a white professor, "Well, but . . . you're not really black. I mean, you're not disadvantaged." In his mind my lack of victim status disqualified me from the race itself. More recently I was complimented by a black student for speaking reasonably correct English, "proper" English as he put it. "But I don't know if I really want to talk like that," he went on. "Why not?" I asked. "Because then I wouldn't be black no more," he replied without a pause.

To overcome his marginal status, the middle-class black had to identify with a degree of victimization that was beyond his actual experience. In college (and well beyond) we used to play a game called "nap matching." It was a game of one-upmanship, in which we sat around outdoing each other with stories of racial victimization, symbolically measured by the naps of our hair. Most of us were middle-class and so had few personal stories to relate, but if we could not match naps with our own biographies, we would move on to those legendary tales of victimization that came to us from the public domain.

The single story that sat atop the pinnacle of racial victimization for us was that of Emmett Till, the Northern black teenager who, on a visit to the South in 1955, was killed and grotesquely mutilated for supposedly looking at or whistling at (we were never sure which, though we argued the point endlessly) a white woman. Oh, how we probed his story, finding in his youth and Northern upbringing the quintessential embodiment of black innocence, brought down by a white evil so portentous and apocalyptic, so gnarled and hideous, that it left us with a feeling not far from awe. By telling his story and others like it, we came to *feel* the immutability of our victimization, its utter indigenousness, as a thing on this earth like dirt or sand or water.

Of course, these sessions were a ritual of group identification, a means by which we, as middle-class blacks, could be at one with our race. But why were we, who had only a moderate experience of victimization (and that offset by opportunities our parents never had), so intent on assimilating or appropriating an identity that in so many ways contradicted our own? Because, I think, the sense of innocence that is always entailed in feeling victimized filled us with a corresponding feeling of entitlement, or even license, that helped us endure our vulnerability on a largely white college campus. . . .

As a middle-class black I have often felt myself *contriving* to be "black." And I have noticed this same contrivance in others—a certain stretching away from the natural flow of one's life to align oneself with a victim-focused black identity. Our particular needs are out of sync with the form of identity available to meet those needs. Middle-class blacks need to identify racially; it is better to think of ourselves as black and victimized than not black at all; so we contrive (more unconsciously than consciously) to fit ourselves into an identity that denies our class and fails to address the true source of our vulnerability.

For me this once meant spending inordinate amounts of time at black faculty meetings, though these meetings had little to do with my real racial anxieties or my professional life. I was new to the university, one of two blacks in an English department of over seventy, and I felt a little isolated and vulnerable, though I did not admit it to myself. But at these meetings we discussed the problems of black faculty and students within a framework of victimization. The real vulnerability we felt was covered over by all the adversarial drama the victim/victimized polarity inspired, and hence went unseen and unassuaged. And this, I think, explains our rather chronic ineffectiveness as a group. Since victimization was not our primary problem—the university had long ago opened its doors to us—we had to contrive to make it so, and there is not much energy in contrivance. What I got at these meetings was ultimately an object lesson in how fruitless struggle can be when it is not grounded in actual need.

At our black faculty meetings, the old equation of blackness with victimization was ever present—to be black was to be a victim; therefore, not to be a victim was not to be black. As we contrived to meet the terms of this formula there was an inevitable distortion of both ourselves and the larger university. Through the prism of victimization the university seemed more impenetrable than it actually was, and we more limited in our powers. We fell prey to the victim's myopia, making the university an institution from which we could seek redress but which we could never fully join. And this mindset often led us to look more for compensations for our supposed victimization than for opportunities we could pursue as individuals.

The discomfort and vulnerability felt by middle-class blacks in the 60's, it could be argued, was a worthwhile price to pay considering the progress achieved during that time of racial confrontation. But what may have been tolerable then is intolerable now. Though changes in American society have made it an anachro-

nism, the monolithic form of racial identification that came out of the 60's is still very much with us. It may be more loosely held, and its power to punish heretics has probably diminished, but it continues to catch middle-class blacks in a double bind, thus impeding not only their advancement but even, I would contend, that of blacks as a group.

The victim-focused black identity encourages the individual to feel that his advancement depends almost entirely on that of the group. Thus he loses sight not only of his own possibilities but of the inextricable connection between individual effort and individual advancement. This is a profound encumbrance today, when there is more opportunity for blacks than ever before, for it reimposes limitations that can have the same oppressive effect as those the society has only recently begun to remove.

It was the emphasis on mass action in the 60's that made the victim-focused black identity a necessity. But in the 80's and beyond, when racial advancement will come only through a multitude of individual advancements, this form of identity inadvertently adds itself to the forces that hold us back. Hard work, education, individual initiative, stable family life, property ownership—these have always been the means by which ethnic groups have moved ahead in America. Regardless of past or present victimization, these "laws" of advancement apply absolutely to black Americans also. There is no getting around this. What we need is a form of racial identity that energizes the individual by putting him in touch with both his possibilities and his responsibilities.

It has always annoyed me to hear from the mouths of certain arbiters of blackness that middle-class blacks should "reach back" and pull up those blacks less fortunate than they—as though middle-class status were an unearned and essentially passive condition in which one needed a large measure of noblesse oblige to occupy one's time. My own image is of reaching back from a moving train to lift on board those who have no tickets. A nobel enough sentiment—but might it not be wiser to show them the entire structure of principles, effort, and sacrifice that puts one in a position to buy a ticket any time one likes? This, I think, is something members of the black middle class can realistically offer to other blacks. Their example is not only a testament to possibility but also a lesson in method. But they cannot lead by example until they are released from a black identity that regards that example as suspect, that sees them as "marginally" black, indeed that holds *them* back by catching them in a double bind.

To move beyond the victim-focused black identity we must learn to make a difficult but crucial distinction: between actual victimization, which we must resist with every resource, and identification with the victim's status. Until we do this we will continue to wrestle more with ourselves than with the new opportunities which so many paid so dearly to win.

B. JOHN E. JACOB
A DOOMED GENERATION?

I suppose I give over a hundred talks a year to groups large and small, but it's rare to come before an audience with as much power as you represent.

So I'm honored to be here and I look forward to this opportunity to present my views on the future prospects for black Americans and to engage in some dialogue with you.

Today I want to begin by briefly sketching what the Urban League is, and going on from there to discuss the plight of black citizens. Along the way, I'd like to look back at some of the things America has done to deal with its racial problems.

And I'd like to look ahead as well, to suggest some of the things we can do to secure the future for black people and for all Americans.

Most of you are familiar with the work of the National Urban League. We have affiliates in 112 cities—and that means most of your districts and states include at least one Urban League.

We're based on three principles—and we've held fast to them since our founding 78 years ago.

One is advocacy on behalf of black citizens and all poor people. We are a repository of research, ideas, and experiences that the nation needs in framing policies that affect the third of our population that is black or poor.

Second, we are a community-based service delivery organization. Urban League job and skills training programs, education and health and housing programs, and a host of others, serve one-and-a-half million people who come to Urban League offices each year.

Currently, we are concentrating on mobilizing black and minority communities around a national Education Initiative designed to radically improve black students' academic achievement. We are also concentrating resources on the plight of female-headed households, teenage pregnancy, crime, and citizenship education.

Third, the National Urban League is a bridge-builder between the races. We are believers in an open, integrated, pluralistic society, and our activities support that goal. Our staffs and boards are integrated, and we work very hard at improving race relations in America.

I am clearly here today in our advocacy role, and I have to tell you that the state of black Americans is very bad. In fact, our future is at risk.

In January, the National Urban League published its annual State of Black America report. It documents continuing black disadvantage.

Let me share with you some of the facts about black life in America. I know that this knowledgeable audience is familiar with them—but I also know that they cannot be repeated often enough.

—Half of all black children grow up in poverty.

—Over a third of all blacks are poor— two million more blacks became poor in the past dozen years.

—Almost two million black workers are jobless—over twelve percent of the black work force, and a rate two-and-a-half times that for whites.

—Black family income is only 58 percent that of whites; the typical black family earns less than the government itself says is needed for a decent but modest living standard.

—Black households have less than one-tenth the wealth of white households.

In this high-tech, information age, black dropout rates in some cities are higher than black graduation rates, and there has been an alarming decline in the numbers of blacks entering college.

In virtually all of those areas, black disadvantage is worse than it has been at any time since the mid-1970s.

At the same time, I should acknowledge the fact that some blacks have made extraordinary progress.

Today, black judges preside over court rooms where civil rights demonstrators were once sentenced in the 1950s. Black executives now help shape policies of corporations that once wouldn't hire blacks. Black professionals live in formerly all-white suburbs and earn middle class incomes.

But they share with their poorer brothers and sisters the bond of blackness— the fact that whether affluent or disadvantaged, all blacks suffer from racism.

Racism need not be violent, like the murder of a black truck driver in Texas by police officers, or the actions of a mob in Howard Beach.

It can take subtler forms that affect all blacks—from the teenage kid denied a job in a downtown store because of racial stereotypes to the son of the black doctor who's stopped by police because he's driving Dad's Mercedes and they just assume a young black behind the wheel of that kind of car stole it.

Recently, we've seen surveys that document the harassment of black managers in corporate America, and their perceptions of a racial ceiling that limits their potential.

So despite the often-proclaimed statements that we are finally a color-blind society, I have to tell you that we are very far . . . very far . . . from achieving that goal.

And let me take this opportunity to say that Congress' action last week in overriding the veto of the Civil Rights Restoration Act helps move us just that little bit closer to our goal.

Your vote to override is important for the future of black people and the entire nation. It endorsed the proposition that federal money should not subsidize discrimination in any of its forms.

And it sends a bi-partisan message that when it comes to civil rights, America will allow no loopholes. . . .

In the 1980s, there was an extraordinary increase in poverty, in homelessness, and in other indexes of disadvantage among blacks and other minorities.

This was due to two factors.

One was the deep cuts in government social programs. The Center on Budget and Policy Priorities studied funding for low-income programs other than entitlements and found that spending was cut by 54 percent after inflation since 1981. Subsidized housing was cut by 81 percent and training and employment services by 68 percent.

A second factor is the economic shift in our society.

The elimination of a substantial part of America's manufacturing base has hit black workers hardest. Studies show they are concentrated in the most vulnerable industries and are more likely to be laid off and less likely to find comparable jobs.

And there has been an extraordinary shrinkage in lower level jobs available to people without high educational credentials. That is the single most important factor in the troubles of the black family. . . .

We've found that black people with skills, education and strong family backgrounds are able to enter the mainstream today. But the other half—blacks without skills and suffering from educational deficiencies and social deficits, are increasingly locked out.

There is a powerful myth today that the answer to such problems is self-help—that it is the sole responsibility of the black community to eradicate dysfunctional behavior and to pull itself into the mainstream.

That's just a myth—without basis in fact or history. I have little patience with the people who tell us to look at other groups that are making it. Black people did not come here voluntarily. No other group came in chains. Today's successful immigrant groups came to these shores with education, with a belief in the American Dream, and with substantial internal community financial resources.

Black people have made it in America despite overwhelming odds—the rise of the new black middle class is proof of that. But far too many of us are trapped in the hopelessness and despair of urban ghettos with little hope to escape. Too many of our kids are seduced by the underground economy and sucked into crack and crime.

While many ask why they don't stop such behavior, I have to ask what kind of society creates an environment of hopelessness and despair that drives young children into self-destructive behavior.

The Urban League knows all about self-help and pulling yourself by your bootstraps. That's what we've been about for 78 years. But we also know that conditions have changed in many of our communities—changed to the point where our efforts cannot possibly succeed without government intervention.

It's all right to talk about pulling yourself by your bootstraps but not when you're talking to people who don't have boots. The conditions that allowed previous generations of black people to pull themselves up have changed. Today's young generation is too concerned with simple survival to think about long-term career choices.

In Chicago's Cabrini public housing project, the big question for kids is: have the gangs stopped shooting so I can go out of the house. We're talking about kids whose parents keep them away from the windows so they won't be hit by stray bullets. We're talking about kids whose classmates tote automatic weapons.

It's a new ball game out there, and those people in positions of power who won't do anything about it and who preach self-help are adding to the problem, not solving it.

The black community today is mobilizing to deal with those issues. Last week I attended a meeting of community leaders drawn from across the nation to find ways to save young black men—America's most endangered group. . . .

With a 28 percent top tax rate, can anyone really argue that a surtax or a third bracket at 35 percent is unreasonable at a time of huge national needs?

Any prudent person invests in the future, and any responsible government does the same. There's a strange notion around that when government builds a bridge it is making a capital investment in the future, but when it invests in a job training program, it is current spending. It's not—it is a long-term investment in human capital.

By not making those investments today, we're increasing tomorrow's deficits. Between 700,000 and 900,000 kids drop out of school every year, and the ultimate cost to society in lost earnings and lost tax revenues comes to $240 billion over their lifetimes! And that doesn't even include the bill for crime, social welfare programs, and other costs.

I find it hard to explain why so many businessmen understand that while others do not. The Committee for Economic Development includes some of the top corporate leaders, and they've urged heavy investments in child development programs and in education.

They point out that one dollar spent in child health programs—the same programs the Administration wants to cut— saves almost $5 in expenditures down the road.

When hard-nosed businessmen start talking about the need for nutrition, health, and educational programs, you know the message is beginning to get across that government action is necessary. Only government can train and educate our young people, keep them healthy, and give them access to the social services they've got to have if they're to make decent lives for themselves. . . .

But today, I do want to suggest that such investments in the nation's future make sense . . . are do-able . . . and should cross party and ideological lines.

Winston Churchill is the model of a conservative statesman, and he once said: "There is no finer investment for any community than putting milk into babies."

And George Will, the conservative columnist, wrote: "It is cheaper to feed the child than jail the man. Persons who do not understand this are not conservatives, just dim."

So I don't want to see the fate of black Americans embroiled in false liberal versus conservative ideological disputes. I would hope that all of us have the sense to understand that government has the responsibility and the ability to solve the social problems that endanger our economy and our society.

And I would hope that all of us have the compassion and the human concern to want to do something about children who face bleak futures and adults who have no jobs, no homes, no hope.

Social and economic policy has been in a state of paralysis over the past decade.

We now find ourselves having to make up for lost time and lost resources. A generation of young black people was lost in the 1980s—doomed to failure and to marginality because they didn't have access to the opportunities they needed to become functioning members of our changing society.

We can't let that wastage of human resources continue. We can't let our society continue to drift apart, separated by unbridgeable gaps in education, income, skills, class and race.

We are at a period in time when the currents of the past and future converge . . . when we are positioned to make decisions and implement policies that determine whether future generations of poor and black people are consigned to the outer borders of society or are drawn into the mainstream.

As Congressmen, as leaders, and as citizens, you have the power to make the right choices and the right decisions.

I have faith that you will.

Steve Jennings/Corbis

Creating music with funky beats and informed by radical politics, Public Enemy—featuring, from left to right, Terminator X, Flavor Flav, and Chuck D—was among the most influential and controversial hip-hop groups of the late 1980s.

AP/Wide World Photos

President Bill Clinton, center, with U.S. Holocaust Memorial Council representatives Harvey Meyerhoff, left, and Nobelist Elie Wiesel, light an eternal flame during the dedication of the U.S. Holocaust Memorial Museum in Washington, D.C., on April 22, 1993.

CULTURE

Cats, the Andrew Lloyd Webber musical inspired by T. S. Eliot's *Old Possum's Book of Practical Cats,* became the longest-running show in Broadway history when it surpassed *A Chorus Line* in June 1997. *Cats* finally ended its run in 2000, after 7,397 performances.

Ho/© Reuters

During the 1990s, skateboarding—long a staple of the youth counterculture, with its own set of fashion codes and slang—gained a measure of mainstream respectability, winning large television audiences for competitions such as the X Games.

In October 1999 (right), Catholics protest the Brooklyn Museum of Art's "Sensation" exhibit, a collection of works by contemporary British artists that offended some New Yorkers, including Mayor Rudolph Giuliani, whose administration attempted but failed to close the exhibit. Trumpet virtuoso Wynton Marsalis (below), performing with the Lincoln Center Jazz Orchestra and the New York Philharmonic in 2001, was the leading American proponent of jazz at the turn of the twentieth century. In 1997 he became the first jazz artist to win the Pulitzer Prize in music.

12.

JAMES R. KINCAID: Mythmaking Among Education Critics

During the 1980s critics of American higher education gained national attention. They included both political figures, such as William Bennett, the U.S. secretary of education, and Lynne Cheney, director of the National Endowment for the Humanities (NEH), as well as academics, notably Allan Bloom of the University of Chicago. These critics argued that higher education in the United States had lost its moorings in the 1960s by embracing the ethic of multicultural diversity, by de-emphasizing the ideals and history of Western civilization, and by questioning the existence of absolute truth. As a consequence, according to the critics, American colleges had produced a generation of students who knew little of their own cultural heritage and who possessed a cynical and self-destructive moral relativism. This turn of events, they believed, contrasted sharply with the lofty goals of American higher education in previous eras. James Kincaid, the Aerol Arnold Professor of English at the University of Southern California, responded to this criticism in an address at the USC Academic Honors Convocation in March 1988. Excerpts of the speech, entitled "The Golden Age of Higher Education—and Other Bunk," are reprinted below.

Source: *Vital Speeches of the Day*, June 1, 1988.

THIS WORD "BUNK," I know, seems almost absurdly ill-chosen for this occasion. Bunk lacks the full-throated rotundity, the walking-on-stilts elevation we expect at an event such as this. While not obscene, bunk is a coarse word, with an unwelcome expressiveness. Using it here risks being taken as satiric, of being supposed to suggest that there is something of bunk about this assemblage. I sprint to assure you that nothing of the sort ever touched ny mind. No, I mean to call up the friendly patriotic vulgarity of the word bunk, the way it evokes a gay-nineties barroom and a simpler past, a past so cozy and assured that Henry Ford could declare with impunity that history itself was bunk.

"Bunk," as we know, means empty, stu-pid claptrap; it also refers to a stinky plant root. This interesting word bunk was fathered by a representative to the 16th United States Congress from the county of Buncombe in North Carolina. Just when every other member felt sure an especially long and tedious debate was ending and amidst roars for the question, our hero, a type we all know well from department meetings and other academic gatherings, rose to speak, indeed insisted on his duty to deliver a few entirely-be-side-the-point-comments on behalf of the people of Buncombe. With our usual American vigor, we lopped off the super-fluous syllable and formed the word bunk. Taking it all together, it is a very useful word, this vacuous, stinking-root talk, the sense of idiotic deviousness demonstrated so well by the member from Buncombe, who wanted to use language to show nothing more than that language can be used, that it can occupy space and time—like jogging. But the pure emptiness conveyed by the term is, as I suggested, belied by a certain rootiness, a sense that some devious purpose is being served after all, whether it's to inflate the importance of the member from Buncombe or to advance sneakily a particular point of view. I have in mind here the usefulness of the term in describing the obfuscating and pernicious effect of golden-age myths on discussions of higher education. The bunkiest of all these, in my view, are the narrative constructions employed by right-wing fundamentalist education critics, like Secretary of Education [William] Bennett, NEH Director Lynne Cheney, Chester E. Finn, Jr. and Diane Ravitch, and the best-selling authors Allan Bloom and E. D. Hirsch, Jr.

These figures have been alarmingly successful in reaching a public apparently eager to believe that our present system functions to close minds, to maintain as securely as possible the ignorance of our students, to dither aimlessly about method as we neglect content, to trash Shakespeare and Plato, to extend the poison of the 60s, to promote a vulgar relativism, and, most damnably, to efface a rich and integrated cultural legacy. In a widely publicized survey and report, entitled most promisingly *What Do [Our] 17-Year-Olds Know?*, Ravitch and Finn have chosen to give us nothing at all on the subject and, in the usual way of bunk, to give us a lot of other stuff instead. I defy anyone to gather from their report any clear sense of what 17-Year-Olds Know. We could, in fact, use such information; it might make us better teachers and administrators to learn something about the culture we are in and the young people we are trying to educate. But this re-

port has no time for such things, driven as it is by the desire to tell us what 17-year-olds don't know. And what they don't know is the great tradition; they no longer are given the keys to the warehouse of facts about western culture, a culture which the authors see rather on the lines of the circulatory system of the body—uniform, and, until the 60s, unbroken. Now, our youth confuse Magellan with the Magna Carta and think Jane Austen is a producer of baked goods like Twinkies. In a speech to the National Press Club, Lynne Cheney laments that "Children were once given Longfellow, Hawthorne, Alcott, Dickens, and Shakespeare," works, she says, "which are regarded as classics" but now "that rich content has diminished."

This is an interesting list of works which are regarded by someone, Cheney apparently, as classics. A nasty person might wonder whether Alcott wasn't shoved into this genteel white men's club to loosen things up a bit, to give a nod to the 60s which are otherwise so despised by these fundamentalists. One might also question the passive voice, the rhetorical attempt to slip by these classics as if they were nominated for that honor by God and not by Cheney or by some small group with an ax to grind.

One notices in all these arguments a moving evocation of an educational past that is rich yet homogeneous, exciting yet absolutely uniform. Bloom sets this past in the 50s; others are more vague, suggesting that the location of this wonderland of agreement and shared knowledge is in some blend of their own remote childhood with an image of Harvard in 1830. Such nostalgic mellowness rests on a view of the past which no history of education I know will bear out even slightly. Indeed, laments for the loss of cultural coherence and the attempt to instill into education a solid core have arisen periodically at least since the Civil War. Every time such questions arise they founder on the issue of just how that coherence can be constituted, on what it rests, whether, in fact, it is desirable. Every time, the very motives of those desiring coherence are called into question; every time the battle is waged inconclusively between those who want a single model for education and those who want diversity and pluralism; every time it becomes apparent that a democratic society can not tolerate the imposition of a single cultural model, certainly not one based on a privileged white male eastern school of the early part of the last century busy legislating a version of culture and heritage that would suit its own ends. One must at least ask whether such a model is likely to answer the needs of our present society. The model proposed by Bloom, Bennett, Cheney, and the rest may be reprehensible on moral and ethical grounds—I think it is. I think it is intolerant, smug, self-serving, and undemocratic. But I also think it is hopelessly unproductive. It won't work, and I hope we are not such fools or so entirely ignorant of history as to give it a try.

Note that the dark side of the conservative golden age myth is always the apocalyptic myth of present catastrophe. The drizzly wetness of the first story cleans the path for the steely-jawed authoritarianism of the second. It has always been so, Thomas Carlyle serving as a good historical example. In this case, we have the specter of Hirsch, supported by a grant from the NEH, actually compiling lists of great facts that might form the basis for making good and sure that future 17-year-olds won't be vacuous as this lot. And how will we be so sure? By testing them, of course, by simple exercises of force. We won't let you pass unless you know who Magellan was. Faced with the impossibility of finding agreement on

what our cultural heritage is or whether it should be so naively propagated, the myth of concern turns to the sheer barbarism of lists. Or, in higher education, the myth shrieks for what Carlyle called captains of industry, no-nonsense leaders, in this case university administrators, who will seize control of a faculty that is seen as silly to begin with and now hopelessly compromised in 60s stuff like popular culture, minority programs, and women's studies. Here is an example of this particular version of bunk, the stinking root that undergirds the preposterous golden age myth. This is from a report issued by The Association of American Colleges in February 1985, entitled "Integrity in the College Curriculum"—I quote:

This generation of academic presidents and deans is required to lead us away from the declining and devalued bachelor's degree that now prevails to a new era of curricular coherence, intellectual rigor, and humanistic strengths. Their visions must be bolder, their initiatives more energetic and imaginative, and the great potential for academic leadership that is latent in the authority of their positions must be asserted forcefully and skillfully. Everywhere there are professors eager to join them, waiting only for some sign of executive leadership.

I don't know of too many professors myself who are looking for General Sherman in the guise of a Dean, waving a list of great things that all should know. To be fair, I also don't know of many Deans or Presidents with such narrow views of education or such a pathological commitment to what bunk calls coherence and integrity. But the authoritarian threat is there, and we would be unwise, I think, to ignore it.

It would be equally unwise to haul out once again the old tired defenses of pluralism and to say that we have some kind of unity in diversity. I think that sort of bunk is at least as smelly as the bunk it is seeking to counter. I think we should regard the present situation as an indication that all is not well, that there is a problem in an educational system that is so fiercely atomized, so baffling to students and, if we admit it, to us. I have very little idea myself of what half the departments in this university actually do, and in one or two cases I don't even know what they *are*.

While I do not want to present my own ignorance as representative, I think we might ask ourselves about our commitment to proliferating specialties, to an additive notion of knowledge and curriculum—when something new comes along make it into a program, if it lasts make it into a department. Are we not, ironically, over-enamored of content, despite what the fundamentalists say? Why are we so wedded to the concept of departments? Why are we so eager to isolate those departments, to insist on the mysterious and entirely separate integrity of each one? Is it possible that we are engaging in a game of academic hide and seek, mostly hide? Does the departmental separation provide us with a means of keeping our most basic assumptions hidden from one another and even from ourselves? Are disciplines simply methodology shielded from questioning? Is there anything other than dead habit that keeps us apart in our separate spheres and that renders to our students an image of the university as a kind of giant shopping mall, with each shopkeeper devoutly interested in his own wares and entirely heedless of his neighbors'? Is it any wonder that students might view the university as divided between shops that offer useful goods in the form of vocational training and professional schools and some that are merely areas for browsing, the expensive antique stores of the

humanities, say. I think we should discuss ways of merging in reference to our competing sets of assumptions about what constitutes truth, evidence, knowledge, culture and cultural positioning, history, and, yes, even cultural coherence. But I think we should discuss these matters democratically, without the assumption that we have or need coherence, without the threat of apocalypse hanging over us, and without yearning for the good old days of Henry Wadsworth Longfellow, Louisa May Alcott and a university populated only by fresh-faced white boys from the best families.

We must, in other words, find ways of conceiving of the issue without invoking the narratives of golden age myths. Such narrative constraints we have found over and over do not lead to happy endings— they do not lead to any endings at all. Such narratives do not end. After a while they subside and we return, slightly ruffled, to our separate cells inside departments, with very little concern for the students who must somehow make sense of this growing multitude of apparently alien disciplines. It seems only reasonable that *we* are the ones who should set about making sense of it. To do so, we need to start with stories other than those of a fall from Eden, stories which allow for some hope, some development, even if that development is not toward coherence. It may be that when we get together to discuss our differences, we won't emerge all aglow with unanimity. It may be that the differences are real differences. But there is much to be gained by an awareness of difference and, I think, by making that difference open and central to our educational structure. Difference itself can be made productive if exposed and nurtured. There is a risk there, of course, and there are no risks at all in bringing up once more the self-stroking bunk about a golden age. But risk is what the future is all about, and the last word on that subject should go to Sheridan's Mrs. Malaprop, who understood much better than Allan Bloom or Lynne Cheney what she was doing: "We will not," says Mrs. Malaprop, "anticipate the past; so mind, young people—our retrospect will be all to the future."

13.

PAUL MONETTE: Living with AIDS

By the mid-1980s, AIDS (acquired immunodeficiency syndrome) had been identified, and blood tests could identify the presence of HIV, the agent of the disease. Because of the nature of its spread in the United States, most Americans came to know the illness as the "gay plague" though in Africa and elsewhere heterosexuals were the disease's predominant victims. Paul Monette, who himself died of AIDS at age 50, was one of the more eloquent chroniclers of gay life; his book Becoming a Man: Half a Life Story, *which describes his youthful struggles with his sexuality and the impact of his HIV-positive diagnosis, won a National Book Award. Having graduated from Yale University in 1967, he taught English and wrote both poetry and light fiction in his early career. When his companion, Roger Horowitz, was diagnosed with HIV, Monette was altered both as a man and as a writer. His* Borrowed Time: An AIDS Memoir, *an extract of which is printed below, is equal parts elegiac lament and wrenching record of the 19-month process they endured together. Horowitz died in 1985, Monette 10 years later.*

Source: *Borrowed Time: An AIDS Memoir*, New York, 1988.

ON WEDNESDAY, August 20, Roger had blood transfused, about three units, as I recall. Though the white count is most consistently affected by AZT [azidothymidine], the red count is also a problem. Many full-blown AIDS patients on long-term AZT have become transfusion-dependent. They have also gotten fairly blasé about the vampire part; but we still thought of transfusion as a grave and unsettling procedure. Yet the new blood perked Roger up considerably for several days, animated and energized him for work. He even talked with Esther Richmond about getting a new will written, the matter unbroached since we'd tucked the '80 version in a drawer.

He was coughing again, but even my radar wasn't especially flashing red. It was more than anything a clearing of the throat, and though in the past that very quality had been part of the ominous slippage toward PCP [*Pneumocystis carinii* pneumonia], I would not see it that way. Or perhaps I couldn't and still go on giving IV twice a day, not to mention keeping up food and fluids and twenty-two pills and Plato.

After one of his Wednesday sessions with Dr. Martin, Roger reported that he had admitted he'd had a good life. I remember how lucidly he repeated the phrase, amazed almost to be saying such a curiously final thing, and with no foreboding of death in the tone, or nothing gloomy at least. But I can't be sure, for I was behind in the death department. Even now, when I'm all caught up, it bewilders me to try to figure what he knew and I didn't. I had an appointment with Martin myself a month after Roger died. The first thing he said was: "He loved you greatly." Then he explained how Roger had gotten beyond the fear of death. Toward the end, he said, Roger's world was one of constricted hopes—Will I have enough energy to work with Fred? Will I be able to eat my supper? "It's impossible to conceive of ourselves without ego," Martin said, but that is where Roger arrived. I can't, of course, know what he must have thought in the hours when he lay there quietly, all but blind. I only know we never seemed any different, not between ourselves. And I felt no shadow of death when he said that his life had been good. Mine too, I thought with a pang of pride.

14.

Ann Richards: Democrats for Michael Dukakis

With popular Republican President Ronald Reagan constitutionally barred from running for a third term, many political pundits believed the Democrats would win back the White House in 1988. The Democratic nominee was Michael Dukakis, the son of Greek immigrants and a three-term governor of Massachusetts who presented himself as a pragmatic and successful politician. Dukakis, however, faced a formidable opponent in the Republican nominee Vice President George Bush. In the fall campaign, Bush asserted that Dukakis held positions on crime and taxes that stood far to the left of the national mainstream, and the characterization of him as a liberal became a kind of political slur. The Dukakis campaign responded by charging that Bush played a larger role in the Iran-Contra scandal than he had previously acknowledged. A highly negative tone sullied the campaign, as personal attacks rather than policy debates dominated the election. Dukakis did not adequately rebut Bush's charges, and Bush won the November election in a landslide. Ann Richards, the governor of Texas, anticipated the negative tone of the fall campaign in her keynote address at the Democratic convention in Atlanta, Georgia, in July 1988. Excerpts from her speech follow.

Source: *Vital Speeches of the Day*, August 15, 1988.

THANK YOU. Thank you very much. Good evening, ladies and gentlemen. Buenas noches, mis amigos! I am delighted to be here with you this evening, because after listening to George Bush all these years, I figured you needed to know what a real Texas accent sounds like.

Twelve years ago Barbara Jordan, another Texas woman, Barbara made the keynote address to this convention, and two women in 160 years is about par for the course.

But, if you give us a chance, we can perform. After all, Ginger Rogers did everything that Fred Astaire did. She just did it backwards and in high heels.

I want to announce to this nation that in a little more than 100 days, the Reagan – Meese – Deaver – Nofziger – Poindexter – North – Weinberger – Watt – Gorsuch – Lavell–Stockman–Haig–Bork–Noriega– George Bush will be over.

You know, tonight I feel a little like I did when I played basketball in the eighth grade. I thought I looked real cute in my uniform, and then I heard a boy yell from the bleachers, "Make that basket, bird legs."

And my greatest fear is that same guy is somewhere out there in the audience tonight, and he's going to cut me down to size.

Because where I grew up there wasn't much tolerance for self-importance—people who put on airs. I was born during the Depression in a little community just outside Waco, and I grew up listening to Franklin Roosevelt on the radio.

Well, it was back then that I came to understand the small truths and the hardships that bind neighbors together. Those were real people with real problems. And they had real dreams about getting out of the Depression. . . .

This Republican Administration treats us as if we were pieces of a puzzle that can't fit together. They've tried to put us into compartments and separate us from each other. Their political theory is "divide and conquer."

They've suggested time and time again that what is of interest to one group of Americans is not of interest to anyone else. We've been isolated, we've lumped into that sad phraseology called "special interests."

They've told farmers that they were selfish, that they would drive up food prices if they asked the Government to intervene on behalf of the family farm, and we watched farms go on the auction block while we bought food from foreign countries. Well, that's wrong.

They told working mothers it's all their fault that families are falling apart because they had to go to work to keep their kids in jeans, tennis shoes and college. And they're wrong.

They told American labor they were trying to ruin free enterprise by asking for 60 days' notice of plant closings, and that's wrong.

And they told the auto industry, and the steel industry, and the timber industry, and the oil industry, companies being threatened by foreign products flooding this country, that you're protectionist if you think the Government should enforce our trade laws. And that is wrong.

When they belittle us for demanding clean air and clean water, for trying to save the oceans and the ozone layer, that's wrong.

No wonder we feel isolated, and confused. We want answers, and their answer is that something is wrong with you.

Well, nothing's wrong with you—nothing wrong with you that you can't fix in November. . . .

We're not going to have the America that we want until we elect leaders who are going to tell the truth—not most days, but every day. Leaders who don't forget what they don't want to remember.

And for eight straight years George Bush hasn't displayed the slightest interest in anything we care about. And now that he's after a job that he can't get appointed to, he's like Columbus discovering America—he's found child care, he's found education.

Poor George, he can't help it—he was born with a silver foot in his mouth.

Well, no wonder—no wonder we can't figure it out—because the leadership of this nation is telling us one thing on TV and doing something entirely different.

They tell us—they tell us that they're fighting a war against terrorists. And then we find out that the White House is selling arms to the Ayatollah.

They tell us that they're fighting a war on drugs, and then people come on TV and testify that the C.I.A. and the D.E.A. and the F.B.I. knew they were flying drugs into America all along. And they're negotiating with a dictator who is shoveling cocaine into this country like crazy. I guess that's their Central American strategy.

Now they tell us that employment rates are great and that they're for equal opportunity, but we know it takes two paychecks to make ends meet today, when it used to take one, and the opportunity they're so proud of is low-wage, dead-end jobs.

And there is no major city in America where you cannot see homeless men sitting in parking lots holding signs that say, "I will work for food."

Now my friends, we really are at a crucial point in American history. Under this Administration we have devoted our resources into making this country a military colossus, but we've let our economic lines of defense fall into disrepair.

The debt of this nation is greater than it has ever been in our history. We fought a world war on less debt than the Republicans have built up in the last eight years. It's kind of like that brother-in-law who drives a flashy new car but he's always borrowing money from you to make the payments.

But let's take what they are proudest of, that is their stand on defense. We Democrats are committed to a strong America. And, quite frankly, when our leaders say to us we need a new weapon system, our inclination is to say, "Well, they must be right."

But when we pay billions for planes that won't fly, billions for tanks that won't fire and billions for systems that won't work, that old dog won't hunt.

And you don't have to be from Waco to know that when the Pentagon makes crooks rich and doesn't make America strong, that it's a bum deal.

Now I'm going to tell you—I'm really glad that our young people missed the Depression and missed the great big war. But I do regret that they missed the leaders that I knew, leaders who told us when things were tough and that we'd have to sacrifice, and that these difficulties might last awhile.

They didn't tell us things were hard for us because we were different, or isolated, or special interests. They brought us together and they gave us a sense of national purpose. They gave us Social Security and they told us they were setting up a system where we could pay our own money in and when the time came for our retirement, we could take the money out.

People in rural areas were told that we deserved to have electric lights, and they were going to harness the energy that was necessary to give us electricity so that my grandmama didn't have to carry that coal oil lamp around.

And they told us that they were going to guarantee that when we put our money in the bank that the money was going to be there, and it was going to be insured, they did not lie to us.

And I think that one of the saving graces of Democrats is that we are candid. We are straight talk. We tell people what we think.

And that tradition and those values live today in Michael Dukakis from Massachusetts.

Michael Dukakis knows that this country is on the edge of a great new era, that we're not afraid of change, that we're for thoughtful, truthful, strong leadership. Behind his calm there's an impatience, to unify this country and to get on with the future.

His instincts are deeply American, they're tough and they're generous, and personally I have to tell you that I have never met a man who had a more remarkable sense of what is really important in life.

And then there's my friend and my teacher for many years, Senator Lloyd Bentsen. And I couldn't be prouder, both as a Texan and as a Democrat, because Lloyd Bentsen understands America— from the barrios to the boardroom. He knows how to bring us together, by regions, by economics, and by example. And he's already beaten George Bush once.

So when it comes right down to it, this election is a contest between those who are satisfied with what they have and those who know we can do better. That's what this election is really all about.

It's about the American dream—those who want to keep it for the few, and those who know it must be nurtured and passed along.

———————◆———————

Jackson is a poet, Cuomo is a poet, and Dukakis is a word processor.
RICHARD NIXON, commenting on Democratic candidates
Jesse Jackson, Mario Cuomo, and Michael Dukakis,
April 15, 1988

15.

PAT ROBERTSON: Republicans for George Bush

For a century following the Civil War, white Southern Protestants voted overwhelmingly for the Democratic Party. Democratic candidates frequently carried 80 percent and in some cases even 90 percent of the vote in Southern states. The source of white Southern loyalty to the Democrats could be traced to the region's deep-seated hostility toward the Republican Party, which most white Southerners associated with Abraham Lincoln and their defeat in the Civil War. In the aftermath of the civil rights era, however, a political earthquake struck the Southern electoral landscape. Northern Democrats' opposition to racial segregation and their support of liberal social welfare programs so alienated Southern Democrats that many Southerners began to defect from the party. In the 1970s, conservative white Southerners, especially evangelical Protestants, increasingly turned to the Republican Party. In 1984, President Ronald Reagan became the first Republican in history to win every Southern state. Two years later, Pat Robertson, a Southern Baptist minister and television evangelist from Virginia, launched the first major effort by a Southern evangelical to win the Republican presidential nomination. Although Robertson ultimately lost the nomination to Vice President George Bush, his strong showing demonstrated just how important the South had become to the Republican Party's national prospects. Robertson's campaign also marked the emergence of social conservatives as a major constituency of the Republican Party. Reprinted below are excerpts from Robertson's endorsement of George Bush at the Republican National Convention in New Orleans, Louisiana, in August 1988.

Source: Republican National Convention Address, New Orleans, August 16, 1988.

FOUR YEARS AGO the keynote speaker at the Democratic National Convention told us that America was a tale of two cities—the "haves" and the "have-nots." The rich and the poor. The upper class and the lower class.

We heard a variation on that message from Jesse Jackson and Teddy Kennedy and every Democrat who spoke last month at their convention in Atlanta.

Ladies and gentlemen, the time has come for truth. The message of the Democratic Party is a message of defeat, di-

vision—and despair. They did not speak for the American people under McGovern or Mondale or Carter, and they do not speak for America today!

But that speaker who compared America to *A Tale of Two Cities* was right in a way he never intended.

THE BEST OF TIMES, THE WORST OF TIMES

That great novel by Charles Dickens begins with a double sentence: "It was the best of times. It was the worst of times."

In 1980 Ronald Reagan and George Bush began a long journey to rescue this country from the "worst of times." From double-digit inflation—soaring interest rates—and widespread unemployment.

As Republicans, our task in 1988 is to continue that journey and build the greatness of America through moral strength.

Exactly two months and 22 days from tonight some 100 million of our fellow citizens will go to their polling places to choose the future course of the United States of America.

Our tale of two cities is really a choice between two paths. Two visions of America. Two philosophies of the future.

When Charles Dickens wrote his epic novel he described in heartrending detail the consequences that the right and wrong choices made on two cities in Europe.

In city number one, under the deceptive slogan liberty, equality, fraternity— the people with revolutionary zeal threw out God, the church, established morality, the established government, their former leaders, sound currency, and some of the private ownership of property. Then they demanded that the new government buy them happiness.

Instead of the government inspired utopia, which the people thought they would get, they got liberal divorce laws and a breakup of families, anarchy, looting, ruinous inflation, and financial chaos.

As the madness fed on itself, they got something much worse—the reign of terror. A time when no one's life was safe from the dreaded guillotine. The second city followed a very different course. There, faith in God was maintained. There was even a spiritual revival under John Wesley. Respect for the rule of law

prevailed. Instead of wild excess, there was self-control and self-restraint. The currency was strong and families were stable. Private property was protected and life was held sacred. With all its faults, England created a strong, stable conservative government that survived with prosperity for a hundred years.

And so, these two cities made choices in 1789 that shaped their future for decades, for generations, to come. And now, 200 years later, America faces its choice.

The Democrats have given us a clear picture of their city. They offer unlimited government, massive transfers of wealth from the productive sector of society to the nonproductive, and ever-increasing regulation of the daily lives of the people and their children.

In the city of the Democratic Party, the liberal mindset reigns supreme. Criminals are turned loose and the innocent are made victims. Disease carriers are protected and the healthy are placed at great risk.

In the Democrat's city, welfare dependency flourishes and no one is held accountable for his or her behavior. Society is always to blame.

In the Democrat's city, the rights of the majority must always take a back seat to the clamorous demands of the special interest minorities. And yet, in their city it is always the majority that must pay the bills, through higher and higher taxes.

Now the Democratic Party has discovered the family. They want us all to be one-big-family. But let's keep in mind that they want you and me to be in one family with Jim Wright as the daddy, Barbara Mikulski as the mommy. And Teddy Kennedy as big brother. I can't speak for you, but I believe I'd rather pick my own relatives.

To build their city, the Democratic Party has selected Michael Dukakis as architect. I submit to you tonight that

Michael Dukakis is the most liberal candidate ever put forward for the presidency by any major party in American history.

THE "L" WORD

In fact, the city the Democrats hope to build is so bad that they are ashamed to mention the word that describes who they are and what they really want to do. They don't want to say it, so they just call it the "L" word.

They know that their programs will require massive new revenue, but in their platform they did not mention once the vehicle they will use to raise money—they just call it the "T" word.

Whether by silence—whether by initials—or whether in a foreign language—it's still tax and spend liberalism and the American people are too smart to fall for it again.

There is another word that the Democrats did not mention once in their platform and not once in the acceptance speech of their candidate. It is a "G" word.

The name of God.

Ladies and gentlemen, our President, Ronald Reagan, was not ashamed to ask the assembled delegates at our convention in Detroit to bow their heads in silent prayer to God. As Americans, we are not ashamed to pledge allegiance to a flag that is a symbol of one nation under God.

And I submit to you that our Party, the Republican Party, assembled here in New Orleans, is not ashamed to write into our National Platform our solemn resolve that the children of this country will once again be allowed to pray to God in the classrooms of America.

As an aside, I should mention that Michael Dukakis is a card carrying member of the ACLU, an organization dedicated to removing all public affirmation of religious faith in America. As President, Michael Dukakis will pack the federal courts with ACLU radicals. If there were no other reason, and there are many, to deny Michael Dukakis the Presidency, this is a reason enough for all of us to vote against him in November. . . .

GOVERNMENT SHOULD SERVE, NOT MASTER

We are Republicans and we believe in government that is our servant, not our master.

We believe that the wisdom of the millions who make up the marketplace is greater than the wisdom of the few who serve in government.

We want a balanced budget, but we believe the way to balance the budget is to cut waste and mismanagement in government, not to raise the taxes on the American people.

There is a word to describe us. It is a "C" word. We are conservatives and we are proud of it!

In November the voters will choose their version of a Tale of Two Cities.

Some people say that they don't care what choice the voters make in November. That it doesn't really matter.

I say to you tonight, We care because it does matter. It matters to us and our children whether we vote Democrat or whether we vote Republican.

And we care whether the successor to a great President, Ronald Reagan, is a liberal who returns us to the failed policies of Jimmy Carter or a principled conservative like George Bush who moves us proudly into the nineteen nineties.

THE "EDUCATION PRESIDENT"

Ladies and gentlemen, George Bush wants to be known as the "Education President." Together we can make our schools the best in the world if we follow a few simple steps: (1) We must guarantee to our children a disciplined, drug-free, crime-free school environment. Tough school principals should be made community heroes not community scapegoats. (2) We must recognize that the so-called new age curriculum of progressive education is a colossal failure and must be replaced. (3) We must place control of education in the hands of parents and teachers in the local communities and take it away from Washington, the Federal Courts, and the liberal leadership of a powerful teachers union. (4) We must give to every parent the maximum freedom to decide what school is best for his or her child. Empowering parents with vouchers and educational choice at the state and local level is an idea whose time has come.

Yet some would say, we can never have better education without stronger families.

In part they are right. In my opinion the breakup of the American family is the number one social problem in our nation today. Half of our marriages end in divorce. Over fifteen million children now live with a single parent. According to press reports, over half of the women with children in the black community do not have any man in residence.

Single women with children are the fastest growing segment of the poor in our land. We speak of the "feminization" of poverty. But what has government done about the problem?

Successive Democratic Congresses have raised the tax burden on parents with children an estimated 245 percent over a twenty year period.

In one year Federal taxpayer's money was used to institute an estimated 225,000 divorce actions. It has been estimated that 30 percent of all divorces in America are caused by misguided welfare laws.

More cruel than all this is the assumption begun by Lyndon Johnson's Great Society programs that the poor did not have to strive, to learn, to compete, to excel.

This attitude fostered dependency, then hopelessness, then despair.

Ladies and gentlemen, we are Republicans and we believe some basic truths:

(1) Government must seek to strengthen families not tear them apart.

(2) Parents are responsible for their own children. If a man fathers a child, that child is not the responsibility of the city, the state, or the federal government. That child is his responsibility and he and the child's mother should be made to look after it.

(3) Women in our society should have complete access to challenging and rewarding careers. If women in our society do the same work as men they should receive the same pay as men for that equal work.

(4) We also need to stop punishing women in our society who choose to be homemakers. If in our society we can afford to give tax deductions and credits to working women with children, we also can afford to give tax deductions and credits to women who want to stay at home and care for their children.

(5) The goal of welfare must be to restore people in crisis to dignity and useful employment . . . not to create a class of government dependents for whom welfare is a way of life. Whatever the Democrats may tell you, that is not the way to "keep hope alive."

But hope is very much alive in America today. It is alive because our vision, the Republican vision, expresses the hopes and the dreams of the vast majority of the American people.

And, as we leave New Orleans, we will go back to our homes confident that we are a party united around a platform that expresses the American spirit—a platform we can be proud to share with our neighbors all over this great nation.

Now, I would like to give a personal, special message to the millions of voters, volunteers, and supporters across America who committed themselves to my campaign. I thank you. I am very proud of you. Now, the time has come for you to make your choice.

This party is about to nominate a man that I have come to respect and admire.

This man can and will lead our nation proudly into the future.

Therefore, tonight I release my delegates and alternates who have come to this convention and urge you and all of my friends across America to give your enthusiastic support to our party, our candidates, and our presidential nominee, George Bush.

As we cast our eyes toward November, we know that a new page of history will be written.

On that page we will inscribe the name of the 41st President of the United States.

His name will be George Bush, Republican. Thank you, and God bless you!

———◆———

No matter how hard he tries to sound like a member of the red-meat right, he seems like an Episcopalian, which he is, at a fundamentalist tent meeting.
MARGARET GARRARD WARNER, reporter, commenting
on presidential candidate George Bush
Newsweek, October 19, 1987

1989

16.

RONALD REAGAN: Farewell Address to the Nation

In January 1989 Ronald Reagan completed his second term as President of the United States. Reagan was the first President since Dwight Eisenhower to complete two full terms in the White House. He was also the oldest serving President in history, leaving the White House just one month shy of his 78th birthday. The Cold War and economic issues largely dominated Reagan's presidency, and his records on economics and foreign relations gave support to both his admirers and his critics. When Reagan entered the White House, the United States suffered from the deepest recession since the Great Depression; and when he left office, the nation was enjoying one of the longest economic expansions since World War II. However, during Reagan's tenure, the United States ran up the largest budget deficits in its history. In foreign affairs, Reagan struck up a surprising friendship with Soviet Premier Mikhail Gorbachev, and the two men began a thaw in American-Soviet relations which ultimately led to the Cold War's end. Conversely, however, Reagan's staunch support for anti-Communist dictators in Latin America and Asia bred anti-Americanism in many less-developed nations. On January 11, 1989, Reagan delivered a farewell address to the nation in a live broadcast from the Oval Office of the White House. Excerpts from his farewell address are printed here.

Source: *Public Papers of the Presidents of the United States*, January 11, 1989.

MY FELLOW AMERICANS:

This is the 34th time I'll speak to you from the Oval Office and the last. We've been together 8 years now, and soon it'll be time for me to go. But before I do, I wanted to share some thoughts, some of which I've been saving for a long time.

It's been the honor of my life to be your President. So many of you have written the past few weeks to say thanks, but I could say as much to you. Nancy and I are grateful for the opportunity you gave us to serve.

One of the things about the Presidency is that you're always somewhat apart. You spend a lot of time going by too fast in a car someone else is driving, and seeing the people through tinted glass—the parents holding up a child, and the wave you saw too late and couldn't return. And so many times I wanted to stop and reach out from behind the glass, and connect. Well, maybe I can do a little of that tonight.

People ask how I feel about leaving. And the fact is, "parting is such sweet sorrow." The sweet part is California and the ranch and freedom. The sorrow—the goodbyes, of course, and leaving this beautiful place.

You know, down the hall and up the stairs from this office is the part of the White House where the President and his family live. There are a few favorite windows I have up there that I like to stand and look out of early in the morning. The view is over the grounds here to the Washington Monument, and then the Mall and the Jefferson Memorial. But on mornings when the humidity is low, you can see past the Jefferson to the river, the Potomac, and the Virginia shore. Someone said that's the view Lincoln had when he saw the smoke rising from the Battle of Bull Run. I see more prosaic things: the grass on the banks, the morning traffic as people make their way to work, now and then a sailboat on the river.

I've been thinking a bit at that window. I've been reflecting on what the past 8 years have meant and mean. And the image that comes to mind like a refrain is a nautical one—a small story about a big ship, and a refugee, and a sailor. It was back in the early eighties, at the height of the boat people. And the sailor was hard at work on the carrier *Midway*, which was patrolling the South China Sea. The sailor, like most American servicemen, was young, smart, and fiercely observant. The crew spied on the horizon a leaky little boat. And crammed inside were refugees from Indochina hoping to get to America. The

Midway sent a small launch to bring them to the ship and safety. As the refugees made their way through the choppy seas, one spied the sailor on deck, and stood up, and called out to him. He yelled, "Hello, American sailor. Hello, freedom man."

A small moment with a big meaning, a moment the sailor, who wrote it in a letter, couldn't get out of his mind. And, when I saw it, neither could I. Because that's what it was to be an American in the 1980's. We stood, again, for freedom. I know we always have, but in the past few years the world again—and in a way, we ourselves—rediscovered it.

It's been quite a journey this decade, and we held together through some stormy seas. And at the end, together, we are reaching our destination. . . .

When you've got to the point when you can celebrate the anniversaries of your 39th birthday you can sit back sometimes, review your life, and see it flowing before you. For me there was a fork in the river, and it was right in the middle of my life. I never meant to go into politics. It wasn't my intention when I was young. But I was raised to believe you had to pay your way for the blessings bestowed on you. I was happy with my career in the entertainment world, but I ultimately went into politics because I wanted to protect something precious.

Ours was the first revolution in the history of mankind that truly reversed the course of government, and with three little words: "We the People." "We the People" tell the government what to do; it doesn't tell us. "We the People" are the driver; the government is the car. And we decide where it should go, and by what route, and how fast. Almost all the world's constitutions are documents in which governments tell the people what their privileges are. Our constitution is a document in which "We the People" tell the government what it is allowed to do. "We the People" are free. This belief has been the underlying basis for everything I've tried to do these past 8 years. . . .

We must keep up our guard, but we must also continue to work together to lessen and eliminate tension and mistrust. My view is that President Gorbachev is different from previous Soviet leaders. I think he knows some of the things wrong with his society and is trying to fix them. We wish him well. And we'll continue to work to make sure that the Soviet Union that eventually emerges from this process is a less threatening one. What it all boils down to is this: I want the new closeness to continue. And it will, as long as we make it clear that we will continue to act in a certain way as long as they continue to act in a helpful manner. If and when they don't, at first pull your punches. If they persist, pull the plug. It's still trust but verify. It's still play, but cut the cards. It's still watch closely. And don't be afraid to see what you see.

I've been asked if I have any regrets. Well, I do. The deficit is one. I've been talking a great deal about that lately, but tonight isn't for arguments, and I'm going to hold my tongue. But an observation: I've had my share of victories in the Congress, but what few people noticed is that I never won anything you didn't win for me. They never saw my troops, they never saw Reagan's regiments, the American people. You won every battle with every call you made and letter you wrote demanding action. Well, action is still needed. If we're to finish the job, Reagan's regiments will have to become the Bush brigades. Soon he'll be the chief, and he'll need you every bit as much as I did. . . .

All great change in America begins at the dinner table. So, tomorrow night in the kitchen I hope the talking begins. And children, if your parents haven't been teaching you what it means to be an American, let 'em know and nail 'em on it. That would be a very American thing to do.

And that's about all I have to say tonight, except for one thing. The past few days when I've been at that window upstairs, I've thought a bit of the "shining city upon a hill." The phrase comes from John Winthrop, who wrote it to describe the America he imagined. What he imagined was important because he was an early Pilgrim, an early freedom man. He journeyed here on what today we'd call a little wooden boat; and like the other Pilgrims, he was looking for a home that would be free.

I've spoken of the shining city all my political life, but I don't know if I ever quite communicated what I saw when I said it. But in my mind it was a tall, proud city built on rocks stronger than oceans, wind-swept, God-blessed, and teeming with people of all kinds living in harmony and peace; a city with free ports that hummed with commerce and creativity. And if there had to be city walls, the walls had doors and the doors were open to anyone with the will and the heart to get here. That's how I saw it, and see it still.

And how stands the city on this winter night? More prosperous, more secure, and happier than it was 8 years ago. But more than that: After 200 years, two centuries, she still stands strong and true on the granite ridge, and her glow has held steady no matter what storm. And she's still a beacon, still a magnet for all who must have freedom, for all the pilgrims from all the lost places who are hurtling through the darkness, toward home.

We've done our part. And as I walk off into the city streets, a final word to the men and women of the Reagan revolution, the men and women across America who for 8 years did the work that brought America back. My friends: We did it. We weren't just marking time. We made a difference. We made the city stronger, we made the city freer, and we left her in good hands. All in all, not bad, not bad at all.

And so goodbye, God bless you, and God bless the United States of America.

17.

GEORGE BUSH: Inaugural Address

The election of 1988 found the United States again in the midst of peace and economic prosperity. After forty years of Cold War tension with the Soviet Union, relations were warming considerably since the selection of Mikhail Gorbachev as Soviet president. After a nasty primary campaign, George Bush captured the Republican Party's nomination. A former naval aviator, Bush was the last World War II veteran to serve as President. Although born in Massachusetts and educated at Yale University, Bush made his career in the private sector as a Texas oilman. He later served two terms in Congress, represented the United States in Beijing as the Ambassador to China, and led the Central Intelligence Agency as its director in the mid-1970s. Following a failed campaign for the Republican Presidential nomination in 1980, he joined Ronald Reagan's winning ticket as running mate and served two terms as Vice President. In the general election, Bush defeated Massachusetts Governor Michael Dukakis, who suffered from his liberal approach to such issues as the death penalty and flag-burning and from harsh negative attacks by the Republicans and their allies. Celebrating the 200th anniversary of the presidency, on January 20, 1989, Chief Justice William Rehnquist administered the oath of office to Bush on the same Bible used at George Washington's first inaugural. With Communist regimes falling throughout eastern Europe, Bush struck a triumphant tone on "democracy's big day," noting that the "nations of the world are moving toward democracy through the door to freedom." Bush also pledged a "kinder" and "gentler" nation, calling the American public to community service by acting as a "thousand points of light." Precisely twelve years later, his son would be inaugurated as the forty-third President of the United States, only the second time in history that a father and son both served as President. The elder Bush's Inaugural Address is reprinted here in full.

Source: *Inaugural Addresses of the Presidents of the United States: From George Washington 1789 to George Bush 1989,* Washington, D.C., 1989.

MR. CHIEF JUSTICE, Mr. President, Vice President Quayle, Senator Mitchell, Speaker Wright, Senator Dole, Congressman Michel, and fellow citizens, neighbors, and friends:

There is a man here who has earned a lasting place in our hearts and in our history. President Reagan, on behalf of our Nation, I thank you for the wonderful things that you have done for America.

I have just repeated word for word the oath taken by George Washington 200 years ago, and the Bible on which I placed my hand is the Bible on which he placed his. It is right that the memory of Washington be with us today, not only because this is our Bicentennial Inauguration, but because Washington remains the Father of our Country. And he would, I think, be gladdened by this day; for today is the concrete expression of a stunning fact: our continuity these 200 years since our government began.

We meet on democracy's front porch, a good place to talk as neighbors and as friends. For this is a day when our nation is made whole, when our differences, for a moment, are suspended.

And my first act as President is a prayer. I ask you to bow your heads:

Heavenly Father, we bow our heads and thank You for Your love. Accept our thanks for the peace that yields this day and the shared faith that makes its continuance likely. Make us strong to do Your work, willing to heed and hear Your will, and write on our hearts these words: "Use power to help people." For we are given power not to advance our own purposes, nor to make a great show in the world, nor a name. There is but one just use of power, and it is to serve people. Help us to remember it, Lord. Amen.

I come before you and assume the Presidency at a moment rich with promise. We live in a peaceful, prosperous time, but we can make it better. For a new breeze is blowing, and a world refreshed by freedom seems reborn; for in man's heart, if not in fact, the day of the dictator is over. The totalitarian era is passing, its old ideas blown away like leaves from an ancient, lifeless tree. A new breeze is blowing, and a nation refreshed by freedom stands ready to push on. There is new ground to be broken, and new action to be taken. There are times when the future seems thick as a fog; you sit and wait, hoping the mists will lift and reveal the right path. But this is a time when the future seems a door you can walk right through into a room called tomorrow.

Great nations of the world are moving toward democracy through the door to freedom. Men and women of the world move toward free markets through the door to prosperity. The people of the world agitate for free expression and free thought through the door to the moral and intellectual satisfactions that only liberty allows.

We know what works: Freedom works. We know what's right: Freedom is right. We know how to secure a more just and prosperous life for man on Earth: through free markets, free speech, free elections, and the exercise of free will unhampered by the state.

For the first time in this century, for the first time in perhaps all history, man does not have to invent a system by which to live. We don't have to talk late into the night about which form of government is better. We don't have to wrest justice from the kings. We only have to summon it from within ourselves. We must act on what we know. I take as my guide the hope of a saint: In crucial things, unity; in important things, diversity; in all things, generosity.

America today is a proud, free nation, decent and civil, a place we cannot help but love. We know in our hearts, not loudly and proudly, but as a simple fact, that this country has meaning beyond what we see, and that our strength is a force for good. But have we changed as a nation even in our time? Are we enthralled with material things, less appreciative of the nobility of work and sacrifice?

My friends, we are not the sum of our possessions. They are not the measure of our lives. In our hearts we know what matters. We cannot hope only to leave our children a bigger car, a bigger bank account. We must hope to give them a sense of what it means to be a loyal friend, a loving parent, a citizen who leaves his home, his neighborhood and town better than he found it. What do we want the men and women who work with us to say when we are no longer there? That we were more driven to succeed than anyone around us? Or that we stopped to ask if a sick child had gotten better, and stayed a moment there to trade a word of friendship?

No President, no government, can teach us to remember what is best in what we are. But if the man you have chosen to lead this government can help make a difference; if he can celebrate the quieter, deeper successes that are made not of gold and silk, but of better hearts and finer souls; if he can do these things, then he must.

America is never wholly herself unless she is engaged in high moral principle. We as a people have such a purpose today. It is to make kinder the face of the Nation and gentler the face of the world. My friends, we have work to do. There are the homeless, lost and roaming. There are the children who have nothing, no love, no normalcy. There are those who cannot free themselves of enslavement to whatever addiction—drugs, welfare, the demoralization that rules the slums. There is crime to be conquered, the rough crime of the streets. There are young women to be helped who are about to become mothers of children they can't care for and might not love. They need our care, our guidance, and our education, though we bless them for choosing life.

The old solution, the old way, was to think that public money alone could end these problems. But we have learned that is not so. And in any case, our funds are low. We have a deficit to bring down. We have more will than wallet; but will is what we need. We will make the hard choices, looking at what we have and perhaps allocating it differently, making our decisions based on honest need and prudent safety. And then we will do the wisest thing of all: We will turn to the only resource we have that in times of need always grows—the goodness and the courage of the American people.

I am speaking of a new engagement in the lives of others, a new activism, hands-on and involved, that gets the job done. We must bring in the generations, harnessing the unused talent of the elderly and the unfocused energy of the young. For not only leadership is passed from generation to generation, but so is stewardship. And the generation born after the Second World War has come of age.

I have spoken of a thousand points of light, of all the community organizations that are spread like stars throughout the Nation, doing good. We will work hand in hand, encouraging, sometimes leading, sometimes being led, rewarding. We will work on this in the White House, in the Cabinet agencies. I will go to the people and the programs that are the brighter points of light, and I will ask every member of my government to become involved. The old ideas are new again because they are not old, they are timeless: duty, sacrifice, commitment, and a patriotism that finds its expression in taking part and pitching in.

We need a new engagement, too, between the Executive and the Congress. The challenges before us will be thrashed out with the House and the Senate. We must bring the Federal budget into balance. And we must ensure that America stands before the world united, strong, at peace, and fiscally sound. But, of course, things may be difficult. We need compromise; we have had dissension. We need harmony; we have had a chorus of discordant voices.

For Congress, too, has changed in our time. There has grown a certain divisiveness. We have seen the hard looks and heard the statements in which not each other's ideas are challenged, but each other's motives. And our great parties have too often been far apart and untrusting of each other. It has been this way since Vietnam. That war cleaves us still. But, friends, that war began in earnest a quarter of a century ago; and surely the statute of limitations has been reached. This is a fact: The final lesson of Vietnam is that no great nation can long afford to be sundered by a memory. A new breeze is blowing, and the old bipartisanship must be made new again.

To my friends—and yes, I do mean friends—in the loyal opposition—and yes, I mean loyal: I put out my hand. I am putting out my hand to you, Mr. Speaker. I am putting out my hand to you, Mr. Majority Leader. For this is the thing: This is the age of the offered hand. We can't turn back clocks, and I don't want to. But when our fathers were young, Mr. Speaker, our differences ended at the water's edge. And we don't wish to turn back time, but when our mothers were young, Mr. Majority Leader, the Congress and the Executive were capable of working together to produce a budget on which this nation could live. Let us negotiate soon and hard. But in the end, let us produce. The American people await action. They didn't send us here to bicker. They ask us to rise above the merely partisan. "In crucial things, unity"—and this, my friends, is crucial.

To the world, too, we offer new engagement and a renewed vow: We will stay strong to protect the peace. The "offered hand" is a reluctant fist; but once

made, strong, and can be used with great effect. There are today Americans who are held against their will in foreign lands, and Americans who are unaccounted for. Assistance can be shown here, and will be long remembered. Good will begets good will. Good faith can be a spiral that endlessly moves on.

Great nations like great men must keep their word. When America says something, America means it, whether a treaty or an agreement or a vow made on marble steps. We will always try to speak clearly, for candor is a compliment, but subtlety, too, is good and has its place. While keeping our alliances and friendships around the world strong, ever strong, we will continue the new closeness with the Soviet Union, consistent both with our security and with progress. One might say that our new relationship in part reflects the triumph of hope and strength over experience. But hope is good, and so are strength and vigilance.

Here today are tens of thousands of our citizens who feel the understandable satisfaction of those who have taken part in democracy and seen their hopes fulfilled. But my thoughts have been turning the past few days to those who would be watching at home, to an older fellow who will throw a salute by himself when the flag goes by, and the women who will tell her sons the words of the battle hymns. I don't mean this to be sentimental. I mean that on days like this, we remember that we are all part of a continuum, inescapably connected by the ties that bind.

Our children are watching in schools throughout our great land. And to them I say, thank you for watching democracy's big day. For democracy belongs to us all, and freedom is like a beautiful kite that can go higher and higher with the breeze. And to all I say: No matter what your circumstances or where you are, you are part of this day, you are part of the life of our great nation.

A President is neither prince nor pope, and I don't seek a window on men's souls. In fact, I yearn for a greater tolerance, an easy-goingness about each other's attitudes and way of life.

There are few clear areas in which we as a society must rise up united and express our intolerance. The most obvious now is drugs. And when that first cocaine was smuggled in on a ship, it may as well have been a deadly bacteria, so much has it hurt the body, the soul of our country. And there is much to be done and to be said, but take my word for it: This scourge will stop.

And so, there is much to do; and tomorrow the work begins. I do not mistrust the future; I do not fear what is ahead. For our problems are large, but our heart is larger. Our challenges are great, but our will is greater. And if our flaws are endless, God's love is truly boundless.

Some see leadership as high drama, and the sound of trumpets calling, and sometimes it is that. But I see history as a book with many pages, and each day we fill a page with acts of hopefulness and meaning. The new breeze blows, a page turns, the story unfolds. And so today a chapter begins, a small and stately story of unity, diversity, and generosity— shared, and written, together.

Thank you. God bless you and God bless the United States of America.

———◆———

Read my lips: no new taxes.
GEORGE BUSH, Presidential nomination acceptance speech
at the Republican National Convention,
August 18, 1988

18.

William Rehnquist: *Webster v. Reproductive Health Services*

In the 1973 case of Roe *v.* Wade, *the U.S. Supreme Court declared that women have a constitutional right to terminate a pregnancy through abortion. The ruling reversed decades of legal restrictions on abortion and struck down all state laws that prohibited abortion. Not surprisingly, the* Roe *decision provoked enormous controversy. Pro-choice groups immediately hailed it as a major accomplishment of the women's movement; pro-life groups derided* Roe *as an immoral and outrageous misreading of the Constitution. Bitter debates over its constitutionality continued for the rest of the twentieth century. In an effort to win more public and political support to their sides, both pro-life and pro-choice groups funded congressional campaigns, ran television advertisements, and held huge rallies and marches. The Supreme Court once again took up the abortion issue in 1989 when it heard the case of* Webster *v.* Reproductive Health Services. *The case involved a Missouri state law enacted in 1986 that barred the use of public facilities for abortion services and mandated fetal viability tests after twenty weeks gestation. In addition, the statute explicitly declared that life begins at conception. The district court struck down these provisions as an unconstitutional violation of* Roe, *a point on which the appellate court concurred, but in its ruling on* Webster, *the Supreme Court found that the Missouri state law did not violate the Constitution, thereby reversing the judgments of the lower courts. Although the* Webster *ruling did not overturn* Roe, *it nevertheless alarmed pro-choice groups because it marked the first time that a majority of the Supreme Court did not explicitly reaffirm the* Roe *decision. Excerpts from the majority opinion on the* Webster *case, delivered by Chief Justice William Rehnquist, are reprinted below.*

Source: *Webster, Attorney General of Missouri*, et al. v. *Reproductive Health Services*, et al., July 3, 1989.

Appellees, state-employed health professionals and private nonprofit corporations providing abortion services, brought suit in the District Court for declaratory and injunctive relief challenging the constitutionality of a Missouri statute regulating the performance of abortions. The statute, inter alia: (1) sets forth "findings" in its preamble that "[t]he life of each human being begins at conception," and that "unborn children have protectable interests in life, health, and well-being," 1.205.1(1), (2), and requires that all state laws be interpreted to provide unborn children with the same rights enjoyed by other persons, subject to the Federal Constitution and this Court's precedents, 1.205.2; (2) specifies that a physician, prior to performing an abortion on any woman whom he has reason to believe is 20 or more weeks pregnant, must ascertain whether the fetus is "viable" by performing "such medical examinations and tests as are necessary to make a finding of [the fetus'] gestational age, weight, and lung maturity," 188.029; (3) prohibits the use of public employees and facilities to perform or assist abortions not necessary to save the mother's life, 188.210, 188.215; and (4) makes it unlawful to use public funds, employees, or facilities for the purpose of "encouraging or counseling" a woman to have an abortion not necessary to save her life, 188.205, 188.210, 188.215. The District Court struck down each of the above provisions, among others, and enjoined their enforcement. The Court of Appeals affirmed, ruling that the provisions in question violated this Court's decision in *Roe* v. *Wade,* 410 U.S. 113, and subsequent cases.

Held: The judgment is reversed. 851 F.2d 1071, reversed.

The Chief Justice delivered the opinion of the Court with respect to Parts I, II-A, II-B, and II-C, concluding that:

1. This Court need not pass on the constitutionality of the Missouri statute's preamble. In invalidating the preamble, the Court of Appeals misconceived the meaning of the dictum in *Akron* v. *Akron Center for Reproductive Health, Inc.,* 462 U.S. 416, 444, that "a State may not adopt one theory of when life begins to justify its regulation of [492 U.S. 490, 491] abortions." That statement means only that a State could not "justify" any abortion regulation otherwise invalid under *Roe* v. *Wade* on the ground that it embodied the State's view about when life begins. The preamble does not by its terms regulate abortions or any other aspect of appellees' medical practice, and 1.205.2 can be interpreted to do no more than offer protections to unborn children in tort and probate law, which is permissible under *Roe* v. *Wade, supra,* at 161–162. This Court has emphasized that

Roe implies no limitation on a State's authority to make a value judgment favoring childbirth over abortion, *Maher* v. *Roe,* 432 U.S. 464, 474, and the preamble can be read simply to express that sort of value judgment. The extent to which the preamble's language might be used to interpret other state statutes or regulations is something that only the state courts can definitively decide, and, until those courts have applied the preamble to restrict appellees' activities in some concrete way, it is inappropriate for federal courts to address its meaning. *Alabama State Federation of Labor* v. *McAdory,* 325 U.S. 450, 460.

2. The restrictions in 188.210 and 188.215 of the Missouri statute on the use of public employees and facilities for the performance or assistance of nontherapeutic abortions do not contravene this Court's abortion decisions. The Due Process Clauses generally confer no affirmative right to governmental aid, even where such aid may be necessary to secure life, liberty, or property interests of which the government may not deprive the individual. *DeShaney* v. *Winnebago County Dept. of Social Services,* 489 U.S. 189, 196. Thus, in *Maher* v. *Roe, supra; Poelker* v. *Doe,* 432 U.S. 519; and *Harris* v. *McRae,* 448 U.S. 297, this Court upheld governmental regulations withholding public funds for nontherapeutic abortions but allowing payments for medical services related to childbirth, recognizing that a government's decision to favor childbirth over abortion through the allocation of public funds does not violate *Roe* v. *Wade.* A State may implement that same value judgment through the allocation of other public resources, such as hospitals and medical staff. There is no merit to the claim that *Maher, Poelker,* and *McRae* must be distinguished on the grounds that preventing access to a public facility narrows or forecloses the avail-

ability of abortion. Just as in those cases, Missouri's decision to use public facilities and employees to encourage childbirth over abortion places no governmental obstacle in the path of a woman who chooses to terminate her pregnancy, but leaves her with the same choices as if the State had decided not to operate any hospitals at all. The challenged provisions restrict her ability to obtain an abortion only to the extent that she chooses to use a physician affiliated with a public hospital. Also without merit is the [492 U.S. 490, 492] assertion that *Maher, Poelker,* and *McRae* must be distinguished on the ground that, since the evidence shows that all of a public facility's costs in providing abortion services are recouped when the patient pays such that no public funds are expended, the Missouri statute goes beyond expressing a preference for childbirth over abortion by creating an obstacle to the right to choose abortion that cannot stand absent a compelling state interest. Nothing in the Constitution requires States to enter or remain in the abortion business or entitles private physicians and their patients access to public facilities for the performance of abortions. Indeed, if the State does recoup all of its costs in performing abortions and no state subsidy, direct or indirect, is available, it is difficult to see how any procreational choice is burdened by the State's ban on the use of its facilities or employees for performing abortions. The cases in question all support the view that the State need not commit any resources to performing abortions, even if it can turn a profit by doing so.

3. The controversy over 188.205's prohibition on the use of public funds to encourage or counsel a woman to have a nontherapeutic abortion is moot. The Court of Appeals did not consider 188.205 separately from 188.210 and 188.215—which respectively prohibit the use of public employees and facilities for such counseling—in holding all three sections unconstitutionally vague and violative of a woman's right to choose an abortion. Missouri has appealed only the invalidation of 188.205. In light of the State's claim, which this Court accepts for purposes of decision, that 188.205 is not directed at the primary conduct of physicians or health care providers, but is simply an instruction to the State's fiscal officers not to allocate public funds for abortion counseling, appellees contend that they are not "adversely" affected by the section and therefore that there is no longer a case or controversy before the Court on this question. Since plaintiffs are masters of their complaints even at the appellate stage, and since appellees no longer seek equitable relief on their 188.205 claim, the Court of Appeals is directed to vacate the District Court's judgment with instructions to dismiss the relevant part of the complaint with prejudice. *Deakins* v. *Monaghan,* 484 U.S. 193, 200.

The Chief Justice, joined by Justice White and Justice Kennedy, concluded in Parts II-D and III that:

1. Section 188.029 of the Missouri statute—which specifies, in its first sentence, that a physician, before performing an abortion on a woman he has reason to believe is carrying an unborn child of 20 or more weeks gestational age, shall first determine if the unborn child is viable by using that degree of care, skill, and proficiency that is commonly exercised by practitioners in the field; but which then provides, in its second sentence, that, in making the viability determination, the physician shall [492 U.S. 490, 493] perform such medical examinations and tests as are neces-

sary to make a finding of the unborn child's gestational age, weight, and lung maturity—is constitutional, since it permissibly furthers the State's interest in protecting potential human life.

(a) The Court of Appeals committed plain error in reading 188.029 as requiring that after 20 weeks the specified test must be performed. That section makes sense only if its second sentence is read to require only those tests that are useful in making subsidiary viability findings. Reading the sentence to require the tests in all circumstances, including when the physician's reasonable professional judgment indicates that they would be irrelevant to determining viability or even dangerous to the mother and the fetus, would conflict with the first sentence's requirement that the physician apply his reasonable professional skill and judgment. It would also be incongruous to read the provision, especially the word "necessary," to require tests irrelevant to the expressed statutory purpose of determining viability.

(b) Section 188.029 is reasonably designed to ensure that abortions are not performed where the fetus is viable. The section's tests are intended to determine viability, the State having chosen viability as the point at which its interest in potential human life must be safeguarded. The section creates what is essentially a presumption of viability at 20 weeks, which the physician, prior to performing an abortion, must rebut with tests—including, if feasible, those for gestational age, fetal weight, and lung capacity—indicating that the fetus is not viable. While the District Court found that uncontradicted medical evidence established that a 20-week fetus is not viable, and that 23 1/2 to 24 weeks' gestation is the earliest point at which a reasonable possibility of viability exists, it also found that there may be a 4-week error in esti-mating gestational age, which supports testing at 20 weeks.

(c) Section 188.029 conflicts with *Roe v. Wade* and cases following it. Since the section's tests will undoubtedly show in many cases that the fetus is not viable, the tests will have been performed for what were in fact second-trimester abortions. While *Roe*, 410 U.S., at 162, recognized the State's interest in protecting potential human life as "important and legitimate," it also limited state involvement in second-trimester abortions to protecting maternal health, id., at 164, and allowed States to regulate or proscribe abortions to protect the unborn child only after viability, id., at 165. Since the tests in question regulate the physician's discretion in determining the viability of the fetus, 188.029 conflicts with language in *Colautti* v. *Franklin,* 439 U.S. 379, 388–389, stating that the viability determination is, and must be, a matter for the responsible attending physician's judgment. And, in light of District Court findings that the tests increase the expenses of abortion, their validity [492 U.S. 490, 494] may also be questioned under *Akron,* 462 U.S., at 434–435, which held that a requirement that second-trimester abortions be performed in hospitals was invalid because it substantially increased the expenses of those procedures.

(d) The doubt cast on the Missouri statute by these cases is not so much a flaw in the statute as it is a reflection of the fact that *Roe*'s rigid trimester analysis has proved to be unsound in principle and unworkable in practice. In such circumstances, this Court does not refrain from reconsidering prior constitutional rulings, notwithstanding stare decisis. E.g., *Garcia v. San Antonio Metropolitan Transit Authority,* 469 U.S. 528. The *Roe* framework is hardly consistent with the notion of a Constitution like ours that is cast in general terms and usually speaks in general principles. The framework's key elements—trimesters and viability—are not found in the Constitution's text, and, since the bounds of the inquiry are essentially indeterminate, the result has been a web of legal rules that have become increasingly intricate, resembling a code of regulations rather than a body of constitutional doctrine. There is also no reason why the State's compelling interest in protecting potential human life should not extend throughout pregnancy rather than coming into existence only at the point of viability. Thus, the *Roe* trimester framework should be abandoned.

(e) There is no merit to Justice Blackmun's contention that the Court should join in a "great issues" debate as to whether the Constitution includes an "unenumerated" general right to privacy as recognized in cases such as *Griswold* v. *Connecticut,* 381 U.S. 479. Unlike *Roe, Griswold* did not purport to adopt a whole framework, complete with detailed rules and distinctions, to govern the cases in which the asserted liberty interest would apply. The *Roe* framework sought to deal with areas of medical practice traditionally left to the States, and to balance once and for all, by reference only to the calendar, the State's interest in protecting potential human life against the claims of a pregnant woman to decide whether or not to abort. The Court's experience in applying *Roe* in later cases suggests that there is wisdom in not necessarily attempting to elaborate the differences between a "fundamental right" to an abortion, *Akron, supra,* at 420, n. 1 a "limited fundamental constitutional right," post, at 555, or a liberty interest protected by the Due Process Clause. Moreover, although this decision will undoubtedly allow more governmental regulation of abortion

than was permissible before, the goal of constitutional adjudication is not to remove inexorably "politically devisive" issues from the ambit of the legislative process, but is, rather, to hold true the balance between that which the Constitution puts beyond the reach of democratic process and that which it does not. Furthermore, the suggestion that legislative bodies, in a Nation [492 U.S. 490, 495] where more than half the population is female, will treat this decision as an invitation to enact abortion laws reminiscent of the dark ages misreads the decision and does scant justice to those who serve in such bodies and the people who elect them.

2. This case affords no occasion to disturb *Roe*'s holding that a Texas statute which criminalized all nontherapeutic abortions unconstitutionally infringed the right to an abortion derived from the Due Process Clause. *Roe* is distinguishable on its facts, since Missouri has determined that viability is the point at which its interest in potential human life must be safeguarded.

Justice O'Connor, agreeing that it was plain error for the Court of Appeals to interpret the second sentence of 188.029 as meaning that doctors must perform tests to find gestational age, fetal weight, and lung maturity, concluded that the section was constitutional as properly interpreted by the plurality, and that the plurality should therefore not have proceeded to reconsider *Roe* v. *Wade.* This Court refrains from deciding constitutional questions where there is no need to do so, and generally does not formulate a constitutional rule broader than the precise facts to which it is to be applied. *Ashwander* v. *TVA* 297 U.S. 288, 346, 347. Since appellees did not appeal the District Court's ruling that the first sentence of 188.029 is constitutional, there is no dispute between the parties over the presumption of viability at 20 weeks created by that first sentence. Moreover, as properly interpreted by the plurality, the section's second sentence does nothing more than delineate means by which the unchallenged 20-week presumption may be overcome if those means are useful in determining viability and can be prudently employed. As so interpreted, the viability testing requirements do not conflict with any of the Court's abortion decisions. As the plurality recognizes, under its interpretation of 188.029's second sentence, the viability testing requirements promote the State's interest in potential life. This Court has recognized that a State may promote that interest when viability is possible. *Thornburgh* v. *American College of Obstetricians and Gynecologists,* 476 U.S. 747, 770–771. Similarly, the basis for reliance by the lower courts on *Colautti* v. *Franklin,* 439 U.S. 379, 388–389, disappears when 188.029 is properly interpreted to require only subsidiary viability findings, since the State has not attempted to substitute its judgment for the physician's ascertainment of viability, which therefore remains "the critical point." Nor does the marginal increase in the cost of an abortion created by 188.029's viability testing provision, as interpreted, conflict with *Akron* v. *Akron Center for Reproductive Health,* 462 U.S. 416, 434–439, since, here, such costs do not place a "heavy, and unnecessary burden" on a woman's abortion decision, whereas the statutory requirement in *Akron,* which related to [492 U.S. 490, 496] previability abortions, more than doubled a woman's

costs. Moreover, the statutory requirement in *Akron* involved second-trimester abortions generally; 188.029 concerns only tests and examinations to determine viability when viability is possible. The State's compelling interest in potential life postviability renders its interest in determining the critical point of viability equally compelling. *Thornburgh, supra,* at 770–771. When the constitutional invalidity of a State's abortion statute actually turns upon the constitutional validity of *Roe,* there will be time enough to reexamine *Roe,* and to do so carefully.

Justice Scalia would reconsider and explicitly overrule *Roe* v. *Wade.* Avoiding the *Roe* question by deciding this case in as narrow a manner as possible is not required by precedent and not justified by policy. To do so is needlessly to prolong this Court's involvement in a field where the answers to the central questions are political rather than juridical, and thus to make the Court the object of the sort of organized pressure that political institutions in a democracy ought to receive. It is particularly perverse to decide this case as narrowly as possible in order to avoid reading the inexpressibly "broader-than-was-required-by-the-precise-facts" structure established by *Roe* v. *Wade.* The question of *Roe*'s validity is presented here, inasmuch as 188.029 constitutes a legislative imposition on the judgment of the physician concerning the point of viability and increases the cost of an abortion. It does palpable harm, if the States can and would eliminate largely unrestricted abortion, skillfully to refrain from telling them so.

19.

Amy Tan: *The Joy Luck Club*

Born in 1952 in Oakland, California, Amy Tan is the daughter of Chinese immigrants. In 1987 she was a successful freelance business writer, with no fiction to her name. That same year she returned with her mother to China, where she met two half-sisters and a new world was revealed to her. This journey of both discovery and self-discovery inspired her first novel, The Joy Luck Club. *In a multiple narrative it presents the frictions of immigrant mothers and their American-born daughters. In the vignette printed below, Waverly Jong takes her American boyfriend, Rich, and her daughter, Shoshana, to visit her very traditional parents.*

Source: *The Joy Luck Club*, New York, 1989.

WHEN I OFFERED Rich a fork, he insisted on using the slippery ivory chopsticks. He held them splayed like the knock-kneed legs of an ostrich while picking up a large chunk of sauce-coated eggplant. Halfway between his plate and his open mouth, the chunk fell on his crisp white shirt and then slid into his crotch. It took several minutes to get Shoshana to stop shrieking with laughter.

And then he had helped himself to big portions of the shrimp and snow peas, not realizing he should have taken only a polite spoonful, until everybody had had a morsel.

He had declined the sautéed new greens, the tender and expensive leaves of bean plants plucked before the sprouts turn into beans. And Shoshana refused to eat them also, pointing to Rich: "He didn't eat them! He didn't eat them!"

He thought he was being polite by refusing seconds, when he should have followed my father's example, who made a big show of taking small portions of seconds, thirds, and even fourths, always saying he could not resist another bite of something or other, and then groaning that he was so full he thought he would burst.

But the worst was when Rich criticized my mother's cooking, and he didn't even know what he had done. As is the Chinese cook's custom, my mother always made disparaging remarks about her own cooking. That night she chose to direct it toward her famous steamed pork and preserved vegetable dish, which she always served with special pride.

"Ai! This dish not salty enough, no flavor," she complained, after tasting a small bite. "It is too bad to eat."

This was our family's cue to eat some and proclaim it the best she had ever made. But before we could do so, Rich said, "You know, all it needs is a little soy sauce." And he proceeded to pour a riverful of the salty black stuff on the platter, right before my mother's horrified eyes.

And even though I was hoping throughout the dinner that my mother would somehow see Rich's kindness, his sense of humor and boyish charm, I knew he had failed miserably in her eyes.

Rich obviously had had a different opinion on how the evening had gone.

When we got home that night, after we put Shoshana to bed, he said modestly, "Well, I think we hit it off *A-o-kay*." He had the look of a dalmatian, panting, loyal, waiting to be petted.

20.

Michael Kinsley: The Collapse of Communism

The Cold War between the United States and Soviet Union came to an end in the late 1980s and early 1990s. After five decades of superpower rivalry, a collapsing Soviet economy forced Premier Mikhail Gorbachev to defuse American–Soviet tensions and end the Cold War. Gorbachev's efforts to reform the Communist system, however, came too late to save the Soviet empire. In the autumn of 1989 Eastern Europe broke away from Soviet control, and in 1991 the Soviet Union itself collapsed. Communist parties disbanded all over the world, and by the end of the 1990s only a handful of Communist countries remained, including North Korea, China, Cuba, Laos, and Vietnam. Even before Soviet Communism came to an end, a debate emerged within the United States over the cause of its demise. Most credited President Ronald Reagan, who they believed forced the Soviets into bankruptcy by daring them to match his massive defense build-up. In contrast, most liberals argued that Communism's fruitless economic policies and repressive political system led to its own failure. In the essay reprinted below, Michael Kinsley, editor of The New Republic *magazine, takes the liberal view, arguing that the inherent flaws of Communism, rather than President Reagan's policies, caused the collapse of the Soviet empire.*

Source: *The New Republic*, December 4, 1989, "Who Killed Communism?"

Jeane Kirkpatrick didn't get it as completely wrong as I had hoped. In her famous 1979 essay, "Dictatorships and Double Standards," she didn't say totalitarian regimes can never evolve toward democracy. What she said is, "There is no instance of a revolutionary 'socialist' or Communist society being democratized," and, "the history of this century provides no grounds for expecting that radical totalitarian regimes will transform themselves."

Nevertheless, the seemingly immutable nature of totalitarian governments, com- pared with authoritarian ones, was a cornerstone of her argument—and the Reagan Administration's initial policy—in favor of friendly relations with friendly dictators and implacable hostility to the Soviet Union.

"We knew, we just knew, all America, that this day would come," said President Bush on November 13 about the amazing events in Berlin. It's nice of him to include us all, but let me confess that I certainly didn't know it would come. And if he knew, he kept it a wonderful surprise. Conservative doctrine had been that it would never come. The mainstream conservative goal—shared by mainstream liberals, with arguments about ways and means—has been containment of communism. The loony right position has been to roll back communism through military action. But the conservative view (unlike that of the father of containment, George Kennan) has never been that a contained communism could collapse of its own internal contradictions.

Quite the opposite. The conservative view has been that communism could always rise above its internal contradictions. Its manifest failure to deliver what it promised would neither persuade its leaders as a matter of logic nor force them as a practical matter to abandon their quest for world domination—let alone their hold on their own societies. Ideologically and economically bankrupt regimes would not merely cling to power but squeeze their people even harder in order to expand. To pluck just one choice passage of many from Jean-François Revel's celebrated 1984 manifesto, *How Democracies Perish:* "a system that has grown so strong despite so many failings, that increasingly dominates the world even when no one wants anything to do with it . . . must nevertheless embody a principle of action and monopolization of power more effective than any mankind has ever known before."

No seer, I too accepted the premise. But I never really understood it. Why were Communists bent on world domination? There have been two sorts of answers, neither satisfactory. One is that they are committed Marxist-Leninist ideologues. That is Ronald Reagan's oft-expressed view, for example. But the Kremlin leaders are not fools. Only a fool could believe in 1989 that Marxism offers the best way to organize society

for prosperity and happiness. Unlike earlier rather durable ideologies, such as the divine right of kings, that is what Marxism was supposed to achieve. And unlike other religions such as Catholicism and Islam, it is supposed to achieve those goals in this world, not the next. It must be awfully hard to get out of bed in the morning and go about your business of world conquest in support of an ideology that has been proved flatly wrong.

Thus the second explanation: sheer power lust. As one friend put it about a colleague (details changed): "The Soviets want to conquer the world for the same reason Sherwood wants to run the accounting department." This was Orwell's theory of totalitarianism in *1984.* O'Brien, representing Big Brother, says to Winston Smith, strapped to the torture table: "Now tell me *why* we cling to power. What is our motive?" Winston starts to say, "You are ruling over us for our own good," when O'Brien interrupts him, turns on the juice, and explains: "We are not interested in the good of others; we are interested solely in power. Not wealth or luxury or long life or happiness: only power, pure power. . . . [N]o one ever seizes power with the intention of relinquishing it. Power is not a means, it is an end," and so on.

This seems cartoonish. Can a society (or even an accounting department) be organized generation after generation, in the face of massive practical failure, to serve mere empty power lust? The most persuasive explanation of Soviet motives is a sort of combination of the other two, with the added factor of momentum. A bureaucracy has grown up that half-believes in an ideology it learned by rote and clings to a less ascetic version of power lust than O'Brien's—one that includes material advantages for itself as the society around it crumbles.

But if the truth is something like that, totalitarianism starts to look a bit more like authoritarianism. And it shouldn't seem so surprising that the material failure of communism should lead fairly directly to its political failure. Or at least that leaders would arise who attempt to reform it beyond recognition. One thing we couldn't have known until very recently, but people like Gorbachev must have understood, is how completely Communists have failed to reinvent humanity. Not only have they failed to remake human nature as Marx predicted, they haven't even managed to sell their own ideology to generations that have grown up completely under their control. Writing in 1982, Kirkpatrick said that this was the big question mark in thinking about whether totalitarianism can evolve. In Poland, East Germany, the Soviet Union, the answer to that question now seems thrillingly clear.

Conservatives, having said the collapse of communism would not happen, now claim credit for it. The congealing party line was inscribed in the *Wall Street Journal*, November 13: "America's victory in the Cold War was consummated by Ronald Reagan." (Hilariously, the *Journal* goes on to call for "a new order," adding:

"Reform of the international monetary system would reflect the seriousness of purpose events now demand.") America's policy of containment undoubtedly hastened the day. But the party line that containment was abandoned in the 1970s and had to be reinvented by Reagan is 99 percent myth.

The record of the 1980s—on the defense buildup, on arms control, on promoting anti-Communist guerrillas, even on Star Wars—is pretty consistently one of Reaganite extremism (or fortitude, if you prefer) later modified or even reversed in the face of liberal opposition. This leaves conservative debaters in a pretty good position to have it both ways: claiming credit, as in Eastern Europe; deflecting blame, as in Nicaragua. To the extent that American policies of the 1980s had any effect at all in producing the current historic developments that no one predicted, what seems to have worked was an inadvertently clever good-cop, bad-cop strategy. Negative incentives for bad behavior don't work without positive incentives for good behavior. We offered the Soviets both. But communism obviously deserves more credit than it has gotten for being able to produce its own collapse.

———————◆———————

The best thing we can do if we want the Russians to let us be Americans is to let the Russians be Russian.
                              GEORGE KENNAN, from the television program
                                   US-Soviet Relations: The First 50 Years,
                                              April 17, 1984

21.

George Bush: Operation Just Cause

Foreign relations with Panama had grown increasingly strained for the United States in the 1980s. Following the death of Panamanian leader Omar Torrijos in 1981, Manuel Noriega consolidated military then civilian power in the Central American nation. In 1989 he annulled the results of the presidential election to rule through a puppet government, establishing a dictatorial regime that was noted for its brutality. A year earlier Noriega had been personally indicted for drug trafficking by a U.S. court, and, though he was formerly on the payroll of the Central Intelligence Agency, in 1989 his privileges with the United States came to an end. In December of that year, after publicly assuming executive power, Noriega declared Panama to be at war with the United States. After Panamanians killed a U.S. Marine, President George Bush ordered the invasion of the country with the express intent of unseating Noriega. The invasion was denounced by both the United Nations General Assembly and the Organization of American States. On the first day of fighting, December 20, the winner of the annulled election became president, and Noriega went into hiding. On January 3, 1990, Noriega was arrested by U.S. forces; in 1992 he was convicted and sentenced to forty years in prison by a U.S. federal court. President Bush delivered the following address to the country in the first days of the invasion.

Source: Address to the Nation, December 20, 1989, George Bush Presidential Library and Museum.

My fellow citizens, last night I ordered U.S. military forces to Panama. No President takes such action lightly. This morning, I want to tell you what I did and why I did it.

For nearly 2 years, the United States, nations of Latin America and the Caribbean have worked together to resolve the crisis in Panama. The goals of the United States have been to safeguard the lives of Americans, to defend democracy in Panama, to combat drug trafficking, and to protect the integrity of the Panama Canal treaty. Many attempts have been made to resolve this crisis through diplomacy and negotiations. All were rejected by the dictator of Panama,

General Manuel Noriega, an indicted drug trafficker.

Last Friday, Noriega declared his military dictatorship to be in a state of war with the United States and publicly threatened the lives of Americans in Panama. The very next day, forces under his command shot and killed an unarmed American serviceman; wounded another; arrested and brutally beat a third American serviceman; and then brutally interrogated his wife, threatening her with sexual abuse. That was enough.

General Noriega's reckless threats and attacks upon Americans in Panama created an imminent danger to the 35,000

American citizens in Panama. As President, I have no higher obligation than to safeguard the lives of American citizens. And that is why I directed our Armed Forces to protect the lives of American citizens in Panama and to bring General Noriega to justice in the United States. I contacted the bipartisan leadership of Congress last night and informed them of this decision, and after taking this action, I also talked with leaders in Latin America, the Caribbean, and those of other U.S. allies.

At the moment, U.S. forces, including forces deployed from the United States last night, are engaged in action in Panama. The United States intends to withdraw the forces newly deployed to Panama as quickly as possible. Our forces have conducted themselves courageously and selflessly. And as Commander in Chief, I salute every one of them and thank them on behalf of our country.

Tragically, some Americans have lost their lives in defense of their fellow citizens, in defense of democracy. And my heart goes out to their families. We also regret and mourn the loss of innocent Panamanians.

The brave Panamanians elected by the people of Panama in the elections last May, President Guillermo Endara and Vice Presidents Calderon and Ford, have assumed the rightful leadership of their country. You remember those horrible pictures of newly elected Vice President Ford, covered head to toe with blood, beaten mercilessly by so-called "dignity battalions." Well, the United States today recognizes the democratically elected government of President Endara. I will send our Ambassador back to Panama immediately.

Key military objectives have been achieved. Most organized resistance has been eliminated. But the operation is not over yet. General Noriega is in hiding. And nevertheless, yesterday a dictator ruled Panama, and today constitutionally elected leaders govern.

I have today directed the Secretary of the Treasury and the Secretary of State to lift the economic sanctions with respect to the democratically elected government of Panama and, in cooperation with that government, to take steps to effect an orderly unblocking of Panamanian Government assets in the United States. I'm fully committed to implement the Panama Canal treaties and turn over the Canal to Panama in the year 2000. The actions we have taken and the cooperation of a new, democratic government in Panama will permit us to honor these commitments. As soon as the new government recommends a qualified candidate, Panamanian, to be Administrator of the Canal, as called for in the treaties, I will submit this nominee to the Senate for expedited consideration.

I am committed to strengthening our relationship with the democratic nations in this hemisphere. I will continue to seek solutions to the problems of this region through dialog and multilateral diplomacy. I took this action only after reaching the conclusion that every other avenue was closed and the lives of American citizens were in grave danger. I hope that the people of Panama will put this dark chapter of dictatorship behind them and move forward together as citizens of a democratic Panama with this government that they themselves have elected.

The United States is eager to work with the Panamanian people in partnership and friendship to rebuild their economy. The Panamanian people want democracy, peace, and the chance for a better life in dignity and freedom. The people of the United States seek only to support them in pursuit of these noble goals. Thank you very much.

1990

22.

MITCHELL KAPOR and JOHN PERRY BARLOW: The Information Age and Open Societies

The closing decades of the twentieth century saw the twilight of the Industrial Age and the dawn of the Information Age. Nowhere was this clearer than in the United States, where, beginning in the late 1970s, the first computer bulletin board systems (BBS) and Internet newsgroups facilitated the sharing of information. Soon, some U.S. government agencies became worried about what was being shared and by whom. In response to the temporary shutdown of one BBS, the Electronic Frontier Foundation (EFF) was formed in 1990 to protect American freedom of speech in cyberspace. In the ensuing decade, the EFF became an influential lobby, helping to pass bills that funded Internet access for all American schools, promoting privacy of communications (including the right to use encryption of electronic data), and opposing unrestricted government surveillance and censorship. The effort to keep cyberspace a free and open society quickly spread to other countries as local computer networks linked up to become the global Internet. Some governments refused to allow their citizens any access to the Internet; others sought to censor unapproved Internet sites and discourse. As wireless access grew in availability everywhere, such strategies seemed doomed to fail. In the selection excerpted here, Mitchell Kapor, designer of Lotus, the first spreadsheet program, and John Perry Barlow, civil libertarian (and onetime lyricist for the Grateful Dead), outline their vision for the Electronic Frontier.

Source: http://www.eff.org

OVER THE LAST 50 years, the people of the developed world have begun to cross into a landscape unlike any which humanity has experienced before. It is a region without physical shape or form. It exists, like a standing wave, in the vast web of our electronic communication systems. It consists of electron states, microwaves, magnetic fields, light pulses and thought itself.

It is familiar to most people as the "place" in which a long-distance telephone conversation takes place. But it is also the repository for all digital or electronically transferred information, and, as such, it is the venue for most of what is now commerce, industry, and broad-scale human interaction. William Gibson called this Platonic realm "Cyberspace," a name which has some currency among its present inhabitants.

Whatever it is eventually called, it is the homeland of the Information Age, the place where the future is destined to dwell.

In its present condition, Cyberspace is a frontier region, populated by the few hardy technologists who can tolerate the austerity of its savage computer interfaces, incompatible communications protocols, proprietary barricades, cultural and legal ambiguities, and general lack of useful maps or metaphors.

Certainly, the old concepts of property, expression, identity, movement, and context, based as they are on physical manifestation, do not apply succinctly in a world where there can be none.

Sovereignty over this new world is also not well defined. Large institutions already lay claim to large fiefdoms, but most of the actual natives are solitary and independent, sometimes to the point of sociopathy. It is, therefore, a perfect breeding ground for both outlaws and vigilantes. Most of society has chosen to ignore the existence of this arising domain. Every day millions of people use ATM's and credit cards, place telephone calls, make travel reservations, and access information of limitless variety . . . all without any perception of the digital machinations behind these transactions.

Our financial, legal, and even physical lives are increasingly dependent on realities of which we have only dimmest awareness. We have entrusted the basic functions of modern existence to institutions we cannot name, using tools we've never heard of and could not operate if we had.

As communications and data technology continues to change and develop at a pace many times that of society, the inevitable conflicts have begun to occur on the border between Cyberspace and the physical world.

These are taking a wide variety of forms, including (but hardly limited to) the following:

I. LEGAL AND CONSTITUTIONAL QUESTIONS

What is free speech and what is merely data? What is a free press without paper and ink? What is a "place" in a world without tangible dimensions? How does one protect property which has no physical form and can be infinitely and easily reproduced? Can the history of one's personal business affairs properly belong to someone else? Can anyone morally claim to own knowledge itself?

These are just a few of the questions for which neither law nor custom can provide concrete answers. In their absence, law enforcement agencies like the Secret Service and FBI, acting at the disposal of large information corporations, are seeking to create legal precedents which would radically limit Constitutional application to digital media.

The excesses of Operation Sun Devil are only the beginning of what threatens to become a long, difficult, and philosophically obscure struggle between institutional control and individual liberty.

II. FUTURE SHOCK

Information workers, forced to keep pace with rapidly changing technology, are stuck on "the learning curve of Sisyphus." Increasingly, they find their hard-acquired skills to be obsolete even before they've been fully mastered. To a lesser extent, the same applies to ordinary citizens who correctly feel a lack of control over their own lives and identities.

One result of this is a neo-Luddite resentment of digital technology from which little good can come. Another is a decrease in worker productivity ironically coupled to tools designed to enhance it. Finally, there is a spreading sense of alienation, dislocation, and helplessness in the general presence of which no society can expect to remain healthy.

III. THE "KNOWS" AND THE "KNOW-NOTS"

Modern economies are increasingly divided between those who are comfortable and proficient with digital technology and those who neither understand nor trust it. In essence, this development disenfranchises the latter group, denying them any possibility of citizenship in Cyberspace and, thus, participation in the future.

Furthermore, as policy-makers and elected officials remain relatively ignorant of computers and their uses, they unknowingly abdicate most of their authority to corporate technocrats whose jobs do not include general social responsibility. Elected government is thus replaced by institutions with little real interest beyond their own quarterly profits.

We are founding the Electronic Frontier Foundation to deal with these and related challenges. While our agenda is ambitious to the point of audacity, we don't see much that these issues are being given the broad social attention they deserve. We were forced to ask, "If not us, then who?"

In fact, our original objectives were more modest. When we first heard about Operation Sun Devil and other official adventures into the digital realm, we thought that remedy could be derived by simply unleashing a few highly competent Constitutional lawyers upon the Government. In essence, we were prepared to fight a few civil libertarian brush fires and go on about our private work.

However, examination of the issues surrounding these government actions revealed that we were dealing with the symptoms of a much larger malady, the collision between Society and Cyberspace.

We have concluded that a cure can lie only in bringing civilization to Cyberspace. Unless a successful effort is made to render that harsh and mysterious terrain suitable for ordinary inhabitants, friction between the two worlds will worsen. Constitutional protections, indeed the perceived legitimacy of representative government itself, might gradually disappear.

We could not allow this to happen unchallenged, and so arises the Electronic Frontier Foundation. In addition to our legal interventions on behalf of those whose rights are threatened, we will:

• Engage in and support efforts to educate both the general public and policy-makers about the opportunities and challenges posed by developments in computing and telecommunications.

• Encourage communication between the developers of technology, government, corporate officials, and the general public in which we might define the appropriate metaphors and legal concepts for life in Cyberspace.

• And, finally, foster the development of new tools which will endow nontechnical users with full and easy access to computer-based telecommunications. . . .

While we expect the Electronic Frontier Foundation to be a creation of some longevity, we hope to avoid the sclerosis which organizations usually develop in their efforts to exist over time. For this reason we will endeavor to remain light and flexible, marshalling intellectual and financial resources to meet specific purposes rather than finding purposes to match our resources. As is appropriate, we will communicate between ourselves and with our constituents largely over the electronic Net, trusting self-distribution and self-organization to a much greater extent than would be possible for a more traditional organization.

We readily admit that we have our work cut out for us. However, we are greatly encouraged by the overwhelming and positive response which we have received so far. We hope the Electronic Frontier Foundation can function as a focal point for the many people of good will who wish to settle in a future as abundant and free as the present.

23.

The *Exxon Valdez* Oil Spill in Alaska

On March 24, 1989, only hours after departing the port of Valdez, Alaska, an oil tanker from the Exxon Corporation bound for California ran aground on Bligh Reef in Prince William Sound. The ruptured tanks of the Exxon Valdez *allowed almost 11 million gallons of crude oil to pour into the Gulf of Alaska, triggering an environmental disaster of epic proportions. In the following months, fanned by strong winds and waves, the heavy slick spread 460 miles, eventually polluting 1,300 miles of shoreline and destroying legions of wildlife—notably salmon, herring, seabirds, sea otters, harbor seals, bald eagles, and killer whales. The enormity of the ecological ruin and the Herculean task of cleanup drew the nation's attention, and thousands of workers and volunteers flooded the area to restore it, an effort that required several summers of labor and $2.1 billion of Exxon funding. Ultimately, the National Transportation Safety Board assigned blame to the corporation, to its incompetent and overworked crew, and to an inadequate system of traffic and regulation, notably that provided by the U.S. Coast Guard. Although there was speculation that the captain of the* Exxon Valdez *was intoxicated at the time of the accident, he was later acquitted of that charge but found guilty of negligence. The ship itself was repaired and recommissioned but legally prohibited from ever reentering Prince William Sound. The following is an excerpt of the final report on the disaster, published by the Alaska Oil Spill Commission almost a year later, in February 1990.*

Source: *Spill: The Wreck of the Exxon Valdez—Final Report,* Alaska Oil Spill Commission, February 1990.

NO ONE ANTICIPATED any unusual problems as the Exxon Valdez left the Alyeska Pipeline Terminal at 9:12 p.m., Alaska Standard Time, on March 23, 1989. The 987-foot ship, second newest in Exxon Shipping Company's 20-tanker fleet, was loaded with 53,094,510 gallons (1,264,155 barrels) of North Slope crude oil bound for Long Beach, California. Tankers carrying North Slope crude oil had safely transited Prince William Sound more than 8,700 times in the 12 years since oil began flowing through the trans-Alaska pipeline, with no major disasters and few serious incidents. This experience gave little reason to suspect impending disaster. Yet less than three hours later, the Exxon Valdez grounded at Bligh Reef, rupturing eight of its 11 cargo tanks and spewing some 10.8 million gallons of crude oil into Prince William Sound.

Until the Exxon Valdez piled onto Bligh Reef, the system designed to carry 2 million barrels of North Slope oil to West Coast and Gulf Coast markets daily had worked perhaps too well. At least partly because of the success of the Valdez tanker trade, a general complacency had come to permeate the operation and oversight of the entire system. That complacency and success were shattered when the Exxon Valdez ran hard aground shortly after midnight on March 24.

No human lives were lost as a direct result of the disaster, though four deaths were associated with the cleanup effort. Indirectly, however, the human and natural losses were immense—to fisheries, subsistence livelihoods, tourism, wildlife. The most important loss for many who will never visit Prince William Sound was the aesthetic sense that something sacred in the relatively unspoiled land and waters of Alaska had been defiled.

Industry's insistence on regulating the Valdez tanker trade its own way, and government's incremental accession to industry pressure, had produced a disastrous failure of the system. The people of Alaska's Southcentral coast—not to mention Exxon and the Alyeska Pipeline Service Company—would come to pay a heavy price. The American people, increasingly anxious over environmental degradation and devoted to their image of Alaska's wilderness, reacted with anger. A spill that ranked 34th on a list of the world's largest oil spills in the past 25 years came to be seen as the nation's biggest environmental disaster since Three Mile Island.

The Exxon Valdez had reached the Alyeska Marine Terminal at 11:30 p.m. on March 22 to take on cargo. It carried a crew of 19 plus the captain. Third Mate Gregory Cousins, who became a central figure in the grounding, was relieved of watch duty at 11:50 p.m. Ship and terminal crews began loading crude oil onto the tanker at 5:05 a.m. on March 23 and increased loading to its full rate of 100,000 barrels an hour by 5:30 a.m. Chief Mate James R. Kunkel supervised the loading. . . .

[Capt. Joseph] Hazelwood spent most of the day conducting ship's business, shopping and, according to testimony before the National Transportation Safety Board (NTSB), drinking alcoholic beverages with the other ship's officers in at least two Valdez bars. Testimony indicated Hazelwood drank nonalcoholic beverages that day at lunch, a number of alcoholic drinks late that afternoon while relaxing in a Valdez bar, and at least one more drink at a bar while the party waited for pizza to take with them back to the ship. . . .

They left Valdez by taxi cab at about 7:30 p.m., got through Alyeska terminal gate security at 8:24 p.m. and boarded ship. . . .

Both the cab driver and the gate security guard later testified that no one in the party appeared to be intoxicated. A ship's agent who met with Hazelwood after he got back on the ship said it appeared the captain may have been drinking because his eyes were watery, but she did not smell alcohol on his breath. Ship's pilot Murphy, however, later indicated that he did detect the odor of alcohol on Hazelwood's breath.

Hazelwood's activities in town that day and on the ship that night would become a key focus of accident inquiries, the cause of a state criminal prosecution, and the basis of widespread media sensation. Without intending to minimize the impact of Hazelwood's actions, however, one basic conclusion of this report is that the grounding at Bligh Reef represents much more than the error of a possibly drunken skipper: It was the result of the gradual degradation of oversight and safety practices that had been intended, 12 years before, to safeguard and backstop the inevitable mistakes of human beings. . . .

At 11:25 p.m. Hazelwood informed the Vessel Traffic Center that the pilot [Murphy] had departed and that he was increasing speed to sea speed. He also reported that "judging, ah, by our radar, we'll probably divert from the TSS [traffic separation scheme] and end up in the inbound lane if there is no conflicting traffic." The traffic center indicated concurrence, stating there was no reported traffic in the inbound lane.

The traffic separation scheme is designed to do just that—separate incoming and outgoing tankers in Prince William Sound and keep them in clear, deep waters during their transit. It consists of inbound and outbound lanes, with a half-mile-wide separation zone between them. Small icebergs from nearby Columbia Glacier occasionally enter the traffic lanes. Captains had the choice of slowing down to push through them safely or deviating from their lanes if traffic permitted. Hazelwood's report, and the Valdez traffic center's concurrence, meant the ship would change course to leave the western, outbound lane, cross the separation zone and, if necessary, enter the eastern, inbound

lane to avoid floating ice. At no time did the Exxon Valdez report or seek permission to depart farther east from the inbound traffic lane; but that is exactly what it did.

At 11:30 p.m. Hazelwood informed the Valdez traffic center that he was turning the ship toward the east on a heading of 200 degrees and reducing speed to "wind my way through the ice" (engine logs, however, show the vessel's speed continued to increase). At 11:39 Cousins plotted a fix that showed the ship in the middle of the traffic separation scheme. Hazelwood ordered a further course change to a heading of 180 degrees (due south) and, according to the helmsman, directed that the ship be placed on autopilot. The second course change was not reported to the Valdez traffic center. For a total of 19 or 20 minutes the ship sailed south—through the inbound traffic lane, then across its easterly boundary and on toward its peril at Bligh Reef. Traveling at approximately 12 knots, the Exxon Valdez crossed the traffic lanes' easterly boundary at 11:47 p.m.

At 11:52 p.m. the command was given to place the ship's engine on "load program up"—a computer program that, over a span of 43 minutes, would increase engine speed from 55 RPM to sea speed full ahead at 78.7 RPM. After conferring with Cousins about where and how to return the ship to its designated traffic lane, Hazelwood left the bridge. The time, according to NTSB testimony, was approximately 11:53 p.m.

By this time Third Mate Cousins had been on duty for six hours and was scheduled to be relieved by Second Mate Lloyd LeCain. But Cousins, knowing LeCain had worked long hours during loading operations during the day, had told the second mate he could take his time in relieving him. Cousins did not call LeCain to awaken him for the midnight-to-4-a.m. watch, instead remaining on duty himself.

Cousins was the only officer on the bridge—a situation that violated company policy and perhaps contributed to the accident. A second officer on the bridge might have been more alert to the danger in the ship's position, the failure of its efforts to turn, the autopilot steering status, and the threat of ice in the tanker lane.

Cousins' duty hours and rest periods became an issue in subsequent investigations. . . . Testimony before the NTSB suggests that Cousins may have been awake and generally at work for up to 18 hours preceding the accident.

Appendix F of this report documents a direct link between fatigue and human performance error generally and notes that 80 percent or more of marine accidents are attributable to human error. Appendix F also discusses the impact of environmental factors such as long work hours, poor work conditions (such as toxic fumes), monotony and sleep deprivation. "This can create a scenario where a pilot and/or crew members may become the 'accident waiting to happen.'. . . It is conceivable," the report continues, "that excessive work hours (sleep deprivation) contributed to an overall impact of fatigue, which in turn contributed to the Exxon Valdez grounding."

Manning policies also may have affected crew fatigue. Whereas tankers in the 1950s carried a crew of 40 to 42 to manage about 6.3 million gallons of oil, according to Arthur McKenzie of the Tanker Advisory Center in New York, the Exxon Valdez carried a crew of 19 to transport 53 million gallons of oil.

Minimum vessel manning limits are set by the U.S. Coast Guard, but without any agencywide standard for policy. The Coast Guard has certified Exxon tankers for a minimum of 15 persons (14 if the

radio officer is not required). . . . [Frank] Iarossi [president of Exxon Shipping Company] and Exxon maintain that modern automated vessel technology permits reduced manning without compromise of safety or function. "Yet the literature on the subject suggests that automation does not replace humans in systems, rather, it places the human in a different, more demanding role. Automation typically reduces manual workload but increases mental workload."

Whatever the NTSB or the courts may finally determine concerning Cousins' work hours that day, manning limits and crew fatigue have received considerable attention as contributing factors to the accident. The Alaska Oil Spill Commission recommends that crew levels be set high enough not only to permit safe operations during ordinary conditions—which, in the Gulf of Alaska, can be highly demanding—but also to provide enough crew backups and rest periods that crisis situations can be confronted by a fresh, well-supported crew.

Accounts and interpretations differ as to events on the bridge from the time Hazelwood left his post to the moment the Exxon Valdez struck Bligh Reef. NTSB testimony by crew members and interpretations of evidence by the State of Alaska conflict in key areas, leaving the precise timing of events still a mystery. But the rough outlines are discernible:

Some time during the critical period before the grounding during the first few minutes of Good Friday, March 24, Cousins plotted a fix indicating it was time to turn the vessel back toward the traffic lanes. About the same time, lookout Maureen Jones reported that Bligh Reef light appeared broad off the starboard bow—i.e., off the bow at an angle of about 45 degrees. The light should have been seen off the port side (the left side of a ship, facing forward); its position off the starboard side indicated great peril for a supertanker that was out of its lanes and accelerating through close waters. Cousins gave right rudder commands to cause the desired course change and took the ship off autopilot. He also phoned Hazelwood in his cabin to inform him the ship was turning back toward the traffic lanes and that, in the process, it would be getting into ice. When the vessel did not turn swiftly enough, Cousins ordered further right rudder with increasing urgency. Finally, realizing the ship was in serious trouble, Cousins phoned Hazelwood again to report the danger and—at the end of the conversation—felt an initial shock to the vessel. The grounding, described by helmsman Robert Kagan as "a bumpy ride" and by Cousins as six "very sharp jolts," occurred at 12:04 a.m. . . .

The vessel came to rest facing roughly southwest, perched across its middle on a pinnacle of Bligh Reef. Eight of 11 cargo tanks were punctured. Computations aboard the Exxon Valdez showed that 5.8 million gallons had gushed out of the tanker in the first three and a quarter hours. Weather conditions at the site were reported to be 33 degrees F, slight drizzle rain/snow mixed, north winds at 10 knots and visibility 10 miles at the time of the grounding.

The Exxon Valdez nightmare had begun. Hazelwood—perhaps drunk, certainly facing a position of great difficulty and confusion—would struggle vainly to power the ship off its perch on Bligh

Reef. The response capabilities of Alyeska Pipeline Service Company to deal with the spreading sea of oil would be tested and found to be both unexpectedly slow and woefully inadequate. The worldwide capabilities of Exxon Corp. would mobilize huge quantities of equipment and personnel to respond to the spill—but not in the crucial first few hours and days when containment and cleanup efforts are at a premium. The U.S. Coast Guard would demonstrate its prowess at ship salvage, protecting crews and lightering operations, but prove utterly incapable of oil spill containment and response. State and federal agencies would show differing levels of preparedness and command capability. And the waters of Prince William Sound—and eventually more than 1,000 miles of beach in Southcentral Alaska—would be fouled by 10.8 million gallons of crude oil. . . .

At 12:26 a.m., Hazelwood radioed the Valdez traffic center and reported his predicament to Bruce Blandford, a civilian employee of the Coast Guard who was on duty. "We've fetched up, ah, hard aground, north of Goose Island, off Bligh Reef and, ah, evidently leaking some oil and we're gonna be here for a while and, ah, if you want, ah, so you're notified." That report triggered a night-long cascade of phone calls reaching from Valdez to Anchorage to Houston and eventually around the world as the magnitude of the spill became known and Alyeska and Exxon searched for cleanup machinery and materials.

Jodie Foster, foreground, and Sir Anthony Hopkins, winners of the Academy Awards for best actress and best actor, respectively, for their performances as FBI agent Clarice Starling and serial killer Hannibal Lecter, in the chilling *The Silence of the Lambs,* which also won the 1991 Oscars for best picture and best director (Jonathan Demme).

After 30 years as host of *The Tonight Show* and king of late-night television, Johnny Carson celebrates his final week with a kiss from Bette Midler (May 21, 1992).

TELEVISION AND FILM

Laura Dern, right, and Ellen DeGeneres, the star of the situation comedy *Ellen,* appear in the April 1997 episode of the show on which DeGeneres' title character "came out" as a lesbian, mirroring the actress-comedienne's own declaration of her sexual orientation.

Two-time Oscar-winning actor Tom Hanks, left, shakes hands at the Venice Film Festival with Steven Spielberg, who won his second Academy Award as best director for the D-Day drama *Saving Private Ryan* (1998), in which Hanks starred. Both Hanks and Spielberg reached new heights of popularity in the 1990s, Hanks becoming a film icon by playing moral characters whose dilemmas are accessible to all and Spielberg directing a series of commercial hits including *Jurassic Park, Schindler's List,* and *Saving Private Ryan.*

Arici Graziano/Corbis Sygma

(Center) Following the success of the first fully computer-generated animated feature, *Toy Story* (1995), the growing use of this new technology led in 1998 to a box-office battle between Disney's *A Bug's Life* and DreamWorks studios' similarly themed *Antz,* two of whose animated stars, Z, left, (voiced by Woody Allen), and Weaver (voiced by Sylvester Stallone) are pictured here. (Bottom) In 2000, CBS spawned a rash of turn-of-the-century "reality television" programming with the success of *Survivor,* the ultimate game show, which marooned 16 contestants on an island near Borneo for 39 days of single-elimination competition that resulted in Richard Hatch, second from the right, taking home the $1 million prize.

Everett Collection

CBS Photo Archive

24.

Barbara Bush: Wellesley College Commencement Speech

In 1990 First Lady Barbara Bush was invited to deliver the commencement address to the graduates of Wellesley College, a private liberal arts college for women in Wellesley, Massachusetts. One-fourth of the graduating class of 600 signed a petition protesting the selection, maintaining that Bush was unqualified because she seemingly rode the coattails of her husband's prominence and was defined not by a career but by the men in her life. The conflict brought up fundamental issues of feminism, as well as the role of a privileged institution facing diversity, which was the theme of the speech by student Christine Bicknell. Also speaking was Raisa Gorbachev, wife of the President of the Soviet Union. Many commentators rushed to defend Bush's choice as homemaker and mother to six children (including two sons who became state governors, one of whom later became president). They also pointed to her advocacy of education and literacy. Many contrasted her appearance with that of the next first lady, Hillary Clinton, who was a generation younger, a Wellesley graduate, and someone who typified the politically driven, career-minded woman who came of age in the 1960s and '70s. Barbara Bush's speech at Severance Green in June 1990 was noted for its self-deprecating humor, and, at its end, she received a standing ovation. Her speech is reprinted below in full.

Source: Mrs. Bush's Remarks at Wellesley College Commencement, June 1, 1990, George Bush Presidential Library and Museum.

I'M REALLY THRILLED to be here today, and very excited, as I know all of you must be, that Mrs. Gorbachev could join us.

These are exciting times. They're exciting in Washington. And I had really looked forward to coming to Wellesley. I thought it was going to be fun. I never dreamt it would be this much fun. So, thank you for that.

More than 10 years ago, when I was invited here to talk about our experiences in the People's Republic of China, I was struck by both the natural beauty of your campus and the spirit of this place. Wellesley, you see, is not just a place, but an idea—an experiment in excellence in which diversity is not just tolerated, but is embraced.

The essence of this spirit was captured in a moving speech about tolerance given last year by a student body president of one of your sister colleges.

She related the story by Robert Fulghum about a young pastor finding himself in charge of some very energetic children, hits upon a game called "Giants, Wizards and Dwarfs." "You have to decide now," the pastor instructed the children, "which you are—a giant, a wizard or a dwarf?" At that, a small girl tugging at his pants leg, asks, "But where do the mermaids stand?" And the pastor tells her there are no mermaids. And she says, "Oh yes there are. I am a mermaid."

Now, this little girl knew what she was, and she was not about to give up on either her identity or the game. She intended to take her place wherever mermaids fit into the scheme of things. Where do the mermaids stand—all of those who are different, those who do not fit the boxes and the pigeonholes? "Answer that question," wrote Fulghum, "and you can build a school, a nation, or a whole world."

As that very wise young woman said, "Diversity, like anything worth having, requires effort." Effort to learn about and respect difference, to be compassionate with one another, to cherish our own identity, and to accept unconditionally the same in others.

You should all be very proud that this is the Wellesley spirit.

Now I know your first choice today was Alice Walker—guess how I know? Known for "The Color Purple." Instead, you got me, known for the color of my hair!

Alice Walker's book has a special resonance here. At Wellesley, each class is known by a special color. For four years, the class of '90 has worn the color purple.

Today, you meet on Severance Green to say goodbye to all of that, to begin a new and a very personal journey, to search for your own true colors. In the world that awaits you beyond the shores of Lake Waban, no one can say what your true colors will be. But this I do know: You have a first-class education from a first-class school, and so you need not, probably cannot, live a paint-by-numbers life.

Decisions are not irrevocable, choices do come back, and as you set off from Wellesley, I hope many of you will consider making three very special choices.

The first is to believe in something larger than yourself, to get involved in some of the big ideas of our time.

I chose literacy because I honestly believed that if more people could read, write, and comprehend, we would be that much closer to solving so many of the problems that plague our nation and our society.

And early on, I made another choice, which I hope you will make as well. Whether you are talking about education, career, or service, you are talking about life and life really must have joy.

It's supposed to be fun. One of the reasons I made the most important decision of my life, to marry George Bush, is because he made me laugh. It's true, sometimes we laugh through our tears, but that shared laughter has been one of our strongest bonds. Find the joy in life because as Ferris Bueller said on his day off—"Life moves pretty fast and if you don't stop and look around once in a while you are going to miss it."

I am not going to tell George you clapped more for Ferris than you clapped for George.

The third choice that must not be missed is to cherish your human connections, your relationships with family and friends. For several years you've had impressed upon you the importance to your career of dedication and hard work, and of course that's true. But as important as your obligations as a doctor, a lawyer, a business leader will be, you are a human being first, and those human connections with spouses, with children, with friends are the most important investment you will ever make.

At the end of your life, you will never regret not having passed one more test, winning one more verdict, or not closing one more deal. You will regret time not spent with a husband, a child, a friend or a parent.

We are in a transitional period right now—fascinating and exhilarating times, learning to adjust to changes and the choices we—men and women—are facing. As an example, I remember what a friend said on hearing her husband complain to his buddies that he had to babysit. Quickly setting him straight, my friend told her husband that when it's your own kids, it's not called babysitting.

Now, maybe we should adjust faster and maybe we should adjust slower. But whatever the era, whatever the times, one thing will never change: Fathers and mothers, if you have children, they must come first. You must read to your children and you must hug your children and you must love your children. Your success as a family, our success as a society, depends not on what happens in the White House but on what happens inside your house.

For over 50 years, it was said that the winner of Wellesley's annual hoop race would be the first to get married. Now they say the winner will be the first to become a CEO. Both of those stereotypes show too little tolerance for those who want to know where the mermaids stand.

So, I want to offer a new legend. The winner of the hoop race will be the first to realize her dream—not society's dream—her own personal dream.

Who knows? Somewhere out in this audience may even be someone who will one day follow in my footsteps and preside over the White House as the president's spouse, and I wish him well.

Well, the controversy ends here, but our conversation is only beginning, and a worthwhile conversation it has been. So, as you leave Wellesley today, take with you deep thanks for the courtesy and the honor you have shared with Mrs. Gorbachev and with me.

Thank you. God bless you. And may your future be worthy of your dreams.

There are only two lasting things we can leave our children: one is roots; the other is wings.

ANONYMOUS

25.

The Americans with Disabilities Act

In the 1950s the national debate over civil rights focused on African Americans; in the 1960s and 1970s it expanded to include women, Latinos, American Indians, and gays and lesbians. In the 1980s the horizon of civil rights expanded once again, this time to include the rights of disabled Americans. In 1986 the National Council on the Handicapped (now the National Council on Disability) called on Congress to pass legislation that would protect the rights of disabled Americans, particularly in ensuring access to public facilities and increasing job opportunities. Although there was wide support for such legislation, business owners lobbied against it. They feared that the act's passage would impose excessive costs on the private sector and curb their right to dismiss employees. After four years of prolonged debate, Congress passed the Americans with Disabilities Act in 1990. In the decade that followed the act had a mixed legacy. It succeeded in forcing hotels, restaurants, movie theaters, universities, and other public facilities to provide adequate access, which constituted a major victory for the disabled. Nevertheless, this legislation did not seem to affect greatly job opportunities, as there was not a significant increase in the number of disabled Americans in the workforce, which proved a great disappointment to the act's supporters. The text of the Americans with Disabilities Act of 1990 is reprinted below in part.

Source: 101 Cong., 2 Session, January 23, 1990, http://www.usdoj.gov/crt/ada/pubs/ada.txt

AMERICANS WITH DISABILITIES ACT of 1990
S. 933
One Hundred First Congress of the United States of America
AT THE SECOND SESSION
Begun and held at the City of Washington on
Tuesday, the twenty-third day of January,
one thousand nine hundred and ninety
An Act
To establish a clear and comprehensive prohibition of
discrimination on the basis of disability.
Be it enacted by the Senate and House of Representatives of
the United States of America in Congress assembled,

SEC. 2. FINDINGS AND PURPOSES.

(a) Findings.—The Congress finds that—

(1) some 43,000,000 Americans have one or more physical or mental disabilities, and this number is increasing as the population as a whole is growing older;

(2) historically, society has tended to

isolate and segregate individuals with disabilities, and, despite some improvements, such forms of discrimination against individuals with disabilities continue to be a serious and pervasive social problem;

(3) discrimination against individuals with disabilities persists in such critical areas as employment, housing, public accommodations, education, transportation, communication, recreation, institutionalization, health services, voting, and access to public services;

(4) unlike individuals who have experienced discrimination on the basis of race, color, sex, national origin, religion, or age, individuals who have experienced discrimination on the basis of disability have often had no legal recourse to redress such discrimination;

(5) individuals with disabilities continually encounter various forms of discrimination, including outright intentional exclusion, the discriminatory effects of architectural, transportation, and communication barriers, overprotective rules and policies, failure to make modifications to existing facilities and practices, exclusionary qualification standards and criteria, segregation, and relegation to lesser services, programs, activities, benefits, jobs, or other opportunities;

(6) census data, national polls, and other studies have documented that people with disabilities, as a group, occupy an inferior status in our society, and are severely disadvantaged socially, vocationally, economically, and educationally;

(7) individuals with disabilities are a discrete and insular minority who have been faced with restrictions and limitations, subjected to a history of purposeful unequal treatment, and relegated to a position of political powerlessness in our society, based on characteristics that are beyond the control of such individuals

and resulting from stereotypic assumptions not truly indicative of the individual ability of such individuals to participate in, and contribute to, society;

(8) the Nation's proper goals regarding individuals with disabilities are to assure equality of opportunity, full participation, independent living, and economic self-sufficiency for such individuals; and

(9) the continuing existence of unfair and unnecessary discrimination and prejudice denies people with disabilities the opportunity to compete on an equal basis and to pursue those opportunities for which our free society is justifiably famous, and costs the United States billions of dollars in unnecessary expenses resulting from dependency and nonproductivity.

(b) Purpose.—It is the purpose of this Act—

(1) to provide a clear and comprehensive national mandate for the elimination of discrimination against individuals with disabilities;

(2) to provide clear, strong, consistent, enforceable standards addressing discrimination against individuals with disabilities;

(3) to ensure that the Federal Government plays a central role in enforcing the standards established in this Act on behalf of individuals with disabilities; and

(4) to invoke the sweep of congressional authority, including the power to enforce the fourteenth amendment and to regulate commerce, in order to address the major areas of discrimination faced day-to-day by people with disabilities. . . .

SEC. 102. DISCRIMINATION.

(a) General Rule.—No covered entity shall discriminate against a qualified individual with a disability because of the disability of such individual in regard to job application procedures, the hiring, advancement, or discharge of employees, employee compensation, job training, and other terms, conditions, and privileges of employment.

(b) Construction.—As used in subsection (a), the term "discriminate" includes—

(1) limiting, segregating, or classifying a job applicant or employee in a way that adversely affects the opportunities or status of such applicant or employee because of the disability of such applicant or employee;

(2) participating in a contractual or other arrangement or relationship that has the effect of subjecting a covered entity's qualified applicant or employee with a disability to the discrimination prohibited by this title (such relationship includes a relationship with an employment or referral agency, labor union, an organization providing fringe benefits to an employee of the covered entity, or an organization providing training and apprenticeship programs);

(3) utilizing standards, criteria, or methods of administration—

(A) that have the effect of discrimination on the basis of disability; or

(B) that perpetuate the discrimination of others who are subject to common administrative control;

(4) excluding or otherwise denying equal jobs or benefits to a qualified individual because of the known disability of an individual with whom the qualified individual is known to have a relationship or association;

(5)(A) not making reasonable accommodations to the known physical or mental limitations of an otherwise qualified individual with a disability who is an applicant or employee, unless such covered entity can demonstrate that the accommodation would impose an undue hardship on the operation of the business of such covered entity; or

(B) denying employment opportunities to a job applicant or employee who is an otherwise qualified individual with a disability, if such denial is based on the need of such covered entity to make reasonable accommodation to the physical or mental impairments of the employee or applicant;

(6) using qualification standards, employment tests or other selection criteria that screen out or tend to screen out an individual with a disability or a class of individuals with disabilities unless the standard, test or other selection criteria, as used by the covered entity, is shown to be job-related for the position in question and is consistent with business necessity; and

(7) failing to select and administer tests concerning employment in the most effective manner to ensure that, when such test is administered to a job applicant or employee who has a disability that impairs sensory, manual, or speaking skills, such test results accurately reflect the skills, aptitude, or whatever other factor of such applicant or employee that such test purports to measure, rather than reflecting the impaired sensory, manual, or speaking skills of such employee or applicant (except where such skills are the factors that the test purports to measure). . . .

SEC. 222. PUBLIC ENTITIES OPERATING FIXED ROUTE SYSTEMS.

(a) Purchase and Lease of New Vehicles.—It shall be considered discrimination for purposes of section 202 of this Act and section 504 of the Rehabilitation Act of 1973 (29 U.S.C. 794) for a public entity which operates a fixed route system to purchase or lease a new bus, a new rapid rail vehicle, a new light rail vehicle, or any other new vehicle to be used on such system, if the solicitation for such purchase or lease is made after the 30th day following the effective date of this subsection and if such bus, rail vehicle, or other vehicle is not readily accessible to and usable by individuals with disabilities, including individuals who use wheelchairs. . . .

SEC. 223. PARATRANSIT AS A COMPLEMENT TO FIXED ROUTE SERVICE.

(a) General Rule.—It shall be considered discrimination for purposes of section 202 of this Act and section 504 of the Rehabilitation Act of 1973 (29 U.S.C. 794) for a public entity which operates a fixed route system (other than a system which provides solely commuter bus service) to fail to provide with respect to the operations of its fixed route system, in accordance with this section, paratransit and other special transportation services to individuals with disabilities, including individuals who use wheelchairs, that are sufficient to provide to such individuals a level of service (1) which is comparable to the level of designated public transportation services provided to individuals without disabilities using such system; or (2) in the case of response time, which is comparable, to the extent practicable, to the level of designated public transportation services provided to individuals without disabilities using such system. . . .

SEC. 226. NEW FACILITIES.

For purposes of section 202 of this Act and section 504 of the Rehabilitation Act of 1973 (29 U.S.C. 794), it shall be considered discrimination for a public entity to construct a new facility to be used in the provision of designated public transportation services unless such facility is readily accessible to and usable by individuals with disabilities, including individuals who use wheelchairs.

SEC. 227. ALTERATIONS OF EXISTING FACILITIES.

(a) General Rule.—With respect to alterations of an existing facility or part thereof used in the provision of designated public transportation services that affect or could affect the usability of the facility or part thereof, it shall be considered discrimination, for purposes of section 202 of this Act and section 504 of the Rehabilitation Act of 1973 (29 U.S.C. 794), for a public entity to fail to make such alterations (or to ensure that the alterations are made) in such a manner that, to the maximum extent feasible, the altered portions of the facility are readily accessible to and usable by individuals with disabilities, including individuals who use wheelchairs, upon the completion of such alterations. Where the public entity is undertaking an alteration that affects or could affect usability of or access to an area of the facility containing a primary function, the entity shall also make the alterations in such a manner that, to the maximum extent feasible, the path of travel to the altered area and the bathrooms, telephones, and drinking fountains serving the altered area, are readily accessible to and usable by individuals with disabilities, including individuals who use wheelchairs, upon completion of such alterations, where such alterations to the path of travel or the bathrooms, telephones, and drinking fountains serving the altered area are not disproportionate to the overall alterations in terms of cost and scope (as determined under criteria established by the Attorney General). . . .

SEC. 302. PROHIBITION OF DISCRIMINATION BY PUBLIC ACCOMMODATIONS.

(a) General Rule.—No individual shall be discriminated against on the basis of disability in the full and equal enjoyment of the goods, services, facilities, privileges, advantages, or accommodations of any place of public accommodation by any person who owns, leases (or leases to), or operates a place of public accommodation. . . .

SEC. 303. NEW CONSTRUCTION AND ALTERATIONS IN PUBLIC ACCOMMODATIONS AND COMMERCIAL FACILITIES.

(a) Application of Term.—Except as provided in subsection (b), as applied to public accommodations and commercial facilities, discrimination for purposes of section 302(a) includes—

(1) a failure to design and construct facilities for first occupancy later than 30 months after the date of enactment of this Act that are readily accessible to and usable by individuals with disabilities, except where an entity can demonstrate that it is structurally impracticable to meet the requirements of such subsection in accordance with standards set forth or incorporated by reference in regulations issued under this title; and

(2) with respect to a facility or part thereof that is altered by, on behalf of, or for the use of an establishment in a manner that affects or could affect the usability of the facility or part thereof, a failure to make alterations in such a manner that, to the maximum extent feasible, the altered portions of the facility are readily accessible to and usable by individuals with disabilities, including individuals who use wheelchairs. Where the entity is undertaking an alteration that affects or could affect usability of or access to an area of the facility containing a primary function, the entity shall also make the alterations in such a manner that, to the maximum extent feasible, the path of travel to the altered area and the bathrooms, telephones, and drinking fountains serving the altered area, are readily accessible to and usable by individuals with disabilities where such alterations to the path of travel or the bathrooms, telephones, and drinking fountains serving the altered area are not disproportionate to the overall alterations in terms of cost and scope (as determined under criteria established by the Attorney General).

(b) Elevator.—Subsection (a) shall not be construed to require the installation of an elevator for facilities that are less than three stories or have less than 3,000 square feet per story unless the building is a shopping center, a shopping mall, or the professional office of a health care provider or unless the Attorney General determines that a particular category of such facilities requires the installation of elevators based on the usage of such facilities. . . .

SEC. 307. EXEMPTIONS FOR PRIVATE CLUBS AND RELIGIOUS ORGANIZATIONS.

The provisions of this title shall not apply to private clubs or establishments exempted from coverage under title II of the Civil Rights Act of 1964 (42 U.S.C. 2000-a(e)) or to religious organizations or entities controlled by religious organizations, including places of worship. . . .

SEC. 402. CLOSED-CAPTIONING OF PUBLIC SERVICE ANNOUNCEMENTS.

Section 711 of the Communications Act of 1934 is amended to read as follows:

"SEC. 711. CLOSED-CAPTIONING OF PUBLIC SERVICE ANNOUNCEMENTS.

"Any television public service announcement that is produced or funded in whole or in part by any agency or instrumentality of Federal Government shall include closed captioning of the verbal content of such announcement. A television broadcast station licensee—

"(1) shall not be required to supply closed-captioning for any such announcement that fails to include it; and

"(2) shall not be liable for broadcasting any such announcement without transmitting a closed caption unless the licensee intentionally fails to transmit the closed caption that was included with the announcement." . . .

SEC. 503. PROHIBITION AGAINST RETALIATION AND COERCION.

(a) Retaliation.—No person shall discriminate against any individual because such individual has opposed any act or practice made unlawful by this Act or because such individual made a charge, testified, assisted, or participated in any manner in an investigation, proceeding, or hearing under this Act.

(b) Interference, Coercion, or Intimidation.—It shall be unlawful to coerce, intimidate, threaten, or interfere with any individual in the exercise or enjoyment of, or on account of his or her having exercised or enjoyed, or on account of his or her having aided or encouraged any other individual in the exercise or enjoyment of, any right granted or protected by this Act.

(c) Remedies and Procedures.—The remedies and procedures available under sections 107, 203, and 308 of this Act shall be available to aggrieved persons for violations of subsections (a) and (b), with respect to title I, title II and title III, respectively. . . .

Congress acknowledged that society's accumulated myths and fears about disability and disease are as handicapping as are the physical limitations that flow from actual impairment.

WILLIAM J. BRENNAN, JR., in a majority opinion of the U.S. Supreme Court, arguing that people with contagious diseases are protected by a law that prohibits discrimination against the handicapped in federally funded programs, March 3, 1987

26.

DANA ROHRABACHER, SIDNEY R. YATES, DICK ARMEY, and MAJOR R. OWENS: Debate on Funding the NEA

In 1965 Congress created the National Endowment for the Arts (NEA) as an independent government agency to provide support for fine arts, literature, music, film, theater, dance, and other activities. The majority of NEA grants were awarded to arts institutions, such as orchestras and museums; to school programs; and to festivals, such as book and film events. There were also endowments for individual artists working on specific projects. Many NEA grants were given in concert with state or local arts agencies, and in the late twentieth century such regional organizations flourished with NEA assistance. By the late 1980s, however, opposition to the NEA developed within Congress. Some members of Congress sought the outright elimination of the agency, others lobbied for monetary and artistic restrictions, while still others rose in defense of full funding. The NEA remained intact, but in the mid-1990s government appropriation was curtailed dramatically. In the excerpts that follow, four congressmen debate the issue in October 1990. In general, arguments against the NEA centered on resistance to federally funding artists whose work many people deemed objectionable (such as those of photographers Robert Mapplethorpe and Andres Serrano) and on acknowledgment of art programs that survive without government assistance. Arguments in support of funding focused on the many successes of the NEA, a defense of the agency's ability to set its own artistic criteria, and its cost efficiencies relative to other government agencies plagued by cost overruns.

Source: *Congressional Record*, 101 Cong., 2 Session, October 11, 1990, "Arts, Humanities, and Museums Amendments of 1990."

A. MR. DANA ROHRABACHER (D) OF CALIFORNIA

Mr. Speaker, today is the culmination of a year-long fight over whether the Federal Government will continue to subsidize art through the National Endowment for the Arts. We will then decide whether Congress will set standards so that the Federal Government is at least not subsidizing obscenity, child pornography, attacks on religion, desecration of the American flag, and any of the other outrages that we have seen in the past.

Mr. Speaker, the Rules Committee has boiled the NEA issue down to three key votes. First, there will be a vote on the Crane amendment to abolish the NEA entirely.

Second, there will be a vote on my amendment to establish not extreme but some commonsense standards for NEA funding. Finally, the bottom-line vote will be on the Williams-Coleman substitute which will, if passed, wipe out all the restrictions that my amendment places on NEA funding. If this substitute passes, it will not matter if my amendment is adopted unanimously. The substitute will eliminate its substance.

The public has been alerted, and the constituents are watching. They know the vote on the gut-the-standard Williams substitute is the key vote.

Every Member of this body has a choice to make. Should there be standards on the spending of Federal dollars concerning the arts? Or should the National Endowment for the Arts be completely unrestricted in doling out our tax dollars to whomever they choose. The Rules Committee has left no middle ground. The debate over the past year has made it clear that our constituents do not want their tax dollars to be wasted on projects that they find morally reprehensible. And they will be watching, and they will know that there is only one way to make the NEA responsible, and that is to vote "yes" on the Rohrabacher amendment and "no" on the William-Coleman substitute which would gut the standards. They will not tolerate the goal of anyone voting for my amendment to set standards and then voting to wipe out those standards with the very next vote.

Mr. Speaker, I would call on my colleagues to vote for meaningful standards to listen to their constituents, to vote for my amendment to set standards and then to eliminate and vote against the gut-the-standards substitute offered by the gentlemen, Messrs. Williams and Coleman.

B. MR. SIDNEY R. YATES (D) OF ILLINOIS

Mr. Chairman, I thank the gentleman for yielding me this time.

Mr. Chairman, I want to continue what the gentleman from Iowa [Mr. Grandy] has been saying about what the National Endowment for the Arts has done over the years.

The gentleman from California [Mr. Rohrabacher] got up earlier and talked about this amendment and said that they were not extreme standards that he was imposing. They are very extreme standards, and if by some chance the House in unwisdom were to accept his amendment, it would smother NEA. It would mean the end of NEA.

Some of you may have seen the broadcast of the Civil War over the last few weeks on PBS. All of those who have seen it have acclaimed it. It was magnificent. I cite that example because the series was made possible by a grant from the National Endowment for the Humanities.

That was a most dramatic and graphic example of the kind of work both the arts and the humanities have made available over the 25 years they have been in existence. They have provided the kind of art for America that the people of America want and like and deserve.

Operas, ballets, plays, special events, both the Endowments have made the funds available that have made this possible, and all through the country there have been grants from the Endowments which are elevating, yes, elevating, the artistic levels and cultural levels of this country, in operas, in plays, in ballet, in lectures, folk art, teaching for children. You listen to some of those who are critical and talk about, as the gentleman from California [Mr. Rohrabacher] did earlier, talk about the outrages, the latest outrages of NEA. What outrages? How many outrages are there? One would think, by the way that he talks and others talk, that there are as many as there are trees in a forest, in one of our national forests. That is not true at all.

In all of the 85,000 grants or more of NEA, there have been a handful of mistakes as there are bound to be. The wonder is that there are not more in the field of culture. What Government agency has not made a mistake? What Government agency has not been held more to account than NEA for its mistakes?

All we hear from the other side is two grants: Mapplethorpe, Serrano; Mapplethorpe, Serrano; Mapplethorpe, Serrano, time and time again, as though their photographs were all that the Endowments for the Arts and the Humanities had ever done. Nothing is further from the truth.

It was also said that we cannot allow tax money to be used for such purposes. One would think that as much money was going into NEA controversial grants as was in a Stealth bomber overrun. That has gone from $75 million a plane to $750 million a plane. The truth is that for Mapplethorpe and Serrano the Federal Government advanced the sum of $45,000 for both of those grants. $45,000, and the Congress last year recaptured the $45,000 by action on this floor. There is no basis for the charge that taxpayers' money is being wasted on pornographic art.

I just want to conclude this by saying that I would hope that the House does not follow the lead of those who want to kill the Endowment in the guise of correcting the defects. The record of the Endowment deserves our praise, not our blame. It deserves our support, not the kind of distorted criticism NEA have received from some Members of the House. I hope the amendments that are restrictive will be defeated.

C. MR. DICK ARMEY (R) OF TEXAS

Mr. Chairman, it has been my observation that every dollar's worth of Government spending of the taxpayers' hardearned money brings with it 1 million dollars' worth of audacity and presumptuousness. In this debate, the most audacious presumption of all is the presumption that without the National Endowment for the Arts, there would not be a participation in and enjoyment of a rejoicing in the arts in the United States.

Mr. Chairman, that presumption is ludicrous. The American people enjoyed the arts, produced the arts, and participated in the arts long, long before the existence of the National Endowment. So if in fact there is going to be Government spending on the arts, it is not a question then of how much art will we have and enjoy, but what will be the nature and the type of the art that we will enjoy?

Mr. Chairman, I would suggest that nobody spends somebody else's money as wisely as they would spend their own, and that is certainly true in this case.

Last year alone there were 18,000 people or organizations that made application to the National Endowment for the Arts. Five thousand of those were granted. Thirteen thousand were not.

Are we to believe that none of those 13,000 artistic endeavors that were denied funding by the U.S. Government's agency ever took place? Are we to believe that each of those 5,000 that were funded should have taken place instead? Are we to believe that none of the 5,000 would have taken place without the grants? . . .

Those of us who question whether or not tax dollars should be used to fund individual artists or organizations in the self-described arts community, or whether such spending should be subject to limits that reflect the sensibilities of the American taxpayer, have been the focus of strident ad hominem attacks. I have had the distinction of being called in the media A "petty moralist," "public pinhead," "troglodyte," "philistine," "bozo," "fascist," and, of course, "censor" by advocates of no-strings-attached Federal spending on art. And I know that some on the other side of this issue have been charged with willfully funding pornography, which never goes over big with the votes back home.

In reasonably addressing the future of the National Endowment for the Arts, we must ask ourselves three fundamental questions:

First, is it the proper role of the Federal Government to grant money to individual artists, arts organizations, and the more traditional fine arts?

Second, if a majority of Members of Congress feel it is the proper role of the Federal Government to fund these individuals and groups, do we have the resources to do it in an era of $200-plus billion deficits?

Third, if funding individual works of arts and performance art is of such high priority, should the Congress have the right to impose standards on works of art which will be funded.

It is no coincidence that freedom of speech is protected by our Constitution's first amendment, for it may be our most important right in America. Anyone who values freedom of expression as deeply as I do should find abhorrent the very existence of a Federal panel charged with determining what art is worthy of funding.

When last year Senator Helms passed his Senate amendment barring certain types of artwork from receiving taxpayer funding, he was branded a censor with lightning speed. The distinction between his proposed denial of funding and the denial of expression was deliberately ignored.

Let's look at this curious contention that withholding tax funds from certain artists is censorship. According to the budget director at the National Endow-

ment for the Arts, the NEA received 17,879 grant applications in fiscal 1989. They chose to fund 4,372 of these. In the language of the demagogs in the arts community who denounce Senator Helms, the NEA censored 13,507 artists last year. Doesn't that have a chilling effect on the arts community?

Throughout last summer's debate, many outside Congress who opposed content restrictions on NEA grants argued that Federal grants were important because they constitute a stamp of approval that enables an artist to receive greater funding in the private sector. Doesn't that scare any of you? Don't you find it frightening that a Government agency is putting its stamp of approval on what is acceptable art, art which is worthy of funding?

Unfortunately, those who cry out for Government funding of individual works of art in one breath and shout "censorship" in the next refuse to acknowledge the inherent contradiction in their actions. The bottom line is the bottom line. They don't want freedom of expression, they want the money. They care less about freedom of expression than they do about the greenback dollar.

If, however, you accept the premise that a Federal agency should spend taxpayers' money to fund individual works of art, you must put it in the context of a Federal budget with competing demands on limited resources. Then the question becomes, "when we have a projected Federal deficit in excess of $200 billion can we afford to spend $180 million on art?"

Some say that figure is a mere drop in the bucket, but how many homeless families could be housed with $180 million? How many scientists could continue researching a cure for AIDS? How many veterans could be given vouchers to allow them to purchase high-quality medical care closer to their homes? How many fledgling democracies might be assisted? How many new law enforcement personnel could be enlisted in our war on drugs? Or how many taxpayers would appreciate some tax relief and deficit reduction?

Surely funding for museums, individual artists, opera productions, city orchestras, and plays would be high on [Abraham] Maslow's Pyramid of Human Needs, which may be why those who take advantage of their availability tend to be the more privileged members of American society. In other words, spending tax dollars to fund works of art amounts to an inequitable transfer of income from lower and middle-class taxpayers to indulge the less urgent needs of society's more privileged class.

It is this Congress' job to prioritize spending, and I would strongly suggest that funding any artistic activity is at or near the bottom of most taxpayers' priorities.

But, if the majority in the House determine that their constituents deem funding for the arts community a national priority, then the question is, "should the National Endowment for the Arts be held accountable for how it spends tax dollars?"

Boom! This is the explosive question at the center of so much heated debate and rhetoric.

One of my distinguished colleagues summed up the conflict earlier this year by saying, "the Federal Government should not diminish the artist's right to offend," but that on the other hand, "Taxpayers have a right to determine how their money should be used."

I cannot see that conflict here. The indisputable right for an artist to offend the public is different from a claimed right to offend the public at public expense. No one ever contended that Andres Serrano should not be free to urinate in a jar and then take a picture of a crucifix submerged in his urine and call it art, but I do not think taxpayers should be forced to pay for it. It is just that simple.

So, how do you protect the taxpayer from such abuse? Obviously, the easiest way is to abolish the agency and rid ourselves of the heart of the problem. Barring that, the answer becomes less clear.

Many artists felt the NEA was being unfairly singled out for congressional oversight during last year's debate when in fact, every agency in the Federal Government is subject to such oversight. What distinguishes the NEA and its grant recipients from all other Government agencies is its assertion that it be exempted from such congressional oversight.

Many advocates of no-strings-attached federal arts funding assert that war is too important to be left to the warriors in the Pentagon. Then they assert that art is more important than war, but art should be left to the artists. And not all artists should determine spending priorities at the NEA, but a small clique on the fringe of the art world, sometimes known as the avant garde, but which I prefer to call the looney left.

I do not believe we should spend NEA money for the enjoyment of artists. I believe we should spend NEA money for the enjoyment of the public, if we spend it at all, and that NEA grants should reflect the public's sensibilities and values.

Obviously, defining what the public's sensibilities and values are is a tricky business. It is a business more easily conducted at local levels, where the sense of community standards is readily identifiable. In this regard, the best way to ensure that Americans are given the opportunity to enjoy works of art, to ensure that rural communities across America can still have access to the fine arts, and to reduce the possibility that tax dollars will be used in a way that denigrates rather than lifts the human spirit may be to grant NEA funds to individual communities for them to spend.

I am very disappointed that Congress has allowed this controversy to continue for much too long and hope that we will do right by the taxpayers today.

D. MR. MAJOR R. OWENS OF NEW YORK

Mr. Chairman, I am proud to speak this afternoon in strong support of reauthorizing the National Endowment for the Arts. One of our former presidents once said:

"Artists stretch the limits of understanding. They express ideas that are sometimes unpopular. In an atmosphere of liberty, artists and patrons are free to think the unthinkable and create the audacious . . . where there's liberty, art succeeds. In societies that are not free, art dies." From whom I quote? Not from one of our liberal Presidents, but from one of the most conservative Presidents of our time, Ronald Reagan.

I stress that point because the debate over the relative merits of the NEA has been centering on the wrong issues. It has been centering on what a very few artists have been doing with their grants and whether or not the works of arts they have created are appropriate or decent. We are not artists. Very few of us would claim to be experts on art. So how can this body sit in judgment over the content of art and even attempt to deem it appropriate or inappropriate or good or bad.

As Mr. Reagan and thousands of other people who are knowledgeable about art assert, artists create art to reflect society, to explore societal ideas and concepts. They do not choose only those ideas which are comfortable and acceptable to us. If they did art would be universally boring. There would be nothing new, nothing daring, nothing to make us think about the art itself and about what it is reflecting.

A person who grew up in the savage ghettos of an inner city, who lived in rundown housing projects and went to school in a crumbling, rat-infested school, is not going to paint pretty pictures of landscapes and fruit bowls, and frolicking kittens. That artist's portrayals are more likely to reflect the experiences of his or her life and the anger of being shut out from the prosperity apparently being realized elsewhere in society.

This art reflects things that are happening in our society, and closing our eyes will not make those things go away. Such art can help us recognize other influences in our culture, and even help us understand them. And if it does not help me or you specifically, you can be sure that it is helping someone, somewhere, who can relate to it.

Artistic freedom enables us to depict images and realities which may or may not be offensive, but which help us explore influences in our culture that we would otherwise not experience. An image or a picture or a book can travel places and affect people all over the world. People who live in remote communities, even in the United States, may have access to a library program which contains books of stories or books of art or musical reproductions which can allow the people in that community to explore the arts and to witness the reflections of people from all corners of the world.

The NEA has financed many programs which promote access to the arts for people who otherwise would not be able to experience art. These programs may include bringing a dance troupe into rural areas on a tour, or it may include sponsoring a musical exploration program for poor students in the inner city.

In my district in central Brooklyn, the NEA has funded many small and worthwhile community programs. One such program is operated through the Bedford Stuyvesant Restoration Corp. This program consists of art workshops, weekend youth programs, art exhibitions from around the world, dance classes and exhibitions, theater productions, writers' workshops, or poetry readings. Students who have participated in these programs have gone on to study at such renowned institutions as the School of the Visual Arts and Pratt Institute. The center received a $36,000 grant from the NEA last year to help fund this multicultural center. With such programs, Restoration has become well known and attracts children and adults from throughout the city to participate in those and many other community-minded programs.

Another cultural program funded by the NEA in my district is New Radio and Performing Arts, a pioneer in the fields of experimental documentaries, contemporary radio drama, and sound experiments for the broadcast media. Endowment support over several years has helped this organization to explore new projects about women poets of color and identify new talents for underrepresented radio themes and contents.

Endowment support to another institution in my district, the Brooklyn Museum, has funded a variety of projects intended to showcase new art forms and smaller programs targeted to the local multiethnic community which seek to increase access to different art forms and encourage exploration of the arts by children.

These and many other worthwhile community programs in my district have been funded by the NEA, and thousands more have been funded nationwide. Mr. Chairman, of more than 80,000 grants, only 20 or 25 have been considered controversial. For this, some Members of this body are advocating that we eliminate the entire program.

Members are rising up in arms because tax dollars have been spent on funding these controversial projects. Mr. Chairman, each taxpayer is responsible for only 62 cents of the total yearly budget for the NEA. Compare that with the cost per taxpayer for each $5 billion B-2 bomber that falls from the sky, or each $20 million rocket that blows up, or the astronomical cost of the $500 billion S&L bailout. Where is the outrage over the cost to the taxpayers of these million and billion dollar black holes?

Members are rising up in arms over supposedly morally repugnant projects being sponsored by the Government. Where is the outrage over the equally morally repugnant problems being created by the Government such as the present situation with the WIC Program which is being cut back to the bare bones, or the housing programs which have been cut more than 60 percent in the past 10 years and caused millions of women and children to live on the streets. And where is the outrage over the morally repugnant waste of Federal funds on the $500 billion S&L bailout, the likes of which we have never seen before and hopefully will never see again. Where is the outrage?

The situation with the National Endowment for the Arts has been blown way out of proportion. There are no rational reasons for restricting this program and there are no reasons at all to eliminate it altogether. This Congress has been stampeded into making wrong and potentially disastrous decisions too frequently in the recent past. We must not bow to these illogical forces. We must fight to preserve this program based not on fear and intimidation, but based on the history and good experiences of this particular program. I urge my colleagues to have courage, and to vote to defend the National Endowment for the Arts reauthorization. Vote for the Williams-Coleman substitute and defeat both the Crane amendment and the Rohrabacher amendment.

27.

HOWELL HEFLIN: The Keating Five of the S&L Scandal

In the 1980s the savings and loan (S&L) industry lobbied Congress to implement sweeping deregulation that would free it from close government scrutiny. To win political support, S&L lobbyists contributed millions of dollars to the campaigns of congressional candidates, many of whom in turn voted for deregulation once elected. Deregulation proved a financial disaster, however, as thousands of S&L's ran up huge debts and hundreds of them filed for bankruptcy, prompting a $500 billion bailout by Congress. When media investigations in the 1990s revealed the influence of S&L contributions on deregulation voting, Congress launched a major internal ethics investigation. Although dozens of senators and representatives had received political contributions from S&L lobbyists, only five senators were singled out for investigation. The group—Democrats Alan Cranston, John Glenn, Dennis DeConcini, and Donald Riegle and Republican John McCain—became known as the "Keating Five" for their close relationship to Charles Keating, president of Lincoln Savings and Loan, who eventually went to prison. Refusing to forget the personal humiliation resulting from the scandal, McCain became the Senate's most outspoken supporter of campaign finance reform, and in 2001 Congress passed the "McCain-Feingold" bill, the first significant campaign finance reform act in a generation. Reprinted below are excerpts from an address on the Senate floor in October 1990 by Senator Howell Heflin of Alabama, who read into the record a press release by the lobby group Common Cause regarding the scandal, which was just beginning to break in the press.

Source: *Congressional Record*, 101 Cong., 2 Session, October 22, 1990, "Ethics Committee Work."

MR. HEFLIN: Mr. President, the proceedings of the Ethics Committee are confidential. This is in accordance with the rules. I do not intend to speak on matters that are confidential in nature, but I do think I should speak to matters that are publicly known relative to the proceedings of the Select Committee on Ethics.

The special counsel to the Ethics Committee made a report on September 10. Since that time, the Ethics Committee has had numerous meetings, several times each week, with meetings averaging around 3 hours each. Some of these meetings have been interrupted because of other important duties and business of the Senate. Each Senator under investigation has now appeared with his attorney before the committee in accordance with a previous agreement. The last Senator and his counsel appeared before the committee on last Thursday, October 18. The committee met again on Friday, October 19. It is the closing days of a session of Congress, there are many competing duties that face individual members of the Ethics Committee. One is on a conference working out differences of budget reconciliation measures which continue to require his absence from the Ethics Committee. Another Senator could not be present for a meeting today, October 22. The committee is scheduled to meet on Tuesday, October 23.

The Ethics Committee does not consider any charge lightly. Each charge has and will be given careful consideration.

I have before me a recent press release from Common Cause, which I will read. In doing so, it is not my purpose to say that it is correct or incorrect, but to say that it should be given careful consideration.

I quote:

On October 13, 1989, Common Cause requested the Senate Select Committee on Ethics to undertake an investigation to determine if activities undertaken in behalf of Charles H. Keating, Jr. and his company, Lincoln Savings and Loan Association, by Senators Alan Cranston (D-CA), Dennis DeConcini (D-AZ), John Glenn (D-OH), John McCain (R-AZ), and Donald Riegle (D-MI) violated Senate ethics rules and standards. On December 22, 1989, the Ethics Committee announced that it had initiated a preliminary inquiry into the matter.

Last week reports surfaced that the Senate Ethics Committee may be getting ready to drop Senators Glenn and McCain from the proceeding. These reports are deeply disturbing. We see no basis for removing Senators Glenn and McCain from this case and believe that any such action by the Senate Ethics Committee would be wholly unwarranted.

Senators Glenn and McCain, along with Senators Cranston, DeConcini, and Riegle, jointly intervened in meetings with the Federal Home Loan Bank Board on behalf of former Lincoln Savings and Loan owner Keating in April of 1987, at a time when Lincoln was approaching insolvency. Each Senator had received substantial financial benefits from Keating, his family and business associates. These included campaign contributions of $34,000 to Senator Glenn and $200,000 in corporate funds to a political action committee (PAC) Glenn controlled. Senator McCain received $112,000 in campaign contributions and substantial free transportation for McCain and his family, including three free trips to Keating's vacation resort in the Bahamas.

For the Senate Ethics Committee to drop Senators Glenn and McCain from this case is to say that there was nothing improper about the meetings that the Senators jointly held with officials of the Federal Home Loan Bank Board. We emphatically disagree. These meetings were held by the Senators to pressure regulatory officials on behalf of the Senators' financial benefactor, Charles Keating. They were meetings that never should have occurred. All five Senators were involved—four in one of the meetings and five in the other—and all five Senators bear responsibility for participating in this improper activity.

In a July 11, 1990, brief filed with the Senate Ethics Committee setting forth the Senate ethics standards applicable in the Keating Five case, former Watergate Special Prosecutor and current Common Cause Chairman Archibald Cox concluded that all five Senators 'not only jointly intervened with the Federal Home Loan Bank Board and Keating's behalf, but their combined intervention took an extraordinary form, seemingly designed [to] put the maximum Senatorial pressure upon the Board to accede to Keating's wishes. Such favors are not available to other citizens.'

The joint meetings attended by the Senators, Cox stated, constituted 'extraordinary pressure upon the FHLBB [Federal Home Loan Bank Board]' and 'an extraordinary favor' to Charles Keating, and make 'each of the five Senators a knowing participant in the fundamental violation regardless of differences in the details of their participation or in the benefits each received.'

The Cox brief stated that 'for even a single Senator to intervene in a particular law enforcement proceeding presents highly delicate ethics questions. Here, the concerted action of the four and then five Senators on April 2 and 9 [1987] even when viewed apart from the financial benefits received, involves such extraordinary use of the office of Senator as to violate the portion of the Code of Ethics [for Government Service] which mandates that a public servant should 'never discriminate unfairly by the dispensing of special favors or privileges to anyone, whether for remuneration or not; . . . '

According to the Cox brief, 'For four or five Senators collectively to use their power and prestige to influence regulatory proceedings for the benefit of a person who confers large financial benefits upon them is, regardless of their subjective motivation, conduct which reasonable persons might construe as influenced by the receipt of the benefits conferred.'

Furthermore, according to the Cox brief, 'One of the most widely known and accepted standards of conduct necessary to preserve confidence in the integrity of our institutions of self-government, including the Senate, forbids a public official or other fiduciary either to act or appear to act in an official capacity in response to gifts or other benefits.' This standard is set forth in the Code of Ethics for Government Service, which provides that any person in government services should '[n]ever accept for himself or his family, favors or benefits under circumstances which might be construed by reasonable persons as influencing the performance of his government duties.'

The Cox brief concluded that '[e]ach of the five,' including Senators McCain and Glenn, 'even if his reported conduct be viewed apart from the others, received money or other benefits from Keating, his family and/or business associates—arranged by Keating—far in excess of the $1,000 campaign contribution that an individual can give to a federal candidate. Each then intervened on behalf of Keating's Lincoln Savings and Loan in an FHLBB inquiry into violations of law risking Lincoln's federally insured deposits. The Code and underlying principle were violated in each of these instances because these circumstances surely 'might lead a reasonable person to contrue the intervention as influenced by the receipt of the favors or benefit.'

In reading this news release, I stated it was not my position to say that it was correct or incorrect; but I do feel that the charges and statements to Common Cause should be given careful and deliberate study and evaluation, as well as the report of special counsel.

There have been many leaks and disclosures concerning the proceedings. Documents have been leaked to the press concerning only three Senators. The leaks have been distorted and misleading in many instances. An analysis of the leaks and the timing of the leaks have convinced me that there has been an organized campaign of leaks. Such an analysis also lends strong suspicion that some of the leaks have come from either members of the committee or their staffs. Why? I ask again the question. Why? The answer obviously is to gain some advantage for some position or person to which the leakers are partisan. The organized campaign has to be for the advantage of a friend or friends, or disadvantage to enemies or for a political advantage. It is interesting to note that the leak of documents have been confined to three Senators and that there have been no leak of documents about the two other Senators. This is supportive of an organized campaign of leaks.

I listened this morning to the statements of Senators McCain, Danforth, Gorton, and Dole. Each belong to the same political party. It is interesting to note that most had prepared statements. Senator Gorton asked for a delay in order that one Senator could come to the floor to make his statement.

I do not believe that the Ethics Committee should be placed in the position of responding to pressure for the benefit of a friend or friends or the disadvantage of enemies or for a party position. The Ethics Committee is organized to be nonpartisan. I have done everything that I possibly can to keep the work of the committee from becoming partisan. I will continue to do so.

The committee owes an obligation to the charged Senators, but it also owes an obligation to the institution as a whole, as well as to the public.

The reason the committee is not meeting today is because of conflicts of work duties. It has scheduled a meeting tomorrow. Hopefully, decisions will be made that are in the best interest of the Senate as an institution with the rights of those accused fully protected.

Thank you, Mr. President.

MR. DANFORTH: Mr. President, will the Senator yield?

MR. HEFLIN: I am not going to yield. I have made a prepared statement. Anything that I might say might get into confidentiality.

———————◆———————

It could probably be shown by facts and figures that there is no distinctly native American criminal class except Congress.
MARK TWAIN, "Pudd'nhead Wilson's New Calendar," in *Following the Equator*, 1897

28.

RICHARD NIXON: The Post-Cold War World

The years 1989–1991 were momentous ones in terms of U.S. foreign policy. The Soviet Union disbanded into a dozen independent nations, and Germany reunited its eastern and western halves. More dramatic to Western observers than the reemergence of these countries, however, were the political changes within them, as Communist regimes gave way to Democratic governments. The Cold War had ended, and American policymakers were suddenly looking out onto a very different world. Former President Richard M. Nixon, whose activity in international affairs was a centerpiece of his administration, attributed the demise of Communism to the aggressive U.S. military buildup by Republican administrations. In the following speech to the Republican Congressional Committee in New York City, Nixon surveys the post-Cold War landscape, declaring that the new global role of the United States is not military or economic but ideological. Still, he argues for continued U.S. military presence in Europe and especially Asia, defending the divisive decision to reestablish relations with China following its repression of prodemocracy demonstrations in Beijing's Tiananmen Square in 1989. The speech was delivered on December 7, 1990, on the forty-ninth anniversary of the Japanese attack on Pearl Harbor that triggered U.S. entry into World War II, and roughly a month before the start of the Persian Gulf War. Nixon supported the U.S. presence in the Gulf in order to protect oil interests, to rebuff the aggressions of Saddam Hussein, and to make certain such aggressors would not reappear in the future.

Source: *Vital Speeches of the Day*, April 1, 1991.

IN HIS BOOK *Great Contemporaries,* Winston Churchill described Lord Rosebery, a nineteenth-century British Prime Minister, as one who had the misfortune of living in a time of great men and small events. Our leaders today do not have that problem. There is no question but that we live in a time of great events.

Nineteen eighty-nine, even more than 1945, which marked the end of World War II, will be remembered as the year of the century for the forces of freedom in the world. Nineteen forty-five marked the defeat of fascism. Nineteen eighty-nine marked the defeat of communism, an even greater threat to peace and freedom.

As a result of what happened in this historic year, we hear today:

The Cold War is over.

The United States and the Soviet Union are no longer adversaries but allies, as we were in World War II.

We are witnessing the end of history—a time when great strategic issues no longer divide us and when we will compete economically rather than militarily and when we can direct our attention to the environment, global warming, world poverty, and other issues where we have common interests.

We are told that we can rely on the United Nations to deal with aggressive nations.

We see an unholy alliance developing between isolationists on the right and the left, who for different reasons say that the United States should withdraw its forces from Europe and Asia and concentrate on solving our problems at home.

Conventional wisdom in the Washington Beltway—the modern version of Plato's Cave—is that we are on the brink of forging a new world order in which all nations will be dedicated to justice and international law.

Before going that far, let us see what has changed, why changes have occurred, what has not changed, and what America's role should be on the world stage now that the Cold War seems to be over.

The changes in 1989 have been breathtaking. The Berlin Wall came down. Germany was united. Communist governments were driven from power in all of the countries in Eastern Europe and except in Romania, this was accomplished peacefully.

The frosting on the cake occurred in our own hemisphere early this year when Violetta Chamorro defeated Daniel Ortega in a free election, the first time this has happened to a communist leader in seventy years.

The most significant changes have occurred in the Soviet Union symbolized by the award of the Nobel Peace Prize to Mikhail Gorbachev. Consider what he has done:

He withdrew the Red Army from Afghanistan.

He did not use the Red Army to keep communist clients in power in Eastern Europe as did Krushchev in 1956 in Hungary and Brezhnev in Czechoslovakia in 1968.

He has allowed West Germany to unite with East Germany.

He has negotiated arms control agreements.

He has adopted political and economic reforms which are so revolutionary that some observers have speculated, that rather than being a dedicated communist and a Russian nationalist, he may be a closet democrat and a closet capitalist at home and a sincere partisan of peace and freedom abroad.

Before reaching those conclusions, let us see why he acted as he did. In 1985, shortly after Gorbachev came to power in the Soviet Union, I asked Hu Yaobang, the Secretary General of the Chinese Communist Party, if he thought Gorbachev would adopt economic reforms in the Soviet Union like those Deng Xiaoping had adopted in China. He replied, "If he doesn't, the Soviet Union will disappear as a great power in the twenty-first century." He was right and Gorbachev knew it.

Look at what he confronted when he came to power six years ago. Everywhere he looked, communism was suffering from terminal illness.

His Third World communist colonies were all liabilities costing huge subsidies from Moscow and in Afghanistan costing lives as well as money.

In Eastern Europe, forces of revolution against Soviet-supported rulers were ready to explode.

At home, the Soviet economy was a basketcase plagued with corruption, alcoholism, and inefficiency.

Abroad, he saw that his major adversary—the United States, under the leadership of President Reagan, had recovered from the malaise of the late seventies, was restoring its military strength, and was embarking on a new weapons system—SDI—which the Soviet Union lacked the resources to match.

Gorbachev had no choice. He had to retrench abroad and reform at home. His first priority, then and now, was to restore the health of the Soviet economy. This was the most revolutionary decision of a Soviet leader since the Russian Revolution which brought the communists to power in 1917. For seventy years, Soviet economic policy had served Soviet foreign policy. Now Soviet foreign policy had to serve Soviet economic policy.

This explains his actions:

He withdrew the Red Army from Afghanistan not only because it was costing men as well as money, but primarily because it helped create a peaceful image for Gorbachev which opened the door for good relations with the West and economic assistance he needed for his desperately sick economy.

He had to choose between using force to keep his puppets in power in Eastern Europe and economic aid from Western Europe. Not surprisingly, he chose Western Europe.

He let East Germany go because he needed financial aid from West Germany.

In the Gulf, he had to choose between his ally Iraq and financial aid from the nations allied against Iraq. Again, not surprisingly, he chose the allies. It has already begun to pay off. Just last week he negotiated a loan of $3 billion from Saudi Arabia, a country which before Iraq invaded Kuwait, had not even recognized the communist government of the Soviet Union.

Whatever the reason, we welcome what he did. He is, without question, very different from the Soviet leaders of the past. He has changed since the time he totally supported Brezhnev's aggressive policies in his relentless climb to power. But it is a change of the head, not the heart. At a time he is using his head, we should not lose ours.

Let us take a hard look at the Soviet Union after six years of Gorbachev's leadership.

His political reforms have been revolutionary. Where there was no freedom of the press, there is now some. Where there was no freedom to criticize Soviet leaders, there is now some. Where there were no free elections, there are now some. But we must bear in mind that while Gorbachev deserves great credit for these reforms, he has also put through legislation which makes him the most powerful Soviet leader since Stalin. All of the evidence points to the conclusion that his goal is not to abandon communism but to save it, not to dismantle the Soviet Union but to preserve it—peacefully if possible, but using force if necessary.

While he deserves credit for his bold political reforms, we must face up to the fact that his economic reforms have been a total failure. For example, while China's per capita income has doubled in the past ten years, Soviet per capita income under Gorbachev has gone down. Bread lines have replaced vodka lines. To get through the winter, Gorbachev has had to go hat-in-hand to get assistance from his new friends in the West. The shopping list he gave Prime Minister Mulroney indicates the depth of his problem. It included pork, beef, flour, powdered milk, and peanut oil.

The results of Gorbachev's policies in the Soviet Union are now clear for everyone to see. To put it bluntly, the Soviet economy is collapsing and the Soviet empire is disintegrating. Fourteen of the fifteen Soviet republics have declared independence from Moscow. The communist idea—the glue that held the Soviet empire together—has lost its potency. Of all the changes in 1989, the most significant is that communism has lost the ideological battle. In the Third World, in Eastern Europe, and most significantly in the Soviet Union, people know that communist socialism doesn't work. The most dramatic proof of this is that while Gorbachev is enormously popular in the United States and in other non-communist countries, he is supported by less than twenty-five percent of the Soviet people. As has been the case in Eastern Europe, instead of a reforming communist as their leader, the people of the Soviet Union want reforms without communism.

This raises the key question. Because of his more benign foreign policy, should we help Gorbachev with his problems at home? The answer is that except for humanitarian aid we should help him only if it serves our interests as well as his.

His economic reforms do not meet that test. It is now obvious that they do not serve his interests. He is trying to combine a command economy with a free market economy. It won't work. There is no halfway house between communism and capitalism. As Andre Sakharov observed shortly before his death,

> "In the absence of radical reforms, to provide aid and technological assistance to the Soviet Union only serves to prop up a failed system and to delay the advent of democracy."

Even if his economic reforms go far enough to work, it does not serve our interest to provide aid to Gorbachev unless he adopts a less threatening defense and foreign policy. While he has announced cuts in his defense budget, his Foreign Minister has stated that the Soviet Union is still spending twenty-five percent of its GNP on defense. In contrast, the United States is spending six percent of its GNP on defense. Even with his cuts in his Soviet military forces, as a result of modernization, they will be leaner but stronger than when Gorbachev came to power six years ago. After the projected cuts in long range nuclear weapons in the START agreement, Gorbachev will still have thirty thousand nuclear weapons, the largest conventional army in the world, and a modern blue-water navy.

There are some who say that if the United States makes further cuts in its defense budget, Gorbachev will follow suit. They are wrong. There is no question but that Gorbachev is a refreshing new kind of Soviet leader. But he is not a philanthropist. We should reduce our nuclear forces and our SDI program only if he agrees to reduce his.

In foreign policy, we should applaud his withdrawing the Red Army from Afghanistan. But except for Nicaragua where the people voted out their communist leader, every one of Gorbachev's communist clients in the Third World is still in power subsidized by as much as $15 billion a year by the Soviet Union.

Before we consider helping Gorbachev, he should help himself by drastically cutting his huge military budget and by cutting off aid and arms sales to Castro and other anti-U.S. communist dictators.

The Cold War may be over in Eastern Europe. It is time for Gorbachev to end the Cold War in the Third World.

What will happen to Gorbachev? Some of the experts give him only a fifty percent chance of staying in power over the next year. I believe the odds are considerably better than that. There are three possible scenarios. He could adopt bolder, free market reforms which might have a chance to rescue the Soviet economy from its enormous crisis. I do not think this is likely because I believe Gorbachev will not be able to bring himself to cut the umbilical cord which unites him with his life-long Marxist ideology. A second possibility is that he could be replaced. This is not likely because there is no one currently on the scene, including Boris Yeltsin, who has the support in the armed forces, the KGB, and the Soviet bureaucracy necessary to bring about a successful coup. The third scenario, and the most likely one, is that Gorbachev, the tough-minded pragmatic politician that he is, will use the extraordinary new powers he has acquired for himself as President of the Soviet Union to crack down on dissident groups—using military force if necessary—and will stay in power by revoking some of the progressive political reforms he has previously initiated. This will cost him some support in the West. But unless he resumes an aggressive foreign policy abroad, most Western political leaders will conveniently ignore the repressive measures he adopts at home to stay in power. As far as the United States is concerned, we should base our defense and foreign policy vis-à-vis the Soviet Union, not on speculations about Gorbachev's intent but on the reality of Soviet capabilities as a nuclear and conventional superpower.

Let us now turn to Europe. We are witnessing the unusual phenomenon of isolationists on the right and left urging that since the Cold War is over, we should withdraw all of our forces from Europe, particularly since the nations of Europe have recovered from the devastation of World War II and should be able to provide for their own defense.

But what would Europe be without an American military presence? Great Britain and France are minor nuclear powers. Germany is an economic superpower without nuclear weapons. The Soviet Union, even without Eastern Europe, will still be a nuclear superpower with the world's largest conventional army. No one can seriously suggest that the British and French would use their nuclear forces to deter a Soviet attack on Germany. With United States forces gone from Europe and NATO dissolved, Germany would have the option of going nuclear or neutral and would be strongly tempted to become a political and economic ally of the Soviet Union. Either of these options is bad for Europe, bad for Germany, and bad for the United States.

We can and should cut our NATO forces substantially because of the dissolution of the Warsaw Pact. But a significant conventional and nuclear U.S. presence in Europe is necessary as insurance against a possible renewal of the Soviet threat and as reassurance for those who fear a resurgent German threat. I do not share the concern that a united Germany would again become an aggressive military power. But despite their public statements, many leaders have that concern.

Let us now look at Asia. Conservative and liberal isolationists say that because there is no longer a Soviet threat, we should bring our forces home from Japan and Korea particularly since they are now rich enough to defend themselves. They are wrong. Keeping an American military presence in Europe is important. Keeping one in Asia is indispensable if we are to have peace in the Pacific. Let us look at Asia without the United States.

You have the Soviet Union, a nuclear superpower which while reducing its forces in Europe has strengthened its naval and nuclear forces in Asia.

You have China which will be a nuclear superpower within ten to twenty years.

You have Japan, an economic superpower without nuclear weapons and without a U.S. defense guarantee. Japan would have no choice but to go nuclear or to make a deal with the strongest of its neighbors, the Soviet Union. Japan can afford to massively increase its defense forces. But even more than is the case with Germany's neighbors in Europe, the

Japanese in Asia are feared by the Koreans, the Chinese, the Philippinos, the Taiwanese, the Malaysians, and the Indonesians, all of whom suffered under Japanese occupation in World War II. A U.S. military presence in Japan and Korea is indispensable if we are to preserve peace in the Pacific.

Let us now look at China. We should continue to deplore the tragedy of Tiananmen Square eighteen months ago. But the Bush Administration is right to restore diplomatic and economic cooperation with the P.R.C. This is in our interest and in the interest of the Chinese people. It is in our interest because China has a veto in the U.N. Security Council and plays an indispensable role in trying to resolve the continuing conflicts in Southeast Asia. And in the non-military area, how can we possibly have a coordinated international initiative on problems of the environment with one-fifth of the world's people not cooperating?

The restoration of a cooperative relationship between China and the United States is without question in the interest of human rights for the Chinese people. China is not a democracy and will not become one in the foreseeable future. But as we saw in Korea and in Taiwan, economic progress inevitably leads to political progress. Economic cooperation, tourism and Chinese students studying in the United States will strengthen the prospects for political reform. That is why Secretary Baker was following the right course in meeting with the Chinese Foreign Minister and why the Administration was justified in supporting the resumption of World Bank loans to China. For the United States to continue to isolate China economically and diplomatically only strengthens the hardliners in China. The only hope for political reform is to re-establish the cooperative relationship we had with China before the tragic events at Tiananmen some eighteen months ago.

Let us now look at the crisis in the Persian Gulf. It is time for some straight talk as to why 400,000 young Americans are spending Christmas in the deserts of Saudi Arabia.

Some liberal pundits and politicians have criticized Bob Dole for saying that we are there for oil and Jim Baker for saying that we are there for jobs. There are more important reasons, but let us not be so hypocritical as to say that preventing an international outlaw from controlling forty percent of the world's oil reserves was not of critical interest to the United States and a justifiable reason for sending forces to the Gulf. Let us suppose that instead of Kuwait this was Nepal, or Upper Volta, or Paraguay being gobbled up by a neighboring state. Does anyone seriously suggest that we would be sending in the Marines to liberate them?

It is equally hypocritical to contend that we are there in support of democracy. None of our Arab allies are democracies and putting the Emir of Kuwait back in power is not going to bring democracy to the Kuwaiti people.

And this is not enough to justify our sending armed forces to the Gulf because Saddam Hussein happened to be a cruel leader. President Bush has been criticized for equating him with Hitler. Whether he is that bad is irrelevant. He is bad enough. His army rapes, loots, and murders the defenseless people of Kuwait. He has held thousands of hostages as human shields. To praise him for releasing hostages he should not have taken in the first place is ludicrous. He has violated international law by using chemical weapons in his war against Iran and even against his own people. If our aim in the Gulf were to punish cruel leaders, we would not be allied with Syria's Hafez Assad who ordered the massacre of 20,000 innocent men, women, and children in the city of Hama in his own country, who has supported international terrorism and possibly the bombing of civilian aircraft, and whose troops have committed brutal atrocities in his campaign to dominate Lebanon.

We are in the Gulf for two major reasons.

Saddam Hussein has unlimited ambitions to dominate one of the most important strategic areas in the world. Because he has oil, he has the means to acquire the weapons he needs for aggression against his neighbors, including at some future time, a nuclear arsenal. If he succeeds in Kuwait, he will attack others and will use whatever weapons he has, including chemical and nuclear to achieve his goals. If we don't stop him now we will have to stop him later when the cost in the lives of young Americans will be infinitely greater. If the Baker diplomatic initiative fails to get him out of Kuwait and if it becomes apparent that sanctions won't work, we must use force as approved by the United Nations resolution. If it comes to that, our diplomats should always remember that where an insatiable aggressor is involved, while war is bad, a bad peace is worse because it can lead to a bigger war.

There is an even more important long-term reason for turning back his aggression. The whole world is heaving a collective sigh of relief as the Cold War appears to be coming to an end. Many believe that we are entering a new era where armed aggression will no longer be an instrument of national policy. We can't be sure that their hopes will be justified. But we can be sure that if Saddam Hussein gains from his aggression against Kuwait there are other potential aggressors in the world who will be tempted to wage war against their neighbors. If we fail to roll back his aggres-

sion—peacefully if possible, by force if necessary—no potential aggressor in the future will be deterred by warnings from the United States or by U.N. resolutions. If we succeed in getting him out of Kuwait and in eliminating his capacity to wage aggressive war elsewhere without sending in American armed forces, potential aggressors will know that when the United States warns against aggression we have the means and the will to back up our warnings.

We all hope that Saddam Hussein will wake up out of his dream world and get out of Kuwait. Some of the Administration's critics sincerely believe that diplomacy and sanctions will eventually convince Saddam Hussein that he should get out of Kuwait. We cannot be sure that they are right, but we can be sure that diplomacy and sanctions will have no chance whatever of succeeding, unless Saddam Hussein knows that if he doesn't get out of Kuwait peacefully, the American people and our allies will be united in using military force to drive him out. His choice is between peace now or suicide later for his country, and possibly for himself.

If we have to resort to force, it will not be just a war about oil. It will not be a war about hostages. It will not be a war about democracy. It will be a war about peace—not just peace in our time, but peace for our children and grandchildren for generations to come. That is why our commitment in the Persian Gulf is a highly moral enterprise.

Now that we have traveled around the world, let us look at the United States. Forty-four years ago in his Iron Curtain speech in Fulton, Missouri, Winston Churchill said,

> "The United States stands at the pinnacle of world power. This is a solemn moment for the American democracy. For with primacy in power is joined an

awe inspiring accountability for the future."

Those words are as true today as they were then. The Soviet threat has declined, but as the crisis in the Gulf demonstrates, the world is still a dangerous place and the United States must continue to play the leading role on the world's stage—not as a world's policeman, but in conflicts like the Gulf where our vital interests are involved. We have to play that role because there is no one else to take our place—not the British, not the French, not the Russians, not the Japanese, and despite some woolly-headed dreaming to the contrary, not the United Nations.

Some question whether we are able to play that role. It is fashionable in some academic circles to say that the United States, like the Soviet Union, is in decline and no longer has the means to play a leading role on the world's stage.

Don't you believe it. We have some awesome problems—drugs, crime, the urban underclass, the deficit. But before World War II, the United States produced twenty-four percent of the world GNP, today we produce twenty-six percent and by the end of the century it will be twenty-eight percent—two and one-half times as much as Japan and five times as much as a united Germany.

The United States today is the world's only complete superpower—economic, military, and political. As Herb Stein has pointed out,

"The United States is a very rich country—not rich enough to do everything, but rich enough to do everything important."

There is a major new factor however, since Churchill spoke those words in 1946. For forty-five years after the end of World War II the United States has carried the major burden of foreign aid, including aid to Japan and Germany who are now our major economic competitors. It is time for other rich countries like Japan and the nations of Western Europe to assume the major portion of that burden since our military power still protects them as well as ourselves. For example, Japan gets sixty percent of its oil from the Persian Gulf. The United States gets ten percent of its oil from the Gulf. At a time when we are doubling our troop strength in the Gulf, Japan should, at the very least, double its economic contribution which now is only $2 billion a year.

This brings us to America's major role in the world today. It is not military or economic. It is ideological.

Communism has been rejected because it didn't work. Freedom is now on trial: will freedom provide the economic and political progress the communists promised and did not produce? Democracy and freedom do not automatically produce progress. Look at the enormous problems in the new democracies in Eastern Europe, and the problems in Brazil and Argentina, which are trying to make the painful transition from command to free-market economies.

The United States is the oldest and most successful democracy in the world. Our challenge is to provide an example for others to follow.

If we are to provide that example, we cannot tolerate a permanent underclass. We cannot tolerate second-rate education. We cannot tolerate poor productivity. We cannot tolerate political gridlock. There are some who say that the answer to our problem is to give more power to government. We reject that proposition. Our answer is for government to adopt policies which give more power to people.

America is a great country. We have become great not because of what government has done for people, but because of what people have done for themselves and their country. Only by policies which make our economy sound, protective, compassionate and free, can we provide an example for others to follow.

It is because I believe our Republican candidates support such policies that I am here today. And that is why I believe that by contributing to their campaigns you are contributing to a better future for America and the world.

As you know, this is the centennial of the birth of one of the greatest of our Presidents, Dwight D. Eisenhower. It is also the centennial of the birth of another giant of the twentieth century—Charles de Gaulle. De Gaulle once said,

> "France is never her true self except when she is engaged in a great enterprise."

I profoundly believe that is true of America; it is true of individuals; it is true of every man and woman in this room.

What is our great enterprise? Exactly forty-nine years ago today, the attack on Pearl Harbor plunged the United States into World War II. Fifty-six million people lost their lives in that war, making the twentieth century the bloodiest in history. Our challenge is to make the twenty-first century a century of peace and to leave our legacy, not just the defeat of communism and fascism, but the victory of freedom.

This is truly a great enterprise worthy of a great people. Only by meeting that challenge can we be true to ourselves.

———————◆———————

The Cold War is behind us. Let us not wrangle over who won it.
MIKHAIL GORBACHEV, June 5, 1990

1991

29.

GEORGE BUSH: Operation Desert Storm

In August 1990 Iraqi forces invaded neighboring Kuwait in an attempt to gain control of its oil reserves, prompting U.S. President George Bush to direct a massive American military buildup in Saudi Arabia to protect against any further Iraqi aggression. The Bush administration officially dubbed the defense of Saudi Arabia "Operation Desert Shield," but the size and scope of the American presence (more than 500,000 American troops had arrived in Saudi Arabia by January 1991) made clear that a powerful offensive capability existed for U.S. forces. Throughout the military buildup, American officials negotiated with Iraqi dictator Saddam Hussein in an effort to persuade him to withdraw from Kuwait. These efforts failed, as did a United Nations' effort to mediate an Iraqi withdrawal. When the United Nations Security Council deadline of January 15, 1991, passed without an Iraqi withdrawal, American and Allied forces launched a massive six-week aerial bombardment that decimated Iraqi supplies, troops, and fortifications in Kuwait and southern Iraq. Excerpts of Bush's speech announcing the opening of the air campaign, known as "Operation Desert Storm," are reprinted here.

Source: *Public Papers of the Presidents of the United States,* January 16, 1991.

JUST 2 HOURS AGO, allied air forces began an attack on military targets in Iraq and Kuwait. These attacks continue as I speak. Ground forces are not engaged.

This conflict started August 2 when the dictator of Iraq invaded a small and helpless neighbor. Kuwait—a member of the Arab League and a member of the United Nations—was crushed; its people, brutalized. Five months ago, Saddam Hussein started this cruel war against Kuwait. Tonight, the battle has been joined. . . .

As I report to you, air attacks are underway against military targets in Iraq. We are determined to knock out Saddam Hussein's nuclear bomb potential. We will also destroy his chemical weapons facilities. Much of Saddam's artillery and tanks will be destroyed. Our operations are designed to best protect the lives of all the coalition forces by targeting Saddam's vast military arsenal. Initial reports from General Schwarzkopf are that our operations are proceeding according to plan.

Our objectives are clear: Saddam Hussein's forces will leave Kuwait. The legitimate government of Kuwait will be restored to its rightful place, and Kuwait will once again be free. Iraq will eventually comply with all relevant United Nation's resolutions, and then, when peace is restored, it is our hope that Iraq will live as a peaceful and cooperative member of the family of nations, thus enhancing the security and stability of the Gulf.

Some may ask: Why act now? Why not wait? The answer is clear: The world could wait no longer. Sanctions, though having some effect, showed no signs of accomplishing their objective. Sanctions were tried for well over 5 months, and we and our allies concluded that sanctions alone would not force Saddam from Kuwait.

While the world waited, Saddam Hussein systematically raped, pillaged, and plundered a tiny nation, no threat to his own. He subjected the people of Kuwait to unspeakable atrocities—and among those maimed and murdered, innocent children.

While the world waited, Saddam sought to add to the chemical weapons arsenal he now possesses, an infinitely more dangerous weapon of mass destruction—a nuclear weapon. And while the world waited, while the world talked peace and withdrawal, Saddam Hussein dug in and moved massive forces into Kuwait.

While the world waited, while Saddam stalled, more damage was being done to the fragile economies of the Third World, emerging democracies of Eastern Europe, to the entire world, including to our own economy.

The United States, together with the United Nations, exhausted every means at our disposal to bring this crisis to a peaceful end. However, Saddam clearly felt that by stalling and threatening and defying the United Nations, he could weaken the forces arrayed against him.

While the world waited, Saddam Hussein met every overture of peace with open contempt. While the world prayed for peace, Saddam prepared for war.

I had hoped that when the United States Congress, in historic debate, took its resolute action, Saddam would realize he could not prevail and would move out of Kuwait in accord with the United Nation's resolutions. He did not do that. Instead, he remained intransigent, certain that time was on his side.

Saddam was warned over and over again to comply with the will of the United Nations: Leave Kuwait, or be driven out. Saddam has arrogantly rejected all warnings. Instead, he tried to make this a dispute between Iraq and the United States of America.

Well, he failed. Tonight, 28 nations—countries from 5 continents, Europe and Asia, Africa, and the Arab League—have forces in the Gulf area standing shoulder to shoulder against Saddam Hussein. These countries had hoped the use of force could be avoided. Regrettably, we now believe that only force will make him leave.

Prior to ordering our forces into battle, I instructed our military commanders to take every necessary step to prevail as quickly as possible, and with the greatest degree of protection possible for American and allied service men and women. I've told the American people before that this will not be another Vietnam, and I repeat this here tonight. Our troops will have the best possible support in the entire world, and they will not be asked to fight with one hand tied behind their back. I'm hopeful that this fighting will not go on for long and that casualties will be held to an absolute minimum.

This is an historic moment. We have in this past year made great progress in ending the long era of conflict and cold war. We have before us the opportunity to forge for ourselves and for future generations a new world order—a world where the rule of law, not the law of the jungle, governs the conduct of nations. When we are successful—and we will be—we have a real chance at this new world order, an order in which a credible United Nations can use its peacekeeping role to fulfill the promise and vision of the U.N.'s founders.

We have no argument with the people of Iraq. Indeed, for the innocents caught in this conflict, I pray for their safety. Our goal is not the conquest of Iraq. It is the liberation of Kuwait. It is my hope that somehow the Iraqi people can, even now, convince their dictator that he must lay down his arms, leave Kuwait, and let Iraq itself rejoin the family of peace-loving nations.

Thomas Paine wrote many years ago: "These are the times that try men's souls."

Those well-known words are so very true today. But even as planes of the multinational forces attack Iraq, I prefer to think of peace, not war. I am convinced not only that we will prevail but that out of the horror of combat will come the recognition that no nation can stand against a world united, no nation will be permitted to brutally assault its neighbor.

No President can easily commit our sons and daughters to war. They are the Nation's finest. Ours is an all-volunteer force, magnificently trained, highly motivated. The troops know why they're there. . . .

And let me say to everyone listening or watching tonight: When the troops we've sent in finish their work, I am determined to bring them home as soon as possible.

Tonight, as our forces fight, they and their families are in our prayers. May God bless each and every one of them, and the coalition forces at our side in the Gulf, and may He continue to bless our nation, the United States of America.

◆

The great, the jewel and the mother of battles has begun.
SADDAM HUSSEIN, speech at the start of the
Persian Gulf War, January 6, 1991

There's no telling what might have happened to our defense budget if Saddam Hussein hadn't invaded Kuwait that August and set everyone gearing up for World War II½. Can we count on Saddam Hussein to come along every year and resolve our defense-policy debates? Given the history of the Middle East, it's possible.
P. J. O'ROURKE, *Parliament of Whores: A Lone
Humorist Attempts to Explain the Entire U.S. Government,* 1991

30.

H. Norman Schwarzkopf: The Persian Gulf War

After the six-week aerial bombardment that began the Persian Gulf War, American ground forces, allied with European and Arab troops, launched Operation Desert Sabre under the command of U.S. General H. Norman Schwarzkopf. Conducted from February 24 to February 27, 1991, this brief but destructive ground offensive ended Iraqi resistance and resulted in the liberation of Kuwait. The decisive and crushing nature of Iraq's defeat stunned the world and created a surge of patriotism in the United States. During the fighting, American and Allied forces suffered some 300 fatalities; the Iraqi army, in contrast, suffered about 100,000 casualties, one of the most disproportionate casualty tolls in the history of warfare and grim testimony to the vast technological superiority of the U.S. military. U.S. President George Bush announced a cease-fire on February 28. The day before the cease-fire Schwarzkopf detailed U.S. military successes at a news conference and fielded questions from the press. Portions of his address are reprinted below.

Source: *Military Review*, September 1991, "Central Command Briefing, Riyadh, Saudi Arabia."

I PROMISED some of you all a few days ago that as soon as the opportunity presented itself, I would give you a complete run-down on what we were doing, and, more important, why we were doing it; the strategy behind what we were doing. . . .

As you recall, we started our deployment on the 7th of August. Basically, what we started out against was a couple of hundred thousand Iraqis that were in the Kuwait theater of operation. I don't have to remind you all that we brought over initially defensive forces, in the form of the 101st, the 82d, the 24th Mechanized Infantry Division, the Third Armored Cavalry, and, in essence, we had them arrayed to the south behind the Saudi Task Force. Also, there were Arab forces over here in this area arrayed in defensive positions. And that, in essence, is the way we started.

In the middle of November, the deci-sion was made to increase the force because by that time huge numbers of Iraqi forces had flowed in the area and generally in the disposition as they're shown right here [indicates map 1], and therefore, we increased the forces and built up more forces. I would tell you that at this time we made a very deliberate decision to align all of those forces within the boundary looking north toward Kuwait. . . . We also at that time had a very active naval presence out in the gulf. And we made sure that everybody understood about that naval presence. One of the reasons why we did that is because it became very apparent to us early on that the Iraqis were quite concerned about an amphibious operation across the shores to liberate Kuwait. . . . They put a very, very heavy barrier of infantry along here and they proceeded to build an extensive barrier that went all the way across the border, down, and around, and up to the side of Kuwait.

Basically, the problem we were faced with was this: When you looked at the troop numbers, they really outnumbered us about 3 to 2. And when you consider the number of combat service support people we had, that's logisticians and that sort of thing, in our armed forces, as far as fighting troops, we were really outnumbered 2 to 1. In addition to that, they had 4,700 tanks versus our 3,500 when the buildup was complete, and they had a great deal more artillery than we do.

I think any student of military strategy would tell you that in order to attack a position, you should have a ratio of approximately 3 to 1 in favor of the attacker. And, in order to attack a position that is heavily dug in and barricaded, such as the one we had here, you should have a ratio of 5 to 1 in the way of troops in the favor of the attacker. So, you can see basically what our problem was at that time. We were outnumbered as a minimum 3 to 2 as far as troops were concerned, we were outnumbered as far as tanks were concerned, and we had to come up with some way to make up the difference.

What we did, of course, was start an extensive air campaign, and I briefed you in quite some detail on that in the past. One of the purposes I told you at that time of that extensive air campaign was to isolate the Kuwaiti theater of operation by taking out all the bridges and supply lines that ran between the north and the southern part of Iraq. That was to prevent reinforcement and supply coming into the southern part of Iraq and the Kuwaiti theater of operation. . . . It was necessary to reduce these forces down to a strength that made them weaker, particularly along the frontline barrier that we had to go through.

We continued our heavy operations out in the sea because we wanted the Iraqis to continue to believe that we were going to conduct a massive amphibious operation. . . . And I think many of you recall the number of amphibious rehearsals we had. . . .

I think this is probably one of the most important parts of the entire briefing I could talk about. As you know, very early on, we took out the Iraqi Air Force. We knew that he had very very limited reconnaissance means. And therefore, when we took out his air force, for all intents and purposes, we took out his ability to see what we were doing down here in Saudi Arabia.

Once we had taken out his eyes, we did what could best be described as the Hail Mary play in football. I think you recall, when the quarterback is desperate for a touchdown at the very end, what he does is, he steps up behind the center, and all of a sudden every single one of his receivers goes way out to one flank, and they all run down the field as fast as they possibly can and into the end zone, and he lobs the ball. In essence that's what we did. When we knew he couldn't see us any more, we did a massive movement of troops all the way out to the west, to the extreme west, because at that time we knew he was still fixed in this area with the vast majority of his forces, and once the air campaign started, he would be incapable of moving out to counter this move, even if he knew we made it.

There were some additional troops out in this area [points to Iraqi territory west of Kuwait], but they did not have the capability or the time to put in the barrier that had been described by Saddam Hussein as an absolutely impenetrable tank barrier that no one would ever get through; I believe those were his words.

So this was absolutely an extraordinary move, I must tell you. I can't recall any

General H. Norman Schwarzkopf points to an Allied troop position at a press conference in Riyadh, Saudi Arabia, on February 27, 1991.

time in the annals of military history when this number of forces have moved over this distance to put themselves in a position to be able to attack. . . .

Not only did we move the troops out there, but we literally moved thousands and thousands of tons of fuel, of ammunition, of spare parts, of water and of food . . . because we wanted to have enough supplies on hand so that if we launched this and if we got into a slugfest battle, which we very easily could have gotten into, we'd have enough supplies to last for 60 days.

This then was the morning of the 24th [points to map 3]. Our plan initially had been to start over here in this area and do exactly what the Iraqis thought we were going to do, and that's take them on head-on into their most heavily defended area. Also, at the same time, we launched amphibious feints and naval gunfire in this area so that they continued to think that we were going to be attacking along this coast, and therefore fixed their forces in this position. Our hope was that by fixing the forces in this position and with this attack through

here in this position, we would basically keep the forces here and they wouldn't know what was going on out in this area. And I believe we succeeded in that very well.

At 4 in the morning, the Marines, the First Marine Division and the Second Marine Division, launched attacks through the barrier system. They were accompanied by the Tiger Brigade, U.S. Army Tiger Brigade of the Second Armored Division. At the same time, over here two Saudi task forces also launched a penetration through this barrier.

But while they were doing that, at 4 in the morning over here [points to far left of map 3], the Sixth French Armored Division, accompanied by a brigade of the 82d Airborne, also launched an overland attack to their objective up in this area, Al Salman airfield, and we were held up a little bit by the weather, but by 8 in the morning, the 101st Airborne Air Assault launched an air assault deep in the enemy territory to establish a forward operating base in this location right here.

Once the 101st had their forward operating base established here, they then went ahead and launched into the Tigris and the Euphrates valley. There's a lot of people who are still saying that the object of the United States of America was to capture Iraq and cause the downfall of the entire country of Iraq.

Ladies and gentlemen, when we were here, we were 150 miles away from Baghdad and there was nobody between us and Baghdad. If it had been our intention to take Iraq, if it had been our intention to destroy the country, if it had been our intention to overrun the country, we could have done it unopposed for all intents and purposes from this position at that time. But that was not our intention. We had never said it was our intention. Our intention was purely to eject the Iraqis out of Kuwait and to destroy the military power that had come in here. . . . The next two days went exactly like we thought they would go. The Saudis continued to make great progress up on the eastern flank . . . turned to come in on the flank heading towards Kuwait City. . . . The 24th Infantry Division made an unbelievable move all the way across into the Tigris and Euphrates valley, and proceeded in blocking this avenue of egress out of, which was the only avenue of egress left because we continued to make sure that the bridges stayed down. So, there was no way out. . . . By this time, we had destroyed or rendered completely ineffective over 21 Iraqi divisions. . . .

Where we are today [points to map 6] is we now have a solid wall across the north of the XVIII Airborne Corps, consisting of the units shown right here attacking straight to the east. We have a solid wall here, again, of the VII Corps, also attacking straight to the east. The forces that they are fighting right now are the forces of the Republican Guard.

Again, today, we had a very significant day when the Arab forces coming from the west and the east closed in and moved in to Kuwait City, where they are now in the process of clearing Kuwait City entirely and assuring that it's absolutely secure. The First Marine Division continues to hold Kuwaiti International Airport; the Second Marine Division continues to be in a position where it blocks any egress out of the city of Kuwait, so no one can leave. To date, we have destroyed over 29—destroyed or rendered inoperable; I don't like to say "destroyed" because that gives you the visions of ab-

solutely killing everyone, and that's not what we are doing, but we have rendered completely ineffective over 29 Iraqi divisions, and the gates are closed. . . .

QUESTIONS AND ANSWERS

THE IRAQI ARMY

I wonder if, in an overview, despite these enormously illustrative pictures, you could say what's left of the Iraqi Army in terms of how long could it be before he could ever be a regional threat, or a threat to the region again.

Well, there's not enough left of it at all for him to be a regional threat to the region, offensive regional threat. As you know, he's got a very large army, but most of the army that is left north of the Tigris-Euphrates Valley is an infantry army. It's not an armored army. It's not an armor-heavy army, which means it really isn't an offensive army.

So it doesn't have enough left, unless someone chooses to rearm them in the future.

DESERTERS AND P.O.W.'S

You said you've got all these divisions along the border which were seriously attrited. It figures to be about 200,000 troops maybe that were there. You've got 50,000 prisoners. Where are the rest of them?

There were a very, very large number of dead in these units, a very, very large number of dead. We even found them when we went into the units ourselves and found them in the trench lines. There were very heavy desertions. At one point, we had reports of desertion rates of more than 30 percent of the units that were along the front here. As you know, we had quite a large number of P.O.W.'s that came across, and so I think it's a combination of desertions, it's a combination of people that were killed, there's a combination of the people that we captured and there's a combination of some other people who are just flat still running.

Did you think that this would turn out—I realize a great deal of strategy and planning went into it—but when it took place, did you think this would turn out to be such an easy cakewalk, as it seems? And, second, what are your impressions of Saddam Hussein as a military strategist?

First of all, if we thought it would have been such an easy fight, we definitely would not have stocked 60 days worth of supplies on these log bases. So, as I told you all for a very, very long time, it is very, very important for a military commander never to assume away the capabilities of his enemy, and when you're facing an enemy that is over 500,000 strong, has the reputation that they've had of fighting for eight years, being combat-hardened veterans, had the number of tanks, and the type of equipment they had, you don't assume away anything. So we certainly did not expect it to go this way.

As far as Saddam Hussein being a great military strategist, he is neither a strategist nor is he schooled in the operational art nor is he a tactician nor is he a general nor is he a soldier. Other than that, he's a great military man—I want you to know that.

———————◆———————

Our strategy in going after this army is very simple. First we are going to cut it off, and then we are going to kill it.
COLIN POWELL, announcing the U.S. Persian Gulf War
aim against the Iraqi army, January 23, 1991

31.

CLARENCE THOMAS: Supreme Court Confirmation

In the spring of 1991 Thurgood Marshall, the first African American justice to serve on the Supreme Court, retired after twenty-four years on the bench. That summer President George Bush nominated as Marshall's replacement Clarence Thomas, a graduate of Yale Law School and a sitting justice on the United States Court of Appeals for the District of Columbia. Like Marshall, Thomas was an African American, but unlike Marshall, Thomas was a conservative Republican. After uneventful hearings before the Senate Judiciary Committee in the fall, Thomas seemed on his way to easy confirmation by the Senate. However, allegations of sexual harassment suddenly emerged against Thomas and sent the hearings into a chaotic uproar. Anita Hill, a black law professor from the University of Oklahoma, alleged that Thomas had made sexually lewd and harassing comments to her when she worked for him at the Department of Education in the early 1980s. Hill's testimony polarized both the Senate and the nation on the question of whether her allegations were true. Some Republicans claimed that Democrats had manufactured the allegations to embarrass Thomas. In contrast, many Democrats thought the dismissal of Hill's charges was evidence of Republican indifference to the issue of sexual harassment. After a bitter debate, Thomas' nomination to the Supreme Court was confirmed by the Senate. The clash brought national attention to the politics of gender and race, as well as to issues of workplace harassment and women in government. Excerpts of Thomas' testimony before the Judiciary Committee are reprinted here.

Source: *Congressional Quarterly Weekly Report,* September 21, 1991, "Where Thomas Stands on Constitutional Questions."

NATURAL LAW

Senators wanted to know whether Thomas would use natural law to decide constitutional issues in cases and whether he would extend his idea of natural law to rights for unborn children or to protections for business against governmental regulation.

My point has been that the framers [of the Constitution] . . . reduced to positive law in the Constitution aspects of life principles that they believed in; for example, liberty. But when it is in the Constitution, it is not a natural right; it is a constitutional right. And that is the important point.

But to understand what the framers meant and what they were trying to do, it is important to go back and attempt to understand what they believed, just as we do when we attempt to interpret a statute that is drafted by this body, to get your understanding. But in constitutional analysis and methodology, as I indicated in my confirmation to the Court of Appeals, there isn't any direct reference to natural law. . . . At no time did I feel nor do I feel now that natural law is anything more than the background to our Constitution. It is not a method of interpreting or a method of adjudicating in the constitutional law area.

"STARE DECISIS," OR LETTING PRECEDENTS STAND

This doctrine holds that principles of law in judicial decisions should be authoritative in later cases, even when a justice might believe the original case was wrongly decided. Some senators fear Thomas would vote to roll back earlier decisions on abortion and civil rights.

I think that the principle of stare decisis . . . is an important link in our system of deciding cases in our system of judicial jurisprudence. . . . We have got to have continuity if there is going to be any reliance, if there is going to be any chain in our case law. I think that the first point in any revisiting of the case is that the case be wrongly decided. . . . But more than that is necessary before one can rethink it or attempt to reconsider it. And I think that the burden is on the individual or on the judge or the justice who thinks that a precedent should be overruled to demonstrate more than its mere incorrectness. And at least one factor that would weigh against overruling a precedent would be the development of institutions as a result of a prior precedent having been in place.

NINTH AMENDMENT

It expressly says that the idea of "rights" is not confined to the Constitution. The high court has rarely mentioned the Ninth Amendment, although individual justices have used it to support Roe v. Wade *and* Griswold v. Connecticut, *a 1965 privacy case from which the*

right to abortion eventually flowed. Thomas had written of his "misgivings about activist judicial use" of the amendment. Senators wanted to know how much weight it should be given.

I think that whatever we do with open-ended provisions such as the Ninth Amendment, that we make sure as judges that those decisions are fettered to analysis or something other than our own predilections or our own views. That would be the concern, the generic concern . . . with any of the open-ended or more open-ended provisions. The court, to my knowledge, has not used the Ninth Amendment, a majority of the court, to decide a particular case. And there has been debate about what the purpose of the Ninth Amendment is. There could be a time when there could be an asserted right under the Ninth Amendment that would come before the court in which there could be found to be a basis for that right in the Ninth Amendment. I don't know. But as scholars do more work and certainly as individuals begin to assert rights and the court begins to consider those, I wouldn't foreclose that from occurring.

CHURCH-STATE SEPARATION

The First Amendment bars government action "establishing" religion. A key case the court uses to decide whether a practice breaches that ban is the 1971 case of Lemon v. Kurtzman, *which involved state aid to parochial schools. The court said the government action is permissible if it meets three tests: It is intended to achieve a secular legislative purpose; its primary effect neither advances nor inhibits religion; and it does not foster excessive government entanglement with religion. Senators wanted to know whether Thomas would make it easier for government to get involved in religion as some senators fear is the inclination of individual justices now on the court.*

I am aware of the tests enunciated in *Lemon v. Kurtzman*. The court has applied the tests with some degree, I think, of difficulty over the years. I have no personal disagreement with the tests, but I say that recognizing how difficult it has been for the court to address just the kind of problem that you have pointed out when the church is on fire or when there is this closeness between the activity of the government and the activity of the church.

I think the wall of separation is an appropriate metaphor. I think we all believe that we would like to keep the government out of our beliefs, and we would want to keep a separation between our religious lives and the government.

EQUAL PROTECTION CLAUSE OF THE CONSTITUTION

Senators wanted to know whether Thomas agreed with Supreme-Court-adopted tests for applying equal protection to laws that are based on race or gender.

I have no reason and had no reason to question or to disagree with the three-tier approach . . . the 'rational basis' test being the least structured or least strict of the tests, the 'heightened scrutiny' test, which has been used in the area of gender and alienage and legitimacy, and the 'strict scrutiny' test, which has been used in the area of fundamental rights and race. I think that those tests attempt in our society to demonstrate the concern that we have for classifications that could infringe on fundamental rights.

DEATH PENALTY

Retiring Justice Thurgood Marshall believes that the death penalty violates the constitutional ban on cruel and unusual punishment. Other justices have voted to uphold state death penalty laws. Congress is weighing bills to ex-pand the federal death penalty to more crimes and to limit death row appeals.

There is nothing that would bother me personally about upholding it in appropriate cases. My concern, of course, would always be that we provide all of the available protections and accord all of the protections available to a criminal defendant who is exposed to or sentenced to the death penalty.

STATUTORY CONSTRUCTION

This concept goes to the heart of how justices construe the work of Congress, and senators wanted to know whether Thomas would tilt toward the administration's view, or a justice's own opinion, of what a law means rather than to congressional statements of legislative intent.

I do not believe that there is room in opinions in our work of judging for the personal predilections, the personal opinions and views of judges. I think in statutory construction, the ultimate goal for us is to determine the will of the legislature, the intent of the legislature, not what we would have replaced the legislative enactment with, if we were in the legislature, and we have no role in legislating.

AFFIRMATIVE ACTION

Thomas said that he opposes race-based affirmative action and that such government preference programs should be based on an individual's disadvantages.

There is a tension, and how far do you go in trying to include people who are left out, and not be unfair to other individuals, and it is one that I had hoped that we could wrestle with in a constructive way. . . . Whether or not I agree with all of them [affirmative action programs]

I think is a matter of record. But the fact that I don't agree with all of them does not mean that I am not a supporter of the underlying effort. I am and have been my entire adult life.

ANTITRUST

A number of bills on antitrust issues are pending before Congress. Thomas was asked generally about antitrust laws and prohibitions on price fixing.

I think that all of our efforts, including the antitrust laws, to keep a free and open economy, one in which there is competitiveness, where the smaller businesses can have an opportunity to compete, and where consumers can benefit from that—those efforts, including the antitrust laws, have been beneficial to our country.

. . . I believe consumers and the country benefit from strong competition. We certainly as consumers benefit when there are new products, when there is development of products, when the quality of the products is improved as a result of competition, and, of course, when there is no temptation toward supra-competitive pricing; in fact, pricing is at the lower levels.

CONTRADICTIONS IN HIS RECORD

Some senators accused Thomas of trying to separate himself from past controversial writings in order to win Senate approval.

I think that various individuals created their own images of me and what they see is that the real person does not fit those images. . . .

I am the same Clarence Thomas. I have been a sitting federal judge for about a year and a half, and the person that you see here is the same sitting federal judge, someone who attempts to be open-minded, who works at it, being impartial, objective, listen and to work through very difficult problems. And a final point: When I was in the executive branch . . . there were battles and there were give and takes. I participated in that, but I am not in the executive branch anymore, I am not a part of the tension between the two political branches.

This is a circus. . . . a high-tech lynching for uppity-blacks who in any way deign to think for themselves, to do for themselves, to have different ideas, and it is a message that, unless you kow-tow to an old order this is what will happen to you, you will be lynched, destroyed, caricatured by a committee of the U.S. Senate, rather than hung from a tree.
    CLARENCE THOMAS, during Senate hearings on his nomination
        to the U.S. Supreme Court, October 11, 1991

Judge Thomas was a man who had used the system to get where he wanted to be, but then felt that everyone else should pull themselves up by their own bootstraps.
    JOYCELYN ELDERS, as quoted in *The New York Times*
        Magazine, January 30, 1994

32.

JOHN MAGINNIS: The Uneasy Appeal of David Duke

In the fall of 1990, former Ku Klux Klan Grand Wizard David Duke ran for the Senate. Incumbent Louisiana Senator J. Bennett Johnston won the election, but Duke carried 44 percent of the vote. Duke's strong showing shocked the nation, and awakened painful memories of the South's long history of white supremacy and racial conflict. Undeterred by his failed Senate bid, Duke mounted a campaign for governor of Louisiana in 1991. In the gubernatorial primary election, Duke finished ahead of incumbent Governor Buddy Roemer, a stunning upset that garnered international attention because of Duke's notorious background. Duke's chances of winning the runoff election seemed very real because his opponent, former Governor Edwin Edwards, had a long history of corruption and lacked popular appeal. The possibility that a former Grand Wizard of the Ku Klux Klan might be elected governor created a media firestorm and made the 1991 Louisiana gubernatorial election the most closely watched in the country. Duke's campaign lost steam when advocacy groups like the National Association for the Advancement of Colored People (NAACP) and major corporations threatened to respond to a Duke victory by mounting an economic boycott of Louisiana, whose economy depends on tourism. On election day, Edwards defeated Duke by a margin of 61 percent to 39 percent. Nevertheless, Duke won slightly over 50 percent of the white vote, which seemed to indicate that racism endured in the deep South. In this essay, Louisiana political columnist John Maginnis explores the roots of Duke's appeal in Louisiana.

Source: *The New Republic*, November 25, 1991, "The Hazards of Duke: Populism and Louisiana's Ghosts."

DAVID DUKE chats with supporters and reporters on the oak-shaded lawn of the antebellum courthouse in Clinton, Louisiana. This is not a rally but a hand-shaking stop of rural parishes during the primary campaign. Aside from the gap-toothed biker with the long beard and the intense, thin-mustached gentleman with the American flag on his sleeve, Duke's supporters appear to be the conservative, small-town, working-class citizens who generally attend his rallies. Then, as Duke speaks, a middle-aged woman in a turquoise dress whispers: "Well, he certainly is the most handsome candidate." When Duke turns to enter the courthouse, she approaches and extends her hand, drawling, "Why, yes, Captain Butler, I remember you." She takes a ring from her finger and presses it into his hand. "I want to make a contribution to your campaign. This is worth about $100." The woman turns and sashays off, and Duke, after staring dumbfounded at the ring for a second, rushes after her. "Ma'am, ma'am, I don't think the Campaign Finance Law will allow me to accept this. Now if you'd like to write a check to the campaign . . ."

In his unsuccessful bid for re-election this year, Louisiana Governor Buddy Roemer relied heavily on television commercials that bore the tag line: "We can't turn back the clock." He had it all wrong. In this state the past, whether in the form of Rhett Butler or otherwise, is always near at hand. Louisiana's clock, which never kept good time to start with, broke sometime in the 1980s when the oil money dwindled and the excessive, corrupt hayride it fueled crashed and burned. The current gubernatorial runoff between David Duke and Edwin Edwards centers not on shaping the future but on digging up the past in search of, if nothing else, someone to blame.

Both lay claim to Huey Long's ghost. The flamboyant, silver-tongued Edwards expanded on Long's vision of spending free-flowing oil revenues on social services for the poor and on lucrative state contracts and patronage to his friends. The oil-bust depression and two subsequent federal trials, however, (including testimony that Edwards paid off Las Vegas collectors with $500,000 in cash stuffed in suitcases) alienated Edwards from the white, working-class end of his base. Until then he'd admitted—even joked about—his gambling and womanizing. But after the trials, the stigma of the high roller and component crook remained, even though Edwards was eventually acquitted of all charges.

In 1987 most of those white, rural Democrats—who had supported Edwards and whose parents had supported Long—turned to the angry agenda of Harvard-educated Representative Buddy Roemer, a former political consultant from rural northwest Louisiana, to cure the excess and corruption of government grown too big. "I love Louisiana," he told campaign audiences, "but I hate Louisiana politics." Like George Bush, Roemer ran from the right but then tried to move his Reaganite revolution to the center to find the real solutions to Louisiana's massive problems. Unlike Bush, the self-absorbed Roemer lacked the people-skills and common sense to hold the center and the right. After the legislature dealt him some bruising setbacks and his second wife left him, Roemer turned to the self-help readings of Robert Fulghum and emerged less interested in the chase of politics. Gone was the zealous, butt-kicking, maverick campaigner. Gone also was his appeal to Huey's old populist flock. Buddy let go of the reins of anger that drove his revolution, and David Duke was there to seize them.

When Duke ran for state representative in 1989, he exchanged his white power spiel for more moderate Reaganism, laced with concern for "our Christian European heritage." He broadened the Reagan brand of conservative populism to include opposition to free trade, especially the recent trade agreement with Mexico. Though a conservative, Duke appeals to many of the children and grandchildren of Long's old populist constituency. Except that today the scapegoats have changed: the rich man is replaced by the welfare cheat, big business by big government. When he announced for governor, Duke said, "I'm a populist like Huey Long. But we need a Huey in reverse, someone from outside the system to bring it back under control."

Duke spent the summer in the countryside, away from the media centers, retracing his steps from his 1990 Senate campaign. His rallies and barbecues attracted big crowds in burgs most statewide candidates never saw: Goldanna, Marthaville, Vivian, Bordelonville, Holly Beach. By the time Roemer made one of his first campaign stops, at the Pickin' and Ginnin' Festival in the cotton town of Rayville, Duke was there to greet him.

"Welcome to Duke Country, governor."

"Thanks, Dave, I thought this was Louisiana."

"Louisiana is Duke Country, governor."

A photographer asked for a picture and captured their frozen smiles. Over the photographer's shoulder, Roemer could see what Duke was talking about. One out of four festival-goers clogging the main drag wore blue Duke stickers or carried Duke placards. The governor walked down the street shaking hands on his way to a meeting with business supporters at the local bank. Duke stood by his campaign booth and the people flocked to him, treating him more like a celebrity than a candidate. "I like what you stand for," said a young woman with Duke-stickered children in tow. "We're all for you down at the gin," said the sunburned cotton farmer.

By fall the rallies moved to the cities and grew larger and more middle class, as computer programmers and nurses joined the ranks of welders and waitresses. "Duke's vote didn't surge in the end," said unsuccessful gubernatorial candidate Sam Jones. "It surfaced." Though it didn't show up in the opinion polls, the Duke vote was there all along, as it was in 1990 when he received 43.5 percent of the vote against U.S. Senator J. Bennett Johnston. Then his showing was attributed to his supporters' fears of unemployment and resentment against federal welfare and affirmative action programs. Voting for Duke was seen as sending the strongest possible message to Washington. Political analysts doubted the same issues would play in the race for governor, with its executive responsibility for a $9 billion budget and management of 75,000 employees.

But by the summer of 1991 Duke's heated rhetoric began filling the vacuum on the right created by the idling Roemer. Duke pushes the same buttons Ronald Reagan did, just as expertly. Like Reagan, he understands the power of the anecdote that oversimplifies a problem and foils any attempt to put it in proportion. . . .

Duke's bond with his audiences immunizes him against his past. Ask a supporter about Duke's Klan and Nazi activities and the typical response is: "Everyone has a past." A pipeline engineer says, "There are things in my past that I'm not proud of." A retired veteran from rural north Louisiana is not bothered by Duke's Klan membership: "Years ago my father and my grandfather all belonged to secret organizations. The KKK was just one of them." An LSU student at a Duke rally in Baton Rouge says, "I'm a Christian and I believe you can change. Three years ago I was lost on alcohol and drugs and I've changed. I think David has changed too." A man along the Rice Festival parade route in Edwards's Cajun hometown of Crowley says, "There are too many people looking at him. If they could prove he was a Nazi, which I doubt, they would have done it by now."

By late in the primary campaign, the more that recent anti-Semitic statements were attributed to Duke, the greater the resentment built against the messenger, the press. "The press never mentions David without calling him a Ku Klux Klan wizard and a Nazi in the first sentence," said a New Orleans woman. "They don't say Edwards was indicted every time they mention him." In a way the local and national press coverage of Duke's past, the documentation of his Klan and Nazi activities, even the condemnation by President George Bush, seem to strengthen the bonds between Duke and his followers. When Duke is attacked, they feel they are being attacked. "He said he's sorry. What more do you want?" said a mechanic in the southwestern town of DeRidder. Also, Louisianans, accustomed to being disparaged for their laissez-faire politics, show wider tolerance for rogue mavericks, from the eighteenth-century pirate Jean Lafitte to modern-day pirates Huey Long and Edwin Edwards. David Duke, the Most Politically Incorrect Man in America, qualifies for that club. . . .

Business leaders are warning that Duke's election would mean economic devastation for a state struggling out of bad times. Several large associations have informed New Orleans tourism officials that they will pull their big national conventions from the city if Duke is elected. Some industrialists say Louisiana would be all but redlined from future plant expansions. That argument will be pounded home by election day, but perhaps with mixed results. Convention tourism is principally a New Orleans industry, and the effects of that and concern for the city do not travel far upriver. Most other state industries are based on natural resources—and are not easily moved. Beyond that, employers fear they carry little influence with their workers' votes, many of whom cheer Duke's opposition to affirmative action. Finally, the more dire the economic warning, the more likely that workers will feel they are being dared to vote for Duke. Never dare the voter.

Edwards says he will not make the mistake of directly attacking Duke and his past, though third-party groups are coming out with ads exposing Duke's false claims of military service and his anti-Semitic statements, including his stated beliefs that the gas chambers of the Holocaust actually were used for delousing. One group, the Coalition Against Racism and Nazism, ran a full-page ad in the *New Orleans Times Picayune* showing before-and-after plastic surgery photos of Duke below the headline: SOME CHANGE IS ONLY SKIN DEEP. The paper's profile of Duke recounted some of the more bizarre incidents from his past, including his alleged involvement in a plot to send mercenaries to overthrow the government of the island of Dominica (Duke later took the Fifth Amendment before a federal grand jury); his celebration, according to friends, of Hitler's birthday until recently; and his authorship, under pen names, of an urban guerrilla manual for black militants and of a soft-porn sex manual for women. But even this help from the press and others leaves Edwards, the veteran attack campaigner, with a problem: he can't attack Duke's record in government because he hardly has one; and he can't attack Duke's positions on issues because they are Reagan's issues, and thus fairly popular with the swing Roemer voter.

Duke has no such problem. He immediately opened up on Edwards's past record of tax increases, environmental neglect, and cronyism. He charges that Edwards is out selling every Cabinet and board position, "some three and four times," though Edwards challenges him to name one instance. At the end of the statewide televised debate last week, Duke held up copies of hundreds of pardons and paroles he said Edwards "sold or gave away. . . ."

Just making the runoff is an important victory for Duke's suddenly rocketing political career. Though he would clearly relish winning, a close second may serve him almost as well. Several congressional districts in Louisiana would make inviting targets in 1992. Also, the timing is natural to enter the spring presidential primaries to take his message national and to expand his fund-raising base (nearly half of his 14,000 individual contributors in this race live outside

Louisiana). By 1996 he could be the best-known Republican presidential candidate next to Dan Quayle, with a popular message, universal name recognition, and his past even further behind him.

Like Huey Long, David Duke is a candidate for hard times. If the national economy is as bad in 1996 as Louisiana's is now, the Republicans' worst mistake would be to underestimate him.

33.

BILL BRADLEY: Support for the Free Trade Agreement

By the early 1990s, Mexico had emerged as one of the United States' leading trading partners. Recognizing Mexico's growing importance to the American economy, the George Bush administration negotiated a sweeping free-trade agreement with Mexico. The agreement, known as the North American Free Trade Agreement (NAFTA), eliminated all trade barriers between the United States, Mexico, and Canada, effectively turning North America into a common market. The treaty, however, faced a major obstacle in the form of Congress. Although many economists hailed NAFTA as a certain economic boon to the United States, the Democratic majority in Congress viewed it warily. Many Democrats feared that NAFTA's passage would devastate working-class Americans by making it easier for corporations to move factories to Mexico, where labor is much cheaper than in the United States. In the speech from April 1991 excerpted below, Senator Bill Bradley of New Jersey broke ranks with his fellow Democrats and called for the passage of the free-trade agreement. Although the Bush administration failed to win Congressional approval for NAFTA in 1991, the election of Bill Clinton to the presidency in 1992 gave it another chance. Like Bradley, Clinton was a pro-NAFTA Democrat, and after weeks of heavy lobbying by Clinton, Congress finally passed NAFTA in an extremely close vote in the fall of 1993.

Source: *Vital Speeches of the Day*, May 15, 1991.

SO WHAT CAN WE SAY about this world? First, we no longer stand unchallenged economically, nor only opposite the U.S.S.R. We spent a lot of our economic productivity during the Cold War on insuring ourselves against a military threat from a Soviet Union whose economic and social foundations were full of termites. Then, just at the time Mikhail Gorbachev, George Bush, and John LeCarre declared the Cold War over; just at the time Germany reunites, and 100,000 So-

viet citizens were permitted to leave; just at the time when we felt we were turning a page of history, Saddam Hussein invaded Kuwait. Was his action the beginning of a new kind of conflict or the end of the old? And was our response the beginning of a new world order or the culmination of the old order?

From the standpoint of the Wilsonian vision for collective security, the war to free Kuwait ranks with World War II and the containment of Soviet expansion in terms of its success. Its message is loud and clear. A dictator who invades another country risks the collective condemnation of the nations of the world and the quick destruction of his army. Yet it may also signal the dawning of an age when even the most skilled collective security cannot prevent the violence that lies ahead. . . .

For newly freed peoples seeking ways to live together peacefully in Central and Eastern Europe, in Africa, within the borders of what is still the Soviet Union, and elsewhere, American leadership depends more on the example of the kind of the country we build than on our military might. And the most powerful example is that of a pluralistic society whose democracy and growing economy takes all its citizens to the higher ground.

But we can't lead by example as long as white Americans build mental walls between themselves and the abysmal living conditions of many black Americans in our cities. We can't lead by example if we allow gangs to turn city neighborhoods into war zones and schools into fortresses so that the 10 percent of the kids who don't want to learn destroy the possibility of learning for the 90 percent who do. We can't lead by example if individuals refuse to take responsibility for their own actions or government bureaucrats remain unaccountable for results. We can't lead by example if it's easier for us to put a man on the moon than to get a low-income pregnant women across town to a doctor. We can't lead by example if we fail to see that crime often causes poverty and destroys the interracial bonds of civil society.

In facing up to the realities of race and ethnicity in America today, we must also observe that the isolation of urban black poverty developed first from our failure to respond to an economic migration of five million people—African Americans

moving from the sharecropping farms of the South to the cities of the North.

Racial, ethnic, and religious conflict is sometimes inseparable from the conflict of economic migration. Open borders to Eastern Europe unleash ethnic fears for the people of homogenous countries in Western Europe. Riots in Marseilles, violence in London, and xenophobia in Germany come from fears of actual and potential migrations from Asia, North Africa, Poland, and the Soviet Union. When large groups of people move from one place to another—things change.

One of the most dramatic economic migrations in the world is occurring along the 2,000-mile border between the United States and Mexico. It's more than "the only frontier between the industrialized and developing worlds." As writer Carlos Fuentes has said, it's also the gulf between 15th Century Spain and 18th Century England. It separates our cultures as well as our economies, but the comparative economic opportunity in the United States increasingly will pull Mexico's best people north, leaving Mexico with the unskilled and America with a massive social problem. That is why understanding the dynamics of economic migration will allow us to control it, forestall its most disruptive economic effects and to lessen the ethnic, racial, and religious tensions that could follow. . . .

Now, nearly 20 million people live in Mexico City choking on air pollution. It was Mexican policies that tried to keep Mexico an anti-American island in a sea of good faith attempts to bridge our differences.

But since President Carlos Salinas, a Harvard-educated economist, took office two years ago, the economic and political changes in Mexico have been as profound as in any country on the globe. Last August, Salinas proposed the most significant step for his country's future, a free-trade agreement with the United States. In February, President Bush and Prime Minister Mulroney of Canada joined Salinas to begin negotiations on a North American free-trade zone.

There is only one thing you really need to know about Mexico to understand why the free-trade agreement is so critical to Salinas: Half of Mexico's 80 million people are under the age of 15. Beginning right now, either jobs will be created below the Rio Grande, in places such as Doctor Coss, or there will be more and more legal and illegal immigration into Texas, California, Oklahoma, Kansas and even to New York and Florida. That economic migration will dwarf the migration of black Americans to the North.

I believe Congress should support a maximum effort to complete the negotiations successfully. It will not be easy. There are legitimate problems but a good free-trade agreement would be of great benefit to the United States. It could add dynamism to our economy, creating thousands of jobs and making us more competitive in world markets. It could transform our southern border and enrich our national culture.

But the Mexican Free Trade Agreement will be controversial. There will be thoughtful and constructive opposition. Such a major development in our economic lives deserves such thorough debate. But if we view the proposed free-trade agreement as one inseparable component of overall reform in Mexico, I cannot see any strong argument for not attempting to get an agreement.

We don't always see Mexico as its people would want us to see them. Opponents of the free-trade pact see Mexico's politics as hopelessly corrupt and undemocratic. Yet Salinas appears to be using his political legitimacy, rather than police power, to bring about reform. And while two-party democracy has not arrived everywhere, it is alive in several states near our border. Opponents of the free-trade pact still see it as a country happily lax in its environmental regulation—yet the mayor of Mexico City told me that he is spending $3.5 billion over four years to clean up the air. Opponents of the trade pact still see Mexico as a stubbornly inefficient, politically stagnant nation unwilling to give up the temporary benefits of inflation, budget deficits, and government ownership of key economic sectors. But Salinas has cut his country's budget deficit by the equivalent of three Gramm-Rudman acts. He has brought inflation down dramatically, reduced tariffs, encouraged foreign investment, and privatized many state enterprises, such as telephones. Opponents of the trade pact see Mexico as inward-looking, and yet Mexico now turns outward, ready to tear down that last frontier between the developing and the industrial world, ready to try to become a first-world nation.

The negotiations over a free-trade pact with Mexico will be a test of whether Americans and Mexicans can overcome their stereotypes and suspicions of each other in pursuit of a larger goal—a more productive economy on both sides of the border. Can we be bold and imaginative enough to create the conditions that will enhance our children's future? Do we have the courage to face the fact that their chances for a better life depends on raising our productivity, which in turn depends on a commitment to quality at home and finding common ground abroad?

Crouching on a street in Panama in December 1989, these soldiers are part of the U.S. invasion force that carried out Operation Just Cause, resulting in the downfall of Panamanian dictator Manuel Noriega. The operation included the dropping of some 4,500 paratroopers, the largest such assault since World War II.

In the wake of the Persian Gulf War of 1991, cars, trucks, buses, and materiel litter the "Highway of Death," the road from Kuwait City to Basra in southern Iraq. American air assaults on the flood of Iraqi troops and personnel fleeing Kuwait in the closing stages of the war were intended to cripple Iraq's future war-making capabilities.

WAR

Cameras and reporters were waiting for U.S. Marines when they landed on the shore of Somalia on December 9, 1992, to participate in the United Nations peacekeeping effort—a reflection of the changing nature of military action in an era of instant global communication.

Smoke rises from a Bosnian Serb ammunition depot within the United Nations-mandated exclusion zone some ten miles from Sarajevo following a North Atlantic Treaty Organization (NATO) air strike on August 30, 1995. American forces participated in the NATO effort to end the fighting in Bosnia and Herzegovina that was eventually quelled by the peace accord negotiated in Dayton, Ohio, in November.

Oleg Stjepanovic—AP/Wide World Photos

In the late twentieth and early twenty-first centuries, technological advances often allowed American forces to fight their battles from afar, using sophisticated weaponry such as the shipborne Tomahawk cruise missile launched against a target in Iraq in September 1996 in response to troop buildups in northern Iraq that threatened the Kurdish population.

U.S. Department of Defense/Getty Images

Anti-Taliban fighters observe U.S. bombing of the cave sanctuaries of the al-Qaeda terrorist organization in Tora Bora Mountains in Afghanistan on December 16, 2001. In response to al-Qaeda's devastating attack on the United States on September 11, American forces invaded Afghanistan, whose ruling Taliban regime had sheltered the terrorist organization.

Reuters NewMedia Inc./Corbis

1992

34.

David Gergen: The Los Angeles Riots

*In 1991 an African American named Rodney King was pulled over for speeding
and reckless driving by Los Angeles police officers. When King resisted arrest, the
police beat him with their batons and kicked him repeatedly. The beating was
captured on videotape and released to the press. The episode received national
attention, and many observers cited the videotape as evidence of endemic police
brutality against African American suspects. In April 1992 the four police officers
involved in the King beating were found not guilty by a white jury in suburban
Los Angeles. News of the innocent verdict outraged African American Los Angeles
residents, particularly those in poorer areas of the city who had long complained of
police brutality and saw the verdict as an example of white racism. Within hours
of the verdict, enraged young African Americans began rioting throughout southcentral Los Angeles. The rioting lasted for more than three days, led to more than
forty deaths, and caused millions of dollars in property damage. In the essay
reprinted below, the state of race relations and the lessons of the Los Angeles riots
are explored by David Gergen, a former speechwriter for Presidents Richard Nixon,
Gerald Ford, and Ronald Reagan.*

Source: *U.S.News & World Report*, May 11, 1992, "The Two Nations of America."

ONE OF THE MOST familiar stories in our
Judeo-Christian heritage is that of Saul
of Tarsus riding toward Damascus,
preparing to persecute the new disciples.
Along the way he is knocked down and
blinded for several days by a heavenly
light, but from his catastrophe he actually comes to see more clearly—and
turns into a man of peace. Is it just possible that the catastrophe our nation experienced last week can help us see
more clearly, too?

Surely, the events in Los Angeles must
open our eyes to some truths we have conveniently tried to ignore. Had it not been
for a chance bystander with a camera, we
would never have seen what can happen
to a black man chased and captured by
white policemen. Had those 81 seconds of
videotape not been seared into our con-

sciousness, we would never have followed the trial proceedings and seen how a jury from which blacks were excluded would shamefully mete out "justice" to white men of the law. Had a volcano of violence not erupted, so wantonly and lawlessly, we might not have understood how our cities are once again boiling cauldrons.

Over the past several years, our political leadership—and too often our media—have engaged in a conspiracy of silence, trying not to talk about what is happening to us as a people. But we can no longer avoid reality. A quarter century after our cities were battered by riots that supposedly prompted a national commitment to racial progress, a wide and bitter chasm continues to exist between blacks and whites. The average family income of blacks today is some 60 percent that of whites, compared with 62.5 percent in 1967. Twice as many blacks continue to be unemployed as do whites.

In his scathing new book, "Two Nations," Andrew Hacker provides a raft of other depressing facts: that 44.8 percent of black children live in poverty today compared with 15.9 percent of whites; that 63.7 percent of black children are born out of wedlock, compared with 14.9 percent of whites; that black women have 635 abortions for every 1,000 babies they bear, compared with 274 for white women, and that 1 out of every 5 black males spends part of his life behind bars. This is the tinderbox that exploded last week.

One might be reassured if the nation were embarked upon a serious, sustained effort to close ranks and raise living standards of minority citizens. But we have been moving in the opposite direction, tired and discouraged. Martin Luther King Jr.'s dream of an integrated society has faded, mocking thousands of black youngsters attending segregated schools named after him. Indeed, there are growing signs that we are dividing even more sharply—race against race, haves against have nots. A recent study found that school segregation is actually increasing in Northern and Western states. From New York and New Jersey to Illinois and California, some 80 percent or more of black and Hispanic students now attend schools with predominantly minority students.

We cannot afford what historian Arthur Schlesinger Jr. has called "the disuniting of America." What has made us special in history is that we have tried so hard—and spilled so much blood—to make equal justice and equal opportunity a living reality, to bring unity from diversity. The economic realities of today only make the case more pressing: It is sobering to realize that half of the new entrants into our work force in the 1990s will be black, Hispanic or Asian.

Fortunately, the challenge before us is not as hopeless as widely believed. Many whites have concluded that blacks will never get off the lower rungs because they are lazy or prone to violence, and that nothing works to help them. The growing body of hard-working, middle-class blacks puts the lie to those pernicious myths. Since 1975, black teenagers have actually increased their high-school completion rate from 66 percent to 78 percent. In her book, "Within Our Reach," Lisbeth B. Schorr also provides plenty of evidence that some programs—yes, *government* programs—actually do work to reduce black poverty. The problem is not that we've done too much but that we've done too little and done it without insisting upon better results.

The verdict in the Rodney King case and the terrible violence that followed need not be a final verdict on America. If we open our eyes to what we are becoming, and then act on it, these terrible days will yet serve a higher purpose.

35.

JESSE JACKSON, JR.: Speech to the Democratic National Convention

Between the Civil War and the Great Depression, the overwhelming majority of African American voters cast their ballots for the Republican party. As the party of President Abraham Lincoln, signer of the Emancipation Proclamation, Republicans naturally appealed to black voters. In 1936, however, President Franklin D. Roosevelt became the first Democrat to win a majority of the black vote. Democrats have maintained the allegiance of African American voters in every election since then. Indeed, by the 1990s, Democrats routinely received 90 percent of the black vote in presidential elections. Bill Clinton aggressively courted African American voters when he ran for president on the Democratic Party ticket in 1992. In particular, Clinton struck an alliance with the Reverend Jesse Jackson, the most influential black Democrat in the country. Jackson first came to national prominence in the 1960s when he worked as an aide to civil rights leader Martin Luther King, Jr. After founding the Rainbow Coalition, a civil rights lobbying organization, Jackson ran for the Democratic presidential nomination in 1984. In the strongest showing ever by an African American candidate, Jackson won several million votes before being defeated by Walter Mondale in the primary. Jackson's influence in the Democratic Party grew even larger in subsequent years. At the Democratic National Convention in July 1992, Jackson's address, printed here, electrified the delegates.

Source: *Vital Speeches of the Day*, August 15, 1992.

CHAIRMAN RON BROWN, you've done a difficult job well. You have brought down barriers. Your work makes us proud. President Bill Clinton, you have survived a tough spring. It will make you stronger for the fall. With your stripes you must heal and make us better. The hopes of many depend upon your quest. Be comforted that you do not stand alone.

Vice President Al Gore comes to this task tested and prepared. He has been a reasoned voice for environmental sanity, a supporter of social justice, an original sponsor of DC statehood. And I, for one, look forward to the vice-presidential debate.

We stand as witnesses to a pregnant moment in history. Across the globe, we feel the pain that comes with new birth. Here, in our country pain abounds. We must be certain that it too leads to new birth, and not a tragic miscarriage of opportunity.

We must turn pain to power, pain into partnership, not pain into polarization.

The great temptation in these difficult days of racial polarization and economic injustice is to make political arguments black and white, and miss the moral imperative of wrong and right. Vanity asks—is it popular? Politics asks—will it win? Morality and conscience ask—is it right?

We are part of a continuing struggle for justice and decency, links in a chain that began long before we were born and will extend long after we are gone. History will remember us not for our positioning, but for our principles. Not by our move to the political center, left or right, but rather by our grasp on the moral and ethical center of wrong and right.

We who stand with working people and poor have a special burden. We must stand for what is right, stand up to those who have the might. We do so grounded in the faith, that what is morally wrong will never be politically right. But if it is morally sound, it will eventually be politically right.

When I look at you gathered here today, I hear the pain and see the struggles that prepared the ground that you stand on. We have come a long way from where we started.

A generation ago—in 1964, Fanny Lou Hamer had to fight even to sit in this convention. Tonight, 28 years later, the chair of the Party is Ron Brown from Harlem; the manager is Alexis Herman, an African American woman from Mobile, Alabama. We have come a long way from where we started.

We are more interdependent than we realize. Not only African Americans benefitted from the movement for justice. It was only when African Americans were free to win and sit in these seats, that Bill Clinton and Al Gore from the new South could be able to stand on this rostrum. We are inextricably bound together in a single garment of destiny. Red, yellow, brown, black and white, we are all precious in God's sight. We have come a long way from where we started.

Tonight we face another challenge. Ten million Americans are unemployed, 25 million on food stamps, 35 million in poverty, 40 million have no health care. From the coal miners in Bigstone Gap, West Virginia to the loggers and environmentalists in Roseburg, Oregon, from displaced textile workers in my home town of Greenville, South Carolina to plants closing in Van Nuys, California, pain abounds. Plants are closing, jobs leaving on a fast track, more are working for less, trapped by repressive anti-labor laws. The homeless are a source of national shame and disgrace.

There is a harshness to America that comes from not seeing and a growing mindless materialism. Our television sets bring the world into our living rooms, but too often we overlook our neighbors.

We have a president who has traveled the world, but has never been to Hamlet, North Carolina. Yet we must not overlook Hamlet.

It was there that 25 workers died in a fire at Imperial Foods, more women than men, more white than black. They worked making chicken parts in vats heated to 400 degrees, with few windows and no fans. The owners locked the doors on the outside. The workers died trapped by economic desperation and oppressive work laws.

One woman came up to me after the fire—she said:

> "I want to work. I don't want to go on welfare. I have three children and no husband. We pluck 90 wings a minute. Now I can't bend my wrist, I got the carpel thing. Then when we're hurt they fire us, and we have no health insurance, and no union to help us. We can't get another job because we're crippled, so they put us on welfare and call us lazy."

I said you are not lazy, and you are not alone.

Her friend, a white woman came up and said:

"I'm 7 months pregnant. We stand in two inches of water with two five-minute bathroom breaks. Sometimes we can't hold our water, and then our bowels, and we faint."

We wept together.

If we keep Hamlet in our hearts and before our eyes, we will act to empower working people. We will protect the right to organize and to strike. We will empower workers to enforce health and safety laws. We will provide a national health care system, a minimum wage sufficient to bring workers out of poverty, paid parental leave. We must build a movement for economic justice across the land.

We face a difficult challenge. Our cities have been abandoned, farmers forsaken, children neglected. Floods in Chicago; fires in Los Angeles. They say they can't find $35 billion for the mayors, but the latest down payment for the S&L bailout was $25 billion. It is time to break the mold.

Now is the time to rebuild America. We must be the party with the plan and the purpose. Four years ago, we fought for a program to reinvest in America, paid for by fair taxes on the rich and savings from the military. This year, Governor Bill Clinton has taken a substantial step in that direction. He has expressed Democratic support for DC statehood, same day on site universal voter registration. He has vowed to challenge corporations to invest at home, retrain their workers and pay their share of taxes. He has made a commitment to raising and indexing the minimum wage. We must build upon that direction and go further still.

In 1932, Franklin Roosevelt ran on a "balance-the-budget" platform in the middle of a recession. Working people in motion pushed him into the New Deal.

The impetus for change will not come top down, it must come bottom up.

The Rainbow Coalition has put forward a "Rebuild America Plan." At its heart is a proposal, with the aid of Felix Rohatyn, one of America's leading experts in public finance, for an American Investment Bank. There are $3 trillion in public and private pension funds, that with government guarantees, could provide $500 billion in seed money, and attract an additional $500 billion, to create a ten-year, $1 trillion plan to rebuild America. Pension funds are the workers money. That money is now used to prop up South Africa, for LBOs [leveraged buyouts], and high risk speculation and greed. We should use the workers' money, with the workers' consent and government guarantees, to secure our future by rebuilding America.

We must have a plan on a scale that corresponds with the size of the problems we face. Taiwan has a $1 trillion plan—it is the size of Pennsylvania. Japan has a $3 trillion plan over ten years. We found the money to help rebuild Europe and Japan after World War II, we found the money to help Russia and Poland. We found $600 billion to bail out the mess left by the buccaneer bankers. Surely we can find the money to rebuild America and put people back to work.

We must have a vision sufficient to correspond with the size of our opportunity. Across the world, walls are coming down. The Cold War is over; the Soviet Union is no more. Russia wants to join NATO. We can change our priorities, reinvest in educating our children, train our workers, rebuild our cities. Today Japan makes fast trains; we make fast missiles. If we change our priorities, and build a high speed national railroad, we could go from New York to Los Angeles in 8 hours. We could make the steel, lay the rail, build the cars and drive them. Scientists can stop devising weapons we don't need and start working on environmental advances we can't live without.

We must have an imagination strong enough to see beyond war. In Israel, Prime Minister Rabin's election is a step toward greater security and peace for the entire region. Rabin's wisdom in affirming negotiation over confrontation, land for peace, bargaining table over battle field has inspired hope, not only in the hearts of democratic Israel, but on the West Bank. Israeli security and Palestinian self-determination are inextricably bound, two sides of the same coin. If peace talks continue, this generation may be able to witness a Middle East tasting the fruits of peace.

In Africa today, democracy is on the march. In Nigeria, we witnessed successful elections last week. But democracy cannot flourish amid economic ruins. Democracy protects the right to vote; it does not insure that you can eat. Today, President Deuf of Senegal, head of development for the Organization of African Unity, is pushing for African development. Like other regions of the world, Africa needs debt relief and credits so it can have the opportunity to grow.

We must understand that development in the Third World and economic prosperity at home are inextricably bound. We can be a force for peace in the Middle East, development to Africa and Latin America, hope in Eastern Europe and the former Soviet Union.

Politics cannot be reduced to a matter of money and ambition. We must stay true to our values, or lose our way.

—In 1939—900 Jews were turned away from the shores of Miami by the U.S. government, sent back to Germany haunted by Hitler.

—In 1942—120,000 Japanese Americans were rounded up and put in American concentration camps.

—In 1992—the U.S. government is turning Haitians away, back into the arms of death, and relaxing sanctions on South Africa.

It was anti-Semitic and wrong in 1939 to lock the Jews out. It was racist and wrong in 1942 to lock the Japanese Americans up. And it is racist and wrong in 1992 to lock the Haitians out and abandon Nelson Mandela in South Africa. South Africa remains a terrorist state. Sanctions should be reimposed until the interim government is established.

We hear a lot of talk about family values, even as we spurn the homeless on the street. Remember, Jesus was born to a homeless couple, outdoors in a stable, in the winter. He was the child of a single mother. When Mary said Joseph was not the father, she was abused. If she had aborted the baby, she would have been called immoral. If she had the baby, she would have been called unfit, without family values. But Mary had family values. It was Herod—the Quayle of his day— who put no value on the family.

We who would be leaders must feel and be touched by people's pain. How can you be a doctor and not touch the sick? How can you be a leader and not touch the hurt? Gandhi adopted the untouchables. Dr. King marched with violent gang members, hoping to turn them to the discipline of non-violence.

Above all, we must reach out and touch our children. Our children are embittered and hurt, but it is not a congenital disease. They were not born that way. They live amidst violence and rejection, in broken streets, broken glass, broken sidewalks, broken families, broken hearts. Their music, their rap, their video, their art reflects their broken world. We must reach out and touch them.

Before the riots in Los Angeles, Representative Maxine Waters and I visited the Imperial Courts and Nickerson Gardens housing projects in Watts, where we spent the night with our children, and then visited the youth detention center with Arsenio Hall and James Almos. We listened to the youth describe their busted and deferred dreams. They suffer 50 percent unemployment, with no prospects of a job or going to college. It costs $5,000 to send them to high school, $34,000 to send them downtown to the youth detention center.

For many of them, jail is a step up. In jail, they are safe from drive-by shootings. In jail, it's warm in the winter, cool in the summer. In jail they get three balanced meals, access to health care, education and vocational training. Everything they should have on the outside they only get on the inside.

Too many of our children see jail as a relief station, and death as a land beyond pain. We must reach out and touch them. Surely, it is better to have dirty hands and clean hearts than clean hands and a dirty heart.

If we reach out, we can win—and deserve to win. We have heard many different arguments about a winning strategy—whether to rally the base or appeal to those who have strayed. But these are not choices. We will win only if we put forth a vision that corresponds with the size of our problems and the scope of our opportunity, if we reach out to those in despair and those who care, reach across the lines that divide by race, region or religion.

As for the Rainbow Coalition, we will continue to build a movement for economic justice in this land. We will work to mobilize working and poor people to change the course of this country. We will join in defeating George Bush in the fall—that is a necessary first step.

We must continue to build. When Roo-sevelt came to office, a movement of working people made a new deal possible. When Kennedy came to office, he did not teach Dr. King about civil rights; Dr. King led a movement that made civil rights unavoidable. When Bill Clinton comes to office, we must build a movement that keeps economic justice at the forefront of the agenda.

I know it's dark. But in the dark the flame of hope still burns.

In LA, they focused on Rodney King beaten by white officers, who were acquitted by an all-white jury. But it was a white man who had the instinct and the outrage to film it and take it public. The media focus was on the white truck driver beaten by black youth. But it was four young black youth who stepped in and saved his life, good samaritans.

In the final analysis it comes down to a question of character. On a small Southern college campus, I once observed a lesson never to be forgotten. I saw a dwarf and a giant walking together—they were an odd couple. He was six feet three, she was three feet tall. When they reached the parting paths, they embraced. He handed her her books and she skipped down the path. It looked to be romantic. I asked the president—what is this I am seeing? He said, I thought you would ask. You see, that is his sister, in fact his twin sister. By a twist of fate he came out a giant, she a dwarf. All the big schools offered him athletic scholarships. The pros offered him money. But he said I can only go where my sister can go. And so he ended up here with us.

Somewhere that young man learned ethics, caring for others. Few of us are driven by a tailwind. Most of us struggle with headwinds. Not all of us can be born tall, some are born short, motherless, abandoned, hungry, orphaned. Somebody has to care. It must be us. And if we do, we will win, and deserve to win.

Keep hope alive.

36.

PAT BUCHANAN: Speech to the Republican National Convention

At the conclusion of the Persian Gulf War, the reelection of President George Bush looked certain. His public approval rating stood at 90 percent, and most of his potential Democratic rivals announced they would not challenge Bush in the 1992 campaign. A weak national economy, however, would prove to be Bush's undoing. In late 1991 Pat Buchanan, a popular political columnist and television commentator who had served in the administrations of Presidents Richard Nixon, Gerald Ford, and Ronald Reagan, launched a dark-horse campaign for the Republican presidential nomination. At first Bush ignored Buchanan's challenge, but when Buchanan began consistently winning 30 percent of the vote in state-by-state primaries, Bush abandoned a "Rose Garden" strategy of campaigning from the White House and took to the campaign trail himself. Although Bush held off the challenge and secured the Republican nomination, Buchanan's strong showing in the primaries revealed that public discontent over the economy was growing, even within Bush's own party. Buchanan's criticism of Bush's handling of the economy hurt the incumbent's campaign and gave Democrats a blueprint to follow in the elections. Buchanan's challenge also reflected social conservatives' disappointment in Bush's failure to pursue antiabortion and school prayer legislation. At the Republican National Convention in Houston, Texas, in August 1992, Buchanan pledged renewed allegiance to Bush, but his strident attacks on the Democrats created only more controversy. In November Bush lost to Governor Bill Clinton of Arkansas. Excerpts of Buchanan's convention speech are reprinted below.

Source: *Vital Speeches of the Day*, September 15, 1992.

WHAT A TERRIFIC CROWD this is. What a terrific crowd. This may even be larger than the crowd I had in Eligay, Georgia. Don't laugh. We carried Eligay.

Listen my friends, we may have taken the long way home, but we finally got here.

The first thing I want to do is to congratulate President Bush, and remove any doubt about where we stand: The primaries are over, the heart is strong again, and the Buchanan brigades are enlisted—all the way to a great comeback victory in November.

My friends, like many of you last month, I watched that giant masquerade ball up at Madison Square Garden—where 20,000 radicals and liberals came dressed up as moderates and centrists—in the greatest single exhibition of cross-dressing in American political history.

One by one, the prophets of doom appeared at the podium. The Reagan decade, they moaned, was a terrible time in America; and they said the only way to prevent even worse times is to entrust our nation's fate and future to the party that gave us McGovern, Mondale, Carter and Michael Dukakis.

Where do they find these leaders? No way, my friends. The American people are not going to go back to the discredited liberalism of the 1960s and the failed liberalism of the 1970s—no matter how slick the package in 1992.

No, the malcontents of Madison Square Garden notwithstanding, the 1980s were not terrible years in America. They were great years. You know it. And I know it. And everyone knows it except for the carping critics who sat on the sidelines of history, jeering at one of the great statesmen of modern time, Ronald Reagan. . . .

But we are here tonight, my friends, not only to celebrate, but to nominate. And an American president has many, many roles.

He is our first diplomat, the architect of American foreign policy. And which of these two men is more qualified for that role? George Bush has been U.N. ambassador, director of the CIA, envoy to China. As vice president, George Bush co-authored and co-signed the policies that won the Cold War. As president, George Bush presided over the liberation of Eastern Europe and the termination of the Warsaw Pact.

And what about Mr. Clinton? Well, Bill Clinton couldn't find 150 words to discuss foreign policy in an acceptance speech that lasted almost an hour. You know, as was said of another Democratic candidate, Bill Clinton's foreign policy experience is pretty much confined to having had breakfast once at the International House of Pancakes.

You know, let's recall what happened. Let us look at the record and recall what happened. Under President George Bush, more human beings escaped from the prison house of tyranny to freedom than in any other four-year period in history.

And for any man, let me tell you for any man to call this the record of failure is the cheap political rhetoric of politicians who only know how to build themselves up by tearing America down, and we don't want that kind of leadership in the United States.

The presidency, my friends, the presidency is also an office that Theodore Roosevelt called America's bully pulpit. Harry Truman said it was preeminently a place of moral leadership. George Bush is a defender of right-to-life, and a champion of the Judeo-Christian values and beliefs upon which this America was founded.

Mr. Clinton, however, has a different agenda.

At its top is unrestricted, unrestricted abortion on demand. When the Irish-Catholic governor of Pennsylvania, Robert Casey, asked to say a few words on behalf of the 25 million unborn children destroyed since Roe v. Wade, Bob Casey was told there was no room for him at the podium at Bill Clinton's convention and no room at the inn.

Yet a militant leader of the homosexual rights movement could rise at that convention and say: "Bill Clinton and Al Gore represent the most pro-lesbian and pro-gay ticket in history." And so they do.

Bill Clinton says he supports school choice—but only for state-run schools. Parents who send their children to Christian schools, or private schools or Jewish schools or Catholic schools need not apply.

Elect me, and you get two for the price of one, Mr. Clinton says of his lawyer-spouse.

And what does Hillary believe? Well, Hillary believes that 12-year-olds should have the right to sue their parents.

And Hillary has compared marriage and the family as institutions to slavery and life on an Indian reservation.

Well, speak for yourself, Hillary.

Friends, my friends, this is radical feminism. The agenda that Clinton and Clinton would impose on America—abortion on demand, a litmus test for the Supreme Court, homosexual rights, discrimination against religious schools, women in combat units—that's change, all right. That's not the kind of change America needs. It's not the kind of change America wants. And it is not the kind of change we can abide in a nation that we still call God's country.

A president of the United States is also America's commander-in-chief. He's the man we authorize to send fathers and sons and brothers and friends into battle.

George Bush was 17 years old when they bombed Pearl Harbor. He left his high school graduation, he walked down to the recruiting office, and signed up to become the youngest fighter pilot in the Pacific war.

And Mr. Clinton? And Bill Clinton?

I'll tell you where he was. I'll tell you where he was.

I'll tell you where he was. When Bill Clinton's time came in Vietnam, he sat up in a dormitory in Oxford, England, and figured out how to dodge the draft.

Let me ask the question of this convention. Which of these two men has won the moral authority to send young Americans into battle? I suggest, respectfully, it is the American patriot and war hero, Navy Lieutenant J. G. George Herbert Walker Bush.

My fellow Americans, my fellow Americans, this campaign is about philosophy, and it is about character; and George Bush wins on both counts.

And it is time all of us came home and stood beside him. . . .

One year ago, my friends, I could not have dreamt that I would be here tonight. I was just one of many panelists on what President Bush calls "those crazy Sunday talk shows." But I disagreed with the president; and so we challenged the president in the Republican primaries and we fought as best we could. From February to June, President Bush won 33 primaries. I can't recall exactly how many we won.

I'll get you the figure tomorrow.

But tonight I want to speak from the heart, to the 3 million Americans who voted for Pat Buchanan for president. I will never forget you, nor the great honor you have done me. But I do believe, I do believe deep in my heart, that the right place for us to be now—in this presidential campaign—is right beside George Bush.

This party is my home. This party is our home, and we've got to come home to it. And don't let anyone tell you any different.

Yes, we disagreed with President Bush, but we stand with him for the freedom of choice religious schools. And we stand with him against the amoral idea that gay and lesbian couples should have the same standing in law as married men and women.

We stand with President Bush for right-to-life, and for voluntary prayer in the public schools.

And we stand against putting our wives and daughters and sisters into combat units of the United States Army. And we stand, my friends, we also stand with President Bush in favor of the right of small towns and communities to control the raw sewage of pornography that so terribly pollutes our popular culture.

We stand with President Bush in favor of federal judges who interpret the law as written, and against would-be Supreme Court justices like Mario Cuomo who think they have a mandate to re-write the Constitution.

My friends, this election is about more than who gets what. It is about who we are. It is about what we believe and what we stand for as Americans. There is a religious war going on in this country for the soul of America. It is a cultural war as critical to the kind of nation we shall be as the Cold War itself, for this war is for the soul of America. And in that struggle for the soul of America, Clinton and Clinton are on the other side, and George Bush is on our side.

And so, to the Buchanan brigades out there, we have to come home, and stand beside George Bush.

In those six months campaigning from Concord, New Hampshire to California, I came to know our country better than I had known it ever before in my life, and I gathered up memories that are going to be with me the rest of my days.

There was that day-long ride through the great state of Georgia in a bus Vice President Bush himself had used in 1988 called Asphalt One. The ride ended in a 9:00 p.m. speech in a tiny town in southern Georgia called Fitzgerald.

There were those workers at the James River Paper Mill, in northern New Hampshire in a town called Groveton—tough, hardy men. None of them would say a word to me as I came down the line, shaking their hands one by one. They were under threat of losing their jobs at Christmas. As I moved down the line, one tough fellow about my age just looked up and said to me, "Save our jobs."

Then there was the legal secretary that I met at the Manchester airport Christmas Day who came running up to me and said, "Mr. Buchanan, I'm going to vote for you." And then she broke down weeping and she said, "I've lost my job, I don't have any money, and they're going to take away my little girl. What am I going to do?"

My friends, these people are our people. They don't read Adam Smith or Edmund Burke, but they came from the same schoolyards and the same playgrounds and town as we came from. They share our beliefs and convictions, our hopes and our dreams. These are the conservatives of the heart. They are our people. And we need to reconnect with them. We need to let them know we know how bad they're hurting. They don't expect miracles of us, but they need to know we care.

There were the people, of Hayfork, a tiny town up in California's Trinity Alps, a town that is now under a sentence of death because a federal judge has set aside 9 million acres for the habitat of the spotted owl—forgetting about the habitat of the men and women who live and work in Hayfork.

And there were the brave people of Koreatown who took the worst of those L.A. riots, but still live the family values we treasure, and who still believe deeply in the American dream.

Friends, in those wonderful 25 weeks of our campaign, the saddest days were the days of that riot in L.A., the worst riot in American history. But out of that awful tragedy can come a message of hope.

Hours after that awful tragedy can come a message of hope.

Hours after that riot ended I went down to the Army compound in south Los Angeles where I met the troopers of the 18th Cavalry who had come to save the city of Los Angeles. An officer of the 18th Cav said, "Mr. Buchanan, I want you to talk to a couple of our troopers." And I went over and I met these young fellas. They couldn't have been 20 years old, and they recounted their story.

They had come into Los Angeles late in the evening of the second day, when the rioting was still going on, and two of them walked up a dark street, where the mob had burned and looted every building on the block but one, a convalescent home for the aged. And the mob was headed in to ransack and loot the apartments of the terrified old men and women inside. The troopers came up the street, M-16s at the ready, and the mob threatened and cursed, but the mob retreated because it had met the one thing that could stop it: force, rooted in justice, and backed by moral courage.

Greater love than this hath no man than that he lay down his life for his friend. Here were 19-year-old boys ready to lay down their lives to stop a mob from molesting old people they did not even know. And as those boys took back the streets of Los Angeles, block by block, my friends, we must take back our cities, and take back our culture, and take back our country.

God bless you, and God bless America.

———————◆———————

The tradition I cherish is the ideal this country was built upon, the concept of religious pluralism, of a plethora of opinions, of tolerance and not the jihad. Religious war, pooh. The war is between those who trust us to think and those who believe we must merely be led.

ANNA QUINDLEN, in response to Pat Buchanan's speech
to the Republican National Convention,
The New York Times, September 6, 1992

37.

JANE O'REILLY: Year of the Woman

One of the most newsworthy aspects of the 1992 Congressional elections was that four women won U.S. Senate seats. They were Dianne Feinstein and Barbara Boxer of California, Carol Moseley-Braun of Illinois, and Patty Murray of Washington. Two other women already held Senate seats: Nancy Kassebaum of Kansas and Barbara Mikulski of Maryland. (A third, Jocelyn Burdick of North Dakota, was appointed to a seat upon the death of her senator husband.) Never before had six women held elected Senate seats at the same time. Convinced that the elections marked a watershed in American political history, observers heralded the results by dubbing 1992 the "Year of the Woman." They pointed out that not only had four women been elected to the Senate but that more women voted in the election than did men. Political scientists predicted that the election would inaugurate a new era of women's participation in politics. Others, however, argued that it would take much longer to break male dominance in Congress; men claimed more than 90 percent of the seats in the House and Senate. In the article reprinted below, Jane O'Reilly, a magazine editor and writer, examines the media's response to the surge in female senators.

Source: *Columbia Journalism Review,* November/December 1992, "Women: The Year of."

THIS YEAR a handful of women won primary elections for United States Senate seats. Eleven, at final count. Even if they all won, and joined the two incumbents and newly appointed senatorial widow Mrs. Jocelyn Burdick—a Democrat from North Dakota—that would be very, very slightly more than 10 percent of the entire Senate. Seventy-two years after women were allowed to vote, the great law of One Woman at a Time appears to have been broken. And lo! 1992 is declared The Year of the Woman! It is, in fact, almost always headlined as The Year of the Woman! singular, in a subliminal reminder that one is enough.

The baseline explanation for The Year of the Woman! was a combination of the response to *Thelma and Louise,* Susan Faludi's *Backlash,* the Clarence Thomas hearings, the congressional banking scandal, redistricting, and incumbency loss of heart. Synergy, if you will, but synergy propelled by a shift, an almost defiant hardening, in political women's confidence. It was as though we had reached the point where we felt we had nothing to lose.

Women are clearly not about to take over the country. But we do think we are capable of it, should try to do it. That women have (almost completely) outgrown our doubts about our place in politics is a story that sounds like baloney to a male editor. It is the kind of news you either get or you don't.

It was this realization that moved about a hundred women writers, reporters, editors, designers, and political activists to publish *The Getting It Gazette* (get it?), a paper for the women delegates to the Democratic convention. It worked so well that we published in Houston, both for the Republican women shut out by their party and for the women gathered outside the convention. To paraphrase Marilyn Quayle, we unleashed our essential natures as women. As women journalists.

As we looked through what passed for coverage of The Year of the Woman!, we were struck first by the way the Democratic convention became an occasion for publishing cute group shots that made the candidates look like giggling sorority girls. Then we recognized the inevitable catfight theme implied in such absurd headlines as this one on a story about Hillary Clinton and Tipper Gore from *The Arizona Republic:* STRONG WOMEN PAIRED ON TICKET, BUT PERSONALITY CLASH TERMED UNLIKELY.

One positive insight gleaned from the clippings was that the predominance of women political reporters at *The New York Times* made a big difference. Anna Quindlen's heroic work has apparently resulted in a readiness at the *Times* to recognize, for example, that Catherine Manegold's piece on the radical feminist Women's Action Coalition (NO MORE NICE GIRLS) was a story on the shift in women's attitudes, *not* a story for the Living section. For the first time, the women editing *Getting It Gazette* occasionally felt we were living in the same country as the editors of the *Times*.

But most of the time we felt we were covering totally different news—for example, the emergence of a distinct movement we dubbed "Femocrats." (The Re-

publican women, ever wary of the F word, preferred to be called "womanists.") They have discovered that women running for office must run almost as hard against the hostility of men in their own party as against the opposition. So they have developed their own fund-raising, campaign-training, and support networks *outside of the two traditional parties.* Emily's List, the fund for Democratic pro-choice women candidates, is one of the most successful non-PAC funds in existence. It has received some coverage—certainly more than The Wish List, its Republican counterpart, which is growing fast on contributions from disaffected Republican moderates. Women candidates are, astonishingly, beginning to be able to raise decent campaign money and are almost at the stage of being able to afford to run hard on their records. That's the news of this Year of the Woman—not "Will Hillary Help or Hurt the Ticket?" or, God help us, which wife has a better cookie recipe?

It's hard to miss the real story on women this year. If a reporter will just listen, there are surprises everywhere. One of our favorite surprises at the *Getting It Gazette* came about this way: we were assigning stories about the state galas at the Democratic convention. A young, untried writer named Janet Reitman wanted to go *anyplace*. We couldn't risk sending her to Femocrat-full Texas or crucial California. "Oh, go to Alabama," we said, and we hoped she would have a good time.

She came back, and with perfect savoir faire reported on the women she had met. Silk dresses, curly hair, law degrees, and no nonsense. "Steel magnolias?" they said to her. "Honey, forget that stuff. We're bitches from hell."

38.

AL GORE: *Earth in the Balance*

In the early 1990s the phenomenon of global warming emerged as a major
national and international issue as scientific research on every continent
confirmed that temperatures had increased worldwide during the previous century.
Although most scientists agreed that global warming was underway, they disagreed
over its cause. Some doubted that the phenomenon had a human cause and
argued that global warming represented a natural environmental phenomenon
over which humans had negligible control. Many other scientists, in contrast,
believed that humans played a significant role and cited the carbon dioxide
emissions produced by industrialization as a major contributory factor. They
warned that if humans did not reduce carbon dioxide emissions, the rise in
temperatures across the planet would eventually create a global environmental
disaster that would include famine, violent weather patterns, and deadly coastal
flooding. In 1992 Al Gore, then a Democratic senator from Tennessee, published
Earth in the Balance, *a provocative book that called on the United States to lead*
the world in reducing carbon dioxide emissions. Gore's book received national
attention later that year when he was elected Vice President. Excerpts from Earth
in the Balance *are reprinted below.*

Source: *Earth in the Balance,* Boston, 1992.

THE U.S. ROLE

As the world's leading exemplar of
free market economics, the United States
has a special obligation to discover effective ways of using the power of market
forces to help save the global environment. Yet even as we correctly point out
the dismal failures of communism, and
even as we push the underdeveloped
world—appropriately, in my view—to
adopt a market-based approach to economics, we have been reluctant to admit
our failure to bring environmental values
into our economic decisions. Further,
the Bush administration has shown little
interest in changing the government
policies that presently distort the princi-

ples of market economics in ways that
encourage the destruction of the environment.

Many U.S. policy-makers seem content
to leave the environmental consequences
of our economic choices in the large
waste-basket of economic theory labeled
externalities. As I stated in Chapter 10,
anything that economists wish to forget
about is called an externality and then
banished from serious thought. For example, consider this analysis by President
Bush's Council of Economic Advisers of
the impact of global warming on agriculture: "The costs of today's agricultural
policies are estimated to be more important in economic terms than even pessimistic estimates of the effects of global

warming, largely because the former must be borne in the present and the latter may occur, if at all, in the relatively distant future."

That's it. As far as the council is concerned, global warming need be given no further thought. Since it has been discounted into insignificance, they figure we can just forget about it. And meanwhile we go on preaching to the rest of the world that our brand of market economics takes everything into account in the most efficient way imaginable.

What if we took a broader view and began incorporating factors affecting the environment into our economic system? How would we do it? Well, here are some specific proposals.

None is likely to be more effective than finding ways to put a price on the environmental consequences of our choices, a price that would then be reflected in the marketplace. For example, if we were to tax the pollution dumped by factories into the air and water, we would get less of it. And we might well notice a sudden increase in the amount of interest companies show in improving the efficiency of their processes in order to reduce the pollution they cause.

To most of us, the principle sounds unassailable: let the polluter pay. But what about when it applies to each of us instead of to a nameless, faceless, corporation? For example, rather than require homeowners to pay higher property taxes to cover the cost of garbage collection, why not lower property taxes and then charge for garbage collection directly—by the pound? Those responsible for creating more garbage would pay more; those who found ways to cut down would pay less. The interest in recycling might rise dramatically. And when choosing between products at the store, people might even start avoiding unnecessary and bulky packaging if they knew it was going to end up in their garbage. There is an economic rule of thumb: whatever we tax, we tend to get less of; whatever we subsidize, we tend to get more of. Currently, we tax work and we subsidize the depletion of natural resources—and both policies have contributed to high unemployment and the waste of natural resources. What if we lowered the tax on work and simultaneously raised it on the burning of fossil fuels? It is entirely possible to change the tax code in a way that keeps the total amount of taxes at the same level, avoids unfairness and "regressivity," but discourages the constant creation of massive amounts of pollution.

Accordingly, I propose:

1. That we create an Environmental Security Trust Fund, with payments into the Fund based on the amount of CO_2 put into the atmosphere. . . .

2. That a Virgin Materials Fee be imposed on products at the point of manufacture or importation based on the quantity of nonrenewable, virgin materials built into the product. . . .

3. The government should adopt a policy of purchasing environmentally appropriate substitutes wherever they are competitive—taking into account full life-cycle costs—with older, less responsible technology. . . .

4. The government must establish higher mileage requirements for all cars and trucks sold in the United States. . . .

5. Efficiency standards throughout the economy—for buildings, for industrial motors and engines, and for appliances must also be strengthened. . . .

6. Utility rate reform must encourage full use of conservation and efficiency measures. . . .

7. Tree planting programs—with carefully selected seedlings appropriate to the areas being planted and careful fol-

low-up to ensure tree survival—should be part of workfare programs in communities where work requirements are attached to welfare payments. . . .

8. Accelerated phaseout of all ozone-destroying chemicals. We should also subsidize the development of truly benign substitutes.

39.

NEIL HOWE and WILLIAM STRAUSS: The New Generation Gap

The discussion of differences between generations became something of an intellectual cottage industry in the 1990s, as the children of the postwar Baby Boom entered midlife and saw their place in the social, cultural, economic, and political limelight threatened by the ascendance of those born after 1961, often called Generation X. Popular music, film, and television helped define the worldview of many in both generations, but the occasional overlap of cultural references did not go far to bridge the gap between those who were mostly in their forties and those who were mostly in their twenties. In the selection reprinted below, excerpted from an article that appeared in The Atlantic Monthly, *Neil Howe and William Strauss compare and contrast the Baby Boomers and the Thirteeners (their name for Generation X), putting their conflict in the context of other generational divides in American history. Howe and Strauss published several books on this theme, beginning with* Generations: The History of America's Future, 1584 to 2069 *(1992).*

Source: *The Atlantic Monthly,* December 1992, "The New Generation Gap."

TWO WORLD VIEWS, reflecting fundamentally different visions of society and self, are moving into conflict in the America of the 1990s. A new generation gap is emerging. In the late 1960s the fight was mainly between twenty-year-olds and the fifty-plus crowd. Today it's mainly between young people and the thirty- to forty-year-olds.

In these gaps, the old 1960s one and the emerging 1990s facsimile, there have been two constants: Each time, the same conspicuous generation has been involved. Each time, that generation has claimed the moral and cultural high ground, casting itself as the apex of civilization and its age-bracket adversaries as

soul-dead, progress-blocking philistines. The first time around, the members of that generation attacked their elders; now they're targeting their juniors.

We're talking about Baby Boomers. Born from 1943 to 1960, today's 69 million Boomers range in age from thirty-two to forty-nine. Defined by its personality type, this generation is somewhat different from the group defined simply by the well-known demographic fertility bulge (1946–1964). At the front end, the grown-up "victory babies" of 1943—peers of Janis Joplin and Bobby Fischer, Joni Mitchell and Geraldo Rivera, Oliver North and Rap Brown, R. Crumb and Angela Davis, Newt Gingrich and Bill

Bradley—include the first Dr. Spock toddlers; the fiery college class of 1965; the oldest Vietnam-era draftcard burners; the eldest among "Americans Under 25," whom *Time* magazine named its "1967 Man of the Year"; and the last twenty-nine-year-olds (in 1972) to hear the phrase "under-thirty generation" before its sudden disappearance. At the back end, the grown-up Eisenhower babies of 1960 are the last-born of today's Americans to feel any affinity with the hippie-cum-yuppie baggage that accompanies the Boomer label.

The younger antagonists are less well known: America's thirteenth generation, born from 1961 to 1981, ranging in age from eleven to thirty-one. Demographers call them Baby Busters, a name that deserves a prompt and final burial. First, it's incorrect: The early-sixties birth cohorts are among the biggest in U.S. history—and, at 80 million, this generation has numerically outgrown the Boom. By the late 1990s it will even outvote the Boom. Second, the name is insulting—"Boom" followed by "Bust," as though wonder were followed by disappointment. The novelist Doug Coupland, himself a 1961 baby, dubs his age-mates "Generation X" or "Xers," a name first used by and about British Boomer-punkers. Shann Nix, a journalist at the *San Francisco Chronicle,* suggests "posties" (as in "post yuppies"), another name that, like Coupland's, leaves the generation in the shadow of the great Boom. . . .

The old generation gap of the late 1960s and early 1970s featured an incendiary war between college kids and the reigning leaders of great public institutions. Back then the moralizing aggressors were on the younger side. And back then Americans in their thirties and early forties (the "Silent Generation," born from 1925 to 1942) stood in between as mentors and mediators.

The new generation gap of the 1990s is different. It features a smoldering mutual disdain between Americans now reaching midlife and those born just after them. This time the moralizing aggressors are on the older side. And this time no generation stands in between.

What separates the collective personalities of Boomers and Thirteeners? First, look at today's mainline media, a hotbed of forty-year-old thinking. Notice how, in Boomers' hands, 1990s America is becoming a somber land obsessed with values, back-to-basics movements, ethical rectitude, political correctness, harsh punishments, and a yearning for the simple life. Life's smallest acts exalt (or diminish) one's personal virtue. A generation weaned on great expectations and gifted in deciphering principle is now determined to reinfuse the entire society with meaning.

Now look again—and notice a countermood popping up in college towns, in big cities, on Fox and cable TV, and in various ethnic side currents. It's a tone of physical frenzy and spiritual numbness, a revelry of pop, a pursuit of high-tech, guiltless fun. It's a carnival culture featuring the tangible bottom lines of life—money, bodies, and brains—and the wordless deals with which one can be traded for another. A generation weaned on minimal expectations and gifted in the game of life is now avoiding meaning in a cumbersome society that, as they see it, offers them little. . . .

BOOMERS

All across America, Americans in their thirties and forties are answering *Rolling-Stone*'s call to "muster the will to remake ourselves into altruists and ascetics." If, a decade earlier, twentysomething hippies evolved into thirtysomething yuppies, the new fortysomethings are now putting (according to the demograpsher Brad Edmondson) "less emphasis on money and more on meaning." How can this be? How can a generation that came of age amid the libidinous euphoria of People's Park now be forming neighborhood associations to push "alcoholics, drug dealers, and wing nuts" out of Berkeley parks and out of their lives? How can a generation that a decade ago went, as Todd Gitlin put it, "from *J'accuse*' to Jacuzzi" now be leaving the Jacuzzi for a cold shower?. . .

Their parents expected Boomers to be, in William Manchester's words, "adorable as babies, cute as grade school pupils and striking as they entered their teens," after which "their parents would be very, very proud of them." In 1965 *Time* magazine declared that teenagers were "on the fringe of a golden era"— and, two years later, described collegians as cheerful idealists who would "lay out blight-proof, smog-free cities, enrich the underdeveloped world, and, no doubt, write finis to poverty and war."

Hardly. Over the next several years Boomers discovered that they were never meant to be doers and builders like their parents. Instead, finding their parents' constructions in need of a major spiritual overhaul, even creative destruction, they triggered a youth-focused "Consciousness Revolution." Along the way, they became what Annie Gottlieb has described as "a tribe with its roots in a time, rather than place or race." That time was the late sixties, when the term "generation gap" gained currency.

The term was coined (and used most frequently) by the hard-charging dads of the "GI Generation," born from 1901 to 1924, a cohort reaching from Walt Disney to George Bush, whose 25 million surviving members today range in age from sixty-eight to ninety-one. Back in the heady days of what the historian

William O'Neill has dubbed "the American High," the GI peers of John F. Kennedy made much of "gaps"—missile gaps, science gaps, poverty gaps. Gaps were something they thought themselves quite good at building bridges across. But not this one. Beginning in the late 1960s the generation gap became a full-fledged age war. . . .

The GI-Boomer age war paralleled the Vietnam shooting war. It crested in 1969, along with draft calls and casualties. A couple of years later—after Ohio's National Guardsmen killed four Kent State students, after student opinion turned solidly against the war, and after Congress amended the Constitution to allow eighteen-year-olds to vote—Boomers began heeding the Beatles' simple "words of wisdom: let it be." The generation gap began to ease, in its outward forms at least, replaced by a grinding pessimism and a gray Boomer drizzle of sex, drugs, unemployment, and a sour (if less confrontational) mood on campus. In politics the Boomers settled in as more apathetic and more just plain illiberal than their rebelled-against parents could ever have imagined.

In the 1970s the GI-versus-Boom clash had a quiet denouement that has proved over time to be at least as consequential as the Boomers' angry demonstrations. No pact was signed, no speeches were made, but something of a deal was struck. On the one hand, Boomers said nothing as GIs then on the brink of retirement proceeded to channel a growing portion of the nation's public resources (over a period from the post-Vietnam peace dividend to the post-Cold War peace dividend) toward their own "entitlements." On the other hand, GIs did not object as Boomers asserted control of the culture. GI leaders (Gerald Ford, Jimmy Carter, Ronald Reagan, George Bush) continued to preside at the pinnacle of government, while their retirement-bound peers became America's first old people to call themselves "senior citizens.". . . No generation in U.S. history—not even that of Jefferson and Madison—can match the GIs' lifetime record of success at getting, holding, and using political power.

At the same time, Boomers—who in the first days of the eighteen-year-old vote were expected to be a political powerhouse, sweeping candidates of their choice into the White House—played the role of political siren, first tempting candidates, then luring them to their demise. It was not until 1992, two decades after George McGovern first begged for their votes, that Boomers finally showed more political clout than the aging GI peers of LBJ and Richard Nixon (and leapfrogged the leaderless Silent Generation, which may become the first generation in American history never to produce a President).

Along the way, the word "yuppie"—a term of derision among others, of self-mocking humor among Boomers—labeled a generation of supposedly sold-out ex-hippies. Introduced in 1981, the word referred to "young upwardly mobile professionals," a group that included only about one out of every twenty Boomers. But a much larger proportion fit the subjective definition: self-immersed, impatient for personal satisfaction, weak in civic instincts. Everything the yuppie did—what he ate, drank, listened to, lived in, and invested for—sent a negative message about GI-style culture and institutions.

Notwithstanding their affluent reputation through the 1980s, Boomers, especially those born in the middle to late 1950s, have not prospered. True, they are roughly keeping pace with the (Silent) generation just before them, at each phase of life. But were it not for the ris-

ing economic power of women (and the two-income household), they would be falling behind. . . .

Although 1990s-edition Boomers are no throwback to the 1960s, they see themselves as they did then (and always have): as the embodiment of moral wisdom. Their aging is taking on a non-apologetic quality—prompting *The New York Times* to relabel them "grumpies" (for "grown-up mature professionals"). The idea of telling other people what to do suits them just fine. They do not inherently dislike government; they simply want to redirect public institutions toward what they consider a socially redemptive purpose. Addressing America's unresolved social issues, from crime and homelessness to health and education, . . .

In one jurisdiction after another, Boomers who once voted for Reaganomics are now engaging in what David Blankenhorn, of the Institute for American Values, calls "a debate about causes and cures," a debate about "what we are prepared to give up." They are pushing for the explicit exercise of public authority—more taxes, zoning, schools, prisons—as long as this authority moves America toward the lofty social standard that Boomers themselves have sanctified. Boomers are stirring to defend values (monogamy, thrift, abstention from drugs) that other generations do not associate with them. The leaders among Boomer blacks, once known for the Afro cut and the black-power salute, are bypassing the rusty machinery of civil-rights legislation pioneered by their elders and are preaching a strict new standard of group pride, family integrity, and community loyalty. . . .

Critics can and do call Boomers smug, narcissistic, self-righteous, intolerant, puritanical. But one commonly heard charge, that of hypocrisy, ill fits a generation that came of age resacralizing America and has kept at it. Always the distracted perfectionists, they apply first a light hand, then (once they start paying attention) a crushingly heavy one. They graze on munchies until they figure it's time to diet, and then they cover themselves with ashes and sackcloth. From Jonathan Schell to Jeremy Rifkin, Charles Murray to Shelby Steele, Steven Jobs to Steven Spielberg, Bill Bennett to Al Gore, Boomers are still doing what they have done for decades: giving America its leading visionaries and wise men— or, depending on your point of view, its preachy didacts.

It is in the shadow of such a generation that Thirteeners are having to come of age.

THIRTEENERS

As they shield their eyes with Ray-Ban Wayfarer sunglasses, and their ears with Model TCD-D3 Sony Walkmen, today's teens and twentysomethings present to Boomer eyes a splintered image of brassy looks and smooth manner, of kids growing up too tough to be cute, of kids more comfortable shopping or playing than working or studying. Ads target them as beasts of pleasure and pain who have trouble understanding words longer than one syllable, sentences longer than three words. Pop music on their Top 40 stations—heavy metal, alternative rock, rap—strikes many a Boomer ear as a rock-and-roll end game of harsh sounds, goin'-nowhere melodies, and clumsy poetry. News clips document a young-adult wasteland of academic nonperformance, political apathy, suicide pacts, date rape trials, wilding, and hate crimes.

Who are they, and what are they up to? On the job, Thirteeners are the reckless bicycle messengers, pizza drivers, yard workers, Wal-Mart shelf-stockers, health-

care trainees, and miscellaneous scavengers, hustlers, and McJobbers in the low-wage/low-benefit service economy. They're the wandering nomads of the temp world, directionless slackers, habitual nonvoters. In school they're a group of staggering diversity—not just in ethnicity but also in attitude, performance, and rewards. After graduation they're the ones with big loans who were supposed to graduate into jobs and move out of the house but didn't, and who seem to get poorer the longer they've been away from home—unlike their parents at that age, who seemed to get richer. . . .

In them lies much of the doubt, distress, and endangered dream of late twentieth-century America. As a group they aren't what older people ever wanted but rather what they themselves know they need to be: pragmatic, quick, sharp-eyed, able to step outside themselves and understand how the world really works. From the Thirteener vantage point, America's greatest need these days is to clear out the underbrush of name-calling and ideology so that simple things can work again. . . .

When they look into the future, they see a much bleaker vision than any of today's older generations ever saw in their own youth. Polls show that Thirteeners believe it will be much harder for them to get ahead than it was for their parents—and that they are overwhelmingly pessimistic about the long-term fate of their generation and nation. They sense that they're the clean-up crew, that their role in history will be sacrificial— that whatever comeuppance America has to face, they'll bear more than their share of the burden. It's a new twist, and not a happy one, on the American Dream.

Trace the life cycle to date of Americans born in 1961. They were among the first babies people took pills not to have. During the 1967 Summer of Love they were the kindergartners who paid the price for America's new divorce epidemic. In 1970 they were fourth-graders trying to learn arithmetic amid the chaos of open classrooms and New Math curricula. In 1973 they were the bell-bottomed sixth-graders who got their first real-life civics lesson watching the Watergate hearings on TV. Through the late 1970s they were the teenage mall-hoppers who spawned the Valley Girls and other flagrantly non-Boomer youth trends. In 1979 they were the graduating seniors of Carter-era malaise who registered record-low SAT scores and record-high crime and drug-abuse rates.

In 1980 they cast their first votes, mostly for Reagan, became the high-quality nineteen-year-old enlistees who began surging into the military, and arrived on campus as the smooth, get-it-done freshmen who evidenced a sudden turnaround from the intellectual arrogance and social immaturity of Boomer students. They were the college class of 1983, whose graduation coincided with the ballyhooed *A Nation at Risk* report, which warned that education was beset by "a rising tide of mediocrity." In 1985 they were the MBA grads who launched the meteoric rise in job applications to Wall Street. And in 1991 they hit age thirty just when turning "thirtysomething" (a big deal for yuppies in the 1980s) became a tired subject—and when the pretentious TV serial with that title was yanked off the air.

Like any generation, Thirteeners grew up with parents who are distributed in roughly equal measure between the two prior generations (Silent and Boom). But also like any generation, they were decisively influenced by the senior parental cohort. Much as GIs shaped the *Sputnik* 1950s for Boomers, the Silent

Generation provided the media producers, community leaders, influential educators, and rising politicians during the R-rated 1970s, the decade that most Thirteeners still regard as their childhood home.

And what did Thirteeners absorb from that generation and that era? Mostly they learned to be cynical about adults whom they perceived to be sensitive yet powerless, better at talking about issues than solving problems. . . .

From Boom to Thirteenth, America's children went from a family culture of *My Three Sons* to one of *My Two Dads*. As millions of mothers flocked into the work force, the proportion of preschoolers cared for in their own homes fell by half. For the first time, adults ranked automobiles ahead of children as necessary for "the good life." The cost of raising a child, never very worrisome when Boomers were little, suddenly became a fraught issue. Adults of fertile age doubled their rate of surgical sterilization. The legal-abortion rate grew to the point where one out of every three pregnancies was terminated. Back in 1962 half of all adults agreed that parents in bad marriages should stay together for the sake of the children. By 1980 less than a fifth agreed. America's divorce rate doubled from 1965 to 1975, just as first-born Thirteeners passed through middle childhood. . . .

From the late 1960s until the early 1980s America's pre-adolescents grasped what nurture they could through the most virulently anti-child period in modern American history. Ugly new phrases ("latchkey child," "throwaway child," and later "boomerang child") joined the sad new lexicon of youth. America's priorities lay elsewhere, as millions of kids sank into poverty, schools deteriorated, and a congeries of elected politicians set a new and distinctly child-hostile course of national overconsumption. Then, when Thirteeners were ready to enter the adult labor force, the politicians pushed every policy lever conceivable—tax codes, entitlements, public debt, unfunded liabilities, labor laws, hiring practices—to tilt the economic playing field away from the young and toward the old. The results were predictable. . . .

Welcome, Thirteeners, to contemporary American life: While older age brackets are getting richer, yours is getting poorer. Where earlier twentieth-century generations could comfortably look forward to outpacing Mom and Dad, you probably won't even be able to keep up. . . . Everywhere they look, Thirteeners see the workplace system rigged against them. As they view it, the families, schools, and training programs that could have prepared them for worthwhile careers have been allowed to rot, but the institutions that safeguard the occupational livelihood of mature workers have been maintained with full vigor. . . .

Like warriors on the eve of battle, Thirteeners face their future with a mixture of bravado and fatalism. Squared off competitively against one another, this melange of scared city kids, suburban slackers, hungry immigrants, desperate grads, and shameless hustlers is collectively coming to realize that America rewards only a select set of winners with its Dream—and that America cares little about its anonymous losers. Sizing up the odds, each Thirteener finds himself or herself essentially alone, to an extent that most elders would have difficulty comprehending. Between his own relative poverty and the affluence he desires, the Thirteener sees no intermediary signposts, no sure, step-by-step path along which society will help him, urge him, congratulate him. Instead, all he sees is an enormous obstacle, with him on one side and everything he wants on the other.

And what's that obstacle? Those damn Boomers.

THE NEW GENERATION GAP

Over the past decade Boomers have begun acting on the assumption that Thirteeners are "lost"—reachable by pleasure-pain conditioning perhaps, but closed to reason or sentiment. In the classroom Boomers instruct the young in "emotional literacy", in the military they delouse the young with "core values" training; on campus they drill the young in the vocabulary of "political correctness." The object is not to get them to understand—that would be asking too much—but to get them to behave. Back in the era of Boomers' youth, when young people did things that displeased older people—when they drank beer, drove fast, didn't study, had sex, took drugs—the nation had an intergenerational dialogue, which, if nasty, at least led to a fairly articulate discourse about values and social philosophy. Today the tone has shifted to monosyllables ("Just say no"). . . .

To date Thirteeners have seldom either rebutted their elders' accusations or pressed their own countercharges. Polls show them mostly agreeing that, yes, Boomer kids probably were a better lot, listened to better music, pursued better causes, and generally had better times on campus. So, they figure, why fight a rap they can't beat? And besides, why waste time and energy arguing? Their usual strategy, in recent years at least, has been to keep their thoughts to themselves. On campus Thirteeners chat pleasantly in P.C. lingo with their "multiculti" prof or dean and then think nothing of spoofing the faculty behind their backs (they can't be totally serious, right?) or playfully relaxing with headphones to the racist lyrics of Ice Cube or Guns N' Roses. But among friends they talk frankly about how to maneuver in a world full of self-righteous ideologues.

Every phase and arena of life has been fine, even terrific, when Boomers entered it—and a wasteland when they left. A child's world was endlessly sunny in the 1950s, scarred by family chaos in the 1970s. Most movies and TV shows were fine for adolescents in the 1960s, unfit in the 1980s. Young-adult sex meant free love in the 1970s, AIDS in the 1990s. Boomers might prefer to think of their generation as the leaders of social progress, but the facts show otherwise. Yes, the Boom is a generation of trends, *but all those trends are negative.* The eldest Boomers (those born in the middle 1940s) have had relatively low rates of social pathology and high rates of academic achievement. The youngest Boomers (born in the late 1950s) have had precisely the opposite: high pathology, low achievement.

Again and again America has gotten fed up with Boom-inspired transgressions. But after taking aim at the giant collective Boomer ego and winding up with a club to bash Boomers for all the damage they did, America has swung late, missed, and (*pow!*) hit the next bunch of saps to come walking by. Constantly stepping into post-Boom desertscapes and suffering because of it, Thirteeners see Boomers as a generation that was given everything—from a *Happy Days* present to a Tomorrowland future—and then threw it all away.

Many a Thirteener would be delighted never to read another commemorative article about Woodstock, Kent State, or the Free Speech Movement. Or to suffer through what Coupland calls "legislated nostalgia"—the celebration of supposedly great events in the life cycle of people one doesn't especially like. Thirteeners fume when they hear Boomers taking

credit for things they didn't do (starting the civil-rights movement, inventing rock-and-roll, stopping the Vietnam War) and for supposedly having been the most creative, idealistic, morally conscious youth in the history of America, if not the world. Even among Thirteeners who admire what young people did back in the sixties, workaholic, values-fixated Boomers are an object lesson in what not to become in their thirties and forties.

Put yourself in Thirteener shoes. Watching those crusaders gray in place just ahead of you—ensconced in college faculties, public-radio stations, policy foundations, and trendy rural retreats—you notice how Boomers keep redefining every test of idealism in ways guaranteed to make you fail. You're expected to muster passions against political authority you've never felt, to search for truth in places you've never found useful, to solve world problems through gestures you find absurd. As you gaze at the seamy underside of grand Boomer causes gone bust, you turn cynical. Maybe you stop caring. And the slightest lack of interest on your part is interpreted as proof of your moral blight. No matter that it was the crusaders' own self-indulgence that let the system fall apart. The "decade of greed" is *your* fault. "Compassion fatigue" is *your* fault. The "age of apathy" has *your* monosyllabic graffiti splattered all over it.

What Thirteeners want from Boomers is an apology mixed in with a little generational humility. Something like: "Hey, guys, we're sorry we ruined everything for you. Maybe we're not such a super-duper generation, and maybe we can learn something from you." Good luck. A more modest Thirteener hope is that Boomers will lighten up, look at their positive side, and find a little virtue in the "Just do it" motto written on their sneaker pumps.

Like two neighbors separated by a spite fence, Boomers and Thirteeners have grown accustomed to an uneasy adjacence. . . .

THE CONSOLATIONS OF HISTORY

Prior to the Missionaries and the Lost, America was home to three earlier pairs of generations matching the Boomer and Thirteener types, dating back to the very first Old World colonists. The experiences of these ancestral pairs give us important clues into how the attitudes and behavior of today's Boomers and Thirteeners could change over the decades ahead.

The lessons to be learned from earlier Boomerlike generations are these: Once they fully occupied midlife, they turned darkly spiritual, seeking the cerebral and the enduring over the faddishly popular. Once in control of public institutions, they stressed character and serenity of soul over process and programs. They approved of social punishments for violators of deeply held values, preaching morality and principle (which, as they grew older, became increasingly associated with age) over fun and materialism (which became increasingly associated with youth). Entering old age, they used their reputation for moral leadership to bring final closure to whatever problem America faced at the time, even at the risk of catastrophe. Whether the peers of Abraham Lincoln or of Sam Adams or of John Winthrop, they had all come of age during eras of spiritual awakening—nothing like the eras of history-bending cataclysm they all presided over as elderly priest-warriors.

History suggests that the Thirteener life-cycle experience is something else altogether. Every time, the Thirteenerlike generations started out life as risk-taking opportunists, picking their way through the social detritus left behind by their Boomerlike predecessors. And every time, reaching midlife at a time of national crisis and personal burnout, they underwent a profound personality transformation. Their risk-taking gave way to caution, their wildness and alienation turned into exhaustion and conservatism, and their nomadic individualism matured into a preference for strong community life. The same unruly rebels and adventurers who alarmed the Colonies during the 1760s later became the crusty old Patrick Henrys and George Washingtons who warned younger statesmen against gambling with the future. The same gold-chasing forty-niners and Civil War brigands whom Oliver Wendell Holmes Jr. called a generation whose "hearts were touched with fire" became the stodgy "Old Guard" Victorians of the Gilded Era. The same gin-fizz "Flaming Youth" who electrified America during the 1920s became the Norman Rockwells and Dwight Eisenhowers who calmed America during the 1950s.

All these generations repeatedly found themselves in situations that are becoming familiar to Thirteeners. When something went right, they always got less than their share of the credit; when something went wrong, they always got more than their share of the blame. In contrast, the Boomerlike generations always found a way to claim more than their share of the credit and accept less than their share of blame. Small wonder, then, that the Boom types kept stepping in and out of generational arguments.

If history tells us that the Boom-Thirteenth quarrel will worsen over the coming decade, it also suggests when and how this new generation gap could resolve itself. The experience of their like-minded ancestors suggests that once Boomers start entering old age, they will ease their attacks on Thirteeners. Once they see their values focus taking firm root in American institutions—and once their hopes are fixed on a new and more optimistic (post-Thirteenth) generation—Boomers will lose interest in the quarrel. As they enter midlife, Thirteen-

ers will likewise tire of goading Boomers. As they change their life tack from risk to caution they will quit trying to argue about Boomer goals and will focus their attention on how to achieve their own goals practically, with no more hurt than is absolutely necessary.

◆

The sense that hipness has got to be a little shopworn can lead to a cross-generational discomfort, one shared by both the baby boomers trying to stretch out the adventure of youth by driving a Jeep Wagoneer and by the twentysomethings who wonder whether they are being led by their nose rings from one bogus trend to the next.

RICHARD LACAYO, "Everybody's Hip
(And That's Not Cool)," *Time*, August 8, 1994

1993

40.

BILL CLINTON: First Inaugural Address

Two years before the 1992 presidential election, President George Bush looked invincible. He had led the successful prosecution of the Persian Gulf War and his approval ratings stood at record levels. However, with the country mired in an economic downturn and with the third-party candidacy of billionaire reformer H. Ross Perot, little-known Arkansas Governor Bill Clinton captured the presidency, winning 43 percent of the vote but decisively defeating Bush in the electoral college. On January 20, 1993, Chief Justice William Rehnquist administered the oath of office. The forty-second president of the United States, Clinton was the third youngest President in the country's history and came to office with an impressive record, but one tarnished by scandal and controversy. Born in Arkansas and educated at Georgetown, Oxford, and Yale universities, Clinton was the nation's youngest governor in 1978 when, at age thirty-two, he was elected in Arkansas. He was the first President since Franklin D. Roosevelt not to serve in the military, and his critics claimed he had dodged the draft during the Vietnam War. Clinton also had a history of sexual controversy, and during the campaign several women came forth with claims of having had extramarital affairs with him. In his First Inaugural Address, Clinton echoed John F. Kennedy's 1961 declaration that a new generation of Americans had assumed the mantle of national leadership. As the first President since the 1920s not encumbered by economic depression, war, or international Communism, Clinton was able to focus his speech on American renewal and reinvention, calling for change not "for change's sake, but change to preserve America's ideals." Clinton's Inaugural Address is reprinted in full here.

Source: *Public Papers of the Presidents of the United States,* January 20, 1993.

TODAY WE CELEBRATE the mystery of American renewal.

This ceremony is held in the depth of winter. But, by the words we speak and the faces we show the world, we force the spring.

A spring reborn in the world's oldest democracy, that brings forth the vision and courage to reinvent America.

When our founders boldly declared America's independence to the world and our purposes to the Almighty, they knew that America, to endure, would have to change.

Not change for change's sake, but change to preserve America's ideals— life, liberty, the pursuit of happiness. Though we march to the music of our time, our mission is timeless.

Each generation of Americans must define what it means to be an American.

On behalf of our nation, I salute my predecessor, President Bush, for his half-century of service to America.

And I thank the millions of men and women whose steadfastness and sacrifice triumphed over Depression, fascism, and Communism.

Today, a generation raised in the shadows of the Cold War assumes new responsibilities in a world warmed by the sunshine of freedom but threatened still by ancient hatreds and new plagues.

Raised in unrivaled prosperity, we inherit an economy that is still the world's strongest, but is weakened by business failures, stagnant wages, increasing inequality, and deep divisions among our people.

When George Washington first took the oath I have just sworn to uphold, news traveled slowly across the land by horseback and across the ocean by boat. Now, the sights and sounds of this ceremony are broadcast instantaneously to billions around the world.

Communications and commerce are global; investment is mobile; technology is almost magical; and ambition for a better life is now universal. We earn our livelihood in peaceful competition with people all across the earth.

Profound and powerful forces are shaking and remaking our world, and the urgent question of our time is whether we can make change our friend and not our enemy.

This new world has already enriched the lives of millions of Americans who are able to compete and win in it. But when most people are working harder for less; when others cannot work at all; when the cost of health care devastates families and threatens to bankrupt many of our enterprises, great and small; when fear of crime robs law-abiding citizens of their freedom; and when millions of poor children cannot even imagine the lives we are calling them to lead—we have not made change our friend.

We know we have to face hard truths and take strong steps. But we have not done so. Instead, we have drifted, and that drifting has eroded our resources, fractured our economy, and shaken our confidence.

Though our challenges are fearsome, so are our strengths. And Americans have ever been a restless, questing, hopeful people. We must bring to our task today the vision and will of those who came before us.

From our revolution, the Civil War, to the Great Depression to the civil rights movement, our people have always mustered the determination to construct from these crises the pillars of our history.

Thomas Jefferson believed that to preserve the very foundations of our nation, we would need dramatic change from time to time. Well, my fellow citizens, this is our time. Let us embrace it.

Our democracy must be not only the envy of the world but the engine of our own renewal. There is nothing wrong with America that cannot be cured by what is right with America.

And so today, we pledge an end to the era of deadlock and drift—a new season of American renewal has begun.

To renew America, we must be bold.

We must do what no generation has had to do before. We must invest more in our own people, in their jobs, in their future, and at the same time cut our massive debt. And we must do so in a world in which we must compete for every opportunity.

It will not be easy; it will require sacrifice. But it can be done, and done fairly, not choosing sacrifice for its own sake, but for our own sake. We must provide for our nation the way a family provides for its children.

Our Founders saw themselves in the light of posterity. We can do no less. Anyone who has ever watched a child's eyes wander into sleep knows what posterity is. Posterity is the world to come—the world for whom we hold our ideals, from whom we have borrowed our planet, and to whom we bear sacred responsibility.

We must do what America does best: offer more opportunity to all and demand responsibility from all.

It is time to break the bad habit of expecting something for nothing, from our government or from each other. Let us all take more responsibility, not only for ourselves and our families but for our communities and our country.

To renew America, we must revitalize our democracy.

This beautiful capital, like every capital since the dawn of civilization, is often a place of intrigue and calculation. Powerful people maneuver for position and worry endlessly about who is in and who is out, who is up and who is down, forgetting those people whose toil and sweat sends us here and pays our way.

Americans deserve better, and in this city today, there are people who want to do better. And so I say to all of us here, let us resolve to reform our politics, so that power and privilege no longer shout down the voice of the people. Let us put aside personal advantage so that we can feel the pain and see the promise of America.

Let us resolve to make our government a place for what Franklin Roosevelt called "bold, persistent experimentation," a government for our tomorrows, not our yesterdays.

Let us give this capital back to the people to whom it belongs.

To renew America, we must meet challenges abroad as well as at home. There is no longer division between what is foreign and what is domestic—the world economy, the world environment, the world AIDS crisis, the world arms race—they affect us all.

Today, as an old order passes, the new world is more free but less stable. Communism's collapse has called forth old animosities and new dangers. Clearly America must continue to lead the world we did so much to make.

While America rebuilds at home, we will not shrink from the challenges, nor fail to seize the opportunities, of this new world. Together with our friends and allies, we will work to shape change, lest it engulf us.

When our vital interests are challenged, or the will and conscience of the international community is defied, we will act—with peaceful diplomacy whenever possible, with force when necessary. The brave Americans serving our nation today in the Persian Gulf, in Somalia, and wherever else they stand are testament to our resolve.

But our greatest strength is the power of our ideas, which are still new in many lands. Across the world, we see them embraced—and we rejoice. Our hopes, our hearts, our hands, are with those on every continent who are building democracy and freedom. Their cause is America's cause.

The American people have summoned the change we celebrate today. You have raised your voices in an unmistakable chorus. You have cast your votes in historic numbers. And you have changed the face of Congress, the presidency, and the political process itself. Yes, you, my fellow Americans have forced the spring. Now, we must do the work the season demands.

To that work I now turn, with all the authority of my office. I ask the Congress to join with me. But no president, no Congress, no government, can undertake this mission alone. My fellow Americans, you, too, must play your part in our renewal. I challenge a new generation of young Americans to a season of service—to act on your idealism by helping troubled children, keeping company with those in need, reconnecting our torn communities. There is so much to be done—enough indeed for millions of others who are still young in spirit to give of themselves in service, too.

In serving, we recognize a simple but powerful truth—we need each other. And we must care for one another. Today, we do more than celebrate America; we rededicate ourselves to the very idea of America.

An idea born in revolution and renewed through two centuries of challenge. An idea tempered by the knowledge that, but for fate, we—the fortunate and the unfortunate—might have been each other. An idea ennobled by the faith that our nation can summon from its myriad diversity the deepest measure of unity. An idea infused with the conviction that America's long heroic journey must go forever upward.

And so, my fellow Americans, at the edge of the 21st century, let us begin with energy and hope, with faith and discipline, and let us work until our work is done. The scripture says, "And let us not be weary in well-doing, for in due season, we shall reap, if we faint not."

From this joyful mountaintop of celebration, we hear a call to service in the valley. We have heard the trumpets. We have changed the guard. And now, each in our way, and with God's help, we must answer the call.

Thank you and God bless you all.

———◆———

It's the economy, stupid.
> JAMES CARVILLE, campaign manager for Bill Clinton, who put up a sign with this saying on it in Clinton's campaign headquarters, emphasizing the importance of the economy as a campaign issue, 1992

41.

The Waco Crisis

By 1990 David Koresh had become the leader of the Branch Davidians, an offshoot group of the Davidian Seventh-day Adventist Church, whose compound was outside Waco, Texas. The reclusive members largely avoided contact with the outside world, but allegations of child abuse and a store of illegal weapons at their compound attracted law enforcement attention. In February 1993 agents of the Bureau of Alcohol, Tobacco, and Firearms (ATF) attempted to enforce a search warrant at the compound and to arrest Koresh. The ATF raid on the compound was followed by a gun battle that left four federal agents and five Branch Davidians dead. After a seven-week siege of the compound, Attorney General Janet Reno authorized the Federal Bureau of Investigation (FBI) to end the siege and seize the compound by force. When the FBI moved against the Branch Davidians on the morning of April 19, a fast-moving fire broke out inside the compound. When the fire was finally suppressed, some eighty Branch Davidians, including Koresh, were dead. The Waco tragedy set off a bitter public debate over who was to blame for the fiasco. Although the federal government claimed that the Branch Davidians started the fire themselves, critics of the government contended that tear gas canisters that the FBI had shot into the compound actually started the fire. Furthermore, many government critics called for Reno's resignation on the charge of incompetence. Paradoxically, when Reno immediately assumed responsibility for the disaster, her public approval ratings went up. The public seemed more impressed by Reno's willingness to shoulder responsibility than by her misjudgments in the effort to end the siege. She ultimately served for another seven and a half years as attorney general.

Source: *National Review*, May 10, 1993, "Conflagration."

SHORTLY AFTER the Waco cult compound had been consumed by fire, Attorney General Janet Reno accepted responsibility for the decision to attack, which she conceded had been an error. That probably represented the general public impression as we went to press. Not surprisingly. It appears that about 80 people died in the fire, including David Koresh, his "wives," and 24 children—a horrible human tragedy by any standard. But how was it brought about?

The initial raid on the compound last February remains a mystery. The justification then given by the Bureau of Alcohol, Tobacco, and Firearms was that the cult was suspected of converting legal semi-automatic weapons into illegal automatic ones. That falls considerably short of murder or robbery, but doubtless it looked ominous. Why, then, did the authorities, federal or local, not arrest Koresh on one of his frequent visits outside the compound? Why was the first step to

Fire engulfs the Branch Davidian compound, near Waco, Texas, April 19, 1993.

go in with all guns blazing? And what was the legal underpinning for this raid?

If there are good answers to these questions, we have yet to hear them. For practical purposes, however, they became moot when Koresh and his followers opened fire, killed four federal officials, and resisted an official siege. From that point, the government had little alternative to arresting Koresh and his accomplices by whatever means necessary. It therefore imposed a siege: cutting off electricity and communications, shining bright lights around the clock, blaring rock music and other loud noises. And when these did not draw the cultists out, the FBI mounted a partial raid, lobbing tear-gas into the compound and breaching its walls. The cult members, thinking this an all-out assault, set fire to their haven with themselves and their children inside. It is a horrible irony that a raid, intended to prevent mass suicide and child abuse, should have led to the death of 24 children in a collective frenzy.

By the siege's end Koresh and his followers were like hijackers who cannot escape but who can murder their hostages (in this case, their own children, but perhaps some adult outsiders too). Seeking the release of hostages by attacking their captors always carries a high risk. If it fails, as it failed tragically here, onlookers think it a mistake. But mounting a siege indefinitely may fail too; the mass suicide at Jonestown was uncoerced. And an assault carried out differently—with greater speed and ruthlessness—might well have succeeded.

The lesson of this episode is not that the use of force was wrong in itself, but that at every stage the government acted incompetently. Its initial raid was overdone and botched; its siege was abandoned, apparently for no good reason; and a slow-motion assault, meant to increase the pressure on cult members, persuaded them that this was the long-awaited Götterdämmerung, giving them both the incentive and the chance to commit mass suicide. If Miss Reno is willing to admit error, let her own up to this catalogue. But we weaken ourselves in the battle against cults of all kinds—reli- gious, political, and terrorist—if we con- clude that force is always too risky, even in surer hands.

42.

Carol Rigolot: Books in an Era of Television

Since the 1940s, no communications medium has had a greater impact on American life than television. Virtually every feature of modern life, from presidential politics to sports to music to education, has been profoundly shaped by television's impact on American society. For example, television played a critical role in the success of the Civil Rights Movement by bringing images of racial violence and injustice into the living rooms of millions of Americans. It played an equally large role in shaping public opinion during the Vietnam War, when images of burning villages and the chaos of guerrilla war helped turn the American public against the war. And it has become in many ways the national town hall, where Americans vicariously share experiences through watching television together. But many observers fear that we may have lost as much as has been gained from television. Book enthusiasts, in particular, warn that television's ubiquitous presence in American life threatens the quantity and quality of reading in the United States. Carol Rigolot, the executive director of the Humanities Council at Princeton University, argues that reading remains as important now as ever for a person to navigate the challenges of modern life. Reprinted below is an address Rigolot delivered to gifted high school students in Tulsa, Oklahoma, in April 1993.

Source: *Vital Speeches of the Day*, September 15, 1993.

A flippant commentator once quipped that "This will never be a civilized coun- try until we expend more money for books than we do for chewing gum." In presenting book awards tonight we may be taking one step in that direction and chalking up a small victory for civiliza- tion. Probably civilization needs all the help it can get.

My Princeton colleague, Alvin Kernan, has recently written a very bleak book called *The Death of Literature* in which he argues that reading has become increas- ingly marginal in a society dominated by television, movies, and videotapes. Prof. Kernan cites a survey according to which 60 percent of all adult Americans have never read a book, while most of the oth- ers read only one book a year. So you can understand why I feel heartened to be part of your book awards ceremony. But I also wonder what you will do with your Princeton prize books. What could en- tice you to read them when there are so many tempting demands on your time? Why would *anybody* read books in a civi- lization of telephones, boom boxes, VCRs, and Nintendo?

When I asked my 14-year-old daughter that question, she reflected for a moment and then replied: "The great thing about books is that they have no commercials!" But are there other qualities? Some of you may remember an episode in *Winnie the Pooh* where Winnie, who loves to eat, indulges in so much honey and condensed milk down in Rabbit's hole that he becomes too large to squeeze back out. He finds himself utterly stuck, with his head outside and his feet inside. Realizing disconsolately that he will have to stay there until he loses weight, he begs of Christopher Robin:

> "Would you read a sustaining Book, such as would help and comfort a Wedged Bear in Great Tightness."

And indeed "for a week Christopher Robin read that sort of book at the North end of Pooh." But Milne doesn't tell us exactly what he means by a Sustaining Book—unless it's *Winnie the Pooh* itself! Not all important or influential books would make us feel good if we were wedged in a rabbit hole. In fact, many would not console us at all, as Franz Kafka, the first existentialist writer, has pointed out.

When Kafka was 20 years old he wondered in a letter if we read books to be happy. And he answered his own question by declaring:

> "Good God, we would also be happy if we had no books, and such books as make us happy we could, if need be, write ourselves."

What we need, Kafka continued,

> "are those books which [. . .] distress us deeply, like the death of one we love better than ourselves, like suicide. A book must be an ice-axe," he concluded, "to break the sea frozen inside us."

When we read Kafka's letter, we understand why his own stories are so disturbing to read! They are all the things he suggests: sharp like ice picks, haunting like grief. Winnie the Pooh would probably not choose Kafka as a Sustaining Book, and yet Kafka is one of the most important authors ever to have written, and none of *us* would want to grow up without having walked around inside his world. Kafka makes us feel new—even if he doesn't necessarily make us feel good. And no one should miss the experience of reading *The Metamorphosis*.

If reading doesn't automatically bring us pleasure, does it have another utility? Sometimes you hear it argued that reading can make us better people, that if people can only be *exposed* to artistic beauty and truth, they will become moral, or, put differently, that if we know what is good, we will *be* good.

This argument is appealing at first glance, but probably not true. Leon Botstein, the president of Bard College, has vigorously attacked it, citing the atrocities that have been committed across time by cultured individuals (including the Nazis). In Botstein's words, literature "is about criticism and critical inquiry" (*The New Republic,* February 11, 1985). It forces us to question, to change, to argue, and to dispute. If literature encourages people to question values, it may sometimes be disruptive to society.

Literature may also be dangerous to individuals. Probably all of us here remember our parents nagging us to turn off the television and read instead. What our parents may not have realized is that reading has not always been considered healthy! In fact, when the printing press was first invented, reading was feared in the same way that too much television is today. Before then, people lived in an oral culture; they listened to stories in groups, or in church, or on the public square. Once books were widely available and could be taken home and read privately, reading became an individual rather than a communal activity. This raised agitated concern about the dangers of solitary reading. In *Don Quixote,* for example, there is a long scene describing the perils of reading alone; people feared that readers might identify so closely with the passions of the characters that they would be tempted to fall in love or commit a crime. Or they might simply go crazy, like Don Quixote himself. This caused lots of worry in the 16th and 17th centuries.

The great scientific thinker, Francis Bacon, warned that too much study could lead to sloth. And for a long time people also feared that reading would damage public health. In 1795 a tract listed the physical consequences of excessive reading:

> "susceptibility to colds, headaches, weakening of the eyes, heat rashes, gut, arthritis, hemorrhoids, asthma, apoplexy, pulmonary disease, indigestion, blocking of the bowels, nervous disorder, migraines, epilepsy, hypochondria, and melancholy."

If reading is so threatening to our mental and physical welfare, why did our parents push it on us? There must be some reasons!

One of the courses Princeton students like best is the "great books" sequence that begins in September with *The Odyssey* and arrives in April at Dostoevsky at the pace of about one masterpiece a week. In the evaluation forms at the end of each semester, students almost always give the authors a grade of 4.8 or 4.9 out of 5. (I like to imagine Homer, Sophocles and Goethe up in Heaven worrying about their evaluations from young American readers!) What is the appeal of these books for contemporary students? What captures their admiration?

I think the answers have to do with the relationship between life and art. The American photographer Aaron Siskind has said that when we look at the world, we "see what we have learned to believe is there, what we have been conditioned to expect." The best example I know of this insight comes from astronomy. My colleagues in astrophysics tell me that in 1054 A.D. the Crab Supernova exploded in the sky before it turned into a black hole. Apparently, for several weeks the night sky was so bright that you could walk around outdoors by the light of this gigantic exploding star. The Chinese saw and recorded the phenomenon. There are some signs that Mesoamericans may also have observed it. But in all of Europe there is no trace that anyone noticed the explosion, for medieval Europeans had no concepts to allow them to assimilate what they were seeing. They believed, following Aristotle, that the heavens were immutable. Since it would be impossible for anything new to occur in the sky, it appears that they simply did not see this otherwise extraordinary change up above.

This incident suggests to me the enormous importance of having minds that are conditioned to look for—and therefore to see—the widest variety of phenomena, ideas, opinions, emotions and possibilities. You may know the Peanuts cartoon where Charlie Brown asks what Snoopy's dream girl would look like. The dog replies: "She'd have round ears like two cookies, big eyes like two more cookies and a nose like a cookie. . ." Obviously Snoopy is projecting onto his dream girl the narrow idea of what he wants to see. If Snoopy could read books, he would have a larger sense of what's possible. He would add a whole gallery of new people to his world, with different kinds of ears, eyes, noses and identities. This would give him more options and a better chance of finding a sweetheart! As we all know, one of the signs of becoming educated is to understand that our options are increasing. Stories can open our imaginations to models and possibilities beyond the ones we know, broadening our imprisoning and simplistic categories. Or they can offer paradigms or models of human experiences, helping us rehearse in advance the predictable patterns and events of life (both the crises and the glories).

One of the ways that all of us try to make sense of our lives is to look back and narrate a coherent autobiography. We structure the events and relationships and feelings into some order with patterns and causes and effects. The more patterns we have at our disposal, the better chance we have of putting our experiences into a wider framework and of coping with mysteries and crises. Stories can also offer perspective on gender roles, generational tensions, injustice, the anguish of decisions, the pain of human relationships. And literature gives us a language in which to articulate our feelings and dilemmas, so we are not afraid of our feelings or trapped by them.

One day, I was talking to a young Polish artist, exiled in the United States, whose views seemed to me particularly insightful. As a citizen of a country that has known occupation and hardship, Ewa believes keenly that the most dangerous thing that can happen to any people is to seek simple solutions to complex issues—to simplify or polarize the world into Manichaean dualities and to miss the fact that reality is actually plural and complex. One of the things she finds most striking in the United States is the number of Americans who crack under strain because we do have sufficient perspective of our defeats; we do not have a wide enough context to realize that temporary set-backs can be overcome in other ways or that good can come from defeat. She believes that we do not always

have the resilience necessary to surmount crises. Reading is one way of discovering plurality, ambiguity, and complexity.

You all know that art imitates life; every television sitcom tries to seem like real life. But I am also convinced that life imitates art. This in my view is the most enriching realization gained from a sojourn among books, and the most serious argument for reading good books. We often, even unconsciously, model aspects of our lives on artistic representations of other lives. We do this when we imitate the Marlboro man or the Pepsi generation: it's the basic tenet of advertising. My students tell me that in *Sports Illustrated* the best looking males are called Adonis for Greek statues. But those are hollow, one-dimensional models. In the cultural baggage of our civilization, there are richer models or patterns. There are individuals in literature whose experience is both a mirror and a model of human dilemmas and quests.

The more you read in the years ahead, the more models you will have. When you find yourself in baffling situations, you will be better able to cope if you can recognize that your dilemma has already been lived—by Ophelia or Antigone or Don Quixote or Aeneas or Dido or Heathcliff. It is not that I wish you the fates of any of these characters, but I am quite convinced that books and paintings enable us to recognize precedents and to put our strivings in a larger context. At certain crucial moments in our lives we surprise ourselves undergoing experiences that we recognize; we become aware of a precedent, a pattern that has been lived by other characters. The awareness of these patterns can place our individual grapplings in a wider context. For the rest of your lives, you will recognize events and scenes that you have read in books.

Reading can also provide some practical skills, besides the more spiritual ones I've described so far. Those of you who are now in high school will have to adjust, in the years after 2001, to things the rest of us cannot even imagine. But all trends suggest that we are evolving from an industrial to an information society, where every occupation will rely on access to data. It is said that the amount of information in the world's libraries and computers used to double every ten years. Now the doubling time has gone down to eight years and is continuing to shrink. There is something terrifying about this statistic; it also underscores the reading and writing skills that will be necessary to sift out and communicate what's valuable. An MIT professor has said that "We are working ourselves out of the manufacturing business and into the thinking business." Employers will need people who can think.

A second trend of our society is the change in outlook from short-term gains to longer-term strategies. This will require employees and citizens who can see issues in their broadest context, who can conceive of multiple alternatives and devise flexible strategies. These are the same capacities we practice when we analyze texts, in which there is not one solution, but rather a network of interpretations from several points of view. Reading calls forth our powers of imagination, comprehension and analysis; it doesn't ask for—or provide—quick and easy solutions.

Finally, a third trend signalled by futurists is that we are becoming an increasingly global economy and culture. People who understand foreign cultures will be the best equipped to succeed in a global economy. Harrison Salisbury, long-time *New York Times* foreign correspondent in China and Russia relates compellingly in his memoirs that the intimate knowledge of the Soviet Union that served him so well as a journalist and commentator on Russian affairs came much more from his reading of Chekhov and Dostoevsky than from any diplomatic communiqués or briefings. The same applies to any foreign or regional culture and to our capacity to enter into new worlds and cultures.

In fact, I am quite convinced that to understand Oklahoma, I would be better off reading literature of the region rather than the guidebooks that were graciously sent to me by the Tulsa Visitor's bureau. If any of you have suggestions of books I should be reading about your region, I hope you will give them to me, so I can read along with you. In the meantime, congratulations on your many successes so far and best wishes for all the good things that lie ahead.

◆

When I go out socially in Washington, I'm careful not to embarrass my dinner companions by asking what they have read lately. Instead I say, 'I suppose you don't have much time to read books nowadays.'
DANIEL BOORSTIN, commenting on the decline in reading, quoted in *The Los Angeles Times Magazine*, September 22, 1991

186

43.

GEORGE F. WILL: Speech Codes on Campus

In the years following the Civil Rights and women's liberation movements of the 1960s and 1970s, the number of female and minority students on college campuses soared. Once largely the preserve of white men, American universities increasingly came to resemble the nation's population as a whole. However, the affirmative action programs that in part made possible the dramatic demographic change on college campuses fell under sharp attack in the 1980s and 1990s. Critics maintained that affirmative action violated white men's rights by giving women and minorities special advantages in the admissions process. The sometimes bitter nature of the debate over affirmative action led many college administrators to pass speech codes that protected women and minorities from verbal harassment. A second controversy soon emerged, however, over the issue of how one defines "harassment," and over whether universities should regulate free speech. In the essay below, political commentator George Will, an influential conservative, asserts that campus speech codes violate the constitutional right to freedom of speech.

Source: *Newsweek*, May 31, 1993, "Compassion on Campus."

WITH COMMENCEMENT season comes a summer respite from attacks on freedom of speech on campuses. Consider the University of Pennsylvania, whose recently resigned president, Sheldon Hackney, is heading for Washington to chair the National Endowment for the Humanities.

Penn's thought police are persecuting a Jewish student because late one night, when he was trying to study and a black sorority group was being noisy beneath his window, he shouted, "Will you water buffaloes get out of here?" The Hebrew word *behama*, meaning water oxen, is a slang put-down meaning dolt. The blacks say their feelings were hurt and—therefore?—he is guilty of "racial harassment." When some other blacks at Penn were offended by a conservative columnist in the student newspaper, they met delivery trucks early one morning and dumped 14,000 copies into the trash bins. Hackney gave this cringingly neutral description of this Brownshirt behavior: the papers "were removed from their regular distribution points." He said two important values, "diversity" and "open expression," needed to be balanced.

Penn State feminists stole 6,000 copies of a conservative paper. Dartmouth blacks collected as "litter" a conservative newspaper distributed in dorms. At Penn, Penn State, Dartmouth and elsewhere blacks, feminists, homosexuals and various ethnic groups are asserting a right not to be annoyed or have their feelings hurt by words.

The menace of this "right" is the subject of Jonathan Rauch's elegant new book, "Kindly Inquisitors: The New Attacks on Free Thought." The right not to be offended, far from promoting civility on campus, is, he says, provoking acrimonious contests to see who can claim to be most, and most frequently, offended, and to decide which groups' being offended matters. Special solicitude is shown to "historically oppressed classes"—basically, everyone except white heterosexual males. Being offended has become a political agenda, even a full-time vocation for some people. They are "thought vigilantes," on the prowl to punish people guilty of thinking proscribed thoughts. So some professors have stopped teaching courses on sensitive subjects (race, ethnicity, sexuality) and some professors tape their classes in case they must defend themselves against a career-threatening charge of "insensitivity."

Religious fundamentalists try to compel "equal time" in school curricula for creationism and evolution. But they are less of a threat than liberals trying to mandate "fairness" for dotty ideas that make some "victim groups" feel good—ideas such as that Greek culture came from Black Africa, or that Iroquois ideas were important to the making of the Constitution.

Speech codes are wielded by inquisitors sniffing for punishable utterances. But Rauch shows the difficulty of writing a rule to proscribe, say, the word "nigger": "Persons shall not use the word 'nigger' in direct conversation with black persons, unless the word is being used demonstratively or illustratively or both parties to the conversation are black or dark-skinned or the intentions are friendly as evinced by signs and gestures attesting to the conversation's mutual congeniality such as smiles, handshakes or affectionate language . . . Nothing in these rules shall be interpreted as proscribing *Huckleberry Finn* except when it is

read aloud to a black person or persons in a taunting or confrontational manner, as evinced by undue emphasis on words such as 'nigger,' 'slave,' 'owner,' or when it is read in other circumstances which a reasonable person might regard as prejudicial and offensive . . ."

That is amusing. The following is not.

At the University of Michigan a student was punished for saying in a classroom discussion that homosexuality is a disease treatable with therapy. Expression of that idea supposedly violated the prohibition of speech that "victimizes" people on the basis of "sexual orientation." At Southern Methodist University a student was sentenced to 30 hours of community service with minority organizations. His crimes included singing "We Shall Overcome" in a sarcastic manner. University of Connecticut rules made punishable "inappropriately directed laughter" and "conspicuous exclusion [of another person] from conversation." At the University of Wisconsin, a speech code forbade utterances that "demean" anyone's "race, sex, religion, color, creed, disability, sexual orientation, national origin, ancestry or age," or which created "an intimidating, hostile or demeaning environment for education." So a student was suspended for telling an Asian-American that "It's people like you—that's the reason this country is screwed up."

Wisconsin's code was declared unconstitutional, as was Michigan's, the guidelines for which gave this example of a punishable offense: "A male student makes remarks in a class like 'Women just aren't as good in this field as men,' thus creating a hostile learning atmosphere for female classmates." The guidelines also said, in Orwellian language, that in order to have "open and vigorous" classroom discussion, students must be protected from "feeling harassed or intimidated." So people could silence others by announcing that they were "feeling" a hostile environment.

Much mischief

But not all sensibilities are equally protected. UCLA suspended a student editor for a cartoon making fun of affirmative action. Then Cal State Northridge disciplined an editor for criticizing UCLA. No one would have been punished for calling critics of affirmative action Neanderthals. When Hackney was criticized for his invertebrate response to the destruction of 14,000 newspapers, a former university president offered this limp defense of him: "Penn is not a public university and is thus not technically bound by the Bill of Rights."

Contemporary liberalism's core value is "compassion." On campuses that means the prevention of the pain caused to "historically oppressed classes" by words they dislike. Many academics, because of their shrill and loopy politics (which permeates and trivializes their scholarship), are irrelevant to the nation's political conversation. So they concentrate on turning their campuses into little lagoons of enforced orthodoxy and policed "sensitivity." They are making much mischief, and many conservatives.

◆

The most stringent protection of free speech would not protect a man in falsely shouting fire in a theater and causing a panic.
OLIVER WENDELL HOLMES, JR., Opinion of the U.S. Supreme Court in *Schenck* v. *U.S.*, 1919, which established that free speech may be abridged when it constitutes a "clear and present" danger

44.

HILLARY CLINTON: Attempts at Health Care Reform

During the 1992 presidential campaign, Governor Bill Clinton of Arkansas promised voters that if they elected him, they would get "two for the price of one." He was speaking of his wife, Hillary, who would become the most politically influential First Lady in history. She would also become one of the most controversial. In 1993 President Clinton appointed his wife to serve as the chairperson of his national task force on health care reform, which caused some consternation. First, critics argued that it was inappropriate for a First Lady to head a major government task force because unlike any other appointee, she could not be fired. Second, many complained that because her task force conducted secret deliberations which no member of the press was allowed to observe, the task force itself was inherently undemocratic. Third, critics argued that Hillary Clinton's views on health care were far to the left of the national mainstream and that her policy proposals would "socialize" a significant percentage of the American economy. In the speech excerpted below, Hillary Clinton (who would be elected to the U.S. Senate from New York in 2000) responded to her critics. In the end, however, criticism of the First Lady and the goals of her task force proved overwhelming. In early 1994 the Democrat-controlled Congress chose not to put Clinton's health care plan to a vote because it lacked the support necessary for passage and they did not want an embarrassing defeat for the President. Furthermore, Republican victories in the 1994 midterm elections guaranteed that Clinton's health care plan would never win congressional passage. The following address, excerpted below, was delivered to the American Medical Association in Chicago, Illinois, in June 1993.

Source: *Vital Speeches of the Day*, July 15, 1993.

ALL OF US respond to children. We want to nurture them so they can dream the dreams that free and healthy children should have. This is our primary responsibility as adults. And it is our primary responsibility as a government. We should stand behind families, teachers and others who work with the young, so that we can enable them to meet their own needs by becoming self-sufficient and responsible so that they, in turn, will be able to meet their families and their own children's needs.

When I was growing up, not far from where we are today, this seemed an easier task. There seemed to be more strong families. There seemed to be safer neighborhoods. There seemed to be an outlook for caring and cooperation among adults that stood for and behind children. I remember so well my father saying to me that if you get in trouble at school, you get in trouble at home—no questions asked—because there was this sense among the adult community that all of them, from my child's perspective, were involved in helping their own and others' children.

Much has changed since those days. We have lost some of the hope and optimism of that earlier time. Today, we too often meet our greatest challenges, whether it is the raising of children or reforming the health care system, with a sense that our problems have grown too large and unmanageable. And I don't need to tell you that kind of attitude begins to undermine one's sense of hope, optimism, and even competence.

We know now—and you know better than I—that over the last decade our health care system has been under extraordinary stress. It is one of the many institutions in our society that has experienced such stress. That stress has begun to break down many of the relationships that should stand at the core of the health care system. That breakdown has, in turn, undermined your profession in many ways, changing the nature of and the rewards of practicing medicine.

Most doctors and other health care professionals choose careers in health and medicine because they want to help people. But too often because our system isn't working and we haven't taken full responsibility for fixing it, that motive is clouded by perceptions that doctors aren't the same as they used to be. They're not really doing what they used to do. They don't really care like they once did. . . .

As you know, the President is in the process of finalizing his proposal for health care reform, and I am grateful to speak with you about the process and where it is today and where it is going. I had originally hoped to join you at your meeting in March in Washington, D.C. And I, again, want to apologize for my absence. I very much appreciated Vice President Gore attending for me, and I also appreciated the kind words from

your executive officials on behalf of the entire association because of my absence.

My father was ill and I spent several weeks with him in the hospital before he died. During his hospitalization at St. Vincent's Hospital in Little Rock, Arkansas, I witnessed firsthand the courage and commitment of health care professionals, both directly and indirectly. I will always appreciate the sensitivity and the skills they showed, not just in caring for my father, not just in caring for his family—which, as you know, often needs as much care as the patient, but in caring for the many others whose names I will never know. I know that some of you worry about what the impact of health care reform will be on your profession and on your practice. Let me say from the start, if I read only what the newspapers have said about what we are doing in our plan, I'd probably be a little afraid myself, too, because it is very difficult to get out what is going on in such a complex process.

But the simple fact is this: The President has asked all of us, representatives of the AMA, of every other element of the health care system, as well as the administration, to work on making changes where they are needed, to keeping and improving those things that work, and to preserving and conserving the best parts of our system as we try to improve and change those that are not.

This system is not working as well as it did, or as well as it could—for you, for the private sector, for the public or for the nation. The one area that is so important to be understood on a macronational level is how our failure to deal with the health care system and its financial demands is at the center of our problems financially in Washington. Because we cannot control health care costs and become further and further behind in our efforts to do so, we find our economy, and particularly the federal budget, under increasing pressure.

Just as it would be irresponsible, therefore, to change what is working in the health care system, it is equally irresponsible for us not to fix what we know is no longer working. So let us start with some basic principles that are remarkably like the ones that you have adopted in your statements, and in particularly in Health Assess America. We must guarantee all Americans access to a comprehensive package of benefits, no matter where they work, where they live, or whether they have ever been sick before. If we do not reach universal access, we cannot deal with our other problems.

And that is a point that you understand that you have to help the rest of the country understand—that until we do provide security for every American when it comes to health care, we cannot fix what is wrong with the health care system. Secondly, we do have to control costs. How we do that is one of the great challenges in this system, but one thing we can all agree on is that we have to cut down on the paperwork and reduce the bureaucracy in both the public and private sectors.

We also have to be sure that when we look at costs, we look at it not just from a financial perspective, but also from a human perspective. I remember sitting in the family waiting area of St. Vincent's, talking to a number of my physician friends who stopped by to see how we were doing. And one day, one of my friends told me that, every day, he discharges patients who need medication to stabilize a condition. And at least once a day, he knows there is a patient who will not be able to afford the prescription drugs he has prescribed, with the result that that patient may decide not to fill the prescription when the hospital supply runs out. Or that patient may decide

that even though the doctor told him to take three pills a day, he'll just take one a day so it can be stretched further.

And even though St. Vincent's has created a fund to try to help support the needs of patients who cannot afford prescriptions, there's not enough to go around, and so every day there is someone who my friend knows and you know will be back in the hospital because of their inability either to afford the care that is required after they leave, or because they try to cut the corners on it, with the net result that then you and I will pay more for that person who is back in the hospital than we would have if we had taken a sensible approach toward what the real costs in the medical system are. That is why we will try, for example, to include prescription drugs in the comprehensive benefit package for all Americans, including those over 65, through Medicare.

We believe that if we help control costs up front, we will save costs on the back end. That is a principle that runs through our proposal and which each of you knows from firsthand experience is more likely to be efficient in both human and financial terms. We will also preserve what is best in the American health care system today.

We have looked at every other system in the world. We have tried to talk to every expert whom we can find to describe how any other country tries to provide health care. And we have concluded that what is needed is an American solution for an American problem by creating an American health care system that works for America. And two of the principles that underlie that American solution are quality and choice.

We want to ensure and enhance quality. And in order to do that, we're going to have to make some changes, and you know that. We cannot, for example, promise to really achieve universal access if we do not expand our supply of primary care physicians, and we must do that. And you will have to help us determine the best way to go about achieving that goal. . . .

I know that many of you feel that as doctors you are under siege in the current system. And I think there is cause for you to believe that, because we are witnessing a disturbing assault on the doctor/patient relationship. More and more employers are buying into managed care plans that force employees to choose from a specific pool of doctors. And too often, even when a doctor is willing to join a new plan to maintain his relationship with patients, he, or she I should say, is frozen out.

What we want to see is a system in which the employer does not make the choice as to what plan is available for the employee, the employee makes that choice for him or herself. But if we do not change and if the present pattern continues, as it will if we do not act quickly, the art of practicing medicine will be forever transformed. Gone will be the patients treasured privilege to choose his or her doctor. Gone will be the close trusting bonds built up between physicians and patients over the years. Gone will be the security of knowing you can switch jobs and still visit your longtime internist or pediatrician or OB/GYN.

We cannot afford to let that happen. But the erosion of the doctor/patient relationship is only one piece of the problem. Another piece is the role that insurance companies have come to play and the role that the government has come to play along with them in second-guessing medical decisions.

I can understand how many of you must feel. When instead of being trusted for your expertise, you're expected to call an 800 number and get approval for even basic medical procedures from a total stranger.

Frankly, despite my best efforts of the last month to understand every aspect of the health care system, it is and remains a mystery to me how a person sitting at a computer in some air-conditioned office thousands of miles away can make a judgment about what should or shouldn't happen at a patient's bedside in Illinois or Georgia or California. The result of this excessive oversight, this peering over all of your shoulder's is a system of backward incentives. It rewards providers for over prescribing, overtesting, and generally overdoing. And worse, it punishes doctors who show proper restraint and exercise their professional judgment in ways that those sitting at the computers disagree with. . . .

Now, adding to these difficulties doctors and hospitals and nurses, particularly, are being buried under an avalanche of paperwork. There are mountains of forms, mountains of rules, mountains of hours spent on administrative minutiae instead of caring for the sick. Where, you might ask yourself, did all this bureaucracy come from? And the short answer is, basically, everywhere.

There are forms to ensure appropriate care for the sick and the dying; forms to guard against unnecessary tests and procedures. And from each insurance company and government agency there are forms to record the decisions of doctors and nurses. I remember going to Boston and having a physician bring into a hearing I held there a stack of forms his office is required to fill out. And he held up a Medicare form and next to it he held up an insurance company form. And he said that they are the same forms that ask the same questions, but the insurance company form will not be accepted by the government, and the government form will not be accepted by the insurance company. And the insurance company basically took the government form, changed the title to call it by its own name and required them to have it filled out. That was the tip of the iceberg.

One nurse told me that she entered the profession because she wanted to care for people. She said that if she had wanted to be an accountant, she would have gone to work for an accounting company instead. But she, like many other nurses, and as you know so well, many of the people in your offices now, are required to be bookkeepers and accountants, not clinicians, not caregivers.

The latest statistic I have seen is that for every doctor a hospital hires, four new administrative staff are hired. And that in the average doctor's office 80 hours a month is now spent on administration. That is not time spent with a patient recovering from bypass surgery or with a child or teenager who needs a checkup and maybe a little extra TLC time of listening and counseling, and certainly not spent with a patient who has to run in quickly for some kind of an emergency.

Blanketing an entire profession with rules aimed at catching those who are not living up to their professional standards does not improve quality. What we need is a new bargain. We need to remove from the vast majority of physicians these unnecessary, repetitive, often even unread forms and instead substitute for what they were attempting to do—more discipline, more peer review, more careful scrutiny of your colleagues. You are the ones who can tell better than I or better than some bureaucrat whether the quality of medicine that is being practiced in your clinic, in your hospital, is what you would want for yourself and your family.

Let us remove the kind of micromanagement and regulation that has not improved quality and has wasted billions of dollars, but then you have to help us substitute for it, a system that the patients of this country, the public of this country, the decision-makers of this country can have confidence in. Now, I know there are legal obstacles for your being able to do that, and we are looking very closely at how we can remove those so that you can be part of creating a new solution in which everyone, including yourself, can believe in.

In every private conversation I've had with a physician, whether it's someone I knew from St. Vincent's or someone I had just met, I have asked: Tell me, have you ever practiced with or around someone you did not think was living up to your standards? And, invariably, the answer is, well, yes, I remember in my training; well, yes, I remember this emergency room work I used to do; yes, I remember in the hospital when so-and-so had that problem. And I've said, do you believe enough was done by the profession to deal with that problem and to eliminate it? And, invariably, no matter who the doctor is, I've been told, no, I don't.

We want you to have the chance so that in the future you can say, yes, I do believe we've been dealing with our problems. It is not something we should leave for the government, and, certainly, we cannot leave it to the patient. That is the new kind of relationship I think that we need to have.

Finally, if we do not, as I said earlier, provide universal coverage, we cannot do any of what I have just been speaking about because we cannot fulfill our basic commitment, you as physicians, us as a society, that we will care for one another. It should no longer be left to the individual doctor to decide to probe his conscience before determining whether to treat a needy patient. I cannot tell you what it is like for me to travel around to hcar stories from doctors and patients that are right on point.

But the most poignant [story] that I tell because it struck me so personally was of the woman with no insurance; working for a company in New Orleans; had worked there for a number of years; tried to take good care of herself; went for the annual physical every year; and I sat with her on a folding chair in the loading dock of her company along with others—all of whom were uninsured; all of whom had worked numbers of years—while she told me at her last physical her doctor had found a lump in her breast and referred her to a surgeon. And the surgeon told her that if she had insurance, he would have biopsied it but because she did not he would watch it.

I don't think you have to be a woman to feel what I felt when the woman told me that story. And I don't think you have to be a physician to feel what you felt when you heard that story. We need to create a system in which no one ever has to say that for good cause or bad, and no one has to hear it ever again.

If we move toward universal coverage, so therefore everyone has a payment stream behind them to be able to come into your office, to be able to come into the hospital, and you will again be able to make decisions that should be made with clinical autonomy, with professional judgment. And we intend to try to give you the time and free you up from other conditions to be able to do that. . . .

Time and again, groups, individuals, and particularly the government, has walked up to trying to reform health care and then walked away.

There's enough blame to go around, every kind of political stripes can be included, but the point now is that we could have done something about health care reform 20 years ago and solved our problems for millions of dollars, and we walked away. Later we could have done something and solved our problems for hundreds of millions, and we walked away.

After 20 years with rate of medical inflation going up and with all of the problems you know so well, it is a harder and more difficult solution that confronts us. But I believe that if one looks at what is at stake, we are not talking just about reforming the way we finance health care, we are not talking just about the particulars of how we deliver health care, we are talking about creating a new sense of community and caring in this country in which we once again value your contribution, value the dignity of all people.

How many more meetings do we need? How many alerts? How many more plans? How many more brochures? The time has come for all of us, not just with respect to health care, but with respect to all of the difficulties our country faces to stop walking away and to start stepping up and taking responsibility. We are supposed to be the ones to lead for our children and our grandchildren. And the way we have behaved in the last years, we have run away and abdicated that responsibility. And at the core of the human experience is responsibility for children to leave them a better world than the one we found.

We can do that with health care. We can make a difference now that will be a legacy for all of you. We can once again give you the confidence to say to your grandsons and granddaughters, yes, do go into medicine; yes, it is the most rewarding profession there is.

So let's celebrate your profession by improving health care. Let's celebrate our children by reforming this system. Let's come together not as liberals or conservatives or Republicans or Democrats, but as Americans who want the best for their country and know we can no longer wait to get about the business of providing it.

Thank you all very much.

Comprising three-by-six-foot panels commemorating loved ones who had died as a result of AIDS (acquired immunodeficiency syndrome), the NAMES Project AIDS Memorial Quilt, displayed here on the Mall in Washington, D.C., in October 1987, became a powerful symbol of the tragic AIDS epidemic that emerged in the 1980s and claimed more than twenty million lives worldwide by the turn of the century.

SCIENCE, MEDICINE, AND TECHNOLOGY

By the late 1990s the use of go-anywhere, talk-anywhere cellular phones had skyrocketed and become ubiquitous in American towns and cities, such as Chicago, where this man talks on a relatively early model in March 1996.

The Palm "handheld" (below) was introduced in 1997. Handheld computers, known as personal digital assistants (PDAs), could carry information and connect to personal computers. PDAs quickly grew in popularity and new software followed.

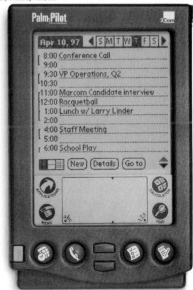

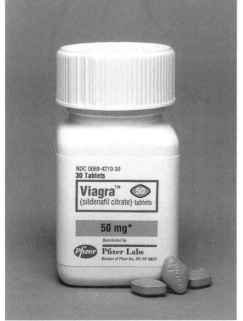

In 1998 Pfizer, Inc., introduced Viagra (left), a prescription drug that is an effective treatment for erectile dysfunction. It also became a popular "lifestyle" drug, capable of stimulating the sexual energy of users. A researcher (center) inserts cultures into petri dishes at the Advanced Cell Technology lab in Worcester, Massachusetts. On November 25, 2001, Advanced Cell Technology announced the successful cloning of a human embryo for the purpose of mining stem cells used to treat disease.

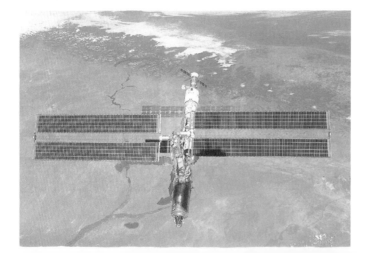

The International Space Station (ISS), photographed by the shuttle orbiter *Atlantis* in February 2001. The result of a partnership of sixteen nations, the ISS was slated, upon completion, to contain six laboratories and offer more opportunity for research than any other spacecraft to date.

45.

Lewis H. Lapham: Presidential Candidate Perot

During the 1992 presidential campaign Texas businessman H. Ross Perot joined the race as an independent, third-party candidate. With a folksy demeanor and disavowal of "politics-as-usual," he boasted one of the largest fortunes in the country, estimated at $3 billion. Although he had never held public office, he claimed that his business experience equipped him for the task of rescuing America from the economic recession of the early 1990s. In the spring of 1992 Perot momentarily led Republican incumbent George Bush and Democratic challenger Bill Clinton in opinion polls, but erratic behavior and charges of eccentricity slowed his campaign. After briefly dropping out of the race, Perot mounted a vigorous fall campaign. On election day he came in a surprisingly strong third place, winning 19 percent of the vote. No third-party candidate had finished as well since Theodore Roosevelt represented the Progressive ("Bull Moose") Party in 1912. Throughout 1993 Perot remained in the news, largely because of his opposition to the North American Free Trade Agreement and his support for a balanced budget amendment. In the following essay, Lewis Lapham, editor of Harper's *magazine, explores the nature of Perot's appeal and the eccentric worldview at the heart of his political philosophy.*

Source: *Harper's Magazine,* July 1993, "Notebook: Music Man."

ANYBODY GLANCING at the television talk shows over the last four or five months would have been hard-pressed to escape the grinning presence of H. Ross Perot, the would-be captain of the American soul who promotes himself—to Larry King and Jay Leno and Charlie Rose and the folks at NBC news—as a political masterpiece. The performance is like that of the crow in Aesop's fable who thinks it can sing as sweetly as the nightingale, but it draws a crowd, and the crowd grows larger and more attentive as President Bill Clinton's approval ratings drift lower in the public-opinion polls. When not otherwise promised to a television host, Perot travels to Washington to teach the Congress the lessons of good government that he learned from his long and careful study of the works of Norman Rockwell. Again the spectacle is grotesque, but what is more grotesque is the deference of the politicians who applaud his screeching as if it were the wisdom of Jefferson or the music of Mozart.

Between late February and early May Perot testified before three congressional committees, and he invariably arrived with a claque of true believers who occupied the back rows of the hearing rooms and provided the silent veneration and spontaneous applause. Also invariably, Perot addressed the members of the committees as if they were schoolchildren arraigned on disciplinary charges before a headmaster determined to make them say their prayers and drink their milk. He established the pose in early March, for the benefit of a committee considering the possibility of congressional reform. Instead of addressing the questions at hand, Perot delivered his standard lecture about a corrupt government squandering the nation's treasure on idle luxuries and useless toys. Portraying the servants of that government (among them all the politicians present in the hearing room) as a crowd of spendthrift fools, he recited his familiar list of complaints about the deficit, foreign lobbyists, extravagant expense accounts, private gymnasiums, idiot welfare programs, cut-rate haircuts, and preferred parking spaces at Washington's National Airport. He ended the lecture with a warning and a threat. If the members of Congress continued to misbehave and failed to heed his sound advice, then on election day the great, good American people would drive them from the temple. Perot knew that this was so because the great, good American people had appointed him their champion and surrogate, and they were not in a mood to tolerate any trifling with their affections. Grinning for the cameras, comforted by the murmuring of the true believers in the back row, delighting in the wonder of his own virtue, Perot said, "I urge you, on behalf of millions of ordinary people who are out there earning a living: Stand on principle. Don't compromise. You will have their support. I can guarantee you. I can deliver if I have to."

What was shocking about the remark was the servile acquiescence with which it was received. Nobody laughed in the man's face. Perot had dressed up the nakedness of his own ambition in the Halloween costume of the public-opinion polls, and he might as well have threatened to summon an army of hooded elves, or Caesar's legions, or the terrible wrath of Ramtha, the ancient warrior from the lost continent of Atlantis who speaks to Shirley MacLaine, but nobody asked him why he wasn't wearing his Batman mask or his wizard's pointed hat. The politicians lacked the courage to laugh because, like President Clinton and the oracles of the Washington news media, they accepted the existence of what they called "the Perot vote" as if it were as real as Mexico and as lucky as a winning lottery ticket. If Perot could attract 19 million votes in last year's presidential election without bothering to declare himself a candidate, and if, four months later, his approval ratings stood at 51 percent (as opposed to 24 percent in September 1992), then clearly his voice was the voice of God. The polls were the polls, and what was the use of objection or dissent to people frightened of both the future and the electorate?. . .

Perot is a charlatan, and the Perot vote represents no interest and no constituency. Like the Bermuda Triangle or the Land of Mordor, it is a fiction, an anthology of grievance or a reservoir of unspecific anger and resentment. Last November it mostly consisted of the disillusion with the purpose as well as the practice of politics, and as President Clinton continues to disavow his campaign promises (bowing or curtsying to almost any corporate lobbyist dressed in a loud voice and an expensive suit), it manifests itself as an inchoate feeling of nostalgia for a world of kings and queens and fairy tales.

During the last six months, I've listened to as many as forty people declare their belief in H. Ross Perot, but aside from their aversion to Bill Clinton and perhaps higher taxes, I can't imagine their agreeing with one another on any specific political theory, program, policy, issue, philosophy, plan, or initiative. Unlike the people who comprised the vote for Governor George Wallace in 1972, or the supporters of Theodore Roosevelt in 1912, they stand for nothing except their own unhappiness. Democracy is about consenting to lose an election, about the balancing of particular interests and the making of always imperfect compromises between the specific constituencies, but Perot's admirers think democracy is a movie by Frank Capra.

Among their disparate company I've counted automobile salesmen, environmentalists, English professors, social engineers, monopolists, remittance men, and friends of Ralph Nader. What they hold in common is an agenda of miscellaneous complaint. Everyone knows what he or she detests (most especially media spokespersons wearing dark suits and red ties), but hardly anyone knows how a caucus works or who paves the roads. On a Friday afternoon in April, over the course of two hours on a train, I met a young woman who said that she voted for Perot because President Clinton had betrayed Kirtland's warbler as well as the spotted owl, and an older man, retired and living in Naples, Florida, who said that he had reduced his interests to three—the Bible, the Social Register, and his gun. At a wedding reception in New York City in early May, I ran across an angry gentleman in a tweed suit who jammed a forefinger into my chest while making repeated and emphatic points about Perot's strength, Perot's decisiveness, Perot's resolve, Perot's grit. Yes, he said, he had considered all the weak-kneed objections, but he was sick of politics, sick of feeling sorry for people who, when you really thought about it, got what they deserved. He didn't think it necessary to specify the tasks to which Perot's grit might be applied, but I was left with the impression that he wouldn't think it amiss if Perot began the work of reclamation by placing the members of

Congress under house arrest or stringing them up by their thumbs. What was wanted was some strong authoritarian medicine to purge the country of its moral relativism (or its limousines, or its liberal media, or its grasping real-estate developers), and Perot clearly was the man to write the prescription.

I suspect that Perot's admirers value him at his true worth. His temperament is apparently that of a vindictive prig, a man who would prefer to conduct the affairs of government as if he were the abbot of a monastery or the warden of a prison. With surprisingly few exceptions, all of his associates—former, current, commercial, and political—testify to his autocratic cast of mind. One is either for him or against him, and anybody who is against him is either a fool or a knave. Certainly he doesn't respond well to even the mildest criticism, and he engages in nominally democratic debate only when he has been assured the privilege of the last word. His pose as the country's candid friend—the honest man speaking truth to power—is so patently false that I'm surprised it doesn't turn rancid in the heat of the television lights. Perot is more accurately described, in G.K. Chesterton's phrase, as the "uncandid candid friend," the smiling and unctuous man who says, "I'm sorry to say we are ruined," but is not sorry at all. He doesn't love what he chastises. The love of country follows from the love of its freedoms, not from the pride in its armies or its gross domestic product. Perot loves his own picture of America, and like the latter-day Puritans who take it upon themselves to examine the citizenry for flaws in its blood, its urine, and its speech, he makes no secret of his sanctimony and intolerance, of his wish to blame, punish, and cast what he trusts will be the first of many stones.

The rising of Perot's image over the horizon of the news suggests that the traditional American political narrative has lost much of its force and most of its coherence. None of the contradictions in Perot's character—the avowed autocrat championing the cause of populist revolt, the humble and plain-spoken servant of the people asking, in effect, to be elected king—dissuades his admirers from the belief that he embodies the country's only hope of regeneration.

Perot picked up the scent of Clinton's weakness as early as February, when Clinton submitted his budget message to Perot's approval before presenting it to Congress. In March Lloyd Bentsen, the secretary of the treasury, made a pilgrimage to Dallas to ask Perot's blessing for the President's crusade against the deficit. Perot ignored the flattery and sharpened the edge of his sarcasm. Within a month of the inauguration he had returned to the talk shows, and to one of the television reporters in attendance he said, "My role is as a grain of sand to the oyster." He canvassed the country as the bringer of bad news, speaking to rapt audiences in California, Texas, Colorado, Florida, Maine, testifying before Congress, presenting two half-hour advertisements for himself on NBC (at a price of $500,000 each), and in answer to questions about the business of state, he relied on his gift for the caustic phrase:

On the North American Free Trade Agreement—"A worn-out inner tube."

Of the Clinton Administration's attempt to stimulate the economy—"Like a faith healer who knows nothing about medicine trying to cure cancer with aspirin."

Of the United States Congress—"It's time to pick up a shovel and clean out the barn."

Of the White House advisers assigned to formulate an energy policy—"Poets, philosophers, and bee-keepers."

Of the secrecy protecting Hillary Clinton's deliberations about health care— "This is not a nuclear bomb program."

The witticisms achieved their intended effect, and as the winter passed into spring, President Clinton worried as much about the Perot vote—its demography, average age, racial composition, throw weight, and mystical significance— as he worried about his budget proposals and the war in Bosnia. In early April, speaking to the American Society of Newspaper Editors at Annapolis, in a tone of voice that was nearly that of a hurt and puzzled child, he was saying that 85 percent of his economic program was "what Ross Perot recommended in the campaign." Clinton didn't know how to placate or appease Perot, and his nervousness was unbecoming in a president. He looked too much like a toadying courtier, and the impression hastened his descent in the public esteem.

By early May Clinton and Perot were exchanging insults in the newspapers (referring to each other as liars and rumormongers), and it had become embarrassingly clear that the gentlemen resembled rival talk-show hosts competing for the same audience. To the extent that authority is invested in persons instead of ideas or institutions, the politician stands on no platform other than the scaffolding of self-dramatization. The rule of love supplants the rule of law, and instead of addressing fellow citizens, the commoner who would be king seeks to recruit fans. . . .

The transformation of politics into soap opera makes nonsense of the sham distinctions between Democrat and Republican, liberal and conservative. Our political discourse becomes synonymous with advertising—a mob of images notable for the strict separation of cause and effect—and the inferior forms of credulity, on a par with astrology and fortune-telling, comprise the tailor's remnants of what was once a public debate. The less that people understand of what politicians do, the more urgent their desire to appoint politicians to the ranks of the immortals.

The founders of the American republic entertained few illusions about the perfection of human nature, but as an advance over the pagan belief in a pantheon of gods and heroes, they proposed the contervailing ideal of a civil government conducted by mere mortals. The proposition was as courageous as it was optimistic, but it doesn't meet the expectations of an age that worships celebrity and defines itself as the sum of its fears.

As the world comes to be seen as a more dangerous and complicated place than was dreamed of in the philosophy of Walt Disney, people become impatient with rulers in whom they all too easily can recognize weaknesses embarrassingly similar to their own. The news broadcasts swell with proofs of catastrophe—murder in the suburbs and riots in the cities, civil war in Bosnia and bankruptcy in Washington—and an anxious public yearns for the shows of omnipotence, not only on the part of its presidents but also from its scientists, its ball players, its divorce lawyers, and its first-term congressmen. Because omnipotence doesn't exist in the state of nature, it must be manufactured, and the supply increases with the demand. The best-seller lists promise the miracles of rescue and deliverance (in the form of diets, exercise machines, and manuals of spiritual recovery), and on the stage of the national political theater the cast of democratic magistrates gives way to a procession of miraculous mandarins offering prayers and sacrifices to the sun or the moon or the deficit. Some of them sing and dance, and some of them, like H. Ross Perot, draw diagrams and astonish Jay Leno with the great news that they also play drums.

———————◆———————

If we did not have such a thing as an airplane today, we would probably create something the size of N.A.S.A. to make one.
H. ROSS PEROT, quoted in *Newsweek,* December 1, 1986

46.

BILL CLINTON: Remarks in Memphis on Urban Renewal

When Bill Clinton was elected President in 1992, he enjoyed enormous popularity among African Americans. Born in Arkansas in 1946, Clinton grew up as a white Southerner under segregation, an experience that left a deep mark on his political career. He idolized the civil rights leader Martin Luther King, Jr., and successfully courted African American support during his winning campaign for governor of Arkansas in 1978. Fourteen years later, when Clinton ran for President, African Americans represented a key constituency of his campaign. As President, Clinton advocated dialogue between the races and widely delivered speeches promoting urban development in depressed black neighborhoods. But, in an unusual step for a liberal politician, Clinton also supported tougher sentences for violent crime. Since the 1960s, many liberals viewed a platform of "law and order" as a veiled agenda of white racism against African Americans. By the fall of 1993, however, as gang violence among young black men in inner cities reached a level of alarm, Clinton argued that fighting crime was itself a civil rights issue, because no Americans suffered more disproportionately from crime than African Americans. In the address excerpted below, Clinton spoke before a black congregation in Memphis, Tennessee, on the issues of crime and urban renewal.

Source: *Public Papers of the Presidents of the United States,* November 13, 1993.

I CAME HERE to support the North American Free Trade Agreement today for a simple reason, and that is that our workers are becoming more productive and more competitive; they have to to survive in the world. But productivity means that the same person can produce more in the same or less time, right? So if fewer people are producing more stuff, the only way you can create more jobs and higher incomes is if you have more customers for the things you're producing.

So that's very important; this trade agreement's important to me. But when you get through all of that, you have to come back to the fact that this country is going to have a very hard time making it unless we do something about this wave of crime and violence that's tearing the heart out of America. And it affects everybody who thinks they're not affected by it. It affects you in many ways by forcing you as taxpayers to pay a lot more money to put people in the penitentiary than you otherwise would. You know, this country now has a higher percentage of people in prison than any other country in the world. Do you know that? That's something we're number one in. And we know in spite of that, a lot of people get out before they should. . . .

In the Washington Post in our Nation's Capital the other day there was an article about children so convinced they would never grow up that at the age of 11, they were planning their funerals. Little girl saying, "Well, now, if I have a funeral, play these hymns at the church," and another one saying, "If I have a funeral, put me in this dress."

Now, it's going to be hard for me or any other President or any Member of Congress to organize this country with the private sector to compete and win in the global economy if we have the kind of public pathology we have today, where children are shooting children with weapons more advanced than the police have.

I come from across the river in Arkansas where we're about to start or maybe they have already started deer season. And some towns, we shut the schools and the factories down at the opening of deer season because nobody shows up anyway. [*Laughter*] I understand all about the right to keep and bear arms, and I was in the woods when I was barely old enough to walk. But I'm telling you, no sane society would allow teenagers to have semiautomatic weapons and go on the streets and be better armed than the police officers. It is crazy. And nobody else does. Only we do. We have to ask ourselves, what are we going to do about this? How did this happen? And I think, frankly, if we're going to find the answers, we're going to have to all check a lot of our baggage at the door. We've got to check our partisan political baggage; we've got to check our racial identities; we've got to check everything at the door. We've just got to be honest children of God and honest Americans and try to analyze how did we get in the fix we're in in this country and what are we going to do about it.

And I have to tell you, I've spent time, I've talked to a lot of young people who were and some who are in gangs. I once had someone go down to the penitentiary and interview every teenager who was there doing a life sentence for murder. Long before I ever thought of running for President I went to south central Los Angeles—which later became famous when it burned down—a couple of years before I ever thought of even getting in this race, just sat in church basements and places like that and talked to people about what was going on. And as nearly as I can determine, what has happened is a combination of the following: Number one, too many of these kids are growing up without family supports, without the structure and value and support they need.

Number two, too many of those kids also have no substitute for the family that's positive. The word "gang" has a bad connotation now. The truth is we all want to be in gangs, if a gang is a group of people that think like you do and do like you do. I mean, what's the difference in the Baptist Church and the Church of God in Christ? They're two different gangs who still want to get to heaven when they die. Right? I mean, really, you think about that. What's the difference in the Democrats and the Republicans? They're two different gangs, and they obey the law, and they vote on election day, and they've got different ideas about how to solve problems. This is very important to understand. We all want to be part of groups. And we get meaning out of our lives from being part of groups, you know?. . .

The third thing that has happened that is different from what happened 30 years ago when people were poor is that you not only have a worse family situation and no other community supports— I mean, 30 years ago, even when kids didn't grow up in intact families in poor neighborhoods, they still lived in places where on every block there was a role model. The person who owned the drugstore lived in the neighborhood. The person that owned the grocery store lived in the neighborhood. The people that filled the churches on Sunday lived in the neighborhoods where they went to church. Now, the third thing that's happened is, weekend drunks have been substituted by permanent drug addicts and drug salesmen. Abuse of alcohol has been replaced by a drug culture that makes some people money destroying other people's lives. It's different. And it is not simple or easy, what to do about it. Mr. Brown's going to talk more about that in a minute.

The fourth thing that has happened is that the central organizing principle of any advanced society has been evaporated, and that is work. Forget about work in and of itself, to earn money and contribute to the rest of our wealth. If you don't have work in neighborhoods and in communities, it is hard for people to organize their lives. It is hard for parents to feel self-esteem. It is hard for them to feel confident giving their kids rules to live by. It is hard for the relationship between the parent and the child to work just right. It is hard for the child to look out and imagine that by working hard things will work out all right.

Now, there are lots of other problems. But I'm convinced that those are the four biggest ones: the breakdown of the family, the breakdown of other community supports, the rise of drugs—it's not just in terms of drug abuse but in terms of a way to get rich—and the absence of work.

And I believe that in order to deal with this, we're going to have to all work together in a whole new national contract. But I believe this is an economic issue. I think it's a public health issue. I think it's a national security issue. And besides that, I'm just tired of trying to explain to myself when I go to bed at night why so many American kids aren't going to make it when they ought to.

So there are things for the Federal Government to do, the President, and the Congress. There are things for the States to do, things for the local folks to do. There are things the private sector has to do. And there are certainly things for the churches to do. But I want to submit to you that there are things that every American citizen's going to have to do.

This family breakdown problem has developed over 30 years. It didn't just happen overnight. The community erosion developed over a long period of time. We cannot rebuild all these institutions overnight, but we can start saving these kids, in the words of a good friend of mine, the same way we lost them, one at a time, which means that there's something for all of us to do here. There is something for all of us to do. And we need both love and discipline. We need both investment in these kids and our future, and we need rules by which people live. We need both. It's not an either/or thing. . . .

I think we ought to pass the crime bill because it offers boot camps instead of penitentiaries for first-time offenders. I think we need to do something to increase the safety of our schools; 160,000 children stay home every day because they're afraid of school. One in five children goes to school every day armed with a knife, a gun, or a club, every day. We've got to change that.

I think we have to provide as much as we can an environment in which the police have a chance to do their job and in which kids are not encouraged to kill each other. . . .

The last thing I would say to you is that we can do these things at the national level. But we have to give these kids hope again. We have to give their families hope again. We have to give their parents who are trying hope again. I stopped in that housing project, like Harold said. It may be one of the poorest places in this town, but I know that most people who live in that housing project do not break the law, do not abuse drugs, and are doing the best they can. And a lot of people forget that. A lot of people forget that. So that's something you're going to have to do. That's your job.

I live in Washington; you live in Memphis. You've got to do that here. You've got to do that. You've got to do it through the churches, through the businesses, through the community groups. You've got to help slowly but surely get this society back to a point where families can be reconstituted, where there can be supports for kids that don't have families so they're in a good gang, not a bad gang. We can do this, folks.

And you know, people have been talking about this for years, but this is the first time in my memory that I think the American people are about fed up, up to their ears in it, scared to death about what's happening to our children and their future, and understand that it affects all the rest of us. We can do this. We can do this.

I'll make this pledge to you: If you'll work on it here, I'll work on it there. I can no longer justify knowing that there's something I can do to make people safer on the streets and our not doing it. I can no longer justify knowing there are things we can do that work to reduce the drug problem and not doing it. I can no longer justify going to bed at night thinking about these children killing other children, thinking about these little kids planning their funerals and not doing something about it. We can do this. And keep in mind, you're working with the same material that's inside you. These are people we're talking about. We can turn this country around if we'll check our divisions at the door, rely on what unites us, and go to work.

———————◆———————

The government of cities is the one conspicuous failure of the United States.
JAMES BRYCE, *The American Commonwealth,* 1888

47.

Street Gangs in California

In the early 1990s violent crime in the United States reached an all-time high, as rates of rape, assault, and robbery soared to unprecedented levels. Although the increase in crime was felt in nearly every region of the country, it particularly affected those living in impoverished urban areas where street gangs had proliferated. In many inner cities, entire neighborhoods became virtual war zones as street gangs fought to defend and expand their territory. No major American city escaped the crime epidemic, and national leaders groped for a response to it. Most observers blamed the crime problem on three main factors: drugs, poverty, and racial injustice. The membership of most street gangs consisted of men of color, particularly African American youths who had been born into broken and impoverished families. The 1992 Los Angeles riots put California in the nation's focus as a state particularly afflicted by gang violence and racial division. In the excerpt below from a 1993 study, the California Attorney General's office explores the roots of gang violence in African American communities.

Source: *Gangs 2000: A Call to Action*, California Department of Justice, 1993.

AFRICAN AMERICAN GANGS began forming in California during the 1920s. They were not territorial; rather, they were loose associations, unorganized, and rarely violent. They did not identify with graffiti, monikers, or other gang characteristics.

These early gangs consisted generally of family members and neighborhood friends who involved themselves in limited criminal activities designed to perpetrate a "tough guy" image and to provide an easy means of obtaining money.

From 1955 to 1965, the African American gangs increased with larger memberships and operated primarily in south central Los Angeles and Compton. This was partly due to more African American youths bonding together for protection from rival gangs.

It was not until the late 1960s when the Crips and the Bloods—the two most vio-

lent and criminally active African American gangs—originated. The Crips began forming in southeast Los Angeles by terrorizing local neighborhoods and schools with assaults and strong-arm robberies. They developed a reputation for being the most fierce and feared gang in the Los Angeles area.

Other African American gangs formed at about the same time to protect themselves from the Crips. One such gang was the Bloods, which originated in and around the Piru Street area in Compton, California; thus, some Bloods gangs are referred to as Piru gangs. The Bloods, which were outnumbered at the time by the Crips three to one, became the second, most vicious African American gang in the Los Angeles area.

Both the Crips and Bloods eventually divided into numerous, smaller gangs (or "sets") during the 1970s. They kept the Crips' and Bloods' (Piru) name, spread throughout Los Angeles County, and began to claim certain neighborhoods as their territory. Their gang rivalry became vicious and bloody.

By 1980, there were approximately 15,000 Crips and Bloods gang members in and around the Los Angeles area. The gangs—or sets—ranged in size from a few gang members to several hundred and had little, if any, organized leadership. The typical age of a gang member varied from 14- to 24-years-old.

Initiation into a gang required the prospective member to "jump in" and fight some of the members already in the gang. Another initiation rite required them to commit a crime within the neighborhood or an assault against rival gang members.

They remained territorial and motivated to protect their neighborhoods from rival gang members. They established unique and basic trademarks such as colors, monikers, graffiti, and hand signs. The color blue was adopted by the Crips as a symbol of gang recognition; red became the color of the Bloods. Monikers—such as "Killer Dog," "12-Gauge," and "Cop Killer"—often reflected their criminal abilities or their ferociousness as gang members. Graffiti identified the gang and hand signs displayed symbols—usually letters—unique to the name of their gang. It was not unusual for members to "flash" hand signs at rival gang members as a challenge to fight. They took great pride in displaying their colors and defending them against rival gangs. They were willing to die for the gang, especially in defense of their colors and neighborhood. It was not until the early 1980s that the era of drive-by shootings began.

They became involved in a variety of neighborhood crimes such as burglary; robbery; assault; and the selling of marijuana, LSD, and PCP. The issue of gang involvement in narcotics trafficking was generally considered to be of a minor nature prior to the 1980s. However, by 1983, African American Los Angeles gangs seized upon the availability of narcotics, particularly crack, as a means of income. Crack had supplemented cocaine as the most popular illicit drug of choice. Prime reasons for the widespread use of crack were its ease of conversion for smoking, the rapid onset of its effect on the user, and its comparatively inexpensive price.

The migration of African American Los Angeles gang members during the 1980s to other United States cities, often for reasons other than some vast gang-inspired conspiracy, resulted in the spread of crack sales and an attendant wave of violence. This spread of crack sales can be traced back to the gang members' family ties in these cities and to the lure of quick profits. These two reasons provided most of the inspiration and motivation for the transplanted gang members.

Considerable diversity is displayed by Crips and Bloods gangs and their members in narcotics trafficking, which allows for different levels of involvement from narcotic selling by adolescents to the more important roles of directing narcotics trafficking activities. In the past, an individual's age, physical structure, and arrest record were often principal factors in determining gang hierarchy; money derived from narcotic sales soon became the symbol which signified power and status.

Crips and Bloods have established criminal networks throughout the country and capitalized on the enormous profits earned from the trafficking and selling of crack cocaine. . . .

The Department of Justice estimates there could be as many as 65,000 African American gang members in California today. The majority of them are still Crips and Bloods gang members. They now range in age from 12 to 35, with some as old as 40. The gangs vary in size from 30 members to as many as 1,000. They continue to fight each other for narcotic-related profits and in defense of territory, and many remain unstructured and informal. A few of them are becoming organized with some definitive gang structure.

Some of the older gang members—known as "Original Gangsters"—who have been in the gang for a long time are often the recruiters and trainers of new gang members. Many are second- and third-generation gang members and have been incarcerated in the California Youth Authority or the California Department of Corrections. Due to their propensity for violence, prison and jail officials have found it necessary to house hardcore members in high-security cell blocks or separate facilities.

Some of the more experienced gang members are beginning to abandon established characteristics, such as wearing the colors blue and red, and are now trying to disguise their gang affiliation by wearing non-descript black and white clothing. Other members continue to rely on the gang trademarks, and neighborhoods abound with graffiti signifying the presence of Crips and/or Bloods gangs.

Some of the gangs have formed alliances with other ethnic gangs, and some Crips and Bloods gangs include Hispanic or Asian gang members. Female gang members are rare, but those who do participate play a minor role in gang activity and are used to rent crack houses or traffic in narcotics. . . .

With gang involvement in the crack market comes a tremendous increase of street-level violence as they battle over the profitable narcotics trade. Violence

is a routine part of doing business, and it is used to terrorize citizens and other gangs resisting their intrusion. They make no effort to distinguish between intended rival gang victims or innocent bystanders.

Besides crack cocaine, African American gang members also sell marijuana and PCP; and some have purchased chemicals for their own production of PCP.

Their use of weapons has evolved to high-powered, large-caliber handguns and automatic and semi-automatic weapons including AK-47 assault rifles and Mac-10s with multiple-round magazines; and they sometimes wear police-type body armor. Gang attacks on police officers have escalated. Gangs—such as the '89 Gangster Crips, Project Crips, Neighborhood Crips, Southside Compton Crips, and the Pueblo Bishop Bloods—have shot at officers during vehicle pursuits, narcotic investigations, robberies, and responses to family disturbances.

Their other crimes range from robberies, burglaries, grand thefts, receiving stolen property, and witness intimidations to assaults with a deadly weapon, drive-by shootings, and murders. In Los Angeles during 1990, there were 135 homicides; 1,416 assaults and batteries; and 775 robberies attributed to Crips and Bloods gang members. . . .

During the April 29 to May 1, 1992, riot in Los Angeles, some of the violence was attributed to the Crips and Bloods. The riot was the worst civil disorder in modern American history. Sixty persons died; some 2,500 were injured; 750 fires were set; 14,000 people were arrested; and upwards of $700 million in damage was done.

Gang members were involved in assaults, attempted murders, murders, arson, and looting. During the riot, two members of the 8-Trey Gangster Crips and two other individuals were seen on national television beating and robbing a truck driver. Twenty-two members of another Crips gang were arrested for looting approximately $80,000 worth of merchandise from electronic stores.

Other Crips and Bloods gang members were responsible for looting many of the 4,500 weapons from gun dealers, sporting goods stores, and pawn shops during the riot. Gang members have indicated they will use the weapons to kill police officers and parole and probation officers via drive-by shootings and ambushes. Gang members have graffitied walls with "187 L.A.P.D." (187 is the California Penal Code Section for homicide); and other gang members have circulated flyers stating, "Open Season on LAPD."

A temporary truce between some of the gang members of the Crips and Bloods occurred in the Los Angeles area following the riot. Many of these gang members are wearing articles of red and blue clothing interweaved to show their unity. These gangs claim the truce will unite their forces to target law enforcement officers; however, to date, there have been no attacks against the officers resulting from this gang alliance.

———————◆———————

It used to be so simple. Bloods hated Crips, Crips hated Bloods. Today, however, the huge profits available from trafficking in cocaine and the proliferation of Asian and Hispanic gangs have made such straightforward rivalries obsolete.

KATHY BRAIDHILL, *Los Angeles Magazine,* 1998

48.

DARCY FREY: Escaping Poverty Through Basketball

Success in sports has long offered a way out of poverty for some Americans. For a talented few, football provided an alternative to the mines and steel mills of Pennsylvania and West Virginia; boxing allowed first young Jews and Italians, then blacks and Hispanics, to fight their way out of the tenements; and baseball offered salvation for farm boys and Latin American immigrants. Few dreams of escape through sports loom larger, though, than the promise of a college basketball scholarship and professional career that have been the brass ring for the predominantly African American youths of the economically depressed inner cities. The world of concrete courts, slumming college coaches, and summer camps sponsored by shoe manufacturers was first chronicled in Rick Telander's book Heaven Is a Playground *(1976) and later in the documentary film* Hoop Dreams *(1994). In this vein, for more than a year, beginning in the summer of 1991, journalist Darcy Frey followed four teenaged basketball stars from the Abraham Lincoln High School of Coney Island, Brooklyn, New York. In telling their story (first in the* Harper's *Magazine article excerpted below and then in the book* The Last Shot*), Frey painted a vivid portrait not just of their dreams for a better life but of the grim, threatening environment of housing projects and of woefully inadequate schools that offer little preparation for the standardized tests that determine scholarship eligibility. Although all four young men went on to play college basketball, only Stephon Marbury, later an NBA all-star, attained the one-in-a-million goal of a professional career.*

Source: *Harper's Magazine*, April 1993, "The Last Shot."

AUGUST 1991

Russell Thomas places his right sneaker one inch behind the three-point line, considers the basket with a level gaze, cocks his wrist to shoot, then suddenly looks around. Has he spotted me, watching from the corner of the playground? No, something else is up: he is lifting his nose to the wind like a spaniel, he is gauging air currents. He waits until the wind settles, bits of trash feathering lightly to the ground. Then he sends a twenty-five-foot jump shot arcing through the soft summer twilight. It drops without a sound through the dead center of the bare iron rim. So does the next one. So does the one after that. Alone in the gathering dusk, Russell works the perimeter against imaginary defenders, unspooling jump shots from all points. Few sights on Brooklyn playgrounds stir the hearts and minds of the coaches and scouts who recruit young men for college basketball teams quite like Russell's jumper; they have followed its graceful trajectory ever since he made varsity at Abraham Lincoln High School, in Coney Island, two years ago. But the shot is merely the final gesture, the public flourish of a private regimen that brings Russell to this court day and night. Avoiding pickup games, he gets down to work: an hour of three-point shooting, then wind sprints up the four-teen flights in his project stairwell, then back to the court, where (much to his friends' amusement) he shoots one-handers ten feet from the basket while sitting in a chair.

At this hour Russell usually has the court to himself; most of the other play-ers won't come out until after dark, when the thick humid air begins to stir with night breezes and the court lights come on. But this evening is turning out to be a fine one—cool and foggy. The low, slanting sun sheds a feeble pink light over the silvery Atlantic a block away, and milky sheets of fog roll off the ocean and drift in tatters along the project walk-ways. The air smells of sewage and saltwa-ter. At the far end of the court, where someone has torn a hole in the chicken-wire fence, other players climb through and begin warming up.

Like most of New York's impoverished and predominantly black neighbor-hoods, Coney Island does not exactly shower its youth with opportunity. In the early 1960s, urban renewal came to Coney Island in the form of a vast tract of housing projects, packed so densely along a twenty-block stretch that a new skyline rose suddenly behind the board-walk and amusement park. The experi-ment of public housing, which has iso-lated the nation's urban poor from the hearts of their cities, may have failed here in even more spectacular fashion because of Coney Island's utter remote-ness. In this neighborhood, on a penin-sula at the southern tip of Brooklyn, there are almost no stores, no trees, no police; just block after block of gray ce-ment projects—hulking, prison-like, and jutting straight into the sea.

Most summer nights an amorphous unease settles over Coney Island as apart-ments become too stifling to bear and the streets fall prey to the gangs and drug dealers. Options are limited: to the south is the stiff gray meringue of the At-lantic; to the north, more than ten miles away, are the Statue of Liberty and the glass-and-steel spires of Manhattan's fi-nancial district. Officially, Coney Island is considered a part of the endless phantas-magoria that is New York City. But on nights like these, as the dealers set up their drug marts in the streets and alley-ways, and the sounds of sirens and gun-fire keep pace with the darkening sky, it feels like the end of the world.

Yet even in Coney Island there are some uses to which a young man's talent, ambition, and desire to stay out of harm's way may be put: there is basket-ball. Hidden behind the projects are dozens of courts, and every night they fill with restless teenagers, there to remain for hours until exhaustion or the hood-lums take over. The high-school dropouts and the aging players who never made it to college usually show up for a physical game at a barren strip of courts by the water known as Chop Chop Land, where bruises and minutes played are accrued at a one-to-one ratio. The younger kids congregate for rowdy games at Run-and-Gun Land. The court there is short and the rims are low, so everyone can dunk, and the only pass ever made is the one inbounding the ball. At Run-and-Gun, players stay on the move for another rea-son: the court sits just below one of the most dreaded projects, where Coney Is-land's worst hoodlums sometimes pass a summer evening "getting hectic," as they say—tossing batteries and beer bottles onto the court from apartment windows fifteen stories above.

The neighborhood's best players—the ones, like Russell, with aspirations—practice a disciplined, team-driven style of basketball at this court by the O'Dwyer projects, which has been dubbed the Garden after the New York Knicks' arena. In a neighborhood ravaged by the commerce of drugs, the Garden offers a tenuous sanctuary. A few years ago, community activists petitioned the housing authority to install night lights. And the players themselves resurfaced the court and put up regulation-height rims that snap back after a player dunks. Russell may be the only kid at the Garden who practices his defensive footwork while holding a ten-pound brick in each hand, but no one here treats the game as child's play. Even the hoodlums decline to vandalize the Garden, because in Coney Island the possibility of transcendence through basketball is an article of faith.

Most evenings this summer I have come to the Garden to watch Russell and his friends play ball. The notion that basketball can liberate dedicated players like these from the grinding daily privations of the ghetto has become a cherished parable, advanced by television sportscasters, college basketball publicists, and sneaker companies proselytizing the work ethic and $120 high-tops. And that parable is conveyed directly to the players at the Garden by the dozens of college coaches who arrive in Coney Island each year with assurances that even if a National Basketball Association contract isn't in the cards, a player's talent and tenacity will at least reward him with a free college education, a decent job, and a one-way ticket out of the neighborhood. But how does this process actually unfold? And what forces stand in its way? How often is basketball's promise of a better life redeemed? It was questions like these that drew me to this court, between Mermaid and Surf avenues.

"Just do it, right?" I glance to my left

and there is Corey Johnson, smiling mischievously, eyes alight. He nods toward the court—players stretching out, taking lay-ups—and it does, in fact, resemble a sneaker commercial. "Work hard, play hard, buy yourself a pair of Nikes, young man," Corey intones. Corey is a deft mimic and he does a superb white TV announcer. "They get you where you want to go, which is out of the ghet-to!" He laughs, we shake hands, and he takes up an observation post by my side.

Corey is Russell's best friend and one of Lincoln High's other star seniors. He, too, expects to play college ball. But he specializes in ironic detachment and normally shows up courtside with his Walkman merely to watch for girls beneath his handsome, hooded eyes.

Basketball newsletters and scouting reports are constantly scrutinizing the players, and practically every day some coach shows up—appraising, coaxing, negotiating, and, as often as not, making promises he never keeps. Getting that scholarship offer is every player's dream—in anticipation, no one steps outside in Coney Island without a Syracuse cap or a St. John's sweatshirt. But in reality only a handful of the neighborhood's players have ever made it to such top four-year programs; most have been turned back by one obstacle or another in high school. Others who have enrolled in college never saw their dream to completion. The list is grim: there was Eric "Spoon" Marbury, who played for the University of Georgia but never graduated, and ended up back in Coney Island working construction; his younger brother Norman "Jou-Jou" Marbury, who lost his scholarship to highly ranked Tennessee because of academic problems in high school; and now David "Chocolate" Harris, a talented player who never even graduated from high school. He dropped out of Lincoln after his freshman year and became a small-time drug dealer. Earlier this summer police found him in an abandoned lot, his hood pulled over his head and a bullet through his skull. He was seventeen. Some of the players warming up at the Garden have written on the tongues of their sneakers, CHOCOLATE: R.I.P.

Stephon—Eric and Norman Marbury's kid brother—is barely fourteen, has yet to begin high school, but already his recruiting has begun. At least one college coach is known to have sent him fawning letters in violation of the National Collegiate Athletic Association rules; street agents, paid under the table by colleges to bring top players to their programs, have begun cultivating Stephon; and practically every high-school coach in the city is heaping him with free gear—sneakers, caps, bags—in an attempt to lure him to his school. At first glance, Stephon doesn't look like the future of anything: he's diminutive, barely five feet nine, with the rounded forehead and delicate features of an infant. He sports a stylish razor cut and a pierced ear, and the huge gold stud seems to tilt his tiny bald head off its axis. Caught somewhere between puberty and superstardom, he walks around with his sneakers untied, the ends of his belt drooping suggestively from his pants, and half a Snickers bar extruding from his mouth.

Basketball is so inextricably woven into the fabric of Coney Island life that almost everyone here can recite a complete oral history of the neighborhood's players. People remember the exact scores of summer tournament games played at this court ten years ago, or describe in rapturous detail the perfect arc that Carlton "Silk" Owens put on his jumper before he was shot in the elbow in 1982. Dog-eared copies of a ten-year-old University of Georgia catalogue with a picture of Spoon Marbury playing with future NBA

great Dominique Wilkins get passed around like samizdat.

Russell, Corey, and Stephon are the natural heirs to this vaunted tradition. But this is a complicated business: given the failures that have preceded them, the new crew is watched by the neighborhood with a certain skittishness, a growing reluctance to care too deeply. Yet Coney Island offers its residents little else on which to hang their pride. So the proceedings here take on a desperate, exalted quality, and by unspoken agreement the misfortunes of bygone players are chalked up to either a lack of will or plain bad luck—both of which make possible the continuance of hope. Silk didn't go pro, it is said, "because that was the year they cut the college draft from three rounds to two." Another player, the explanation goes, had that pro game, went to the hoop both ways, "but he was done in by a shyster agent."

Still, the suspicion lingers that something larger and less comprehensible may be at work. Ten years ago, the Long Island City projects in Queens produced New York's best players, but the drug industry and the collapse of that neighborhood into violence, broken families, and ever-greater poverty put an end to its dynasty. In recent years the torch has passed to Coney Island, which struggles to avoid a similar fate.

SEPTEMBER

Abraham Lincoln High School is a massive yellow-brick building of ornate stonework and steel-gated windows a few blocks north of the boardwalk. As Coney Island has deteriorated, so has Lincoln High, though the school itself sits about a mile from the projects at the end of Ocean Parkway, a stately, tree-lined boulevard. Across the parkway are Brighton Beach and several other Jewish neighborhoods, but the kids from those areas are usually sent elsewhere for their education, as Lincoln has become, little by little, a ghetto school for the projects.

A malaise has set in at Lincoln, as it has at so many inner-city public schools. Students regularly walk in and out of class, sleep at their desks, throw projectiles through doorways at friends in the hall. In the teachers' cafeteria, conversation often reverts to pension plans and whether the 2,500 Lincoln kids are as bad as last year or worse. The first day I dropped by, there was much commotion because the locker of a student was found to contain a handgun. On my second visit, the weapon in question was a six-inch knife. After one student was sent to the hospital with a neck wound requiring forty stitches, even some of the most peaceable kids began carrying X-Acto knives for protection.

Spectators at games in the New York Public School Athletic League (PSAL) are often frisked at the door by guards with metal detectors. Still, incidents occur. In the middle of the 1982 semifinals, between Alexander Hamilton and Ben Franklin, an off-duty security guard chased a knife-wielding fan directly onto the court and put a gun to his head while the crowd and players ran screaming for the exits. And then there is that ritual of basketball in the urban public schools: the pregame *passeggiata* of the neighborhood's drug dealers. During warm-ups in certain gyms, the steel doors will swing open and slowly, conspicuously, daring the security guards to stop them, the dealers will make their entrance, signaling to friends in the bleachers while strolling around the court draped in leather, fur, and several pounds of gold.

Into this chaos walk the college coaches—pin-striped and paisley-tied, bearing four-color photos of sold-out college arenas and statistics on how many games their teams play on national television. Usually they precede their visits by dropping the players brief notes, like the one from a Fordham coach to a Lincoln player describing how one of the college's basketball stars became rich beyond his wildest dreams. "This could be you someday," the coach wrote. "See how Fordham can change your life?" The coach signed off with the salutation, "Health, Happine$$, and Hundred$."

The recruiting circus has been a fact of life for Russell and his friends ever since they were in junior high. Directly across the street from Lincoln sits William Grady Tech—another powerhouse PSAL team—and the two schools compete zealously for the pool of talent coming out of the Coney Island projects. Lincoln players often refer to Grady as "the best team money can buy." Grady players claim that Lincoln tries to lure them away with sneakers and promises to "pass them along" in their classes. Coaches at both schools deny such allegations, but it is a fact that thirteen-year-old Coney Island athletes are encouraged to shop for high schools the way the seniors pick colleges—according to which school will give them the most playing time, the best chance to win a city title, and the exposure to get recruited to the next level.

According to NCAA rules, students who want to play sports at a four-year, Division I school, those with the nation's top athletic programs, must enter college having maintained at least a 70 average in high school and having received a combined score of 700 on the math and verbal sections of the SATs—the last an insurmountable obstacle to many black players with poor educations and little experience taking standardized tests. Failing that, a player must earn a two-year degree at a junior college before moving on to a four-year school. Many Division I coaches, however, refuse to recruit junior-college players, considering them damaged goods. So players who don't go directly to a four-year school often never get to play top college ball or earn their bachelor's degrees.

The first time Russell took the SATs, he received a combined score somewhere in the mid-500s. (You receive 400 points for signing your name.) This year he gave up his lunch period to study, and lately he's been carrying around a set of vocabulary flash cards, which he pulls out whenever there isn't a basketball in his hands. By dint of tremendous effort, Russell had also brought his average up to 78—the highest on the team. These are extraordinary developments for someone whose schooling over the years has been so bad that he had never, until recently, finished a book or learned the fundamentals of multiplication, even as he was being called upon to answer reading-comprehension and algebra questions on the SATs. "I used to think there were smart people and dumb people, but that's not true," Russell says forcefully. "Everybody's got the same brain. They say a human mind can know a thousand words—it's like a little computer! But you got to practice." He pauses. "But how come it's always the guys who don't study who get their 700s? Seems like the guys who work hard always get screwed. But oh, well."

From across the football field, the chants and cries of cheerleading practice travel toward us with perfect clarity. Russell shades his eyes with his hands and watches a tumble of cartwheels. "It's nice out here, isn't it? All the trees and everything? Out where I live there's nothing but total corruption and evilness, drugs and stolen cars. All my friends be getting arrested, shot at . . . " It is not too much to say that basketball saved Russell. In junior high he was trouble, sometimes leaving home for long stretches to hang

out on the streets with his friends. But he was spotted playing ball in the parks by one of Lincoln's unofficial recruiters, who persuaded him to enroll. In high school he gained confidence and won the hearts of teachers who admired his efforts while growing increasingly appalled by what he had never been taught. Now after school, while certain of his classmates walk over to Brighton Beach to hold up pensioners at gunpoint, Russell goes straight home, takes his vitamins, does his push-ups, and combs through college-recruiting brochures until bedtime. His dream is not to become a pro, he tells me, but "to graduate college, start me a nice little family, and get me a nice little job as a registered nurse."

This is what this whole basketball business is about, isn't it? By playing ball and playing by the rules, a kid like Russell is saved from the streets—saved too from that unshakable belief in his own insignificance—and set on a path that could change his life.

OCTOBER

Stephon does not suffer from the usual array of adolescent insecurities, but why should he? As a freshman, he arrived at Lincoln already a legend, and his performance later today, during the season's first official practice, will do nothing to lower his profile. Hopes for this year's team are running so high that everyone gathers in the gym to see for himself: students, teachers, other coaches, and a reporter for *Newsday* who will cover the team all season.

Bobby Hartstein, head coach of the Lincoln team, sounds overjoyed—and vastly relieved. Lincoln has had great players before, but never a virtual child prodigy like Stephon.

The Marbury story *is* a good one, though it may never be written to the father's liking. After starring at Lincoln, Eric went on to play for the University of Georgia, but he failed to graduate before his scholarship ran out and was now back in Coney Island. Donnie, the second son, displayed even greater promise, but he didn't have a 70 average in high school and had to do time at two junior colleges. After two years, he moved on to Texas A&M, where he led the Southwest Conference in scoring. But he too never graduated and was passed over in the college draft; now he's out in Utah, at another college, trying to finish his degree. Then came Norman. If ever Coney Island had produced pro material, it was he. The first public-school player in New York ever to be named all-city three years in a row, Norman was a dazzler—fast, strong, with a deadly outside shot and the ability, on drives to the basket, to take on the largest foes. He had his pick of top programs and eventually signed with Tennessee, which had assured him that if he chose their school, he could still attend for free even if he didn't make 700; he would simply have to sit out his freshman season, as the NCAA rules require. But in the summer of 1990, just weeks before he was set to leave for Knoxville, he came up 40 points short of 700 on his final SAT attempt. Tennessee broke its promise and withdrew its offer. Norman, Coney Island's finest product to date, packed his bags for a junior college in Florida. (He now plays for a Salt Lake City junior college.)

For years Donald Marbury had watched his boys fall short. Now he was down to his last—and most talented—son.

NOVEMBER

I have yet to hear Corey talk much about colleges, so I ask him where he wants to play. "Oh, I'm thinking about some southern schools: Florida State,

North Carolina, maybe Virginia. I hate it when it gets sharp and brisk out like this. My one rule is, I won't go anyplace where I got to wear one of them Eskimo coats." Corey's recruiting hasn't even begun, but he's already established the proper hedonistic frame of mind.

"Still got to pass those SATs," Russell warns.

"I'm not scared," Corey replies. "I do well on tests. Anyway, this should be our year to relax."

"That test is *hard*," says Stephon from the backseat. "I looked at it once and almost fainted. I read somewhere that David Robinson got a 1300. Is that possible?"

"I heard there are players who get other guys to take the test for them," Russell says. "How do they get away with that? Find someone who looks like them?"

This is not a good sign. One of Russell's friends at Grady, who had scored lower than he on practice tests, suddenly got his 700 and signed with a top program. Some Lincolnites have begun wondering whether Grady players are using stand-ins to take the test.

The NCAA and the college basketball industry have done much soul-searching in recent years over the SAT requirement, as well they should. A combined score of 700 may not seem like a terribly rigorous standard, but given the quality of the Lincoln players' schooling, it's not surprising that they don't know a synonym for *panache* or how to make the most of what they do know; they've never been told, for example, to avoid guessing and answer only the questions they're sure of—the kinds of test-taking tips suburban kids learn on their first day in a Stanley Kaplan review course. Russell's school average, now over 80, says a lot more about his determination to succeed, but that alone will get him nowhere.

One day in study hall, I watched Corey sitting in the back, bent over his desk, while all around him his classmates wreaked havoc, throwing spitballs and jumping from desk to desk. At the end of the period I asked what he had accomplished and he handed me a poem about life in Coney Island that ended, "A place meant for happiness, sweet love and care—/ Something any human desires to share./ Yet it seems to haunt instead of praise/ The foundation and center of our bitter days."

When I had finished reading, Corey said to me, "I'm going to be a writer—you know, creative writing, poetry, free-associative stuff. I just play ball to take up time." Corey was tremendously prolific, dashing off a new poem for every girl he met. But having successfully merged his twin passions—writing and romance—he never left time for his homework. He did the assignments he liked, ignored the rest, and, though he never caused trouble in class, had a 66 average and was one failed test away from losing his high-school eligibility. Already Division I coaches had identified him as a gifted player whose grades could be his undoing.

In Coney Island, girls and the distractions of friends represent such a threat to a college career that the neighborhood's talented athletes are often urged to give up the rights and privileges of adolescence and attend a high school far from home. They will be lonely, but they will stay on the straight and narrow. Corey's older brother Louis took this strategy one step further, going into seclusion at an all-boys school, then spending an extra year at a prep school that serves as a sort of academic rehab clinic for basketball players. Not coincidentally, he passed his SATs and became the first of the six Johnson boys to make it to a Division I program, the University of Buffalo.

Louis was so dedicated to his craft that he would practice his shot under the Garden lights until 4:00 A.M. Everyone wishes Corey were equally single-minded. But Corey's sensibility is too quirky for that, and therein lies a danger. If Corey lived twenty-five miles north in, say, Scarsdale, he'd play the offbeat writer whose poor grades earn him a four-year sentence at Colgate, to be served while his classmates all go Ivy. But Corey fools around in an arena where there are no safety schools or safety nets. All of which presents a sad bit of irony: inner-city kids are always accused of doing nothing but throwing a ball through a hoop. Then along comes someone like Corey who takes pleasure in a million other things. (When the Lincoln team runs wind sprints on the outdoor track, Corey gladly takes the outside lane so he can run his hands through the canopy of leaves above his head.) In Coney Island, however, you ignore your basketball talent at great risk—athletic scholarships being significantly easier to come by than those for ghetto poets.

DECEMBER

Here they are, playing by all the rules: They stay in school—though their own school hardly keeps its end of the bargain. They say no to drugs—though it's the only fully employed industry around. They don't get into trouble with the NCAA—though its rules seem designed to foil them, and the coaches who break the rules go unpunished. They even heed their parents' wishes—and often pay a stiff price.

Of course none of them is perfect: Russell panics about his SATs and the choices he must make, and has trouble owning up to it; Corey won't apply himself and kids himself into thinking it won't matter; Stephon has—what shall we call it?—an attitude that needs some adjustment. But they operate in an environment that forgives none of the inevitable transgressions of adolescence and bestows no second chances.

Which makes this process of playing for a scholarship not the black version of the American dream, as some would suggest, but a cruel parody of it. In the classic parable you begin with nothing and slowly accrue your riches through hard work in a system designed to help those who help themselves. Here you begin with nothing but one narrow, treacherous path and then run a gauntlet of obstacles that merely reminds you of how little you have: recruiters pass themselves off as father figures, standardized tests humiliate you and reveal the wretchedness of your education, the promise of lucrative NBA contracts reminds you of what it feels like to have nothing in this world.

Jou-Jou, Silk, Chocolate, Spoon, Spice, Ice, Goose, Tiny, T, Stretch, Space, Sky: all of them great Coney Island players, most of them waiting vainly for a second chance, hanging out in the neighborhood, or dead. And here come Russell, Corey, and Stephon in my car, riding down Mermaid Avenue in the bone chill and gloom of this December night, hoping for the best, and knowing that in this particular game failure is commonplace, like a shrug, and heartbreak the order of the day.

———————◆———

In a very special way basketball has blended with our self-image. Black male arrogance, intelligence, greed, toughness, weakness, and innovation are all displayed in this sport. Since the sport's invention 100 years ago Black players have been depicted as clowns, role models, and threats to its survival and, ultimately, the game's very soul.

NELSON GEORGE, *Elevating the Game: The History and Aesthetics of Black Men in Basketball,* 1992

49.

JAMES HOWARD KUNSTLER: *The Geography of Nowhere*

In the decades following World War II, residential developers and legions of homeowners were buoyed by the seemingly endless supply of new, inexpensive housing that spread radially from American cities into the surrounding countryside. By the early 1990s, however, metropolitan sprawl had become a bugbear for city planners, who were unable to exorcise it, partly because they lacked comprehensive, regional authority. James Howard Kunstler's 1993 book, The Geography of Nowhere, *traced the history of housing styles in the United States: from early colonial and Georgian, through the nineteenth-century boom in Greek Revival and Victorian, and finally, in the early twentieth century, to the low-lying California bungalow and Prairie house. In Kunstler's view this proud history reached a disastrous crescendo after World War II—at the intersection of mass production, motorized access, and ready financing—in a cacophony of suburban tract housing that has created a blight on the American landscape. "Eighty percent of everything ever built in America has been built in the last fifty years," Kunstler announces, "and most of it is depressing, brutal, ugly, unhealthy, and spiritually degrading." The excerpt that follows is from Kunstler's chapter entitled, "A Place Called Home."*

Source: *The Geography of Nowhere: The Rise and Decline of America's Man-Made Landscape,* New York, 1993.

AT REGULAR INTERVALS, the United States Government reports the number of "housing starts" as a barometric indicator of how the nation's economic weather is blowing, fair or foul. The more housing starts, the better for the economy, the better for our civilization, so the thinking goes. More families will move into "decent" housing, and more paychecks will go into the pockets of building contractors and cement truck drivers. In 1992, there were 1,200,000 housing starts.

It's a figure that ought to send chills up the spine of a reflective person because these housing starts do not represent newly minted towns, or anything describable as real or coherent communities. Rather, they represent monoculture tract developments of cookie-cutter bunkers on half-acre lots in far-flung suburbs, or else houses plopped down in isolation along country roads in what had been cornfields, pastures, or woods. In any case, one can rest assured that they will only add to the problems of our present economy and of American civilization. They will relate poorly to other things around them, they will eat up more countryside, and they will increase the public fiscal burden.

There must have been a time when people looked forward to the erection of a new house in town, or even at the edge of town. By town, I mean something akin to a living organism composed of different parts that work together to make the whole greater than the sum of its parts—that is, a community. A new building would be expected to add value and richness to this community, as a new child is eagerly awaited by members of a family.

All that has changed in the last fifty years. Our towns no longer have boundaries, but sprawl out of their old containers into the countryside, where the functions of the town—markets, restaurants, law offices, hair salons, TV repair shops—tend to destroy open space without adding up to a community. The separate buildings exist in physical discontinuity with each other and their surroundings, and they promote further discontinuities of meaning and context, especially when they are decorated with symbols intended to snag the attention of passing motorists—and this is true for houses as well as carpet stores and used car lots. Today, when the bulldozers show up to clear the homesites, we greet them with a groan of despair—oh no, not another development!—and with a conviction that whatever gets built will be painful to see, bad for the biosphere, and socially pernicious. One looks upon new home construction as the cancer patient must contemplate the spread of malignant cells through his healthy tissue.

It must be emphasized that the crisis of the American home is not one of interior organization or technical innovation—these problems have largely been solved—but of how it relates or fails to relate to a town. It happens that the symptoms of this disease are most apparent in the way houses look on the outside. All the doodads (to borrow a term from architect Robert Venturi) tacked on to liven them up not only fail to conceal the fundamental illness but make it more obvious. The models costing half a million dollars are as bad as those costing $100,000, and for the same reasons, though they may be more spacious and include luxurious equipment for bathing and cooking. This is quite an extraordinary thing. It can only be possible where people feel no connection or allegiance to their locality—and, in fact, Americans move relentlessly, every four years on the average.

Quickest to uproot themselves are the educated classes, generally to advance their corporate careers. In an earlier era, these would have been the people who stayed put long enough to become stewards, official or otherwise, of that complex of values known as pride of place. They would have owned the business blocks downtown, and taken care of them. They would have built the churches, the libraries, the town bandshell, the ballfields. And they would have built houses for their own families that embodied the ideas of endurance and continuity. Today, this class of citizen is in the service of the large corporations whose very survival is predicated on destroying local economies and thus local communities. So it is somehow just that their hirelings should live in places of no character, no history, and no community.

The tragic thing is that there existed in America a fine heritage of regional home-building traditions, rich with values and meanings, and we threw it all away. Vestigial symbols of that tradition remain—the screw-on plastic shutters, fanlights with pop-in mullions, vinyl clapboards, the fakey front portico too narrow to put a chair on—but the building culture from which these details derive is as lost as the music of the Aztecs. . . .

Across the rural northeast, where I live, the countryside is littered with new houses. It was good farmland until recently. On every county road, every unpaved lane, every former cowpath, stand new houses, and each one is somebody's version of the American Dream. Most are simple raised ranches based on tried-

and-true formulas—plans conceived originally in the 1950s, not rethought since then, and sold ten thousand times over.

These housing "products" represent a triumph of mass merchandising over regional building traditions, of salesmanship over civilization. You can be sure the same houses have been built along a highway strip outside Fresno, California, at the edge of a swamp in Pahokee, Florida, and on the blizzard-blown fringes of St. Cloud, Minnesota. They might be anywhere. The places they stand are just different versions of nowhere, because these houses exist in no specific relation to anything except the road and the power cable. Electric lighting has reduced the windows to lame gestures. Tradition comes prepackaged as screw-on aluminum shutters, vinyl clapboards, perhaps a phony cupola on the roof ridge, or a plastic pediment over the door—tribute, in sad vestiges, to a lost past from which nearly all connections have been severed. There they sit on their one- or two- or half-acre parcels of land—the scruffy lawns littered with the jetsam of a consumerist religion (broken tricycles, junk cars, torn plastic wading pools)—these dwellings of a proud and sovereign people. If the ordinary house of our time seems like a joke, remember that it expresses the spirit of our age. The question, then, is: what kind of joke represents the spirit of our age? And the answer is: a joke on ourselves.

Lately among these houses a new fashion has arisen of sticking humorous painted plywood cutouts on the front lawn. Four-by-eight-foot plywood sheets lend themselves nicely to this sort of sculptural treatment. The prototype was a life-sized cutout of a fat woman bending over, as though weeding the flower beds, so that her bloomers are exposed to all passersby—presumably motorists. Soon she was joined by a male compan-

ion, also weeding and bent over so as to expose the crack at the top of his butt over low-slung pants. A year or so later, a new character appeared: a mischievous child of about two with his diapers dangling around his knees in the act of peeing. Commonly this impish figure was displayed against the foundation shrubs, with the implication that the house itself was being peed on. Probably unconsciously, the homeowner had surpassed his own humorous intentions. This is what comes of living in houses without dignity.

These plywood cutouts are common lawn decorations in our part of the country, as birdbaths were thirty years ago. One can't pass these cartoon-like displays without thinking of television—indeed, of how much television has to do with the way houses look in the present landscape. The American house has been TV-centered for three generations. It is the focus of family life, and the life of the house correspondingly turns inward, away from whatever occurs beyond its four walls. (TV rooms are called "family rooms" in builders' lingo. A friend who is an architect explained to me: "People don't want to admit that what the family *does* together is watch TV.") At the same time, the television is the family's chief connection with that outside world. The physical envelope of the house itself no longer connects their lives to the outside in any active way; rather, it seals them off from it. The outside world has become an abstraction filtered through television, just as the weather is an abstraction filtered through air conditioning.

The car, of course, is the other connection to the outside world, but to be precise it connects the inhabitants to the inside of their car, not to the outside world per se. The outside world is only an element for moving through, as submarines move through water.

As the outside world became more of an abstraction, and the outside of the house lost its detail, it began to broadcast information about itself and its owners in the abstracted language of television, specifically of television advertising, which is to say a form of communication based on simplifications and lies. As in television advertising, the lies have to be broad and simple because the intended audience is a passing motorist who will glance at the house for a few seconds. So, one dwelling has a fake little cupola to denote vaguely an image of rusticity; another has a fake portico à la *Gone With the Wind,* with skinny two-story white columns out of proportion with the mass of the house, and a cement slab too narrow to put a rocking chair on, hinting at wealth and gentility; a third has the plastic pediment over the door and brass carriage lamps on either side, invoking "tradition." The intent is to create associations that will make the house appear as something other than the raised ranch it actually is, something *better,* older, more enduring, resonant with history and taste.

It must be obvious that there are honest ways to design a dwelling that confer meaning and sensual appeal. But they involve more complicated procedures than the two-second visual pitch to a passing motorist using cartoonish symbolism. And the task is made inordinately more difficult when each house is disposed on its own acre, with only a schematic connection to the land in the form of "landscaping" with shrubs, and no relation whatever to other buildings—even if there are some nearby. It is also difficult when the street is degraded by a lot of automobile traffic.

Americans wonder why their houses lack charm. The word *charm* may seem fussy, trivial, vague. I use it to mean explicitly *that which makes our physical surroundings worth caring about.* It is not a trivial matter, for we are presently suffering on a massive scale the social consequences of living in places that are not worth caring about. Charm is dependent on connectedness, on continuities, on the relation of one thing to another, often expressed as tension, like the tension between private space and public space, or the sacred and the workaday, or the interplay of a space that is easily comprehensible, such as a street, with the mystery of openings that beckon, such as a doorway set deeply in a building. Of course, if the public space is degraded by cars and their special needs—as it always is in America, whether you live in Beverly Hills or Levittown—the equation is spoiled. If nothing is sacred, then everything is profane.

The equation is also spoiled when buildings cease to use the basic physical vocabulary of architecture—extrusions and recesses—and instead resort to tacked-on symbols and signs. One is a real connection with the real world; the other is an appeal to second-hand mental associations. (I saw a wonderful example of this in Vermont: a two-story building on a rural highway that had a gigantic sign on it, with letters four-feet high. The sign said COUNTRY STORE, as though passing strangers had to be informed in written words that they were in the country. The woods and meadows on each side of the road were not enough to get across the point.)

This habit of resorting to signs and symbols to create the illusion of charm in our everyday surroundings is symptomatic of a growing American character disorder: the belief that it is possible to get something for nothing. The germ of this disorder probably has been with us a very long time, because this was such a bountiful land. But our economic luck in the aftermath of World War II accelerated the syndrome. Life was so easy here for so many for such a long time that Americans somehow got the idea that you merely had to wish something was so in order to make it so. The culture of advertising—which bombarded Americans daily, hourly—eroded our capacity to distinguish between the truths and the lies. And not even in moral terms, but on the practical level. You could label a house "traditional" and someone would accept it, even if all the traditional relationships between the house and its surroundings were obliterated. You could name a housing development Forest Knoll Acres even if there was no forest and no knoll, and the customers would line up with their checkbooks open. Americans were as addicted to illusion as they were to cheap petroleum. They had more meaningful relationships with movie stars and characters on daytime television shows than they did with members of their own families. They didn't care if things were real or not, if ideas were truthful. In fact, they preferred fantasy. They preferred lies. And the biggest lie of all was that the place they lived in was *home*. . . .

The mobility that Americans prize so highly is the final ingredient in the debasement of housing. The freedom to pick up and move is a premise of the national experience. It is the physical expression of the freedom to move upward socially, absent in other societies. The automobile allowed this expression to be carried to absurd extremes. Our obsession with mobility, the urge to move on every few years, stands at odds with the wish to endure in a beloved place, and no place can be worthy of that kind of deep love if we are willing to abandon it on short notice for a few extra dollars. Rather, we choose to live in Noplace, and our dwellings show it. In every corner of the nation we have built places unworthy of love and move on from them without regret. But move on to what? Where is the ultimate destination when every place is Noplace?

◆

Seventy-two suburbs in search of a city.
                    Attributed to both DOROTHY PARKER and ALEXANDER
                         WOOLLCOTT, characterizing Los Angeles

1994

50.

Roy Beck: Small Towns, New Immigrants

Between the 1920s and the 1960s the United States sharply curtailed immigration. The decision to reduce immigration stemmed from two major trends: 1) the United States possessed a surplus of domestic labor, and 2) a national consensus had developed that saw heavy immigration as a threat to America's cultural unity. In the 1960s, however, after four decades of restricted immigration, government policy toward immigration was reversed. A growing appreciation of cultural diversity coupled with a significant labor shortage prompted Congress to relax immigration laws and encourage a new wave of immigrants to enter the country. In the late 1980s and early 1990s more than one million immigrants were entering the United States annually, some legally and others illegally. Although most settled in large urban areas, a growing number located in small towns in the interior of the country. This influx sparked a renewed fear in some people that immigrants threatened the nation's cultural unity, and many Americans began to call for a reinstitution of restrictions on immigration. Others, in contrast, argued that the immigrants assimilated quickly into American society and provided a workforce crucial to the growth of the national economy. In an essay for the The Atlantic Monthly, *Roy Beck, an editor for the journal* The Social Contract, *explored the impact of immigration on a small town in Wisconsin in the early 1990s. Excerpts are reprinted below.*

Source: *The Atlantic Monthly*, April 1, 1994, "The Ordeal of Immigration in Wausau."

IT ALL BEGAN SIMPLY enough, when a few churches and individuals in Wausau, Wisconsin, decided to resettle some Southeast Asian refugees during the late 1970s. To most residents, it seemed like a nice thing to do. Nobody meant to plant the seeds for a social transformation. But this small and private charitable gesture inad- vertently set into motion events that many residents today feel are spinning out of control. Wausau—the county seat of the nation's champion milk-producing county—has learned that once the influx starts, there's little chance to stop it. Re- gardless of how many newcomers failed to find jobs in this north-central Wisconsin city of 37,500, or how abraded the social fabric became, the immigrant population just kept growing.

In little more than a decade the immigrant families' children have come to make up almost a quarter of the elementary schools' enrollment, crowding facilities past their limits—and there's no peak in sight. The majority of immigrant students are Southeast Asians, and most of these are from the nomadic Hmong mountain tribes of Laos, which unsuccessfully tried to prevent a Communist takeover of their homeland some twenty years ago. Seventy percent of the immigrants and their descendants are receiving public assistance, because the local labor market has not been able to accommodate them. Religious and other private agencies—which, through federal agreements, create most of the refugee streams into American communities—are pledged to care for the newcomers for only thirty days.

Native-born taxpayers must shoulder most of the rising costs of providing more infrastructure, public services, teachers, and classrooms for the burgeoning community of immigrants, who make up relatively little of the tax base. In 1992 alone the Wausau school district's property-tax rate rose 10.48 percent—three times as much as taxes in an adjoining school district with few immigrants.

"At first, most saw the new residents as novel and neat; people felt good about it," Fred Prehn, a dentist and the father of two school-age children, told me during a visit I made to Wausau some months ago. At the time we spoke, he was the senior member of Wausau's school board. "Now we're beginning to see gang violence and guns in the schools. Immigration has inspired racism here that I never thought we had." Prehn accused religious agencies of swelling the immigrant population without regard to the city's capacity for assimilation. He said that the numbers and concentration of newcomers had forced the school board into a corner from which busing was the only escape. English was becoming the minority spoken language in several schools. Many native-born parents feared that their children's education was being compromised by the language-instruction confusion; many immigrant parents complained that their children couldn't be assimilated properly in schools where the immigrant population was so high. For two years citizens were polarized by the prospect of busing—something that would have been inconceivable in 1980. Divisions deepened last September, when the school board initiated the busing, and again in December, when voters recalled Prehn and four other board members, replacing them with a slate of anti-busing candidates. Community divisions are likely to persist, since busing supporters threaten lawsuits if the new board ends the busing.

Even more of a shock has been the emergence of organized gang activity. Wausau Detective Sergeant Paul Jicinsky told me that Asian gangs of thieves, centered in St. Paul and Milwaukee, have recruited immigrant youths in Wausau. Most small Wisconsin cities started Asian-refugee resettlement programs at the prodding of government and religious leaders a decade or so ago, and most are now part of a Crime Information Exchange that, Jicinsky said, had been established almost exclusively to keep track of Asian gang activity in Minnesota and Wisconsin. Hmong parents, lamenting that their difficulty with English impedes their exercise of authority over their children, were at the forefront of those asking the police to combat gang activity. The cycle of community tensions spins

round as native youths link up with outside white gangs to respond to Asian
gangs. Compared with the urban core of
many big cities, Wausau remains quite a
peaceful place. But the comparison that
matters for most residents is with the
Wausau that used to be. "We don't want
to become another California," a Wausau
businessman told me. It's a fear often expressed as residents grapple with the
problems familiar to America's congested coastal urban areas after nearly
three decades of federally sponsored
mass immigration and refugee resettlement.

At the same time, frustration grows
among immigrants whose economic assimilation is dramatically incomplete.
That frustration, in combination with resentment among natives over taxes and
busing, seems to be the cause of inter-
ethnic violence among the young. The violence takes varied forms. A dance at
Wausau East High School, for instance,
had to be canceled just as it was starting
because of a fight between immigrant
and native girls, which was serious
enough that an ambulance had to be
called. Mayor John D. Hess, in a newsletter to all residents, wrote, "Is there a
problem with groups/gangs of school
age kids in Wausau? Emphatically, yes.
The number of incidents involving
group violence leads all of us to believe
that groups of school age kids are organizing for whatever reasons. . . . Is there a
problem relating to racial tensions in
Wausau? Emphatically, yes."

The 1980 U.S. Census found Wausau
to be the most ethnically homogeneous
city in the nation, with less than one percent of the population other than white.
"This was a very nice thriving community; now immigration problems have divided the town and changed it drastically," Sandy Edelman, a mother of
preschool-age children, told me. "Neigh-

borhood is pitted against neighborhood.
When we were moving here, a few years
ago, I had this image of children walking to school. It was paradise, we
thought. We never thought it was possible there ever could be busing in these
schools."

A MIDDLE-CLASS DREAM

Although Wausau is not marked by
splashy displays of wealth, the word "paradise" crops up in wistful descriptions of
the recent past by all types of residents,
including immigrants. They obviously
aren't talking about some idyllic South
Seas utopia. What they have in mind
seems to be a kind of pragmatic middle-
class American dream, in which labor
produced a comfortable standard of living in a community that was under the
control of its residents and where there
existed a safe, predictable domestic tranquillity in which to rear children and
nearby open spaces for north-country
recreation. It was a way of life created by
the descendants of German and Polish
immigrants and New England Yankee migrants, who by 1978 had spent roughly a
century getting used to one another and
creating a unified culture.

On my visit to Wausau, I found some
anger. But the overwhelming emotion
seemed to be sadness about a social revolution that the community as a whole
had never requested or even discussed.
While most residents spoke well of the
immigrants as individuals, they thought
that the volume of immigration had
crossed some kind of social and economic threshold. Many sensed that their
way of life is slipping away, overwhelmed
by outside forces they are helpless to
stop.

Wausau leaders describe their city
prior to 1978 as one with no social tensions and only traces of crime. Residents

enjoyed a long tradition of progressive politics, education, and business. A healthy match between the labor force and well-paying jobs was the result of a diverse economy heavily reliant on the Wausau Insurance Companies and the manufacture of windows, paper, cheese, electric motors and generators, fast-food-outlet exhaust fans, and garden tools.

In the eyes of some residents, though, this "paradise" may well have been boring. "This was a rather sterile community, and we needed ethnic diversity," says Phyllis A. Bermingham, the director of the county department that administers the jobs program for welfare recipients. "I'm glad Wausau had major refugee resettlement. It has added so much variety." Sue Kettner, who is in charge of refugee services at a family-planning agency, says, "I have a dream that Wausau will become uniquely cosmopolitan and take advantage of its diversity." The until-recently "sterile" and homogeneous Wausau-area schools now enroll students from Laos, Cambodia, Thailand, Vietnam, China, the Philippines, Korea, Japan, Norway, Albania, Egypt, the former East Germany, the former Yugoslavia, and the former Czechoslovakia.

The idea of a moratorium on immigration comes up often in discussions in Wausau. But many people told me that they don't raise the idea in public, because they believe that religious, media, and government leaders would readily label any kind of criticism of immigration a manifestation of racism. From 1924 until 1965 the nation's immigration laws prevented foreign migration from reshaping the social landscape of American communities. The laws no longer do. Wausau is but one example of the results of radically modified laws, and many residents are astonished at the rapidity and relentlessness of change.

From a few dozen refugees in 1978, Wausau's immigrant community grew to 200 by 1980, doubled from there by 1982, and doubled again by 1984. Since then it has more than quintupled, to reach roughly 4,200. Even if the influx slows, Southeast Asians may become the majority population in Wausau well within the present residents' lifetimes. In this, Wausau is not unique but only an indicator of the demographic effects of current immigrant streams in the nation as a whole. . . .

Wausau's experience, although relatively uncommon in the Midwest, is quite common among American communities of the 1980s and 1990s. The majority of U.S. population growth since 1970 has come from immigrants and their descendants. They will probably contribute two thirds of the growth during this decade and nearly all of it after the turn of the century if federal policies remain the same.

FALSE PROMISES

On a main road into downtown, an ALL-AMERICAN CITY sign reminds residents and visitors alike that Wausau is not inherently incapable of rising to the challenge of assimilating new residents. It was doing a fine job in 1984, when it won the award commemorated by the sign.

Nearby is another sign. WELCOME HOME TO WAUSAU, this one says, in the homespun way of small cities. It is more than a cliche to say that many natives no longer feel at home here, even as newcomers feel less than welcome. It is noteworthy, however, that when natives told me longingly of a lost "home," most seemed to refer not to the Wausau of 1978, before the refugee influx, but to the Wausau of 1984, when the influx was at a level that still constituted a delightful spice and community relations were harmonious.

John Robinson, who was the mayor of Wausau from 1988 to 1992, acknowledges that no government entity at any stage of Wausau's transformation talked to residents about immigration rates or developed community-wide planning for projecting future changes or deciding whether current trends should be allowed to continue. "The Southeast Asian evolution in Wausau was not a planned process," Robinson told me. "It was sort of a happening. Could the city have planned differently? Yes. But until there is a real need staring you in the face, you don't always reach out and address it." Robinson, who was a young city councilman from 1974 to 1981 and a member of the legislature from 1981 to 1988, says he isn't sure the city could have changed anything even if officials had spoken out against continuing federal refugee resettlement.

In 1984 Wausau's welcome of Southeast Asians was still bighearted enough, and its relations between cultures congenial enough, for Wausau to be designated an All-American City. Youa Her, an educated, articulate leader of the early wave of Hmong settlers, made one of Wausau's presentations to the national panel of judges. The thirty-four-year-old woman's description of Wausau's generosity reportedly left the panelists with tears in their eyes.

Nobody is exactly sure when and how everything started to go sour. But it was probably around the time of the award—certainly before Youa Her's tragic death, in January of 1986, of tubercular meningitis. Newspapers from those years reveal a community increasingly sobered by the realization that what appeared to be a short-term, private charitable act had no apparent end and was starting to entail a lot of local public costs. Many na-tives resent that nobody ever leveled with them about costs or where trends would lead, and they feel they were misled by the local media and by federal, state, and religious leaders.

During the late 1970s residents had assumed that the congregations would cover any costs of caring for the refugees they were sponsoring. After all, it was their project. One sponsor reinforced that notion, telling a reporter, "[Sponsorship] is not something that will last three days or three months or three years. It can be something to last a lifetime."

But the churches' financial commitment was actually rather shallow and short-lived, as Jean Russell, of the county welfare department, explains it. "At the beginning it was good Christian people wanting to do something for somebody. What they did was pick the refugees up at the airport and drive them to our office. The churches did help some, but the Hmong couldn't make it without social services." (The Hmong are not unusual in this regard. A 1991 U.S. Department of Health and Human Services study indicated that nationwide about two thirds of all Southeast Asian refugees who have arrived since 1986 remain on public assistance.)

Wausau residents were assured, though, that they had no reason to worry about increased welfare costs. In 1979 Susan G. Levy, the coordinator for the state's resettlement assistance office, explained that local taxpayers would not be adversely affected by private sponsors' generosity in inviting refugees, because the federal government would pick up the welfare tab.

As long as the flow was meager, Wausau's economy did fairly well at providing jobs to keep the immigrants off the welfare rolls. "Refugees Are Very Adaptable, State Officials Say" was one 1979 headline in the local paper. In June of 1980 the paper reported that 80 percent of the city's refugees became self-supporting within about three years: "Wausau's 200 Asian refugees doing well, more sponsors needed."

Promoters seemed certain that anything that was good and worked on one scale would be even better on a larger scale. Milton Lorman, a state representative from Fort Atkinson, urged Wisconsin to speed the flow of refugees. "The Statue of Liberty symbolizes the historic support of this country for immigrant rights," he said. "Wisconsin, as a state settled by immigrants, proves that this dream works."

But by May of 1982 an important threshold of danger had been crossed. One headline read, "Most refugees now receiving AFDC, relief aid." The immigrant population in Wausau had doubled since 1980, and the nation was in recession. That spring the federal government cut back its welfare assistance to new refugees. In the years that followed, federal and state governments—having enticed communities to take in immigrants—withdrew more and more support, leaving local taxpayers to bear most of the cost. "The federal government was a silent partner and then became a non-existent partner," John Robinson laments.

Youa Her in late 1984 accepted the idea of economic limitations. "Anybody that calls," she said, "we'll tell them to think it over and not to be so hurried [to move to Wausau]." Choj Hawj, who was the elected leader of the Hmong Association at the time, said, "When I look to the economy and the population of Wausau city, we don't want any more to come until things look up."

The former school-board member Fred Prehn recalls that Youa Her was also concerned about proportionality and the effect of continued immigration on social relationships. He says she thanked city leaders for how well Wausau had provided for her people. But she warned them not to let the Hmong become more than five percent of the population, Prehn says; if their numbers went much higher, the natives might start to resent the immigrants, and hostility would begin to replace hospitality.

A month after Her's death Robert Nakamaru, a college professor, addressed the proportionality issue at an event that was intended in part to soothe emerging ethnic tensions. "When there are just a handful, they are seen as quaint," Nakamaru said of the immigrants. "But there is a point where a minority reaches a critical mass in the perception of the majority. Wausau is getting close to that point." Since then the city's immigrant population has quadrupled. . . .

A COOLING-OFF PERIOD

For twenty-eight years Billy Moy's One World Inn served Chinese food in a former train depot on an island in the Wisconsin River. Bridges connecting the western half of Wausau to its downtown, on the east side, route traffic past the depot. Before his retirement last year Billy Moy, who arrived in Wausau as a Chinese refugee, sat with me in a darkened back room and told the kind of colorful escape and success stories that traditionally have evoked warmhearted responses from Americans. As a teenager he fled the Chinese Communists in 1951 and arrived by train in Wausau in 1952. After years of hard work, perseverance, and saving, and six years in the U.S. Army reserves, Moy bought the island depot and turned it into his restaurant in 1965.

"I didn't know a word of English when I arrived," Moy told me. In that he was like many of the refugees arriving today. But his reception and his freedom to move into the economic mainstream were far different. Why? One explanation may be that Moy had more education than the Hmong, whose people didn't even have a written language until recent decades. More important, perhaps, he was a novelty in Wausau, rather than a member of a mass of newcomers which natives may find threatening. "I started with first-grade English and high school math," Moy said. "People were very nice, especially the teachers. Kids never harassed me. Never a bad word. I guess it was because I was the only one." Fred Prehn went to school with Moy's son during the 1960s and 1970s and recalls that the young Moy was the only minority student. That son now has an M.B.A. and is a business analyst in Milwaukee.

But today's economy has not offered as many opportunities to the large number of refugees of the eighties and nineties, Mary C. Roberts, of the Marathon County Development Corporation, told me. "The Southeast Asian unemployment rate is high," Roberts said. "I think it is kind of irresponsible for churches to bring more in without at least the equivalent of one job pledged per family. Churches look at this just from the humanitarian angles and not the practical."

Various Wausau residents told me they favor a "cooling-off period" before more refugees are resettled in their city. Few residents know it, but such a period played a major role in creating the homogeneous Wausau they now consider the norm. After the turn of the century, immigration caused a social upheaval in Wausau. Back then the Germans and the Yankees were distinct ethnic groups, neither of which found particular strength in diversity. From 1880 to the start of the First World War, Germans streamed into Wausau, eventually overwhelming its New England Yankee founders. Jim

Lorence, a local historian, says that the Germans became the predominant ethnic group around 1910. By the end of the decade the immigrants had turned the once conservative Republican town into a Socialist powerhouse. After the November 1918 elections, nearly every county office and both of the county's seats in the state assembly were filled by German-elected Socialists, Lorence says. Amid the political turmoil, natives felt like foreigners in their own home town. Around the nation this period was a time of sweatshops, worsening inner-city squalor, and ethnic hatred that propelled the Ku Klux Klan to its greatest popularity ever. The KKK, however, never got a strong foothold in Wausau, Lorence says.

The federal government in 1924 responded to the problems in a way that had a profound effect on the future development of Wausau and the nation. Congress lowered immigrant admissions to a level more palatable to local labor markets, according to the labor economist Vernon Briggs, of Cornell University. In his recent book, *Mass Immigration and the National Interest,* he describes how the 1924 law gave the country a much-needed forty years to assimilate the new immigrants. The KKK's power receded nationally, and cultural wounds began to heal. Labor markets gradually tightened. That helped stimulate improvements in technology and productivity which supported the middle-class wage economy that Americans took for granted until the 1970s—when the labor supply ballooned owing to renewed mass immigration, the entry of the Baby Boomers into the job market, and a radical increase in the number of married women in the workplace. Since then wages have declined and disparities of wealth have widened. . . .

Congress began to take part in the discussion about a cooling-off period late last year, when Senator Harry Reid and

Representative James Bilbray, both Democrats from Nevada, introduced comprehensive immigration-reform bills that would cut the number of legal immigrants by roughly two thirds, to 300,000 and 350,000 a year. (The U.S. average from 1820 to 1965 was 297,000.) In February, Representative Bob Stump, an Arizona Republican, introduced a "moratorium" bill that would reduce immigration even further. The last time Congress cut the flow of immigrants, in the 1920s, Wausau began to experience social healing, Jim Lorence says. Though it took another thirty years for the major divisions between the German immigrants and the native Yankees to disappear, the disparate ethnic groups slowly began to achieve a unified and harmonious culture—the paradigm of a recoverable paradise.

51.

RICHARD BROOKHISER: The Whitewater Scandal

When Bill Clinton won the presidency in 1992, he planned to devote his first term to reforming health care, welfare, and the national economy. By 1994, however, a scandal from his years as governor of Arkansas threatened to derail his legislative agenda. While governor in the late 1970s, Clinton and his wife, Hillary, had bought shares in the Whitewater Development Corporation, a real-estate venture run by their friends and political allies, James and Susan McDougal. The venture failed, but rumors of wrongdoing surrounded the Whitewater development and followed Clinton into the White House. During Clinton's first term, Janet Reno, his attorney general, appointed a special prosecutor to investigate the scandal. Despite a long and costly investigation, Kenneth Starr, the special prosecutor, never found hard evidence of illegal activity by Clinton. During his Whitewater investigation, however, Starr inadvertently ran across the fact that Clinton had conducted a sexual relationship with a White House intern, Monica Lewinsky. Starr shifted the entire focus of the Whitewater investigation to Clinton's sexual behavior and the question of whether the president committed perjury in his denial of the affair. Ultimately, in 1998, Starr's report prompted the House of Representatives to impeach Clinton. In the Senate trial, Clinton won an acquittal and served out the remainder of his term in the White House. In the National Review *magazine article excerpted below, senior editor Richard Brookhiser describes the roots of the Whitewater scandal.*

Source: *National Review,* March 21, 1994, "Whitewater Runs Deep."

THE PIGGYBANK

Whitewater first came to public attention in a March 8, 1992, story in the *New York Times.* (It would be about the last time the *Times* was ahead of the curve on the case.) The story reported that the Clintons had taken tax deductions in the mid Eighties on interest payments for loans that had in fact been paid for them by the Whitewater Development Corporation, a real-estate scheme in northern Arkansas which they half-owned. Clinton, who had struggled through the Gennifer Flowers scandal only weeks earlier, asked James Lyons, a friendly lawyer, to look through his Whitewater records, such as they were. On March 28, Lyons reported that the Clintons had lost $68,900 on the venture. Reasoning that bad investors can't be tax cheats, the press let the story drop.

By the fall of 1992, the Resolution Trust Corporation, which is charged with cleaning up the S&L mess, was looking at Whitewater's other owners, James and Susan McDougal. James McDougal had known Bill Clinton since the late Sixties. The two couples formed the Whitewater partnership shortly before Clinton was first elected governor in 1978. Four years later, McDougal bought Madison Guaranty, a small thrift. It got bigger. McDougal acquired a blue Bentley, and the nickname "Diamond Jim." Susan's nickname was "Hot Pants," because that's what she wore on commercials promoting Whitewater. In 1989, Madison Guaranty went under, at a cost to taxpayers of $60 million.

An RTC document named the Clintons as potential witnesses to the deeds of McDougal and his "shell corporations." The Bush Justice Department would not give the matter top priority in the homestretch of a presidential campaign, and the Clinton Justice Department let it lie. But in October 1993, the RTC prodded Justice again, and Whitewater once more became a matter of public discussion.

One subject the media have discussed has been favors McDougal allegedly did for the Clintons. Representative Jim Leach (R., Iowa) has called Madison "a private piggybank." Most of the crooked S&Ls of the Eighties benefitted their

owners. But Madison Guaranty also extended itself for an array of well-connected Arkansans, including the Clintons. McDougal has claimed that in 1984, Clinton complained that he was hard up. "I asked him how much he needed, and Clinton said about $2,000 a month." Madison Guaranty put Hillary Clinton on a $2,000 a month retainer, paid through the Rose Law Firm where she worked—an arrangement that lasted for 15 months. The White House denies that Clinton sought business for his wife.

A year later, McDougal helped Clinton retire a big bank loan, possibly with the unwitting help of Madison's depositors. In the last days of the 1984 gubernatorial campaign Clinton, feeling a case of election jitters, borrowed $50,000 from a tiny bank in eastern Arkansas, run by a member of his staff. After Clinton won, he asked McDougal to "knock out the deficit." Madison held a fund-raiser in April 1985 which raised $35,000 for Clinton, but investigators suspect that $12,000 of that money—four certified checks for $3,000 apiece—was fraudulently raised. One of the "contributors" whose name appears on one of the checks denies he ever gave $3,000 to Clinton in 1985, for the excellent reason that he was a Republican college student at the time.

More serious are the favors the Clintons may have done for McDougal. The feds were taking a grim view of Madison Guaranty by 1984; the Federal Home Loan Bank Board called its lending practices "unsafe and unsound." In April 1985—the same month as the fund-raiser—Hillary Clinton earned her retainer by proposing a rescue plan for Madison to the Arkansas Securities Department. (The plan proposed that Madison be allowed to sell preferred stock, and offered, as proof of its health, an optimistic audit by Madison's accounting firm.) As luck would have it, the commissioner of the Securities Department whom Hillary's husband had just appointed was Beverly Bassett (now Beverly Bassett Schaffer), a big-hair woman who had done work for Madison Guaranty in an earlier incarnation as a securities lawyer. It doesn't get any tighter than this. In a letter addressed "Dear Hillary," Bassett okayed the plan.

Madison never got around to issuing any stock, and in the fall of 1985 the feds scheduled an audit for early next year. Enter now David Hale, a municipal judge in Little Rock who ran Capital Management, an investment firm backed by the Small Business Administration for the purpose of aiding disadvantaged entrepreneurs. Hale now claims that in February 1986, in a meeting at the State Capitol, Governor Clinton asked: "Are you going to be able to help Jim and me out?"

"That's just the way business is done in Arkansas," Hale adds.

The White House says that Hale, who is under indictment for fraud, is a liar out to "save his butt." What partly supports Hale, however, is that Capital Management in fact loaned $300,000 to that disadvantaged entrepreneur, Susan McDougal, and almost half of that money ended up in Whitewater's account, where it was used to buy 810 acres from International Paper.

These activities have to be set in the context of the Clintons' political and personal situation. In 1992 Bill Clinton looked like an unstoppable figure, a political Terminator. But he had been stopped once, in 1980, when he lost his first re-election bid for governor. He never took a race for granted after that. The Clintons' personal finances did not become comfortable until Hillary began landing on corporate boards in the late Eighties. A friend with Jim McDougal's cash flow was a friend indeed. McDougal

went to bat for the Clintons, at times—allegedly—out of order. Did they do the same for him?

THE FOUR LAWYERS

In a 1992 debate before the Illinois primary, Jerry Brown said Clinton's "wife's law firm is representing clients before state . . . agencies, his appointees." Clinton replied that the Rose Law Firm was "the oldest law firm in America, west of the Mississippi," and that Brown ought to be "ashamed" of himself "for jumping on my wife." The Rose Law Firm is old, yet, as we have seen, Brown's statement was true. What else had Mrs. Clinton and the partners who crossed the Mississippi with her to Washington—William Kennedy III, Webster Hubbell, and Vincent Foster—been up to?

One old case throws an ironic light on present policy debates. In 1989 Beverly Enterprises, a national nursing-home business, decided to sell 45 nursing homes in Iowa. Beverly Enterprises is indirectly controlled by the Stephens family, Little Rock banking kingpins; William Kennedy III of the Rose Law Firm (now associate counsel in the White House) handled the deal. On one day in August 1989 the nursing homes—which an Iowa judge has since ruled were worth about $47 million at the time—were sold to a Texas businessman, who re-sold them to a charitable company he controlled, backed by Iowa state tax-exempt bonds. Final sale price: $63.5 million. Not bad for a day's work. Rose Law could have collected as much as a million dollars for shuffling the papers, to be divided in bonuses among its partners, including Hillary Rodham Health Care. Meanwhile, the nursing homes, in order to pay off their debt, were forced to raise fees.

The nursing-home deal, all perfectly legal, offered a foretaste of the Clinton health plan: everyone was screwed, except the large medical corporations and the lawyers. But some Little Rock legal practitioners skated on slimmer ice.

Also in 1989, the Federal Deposit Insurance Corporation decided to sue the accounting firm that had presented a clean bill of health for Madison Guaranty to the Arkansas Securities Department in 1985. Vince Foster, another partner at Rose Law and later deputy White House counsel, wrote the FDIC offering Rose's services as outside counsel, declaring, in a careful present tense, that "the firm does not represent any savings-and-loan association in state or federal regulatory matters." Foster's statement was true, but so narrowly as to be false. The Rose Law Firm did not represent any S&Ls in 1989, but it had represented Madison Guaranty four years earlier—and in the matter under investigation. One seventeenth-century Jesuit, acting undercover in a Protestant country, when interrogated by the authorities denied that he was a priest, adding silently to himself, ". . . of Apollo." What was good enough for the Jesuits was good enough for the FDIC. Webb Hubbell, a Rose partner who is now associate attorney general—and hence number three

man at the Justice Department—handled the FDIC's case, settling the accountants' liability for the $60 million debacle at $1 million.

Two years earlier, two Rose Law Firm partners had handled a similar case for the Federal Savings and Loan Insurance Corporation, in similar style. The feds were pursuing a bond trader who they claimed had defrauded a defunct Illinois S&L, First American of Oak Brook. The Rose Law Firm offered itself successfully as outside counsel, and assigned Vince Foster and Hillary Clinton to the case. No one seems to have mentioned their connection to the bond trader: Dan Lasater, a restaurateur and cocaine smuggler who was a friend of the Clinton family. Lasater met the Clintons because his box at the Hot Springs race track was next to that of Virginia Kelley, Bill Clinton's mother. Lasater ended up paying $200,000, in return for dismissal of the $3.3 million suit.

Vince Foster is gone, of course, but the other three lawyers are still on call. With so much legal advice available, you would think Bill Clinton—himself a lawyer—would have handled his troubles more adroitly. But maybe he is doing exactly what they tell him.

———————◆———————

Whitewater is not about cover-ups, it's about screw-ups.
David Gergen, *The Washington Post,* March 6, 1994

52.

CIA Turncoat Aldrich Ames

In April 1994 a federal court convicted Aldrich Ames, a former analyst for the Central Intelligence Agency (CIA), of espionage for trading national security information to the Soviet Union and then Russia for money. Ames was the highest-ranking officer in the CIA's history to be found guilty of treason. The Ames case was a serious blow to CIA integrity and prompted new questions about the agency's competence. Founded in the 1940s as part of U.S. policy of containing Communism during the Cold War, the CIA was originally mandated to provide the White House with secret intelligence on the Soviet Union and other adversaries. It analyzed foreign intelligence, recruited double agents, and infiltrated spies into foreign governments. In the 1970s, a Senate investigation into CIA activities revealed that the agency had also taken part in numerous foreign coups and political assassinations. Those revelations shocked the public and prompted Congress to restrict severely both the CIA's budget and its foreign activities. The public fallout from the scandals demoralized many CIA analysts and field agents, and employee recruitment and retention became a problem. By the 1990s the agency seemed to have rebuilt its public reputation, only to have the Ames scandal shake it once again. In November 1994 the Senate Select Committee on Intelligence released its assessment of the Ames espionage case and its implications for the U.S. intelligence community. Reprinted below, excerpts of this document include a brief overview of the case against Ames, details of the treason, and recommendations for policy changes within the CIA.

Source: *An Assessment of the Aldrich H. Ames Espionage Case and Its Implications for U.S. Intelligence,* Washington, D.C., 1994.

INTRODUCTION

On February 21, 1994, agents from the Federal Bureau of Investigation (FBI) arrested a 52-year-old employee of the Central Intelligence Agency (CIA), Aldrich Hazen Ames, outside his Arlington, Virginia, residence, on charges of conspiracy to commit espionage on behalf of Russia and the former Soviet Union. According to the affidavit supporting the arrest warrant, these activities had begun in April 1985, and continued to the time of

the arrest. Ames's wife, Maria del Rosario Casas Ames, was arrested inside the residence on the same charges shortly after her husband was taken into custody.

Announced publicly the following day, the arrests prompted outrage and alarm across the country. Ames had been an employee of [the] CIA for 31 years, with most of his career spent in the Directorate of Operations, which is responsible for carrying out CIA clandestine operations around the globe. While the precise extent of Ames's espionage activities was unclear at the time of his arrest, Justice Department officials confirmed that Ames was believed to have caused the death or imprisonment of a number of Soviets who had been sources of the CIA and FBI. There were calls in Congress for curtailing aid to Russia, and legislative proposals were introduced within days of the arrests to bolster government security practices. A CIA team was sent to Moscow to speak with the Russian intelligence services, but returned empty handed.

President Clinton directed that the senior intelligence officer at the Russian Embassy in Washington be expelled from the United States in retaliation, while at the same time cautioning against treating the episode as a cause for disrupting the fragile political relationship with Russia.

The affidavit made public at the time of the arrests also confirmed that Ames had received substantial payments for the information he had provided—money that he had used years earlier to purchase a new Jaguar automobile and a $540,000 home, with cash, in Arlington. Apparently, these seemingly large expenditures by an employee making less than $70,000 a year had not raised questions at the CIA.

The Senate Select Committee on Intelligence (hereinafter "the Committee") received its initial briefing regarding the case on the day the arrests were publicly announced. The facts contained in the affidavit supporting the arrest and search warrants were summarized by representatives of the FBI. While recognizing the need to avoid actions that might complicate or hamper the ongoing FBI investigation and ultimately the Justice Department's prosecution of the case, the Committee was deeply concerned that Ames had been able to carry out his espionage activities without detection for a period of nine years, despite the presence of circumstances which indicated a security problem. What had gone wrong?

To answer this question, the Chairman and Vice Chairman of the Committee wrote to Frederick P. Hitz, the Inspector General of the CIA on February 23, 1994, requesting a comprehensive investigation of the Ames case. On March 1, the Committee met in closed session with Mr. Hitz to discuss the plans to investigate the Ames case.

In the meantime, the Committee continued to receive off-the-record briefings from the FBI and CIA regarding the progress of the ongoing investigation. The searches of Ames's office and residence conducted after the arrests yielded additional evidence of his relationship with the KGB and, since 1991, with its successor intelligence service, the SVR. Indeed, it appeared that Ames may have received approximately $2.5 million for the information he provided. It was clear the case represented a security breach of disastrous proportions.

On March 10, 1994, the Committee heard testimony in executive session from Director of Central Intelligence, R. James Woolsey, about the interim actions he was taking in light of the Ames case. This testimony was supplemented by a letter from the Director on March 24, 1994, advising the Committee that he would not promote, advance to a more responsible position, or provide any job-related recognition to, those responsible for supervising Ames or for dealing with issues related to the Ames investigation until the Inspector General had submitted his report on the case. Additional steps to tighten security at the CIA were also outlined in the letter.

On April 13, 1994, the Committee held another closed session regarding the Ames case specifically to obtain the response of the CIA to certain stories which had appeared in the press. In particular, CIA witnesses denied press accounts that Ames had been warned by a superior that he was under investigation for espionage.

On April 28, 1994, Ames and his wife, Rosario, pled guilty to charges stemming from their espionage activities. Entered into the record at the time the pleas were made was an agreed-upon "Statement of Facts" which provided new details regarding the Ameses' espionage activities. Meetings with the Soviets in Washington, D.C., Vienna, Bogota, and Caracas were acknowledged for the first time. Ames also acknowledged that as of May 1, 1989, he had been paid over $1.8 million by the KGB and that $900,000 more had been set aside for him.

In a statement read to the court at the time the plea agreements were entered, Ames admitted having compromised "virtually all Soviet agents of the CIA and other American and foreign services known to me" and having provided to the Soviet Union and to Russia a "huge quantity of information on United States foreign, defense and security policies." Ames went on to say:

> For those persons in the former Soviet Union and elsewhere who may have suffered from my actions, I have the deepest sympathy even empathy. We made similar choices and suffer similar consequences.

As part of their plea agreements, both defendants agreed to cooperate fully with the government to explain the nature and extent of their espionage activities. Both signed agreements forfeiting the proceeds of their espionage activities to the U.S. Government. Ames was sentenced to life in prison, his wife later received 63 months in prison.

With a trial of the Ameses obviated by the plea agreements, the Committee was no longer constrained in its inquiry by the possibility of interfering with the criminal prosecution. At closed hearings held on May 6, June 16, and June 28, the Committee focused upon Ames's espionage activities as well as the handling of the case by the CIA and FBI. On July 18 a full day was devoted to a staff briefing by representatives of the CIA and FBI, who covered the case from start to finish.

These proceedings were supplemented by an interview of Ames by Chairman [Senator Dennis] DeConcini which occurred on August 5, 1994, at a secure facility in Northern Virginia. In mid August, copies of the transcripts of the debriefings of Ames by the FBI were provided to the Committee, as well as copies of the interview summaries performed by the FBI during the criminal investigation.

On September 24, 1994, the Inspector General of the CIA submitted the report of his investigation to the Committee. Over 450 pages in length, the report provided a comprehensive, thorough, and candid assessment of how the CIA had handled the Ames case. Based upon interviews with over 300 people, including several interviews with Ames himself, and documentary evidence totaling over 45,000 pages, the report provided a wealth of new information. The Committee, in fact, relied heavily on this extraordinary report in the preparation of this report.

FACTUAL SUMMARY OF THE AMES CASE

AMES'S ESPIONAGE AND THE GOVERNMENT'S ATTEMPTS TO CATCH A SPY

1 APRIL 1985 TO JULY 1986

Ames Offers His Services

With his considerable knowledge of Soviet operations and experience in clandestine operations, Aldrich Ames conceived of a plan to obtain money from the Soviets without being detected by the CIA or the FBI.

As summarized in the previous section, Ames routinely assisted another CIA office which assessed Soviet embassy officials as potential intelligence assets. His SE [Soviet-East European] Division manager agreed to and sanctioned his work in this area in late 1983 or early 1984, even though Ames was in a counterintelligence job which gave him access to both former and active CIA operational cases involving Soviet intelligence officers. Ames initially coordinated his contacts with the FBI, and he worked out the operational details with the local CIA office responsible for such operations.

According to Ames, he contacted selected Soviet officials using an assumed name and fake job description identifying himself as a Soviet Union expert with the Intelligence Community Staff.

Using this cover, he met with a particular Soviet official for almost a year. When this official returned to Moscow, he suggested Ames continue his contacts with a Soviet Embassy official Sergey Dmitriyevich Chuvakhin, a member of the Soviet Ministry of Foreign Affairs who specialized in arms control matters. In April 1985, Ames arranged a meeting with Chuvakhin. Chuvakhin thought the meeting was to discuss broad U.S.-Soviet security concerns, and the CIA thought Ames was meeting with Chuvakhin to assess the Soviet as a possible source for U.S. intelligence. In fact, Ames planned to offer the Soviets classified information in exchange for money.

Ames entered the Soviet Embassy in Washington, D.C. on 16 April 1985, and handed an envelope to the duty officer at the reception desk, while asking for Chuvakhin by name. The message was addressed to the Russian officer he knew to be the most senior KGB officer at the embassy. Although unspoken, it was implied that Ames wanted the letter delivered to the KGB officer. The duty officer nodded his understanding. Ames then had a short conversation with Chuvakhin and departed the embassy.

Inside the envelope left with the duty officer at the Soviet Embassy was a note which described two or three CIA cases involving Soviets who had approached the CIA to offer their services. The CIA believed each to be controlled by the KGB, (i.e. "double agents") and thus, Ames thought that disclosing to the KGB that these Soviets were working with the CIA was "essentially valueless information." Nonetheless, he thought providing such information would establish his bona fides as a CIA insider. (Later, Ames disclosed to the KGB that, in fact, the CIA believed these Soviets were controlled "double agents.")

To further establish his bona fides, Ames included a page from an internal SE Division directory with his true name highlighted. He also listed an alias he had assumed when meeting Soviet officials earlier in his career. Finally, he requested a payment of $50,000. Ames has stated he did not ask for a follow up meeting or suggest possible future means of communication with the KGB in this initial letter. Several weeks later, however, Chuvakhin scheduled another luncheon with Ames. According to Ames, he entered the Soviet Embassy on May 15, 1985, and asked for Chuvakhin, but instead was escorted to a private room.

A KGB officer came in and passed him a note which said that the KGB had agreed to pay him $50,000. The KGB note also stated that they would like to continue to use Chuvakhin as an intermediary between the KGB and Ames. Two days later, on 17 May, Ames met

Chuvakhin and received a payment of $50,000 cash.

Motivation for Continuing His Espionage Activities

Ames has admitted that his motivation to commit treason changed over time. Because of his perception of his growing financial problems, Ames say[s] he initially planned a one time "con game" to provide the Soviets with the identities of their own double agent operatives, in return for a one-time payment of $50,000 to cover his debts. He guessed the KGB would pay him the $50,000 and thought this would solve most of his outstanding financial problems.

What motivated Ames to continue the relationship with the KGB after the $50,000 payment is not altogether clear, even to Ames himself. In an interview with Senator DeConcini, Ames observed that he viewed his request for $50,000 as a "one time deal." Ames stated that ". . . (a)t that time in May when I had got the money, I figured I was finished." Ames elaborated in the interview:

> I'm still puzzled as to what took me to the next steps. The main factor, on balance I think, was a realization after I had received the $50,000, was a sense of the enormity of what I had done. I think I had managed under the stress of money and thinking, conceiving the plan I had carried out in April, I saw it as perhaps a clever, . . . not a game, but a very clever plan to do one thing. . . . (I)t came home to me, after the middle of May, the enormity of what I had done. The fear that I had crossed a line which I had not clearly considered before. That I crossed a line I could never step back. And . . . I think in retrospect, it is very difficult for me to reconstruct my thoughts at the time. Before April, I can very well. It was a very rational, clever plan, cut between the

middle of May and the middle of June . . . it was as if I were sleepwalking. I can't really reconstruct my thinking. It was as if I were in almost a state of shock. The realization of what I had done. But certainly underlying it was the conviction that there was as much money as I could ever use. If I chose to do that.

Ames has also told FBI investigators involved in his debriefings that, in retrospect, he left his initial communication with the Soviets open ended so that they would expect his continued cooperation. After the KGB paid him the $50,000, according to an FBI official, Ames "decided that he wasn't going to stop at that point."

Increased Espionage Activities

Ames's next step dealt a crippling blow to the CIA's Soviet operations. According to interviews with Ames, without any prompting or direction by the KGB or any promise of additional money, he met again with Chuvakhin on June 13, 1985, and provided copies of documents which identified over ten top-level CIA and FBI sources who were then reporting on Soviet activities. CIA officials have testified that Ames provided the "largest amount of sensitive documents and critical information, that we know anyway, that have ever been passed to the KGB in one particular meeting . . ." Ames wrapped up five to seven pounds of message traffic in plastic bags and hand carried them out of the CIA Headquarters building for delivery to the KGB, knowing that the CIA no longer examined packages carried out of the building by Agency employees. Ames would use this simple and straightfoward method at both CIA Headquarters and during his Rome assignment to provide information to the KGB. In court documents filed for this case, Ames admitted he disclosed the identities of Russian military and intelligence officers who were cooperating with the CIA and friendly foreign intelligence services. Some of these officials held high level jobs within the Soviet military and intelligence services. For example, the court documents stated, one particular asset was "a KGB officer stationed in Moscow who had provided valuable intelligence including the revelation that the KGB used an invisible substance referred to as 'spy dust' to surveil U.S. officials in Moscow." Ames has also admitted that part of his rationale for exposing these operations to the KGB was because he sought to protect his own role as KGB informant by eliminating those KGB assets who could be in the best position to tell the CIA of Ames's espionage.

The CIA Recognizes a Problem

In the months ahead, the CIA would begin to learn of the loss of the sources identified by Ames on June 13, 1985.

But unbeknownst to the CIA, at virtually the same time Ames began his relationship with the KGB, a former CIA employee, who had had access to some of the same Soviet cases which were disclosed by Ames, was himself cooperating with the Soviets.

Edward Lee Howard

The CIA had hired Edward Lee Howard in 1981, and as part of his training for an initial assignment in Moscow, Howard had been given access to the details of certain CIA operations in the Soviet Union, including identifying information on several CIA sources. In 1983, after Howard made damaging admissions during a polygraph examination which indicated serious suitability problems, the CIA abruptly terminated Howard's

employment with the CIA. His bitterness toward the CIA gradually increased over the next year. Late in 1984, Howard decided to retaliate by compromising several CIA operations to the KGB. He is believed to have met with the KGB in January 1985, and again several months later in May 1985, and presumably disclosed the details of several CIA operations.

For CIA officials, the recognition of the source and extent of the losses of its Soviet operations took months to piece together. In May 1985—several weeks before Ames passed his list of sources to the KGB—officials in the Directorate of Operations began to sense a possible security problem when a CIA source was suddenly recalled to the Soviet Union. Later that summer, the CIA became aware that a Soviet source handled by British intelligence had been recalled to Moscow and was accused of spying.

Then on June 13, 1985, the same day that Ames gave the list of CIA and FBI sources to the KGB in Washington, the KGB thwarted a planned meeting between one of the sources disclosed by Ames and a CIA officer in the Soviet Union, indicating to CIA officials that the Soviet asset had been compromised. (Although it is now presumed that Howard had enabled the KGB to identify this source, the source was also among those identified by Ames in his 13 June 1985 transmittal to the KGB.)

The CIA began to focus on Howard as the source of these compromises in August 1985 when a high-level KGB defector, Vitaly Yurchenko, told [the] CIA he had seen cables in 1984 which identified a former CIA employee named "Robert" as a KGB source. Soon afterward, as a result of the debriefings of Yurchenko, the CIA determined that "Robert" was, in fact, Edward Lee Howard.

While Yurchenko was being debriefed in Washington, Howard was meeting with the KGB in Vienna. At that meeting the KGB warned him that one of their officers with knowledge of his case was missing. On September 21, 1985, two days after a meeting with the FBI where he was confronted with Yurchenko's allegations, Howard eluded FBI surveillance and fled the United States for Helsinki, Finland, and ultimately settled in the Soviet Union. He has effectively eluded U.S. authorities ever since.

More Losses Surface

As the Howard case was unfolding, the CIA learned in September 1985 that a source in Moscow had been arrested for espionage. In October 1985, the CIA learned that a second intelligence asset in a European country, who returned to Moscow in August on home leave, had never returned to his post. In December of that year, the CIA learned that this asset had also been arrested. In January of 1986, the CIA learned that a third source posted in a European country had been taken into custody by Soviet authorities in November and returned to Moscow. These assets, whose arrests were reported in the fall of 1985, were regarded among the most important CIA human sources at the time. All of these sources were later executed.

According to a CIA analysis, Howard had known of none of these agents. Thus, while Howard's treachery had initially clouded the picture, it was clear to the SE Division of the Directorate of Operations by the end of 1985 that the defection of Howard alone could not explain the disastrous events which were unfolding.

Indeed, throughout 1986, CIA continued to learn of Agency operations that had been compromised to the Soviets. As one CIA officer put it, "they were wrapping up our cases with reckless abandon."

This was, by all accounts, highly unusual behavior for the KGB. If the KGB had recruited an agent within the CIA, the last thing they would likely do—according to the prevailing wisdom among the Agency's professional "spy catchers"— would be to draw attention to the agent by suddenly "rolling up" all the cases he knew about. According to the CIA IG [Inspector General] report, Ames says that his KGB handlers recognized the dangers of what they had done. They told Ames that they regretted putting him in such a position, but believed their political leadership felt they had little choice but to take those steps.

In all, there were over 20 operations compromised to the Soviets during this period, less than half of which could plausibly be attributed to Edward Lee Howard. In addition, other U.S. intelligence activities which had clearly not been known to Howard were also compromised during this time period. The compromise of the identities of these intelligence agents amounted to a virtual collapse of the CIA's Soviet operations. . . .

Ames Continues His Double Life

While the CIA attempted to sort out what had gone so drastically wrong with its Soviet operations, Ames continued to provide the KGB with classified information from May 1985 until he left for an overseas assignment in Rome in July 1986. Ames met repeatedly with Chuvakhin, his intermediary, and passed a wealth of detail about Soviets targeted by the CIA, double agent operations, the identity of other CIA agents, background information on his past tours, and CIA modus operandi. In the end, the FBI identified over 14 occasions between May 1985 and July 1986 when Chuvakhin met with Ames, although Ames believes there were probably a few more meetings which were not detected by the Bureau.

In order to maintain a plausible cover for his frequent lunches with Chuvakhin, Ames filed reports with the CIA which summarized his meetings, and he met occasionally with CIA and FBI officials to discuss the progress of his recruitment operation targeted against Chuvakhin.

According to testimony from CIA officials, Ames was walking a difficult line:

> Rick was trying to play a funny game, you know, because in one sense he was—he wanted to make it look good enough so that everybody would want to continue the operation, but on the other hand not to make it look so good that people would start to focus on it. And not to make it look so good that when Rick decided to withdraw from it, that someone else would want to take over the case.

By July 1985, Ames stopped reporting to the FBI and the CIA on his meetings with Chuvakhin. He verbally reported some of his contacts to the CIA office he was supporting, and the CIA office passed on the relevant operational details to the FBI. The FBI was aware that the meetings continued and requested that the CIA follow-up to ensure that Ames submitted formal reports of the meetings, as required by both organizations. The FBI presumed that the CIA knew of the meetings and that Ames was simply slow in getting the paper work done. According to FBI officials:

> There were two or three times that our people either went over there and finally actually sent a communication over asking CIA why aren't we receiving any of the reports of these meetings. But the reports were never forthcoming and neither CIA nor FBI, followed up. Also, the reports that were made were not shown to his current bosses in SE.

The CIA did attempt to get Ames to provide reports of his meetings with Chuvakhin after he had been reassigned to Rome, but Ames never responded and no further action appears to have been taken.

In fact, there appears to have been a breakdown in the monitoring of Ames's operational relationship with Chuvakhin. Ames's immediate supervisor in SE Division had given his approval for the contacts between Ames and the Soviet Embassy official in early 1984. On the other hand, this manager did not have supervisory authority over the operation against Chuvakhin, a role correctly assumed by the officers in the CIA field office responsible for monitoring CIA contacts with Soviets within the U.S. (These officers had also approved Ames's contacts with Chuvakhin.) Yet the field officers did not monitor his contacts closely, and did not keep Ames's SE Division management well informed about the case, or alert Ames's direct supervisors when Ames failed to report regularly on his meetings.

Senior SE Division supervisors in 1985 who were in positions to know both about Ames's counterintelligence role at headquarters, as well as about CIA field office operations targeted against Soviet Embassy officials in Washington, have stated that they were unaware of his meetings with Soviet Embassy officials and would have disapproved such meetings had they known of them, in light of Ames's sensitive position in the counterintelligence branch.

Ames received, in addition to the initial payment of $50,000, regular cash payments during his subsequent luncheons with Chuvakhin, in amounts ranging between $20,000 and $50,000. At some point between October and December 1985, the Soviets told him he would be paid an additional $2 million, above and beyond the recurring cash payments. He was advised that the Soviets would hold the money for him. Ames has said he did not solicit this money and never made any additional request for money beyond his first meeting, but that the KGB promise of $2 million "sealed his cooperation."

Ames maintained several local bank accounts in his name, as well as in his new wife's name, where he would regularly deposit the cash he received from the Soviets. When Ames received a payment from the KGB, he generally broke it down into smaller cash deposits—in increments under $10,000 in order to avoid bank reporting requirements which might have led to inquiries by banking regulators.

Sometime after his marriage to Rosario, Ames developed a cover story to explain his increased wealth in order to hide the true source of the funds. His co-workers recalled that Ames did not dispel the notion that Rosario came from a wealthy and established family in Colombia. Ames explained to several colleagues that Rosario had a share of the inheritance and the family business, which continued to generate substantial revenue. Ames claims that he did not express this in the presence of Rosario or close friends since they would know that this was untrue. However, at least one colleague recalls Rosario being present during conversations in Rome when Ames discussed Rosario's family wealth. . . .

EXCERPTS FROM
COMMITTEE'S CONCLUSIONS
AND RECOMMENDATIONS

Over the months since his arrest, it has become clear that Aldrich Hazen Ames caused more damage to the national security of the United States than any spy in the history of the CIA.

Obviously, something went terribly wrong. For a CIA officer to carry on espionage activities without detection for almost nine years indicates, on its face, a failure of the system. As the Committee began to look into this failure, we found a bureaucracy which was excessively tolerant of serious personal and professional misconduct among its employees, where security was lax and ineffective. And we found a system and a culture unwilling and unable—particularly in the early years of Ames's betrayal—to face, assess, and investigate the catastrophic blow Ames had dealt to the core of its operations. The system which permitted Ames's prolonged betrayal must be changed. The country cannot afford such calamities in the future.

In the discussion which follows, the Committee sets forth where we believe the system failed and what we believe should be done to correct it. In the end, regardless of what the Committee may recommend or what Congress may enact, fundamental change will come only if the Director of Central Intelligence, supervisors at all levels, and the employees of the CIA bring it about. The leadership must come from within. It is clear, given the immense national security interests at stake, that there was "gross negligence"—both individually and institutionally—in creating and perpetuating the environment in which Ames was able to carry out his espionage activities for nine years without detection.

As this report documents, the failures evident in the Ames case were numerous and egregious. While it might be argued that the majority of individuals cited by the Inspector General were guilty of acts of omission rather than commission, the seriousness of these omissions cannot be overstated. The failures of the individuals cited by the Inspector General led to the loss of virtually all of CIA's intelligence assets targeted against the Soviet Union at the height of the Cold War. Ten of these agents were executed.

If there is not a higher standard of accountability established by DCIs, then a repeat of the Ames tragedy becomes all the more likely. Management accountability within the Intelligence Community should be no less than the highest levels found elsewhere in the Executive branch.

Having noted in strong terms the magnitude of CIA's failures, the Committee would be remiss not to point out what went right. A traitor, responsible for heinous acts of espionage, was identified and convicted. He has been imprisoned for life. In the end, this was accomplished by the work of a small group of CIA and FBI personnel who took part in what became a long and arduous inquiry—for some, lasting almost nine years. At least one member of this group appears to have pushed from the very beginning to get to the bottom of the 1985 compromises. It was his impetus that eventually put the investigation back on track in 1991.

THE FAILURE TO DEAL WITH SUITABILITY PROBLEMS

From the outset of his career at the CIA, Ames demonstrated serious suitability problems which, over the years, should have led his supervisors to reassess his continued employment. These problems included drunkenness, disregard for security regulations, and sloppiness towards administrative requirements. In the years immediately before he began to commit espionage and during the rest of his career, his supervisors were aware of his personal and professional deficiencies, but did not make his problems part of his official record, nor act effectively to correct them. Despite his recognized unsuitability, there is little evidence that his assignments, activities, or access to sensitive information were in any way limited as a result.

In April 1993, when CIA headquarters asked Ames's supervisors in Mexico City whether Ames qualified for a staff position in another Latin American country, they recommended against it, citing his alcohol problem, his failure to financial accountings [sic], and his generally poor performance. Nevertheless, six months later, when a former supervisor of Ames requested him to fill a position in the SE Division at headquarters—the most sensitive element of the Directorate of Operations—there is no indication that Ames's alcohol problem or poor performance were ever noted. Indeed, Ames was placed in a position which provided him access to the identities of virtually all of the Soviet intelligence officers by the CIA without his new supervisors being aware of the problems he had had in Mexico City.

The alcohol abuse counseling that Ames ultimately did receive upon his return to headquarters amounted to one conversation with a counselor, who, according to Ames, told him that his case was not a serious one when compared to many others in the Directorate of Operations.

In 1983, during the assignment in Mexico City, Ames also began an extramarital relationship with a Colombian national. Rosario Casas Depuy (hereinafter "Rosario"), herself a recruited asset of the CIA. Over time, the seriousness of their relationship became apparent to several of Ames's colleagues, but this never led to any action by Ames's supervisors, despite the fact that CIA regulations prohibit sexual relationships with recruited assets and require that reports of "close and continuing" relationships with foreign nationals be submitted by employees. Despite the security implications of this relationship, the violation of Agency regulations was ignored.

In fact, Ames did not file an official report concerning his relationship with

Rosario until April 1984, four months after she came to the United States to live with him. Indeed, it appears that until their marriage in August 1985, Ames (still married to his first wife) and Rosario continued to live together, with[out] any perceptible concern being registered by the CIA. While the counter-intelligence staff recommended in February 1985, that in view of the anticipated marriage, Ames be moved to a less sensitive position, nothing changed. Ames continued in the same position.

Over his career, Ames repeatedly demonstrated carelessness and disdain for security requirements. In 1975, while on his way to meet a CIA source in New York, Ames left a briefcase of classified materials identifying the source on a subway train. Although the briefcase was ultimately recovered, it might well have compromised the source's relationship with the CIA. In Rome, he was known to prepare classified reports at home. During his assignments at CIA headquarters between 1989 and 1994, he was occasionally found in other CIA offices where he had no reason to be, and with materials he had no reason to have.

He was equally negligent throughout his career in complying with the administrative requirements imposed on officers of the Directorate of Operations, such as submitting financial accountings for the cases he was handling.

Despite these and other incidents, Ames never received a single official reprimand during his 31-year career at the CIA. Indeed, most of the incidents and shortcomings which have come to light since Ames was arrested were never made a matter of official record. Once on board, his fitness to serve in the Directorate of Operations was never reevaluated.

It is the Committee's perception, which the Ames case confirms, that the Directorate of Operations has been far too willing to dismiss or ignore flagrant examples of personal misconduct among its officers. Security concerns are too often dismissed as the bureaucratic whining of small-minded administrators. All too often an officer who has been through training, gone through the polygraph examination, and had an overseas assignment, is accepted as a "member of the club," whose fitness for assignments, promotions, and continued service becomes immune from challenge.

Director Woolsey, in a recent speech, said that the "culture" of the directorate must be changed. The Committee shares that view. Such change will not come solely by changing regulations or personnel. It will come only when supervisors at every level of the directorate take seriously their responsibilities as managers. Personal misconduct should be documented. Officers who do not meet acceptable standards of personal behavior should not be assigned to sensitive positions nor qualify for supervisory positions. Personal shortcomings should be factored into consideration of promotions and bonus awards. While officers with personal problems should be given an opportunity, as well as appropriate assistance, to rehabilitate themselves, failing that, their employment with the directorate, if not the Agency, itself, should be terminated.

FAILURE TO RESTRICT THE ASSIGNMENTS AND ACCESS OF SUSPECTS IN COUNTERINTELLIGENCE CASES

The Ames case reveals glaring weakness in the CIA's procedures for dealing with the career assignments of employees who are under suspicion for compromising intelligence operations. The CIA failed to restrict Ames's assignments and access even after information surfaced in 1989 which indicated Ames was a possible counterintelligence problem.

In September 1989, after a poor tour in Rome, which was known to the managers in the SE Division, his SE superiors allowed Ames to return to the SE Division and assigned him to the office supporting to all Soviet and East European operations in Europe, a position affording him broad access to sensitive information. He remained assigned to the SE Division until August 1990. During this period, investigators learned about Ames's unexplained affluence and developed information regarding several large bank deposits and a particularly large currency exchange. Yet none of this appears to have had any bearing on Ames's continued assignment or access during this period.

In October 1990, SE Division managers reassigned Ames to the Counterintelligence Center (CIC) because he had performed poorly and they wanted him out of the Division. Apparently, supervisors in the CIC knew Ames was a poor performer and were aware that questions had been raised about his unexplained affluence. Yet they believed they could manage the problem. After his arrest, these officials recognized that Ames's position had given him access to data which identified virtually every double agent operation controlled by the United States. It is unclear how or why his CIC supervisors did not ascertain or evaluate the extent of his access at the time.

In April 1991, while Ames was assigned to the CIC, the Office of Security carried out an updated background investigation of Ames. The results of this investigation were evaluated and shared with the investigator assigned to the special task force. Reflecting interviews with his co-workers in Rome and his Arlington, Virginia, neighbors, the investigation produced information that Ames had frequent contacts in Rome with Soviet and East European officials not fully explained by his work requirements, frequently violated security regulations by leaving his safe open and doing classified work at home, and lived far beyond his CIA salary in both Rome and Arlington. (One of those interviewed went so far as to say that he would not be surprised if Ames were a spy.)

Inexplicably, the CIA security officer who reviewed the investigative report evaluated it as "raising no CI concerns," and the task force investigator assigned to the case did not regard the report as providing any new information. Ames retained his security clearance and his job in the Counterintelligence Center, and no further action was taken to follow-up on the information developed in his report. Indeed, the special task force members viewed the investigative report, together with the favorable results of the April 1991, polygraph, as giving Ames "a clean bill of health."

In September 1991, despite having been "booted out" of the SE Division a year earlier, and despite the special task force inquiry then underway, Ames was allowed to return to the SE Division to conduct a special study of the KGB. While the study itself did not call for particularly sensitive access, Ames once again was given access to the personnel and records of the SE Division.

Recommendation: The Director of Central Intelligence should establish procedures to inform current and prospective supervisors about employees under suspicion in counterintelligence cases. While the need to protect the secrecy of the investigation is essential, as well as the need to protect the employees themselves from unfair personnel actions, the assignment of employees under suspicion without frank consultations at the supervisory level increases the likelihood of serious compromises and leads to conflict between CIA elements.

Recommendation: The Director of Central Intelligence should issue procedures to require, in any case in which an employee is under suspicion for espionage or related activities, that a systematic evaluation be made of the employee's access to classified information, and that appropriate and timely actions be taken to limit such access. While care must obviously be taken to ensure that such actions do not tip off the employee that he or she is under suspicion, the failure to evaluate the access of an employee in these circumstances may eventually result in damage that might have been prevented.

CONTROL OF CLASSIFIED DOCUMENTS AND MATERIALS

The Ames case also demonstrated gaps in the control of sensitive classified information. Ames was able—without detection—to walk out of CIA headquarters and the U.S. Embassy in Rome with bags and envelopes stuffed with classified documents and materials. Many of the classified documents he passed to his KGB handlers were copies of documents that were not under any system of accountability. Ames did not even have to make copies of them. In his last job in the Counternarcotics Center at the CIA, Ames was able to "download" a variety of classified documents onto computer discs and then simply remove them to his home. When he attended a conference in Turkey in 1993, he brought a lap-top computer to do work in his hotel room. This apparently raised no security concern among those familiar with the incident. He was also able to visit offices he had no reason to be in, and gain access to information he had no business seeing.

In the late 1970s, the CIA instituted a policy calling for random and unannounced spot-checks of personnel leaving Agency compounds. But the policy was discontinued soon thereafter due to the inconvenience caused to those subject to such searches.

Ames recounted later that his KGB handlers were amazed at his ability to gain access to sensitive operations and take large bundles of classified information out of CIA offices without arousing suspicion, a sad commentary on the laxness of security at the CIA.

Recommendation: The Director of Central Intelligence should reinstate the policy making persons leaving CIA facilities subject to random searches of their person and possessions, and require that such searches be conducted unannounced and periodically at selected locations. Such searches should be conducted frequently enough to serve as a deterrent without unduly hampering the operation of the facilities involved.

Recommendation: The Director of Central Intelligence should institute computer security measures to prevent employees from being able to "download" classified information onto computer diskettes and removing them from CIA facilities. In addition, existing policies for the introduction, accountability, dissemination, removal, and destruction of all forms of electronic media should be reevaluated. The ability of the CIA's security managers to "audit" specific computer-related functions in order to detect and monitor the actions of suspected offenders should be upgraded.

Recommendation: The Director of Central Intelligence should institute a policy requiring employees to report to their supervisor any instance in which a CIA employee attempts to obtain classified information which the CIA employee has no apparent reason to know. In turn, supervisors should be required to report to the CIA Counterintelligence Center any such case where a plausible explanation for such a request cannot be ascertained by the supervisor.

Recommendation: The Director of Central Intelligence should institute new policies to improve the control of classified documents and materials within the CIA. In particular, the Directorate of Operations should undertake an immediate and comprehensive review of its practices and procedures for compartmenting information relating to clandestine operations to ensure that only those officers who absolutely need access can obtain such information. Further, the Director should establish and maintain a detailed, automated record of the access granted to each of its employees.

COORDINATION OF SECURITY AND COUNTERINTELLIGENCE

The Ames case demonstrated a serious division between security and counterintelligence activities in the CIA. Even though an investigator from the Office of Security (OS) participated in the investigation of the 1985–86 compromises under the auspices of the Counterintelligence Center (CIC), he failed to coordinate properly with OS with respect to Ames's 1991 polygraph examination. OS had initiated a background investigation of Ames in March 1991, but went ahead with the polygraph in April without the benefit of the background investigation. As it turned out, the background investigation provided significant information about Ames that was largely ignored by

the investigator assigned to the CIC in light of Ames's passing the polygraph examination.

Citing senior security officials, the Inspector General's report noted there had always been a "fault line" in communications between the CIC and its predecessors, and the OS. The CIC had not always shared information regarding its counterintelligence investigations and had failed to make use of OS's investigative expertise. Indeed, the search to find the cause of the 1985 compromises might have moved more quickly from analysis to investigation if there had been better coordination between security and counterintelligence.

The Inspector General's report also found "a gradual degradation" of the resources and authority given the security function since 1985, concluding that "this degradation has adversely affected the Agency's ability to prevent and deter activities such as those engaged in by Ames . . ." The Committee shares the view that this decline has been too great and too precipitous.

THE NEED FOR CONTINUED FOLLOW-UP

Many of the problems identified by the Committee are deep-seated and pervasive, and will not be solved easily or quickly. Yet these problems are too important and too integral to the functioning of an agency with important national security responsibilities not to merit continuing and intensive scrutiny by both CIA managers and the congressional oversight committees.

Memories of the "Camelot" Administration of
John F. Kennedy were rekindled by the deaths in
1994 and 1999, respectively, of Jacqueline
Kennedy Onassis and her son, John F. Kennedy,
Jr., both shown here in 1989 beneath a portrait of
the former President.

A San Francisco house lies in ruin following the Loma
Prieta earthquake, one of the most lethal quakes in
American history, which struck the Bay Area during the
evening rush hour on October 17, 1989, registering 7.1
on the Richter scale, killing some 60 people, and causing
extensive property damage (including the collapse of a
portion of the San Francisco-Oakland Bay Bridge).

SOCIETY

A National Guardsman stands watch in Los Angeles in late April 1992 during rioting that raged in reaction to the
acquittal of white Los Angeles policemen who had been captured on videotape a year earlier beating an African
American, Rodney King; some fifty people died in the riots.

Gathering in Washington, D.C., on October 16, 1995, to pledge themselves to self-reliance and respect for women and to bring attention to continuing racism and economic inequity, hundreds of thousands of African American men (estimates ranged from 400,000 to one million) participated in the Million Man March championed by the Nation of Islam's controversial leader Louis Farrakhan.

Doug Mills—AP/Wide World Photos

Flanked by defense attorneys F. Lee Bailey, left, and Johnnie Cochran, right, former football star and actor O. J. Simpson celebrates on October 3, 1995, as he is found not guilty of the murder of ex-wife Nicole Brown Simpson and her friend Ronald Goldman.

AFP/Corbis

Students from Columbine High School in suburban Denver, Colorado, grieve and console one another on April 21, 1999, the day after fellow students Eric Harris and Dylan Klebold went on a shooting spree that left twelve Columbine students and one teacher dead and twenty-one wounded before the assailants took their own lives in the worst of several shootings at schools in the 1990s.

Najlah Feanny/Corbis Saba

53.

Contract with America

In November 1994, the Republican Party won control of both the House of Representatives and the Senate. It was a victory of historic proportions; Republicans had not held a majority in both houses of Congress since 1954. Moreover, since 1932 Republicans had controlled the House of Representatives only twice. Much of the credit for the Republicans' victory was given to Representative Newt Gingrich of Georgia. A former history professor, Gingrich had spent the better part of two decades laying the groundwork for a Republican congressional majority. When President Bill Clinton's popularity plummeted in the summer and fall of 1994, Gingrich skillfully positioned House Republicans as a viable alternative to what he described as Clinton's "failed" liberal policies. Their program for change was encapsulated in the "Contract with America," reprinted below. In the aftermath of the 1994 midterm elections, Gingrich was elected Speaker of the House by his fellow House Republicans. His tenure as House Speaker, however, soon faltered. His abrasive personality alienated voters, and Clinton went on to win reelection in 1996. Although Republicans still held control of the House of Representatives, in December 1998 they rebelled against Gingrich, and he was forced to resign as House Speaker.

Source: http://www.house.gov

As Republican Members of the House of Representatives and as citizens seeking to join that body we propose not just to change its policies, but even more important, to restore the bonds of trust between the people and their elected representatives. That is why, in this era of official evasion and posturing, we offer instead a detailed agenda for national renewal, a written commitment with no fine print.

This year's election offers the chance, after four decades of one-party control, to bring to the House a new majority that will transform the way Congress works. That historic change would be the end of government that is too big, too intrusive, and too easy with the public's money. It can be the beginning of a Congress that respects the values and shares the faith of the American family. Like Lincoln, our first Republican president, we intend to act "with firmness in the right, as God gives us to see the right." To restore accountability to Congress. To end its cycle of scandal and disgrace. To make us all proud again of the way free people govern themselves.

On the first day of the 104th Congress, the new Republican majority will immediately pass the following major reforms, aimed at restoring the faith and trust of the American people in their government:

• FIRST, require all laws that apply to the rest of the country also apply equally to the Congress;

• SECOND, select a major, independent auditing firm to conduct a comprehensive audit of Congress for waste, fraud or abuse;

• THIRD, cut the number of House committees, and cut committee staff by one-third;

• FOURTH, limit the terms of all committee chairs;

• FIFTH, ban the casting of proxy votes in committee;

• SIXTH, require committee meetings to be open to the public;

• SEVENTH, require a three-fifths majority vote to pass a tax increase;

• EIGHTH, guarantee an honest accounting of our Federal Budget by implementing zero base-line budgeting.

Thereafter, within the first 100 days of the 104th Congress, we shall bring to the House Floor the following bills, each to be given full and open debate, each to be given a clear and fair vote and each to be immediately available this day for public inspection and scrutiny.

1. THE FISCAL RESPONSIBILITY ACT: A balanced budget/tax limitation amendment and a legislative line-item veto to restore fiscal responsibility to an out-of-control Congress, requiring them to live under the same budget constraints as families and businesses.

2. THE TAKING BACK OUR STREETS ACT: An anti-crime package including stronger truth-in-sentencing, "good faith" exclusionary rule exemptions, effective death penalty provisions, and cuts in social spending from this summer's "crime" bill to fund prison construction and additional law enforcement to keep people secure in their neighborhoods and kids safe in their schools.

3. THE PERSONAL RESPONSIBILITY ACT: Discourage illegitimacy and teen pregnancy by prohibiting welfare to minor mothers and denying increased AFDC for additional children while on welfare, cut spending for welfare programs, and enact a tough two-years-and-out provision with work requirements to promote individual responsibility.

4. THE FAMILY REINFORCEMENT ACT: Child support enforcement, tax incentives for adoption, strengthening rights of parents in their children's education, stronger child pornography laws, and an elderly dependent care tax credit to reinforce the central role of families in American society.

5. THE AMERICAN DREAM RESTORATION ACT: A $500 per child tax credit, begin repeal of the marriage tax penalty, and creation of American Dream Savings Accounts to provide middle class tax relief.

6. THE NATIONAL SECURITY RESTORATION ACT: No U.S. troops under U.N. command and restoration of the essential parts of our national security funding to strengthen our national defense and maintain our credibility around the world.

7. THE SENIOR CITIZENS FAIRNESS ACT: Raise the Social Security earnings limit which currently forces seniors out of the work force, repeal the 1993 tax hikes on Social Security benefits and provide tax incentives for private long-term care insurance to let Older Americans keep more of what they have earned over the years.

8. THE JOB CREATION AND WAGE ENHANCEMENT ACT: Small business incentives, capital gains cut and indexation, neutral cost recovery, risk assessment/cost-benefit analysis, strengthening the Regulatory Flexibility Act and unfunded mandate reform to create jobs and raise worker wages.

9. THE COMMON SENSE LEGAL REFORM ACT: "Loser pays" laws, reasonable limits on punitive damages and reform of product liability laws to stem the endless tide of litigation.

10. THE CITIZEN LEGISLATURE

ACT: A first-ever vote on term limits to replace career politicians with citizen legislators.

Further, we will instruct the House Budget Committee to report to the floor and we will work to enact additional budget savings, beyond the budget cuts specifically included in the legislation described above, to ensure that the Federal budget deficit will be less than it would have been without the enactment of these bills.

Respecting the judgment of our fellow citizens as we seek their mandate for reform, we hereby pledge our names to this Contract with America.

———◆———

In every election in American history both parties have their clichés. The party that has the clichés that ring true wins.
NEWT GINGRICH, *International Herald Tribune,*
August 1, 1988

54.

RALPH NADER: The Flip Side of Free Trade

In the last two decades of the twentieth century, the United States negotiated an ambitious series of international free-trade agreements. These pacts reduced trade barriers and promoted the international exchange of goods and services, a policy that came to be known as globalization. The federal government defended free trade on the grounds that it encouraged the economic growth of all the nations involved and promoted the spread of high-tech industries, an area in which the United States enjoyed a competitive advantage. Advocates of free trade contended that it brought closer relations with neighboring Canada and Mexico, both of which joined the United States in signing the landmark North American Free Trade Agreement (NAFTA) in 1992. Critics, however, charged that trade pacts like NAFTA protected corporate polluters, caused the loss of blue-collar jobs, and undermined national sovereignty. No public figure took a more prominent role in the campaign against globalization than activist Ralph Nader. He first came to national attention in the 1960s as a preeminent spokesman for consumer interests when he exposed serious safety problems in American automobiles. In the 1990s Nader turned his attention to the issues of free trade and workers' rights, and in 2000 he mounted a presidential campaign as the nominee of the Green Party. In the following two essays for The Nation *magazine, Nader attacked global free-trade groups for their elitist lack of accountability and detrimental impact on labor and the environment. Nader wrote these essays in the final months of 1994, just before the World War II-era GATT (General Agreement on Tariffs and Trade) was replaced by a stronger international body, the World Trade Organization.*

Sources: *The Nation,* October 10, 1994.

The Nation, December 5, 1994.

A. DROP THE GATT

Ignoring the rising public pressure to postpone the matter until next year, the Clinton Administration is about to send a seriously flawed World Trade Organization agreement to Congress for approval under fast-track procedures allowing no amendments. The W.T.O. pact, a creation of the Uruguay Round of the General Agreement on Tariffs and Trade (GATT), is more than an economic document. It is a system of international governance with powerful legislative, executive and judicial authority over member nations. As such, any evaluations of the W.T.O. regime should use the democratic yardsticks we apply domestically.

Such an inquiry seems to have escaped the self-described free traders at *The New York Times* and *The Washington Post* as well as other national media. Practicing the official-source journalism that uncritically reports the Administration's inflated estimates of the pact's economic benefits, the *Times* and the *Post* routinely turn their backs on the troubling political and legal issues raised by the W.T.O.'s secrecy, inaccessibility and its one-nation-one-vote/no-veto system of decision-making that gives St. Kitts, Luxembourg and Singapore equal power with the United States.

A gauge of the extent of this indifference was the media's treatment of a remarkable public letter sent to President Clinton on September 14 by fifty-one leaders of major news organizations and journalism groups. The signers urged the President to open World Trade deliberations to the American public and press. The letter, signed by such people as Greg Favre, president of the American Society of Newspaper Editors, Lawrence Beaupre, vice president of the Associated Press Managing Editors Association, and Bill Kovach, curator of the Nieman Foundation, listed five anti-democratic areas of concern.

They include a lockout of the press and the public from W.T.O. tribunals; suppression of the briefs and other documents presented by governments that are parties to disputes before these tribunals; denial of citizens' rights to petition; the absence of conflict-of-interest standards for the tribunals' three trade specialists, who act as judges and may simultaneously pursue private business careers; and a prohibition of any independent appeals of W.T.O. tribunal decisions. The perfunctory internal appeals process within the W.T.O. is secret. The letter was circulated by John Seigenthaler, chairman of the Freedom Forum First Amendment Center at Vanderbilt University, who told Clinton, We must "restore democratic openness to this crucial

process. To do otherwise would break a sacred pact with the American people."

This unprecedented appeal to the President was not considered worthy of even a squib by the *Times* or the *Post*. Nor did any columnist or editorial writer mention this criticism of the W.T.O. agreement by their colleagues. (To be fair, the *Times* was preoccupied that day with producing ten articles on the predictable termination of the baseball season.)

As the letter to the President pointed out, serious issues of sovereignty and democracy are at stake. Membership in the W.T.O. would commit the United States to make its laws and regulations conform to the W.T.O.'s decisions and rules. That means adhering to a regime that places trade *über alles,* that subordinates all nontrade values and policies—such as consumer, environment and workplace standards—to the imperatives of foreign commerce. Noncompliance may be punished by perpetual trade fines or sanctions. And the W.T.O. regime will be enforced by closed, secretive W.T.O. tribunals without citizen or even subnational (i.e., state and local) input.

This structural bias favoring commerce would produce two dynamics. One is well described in reports earlier this year by the European Union, Japan and Canada spotlighting the federal and state laws in the United States that they believe would be illegal under the W.T.O. and therefore challengeable before the Geneva tribunals. On their list are laws regulating food safety, fuel efficiency, clean air, recycling and many other matters, including the Nuclear Nonproliferation Act of 1978.

The second dynamic is a pull-down effect. The Uruguay Round agreement's provisions on nontariff trade barriers do not penalize any country that treats its workers, consumers or environment too harshly. Except for products made by prison labor, anything goes, including materials made by child labor. Nations likely to be found in violation are those with strong consumer, labor and environmental standards that are challenged as barriers to imports. Food labeling and pesticide control laws can fall into this category and enable the E.U. or countries like Brazil to prevail against the United States before the tribunals on charges of trade violations. The result will be a weakening of living standards and a chilling of proposed environmental advances, which is just what the global corporations that shaped the Uruguay Round's provisions want as they seek nations with lower labor costs and permissive laws.

Since the W.T.O.'s terms do not require nations to decide on membership until July 1995, there is no need for Congress to rush to judgment on a trade pact that was conceived and negotiated secretly. More time is needed to let the American people know just what our country is getting into. They should be given a chance to tell Congress what they think before the W.T.O.'s international autocracy further diminishes our modest democracy.

B. GATT HYPOCRISY

Usually, politicians victorious in November wait until at least January to break their promises. Newt Gingrich, the next Speaker of the House, is determined to do it right after Thanksgiving by marshaling his Republican troops behind the World Trade Organization (W.T.O.) agreement.

In the last election Gingrich campaigned for (1) balancing the budget, (2) devolving power from Washington to the states, (3) reducing the size of the federal government, (4) giving more power to the people and (5) deregula-

tion. By championing the W.T.O., also known as the Uruguay Round of the General Agreement on Tariffs and Trade (GATT), Gingrich endorses (1) a Senate budget-busting waiver of $31 billion, due to tariff revenue reductions under the agreement, (2) ceding power to the W.T.O. in Geneva to invalidate U.S. laws or impose perpetual trade fines, (3) replacing democratic powers residing in the U.S. government with the autocratic authority of a world government, (4) stripping citizens of any voice in or control over the decisions of the W.T.O., with its one nation, one vote, that permits two dictatorships to outvote the United States and (5) enabling the foreign regulation of U.S. health, safety and other living standards.

By contrast, in the Senate, Gingrich's fellow Republicans Jesse Helms, Strom Thurmond, Larry Craig and, with cagey ambiguity, Larry Pressler and Phil Gramm, have serious reservations about the W.T.O. They object to its budget-busting, to Clinton's pork provisions in it, to its being treated as a trade agreement rather than a treaty requiring a two-thirds Senate ratification vote, and to the sovereignty-invading powers it gives to secretive and dictatorial supranational tribunals.

Senate Republican leader Bob Dole has expressed similar concerns, but he is under conflicting pressures—from the party's right wing and from his constituents in Kansas opposing GATT, and from the multinational corporation-Wall Street crowd, which urges its quick approval. Dole is hearing from both Republican and Democratic senators that the vote should not be taken as scheduled, on December 1, during the lame-duck session of Congress. Under its own terms, the pact does not need to be voted on until July 1995.

There is a serious ethical question

about a lame-duck session voting on such a consequential system of international governance without any right of amendment. Many of these lame ducks are negotiating for jobs with law firms, trade associations and lobbying groups, creating potential conflicts of interest.

Earlier this year, state and county officials raised the issue of what the federal government would do when state and local laws are invalidated by the W.T.O.'s closed tribunals in Geneva. State attorneys general were upset that under the agreement they could not go to Geneva to defend their health, safety, tax and other laws challenged by a foreign government; only federal officials may argue for the states. The Administration promised to consult with them on how the United States would go about conforming state and local laws to the W.T.O.'s dictates. But the state officials' key demand, that only Congress may pre-empt local laws—rather than the executive branch, flexing its muscle with threats to withhold highway aid and similar sanctions—was rejected by U.S. Trade Representative Mickey Kantor.

Protests against GATT by all the national trade unions and environmental groups, by all but one of the major consumer groups and by church, family farm and animal rights associations have received very little press attention in the past year. But now that there are sharp divisions between Republican senators and between presidential aspirants Dole and Gramm, the national media may start giving this issue proper coverage, informing the public about the proposed autocratic regime of the World Trade Organization.

———————◆———————

GATT represents the New World Order in trade.
MICKEY KANTOR, U.S. Trade Representative,
September 18, 1994

1995

55.

BILL CLINTON: State of the Union

In the midterm elections of November 1994, Republicans won control of both houses of Congress. The new Republican majority in the House of Representatives was especially historic, because Republicans had not held control of the House for forty years. The election results were widely viewed as a repudiation of President Bill Clinton, the Democrat elected two years previously. Clinton had campaigned as a moderate "New Democrat" in 1992, but during his first two years as President, he governed largely as a traditional liberal Democrat, exemplified by his ambitious plan to adopt a single-payer health care system. After the 1994 midterm elections, many political commentators foresaw the end of the Clinton presidency and predicted an easy win for the Republican candidate in 1996. Clinton, however, changed course dramatically in 1995. With the declaration "the era of big government is over," he adopted Republican positions on taxes and the economy. Clinton's repackaging as a political centrist won the approval of the electorate, and in 1996 he won a second term as President. Clinton's 1995 State of the Union address, in which he first signaled his turn to the political center, is excerpted below.

Source: *Public Papers of the Presidents of the United States,* January 24, 1995.

MR. PRESIDENT, Mr. Speaker, Members of the 104th Congress, my fellow Americans: Again we are here in the sanctuary of democracy, and once again our democracy has spoken. So let me begin by congratulating all of you here in the 104th Congress and congratulating you, Mr. Speaker.

If we agree on nothing else tonight, we must agree that the American people certainly voted for change in 1992 and in 1994. And as I look out at you, I know how some of you must have felt in 1992. [*Laughter*]

I must say that in both years we didn't hear America singing, we heard America shouting. And now all of us, Republicans and Democrats alike, must say, "We hear you. We will work together to earn the jobs you have given us." For we are the keepers of a sacred trust, and we must be faithful to it in this new and very demanding era. . . .

We are moving from an industrial age built on gears and sweat to an information age demanding skills and learning and flexibility. Our Government, once a champion of national purpose, is now seen by many as simply a captive of narrow interests, putting more burdens on our citizens rather than equipping them to get ahead. The values that used to hold us all together seem to be coming apart.

So tonight we must forge a new social compact to meet the challenges of this time. As we enter a new era, we need a new set of understandings, not just with Government but, even more important, with one another as Americans.

That's what I want to talk with you about tonight. I call it the New Covenant. But it's grounded in a very, very old idea, that all Americans have not just a right but a solemn responsibility to rise as far as their God-given talents and determination can take them and to give something back to their communities and their country in return. Opportunity and responsibility: They go hand in hand. We can't have one without the other. And our national community can't hold together without both.

Our New Covenant is a new set of understandings for how we can equip our people to meet the challenges of a new economy, how we can change the way our Government works to fit a different time, and, above all, how we can repair the damaged bonds in our society and come together behind our common purpose. We must have dramatic change in our economy, our Government, and ourselves.

My fellow Americans, without regard to party, let us rise to the occasion. Let us put aside partisanship and pettiness and pride. As we embark on this new course, let us put our country first, remembering that regardless of party label, we are all Americans. And let the final test of everything we do be a simple one: Is it good for the American people?. . .

More important, I think we all agree that we have to change the way the Government works. Let's make it smaller, less costly, and smarter; leaner, not meaner. [*Applause*]

I just told the Speaker the equal time doctrine is alive and well. [*Laughter*]

The New Covenant approach to governing is as different from the old bureaucratic way as the computer is from the manual typewriter. The old way of governing around here protected organized interests. We should look out for the interests of ordinary people. The old way divided us by interest, constituency, or class. The New Covenant way should unite us behind a common vision of what's best for our country. The old way dispensed services through large, top-down, inflexible bureaucracies. The New Covenant way should shift these resources and decisionmaking from bureaucrats to citizens, injecting choice and competition and individual responsibility into national policy. The old way of governing around here actually seemed to reward failure. The New Covenant way should have built-in incentives to reward success. The old way was centralized here in Washington. The New Covenant way must take hold in the communities all across America. And we should help them to do that. . . .

Last year I introduced the most sweeping welfare reform plan ever presented by an administration. We have to make welfare what it was meant to be, a second chance, not a way of life. We have to help those on welfare move to work as quickly as possible, to provide child care and teach them skills, if that's what they need, for up to 2 years. And after that, there ought to be a simple, hard rule: Anyone who can work must go to work. If a parent isn't paying child support, they should be forced to pay. We should suspend drivers' license, track them across State lines, make them work off what they owe. That is what we should do. Governments do not raise children, people do. And the parents must take responsibility for the children they bring into this world. . . .

Middle class values sustain us. We must expand the middle class and shrink the under class, even as we do everything we can to support the millions of Americans who are already successful in the new economy.

America is once again the world's strongest economic power: almost 6 million new jobs in the last 2 years, exports booming, inflation down. High-wage jobs are coming back. A record number of American entrepreneurs are living the American dream. If we want it to stay that way, those who work and lift our Nation must have more of its benefits.

Today, too many of those people are being left out. They're working harder for less. They have less security, less income, less certainty that they can even afford a vacation, much less college for their kids or retirement for themselves. We cannot let this continue. If we don't act, our economy will probably keep doing what it's been doing since about 1978, when the income growth began to go to those at the very top of our economic scale and the people in the vast middle got very little growth, and people who worked like crazy but were on the bottom then fell even further and further behind in the years afterward, no matter how hard they worked. . . .

In the past, the minimum wage has been a bipartisan issue, and I think it should be again. So I want to challenge you to have honest hearings on this, to get together, to find a way to make the minimum wage a living wage.

Members of Congress have been here less than a month, but by the end of the week, 28 days into the new year, every Member of Congress will have earned as much in congressional salary as a minimum wage worker makes all year long.

Everybody else here, including the President, has something else that too many Americans do without, and that's health care. Now, last year we almost came to blows over health care, but we didn't do anything. And the cold, hard fact is that, since last year, since I was here, another 1.1 million Americans in working families have lost their health care. And the cold, hard fact is that many millions more, most of them farmers and small business people and self-employed people, have seen their premiums skyrocket, their copays and deductibles go up. There's a whole bunch of people in this country that in the statistics have health insurance but really what they've got is a piece of paper that says they won't lose their home if they get sick.

Now, I still believe our country has got to move toward providing health security for every American family. But I know that last year, as the evidence indicates, we bit off more than we could chew. So I'm asking you that we work together. Let's do it step by step. Let's do whatever we have to do to get something done. Let's at least pass meaningful insurance reform so that no American risks losing coverage for facing skyrocketing prices, that nobody loses their coverage because they face high prices or unavailable insurance when they change jobs or lose a job or a family member gets sick. . . .

And I would like to say a special word to our religious leaders. You know, I'm proud of the fact the United States has more houses of worship per capita than any country in the world. These people who lead our houses of worship can ignite their congregations to carry their faith into action, can reach out to all of our children, to all of the people in distress, to those who have been savaged by the breakdown of all we hold dear. Because so much of what must be done must come from the inside out and our religious leaders and their congregations can make all the difference, they have a role in the New Covenant as well. . . .

We all gain when we give, and we reap what we sow. That's at the heart of this New Covenant. Responsibility, opportunity, and citizenship, more than stale chapters in some remote civic book, they're still the virtue by which we can fulfill ourselves and reach our God-given potential and be like them and also to fulfill the eternal promise of this country, the enduring dream from that first and most sacred covenant. I believe every person in this country still believes that we are created equal and given by our Creator the right to life, liberty and the pursuit of happiness. This is a very, very great country. And our best days are still to come.

———————◆———————

A government big enough to give you everything you want is a government big enough to take from you everything you have.
GERALD FORD, addressing Congress, August 12, 1974

It is perfectly true that the government is best which governs least. It is equally true that the government is best which provides most.
WALTER LIPPMANN, *A Preface to Politics,* 1913

56.

MADELEINE K. ALBRIGHT: The United States in the United Nations

In November 1919 the Senate rejected American membership in the League of Nations. This action stemmed from the Senate's fear that United States involvement in an international governing body would undermine American sovereignty and would mark a radical departure from the country's traditional policy of isolationism. The debate over American internationalism, however, did not end in 1919. The Japanese attack on Pearl Harbor, Hawaii, in 1941 demonstrated that isolationism was impossible even if the United States avoided involvement in international organizations. Consequently, at the close of World War II, the United States led the way in the creation of the United Nations, even establishing its headquarters in New York City. By the mid-1990s, however, many Americans began to argue that the United States would be better off acting alone in foreign affairs, rather than in concert with the United Nations. In the address reprinted below from January 1995, Madeleine Albright explains why she believes American involvement in the United Nations is mutually beneficial for both the United Nations and the United States. At the time of the address, Albright was U.S. ambassador to the United Nations. She subsequently served as secretary of state, the first woman to hold that position.

Source: *Vital Speeches of the Day,* April 1, 1995.

THE WHIRLIGIG OF CHANGE has been in particular evidence where I work—promoting and defending American interests at the U.N.

Consider that only two years ago, shortly before he left office, President Bush observed that:

> "The U.N. . . .(is) emerging as a central instrument for the prevention and resolution of conflicts and the preservation of peace."

About the same time, former President Reagan called for

> "a standing U.N. force—an army of conscience—equipped and prepared to carve out humanitarian sanctuaries through force if necessary."

In historical terms, that was yesterday. Yet today, some of the loudest voices propound sentiments far different:

The U.N. is "the longtime nemesis of millions of Americans," says one leader on Capitol Hill. It is "a totally incompetent instrument anyplace that matters," says another. Bills have been introduced in both the House and Senate designed not to reform U.N. peacekeeping, but to kill it.

The goal, in the view of one advocate, is to bring "the U.N. back to where it was when it was created."

What a curious ambition.

Tonight, I want to discuss what the consequences would be for America if that great leap backward were taken. I want also to outline a forward-looking vision of American leadership at the U.N.; a vision that reflects past lessons, current capabilities, future challenges and enduring principles.

The U.N. is fifty years old this year. I doubt I am alone in this room in remembering that on my fiftieth birthday, celebration took a back seat to reflection—and new resolve. The power of the United Nations Charter—which Americans wrote—can be found not only in its eloquence, but in its origins. The authors of those lofty ideals understood well the lethal nature of isolationism's siren call. They had seen arise in Europe and Asia after World War I great evil; they had seen the world react passively to savage crimes; they had seen leaders back away repeatedly from the *possibility* of war, and thereby assure the *reality* of war.

The battle-hardened generation of Roosevelt, Churchill and De Gaulle viewed the U.N. as a practical response to an inherently contentious world; a necessity not because relations among states could ever be brought into perfect harmony, but because they cannot.

From the day we signed the U.N. Charter, Americans—Republican and Democrat—have viewed the U.N. not as an end in itself, but as one instrument, among many, for advancing U.S. goals.

In the words of President Truman:

> "We support the U.N. and keep this contract because the Charter expresses our fundamental aims in the world . . . to attain peace with justice, to assure freedom and to bring about economic and social progress for ourselves and all people."

Let me assure you tonight. This Administration will not allow the hullabaloo over a more recent contract to cause the Charter of the United Nations, the contract of Truman and Vandenberg and Dulles and FDR and Eleanor Roosevelt and the generation that triumphed over the Nazis, to be ripped to shreds.

Our generation is privileged to live in an era when our fundamental aims are not opposed by another superpower. But threats and conflicts continue to arise that engage our interests. Among these threats are:

—efforts by rogue regimes to build or acquire weapons of mass destruction;

—attempts by regional powers hostile to U.S. interests to dominate their respective regions through aggression, intimidation or terror;

—transnational criminal enterprises, which thrive where national governments are either weak or complicit; and

—what Leslie Gelb described recently as the "teapot wars"; internal conflicts among ethnic, national, religious or tribal groups that undermine regional stability, impede democratic reform and stifle economic growth.

Because we face a multiplicity of threats, we need a multiplicity of options. The ultimate guarantor of our security remains our capacity to act forcefully and, if we must, unilaterally.

Our military must remain modern, mobile, ready and strong and, as President Clinton pledged in his address two nights ago—it will.

We must maintain vigorous alliances—and we are.

And we must conduct strong, steady and creative diplomacy and—under the leadership of Secretary of State Christopher—that is exactly what we are doing.

In this new era, our energies remain focused on issues central to our security and economic well-being:

—trade agreements that will create new American jobs;

—cooperation among the major powers, especially on the control of nuclear weapons;

—creation of a secure, integrated and fully democratic Europe;

—stability in other key regions, such as the Middle East and the Korean peninsula; and

—continued momentum towards democracy and market economies.

In pursuing these and other goals, we must be prepared to act alone, for our willingness to do so is often the key to effective joint action. But the recent debate between the proponents of unilateral and multilateral action assumes a false choice. Multilateralism is a means, not an end. . . .

In the late 1940's and early 1950's, there were many who called for the U.S. to abandon the U.N. because it had failed to prevent the Korean war. There is a similar frustration now because the U.N. was unable to halt Rwandan genocide, transform Somalia or bring peace with justice to the Balkans.

We are finding that few international conflicts offer the clarity provided by Iraq's invasion of Kuwait—where the aggression was clear, the stakes included oil and the possibility of a madman equipped with nuclear arms, the military terrain was favorable, the enemy was isolated, the finest armed forces in the world—ours—were fully engaged, and the bills were being paid by someone else. Increasingly, threats to stability are not clear, but devilishly complex: violence caused not by international aggression, but by civil war; fragile ceasefires that do not hold; extremist political movements within strategic states; or ethnic violence that spills unpredictably across national lines.

On Capitol Hill, prescriptions now circulating for responding to these challenges would remove the U.N. as an option. The rationale is bewildering. Sponsors say the cost of U.N. peace operations is too high; and that the readiness of our armed forces is harmed by their support for what the U.N. does. The irony is that if we put the U.N. out of business, our costs will go up, not down, for our interests will require that we act on our own *more* often; and the wear and tear on our military will be *greater,* not less.

Those who advocate, in the words of one, "ending U.N. peacekeeping as we know it," should consider with care what would happen if they got their wish.

We could expect:

First, that existing peace operations would be disrupted at great peril to world peace. I can think of few quicker ways to undermine global stability than to rip U.N. peacekeepers out of Cyprus, Lebanon, Kashmir and the border between Kuwait and Iraq.

Second, the U.N. operation in former Yugoslavia, UNPROFOR, would become unsustainable.

UNPROFOR now accounts for more than half the costs and personnel of U.N. peacekeeping. Closing it down would be the only way to reduce dramatically short term costs. But despite its shortcomings, UNPROFOR has a purpose. Its precipitous withdrawal could cause the resumption of full-scale war, sever the humanitarian lifeline that keeps hundreds of thousands of civilians alive, cause new outflows of refugees and imperil further the survival of a viable, multi-ethnic Bosnian state.

Withdrawal under non-permissive conditions, moreover, would likely endanger the peacekeepers and those—including American troops—called upon to assist them. The result would be greater risk and higher cost than maintaining UNPROFOR.

Third, there would be no new or expanded U.N. peace operations. In some cases, this would represent dollars saved. But successful operations, such as those in Namibia, El Salvador, Cambodia and

Mozambique, reduce long term costs. They permit refugees to return home and create conditions under which domestic economies may rebuild. As Representative Ben Gilman recently wrote to the President, the cost of an expanded peace operation in Angola would certainly not exceed the amount currently devoted to humanitarian relief.

In Haiti, if we are unable to make a transition, as now planned, from the current multinational force to a U.N. force, we will face the choice between carrying on alone—at far greater expense to us than under the U.N.—or abandoning Haiti's democratic government before it has the means to maintain internal order. This latter course would damage American credibility, invite a coup and risk a return to brutal human rights violations and desperate attempts by migrants to flee aboard unseaworthy vessels to our shores.

Fourth, monitoring the actions of major regional powers would be more difficult. Today, for example, small U.N. observer missions provide a useful window on events in Georgia and Tajikistan, where Russian peacekeeping forces are deployed. Verifying that peacekeeping is being conducted in accordance with international principles and with respect for the sovereignty of local governments would be complicated by the lack of a U.N. presence.

Finally, if America pulls the plug on U.N. peacekeeping, our ability to lead at the U.N. will be damaged seriously. Our influence would surely diminish over decisions ranging from maintaining sanctions against rogue states to U.N. reform to ensuring greater balance within the General Assembly on resolutions affecting the Middle East. And our ability to argue that other nations should meet their obligations to the U.N. and to international law would be undermined.

The question arises: why has such ill-advised legislation been introduced? The answer, I think, is frustration. There is a perception that the United States is somehow being played for a sucker; that we are turned to constantly for help by those who are unwilling to pay their own way or to take their own fair share of risks. This perception is not new. In the years immediately following World War II, similar emotions prompted opposition to American participation in NATO, to the Marshall Plan and aid to Greece and Turkey. When President Roosevelt devised lend lease to save a Great Britain bombarded daily by Nazi planes—the predictable complaints were heard: we can't afford it; the British already owe us money; this is Europe's battle, not our own.

Such feelings are understandable, and often play well at home. But they miss a very basic fact. In each instance, when we have come to the aid of others, we have acted also in America's best interests. That was true of lend lease; it was true of the costly, but necessary, steps we took to contain Communist aggression; it is true of our participation in, and support for, United Nations peacekeeping and enforcement of U.N. resolutions against the likes of Serbia and Iraq. America is not just another country; we are a global power with global interests; and if we do not lead, we cannot expect that others will. Our position in the world may, to some, be grounds for complaint; but to most Americans, it is grounds for pride.

Our interests would not be served by destroying U.N. peacekeeping or by making it more difficult for us to gain support for our objectives at the U.N. We do, however, need a better mechanism for ensuring that Congress has an appropriate role in decisions that result in new, unforeseen and unbudgeted financial obligations. This includes the range of deployments of our armed forces from defense missions to sanctions enforcement to humanitarian relief to participation in U.N. operations. The Administration is committed to working with the Congress to develop such a mechanism. . . .

Today, under President Clinton, we are called upon to develop a new framework for protecting our territory, our citizens and our interests in a dramatically altered world. In devising that framework, we will make full use of our own reserves of military and economic power. We will invite help from old friends and new. We will look beyond the horizon of the short term, recognizing that even seemingly distant problems and conflicts may, one day, come home to America. And we will work to develop a consensus within our own country about the appropriate role for international organizations in promoting our objectives.

Let us not forget. Even before America was a country, it was an idea. We are the inheritors of a tradition that dates back not to the courtly intrigues of inbred royalty, or to the depredations of rapacious empire, but to the architects of human liberty.

My own family came to these shores as refugees. Because of this nation's generosity and commitment, we were granted asylum after the Communist takeover of Czechoslovakia. The story of my family has been repeated in millions of variations over two centuries in the lives not only of immigrants, but of those overseas who have been liberated or sheltered by American soldiers, empowered by American assistance or inspired by American ideals.

We have a responsibility in our time, as our predecessors did in theirs, to build a world not *without* conflict, but in which conflict is effectively contained; a world, not *without* repression, but in which the sway of freedom is enlarged; a world not *without* lawless behavior, but in which the law-abiding are progressively more secure.

That is what President Clinton has referred to, in a broader context, as a covenant with the future.

That is our mandate in this new era.

Thank you very much.

Yes, I do, but it is better for aged diplomats to be bored than for young men to die.

WARREN ROBINSON AUSTIN, responding to the question of whether he had become tired during the apparently interminable debates at the United Nations

57.

WILLIAM J. BENNETT: Immigration in California

In 1994 California voters passed Proposition 187, a ballot initiative that stripped illegal aliens of public services, including education and health care. The principal targets of Proposition 187 were Mexican immigrants who illegally crossed into California every year by the thousands. The massive influx of Mexican immigrants to the United States (both legal and illegal) began in the 1960s and 1970s but grew to greater proportions in the 1980s and 1990s, setting off a contentious political debate within the United States. This immigration was largely a result of widespread poverty in Mexico and economic opportunity in the United States, spurred by American business demands for low-wage labor, which Mexican immigrants provided. As the most populous state in the country and with a seemingly porous border with Mexico, California quickly emerged at the forefront of an anti-immigrant backlash. Supporters of Proposition 187 argued that illegal aliens placed a burdensome drain on state services and cost California taxpayers millions of dollars every year. On the other hand, opponents of Proposition 187 argued that disallowing public services would not deter illegal immigration but only worsen poverty in California. William Bennett, former secretary of education during the Ronald Reagan administration, was among the first Republican leaders to oppose Proposition 187, despite the fact that many California Republicans supported it.

Source: *Current*, February 1995, "Making Americans: Immigration and Tolerance."

PROPOSITION 187, California's ballot initiative which deprives illegal aliens of such publicly funded services as education and health care, won an overwhelming victory last month. A handful of states have expressed interest in putting similar measures on the ballot. Legislation may be introduced in the 104th Congress that would reduce legal immigrant quotas by as much as 50 percent. And some prominent conservatives are now arguing for a moratorium on legal immigration.

Just a few years ago, immigration issues went virtually unmentioned; soon they will be near the top of the national political agenda. For the first time in decades, the GOP will decide immigration policy—and at a time when Republicans are engaged in a vigorous debate about what direction to go. The new majority party now has an opportunity to craft legislation that is responsible, effective and consonant with the best aspects of the American character.

The most contentious part of the entire immigration debate is illegal immigration. When Jack Kemp and I came out in opposition to Proposition 187, we knew we were going against strong and deep political currents. But I believed then and I believe now that the proposition is meretricious, shortsighted (i.e., throwing 300,000 children out of school and onto the streets) and employs means that are profoundly anti-conservative and pernicious (to wit: charging private citizens with the duty of identifying people they "suspect" to be illegal and requiring them to turn the names over to state and federal authorities). It is worth noting that there are already reports from California that Proposition 187 is creating fear among legal immigrants and massive confusion in courts and schools, and among doctors, police officers and social service providers.

Illegal immigration is a very serious problem, and all Americans, especially Californians, are right to be upset and angry. Every sovereign nation has the right and the duty to control its borders. We need to put into place policies that will curb illegal immigration and assist the states in their efforts to do the same. These measures should include beefing up border patrols and deploying them more intelligently; expediting the deportation process, particularly for illegal immigrants convicted of a crime; cracking down on fraudulent immigration documents; overhauling the Immigration and Naturalization Service; changing some of the requirements for immigration sponsorship; and reducing the number of employment eligibility documents. A number of these proposals have been recommended by the House Republican Task Force on Illegal Immigration and the new Republican majority will, I hope, act on them. . . .

But the larger and more important issue before Congress and the country is *legal* immigration. While there are some minor reforms worth examining, my views on legal immigration are guided by an explicit underlying conviction: Legal immigrants are a net plus for America and hence current policy is essentially vi-

able. In this, the distinction between legal and illegal is fundamental. And making this distinction is critical to policy.

Studies show that legal immigrants are often self-selected on the basis of industry, hard work, self-reliance and a respect for time-honored American principles. They hold strong family values and deeply rooted religious faith. And immigrants are making important contributions to America in the fields of science, engineering, biotechnology, computer hardware and software, to mention just a few.

The Manhattan Institute and the Urban Institute have provided important empirical evidence about immigration. In 1993, the United States admitted just over 900,000 legal immigrants. While recent decades have seen large numbers of immigrants arrive in this country, their numbers are half what they were during the last wave of immigration. Eight percent of our population is foreign-born, compared with double that figure at the turn of the century. Contrary to popular opinion, immigration does not cause higher unemployment rates for U.S. workers (in part because of the jobs immigrants create with new businesses they start). Except for refugees, immigrants who arrived in the past decade receive welfare payments at lower rates than native-born Americans. They are a huge net contributor to Social Security, and annual taxes paid by immigrants more than offset their costs to society, generating a net annual surplus of $25 billion to $30 billion.

In one of the most comprehensive studies ever done on the link between crime and legal immigration, economists Kristin Butcher and Anne Morrison Piehl find "no evidence that immigrants are more likely to engage in criminal activity than natives. In the individual data, in fact, whether or not one controls for other demographic characteristics, immigrants are significantly less likely to commit crime. . . . [We] find no evidence that areas with high levels of immigration have experienced disproportionate growth in criminal activity over the last decade."

Historians have noted that during the 19th century there were real questions about whether the Irish, Italians, Chinese and Polish immigrants were capable of being assimilated. The Irish were despised "for their ignorance, poverty and superstition." German immigrants were considered an affront to American culture, in part because they wanted to preserve their traditions and language. In the early part of this century, Jewish immigrants were among the least skilled of all immigrant groups that arrived.

There are two important historical facts to keep in mind. The first is that during times of economic uncertainty and social disrepair, immigrants are always among the first (and easiest) targets of public antipathy. The second is that virtually every group that has come to America's shores has been spurned upon its arrival, and anti-immigration sentiments have run through public opinion polls for as long as we have had reliable information. Yet these groups have not only assimilated, they have become welcome and valuable members of American society. (Recent public opinion surveys show that the once-despised Irish now consistently rate as the nationality which most benefits this nation).

The immigration issue evokes the strongest passions in the cultural, and not the economic, arena. Indeed, immigration cannot be fully understood outside a larger cultural context. There is an alarming reluctance in our schools and universities to affirm, advance and transmit our common American culture. And while it has profound implications for immigration, I believe contemporary American society's most serious problems are more fundamental than, and different from, immigration. Our problem does not have to do with legal immigration but with assimilation—and assimilation not just for people born in foreign lands but for the people born in this nation.

Cultural anthropologist David Murray has referred to new-born children as the "ultimate undocumented aliens." By that he means that children are not born with any culture or society; they must be helped to become citizens every bit as urgently as, say, refugees from Southeast Asia. If we fail the American-born children, they will be the aliens who overwhelm us. And this is precisely what we are seeing happen today.

Because of American diffidence and neglect, many children are not being acculturated and socialized. The repayment for that neglect is now being played out on our urban streets, in hospital emergency rooms, in our courts and our classrooms. In too many places, republican virtues are not being inculcated.

The advocates for ending immigration argue that immigrants pose a cultural threat to America and that our society is no longer capable of assimilating them. But pinning the blame on immigrants for America's social decay is a dodge and a distraction. And it happens to be exactly wrong. One can make a strong argument that many new immigrants have been corrupted by those same degraded aspects of American culture that trouble so many American parents.

It's time we get on with the real work that needs to be done: Revivify our character-forming institutions and put an end to misguided government-sponsored policies that foster social fragmentation, resegregation and racial tension. The argument for dismantling the current welfare state and stopping its corrupting dependency has received an extensive public hearing. But there are three other areas that bear on this issue.

Bilingualism: Mastery of English is a key to individual opportunity in America. Teaching English to those whose native language is not English is a continuation of the struggle to provide for all Americans the opportunity to participate fully in our political, economic and social life. Having a common language is an essential condition of a unified nation. We should not be bashful about proclaiming fluency in this language as a critical educational goal, and we should not be timid in reforming our policies so as to secure it.

Multiculturalism: One of the arguments that the anti-immigration advocates rely on is that immigrants promote ethnic separatism and their foreign culture will contaminate our culture. In fact, radical multiculturalism has its origins in America and finds its intellectual home in America's elite universities. Francis Fukuyama has pointed out that "the ideological assault on traditional family values . . . was not the creation of recently arrived Chicano agricultural workers or Haitian boat people, much less of Chinese or Korean immigrants." Rather, he says, it "originated right in the heart of America's well-established white, Anglo Saxon community."

Counting by Race: Quotas, race norming, racial gerrymandering and set-asides undercut the founding American principle of equality under the law. These policies judge individuals on the color of their skin, not on the "content of their character," and they have the effect of prying Americans apart. We need to reestablish a principle that many of us thought we settled three decades ago: the moral case for putting a de jure end to racial discrimination and preferences. A good place to advance the cause is in California, where right now a group is undertaking an effort to place a civil rights initiative on the primary election ballot in 1996. Called the California Civil Rights Initiative, it is a constitutional amendment prohibiting the state and its "subdivisions" (colleges, agencies, or local governments) from "us[ing] race, color, ethnicity, national origin, sex or religion as a criterion for either discriminating against, or granting preferential treatment to, any individual or group in the operation of the state's system of public employment, public education or public contracting."

"The first step in liquidating a people is to erase its memory," the historian Milan Hubl says in Milan Kundera's "The Book of Laughter and Forgetting." "Destroy its books, its culture, its history. Then have somebody write new books, manufacture a new culture, invent a new history. Before long the nation will begin to forget what it is and what it was."

Our collective cultural task is to remember what we were and what we still are. If we once again get that right, then immigrants will fit in and flourish, as they always have. If we keep getting it wrong, then it won't really matter where the people come from. For whatever their place of origin, they will be citizens without a culture, and they will bear children without a future.

58.

BILL CLINTON: The Oklahoma City Bombing

On April 19, 1995, a truck-bomb attack on the Alfred P. Murrah Federal Building in Oklahoma City, Oklahoma, killed 168 people. At that time it was the worst terrorist attack in American history. Timothy McVeigh, a Gulf War veteran turned right-wing extremist, was later convicted of planning and implementing the attack, and sentenced to death; he was executed at a federal prison in Indiana in June 2001. President Bill Clinton spoke at a nationally televised memorial service in Oklahoma City a few days after the attack. In the wake of the 1994 midterm elections—when Republicans gained a majority in Congress—the Democratic President's national popularity had sunk to an all-time low. However, Clinton's emotional meeting with the victims' families in Oklahoma City and his moving speech at the memorial service won praise throughout the country. Following the attack, the spectre of homegrown, antigovernment extremists also cast scrutiny on the partisan rhetoric of House Speaker Newt Gingrich and members of the Republican Congress who spoke bluntly about the dangers of a large federal government. Gingrich's popularity began a long decline that ultimately led to his forced resignation as House Speaker in November 1998. In contrast, after the Oklahoma City speech, Clinton's popularity grew rapidly, and in 1996 he won reelection to a second term as President. His speech is reprinted here in full.

Source: *Public Papers of the Presidents of the United States,* April 23, 1995.

THANK YOU very much. Governor Keating and Mrs. Keating, Reverend Graham, to the families of those who have been lost and wounded, to the people of Oklahoma City who have endured so much, and the people of this wonderful State, to all of you who are here as our fellow Americans: I am honored to be here today to represent the American people. But I have to tell you that Hillary and I also come as parents, as husband and wife, as people who were your neighbors for some of the best years of our lives.

Today our Nation joins with you in grief. We mourn with you. We share your hope against hope that some may still survive. We thank all those who have worked so heroically to save lives and to solve this crime, those here in Oklahoma and those who are all across this great land and many who left their own lives to come here to work hand in hand with you.

We pledge to do all we can to help you heal the injured, to rebuild this city, and to bring to justice those who did this evil.

This terrible sin took the lives of our American family: innocent children, in that building only because their parents were trying to be good parents as well as good workers; citizens in the building going about their daily business; and many there who served the rest of us, who worked to help the elderly and the disabled, who worked to support our farmers and our veterans, who worked to enforce our laws and to protect us. Let us say clearly, they served us well, and we are grateful. But for so many of you they were also neighbors and friends. You saw them at church or the PTA meetings, at the civic clubs, at the ball park. You know them in ways that all the rest of America could not.

And to all the members of the families here present who have suffered loss, though we share your grief, your pain is unimaginable, and we know that. We cannot undo it. That is God's work.

Our words seem small beside the loss you have endured. But I found a few I wanted to share today. I've received a lot of letters in these last terrible days. One stood out because it came from a young widow and a mother of three whose own husband was murdered with over 200 other Americans when Pan Am 103 was shot down. Here is what that woman said I should say to you today: "The anger you feel is valid, but you must not allow yourselves to be consumed by it. The hurt you feel must not be allowed to turn into hate but instead into the search for justice. The loss you feel must not paralyze your own lives. Instead, you must try to pay tribute to your loved ones by continuing to do all the things they left undone, thus ensuring they did not die in vain." Wise words from one who also knows.

You have lost too much, but you have not lost everything. And you have certainly not lost America, for we will stand with you for as many tomorrows as it takes.

If ever we needed evidence of that, I could only recall the words of Governor and Mrs. Keating. If anybody thinks that Americans are mostly mean and selfish, they ought to come to Oklahoma. If anybody thinks Americans have lost the capacity for love and caring and courage, they ought to come to Oklahoma.

To all my fellow Americans beyond this hall, I say, one thing we owe those who have sacrificed is the duty to purge ourselves of the dark forces which gave rise to this evil. They are forces that threaten our common peace, our freedom, our way of life.

Let us teach our children that the God of comfort is also the God of righteousness. Those who trouble their own house will inherit the wind. Justice will prevail.

Let us let our own children know that we will stand against the forces of fear. When there is talk of hatred, let us stand up and talk against it. When there is talk of violence, let us stand up and talk against it. In the face of death, let us honor life. As St. Paul admonished us, let us not be overcome by evil but overcome evil with good.

Yesterday Hillary and I had the privilege of speaking with some children of other Federal employees, children like those who were lost here. And one little girl said something we will never forget. She said we should all plant a tree in memory of the children. So this morning before we got on the plane to come here, at the White House, we planted that tree in honor of the children of Oklahoma. It was a dogwood with its wonderful spring flower and its deep, enduring roots. It embodies the lesson of the Psalms that the life of a good person is like a tree whose leaf does not wither.

My fellow Americans, a tree takes a long time to grow, and wounds take a long time to heal. But we must begin. Those who are lost now belong to God. Some day we will be with them. But until that happens, their legacy must be our lives.

Thank you all, and God bless you.

59.

JOYCE CAROL OATES: Where Timothy McVeigh Went

When news spread across the country that a truck-bomb explosion in Oklahoma City had killed 168 people, many Americans assumed that foreign terrorists had perpetrated the attack. To the nation's surprise, however, federal and state authorities soon identified Timothy McVeigh as the prime suspect in the crime. A veteran of the United States Army, McVeigh served with distinction in the Persian Gulf War. After the war, McVeigh became embittered toward the federal government and entered the circles of antigovernment extremists on the fringes of the American political landscape. With overwhelming evidence against him, McVeigh was eventually convicted in federal court, sentenced to death, and, in June 2001, executed at a federal prison. In the essay reprinted below, the novelist Joyce Carol Oates describes McVeigh's hometown in upstate New York and looks for clues as to how a child of small-town America could become a mass murderer.

Source: *The New Yorker*, May 8, 1995, "American Gothic."

TIMOTHY JAMES MCVEIGH, the chief suspect in the recent bombing in Oklahoma City, grew up in the western corner of New York state, in Pendleton, a rural community of small farms and suburban homes twenty miles north of Buffalo and five miles southwest of Lockport. Pendleton is barely even a town, lacking its own post office, commercial center, and coherent identity. It's more a region than a community, farmland interspersed with ranch houses of modest dimensions, often with flagpoles in the front yards (as in front of the McVeigh family's home). Here and there are the remains of old, weatherworn farmhouses, perhaps an old, rotted barn, coop, or silo—relics of an era so seemingly remote in 1995 that they might be from another century. Pendleton, like nearby Millersport, Rapids, Wrights Corners, and Cambria Center is a place of such minimal visual identity that one suspects that lives here are intensely inward—in the way, that is, of contemporary "inwardness," a function not of the inner self, or soul, but of the media. If you seek identity in such places, you will take it from stylized, generic, action-oriented television or film images, not from the community. There is no community. By tradition, western New York state has been a region of hunters, fishermen, "sportsmen." Now that wildlife has been severely depleted, and hunting strictly regulated, gun lovers are often obliged to travel some distance to use their guns both passionately and legally.

In the mythos of the surrounding countryside, Lockport, with its twenty-five thousand inhabitants, is *the* city. When Timothy McVeigh spent time there, he would have been identified as "from the country"—the vague, just slightly pejorative designation given such boys and girls, as if identity might be a matter of geography and distance. Until April 22nd, Lockport's most notable citizens were, arguably, the late William E. Miller (Barry

Goldwater's running mate in the 1964 election), the late William G. Morgan, inventor of volleyball, and lately Dominic (Mike) Cuzzacrea, world-record holder for marathon running while flipping a pancake. It's a city of vertiginously steep hills built on the banks of the Erie Barge Canal—Lockport's predominant feature—which cuts through it in a deep swath and divides it approximately in two. (The well-to-do sector is generally south of the canal, sloping upward; Lowertown, steeply downhill, has always been working-class, semi-industrial, relatively undeveloped.) Uptown are elegant mansions and walled "estates" dating as far back as the eighteen-fifties. Within its city limits, Lockport has changed very little since the nineteen-fifties, a decade of local prosperity. As soon as you cross the city limits, however, you're in Lockport Mall—Fast Food—Gas Station Hell, U.S.A.

Shabby not only at its edges, Lockport still exudes an air of romance. It might have been imagined in a more innocent time by Thornton Wilder or Edward Hopper, appropriated now by David Lynch. In the canal area, it seems to possess on even the sunniest days a faint sepia cast, as in an old photograph. Downtown Main Street has a look of malnourished "urban renewal"—reasonably new buildings juxtaposed with aged buildings, structures under perennial renovation, For Sale/For Lease signs, vacant lots in what would seem to be prime real-estate territory. It is the Barge Canal that draws one's attention, though. To walk along the canal's high banks, on cracked and littered pavement, gazing down at the foaming, black water below, is mesmerizing. Framed by dizzyingly steep, stark stone walls, the canal has the look of a nightmare domesticated by frequent viewings, like German woodcuts in an edition of the Grimms' fairy tales.

In Pendleton, at Star Point Central High School, Timothy McVeigh is said to have had an undistinguished, virtually anonymous career. The iconographic image of the fanatic, the madman, the lover of guns and explosion fantasies, the coolly plotting terrorist, is difficult to derive from such a modest, homogeneous American background. D. H. Lawrence described the essential American soul as "hard, isolate, stoic, and a killer," but this seems a romantic exaggeration in our media-processed time. To grow up in Pendleton, New York, is to know oneself distinctly marginal; wherever the fountainheads of significance, let alone power, they are surely not here, nor are they even within easy driving distance. The way to the marginal personality, like Timothy McVeigh's, must be through identification with power. When not isolates, such men (yes, they are nearly always men) join paramilitary groups or para-religious cults, for which they are often willing to die. In these groups, one is both nowhere and at the very center of power: the "power," at least, to destroy.

To visit such wholly American places as Pendleton and Lockport is to be granted a revelation: how little where we have lived, with whom we have lived, and of whom we are born has any longer to do, in the public sense, with who we are. What connection is there between place of origin and destiny? Where Timothy McVeigh came from is of relatively little significance set beside where, as a young man, he went: into the United States Army and the Gulf War, to a semi-rural paramilitary organization called the Michigan Militia, and, it now appears, to Oklahoma City and the Alfred P. Murrah Federal Building, with a crude homemade bomb, on April 19, 1995. Where we come from in America no longer signifies—it's where we go, and what we do when we get there, that tells us who we are.

60.

TED KACZYNSKI: The Unabomber Manifesto

Since May 1978 a terrorist later known as the Unabomber had been mailing letter bombs with regularity to university professors and corporate employees who worked in technological fields. After a brief period of inactivity beginning in the late 1980s, letter bombs resumed in the early 1990s, when the bomber first made known his anarchist motives: ending the influence of technology on modern life. During the span of seventeen years, the bombings resulted in three deaths and twenty-three injuries. In April 1995 the Unabomber promised to stop mailing bombs if, by a given time, a major newspaper or magazine would publish his 35,000-word manifesto, a radical diatribe against technology. Using the massive tome to piece together clues of the criminal's identity and whereabouts, federal agents intensified the manhunt. On September 19, 1995, after much deliberation among the news media over a criminal ultimatum, The Washington Post, *with assistance from* The New York Times, *published the manifesto in an eight-page supplement, a few months shy of the bomber's stated deadline. The published text jarred the memory of David Kaczynski, who saw in it strong similarities to the writing of his brother, Theodore, a former mathematics professor at the University of California, Berkeley, who was educated at Harvard University and the University of Michigan. In April 1996 FBI agents arrested Ted Kaczynski at his cabin home in rural Montana, where a typed original of the manifesto was discovered. In January 1998 Kaczynski pleaded guilty to the bombings and was sentenced to life in prison. The introduction to Kaczynski's manifesto is reprinted below.*

Source: Berkeley, Jolly Roger Press, 1995.

INDUSTRIAL SOCIETY AND THE FUTURE

1. The Industrial Revolution and its consequences have been a disaster for the human race. They have greatly increased the life-expectancy of those of us who live in "advanced" countries, but they have destabilized society, have made life unfulfilling, have subjected human beings to indignities, have led to widespread psychological suffering (in the Third World to physical suffering as well) and have inflicted severe damage on the natural world. The continued development of technology will worsen the situation. It will certainly subject human beings to greater indignities and inflict greater damage on the natural world, it will probably lead to greater social disruption and psychological suffering, and it may lead to increased physical suffering even in "advanced" countries.

2. The industrial-technological system may survive or it may break down. If it survives, it MAY eventually achieve a low level of physical and psychological suffering, but only after passing through a

long and very painful period of adjustment and only at the cost of permanently reducing human beings and many other living organisms to engineered products and mere cogs in the social machine. Furthermore, if the system survives, the consequences will be inevitable: There is no way of reforming or modifying the system so as to prevent it from depriving people of dignity and autonomy.

3. If the system breaks down the consequences will still be very painful. But the bigger the system grows the more disastrous the results of its breakdown will be, so if it is to break down it had best break down sooner rather than later.

4. We therefore advocate a revolution against the industrial system. This revolution may or may not make use of violence; it may be sudden or it may be a relatively gradual process spanning a few decades. We can't predict any of that. But we do outline in a very general way the measures that those who hate the industrial system should take in order to prepare the way for a revolution against that form of society. This is not to be a POLITICAL revolution. Its object will be to overthrow not governments but the economic and technological basis of the present society.

5. In this article we give attention to only some of the negative developments that have grown out of the industrial-technological system. Other such developments we mention only briefly or ignore altogether. This does not mean that we regard these other developments as unimportant. For practical reasons we have to confine our discussion to areas that have received insufficient public attention or in which we have something new to say. For example, since there are well-developed environmental and wilderness movements, we have written very little about environmental degradation or the destruction of wild nature, even though we consider these to be highly important.

———————◆———————

The real problem is not whether machines think but whether men do.
B. F. SKINNER, *Contingencies of Reinforcement,* 1969

61.

GERTRUDE HIMMELFARB: The Pitfalls of Postmodernism

In the 1960s and 1970s, the French philosophy of postmodernism began to make major inroads among American academics, particularly those in the humanities. According to simplified postmodernist theory, all truth is relative, and hence there are no moral or intellectual absolutes. A natural conclusion of postmodernism is that if all truth is relative, then no one perspective is superior to any other. Postmodernism was controversial almost immediately upon its arrival in American academic circles. Critics of postmodernism contended that it substituted ideological polemics and moral relativism for intellectual rigor. They also maintained that the postmodernist rejection of objective truth undermined scholarly standards, because it encouraged academics to embrace subjectivity in their research, writing, and teaching. In the 1990s one of the leading academic opponents of postmodernism was cultural critic and historian Gertrude Himmelfarb of the City University of New York.

Source: *Commentary*, September 1995, "Academic Advocates."

RECENT DISCUSSIONS of academic freedom have focused on one particularly egregious case of professorial racism and anti-Semitism. In class and in public lectures, Professor Leonard Jeffries, then the chairman of the black-studies program at the City College of New York, expounded his theories of the genetic supremacy of blacks and of the responsibility of Jews for the slave trade. In 1992 City College removed him from the chairmanship, but he was reinstated after a federal court found that the school had violated his right to free speech. This April that court decision was reversed, and Jeffries has now stepped down as chairman, though he continues to be a tenured professor.

The academic and legal communities, to say nothing of civil-rights organizations, have tied themselves in knots trying to sort out the issues raised by the Jeffries case. Would there have been a problem if the professor had preached his doctrines only outside the university and not within? Or in the university (in a meeting of a black-student organization, for example) but not in the classroom? Or in the classroom while permitting other views to be heard and assuring students they would not be penalized for expressing such views? Or in a private rather than a public university?

Or—and this is the more fundamental issue—what was the ground for moving against Jeffries in the first place? Was it the political nature of his ideas, threatening the civility of discourse that is supposed to prevail in the university, and (in the language of sexual-harassment cases) creating a "hostile environment" for whites and Jews, thus jeopardizing their civil rights? Or was it the untruth of his ideas—their unscientific, nonhistorical character?

The last question is the most vexatious. For it raises the familiar argument: who is to say what is true and untrue? A professor cites his authorities; so do his opponents. If those authorities conflict, is that not the nature of all scholarly inquiry? Is it not the basic assumption of academic freedom—indeed, of freedom in general—that truth emerges only from the conflict of ideas? Surely this is the great lesson we all learned from John Stuart Mill: that truth depends on the "collision of adverse opinions," that an undisputed truth is "a dead dogma, not a living truth," and that adverse opinions are so essential to truth that they should be artificially contrived, if necessary, by "the most skillful devil's advocate."

"Devil's advocate"—that describes the role of all too many of our professors today. The Jeffries case is only the tip of the iceberg. Precisely because it deals with such sensitive issues as racism and anti-Semitism, it obscures a larger problem that bedevils the university: the problem of advocacy in general. Not just the advocacy of patently and outrageously offensive doctrines; rather, the advocacy of any views that a professor might hold on any subject.

In most universities, professors have become accustomed to expressing their opinions freely on all sorts of matters about which they may or may not have any professional competence. They do so as uninhibitedly in classrooms and lecture halls as in the media and public forums. Moreover, not only do they feel free to express their opinions; they feel free to promote causes, interests, and organized activities of every kind. At issue is not the professor who, in a class on Shakespeare, presents his own interpretation of *Hamlet*; it is the professor who, in a class on Shakespeare, presents his

own view of homosexuality and gay rights, or who so distorts *Hamlet* as to make it seem a tract about homosexuality and gay rights.

The professor as advocate. Is this what academic freedom is about? Originally intended to protect professors in their scholarly pursuit of truth within the university, while ensuring their political rights as citizens outside the university, the doctrine is now invoked to allow professors to express their political views in the classroom, without regard for either scholarship or truth. Although this is not the first time that advocacy in this sense has reared its head in the university, it is the first time it has done so with the approval of so many professors in so many disciplines—and not in the name of truth but in a show of disrespect for the very idea of truth.

Even Marxists in their heyday were not so dismissive of truth. They were, to be sure, contemptuous of those "bourgeois truths" that parade under the names of freedom, justice, law, and culture. These were said to represent the "social consciousness" of the ruling class, the "superstructure" that gives a specious legitimacy to capitalist property, production, and social relations. But Communism, Marx had explained, would bring with it not another such superstructure but truth itself, because Communism, being the "real movement" of history, could be depicted by a "real, positive science." It was in the name of that "science"—in other words, of truth—that Marxist professors assumed the mantle of advocacy, determined not merely to "interpret" the world but to "change" it.

Today a good many professors accept the Marxist indictment of bourgeois society and culture while rejecting any notion of a "real, positive science" or any other kind of truth. In the now-familiar race/class/gender trinity that has replaced Marx's monolithic class doctrine, there is no room for transcendent truth or knowledge.

For a while, in the new multicultural order, it was possible to envision a flourishing of scholarship inspired by the different perspectives of newly "empowered" groups. Black historians, feminist historians, ethnic historians, gay and lesbian historians would pursue their own interests in the traditional way, as scholars rather than advocates. But as each group has tried to overcome its own "marginality" by "mainstreaming" itself into the center of the curriculum, the competing, often conflicting, pressures and passions have made advocates of all but the most resolute scholars.

Recently another movement has emerged to give credibility to the practice of advocacy. This is postmodernism, which has swept through the academic disciplines—literature most conspicuously, but also history, philosophy, anthropology, the law. Postmodernism is the most influential, and perhaps the most enduring, of all the fashions that have afflicted the university in recent times. This is not to say that all professors have become postmodernists. But the basic tenets of the creed have pervaded the academy to the point where most young professors, and a good many older ones, accept them almost unthinkingly.

The animating spirit of postmodernism is a radical skepticism and relativism that rejects any idea of truth, knowledge, reason, or objectivity. More important, it refuses even to aspire to such ideas, on the ground that they are not only unattainable but undesirable— that they are, by their very nature, authoritarian and repressive.

This is very different from the skepticism and relativism that scholars have always brought to their trade. Historians, most notably, have always had a healthy dose of both. They have been acutely aware of the limitations of their discipline: the deficiency of the historical record, the selectivity inherent in the writing of history, the fallibility and subjectivity of the historian, and thus the imperfect, tentative, and partial (in both senses of the word) nature of every historical work.

But professional historians have always made the most strenuous efforts to curb and control these deficiencies. This is what is meant by the "discipline" of history, and why until recently the keystone of every graduate program has been a required course on "methodology," instructing students in the proper use of sources, the need for substantiating and countervailing evidence, the conventions of documentation and citation.

Today, such courses are very nearly obsolete, and the very idea of a discipline of history is regarded as disingenuous or hypocritical. Similarly, the idea of fact (the word now appears almost invariably in quotation marks) is derided, as are the ideas of truth, objectivity, and reality. What passes as history, like all forms of knowledge, is presumed to be a "construct" of the "hegemonic" class. There is no truth to be derived from history—not even partial, incremental, contingent truths. There is no objectivity—not even an approximation of it or any reason to strive toward it. There are not even any events—only "texts" to be interpreted in accord with the historian's interest and disposition, just as the text of a poem may be an occasion for the free-floating imagination of the literary critic.

It is in this spirit that all the humanities have been relativized, subjectified, "problematized" (as the deconstructionists say)—and thus politicized. For if there is no reality, no truth, no facts, no objectivity, then there are only will and power. "Everything is political," the popular slogan has it. Every professor—indeed, every student—is presumed to be, consciously or not, an advocate.

This is the intellectual rationale that lies behind the practice of advocacy. Not all advocates are postmodernists, but those who pride themselves on being "engaged" can take comfort in a learned and sophisticated theory, couched in an appropriately arcane language, that makes advocacy intellectually reputable and morally commendable.

Certainly this is the view that emerged in Pittsburgh this June at a conference on advocacy organized by the Modern Language Association (MLA) and sponsored by fifteen leading professional associations. The overwhelming consensus of the participants (I was among the few dissenters) was that advocacy in the classroom is not only proper; it is natural and inevitable. Professors, the argument went, obviously have opinions on all sorts of subjects. Is it not better for them to express those opinions openly rather than surreptitiously? Is not advocacy a necessary part of the competition of ideas that is the driving force of scholarship? And is not advocacy an essential component of the new inclusive, multicultural university, where diverse groups are for the first time asserting themselves? If advocacy were limited, would this not inhibit, even repress, these new constituencies?

Some of the speakers qualified their enthusiasm. Advocacy, they allowed, should not mean indoctrination; students should feel free to disagree with a professor and not be penalized if they do so; although no professor is obliged to present a "balanced view," the curriculum as a whole should provide balance; civility, rather than objectivity, should be the goal of the scholar; and—a cautionary note—professors should be wary of expressing views that might bring complaints of harassment from students.

But there were also those who spurned such compromises. "I let my students know," one professor declared, "where I'm coming from, and also that they're free to write papers which disagree with positions I've taken in class. But those papers had better be very, very good because I'll read them with a more critical eye than the ones I agree with." "Neutrality," said the head of a women's-studies department, "is not something I want to encourage in my students"—or in the classroom, where she declines to present the views of anti-feminists. Still another professor spoke of the "transformative" experience of her students, whose term papers were based on their work at rape-crisis centers, battered-women's shelters, and AIDS clinics. Asked whether that experience would be equally valuable if they had worked at a pro-life center or at a branch of the NRA, she replied that that was "not the same thing."

This notion of advocacy, which is as intolerant of others' opinions as it is indulgent of one's own, was reflected in another talk at the MLA conference by a philosophy professor, who insisted that politics is as relevant in the sciences as in the arts. He himself, he said, was frankly a "partisan," in contrast to those who merely appeared to favor neutrality but in reality were "dogmatists"; the latter were the true enemies of the "open classroom."

If feminists tend to be most outspoken in supporting and practicing advocacy, it is because they believe most fervently in the principle, "Everything is political." Since women are the victims of an oppressive, patriarchal power structure (so the argument goes), they are obliged to be no less political in combating that power structure. Theirs is the class struggle "engendered," as it were. Moreover, every aspect of their lives is implicated in the struggle. Hence the corollary principle: "the personal is political."

The personal has always been high on the agenda of women's-studies courses. As *Mother Jones,* hardly a magazine hostile to feminism, reports of an informal survey of such courses: "In many classes discussions alternate between the personal and the political, with mere pit stops at the academic." On the theory that female students have been deprived not only of power but of the very awareness of their powerlessness, many women's-studies courses are devoted to "consciousness-raising." Thus, the classes are sometimes little more than rap sessions, or, at a more elevated level, group-therapy sessions, in which students and professor alike dwell on their own experiences, feelings, and grievances. Even courses ostensibly devoted to the history or literature of women in earlier times often infuse those subjects with the sentiments of a latter-day feminism, stripping away the "false consciousness" imposed by the regnant patriarchy and restoring the "voice" women never had.

Recently, the personal has taken on a new urgency at our universities and is invading courses and subjects far removed from women's studies. Out of postmodernism, with its suspicion of logic as "logocentric," of reason as "phallocentric," of objectivity as "authoritarian," there has emerged a new subjectivism—a new "personalism," one might call it—that exalts the scholar's own feelings, sensations, emotions, and private experiences.

This trend has been described in articles bearing such provocative titles as "The I's Have It," "Dare We Say 'I'?," and "Don't Leave Out the Juicy Things" (meaning the personal things). The point is not that professors have taken to writing their autobiographies. Rather,

they are being autobiographical no matter what they may happen to be writing about: Japanese society, primitivism and Western culture, the story of a Mexican peddler, the analysis of a French painter. The personalist mode exhibits itself not in an occasional intrusion of reminiscences or experiences but as a dominating presence. The traditionally impersonal voice of the scholar—the "footnote voice," as it has been disparagingly called—has been replaced by the triumphal "I." "George Eliot, *c'est moi,*" announces a recent biographer of the great 19th-century novelist.

The new "personalism" has progressed far enough to invite some derisory comments. "The ideology of . . . Miss Piggy," one critic calls it. Another complains that professors have become "self-absorbed and confessional." Still another speaks of the scholars' "nouveau solipsism." Such solipsism, or narcissism, seems to be far removed from political advocacy. Yet it is itself an invitation to any kind of advocacy, now justified by the ultimate authority, the sensibility of the professor. At the very least, it is another way of imposing the professor's agenda upon the student, who is once again made hostage to the professor's preoccupations.

As we depart ever more from the traditional conception of the university, it is important to reflect on the momentum of ideas that has brought us to this point. For these ideas affect not only our views about advocacy—*how* professors communicate with students and with the scholarly community—but also our views about scholarship itself—*what* is being communicated, what we take to be the nature of the scholarly enterprise and the function of the university.

In the absence of any idea—or ideal—of truth, or objectivity, or disinterested knowledge, how is one to judge scholarly merit? What safeguards are there against willful ignorance and deception? If everything is political, if, indeed, the personal is political, we are truly in the condition depicted by Nietzsche: "Nothing is true; everything is permitted." This is a prescription not for academic freedom, but for intellectual and moral nihilism. Fortunately, we are not yet in that condition. Not all professors, perhaps not most professors, subscribe to the new doctrines, and not all who do act upon them. But there is no doubt that relativism and subjectivism are more pervasive than ever and have been carried to extremes that would not have been tolerated only a few years ago.

In *A History of the World in 10½ Chapters* by the English novelist and essayist Julian Barnes, the narrator explains why a world bereft of the idea of truth would be humanly, morally intolerable:

> We all know objective truth is not obtainable; that when some event occurs we shall have a multiplicity of subjective truths which we assess and then fabulate into history, into some God-eyed version of what "really" happened. . . . But while we know this, we must still believe that objective truth is obtainable; or we must believe that it is 99 per cent obtainable; or if we can't believe this we must believe that 43 per cent objective truth is better than 41 per cent. We must do so, because if we don't we're lost, we fall into beguiling relativity, we value one liar's version as much as another liar's, we throw up our hands at the puzzle of it all, we admit that the victor has the right not just to the spoils but also to the truth.

———◆———

[T]he most educationally effective way to deal with present conflicts over education and culture is to teach the conflicts themselves. And not just teach the conflicts in separate classrooms, but structure them into the curriculum, using them to give the curriculum the coherence that it badly lacks.

GERALD GRAFF, "Teach the Conflicts," 1990

62.

Henry Louis Gates, Jr.: The Trial of O. J. Simpson

Race was a central theme in two of the most publicized events of 1995: the trial of O. J. Simpson and the Million Man March. Simpson, a legendary former National Football League running back, was accused of murdering his ex-wife and her companion in Los Angeles in the summer of 1994. Both of the victims were white, whereas Simpson is black. Despite substantial incriminating evidence against Simpson, the predominantly African American jury found him not guilty in less than four hours of deliberations. Many whites condemned the verdict as an example of reverse racism, while many blacks celebrated it as a victory over police harassment of African Americans. The stark difference in black and white responses to the verdict seemed to symbolize a deeper racial division within the country than many Americans realized. Two weeks after the Simpson verdict, Nation of Islam leader Louis Farrakhan held a march on Washington, D.C., in which he invited a million African American men to attend. Farrakhan's history of anti-Semitic and anti-white rhetoric made him a controversial figure. In the essay reprinted below, Henry Louis Gates, Jr., of Harvard University, surveys the responses of African American intellectuals to the Simpson trial and the Million Man March.

Source: *The New Yorker*, October 23, 1995, "Thirteen Ways of Looking at a Black Man."

"Every day, in every way, we are getting meta and meta," the philosopher John Wisdom used to say, venturing a cultural counterpart to Émile Coué's famous mantra of self-improvement. So it makes sense that in the aftermath of the Simpson trial the focus of attention has been swiftly displaced from the verdict to the reaction to the verdict, and then to the reaction to the reaction to the verdict, and, finally, to the reaction to the reaction to the reaction to the verdict—which is to say, black indignation at white anger at black jubilation at Simpson's acquittal. It's a spiral made possible by the relay circuit of race. Only in America.

An American historian I know registers a widespread sense of bathos when he says, "Who would have imagined that the Simpson trial would be like the Kennedy assassination—that you'd remember where you were when the verdict was announced?" But everyone does, of course. The eminent sociologist William Julius Wilson was in the red-carpet lounge of a United Airlines terminal, the only black in a crowd of white travellers, and found himself as stunned and disturbed as they were. Wynton Marsalis, on tour with his band in California, recalls that "everybody was acting like they were above watching it, but then when it got to be ten o'clock—zoom, we said, 'Put the verdict on!' " Spike Lee was with Jackie Robinson's widow, Rachel, rummaging though a trunk filled with her husband's belongings, in preparation for a bio-pic he's making on the athlete. Jamaica Kincaid was sitting in her car in the parking lot of her local grocery store in Vermont, listening to the proceedings on National Public Radio, and she didn't pull out until after they were over. I was teaching a literature seminar at Harvard from twelve to two, and watched the verdict with the class on a television set in the seminar room. That's where I first saw the sort of racialized response that itself would fill television screens for the next few days: the white students looked aghast, and the black students cheered. "Maybe you should remind the students that this is a case about two people who were brutally slain, and not an occasion to celebrate," my teaching assistant, a white woman, whispered to me.

The two weeks spanning the O. J. Simpson verdict and Louis Farrakhan's Million Man March on Washington were a good time for connoisseurs of racial paranoia. As blacks exulted at Simpson's acquittal, horrified whites had a fleeting sense that this race thing was knottier than they'd ever supposed—that, when all the pieties were cleared away, blacks really *were* strangers in their midst. (The unspoken sentiment: *And I thought I knew these people.*) There was the faintest tincture of the Southern slaveowner's disquiet in the aftermath of the bloody slave revolt led by Nat Turner—when the gentleman farmer was left to wonder which of his smiling, servile retainers would have slit *his* throat if the rebellion had spread as was intended, like fire on parched thatch. In the day or so following the verdict, young urban professionals took note of a slight *froideur* between themselves and their nannies and babysitters—the awkwardness of an unbroached subject. Rita Dove, who recently completed a term as the United States Poet Laureate, and who believes

that Simpson was guilty, found it "appalling that white people were so outraged—more appalling than the decision as to whether he was guilty or not." Of course, it's possible to overstate the tensions. Marsalis invokes the example of team sports, saying, "You want your side to win, whatever the side is going to be. And the thing is, we're still at a point in our national history where we look at each other as sides."

The matter of side-taking cuts deep. An old cartoon depicts a woman who has taken her errant daughter to see a child psychiatrist. "And when we were watching 'The Wizard of Oz,' " the distraught mother is explaining, "she was rooting for the wicked witch!" What many whites experienced was the bewildering sense that an entire population had been rooting for the wrong side. "This case is a classic example of what I call interstitial spaces," says Judge A. Leon Higginbotham, who recently retired from the federal Court of Appeals, and who last month received the Presidential Medal of Freedom. "The jury system is predicated on the idea that different people can view the same evidence and reach diametrically opposed conclusions." But the observation brings little solace. If we disagree about something so basic, how can we find agreement about far thornier matters? For white observers, what's even scarier than the idea that black Americans were plumping for the villain, which is a misprision of value, is the idea that black Americans didn't recognize him *as* the villain, which is a misprision of fact. How can conversation begin when we disagree about reality? To put it at its harshest, for many whites a sincere belief in Simpson's innocence looks less like the culture of protest than like the culture of psychosis.

Perhaps you didn't know that Liz Claiborne appeared on "Oprah" not long ago and said that she didn't design her clothes for black women—that their hips were too wide. Perhaps you didn't know that the soft drink Tropical Fantasy is manufactured by the Ku Klux Klan and contains a special ingredient designed to sterilize black men. (A warning flyer distributed in Harlem a few years ago claimed that these findings were vouchsafed on the television program "20/20.") Perhaps you didn't know that the Ku Klux Klan has a similar arrangement with Church's Fried Chicken—or is it Popeye's?

Perhaps you didn't know these things, but a good many black Americans think they do, and will discuss them with the same intentness they bring to speculations about the "shadowy figure" in a Brentwood driveway. Never mind that Liz Claiborne has never appeared on "Oprah," that the beleaguered Brooklyn company that makes Tropical Fantasy has gone as far as to make available an F.D.A. assay of its ingredients, and that those fried-chicken franchises pose a threat mainly to black folks' arteries. The folklorist Patricia A. Turner, who has collected dozens of such tales in an invaluable 1993 study of rumor in African-American culture, "I Heard It Though the Grapevine," points out the patterns to be found here: that these stories encode regnant anxieties, that they take root under particular conditions and play particular social roles, that the currency of rumor flourishes where "official" news has proved untrustworthy.

Certainly the Fuhrman tapes might have been scripted to confirm the old saw that paranoids, too, have enemies. If you wonder why blacks seem particularly susceptible to rumors and conspiracy theories, you might look at a history in which the official story was a poor guide to anything that mattered much, and in which rumor sometimes verged on the truth. Heard the one about the L.A. cop who hated interracial couples, fantasized about making a bonfire of black bodies, and boasted of planting evidence? How about the one about the federal government's forty-year study of how untreated syphilis affects black men? For that matter, have you ever read through some of the F.B.I.'s COINTELPRO files? ("There is but one way out for you," an F.B.I. scribe wrote to Martin Luther King, Jr., in 1964, thoughtfully urging on him the advantages of suicide. "You better take it before your filthy, abnormal, fraudulent self is bared to the nation.")

People arrive at an understanding of themselves and the world through narratives—narratives purveyed by schoolteachers, newscasters, "authorities," and all the other authors of our common sense. Counternarratives are, in turn, the means by which groups contest the dominant reality and the fretwork of assumptions that supports it. Sometimes delusion lies that way; sometimes not. There's a sense in which much of black history is simply counternarrative that has been documented and legitimatized, by slow, hard-won scholarship. The "shadowy figures" of American history have long been our own ancestors, both free and enslaved. In any case, fealty to counternarratives is an index to alienation, not to skin color. . . .

Yet you need nothing so grand as an epistemic rupture to explain why different people weigh the evidence of authority differently. In the words of the cunning Republican campaign slogan, "Who do you trust?" It's a commonplace that white folks trust the police and black folks don't. Whites recognize this in the abstract, but they're continually surprised at the *depth* of black wariness. They shouldn't be. Norman Podhoretz's soul-searching 1963 essay, "My Negro Problem, and Ours"—one of the frankest accounts we have of liberalism and race sentiment—tells of a Brooklyn boyhood spent under the shadow of carefree, cruel Negro assailants, and of the author's residual unease when he passes groups of blacks in his Upper West Side neighborhood. And yet, he notes in a crucial passage, "I know now, as I did not know when I was a child, that power is on my side, that the police are working for me and not for them." That ordinary, unremarkable comfort—the feeling that "the police are working for me"—continues to elude blacks, even many successful blacks. Thelma Golden, the curator of the Whitney's "Black Male" show, points out that on the very day the verdict was announced a black man in Harlem was killed by the police under disputed circumstances. As older blacks like to repeat, "When white folks say 'justice,' they mean 'just us.'"

Blacks—in particular, black men—swap their experiences of police encounters like war stories, and there are few who don't have more than one story to tell. "These stories have a ring of cliché about them," Erroll McDonald, Pantheon's executive editor and one of the few prominent blacks in publishing, says, "but, as we all know about clichés, they're almost always true." McDonald tells of renting a Jaguar in New Orleans and being stopped by the police—simply "to show cause why I shouldn't be deemed a problematic Negro in a possibly stolen car." Wynton Marsalis says, "Shit, the police slapped me upside the head when I was in high school. I wasn't Wynton Marsalis then. I was just another nigger standing out somewhere on the street whose head could be slapped and did get slapped." The crime novelist Walter Mosley recalls, "When I was a kid in Los Angeles, they used to stop me all the time, beat on me, follow me around, tell me that I was stealing things." Nor does

William Julius Wilson—who has a son-in-law on the Chicago police force ("You couldn't find a nicer, more dedicated guy")—wonder why he was stopped near a small New England town by a policeman who wanted to know what he was doing in those parts. There's a moving violation that many African-Americans know as D.W.B.: Driving While Black.

So we all have our stories. In 1968, when I was eighteen, a man who knew me was elected mayor of my West Virginia county, in an upset victory. A few weeks into his term, he passed on something he thought I should know: the county police had made a list of people to be arrested in the event of a serious civil disturbance, and my name was on it. Years of conditioning will tell. Wynton Marsalis says, "My worst fear is to have to go before the criminal-justice system." Absurdly enough, it's mine, too.

Another barrier to interracial comprehension is talk of the "race card"—a phrase that itself infuriates many blacks. Judge Higginbotham, who pronounces himself "not uncomfortable at all" with the verdict, is uncomfortable indeed with charges that Johnnie Cochran played the race card. "This whole point is one hundred per cent inaccurate," Higginbotham says. "If you knew that the most important witness had a history of racism and hostility against black people, that should have been a relevant factor of inquiry even if the jury had been all white. If the defendant had been Jewish and the police officer had a long history of expressed anti-Semitism and having planted evidence against innocent persons who were Jewish, I can't believe that anyone would have been saying that defense counsel was playing the anti-Semitism card." Angela Davis finds the very metaphor to be a problem. "Race is not a card," she says firmly. "The whole case was pervaded with issues of race."

Those who share her view were especially outraged at Robert Shapiro's famous post-trial rebuke to Cochran—for not only playing the race card but dealing it "from the bottom of the deck." Ishmael Reed, who is writing a book about the case, regards Shapiro's remarks as sheer opportunism: "He wants to keep his Beverly Hills clients—a perfectly commercial reason." In Judge Higginbotham's view, "Johnnie Cochran established that he was as effective as any lawyer in America, and though whites can tolerate black excellence in singing, dancing, and dunking, there's always been a certain level of discomfort among many whites when you have a one-on-one challenge in terms of intellectual competition. If Edward Bennett Williams, who was one of the most able lawyers in the country, had raised the same issues, half of the complaints would not exist."

By the same token, the display of black prowess in the courtroom was heartening for many black viewers. Cornel West says, "I think part of the problem is that Shapiro—and this is true of certain white brothers—has a profound fear of black-male charisma. And this is true not only in the law but across the professional world. You see, you have so many talented white brothers who deserve to be in the limelight. But one of the reasons they are not in the limelight is that they are not charismatic. And here comes a black person who's highly talented but also charismatic and therefore able to command center stage. So you get a very real visceral kind of jealousy that has to do with sexual competition as well as professional competition."

Erroll McDonald touches upon another aspect of sexual tension when he says, "The so-called race card has always been the joker. And the joker is the history of sexual racial politics in this country. People forget the singularity of this issue—people forget that less than a century ago black men were routinely lynched for merely glancing at white women or for having been *thought* to have glanced at a white woman." He adds, with mordant irony, "Now we've come to a point in our history where a black man could, potentially, have murdered a white woman and thrown in a white man to boot—and got off. So the country has become far more complex in its discussion of race." This is, as he appreciates, a less than perfectly consoling thought. . . .

Of course, the popular trial of Nicole Brown Simpson—one conducted off camera, in whispers—has further occluded anything recognizable as sexual politics. When Anita Hill heard that O. J. Simpson was going to be part of the Million Man March on Washington, she felt it was entirely in keeping with the occasion: a trial in which she believed that matters of gender had been "bracketed" was going to be succeeded by a march from which women were excluded. And, while Minister Louis Farrakhan had told black men that October 16th was to serve as a "day of atonement" for their sins, the murder of Nicole Brown Simpson and Ronald Goldman was obviously not among the sins he had in mind. Bell Hooks argues, "Both O. J.'s case and the Million Man March confirm that, while white men are trying to be sensitive and pretending they're the new man, black men are saying that patriarchy must be upheld at all costs, even if women must die." She sees the march as a congenial arena for Simpson in symbolic terms: "I think he'd like to strut his stuff, as the patriarch. He is the dick that stayed hard longer." ("The surprising thing is that you won't see Clarence Thomas going on that march," Anita Hill remarks of another icon of patriarchy.) Farrakhan himself prefers metaphors of military mobilization, but the exclusionary politics of the event has clearly distracted from its ostensible message of solidarity. "First of all, I wouldn't go to no war and leave half the army home," says Amiri Baraka, the radical poet and playwright who achieved international renown in the sixties as the leading spokesman for the Black Arts movement. "Logistically, that doesn't make sense." He notes that Martin Luther King's 1963 March on Washington was "much more inclusive," and sees Farrakhan's regression as "an absolute duplication of what's happening in the country," from Robert Bly on: the sacralization of masculinity.

Something like that dynamic is what many white feminists saw on display in the Simpson verdict; but it's among women that the racial divide is especially salient. The black legal scholar and activist Patricia Williams says she was "stunned by the intensely personal resentment of some of my white women friends in particular." Stunned but, on reflection, not mystified. "This is Greek drama," she declares. "Two of the most hotly contended aspects of our lives are violence among human beings who happen to be police officers and violence among human beings who happen to be husbands, spouses, lovers." Meanwhile, our attention has been fixated on the rhetorical violence between human beings who happen to disagree about the outcome of the O. J. Simpson trial. . . .

There are some for whom the question of adaptation is not entirely abstract. The performance artist and playwright Anna Deavere Smith has already worked on the 911 tape and F. Lee Bailey's cross-examination of Mark Fuhrman in the drama classes she teaches at Stanford. Now, with a dramaturge's eye, she identifies what she takes to be the climactic moment: "Just after the verdict was read I will always remember two sounds and one image. I heard Johnnie Cochran go 'Ugh,' and then I heard the weeping of Kim Goldman. And then I saw the image of O. J.'s son, with one hand going upward on one eye and one hand pointed down, shaking and sobbing. I couldn't do the words right now; if I could find a collaborator, I would do something else. I feel that a choreographer ought to do that thing. Part of the tragedy was the fact of that 'Ugh' and that crying. Because that 'Ugh' wasn't even a full sound of victory, really." In "Thirteen Ways of Looking at a Blackbird" Wallace Stevens famously said he didn't know whether he preferred "The beauty of inflections / Or the beauty of innuendoes, / The blackbird whistling / Or just after." American culture has spoken as with one voice: we like it just after.

Just after is when our choices and allegiances are made starkly apparent. Just after is when interpretation can be detached from the thing interpreted. Anita Hill, who saw her own presence at the Clarence Thomas hearings endlessly analyzed and allegorized, finds plenty of significance in the trial's reception, but says the trial itself had none. Naturally, the notion that the trial was sui generis is alien to most commentators. Yet it did not arrive in the world already costumed as a racial drama; it had to be racialized. And those critics—angry whites, indignant blacks—who like to couple this verdict with the Rodney King verdict should consider an elementary circumstance: Rodney King was an unknown and undistinguished black man who was brutalized by the police; the only thing exceptional about that episode was the presence of a video camera. But, as Bell Hooks asks, "in what other case have we ever had a wealthy black man being tried for murder?" Rodney King was a black man to his captors before he was anything else; O. J. Simpson was, first and foremost,

O. J. Simpson. Kathleen Cleaver observes, "A black superhero millionaire is not someone for whom mistreatment is an issue." And Spike Lee acknowledges that the police "don't really bother black people once they are a personality." On this point, I'm reminded of something that Roland Gift, the lead singer of the pop group Fine Young Cannibals, one told a reporter: "I'm not black, I'm famous."

Simpson, too, was famous rather than black; that is, until the African-American community took its lead from the cover of *Time* and, well, blackened him. Some intellectuals are reluctant to go along with the conceit. Angela Davis, whose early-seventies career as a fugitive and a political prisoner provides one model of how to be famous *and* black, speaks of the need to question the way "O. J. Simpson serves as the generic black man," given that "he did not identify himself as black before then." More bluntly, Baraka says, "To see him get all of this God-damned support from people he has historically and steadfastly eschewed just pissed me off. He eschewed black people all his life and then, like Clarence Thomas, the minute he gets jammed up he comes talking about 'Hey, I'm black.' " And the matter of spousal abuse should remind us of another role-reversal entailed by Simpson's iconic status in a culture of celebrity: Nicole Brown Simpson would have known that her famous-not-black husband commanded a certain deference from the L.A.P.D. which she, who was white but not yet famous, did not.

"It's just amazing that we in the black community have bought into it," Anita Hill says, with some asperity, and she sees the manufacture of black-male heroes as part of the syndrome. "We continue to create a superclass of individuals who are above the rules." It bewilders her that Simpson "was being honored as someone who was being persecuted for his politics,

when he had none," she says. "Not only do we forget about the abuse of his wife but we also forget about the abuse of the community, his walking away from the community." And so Simpson's connection to a smitten black America can be construed as yet another romance, another troubled relationship, another case study in mutual exploitation.

Yet to accept the racial reduction ("WHITES V. BLACKS," as last week's *Newsweek* headline had it) is to miss the fact that the black community itself is riven, and in ways invisible to most whites. I myself was convinced of Simpson's guilt, so convinced that in the middle of the night before the verdict was to be announced I found myself worrying about his prospective sojourn in prison: would he be brutalized, raped, assaulted? Yes, on sober reflection, such worries over a man's condign punishment seemed senseless, a study in misplaced compassion; but there it was. When the verdict was announced, I was stunned—but, then again, wasn't my own outrage mingled with an unaccountable sense of relief? Anna Deavere Smith says, "I am seeing more than that white people are pissed off and black people are ecstatic. I am seeing the difficulty of that; I am seeing people having difficulty talking about it." And many are weary of what Ishmael Reed calls "zebra journalism, where everything is seen in black-and-white." Davis says, "I have the feeling that the media are in part responsible for the creation of this so-called racial divide—putting all the white people on one side and all the black people on the other side."

Many blacks as well as whites saw the trial's outcome as a grim enactment of Richard Pryor's comic rejoinder "Who are you going to believe—me, or your lying eyes?" "I think if he were innocent he wouldn't have behaved that way," Jamaica Kincaid says of Simpson, taking note of his refusal to testify on his own behalf. "If you are innocent," she believes, "you might want to admit you have done every possible thing in the world—had sex with ten donkeys, twenty mules—but did not do this particular thing." William Julius Wilson says mournfully, "There's something wrong with a system where it's better to be guilty and rich and have good lawyers than to be innocent and poor and have bad ones."

The Simpson verdict was "the ultimate in affirmative action," Amiri Baraka says. "I *know* the son of a bitch did it." For his part, Baraka essentially agrees with Shapiro's rebuke of Cochran: "Cochran is belittling folks. What he's saying is 'Well, the niggers can't understand the question of perjury in the first place. The only thing they can understand is, 'He called you a nigger.' " He alludes to *Ebony's* fixation on "black firsts"—the magazine's spotlight coverage of the first black to do this or that—and fantasizes the appropriate *Ebony* accolade. "They can feature him on the cover as 'The first Negro to kill a white woman and get away with it,' " he offers acidly. Then he imagines Farrakhan introducing him with just that tribute at the Million Man March. Baraka has been writing a play called "Othello, Jr.," so such themes have been on his mind. The play is still in progress, but he *has* just finished a short poem:

Free Mumia!
O.J. did it
And you know it.

"Trials don't establish absolute truth; that's a theological enterprise," Patricia Williams says. So perhaps it is appropriate that a religious leader, Louis Farrakhan, convened a day of atonement; indeed, some worry that it is all too appropriate, coming at a time when the resurgent right has offered us a long list of sins for which black men must atone. But the crisis of race in America is real enough. And with respect to that crisis a mass mobilization is surely a better fit than a criminal trial. These days, the assignment of blame for black woes increasingly looks like an exercise in scholasticism; and calls for interracial union increasingly look like an exercise in inanity. ("Sorry for the Middle Passage, old chap. I don't know *what* we were thinking." "Hey, man, forget it—and here's your wallet back. No, really, I want you to have it.") The black economist Glenn Loury says, "If I could get a million black men together, I wouldn't march them to Washington, I'd march them into the ghettos."

But because the meanings of the march are so ambiguous, it has become itself a racial Rorschach—a vast ambulatory allegory waiting to happen. The actor and director Sidney Poiter says, "If we go on such a march to say to ourselves and to the rest of America that we want to be counted among America's people, we would like our family structure to be nurtured and strengthened by ourselves and by the society, that's a good point to make." He sees the march as an occasion for the community to say, "Look, we are adrift. Not only is the nation adrift on the question of race—we, too, are adrift. We need to have a sense of purpose and a sense of direction." Maya Angelou, who agreed to address the assembled men, views the event not as a display of male self-affirmation but as a ceremony of penitence: "It's a chance for African-American males to say to African-American females, 'I'm sorry. I am sorry for what I did, and I am sorry for what happened to both of us.' " But different observers will have different interpretations. Mass mobilizations launch a thousand narratives—especially among subscribers to what might be called the "great event" school of history. And yet Farrakhan's recurrent calls for individual accountability consort oddly with the absolution, both juridical and populist, accorded O. J. Simpson. Simpson has been seen as a symbol for many things, but he is not yet a symbol for taking responsibility for one's actions.

All the same, the task for black America is not to get its symbols in shape: symbolism is one of the few commodities we have in abundance. Meanwhile, Du Bois's century-old question "How does it feel to be a problem?" grows in trenchancy with every new bulletin about crime and poverty. And the Simpson trial spurs us to question everything except the way that the discourse of crime and punishment has enveloped, and suffocated, the analysis of race and poverty in this country. For the debate over the rights and wrongs of the Simpson verdict has meshed all too well with the manner in which we have long talked about race

and social justice. The defendant may be free, but we remain captive to a binary discourse of accusation and counter-grievance, of victims and victimizers. It is a discourse in which O. J. Simpson is a suitable remedy for Rodney King, and reductions in Medicaid are entertained as a suitable remedy for O. J. Simpson: a discourse in which everyone speaks of payback and nobody is paid. The result is that race politics becomes a court of the imagination wherein blacks seek to punish whites for their misdeeds and whites seek to punish blacks for theirs, and an infinite regress of score-settling ensues—yet another way in which we are daily becoming meta and meta. And so an empty vessel like O. J. Simpson becomes filled with meaning, and more meaning—more meaning than any of us can bear. No doubt it is a far easier thing to assign blame than to render justice. But if the imagery of the court continues to confine the conversation about race, it really will be a crime.

◆

The televising of trials would cause the public to equate the trial process with the forms of entertainment regularly seen on television and with the commercial objectives of the television industry.

EARL WARREN, opinion on the U.S. Supreme Court,
Billie Sol Estes v. *Texas,* June 7, 1965

63.

CHARLES McGRATH: The Prime-Time Novel

Television's huge impact on American life has long been recognized, but from the medium's inception there have been those who have questioned the quality of its programming. Some of its defenders locate television's "golden era" in the period from the late 1940s to the mid-1950s, when the large demand for new programs resulted in a proliferation of anthology dramas such as the NBC Television Playhouse *and the* Kraft Television Theater. *These teleplays required a constantly changing supply of actors, writers, and directors, affording opportunities to innovate that were less available on the stage and in film. As the television-watching habit became ingrained, however, many critics believe the networks began limiting innovation and producing less-demanding programs that simply would not drive away viewers. Although some have reevaluated the programming of the 1960s, many argue that lowest-common-denominator values ruled the airwaves. In response to new government regulation of programming and advertising in the early 1970s (and later to the advent of cable television), the networks rethought their approach, creating programs that appealed to narrower demographic groups. In the process, more sophisticated programs were created and "quality" television reemerged with shows such as* All in the Family *(1971–79) and* Hill Street Blues *(1981–87), driven by producer-auteurs such as Norman Lear and Steven Bochco. In the article excerpted below, Charles McGrath, the editor of* The New York Times Book Review, *points to several programs from the mid-1990s as examples of a new golden era in which the best television programs provide viewers with many of the same satisfactions that readers found in serialized novels.*

Source: *The New York Times Magazine*, October 22, 1995, "The Triumph of the Prime-Time Novel."

NEW YORK CITY, perhaps more than any other place on earth, harbors large pockets of people who brag about being too busy to watch TV. Many of them are lying—at least a little. On average, 54.4 million Americans tune in every night, remember. Some of them are even card-carrying intellectuals who, if they haven't graduated yet to a 60-inch screen with wall projection and Dolby sound, nevertheless keep a little cable-ready Sony wedged up there in the bookcase, next to the Rilke and Heidegger. If you're telling the truth, though—if you *really* haven't looked lately—you should give it another chance. You're missing out on something. TV is actually enjoying a sort of golden age—it has become a medium you can consistently rely on not just for distraction but for enlightenment.

I should quickly explain here that by TV I don't mean all TV, or even most of it. I don't mean the tabloid exposés of Sally, Ricki, Geraldo and the rest. I don't mean the sitcoms, which, with a few exceptions like "Home Improvement," seem increasingly devoted to the theme of dysfunction and to be stuck on the premise of cramming as many unlike people as possible into a single household. I don't mean the prime-time soaps, like "Melrose Place" and "Beverly Hills 90210," though I watch them faithfully.

And I especially don't mean highbrow TV like "Masterpiece Theater," with its attempts to translate three-decker Victorian novels onto the tube. As last season's "Martin Chuzzlewit" demonstrated—not to mention the disastrous "Middlemarch" of the season before—TV, no matter how well intentioned or generously budgeted, probably isn't capable of successfully dramatizing such large-scale literary creations, at least not in just a few hourly installments. . . .

The TV shows I have in mind are the weekly network dramatic series. These shows are flourishing in a way that they haven't since the very early days of the medium, and have grown in depth and sophistication into what might be thought of as a brand-new genre: call it the prime-time novel.

To watch network TV still requires a fair amount of patience. Even when you tune in to the best shows you have to endure the constant onslaught of commercial interruptions, and commercials, it has to be said, have not improved over the years. (It helps if you picked up the television habit back in your childhood, during those blissful, cartoon-saturated Saturday mornings spent in front of the old cathode-ray-tubed RCA, while your mother banged the vacuum around your feet and sighed about all the fresh air you were missing—you learned how to tune out.) Yet for all its commercialism, network TV now is less under the thumb of the money men than either the movies or the Broadway theater, if only

because with any given episode there's so much less at stake financially. TV, as a result, is frequently more daring and less formulaic than either the stage or the big screen, both of which have to make back huge investments very quickly. Television can afford to take chances, and often enough it does. And TV of late has, ironically, become much more of a writer's medium than either movies or Broadway, which are more and more preoccupied with delivering spectacle of one kind or another. (TV is more of a writer's medium than a lot of magazines, for that matter.)

This state of affairs has come about not through any great wisdom or cultural aspirations on the part of the executives who run the networks—these people have M.B.A.'s, after all, not degrees in comp lit. It has happened, rather, because of the very nature of the medium (spectacle doesn't show up well on the small screen, and it's too expensive anyway) and because of the almost accidental fact that the people who create and who produce most shows are also the people who write them, or else they're former writers. In any case, it's generally the writers, not the directors or the editors, who have the final cut. Think of what Hollywood would be like if the novelist Richard Price, say, got to tell Spike Lee what to do.

TV will never be better than reading, thank goodness. It's hard to imagine a tube, however small, that could approximate the convenience and portability—the companionability—of a book. And images and spoken words, no matter how eloquent, lack the suggestiveness, the invitation to something deeper, of words on a page. But on television these days, if you listen hard enough, you can often hear dialogue of writerly quality—dialogue, that is, that's good enough to be in a book. And there are ways in which

TV has actually taken over some of the roles that books used to fill. A few of the more inventive TV series, for example, have become for our era the equivalent of the serial novel, unfolding epic stories installment by installment, and sweeping all of us up in shared anxiety and in a lot of group sighing and head shaking over what fate or (it's the same thing) the author has in store.

TV drama is also one of the few remaining art forms to continue the tradition of classic American realism, the realism of Dreiser and Hopper: the painstaking, almost literal examination of middle- and working-class lives in the conviction that truth resides less in ideas than in details closely observed. More than many novels, TV tells us how we live now.

Much of the TV drama I'm talking about—shows like "E.R.," "Chicago Hope," "Homicide: Life on the Streets," "N.Y.P.D. Blue," "Law and Order," "Picket Fences" and the lamentably canceled "My So-Called Life"—is rooted in the formulas set down in the earliest days of the medium: the cop show, for example, or the doc show. The first generation of great TV writers, the Gore Vidals and Paddy Chayefskys, consciously based their work on literary models, and on classical dramatic principles in particular. The current generation is no less literary ("Homicide"'s Henry Bromell used to write short stories for *The New Yorker*), but to a considerable extent the best new shows owe their form and content to nothing other than TV itself. You could make a case, I suppose, that the great innovation of contemporary TV—the device, first used by "Hill Street Blues" in 1981, of telling several stories at once—was inspired at least in part by Elmer Rice's 1929 play, "Street Scene," which simultaneously told the stories that unfolded in a single day in the life of sev-

eral families living in a New York tenement. You could also argue, much more convincingly, that some of the better writing on the good shows now could never have happened without the example of novelists like Elmore Leonard and George V. Higgins. The real influence, however, is simply earlier cop and doc shows like "Naked City" and "Ben Casey," whose tricks the latest crop of writers have borrowed and whose formulas they've enriched and complicated. Many of these shows, in fact, work by combining several familiar TV genres: doc show plus soap opera, for example ("E.R."), or cops-and-robbers plus midlife-crisis comedy ("N.Y.P.D. Blue").

What's surprising is that by operating within the ancient conventions, and sometimes right at the very edges of them, these shows often manage a considerable degree of originality. And they frequently attain a kind of truthfulness, or social seriousness, that movies, in particular, seem to be shying away from these days. A TV executive I know is fond of pointing out that an issue-oriented film like "Silkwood" or "Norma Rae" could not be made today, that nobody would finance such a project; his implication is that people who care about radiation and about the labor movement are now working for TV instead of for Hollywood. In truth, TV might not make "Silkwood" or "Norma Rae" either, and yet in some series characters like Norma Rae and Karen Silkwood would not seem the least out of place.

Few shows have ever been as issue-oriented as "Law and Order" (NBC, Wednesday night). Its seriousness, in fact—its way of looking at contemporary issues from several sides at once—is what most recommends this program, which in other respects has an almost antediluvian quality. No jumpy, hand-held-camera shots, that is; no overlapping dialogue; no complicated ensemble plots. Each episode proceeds in a stately Aristotelian fashion, following the two-part formula invoked by the introductory voice-over: "In the criminal justice system, the people are represented by two separate yet equally important groups: the police, who investigate crime, and the district attorneys, who prosecute the offenders. These are their stories.". . .

What these characters (the lawyers especially) mostly do is talk. They talk about "perps" and victims and witnesses, naturally, but they also talk a lot about rights and about the system and about the urgent and sometimes unresolvable dilemmas that the writers send their way with such uncanny regularity. "Law and Order" depends on stories more than characters, and it's known in the industry for its speed in responding to real-life events and incorporating them into the show's plots; sometimes it takes as little as eight weeks for a script to be developed and to make its way onto the air. Last season alone there were stories involving abortion rights and affirmative action; a murder, very similar to a famous Westchester case, in which a young man, suffering an alcoholic blackout, killed two people he mistakenly took to be his parents, and the apprehension and conviction of a Katherine Ann Power-like fugitive (who, in a nice touch, was represented by William Kunstler himself, his shaggy gray locks streaming behind him and his glasses perched unslippably on that majestic furrowed dome). Still unresolved (though a solution has been promised this season) is a two-year-old murder case eerily reminiscent of the Malcolm X assassination. This one includes characters modeled on Louis Farrakhan and Coretta Scott King. It has raised the specter of race riots in New York, and turns on the issue of a lone gunman versus a conspiracy of

shooters. It has everything except the Michigan militia.

The very best of the TV dramas, however, aren't quite as earnest and explicit as "Law and Order" tends to be; they're informative in another, more subliminal way. For instance, if you watch enough "E.R.," the hit show set in the busy emergency ward of a Chicago hospital (NBC, Thursday night), you can, without even knowing it, learn a lot about medicine. I'd like to think that in a personnel shortage I could pitch right in. . . .

Though "E.R." follows the "Hill Street"-honed formula of overlapping several self-contained plots with one or more longer-running stories that take several weeks to unfold, it somehow manages a nearly opposite effect with time. Instead of slowing TV time down, as "Hill Street" did, and making it resemble novelistic time, a typical episode of "E.R." crams into 48 minutes so much incident and so many people that the effect is a kind of hyper-reality, an adrenaline rush. "E.R." has lots of compelling characters: Dr. Benton, the intense, dignified black surgeon who can cure everything, it seems, except his own inner hurt; Dr. Greene, the sensitive resident whose marriage is falling apart and whose career suddenly looked bleak after he botched a delivery; Dr. Ross, the womanizing pediatrician; Nurse Hathaway, troubled and depressed and for a while sneaking too many pills from the drug cabinet. But mostly we get to know them not, as on the old "St. Elsewhere"— which used to be *the* state-of-the-art medical drama—by spending a lot of quality time, so to speak, hanging out with them, but, rather, by catching up with them in snatches as they race from one crisis to the next. The result, often, is a kind of intensity delivered on the run.

A small episode in last season's finale, involving an end-stage AIDS patient, his mother and his lover, and their letting him go, can't have taken up more than a few minutes of air time; yet in its brevity and directness, and in the honesty of its details, it was a more affecting evocation of the AIDS crisis than Jonathan Demme's overblown "Philadelphia," say. Its power came from the fact that this little moment happened in the middle of a lot of other moments—almost as in life. Similarly, a brief, silent stretch at the end of the botched-delivery episode, when Dr. Greene, exhausted, fighting tears, rides the El home in a cold winter dawn, achieved a remarkably understated eloquence. The show has a knack for dramatizing private moments—for sneaking up on them when both we and the characters are most worn down and vulnerable.

But the real reason for "E.R."'s success, I think, is that it recognizes that such private moments are so few and so hasty, and that most of us are overinvolved in an activity that has traditionally been given short shrift on TV, and in print and on the movie screen as well. I mean work, of course. In movies these days, if people have jobs at all it's in fields like architecture or publishing—professions, it would seem, that don't demand you do very much. In contemporary American novels, what people mostly do, besides sort out their relationships, is write or teach. Not the least of the qualities recommending Richard Ford's new novel, "Independence Day," is that, for a change, the protagonist actually goes to the office every day and toils at an ordinary middle-class desk job—or desk-and-car job. (He's a real-estate agent.)

Work, along with class, has somehow become an overlooked little secret in a lot of American art, popular or high, something to be avoided or ignored. Robert Benton's "Nobody's Fool" is one of the few recent Hollywood movies with a working-class theme, and though it was in many ways a careful and thoughtful effort, by casting Paul Newman as the story's hero, a hard-drinking underemployed construction worker, it inevitably invested blue-collar life with a sheen of glamour. Newman's work clothes looked like something he had ordered from the Lands' End catalogue.

TV sitcoms like "Roseanne" and "Married With Children" have lately embraced both work and class, offering us a raucous, newly liberated view of blue-collar family life. But shows like "E.R." have gone one step further. They've remembered that for a lot of us work is where we live most of the time; that, like it or not, our job relationships are often as intimate as our family relationships, and that work is often where we invest most of our emotional energy. Even if we don't work in hospitals or in station houses, we can recognize these TV workplaces as being very similar to our own—with their annoyances and reassuring rituals, crises and the endless time between filled with talk of everything and nothing.

The workplace where I've found myself most at home lately—after my day job, that is—is the 15th Precinct, the home of "N.Y.P.D. Blue," the Emmy winner created by Steven Bochco and David Milch, who also worked together on "Hill Street Blues." . . . "N.Y.P.D. Blue" is filmed almost entirely in Hollywood, but by using some well-chosen New York City exteriors and just a few station-house sets—a poorly lighted stairwell, a squad room, a room where suspects are interviewed and a dingy men's room (where many of the most intimate and revealing scenes take place)—the show has managed to evoke the authentic look and feel of New York and its police force.

"N.Y.P.D. Blue" is full of cases, many of them based on the recollections of Bill

Clark, a retired New York City detective who works as a consultant on the program and has also collaborated with Milch on a book about the series' beginnings. The show has perfected the old "Hill Street" formula of braiding into one 48-minute installment one or two self-contained subplots and a longer story that may take several episodes to unfold, so that the viewer is simultaneously satisfied and left hanging. In any given week the show overflows with narrative—stories about "skels," "mungo guys," junkies, rapists and thieves, and about the private lives of the cops who pursue them.

It is not plot, however, that drives the show as much as it is characters, in particular Andy Sipowicz, the bald, thick-chested, volatile but repressed detective who, in Dennis Franz's masterly portrayal, has invested both the wisecrack and the slow burn with a rare kind of eloquence. Franz, it should be noted, is not exactly breaking new ground here: this is the 27th time he has played a cop. According to Milch, everyone on the set marvels at how little he needs to prepare for his scenes, how he never has to think about them. Effortlessness, or the appearance of effortlessness, is actually a hallmark of the best TV acting, as opposed to movie acting, in which so often we're meant to see (or, at any rate, are never allowed to forget) the personality of the actor underneath the role. Think Meryl Streep in just about any of her pictures or, at another extreme, Bruce Willis in just about any of his. Franz *is* Sipowicz, and the difference is that TV allows him to inhabit the role in ways that the big screen would not—in dozens and dozens of small moments, for example, and by reacting to other characters as well as by being the focus of a scene. Sometimes, for minutes on end, all he does is *listen*— in anger or disbelief or with enormous

weariness. The difference, in its way, is as great as the difference between screen acting and stage acting. . . .

What makes Sipowicz so affecting— and so funny—is not just his lumbering dignity but the fact that we have seen him change. Down a long corridor of Tuesday nights, we've watched him struggle with the bottle, with rage (especially in cases involving children) and with his own barely concealed racism and homophobia. We've seen him make peace with his estranged son, and we've seen him, with agonizing slowness and one terrifying drunken slip-up, fall in love with, move in with, and even propose to and marry, Sylvia Costas, the long-suffering assistant district attorney whom he insulted in the show's very first episode after she failed to convict a mobster he had arrested and then implied that the problem, in part, was that Sipowicz had lied on the stand. (When she upbraids him, his response is to grab his crotch.)

And it's not just Sipowicz who changes, of course. Detective Medavoy, a bundle of nerdish anxieties, becomes, after an uncharacteristic moment of boldness, more and more silent, flushed and awkwardly neurotic, and eventually blows his romance with the sultry but bighearted station-house receptionist, Miss Abandando. Detective Martinez, the young rookie, screws up his courage over an entire season and is eventually rewarded by getting a date with Detective Lesniak. Lieutenant Fancy and his younger brother, who are black, quarrel and then reconcile over the issue of how best to get along in a police force run by white folks.

All these alterations, some great, some small, happen incrementally, over weeks of episodes—the way such things happen in life, and not the way they typically happen in movies, for example, or even in books. To think of a character in recent

American fiction who actually evolves this way—who ages and changes before our eyes—you may have to go back to Harry Angstrom, in Updike's "Rabbit" novels. In so many contemporary books, you get just a few days or weeks in the lives of the characters, or a year or two at most. There isn't room enough for a whole lot to happen.

Milch, who as an undergraduate at Yale studied writing with Robert Penn Warren, has said on several occasions that Warren's greatest lesson was that the secret subject of any story is what we learn, or fail to learn, over time. And it's time—hours and hours of it, stretched out over a 22-week season—that is both the great advantage of "N.Y.P.D. Blue" (compared with the two or three hours at most that are available to plays or to movies) and its great discovery. The show uses time the way serial novels used to, incorporating the intervals between installments, and the tension between what we've learned and what we fear or hope, into the experience of the story itself.

I had several morning-after conversations last year with a friend of mine, another faithful viewer, about whether or not [Sipowicz's partner Bobby] Simone's new girlfriend, Detective Russell, was a secret alcoholic—discussions not dissimilar, I imagine, to the ones serial readers must have had in 1841 while they waited for the news about what had happened to Dickens's Little Nell. . . .

The other trick "N.Y.P.D. Blue" may have learned from the serial novel, and from Dickens in particular, is that lesser characters can sometimes claim center stage without necessarily taking on new attributes. They can do it, in fact, by simply becoming truer to their limited natures, as happened last season with Medavoy and Abandando, who, as Milch says, took even the writers by surprise. Nobody was prepared for this unlikely romance,

or for how low the self-immolating Medavoy would eventually sink. "N.Y.P.D. Blue" has erased some of the traditional boundaries between subplot and main plot—the show is all one big plot that takes weeks and weeks to resolve—but it has also learned how to play characters who change against those who cannot. It has learned, in fact, a great Dickensian lesson: it is in the nature of adversity to turn most of us into caricatures.

"E.R." and "N.Y.P.D. Blue" are still TV shows, to be sure. People occasionally die on "E.R.," but more often they get better; in any case, few suffer much. The wards are always humming, the nurses and orderlies cheerful and polite. Nobody is seen paying a bill, or even filling out an insurance form, for that matter. And the cases on "N.Y.P.D. Blue" are almost always "cleared," as the cops say, and most often not by means of tedious, time-consuming legwork but, rather, by the much more efficient expedient of picking up a couple of skels and then playing good cop-bad cop with them until they break down and confess. I've never seen anybody on this show exercise his constitutional right and clam up until he can consult a lawyer.

It almost goes without saying that neither "E.R." nor "N.Y.P.D. Blue," for all their daring in other ways ("N.Y.P.D.," in particular, has repeatedly pushed the network censors way over the usual line when it comes to language and nudity), has dramatized one of the most basic and elemental acts of private life in America—namely, TV watching itself. Except for Sipowicz (who shoots the tube out one night in a drunken rage), nobody on these shows seems to even own a television set; I've never seen a character looking at one, not even the poor sick kids, bored silly, in the "E.R." children's ward. (They have to make do with Gameboys instead.)

The only way TV makes its presence known in these prime-time dramas is in the form of newspeople pushing their way into the station-house lobby or clamoring, vulturelike, outside the emergency-room entrance; in all of these confrontations, the camera is always seen as an antagonist, a disrupter of business and a falsifier of truth. In one episode of "Homicide: Life on the Street"—the innovative cop drama that the film director Barry Levinson is the co-producer of— the show's writers even experimented with the device of having obnoxious newscasters, with hand-held cameras, seem to waylay the characters with pointless questions between scenes.

The failure of TV drama to take itself into account is one of the great oddities of the medium. It's only on the comedies like "Roseanne" that the characters regularly do what the rest of us do: come home, give a quick wave to the spouse and the kids and then grab the newspaper to see what's on that night.

The most realistic TV family of all, of course, is Homer and Marge and the gang: the Simpsons, who not only put in hours in front of the tube, while pizza crusts and spent soda and beer cans mount up around them, but have formed most of their ideas about the world from what they see on television. TV may, in fact, be all that holds the Simpson family together.

Watching television is in many ways a private, solitary activity—almost like reading. But watching television is also what we do as a nation; millions and millions of us tune in together, like Homer and Marge, at the same time, to the same shows. Television is something, maybe the only thing, that all of us have in common. In my own case, I was never so grateful for TV as when, during a period in my life not long ago, I was working at a job that required me to spend 12 or 14 hours a day reading, or else talking to people about what they had written. By the time I got home, cranky and bleary-eyed, my wife and children were often asleep, but my faithful companion in the den never failed to brighten at my arrival. It gave me the news and the scores, sang all the new songs to me and generally kept me abreast of all the life I was missing. Most of all it told me stories. When I went back to work the next day I had something to talk about—how Andy was doing, whether Doc Greene and his wife would get back together—and I felt connected.

It's tempting to imagine a time when TV, which is one of the things routinely blamed for the breakup of the American family, could bring us all together again, the way it did a few years ago when we paused as a nation to consider who really killed J.R. TV could give us the news not just by reporting but by telling us even better, more affecting stories and by introducing us to richer, more complicated characters, about whom we could care even more deeply. It could happen.

But I'm not holding my breath. . . .

64.

BRUCE SPRINGSTEEN: "Youngstown"

Beginning in the 1970s the American steel industry entered a period of prolonged decline brought about largely by improved foreign competition and inefficiency resulting from the failure to modernize. The unemployment, dislocation, and disappointment that became increasingly prevalent in traditional mill towns such as Youngstown, Ohio, once the second most productive steelmaking city in the United States, is the subject of this selection by Bruce Springsteen. Bursting upon the national scene in 1975 with his simultaneous appearance on the covers of Time *and* Newsweek *magazines as rock's "next big thing," Springsteen has long poetically chronicled blue-collar life—often finding the promise of the American Dream to be hollow—and celebrated community. This song is taken from Springsteen's 1995 album,* The Ghost of Tom Joad, *a cycle of socially conscious songs at least partly inspired by John Steinbeck's novel* The Grapes of Wrath. *The Jenny referred to in the chorus alludes to the Jeanette blast furnace of the Brier Hill Works.*

Source: *The Ghost of Tom Joad,* Columbia Records, 1995.

YOUNGSTOWN

By Bruce Springsteen

Here in northeast Ohio
Back in 1803
James and Dan Heaton
Found the ore that was linin' Yellow Creek
They built a blast furnace
Here along the shore
And they made the cannonballs
That helped the Union win the war

Here in Youngstown
Here in Youngstown
My sweet Jenny I'm sinkin' down
Here darlin' in Youngstown

Well my daddy worked the furnaces
Kept 'em hotter than hell
I come home from 'Nam, worked my way to scarfer
A job that'd suit the devil as well

Taconite, coke and limestone
Fed my children and made my pay
Them smokestacks reachin' like the arm of God
Into a beautiful sky of soot and clay

Here in Youngstown
Here in Youngstown
My sweet Jenny I'm sinkin' down
Here darlin' in Youngstown

Well my daddy come on the Ohio works
When he come home from World War Two
Now the yard's just scrap and rubble
He said "Them big boys did what Hitler couldn't do"
These mills they built the tanks and bombs
That won this country's wars
We sent our sons to Korea and Vietnam
Now we're wondering what they were dying for

Here in Youngstown
Here in Youngstown
My sweet Jenny I'm sinkin' down
Here darlin' in Youngstown

From the Monongahela Valley
To the Mesabi iron range
To the coal mines of Appalachia
The story's always the same
Seven hundred tons of metal a day
Now sir you tell me the world's changed
Once I made you rich enough
Rich enough to forget my name

And Youngstown
And Youngstown
My sweet Jenny I'm sinkin' down
Here darlin' in Youngstown

When I die I don't want no part of heaven
I would not do heaven's work well
I pray the devil comes and takes me
To stand in the fiery furnaces of hell

1996

65.

Overview of the Telecommunications Act

The Telecommunications Act of 1996, signed by President Bill Clinton in February of that year, was essentially a long-awaited update to the Communications Act of 1934. In the nearly sixty-two years since that first bill went into effect, methods of communication in America had changed radically, particularly at the end of the century with the adoption of new digital forms of connection. It was also a milestone for deregulation, and it created a flurry of mergers, acquisitions, and divestitures among the giants of the telecommunications industry, as well as the rapid rise and fall of many small entrepreneurs. In essence the Telecommunications Act allowed for greater competition among local telephone, long-distance telephone, and cable television markets, which existed for the most part as regulated monopolies. Beyond these base industries, however, the act had far-reaching effects on such businesses as traditional radio stations and other radio spectrum users, Internet providers and broadcasters, computer hardware manufacturers, and software developers. The act also opened new doors for a number of emerging technologies, such as digital television, wireless and satellite services, and subscription programming. The following is an overview of the act that was provided by the Benton Foundation, which is an organization that evaluates digital communications policies and their effects on society.

Source: Benton Foundation, 1996, "The Telecommunications Act of 1996 and the Changing Communications Landscape."

ON FEBRUARY 8 President Clinton signed the Telecommunications Act of 1996 into law in a ceremony at the Library of Congress—the only time a bill has ever been signed into law there—highlighting the Act's effect on information and educational resources.

The 1996 Act updates the Communications Act of 1934 and provides a new, national policy framework that relies on competition and market forces to advance the deployment of communications infrastructures throughout the country. It includes special provisions for public schools and libraries. The 1996 Act touches almost every aspect of communications including:

• Telephone services including local, long-distance, and wireless

• Free, over-the-air broadcast television

• Cable television

• Content and programming on television and computer networks including the Internet.

In this briefing we examine a number of aspects of the Act and their place in the changing communications landscape. Although there has been much focus on the deregulatory aspects of the Act, there are a number of provisions that actually increase regulation. The Act also promises that all Americans will be served by telecommunications systems. Importantly, the public still has a number of opportunities to shape the new landscape through input to the implementation decisions being made at the federal, state, and local levels.

In particular, the work of delivering the promised benefits of new computer and information technologies now moves to the Federal Communications Commission (FCC) and to state and local governments. The FCC is deciding what telecommunications services should be made available to all Americans regardless of market forces and is devising a plan to discount those services for public schools and libraries. State and local governments, and the input of public interest advocates, will be crucial in implementing equitable policies.

Important decisions will be made in the months ahead that will help determine the actual structure of the new communications system. Will it allow a diverse range of new voices to reach the public rather than merely extending the reach of the current mass media? Will the new communications byways allow

noncommercial expression as well as serving commercial interests?

The answers depend, in part, on how effectively nonprofit organizations, advocacy groups, public institutions, and state and local governments assert their views of the public interest. "The passage of this bill is not the end, it's just the beginning," says Andrew Blau, director of the Communications Policy Project at the Benton Foundation. "The key issues that will determine whether this Act advances the public interest are still up for grabs."

I. TELEPHONE SERVICE: CONNECTING EACH TO ALL

In the past, the connection of a telephone wire from a local phone company to the home has meant the family's ability to speak with friends and family, to contact businesses and make purchases, to participate in the democratic process by having access to public officials at every level of government, to alert emergency services in times of crisis, and to reach current or potential employers. The importance of these functions in everyone's daily life justified a national policy priority to connect every household to the telephone network.

Today the connection to the network remains important for all these reasons, but for many more as well. In a time when we increasingly use information as a commodity, telecommunications are becoming increasingly important for the delivery of that commodity. The continuing convergence of communication and computer technologies allows information to be dispersed with greater ease and speed in a wide variety of formats (voice, data, image, and video) to the audience of our own choosing (broadcast, narrowcast, or point-to-point).

Approximately 94 percent of all American households have telephone service.

For most of the 6 percent that remain unconnected, phone rates are the major barrier for getting on and staying on the network. . . .

A. LOCAL TELEPHONE SERVICE: FROM MONOPOLY TO COMPETITION

Regional Bell Operating Companies (RBOCs), or "Baby Bells," and other local exchange carriers (LECs) currently provide more than 95 percent of local phone service in this country. The 1996 Act attempts to create competitive local telecommunications markets that would eliminate the last bottleneck in telecommunications services. The "local loop," the connection from the home or business to the local switch, has been controlled by a local monopoly for nearly 100 years. The 1996 Act outlines the rules by which RBOCs will have to open up their networks so that competitors can interconnect and offer comparable services to local subscribers.

In April 1996 the FCC issued a Notice of Proposed Rulemaking to allow the public to comment on the establishment of regulations to implement interconnection requirements. Under the Act RBOCs must:

• Negotiate interconnection agreements in good faith;

• Provide interconnection to their networks on just, reasonable, and nondiscriminatory terms and conditions;

• Provide access to each separate network element such as subscriber numbers, databases, or signaling systems;

• Offer resale of their telecommunications services at wholesale rates;

• Provide reasonable public notice of changes to their networks; and

• Provide physical collocation (facilities sharing), or virtual collocation if physical collocation is impractical.

Proponents of these provisions argue that greater competition in the local loop will lead to lower prices and increased services for consumers. Such competition could come from wireless services as well as other wire-based providers such as: small local service providers unaffiliated with the RBOCs and incumbent LECs, RBOCs operating outside of their service areas, long-distance providers, and new entrants into telecommunications such as cable TV and utility companies. AT&T, for example, has filed petitions in each of the 50 states to provide local telephone service. A small number of cable companies and utility companies have also announced plans to provide local service.

Some public interest advocates speculate that this competition may never be realized without proper safeguards. They believe that in the interim customers may see higher rates instead of the promised lower rates. Potential scenarios for competition that should be monitored include:

• *Wireless Service.* In some nations where potential subscribers might have to wait years for new service, wireless telephone services are proliferating because of the ease and decreased expense of connecting new customers. A "wireless local loop" could arise in the U.S. as well if sufficient radio spectrum, the medium that wireless services transmit on, is allocated for personal telephony. The spectrum has many potential users however: broadcast television and radio use large portions of spectrum and some television stations are asking for more. Terrestrial and orbital satellite systems are becoming popular for providing video services to the home. National defense organizations have spectrum allotments. Public safety organizations such as police, fire, and other emergency services use dedicated frequencies to coordinate responses. Utility companies want spectrum so that meters can be checked without having to send someone to the home to do it; even taxicab services are coordinated in our cities using portions of the spectrum. In short, there simply isn't enough spectrum available for all these services.

• *Local Service Providers Unaffiliated with the RBOCs.* Competing local phone companies exist, but, at present, provide service to a small percentage of subscribers. Many fear that these companies will target only the highest volume customers, especially large businesses, and ignore low volume customers, especially in low-income areas. If people are to believe in the mantra of market forces—that competition means lower prices—then they should also be wary that companies may pursue the customers who will offer them the greatest returns. Customers in high-cost or low-income areas may not see the benefits of competition for some time to come.

• *Competition from Other RBOCs.* At first, this seemed like the most likely source of competition in the local market. A neighboring RBOC, with facilities already in place, would begin to compete across the state lines that separate the RBOCs. As the RBOC gained more of the market share in an area, presumably, they would expand their infrastructure into that area. In the past few months, however, four of the seven RBOCs have announced plans to merge. Their strategy may be to protect their core business, local telephone service, and expand into long-distance service as well. A customer could receive local and long-distance service from one provider (once the norm in telecommunications when AT&T was the sole provider), but may not necessarily see any relief in their bill.

• *Long-Distance Carriers.* As noted earlier, AT&T has petitioned each state to

be allowed to provide local telephone service. With name recognition in some areas greater than that of the local provider, AT&T and others may have a good chance to lure some customers away with the same one-stop-shopping offers that local RBOCs will make. These companies will not necessarily be building their own facilities in local areas. They will buy local service wholesale from RBOCs and sell it retail to customers.

• *Cable and Utility Companies.* Perhaps the only players with an infrastructure that rivals that of the RBOCs are cable, power, gas, and other utility companies. They can use their current right-of-way access to connect with a large portion of American households. Most cable systems today, however, allow for a great deal of information to flow towards the home, but allow little data to flow back the other way. These companies will have to make heavy investments in new facilities to provide telephony services. Many cable companies are already carrying large debts and may be unable to make this transition. Another problem may be customer confidence. Telephone service needs to be more reliable than cable TV. Many customers may ask, "What does the cable company (or the gas company or the electric company) know about telephone service?"

Ironically, in the wake of the 1996 Act, RBOCs are asking to raise local telephone rates by about $10 a month over a five-year period. These rate hikes, RBOCs say, will be offset by decreased long-distance bills (which represent over 50 percent of consumers' telephone bills) and cheaper add-on services such as call-waiting and caller ID. Long-distance rates, however, may not decline sufficiently to offset local rate increases. Without lower long-distance rates, the basic, no-frills subscriber will see substantially increased phone bills if the requested rate hikes are enacted.

B. UNIVERSAL SERVICE: THE GUARANTEE THAT EACH IS CONNECTED TO ALL

The 1996 Act sets forth—for the first time in federal legislation—explicit principles and mechanisms designed to guarantee that some set of telecommunications services are available to all at affordable rates. According to the Act, this "universal service" package will be established by the FCC and should evolve over time to take into account advances in telecommunications and information technologies and services. The Act also identifies schools, libraries, and health care providers as important institutions in extending the benefits of telecommunications services to all. The Act targets these institutions for preferential rates for basic service and mandates a plan for deploying advanced services at these sites as well. . . .

II. BROADCAST SPECTRUM: MAKING "FREE TV" MORE COMPETITIVE

Another important medium for the delivery of information is broadcast spectrum. Many industries and services are dependent on the spectrum allocation decisions made at the FCC including broadcast television and radio, private radio communications (such as police and taxi dispatch), wireless telephones, and terrestrial and orbital satellites. Potential new users include utility companies, Internet providers, and wireless computer networks. These industries all compete to convince the FCC that their services are in the public interest. These industries, and most companies within each industry, vie for a bigger slice of the spectrum pie. Since there are so many competing interests, spectrum is considered a scarce resource even though emerging digital technologies allow for more efficient use of it.

The Telecommunications Act goes a long way to make broadcast television more competitive with cable services or new satellite services which are becoming the primary delivery systems for video programming.

• The Act allows the FCC to double the spectrum allocated to current television broadcasters to facilitate a transition to digital television. Digital television technology allows TV stations to broadcast sharper pictures with CD-quality sound (rivaling the quality experienced at a movie theater) or to broadcast many more channels simultaneously. Hence, for each channel 2 across the country, there may be a channel 2a, 2b, 2c, 2d, and 2e with five different shows, targeting five different audiences. If the broadcasters can offer greater audience definition, these programs may become more attractive for potential advertisers.

• The Act allows broadcasters more flexibility with what they can do with the additional spectrum allocation. They are not mandated to offer free, over-the-air broadcasts; they may offer subscription and pay-per-view programming, wireless telephone service, paging, data transmission, or any other service. In return, the broadcasters would have to pay fees to the FCC based on the value of the spectrum if it were to be auctioned. These provisions create new revenue streams for broadcasters who can branch out into new information services.

• The Act allows owners to purchase more stations even within the same market, allows TV and radio cross-ownership, allows broadcast and cable cross-ownership, and allows existing networks to begin new affiliate networks. Although the intent of the Act may be to encourage greater competition, the same mechanisms that encourage competition also allow large media conglomerates to enjoy economies of scale and scope. Under some scenarios, this may result in a small handful of large corporations controlling the medium a household receives its video programming from—no matter which medium the family may choose.

• Along with all of this, broadcasters may receive licenses with longer durations and relaxed renewal processes. Hence, the owner would have more confidence in the stability of the license and will have a more solid business plan when seeking capital. In a May joint filing to the FCC, the Center for Media Education and the Media Access Project argued that "[t]he public interest will be harmed by an increase in license terms unless there are corresponding requirements to insure that broadcasters meet their public interest trustee obligations." The groups argue that the FCC should better define a broadcaster's obligation to air children's educational television and locally originated programming.

Broadcasters receive all this when they are providing fewer and fewer of the public interest services that are supposed to make them special in the eyes of policymakers and earned them rights to free spectrum. For example:

• Children's educational television has all but disappeared on commercial stations.

• Candidates for political office spend millions buying ads to include the public in election decisions and, in the process, become more beholden to fundraising than leading.

• Public outcries for less violent programming are paid lip service at best.

• Community-originated programming finds fewer and fewer outlets for broadcast.

The Act does not make the obligations broadcasters owe to their communities any clearer, but makes clear that any of the obligations that apply to the current licenses will also apply to the new "digital" licenses.

Bob Dole called this plan "corporate welfare" and delayed the passage of the 1996 Act over this issue. The Telecommunications Act of 1996 was passed with an agreement that the FCC would not move forward on its plan to issue licenses to incumbent broadcasters before Congress revisited the issue. Preliminary moves to auction the spectrum in question have not gone far. Senate Commerce Committee member John McCain (R-Ariz.), who favors a plan to force broadcasters to bid for the additional spectrum, has said he "would never underestimate the incredible clout of the National Association of Broadcasters," the broadcast lobby in Washington, DC.

The present allocation scheme at the FCC will take away spectrum licenses from a class of small broadcasters called Low Power Television (LPTV). LPTV stations serve small geographic areas across the country. Nearly 90 percent of the minority-owned broadcast television stations are LPTV. They serve diverse ethnic communities with programming in Spanish, Korean, and many other languages.

Many public interest advocates believe that there should be some sort of payback for the public. The public will have to reinvest billions of dollars in television receivers in order to gain access to digital television. Are clearer pictures and CD-quality sound—the public's supposed payback in this transition—worth it? Many argue that broadcasters should have to pay for additional spectrum with a portion of the proceeds going to fund public service media—public television and radio broadcasters, wiring public classrooms and libraries to advanced computer networks like the Internet, educational programming for children—or broadcasters should be subject to well-defined, well-enforced public interest obligations such as free air time for political candidates, educational programming for children, and access for community programmers. The battle to gain these returns will be fought in Congress and at the FCC within the next year.

III. CABLE TELEVISION: UNREGULATED RATES AND COMPETITION FROM THE LOCAL PHONE COMPANIES

Over 50 years ago, cable TV was invented to provide clearer reception of broadcast stations. Cable TV lines now pass by approximately 90 percent of American households and approximately 60 percent of American homes subscribe to cable services. Broadcast stations are still transmitted along these lines, but now a host of other channels are included offering entertainment, news, public affairs, children's programming, ethnic programming, and much more.

The 1996 Telecommunications Act repeals many of the major provisions of the 1992 Cable Act which regulated the rates of cable television. On April 1, 1999, all rate regulation is repealed except for the "basic tier" of cable programming. . . .

The Act repeals the FCC's "telco-cable cross-ownership" restrictions. Local telephone companies are authorized to offer video services either by distributing programming as a cable television system or by establishing an "open video system" (OVS) to deliver video programming to the home. An OVS operator must make the majority of the system's channels available for programming by others, but is itself permitted to program up to one-third of the channels. . . .

IV. OBSCENE AND VIOLENT PROGRAMMING: SPEECH RIGHTS ON COMPUTER NETWORKS AND THE "V-CHIP"

A. COMMUNICATIONS DECENCY ACT OF 1996

The Telecommunications Act of 1996 contains the controversial "Communications Decency Act of 1996" (CDA). Most of the controversy centers around provisions aimed at limiting minors' access to objectionable material on the Internet and the effects those provisions will have on First Amendment rights for all Internet users.

The 1996 Act revises provisions of the Communications Act of 1934 prohibiting obscene or harassing telephone calls and conversation to apply to obscene or harassing use of any telecommunications facility and increases the penalties for violations. The Act also prohibits using a telecommunications device to:

• Make or initiate any communication that is obscene, lewd, lascivious, filthy, or indecent with intent to annoy, abuse, threaten, or harass another person.

• Make or make available obscene communication.

• Make or make available an indecent communication to minors.

The Act amends the federal criminal code to specify that current obscenity statutes prohibit using a computer to transmit obscene material—including material concerning abortion—or for any indecent or immoral use. The Act prohibits using any telecommunications facility to persuade a minor to engage in prostitution or any sexual act for which any person may be criminally prosecuted.

Exemptions to prosecution include:

• Persons providing access or connection to a telecommunications facility, system, or network not under such person's control.

• Employers are not responsible for actions of employees unless the employee's conduct is within the scope of employment and is known, authorized, or ratified by the employer.

• In regard to prohibited communications and minors, a person is not liable if they have taken appropriate actions to prevent access by minors or have restricted access by requiring use of a verified credit card, debit account, or adult access code or personal identification number.

• The Act provides that no provider or user of an interactive computer service shall be held liable for any voluntary action taken to restrict access to, or to enable information content providers to restrict access to, material that the user or provider considers to be objectionable, whether or not such material is constitutionally protected. This provision may allow online service providers to act as censors on their systems limiting the online speech rights of their subscribers.

If the universal service provisions of the Telecommunications Act assist libraries and schools in getting online, the CDA provisions may determine what these institutions make available online and the degree to which they are responsible for materials that users access through their facilities. The Act restricts the transmission of "indecent" material, yet it relies upon a very broad definition of indecent, which courts have traditionally ruled is protected speech under the First Amendment. "Indecent" is a vague legal term and could be stretched to include health information (for example, sex education and online forums about breast cancer), art, and cultural materials. These institutions could be held legally liable for making information

available to minors through their controlled facilities, and there have been suggestions that Congressional proponents of these measures intended to keep them responsible in order to create publicly accountable "choke points" for controversial materials.

A number of public interest groups—including the American Library Association, the Center for Democracy and Technology, and People for the American Way—are challenging these provisions as overbroad and unconstitutional. They argue that if libraries and schools are to reflect and transmit American culture in the digital age, they must ensure that their holdings and services reflect a diverse set of views, images, and experience.

B. THE "V-CHIP" AND VIEWER CONTROL

An entire section of the 1996 Act addresses televised violence. The "V-chip" is a proposed technological fix for reducing children's exposure to violent video programming. The chip would allow parents to program their televisions to block programs with violent content. All televisions sold in the United States must include the V-chip by 1998.

The broadcast television industry has one year to establish ratings for objectionable programming and to begin broadcast of those ratings. In February television executives pledged to label programs by January 1997. Jack Valenti, the man who devised the rating system for the motion picture industry, was selected to devise a ratings system for television programming. If the FCC determines that the television industry has failed in implementing a ratings system, the Commission is required to convene an advisory committee which will have one year to recommend a rating system.

Several groups have already announced their intent to file constitutional challenges to the indecency and V-chip portions of the Act. With regard to the V-chip provisions, these groups see the voluntary ratings of commercially-vested interests as insufficient and the possible ratings by a government agency as unconstitutional. A third option would allow independent organizations to make their own rating systems available for parents and to grant these ratings "must-carry"-type rights.

66.

Bob Dole: Acceptance Speech

In the summer of 1996, Senator Bob Dole of Kansas accepted the Republican nomination for President. The nomination capped one of the most remarkable careers in American political history. While serving as a U.S. Army officer in Italy during World War II, Dole was grievously injured by a German artillery shell. Dole lost the use of his right arm, but made a remarkable recovery. He spent eight years in Congress, then won election to the U.S. Senate in 1968. Twice he failed to gain the Republican nomination for President, first in 1980, then again in 1988. Finally, in 1996, he won the nomination after weathering primary challenges from conservative journalist Pat Buchanan, former Tennessee Governor Lamar Alexander, and millionaire businessman Steve Forbes. Although Dole was witty and experienced, his acerbic personality and awkward public speeches failed to connect with most voters during the general election campaign. He also suffered from close association with his fellow Republican Newt Gingrich, who had grown deeply unpopular during his two years as Speaker of the House of Representatives. On election day, Dole lost to Bill Clinton, the incumbent President, by a margin of 49 percent to 42 percent (populist independent Ross Perot carried 7 percent of the vote). Reprinted below are portions of Dole's acceptance speech on August 15, 1996, at the Republican National Convention in San Diego, California.

Source: Acceptance Speech for the Republican Presidential Nomination, San Diego, August 15, 1996.

THANK YOU very much, what a night. Thank you California. And thank you San Diego for hosting the greatest Republican convention of them all. Thank you President Ford and President Bush and God bless you Nancy Reagan for your moving tribute to President Reagan. By the way, I spoke to President Reagan this afternoon and I made him a promise that we would win one more for the Gip-per. And he appreciated it very much.

Ladies and gentlemen, delegates to the convention, and fellow citizens: I cannot say it more clearly than in plain speaking. I accept your nomination to lead our party once again to the presidency of the United States. And I am profoundly moved by your confidence and trust, and I look forward to leading America into the next century.

But this moment, but this is not my moment, it is yours. It is yours, Elizabeth. It is yours, Robin. It is yours, Jack and Joanne Kemp. And do not think that I have forgotten whose moment this is above all. It is for the people of America that I stand here tonight, and by their generous leave. And as my voice echoes across darkness and desert, as it is heard over car radios on coastal roads, and as it travels above farmland and suburb, deep into the heart of cities that, from space look tonight like strings of sparkling diamonds, I can tell you that I know whose moment this is: It is yours. It is yours entirely.

And who am I, and who am I, that stands before you tonight? I was born in Russell, Kansas, a small town in the middle of the prairie surrounded by wheat and oil wells. As my neighbors and friends from Russell, who tonight sit in the front of this hall, know well, Russell, though not the West, looks out upon the West. And like most small towns on the plains, it is a place where no one grows up without an intimate knowledge of distance. And the first thing you learn on the prairie is the relative size of a man compared to the lay of the land. And under the immense sky where I was born and raised, a man is very small, and if he thinks otherwise, he's wrong.

I come from good people, very good people, and I'm proud of it. My father's name was Doran, my mother's name was Bina. I loved them, and there is no moment when my memory of them and my love for them does not overshadow anything I do, even this, even here. And there is no height to which I have risen that is high enough to allow me to forget them, to allow me to forget where I came from and where I stand, and how I stand, with my feet on the ground, just a man, at the mercy of God.

And this perspective has been strengthened and solidified by a certain wisdom that I owe not to any achievement of my own, but to the gracious compensations of age. And I know that in some quarters I may not, I may be expected to run from the truth of this. But I was born in 1923, facts are better than dreams, and good presidents and good candidates don't run from the truth. I do not need the presidency to make or refresh my soul. That false hope I will gladly leave to others, for greatness lies not in what office you hold, but in how honest you are, in how you face adversity, and in your willingness to stand fast in hard places.

Age has its advantages. Let me be the bridge to an America that only the unknowing call myth. Let me be the bridge to a time of tranquillity, faith, and confidence in action. And to those who say it was never so, that America has not been better, I say, you're wrong, and I know, because I was there. And I have seen it. And I remember. And our nation, though wounded and scathed, has outlasted revolution, civil war, world war, racial oppression and economic catastrophe. We have fought and prevailed on almost every continent and in almost every sea. We have even lost, but we have lasted, and we have always come through.

What enabled us to accomplish this has little to do with the values of the present. After decades of assault upon what made America great, upon supposedly obsolete values. What have we reaped? What have we created? What do we have? What we have in the opinion of millions of Americans is crime and drugs, illegitimacy, abortion, the abdication of duty, and the abandonment of children. And after the virtual devastation of the American family, the rock upon this country—on which this country was founded, we are told that it takes a village, that is, the collective, and thus, the state, to raise a child. The state is now more involved than it has ever been in the raising of children, and children are now more neglected, abused, and more mistreated than they have been in our time. This is not a coincidence, and, with all due respect, I am here to tell you, it does not take a village to raise a child. It takes a family to raise a child.

If I could by magic restore to every child who lacks a father or a mother, that father or that mother, I would. And though I cannot, I would never turn my back on them, and I shall as president promote measures that keep families whole. I am here to tell you that permissive and destructive behavior must be opposed, that honor and liberty must be restored, and that individual accountability must replace collective excuse. And I am here to say to America, do not abandon the great traditions that stretch to the dawn of our history, do not topple the pillars of those beliefs—God, family, honor, duty, country—that have brought us through time and time and time and time again.

To those who believe that I am too combative, I say, if I am combative, it is for love of country. It is to uphold a standard that I was born and bred to defend. And to those who believe that I live and breathe compromise, I say that in politics, honorable compromise is no sin. It's what protects us from absolutism and intolerance. But one must never compromise in regard to God, and family, and honor, and duty and country. I am here to set a marker, so that all may know that it is possible to rise in politics with these things firmly in mind, not compromised, and never abandoned, never abandoned. For the old values endure. And though they may sleep and though they may fal-

ter, they endure. I know this is true. And to anyone who believes that restraint, honor, and trust in the people cannot be returned to the government, I say, follow me. . . .

Now, which is more important? Wealth or honor? It is not, as was said by the victors four years ago, "the economy, stupid." It's the kind of nation we are. It's whether we still possess the wit and determination to deal with many questions, including economic questions, but certainly not limited to them. All things do not flow from wealth or poverty. I know this first hand, and so do you. All things flow from doing what is right. The triumph of this nation, the triumph of this nation lies not in its material wealth but in courage, sacrifice and honor. We tend to forget this when our leaders forget it, and we tend to remember it when they remember it.

The high office of the presidency requires not a continuous four-year campaign for re-election, but, rather, broad oversight and attention to three essential areas—the material, the moral, and the nation's survival, in that ascending order of importance. And in the last presidential election, you, the people, were gravely insulted. You were told that the material was not only the most important of these three but, in fact, really the only one. I don't hold to that for a moment. No one can deny the importance of material well being. And in this regard it is time to recognize that we have surrendered too much of our economic liberty.

I do not appreciate the value of economic liberty nearly as much for what it has done in keeping us fed as to what it's done in keeping us free. The freedom of the marketplace is not merely the best guarantor of our prosperity, it is the chief guarantor of our rights. And a government that seizes control of the economy for the good of the people, ends up seizing control of the people for the good of the economy.

And our opponents portray the right to enjoy the fruits of one's own time and labor as a kind of selfishness against which they must fight for the good of the nation. But they are deeply mistaken, for when they gather to themselves the authority to take the earnings and direct the activities of the people, they are fighting not for our sake, but for the power to tell us what to do.

And you now work from the first of January into May just to pay your taxes, so that the party of government can satisfy its priorities with the sweat of your brow, because they think that what you would do with your own money would be morally and practically less admirable than what they would do with it. And that has simply got to stop. It's got to stop in America. It is demeaning to the nation that within the Clinton administration a corps of the elite who never grew up, never did anything real, never sacrificed, never suffered and never learned, should have the power to fund with your earnings their dubious and self-serving schemes. . . .

And make no mistake about it: my economic program is the right policy for America and for the future and for the next century. And here's what it'll mean to you. Here's what it will mean to you. It means you will have a president who will urge Congress to pass and send to the states for ratification a balanced budget amendment to the Constitution. It means you will have a president and a Congress who will have the will to balance the budget by the year 2002. It means you will have a president who will reduce taxes 15 percent across-the-board for every taxpayer in America. It will include a $500 per child tax credit for lower- and middle-income families. Taxes for a family of four making $35,000

would be reduced by more than half—56 percent to be exact. And that's a big reduction. It means you'll have a president who will help small businesses—the businesses that create most new jobs—by reducing the capital gains tax rate by 50 percent. Cut it in half. It means you will have a president who will end the IRS as we know it. It means you will have a president who will expand Individual Retirement Accounts, repeal President Clinton's Social Security tax increase, provide estate tax relief, reduce government regulation, reform our civil justice system, provide educational opportunity scholarships, and a host of other proposals that will create more opportunity, and security for all Americans and all across America. . . .

I will speak plainly on another subject of importance. We are not educating all of our children. Too many are being forced to absorb the fads of the moment. Not for nothing are we the biggest education spenders and among the lowest education achievers among the leading industrial nations. The teachers' unions nominated Bill Clinton in 1992, they are funding his re-election now, and they, his most reliable supporters, know he will maintain the status quo. And I say this, I say this not to the teachers, but to their unions. I say this, if education were a war, you would be losing it. If it were a business, you would be driving it into bankruptcy. If it were a patient, it would be dying.

And to the teachers unions I say, when I am president, I will disregard your political power, for the sake of the parents, the children, the schools and the nation. I plan to enrich your vocabulary with those words you fear—school choice and competition and opportunity scholarships—all this for low and middle income families so that you will join the rest of us in accountability, while others compete with you for the commendable privilege of giving our children a real education. . . .

And for those who say that I should not make President Clinton's liberal judicial appointments an issue of this campaign, I have a simple response. I have heard your argument: the motion is denied.

I save my respect for the Constitution, not for those who would ignore it, violate it, or replace it with conceptions of their own fancy. My administration will zealously protect civil and constitutional rights, while never forgetting that our own primary duty is protecting law-abiding citizens—everybody in this hall.

I have no intention of ignoring violent—I said violent—criminals, understanding them, or buying them off. A nation that cannot defend itself from outrage does not deserve to survive. And a president who cannot lead against those who prey upon it does not deserve to be president of the United States of America. I am prepared to risk more political capital in defense of domestic tranquility than any president you have ever known. The time for such risk is long overdue. . . .

And on my first day in office, I will put America on a course that will end our vulnerability to missile attack and rebuild our armed forces. It is a course, it is a course President Clinton has refused to take. On my first day in office, I will put terrorists on notice: If you harm one American, you harm all Americans. And America will pursue you to the ends of the earth. In short, don't mess with us if you're not prepared to suffer the consequences. And furthermore, the lesson has always been clear. If we are prepared to defend—if we are prepared to fight many wars, and greater wars, and any wars that come—we will have to fight fewer wars, and lesser wars, and perhaps

no wars at all. It has always been so, and will ever be so. . . .

And when I am president, every man and every woman in our Armed Forces will know the president is their commander in chief—not Boutros Boutros Ghali or any other U.N. secretary general. This I owe not only to the living but to the dead, to every patriot, to every patriot grave, to the ghosts of Valley Forge, of Flanders Field, of Bataan, of Chosin Reservoir, Khe Sanh, and the Gulf. This I owe to the men who died on the streets of Mogadishu not three years ago, to the shadows of the bluffs of Normandy, to the foot soldiers who never came home, to the airmen who fell to earth, and to the sailors who rest perpetually at sea.

This is not an issue of politics, but far graver than that. Like the bond of trust between a parent and a child, it is the lifeblood of the nation. It commands not only sacrifice but a grace in leadership embodying both caution and daring at the same time. And this we owe not only to ourselves. Our allies demand consistency and resolve, which they deserve from us as we deserve it from them. But even if they falter, we cannot, for history has made us the leader, and we are obliged by history to keep the highest standard possibl[e].

And in this regard may I remind you of the nation's debt to Presidents Nixon, Ford, Reagan and Bush. President Nixon engaged China and the Soviet Union with diplomatic genius. President Ford, who gave me my start in 1976, stood fast in a time of great difficulty, and with the greatest of dignity. Were it not for President Reagan, the Soviet Union would still be standing today. He brought the Cold War to an end—not, as some demanded, through compromise and surrender—but by winning it. That's how he brought the Cold War to an end. President Bush, with a mastery that words fail to convey, guided the Gulf War coalition and its military forces to victory. A war that might have lasted years and taken the lives of tens of thousands of Americans passed so swiftly and passed so smoothly that history has yet to catch its breath and give him the credit he is due. History is like that. Whenever we forget its singular presence it gives us a lesson in grace and awe.

And when I look back upon my life, I see less and less of myself, and more and more of history of this civilization that we have made, that is called America. And I am content and always will be content to see my own story subsumed in great events, the greatest of which is the simple onward procession of the American people.

What a high privilege it is to be at the center in these times, and this I owe to you, the American people. I owe everything to you, and to make things right and to close the circle I will return to you as much as I possibly can. It is incumbent upon me to do so, it is my duty and my deepest desire. And so tonight, I respectfully, I respectfully ask for your blessing and your support. The election will not be decided—the election will not be decided—by the polls or by the opinion-makers or by the pundits. It will be decided by you. It will be decided by you.

And I ask for your vote so that I may bring you an administration that is able, honest and trusts in you. For the fundamental issue is not of policy, but of trust—not merely whether the people trust the president, but whether the president and his party trust the people, trust in their goodness and their genius for recovery. That's what the election is all about. For the government, the government cannot direct the people, the people must direct the government.

This is not the outlook of my opponent—and he is my opponent, not my enemy. Though he has of late tried to be a good Republican—and I expect him here tonight—there are certain distinctions that even he cannot blur. There are distinctions between the two great parties that will be debated, and must be debated, the next 82 days. He and his party who brought us the biggest tax increase in the history of America.

We are the party of lower taxes and greater opportunity. We are the party whose resolve did not flag as the Cold War dragged on, we did not tremble before a Soviet giant that was just about to fall, and we did not have to be begged to take up arms against Saddam Hussein. We're not the party that, as drug use has soared among the young, hears no evil, sees no evil, and just cannot say, "just say no." We are the party that trusts in the people. I trust in the people. That is the heart of all I have tried to say tonight.

My friends, a presidential campaign is more than a contest of candidates, more than a clash of opposing philosophies. It is a mirror held up to America. It is a measurement of who we are and where we come from, and where we're going. For as much inspiration as we may draw from a glorious past, we recognize America preeminently as a country of tomorrow. For we were placed here, for a purpose, by a higher power, there's no doubt about it. Every soldier in uniform, every school child who recites the Pledge of Allegiance, every citizen who places her hand on her heart when the flag goes by, recognizes and responds to our American destiny.

Optimism is in our blood. I know this as few others can. There was once a time when I doubted the future. But I have learned as many of you have learned that obstacles can be overcome, and I have unlimited confidence in the wisdom of our people and the future of our country.

Tonight, I stand before you, tested by adversity, made sensitive by hardship, a fighter by principle and the most optimistic man in America. My life is proof that America is a land without limits. With my feet on the ground, and my heart filled with hope, I put my faith in you and in the God who loves us all. For I am convinced that America's best days are yet to come. May God bless you. And may God bless America. Thank you very much.

———◆———

Sometimes I think we're the only two lawyers in Washington who trust each other.

ELIZABETH DOLE, speaking of her husband,
Bob Dole, *Newsweek*, August 3, 1987

Financier Ivan Boesky, center, in New York City in 1987, was a focal point of the insider trading scandals that shook Wall Street in the 1980s. Fined $100 million and sentenced to three years in prison, Boesky detailed widespread corruption that led to charges against large securities firms, including Drexel Burnham Lambert Inc., and its "junk-bond" trader Michael Milken.

BUSINESS AND LAW

McDonald's Happy Meal® promotion for the 1988 Summer Olympic Games in Seoul, South Korea. Corporate partnerships with large media events such as the Olympics or the release of blockbuster films became commonplace in the 1980s and '90s, especially with fast-food chains that offered event-related collectible toys.

Then Supreme Court nominee Clarence Thomas looks on during confirmation hearings by the Senate Judiciary Committee on October 11, 1991. Allegations of sexual harassment brought by former assistant Anita Hill turned the routine hearings into a national debate on gender relations in the workplace.

On November 2, 1998, the videotaped testimony of Microsoft chairman Bill Gates was played for the federal court hearing the antitrust case against the software giant. The trial lasted for 30 months and resulted in a court order to break up the company. In 2001 an appeals court overturned the order but still found the company in violation of the Sherman Antitrust Act.
© Reuters

A caravan of webvan.com trucks (center) rolls into San Francisco in 1999. Webvan.com, an Internet company that offered on-line grocery shopping and home delivery, enjoyed a rapid rise on the stock market in the late 1990s but, like many Internet startups of the time, suffered a calamitous fall. By mid-summer 2001, webvan.com was out of business. (Below) In Boston, on December 14, 1999, Massachusetts officials display a facsimile check for $99.7 million, the first installment of the state's share of the settlement of more than $200 billion to be paid by the tobacco industry to 46 states. Two years earlier, Florida, Minnesota, Mississippi, and Texas had sued "Big Tobacco" for the cost of smoking-related health care and settled for $40 billion.

John T. Barr—AP/Wide World Photos

Jennifer Taylor—AP/Wide World Photos

67.

Geoffrey Bible, Linda Himelstein, David Greising, and Lori Bongiorno: The Case Against Big Tobacco

The first confirmed connection between tobacco and lung cancer came in 1950 when a medical report revealed that a significant percentage of all lung cancer patients smoked cigarettes, pipes, or cigars. Subsequent studies further strengthened the connection, and in 1964 the Surgeon General issued the first public health warning against smoking. By the 1970s Congress had banned tobacco advertising on television and authorized health warning labels on tobacco products. The clamor over the legal liability of tobacco companies reached a climax in the 1980s and 1990s when cancer-stricken smokers began to file lawsuits against the companies. The debate hinged on the companies' use of nicotine, a substance that promoted tobacco addiction. In 1992 the Supreme Court declared that smokers could sue tobacco companies for their health care costs, and in the mid-1990s attorneys general in states across the country sued the major tobacco companies to recover Medicaid expenses incurred in the treatment of smokers. Meanwhile, investigative reports by television and print journalists revealed that tobacco companies spiked the level of nicotine in cigarettes to increase their addictive power. Tobacco companies at first strenuously denied the allegations, but when internal documents proved that they had in fact manipulated nicotine levels, the corporations sought a legal settlement with state prosecutors. In 1998 the tobacco industry and forty-six state attorneys general signed a settlement agreement that projected payments in excess of $200 billion and included a complete ban on all tobacco advertising that targeted young people. Reprinted below are an interoffice memo of Philip Morris Companies Inc. and a Business Week *magazine article from the following month, both written in the wake of one of the first tobacco lawsuit settlements, by the Liggett Group Inc. in March 1996.*

Sources: http://www.legacy.library.ucsf.edu/

Business Week, April 1, 1996, "The Smell of Blood."

A. GEOFFREY BIBLE

PHILIP MORRIS MEMO

I AM PLEASED to tell you that Philip Morris U.S.A. has begun placing the attached full-page ad in newspapers nationwide to let people know once again that we reject the charge that we "manipulate" nicotine in cigarettes.

There is nothing mysterious or newsworthy about the "tar" and nicotine content of cigarettes; the ratings appear in all cigarette ads. We work hard to make sure our products are consistently the finest available, and that means we emphasize quality control in the manufacturing process. As our ad says, quality control is not "manipulation."

I am delighted by the strong spirit I see in our organization. Let me repeat that despite a week of sensational headlines, our commitment to the company, its employees and our strategies has not changed. Nor has our approach to our critics. We will set the record straight and we intend to prevail in the courts of law.

B. LINDA HIMELSTEIN, DAVID GREISING, LORI BONGIORNO
LIGGETT GROUP SETTLEMENT

Big lawsuits tend to be ponderous, especially if they involve the tobacco industry. But antitobacco forces have been in a frenzy ever since Mar. 13, when Liggett Group Inc. became the first company to settle lawsuits alleging that cigarette makers concealed what they knew about the dangers of smoking. Subpoenas are out to former industry employees, new witnesses are surfacing, potential plaintiffs have stepped forward, and prosecutors are intensifying their criminal inquiries. "There's the smell of blood in the air," says John P. Coale, a lawyer representing the so-called Castano class action, a case brought on behalf of all addicted smokers that Liggett settled.

Cigarette makers, whose once united front against critics has been destroyed by Liggett's gambit, clearly don't see it that way. "The settlement does not represent any change of tactics or strategy on the part of the companies, nor do we plan to do anything but vigorously defend the cases," says Daniel W. Donahue, deputy general counsel at R.J. Reynolds Tobacco Co. Some go so far as to predict that the settlement will ultimately fail—after a mandatory court review. Brown & Williamson Tobacco Corp. says its legal strategy is unchanged by recent events, and Lorillard Tobacco Co. declines all comment.

CRIMINAL? Still, the pressure against the industry is intensifying. On Mar. 18, the Food & Drug Administration released affidavits from three former Philip Morris employees—Ian L. Uydess, Jerome K. Rivers, and William A. Farone—stating that Philip Morris deliberately manipulates nicotine levels in its cigarettes to assure smokers a nicotine jolt. That may contradict testimony by tobacco executives. Philip Morris and its brethren admit they sometimes adjust nicotine levels—but they say it's only to improve taste and maintain product quality. "On the assertions of monitoring nicotine, [the affidavits] are 100% absolutely completely false," says a Philip Morris spokesman.

What worries many analysts is the prospect of criminal liability for the industry and its executives. Critics have charged for years that tobacco companies misled the public and concealed what they knew about the risks associated with smoking. But no jury has ever sided with a plaintiff on such claims. "It's not as if we've been hiding the fact that nicotine is part of the smoking experience," says RJR's Donahue. "If we were, we've done a damn poor job of it."

A criminal indictment or conviction, however, could change jurors' minds. In Washington, the Justice Dept. is probing whether tobacco executives committed perjury in 1994, when they testified before Congress that they didn't believe nicotine was addictive. In New Orleans, in a case focusing on allegations that a low-level Brown & Williamson employee was involved in a plan to smuggle cigarettes into Canada, indictments could be filed "within weeks," says Eddie J. Jordan Jr., the U.S. Attorney in New Orleans. The company says that it and its senior executives are not targets of the probe. Nonetheless, says Gary Black, a tobacco analyst at Sanford C. Bernstein & Co., "if you see an indictment that charges a tobacco company with a criminal act, it poisons the jury, and it could poison judges." Meanwhile, three other grand juries are also looking into Big Tobacco's practices. In Manhattan, the feds are investigating the companies for securities fraud. Additional federal inquiries are under way in Brooklyn, N.Y., and Alexandria, Va. And investigations are coming on all fronts. On Mar. 18, Uydess and Rivers were subpoenaed by the Mississippi Attorney General as part of that state's bid to recoup money spent on smoking-related illnesses. Uydess, a former scientist, and Rivers, a cigarette plant manager, will be deposed on Apr. 22 and 24 in Pascagoula.

The pair could well be joined by others. In the past week, roughly a dozen defectors from several companies have gotten in touch with various states and their lawyers to offer information, according to prosecutors and plaintiffs' lawyers. For instance, on Mar. 18, a former tobacco company salesman telephoned Trey Bobinger, an assistant attorney general in Mississippi, to reveal what he knew about how manufacturers control the nicotine levels in their products. "People are now voicing concerns about things about which they have personal knowledge," says Bobinger.

RENEGADE. Tobacco foes are hoping cash will prompt other defectors to speak out. Action on Smoking & Health, a consumer group in Washington, plans soon to offer a $100,000 award for information leading to the arrest of company executives who may have misled the public about the effects of smoking.

Several more states, including Washington and Texas, are now deciding whether to join the fray. "Every state attorney general is grappling with what to do about the issue," says James E. Tierney, a former attorney general in Maine who works with antitobacco lawyers and helps coordinate states' antitobacco activities. "I mean all 50."

Plaintiffs have renegade investor Bennett S. LeBow to thank for their current good fortune. As part of a bid to force a merger with RJR's tobacco unit, LeBow, CEO of Brooke Group, which owns Liggett, cut deals with class action lawyers and states on Mar. 13 that would also apply to any company that acquired Liggett. On Apr. 17, RJR shareholders vote on a LeBow slate of directors for Nabisco Holdings Corp.

Some shareholders aren't willing to wait. On Mar. 19, New York Comptroller H. Carl McCall announced that the state's $75 billion pension fund would make no further investments in tobacco stocks. "We need to limit our exposure," he says. But others are more sanguine. Donald A. Yacktman, president of Yacktman Asset Management Co., which owns 700,000 RJR shares, is convinced LeBow's strategy will fail. And he believes lawyers and shareholders are overreacting. "This seems to be the normal manic-depressive reaction to an event," says Yacktman. Or maybe it's just a new kind of nicotine rush—one that could leave tobacco executives in a pile of trouble.

68.

The Child Pornography Prevention Act

Although the Internet brought many benefits to American life in the 1990s, one of its most disturbing and unwelcome consequences was the proliferation of child pornography. Sexually explicit photographs of children had existed before the arrival of computers, but the Internet greatly facilitated their dissemination. Almost immediately, pedophiles used the emerging medium to acquire and spread child pornography, operating largely beneath the knowledge of local and federal authorities, who consequently responded slowly to the problem. By the mid-1990s, however, investigations by various journalists and federal authorities revealed that a stunningly large number of child pornography sites were available on the Internet. In 1996 Congress responded by passing a federal law that expanded the prohibition on child pornography to include the use of computers and other technologies. Although the federal courts subsequently struck down the act on constitutional grounds, popular opinion remained strongly supportive of a complete ban on the possession and distribution of pornographic materials involving children. The opening section of the Child Pornography Prevention Act of 1996 is reprinted below.

Source: http://www.access.gpo.gov/nara/nara005.html

H.R. 3610

Sec. 121. This section may be cited as the "Child Pornography Prevention Act of 1996".

Subsection 1. Findings.

Congress finds that—

(1) the use of children in the production of sexually explicit material, including photographs, films, videos, computer images, and other visual depictions, is a form of sexual abuse which can result in physical or psychological harm, or both, to the children involved;

(2) where children are used in its production, child pornography permanently records the victim's abuse, and its continued existence causes the child victims of sexual abuse continuing harm by haunting those children in future years;

(3) child pornography is often used as part of a method of seducing other children into sexual activity; a child who is reluctant to engage in sexual activity with an adult, or to pose for sexually explicit photographs, can sometimes be convinced by viewing depictions of other children "having fun" participating in such activity;

(4) child pornography is often used by pedophiles and child sexual abusers to stimulate and whet their own sexual appetites, and as a model for sexual acting out with children; such use of child pornography can desensitize the viewer to the pathology of sexual abuse or exploitation of children, so that it can become acceptable to and even preferred by the viewer;

(5) new photographic and computer imagining technologies make it possible to produce by electronic, mechanical, or other means, visual depictions of what appear to be children engaging in sexually explicit conduct that are virtually indistinguishable to the unsuspecting viewer from unretouched photographic images of actual children engaging in sexually explicit conduct;

(6) computers and computer imaging technology can be used to—

(A) alter sexually explicit photographs, films, and videos in such a way as to make it virtually impossible for unsuspecting viewers to identify individuals, or to determine if the offending material was produced using children;

(B) produce visual depictions of child sexual activity designed to satisfy the preferences of individual child molesters, pedophiles, and pornography collectors; and

(C) alter innocent pictures of children to create visual depictions of those children engaging in sexual conduct;

(7) the creation or distribution of child pornography which includes an image of a recognizable minor invades the child's privacy and reputational interests, since images that are created showing a child's face or other identifiable feature on a body engaging in sexually explicit conduct can haunt the minor for years to come;

(8) the effect of visual depictions of child sexual activity on a child molester or pedophile using that material to stimulate or whet his own sexual appetites, or on a child where the material is being used as a means of seducing or breaking down the child's inhibitions to sexual abuse or exploitation, is the same whether the child pornography consists of photographic depictions of actual children or visual depictions produced wholly or in part by electronic, mechanical, or other means, including by computer, which are virtually indistinguishable to the unsuspecting viewer from photographic images of actual children;

(9) the danger to children who are seduced and molested with the aid of child sex pictures is just as great when the child pornographer or child molester uses visual depictions of child sexual activity produced wholly or in part by electronic, mechanical, or other means, including by computer, as when the material consists of unretouched photographic images of actual children engaging in sexually explicit conduct;

(10)(A) the existence of and traffic in child pornographic images creates the potential for many types of harm in the community and presents a clear and present danger to all children; and

(B) it inflames the desires of child molesters, pedophiles, and child pornographers who prey on children, thereby increasing the creation and distribution of child pornography and the sexual abuse and exploitation of actual children who are victimized as a result of the existence and use of these materials;

(11)(A) the sexualization and eroticization of minors through any form of child pornographic images has a deleterious effect on all children by encouraging a societal perception of children as sexual objects and leading to further sexual abuse and exploitation of them; and

(B) this sexualization of minors creates an unwholesome environment which affects the psychological, mental and emotional development of children and undermines the efforts of parents and families to encourage the sound mental, moral and emotional development of children;

(12) prohibiting the possession and

viewing of child pornography will encourage the possessors of such material to rid themselves of or destroy the material, thereby helping to protect the victims of child pornography and to eliminate the market for the sexual exploitative use of children; and

(13) the elimination of child pornography and the protection of children from sexual exploitation provide a compelling governmental interest for prohibiting the production, distribution, possession, sale, or viewing of visual depictions of children engaging in sexually explicit conduct, including both photographic images of actual children engaging in such conduct and depictions produced by computer or other means which are virtually indistinguishable to the unsuspecting viewer from photographic images of actual children engaging in such conduct. . . .

69.

Max Gitter: The Olympic Bombing and Press Leaks

During the 1996 Summer Olympics in Atlanta, Georgia, a bomb exploded amid a crowd of spectators, killing one and injuring many others. The Federal Bureau of Investigation (FBI) took up the case and began an intensive scrutiny of potential suspects. Although suspicion focused initially on right-wing extremist groups who held grudges against the federal government, the FBI soon turned its attention to Richard Jewell, a local security guard. Although the FBI had no evidence linking Jewell to the crime, he fit one of the potential personality profiles the FBI had drawn up of the bomber. The FBI subjected Jewell to hours of intensive questioning, which turned up nothing. Frustrated by their lack of progress, the FBI attempted to place pressure on Jewell by leaking to the press the fact that he was a suspect. As expected, a media circus soon developed, and Jewell fell under round-the-clock scrutiny by journalists. He still refused to admit wrongdoing, and in time even the FBI realized that he was innocent. The FBI's use of media leaks to hound an innocent man shocked Americans and elicited sharp condemnation on editorial pages across the country. The FBI never apprehended the real bomber, though fugitive Eric Robert Rudolph was formally charged with the crime in 1998. In the essay reprinted below, Max Gitter, a lawyer and contributor to The New Republic *magazine, discusses the Jewell case and condemns the use of leaks as a form of insider trading.*

Source: *The New Republic,* November 25, 1996, "Bad Plumbing."

Most people feel sorry for Richard Jewell, the FBI's now-exonerated suspect in the Atlanta Olympics bombing. They pity him for his ordeals with agents who went to great lengths to trick him into confessing. But they also doubt that Jewell has a case against the FBI. After all, it is virtually impossible to sue a government agency. And Jewell will have an equally hard time suing the press, the argument goes, because he was already a public figure when he was tagged as a suspect.

But Jewell may have a way out, if he tries a novel strategy. The media will defend themselves against claims of malice by saying they relied on some authoritative, if anonymous, government source who told them Jewell was a suspect. The FBI and other government investigators have, of course, denied they leaked the story. If they are right, Jewell can sue the *Atlanta Journal-Constitution* for recklessness. But surely Jewell will try for pre-trial discovery, which should expose who leaked the story.

Jewell might stand a chance against the government, moreover, if he focuses his case not so much on this particular leak as on the Justice Department's long history of failing to pursue leakers in its midst. (When was the last time you read about an indictment of a prosecutor or FBI agent for leaking grand jury materials to the press?) His suit against the government might fare better if he portrayed the Justice Department as creating an environment that routinely overlooks, and tacitly encourages its employees to violate, the rules concerning leaks. It creates a permissive atmosphere, analogous to the "hostile working environment" in sexual harassment cases.

This strategy could get at an intractable and chronic problem: the damage to people's rights and reputations wrought by government leaks.

Government leaks are normally challenged by defense attorneys during ongoing investigations or prosecutions. But judges are extremely reluctant even to investigate the government at that stage for fear of jeopardizing a pending case. As a defense attorney during the financial scandals of the late '80s, I witnessed firsthand what typically happens—nothing. Despite massive, continuing leaks about what should have been secret SEC [Security and Exchange Commission] and grand jury investigations—some of which could have come from government sources—defendants could only get courts to defer the problem of leaks until after trial. When the proceedings were over, however, the leaks were never pursued. Defendants who were vindicated wanted only to put the entire matter behind them. And there was little public sympathy for convicted financiers claiming their rights were impinged by some government agent who, after all, did help put the rich felon in jail.

The Jewell case is different. Judging by his press conference, he does not want to put the case behind him. And public sympathy is with Jewell. It is the perfect occasion to address the plight of the accused—and the unaccused—who are made to suffer.

Let's be clear, first of all, that leaks violate the law and seriously prejudice suspects and defendants. Federal statutes prohibit disclosure of information on grand jury investigations. The Constitution guarantees due process as well as a secret grand jury proceeding for serious criminal charges. As any criminal defense attorney can attest, leaks to the media prejudice the potential jury pool. (Indeed, many argue that that is precisely why prosecutors engage in leaks.) Leaks and the resulting media coverage can even affect judges. An unusually high percentage of convictions in the Wall Street scandals were reversed. The leaks, the consequent media frenzy and the public's outrage undoubtedly inhibited some judges from dismissing at the outset attenuated indictments and overreaching prosecutorial theories.

Can anything be done about these kinds of leaks? Well, maybe. Laws against leaking are almost never enforced, for obvious reasons: each of the two principal institutions in our society that expose wrongful conduct has a conflict. The media have a vested interest in ensuring a continuing flow of leaks and go to great lengths to keep the identity of leakers secret. Similarly, every government agency has an interest in protecting its own. Self-investigation by government agencies is notoriously unreliable. No one was indicted, fired, suspended or even identified for leaking stories about the financial investigations in the '80s.

What is needed is an independent force, such as an invigorated Office of Professional Responsibility in the Justice Department, with the teeth and the will to pursue leakers and a real prospect of public recognition for successfully performing that job. Neither that nor any other reform is likely to occur without a transformation in public attitudes. The leakers of government investigations must be deglorified.

After the Pentagon Papers and Watergate, the media persuaded society that government leaks are essential to democratic functioning. But this position has little merit in a criminal investigation, where it tramples due process and privacy rights. The public, the media and the courts need to understand that leakers are not always courageous whistleblowers; in many cases, they are opportunistic abusers of positions of trust.

The legal and ethical posture of an FBI agent, a Georgia state investigator or a prosecutor who leaks information about a pending investigation is the same as that of a person who passes on "tips" or inside information about a corporate takeover. The seminal Supreme Court case about insider trading, *Dirks* v. *SEC*, made clear that a person who acquires confidential financial information through a position of trust and then conveys that information to another for personal gain is guilty of insider trading. And so, for example, an employee of a law firm is guilty of insider trading if he learns of a possible takeover and then passes that confidential information to a friend in hopes of gaining either a direct immediate benefit, such as a share of the financial gains, or what is called a "reputational" benefit, such as enhanced stature in the eyes of the "tippee" and the possibility of one day obtaining a favor from the tippee.

Like the law firm employee, the government leaker acquires confidential information through a position of trust. He then offers that information to the media either for an immediate gain, such as winning a prosecution by prejudicing the jury pool, or some "reputational" benefit, such as cultivating a relationship with a reporter who might later write a favorable story. The media's "defense" of government leaks—that they inform the public early about potential prosecutions—also has a parallel in the case of the inside trader: many economists believe that insider trading is beneficial because it sends "signals" to the market that raise the price of a takeover stock, thereby helping those who otherwise would sell at too low a price.

If we start calling these leakers what they are—insider traders—perhaps their standing with the public will be diminished. Only then will the incidence of such leaks be reduced.

1997

70.

DENNIS O'BRIEN: The High Cost of Higher Education

Gaining a college education was traditionally a luxury in American life. Before World War II, the vast majority of college graduates were white men of middle- and upper-middle-class backgrounds. In the aftermath of the war, however, college enrollment soared. The first wave of new college students included returning servicemen, who paid for their educations with federal subsidies (known generally as the G.I. Bill). In the 1960s and 1970s the number of female and minority college students skyrocketed as well. With the ranks of college graduates swelling, many white-collar employers found it possible to require a college degree for all job applicants. Where once a high school diploma afforded access to desirable jobs, it now became clear that a college degree was a necessity in the modern workplace. In turn, the growing importance of a college education led even more high school students to apply to college. By the 1990s the American university system enrolled vastly more students than any other university system in the world. At the same time, however, college tuition bills hit all-time highs. In the essay excerpted below, Dennis O'Brien of the University of Rochester explores the long-term implications of these pressures, which may result in one of two business models: a command economy, with a standardized curriculum and fixed faculty, or a demand economy, with a free-market curriculum and revolving faculty.

Source: *Commonweal*, March 28, 1997, "A 'Necessary' of Modern Life? A Very Expensive College Education."

IN 1844, Middlebury College in Vermont sued one Lyman Chandler for nonpayment of tuition. The college lost. The final verdict was rendered by the Vermont Supreme Court. Mr. Justice Royce summed up: "A collegiate education is not ranked among the necessaries for which an infant can render himself liable for contract." The statement inhabits the realm of common law. Chandler was an "infant"—he was fifteen when he originally enrolled, and thus below the age of majority. Under common law, minors could validly contract for "necessaries": food, lodging, clothing. Was higher education a "necessary"? The court noted that a "common school" education was a necessary since it was "essential to the intelligent discharge of civil, political, and religious duties," but college studies, "though they tend greatly to elevate and adorn personal character, are a source of much private enjoyment, and may justly be expected to prove of public utility . . ., are far from being necessary in the legal sense." As the court observed: "The mass of our citizens pass through life without [collegiate education]."

Tuition at Middlebury in 1844 was $20 per quarter (plus $7 for room, sweeping $4, library $2, board in town $50). Chandler couldn't afford it. In 1996–97, Middlebury's comprehensive fee—which includes room, board, and fees—exceeds $28,000 (sweeping thrown in). Could Chandler—can anyone!—afford it? (Middlebury must think so, since it has announced plans to expand the size of its student body.)

I mention this mini-bit of history to give perspective on the issue of the high price of higher education. Reflection all the way back to *Middlebury* v. *Chandler* indicates the absolutely radical change in the place and price of higher education. Using the wholesale price index as at least a rough measure, costs have risen by a factor of about ten since the 1840s. That should peg current costs at Middlebury at $2490. But a Middlebury education is now over *one hundred times* more expensive than when Chandler could not afford tuition. Neither could most citizens in the nineteenth century, and most would have agreed with the Vermont justices that it was not a "necessary."

It is sobering to consider that higher education has *always been unaffordable*. . . . (Before World War II less than 5 percent of the U.S. population had college degrees; today 50 percent of the college-age population receives "postsecondary" instruction.) What changed everything was the G.I. Bill. For the first time in American history, lots of people could afford higher education. Once properly imbued with the college spirit, the G.I.-Bill generation and after were determined that their children should have the same advantage.

If college became somewhat more affordable through government largess (G.I. Bill, vast expansion of public higher education), social perception also changed: college education came to be seen as a "necessary" for economic and social reasons. Sociologist David Riesman claimed that a college degree—any college—is *the* American passport to the middle class. If higher education is perceived as establishing a life position, not a personal adornment, one can even change the philosophy of funding. Like housing, education is a life necessity to be subsidized (in public housing/public education or government grants and/or long-term loans).

Despite the fact that higher education has a long history of unaffordability—recently tempered by government subsidy—I think that the current situation is different and drastic. When discussing the extraordinarily high cost of higher education today, it is not cost alone that is an issue; it is the cost plus the social demand. When no one wanted to go—or even dreamed of affording tuition—the "high cost" was, in a sense, a nonissue. In the meanwhile, colleges and universities have become somewhere near one hundred times more complex and sophisticated. Middlebury *circa* 1844 had 1,500 books in the library, no scientific equipment, no gymnasium, and five ministerial faculty. Contemporary colleges have extensive libraries—often in the millions of volumes—cyclotrons, computers, football stadia, and cadres of highly trained specialist faculty. No wonder they are more expensive. . . .

If the current *price* structure of higher education annoys tuition payers and taxpayers, what are possible scenarios for the future?

• *Private colleges will be utterly priced out of the market.* That's unlikely for the really high-priced institutions. Princeton is nowhere near setting a "market clearing price" (the price that is so high that it exhausts the number of potential buyers). This is a sempiternal truth for institutions of high prestige. Someone will pay (almost) anything for Ivy-ish credentials. The pressure in the private realm is on second-tier, often moderately priced institutions of lesser "prestige." Their competition is the public institution in the next county which is currently a real bargain. However. . . .

• *Public universities will boost tuition.* A harried public university president told me that his budget had been cut so drastically that he no longer considered his institution a state university, even a state-supported university—"state-located" was the best he could suggest. Given the closing down of the state treasury, public institutions have already and will continue to increase tuition sharply. Out-of-state tuition for some of the flagship state universities is already at $10,000—at a level with the modest-priced privates.

• *Private and public higher education will become financially similar.* United States private universities already are heavily dependent on government funding. A major research university may receive— through research funding, government grants-in-aid to students, and federal loan programs—more than half its aggregate income from direct or indirect government sources. *Public* universities, on the other hand, often receive only modest funding from their home state. The University of Vermont gets about 16 percent of its budget from the state; only 25 percent of UCLA's budget is state-funded. If the state does not/will not fund, high-tuition *public* education is the likely result. . . .

There are two opposite scenarios for greater efficiency in higher education: command economy or demand economy. Saint John's College in Annapolis, Maryland, approximates a command economy: there is a fixed four-year curriculum, all faculty teach across the curriculum, all students take the same course of study. Theoretically this is 100-percent efficient, no redundancy. At the opposite pole is a demand, free-market curriculum. Community colleges approximate this model. . . . Of the two models, I expect the free-market model to prevail since a command model requires the sort of philosophical consensus that modern universities find virtually impossible to reach. Thus, it is reasonable to forecast:

• *More adjunct faculty*: part-time instructors employed on an as-needed basis. This avoids long-term, costly tenure contracts and present fringe benefits. This cost-cutting strategy is already widely practiced, and regarded as "scandalous" by traditionalists.

• *Out-sourcing*: a refinement of adjunct faculty. Instead of a labor market of freelance adjuncts, some bright soul will create the Einstein Consortium, so that colleges can out-source physics as they do food service.

• *Programmed instruction*: technology has a history of replacing costly services. Programmed instruction in the past has been awkward and amateurish. No more. I have reviewed a CD-rom precalculus course offered for credit in one state college system. It has compelling graphics and contains everything, including the homework and final exam.

• *Microsoft U.*: Bill Gates announces the opening of fifty colleges in the

major cities—all instruction on sophisticated computers and interactive television.

It all sounds implausible? Nothing

could have been more implausible to
Lyman Chandler than half the "common
school" graduates attending colleges at
one hundred times the price.

71.

DEB PRICE: Ellen DeGeneres Comes Out on Television

*In the mid-1990s Ellen DeGeneres, a popular stand-up comic, became the star of a
television sitcom called* Ellen. *As the show's popularity grew, the tabloid press
spread rumors about her sexual orientation. Although she was in fact a lesbian,
DeGeneres initially kept her sexual identity private. No star of a television sitcom
had ever before come out as a lesbian, and many people believed that public
prejudice against homosexuals and lesbians would wreck the career of any actor or
actress who was openly gay. In the spring of 1997, DeGeneres decided to make
public her sexual orientation and to do so on her show. Word of her intentions
leaked before the episode aired, generating enormous public anticipation and
comment. Conservative religious groups threatened to boycott both the program's
network, the American Broadcasting Corporation, and any advertisers that aired
commercials during the show. When the episode finally was televised, it attracted an
extraordinarily large audience of forty-two million viewers, and advertisers competed
to buy commercial time during the* Ellen *time slot. The media's response to the
episode was overwhelmingly positive, and many social observers viewed DeGeneres
as a pioneer in the acceptance of gay characters by mainstream audiences. In the
essay excerpted below, Deb Price, a columnist for* The Detroit News, *analyzes the
social impact of DeGeneres' "coming out" on national television.*

Source: *The Detroit News,* May 16, 1997, "Ellen DeGeneres Paved the Way for Other Gays to Tell the
World the Truth."

EVERYBODY KNOWS about Ellen. "And
there's no reason to discuss it ever
again." That's the sound of fresh pain
talking. That's the sound of a bewildered
parent, Ellen's television dad.

But luckily for us viewers, ABC was
savvy enough to realize that Ellen's com-
ing-out was merely the beginning of a
great many overdue conversations. The
network followed the Big, History-Mak-
ing Ellen Episode with a pair of worthy
encores. They beautifully captured the

strange, unsettling, but often quite wonderful things that happen when lines of
communication remain open long
enough to take a discussion beyond the
simple proclamation "I am gay." After
working through a lot of fears and confusion a gay person takes the first few
tentative steps out of the closet—only to
run smack-dab into the fears and confusion of straight friends, relatives and colleagues. So, as sweet, wholesome, homo-
sexually inexperienced Ellen Morgan dis-

covered, anyone who comes out is instantly turned into an educator.

There was Ellen, valiantly keeping her wits and her wit about her as she fielded some truly oddball questions about being gay. There was Ellen, struggling to keep difficult conversations alive while simultaneously correcting anyone under the impression that only heterosexuality is normal. And there was Ellen, quickly harnessed with the age-old presumption that anyone gay has the Triple X sex life of a porn queen.

In the hands of a different creative team, the back-to-back Ellen follow-ups easily could have lapsed into tawdry, smirky bids for cheap laughs that reinforce stereotypes—in other words, pretty much television as usual. But instead they maintained the superb quality of Ellen's lesbian debut—sensational in all the best senses.

What both encores did magnificently was depict the almost surreal experience of suddenly being openly gay in our rapidly changing world, where heterosexual responses are anything but fixed or predictable:

Ellen's dad, a toy train hobbyist, got teary-eyed because his daughter didn't end up fitting the life that he had all laid out for her in his tiny model village. And Ellen coped. On career day, school kids grilled her about how much a lesbian makes and whether you have to go to college to be one. Again, Ellen coped. Ellen's giddily supportive co-workers started pushing "homo-licious gay-puccino" at the bookstore cafe. Ellen sipped, coped and told them to call it "cinnamon coffee."

If there's ever a how-to course on Becoming a Gay Role Model, these episodes should be training films. Ellen pushed beyond her discomfort with confrontations to nudge her parents into working through their negative reactions. They, in turn, became textbook examples of Getting Over It, with Ellen's dad shouting, "She's here! She's queer! Get used to it!"

Even more than her interactions with her parents, though, Ellen's dealings with her pal Paige illustrated why coming out is terrifying but worth all its risks. Paige reacted to the Big News by getting squeamish. Even sharing a box of popcorn with Ellen felt too weird, too intimate. Ellen was hurt but didn't let go of their friendship. And Paige's better instincts finally kicked back in: "You're my best friend, and I love you—gay, straight or whatever."

◆

As a "close-up" medium whose dramatic and social locus is the home, television addresses the inner life by minimizing the heroic while maximizing the private and personal aspects of existence.
                    GEORGE LIPSITZ, *Time Passages: Collective Memory and American Popular Culture,* 1990

72.

Frank Deford: The Best Golfer in the World

After one of the greatest amateur careers in the history of golf, Tiger Woods became the preeminent player on the professional circuit in the late 1990s. The son of an African American father and a Thai mother, he also became the first golfer of either African American or Asian descent to win the prestigious Masters Tournament. Moreover, in 2001 Woods became the first player to win consecutively the four modern major tournaments of golf (the Masters, the U.S. Open, the British Open, and the PGA Championship), a feat known as the Grand Slam. He also holds the record for single-season earnings with more than $9 million. In the article reprinted here Frank Deford, noted American sportswriter, humorously enumerates Woods' dominance of the sport in the 1990s.

Source: *Newsweek*, June 2, 1997, "The Lost Generation."

You're The Second-Best Golfer in the world. You're Faldo or Price or Els or Montgomerie or Lehman or Norman or. . .

Whoever.

Whatshisname.

You're The Second-Best Golfer in the world and you thought you had a really rich contract with Titleist or Callaway or somebody, but now it's chump change compared to what HE's got.

But then, you're The Second-Best Golfer in the world and nobody even cares anymore what ball you're playing.

Or what you're wearing.

Or what you're hitting with.

Or, for that matter: what your name is.

You're The Second-Best Golfer in the world, and when the guy next to you on the airplane finds out what you do for a living, he asks you if you know HIM.

And what's HE really like?

And what's Fluff, HIS caddie, really like?

You're The Second-Best Golfer in the world and when you arrive at the tournament, everybody tells you, isn't it wonderful because HE will actually play here this week.

You're The Second-Best Golfer in the world, and while you're certainly not as stupid as Fuzzy, you are human, you're one of the boys, and did-you-hear-the-one-about, and now, can you believe this, all of a sudden, because of HIM, *you're the minority?*

You're The Second-Best Golfer in the world, and you remember when you made your first 36-hole cut at a tournament, won $640 for finishing tied for 24th place, went out and applied for an American Express card.

Now you've moved up to the Platinum card, but all of a sudden HE *is* the American Express card. And you can't even leave home without HIM.

You're The Second-Best Golfer in the world, and you hit it right on the button, perfect, right down the middle, 270 yards, and that leaves you only 60 yards

Tiger Woods receives the legendary green jacket upon winning the 1997 Masters Tournament at the Augusta (Georgia) National Golf Club.

You're The Second-Best Golfer in the world, but away from a tournament city, you can't even get a good table at a steakhouse, because nobody knows you from the Culligan Man, but already HIS mother has a Q-rating higher than Tea Leoni or Craig T. Nelson and HIS father just sold his book to Miramax.

Starring Bill Cosby, no doubt. With Wilford Brimley as Fluff.

You're The Second-Best Golfer in the world and you finally got a deal to represent a resort in Florida with a certified PGA course and a mall. Already, though, HE's got a deal representing a whole country.

Thailand.

I forget: Is Asia just a tour or is it a whole continent, too?

You're The Second-Best Golfer in the world, so why are you already looking ahead to the senior tour on ESPN2?

You're The Second-Best Golfer in the world, and you've reached a point where maybe you win a couple more majors, and they mention you in the same breath as Snead or Nelson, but all of a sudden you realize nobody even heard of Snead of Nelson anymore.

Also, for that matter, now, nobody anymore ever heard of Jones or Hogan or Nicklaus.

You're The Second-Best Golfer in the world and nobody even stays still and quiet when you putt out, because they've got to run to get a good spot so they can shout "You The Man" louder than the other butt-kissing, putter-sniffing guys when HE tees off.

You're The Second-Best golfer in the world, longtime par-busting star of the tour, and suddenly you realize there is no

short of HIM, because he kinda misplayed his drive.

But, anyway, you absolutely are The Second-Best Golfer in the world, and, after all, you're playing a game for mature, thinking men, where physical prowess is only part of the act, and you've miscalculated with the four-iron and put the approach short in the trap, whereas HE faded the eight-iron hole high, two feet straight in for the birdie.

You're The Second-Best Golfer in the world, and HE doesn't even know you're the guy paired with him today, but already you're thinking that maybe, just maybe, HE can't play a Scottish links course all that well the first time, in a few weeks, so there's at least one tournament all year I got an outside chance in.

If the wind really blows like a madman off the Firth of Forth.

And HE doesn't like the food.

You're The Second-Best Golfer in the world, and your agent keeps telling you that if you just put a little snap in your best Arnold Palmer anecdotes, you can maybe get a shot on Leno or Letterman, or, for sure, a pop on Tom Snyder . . . but HE's already done Oprah and Barbara Walters and turned down the president.

"tour." It is just HIS show.

But then, you're The Second-Best Golfer in the world, and suddenly you understand: there is no second-best golfer in the world.

And, you're the second-best golfer in all the world of golf, and then you realize there is no golf anymore. It is just HIM, playing around.

It is just Tiger Woods.

Alone.

And this is the way it's going to be for another 20 years.

Mind if I play through?

———◆———

My dad once told me, 'No matter what anyone says or writes, really, none of those people have to hit your little four-foot putt. . . . You have to go do it yourself.'

TIGER WOODS, *Quotable Tiger,* 2001

73.

Boris Gulko: Chess: Man Versus Machine

At the time the computer was invented in the mid-twentieth century, chess enthusiasts speculated that one day a chess-playing computer would defeat human chess players, even world champions. In the 1950s programmers began to design chess-playing computers, but it took decades before any could challenge even moderately talented humans. In the mid-1990s the IBM corporation designed "Deep Blue," which they described as the greatest chess-playing computer of all time. "Deep Blue" was in fact so good that Garry Kasparov, widely considered the greatest chess player of all time, agreed to play the computer in a series of public matches. In a stunning upset, "Deep Blue" defeated Kasparov. In the essay below Boris Gulko analyzes the results of the Kasparov-"Deep Blue" matches. Gulko won the Soviet Union's national chess championship in 1977, then immigrated to the United States, where he became the United States national chess champion in 1994. In 1996 he served on the U.S. national chess team at the Summer Olympic Games in Atlanta, Georgia.

Source: *Commentary,* July 1997, "Is Chess Finished?"

NOT SINCE American Patriot missiles knocked Iraqi Scuds out of the skies in the Persian Gulf war has a scientific achievement stirred so much public wonderment. I am referring, of course, to the defeat of world chess champion Garry Kasparov in New York at the hands of IBM's computer, Deep Blue.

In the weeks since this extraordinary event, two opposing opinions have arisen about its significance. On one side are those who see the match as a major milestone in history, the dawn of the age of artificial intelligence. As *Newsweek* put it before the encounter even got underway, "we stand at the brief corona of an eclipse—the eclipse of certain human mastery by machines that humans have created." And the critic Charles Krauthammer, in a cover story in the *Weekly Standard* (May 26, 1997) written after Kasparov was crushed, asserted that in one of its games Deep Blue had passed the famous Turing test for the existence of machine intelligence, its output, at least in the restricted realm of chess, being indistinguishable from that of the human mind. "We have just seen the ape straighten his back, try out his thumb, utter his first words, and fashion his first arrow."

On the opposite side are those who downplay the meaning of the human defeat. "Deep Blue is just a machine," wrote the Yale University computer scientist David Gelernter in *Time* (May 19, 1997). While the IBM device represents, in Gelernter's words, a "beautiful and amazing technological achievement," all its programmers did was to solve a problem which, though admittedly "much harder than adding numbers," nevertheless amounted to raw calculation. As for intelligence, Deep Blue "doesn't have a mind any more than a flowerpot has a mind."

In my opinion, both these views are wide of the mark. Deep Blue's victory is far from the stupendous feat which some pundits (and IBM publicists) have cracked it up to be, and the fact that it succeeded in beating the world champion by a score of 3½ to 2½ tells us little about the machine's intelligence *or* about its impressive ability to calculate. As it happens, the computer played a mediocre game at best. The only questions raised by the match concern the shockingly bad form of Garry Kasparov, the greatest chess master ever to have walked the earth.

The effort to program computers to play chess began in earnest in the 1950's, and there can be no question that over the past four decades, considerable progress has been made. Fantastic increases in the speed of microprocessors and refinements in programming have combined to bring computers to a level I myself would characterize as decent—if still not on a par with top-level championship chess. I know, from much personal experience, whereof I speak.

Beginning in 1989, an annual tournament, the Harvard Cup (so named by the Harvard students who organized it), has pitted a team of top grandmasters against the best computers in the world, including, on one occasion, Deep Thought and Chiptest, two of Deep Blue's precursors. I have participated in all but one of these events. From early on, both the strengths and the glaring weaknesses of our silicon opponents have been plain to see.

Just as Gelernter and others have pointed out, the computers' major advantage in encounters with human beings is calculation. It has been established that the total number of possible

chess games which can develop from the starting position on the board not only exceeds the number of atoms in the known universe, but does so by a wide margin. As computers play, they sort through as many positions as they can generate in the time allotted to them, a task which (like humans) they necessarily perform incompletely, but with incredible speed and thoroughness. Deep Blue is said to examine 200 million positions a second. Against this advantage, however, one must place certain deficiencies: computers lack essential traits like intuition, imagination, and, most fundamentally, a capacity to plan.

The ability to calculate is at a premium in chaotic, open positions, where one's pieces are not hemmed in by one's own pawns but instead are thrust into the fray. There the computer excels. For the human player, the trick is thus to steer the game into quiet channels in which everything hinges on the formulation of a long-term strategy which can be carried out (in a general and not wholly precise way) over the next dozen or more moves, far deeper into the future than the computer can see.

At the Harvard Cup tournaments and in the many previous encounters between computers and human beings, the machines proved very dangerous in chaotic positions and managed to score a number of sensational wins. But in positions where tactics recede in importance and strategic planning comes to the fore, they were shorn of their strength. Not that the machines ever made crude errors, but they played purposeless computer moves against purposeful human players, and the asymmetrical nature of the competition told on their scores.

In the first year of the Harvard Cup, the computers garnered a total of one victory and one draw in sixteen games.

As processing speed bounded upward, their chess play improved, but also leveled off. In 1994, their best year, the computers won thirteen and drew eleven of 48 games; in 1995, even as similar programs were deployed on more powerful hardware, their share of victories and draws fell. Given their tactical prowess, one certainly had to treat them with respect, but chess with any sort of interesting intellectual content, i.e., containing any form of strategic planning, they simply did not play.

Which brings us back to Deep Blue. Has the IBM team broken some kind of barrier? Do Deep Blue's hundreds of specialized accelerator chips deliver something new, something of which grandmasters, as Kasparov himself has said, must be "afraid"? Judging by what I saw in New York, my own answer is an unequivocal no, and in this I am hardly alone. Many grandmasters, in fact, were struck by the appallingly low level of the play on *both* sides. The Indian wizard, Viswanathan Anand, spoke of the match's "disappointing" chess, and to the American grandmaster Patrick Wolff, the computer in some situations played like a "numskull."

Indeed, nothing in New York was a departure from the usual machine chess of the kind witnessed at the Harvard Cup. In some positions Deep Blue excelled at calculation, but in others it made moves that were aimless and just plain dull. What is unaccountable, however, is that Kasparov played even worse, and without a trace of the blinding bolts of brilliance we have been accustomed to see issue forth from him.

Kasparov lost two games in the match. Of the first defeat, in the second round, Charles Krauthammer has written that the computer played "Brilliantly. Creatively. Humanly." I would call this a gigantic stretch. As we know from the in-

stantaneous nature of its responses to Kasparov's play, the first nineteen moves the computer spit out in this game were drawn from its vast database of chess openings; its microprocessor array was, in effect, still asleep. The task Deep Blue performed here is roughly comparable in complexity to what a computer does when searching through an electronic card catalog at a library, which is to say not very complex at all.

Only on move twenty, after Kasparov played a move that was not in its memory, did Deep Blue's calculating engine engage: it paused and began to "think" for the first time in the game. The computer liked what it found. Not only had Kasparov allowed it to come through the treacherous shoals of the opening without having to calculate and possibly go astray, but he had acquiesced in a cramped and futureless position which he then proceeded to worsen with a few less than optimal moves.

Yet even after Kasparov found himself in a truly horrendous bind, the computer made an entirely pointless move. Although not of the type that did damage to its own position, this was one of many moments showing that the computer was playing without any sort of discernible plan. If anything, game two was an astonishing display of the difficulty even a brute capable of assessing millions of positions a second will encounter in mastering the mysteries of chess; after acquiring a winning position, Deep Blue committed two errors in its own domain of calculation, the second of which gave Kasparov the chance to force a draw.

Unfortunately, instead of seizing the moment, the champion resigned, perhaps the only case in history where a player of his caliber surrendered unnecessarily in a drawn position. But Kasparov's premature capitulation should not obscure the fact that in its most praised game (as indeed throughout the match), Deep Blue made senseless if typically computer-like moves and was thus far from passing the Turing test for artificial intelligence. . . .

What really happened to Garry Kasparov in this match is something I cannot adequately explain. There is some evidence to suggest that the same champion who shows no mercy whatsoever when dispatching ordinary mortals does have special psychological difficulties meting out similar punishment to machines. In 1994, Kasparov suffered a loss in an elimination tournament in London while playing against the computer Chess Genius, a defeat he accompanied with much talk about the computer's unprecedented and phenomenal strength. But in fact Chess Genius was not the giant-killer it seemed to Kasparov. Two rounds later, Viswanathan Anand prevailed over Chess Genius with ease, using only four of the 25 minutes allotted him.

If Kasparov has another flaw, it is his curiosity; he is a relentless seeker after "truth" in chess. This, indeed, is one source of his power in competition with his fellow man. Against computers, however, he seems to favor moves designed to elicit information about how the program is constructed rather than going directly for the jugular.

Such complexes aside, there may be still another and simpler explanation for Kasparov's failure in New York: a chess player can have a bad day or, in this case, a bad week. . . .

Chess may be just a game, but it is also an art, and it is in the human dimensions of that art—the haphazard trajectory of imagination, the expression of passion, and the struggle of personalities—where not only the beauty but the actual strength of grandmaster play resides. Convinced of this as I am, I doubt that the kind of computers we know today will play chess any time soon on the level that Garry Kasparov displays when he is in form.

Of course, with the world champion losing to a machine, the activity to which I and others have devoted our lives has unquestionably suffered a blow to its reputation. But I am reminded again of how we all marveled at those Patriot missiles during the Persian Gulf war—a perfect 33 out of 33 attempted interceptions, General Schwarzkopf bragged at the time. Only on subsequent analysis did we learn that the Patriots failed to bring down more than a tiny fraction of the total number of Scuds launched by Saddam Hussein.

She hung up and I set out the chess board. . . . and played a championship tournament game between Gortchakoff and Meninkin, seventy-two moves to a draw, a prize specimen of the irresistible force meeting the immovable object, a battle without armor, a war without blood, and as elaborate a waste of human intelligence as you could find anywhere outside an advertising agency.

RAYMOND CHANDLER, *The Long Goodbye*, 1953

74.

Kurt L. Schmoke: Welfare Reform

Since the passage of President Lyndon B. Johnson's Great Society legislation in the 1960s, one of the most controversial issues in American politics has been welfare. Supporters of welfare argue that the government has a moral obligation to provide a social safety net for its poorest citizens. Critics of welfare, however, assert that it creates a web of dependency that traps its recipients in poverty. By the early 1990s, calls for welfare reform reached a crescendo. In his 1992 campaign for President, Bill Clinton took a middle position between the critics and supporters of welfare, as he pledged to "mend welfare, not end it." In the spring of 1996, the Republican-controlled Congress passed the most sweeping welfare reform law in history, cutting off welfare payments to adults after they had spent two years on welfare rolls. The bill received wide popularity among moderate and conservative voters, and, with his reelection campaign only months away, Clinton signed the bill into law. Clinton's support for welfare reform deeply divided the Democratic Party. Although many moderate Democrats applauded the bill, many liberal Democrats accused Clinton of betraying the Democratic Party's principles in his drive to get reelected. Welfare reform, however, was one of the most popular measures of Clinton's first term as President. In November 1996 Clinton won reelection, and by the end of his second term, welfare rolls reached their lowest level in thirty years. Kurt Schmoke, the mayor of Baltimore, Maryland, delivered the following address to the United Way of America's National Conference on Welfare Reform in September 1997.

Source: *Vital Speeches of the Day*, November 15, 1997.

Good afternoon. I want to begin these remarks with a simple thank you for the invitation to speak to you today. I also want to thank the United Way of America for sponsoring this important conference. More fundamentally, I thank you for all that you do nationally and locally in so many ways to help people in need and to raise public consciousness about issues that affect them. This conference is but one reflection of that commitment.

And it comes at a pivotal time: a little more than a year after President Clinton made good his promise to "end welfare as we know it" by signing into law "The Personal Responsibility and Work Opportunity Reconciliation Act of 1996."

As most of you are all too aware, under the law almost all adult welfare recipients must find work or be in some kind of "work activity" within two years, or they lose their benefits.

Moreover, they face a lifetime public assistance limit of five years.

At the signing ceremony, President Clinton heralded the new law as "the beginning of a new era in which welfare will become what it was meant to be: a second chance, not a way of life." This conference gives us an opportunity to take a hard look at whether welfare reform will become what it was meant to be. Will it truly help people move from dependence to independence and enable them to achieve a better life for themselves and their children? Or will it drive them deeper into poverty and hopelessness?

With these questions hovering in the background, I've been asked to share reflections about how cities are faring under welfare reform one year into the law. My remarks will focus on Baltimore, but I believe they can apply to many other big cities as well.

Frankly, when I was thinking about what I was going to say to you this afternoon, I wasn't quite sure what my main message should be. Should I tell you about things people like to count? I could tell you that between January 1996 and August 1997, Baltimore City's welfare caseload dropped 21 percent—from almost 99,000 to a little over 78,000. If numbers were your indicator of success, the obvious conclusion would be, "Yes, welfare reform is working."

But as a former football player, I know that declaring success at this point is like declaring victory in the first quarter of the game. With welfare reform only in its "first quarter," the final outcome is nearly impossible to predict.

The mixed messages I am getting from my agency heads underscore the difficulty of trying to measure the success of welfare reform at this stage. Let me tell you about some of these conversations.

When I talk to my social services people they point to the drop in the caseload. They cite the number of welfare recipients participating in job readiness, job search, work experience and grant diversion programs—almost 8,000 as of

August of this year. They tell me about agreements and contracts signed with 27 new partners in the public and private sectors to provide job placement services for welfare recipients. Tallying up such facts and figures, their assessment is that the City is making significant "progress" in implementing welfare reform.

When I talk to my employment development people I'm hearing a story with a slightly different slant. Sure, they tell me of the hundreds of welfare recipients who have gone through job training in the past year, and of the 2,500 who have found employment. And they're even proud to provide individual portraits of some of these individuals.

People like Dana, a single mother of three, who already had obtained her GED, knew WordPerfect, and typed 50 words a minute. She was assigned to train as an office clerk at a City agency, and within six weeks, was offered a full-time position. Or Lisa who used the services of one of the two full-scale career centers the City has set up for welfare recipients and attended the local community college. Lisa now has a job at Bell Atlantic, earning $19 an hour.

But my employment development people also say that such individual success stories shouldn't seduce us into thinking that moving people to self-sufficiency is an easy task. Another set of figures provides a more telling story.

To meet federal and state requirements, about 14,000 City welfare recipients must be in a job or work-related activity by January 1, 1999. Yet, an increase of only 2,800 jobs is projected for Baltimore in the types of industries and businesses that can absorb low-skill entry-level workers. And that's between 1997 and the year 2000.

What's more, with Baltimore's unemployment rate the highest of any jurisdiction in the Baltimore metropolitan area

(8.5% as of July), people trying to get off welfare will face some stiff competition.

From such figures, it's obvious that on its own, Baltimore City cannot find jobs or work experiences for the large numbers of people who will be leaving the welfare rolls. A regional approach to employment will be required. That's not all. To bridge the gap between all these new job seekers and the private sector jobs that are available, we also are going to have to find a way to create more subsidized jobs.

My employment development people also remind me that the Lisas and Danas represent welfare reform's first wave—in relative terms, the easy cases. Both women had skills, motivation, a strong work ethic, and a support network. Each could easily be a "poster child" for welfare reform.

As the welfare rolls continue to drop, such "poster children" will be harder to find. Those left represent the toughest cases. Of those 14,000 welfare recipients who must get jobs or be engaged in work related activities by January 1, 1999: 52% have no high school diploma; 26% have been on the rolls for more than five years and have little or no prior work experience; an estimated 16% have drug or alcohol related problems; and 50% will require subsidized child care.

Even in a booming economy, finding jobs for such a population is highly problematic. I think we all know what will happen during an economic downturn.

When I speak to my homeless relief advisers, I get another set of perceptions, and another set of numbers. They point to an upsurge in requests for emergency shelter—from 3,000 in the first half of 1996 to 5,000 in the first half of 1997, a 40 percent increase. And they tell me that families and individuals are overwhelming the city shelters. Over the past two months, shelter operators have had to turn away people because there were no more beds available. The last time this happened was in the 1980s.

According to my homeless relief advisers, the anecdotal evidence points to some connection between what they are seeing at the shelters and the new welfare law—either because people have lost their benefits as a result of sanctions, or they didn't apply for benefits because they thought they couldn't get them, or they have had their benefits cut off from some other jurisdiction and have moved to Baltimore.

Further anecdotal evidence from another source: I recently met with a group of ministers who told me that more people are using their churches' food pantries and feeding programs than a year ago.

I fear that what we're seeing in these feeding programs and in our shelters may be part of the face of this new welfare reform.

It's a complicated face.

Like many big city mayors, I supported the need for welfare reform. We must move people from welfare to work. This nation was built on the work ethic, and work is one of the things that gives life meaning and purpose.

I agree with the President that the welfare system ought to be one that is transitional and moves people to independence, not to prolonged dependence. And I have been working diligently with my agency heads to try to make welfare reform work, as I promised the President that I would.

Our efforts to help move people from welfare to work are not confined to the City's Department of Social Services and the Office of Employment Development, our lead agencies in welfare reform. Nearly every City agency is involved. . . .

So yes, we in Baltimore welcome welfare reform and yes, we are responding vigorously to the challenge it poses. At the same time, I think we have to be realistic about what it takes to make welfare reform work in a city like Baltimore.

What does it take?

We must be able to offer people without skills the ability to get training. A job search without skills doesn't lead to very much. We must increase our support services, such as child care, job counseling, and drug treatment. And we must develop more innovative ways to address the transportation issue.

We need the sustained participation of private businesses in hiring and helping to train people who have been in a state of dependency for so long. Private businesses don't have to do it all, of course. But they have to do more.

We need the United Way and other organizations in the nonprofit sector to continue to keep the issue of welfare reform on the national radar screen. The United Way's statement on welfare reform and its implications for charities is a fine example of your efforts in this regard.

As we go forward with implementing the welfare reform law, we must be willing to reexamine certain of its provisions to ensure that there is an adequate safety net for vulnerable children. Neglect of little children must not be the legacy of welfare reform in America or in the City of Baltimore.

And if it turns out that five years is far too short a time frame in which to achieve self-sufficiency, if the economy falters, if the unpredictable occurs, we must not allow the ideology of welfare reform to override the need to make pragmatic adjustments in the law.

As we undertake this bold national experiment to "end welfare as we know it," we are learning as we go along. And we must be courageous enough to change what we find doesn't work, even as we applaud what works.

When President Clinton signed the welfare reform bill, I said that my worries about the daunting challenge of moving so many people from prolonged dependence to self-sufficiency were giving me a lot of sleepless nights. Well, let me tell you, my rest isn't easy yet.

Despite the statistics, despite our real success stories, despite our earnest efforts, we still have a long way to go before we can declare welfare reform an unequivocal success. As this old football player said earlier, you don't declare victory in the first quarter of the game.

I leave you with one other thought about this bold national experiment: We must never forget that the raw materials of this experiment are real people's lives.

———————◆———————

I will be the first to say that adults in our society need to take responsibility for themselves if they possibly can. But until we come to a real understanding of the structural problems in our economy and society that are getting in our way, we will continue to legislate by bumper stickers and slogans.
PAUL WELLSTONE, *The Nation*, April 17, 1997

75.

Margaret Warner, Ron Unz, and James Lyons: Debating Bilingual Education

The bilingual education movement gained steam in 1974 with the passage of the Bilingual Education Act and the Equal Education Opportunity Act, which mandated that all federally funded schools meet the "special educational needs" of students not proficient in English. In many districts, bilingual education was installed so that young students could first learn basic academic subjects in their native language before acquiring English as a second language. In the years following, however, the numbers of students in these programs swelled, and critics pointed to alarming dropout rate and lack of English-language proficiency, despite increases in funding. States with significant percentages of Spanish speakers, such as California, became battlegrounds over the issue of bilingual education. Those on both sides of the issue believed their position led to more successful students while their opponents' position only served to isolate nonnative speakers. In 1998 the passage of California's Proposition 227 mandated the abolition of bilingual education in the public school system, requiring all instruction to be delivered in English. Similar ballot measures began appearing in other states, passing in Arizona in 2000. The following debate was broadcast on The NewsHour with Jim Lehrer *television program on September 21, 1997, and was conducted by Margaret Warner,* NewsHour *correspondent. The transcript is reprinted below.*

Source: *The NewsHour with Jim Lehrer,* September 21, 1997, "Double Talk? The Debate over Bilingual Education."

MARGARET WARNER, Debate moderator: Nationally, the controversy over bilingual education has boiled down to an even starker question, whether to preserve it at all. About 6 percent of the nation's school population—some 3.1 million children—are enrolled in some sort of bilingual education. The federal government spends $178 million to support bilingual programs, a fraction of the billions spent on bilingual education by states and localities. But several bills have been introduced in this Congress to abolish or drastically curtail federal support for bilingual education, and in Califor-nia, a group called English for the Children is collecting signatures for a ballot referendum in next year's election. It would require all public school instruction to be conducted in English. With us now are Ron Unz, chairman of the English for the Children, the committee sponsoring the California ballot initiative, and James Lyons, executive director of the National Association of Bilingual Education. Mr. Unz, why do you believe that bilingual education should be scrapped?

RON UNZ, Anti-Bilingual Education Activist: Well, the overwhelming practical evidence is that bilingual education has failed on every large scale case that's been tried in the United States, in particular in California. The origins of this initiative was the case last year of a lot of immigrant Latino parents in downtown LA, who had to begin a public boycott of their local elementary school to try to force the school to give their children the right to be taught English, which the school was denying. And I think that really opened my eyes to the current state of the program in California, where the statistics are dreadful.

MARGARET WARNER: Mr. Lyons.

JAMES LYONS, National Association for Bilingual Education: It is not the case that bilingual education is failing children. There are poor bilingual education programs, just as there are poor programs of every type in our schools today. But bilingual education has made it possible for children to have continuous development in their native language, while they're in the process of learning English, something that doesn't happen overnight, and it's made it possible for children to learn math and science at a rate equal to English-speaking children while they're in the process of acquiring English.

MARGARET WARNER: Mr. Unz, what about that point that for these children who don't speak English well they will fall behind in the basic subjects if they can't be taught those in Spanish, or whatever language? I shouldn't say just Spanish, but whatever their family's language is.

RON UNZ: That's a very reasonable point. And to the extent that we're talking about older children, 14 or 15 year olds who come to the United States, don't know any English and are put in the public schools I think a very reasonable case can be made for bilingual education. I don't know if it's correct, but at

least you can make a case for it. But most of the children we're talking about enter California or America public schools when they're five or six or seven. At the age of five years old, the only academic subjects a child is really doing is drawing with crayons or cutting and, you know, with paper and that type of thing. And at that age children can learn another language so quickly and easy that the only reasonable thing to do is to put them in a program where they're taught English as rapidly as possible and then put into the mainstream classes with the other children so they can move forward academically.

MARGARET WARNER: There is something to that point, isn't there, Mr. Lyons, that very young children do absorb languages very quickly?

JAMES LYONS: They absorb certain facets of language very quickly. They learn to speak in an unaccented form like a native English speaker. But the research shows that actually adults are much more efficient and quicker language learners than children because they're working from a broader linguistic base, a greater conceptual base. I really take objection to what Mr. Unz is saying; that children at the age of five, six, and seven are only coloring and cutting out paper. That isn't going to lead to the high standards.

When I go into elementary schools, first, second, and third grade, I see schools that are focused on teaching literacy skills, certainly by the third grade, that's a national goal. I see schools that are teaching children about life around them. The point of the matter is, is that bilingual education provides children with continuous development in an intelligible way while they're in the process of acquiring a language.

MARGARET WARNER: All right. Let me stay with you for a minute, Mr. Lyons. Let me just ask you something. I think and polls show that many Americans say if a child comes here from another country, they can certainly understand why this is necessary. But I think a majority of students in bilingual ed—the younger students—were all born in the U.S.

GENERATIONS OF LIMITED ENGLISH PROFICIENCY

JAMES LYONS: That's absolutely correct. A majority still—just the bare majority of the children who are limited English proficient—and actually only about a third of those children ever received bilingual education programming. But those children are native born. One of the reasons that they are limited English proficient is their parents, who were non-English language background people, didn't succeed in the English only programs, which were the only programs in this country prior to the period that we're talking about today.

MARGARET WARNER: What about that point, Mr. Unz?

RON UNZ: Well, most of these parents actually are immigrants, themselves. In other words, they came here five or ten or fifteen years ago, and their children either were born here, or their children came with them at a very young age. So, in other words, the children, themselves, are often native born, but the parents are almost always first generation immigrants.

MARGARET WARNER: All right. Let me stay with you for a minute. You called this a failed system. What is your definition of success or failure?

RON UNZ: Well, let's look at the numbers in California—and they really are horrifying. A quarter of all the children in California public schools are classified as not knowing English, limited English proficiency. Of the ones who don't know

English in any given year only 5 or 6 percent learn English. Since the goal of the system, obviously, should be make sure that these children learn English, we're talking about a system with an annual failure rate of 95 percent. Now, when we're talking about little children, everybody I know who's come here from other countries—I work in Silicon Valley—I'm in the software business—many of my friends are foreign immigrants. They came here when they were a variety of different ages. All of them agree that little children or even young teenagers can learn another language quickly, though only 5 percent of these children in California are learning English each year. And that's what I define as failure.

MARGARET WARNER: Do you agree with that, either that definition of success, which is that it's learning English, is that the purpose of bilingual education? And secondly, do you agree that it's not doing the job?

JAMES LYONS: Well, the first point is I think we need a broader definition than simply learning English. The child who learns English but doesn't learn any of the other academic subjects taught in school is not going to succeed. But even if we use the restricted definition that Mr. Unz is proposing of learning English—and he's basing this on the "re-designation rates" of children who are re-designated annually as fully English proficient, as opposed to limited English proficient—it isn't bilingual education that's to blame. One third of the children in California who are limited English proficient are receiving bilingual education. Two thirds are not. And if you compare the re-designation rates of schools that provide a lot of bilingual education versus the English only kind of programs that Mr. Unz wants, you find the schools that are using native language as the medium of instruction do much better.

MARGARET WARNER: Let me stay with you, Mr. Lyons, for a minute, and ask you about something that came up in Betty Ann's taped piece, which is that some parents who want the children in bilingual ed actually say they wanted in part to maintain the family's original language. Is that a purpose of bilingual education, as well as a transition to English? Do you think it's also to maintain a kind of dual cultural identity?

JAMES LYONS: I think the notion of maintaining the ability to communicate in the family is terribly important. It's not the primary objective. I remember a television producer, in fact, who told me her life story, the fact that she brought home a note when she was five years old from the kindergarten teacher saying, please, do not let Juliet speak Italian anymore, she told me that that was—her grandmother lived with her family, lived in the same home—that that was the very last day, she said, that "I ever spoke to my grandmother. And it was the last day that my grandmother ever spoke to me. And my grandmother lived in the house with my family for seven years from that point forward." That isn't what we want in America. I think we want families that can communicate across generations, grandparents and grandchildren.

MARGARET WARNER: Mr. Unz, do you think that's a proper role for public education, to help these children remain essentially in linguistic contact with their families?

"FAMILY CULTURE, FAMILY TRADITION AND FAMILY LANGUAGE ARE THE RESPONSIBILITY OF THE FAMILY"

RON UNZ: I think family culture, family tradition, and family language are the responsibility of the family. They should be the ones making the decision as to how much or how little of these cultural traditions should they maintain. The responsibility of the American public education system is to give young children the tools they need to become assimilated, productive members of society. And one of the most important tools is a knowledge of reading and writing and speaking English.

Right now hundreds of thousands of the children in California and around the United States are leaving the public schools illiterate in English because of the schools' refusal to teach them English at a young age. Think about what it means when a child leaves the public schools as a teenager or as a graduate not knowing how to read or write English at anything more than a second or third grade level. They can never get a job. They can never be successful. And that's where a lot of the problems like crime and gangs come from because the schools are failing in their responsibility because of the completely mis-perceived, mis-structured educational theory which just doesn't work in practice.

MARGARET WARNER: And how do you answer that basic question, which that superintendent in Betty Ann's piece also raised, these kids leave school, they can't compete in an English environment?

JAMES LYONS: And many of those children not only have been in bilingual education; they are English language background children. We have children who are graduating today after 13 years in public schooling unable to read, unable to write. Is bilingual education to blame? No, it's not. It can't be, because these children were never in a bilingual education program, and, in fact, they're native English speakers. I think we're confusing what is the cause of the problem. We have poor schools throughout this country in virtually every state of the union. Bilingual education are part of the poor schools in some places; in other places they're allowing children to achieve everything that they need to achieve and to excel, go on to college.

76.

Makah Indians Allowed to Hunt Whales

For two hundred years whalers devastated whale populations around the world, in some cases hunting breeds to the point of extinction. In the 1970s an international consensus emerged to curb commercial whaling, and in 1985/86 the International Whaling Commission (IWC) declared a moratorium on commercial whaling. Not all whalers harvested whales for profit, however. In particular, aboriginal peoples in Russia, Canada, and the United States hunted whales for sustenance and as part of community rituals stretching back thousands of years, often using traditional methods. Despite their support for the IWC, a number of governments feared its zeal to protect whale populations infringed on the cultural and religious practices of native peoples. Several countries lobbied for a limited exception to be made on behalf of noncommercial aboriginal whalers. Reprinted below is a 1997 press release by the IWC that dealt with one such agreement with the Makah Indian tribe of Washington state. Some environmental groups accuse tribal whalers of violating the agreement's ban on selling the whale meat and on limiting the number of whale hunts. The issue remains hotly debated, particularly in the Pacific coastal states of Alaska and Washington, where the goals of environmentalists and the cultural practices of aboriginal peoples coexist uneasily.

Source: U.S. Delegation News Release, October 23, 1997, "Whaling Commission Approves Combined Russian-Makah Gray Whale Quota."

THE INTERNATIONAL WHALING Commission today adopted a quota that allows a five-year aboriginal subsistence hunt of an average of four non-endangered gray whales a year for the Makah Indian Tribe, combined with an average annual harvest of 120 gray whales by Russian natives of the Chukotka region.

A combined quota accommodates the needs of the two aboriginal groups hunting whales from a single stock. The commission adopted the combined quota by consensus, thereby indicating its acceptance of the United States' position that the Makah Tribe's cultural and subsistence needs are consistent with those historically recognized by the IWC. The Makah Tribe, located on the remote northwest tip of Washington state, expects to start its subsistence hunt in the fall of 1998 under government supervision. The Makah quota will not involve commercial whaling.

"The United States has fulfilled its moral and legal obligation to honor the Makah's treaty rights. The right to conduct whaling was specifically reserved in the 1855 U.S.-Makah Treaty of Neah

Bay," said Will Martin, alternate U.S. commissioner to the International Whaling Commission, and deputy assistant secretary for international affairs for the National Oceanic and Atmospheric Administration.

The two countries agreed to submit a joint request for an average of 124 gray whales a year, of which 120 are for Russia's Chukotka people, and four are for the Makah Tribe. The United States and Russia tabled the joint resolution after many countries suggested that the two nations work together to address the needs of both native groups while reducing the overall quota. In preliminary proceedings, the Russian government had outlined its need for 140 gray whales a year and the Makah Tribe had outlined its need for up to five gray whales a year.

Over a five-year period, the joint quota will reduce the number of whales taken by 80 from the existing Russian 140-whale annual quota. The Commission's Scientific Committee will conduct an annual review of the gray whale stock and can recommend changes to the quota. "The approval of this joint gray whale quota reduces the overall number of whales taken while addressing the needs of the native groups," said Martin.

The Makah request is unique among native peoples, in that the tribe's 1855 Treaty of Neah Bay is the only Indian treaty in the United States that expressly reserves a tribal right to go whaling. "We are pleased that the commission has recognized the cultural and subsistence need of the Makah Tribe," said Marcy Parker, Makah Tribal Council member, and member of the U.S. delegation. "We will now develop a management plan and are committed to being a responsible co-manager of the gray whale resource in our usual and accustomed whaling grounds."

The Makah have a 1,500-year whaling tradition. Tribal whaling ceased in the early 1900's after commercial whalers had decimated whale stocks and government assimilation programs forced tribal members to abandon their intricate whaling rituals and pursue an agrarian lifestyle. Today, almost half of the Makah people live below the poverty line, unemployment is nearly 50 percent, and their subsistence fish and shellfish resources are dwindling to all-time lows.

"We appreciate the support and dedication the United States government has shown the Makah Tribe in our request to resume our centuries-old whaling heritage. The Makah tribal members will now be able to again perform important whaling rituals and receive sustenance from this important and traditional marine resource. Today will mark one of the most significant events in our history with western civilization that will now be passed on through our oral traditions as a positive move toward cultural revival of vital missing links once thought lost to our people," said Parker.

The Makah Tribe will not use commercial whaling equipment, but will combine humane hunting methods with continued traditional hunting rituals, including using hand-crafted canoes. The U.S. government's environmental assessment of the hunt found it will not adversely affect the gray whale stock's healthy status, which is currently at more than 22,000. The gray whale was taken off the U.S. Endangered Species Act list in 1994.

In a related action, the commission approved on Wednesday a combined quota of bowhead whales to meet the needs of the Eskimos in Alaska and Russia. The combined quota allows an average of 56 bowhead whales to be landed each year. The Alaska Eskimos have been conducting aboriginal subsistence hunts with approval of the International Whaling Commission since the commission began regulating such hunts in the 1970's.

"We are pleased that the commission continues to recognize the importance of the bowhead whale hunt to Alaskan Eskimos," said Martin. "The central focus of the bowhead hunt in the culture of the Eskimos is well known.

The 39-member International Whaling Commission is the sole international body with authority to regulate all forms of whaling. Under the commission's whaling regulations, native communities are allowed quotas for subsistence and cultural purposes. Such quotas prohibit the sale of any edible whale products from aboriginal subsistence hunts.

———————◆———————

The more I dive into this matter of whaling, and push my researches up to the very springhead of it, so much the more am I impressed with its great honourableness and antiquity; and especially when I find so many great demigods and heroes, prophets of all sorts, who one way or other have shed distinction upon it, I am transported with the reflection that I myself belong, though but subordinately, to so emblazoned a fraternity.
HERMAN MELVILLE, *Moby Dick*, 1851

1998

77.

ALAN GREENSPAN: The Role of Free Markets

In the spring of 1998, the United States was in the midst of the greatest economic expansion of the twentieth century. The boom began in the early 1990s and had many causes. Chief among them was the collapse of the Soviet Union in 1991, which shattered what was left of Communism's credibility and accelerated the global embrace of free-market capitalism. For half a century the superpower rivalry between the United States and Soviet Union represented the economic clash between Communism and capitalism. During the Great Depression of the 1930s, many intellectuals concluded that market capitalism was inherently too unstable and too predatory to ever sustain an economy over the long haul. They argued that only the centrally planned economic system advocated by Communism could maintain economic stability on a permanent basis. The last half of the twentieth century, however, proved just the reverse to be true. Communism failed utterly to promote growth and maintain economic stability. Countries that embraced Communist economic systems, such as the Soviet Union and Cuba, were bankrupt by the 1990s. Market capitalism, in contrast, succeeded in both maintaining worldwide economic growth and in expanding the size of the middle class to an extent unseen in economic history. In the April 1998 address excerpted below, Alan Greenspan, the chairman of the United States Federal Reserve Board, analyzes the growth and expansion of market capitalism.

Source: *Vital Speeches of the Day,* May 1, 1998.

THE CURRENT TURMOIL in East Asia is easy to categorize as one of many such crises over the decades. Nonetheless, it appears to be an important milestone in what evidently has been a significant and seemingly inexorable trend toward market capitalism and political systems that stress the rule of law. The shifts have been gradual but persistent.

Markets today are responding far more rapidly to subtle changes in consumers' values and choices than ever before. While advancing technology has always been a factor sensitizing markets to changing consumer tastes, what is so striking in recent years is how pervasive that force has become. Just-in-time inventory systems have enabled production to more rapidly adjust to changing consumption. Satellite coordinated trucking moves goods to destinations of optimal use. Bar coding has facilitated a major revolution in retailing. For supermarkets, for example, checkout scanning devices have facilitated the creation of a variety of wares reflecting the most current consumer wants.

Those producers who cannot keep up with this technologically driven surge to efficiency fall by the wayside. Those exceptionally skilled in advanced engineering and computer programming, for example, are rewarded with significantly higher levels of income relative to the less facile. It is difficult to prove, but arguably luck, the great random leveler in the market place, appears to play an ever smaller role in determining success and failure in today's just-in-time, high quality, productive systems. Those systems appear to be especially rewarding to financial skills. The advent of computer and telecommunications technology has spawned a vast proliferation of new financial derivatives products crafted by mathematicians and finance technicians who had never previously found favor on either Wall or Lombard Streets. The above-average earnings they receive reflect the increasing value added created by financial institutions, which, in turn, results from their enhanced ability to marshal savings to support investment in the most productive physical capital.

Not unexpectedly, as the share of Gross Domestic Product has shifted persistently to conceptual products and services from those requiring physical brawn to produce, the wage premium for skills and education has risen significantly, especially during the past two decades. As one might surmise, the shift arguably has led to the sharply higher college enrollments that we see here in the United States and elsewhere. But the resulting increased supply of skills has apparently generally not been sufficient to offset the increasing demand, as net returns to education, at least until quite recently, have continued to rise.

Left to its own devices, this new high-tech competitive system appears to exhibit little leeway for inefficiency. Inefficiencies expose potential unexploited profit opportunities, that in full, open, and effectively competitive markets induce new resources to be brought to bear to eliminate bottlenecks and other, less than optimum, uses of capital.

Of course, little of this is new. Market economies have succeeded over the centuries by thoroughly weeding out the inefficient and poorly equipped, and by granting rewards to those who could anticipate consumer demand and meet it with minimum use of labor and capital resources. But the newer technologies are goading this process. For good or ill, an unforgiving capitalist process is driving wealth creation. It has become increasingly difficult for policymakers who wish to practice, as they put it, a more "caring" capitalism to realize the full potential of their economies. Their choices have become limited. To the extent they block themselves or portions of their population from what they perceive as harsh competitive pressures, they must accept a lower average standard of living for their populace. As a consequence, increasingly, nations appear to be opting to open themselves to competition, however harsh, and become producers that can compete in world markets. Not irrelevant to the choice is that major advances in telecommunications have made it troublesome for politicians and policymakers to go too far in preempting market forces when the material affluence of market-based economies has become so evident to ubiquitous television watchers, their constituents, around the world.

It was not always thus. In the first decades following World War II, before the advent of significant advances in computer and telecommunications technologies, market economies appeared less daunting. Adjustments were slower. International trade comprised a far smaller share of domestic economies. Tariff walls blocked out competition, and capital controls often constrained cross-border currency flows. In retrospect, the economic environment appeared less competitive, more tranquil, and certainly less threatening to those with only moderate or lesser skills. Indeed, before computer technology automated many repetitive tasks, the unskilled were able to contribute significant value added and earn a respectable wage relative to the skilled.

In this less demanding world, governments were able to construct social safety nets and engaged in policies intended to redistribute income. Even though such initiatives often were recognized as adding substantial cost to labor and product markets, and thereby reducing their flexibility, they were not judged as meaningful impediments to economic growth. In economies not broadly subject to international trade, competition was not as punishing to the less efficient as it is today. To be sure, average standards of living were less than they could have been, and the composition of output was far less sensitive to changing consumer tastes than is the case in today's high-tech environment. There is clearly a significant segment of society that looks back at that period with affectionate nostalgia.

But maintaining the kind of safety net that, for example, is prevalent in most continental European countries where high unemployment appears chronic is proving increasingly problematic in today's altered environment. Govern-

ments of all persuasions still may choose to help people acquire the skills they need to utilize new technologies. And they generally endeavor to support the incomes of those who have been less able to adapt. But technology and competition are extracting a high price for the more intrusive forms of intervention that impair market incentives to work, save, invest, and innovate.

International competitive pressures are narrowing the choices for economies with broad safety nets: the choice of accepting shortfalls in standards of living, relative to the less burdened economies, or loosening the social safety net and acquiescing in the greater concentrations of income that seem to be associated with our high-tech environment. Erecting trade barriers to shut off cross-border competition leads to the loss of the great advantages of the international division of labor and cannot be considered a realistic alternative for societies choosing to realize the full benefits of technological advances. Fortunately, for the moment at least, there appears limited sentiment in Europe or elsewhere to move in that direction.

Clearly, the synergies of transistor, laser, and satellite technologies have created a computer and telecommunications revolution over the last half century that is altering the way people interact with each other and with their institutions. We are adding to our knowledge of which economic and political systems contribute to welfare and wealth and which do not.

This process, of course, has been ongoing especially since the advent of the Industrial Revolution when the emergence of significant wealth creation first offered meaningful alternatives. But in the post-World War II years most of what had been open to conjecture and debate throughout the nineteenth century and first half of the twentieth, is gradually being settled by the sharp realities of recent experience.

I am not alleging that the human race is about to irreversibly accept market capitalism as the only relevant form of economic and social organization and that this great debate is over. There remains a large segment of the population that still considers capitalism and its emphasis on materialism, in all its forms, degrading to man's spiritual nature. In addition, even some of those who seek material welfare view competitive markets as subject to manipulation by mass promotion and advertising that drives consumers to desire and seek superficial and ephemeral values. Some governments even now attempt to override the evident preferences of their citizens, by limiting their access to foreign media because they judge such media will undermine their culture. Finally, there remains a latent protectionism, in the United States and elsewhere, which could emerge as a potent force against globalization should the current high-tech world economy falter.

Moreover, I certainly have no doubt that in the event of problems in today's new, more Spencerian, form of capitalism, governments would increase their interventions in an endeavor to alter market results.

And, as history amply demonstrates, most recently in East Asia, market—or mostly market—systems can produce crises that tempt government intervention. Such crises arise on occasion when confidence unexpectedly fails and is replaced by fear and a loss of trust, inducing a vicious cycle of retrenchment in economic activity and government endeavors to counter it. Nonetheless, in light of the record of failures of intrusive intervention over recent decades, it is difficult to imagine such activism persisting much beyond any immediate crisis. . . .

To get a better sense of the forces that are driving the world's economies, especially in the second half of the twentieth century, it is useful to understand why the Soviet experiment in central planning failed. Indeed, it is not an exaggeration to state that from this failure we have learned as much about why our free capitalist systems work, as about why central planning does not. The Soviet economic failure was so unambiguous that it proffered a new set of standards to better gauge alternative economic paradigms. It, for example, afforded us a far better understanding of why some of the mercantilistic capitalist economies of East Asia worked for awhile but then did not.

Centrally planned economic systems, such as that which existed in the Soviet Union, had great difficulty in creating wealth and rising standards of living. In theory, and to a large extent in practice, production and distribution were determined by specific instructions—often in the form of state orders—coming from the central planning agencies to the various different producing establishments, indicating from whom, and in what quantities, they should receive their raw materials and services, and to whom they should distribute their final outputs.

Without an effective market clearing mechanism, the consequences of such a paradigm, as one might readily anticipate, were both huge surpluses of goods that were not wanted by the populace, and huge shortages of products that consumers desired, but were not produced in adequate quantities. The imbalance of demand over supply of these latter products inevitably required rationing or its equivalent—standing in queues for limited quantities of goods and services.

One might think that the planning authorities should have been able to adjust to these distortions. They tried. But they faced insurmountable handicaps in that they did not have access to the immediate signals of price changes that so effectively facilitate the clearing of markets in capitalist economies. Movements in prices give incentives to adjust the allocation of physical resources to accommodate the changing technology of production and the shifting tastes of consumers.

Among the key prices central planning systems lacked were the signals of finance—equity values and the broad array of interest rates. In a centrally planned system, finance plays a decidedly minor role. Since the production and distribution of goods and services are essentially driven by state orders and rationing, finance amounts to little more than a system for record keeping. While there are pro-forma payment transfers among state-owned enterprises, few if any actions are driven by them. Payment arrears, or even defaults, are largely irrelevant in the sense that they are essentially intracompany transactions among enterprises owned by the same entity, that is, the state.

Under central planning there are no credit standards, no interest rate risks, no market value changes—none of the key financial signals that determine in a market economy who gets credit and who does not, and hence who produces what and sells to whom. In short, none of the financial infrastructure that converts the changing valuations of consumers and shifting efficiencies of capital equipment into market signals that direct production for profit is available. But it didn't matter in the Soviet-bloc economies. Few decisions in those centrally planned systems were affected by the lack of a developed financial system. . . .

Centrally planned economies tend to be frozen in time. They cannot readily accommodate innovation, new ideas, new products, and altered specifications.

In sharp contrast, market economies are driven by what Professor Joseph Schumpeter, a number of decades ago, called "creative destruction." By this he meant newer ways of doing things, newer products, and novel engineering and architectural insights that induce the continuous obsolescence and retirement of factories and equipment and a reshuffling of workers to new and different activities. Market economies in that sense are continuously renewing themselves. Innovation, risk-taking, and competition are the driving forces that propel standards of living progressively higher. . . .

Many Asian policymakers are learning that government-directed investments, backed by government inducements to banks to finance them, can lead to substantial gains in output for a number of years in economies with low real wages and low productivity (as it did in the Soviet Union). Eventually and inevitably, however, such a regime leads to establish facilities that produce goods and services that domestic consumers and export customers apparently no longer want. The consequent losses to companies, and the resultant buildup of nonperforming bank loans, hobble financial intermediation and the economy.

There has been, to be sure, much pain and periodic backtracking among a number of the nations that discarded the mantle of some forms of central planning or mercantilist capitalism. There will doubtless be more. But as a consequence of the experience of the last half century, market capitalism has clearly become ascendant, at least for now. Advancing technologies have spurred the competitive forces of the market to accelerate the rise in consumer wealth and living standards. So long as material well-being holds a high priority in a nation's value system, the persistence of technological advance should foster this process. If we can continue to adapt to our new frenetic high tech economy, that is not a bad prospect for the next century.

Lt. Col. Oliver North takes the oath before testifying during the joint House-Senate hearings on the Iran-Contra Affair, July 7, 1987.

Jesse Jackson, who lost the presidential nomination to Massachusetts Governor Michael Dukakis, addresses the Democratic National Convention, in Atlanta, Georgia, July 19, 1988.

POLITICS

Texas billionaire H. Ross Perot, the third-party candidate who won 19 percent of the vote in the 1992 presidential election, points to a chart during a 30-minute commercial for his candidacy.

John Duricka—AP/Wide World Photos

(Top) Representative Newt Gingrich of Georgia addresses fellow Republican congressional candidates during a rally for the "Contract with America," the platform they used to capture a majority in the House of Representatives during the 1994 midterm elections. (Center) In a still image from television in November 1996, President Bill Clinton embraces Monica Lewinsky, the White House intern at the center of the political maelstrom that led to the impeachment of the President. (Bottom) Volunteers examine a ballot during the hand recount of votes in a Florida county; the 2000 presidential election hung in the balance until the U.S. Supreme Court ruled on the legitimacy of the recount in Florida, whose electoral votes determined that Republican George W. Bush and not Democrat Al Gore became the forty-third President.

APTV/AP Wide World Photos

Mayer Robert/Corbis Sygma

78.

School Voucher Program in Wisconsin

In the 1990s many states held internal debates over public school financing and other reforms, principally how to address inequities between rich and poor educational districts and how to best deal with schools of subpar quality. Several states held referendums or allowed pilot programs built around the use of school vouchers, taxpayer-funded credits that public school students could spend at an alternative school of their choice, public or private. Since many private schools were affiliated with a religion, there was concern that the use of vouchers violated the First Amendment of the Constitution, which established a separation between church and state. Voucher opponents included civil libertarians, leading Democrats, and teachers' unions, which viewed voucher programs as attacks on public schooling. Proponents of school choice argued that these programs forced bad schools to be accountable for their failures and gave disadvantaged students better educational opportunities. A major victory for school choice occurred in June 1998 when the Wisconsin Supreme Court decided in favor of the Milwaukee Parental Choice Program (MPCP), which began using tuition vouchers in 1990. The MPCP passed the court's three-pronged test, demonstrating that it had secular purpose, neither advanced nor inhibited religion, and did not create excessive entanglement between government and religion. For the judges, a crucial distinction of the Milwaukee program was that the money was given to the parents of students rather than to the schools themselves. In November 1998 the U.S. Supreme Court allowed the Wisconsin Supreme Court decision to stand when it decided not to hear an appeal. The majority opinion in the Wisconsin ruling of June 1998 was delivered by Donald W. Steinmetz and is excerpted below.

Source: Supreme Court of Wisconsin, Case No. 97-0270, June 10, 1998.

1. This case raises a number of issues for review:

(1) Does the amended Milwaukee Parental Choice Program (amended MPCP) violate the Establishment Clause of the First Amendment to the United States Constitution? Neither the court of appeals nor the circuit court reached this issue. We conclude that it does not.

(2) Does the amended MPCP violate the religious establishment provisions of Wisconsin Constitution art. I, § 18? In a divided opinion, the court of appeals held that it does. We conclude that it does not.

(3) Is the amended MPCP a private or local bill enacted in violation of the procedural requirements mandated by Wis. Const. art. IV, § 18? The court of appeals did not reach this question, and the circuit court held it is. We conclude that it is not.

(4) Does the amended MPCP violate

the uniformity provision of Wis. Const. art. X, § 3? The court of appeals did not reach this issue, and the circuit court concluded that the amended MPCP does not violate the uniformity clause. We also conclude that it does not.

(5) Does the amended MPCP violate Wisconsin's public purpose doctrine, which requires that public funds be spent only for public purposes? The court of appeals did not reach this issue, and the circuit court concluded that the amended MPCP does violate the public purpose doctrine. We conclude that it does not.

(6) Should children who were eligible for the amended MPCP when this court's injunction issued on August 25, 1995, and who subsequently enrolled in private schools, be eligible for the program if the injunction is lifted? Neither court below addressed this issue. We conclude that they should.

2. This case is before the court on petition for review of a published decision of the court of appeals, *Jackson* v. *Benson*, 213 Wis. 2d 1, 570 N.W.2d 407 (Ct. App. 1997). The court of appeals, in a 2–1 decision, affirmed an order of the Circuit Court for Dane County, Paul B. Higginbotham, Judge, granting the Respondents' motion for summary judgment. The majority of the court of appeals concluded that the Milwaukee Parental Choice Program, Wis. Stat. §119.23, as amended by 1995 Wis. Act 27, §§ 4002–4009 (amended MPCP), was invalid under Article I, § 18 of the Wisconsin Constitution because it directs payments of money from the state treasury for the benefit of religious seminaries. The majority of the court of appeals declined to decide whether the amended MPCP violates the Establishment Clause of the First Amendment or other provi-

sions of the Wisconsin Constitution. In dissent, Judge Roggensack concluded that the amended MPCP did not violate either the federal or state constitution. The State appealed from the decision of the court of appeals. We granted the State's petition for review and now reverse the decision of the court of appeals. We also conclude that the amended MPCP does not violate the Establishment Clause or the Wisconsin Constitution.

3. We are once again asked to review the constitutionality of the Milwaukee Parental Choice Program provided in Wis. Stat. §119.23 (1995–96). The Wisconsin legislature enacted the original Milwaukee Parental Choice Program (original MPCP) in 1989. *See* 1989 Wis. Act 336. As amended in 1993, the original MPCP permitted up to 1.5 percent of the student membership of the Milwaukee Public Schools (MPS) to attend at no cost to the student any private nonsectarian school located in the City of Milwaukee, subject to certain eligibility requirements.

4. Under the original MPCP, the legislature limited the students eligible for participation in the original program. To be eligible for the original MPCP, a student (1) had to be a student in kindergarten through twelfth grade; (2) had to be from a family whose income did not exceed 1.75 times the federal poverty level; and (3) had to be either enrolled in a public school in Milwaukee, attending a private school under this program, or not enrolled in school during the previous year. *See* Wis. Stat. §119.23(2)(a) (1)–(2)(1993–94).

5. The legislature also placed a variety of qualification and reporting requirements on private schools choosing to participate in the original MPCP. To be eligible to participate in the original MPCP, a private school had to comply with the anti-

discrimination provisions imposed by 42 U.S.C. § 2000d and all health and safety laws or codes that apply to Wisconsin public schools. *See id.* at §119.23(2)(a) (4)–(5). The school additionally had to meet on an annual basis defined performance criteria and had to submit to the State certain financial and performance audits. *See id.* at §119.23(7), (9).

6. Under the original MPCP, the State Superintendent of Public Instruction was required to perform a number of supervisory and reporting tasks. The legislature required the State Superintendent to submit an annual report regarding student achievement, attendance, discipline, and parental involvement for students in the program compared to students enrolled in MPS in general. *See id.* at §119.23(5)(d). The original MPCP further required the State Superintendent to monitor the performance of students participating in the program, and it empowered him or her to conduct one or more financial and performance audits of the program. *See id.* at §119.23(7)(b), (9)(a).

7. Under the original MPCP, the State provided public funds directly to participating private schools. For each student attending a private school under the program, the State paid to each participating private school an amount equal to the state aid per student to which MPS would have been entitled under state aid distribution formulas. *See id.* at §119.23(4). In the 1994–95 school year, this amount was approximately $2,500 per participating student. The amount of state aid MPS received each year was reduced by the amount the State paid to private schools participating in the original program. *See id.* at §119.23(5)(a).

8. The original MPCP withstood a number of state constitutional challenges in *Davis* v. *Grover,* 166 Wis. 2d 501, 480 N.W.2d 460 (1992). In *Davis,* this court

first held that the original program, when enacted, was not a private or local bill and therefore was not subject to the prohibitions of Wis. Const. art. IV, § 18. *See id.* at 537. The court then held that the program did not violate the uniformity clause in Wis. Const. art. X, § 3 because the private schools did not constitute "district schools" simply by participating in the program. *See id.* at 540. The court finally held that the program, although it applied only to MPS, served a sufficient public purpose and therefore did not violate the public purpose doctrine. *See id.* at 546.

9. During the 1994–95 school year, approximately 800 students attended approximately 12 nonsectarian private schools under the original program. For the 1995–96 school year, the number of participating students increased to approximately 1,600 and the number of participating nonsectarian private schools increased to 17.

10. In 1995, as part of the biennial budget bill, the legislature amended in a number of ways the original MPCP. *See* 1995 Wis. Act 27, §§ 4002-4009. First, the legislature removed from Wis. Stat. §119.23(2)(a) the limitation that participating private schools be "nonsectarian." *See* 1995 Wis. Act 27, § 4002. Second, the legislature increased to 15 percent in the 1996–97 school year the total percentage of MPS membership allowed to participate in the program. *See id.* at § 4003. Third, the legislature deleted the requirement that the State Superintendent conduct annual performance evaluations and report to the legislature, and it eliminated the Superintendent's authority to conduct financial or performance evaluation audits of the program. *See id.* at §§ 4007m and 4008m.

11. Fourth, the legislature amended the original MPCP so that the State, rather than paying participating schools di-

rectly, is required to pay the aid to each participating student's parent or guardian. Under the amended MPCP, the State shall "send the check to the private school," and the parent or guardian shall "restrictively endorse the check for the use of the private school." *Id.* at § 4006m. Fifth, the amended MPCP places an additional limitation on the amount the State will pay to each parent or guardian. Under the amended MPCP, the State will pay the lesser of the MPS per student state aid under Wis. Stat. §121.08 or the private school's "operating and debt service cost per pupil that is related to educational programming" as determined by the State. *See id.* The amended MPCP does not restrict the uses to which the private schools can put the state aid. Sixth, the legislature repealed the limitation that no more than 65 percent of a private school's enrollment consist of program participants. *See id.* at § 4003. Finally, the legislature added an "opt-out" provision prohibiting a private school from requiring "a student attending the private school under this section to participate in any religious activity if the pupil's parent or guardian submits to the teacher or the private school's principal a written request that the pupil be exempt from such activities." *Id.* at § 4008e.

12. The Respondents, Warner Jackson, et al. and Milwaukee Teachers Education Association (MTEA), et al. filed two original actions in August 1995. Together the lawsuits challenged the amended MPCP under the Establishment Clause of the First Amendment; Wis. Const. art. I, § 18; art. X, § 3; art. IV, § 18; and the Wisconsin public purpose doctrine. On August 15, 1996, the National Association for the Advancement of Colored People (NAACP) filed a separate lawsuit, alleging the same claims as the first two lawsuits and adding a claim that, on its face, the amended MPCP violated the Equal Protection Clause of the Fourteenth Amendment and Wis. Const. art. I, § 1. The NAACP then filed a motion to consolidate the lawsuits. The circuit court consolidated the cases, but bifurcated the proceedings so that the equal protection claims would be heard only if the amended MPCP was upheld.

13. The State filed, under Wis. Stat. §(Rule) 809.70, a petition for leave to commence an original action, seeking from this court a declaration that the amended MPCP was constitutional. This court accepted original jurisdiction and entered a preliminary injunction staying the implementation of the amended program, specifying that the pre-1995 provisions of the original program were unaffected. Following oral argument, this court split three-to-three on the constitutional issues, dismissed the petition, and effectively remanded the case to the circuit court for further proceedings. *See State ex rel. Thompson* v. *Jackson,* 199 Wis.2d 714, 720, 546 N.W.2d 140 (1996)(per curiam).

14. Following remand, the circuit court partially lifted the preliminary injunction, thereby allowing the State to implement all of the 1995 amendments except the amendment allowing participation by sectarian private schools. In January 1997, the circuit court granted the Plaintiffs' motions for summary judgment, denied the State's motion for summary judgment, and invalidated the amendments to the MPCP. The circuit court held that the amended MPCP violates the religious benefits and compelled support clauses of Wis. Const. art. I, § 18, the public or local bill prohibitions of Wis. Const. art. IV, § 18, and the public purpose doctrine as the program applied to sectarian schools. The circuit court also found that the amended program did not violate the uniformity clause in Wis. Const. art. X, § 3 or the public purpose

doctrine as it applied to the nonsectarian private schools. Because the circuit court invalidated the amended MPCP on state constitutional grounds, the court did not address the question whether the program violates the Establishment Clause. The State appealed from the circuit court's order, and the court of appeals, with Judge Roggensack dissenting, affirmed.

15. A majority of the court of appeals held that the amended MPCP violates the prohibition against state expenditures for the benefit of religious societies or seminaries contained in Wis. Const. art. I, § 18. The court of appeals, therefore, struck the amended MPCP in its entirety and found it unnecessary to reach the other state and the federal constitutional issues. The State appealed to this court, and we granted the State's petition for review.

16. In the circuit court, the Respondents challenged the amended MPCP under the Establishment Clause of the First Amendment; Wis. Const. art. I, § 18; art. X, § 3; art. IV, § 18; and the Wisconsin public purpose doctrine. We address each issue in turn.

17. Before we begin our analysis of the amended MPCP, we pause to clarify the issues not before this court. In their briefs and at oral argument, the parties presented information and testimony expressing positions pro and con bearing on the merits of this type of school choice program. This debate largely concerns the wisdom of the amended MPCP, its ef-ficiency from an educational point of view, and the political considerations which motivated its adoption. We do not stop to summarize these arguments, nor to burden this opinion with an analysis of them, for they involve considerations not germane to the narrow constitutional issues presented in this case. In the absence of a constitutional violation, the desirability and efficacy of school choice are matters to be resolved through the political process. This program may be wise or unwise, provident or improvident from an educational or public policy viewpoint. Our individual preferences, however, are not the constitutional standard. . . .

IX. Conclusion

114. In conclusion, based upon our review of both the statute now before us and the stipulated facts, we conclude that the amended MPCP does not violate the Establishment Clause of the First Amendment; Wis. Const. art. I, § 18; art. IV, § 18; art. X, § 3; or the Wisconsin public purpose doctrine. We therefore reverse the decision of the court of appeals and remand the matter to the circuit court with directions to grant the State's motion for summary judgment, to dismiss the NAACP's facial equal protection claim, and to dissolve the injunction barring the implementation of the amended MPCP.

By the Court.—The decision of the court of appeals is reversed, and the cause is remanded to the circuit court for further proceedings consistent with this opinion.

79.

Kenneth W. Starr: The Starr Report

When Bill Clinton ran for President in 1992, he was besieged with allegations of marital infidelity. On Super Bowl Sunday 1992, Clinton and his wife Hillary appeared on the CBS television program 60 Minutes to respond to the allegations. Clinton claimed that while he had "caused pain" in his marriage in the past, he and his wife had a solid marriage. Voters seemed unconcerned by the allegations, and Clinton went on to win the 1992 presidential election. Two years later, an Arkansas woman, Paula Jones, accused Clinton of sexually harassing her while he was governor of Arkansas. Once again, the allegations had little impact on Clinton's popularity, and in 1996 he won reelection as president. In January 1998 a new and far more damaging allegation of sexual impropriety emerged against Clinton. While serving as independent counsel for an investigation into Clinton's financial dealings as governor (known generally as the "Whitewater" investigation), Kenneth Starr learned that Clinton was involved in a sexual relationship with a former White House intern, Monica Lewinsky. Word of Starr's revelation soon leaked to the press and set off a year-long media firestorm. Clinton initially denied the allegations, but, when DNA evidence surfaced that proved the affair, Clinton reversed course. In a nationally televised address in August 1998, he admitted to the relationship with Lewinsky, but denied lying under oath. The House of Representatives impeached Clinton on the grounds of perjury and sexual misconduct in December 1998 but Clinton won acquittal in a Senate trial in January 1999. Reprinted below are portions of Starr's official report on the Clinton-Lewinsky affair.

Source: http://www.house.gov

INTRODUCTION

As required by Section 595(c) of Title 28 of the United States Code, the Office of the Independent Counsel ("OIC" or "Office") hereby submits substantial and credible information that President William Jefferson Clinton committed acts that may constitute grounds for an impeachment.

The information reveals that President Clinton:

• lied under oath at a civil deposition while he was a defendant in a sexual harassment lawsuit;

• lied under oath to a grand jury;

• attempted to influence the testimony of a potential witness who had direct knowledge of facts that would reveal the falsity of his deposition testimony;

• attempted to obstruct justice by facilitating a witness's plan to refuse to comply with a subpoena;

• attempted to obstruct justice by encouraging a witness to file an affidavit that the President knew would be false, and then by making use of that false affidavit at his own deposition;

• lied to potential grand jury witnesses, knowing that they would repeat those lies before the grand jury; and

• engaged in a pattern of conduct that was inconsistent with his constitutional duty to faithfully execute the laws.

The evidence shows that these acts, and others, were part of a pattern that began as an effort to prevent the disclosure of information about the President's relationship with a former White House intern and employee, Monica S. Lewinsky, and continued as an effort to prevent the information from being disclosed in an ongoing criminal investigation.

FACTUAL BACKGROUND

In May 1994, Paula Corbin Jones filed a lawsuit against William Jefferson Clinton in the United States District Court for the Eastern District of Arkansas. Ms. Jones alleged that while he was the Governor of Arkansas, President Clinton sexually harassed her during an incident in a Little Rock hotel room. President Clinton denied the allegations. He also challenged the ability of a private litigant to pursue a lawsuit against a sitting President. In May 1997, the Supreme Court unanimously rejected the President's legal argument. The Court concluded that Ms. Jones, "[l]ike every other citizen who properly invokes [the District Court's] jurisdiction . . . has a right to an orderly disposition of her claims," and that therefore Ms. Jones was entitled to pursue her claims while the President was in office. A few months later, the pretrial discovery process began. . . .

On January 17, 1998, President Clinton was questioned under oath about his relationships with other women in the workplace, this time at a deposition. Judge Wright presided over the deposition. The President was asked numerous questions about his relationship with Monica Lewinsky, by then a 24-year-old former White House intern, White House employee, and Pentagon employee. Under oath and in the presence of Judge Wright, the President denied that he had engaged in a "sexual affair," a "sexual relationship," or "sexual relations" with Ms. Lewinsky. The President also stated that he had no specific memory of having been alone with Ms. Lewinsky, that he remembered few details of any gifts they might have exchanged, and indicated that no one except his attorneys had kept him informed of Ms. Lewinsky's status as a potential witness in the Jones case.

THE INVESTIGATION

On January 12, 1998, this Office received information that Monica Lewinsky was attempting to influence the testimony of one of the witnesses in the Jones litigation, and that Ms. Lewinsky herself was prepared to provide false information under oath in that lawsuit. The OIC was also informed that Ms. Lewinsky had spoken to the President and the President's close friend Vernon Jordan about being subpoenaed to testify in the Jones suit, and that Vernon Jordan and others were helping her find a job. The allegations with respect to Mr. Jordan and the job search were similar to ones already under review in the ongoing Whitewater investigation.

After gathering preliminary evidence to test the information's reliability, the OIC presented the evidence to Attorney General Janet Reno. Based on her review of the information, the Attorney General determined that a further investigation by the Independent Counsel was required.

On the following day, Attorney General Reno petitioned the Special Division of the United States Court of Appeals for the District of Columbia Circuit, on an expedited basis, to expand the jurisdiction of Independent Counsel Kenneth W. Starr. On January 16, 1998, in response to the Attorney General's request, the Special Division issued an order that provides in pertinent part:

The Independent Counsel shall have jurisdiction and authority to investigate to the maximum extent authorized by the Independent Counsel Reauthorization Act of 1994 whether Monica Lewinsky or others suborned perjury, obstructed justice, intimidated witnesses, or otherwise violated federal law other than a Class B or C misdemeanor or infraction in dealing with witnesses, potential witnesses, attorneys, or others concerning the civil case Jones v. Clinton. . . .

THE SIGNIFICANCE OF THE EVIDENCE OF WRONGDOING

It is not the role of this Office to determine whether the President's actions warrant impeachment by the House and removal by the Senate; those judgments are, of course, constitutionally entrusted to the legislative branch. This Office is authorized, rather, to conduct criminal investigations and to seek criminal prosecutions for matters within its jurisdiction. In carrying out its investigation, however, this Office also has a statutory duty to disclose to Congress information that "may constitute grounds for an impeachment," a task that inevitably requires judgment about the seriousness of the acts revealed by the evidence.

From the beginning, this phase of the OIC's investigation has been criticized as an improper inquiry into the President's personal behavior; indeed, the President himself suggested that specific inquiries into his conduct were part of an effort to "criminalize my private life." The regret-table fact that the investigation has often required witnesses to discuss sensitive personal matters has fueled this perception.

All Americans, including the President, are entitled to enjoy a private family life, free from public or governmental scrutiny. But the privacy concerns raised in this case are subject to limits, three of which we briefly set forth here.

First. The first limit was imposed when the President was sued in federal court for alleged sexual harassment. The evidence in such litigation is often personal. At times, that evidence is highly embarrassing for both plaintiff and defendant. As Judge Wright noted at the President's January 1998 deposition, "I have never had a sexual harassment case where there was not some embarrassment." Nevertheless, Congress and the Supreme Court have concluded that embarrassment-related concerns must give way to the greater interest in allowing aggrieved parties to pursue their claims. Courts have long recognized the difficulties of proving sexual harassment in the workplace, inasmuch as improper or unlawful behavior often takes place in private. To excuse a party who lied or concealed evidence on the ground that the evidence covered only "personal" or "private" behavior would frustrate the goals that Congress and the courts have sought to achieve in enacting and interpreting the Nation's sexual harassment laws. That is particularly true when the conduct that is being concealed—sexual relations in the workplace between a high official and a young subordinate employee—itself conflicts with those goals.

Second. The second limit was imposed when Judge Wright required disclosure of the precise information that is in part the subject of this Referral. A federal judge specifically ordered the President, on more than one occasion, to provide the requested information about relationships with other women, including Monica Lewinsky. The fact that Judge Wright later determined that the evidence would not be admissible at trial, and still later granted judgment in the President's favor, does not change the President's legal duty at the time he testified. Like every litigant, the President was entitled to object to the discovery questions, and to seek guidance from the court if he thought those questions were improper. But having failed to convince the court that his objections were well founded, the President was duty bound to testify truthfully and fully. Perjury and attempts to obstruct the gathering of evidence can never be an acceptable response to a court order, regardless of the eventual course or outcome of the litigation.

The Supreme Court has spoken forcefully about perjury and other forms of obstruction of justice: In this constitutional process of securing a witness'[s] testimony, perjury simply has no place whatever. Perjured testimony is an obvious and flagrant affront to the basic concepts of judicial proceedings. Effective restraints against this type of egregious offense are therefore imperative. The insidious effects of perjury occur whether the case is civil or criminal. Only a few years ago, the Supreme Court considered a false statement made in a civil administrative proceeding: "False testimony in a formal proceeding is intolerable. We must neither reward nor condone such a 'flagrant affront' to the truth-seeking function of adversary proceedings. . . . Perjury should be severely sanctioned in appropriate cases." Stated more simply, "[p]erjury is an obstruction of justice."

Third. The third limit is unique to the President. "The Presidency is more than an executive responsibility. It is the inspiring symbol of all that is highest in American purpose and ideals." When he took the Oath of Office in 1993 and again in 1997, President Clinton swore that he would "faithfully execute the Office of President." As the head of the Executive Branch, the President has the constitutional duty to "take Care that the Laws be faithfully executed." The President gave his testimony in the Jones case under oath and in the presence of a federal judge, a member of a co-equal branch of government; he then testified before a federal grand jury, a body of citizens who had themselves taken an oath to seek the truth. In view of the enormous trust and responsibility attendant to his high Office, the President has a manifest duty to ensure that his conduct at all times complies with the law of the land.

In sum, perjury and acts that obstruct justice by any citizen—whether in a criminal case, a grand jury investigation, a congressional hearing, a civil trial, or civil discovery—are profoundly serious matters. When such acts are committed by the President of the United States, we believe those acts "may constitute grounds for an impeachment."

◆

It's a sad story. Our job is not to get Clinton out. It is just to give information.
BRETT KAVANAUGH, staff of independent counsel
Kenneth W. Starr, quoted by Bob Woodward in
Shadow: Five Presidents and the Legacy of Watergate, 1999

80.

JOSEPH LIEBERMAN: Reaction to the Clinton-Lewinsky Affair

In August 1998 President Bill Clinton admitted to having had a sexual affair with Monica Lewinsky, a White House intern. The Clinton-Lewinsky affair first received public notice in January 1998 when Kenneth Starr, special prosecutor for the "Whitewater" investigation (concerning Clinton's financial dealings while governor of Arkansas), subpoenaed Lewinsky. For nearly eight months Clinton denied the existence of an affair with Lewinsky, until DNA taken from a stain on a dress owned by Lewinsky proved beyond doubt that a sexual relationship had in fact transpired between the two. By admitting to the affair, Clinton also admitted that he had lied to cover up the affair. Republicans asserted that Clinton's lies merited impeachment, whereas Clinton's fellow Democrats maintained that the affair was a private matter that had not impeded Clinton's execution of his duties as president. In December 1998 the Republican-controlled House of Representatives voted to impeach the president. In January 1999, however, the Republican-controlled Senate did not convict Clinton, thus allowing him to serve out the remainder of his term. Despite the fact that the Democrats had almost unanimously supported Clinton throughout the controversy, many of his fellow party members felt betrayed by his behavior. Joseph Lieberman, a prominent and respected senator from Connecticut who would be the Democratic nominee for Vice President in 2000, expressed his party's disappointment and anger toward Clinton in a speech on the floor of the U.S. Senate in September 1998.

Source: *Vital Speeches of the Day*, October 1, 1998.

MR. PRESIDENT, I rise today to make a most difficult and distasteful statement, for me, probably the most difficult statement I have made on this floor in my ten years in the Senate.

On August 17th, President Clinton testified before a Grand Jury convened by the Independent Counsel and then talked to the American people about his relationship with Monica Lewinsky, a former White House intern. He told us that the relationship was "not appropriate," that it was "wrong," and that it was "a critical lapse of judgement and a personal failure" on his part. In addition, after seven months of denying that he had engaged in a sexual relationship with Ms. Lewinsky, the President admitted that his "public comments . . . about this matter gave a false impression." He said, "I misled people."

My immediate reaction to this statement was deep disappointment and personal anger. I was disappointed because the President of the United States had just confessed to engaging in an extramarital affair with a young woman in his employ and to willfully deceiving the nation about his conduct. I was personally angry because President Clinton had by his disgraceful behavior jeopardized his Administration's historic record of accomplishment, much of which grew out of the principles and programs that he and I and many others had worked on together in the New Democratic movement. I was also angry because I was one of the many people who had said over the preceding seven months that if the President clearly and explicitly denies the allegations against him, then, of course, I believe him.

Since that Monday night, I have not commented on this matter publicly. I thought I had an obligation to consider the President's admissions more objectively, less personally, and to try to put them in a clearer perspective. And I felt I owed that much to President Clinton, for whom I have great affection and admiration, and who I truly believe has worked tirelessly to make life tangibly better in so many ways for so many Americans.

But the truth is, after much reflection, my feelings of disappointment and anger have not dissipated. Except now these feelings have gone beyond my personal dismay to a larger, graver sense of loss for our country, a reckoning of the damage that the President's conduct has done to the proud legacy of his presidency, and ultimately an accounting of the impact of his actions on our democracy and its moral foundations.

The implications for our country are so serious that I feel a responsibility to my constituents in Connecticut, as well as to my conscience, to voice my concerns forthrightly and publicly, and I can think of no more appropriate place to do so than the floor of this great body. I have chosen to speak particularly at this time, before the Independent Counsel files his report, because while we do not know enough to answer the question of whether there are legal consequences from the President's conduct, we do

know enough to answer a separate and distinct set of questions about the moral consequences for our country.

I have come to this floor many times in the past to speak with my colleagues about my concerns, which are widely-held in this chamber and throughout the nation, that our society's standards are sinking, that our common moral code is deteriorating, and that our public life is coarsening. In doing so, I have specifically criticized leaders of the entertainment industry for the way they have used the enormous influence they wield to weaken our common values. And now because the President commands at least as much attention and exerts at least as much influence on our collective consciousness as any Hollywood celebrity or television show, it is hard to ignore the impact of the misconduct the President has admitted to on our children, our culture and our national character.

To begin with, I must respectfully disagree with the President's contention that his relationship with Monica Lewinsky and the way in which he misled us about it is "nobody's business but" his family's and that "even presidents have private lives," as he said. Whether he or we as a people think it fair or not, the reality in 1998 is that a president's private life is public. Contemporary news media standards will have it no other way. Surely this President was given fair warning of that by the amount of time the news media has dedicated to investigating his personal life during the 1992 campaign and in the years since.

But there is more to this than modern media intrusiveness. The President is not just the elected leader of our country, he is, as presidential scholar Clinton Rossiter observed, "the one-man distillation of the American people," and "the personal embodiment and representative of their dignity and majesty," as President

Taft once said. So when his personal conduct is embarrassing, it is so not just for him and his family. It is embarrassing for us all as Americans.

The President is also a role model, who, because of his prominence and the moral authority that emanates from his office, sets standards of behavior for the people he serves. His duty, as the Rev. Nathan Baxter of the National Cathedral here in Washington said in a recent sermon, "is nothing less than the stewardship of our values." So no matter how much the President or others may wish to "compartmentalize" the different spheres of his life, the inescapable truth is that the President's private conduct can and often does have profound public consequences.

In this case, the President apparently had extramarital relations with an employee half his age, and did so in the workplace, in vicinity of the Oval office. Such behavior is not just inappropriate. It is immoral. And it is harmful, for it sends a message of what is acceptable behavior to the larger American family, particularly to our children, which is as influential as the negative messages communicated by the entertainment culture. If you doubt that, just ask America's parents about the intimate and often unseemly sexual questions their young children have been asking and discussing since the President's relationship with Ms. Lewinsky became public seven months ago.

I have had many of those conversations in recent days, and from that I can conclude that many parents feel much as I do, that something very sad and sordid has happened in American life when I cannot watch the news on television with my ten-year-old daughter anymore.

This is, unfortunately, familiar territory for America's families in today's anything-goes culture, where sexual promiscuity is too often treated as just another lifestyle choice with little risk of adverse consequences. It is this mindset that has helped to threaten the stability and integrity of the family, which continues to be the most important unit of civilized society, the place where we raise our children and teach them to be responsible citizens, to develop and nurture their personal and moral faculties.

President Clinton is well aware of this threat and the broad public concern about it. He has used the bully pulpit over the course of his presidency to eloquently and effectively call for the renewal of our common values, particularly the principle of personal responsibility, and our common commitment to family. And he has spoken out admirably against sexual promiscuity among teenagers in clear terms of right and wrong, emphasizing the consequences involved.

All of which makes the President's misconduct so confusing and so damaging. The President's relationship with Miss Lewinsky not only contradicted the values he has publicly embraced over the past six years; it has compromised his moral authority at a time when Americans of every political persuasion agree that the decline of the family is one of the most pressing problems we as a nation are facing.

Nevertheless, I believe the President could have lessened the harm his relationship with Ms. Lewinsky has caused if he had acknowledged his mistake and spoken with candor about it to the American people shortly after it became public in January. But as we now know, he chose not to do this. His deception is particularly troubling because it was not just a reflexive and understandably human act of concealment to protect himself and his family from the "embarrassment of his own conduct," as he put it, when he was confronted with it in his deposition in the Paula Jones case, but rather the intentional and premeditated decision to do so.

In choosing this path, I fear that the President has undercut the efforts of millions of American parents who are naturally trying to instill in our children the value of honesty. As most any mother or father knows, kids have a singular ability to detect double standards. So we can safely assume that it will be that much more difficult to convince our sons and daughters of the importance of telling the truth when the most powerful man in the nation evades it. Many parents I have spoken with in Connecticut confirm this unfortunate consequence.

The President's intentional and consistent misstatements may also undercut the trust that the American people have in his word, which would have substantial ramifications for his presidency. Under the Constitution, as presidential scholar Richard Neustadt has noted, the President's ultimate source of authority, particularly his moral authority, is the power to persuade, to mobilize public opinion and build consensus behind a common agenda, and at this the President has been extraordinarily effective. But that power hinges on the President's support among the American people and their faith and confidence in his motivations, his agenda, and ultimately his personal integrity. As Teddy Roosevelt once explained, "My power vanishes into thin air the instant that my fellow citizens who are straight and honest cease to believe that I represent them and fight for what is straight and honest; that is all the strength I have."

Sadly, with his deception, President Clinton may have weakened the great power and strength of which President Roosevelt spoke. I know this is a concern that many of my colleagues share, that the President has hurt his credibility and

therefore, perhaps, his chances of moving his agenda forward. But I believe that the harm the President's actions have caused extend beyond the political arena. I am afraid that the misconduct the President has admitted may be reinforcing one of the most destructive messages being delivered by our popular culture—namely that values are essentially fungible. And I am afraid that his misconduct may help to blur some of the most important bright lines of right and wrong left in our society.

I do not raise these concerns as self-righteous criticism. I know that the President is far from alone in the wrongdoing he has admitted. We as humans are all imperfect. We are all sinners. Many have betrayed a loved one, and most of us have told lies. Members of Congress have certainly been guilty of such behavior, as have some previous Presidents. We try to understand the profound complexity and difficulty of personal relationships, which gives us pause before passing judgement on them. We all fall short of the standards our best values set for us. Certainly I do.

But the President, by virtue of the office he sought and was elected to, has traditionally been held to a higher standard. This is as it should be, because the American president is not, as I quoted earlier, just the one-man distillation of the American people but the most powerful person in the world, and as such the consequences of misbehavior by a President, even private misbehavior, are much greater than that of an average citizen, a CEO, or even a Senator. That is what I believe presidential scholar James Barber, in his book, *The Presidential Character,* was getting at when he wrote that the public demands "a sense of legitimacy from, and in, the Presidency . . . There is more to this than dignity, more than propriety. The President is expected to personify our betterness in an inspiring way, to express in what he does and is (not just what he says) a moral idealism which, in much of the public mind, is the very opposite of politics."

Just as the American people are demanding of their leaders, though, they are also fundamentally fair and forgiving, which is why I was so hopeful the President could begin to repair the damage done with his address to the nation on the 17th. But like so many others, I came away feeling that he, for reasons that are thoroughly human, had squandered a great opportunity that night. He failed to clearly articulate to the American people that he recognized how significant and consequential his wrongdoing was and how badly he felt about it. He also failed to show that he understood his behavior has diminished the office he holds and the country he serves, and that it is inconsistent with the mainstream American values that he has advanced as President. And he failed to acknowledge that while Mr. Starr, Ms. Lewinsky, Mrs. Tripp, and the news media have all contributed to the crisis we now face, his presidency would not be in peril if it had not been for the behavior he himself described as "wrong" and "inappropriate."

Because the conduct the President has admitted to was so serious and his assumption of responsibility on August 17th so inadequate, the last three weeks have been dominated by a cacophony of media and political voices calling for impeachment, or resignation, or censure, while a lesser chorus implores us to "move on" and get this matter behind us.

Appealing as the latter option may be to many people who are understandably weary of this crisis, the transgressions the President has admitted to are too consequential for us to walk away and leave the impression for our children and for our posterity that what President Clinton acknowledges he did within the White House is acceptable behavior for our nation's leader. On the contrary, as I have said at length today, it is wrong and unacceptable and should be followed by some measure of public rebuke and accountability. We in Congress—elected representatives of all the American people—are surely capable institutionally of expressing such disapproval through a resolution of reprimand or censure of the President for his misconduct, but it is premature to do so, as my colleagues of both parties seem to agree, until we have received the report of the Independent Counsel and the White House's response to it.

In the same way, it seems to me, talk of impeachment and resignation at this time is unjust and unwise. It is unjust because we do not know enough in fact and will not until the Independent Counsel reports and the White House responds to conclude whether we have crossed the high threshold our Constitution rightly sets for overturning the results of a popular election in our democracy and bringing on the national trauma of removing an incumbent President from office. For now, in fact, all we know for certain is what the President acknowledged on August 17th. The rest is rumor, speculation, or hearsay—much less than is required by Members of the House and Senate in the dispatch of the solemn responsibilities that the Constitution gives us in such circumstances.

I believe that talk of impeachment and resignation now is unwise because it ignores the reality that while the Independent Counsel proceeds with his investigation, the President is still our nation's leader, our Commander-in-Chief. Economic uncertainty and other problems here at home, as well as the fiscal and political crises in Russia and Asia and the growing threats posed by Iraq, North Korea, and worldwide terrorism, all demand the President's focused leadership. For that reason, while the legal process moves forward, I believe it is important that we provide the President with the time and space and support he needs to carry out his most important duties and protect our national interest and security.

That time and space may also give the President additional opportunities to accept personal responsibility for his behavior, to rebuild public trust in his leadership, to recommit himself to the values of opportunity, responsibility and community that brought him to office, and to act to heal the wounds to our national character.

In the meantime, as the debate on this matter proceeds, and as the investigation continues, we would all be advised to heed the wisdom of Abraham Lincoln's second annual address to Congress in 1862. With the nation at war with itself, Lincoln warned, "If there ever could be a proper time for mere catch arguments, that time is surely not now. In times like the present, men should utter nothing for which they would not willingly be responsible through time and eternity."

I believe we are at such a time again today. With so much at stake, we too must resist the impulse toward "catch arguments" and reflex reactions. Let us proceed in accordance with our nation's traditional moral compass, yes, but in a manner that is fair and at a pace that is deliberate and responsible. Let us as a nation honestly confront the damage that the President's actions over the last seven months have caused, but not to the exclusion of the good that his leadership has done over the past six years nor at the expense of our common interests as Americans. And let us be guided by the conscience of the Constitution, which calls on us to place the common good above any partisan or personal interest, as we now work together to resolve this serious challenge to our democracy. Thank you.

Now, I have to go back to work on my State of the Union speech. . . . But I want to say one thing to the American people. I want you to listen to me. I'm going to say this again. I did not have sexual relations with that woman, Miss Lewinsky.

BILL CLINTON, during a White House press conference on education, January 26, 1998

81.

The Digital Millennium Copyright Act

The rise of the Internet in the 1990s opened vast new opportunities for the exchange of ideas and information, which brought with them a new generation of security problems. Via the Internet, criminals were able to "hack" into individual or business computer files and steal or alter private data. Copyright protection was another area of confusion and concern. Traditionally, copyright laws focused on published material, but the Internet made possible the electronic reproduction of virtually any document. The inadequacy of existing laws particularly alarmed businesses that needed copyright protection, such as book publishers, music recording companies, software publishers, and filmmakers. In response to these concerns, Congress passed the Digital Millennium Copyright Act in 1998. The act, among other points, banned the use of software that circumvented copyright protections in computer programs. Although many hailed the act as a wise step in protecting fundamental copyrights, some critics charged that it suppressed free speech and unfairly limited the freedom of computer scientists and researchers. Others warned that the act would ultimately backfire, claiming that it would deter research to study flaws in computer security programs. Excerpts from the Digital Millennium Copyright Act are reprinted below.

Source: U.S. Copyright Office Summary, December 1998.

TITLE I: WIPO TREATY IMPLEMENTATION

TECHNOLOGICAL PROTECTION AND COPYRIGHT MANAGEMENT SYSTEMS

Each of the [1996 World Intellectual Property Organization] WIPO treaties contains virtually identical language obligating member states to prevent circumvention of technological measures used to protect copyrighted works, and to prevent tampering with the integrity of copyright management information. These obligations serve as technological adjuncts to the exclusive rights granted by copyright law. They provide legal protection that the international copyright community deemed critical to the safe and efficient exploitation of works on digital networks.

CIRCUMVENTION OF TECHNOLOGICAL PROTECTION MEASURES

General approach

Article 11 of the WCT [WIPO Copyright Treaty] states:

Contracting Parties shall provide adequate legal protection and effective legal remedies against the circumvention of effective technological measures that are used by authors in connection with the exercise of their rights under this Treaty or the Berne Convention and that restrict acts, in respect of their works, which are not authorized by the authors concerned or permitted by law.

Article 18 of the WPPT [WIPO Performances and Phonograms Treaty] contains nearly identical language.

Section 103 of the DMCA [Digital Millennium Copyright Act] adds a new chapter 12 to Title 17 of the U.S. Code. New section 1201 implements the obligation to provide adequate and effective protection against circumvention of technological measures used by copyright owners to protect their works.

Section 1201 divides technological measures into two categories: measures that prevent unauthorized *access* to a copyrighted work and measures that prevent unauthorized *copying*[2] of a copyrighted work. Making or selling devices or services that are used to circumvent either category of technological measure is prohibited in certain circumstances, described below. As to the act of circumvention in itself, the provision prohibits circumventing the first category of technological measures, but not the second.

This distinction was employed to assure that the public will have the continued ability to make fair use of copyrighted works. Since copying of a work may be a fair use under appropriate circumstances, section 1201 does not prohibit the act of circumventing a technological measure that prevents copying. By contrast, since the fair use doctrine is not a defense to the act of gaining unauthorized access to a work, the act of circumventing a technological measure in order to gain access is prohibited.

Section 1201 proscribes devices or services that fall within any one of the following three categories:

- they are primarily designed or produced to circumvent;
- they have only limited commercially significant purpose or use other than to circumvent; or
- they are marketed for use in circumventing.

No mandate

Section 1201 contains language clarifying that the prohibition on circumvention devices does not require manufacturers of consumer electronics, telecommunications or computing equipment to design their products affirmatively to respond to any particular technological measure. (Section 1201(c)(3)). Despite this general 'no mandate' rule, section 1201 (k) does mandate an affirmative response for one particular type of technology: within 18 months of enactment, all analog videocassette recorders must be designed to conform to certain defined technologies, commonly known as Macrovision, currently in use for preventing unauthorized copying of analog videocassettes and certain analog signals. The provision prohibits rightholders from applying these specified technologies to free television and basic and extended basic tier cable broadcasts.

Savings clauses

Section 1201 contains two general savings clauses. First, section 1201 (c)(1) states that nothing in section 1201 affects rights, remedies, limitations or defenses to copyright infringement, including fair use. Second, section 1201(c)(2) states

---

2. "Copying" is used in this context as a short-hand for the exercise of any of the exclusive rights of an author under section 106 of the Copyright Act. Consequently, a technological measure that prevents unauthorized distribution or public performance of a work would fall in this second category.

that nothing in section 1201 enlarges or diminishes vicarious or contributory copyright infringement.

Exceptions

Finally, the prohibitions contained in section 1201 are subject to a number of exceptions. One is an exception to the operation of the entire section, for law enforcement, intelligence and other governmental activities. (Section 1201(e)). The others relate to section 1201(a), the provision dealing with the category of technological measures that control access to works.

The broadest of these exceptions, section 1201 (a)(1)(B)-(E), establishes an ongoing administrative rule-making proceeding to evaluate the impact of the prohibition against the act of circumventing such access-control measures. This conduct prohibition does not take effect for two years. Once it does, it is subject to an exception for users of a work which is in a particular class of works if they are or are likely to be adversely affected by virtue of the prohibition in making noninfringing uses. The applicability of the exemption is determined through a periodic rulemaking by the Librarian of Congress, on the recommendation of the Register of Copyrights, who is to consult with the Assistant Secretary of Commerce for Communications and Information.

The six additional exceptions are as follows:

1. *Nonprofit library, archive and educational institution exception* (section 1201(d)). The prohibition on the act of circumvention of access control measures is subject to an exception that permits nonprofit libraries, archives and educational institutions to circumvent solely for the purpose of making a good faith determina-

tion as to whether they wish to obtain authorized access to the work.

2. *Reverse engineering* (section 1201(f)). This exception permits circumvention, and the development of technological means for such circumvention, by a person who has lawfully obtained a right to use a copy of a computer program for the sole purpose of identifying and analyzing elements of the program necessary to achieve interoperability with other programs, to the extent that such acts are permitted under copyright law.

3. *Encryption research* (section 1201(g)). An exception for encryption research permits circumvention of access control measures, and the development of the technological means to do so, in order to identify flaws and vulnerabilities of encryption technologies.

4. *Protection of minors* (section 1201(h)). This exception allows a court applying the prohibition to a component or part to consider the necessity for its incorporation in technology that prevents access of minors to material on the Internet.

5. *Personal privacy* (section 1201 (i)). This exception permits circumvention when the technological measure, or the work it protects, is capable of collecting or disseminating personally identifying information about the online activities of a natural person.

6. *Security testing* (section 1201 (j)). This exception permits circumvention of access control measures, and the development of technological means for such circumvention, for the purpose of testing the security of a computer, computer system or computer network, with the authorization of its owner or operator.

Each of the exceptions has its own set of conditions on its applicability, which are beyond the scope of this summary.

TITLE II: ONLINE COPYRIGHT INFRINGEMENT LIABILITY LIMITATION

Title II of the DMCA adds a new section 512 to the Copyright Act to create four new limitations on liability for copyright infringement by online service providers. The limitations are based on the following four categories of conduct by a service provider:

1. Transitory communications;
2. System caching;
3. Storage of information on systems or networks at direction of users; and
4. Information location tools.

New section 512 also includes special rules concerning the application of these limitations to nonprofit educational institutions.

Each limitation entails a complete bar on monetary damages, and restricts the availability of injunctive relief in various respects. (Section 512 (j)). Each limitation relates to a separate and distinct function, and a determination of whether a service provider qualifies for one of the limitations does not bear upon a determination of whether the provider qualifies for any of the other three. (Section 512(n)).

The failure of a service provider to qualify for any of the limitations in section 512 does not necessarily make it liable for copyright infringement. The copyright owner must still demonstrate that the provider has infringed, and the provider may still avail itself of any of the defenses, such as fair use, that are available to copyright defendants generally. (Section 512 (l)).

In addition to limiting the liability of service providers, Title II establishes a procedure by which a copyright owner can obtain a subpoena from a federal court ordering a service provider to disclose the identity of a subscriber who is allegedly engaging in infringing activities. (Section 512(h)).

Section 512 also contains a provision to ensure that service providers are not placed in the position of choosing between limitations on liability on the one hand and preserving the privacy of their subscribers, on the other. Subsection (m) explicitly states that nothing in section 512 requires a service provider to monitor its service or access material in violation of law (such as the Electronic Communications Privacy Act) in order to be eligible for any of the liability limitations. . . .

TITLE III: COMPUTER MAINTENANCE OR REPAIR

Title III expands the existing exemption relating to computer programs in section 117 of the Copyright Act, which allows the owner of a copy of a program to make reproductions or adaptations when necessary to use the program in conjunction with a computer. The amendment permits the owner or lessee of a computer to make or authorize the making of a copy of a computer program in the course of maintaining or repairing the computer. The exemption only permits a copy that is made automatically when a computer is activated, and only if the computer already lawfully contains an authorized copy of the program. The new copy cannot be used in any other manner and must be destroyed immediately after the maintenance or repair is completed.

TITLE IV: MISCELLANEOUS PROVISIONS

EPHEMERAL RECORDINGS FOR BROADCASTERS

Section 112 of the Copyright Act

grants an exemption for the making of "ephemeral recordings." These are recordings made in order to facilitate a transmission. Under this exemption, for example, a radio station can record a set of songs and broadcast from the new recording rather than from the original CDs (which would have to be changed "on the fly" during the course of a broadcast).

As it existed prior to enactment of the DMCA, section 112 permitted a transmitting organization to make and retain for up to six months (hence the term "ephemeral") no more than one copy of a work if it was entitled to transmit a public performance or display of the work, either under a license or by virtue of the fact that there is no general public performance right in sound recordings (as distinguished from musical works).

The Digital Performance Right in Sound Recordings Act of 1995 (DPRA) created, for the first time in U.S. copyright law, a limited public performance right in sound recordings. The right only covers public performances by means of digital transmission and is subject to an exemption for digital broadcasts (i.e., transmissions by FCC licensed terrestrial broadcast stations) and a statutory license for certain subscription transmissions that are not made on demand (i.e. in response to the specific request of a recipient).

Section 402 of the DMCA expands the section 112 exemption to include recordings that are made to facilitate the digital transmission of a sound recording where the transmission is made under the DPRA's exemption for digital broadcasts or statutory license. As amended, section 112 also permits in some circumstances the circumvention of access control technologies in order to enable an organization to make an ephemeral recording. . . .

WEBCASTING AMENDMENTS TO THE DIGITAL PERFORMANCE RIGHT IN SOUND RECORDINGS

As discussed above, in 1995 Congress enacted the DPRA, creating a performance right in sound recordings that is limited to digital transmissions. Under that legislation, three categories of digital transmissions were addressed: broadcast transmissions, which were exempted from the performance right; subscription transmissions, which were generally subject to a statutory license; and on-demand transmissions, which were subject to the full exclusive right. Broadcast transmissions under the DPRA are transmissions made by FCC-licensed terrestrial broadcast stations.

In the past several years, a number of entities have begun making digital transmissions of sound recordings over the Internet using streaming audio technologies. This activity does not fall squarely within any of the three categories that were addressed in the DPRA. Section 405 of the DMCA amends the DPRA, expanding the statutory license for subscription transmissions to include webcasting as a new category of "eligible nonsubscription transmissions."

In addition to expanding the scope of the statutory license, the DMCA revises the criteria that any entity must meet in order to be eligible for the license (other than those who are subject to a grandfather clause, leaving the existing criteria intact.) It revises the considerations for setting rates as well (again, subject to a grandfather clause), directing arbitration panels convened under the law to set the royalty rates at fair market value.

This provision of the DMCA also creates a new statutory license for making ephemeral recordings. As indicated above, section 402 of the DMCA amends section 112 of the Copyright Act to permit the making of a single ephemeral recording to facilitate the digital transmission of sound recording that is permitted either under the DPRA's broadcasting exemption or statutory license. Transmitting organizations that wish to make more than the single ephemeral recording of a sound recording that is permitted under the outright exemption in section 112 are now eligible for a statutory license to make such additional ephemeral recordings. In addition, the new statutory license applies to the making of ephemeral recordings by transmitting organizations other than broadcasters who are exempt from the digital performance right, who are not covered by the expanded exemption in section 402 of the DMCA.

ASSUMPTION OF CONTRACTUAL OBLIGATIONS UPON TRANSFERS OF RIGHTS IN MOTION PICTURES

Section 416 addresses concerns about the ability of writers, directors and screen actors to obtain residual payments for the exploitation of motion pictures in situations where the producer is no longer able to make these payments. The guilds' collective bargaining agreements currently require producers to obtain assumption agreements from distributors in certain circumstances, by which the distributor assumes the producer's obligation to make such residual payments. Some production companies apparently do not always do so, leaving the guilds without contractual privity enabling them to seek recourse from the distributor.

The DMCA adds a new chapter to Title 28 of the U.S. Code that imposes on transferees those obligations to make residual payments that the producer would be required to have the transferee assume under the relevant collective bargaining agreement. The obligations attach only if the distributor knew or had reason to know that the motion picture was produced subject to a collective bargaining agreement, or in the event of a court order confirming an arbitration award under the collective bargaining agreement that the producer cannot satisfy within ninety days. There are two classes of transfers that are excluded from the scope of this provision. The first is transfers limited to public performance rights, and the second is grants of security interests, along with any subsequent transfers from the security interest holder.

It grieves me to think how far more profound and reverent a respect the law would have for literature if a body could only get drunk on it.

MARK TWAIN, speech commenting on the lack of international copyright law, 1881

82.

HELENE GOLDBERG: Radio Therapy

Despite an enormous variety of modern audiovisual entertainment options ranging from television and movies to compact discs and the Internet, radio remained a potent force in American culture. One reason for radio's enduring success was the talk-radio format, which experienced renewed popularity in the 1990s. A number of talk-show hosts, such as Rush Limbaugh, Don Imus, and Howard Stern, became household names, which in some cases led to controversy. Critics chided "shock jocks" such as Stern for lewd and coarse discussions of women and sex. Conversely, some talk-show hosts were criticized for being too conservative. Dr. Laura Schlessinger (Ph.D. in physiology), who dispensed advice on her nationally syndicated radio show, became a lightning rod for criticism when she publicly condemned same-sex unions, unwed mothers, and extramarital sex. Despite such criticism, Schlessinger remained highly popular with radio listeners. Her defenders contended that she represented traditional values in a time of rapid social change and cultural upheaval. Moreover, they claimed that Schlessinger exposed a culture of victimization that prevents people from taking charge of their own lives and from assuming responsibility for their actions. The debate over Schlessinger showed no signs of ending as the century came to a close. In the essay excerpted below, Helene Goldberg, a psychologist and contributor to Tikkun *magazine, takes issue with Schlessinger's psychological techniques and self-help advice.*

Source: *Tikkun,* November–December 1998, "Analyzing Dr. Laura."

DR. LAURA has the largest and most lucrative psychotherapy practice in the world. Every day 18 million people tune in to one of the 450 radio stations that carry her syndicated program. . . .

Her listeners tune in avidly to hear her harangue troubled callers for being wimps and whiners. And Laura hates whiners (unless she's doing the whining). To tell the truth, she doesn't have much patience for most of her callers. She is unable to listen for more than a few seconds without making someone sound foolish, weak, or evil. While other pop therapists urge attention toward the "inner child," Laura is more in tune with her own "inner harpy." She can do without empathy too. She is a scold and her listeners seem to love it. In a field that often valorizes ambiguity and complexity, Laura speaks with the certainty of a seer or a demagogue. She is the anti-shrink. She has no patience for the current psychobabble of victims and survivors. What is the point of understanding a problem? Just GET OVER IT.

Some of her simplicity seems refreshing, especially when applied to others. It is reassuring that no matter how intractable our own problems might seem, other people's problems are just plain dumb. Dr. Laura's approach: If you are a drug addict, stop. Don't get pregnant if you are not married. Don't even think of having an abortion. If you are poor, get a job. If you are a mother, however, quit your job and stay home with your kids. If you are a single mother: a) see above—don't be, or b) get a job that allows you to support you and your family and still allows you to stay home with your kids (being a radio shrink fills the bill), or c) give the children up for adoption to a good religious heterosexual family. It's OK to be homosexual, but don't try to raise kids (heterosexuals make better parents). Don't let your kids have sex or take drugs. If they do, cut them off. If you had an abusive childhood, get over it. How much simpler than spending months or years exploring and understanding these issues in order to solve them. Laura does it all in few minutes: just long enough to assign blame.

Though the predicaments her listeners bring run the gamut of human problems, Laura's advice rings but a single note: She offers a simplistic morality; Dr. Laura proclaims that the right ethical choice is easy. Again and again she condemns her listeners for putting their immediate expediency before their values; for blinding themselves to their own weaknesses; for whining about having chosen the wrong partner. . . .

Laura draws her listeners by toying with their hunger to believe that for all their personal pain and confusion and the suffering they see around them, their world is comprehensible, just, and moral. Laura's self-righteous indignation plays on a universal hope for a moral universe, a hope that becomes more desperate as society turns its back on its own moral obligation to help those in need. The truth is that the less humane our society gets, the more need we feel to justify its authority. Just as children of abusive parents find it less threatening to blame themselves than their parents, people who suffer the most are first to blame themselves for their pain. The victim—and victims almost universally believe they must deserve their suffering—complies with the injustice.

People call Laura because they are in pain and need help, but they also believe that they don't deserve to be helped. Thus when Laura twists the knife a little deeper into a suffering caller, blaming the victim, she absolves the rest of us for a moment from our own guilt. She also confirms our belief that we don't really deserve help. She constantly reminds us that "God helps those who help themselves." But what about the helpless? The price of her absolution is that we too turn our backs on those in need, and, at the same time, deny our own inner cries for help. Every problem is an occasion for swift response—something to be eliminated, not understood. Her anti-psychological rapier slashes through our Gordian tangle of guilt but leaves us scarred in the process.

Laura's enormous popularity bolsters a widespread and disturbing movement in our country to trivialize psychological problems. Her powerful appeal mirrors two prevailing and dangerous deceptions. First is the mistaken belief that emotional problems are, on the whole, malingering or a result of moral laxity. Many of her callers may share Laura's scorn for complex psychological explanations, but they still suffer from failed relationships and yearn for love and community. They feel bad and they turn to Laura for help they are not sure they deserve. Laura's smug piety affirms the possibility of a better life if they'll only accept full personal blame for their problems. Their guilt over their own suffering leaves them exquisitely susceptible to Laura's attacks.

The second deception Laura's success feeds on is that long term psychotherapy is ineffective. It has become an oft-repeated and acceptable deceit that psychotherapy is mere quackery; this position is upheld not only by the uneducated, but is gaining acceptance in cynical academic circles as reflected in the writings of Frederick Crews and Jeffrey Masson. Laura encourages her listeners to believe that her invectives and platitudes are the best help they can hope for, and that the expense of real psychotherapy is a self-indulgence—a waste of time and money.

Now it is true that not all therapists are equally good, but the truth is that there is an enormous body of reputable research that confirms that psychotherapy and psychiatry are remarkably effective treatments for the entire gamut of emotional problems. In an extensive survey organized by Consumer Reports, over 90 percent of those who used the services of a psychotherapist for problems ranging from everyday unhappiness to severe mental illness said that they were helped. Contradicting Laura's contempt for long-term psychotherapy, the survey confirmed that those who stayed in therapy the longest were helped the most. Further studies show that, on the whole, psychotherapy is often more effective than many other common medical interventions. Even the most serious mental illnesses respond to a combination of therapy and psychopharmacology. . . .

How sad then that many people's only experience with psychotherapy is the radio ravings of Dr. Laura, and that they have to settle for her platitudes rather than get real assistance.

◆

Half his listeners swear by him; half swear at him.
JOHN MCCOLLISTER, characterizing radio talk show host
Rush Limbaugh, *The Saturday Evening Post,* 1993

83.

The Rise of Hip-Hop

By the late 1990s, rap (the lyrics) and hip-hop (the backing sounds and the overarching cultural movement associated with the two) had displaced country and western as America's best-selling music. Although hip-hop had originated in the poor, predominantly African American community in the South Bronx section of New York City in the late 1970s, by the end of the twentieth century more than two-thirds of hip-hop's audience was white and suburban. So ubiquitous was rap that the February 8, 1999, cover of Time *magazine proclaimed "Hip-Hop Nation." Almost from hip-hop's inception, mainstream media and many people, both black and white, criticized the violence and misogyny at the heart of much rap (especially the subgenre of gangsta [gangster] rap). No song aroused more controversy than "Cop Killer" (technically a "thrash-metal" song), released by Ice-T and Body Count in 1992. A psychopath's promise to respond murderously to police brutality, it was condemned by President George Bush. But in its twenty-year-plus history, rap has taken on much broader subject matter, from calls to political action, such as "Don't Believe the Hype" (1989) by Public Enemy (whose Chuck D famously characterized rap as the "black CNN"), and celebrations of roots and community, such as Arrested Development's "Tennessee"(1992), to positive affirmations like Lauryn Hill's "Everything Is Everything" (1998)—all of which are excerpted here.*

Sources: Reach Global Songs and Songs of Universal, Inc., 1988.
EMI Blackwood Music Inc. and Arrested Development, 1992.
Sony/ATV Music Publishing, 1998.

A. DON'T BELIEVE THE HYPE

By Carlton Ridenhour [Chuck D],
Hank Shocklee, and Eric Sadler for
Public Enemy

Back
Caught you lookin' for the same thing
It's a new thing—check out this I bring
Uh Oh the roll below the level
'Cause I'm livin' low next to the bass, C'mon
Turn up the radio
They claim that I'm a criminal
By now I wonder how
Some people never know
The enemy could be their friend, guardian

I'm not a hooligan
I rock the party and
Clear all the madness, I'm not a racist
Preach to teach to all
'Cause some they never had this
Number one, not born to run
About the gun . . .
I wasn't licensed to have one
The minute they see me, fear me
I'm the epitome—a public enemy
Used, abused without clues
I refused to blow a fuse
They even had it on the news
Don't believe the hype . . .

B. TENNESSEE

By Speech [Todd Thomas] and Tarre Jones for
Arrested Development

Lord it's obvious we got a relationship
Talkin to each other every night and day
Although you're superior over me
We talk to each other in a friendship way
Then outta nowhere you tell me to break
Outta the country and into more country
Past Dyesburg into Ripley
Where the ghost of childhood haunts me
Walk the roads my forefathers walked
Climbed the trees my forefathers hung from
Ask those trees for all their wisdom
They tell me my ears are so young (home)
Go back to from whence you came (home)
My family tree my family name (home)
For some strange reason it had to be (home)
He guided me to Tennessee (home)

[Chorus]
Take me to another place
Take me to another land
Make me forget all that hurts me
Let me understand your plan

Now I see the importance of history
Why people be in the mess that they be
Many journeys to freedom made in vain
By brothers on the corner playin ghetto games
I ask you lord why you enlightened me

Without the enlightment of all my folks
He said cuz I set myself on a quest for truth
And he was there to quench my thirst
But I am still thirsty . . .
The lord allowed me to drink some more
He said what I am searchin for are
The answers to all which are in front of me
The ultimate truth started to get blurry
For some strange reason it had to be
It was all a dream about Tennessee

C. EVERYTHING IS EVERYTHING

By Lauryn Hill and Johari Newton for Lauryn Hill

I philosophy
Possibly speak tongues
Beat drum, Abyssinian, street Baptist
Rap this in fine linen, from the beginning
My practice extending across the atlas
I begat this
Flipping in the ghetto on a dirty mattress
You can't match this rapper slash actress
More powerful than two Cleopatras
Bomb graffiti on the tomb of Nefertiti
MCs ain't ready to take it to the Serengeti
My rhymes is heavy like the mind of sister Betty
L-Boogie spars with stars and constellations
Then came down for a little conversation
Adjacent to the king, fear no human being
Roll with cherubims to Nassau Coliseum
Now hear this mixture, where Hip Hop meets scripture
Develop a negative into a positive picture

[Chorus]
Now Everything Is Everything
What is meant to be, will be
After winter, must come spring
Change, it comes eventually

1999

84.

James K. Glassman and Kevin A. Hassett: Why Stocks Are a Good Buy

Between 1981 and 1999, the Dow Jones Industrial Average (DJIA) increased more than tenfold, culminating in an all-time high of just over 11,000. The extraordinary increase in stock market values had enormous ramifications for the economy. Stock ownership more than doubled during the 1990s, which meant that by the end of the decade about half of all adult Americans owned stocks. In response to intense public interest in stocks, cable television networks created new channels devoted solely to covering the market. The Wall Street Journal *achieved the largest circulation of any newspaper in the nation. Millions of Americans came to view the stock market as an opportunity to earn money relatively easily. Increasingly, people spoke of a new, "recession-proof" stock market that would grow vastly beyond even the 11,000 level. James Glassman and Kevin Hassett, both market analysts, laid out the case for a long-term increase in the stock market in their book* Dow 36,000 *(1999), which is excerpted below. Although the DJIA fell by more than four thousand points in the year and a half following its January 2000 peak and millions of investors left the market, Glassman and Hassett continued to maintain that stock purchases remained an excellent long-term investment.*

Source: *Dow 36,000: The New Strategy for Profiting from the Coming Rise in the Stock Market*, New York, 1999.

Never before have so many people owned so much stock. They depend on their shares not just to enjoy a comfortable retirement, but also to pay tuition, to buy a house or a car, to help their children, to take a long vacation, or simply to lead a good life.

Today, half of America's adults are shareholders—up from one-fifth in 1990 and just one-tenth in 1965. Stocks are the largest single asset that families own, topping even the net value of their homes.

But investors—many of them novices—are as frightened as they are enthusiastic. The market has been a great boon, but it remains a great and ominous mystery.

It should not be. This book will give you a completely different perspective on stocks. It will tell you what they are really worth—and give you the confidence to buy, hold, and profit from your investments. It will convince you of the single most important fact about stocks at the dawn of the twenty-first century: They are cheap. . . .

For too long, the value of stocks has been seriously underrated.

Consider dividends, which are the part of a company's earnings that it gives out in cash, usually in the form of quarterly checks, to its shareholders. Most stocks today pay what the experts say are paltry dividends. But the truth about dividends is that they increase as earnings increase—and over time, these increases compound so that even tiny dividends today will provide shareholders with loads of cash in the long term.

Take General Electric Co., a giant diversified corporation with interests ranging from lightbulbs to broadcasting to jet engines to plastics to consumer finance. GE is superbly managed but hardly the sort of fresh, go-go business associated with parabolic growth. After all, it is more than a century old. In Chapter 13, we will closely examine GE, but here are the highlights on the company's dividends.

First, we took the price of GE in 1989 and adjusted it for splits that occurred later. (When a company splits its stock, it issues new shares to current owners, but the value of their total holdings does not change. For instance, if you own 100 shares with a market price of $100 each, and the stock splits two-for-one, you will own 200 shares with a market price of about $50 each.)

In 1989, you could have bought a share of GE for $11, after accounting for splits. At the time, the stock was paying an annual dividend of 41 cents, or 3.7 percent of the share price. The dividend rose each year, so that, by the start of 1999, it was $1.40—or more than three times the annual dividend ten years earlier.

In other words, in 1999, your GE stock was paying you a dividend return—in that year alone—of 12.7 percent on your original investment, or well over twice the rate of a ten-year Treasury bond, and rising. At this pace, in another twenty years, GE will be paying an annual dividend that represents a 50 percent return on your initial investment!

GE is a profitable company that passes on its gains to shareholders, but it is not exceptional. In the year 1999 alone, dividends on a share of Philip Morris exceed the stock's 1980 purchase price.

This is the difference between what bonds and stocks put into your pockets: Bonds may make higher interest payments to start, but over time stocks outstrip them because the profits of healthy firms increase, and so do their dividends.

For example, over the twenty years starting in 1977, a $1,000 investment in American Brands, a modest consumer products company that later sold some divisions and changed its name to Fortune Brands, put five times as much money (in dividends alone) into the pockets of its shareholders as a $1,000 investment at the same time in a long-term Treasury bond.

Our research found that, since 1946, dividends have risen, on average, more than 6 percent a year. The after-tax earnings that companies report to shareholders have risen more than 7 percent. Something growing that fast doubles about every ten years through the miracle of compounding.

Those growth rates are at the heart of our theory about rising stock prices. They have largely been ignored by analysts, who prefer to judge stocks by backward-looking valuation techniques that, much of the time, have argued against investing in stocks at all.

The measures you see in the stock tables and hear mentioned on television have been so wrong for so long that it is hard to see why anyone continues to pay attention to them. But old ideas die hard.

New ideas, on the other hand, disturb. On March 30, 1998, we unveiled our theory in *The Wall Street Journal* under the headline, "Are Stocks Overvalued? Not a Chance." At the time, the Dow stood at 8782, and we said we were comfortable then, as now, with the index rising to 36,000 or even higher.

The article provoked criticism because it challenged the cherished assumptions of the financial establishment—for example, that dividend yields of 2 percent are too low and that P/E ratios of 25 are too high. But the truth is that clinging to the conventional wisdom can be very costly to investors.

(Don't worry. We'll explain all the jargon. For example, a "price-to-earnings ratio" indicates how many dollars an investor has to pay today for one dollar's worth of a company's profits. The average P/E since 1872 has been 14. A high P/E indicates that a stock is popular—some would say *too* popular—with investors.)

At the same time, our views have led some professionals to begin reconsidering the old rules of the stock market. After our *Wall Street Journal* piece, Byron Wien, the respected Morgan Stanley strategist, wrote a letter to his clients laying out our arguments—for example, that "the fair-market P/E multiple of the market could reach 100." The article, he said, "did start me thinking."

It's smart to be skeptical when someone (like us) claims that "this time it's different"—that something new is happening in the stock market. But, as Wien points out, there have been times "when recognizing that something was, in fact, different paid off significantly."

Still, a more common response to our ideas by the financial establishment was anger and resentment. Following our second piece in *The Wall Street Journal*—on March 17, 1999, just after the Dow passed 10,000—Bob Brusca, then chief economist at Nikko Securities, was quoted in the *New York Post* as saying "This stupid article does not make any sense." . . .

One reason that stock ownership is soaring—from 10 percent of adults in 1965 to 21 percent in 1990 to 43 percent in 1997 to an estimated 50 percent today—is that Americans have begun to understand that equities offer both high returns and, over the long term, low risk.

Another reason is that with low-cost mutual funds and tax-advantaged retirement accounts, it has never been easier to invest. In 1980, just 6 million families owned mutual funds; by 1998, that figure had jumped to 44 million, or two out of five households. From 1980 to 1998, assets held in stock mutual funds have increased from $44 million to $3 trillion. The average fund-holding family has $98,000 socked away in stocks, bonds, and money market funds. Meanwhile, 401(k) retirement plans are also booming. More than 25 million Americans participate, and total assets top $1.4 trillion.

But, with all this money sunk into mysterious equities—which, to many investors, are simply names and numbers on the stock pages—no wonder Americans are worried. This book should allay the fears. Armed with the knowledge of what your stocks are really worth, you can resist the daily drumbeat of news reporting that previously would shake your faith in what you own.

The press and the financial analysts are continually saying that stocks are overvalued, and they have continually been wrong. By contrast, Warren Buffett, chairman of Berkshire Hathaway, Inc., and the most successful investor of the past century, told investors at his company's 1998 annual meeting in Omaha: "The market is not overvalued, in our view, if two conditions are met: namely, number one, that interest rates stay at or near present levels or go lower and, number two, that corporate profitability stays close to current levels."

We concur, but take a slightly more optimistic view. Profit growth can revert to historical levels and interest rates can actually rise—as long as real (or after-inflation) rates stay roughly where they are. In that case, stocks are not overvalued. In fact, they are significantly *undervalued*. In the pages ahead, you will hear our argument, which goes like this:

1. Over the long term, a diversified portfolio of stocks is no more risky, in real terms, than an investment in bonds issued by the United States Treasury.

2. Stocks have historically paid shareholders a large premium—about seven percentage points more than bonds. (In other countries, the premium has been only slightly smaller. In Britain, for example, writes Martin Wolf of the *Financial Times*, it has been about six percentage points since 1918.)

3. This equity premium, based on the erroneous assumption that the market is so risky that anyone who invests in it should get higher returns as compensation, gives investors a delightful unearned dividend.

4. Evidence abounds that investors are catching on, realizing that the equity premium is unnecessary. So they are bidding up the price of stocks to take advantage of this terrific deal.

5. If there is no risk premium, then, over time, stocks and bonds should put about the same amount of money into the pockets of the people who buy them.

6. Therefore, the correct valuation for stocks—the perfectly reasonable price—is one that equalizes the total flow of cash from stocks and bonds in the long run.

7. Several complementary approaches show that the P/E that would equalize cash flows is about 100.

8. The Dow Jones industrial average was at 9000 when we began writing this book, and its P/E was about 25. So, in order for stocks to be correctly priced, the Dow should rise by a factor of four—to 36,000.

9. The Dow should rise to 36,000 immediately, but to be realistic, we believe the rise will take some time, perhaps three to five years.

10. In the meantime, as we show in the second part of the book, you can profit by taking our approach to your investment planning and your stock portfolio.

In other words, stocks are an exceptional investment. They are just as risky as bonds over long periods of time, and their returns—at least for now—are much higher.

◆

The more kites that are up, the more string they need, and when it runs out, the bigger the loss. . . . no one ever got a balloon up quite as high or hit bottom as hard as I did. I figure the lessons I learned were worth the money. Wounds made by these gambles soon heal, and before long the boys are back, looking at the board again.

SUE SANDERS, commenting on her involvement
in the stock market, *Our Common Herd,* 1940

85.

CANDACE CORLETT: Marketing to Older Women on the Internet

In 1990 few Americans had heard of the Internet, yet just a few years later the term was a household word. Much like the spread of the personal computer in the 1980s, use of the Internet expanded quickly in the 1990s as millions of Americans subscribed to Internet service providers. Its growth affected virtually every feature of American life, from politics and business to culture and entertainment. Almost immediately, advertisers realized the enormous marketing possibility of the Internet: it afforded a fast and inexpensive method of reaching millions of new consumers through a vibrant, emerging medium. The first demographic group to use the Internet on a regular basis consisted of young people under the age of thirty, and advertisers naturally turned their attention to them first. As the Internet took hold among older users, advertisers began to tailor new marketing strategies to different ages, incomes, and social backgrounds. In an address before business researchers in May 1999, Candace Corlett, the president of a market research company, discussed advertising strategies for reaching Internet users who were female and over age fifty. Excerpts of her speech are reprinted below.

Source: *Vital Speeches of the Day,* October 15, 1999.

THE BABY BOOMERS have been turning 50 for only two years and already they have stirred an enormous amount of activity in industry. Baby boomers are not a generation to be ignored. What's that song, "I know what I want and I want it now." You can almost see them stamping their feet and demanding new products and services: skin creams to erase lines, medications to manage menopause, biotechnology to replace damaged body parts. That is why we are all here today, because the 50-plus population, even before the onslaught of the baby boomers, is a significant target audience and now it is really getting attention. Why?

First, the demographics are just too compelling to ignore any longer. The population has shifted to the point where consumers over 50 . . .

- Represent 38% of the total U.S. adult population
- They are 70 million people strong
- They control 55% of the discretionary spending in our economy
- 77% of the U.S. assets are in their name, and
- 80% of the U.S. savings dollars are in their name

As for women, they live longer than men so the over 50 population skews to 52% women vs. 48% men.

Quite frankly, marketers don't exactly know what to do about these consumers over 50 who are re-defining aging. Our image of retirement is a life of leisure, but most of today's retirees have full calendars doing volunteer work, minding grandchildren, traveling, working and pursuing their hobbies.

This is a new generation of aging Americans that is defying the stereotype of "senior citizens." They are not "old" as we have known it. They retire but then they get new jobs . . . and new careers. They get re-born to nutrition and physical fitness.

They don't sit home watching TV, they roam the world with the Elderhostel and Walking Tours. They are not technologically challenged. Quite the contrary, they embrace the marvel of the Internet.

They have money to spend but they are discriminating consumers. Remember that this is the generation that learned from consumer advocates Ralph Nader and Betty Furness to demand service, information and value. They have also spent many years exposed to advertising and quite frankly, by now they are pretty jaded to advertising.

The statistics on ownership of computers and Internet usage change faster than the auditors can audit them, but one consistent message is that computers and the Internet work for the older as well as the younger population.

• 68% of on-line buyers are over 40

• 65% growth in on-line usage since 1997

• 38 hours a month on-line, more than any other demographic

At a conference on Internet retailing, a representative from the Gap said that their on-line customer is much older than the in-store customer. How could that be if the Internet is the world of youth? Quite simple if you think about it: young people go to the stores to socialize, to meet friends and find dates. Older customers don't need that kind of socialization and are quite happy to order from home without the fuss of try-ons, crowds, lines and young people hanging around trying to meet other young people. . . .

Now that we have shattered your stereotypes, without further delay: here are 3 steps to successful Internet marketing to women over 50:

STEP #1. DEFINE YOUR TARGET AUDIENCE

50-plus is not a homogenous market. It is as diverse as 18 to 49 and you need to clearly understand which group is going to be most responsive to what you have to sell.

The GI Generation is the oldest segment. Born between 1909 and 1925 they are currently 74 to 90 years of age and there are 9 million women in this age group.

They are the generation of women that went to work while the men fought the great wars. They then returned to tending families in the newly created suburbs. Their husbands went to school on the GI bill and their first homes were acquired with GI housing loans. The majority were grateful to and dependent upon a husband-provider who was employed for decades by a solid company. The company and the United States government were viewed as their benefactors and they in return became team players, loyal to country and company. They are described as the population that "Works Within the System."

It is this generation that is forcing us to re-think the meaning of longevity, their own as well as ours. This is an active audience for many products and services including every health care innovation that prolongs the good life, from joint replacements, expensive prescriptions and technology. . . .

STEP #2. GET TO KNOW THEM

The core target audience for marketing to women is 48 million women be-

tween the ages of 40 and 73. They are characterized by:
- The liberation of women
- Identities apart from family and children
- Seeking personal fulfillment
- Freedom to choose

What distinguishes them from earlier generations of older women is the freedom to choose, if and how many children they have, pursue degrees or not, earn their own income, stay in a marriage, stay in shape, go gray or stay a redhead. And now it is theirs to choose how they will age.

But the huge contradiction is very few businesses are talking to them. Does anyone know why? Are we afraid that aging is contagious? Is there a stigmata [sic] associated with these women? If she wears your products, will it be un-trendy, old?

If you are smart enough to go get them you first want to be sure you have the pieces that will make you successful.

There are seven indicators that transform someone from youth into a mature market consumer. The transformation happens for some women in their late 40s if children have left the nest. For others it occurs in their late 60s, particularly if they started working later in life or had children later in life. The actual age is less important than their state of mind. But the result is shifting attitudes that you need to appreciate before you can motivate the mature market woman.

Lifestyles Change

Something happens to dramatically change the lifestyle. Children leave the nest. The large family home is traded for an easier maintenance home. Retirement happens. Significant changes such as these are catalysts for a new life stage.

The Self Regains Importance

Somewhere along the road of aging a person stops and decides "It's time for me now." The self becomes more important than the demands of the children, community, career. A sense awakens that whispers "Now it's time for me."

Spirits are Renewed

There is something uplifting about taking time for yourself. Turning 50 or 65 or 70 can be downright depressing. But most people rebound and decide to live full rich senior lives.

New Time Needs to Be Filled

It may be hard for many of you to imagine people being so anxious about free time, but remember the people who are in their 50s and 60s today are used to being busy, over-committed, stressed. Now they are intense about keeping busy, active and involved. They are looking to publications and industry to provide them with ideas on how to fill their time.

Money Has New Dimensions

Certainly the end of mortgages and tuition payments bring immense financial relief and it does not have to be a six-figure bank account to create a sense of wealth, just having some money left over each week gives people a new sense of freedom to spend.

Bodies Send New Messages

People are very candid about the messages they receive from their bodies. Certain parts just don't work as well as they used to, but that doesn't mean that they stopped doing. Today's mature population counts on medications, exercise, better eating and product innovations to help compensate for an aging body. In general, as long as older people are free from pain, they consider themselves to be in good health.

Purchases are Viewed with New Perspective

Aging brings release from peer pressure. Older consumers need to keep up with no one. They may choose to vacation in a four star resort and then seek out budget motels with the best senior discounts for weekend travel. They lived through the '70s, during the birth of consumer activism and protection. Now that they have more time available they comparative shop and devour information before they purchase. Most important of all, the mature market is an informed, seasoned consumer. They look for information to guide their purchases. Remember, they grew up with Ralph Nader and Betty Furness teaching them; they will not be fooled. They demand information about what they are buying and the Internet is the ideal place to give it all to them. Let them choose how much or how little they want.

STEP #3. SPEAK SO THEY WILL HEAR

Talk about what is of interest to them. Do not be afraid to bring the hush-hush topics out of the closet, and on the Internet you have the option to talk about these topics in private. . . .

Menopause was a taboo topic but it has come out of the closet. Menopause talk is everywhere. Best-sellers, newspaper and magazine articles address menopause, and hormone replacement manufacturers take their message directly to the consumer in Rx advertising. And Wyeth Ayerst sends a complimentary subscription of their *Seasons* magazine to anyone who receives a prescription of their estrogen products.

There is a lack of information available to women on how to make the most of aging. It is their topic and the magazines have left it to you to fill the gap.

Once you are talking about what they want to listen to then you need to watch your attitude.

PROMOTE THE UPSIDE OF AGING

People are all too familiar with the downside of aging. You don't need to remind them. Sell to them with the promise of the second stage of life!

Vitality—This will be the aspirational benefit of living a long, fulfilling life. Without vitality, aging is dreadful.

Club Med certainly evokes an image of young, single, free spirited and adventuresome people. Few of these traits are generally associated with the older market. However, Club Med saw their business as resorts and the 50 plus population includes frequent travelers who love resorts. With smart copy edits and a well-targeted brochure, Club Med launched "Forever Young" [and] captured the vitality that attracts the older traveler.

Glow—is the color of vitality. Everything that is good will glow—the glow of good health, the glow of skin, restored glow to hair.

Growth—is what aging people want in all its forms, except of course, girth. Personal growth, financial growth, muscle growth, hair growth.

Copy—"First" will replace "new" as the attention-grabbing, neon-letter word. New millennium aging people want to experience firsts: first sports car, first cross-country trip, first investment portfolio, first college course, first grandchild, first simulated space flight. Retirement will be a time of firsts.

Now, "begin," "start" will be call-to-action words. These words will be the most compelling motivation because they subtly suggest doing it now while you still can. Words like "fast" and "instantly," which suggest speed and frenzy, will be much less important to an audience that wants to do things at a more reasonable (not slower) pace that allows them to savor the experience.

"On my terms," and any derivation of this phrase, will be an important re-assurance. One of the joys of aging is freedom from peer pressure. "Copy" will encourage individualism and offer customization.

Graphics—Small tightly spaced type is illegible. LARGE BOLD TYPE IS OFFENSIVE. Somewhere in-between there is a legible point type size with enough white space around it to encourage reading.

Models—Ageless Models—Surprise! There is such a thing as an ageless model. Is she/he 44, 55, or a well-preserved 61? Only their physician needs to know for sure. Consumers won't care. As long as the model looks over 45 there is credibility.

New Lifestyles

Think twice about the cozy, silver-haired couple. Among the 50 plus population the majority are widowed, divorced or legally separated. Half of the rest wish that they were. The use of couples in advertising will be reserved for luxury goods, like diamond rings. The best people to reflect the over 50 audience will be mixed groups of an uneven number of men and women, followed by mothers and daughters, sisters and menfolk.

Toss out all those shots of golf carts. The new generation does not want to be confined to a golf cart. That's the dream of over-worked 45 year olds, not of active retirees. Golf carts will be replaced by active pleasure symbols, like sailboats, bicycles, hiking boots and walking sticks, carpentry tools, even motorcycle repair kits.

AGEISM IN ADVERTISING

The final caveat—watch out for ageism in advertising. Insensitivity to aging will replace racism and sexism as the most fatal offense. This is going to be a real challenge for creative executives in their 20s and 30s. It will take at least two decades of sensitivity training to program our youth culture to instinctively think in terms of the positive experiences of aging. Will it ever be fun to get old? Of course not; but if advertising can make it appear fun to be a teenager or starting out young and single in your 20s, then why not the 50s, 60s, or 70s.

Never before has an older generation been conversant with so many divergent ideas and dissenting values. . . . It is the generation whose cultural repertory blithely mixed and matched Western political ideology with Asian religions, Native American lore with high tech, psychotherapy with psychedelic drugs.
THEODORE ROSZAK, *Longevity Revolution: As Boomers Become Elders*, 2001

[G]lobal aging will be the leitmotif of the twenty-first century.
PAUL WALLACE, *Agequake: Riding the Demographic Rollercoaster Shaking Business, Finance and Our World*, 1999

86.

Native American Tribal Gambling

Legalized gambling in the United States expanded dramatically in the 1980s. The continued prosperity of Las Vegas, Nevada, where gambling had flourished since the 1930s, the rejuvenation of Atlantic City, New Jersey (largely through the introduction of casino gaming in 1978), and the widespread success of state lotteries all suggested that the economic benefits of gambling far outweighed the perceived social ills. Native American communities, long hampered by poverty and unemployment, also turned to casino gambling in the late 1980s as a means of breaking their cycle of economic malaise. In 1996 Congress authorized a study of the social and economic implications of gambling in the United States. The results of the study—published in 1999 and excerpted below—paid special attention to the impact of casino gambling on Native American communities and the latter's relationship with federal and state governments.

Source: *National Gambling Impact Study Commission Report,* June 18, 1999.

GROWTH OF TRIBAL GAMBLING

Large-scale Indian casino gambling is barely a decade old. Its origins trace back to 1987, when the U.S. Supreme Court issued its decision in *California* v. *Cabazon Band of Mission Indians.* This decision held that the state of California had no authority to apply its regulatory statutes to gambling activities conducted on Indian reservations. In an effort to provide a regulatory framework for Indian gambling, Congress passed the *Indian Gaming Regulatory Act* (IGRA) in 1988. IGRA provides a statutory basis for the regulation of Indian gambling, specifying several mechanisms and procedures and including the requirement that the revenues from gambling be used to promote the economic development and welfare of tribes. For casino gambling—which IGRA terms "Class III" gambling—the legislation requires tribes to negotiate a compact with their respective states, a provision that has been a continuing source of controversy and which will be discussed at length later in this chapter.

The result of those two developments was a rapid expansion of Indian gambling. From 1988, when IGRA was passed, to 1997, tribal gambling revenues grew more than 30-fold, from $212 million to $6.7 billion. By comparison, the revenues from commercial casino gambling (hereinafter termed "commercial gambling") roughly doubled over the same period, from $9.6 billion to $20.5 billion in constant 1997 dollars.

Since the passage of IGRA, tribal gambling revenues consistently have grown at a faster rate than commercial gambling revenues, in large part because a relatively small number of the Indian gambling facilities opened in densely populated markets that previously had little, if any, legalized gambling. . . .

As was IGRA's intention, gambling revenues have proven to be a very important source of funding for many tribal governments, providing much-needed improvements in the health, education, and welfare of Native Americans on reservations across the United States. Nevertheless, Indian gambling has not been a panacea for the many economic and social problems that Native Americans continue to face.

Only a minority of Indian tribes operate gambling facilities on their reservations. According to the Bureau of Indian Affairs (BIA), there are 554 federally recognized tribes in the United States, with 1,652,897 members, or less than 1 percent of the U.S. population. In 1988, approximately 70 Indian casinos and bingo halls were operating in a total of 16 states; in 1998, approximately 260 facilities were operating in a total of 31 states. . . . Of these 554 tribes, 146 have Class III gambling facilities, operating under 196 tribal-state compacts.

More than two-thirds of Indian tribes do not participate in Indian gambling at all. Some tribes, such as the Navajo Nation, have rejected Indian gambling in referenda. Other tribal governments are in the midst of policy debates on whether or not to permit gambling and related commercial developments on their reservations.

The reasons for opposition are varied, but a common theme among many opposed to Indian gambling is a concern that gambling may undermine the "cultural integrity" of Indian communities.

For the majority of tribes with gambling facilities, the revenues have been modest yet nevertheless useful. However, not all gambling tribes benefit equally. The 20 largest Indian gambling facilities account for 50.5 percent of total revenues, with the next 85 accounting for 41.2 percent. Additionally, not all gambling facilities are successful. Some tribes operate their casinos at a loss and a few have even been forced to close money-losing facilities.

TRIBAL SOVEREIGNTY AND INDIAN GAMBLING

Under the U.S. Constitution and subsequent U.S. law and treaties with Indian nations, Native Americans enjoy a unique form of sovereignty. Chief Justice John Marshall, who was instrumental in defining the constitutional status of Indians, described the legal relationship between the federal government and the tribes as "unlike that of any other two people in existence." Two centuries of often contradictory federal court decisions and Congressional legislation have ensured that the definition and boundaries of tribal sovereignty remain in flux. Differing perspectives on the nature and extent of that sovereignty—in particular, the relationship of Indian tribes to the state governments in which they reside—lie at the heart of the many disputes about Indian gambling.

The authority for tribal governmental gambling lies in the sweep of U.S. history and the U.S. Constitution. The Commerce Clause of the U.S. Constitution recognizes Native American tribes as separate nations. The Supreme Court so held in the early years of the Nation's history. In *Cherokee Nation* v. *Georgia*—the Court held that an Indian tribe is a "distinct political society . . . capable of managing its own affairs and governing itself." A year later in *Worcester* v. *Georgia*—Chief Justice Marshall, writing for the Court, held that Indian tribes are distinct, independent political communities "having territorial boundaries, within which their authority [of self-government] is exclusive . . . " By entering into treaties, the Court held, Indian tribes did not "surrender [their] independence—[their] right to self-government . . . "

These principles of federal law have been repeatedly reaffirmed by the Supreme Court. Thus, it is broadly understood that "[t]he sovereignty retained by tribes includes 'the power of regulating their internal and social relations'"—and that this authority includes the "power to make their own substantive law in internal matters . . . and to enforce that law in their own forums." And under settled law these rights include the right to engage in economic activity on the reservation, through means that specifically include the right to conduct gambling on reservation lands.

As a result of these principles, state law generally does not apply to Indians on the reservation. . . .

The federal government's unique obligation toward Indian tribes, known as the trust responsibility, is derived from their unique circumstances; namely that Indian tribes are separate sovereigns, but are subject to federal law and lack the lands and other resources to achieve self-sufficiency. . . . The trust responsibility is the obligation of the federal government to protect tribes' status as self-governing entities and their property rights.

However, Congress may limit tribal sovereignty. The Congressional power over Indian affairs is plenary, subject to constitutional restraint. Congress may use its plenary power to "limit, modify or eliminate the powers of local self-government which the tribes otherwise possess." But, federal law now recognizes that Congressional acts are subject to judicial review to determine whether such enactments violate Indian rights and whether they are constitutional. . . . In short, Indian rights are no longer excluded from the protection of the Constitution.

In these decisions, the Supreme Court also articulated the standard of review under which the constitutionality of Indian legislation is to be tested. That standard requires that the legislation "be tied rationally to the fulfillment of Congress' unique obligation toward the Indians . . ." Applying this standard, the Supreme Court has critically examined federal legislation affecting Indians to determine whether it comports with constitutional limits imposed on Congressional power. As a result of that analysis, the Court has set aside those enactments that contravene the Fifth Amendment—or has held the United States liable to pay just compensation.

FEDERAL POLICY: FAILURE OF THE "TRUST RESPONSIBILITY" AND ALTERNATIVE REVENUE SOURCE TO INDIAN GAMBLING

The statistics are disheartening. According to U.S. government figures, the rates of poverty and unemployment among Native Americans are the highest of any ethnic group in the U.S., whereas per capita income, education, home ownership, and similar indices are among the lowest. Statistics on health care, alcoholism, incarceration, and so forth, are similarly bleak. . . .

The poor economic conditions in Indian country have contributed to the same extensive social ills generated in other impoverished communities including high crime rates, child abuse, illiteracy, poor nutrition, and poor health care access.

But with revenues from gambling operations, many tribes have begun to take unprecedented steps to begin to address the economic as well as social problems on their own. For example, through gambling tribes have been able to provide employment to their members and other residents where the federal policies failed to create work. This has resulted in dramatic drops in the extraordinarily high unemployment rates in many, though not all, communities in Indian country and a reduction in welfare rolls and other governmental services for the unemployed.

Tribes also use gambling revenues to support tribal governmental services including the tribal courts, law enforcement, fire protection, water, sewer, solid waste, roads, environmental health, land-use planning and building inspection services, and natural resource management. They also use gambling revenues to establish and enhance social welfare programs in the areas of education, housing, substance abuse, suicide prevention, child protection, burial expenses, youth recreation, and more. Tribes have allocated gambling funds to support the establishment of other economic ventures that will diversify and strengthen the reservation economies. Gambling revenues are also used to support tribal language, history, and cultural programs. All of these programs have historically suffered from significant neglect and underfunding by the federal government. Although the problems these programs are aimed at reducing continue to plague Indian communities at significant levels, gambling has provided many tribes with the means to begin addressing them. There was no evidence presented to the Commission suggesting any viable approach to economic development across the broad spectrum of Indian country, in the absence of gambling.

THE MOVE TOWARD SELF-DETERMINATION

Over the past two centuries, the policy of the U.S. government toward the Indian tribes has oscillated between recognition of their separate status and attempts to culturally assimilate them into the broader society. Federal policy toward Indians in the first half of this century emphasized the latter and was characterized by an effort to reduce their separate status, culminating in the so-called Termination Policy of the 1950's. Under the Termination Policy, several Indian reservations were broken up and the land divided among members and some tribes were "terminated" and declared no longer in existence. This policy was reversed in the 1960's and 1970's when Native American self-awareness and political movements expanded. At the same time, there was growing public awareness of the difficult economic and social conditions on reservations. As a result of these developments, the federal government's policy toward Native Americans shifted toward enhancing tribal self-determination and placing a greater emphasis on promoting economic and social development on the reservations. . . .

REVIEW OF REGULATIONS

IGRA provides a regulatory framework for the conduct of gambling on Indian lands. It divides the gambling into three classes, each with a separate treatment:

• Class I consists of traditional tribal games and social games for prizes of nominal value, all of which are subject solely to tribal regulation;

• Class II consists of bingo, instant bingo, lotto, punch cards, and similar games and card games legal anywhere in the state and not played against the house. A tribe may conduct or license and regulate Class II gambling if it occurs in a "state that permits such gaming for any purpose by any person" and is not prohibited by federal law;

• Class III consists of all other games, including electronic facsimiles of games of chance, card games played against the house, casino games, pari-mutuel racing, and jai alai. Class III games may be conducted or licensed by a tribe in a state that permits such gambling for any purpose or any person, subject to a state-tribal compact. The compact may include tribal-state allocations of regulatory authority; terms of criminal justice cooperation and division of labor; payments to the state to cover the costs of enforcement or oversight; tribal taxes equal to those of the state; procedural remedies for breach of the compact; and standards for the operation of gambling, including licensing.

Class II Tribal/Federal (NIGC) Regulation

One of IGRA's provisions was the establishment of the National Indian Gaming Commission (NIGC), which was given certain regulatory and investigative functions regarding Indian gambling. Originally the NIGC's responsibilities were focused largely on Class II facilities, but the rapid growth in Class III operations has resulted in a shift of its emphases toward this sector of Indian gambling. . . .

Given the often opposing viewpoints between tribes and state governments, IGRA's requirement that the two parties negotiate compacts for Class III gambling has been the source of continuing controversy. On one hand, the federal courts have ruled that Indian tribes have a right to establish gambling facilities on their reservations; on the other hand, IGRA requires that compacts be negotiated between the tribes and the states, obviously requiring the state's consent. Clearly, some form of mutual agreement is required. Although most states and tribes seeking to open gambling facilities have managed to successfully negotiate compacts, many have not. When an impasse develops, each side commonly accuses the other of not negotiating "in

good faith" and there is no accepted method of resolution.

ELEVENTH AMENDMENT IMMUNITY FOR STATES

IGRA contains a provision for resolving such impasses, at least when it has been the state that is accused of not negotiating in good faith: the tribe may sue the state in federal court. However, in *Seminole Tribe of Florida* v. *Florida,* a federal court found that this violated the Eleventh Amendment's guarantee of state sovereign immunity.

This decision, which covers a plethora of legal issues, has been widely interpreted. It did not, however, declare invalid nor set aside any part of the Act, nor did it set aside any Class III gambling pacts already negotiated. Obviously, states and tribes may continue to voluntarily enter into new compacts.

One immediate and continuing effect of the *Seminole* decision is that a tribe has no judicial recourse if it believes a state has failed to comply with IGRA's "good faith" provisions. The *Seminole* decision contributed to a stalemate in negotiations between a number of tribal and state governments, a stalemate that continues nearly three years after the *Seminole* decision.

STATE CRITICISM OF IGRA

Many states are unhappy with several of IGRA's provisions. In testimony before the Commission, representatives of the states have raised a number of areas of concern regarding Indian gambling, including: (1) The federal government does not actively and aggressively enforce IGRA on the reservations, and the states are unable to enforce it on their own; (2) IGRA requires states to negotiate in good faith but does not place the same requirement on tribes; and (3) the scope of gambling activities allowed to tribes is not clearly defined under IGRA. . . .

In an attempt to resolve the impasse caused by the *Seminole* decision and provide a mechanism for resolving state-tribal disputes regarding compacts, the Bureau of Indian Affairs published an "Advanced Notice of Proposed Rulemaking" (hereinafter, "ANPR") on May 10, 1996. The proposed procedures are a complex and lengthy series of steps involving repeated consultation with the respective tribes and states, but the key element is a provision that would allow the Secretary of the Interior to approve a tribe's request to operate gambling facilities, even if the state and tribe have been unable to agree on a compact. Tribes have strongly supported the ANPR because it would replace the remedy nullified by the *Seminole* decision; states have strongly opposed the proposal as an infringement on their sovereignty. . . .

OTHER MECHANISMS

Other mechanisms have been proposed for resolving the problems underlined by the *Seminole* case. For example, the Department of Justice might prosecute tribes in federal courts only when the state has acted in good faith or by suing states on behalf of the tribes when it determines that the states are refusing to comply with their obligations under IGRA. One scholar has argued for expansion of federal jurisdiction to allow for federal resolution of state-tribal disputes. Senator Daniel Inouye (D-Hawaii) has suggested that both states and tribes agree to waive their sovereign immunity on this issue. No proposal, however, has

secured the agreement of tribes and states.

OTHER ISSUES FOR CONSIDERATION

TAXATION

Few topics regarding Indian gambling have generated more controversy and heated dispute than the subject of taxation.

As governmental entities, tribal governments are not subject to federal income taxes. Instead, the Internal Revenue Service classifies tribal governments as non-taxable entities. As Indian casinos are owned and often operated by the tribes, the net revenues from these facilities go directly into the coffers of the tribal governments. Some proponents of Indian gambling argue that these revenues are thus taxed at a rate of 100 percent.

As noted above, IGRA requires that the revenues generated by Indian gambling facilities be used for tribal governmental services and for the economic development of the tribe. To the extent that the revenues are used for these purposes, they are not subject to federal taxes. The major exception concerns per-capita payments of gambling revenues to eligible tribal members. According to IGRA, if any gambling revenues remain after a tribe's social and economic development needs have been met, and its tribal government operations have been sufficiently funded, then per-capita distributions can be made to eligible tribal members, if approval is granted by the Secretary of the Interior. Individuals receiving this income are then subject to federal income taxes as ordinary income.

State income taxes, however, do not apply to Indians who live on reservations and who derive their income from tribal enterprises. State income tax does apply to non-Indians working at Indian casinos, and to Indians living and working off the reservations, as well as to those Indians who live on reservations but who earn their income at non-tribal operations off the reservations.

In general, state and local government taxes do not apply to tribes or tribal members living on reservations. However, many of the state-tribal compacts that have been negotiated contain provisions for payments by the tribes to state governments, which may or may not then allocate some of the proceeds to local governments. . . .

RECOMMENDATIONS

6.1 The Commission acknowledges the central role of the National Indian Gaming Commission (NIGC) as the lead federal regulator of tribal governmental gambling. The Commission encourages the Congress to assure adequate NIGC funding for proper regulatory oversight to ensure integrity and fiscal accountability. The Commission supports the NIGC's new Minimum Internal Control Standards, developed with the help of the National Tribal Gaming Commissioners and Regulators, as an important step to ensure such fiscal accountability. The Commission recommends that all Tribal Gaming Commission work ensures that the tribal gambling operations they regulate meet or exceed these Minimum Standards, and that the NIGC focus special attention on tribal gambling operations struggling to comply with these and other regulatory requirements.

6.2 The Commission recommends that IGRA's classes of gambling be clearly defined so that there is no confusion as to what forms of gambling constitute Class II and Class III gambling activities.

Further, the Commission recommends that Class III gambling activities should not include any activities that are not available to other persons, entities or organizations in a state, regardless of technological similarities. Indian gambling should not be inconsistent with the state's overall gambling policy.

6.3 The Commission recommends that labor organizations, tribal governments, and states should voluntarily work together to ensure the enforceable right of free association—including the right to organize and bargain collectively—for employees of tribal casinos. Further, the Commission recommends that Congress should enact legislation establishing such worker rights only if there is not substantial voluntary progress toward this goal over a reasonable period of time. . . .

6.7 The Commission recommends that tribal and state sovereignty should be recognized, protected, and preserved.

6.8 The Commission recommends that all relevant governmental gambling regulatory agencies should take the rapid growth of commercial gambling, state lotteries, charitable gambling, and Indian gambling into account as they formulate policies, laws, and regulations pertaining to legalized gambling in their jurisdictions. Further, the Commission recommends that all relevant governmental gambling regulatory agencies should recognize the long overdue economic development Indian gambling can generate.

6.9 The Commission has heard substantial testimony from tribal and state officials that uncompacted tribal gambling has resulted in substantial litigation. Federal enforcement has, until lately, been mixed. The Commission recommends that the federal government fully and consistently enforce all provisions of the IGRA.

6.10 The Commission recommends that tribes, states, and local governments should continue to work together to resolve issues of mutual concern rather than relying on federal law to solve problems for them.

6.11 The Commission recommends that gambling tribes, states, and local governments should recognize the mutual benefits that may flow to communities from Indian gambling. Further, the Commission recommends that tribes should enter into reciprocal agreements with state and local governments to mitigate the negative effects of the activities that may occur in other communities and to balance the rights of tribal, state and local governments, tribal members, and other citizens. . . .

6.13 The Commission recommends that Congress should specify a constitutionally sound means of resolving disputes between states and tribes regarding Class III gambling. . . .

6.15 The Commission recommends that tribal governments should be encouraged to use some of the net revenues derived from Indian gambling as "seed money" to further diversify tribal economies and to reduce their dependence on gambling.

———————◆———————

The gambling known as business looks with austere disfavor upon the business known as gambling.
                                    AMBROSE BIERCE, *The Devil's Dictionary,* 1906

To a people whose culture, economy, and governance were based on ideas of the Enlightenment and what has come to be known as liberal democracy, the ways and worldviews of the Indians were anomalous at best, threatening at worst.
                                    W. DALE MASON, *Indian Gaming: Tribal Sovereignty and American Politics,* 2000

Arguably the greatest player in the history of professional basketball, five-time league Most Valuable Player Michael Jordan embraces the trophy for the 1990–91 National Basketball Association championship, the first of six titles the Chicago Bulls would win with Jordan, who led the league in scoring ten times. During his career Jordan also became the most recognized athlete in the world, thanks in part to an aggressive marketing strategy that had him endorsing a myriad of commercial products.

Shortstop Cal Ripken, baseball's "Iron Man," acknowledges the crowd at Baltimore's Camden Yards on September 6, 1995, after starting his 2,131st consecutive game for the Baltimore Orioles, eclipsing Hall of Famer Lou Gehrig's major league record and extending it to 2,632 games before ending his twenty-one year career in 2001.

SPORTS

The U.S. women's football (soccer) team celebrates winning the gold medal in the 1996 Summer Olympics, setting the stage for their triumph at the Women's World Cup in 1999. Their victory was viewed by many as the culmination of developmental football programs at the youth and collegiate levels and a payoff for initiatives to provide opportunities for women's sports.

On the last day of the 1998 season, the scoreboard at Busch Stadium in St. Louis, Missouri, shows the final score of the home run race between Chicago Cubs slugger Sammy Sosa and Cardinal Mark McGwire. After a prolonged strike in 1994 that canceled the World Series and soured many fans on baseball, the excitement of McGwire and Sosa's summer-long battle to break Roger Maris' Major League single-season home run record rejuvenated interest in the "national pastime."

Ed Reinke—AP/Wide World Photos

Sisters Serena (below left) and Venus Williams show off their trophies after the championship match of the 2001 U.S. Open. Venus defeated her sister to win her second straight U.S. Open title.

Reuters NewMedia Inc./Corbis

Doug Pensinger—Allsport/Getty Images

Lance Armstrong (above) of the U.S. Postal Service team celebrates his victory in the 2001 Tour de France during the final stage through Paris. It was Armstrong's third consecutive triumph in cycling's most storied race.

87.

Arturo Vargas: Latino Voters

During the 1990s, the size of the Latino population in the United States soared. Most of the increase was the result of immigration, particularly from Mexico and Central America. The 2000 census revealed that for the first time in American history, Hispanics had surpassed African Americans in population, thus becoming the largest minority group in the country. Though comprising a diversity of national origin, Latinos made their presence felt throughout American society in the last decades of the twentieth century, from sports and music to language and culture. In the 1990s Latinos entered politics as never before: the number of Latino officeholders more than doubled, and Latino voting rates increased similarly. Although in that decade Latinos voted for Democratic candidates in national elections by a margin of two to one, Republicans made significant inroads at the state level. For example, Texas Governor George W. Bush won close to half the Latino vote in the 1998 gubernatorial election. Both Bush and Al Gore courted Latino voters in the tightly contested presidential election of 2000. Arturo Vargas, executive director of the National Association of Latino Elected and Appointed Officials, delivered the following speech in Colorado Springs, Colorado, in September 1999. Excerpted below, his address examines the impact of Latino voters on the American political landscape.

Source: *Vital Speeches of the Day,* January 1, 2000.

I want to thank Phil Burgess, president of the Center for the New West, and Sol Trujillo, who is chairman of the Center's board and chairman and CEO of US West, for inviting me to be with you here this evening, and to speak about a topic that I think is very timely: the role of Latinos in American politics.

And I have to tell you, it is somewhat frightening to see two white, middle-aged men speaking better Spanish than your own niece and nephews.

Yet I believe it says a great deal about what is happening today with respect to Latinos and American politics. There are (and I do this for the benefit of my friends in the media) five main points I want to make with respect to this topic.

First, the impact of Latinos in the electorate is largely based upon the increase of Latinos in the general population.

Second, there has been a steady and consistent increase in Latino participation in voting since 1992, and much of this has been a result of a significant contribution of new citizens, newly naturalized citizens, who have had a demonstrable impact on the Latino electorate and their behavior.

Third, the political hostility toward immigrants and Latinos contributed to the increase of legal permanent residents applying for U.S. citizenship and participating in voting, which set the stage for an overwhelming support for Democrats from Latinos from 1994 through 1998.

Fourth, the concentration of Latinos in strategic states make their role in the Presidential election very important.

And, lastly, the next election will be a true test of whether this trend of increased Latino voter participation holds, and also will be a major opportunity for the Republican Party to make up some lost ground with Latinos.

In 1990, the Census Bureau counted 22.1 million Hispanics in the continental United States. When we (NALEO) count the number of Latinos in elected office, we include only the 50 states. We do not include elected officials in Puerto Rico. The 1990 census represented a 50% increase over 1980. Half of this increase was due to immigration. Half of that increase was due to natural factors, the difference of births or deaths.

Two weeks ago, the U.S. Census Bureau released population growth estimates from 1990 through 1998, and reported a 36% increase in the Latino population during this period. About 7.9 million Latinos were added to the U.S. population. Latinos now account for about 11% of the U.S. population, and in about five years, Latinos are expected to surpass African-Americans and become the second largest population group in the United States.

Latinos are a large and growing population as well as incredibly diverse: 63% of Latinos are of Mexican origin, about 14% are of Puerto Rican origin, 6% are of Cuban origin, and about 12% are of Central and South American origin.

In the West, the Latino population is overwhelmingly of Mexican origin with a strong and growing Central American population, particularly in California. In fact, Los Angeles has the largest concentration of Salvadorenos of anywhere outside of El Salvador, second only to Washington, D.C., and followed by Houston. The Latino population's diversity also is geographic. Latinos live in each of the 50 states, yet we are concentrated in a handful of states. Latinos also are incredibly diverse politically, which I will discuss shortly. Latinos are also a youthful population, which has a fundamental impact on Latino voting strength. Nationally, Latinos have a median age of about 26 years, compared to a median of 36 years for the Anglo population in the United States.

Thus, of every 100 Latinos, 40 of them are unable to vote because they are under 18. Of the remaining 60, about 40% of them cannot vote because they are not U.S. citizens. And when issues such as low levels of educational attainment, low levels of income, and low home ownership rates, are factored in, it is not hard to understand why 5% of the U.S. electorate is made up of Latinos while the U.S. population is 11%. Thus, when people claim, "Well, Latinos don't vote," this represents, I think, a lack of understanding about the nature of the Latino population. Often, Latinos do not vote because they cannot vote. Many are too young and many others are not citizens. Now, the age factor will adjust over time. The citizenship factor has been changing, and I will talk about that in a few seconds as well. Yet despite these factors that inhibit voting, there nevertheless has been a steady and consistent increase in Latino voting strength. . . .

How did Latinos vote? Well, in 1992, 65% voted for Clinton, and 25% for Bush. Nineteen ninety-four was the year of the Republican landslide, but it also was the year of Proposition 187 in California, which I believe really became the defining moment for Latino politics this decade. . . .

About 700,000 more Latinos voted in 1996 than in 1992, while the number of non-Latinos voting declined in absolute numbers. Thus, a phenomenon which is occurring is that as more Latinos are voting, more non-Latinos are not voting, which increases the overall Latino percentage of the electorate and makes the impact of Latinos so much stronger at the voting polls. Nineteen ninety-six also was the election that saw the strongest Latino support for a Democrat candidate. Clinton received about 71% of the Latino vote, while Dole received 21%, the lowest for a Republican candidate.

And there is a gender gap among Latinos, just as there is among non-Latinos. Eighty percent of Latinas voted for Clinton, and 60% of Latinos voted for Clinton. Fifty-three percent of the electorate in the Latino community is made up of women; the gender gap is even more pronounced among Latinos than among non-Latinos. . . .

Naturalized citizens are having a real impact on who Latino voters overall are. Many observers of Latino political behavior who have been following these trends in the Latino community believe that the increase in the interest in naturalization is a reaction, in fact, to Proposition 187 in California and to the welfare legislation passed by Congress in 1995 that denied benefits to legal, permanent residents. Not undocumented immigrants, but to legal, permanent residents.

Many of these citizens during this period of overt hostility toward immigrants, and Latinos specifically, sought out U.S. citizenship, I believe, as an act of self-defense, out of anger, out of fear, and out of a real desire to play a role in politics. And they have had an impact on the Latino vote overall. Eighty percent of the new voters voted for Clinton and only 5% of the new voters voted for Dole. . . .

A new generation has emerged, although not necessarily permanently, a generation of Latino voters who vote religiously and vote to support Democratic candidates. In the 1998 elections, Latino

support helped in Congressional, state legislative and statewide races throughout the State of California and in the West. Again, the Tomas Rivera Policy Institute reported that [California Governor Pete] Wilson's high negatives among Latinos really dragged down Republican candidates. In fact, in a 1997 special election for a state legislative race in a heavily Latino and heavily immigrant district where all the candidates were Latinos, the one who won in a landslide used the message that he was the best candidate to oppose Pete Wilson's policies.

Now, he was going to be one of 80 members of a legislature, but his campaign was, "I'm the best one to go up against Pete Wilson," and he won in a landslide in a Latino district.

Gubernatorial candidate Gray Davis also was a huge beneficiary of the Latino vote. Eight-one percent of Latinos voted for Davis; 77% of Latinos voted for U.S. Senator Barbara Boxer. Cruz Bustamante, the first Latino to win a statewide race since 1871, was elected Lt. Governor. . . .

A critical element in producing Latino voters is organized labor. I encourage you to look at the role of labor unions in not just organizing Latinos to join labor unions, but organizing Latinos to turn out at the polls. Unions have had a demonstrable impact on California races and could be pivotal in the 2000 election.

Of course, there are notable exceptions to the Latino Democratic landslide, obviously George W. Bush in Texas is one of these exceptions. There are estimates that he received anywhere from 39% to 49% of the Latino vote in 1998. Some argue that Latino turnout in Texas was low to begin with, so it was only his hardcore supporters who turned out. So the percentage of Latino support that Bush received may not necessarily represent his strength throughout all the Latino community. Yet the bottom line is the Governor is popular among Latinos in Texas, and he had coattails as well. Tony Garza won statewide in the state of Texas as a Republican, and he now sits on the Texas Railroad Commission. California elected three Republican Latinos to the State Assembly, joining the one who was elected in 1996. There are now four Latinos in the Assembly who are Republican, and 13 who are Democrat. And there are two caucuses: the Latino Legislative Caucus that is Democrat, and a Hispanic Republican Caucus. Great diversity for the community that I think is very healthy. . . .

The Republican strategy is really to try to get at least 40% of the Hispanic vote. If Republicans get 40% of the vote, they believe they will have been successful. They claim that they are going to work hard for the Latino vote. They are going to put money into TV ads, something that we have not seen nationally since the 1988 race between George Bush and Michael Dukakis. Bush is attractive to the Latinos. He has a base in Texas, and his brother (Gov. Jeb Bush) is very popular among Latinos in Florida where he received 67% of the Latino vote. Bush is also consciously distancing himself in California from Pete Wilson. I have yet to see George W. Bush and Pete Wilson in the same room, and to me it is no surprise. George W. Bush opposes English Only. He supports vouchers, which in fact are popular among Latinos, and he has worked well with Hispanic leaders in Texas. . . .

I think the debates over the Census and sampling were harmful to the Republican Party. The Census is an issue that is very keen in the Latino community. Latino organizations and Latino leaders made the census a priority in 1970, 1980 and 1990, and we will again in the year 2000.

Latino organizations and leaders are engaging in comprehensive outreach efforts to educate Latinos about the importance of being counted in the Census. Whenever anybody puts himself in the position of appearing not to advocate for a full Census count, it sends a strong message to Latinos that you are not on their side.

There are a couple of other issues before Congress this session that also could hurt the image of the Republican party among Latinos. The restructuring of the INS is being proposed in a way that my organization opposes—my board of directors, which is 20% Republican—opposes. Congress is proposing to cut funds for bilingual education, which has strong support among Latinos. . . .

The big question is, will the trend of voter participation among Latinos continue in the year 2000? There are some indications that the factors contributing to low voter turnout overall, the good old American political apathy, may be catching up to Latinos and affecting them as well.

The sting of Proposition 187, welfare reform, Proposition 227 may be fading. And other than in Arizona, where there is another initiative to eliminate bilingual education, there do not seem to be emerging other wedge issues that may be galvanizing Latinos like they were in 1994, 1996 and 1998.

Ultimately, I believe, the candidate who can best convey a message to Latinos on the most important issues that they care about will have the advantage.

The most important issues for Latinos today are crime and drugs, education, and economic opportunity. Look for continued outreach to new voters. Look for the use of Spanish-language media to reach these voters.

As the Presidential race unfolds, Latinos are settling into a position where we have worked very, very hard to be. We want to be in a place where our vote is not taken for granted by Democrats or Republicans; where candidates consciously reach out to Latino voters and work hard to convince us that they offer the better alternative to advance our interests, and that political parties think twice about pursuing policies that will alienate Latinos.

This is essentially where we want to be. We are not there yet, but I think we are well on our way. Thank you.

88.

ANDREW SULLIVAN: Hate Crimes

In addition to ending public segregation, the Civil Rights Movement of the 1950s and 1960s created a new public consciousness of the role of race and discrimination in American life. In the movement's aftermath, there grew a widespread belief that the federal government had an obligation to preserve and promote equality. Controversy soon arose, however, over the question of how the government should go about doing so. The adoption of affirmative action programs and federally mandated school busing in the 1970s shattered the national consensus on civil rights and set off a debate over the government's role. The debate continued into the 1990s, when Congress passed hate crime legislation categorizing as a civil rights violation "crimes that manifest evidence of prejudice based on race, religion, sexual orientation, or ethnicity." Critics charged that motives for crime were often too elusive to categorize and that such legislation created inequalities in the criminal justice system. Others cited the 1998 murder of James Byrd, a black man, by three white supremacists in Texas, or the 1998 killing of Matthew Shepard, a gay college student in Wyoming, as evidence of the need for hate crimes legislation. Andrew Sullivan, former editor of The New Republic *magazine, addressed the issue in an essay entitled "What's So Bad About Hate?" for the* The New York Times Magazine. *It is excerpted here.*

Source: *The New York Times Magazine*, September 26, 1999, "What's So Bad About Hate?"

I WONDER what was going on in John William King's head two years ago when he tied James Byrd, Jr.'s feet to the back of a pickup truck and dragged him three miles down a road in rural Texas. King and two friends had picked up Byrd, who was black, when he was walking home, half drunk, from a party. As part of a bonding ritual in their fledgling white supremacist group, the three men took Byrd to a remote part of town, beat him, and chained his legs together before attaching them to the truck. Pathologists at King's trial testified that Byrd was probably alive and conscious until his body finally hit a culvert and split in two. When King was offered a chance to say something to Byrd's family at the trial, he smirked and uttered an obscenity.

We know all these details now, many months later. We know quite a large amount about what happened before and after. But I am still drawn, again and again, to the flash of ignition, the moment when fear and loathing became hate, the instant of transformation when King became hunter and Byrd became prey.

What was that? And what was it when Buford Furrow, Jr., longtime member of the Aryan Nations, calmly walked up to a Filipino-American mailman he happened to spot, asked him to mail a letter, and then shot him at point-blank range? Or when Russell Henderson beat Matthew Shepard, a young gay man, to a pulp, removed his shoes, and then, with the help of a friend, tied him to a post, like a dead coyote, to warn off others?

For all our documentation of these crimes and others, our political and moral disgust at them, our morbid fascination with them, our sensitivity to their social meaning, we seem at times to have no better idea now than we ever had of what exactly they were about. About what that moment means when, for some reason or other, one human being asserts absolute, immutable superiority over another. About not the violence, but what the violence expresses. About what—exactly—hate is. And what our own part in it may be.

I find myself wondering what hate actually is in part because we have created an entirely new offense in American criminal law—a "hate crime"—to combat it. And barely a day goes by without someone somewhere declaring war against it. Last month President Clinton called for an expansion of hate-crime laws as "what America needs in our battle against hate." A couple of weeks later, Senator John McCain used a campaign speech to denounce the "hate" he said poisoned the land. New York's mayor, Rudolph Giuliani, recently tried to stop the Million Youth March in Harlem on the grounds that the event was organized by people "involved in hate marches and hate rhetoric."

The media concur in their emphasis. In 1985, there were eleven mentions of "hate crimes" in the national media database Nexis. By 1990, there were more than a thousand. In the first six months of 1999, there were seven thousand. "Sexy fun is one thing," wrote a *New York Times* reporter about sexual assaults in Woodstock '99's mosh pit. "But this was an orgy of lewdness tinged with hate." And when Benjamin Smith marked the Fourth of July this year by targeting blacks, Asians, and Jews for murder in Indiana and Illinois, the story wasn't merely about a twisted young man who had emerged on the scene. As the *Times* put it, "Hate arrived in the neighborhoods of Indiana University, in Bloomington, in the early-morning darkness."

But what exactly was this thing that arrived in the early-morning darkness? For all our zeal to attack hate, we still have a remarkably vague idea of what it actually is. A single word, after all, tells us less, not more. For all its emotional punch, "hate" is far less nuanced an idea than prejudice, or bigotry, or bias, or anger, or even mere aversion to others. Is it to stand in for all these varieties of human experience—and everything in between? If so, then the war against it will be so vast as to be quixotic. Or is "hate" to stand for a very specific idea or belief, or set of beliefs, with a very specific object or group of objects? Then waging war against it is almost certainly unconstitutional. Perhaps these kinds of questions are of no concern to those waging war on hate. Perhaps it is enough for them that they share a sentiment that there is too much hate and never enough vigilance in combating it. But sentiment is a poor basis for law and a dangerous tool in politics. It is better to leave some unwinnable wars unfought. . . .

And why is hate for a group worse than hate for a person? In Laramie, Wyoming, the now-famous "epicenter of homophobia," where Matthew Shepard was brutally beaten to death, vicious murders are not unknown. In the previous twelve months, a fifteen-year-old pregnant girl was found east of the town with seventeen stab wounds. Her thirty-eight-year-old boyfriend was apparently angry that she had refused an abortion and left her in the Wyoming foothills to bleed to death. In the summer of 1998, an eight-year-old Laramie girl was abducted, raped, and murdered by a pedophile, who disposed of her young body in a garbage dump. Neither of these killings was deemed a hate crime, and neither would be designated as such under any existing hate-crime law. Perhaps because of this, one crime is an international legend; the other two are virtually unheard of.

But which crime was more filled with hate? Once you ask the question, you realize how difficult it is to answer. Is it more hateful to kill a stranger or a lover? Is it more hateful to kill a child than an adult? Is it more hateful to kill your own child than another's? Under the law before the invention of hate crimes, these decisions didn't have to be taken. But under the law after hate crimes, a decision is essential. A decade ago, a murder was a murder. Now, in the era when group hate has emerged as our cardinal social sin, it all depends.

The supporters of laws against hate crimes argue that such crimes should be disproportionately punished because they victimize more than the victim. Such crimes, these advocates argue, spread fear, hatred, and panic among whole populations and therefore merit more concern. But of course all crimes victimize more than the victim and spread alarm in the society at large. Just think of the terrifying church shooting in Texas

only two weeks ago. In fact, a purely random murder may be even more terrifying than a targeted one, since the entire community and not just a part of it feels threatened. High rates of murder, robbery, assault, and burglary victimize everyone, by spreading fear, suspicion, and distress everywhere. Which crime was more frightening to more people this summer: the mentally ill Buford Furrow's crazed attacks in Los Angeles, killing one, or Mark Barton's murder of his own family and several random day-traders in Atlanta, killing twelve? Almost certainly the latter. But only Furrow was guilty of "hate."

One response to this objection is that certain groups feel fear more intensely than others because of a history of persecution or intimidation. But doesn't this smack of a certain condescension toward minorities? Why, after all, should it be assumed that gay men or black women or Jews, for example, are as a group more easily intimidated than others? Surely in any of these communities there will be a vast range of responses, from panic to concern to complete indifference. The assumption otherwise is the kind of crude generalization the law is supposed to uproot in the first place. And among these groups, there are also likely to be vast differences. To equate a population once subjected to slavery with a population of Mexican immigrants or third-generation Holocaust survivors is to equate the unequatable. In fact, it is to set up a contest of vulnerability in which one group vies with another to establish its particular variety of suffering, a contest that can have no dignified solution.

Rape, for example, is not classified as a hate crime under most existing laws, pitting feminists against ethnic groups in a battle for recognition. If, as a solution to this problem, everyone except the white straight able-bodied male is regarded as a possible victim of a hate crime, then we have simply created a two-tier system of justice in which racial profiling is reversed, and white straight men are presumed guilty before being proved innocent, and members of minorities are free to hate them as gleefully as they like. But if we include the white straight male in the litany of potential victims, then we have effectively abolished the notion of a hate crime altogether, for if every crime is possibly a hate crime, then it is simply another name for crime. All we will have done is widened the search for possible bigotry, ratcheted up the sentences for everyone, and filled the jails up even further. . . .

The truth is, the distinction between a crime filled with personal hate and a crime filled with group hate is an essentially arbitrary one. It tells us nothing interesting about the psychological contours of the specific actor or his specific victim. It is a function primarily of politics, of special-interest groups carving out particular protections for themselves, rather than a serious response to a serious criminal concern. In such an endeavor, hate-crime law advocates cram an entire world of human motivations into an immutable, tiny box called hate and hope to have solved a problem. But nothing has been solved, and some harm may even have been done.

In an attempt to repudiate a past that treated people differently because of the color of their skin or their sex or religion or sexual orientation, we may merely create a future that permanently treats people differently because of the color of their skin or their sex, religion, or sexual orientation. This notion of a hate crime, and the concept of hate that lies behind it, takes a psychological mystery and turns it into a facile political artifact. Rather than compounding this error and extending it even further, we should seriously consider repealing the concept altogether.

To put it another way: violence can and should be stopped by the government. In a free society, hate can't and shouldn't be. The boundaries between hate and prejudice and between prejudice and opinion and between opinion and truth are so complicated and blurred that any attempt to construct legal and political fire walls is a doomed and illiberal venture. We know by now that hate will never disappear from human consciousness; in fact, it is probably, at some level, definitive of it. We know after decades of education measures that hate is not caused merely by ignorance and, after decades of legislation, that it isn't cured entirely by law.

To be sure, we have made much progress. Anyone who argues that America is as inhospitable to minorities and to women today as it has been in the past has not read much history. And we should of course be vigilant that our most powerful institutions, most notably the government, do not actively or formally propagate hatred, and insure that the violent expression of hate is curtailed by the same rules that punish all violent expression.

But after that, in an increasingly diverse culture, it is crazy to expect that hate, in all its variety, can be eradicated. A free country will always mean a hateful country. This may not be fair, or perfect, or admirable, but it is reality, and while we need not endorse it, we should not delude ourselves into thinking we can prevent it. That is surely the distinction between toleration and tolerance. Tolerance is the eradication of hate; toleration is coexistence despite it. We might do better as a culture and as a polity if we concentrated more on achieving the latter than the former. We would certainly be less frustrated.

And by aiming lower, we might actually reach higher. In some ways, some expression of prejudice serves a useful social purpose. It lets off steam; it allows natural tensions to express themselves incrementally; it can siphon off conflict through words rather than actions. Anyone who has lived in the ethnic shouting match that is New York City knows exactly what I mean. If New Yorkers disliked each other less, they wouldn't be able to get on so well. We may not all be able to pull off a Mencken—bigoted in words, egalitarian in action—but we might achieve a lesser form of virtue: a human acceptance of our need for differentiation without a total capitulation to it.

Do we not owe something more to the victims of hate? Perhaps we do. But it is also true that there is nothing that government can do for the hated that the hated cannot better do for themselves. After all, most bigots are not foiled when they are punished specifically for their beliefs. In fact, many of the worst haters crave such attention and find vindication in such rebukes. Indeed, our media's obsession with "hate," our elevation of it above other social misdemeanors and crimes, may even play into the hands of the pathetic and the evil, may breathe air into the smoldering embers of their paranoid loathing. Sure, we can help create a climate in which such hate is disapproved of—and we should. But there is a danger that if we go too far, if we punish it too much, if we try to abolish it altogether, we may merely increase its mystique, and entrench the very categories of human difference that we are trying to erase.

For hate is only foiled not when the haters are punished but when the hated are immune to the bigot's power. A hater cannot psychologically wound if a victim cannot psychologically be wounded. And that immunity to hurt can never be given; it can merely be achieved. The racial epithet only strikes at someone's core if he lets it, if he allows the bigot's definition of him to be the final description of his life and his person—if somewhere in his heart of hearts, he believes the hateful slur to be true. The only final answer to this form of racism, then, is not majority persecution of it but minority indifference to it. The only permanent rebuke to homophobia is not the enforcement of tolerance but gay equanimity in the face of prejudice. The only effective answer to sexism is not a morass of legal proscriptions but the simple fact of female success. In this, as in so many other things, there is no solution to the problem. There is only a transcendence of it. For all our rhetoric, hate will never be destroyed. Hate, as our predecessors knew better, can merely be overcome.

Hate crimes are a form of terrorism. They have a psychological and emotional impact which extends far beyond the victim. They threaten the entire community, and undermine the ideals on which the nation was founded.

Edward M. Kennedy, 1998

89.

Brooklyn Museum v. City of New York and Rudolph Giuliani

In September 1999 the Brooklyn Museum of Art prepared to host a display of the "Sensation" exhibit, a collection of works by contemporary British artists. The exhibit included many shocking images and artworks, including a picture of the Virgin Mary covered in elephant dung. The Royal Academy of Art in London first mounted the exhibit in 1997, at which time it attracted record crowds and considerable controversy. Home to one of the largest art collections in the United States, the Brooklyn Museum had a history of displaying controversial works, and it possessed major influence in the international art community. It also had a long-standing practice of promoting educational art programs for public schools. When New York City Mayor Rudolph Giuliani learned of the nature of "Sensation," his office attempted to prevent its exhibition in New York. Catholic leaders accused the exhibit of denigrating Catholicism, Congress condemned the museum's board as violators of public decency, and protesters flocked to the museum's doors. Giuliani even threatened to cut off all public funding for the museum. Despite the pressure, the museum's board not only refused to back down, it sued the city and Mayor Giuliani to prevent them from blocking the exhibit's display. The suit succeeded and the exhibit ran until January 2000. Giuliani responded by establishing a decency panel to monitor art exhibits in the city's museums. The decision in favor of the museum was rendered by U.S. District Judge Nina Gershon. Portions of her ruling are reprinted below.

Source: United States District Court, Eastern District of New York, 99 CV 6071.

THE MAYOR of the City of New York has decided that a number of works in the Brooklyn Museum's currently showing temporary exhibit "Sensation: Young British Artists from the Saatchi Collection" are "sick" and "disgusting" and, in particular, that one work, a painting entitled "The Holy Virgin Mary" by Chris Ofili, is offensive to Catholics and is an attack on religion. As a result, the City has withheld funds already appropriated to the Museum for operating expenses and maintenance and, in a suit filed in New York State Supreme Court two days after the Museum filed its suit in this court, seeks to eject the Museum from the City-owned land and building in which the Museum's collections have been housed for over one hundred years.

The Museum seeks a preliminary injunction barring the imposition of penalties by the Mayor and the City for the Museum's exercise of its First Amendment rights. The City and the Mayor move to dismiss the Museum's suit in this court, insofar as it seeks injunctive and declaratory relief, on the ground that this court must abstain from exercising jurisdiction in favor of the New York court action, in which, they argue, the

Museum may assert, by way of defense and counterclaim, its First Amendment claims. For the reasons that follow, defendants' motion is denied, and plaintiff's motion is granted. . . .

III. THE CONTROVERSY OVER THE SENSATION EXHIBIT

The Sensation Exhibit was first shown in 1997 at the Royal Academy of Art in London, where it drew record crowds for a contemporary art exhibit and generated controversy and some protest demonstrations. The Brooklyn Museum's Director, Arnold Lehman, viewed the Exhibit in London and decided to attempt to bring it to New York after its scheduled showing at a museum in Berlin. The Exhibit includes approximately ninety works of some forty contemporary British artists, a number of whom have received recognition by the artistic community. Chris Ofili, Damien Hirst, and Rachel Whiteread, for example, have received the Turner Award from the Tate Gallery. After being shown in Brooklyn, the Exhibit is scheduled to be shown at the National Gallery of Australia, and the Toyota City Museum outside of Tokyo.

Mr. Lehman's efforts to bring the Exhibit to Brooklyn continued through 1998, and plans were finalized in April 1999. Mr. Lehman, starting in 1998, kept the Museum's Board of Trustees informed of his efforts, and of the Exhibit's controversial nature. The Mayor of the City is an *ex officio* member of the Board, but his representative did not attend certain meetings at which the Exhibit was discussed, although minutes of the meetings were sent to him. The Commissioner of the City's Department of Cultural Affairs, Schuyler Chapin, also is an *ex officio* member of the Board of Trustees. His designated representative did attend meetings regularly and re-

ceive minutes of Board meetings. On or about March 10, 1999, Mr. Lehman gave Commissioner Chapin a copy of the catalog for the Exhibit and discussed its content. The catalog includes photographs and descriptions of virtually all of the works in the Exhibit, including every work that the City now finds objectionable. For example, it contains a full page color photograph of "The Holy Virgin Mary" and a description of the materials of which it is made, including elephant dung. On or about April 6, 1999, Mr. Lehman sent letters to members of the Board of Trustees, including Commissioner Chapin and other public officials, stating that the Exhibit was controversial, and he set forth the Museum's plans to charge an admission fee for the Exhibit and to require that all children be accompanied by an adult. The letters specifically described the work of the artist Damien Hirst, recognized "for his sections of various animals (sharks, lambs, etc.) individually preserved and presented in sealed, formaldehyde-filled glass containers." The Museum issued a similar press release on about the same date. A *New York Times* article on April 8, 1999, entitled "British Outrage Heads for Brooklyn," described reactions of shock and condemnation, together with protests, that the Exhibit had generated in London, as well as accusations by detractors that the Exhibit promoted the commercial interests of Charles Saatchi, owner of all of the works in the Exhibit. The article described some of the controversial works in the Exhibit, including that of Hirst.

Commissioner Chapin, in a letter dated April 14, thanked Mr. Lehman for his "fascinating letter" about the Exhibit, which, he wrote, seemed designed to "shake up New York's art world." Commissioner Chapin voiced no objection to the Museum's planned admission policies and promised to convey "any thoughts about funding he might have." There is no evidence that the Mayor himself was personally aware of the specific contents of the Exhibit.

The Exhibit was scheduled to open to the public at the Museum on October 2, 1999. City officials first began raising objections to the Exhibit on September 22. On that date, Commissioner Chapin, stating that he was acting on behalf of the Mayor, advised Mr. Lehman by telephone that the City would terminate all funding to the Museum unless it canceled the Exhibit. Commissioner Chapin specifically referred to the fact that the Mayor found objectionable "The Holy Virgin Mary" by Chris Ofili. (All of the five Ofili works in the Exhibit use elephant dung together with other materials. In addition, on the painting entitled "The Holy Virgin Mary," there are small photographs of buttocks and female genitalia scattered on the background.) The Mayor explained his position publicly that day, taking particular exception to "The Holy Virgin Mary." The Mayor stated that this work "offends me" and "is sick," and he explained his decision to terminate City funding as follows:

> You don't have a right to a government subsidy to desecrate someone else's religion. And therefore we will do everything that we can to remove funding from the [Museum] until the director comes to his senses. And realizes that if you are a government subsidized enterprise then you can't do things that desecrate the most personal and deeply held views of the people in society.

The Mayor also referred to a Hirst work of two pigs in formaldehyde as "sick stuff" to be exhibited in an art museum.

The following day, the Mayor accused the Museum of violating the Lease by mounting an exhibit which was inaccessi-ble to schoolchildren and by failing to obtain his permission to restrict access to the Exhibit, which he made clear he would not give because of his view that taxpayer-funded property should not be used to "desecrate religion" or "do things that are disgusting with regard to animals." In a letter from New York City Corporation Counsel Michael D. Hess to Mr. Lehman, dated September 23, 1999, Mr. Hess stated that "[t]he Mayor will not approve a modification of the Contract to allow [the Museum] to restrict admission to the museum. In light of the fact that [the Museum] has already determined that it would be inappropriate for those under 17 years of age to be admitted to the exhibit without adult supervision (a determination with which the City does not disagree), [the Museum] cannot proceed with the exhibit as planned."

The Mayor and other senior City officials continued, and escalated, their attacks on the Exhibit and their threats to the Museum, vowing to cut off all funding, including construction funding, to seek to replace the Board of Trustees, to cancel the Lease, and to assume possession of the Museum building, unless the Exhibit were canceled. The Mayor asserted on September 24 that he would not "have any compunction about trying to put them out of business, meaning the board." On September 28, the Mayor publicly stated that taxpayer dollars should not "be used to support the desecration of important national or religious symbol, of any religion." A City press release that day denounced "an exhibit which besmirches religion and is an insult to the community." The press release announced that, in response to the Museum Board's formal decision that day to proceed with the Exhibit, the City would end its funding of the Museum immediately. In his deposition, Deputy Mayor Joseph Lhota acknowledged that he had earlier told the Chairman of the Museum's Board of Trustees, Robert Rubin, that all City funding to the Museum would be canceled unless the Museum agreed to remove "The Holy Virgin Mary" from the Exhibit.

In response to the City's threats, including explicit statements by senior officials that the City would withhold its monthly payment of $497,554 due on October 1, 1999, the Museum commenced this action against the City and the Mayor on September 28, 1999, pursuant to 42 U.S.C. § 1983, seeking declaratory and injunctive relief, to prevent the defendants from punishing or retaliating against the Museum for displaying the Exhibit, in violation of the Museum's rights under the First and Fourteenth Amendments, including cutting off funding, terminating the lease, seizing the building or attempting to fire the Board of Trustees. The City has in fact withheld the scheduled October payment to the Museum. Plaintiff filed an amended complaint on October 1, 1999, adding claims for damages against the defendants, and claims of violation on the Equal Protection Clause and state and local law. . . .

THE FIRST AMENDMENT CLAIM: THE MUSEUM'S MOTION FOR A PRELIMINARY INJUNCTION

STANDARD FOR ISSUING A PRELIMINARY INJUNCTION

A party seeking a preliminary injunction must ordinarily demonstrate (a) irreparable harm and (b) either (1) likelihood of success on the merits or (2) sufficiently serious questions going to the merits to make them a fair ground of litigation and a balance of hardships tipping decidedly in its favor. *Time Warner Cable of New York City* v. *Bloomberg L.P.,* 118

F.3d 917, 923 (2d Cir. 1997). The defendants argue that the second, lesser standard is inapplicable to them as governmental actors, but the kind of governmental conduct entitled to a "higher degree of deference" and therefore requiring a showing of a likelihood of success on the merits, *see Able* v. *United States,* 44 F.3d 128, 131 (2d Cir. 1995) (per curiam), is not involved in this case, where defendants essentially rely on the Lease, which restates the purposes of the enabling legislation, and the Contract.[3] In any event, as will be seen, the Museum easily establishes a likelihood of success on the merits. . . .

THE MUSEUM'S LIKELIHOOD OF SUCCESS ON ITS FIRST AMENDMENT CLAIM

"If there is any fixed star in our constitutional constellation, it is that no official, high or petty, can prescribe what shall be orthodox in politics, nationalism, religion, or other matters of opinion. . . ." *West Virginia State Bd. of Ed.* v. *Barnette,* 319 U.S. 624, 642 (1943). In keeping with that principle, the First Amendment bars

---

3. In *Able,* the Court found only the likelihood of success standard applicable where challenged governmental conduct was taken pursuant to "legislation or regulations developed through presumptively reasoned democratic processes," for such conduct is "entitled to a higher degree of deference and should not be enjoined lightly." 44 F.3d at 131. *See Association of Legal Aid Attorneys* v. *City of New York,* 1997 WL 620831, *2 (S.D.N.Y. 1997) (denying lesser standard where governmental action was taken in an effort to meet a statutory obligation). In contrast, where the challenged governmental action is not the result of such processes, either standard may be used. Thus, in *Time Warner,* the Court found both standards applicable where the governmental action was not taken pursuant to the "exercise of governmental regulatory authority" but was "'proprietary' in nature." 118 F.3d at 923-24. And in *Haitian Centers Council, Inc.,* v. *McNary,* 969 F.2d 1326, 1339 (2d Cir. 1992), vacated as moot sub nom. *Sale* v. *Haitian Centers Council, Inc.,* 509 U.S. 918 (1993), the Court noted that "Congress' broad grant of authority in the INA" is not sufficient, in the absence of specific statutory authority, to require a showing of likelihood of success where plaintiffs challenged conduct of the Immigration and Naturalization Service.

government officials from censoring works said to be "offensive," *Texas v. Johnson,* 491 U.S. 397, 414 (1989), "sacrilegious," *Joseph Burstyn, Inc. v. Wilson,* 343 U.S. 495, 531 (1952), "morally improper," *Hannegan v. Esquire,* 327 U.S. 146, 149 (1946), or even "dangerous," *Regan v. Taxation with Representation of Washington,* 461 U.S. 540, 548 (1983). "If there is a bedrock principle underlying the First Amendment, it is that the government may not prohibit the expression of an idea simply because society finds the idea itself offensive or disagreeable." *Texas v. Johnson,* 491 U.S. at 414. . . .

The City and the Mayor argue that they can avoid an injunction based upon the First Amendment because the showing of the Sensation Exhibit violates the Museum's statutory purposes and the terms of its Lease and Contract with the City. According to defendants, the withholding of financial support does not reflect a violation of the First Amendment but only an effort to vindicate the City's contractual rights. As in the *Cuban Museum* case [*Cuban Museum of Arts and Culture, Inc. v. City of Miami,* 766 F. Supp. 1121 (S.D. Fla, 1991)], this claim is pretextual. In addition, it is without evidentiary basis. The language of the statutes, the Lease and the Contract, and the undisputed evidence as to how the City itself has viewed these documents, shows a high likelihood that the Museum will defeat any claims that it is acting in

violation of its statutory and contractual purposes as an art museum providing the public with enjoyment and education about art.

Whether the art shown is perceived as offensive or respectful, vulgar or banal, "good" art or "bad" art, the Mayor and the City offer no basis for the court to conclude that the Exhibit falls outside the broad parameters of the enabling legislation.[4] Nor is there any basis for the City's accusation that the Museum has failed in its duty to educate.[5] As for the defendants' emphasis on the unsuitability of the Sensation Exhibit for children, they acknowledge that there is nothing in the Lease or Contract which requires that every exhibit be suitable for schoolchildren of all ages. Nor is there anything which prevents the Museum from imposing reasonable restrictions on the access of schoolchildren to certain exhibits, in order to accommodate the Museum's undisputed right to display what Deputy Mayor Lhota called "mature" works of art.[6]

There is also no language in the Lease or Contract that gives the Mayor or the City the right to veto works chosen for exhibition by the Museum. The Contract

---

4. The enabling Act describes the purposes of the Brooklyn Institute of Arts and Sciences to include "the establishment and maintenance of museums and libraries of art and science" for the provision of "popular instruction and enjoyment." The Brooklyn Museum boasts the second largest collection of art in the United States. It has vast, diverse permanent collections and every year offers many temporary exhibits. The Sensation Exhibit, despite its controversial nature, has been recognized by other prominent museums as worthy of public display, and some of its individual artists have been recognized with prestigious awards and exhibitions in prominent museums.

5. The Museum's extensive educational programs are undisputed. It is implementing several educational programs in conjunction with the Sensation Exhibit itself, including lectures, films, and panel discussions with critics and scholars. The Museum is also hosting an open public dialogue, entitled "Fast, Cheap and Out of Control? The Sensational and the Serious in Contemporary Art" to discuss the merits of the sensational aspects of the Exhibit. In addition, the Museum has volunteers to answer questions in the galleries, and a Student Critic Program for thirteen- to seventeen-year-olds.

6. In fact, the Lease and Contract state that the "public and private schools" of the City shall have access to the Museum at "reasonable times," thus seemingly acknowledging that the Museum may, under certain conditions, need to place restrictions on the access of schoolchildren. That the Brooklyn Museum is not limited to showing works suitable for children is further evidenced by the existence of the now independent Brooklyn Children's Museum, separately financed by the City, which was originally part of the Brooklyn Institute of Arts and Sciences, and is designed to cater to the needs of children.

provides for the City to make maintenance payments to the Museum, without stating any conditions regarding the content of the Museum's artworks. The inability of the City and the Mayor to identify any standard for what constitutes a Lease or Contract violation, other than the Mayor and Deputy Mayor's personal views, reinforces the conclusion that it has never been contemplated that the City or the Mayor would have veto power over the Museum's decisions as to what to display.[7] Deputy Mayor Lhota testified that there are no rules, regulations or procedures or even an *ad hoc* method for determining whether the City would view a particular work as inappropriate. The City's Procedures Manual confirms this.

That the advertising for the Exhibit cautions viewers that "the contents of the exhibition may cause shock, vomiting, confusion, panic, euphoria and anxiety" is not, as the City urges, an admission by the Museum that the Exhibit violates the Lease and Contract. Taking the advertising at face value (although the City has also argued that it is a crude effort to attract attention to the Exhibit), the City fails to show that art that is considered shocking, provocative, or disturbing gives rise to a violation of the Lease or the Contract.

The City and the Mayor argue that, if the court enjoins the withholding of its subsidy, the Museum will be free, under the protection of the First Amendment, to do anything at all, even transform itself into, for example, a museum of pornography. That, of course, is absurd. The Museum has been publicly supported for over one hundred years as a broad-based *art* museum. If it now sold its collections and became a pornography museum, the withholding of operating subsidies and the claims of a Lease or Contract violation would arise under vastly different facts from those presented here. The City and the Mayor have not shown that the funding provided has not been spent for the purpose authorized.

Finally, the City and the Mayor argue that they have a "duty" to withdraw support for the Museum because it showed paintings that are offensive and that desecrate religion in a public building. Given the Mayor's emphasis on the anti-Catholic sentiment he finds in the Ofili work, and despite the defendants' explicit disavowal of reliance on the Establishment Clause on oral argument, it is important to note the requirement that government remain neutral with regard to religious expression, whether "it manifest a religious view, an antireligious view, or neither." *Rosenberger* v. *Rectors and Visitors of the University of Virginia*, 515 U.S. 819, 841 (1995). In *Rosenberger*, the Supreme Court held unconstitutional a state university's denial of funding to a student journal solely because the journal espoused a Christian viewpoint. *See generally Joseph Burstyn, Inc.*, 343 U.S. 495.

It is undisputed that the Museum's permanent collections contain many reverential depictions of the Madonna as well as other religious paintings and ritual objects. Just as there is no suggestion that the Museum is violating the Establishment Clause and endorsing religion by showing these works, *see, e.g., Agostini* v. *Felton*, 521 U.S. 203 (1997) and *Lemon* v. *Kurtzman*, 403 U.S. 602 (1971), there can equally be no suggestion that the

---

7. Deputy Mayor Lhota said he would ask himself three questions when considering whether art should be allowed in the Museum: First, whether he would want his eight-year-old daughter to see it; second, does it desecrate anyone's religion; and third, will anyone who believes in animal rights be offended. However, he disavowed that an affirmative answer to any one of these questions would preclude the work from being displayed in the Museum, and he acknowledged that the Museum could show "controversial" works of art or works of art that are "mature," which he defined as works unsuitable for viewing by his eight-year-old daughter.

Museum is violating the Establishment Clause by showing Mr. Ofili's work. The question of endorsement is evaluated from the perspective of the "objective observer." *See Wallace v. Jaffree*, 472 U.S. 38, 76 (1985) (O'Connor, J., concurring). The Brooklyn Museum contains art from all over [the] world, from many traditions and many centuries. No objective observer could conclude that the Museum's showing of the work of an individual artist which is viewed by some as sacrilegious constitutes endorsement of anti-religious views by the City or the Mayor, or for that matter, by the Museum, any more than that the Museum's showing of religiously reverential works constitutes an endorsement by them of religion. The suggestion that the Mayor and the City have an obligation to punish the Museum for showing the Ofili work turns well-established principles developed under the Establishment Clause on their head. If anything, it is the Mayor and the City who by their actions have threatened the neutrality required of government in the sphere of religion.

CONCLUSION

The City's motion to dismiss is denied. As the Museum has established irreparable harm and a likelihood of success on its First Amendment claim, its motion for a preliminary injunction is granted.

One person's art may be another person's vice, but it also may be somebody's pornography industry.

Editorial, *Commonweal*, November 9, 1990

90.

D. STANLEY EITZEN: American Sport at the End of the Twentieth Century

No industry experienced more rapid growth in the twentieth century than the business of American sports. At the beginning of the century, three spectator sports dominated the public mind: baseball, horse racing, and boxing. By century's end, dozens of American sports commanded millions of fans and generated billions of dollars in total revenue. During this period sports also became a major focus of social change. The racial integration of professional baseball, for example, anticipated by two decades the civil rights legislation of the 1960s. The growing popularity of women's team sports, particularly soccer and basketball, resulted directly from the women's liberation movement of the 1970s. The public's fascination with sports shows no signs of waning any time soon. Indeed, the Super Bowl, the championship game of professional football, annually attracts over 500 million television viewers worldwide. The rise of sports as big business even includes amateur sports, particularly at the college and Olympic levels. College football games routinely attract tens of thousands of spectators, and several college stadiums seat over 100,000. In the address reprinted below, D. Stanley Eitzen, professor emeritus at Colorado State University, examines what sports tell us about American society. The speech was given at a symposium in Fort Collins, Colorado, in November 1998.

Source: *Vital Speeches of the Day*, January 1, 1999.

WE ARE HERE to consider sport through the assorted lenses of sociologists, sports journalists, and sports practitioners. For my contribution I will present a brief overview, focusing on several paradoxes that are central to sport as it has come to be.

Paradox: While seemingly a trivial pursuit, sport is important. On the one hand, sport is entertainment, a fantasy, a diversion from the realities of work, relationships, and survival. But if sport is just a game, why do we take it so seriously? Among the many reasons, let's consider four: First, sport mirrors the human experience. The introductory essay in a re-

cent issue of *The Nation*, which was devoted to sport, said this:

> Sport elaborates in its rituals what it means to be human: the play, the risk, the trials, the collective impulse to games, the thrill of physicality, the necessity of strategy; defeat, victory, defeat again, pain, transcendence and, most of all, the certainty that nothing is certain—that everything can change and be changed.

Second, sport mirrors society in other profound ways as well. Sociologists, in particular, find the study of sport fascinating because we find there the basic elements and expressions of bureaucratization, commercialization, racism, sexism, homophobia, greed, exploitation of the powerless, alienation, and the ethnocentrism found in the larger society. Of special interest, too, is how sport has been transformed from an activity for individuals involved in sport for its own sake, to a money-driven, corporate entity where sport is work rather than play, and where loyalty [to] players, coaches and owners is a quaint notion that is now rarely held. Also, now athletes are cogs in a machine where decisions by coaches and bureaucracies are less and less player-centered. I am especially concerned with the decisions made by big-business bureaucracies (universities, leagues, cartels such as the NCAA, corporations, and sports conglomerates such as Rupert Murdoch's empire, which just in the U.S. includes ownership of the Los Angeles Dodgers, the Fox network, FX, 22 local cable channels, the New York Post, 20 percent of L.A.'s Staples center, a sports arena now under construction, and the partial rights to broadcast NFL games for eight years and major league baseball for five years). Another powerful sports conglomerate is the Walt Disney Corporation which owns the Mighty Ducks of Anaheim, 25 percent of the Anaheim Angels and the option to buy the rest from Gene Autry's estate, ABCTV, ESPN, and like Murdoch, partial rights for eight years of NFL games and five years of major league baseball. While we're at it, let's list the Time Warner sports empire, where Ted Turner is the major player: this sports empire includes ownership of the Atlanta Braves, Atlanta Hawks, Atlanta Thrashers, the Goodwill Games, World Championship Wrestling, Turner Field plus the Atlanta arena now under construction, Sports Illustrated, Time Magazine, CNN, HBO, TNT, TBS, and Warner Brothers. They have a four-year deal as the NBA's cable partner. Obviously, sport is not a trivial pursuit by these media moguls.

A third reason why sports are so compelling is that they combine spectacle with drama. Sports, especially football, involve pageantry, bands forming a liberty bell or unfurling a flag as big as the football field, and militaristic displays with the drama of a situation where the outcome is not perfectly predictable. Moreover, we see excellence, human beings transcending the commonplace to perform heroic deeds. There is also clarity—we know, unlike in many other human endeavors, exactly who won, by how much, and how they did it.

Finally, there is the human desire to identify with something larger than oneself. For athletes, it is to be part of a team, working and sacrificing together to achieve a common goal. For fans, by identifying with a team or a sports hero, they bond with others who share their allegiance; they belong and they have an identity. This bond of allegiance is becoming more and more difficult as players through free agency move from team to team, as coaches are hired and fired and many times when coaches are successful they break their contracts to go to a more lucrative situation, leaving their players, assistants, and fans in their wake. The owners of many professional teams blackmail their cities for more lucrative subsidies or they'll move, which they sometimes do, leaving diehard fans without teams.

Paradox: Sport has the capacity to build character as well as encourage bad character. On the one hand, sports participation encourages hard work, perseverance, self-discipline, sacrifice. Following the rules, obeying authority, and working with teammates to achieve a common goal. Sport promotes fair play. Of the many examples of ethical behavior in sport, let me cite one. A month after Rockdale County (Georgia) won the state basketball championship in

1987, the coach Cleveland Stroud found that he had unknowingly used an ineligible player. Although the player in question was in the game only a minute or two and had not scored, Stroud notified the authorities of the infraction. As a result, the only state championship in the school's history was forfeited. Coach Stroud said, "you've got to do what's honest and right. People forget the scores of basketball games; they don't ever forget what you're made of." There are countless examples where competitors show respect for one another, where sportsmanship rules.

But for all of the honor and integrity found in sport there is also much about sport that disregards the ideals of fair play. Good sportsmanship may be a product of sport, but so is bad sportsmanship. Let me cite a few examples: (1) trashtalking and taunting opponents; (2) dirty play (a recent article in Sports Illustrated documented dirty play in the NFL, citing the ten worst offenders, saying that "there's a nasty breed of players who follow one cardinal rule: Anything goes, and that means biting, kicking, spearing, spitting, and leg-whipping"); (3) coaches who teach their players how to hold and not get caught; (4) faking being fouled so that a referee who is out of position will call an undeserved foul on the opponent; (5) trying to hurt an opponent; (6) coaches rewarding players for hurting an opponent; (7) throwing a spitter or corking a bat; (8) using illegal drugs to enhance performance; (9) crushing an opponent (a Laramie, Wyoming, girls junior high basketball team won a game a few years ago by a score of 81–1, using a full-court press the entire game); (10) fans yelling racial slurs; (11) coaches who, like Pat Riley of the Miami Heat, demand that their players not show respect for their opponents (Riley fines his players $1,500 if they help an opposing player get off the floor); (12) coaches who are sexist and homophobic, calling their male players pussies or fags if they are not aggressive enough; (13) a male locker room culture that tends to promote homophobia, sexism, and aggressive behaviors, and (14) coaches who recruit illegally, who alter transcripts and bribe teachers to keep players eligible, and who exploit players with no regard for their health or their education.

What lesson is being taught and caught when a coach openly asks a player to cheat? Consider these two examples. A few years ago, the Pretty Prairie Kansas High School had twin boys on his team. One of the twins was injured but suited up for a game where his brother was in foul trouble at half time. The coach had the twins change jerseys so that the foul-plagued twin would be in the second half with no fouls charged to the player's number he was now wearing.

In another instance, a high school football coach in Portland sent a player into the game on a very foggy night. The player asked: "Who am I going in for?" "No one," the coach replied, "the fog is so thick the ref will never notice you."

My point is that we live in a morally distorted sports world—a world where winning often supersedes all other considerations, where moral values have become confused with the bottom line. In this in-your-face, whip-your-butt climate, winning-at-any-price often becomes the prevailing code of conduct. And when it does, I assert, sport does build character, but it is bad character. When we make the value of winning so important that it trumps morality, then we and sport are diminished.

Paradox: While the nature of sport is competition where ability tells, the reality is that race restricts. Just as in other social realms, we find in sport that the ascribed status of race gives advantage to some and disadvantage to others. Let's look at racism in sport, focusing on African Americans since they are the dominant racial minority in American sport.

At first glance, its seems impossible that Blacks are victims of discrimination in sport since some of them make huge fortunes from their athletic prowess, such as Michael Jordan, who makes an estimated $80 to $90 million a year in salary, endorsements, and public appearances, and Tiger Woods, who, although just beginning his professional career, makes $30 to $40 million annually. Moreover, it is argued that Blacks in sport are not victims of discrimination because, while only constituting 12 percent of the general population, they comprise 65 percent of the players in professional football, 80 percent of professional basketball players, and 18 percent of the players in major league baseball (and where Latinos constitute another 18 percent). Also about 60 percent of the football and basketball players in big-time college programs are African Americans.

Despite these empirical facts that seem to contradict racism in sport, it is prevalent in several forms. Let me cite some examples. First, Blacks are rarely found in those sports that require the facilities, coaching, and competition usually provided only in private—and typically racially segregated—clubs; sports such as swimming, golf, skiing, and tennis. Black athletes also are rarely found where it takes extraordinary up-front money, usually from corporate sponsors, to participate such as in automobile racing.

But even in the team sports where African Americans dominate numerically, there is evidence of discrimination. Sociologists have long noted that Blacks tend to be relegated to those team positions where the physical attributes of strength, size, speed, aggressiveness, and "instinct" are important but that they are underrepresented at those playing positions that require thinking, leadership and are the most crucial for outcome control. This phenomenon, known as stacking, continues today, at both the college and professional levels in football and baseball.

African Americans are also underrepresented in nonplaying leadership positions. At the professional level team ownership is an exclusively all-White club. In the league offices of the NCAA, major league baseball, the NBA, and the NFL, the employees are disproportionately White. The same is true, of course, for head coaches in big-time college and professional sports.

African Americans are also underrepresented in ancillary sports positions such as Sports Information Director, ticket managers, trainer, equipment manager, scout, accountant, sportswriting, and sports broadcasting, especially play-by-play announcing.

Another consistent finding by sociologists is a form of discrimination known as "unequal opportunity for equal ability." This means that the entrance requirements for Blacks to college scholarships or to the professional leagues are more rigorous than they are for Whites. In essence, Black players must be better than White players to succeed in the sports world. In baseball, for example, Blacks consistently have higher statistics (batting average, home runs, stolen bases, earned run average) than Whites. What's happening here is that superb Black athletes are not discriminated against but the substars do experience discrimination. The findings clearly indicate that the undistinguished Black player is less likely to play regularly than the equally undistinguished White player. As sociologist Jonathan Brower has said, "in sport mediocrity is a white luxury."

Paradox: Schools emphasize sports because of the personal and social benefits for participants, yet these same schools have generally resisted efforts by girls and women for participation and resources equal to that of boys and men. Research shows many benefits from sports for girls and women. When female athletes are compared to their non-athlete peers, they are found to have higher self-esteem and better body image. For high school girls, athletes are less likely than nonathletes to use illicit drugs; they are more likely to be virgins; if sexually active they are more likely to begin intercourse at a later age; and they are much less likely to get pregnant. These advantages are in addition to the standard benefits of learning to work with teammates for a common goal, striving for excellence, and the lessons of what it takes to win and how to cope with defeat. Yet, historically, women have been denied these benefits. And, even today, the powerful male establishment in sport continues to drag its collective feet on gender equity.

Title IX, passed in 1972, mandated gender equity in school sports programs. While this affected schools at all levels, I'll focus on the college level because this is where women have met the most resistance. Since 1972 women's intercollegiate programs have made tremendous strides, with participation quadrupling from 30,000 women in 1971 to 116,272 in 1996. Athletic scholarships for women were virtually unknown in 1972, now women athletes receive 35 percent of the athletic scholarship money that is distributed. These increases in a generation represent the good news concerning gender equity in collegiate sport. The bad news, however, is quite significant. Looking at the data for big-time schools for the 1995–96 school year, we find the following disparities by gender:

1. Head coaches of women's teams were paid 63 cents for every dollar earned by coaches of men's teams (and this inequity does not include many of the extras the coaches of men's teams are more likely than the coaches of women's teams to receive—lucrative radio and television deals, endorsements, cars, country club memberships, sweetheart business deals, and housing allowances).

2. Only seven schools met the proportionality test for equity—i.e., the number of women athletes should be within 5 percent of the proportion of women undergraduates enrolled. The average negative gap was 16 percent.

3. The average gender composition of an athletic department was 292 male athletes and 163 female athletes (65 percent male and 35 percent female), with a similar disproportionate distribution of scholarships.

4. The recruiting budget was skewed in favor of males with a 76 percent/24 percent ratio.

5. Operational expenditures were distributed even more unevenly at 78 percent/22 percent. And, most telling, it was not uncommon for a school with a big-time football program to spend twice as much on its football team as it spent on all its women's sports combined.

6. In a most ironic twist, in 1972, when Title IX was enacted, more than 90 percent of women's teams were coached by women. But now that participation for women has quadrupled, the percentage of women's teams coached by women has dropped to 48 percent.

7. At the administrative level, women hold 36 percent of all administrative jobs in women's programs and only 19 percent of all women's programs are actually headed by a female administrator.

Clearly, as these data show, gender equity is not part of big-time college sports programs. In my view, universities must address the question: Is it appropriate for a college or university to deny women the same opportunities that it provides men? Shouldn't our daughters have the same possibilities as our sons in all aspects of higher education? Women are slightly more than half of the undergraduates in U. S. higher education. They receive half of all the master's degrees. Should they be second-class in any aspect of the university's activities? The present unequal state of affairs in sport is not inevitable. Choices have been made in the past that have given men advantage in university sports. They continue to do so, to the detriment of not only women's sports but also the so-called minor sports for men.

These are a few paradoxes concerning contemporary sport in the United States. There are more but I'll let my colleagues and the other panelists speak directly or indirectly to them. Let me conclude my remarks with this statement and a plea. We celebrate sport for many good reasons. It excites and it inspires. We savor the great moments of sport when an athlete does the seemingly impossible or when the truly gifted athlete makes the impossible routine. We exult when a team or an athlete overcomes great odds to succeed. We are touched by genuine camaraderie among teammates and between competitors. We are uplifted by the biographies of athletes who have used sport to get an education that they would have been denied because of economic circumstance or who have used sport to overcome delinquency and drugs. But for all of our love and fascination with sport and our extensive knowledge of it, do we truly understand it? Can we separate the hype from the reality and the myths from the facts? Do we accept the way sport is organized without questioning? Unfortunately for many fans and participants alike there is a superficial, uncritical, and taken-for-granted attitude concerning sport. Sportswriter Rick Reilly of Sports Illustrated has written that "sport deserves a more critical examination. We need to ask more probing questions about sport." That has always been my goal; it continues to be my goal; and I hope that it is yours as well.

To be perfectly honest, what I'm really thinking about are dollar signs.
TONYA HARDING, after winning the U.S. women's national figure
skating championship following the withdrawal of favored
Nancy Kerrigan, who was injured in an attack later
revealed to have been planned by Harding's husband,
quoted in *The New York Times,* January 15, 1994

2000

91.

Daniel P. Jordan: The Thomas Jefferson and Sally Hemings
Paternity Debate

Rumors that Thomas Jefferson had an affair with Sally Hemings, one of his slaves, began during his presidency. Jefferson himself neither admitted nor denied the allegations, and the general public viewed the matter as unsubstantiated political mudslinging. Until the late twentieth century, historians largely upheld that verdict, though in the 1870s two pieces of contradictory evidence had surfaced. On one hand, one of Hemings' sons claimed in a newspaper interview that Jefferson was his father; on the other, a new biography of Jefferson reported that his nephew was the father of all or most of Hemings' children. Published in 1968, Winthrop Jordan's White Over Black: American Attitudes Toward the Negro, 1550–1812 *added new fuel to the argument with its observation that Hemings had become pregnant only when Jefferson (who was away from home more than he was there) was in residence at Monticello. Increasingly the matter was debated in the context of the growing awareness of Jefferson's negative views of African Americans, as historians struggled to reconcile the image of Jefferson the democratic idealist with Jefferson the slaveholder. In this light, the nature of the alleged relationship became the focus of new debate. Was it a matter of love, rape, or something else? Still, the notion of a Jefferson-Hemings relationship remained a matter of conjecture and debate until 1998, when a DNA study of Hemings' descendants revealed that they were also descendants of the Jefferson family. The DNA results strongly suggested that Jefferson had indeed had a relationship with Hemings. The Jefferson Foundation at Monticello, Virginia, responded to the DNA results in a formal public statement, which is reprinted below.*

Source: Statement on the TJMF Research Committee Report on Thomas Jefferson and Sally Hemings, Thomas Jefferson Foundation, January 26, 2000.

When the DNA study was released on the evening of October 31, 1998, the Thomas Jefferson Foundation (TJMF) responded immediately. Within twenty-four hours, we held a press conference with Dr. Eugene Foster (principal author of the study), posted a statement on our web site, and instructed our interpreters to initiate conversations with our visitors about the study. The Foundation also pledged that it would evaluate the scientific results—and all other relevant evidence—in a systematic and comprehensive way, and that we would, in the Jeffersonian tradition, "follow truth wherever it may lead."

Shortly thereafter, I appointed a staff research committee that included four Ph.D.'s (one with advanced study in genetics) and an M.D. The mandate was straightforward: (1) to gather and assess critically all relevant evidence about the relationship between Thomas Jefferson and Sally Hemings; (2) to consult with outside experts as well as with two long-standing TJMF advisory committees, comprised of scholars, public historians, and museum professionals who provide counsel for the Foundation's International Center for Jefferson Studies and about African-American interpretation at Monticello; and (3) to report its findings and recommendations to me in written form and in a timely manner. The committee, headed by Dr. Dianne Swann-Wright, responded in a manner that was scholarly, meticulous, and thorough. The committee's report is attached. I believe it represents the most extensive compilation ever of what is known and not known about this complex and consequential topic. It also reflects the Foundation's abiding belief in sharing serious research with the broadest possible audiences.

I concur with the committee's findings. Although paternity cannot be established with absolute certainty, our evaluation of the best evidence available suggests the strong likelihood that Thomas Jefferson and Sally Hemings had a relationship over time that led to the birth of one, and perhaps all, of the known children of Sally Hemings. We recognize that honorable people can disagree on this subject, as indeed they have for over two hundred years. Further, we know that the historical record has gaps that perhaps can never be filled and mysteries that can never be fully resolved. Finally, we stand ready to review any fresh evidence at any time and to reassess our understanding of the matter in light of more complete information.

But for now, we will move forward to implement the findings of the research committee in a way that reflects the Foundation's ongoing commitment to scholarship. From the beginning, we have treated the Thomas Jefferson-Sally Hemings relationship as a research issue, and we will continue to do so. We believe it offers opportunities for the Thomas Jefferson Foundation, and that it will advance our firm belief in telling a story here that is accurate and honest—and thus inclusive—about Jefferson's remarkable life and legacy in the context of the complex and extraordinary plantation community that was Monticello.

It seems, then, that Jefferson defenders, in their reliance on stereotypes about carpetbaggers, former slaves, and slave narratives, took a shortcut and as a result created what can only be called bad history. . . . All of the ink that has been spilled purveying the notion that S. F. Wetmore invented the idea, or put Madison Hemings up to saying, that he was the son of Thomas Jefferson, turns out to have been just that: spilled ink.

ANNETTE GORDON-REED, *Thomas Jefferson and Sally Hemings: An American Controversy*, 1997

92.

George Marotta: The Stock Market Bubble

In the 1990s the U.S. stock market underwent an unprecedented expansion that surpassed even the boom years of the 1920s and helped to fuel the longest peacetime economic expansion in American history. After a brief recession in the early 1990s, the American economy grew robustly for the rest of the decade as the fledgling Internet and high-technology industries promoted a general expansion of the economy. Consumer confidence surged and investor confidence followed close behind. By the end of the 1990s, many market analysts declared that a "new economy" had been created, one that could not be gauged by traditional tools of valuation. Some even speculated that this new economy was recession-proof. There were market analysts, however, who took a more pessimistic view, arguing that the rules of the "old" economy still applied and that stock price overvaluation would create a market crash. The crux of the debate rested on the question of whether optimism about the market had created artificially inflated stock values or whether the stock values simply reflected the strength of the economy. In the March 2000 speech reprinted below, George Marotta, a research fellow at the Hoover Institution of Stanford University, takes the pessimistic view, which subsequently would be vindicated by the stock market's collapse in 2001.

Source: *Vital Speeches of the Day*, April 15, 2000.

THE DOW JONES Industrial Average [DJIA] is now trading at a level of 10,000. Some believe that it is hugely over-valued, that we are in a bubble, and that a big correction is overdue. Others believe the contrary, that it is actually undervalued and should continue to go higher. Which school is correct? Let's examine the arguments and then you can be the judge.

The U.S. economy over the past decade has been the envy of the world. Times have never been better, due largely to five fabulous years of stock market advance. Also, the economy in general is picture perfect with unemployment at 4 percent and inflation at 2 percent.

Economists have a simple tool to measure the health of the economy. It is called the "misery" index. It is the addi-tion of unemployment and inflation. Today, the misery index is at a very, very low level of 6. It wasn't always this rosy. I recall the misery index hit a level of 22 at the end of the 1970s, largely due to the high inflation and unemployment induced by the energy crisis.

Today, we are in the longest economic growth period since the end of World War II—107 months reached just last month. The economy raced ahead during the last quarter of 1999 at a rate of seven percent—the strongest in three years.

THE U.S. STOCK MARKET

Since the collapse of the Berlin Wall in 1989 and the demise of the Soviet Union in 1991, the U.S. stock market (the primary tool of our capitalistic society) has been celebrating the victory of free markets over communism. The prices of stocks have appreciated at a very rapid rate over the past five years, gaining over 20 percent annually during that period— one of history's best records.

Last year, the NASDAQ over-the-counter index rose an incredible 85 percent, compared with 25 percent for the Dow Jones Industrial Average. Most of the technology companies are traded on the NASDAQ market. The market value of all technology companies now totals 30 percent of all traded stocks, up from just 10 percent a decade ago.

Also for the first time, the market value of stocks on the over-the-counter market now exceed those on the New York Stock Exchange in value. Most of the "old" economy stocks are traded on the NYSE and companies of the "new" economy trade on the over-the-counter market. NASDAQ stocks are more highly valued than the NYSE stocks as they sell for 31 times their annual earnings compared with 23 times the annual earnings of companies on the New York exchange.

Forty-three percent of U.S. households or about 76 million Americans today own common stocks. That's an increase of 126 percent since 1982. The stock market advance is largely being fueled by baby boomers who are putting money away for their retirement.

Most retirement monies go into mutual funds, which often exceeds $20 billion a month.

All mutual funds reached a value of $1 trillion in 1995. Today, there is $4 trillion in 7,000 equity (common stock) funds alone.

At a level of 10,000, the most commonly quoted Dow Jones Industrial Index is near its highest level in history, which was reached in mid-January 2000 at a level of 11,750. The market has come a long way since August 1982 when the Dow was 777. The market made two major corrections since 1982. The first was the October 1987 bear market which dropped the Dow from 2,722 to 1,738. The second was the Kuwait War 1990 period when the Dow corrected from 2,999 to 2,384.

The ten largest common stocks in terms of market valuation are Microsoft, Cisco, General Electric, Intel, Exxon-Mobil, Wal-Mart, Lucent, Oracle, IBM, and Citigroup. Six of the ten are computer/technology stocks that were not among the top ten a decade ago. The top ten stocks in market value are the top ten stocks in the Standard & Poors 500 Stock Index. These top ten represent 26 percent of the market value of the 500 stocks.

On November 1, 1999, four "old economy" stocks were dropped from the Dow Jones Industrial Average to make way for "new economy" stocks which included Microsoft and Intel.

FOREIGN STOCK MARKETS

The U.S. stock market is the largest in the world and represents almost 40 percent of the value of all publicly-traded stocks in the world. The next largest stock market is Japan followed by the United Kingdom, Germany and France.

European stock markets have had similar good returns (as did the U.S. market), earning a total return of about 20 percent annually for the past five years. The European Union and the new Euro currency are revolutionizing that economy. The fourteen-member EU is creating an economy that is almost as large as the United States. Their goal is to create the economies-of-scale to better compete with the U.S. and Japan, to improve their grow rate, to reduce unemployment, to cut prices, and generally to improve their standards of living. Also, Europe is fast moving toward the "new" economy with some thinking that they are about 5 years behind the U.S. Sweden, Germany and France all have had better stock markets than the U.S. over the past year.

Japan is very slowly recovering from a decade-long recession. Their stock market dropped steadily from 1990 and a high of almost 40,000 in the Nikkei average to its present level of 20,000 (having risen steadily over the past two years from a low of 13,000). Last year, Japanese stocks rose more than U.S. stocks.

The Southeast Asia, Russian, and Mexican currency crises are largely over. In Southeast Asia in 1997, a currency meltdown and lack of confidence in Thailand spread to Malaysia, Indonesia, Hong Kong, Taiwan and South Korea. Their recovery is adding to the general advance in economies throughout the world. In fact, improved economies around the world is adding to the demand for oil which has risen from $13 a barrel to $31. If the price of U.S. gasoline rises to $2.50 a gallon this summer that will certainly add to an increase in inflation.

Lagging stock markets are found in Russia and Africa and in some emerging-market countries. Some former Third World countries are still making the transition from a farming to an industrial society, but many are dramatically altering and modernizing their national economic policies to benefit from the rapid growth of world trade. The market value of common stocks in the emerging-market countries has vaulted from a few percentage points to about twelve percent of total world valuation today.

WEALTH EFFECT

In January 2000, the value of all publicly traded stocks in the U.S. reached a new high of $13.8 trillion (this figure is obtained from the Wilshire 5000 index). The rising stock market is creating for Americans a feeling of prosperity and wealth which results in their increased spending.

Over the past five years, the total stock market capitalization has gone from $4.5 trillion at the end of 1994 to $13.5 trillion at the end of 1999. Divide this $9 trillion in new wealth by a population of 270 million and you get $33,333 for every man, woman and child. Of course, wealth is not that evenly divided, but you get the idea. Assuming equal distribution and a family of three, equity values have added $100,000 to the wealth of every family in just five years.

Federal Reserve Board Chairman Greenspan estimates that every $100 increase in stock wealth is translated into 3 or 4 dollars of increased consumer spending. As consumer spending makes up 70 percent of our GDP, he worries that this could have a big effect on pushing the economy into an inflationary mode.

THE BAD NEWS

The bad news is that we could be in a stock market bubble that if corrected quickly could bring to a halt, not only the prosperity of our country, but could seriously affect the world economy. Let's examine some common stock market statistics.

Market Capitalization: The market capitalization of all publicly traded stocks is now 160 percent of the annual Gross Domestic Product. It usually averages just 40 percent and only reached about 80 percent twice—before the 1929 crash and the 1987 market correction. From its peak in 1929, the DJIA fell 89 percent by mid-1932.

P/E Ratio: This average is currently very high for both the Dow, the S&P 500, and the NASDAQ indices. It represents the price of stock over last year's earnings, and from 1926 through 1994 it has averaged about 14. The Dow P/E is currently 65 percent higher than average and the S&P 500 is 121 percent higher. The eight largest NASDAQ capitalization stocks are trading at a price-earnings ratio of 50 which is 251 percent higher than average.

Dividend Yield: Dividend payment divided by stock price is the dividend yield. Yield on the Dow is now 1.4 percent whereas the average has been about 4 percent.

Price to Book Ratio: The book value per share divided into stock price is now 6, whereas the average has been about 2.

Average Length of Markets: Historically bull markets last three years and bear markets a little over one year. This current bull market is very aged at nine years.

Cash Reserves in Mutual Funds: Liquid reserves (or cash) now average only four percent of total assets in equity mutual funds, compared with a longtime average of about ten percent of assets. In case of a prolonged downturn, mutual funds may not be able to pay departing investors without having to sell securities which would magnify a downturn. Low cash level often occurs at market peaks; for example it was 4.5 percent in January 1973 before a severe two-year correction. In 1996 when cash reserves fell to 7 percent that was the lowest level in the previous 17 years.

Popularity of Growth and Index Funds: Investors may not realize the risk involved in investing in all-stock index funds. These funds are invested in companies on a market-weighted basis which means that a large percentage of monies are going into the few largest companies. For example, last year seven companies in the S&P 500 index contributed half of

that index's 25 percent gain: Microsoft, Cisco, GE, Wal-Mart, Nortel, Oracle, and AOL. Technology's equity market capitalization has doubled in the last four years. Last year, $131 billion went into aggressive and growth funds and the value of stock funds value rose from $3 trillion to $4 trillion. Sixty percent of mutual fund assets are now in common stocks versus only 22 percent in 1984 (a year in which sixty percent of assets were in money-market funds). The mutual fund which attracted the most money last year was the Vanguard S&P 500 Index fund which now totals $104 billion.

Irrational Expectations: A survey by Montgomery Securities of San Francisco reveals that investors are expecting returns of 34 percent annually over the next decade. Whereas, from 1926 through 1994, stocks have appreciated at an annual average rate of 11 percent.

Boomers' Inexperience: A major driving force behind the rising stock market are boomers investing for their retirement. However, few boomers have experienced a prolonged bear market such as the 1973-1974 downturn which dropped stocks 45 percent. It took 8 years for the market to recoup that loss. (Those born in 1945 were 28 in 1973 and were not saving seriously for retirement at that age.) Many investors today are not aware what a prolonged bear can do to their intentions to act like long-term investors. The 1987 dip was 35 percent but was short-lived. More recent downturns were of the 20 or 10 percent magnitude which just convinces investors that it is prudent to buy on such dips—which causes the market to go even higher. Investors today behave as if the Dow will never plunge again.

Savings Rate: The U.S. experienced a zero saving rate in 1999. Spending increased at 6 percent while incomes rose only 5 percent. That proves that consumers' spending patterns are being expanded by the rising stock market.

CONCLUSION

There is a big argument going on today regarding the stock market. There are those who say that the old measurements do not apply, that we are in a "new" economy, and that things are different this time. They argue that the good news justifies current market levels because inflation is low, unemployment is low, productivity is increasing, stocks provide a better annual return than bonds over the long term, companies are buying back their own stock, tax laws make capital gains preferable to dividends, and the stock market is on its way to a level of 36,000 in the Dow average.

On the other hand, the market is very "pricey" when old-fashioned measures of stock market valuation are examined. There are other disturbing signs which may point to a "top" in this market. For example, the two largest stock markets are planning to offer shares in themselves to the public after 18 years of the broadest financial advance in history.

Because of our decade-long economic advance, there is a growing belief that the New Economy will provide perpetual prosperity and recessions will become a thing of the past. Another sign of a top is the fact that the head of Amazon.com was selected Man of the Year by *Time* magazine, and the *Reader's Digest* magazine just carried an article by James Glassman, author of *Dow 36,000!* The Initial Public Offering craze continues with new untried companies gaining a 100 percent pop on their first trading day. (However, since 1993, three-fourth's of internet-related companies now trade below their offering price; i.e., E-toys, Priceline, E-trade and Value America.) Another ominous sign is that some Americans are giving up their secure employment to become day traders.

The Dow average now stands at about the 10,000 level. If the stock market corrects, what level of support should we expect? Well, if the Dow were trading at valuations which prevailed from 1926 through 1994, it would now be at about the 6,000 level. If it were selling at valuations which prevailed at the beginning of this bull market in 1982, the Dow average would be at the 4,000 level.

The Japanese believe that the U.S. is now in a huge bubble. How do they know? They've been there and they have suffered for a whole decade and their market is still half of what it was in 1990. Market guru John Templeton said that bull markets are born on pessimism, grow on skepticism, mature on optimism, and die on euphoria. Are we there yet?

———————◆———————

When the bubble bursts, the new economy will just be a bad memory. . . . A lot of these dot.coms are worth a corner lemonade stand and are putting real companies out of business. What are you going to tell people who lose much of their retirement savings in their 401K when there's a downturn?

DEAN BAKER, economist,
March 16, 2000

93.

The Vermont Civil Union Act

Decisions by the U.S. Supreme Court in 1967 and 1978 affirmed that marriage is one of the basic human rights. This right, which in the United States carries with it more than one thousand separate benefits and privileges from the federal government and typically another four hundred from state governments, was actively pursued by gay and lesbian couples in the 1990s. The attempt by three same-sex couples in Hawaii to obtain marriage licenses in 1990 sparked debate about the individual's right to marry and the definition of marriage itself. In 1996 Congress passed the Defense of Marriage Act, which restricted federal marriage benefits to heterosexual unions; however, that same year courts in Hawaii ruled that marriage rights and privileges must be extended to every citizen. Only two years later, though, Hawaiian voters approved an amendment to the state constitution allowing the legislature to forbid same-sex marriages. By 2001 similar restrictive marriage laws had been enacted in thirty-six states. Defying this trend, the Vermont Civil Union Act of 2000 (summarized below) followed a ruling by the state supreme court that extended the rights and benefits of marriage to same-sex couples. Yet even as it brought these privileges, the new Vermont law still affirmed the traditional definition of marriage as a heterosexual union.

Source: Brief Summary of H. 847 as Passed by the General Assembly, Montpelier, 2000.

THE PURPOSE of the act is "to respond to the constitutional violation found by the Vermont Supreme Court in *Baker* v. *State,* and to provide eligible same-sex couples the opportunity to 'obtain the same benefits and protections afforded by Vermont law to married opposite-sex couples' as required by Chapter I, Article 7 of the Vermont Constitution."

The act also provides eligible blood-relatives and relatives related by adoption the opportunity to establish a reciprocal beneficiaries relationship so they may receive certain benefits and protections and be subject to certain responsibilities that are granted to spouses.

Civil union status is available to two persons of the same sex who are not re-lated to one another. Parties to the civil union must be at least 18 years old and competent to enter a contract. To enter a civil union, a person may not already be a party to another civil union or a marriage.

Parties to a civil union will have all of the same benefits, protections and responsibilities under law, whether they derive from statute, administrative or court rule, policy, common law or any other source of civil law, as are granted to spouses in a marriage.

The family court will have jurisdiction over all proceedings relating to the dissolution of civil unions. The dissolution of civil unions will follow the same procedures, and be subject to the same substantive rights and obligations that are involved in the dissolution of marriage, including any residency requirements.

To establish a civil union, a couple may apply for a civil union license at their town clerk's office. If the couple meets the requirements for establishing a civil union, the clerk will issue the couple a civil union license. Within 60 days of issuance of the license, a couple must have the civil union certified by an authorized person. Persons authorized to certify a civil union include judges, justices of the peace and clergy.

Nonresidents may obtain a civil union license from any town clerk in the state rather than having to obtain the license from a town clerk in the county in which the civil union is going to be certified.

Town clerks will provide persons who apply for a civil union license with information prepared by the secretary of state that advises such persons of the benefits, protections and responsibilities of a civil union, and that Vermont residency may be required for dissolution of a civil union in Vermont.

Insurers must make available dependent coverage to parties to a civil union that is equivalent to that provided to married persons. An individual or group health insurance policy which provides coverage for a spouse or family member of the insured shall also provide the equivalent coverage for a party to a civil union.

Employers are not required to provide coverage to parties to a civil union. Insurers will be required to offer equivalent coverage, but the employer then decides whether to purchase the group health insurance for its employees and which employees are eligible for the insurance.

For the purpose of state income taxes, parties to a civil union will be taxed in the same manner as married persons. However, Vermont estate taxes are treated differently because the state's estate taxes are not piggybacked on the federal estate taxes.

"Marriage" is defined as the legally recognized union of one man and one woman in both the marriage chapter and the civil union chapter in the domestic relations title.

Two persons who are blood-relatives or relatives related by adoption and prohibited from establishing a civil union or marriage with one another may establish a reciprocal beneficiaries relationship. Persons must be at least 18 years old and competent to enter a contract. They may not be a party to another reciprocal beneficiaries relationship, a civil union or a marriage. Each person must consent to the relationship without force, fraud or duress.

Two persons who meet the criteria may establish a reciprocal beneficiaries relationship by presenting a signed, notarized declaration of a reciprocal beneficiaries relationship to the commissioner of health, and paying a filing fee of $10.00.

Reciprocal beneficiaries may receive the benefits and protections, and be subject to the responsibilities that are granted to spouses in the following specific areas: (1) Hospital visitation and medical decision-making; (2) Decision-making relating to anatomical gifts; (3) Decision-making relating to disposition of remains; (4) Durable power of attorney for health care and terminal care documents; (5) Patient's bill of rights; (6) Nursing home patient's bill of rights; and (7) Abuse prevention.

Either party to a reciprocal beneficiaries relationship may terminate the relationship by filling a signed, notarized declaration with the commissioner. Within 60 days of the filing of the declaration and payment of the fee by a party to a reciprocal beneficiaries relationship, the commissioner shall file the declaration and issue a certificate of termination of a reciprocal beneficiaries relationship to each party of the former relationship.

If a party to a reciprocal beneficiaries relationship enters into a valid civil union or a marriage, the reciprocal beneficiary relationship shall terminate, and the parties shall no longer be entitled to the benefits, protections and responsibilities of the reciprocal beneficiaries relationship.

A Civil Union Review Commission is established for two years. The commission will be comprised of 11 members, consisting of two members of the House designated by the Speaker of the House, who shall be of different political party affiliations; two members of the Senate designated by the Senate Committee on Committees, who shall be of different political party affiliations; four members appointed by the Governor representing the public, one of whom shall be an at-torney familiar with Vermont family law; one member appointed by the Chief Justice of the Vermont Supreme Court; the chair of the Human Rights Commission or his or her designee; and the Attorney General or his or her designee.

The commission will prepare and implement a plan to inform members of the public, state agencies, and private and public sector businesses and organizations about the act, as well as collect information about the implementation, operation, and effect of the act, and report to the general assembly and the governor with its findings, conclusions and recommendations.

The findings, purpose and the commission sections of the act take effect upon passage. The insurance sections of the act take effect January 1, 2001. The tax sections of the act take effect January 1, 2001. The rest of the act takes effect July 1, 2000.

———◆———

'Separate but equal' was a failed and pernicious policy with regard to race; it will be a failed and pernicious policy with regard to sexual orientation.
ANDREW SULLIVAN, *The New Republic,* May 8, 2000

94.

The Columbine High School Murders

Beginning in the 1970s, gun violence in American schools emerged as a major national issue. By the 1990s the problem was not confined to the inner cities or even to cities in general. School shootings had occurred in Mississippi and Kentucky in 1997, and in Arkansas and Oregon in 1998. In the spring of 1999, however, the issue took on special urgency when the worst school shooting incident in American history occurred at a wealthy public school in Littleton, Colorado, a suburb of Denver. On April 20, two students at Columbine High School, Eric Harris and Dylan Klebold, entered their school with semiautomatic rifles, pistols, and several explosives. In less than twenty minutes, they killed twelve fellow students and a teacher and had wounded twenty-one others. The violence came to an end when Harris and Klebold took their own lives. News of the Columbine tragedy stunned the nation. There was also strong criticism of a slow police response. Despite the fact that the shooting ended by noon, police and sheriff's deputies, believing there was continuing danger, did not move into the shooting area until several more hours had passed, during which time some victims bled to death. In the larger view, the Columbine massacre set off a national debate on how to end gun violence in schools. A growing number of schools throughout the nation invested in private security forces and metal detectors. Reprinted below is the official Jefferson County Sheriff's Office account of the events at Columbine High School on April 20, 1999.

Source: Jefferson County Colorado Sheriff's Office Report, May 15, 2000.

DEAR CITIZEN:

The investigation of the shootings that occurred at Columbine High School on April 20, 1999, has been completed. The conclusions of the investigation are contained in this report, which we now submit to our community.

What follows is the account of a spring day last year, when two Columbine students attacked their classmates and teachers with an arsenal of firearms and explosives. Within the span of 16 minutes, the gunmen had killed 13 people and wounded 21 others. A savage act of domestic terrorism, their crime is the deadliest school shooting in the history of the United States.

Because the shootings ravaged many lives, we feel an obligation, in the interest of public safety, to document the final moments of the deceased and provide the public with a shared understanding of that day. This report explains how the crime was planned and committed. It also describes the work of those who answered the call for help. By day's end on April 20, the responders numbered nearly 1,000 and represented the entire law enforcement, fire and medical services community of metropolitan Denver.

In preparing this report, we have relied on the work of approximately 80 investigators from all levels of government. Under the direction of the Jefferson County Sheriff's Office, the investigators contacted students, teachers and others who might have information about the crime. In all, investigators completed more than 4,400 leads. They examined videotapes, 911 recordings, ballistic reports, medical and autopsy reports, and physical evidence collected at the scene and the conspirators' residences.

Although the investigation approached conclusion in January 2000, the case remains classified as "open" in the event new information comes to light. To protect our ability to pursue this case further should the opportunity present itself—and to preserve the privacy of witnesses who are not yet in the public eye—we have excluded certain names and details from this report. Whenever possible, however, we have presented full documentation to provide a complete understanding of these events. We have chosen to present this report in CD-ROM format so that audio and video recordings may be included.

Among the significant findings of the 10-month investigation into the Columbine shootings are these:

1. Initial 911 calls included mention of a shooter on the high school roof. The man witnesses saw was an air conditioning repairman, who hid on the roof during the shootings. He was not involved in the crime.

2. The gunmen fired their first shots at about 11:19 a.m. and injured the last victim at 11:35 a.m. By shortly after noon, the killers, Eric Harris and Dylan Klebold, had died at their own hands.

3. The gunmen were in the library for 7½ minutes. In that time, they shot and killed 10 people and wounded 12 more.

They carried more than enough ammunition to kill all 56 people in the library.

4. Physical evidence does not indicate the presence of a third shooter. No known evidence suggests that anyone had prior knowledge of the killers' plans.

5. Surveillance videotapes clearly demonstrate that two 20-pound propane bombs were placed in the cafeteria the morning of April 20, 1999, and not the night before as has been rumored. No bomb was hidden in the kitchen.

6. According to their writings and videotapes, the gunmen planned to kill far more people. Had the two bombs in the cafeteria functioned properly, all 488 people in the room may have died.

7. The murderers carried two 20-lb. propane bombs, all of the pipe bombs, CO_2 bombs and other explosive devices into the school with them on April 20. They carried those devices in duffel bags and backpacks or in ammunition pouches strapped to their bodies. The remaining explosives were left in their cars.

8. In their yearbooks, videotapes, journals and computer files, Klebold and Harris listed 67 people they disliked for various reasons. Only one of those individuals was actually injured, and there is no evidence that he was specifically targeted on April 20.

9. Based on their writings, Klebold and Harris expected the bomb they placed south of the school near Wadsworth Boulevard to divert attention from the school for a longer period of time. The failure of the cafeteria bombs to detonate and the arrival of responding officers apparently caused the gunmen to re-evaluate their planned attack, since they had never listed the school library as a destination point.

10. On April 20, officers contacted suspicious persons near Columbine High School as well as friends and acquaintances of Harris and Klebold. Based on

some media portrayals, many believed those persons had been arrested or were involved in the crime. In fact, all of those people were interviewed and released.

In addition to providing information about the crime and law enforcement response, this report acknowledges staff from numerous government, mental health and nonprofit agencies who came forward to serve our grieving community. In response to the shootings, our community has received unparalleled support from professionals throughout the nation and the Denver metropolitan area.

Upon receiving a briefing about the law enforcement response to this horrible crime, U.S. Attorney General Janet Reno commented that these professionals had "shown the nation and the world America's finest in crisis." We agree, and wish to express our deep appreciation for their assistance.

While this report establishes a record of the events of April 20, it cannot answer the most fundamental question— WHY? That is, why would two young men, in the spring of their lives, choose to murder faculty members and classmates? The evidence provides no definitive explanation, and the question continues to haunt us all.

While our community struggles with that question and grieves those who were lost, we remain united in one hope—that our nation shall never see anything resembling the tragedy at Columbine High School again.

John P. Stone, Sheriff
John A. Dunaway, Undersheriff

———————◆———————

As the country watched Littleton last week, we seemed to be hurtling toward a National Moment, a late-'90s version of, say, the sinking of the Maine, *or the Kent State shootings during Vietnam, or Rock Hudson's death. These moments can be dangerous, as such soul searching quickly turns into lawmaking. History may remember last week because of what happens in the next few weeks, so let's try to get it right.*

JOHN CLOUD, "What Can the Schools Do?"
Time, May 3, 1999

95.

Bob Costas: The Traditions of Baseball

Major League Baseball experienced all-time highs and lows in the roller-coaster decade of the 1990s. In 1994 a bitter and protracted labor dispute between the baseball players' union and team owners culminated in a season-ending strike. For the first time in ninety years, no World Series was held. The strike finally ended in the spring of 1995, but public resentment toward both the players and owners festered. Ballpark attendance fell by 25–30 percent, and many fans claimed they would never return to the sport. Despite such apathy, fan interest slowly returned, and it surged in 1998 when Mark McGwire of the St. Louis Cardinals and Sammy Sosa of the Chicago Cubs both broke the single-season home run record of Roger Maris (sixty-one), which had stood for thirty-seven years. At the season's end, the record was reset by McGwire with seventy home runs, many of which were covered live on national television. Fan attendance approached pre-1994 levels, and many baseball commentators expressed the hope that the game would reestablish itself as the national pastime. Problems remained, however. The sport struggled with a financial imbalance between wealthy teams from major metropolises and poorer teams from small-market towns. Bob Costas, a sports broadcaster for the National Broadcasting Company (NBC), emerged as one of the most articulate supporters of reforming the game. Excerpts from an American Enterprise *interview with Costas conducted by Curt Smith are reprinted below.*

Source: *American Enterprise,* June 2000, "Live with TAE: Interview."

Thomas Wolfe once wrote, referring to baseball, "Almost everything I know of spring is in it." That is not nearly as true today. Why?

For millions of Americans, baseball still has a real hold on their hearts and imagination, but it's unrealistic to assume that baseball is going to hold quite the place in American culture that it used to. That doesn't mean that it needs to surrender everything that's essential about it.

What disturbs me is that baseball in recent years has seemed to be panic-stricken, so intent on catching the shifting winds of pop culture that it's willing to distort the essence of the game.

Baseball's best bet is to accentuate the differences between it and other sports, and the greatest strength of baseball is its timelessness. Modern proof of that is the success of all the new retro ballparks: these throwbacks to old feelings are the closest thing to an unmitigated success that baseball has experienced over the last ten years.

The results of other supposedly inspired changes—divisional realignments, expanded playoffs, the wild card, interleague play—are mixed at best and disastrous at worst.

In Fair Ball: A Fan's Case for Baseball,

you talk about the distinction—which baseball has failed to recognize—between "mere change and real progress."

Baseball has changed willy-nilly over the past several years and has managed, with the help of a compliant press, to frame the argument as a question of whether you're a progressive or a baseball conservative; whether you embrace change or you're resistant to change.

These are just mindless buzzwords. No intelligent person isn't willing to change if the change represents an improvement over what went before. But in baseball's case, if you're going to expand the playoffs, is the wild card the best way to do it—if in the process you destroy the meaning and drama of the regular season?

If you're going to play inter-league games, and I have no problem with that in concept, is it right to have the same divisions constantly match up against each other so that Mark McGwire and the Cardinals never come to Fenway Park? Derek Jeter and the Yankees never come to Cincinnati?

Or would it be better to rotate the inter-league games so that they felt more special? So that Ken Griffey, Jr., now in the National League, came to an American League city only once every three years; so that the games between the Yankees and Mets, instead of becoming annual affairs, were really something that was anticipated; so that the distinction between the leagues was maintained, but at the same time the novelty and appeal of inter-league games was also highlighted?

Does the record not show that when it comes to baseball, tradition sells?

Tradition does sell when it comes to baseball, and tradition should be respected in baseball more so than in other sports because it's an important part of baseball's appeal. Even when baseball modernizes, its best bet is to incorporate some element of timelessness, some element of baseball's historic appeal.

The reason I object to the label "traditionalist," though, is that in the present argument being called a traditionalist is akin to being labeled a member of the "Flat Earth Society."

I have no problem at all with baseball changing. Baseball has changed in the past, but not every change is progress. Take a couple of changes that occurred at roughly the same time.

In 1969, baseball, which had gone in the space of less than a decade from the 16 teams that it had for the better part of a century to 24 teams, decided it would split into two six-team divisions per league. So instead of a single pennant race, leading directly into the World Series, they went to Eastern and Western divisions in each league, and they played a league championship series at the conclusion of the regular season and then the World Series.

That was a practical and sensible change brought about by changing circumstances, and while it wasn't exactly the same as the baseball that had preceded it, it preserved the essence of the baseball everyone knew. Those divisional races felt like pennant races.

At about the same time, new ballparks cropped up all around baseball. Some of them were domed stadiums. All of the new parks had artificial turf. Does anybody, in retrospect, believe that was a good idea? It was progress. It certainly was modern. But it didn't improve baseball in any way. . . .

The length of pro baseball and football games is in large part due to television time-outs. Is there any chance the networks would reduce the length of these time-outs?

Under the present circumstances, there's no chance of that because the rights fees are too high, and those funds have to be recouped somehow.

On the other hand—and this may sound pie in the sky—but if baseball valued its own product enough to accept lower rights fees, so that they were able to play some World Series games in the daytime (which they should do just for the sake of the beauty and tradition), and if they were willing to contract the playoffs so that the games started earlier in October, then television would be willing to show fewer commercials.

There are other ways to shorten baseball games. Call the rule-book strike zone. Encourage pitchers not to dawdle with nobody [sic] on base, and batters not to step out of the batter's box after each and every pitch.

Every athlete in sports today has grown up watching television, and they've been conditioned by television to pose. And all this posing drags the game out.

Hispanics now dominate many baseball statistics, especially in the American League. How does the increased presence of non-English-speaking players affect baseball's mass appeal?

The more great players you bring to the game, the better. With baseball no longer reigning supreme as the unquestioned national pastime, and therefore losing a lot of great athletes, especially African-American athletes, to other team sports, you ought to go wherever you can find additional pools of talent: not just Latin America but increasingly now Asia. It's all to the good.

I can't imagine a baseball fan who doesn't think that baseball is all the better for every Pedro Martinez and Sammy Sosa it can find. . . .

In city after city, owners threaten to move unless governments build them new stadiums. Is this a legitimate use of taxpayer dollars?

Under the right conditions. It's legitimate if it's a public-private partnership, rather than just a grab of public funds by wealthy owners who are playing on the emotions of sports fans. And as long as stipulations are in place that say a certain percentage of the seats must, by law, be kept affordable. It's crazy to spend public funds on a ballpark that's going to be loaded with luxury boxes for high rollers, but where there aren't five-dollar tickets so the average guy can bring his family several times a year.

You wouldn't spend public funds on a library or a museum and then have an admission charge that effectively locked out a huge percentage of the populace.

Part of the appeal of sports, maybe baseball in particular, used to be that it was one of the few places where a cab driver was likely to find himself sitting next to a bank president. At present, that's not very likely to happen. . . .

Are professional sports just entertainment, or do they have any ability to teach lessons which can make spectators better citizens?

Sports has always been entertainment. It's always been a business. But there was a time when the game itself had some value. I guess it still can, but it's pretty hard to find the pearl in the oyster.

96.

BARRY R. MCCAFFREY: Do Not Legalize Drugs

Perhaps no twentieth-century social problem posed a more vexing challenge than that of drug abuse. In the 1960s drug use dramatically escalated, bringing with it severe social consequences. Addiction rates soared, crime rates rose, and a sense of public alarm took hold. Despite the grave nature of illicit drug use, the federal government seemed unable to respond effectively to stem its spread, though not from a lack of action. In the 1970s and 1980s the government "declared war" on drugs, imposed increasingly strict prison sentences for drug possession, gave the Drug Enforcement Administration wide powers to stop the flow of narcotics into the United States, and established the office of "drug czar" to manage the government's antidrug policy. Yet, despite these expensive measures, the drug problem continued to plague American society. Dismayed by the government's inability to curb drug use, some observers declared that the war on drugs had failed and that the government should reverse its policies and try decriminalization as a solution. This proposal to legalize drugs received strong criticism from both policymakers and the general public. Excerpted below is testimony that Barry McCaffrey, director of the White House Office of National Drug Control Policy (ONDCP), gave in June 1999 before a Congressional subcommittee on the issue of decriminalizing drugs.

Source: Testimony before the U.S. House of Representatives Subcommittee on Criminal Justice, Drug Policy, and Human Resources, Washington, D.C., June 16, 1999.

WHAT PROPONENTS OF LEGALIZATION REALLY WANT: EASY ACCESS TO ALL DRUGS OF ABUSE

PROPONENTS OF LEGALIZATION know that the policy choices they advocate are unacceptable to the American public. Because of this, many advocates of this approach have resorted to concealing their real intentions and seeking to sell the American public legalization by normalizing drugs through a process designed to erode societal disapproval.

For example, ONDCP has expressed reservations about the legalization of hemp as an agricultural product because of the potential for increasing marijuana growth and use. While legitimate hardworking farmers may want to grow the crop to support their families, many of the other proponents of hemp legalization have not been as honest about their goals. A leading hemp activist is quoted in the *San Francisco Examiner* and on the Media Awareness Project's homepage (a group advocating drug policy reforms) as saying he "can't support a movement or law that would lift restrictions from industrial hemp and keep them for marijuana." If legalizing hemp is solely about developing a new crop and not about eroding marijuana restrictions, why does this individual only support hemp dereg-ulation if it is linked to the legalization of marijuana?

Similarly, when Ethan Nadelmann, Di-rector of the Lindesmith Center (a drug research institute), speaks to the main-stream media, he talks mainly about is-sues of compassion, like medical mari-juana and the need to help patients dying of cancer. However, Mr. Nadel-mann's own words in other fora reveal his underlying agenda: legalizing drugs. Here is what he advocates:

> *Personally, when I talk about legaliza-tion, I mean three things: the first is to make drugs such as marijuana, cocaine, and heroin legal. . . .*
>
> *I propose a mail order distribution system based on a right of access. . . .*
>
> *Any good non-prohibitionist drug policy has to contain three central ingredients. First, possession of small amounts of any drug for personal use has to be legal. Sec-ond, there have to be legal means by which adults can obtain drugs of certified quality, purity and quantity. These can vary from state to state and town to town, with the Food and Drug Administration playing a supervisory role in controlling quality, pro-viding information and assuring truth in advertising. And third, citizens have to be empowered in their decisions about drugs. Doctors have a role in all this, but let's not give them all the power.*
>
> *We can begin by testing low potency co-caine products—coca-based chewing gum or lozenges, for example, or products like Mar-iani's wine and the Coca-Cola of the late 19th century—which by all accounts were as safe as beer and probably not much worse than coffee. If some people want to distill those products into something more potent, let them. . . .*

International financier George Soros, who funds the Lindesmith Center, has advocated: "If it were up to me, I would establish a strictly controlled distributor network through which I would make most drugs, excluding the most danger-ous ones like crack, legally available." William F. Buckley, Jr. has also called for the "legalization of the sale of most drugs, except to minors."

Similarly, when the legalization com-munity explains their theory of harm re-duction—the belief that illegal drug use cannot be controlled and, instead, that government should focus on reducing drug-related harms, such as overdoses—the underlying goal of legalization is still present. For example, in a 1998 article in *Foreign Affairs*, Mr. Nadelmann expressed that the following were legitimate "harm reduction" policies: allowing doctors to prescribe heroin for addicts; employing drug analysis units at large dance parties, known as raves, to test the quality of drugs; and "decriminalizing" possession and retail sale of cannabis and, in some cases, possession of "hard drugs."

Legalization, whether it goes by the name harm reduction or some other trumped up moniker, is still legalization. For those who at heart believe in legal-ization, harm reduction is too often a lin-guistic ploy to confuse the public, cover their intentions and thereby quell legiti-mate public inquiry and debate. Chang-ing the name of the plan doesn't consti-tute a new solution or alter the nature of the problem. . . .

FALLACY: DRUG LEGALIZATION WILL NOT INCREASE DRUG USE.

REALITY: DRUG LEGALIZATION WOULD SIGNIFICANTLY INCREASE THE   HUMAN   AND   ECONOMIC COSTS ASSOCIATED WITH DRUGS.

Proponents argue that legalization is a cure-all for our nation's drug problem. However, the facts show that legalization is not a panacea but a poison. In reality, legalization would dramatically expand America's drug dependence, significantly increase the social costs of drug abuse, and put countless more innocent lives at risk. . . .

During the 1970s, our nation engaged in a serious debate over the shape of our drug control policies. (For example, within the context of this debate, between 1973 and 1979, eleven states "decriminalized" marijuana). During this timeframe, the number of Americans supporting marijuana legalization hit a modern-day high. While it is difficult to show causal links, it is clear that during this same period, from 1972 to 1979, marijuana use rose from 14 percent to 31 percent among adolescents, 48 percent to 68 percent among young adults, and 7 percent to 20 percent among adults over twenty-six. This period marked one of the largest drug use escalations in American history.

A similar dynamic played out nationally in the late 1800s and early 1900s. Until the 1890s, today's controlled substances—such as marijuana, opium, and cocaine—were almost completely unregulated. It was not until the last decades of the 1800s that several states passed narcotics control laws. Federal regulation of narcotics control did not come into play until the Harrison Act of 1914.

Prior to the enactment of these laws, narcotics were legal and widely available across the United States. In fact, narcotics use and its impacts were commonplace in American society. Cocaine was found not only in early Coca-Cola (until 1903) but also in wine, cigarettes, liqueur-like alcohols, hypodermic needles, ointments, and sprays. Cocaine was falsely marketed as a cure for hay fever, sinusitis and even opium and alcohol abuse. Opium abuse was also widespread. One year before Bayer introduced aspirin to the market, the company also began marketing heroin as a "nonaddictive," no prescription necessary, over-the-counter cure-all.

During this period, drug use and addiction increased sharply. While there are no comprehensive studies of drug abuse for this period that are on par with our current *National Household Survey on Drug Abuse* and *Monitoring the Future* studies, we can, for example, extrapolate increases in opium use from opium imports, which were tracked. Yale University's Dr. David Musto, one of the leading experts on the patterns of drug use in the United States, writes: "The numbers of those overusing opiates must have increased during the nineteenth century as the per capita importation of crude opium increased from less than 12 grains annually in the 1840s to more than 52 grains in the 1890s." Only in the 1890s when societal concerns over and disapproval of drug use began to become widespread and triggered legal responses did these rates level off. Until this change in attitudes began to denormalize drug use, the United States experienced over a 400 percent increase in opium use alone. This jump is even more staggering if one considers that during this period other serious drugs, such as cocaine, were also widely available in every-day products.

Moreover, while we do not believe that the period of prohibition on alcohol is directly analogous to current efforts against drugs, our experiences with alcohol prohibition also raise parallel concerns. While prohibition was not without its flaws, during this period alcohol usage fell to between 30 to 50 percent of its pre-prohibition levels. From 1916 to 1919 (just prior to [when] prohibition went into effect in 1920), U.S. alcohol consumption averaged 1.96 gallons per person per year. During prohibition, alcohol use fell to a low of .90 gallons per person per year. In the decade that followed prohibition's repeal, alcohol use increased to a per capita annual average of 1.54 gallons and has since steadily risen to 2.43 gallons in 1989. Prohibition also substantially reduced the rates of alcohol-related illnesses.

The United States has tried drug legalization and rejected it several times now because of the suffering it brings. The philosopher Santayana was right in his admonition that "those who cannot remember the past are condemned to repeat it." Let us not now be so foolish as to once again consider this well worn, dead-end path.

THE IMPACT ON YOUTH

Most importantly the legalization of drugs in the United States would lead to a disproportionate increase in drug use among young people. In 1975, the Alaskan Supreme Court invalidated certain sections of the state's criminal code pertaining to the possession of marijuana. Based on this finding, from 1975 to 1991, possession of up to four ounces of the drug by an adult who was lawfully in the state of Alaska became legal. Even though marijuana remained illegal for children, marijuana use rates among Alaskan youth increased significantly. In response, concerned Alaskans, in particular the National Federation of Parents for Drug-Free Youth, sponsored an antidrug referendum that was approved by the voters in 1990, once again rendering marijuana illegal.

In addition to the impact of expanded availability, legalization would have a devastating effect on how our children see drug use. Youth drug use is driven by attitudes. When young people perceive drugs as risky and socially unacceptable youth drug use drops. Conversely, when children perceive less risk and greater acceptability in using drugs, their use increases. If nothing else, legalization would send a strong message that taking drugs is a safe and socially accepted behavior that is to be tolerated among our peers, loved ones and children. Such a normalization would play a major role in softening youth attitudes and, ultimately, increasing drug use.

The significant increases in youth drug use that would accompany legalization are particularly troubling because their effects would be felt over the course of a generation or longer. Without help, addictions last a lifetime. Every additional young person we allow to become addicted to drugs will impose tremendous human and fiscal burdens on our society. Legalization would be a usurious debt upon our society's future—the costs of such an approach would mount exponentially with each new addict, and over each new day.

THE IMPACT OF DRUG PRICES

If drugs were legalized, we can also expect the attendant drop in drug prices to cause drug use rates to grow as drugs become increasingly affordable to buy. Currently a gram of cocaine sells for between $150 and $200 on U.S. streets. The cost of cocaine production is as low as $3 per gram. In order to justify legalization, the market cost for legalized cocaine would have to be set so low as to make the black market, or bootleg cocaine, economically unappealing. Assume, for argument sake, that the market price was set at $10 per gram, a three hundred percent plus markup over cost, each of the fifty hits of cocaine in that gram could retail for as little as ten cents.

With the cost of "getting high" as low as a dime (ten cents)—about the cost of a cigarette—the price of admission to drug use would be no obstacle to anyone even considering it. However, each of these "dime" users risks a life-long drug dependence problem that will cost them, their families, and our society tens of thousands of dollars.

In addition to the impact on youth, we would also expect to see falling drug prices drive increasing drug use among the less affluent. Among these individuals the price of drug use—even at today's levels—remains a barrier to entry into use and addiction. The impact of growing use within these populations could be severe. Many of these communities are already suffering the harms of drug use—children who see no other future turning to drugs as an escape, drug dealers driving what remains of legitimate business out of their communities, and families being shattered by a loved one hooked on drugs. Increased drug use would set back years of individual, local, state and federal efforts to sweep these areas clean of drugs and build new opportunities. . . .

FALLACY: DRUGS ARE HARMFUL BECAUSE THEY ARE ILLEGAL.

REALITY: DRUGS ARE HARMFUL NOT BECAUSE THEY ARE ILLEGAL; THEY ARE ILLEGAL BECAUSE THEY ARE HARMFUL.

Critics argue that the harm to our society from drugs, such as the costs of crime, could be reduced if drugs were legalized. The logic is flawed. By increasing the availability of drugs, legalization would dramatically increase the harm to innocent people. With more drugs and drug use in our society, there would be more drug-related child abuse, more drugged driving fatalities, and more drug-related workplace accidents. None of these harms are caused by law or law enforcement but by illegal drugs.

Even with respect to the crime-related impact of drugs, drug-related crimes are driven far more by addiction than by the illegality of drugs. Law enforcement doesn't cause people to steal to support their habits; they steal because they need money to fuel an addiction—a drug habit that often precludes them from earning an honest living. Even if drugs were legal, people would still steal and prostitute themselves to pay for addictive drugs and support their addicted lifestyles. Dealers don't deal to children because the law makes it illegal; dealers deal to kids to build their market by hooking them on a life-long habit at an early age, when drugs can be marketed as cool and appealing to young people who have not matured enough to consider the risks. Make no mistake: legalizing drugs won't stop pushers from selling heroin and other drugs to kids. Legalization will, however, increase drug availability and normalize drug-taking behavior, which will increase the rates of youth drug abuse.

For example, although the Dutch adopted a more tolerant approach to illegal drugs, crime is in many cases increasing rapidly in Holland. The most recent international police data (1995) shows that Dutch per capita rates for breaking and entering, a crime closely associated with drug abuse, are three times the rate of those in Switzerland and the United States, four times the French rate, and 50 percent greater than the German rate. "A 1997 report on hard-drug use in the Netherlands by the government-financed Trimbos Institute acknowledged that 'drug use is considered the primary motivation behind crimes against property'— 23 years after the Dutch [drug] policy was supposed to put a brake on that." Moreover, *Foreign Affairs* recently noted that in areas of Holland where youth cannabis smokers are most prevalent, such as Amsterdam, Utrecht and Rotterdam, the rates of juvenile crime have "witnessed skyrocketing growth" over the last three to four years. Statistics from the Dutch Central Bureau of Statistics indicate that between 1978 and 1992, there was a gradual, steady increase in violence of more than 160 percent.

In contrast, crime rates in the United States are rapidly dropping. For example, the rate of drug-related murders in the United States has hit a ten-year low. In 1989, there were 1,402 drug-related murders. By 1997 that number fell to 786. In 1995, there were 581,000 robberies in the United States. By 1997, that number fell to roughly 498,000.

America's criminal justice system is not the root cause of drug-related crime. It is the producers, traffickers, pushers, gangs and enforcers who are to blame, as are all the people who use drugs and never think about the web of criminality and suffering their drug money supports.

97.

E. J. Dionne, Jr.: Suburban Politics

The 2000 presidential election was the closest in modern American history. Throughout the campaign, Texas Governor George W. Bush, the Republican nominee, and Vice President Al Gore, the Democratic nominee, ran neck and neck in the polls. With most rural Americans favoring Bush, and most urban Americans favoring Gore, it was clear to both sides that the election would be decided in the suburbs. The two campaigns' decision to focus on the suburbs proved well-founded: suburbanites would cast over 50 percent of the national vote in the 2000 election. The rise of the suburbs as a key battleground in American politics began long before the 2000 election. Suburbia first blossomed in the 1950s with the construction of the interstate highway system that facilitated the massive exodus of rural and urban residents, and in the decades that followed the suburbs bloomed even brighter. As they grew in population, the suburbs also grew in political influence. By the 1990s they stood atop the American political pyramid, but neither the Republicans nor the Democrats possessed a monopoly on suburban political allegiances. In the essay that follows, Washington Post *columnist E. J. Dionne analyzes the campaign issues that mean the most to suburban voters.*

Source: *The Washington Post*, September 29, 2000, "Suburban Prize."

PORING OVER the numbers on American life 40 years ago, the great journalist Theodore H. White saw the American future. "Americans were abandoning the city and deserting the countryside, said the 1960 census," he wrote. "It also told where they were going: to the suburbs."

And they kept on going. The entirely true cliche about American politics after the census three decades later was that the 1992 election was to be our first in which a majority of the votes were cast not from the countryside, not from the city, but from the suburbs. Republicans assumed that Suburban Nation would inevitably be Republican Nation.

Not an implausible idea, but it was wrong. Our first two suburbanized elections went to Bill Clinton, and Al Gore has a fair chance of winning the third.

What went haywire with the expectation of Republican dominance? For starters, all suburbs aren't the same. John McGovern, campaign manager for Republican congressional candidate Mark Kirk in the district just north of here, compares the old suburbs of Lake Forest and Winnetka with the fast-growing suburbs of Arlington Heights and Vernon Hills.

"You're talking about two cultures," he said—the differences between old and new wealth. And some suburbs are far richer than others, which affects how they vote.

"All these suburbs are politically diverse," McGovern says. "But in the older suburbs, the voters tend to temper their fiscal conservativism with civic and social activism. As a result, a lot of them split their tickets. The newer suburbs have seen tremendous growth and have attracted a lot of new residents. The voters there tend to be more suspicious of big government. They split tickets too but are more reliably Republican."

Nor did the issues work out as Republicans might have hoped. Rep. John Edward Porter, a Republican who is retiring and is strongly backing Kirk, his former aide, says voters in his district have "three litmus tests." They are: "Do you support gun control? Are you pro-choice [on abortion]? Are you pro-environment?"

Kirk passes all three, but they are not an ideal set of issues for George Bush, nor for a Republican Congress dominated by conservative southerners. Porter jokes that he blames "my old friend George McGovern" for the problem Republicans now confront.

The very liberal 1972 Democratic presidential nominee, Porter says, drove southern conservatives out of the Democratic Party. "The whole South said goodbye to the Democratic Party," he says, "and a whole large conservative constituency came over to the Republicans." What appeals to those southern Republicans does not necessarily appeal here.

Sen. Richard Durbin, an Illinois Democrat, says Bush has a problem with voters in these parts on both abortion and gun control: "There is a skepticism about a Republican out of the South who is wrong on these two issues."

Durbin became active in politics in the mid-1960s and says today's suburbs are a world away from the solid Republican bastions they once were. "When you talked about the North Shore, it was a desert for Democrats," he said of the affluent precincts north of Chicago where he and many other Democrats now do just fine.

Illinois' Republican senator, Peter Fitzgerald, transcended the litmus test by winning in 1998 as a strong foe of abortion. Yet Fitzgerald is under no illusions about how his views on the issue play among suburban voters. "The Republican Party is split in its base in the suburbs between the pro-life and pro-choice sides," he says.

Fitzgerald pulled off his victory because of what Durbin delicately calls "a whirlwind of controversy" around ethical problems that confronted the Democrat he defeated, then-Sen. Carol Moseley-Braun. Fitzgerald draws hope for Bush from his experience. Bush, he says, will be helped by attacks on Clinton and Gore around questions of "ethics and integrity" among "clean government" suburbanites.

Perhaps. But Sam Popkin, a political scientist at the University of California at San Diego, who is helping the Gore campaign, says Republicans misunderstand suburbanites if they see them as pure anti-tax, anti-government voters. "They want suburban-oriented government, not no government." Referring to the famously liberal Republican governor of New York and the famously conservative Republican president, Popkin added: "They want Rockefeller, not Reagan."

That may be the definitive comment on how the suburbanization of America has, in fact, turned the country more Republican by pushing Democrats to behave more like the liberal Republicans of old. As Durbin points out, suburban voters support government to solve problems they care about such as rising gas prices and defective tires. They favor spending on education and health care.

And many suburbanites would like government to wage war on sprawl and traffic jams.

But they retain, Durbin says, "a healthy skepticism about new programs, and how big they're going to be and how effective they're going to be."

A Bush victory would disprove all theories about how out of touch with suburbanites Republicans have become. But if Gore wins, Republicans will have to wonder how they allowed their own progressive tradition—a tradition much appreciated in the suburbs—to become an adjunct to the Democratic Party.

98.

Robert D. Putnam: Reviving the American Community

Suburbanization brought many advantages to American life. Suburbs offered an apparent refuge from the noise, pollution, crime, and cramped quarters of the city. Equally important, they offered millions of middle- and working-class people the opportunity to own houses for the first time. Suburbanization proved so popular that by the 1990s one in every two Americans lived in the suburbs. At the same time, however, social commentators saw drawbacks. The rapid flight of the middle class from cities contributed to urban decay, to a stark economic division between the prosperous suburbs and the impoverished inner city, and then to urban sprawl, which in turn created a divide among the suburbs themselves, as inner-ring suburbs became poorer and outer-ring suburbs grew wealthy. Urban sprawl also eroded the traditional conception of the neighborhood. Unlike the residents of long-standing urban neighborhoods, suburbanites often had shallow roots in their community and typically knew only a handful of their neighbors. By the end of the century, many suburbanites longed for a renewed sense of community and civic unity. In his book Bowling Alone: The Collapse and Revival of American Community, *social critic Robert Putnam explores efforts to reestablish community links, or social capital, in modern American society. Excerpts from his book are reprinted below.*

Source: *Bowling Alone: The Collapse and Revival of American Community,* New York, 2000.

Philosophers from Aristotle and Rousseau to William James and John Dewey have begun discussions of civics with the education of youth. They have pondered the essential virtues and skills and knowledge and habits of democratic citizens and how to instill them. That starting point is especially appropriate for reformers today, for the single most important cause of our current plight is a pervasive and continuing generational decline in almost all forms of civic engagement. Today's youth did not initiate the erosion of Americans' social capital—their parents did—and it is the obligation of Americans of all ages to help rekindle civic engagement among the generation that will come of age in the early years of the twenty-first century.

So I set before America's parents, educators, and, above all, America's young adults the following challenge: *Let us find ways to ensure that by 2010 the level of civic engagement among Americans then coming of age in all parts of our society will match that of their grandparents when they were that same age, and that at the same time bridging social capital will be substantially greater than it was in their grandparents' era.* One specific test of our success will be whether we can restore electoral turnout to that of the 1960s, but our goal must be to increase participation and deliberation in other, more substantive and fine-grained ways, too—from team sports to choirs and from organized altruism to grassroots social movements.

The means to achieve these goals in the early twenty-first century, and the new forms of connectedness that will mark our success, will almost surely be different from those of the mid-twentieth century. For this reason, success will require the sensibility and skills of Gen X and their successors, even more than of baby boomers and their elders. Nevertheless, some "old-fashioned" ideas are relevant. Take civics education, for example. We know that knowledge about public affairs and practice in everyday civic skills are prerequisites for effective participation. We know, too, that the "civics report card" issued by the U.S. Department of Education for American elementary and high school students at the end

of the twentieth century was disappointing. So improved civics education in school should be part of our strategy—not just "how a bill becomes a law," but "How can I participate effectively in the public life of my community?" Imagine, for example, the civic lessons that could be imparted by a teacher in South Central Los Angeles, working with students to *effect* public change that her students think is important, like getting lights for a neighborhood basketball court.

We know other strategies that will work, too. A mounting body of evidence confirms that community service programs really do strengthen the civic muscles of participants, especially if the service is meaningful, regular, and woven into the fabric of the school curriculum. Episodic service has little effect, and it is hard to imagine that baby-sitting and janitorial work—the two most frequent types of "community service" nationwide, according to one 1997 study—have much favorable effect. On the other hand, well-designed service learning programs (the emerging evidence suggests) improve civic knowledge, enhance citizen efficacy, increase social responsibility and self-esteem, teach skills of cooperation and leadership, and may even (one study suggests) reduce racism. Interestingly, voluntary programs seem to work as well as mandatory ones. Volunteering in one's youth is . . . among the strongest predictors of adult volunteering. Intergenerational mentoring, too, can serve civic ends, as in Boston's Citizen Schools program, which enables adult volunteers to work with youth on tangible after-school projects, like storywriting or Web site building.

Participation in extracurricular activities (both school linked and independent) is another proven means to increase civic and social involvement in later life. In fact, participation in high school music groups, athletic teams, service clubs, and the like is among the strongest precursors of adult participation, even when we compare demographically matched groups. From a civic point of view, extracurricular activities are anything but "frills," yet funding for them was decimated during the 1980s and 1990s. Reversing that perverse development would be a good start toward our goal of youthful reengagement by 2010. Finally, we know that smaller schools encourage more active involvement in extracurricular activity than big schools—more students in smaller schools have an opportunity to play trombone or left tackle or King Lear. Smaller schools, like smaller towns, generate higher expectations for mutual reciprocity and collective action. So deconcentrating megaschools or creating smaller "schools within schools" will almost surely produce civic dividends.

Our efforts to increase social participation among youth must not be limited to schooling. Though it is not yet easy to see what the Internet-age equivalent of 4-H or settlement houses might be, we ought to bestow an annual Jane Addams Award on the Gen X'er or Gen Y'er who comes up with the best idea. What we need is not civic broccoli—good for you but unappealing—but an updated version of Scouting's ingenious combination of values and fun. I challenge those who came of age in the civically dispiriting last decade of the twentieth century to invent powerful and enticing ways of increasing civic engagement among their younger brothers and sisters who will come of age in the first decade of the twenty-first century. . . .

Politics and government is the domain where our voyage of inquiry about the state of social capital in America began, and it is where I conclude my challenges to readers who are as concerned as I am about restoring community bonds in America. Nowhere is the need to restore connectedness, trust, and civic engagement clearer than in the now often empty public forums of our democracy. So I challenge America's government officials, political consultants, politicians and (above all) my fellow citizens: *Let us find ways to ensure that by 2010 many more Americans will participate in the public life of our communities—running for office, attending public meetings, serving on committees, campaigning in elections, and even voting.* It is perhaps foolhardy to hope that we could reverse the entire decline of the last three to four decades in ten years, but American democracy would surely feel the beneficent effects of even a partial reversal.

Campaign reform (above all, campaign finance reform) should be aimed at increasing the importance of social capital—and decreasing the importance of financial capital—in our elections, federal, state, and local. Since time is distributed more equally across the population than money, privileging time-based participation over check-based participation would begin to reverse the growing inequality in American politics. Government authority should be decentralized as far as possible to bring decisions to smaller, local jurisdictions, while recognizing and offsetting the potential negative effect of that decentralization on equality and redistribution. Indeed, liberals alert to the benefits of social capital should be readier to transfer governmental authority downward in exactly the same measure that compassionate conservatives should be readier to transfer resources from have to have-not communities. Decentralization of government resources and authority to neighborhood councils has worked in cities like Minneapolis, Portland, and Seattle, creating new social capital in the form of potluck dinners, community gardens, and flea markets, though deft design is needed to be sure that the balance between bridging and bonding does not tip too far toward urban fragmentation.

Policy designers of whatever partisan persuasion should become more social capital-savvy, seeking to do minimum damage to existing stocks of social capital even as they look for opportunities to add new stocks. How about a "social-capital impact statement" for new programs, less bureaucratic and legalistic than environmental impact statements have become, but equally effective at calling attention to unanticipated consequences? For example, the greatest damage to social capital in the inner city of Indianapolis, Indiana, in the last half century was the unintended disruption of neighborhood networks when those neighborhoods were pierced by Interstate 65 in the early 1960s. The Front-Porch Alliance created by former mayor Stephen Goldsmith more than a quarter century later was a worthy effort to help restore some Indianapolis neighborhood institutions, but Goldsmith himself would be the first to say that it would have been better to avoid the damage in the first place.

In all the domains of social-capital creation that I have discussed here all too briefly, social capitalists need to avoid false debates. One such debate is "top-down versus bottom-up." The roles of national and local institutions in restoring American community need to be complementary; neither alone can solve the problem. Another false debate is whether government is the problem or the solution. The accurate answer, judging from the historical record . . . is that it can be both. Many of the most creative investments in social capital in American history—from county agents and the 4-H to community colleges and the March of Dimes—were the direct result of government policy. Government may be responsible for some small portion of the declines in social capital I have traced in this volume, and it cannot be the sole solution, but it is hard to imagine that we can meet the challenges I have set for America in 2010 without using government.

The final false debate to be avoided is whether what is needed to restore trust and community bonds in America is individual change or institutional change. Again, the honest answer is "Both." America's major civic institutions, both public and private, are somewhat antiquated a century after most of them were created, and they need to be reformed in ways that invite more active participation. Whether the specific suggestions I have made for institutional reform are persuasive or not is less important than the possibility that we may have a national debate about how to make our institutions more social capital-friendly. In the end, however, institutional reform will not work—indeed, it will not happen—unless you and I, along with our fellow citizens, resolve to become reconnected with our friends and neighbors. Henry Ward Beecher's advice a century ago to "multiply picnics" is not entirely ridiculous today. We should do this, ironically, not because it will be good for America—though it will be—but because it will be good for us.

99.

CLOTAIRE RAPAILLE: How Americans Think

From the earliest days of the republic, how Americans think and what they want from their lives has been a central preoccupation for entrepreneurs as well as politicians and intellectuals. The methods used to answer these questions have grown increasingly sophisticated as opinion polls, market research, and focus groups have been employed to gauge public reaction not just to soft drinks but to the specific language used in government policy. Yet, at the turn of the twenty-first century, among the most interesting analyses of the wants and needs of Americans came from Clotaire Rapaille, a medical anthropologist who abjured statistics to study instead the influence of cultural archetypes on opinion. Borrowing from Freudian psychology and the Jungian notion of the collective unconscious, he examined the cultural basis of early associations with ideas and objects to understand how these "emotional memories" affect later decision making. He has used this approach in the service of business, industry, and politics (the 1988 Presidential campaign of George Bush, for example), and it was instrumental to the design of DaimlerChrysler's hugely successful automobile the PT Cruiser. In the tradition of foreign observers from Alexis de Tocqueville to Aleksandr Solzhenitsyn, the French-born Rapaille (whose accent remains pronounced) offered insights into American character in the interview with National Public Radio excerpted below.

Source: Interview: Clotaire Rapaille, NPR, 2000.

I don't think Americans want a message, and that is what is really frightening, in some ways. They want good entertainment. Bill Clinton was a master of entertainment. You know, the archetype, for me, of Bill Clinton is [a] cheap entertainer. [He] is cheap because [he] only makes, like, $200,000 a year when Oprah Winfrey make[s] several million dollars. So compare[d] with other entertainer[s], he is cheap. But [he's] a great entertainer. And there is a new story all the time. It's better than any soap opera that you can imagine. This is going to be difficult to match. Gore is kind of boring, Mr. Bush is boring, too. This is what is wrong with these two people.

Dr. Rapaille, aren't you worried people will listen to you and say, 'Gee, this guy's making a joke of us'?

I'm not making a joke. This is a reality. You know, I'm personally fascinated and very interested in foreign policy . . . I'm a new American, and I choose to become American and I love this country and I think that America has a role to play in the world. And if we don't play this role, the world is going to be in bad shape. But American people don't care about foreign policy. And so you see that's the major problem.

Second, Americans don't like intelligent people. I mean, when you are too

Carefully designed with a retro 1930s look, DaimlerChrysler's PT Cruiser caught the fancy of many Americans in 2000.

car with—a convertible car, the message might be, 'Please rape me.' And you don't want to send this message. You want to have a big car, powerful car, like a tank with a machine gun. And the message is 'Don't mess with me.' . . .

But then the inside. The inside is completely different. If the outside is "Mad Max," the inside should be the Ritz-Carlton. 'I want the Ritz-Carlton inside.' 'I want cup holders that can warm up my coffee' . . . I want luxury.

intelligent you're frightening people. If you say, 'Well, I was the last of my class, I almost flunk[ed] everything,' people love you. I wrote 10 books and I'm hiding it because people say, 'Who is this guy? Ten books? Oh, well, how arrogant he is.'. . . You have to be street smart and Mr. Clinton is . . . He understand[s] the way people react. He can lie and be re-elected, which is a very big surprise for the rest of the world, but not for us because he's one of us in many ways.

One of your great attributes, as someone who studies American people, is this sense of street smarts, which translates into all kinds of products, most spectacularly this summer this car—the Chrysler PT Cruiser.

First of all, we have a different code in America for outside of the car and inside of the car. So we realize that the outside code for a car in America is "Mad Max."

"Mad Max"? You talking about the Australian movie where Mel Gibson runs around . . .

Absolutely. It's a war out there. And you have to send the right message. And the message is not—like, if you have a little

In the middle of the jungle with your big . . .

Absolutely. Because when you want to keep everybody away from you you want to be inside and feel comfortable. In the PT Cruiser, you have more than 50 different positions for the seat, including taking everything out and transforming that into a minivan . . . So that was a key discovery for them, to realize that most of the time they were using some round shape outside but more feminine, more inside kind of code outside the car and they were sending the wrong message.

Dr. Rapaille, if I may, you said you've become an American citizen, I guess, fairly recently?

Yes. Correct. Six years ago.

Six years ago. And you also said that you like foreign policy but Americans don't.

Yes.

You're an intellectual and Americans don't like intellectuals.

Correct. Yeah.

Why did you bother to become an American?

Oh, this is very key for me. I think American culture is a very adolescent culture and adolescent culture means [that] we have big dreams, big hopes. 'I don't know what I'm going to do but let's do it.' And I love that. I love this dimension. . . . France [is] not an adolescent culture. It's the opposite, you know. And these people they always criticize everything. They never want to do anything. They have an idea and an idea is enough. You know, 'Oh, I had a great idea.' 'What did you do with it?' 'I was supposed to do something with an idea?' Well, it's an idea. It's a great idea. That's it.

And so I was so tired of that so I decided, you know, I'm not going to spend my life in a culture like that. I'd rather be part of an adolescent culture than a senile culture.

100.

Leon James and Diane Nahl: Road Rage

Perhaps no nation has embraced automobiles with as much enthusiasm as has the United States. Since the 1920s the United States has led the world in the rates of car ownership, miles of paved roads, and number of licensed drivers. The American passion for the automobile, however, has not come without costs. The number of fatal car accidents in the United States dwarfs that of other nations, and on average American drivers spend more time in traffic in a month than most people in other countries do in a year. In the 1990s a newly named phenomenon added yet another challenge to American drivers: road rage. As streets became more crowded, they also became more dangerous. Opinion polls have reported that road rage and aggressive driving are major daily concerns of the driving public. In their book Road Rage and Aggressive Driving: Steering Clear of Highway Warfare *(2000), professors Leon James and Diane Nahl analyze the sources of road rage and recommend safe driving techniques. Excerpts from their book are reprinted below.*

Source: *Road Rage and Aggressive Driving*, Amherst, 2000.

DRIVING IN TRAFFIC routinely involves events and incidents. Events are normal sequential maneuvers such as stopping for lights, changing lanes, or braking. Incidents are frequent but abnormal events. Some of these are dangerous and frightening, such as near-misses or violent exchanges, while others are merely annoying or depressing, such as being insulted by a driver or forgetting to make a turn. Driving events and incidents are sources of psychological forces capable of producing powerful feelings and irrational thought sequences. Driving is a dramatic activity performed by millions on a daily basis. The drama stems from high risk, interactivity, and unpredictability. Predictability creates safety, security, and escape from disaster. Unpredictability creates danger, stress, and crashes.

For many, driving is linked to a value of freedom of locomotion. On one hand, we can get into our cars and drive where we please, the very symbol of freedom and independence. But on the other hand, we encounter restrictions and constrictions—regulations, congestion, and the unexpected actions of other motorists that prevent us from driving as we wish. The following list identifies fifteen conflicting aspects of driving that act as stressors. The list represents emotional challenges that are common occasions for expressing hostility and aggressiveness on highways and streets:

1. *Immobility:* Most of the body remains still and passive during driving, unlike walking, where the entire body exerts effort and remains continuously active. Tension tends to build up when the body is physically constricted.

2. *Restriction:* Motor vehicles are restricted to narrow bands of highway and street lanes. In congested traffic, progress will inevitably be continually blocked by numerous other cars. Being prevented from going forward when you expect to arouses frustration, and along with it anxiety and an intense desire to escape the restriction. This anxiety prompts drivers to perform risky or aggressive maneuvers to get away or get ahead.

3. *Regulation:* Driving is a highly regulated activity. Government agencies and law enforcement officers tell drivers how fast and where they may drive, but cars and trucks have powerful engines capable of going much faster than is allowed. Drivers are punished for violating regulations. This regulation, though lawful and obviously necessary, feels like an imposition and arouses a rebellious streak in many, which then prompts them to disregard whatever regulations seem to be wrong or inconvenient.

4. *Lack of personal control:* Traffic follows the objective laws that govern flow patterns, like those we see in rivers, pipes, blood vessels, and streaming molecules. In congested traffic the flow depends on the available spaces between the cars. When one car slows down, hundreds of other cars behind run out of space and drivers must tap their brakes to slow down, or stop altogether. No matter how we drive, it is impossible to beat these traffic waves, whose cause may start miles away. This lack of personal control over traffic events is frustrating and often leads to venting anger on whoever is around—usually another driver or a passenger.

5. *Being put in danger:* Drivers love their cars and car repairs are expensive. Even a scratch is aggravating because it reduces the car's value. Congested traffic filled with impatient and aggressive drivers can create hair-raising close calls and hostile incidents, sometimes within a few minutes of each other. This results in physiological stress, along with many negative emotions—fear, resentment, rage, a sense of helplessness, and a depressed mood.

6. *Territoriality:* The car is symbolically associated with individual freedom and self-esteem, promoting an attitude of defensiveness and territoriality. Our car is our castle and the space around the car is our territory. When other drivers invade our space and threaten our castle, we often respond with hostility, even with warlike postures and aggressive reactions to routine incidents. We often perceive such incidents as skirmishes and battles. For many motorists, driving has become a dreaded emotional roller coaster.

7. *Diversity:* There are currently 177 million licensed drivers in the United States and they represent a breadth of experience, knowledge, ability, style, and purposes for being on the road. These social differences reduce predictability

because drivers with different skills and purposes don't behave according to the expected norms. Motorists' confidence is shaken by unexpected events, and driving becomes more complex and more emotionally challenging.

8. *Multitasking:* The increase in dashboard complexity and other in-car activities like talking on the phone or checking e-mail challenge our ability to remain alert and focused behind the wheel. Moreover, we become more irritated at others—and they at us—when our attention as drivers is perceived to be lacking due to multitasking behind the wheel.

9. *Denial:* Typically, most driving is automatic, using unconscious habits learned and compiled over years. Drivers tend to exaggerate their own excellence, overlooking their many mistakes. When passengers complain or when other drivers are threatened by these errors, there is a strong tendency for the individual to deny such mistakes and to see complaints as exaggerated, hostile, or unwarranted. This denial causes us to feel indignant and self-righteous enough to wish to punish and retaliate.

10. *Negativity:* When learning to drive, we don't just learn to manipulate the vehicle; we also acquire an overly critical attitude toward other drivers. As children we're exposed to the judgmental behavior of our parents and other adults as they drive us around. It's also reinforced in movies portraying drivers behaving badly. This culture of mutual hostility among motorists promotes an active and negative emotional life behind the wheel.

11. *Self-serving bias:* Driving incidents are not neutral; someone is always considered to be at fault. The tendency to attribute fault to others is natural, but it influences our memory of what happened, and we easily lose objectivity and judgment in a dispute.

12. *Venting:* Our culture permits and even encourages venting anger. It's supposed to be healthy to "let it out" instead of keep it inside. But venting has its own logic, and vented anger tends to expand until it breaks out into overt hostility. Venting is felt as an energizing "rush." This seductive feeling is short-lived, and is accompanied by a stream of anger-inspiring thoughts that impair judgment and tempt us into rash and dangerous actions. Habitual venting can have serious physical consequences by weakening the immune system. But motivation and self-training can help drivers learn not to explode.

13. *Unpredictability:* Streets and highways create an environment of drama, danger, and uncertainty. Competition, hostility, and stress further intensify negative emotions. Even noise and smells aggravate feelings of frustration and resentment. The driving environment requires constant emotional adjustment to unexpected, tedious, brutish, and dangerous occurrences.

14. *Isolation:* Motorists cannot communicate. There is no easy way of saying, "Oops, I'm sorry!" as we can in a bank line. This leads to ambiguity and misunderstanding: "Did he just flip me off or was that an apology?" It would be helpful if vehicles were equipped with an electronic display allowing drivers to flash appropriate prerecorded messages that facilitate coordination and positive interaction in driving.

15. *Emotional challenges:* Traditionally, driver education teaches students some general principles of safety, with a few hours of supervised hands-on experience behind the wheel or on a driving simulator. Developing awareness of common and problematic driving behaviors and the application of sound judgment and emotional self-control have not been part of the training. Most nonprofes-

sional drivers today are insufficiently trained in cognitive and affective skills. Cognitive skills are good habits of thinking and judgment in challenging situations. Affective skills are good habits of attitude and motivation in challenging situations. Drivers often lack the emotional intelligence coping skills essential for driving on today's roads, including how to:

- cool off when angered or frustrated;
- retain focus when multitasking;
- cooperate with the traffic flow and not hinder it;
- allocate sufficient time for the trip;
- feel responsible for obeying traffic regulations; and
- be a supportive, noncompetitive, compassionate driver.

The common element in all fifteen driving stressors is anger, possibly the most frequent of human emotions. Anger has always been closely linked to aggressive behavior. It is common to relate aggressiveness to social and environmental factors, in addition to individual personality factors. For instance, under certain critical conditions, congestion on highways and anonymity in cars interact with faulty attitudes and inadequate coping skills to produce aggressive traffic behavior. These apparent triggering conditions are unpredictable and hold symbolic meaning to the interactants, who may report having felt insulted or threatened.

Sigmund Freud held a Darwinian theory of human aggression, still popular today, that views anger as a biological instinct. Aggression and violence are ultimately forces of self-destructiveness in the innate struggle between life and death. Aggressiveness and assertiveness are clearly different in intention, but sometimes they are difficult to distinguish behaviorally. In our society, competition and disagreement are often used

as mechanisms for establishing identity, as in athletics and the marketplace. Biological theories of aggressiveness have also been used to rationalize aggressive driving. According to a U.K. study, an increase in road rage incidents occurred throughout the various layers of society: young and old, men and women, the public and law enforcement alike. Furthermore, road rage behavior could not be predicted on the basis of personality or reputation, so that those committing violent roadway behavior do so uncharacteristically. . . .

The anger we feel behind the wheel may have either (or both) of two sources: another driver's behavior or some earlier event unrelated to driving. *Displaced anger* is a common defense mechanism used in many situations. On the road, displaced anger seems to be triggered by a driving incident, and the other driver becomes the enemy target. Some drivers seek medical help after a scary driving incident, even when not obviously injured. These symptoms of post-traumatic stress disorder can last for months, even years, according to Dr. Arnold Nerenberg, a noted road rage psychotherapist. There are few self-referrals at the Harborview Anger Management clinic, according to Dr. Maiuro:

> People exhibiting road rage often do not seek help because of their limited self-awareness and a tendency to see the "other guy" (perceived as provocative and deserving of retaliation) as the problem. Consequently, self-referral to programs such as ours is rare, and an afflicted driver usually arrives for help at the request of a traffic court judge, lawyer, or family member concerned about the person's own safety and the risk to others.

Our research in Hawaii shows that aggressive drivers resist change primarily because they deny that they have a driv-

ing problem. Our three-step program for
recovery from aggressive driving begins
with the most difficult step, "I acknowledge that I need to retrain myself as a

driver." The hallmark of today's driving
culture is denying aggressiveness or calling it assertive, efficient, or progressive
instead.

101.

JOHN MCCAIN: Ban the Soft Money

*By the 1990s many Americans had concluded that campaign contributions from
corporations and political lobbying groups had corrupted the country's electoral
process. Politicians seemed to spend too much time and energy soliciting campaign
donations to finance their reelection instead of taking care of the nation's business.
In addition, many observers believed that corporate and special interest
contributions influenced politicians' votes at the expense of the public interest.
John McCain, a U.S. senator from Arizona, responded to this public discontent by
mounting a presidential campaign committed to reforming the campaign-funding
system. During the 2000 primary campaign, McCain lost the Republican
nomination to Texas Governor George W. Bush but succeeded in placing
campaign-funding reform at the top of the American political agenda. Both parties
adopted reform platforms during the general campaign, and in the aftermath of
the election, McCain led the way in calling on Congress to pass legislation on the
issue. He targeted in particular "soft money" donations, unregulated campaign
contributions made by special interest groups directly to political parties, often in
huge sums. Shortly after the general election, McCain laid out his argument
against "soft money" in a* Washington Post *opinion piece from November 2000,
reprinted below. In 2001 Congress passed his campaign finance reform bill.*

Source: *The Washington Post,* November 19, 2000.

ALTHOUGH THE FORMAL campaign for the
presidency ended on Nov. 7, it's evident
to even the most indifferent observer of
current events that the presidency is still
being contested—vigorously contested by
both legal and political means. The public is understandably concerned not only
about the outcome but also about how it
is achieved.

Whoever takes office in January will,
regrettably and not deservedly, enter office with widespread partisan questions
about his legitimacy. I believe the next

president has earned and should be accorded the respect of all Americans, and
a fair chance to lead this great nation. I
am confident that we will determine who
won Florida, and that he won it fairly.
But many aggrieved partisans who supported the losing candidate will not, I
fear, be quick to share my confidence.
That is the new fact of our political life
produced by the incredibly narrow margin of victory in this election, and by the
resulting confusion and hard feelings in
Florida.

The harsh partisanship of recent years that has contributed to the American people's diminished esteem for public officials could grow worse, causing people's faith in government's ability to serve their needs to decline correspondingly. The next president will have to embark immediately on a series of confidence-building measures that might encourage Congress to help him find bipartisan solutions to difficult national problems, allay the suspicions of half the electorate and give hope to all Americans that, just maybe, those of us privileged to govern America are capable under trying circumstances of putting the nation's interests before our own.

Patriots of both parties have offered sensible suggestions toward that end, from the new president's choosing respected members of the other party to serve in his Cabinet to reconciling, with fair compromises, some of the policy priorities of both parties. But let me offer one measure that I think would greatly enhance the prospects for bipartisan progress on the nation's business, help the new president confound expectations of ineffectiveness and begin restoring Americans' faith in the credibility of their leaders.

When all the money that washed through this election cycle is counted, $4 billion or more will have been spent on federal and state campaigns, half again as much as was spent on all races in 1996. Voter turnout, up slightly from 1996, was still only a little more than half of all eligible voters. Most discouraging was the abysmally low turnout among voters age 18 to 29—just 38 percent.

Clearly, the rushing stream of cash, coming in the form of huge, unlimited contributions known as soft money, has done precious little to encourage participation in our democratic processes. On the contrary, it has increased public in-

difference and cynicism by, among other things, underwriting much of the negative advertising that is intended to drive down voter turnout.

More troubling than the public's widespread neglect of its most fundamental civic responsibility—voting—is its deeply rooted perception, to the point that it has become part of American folklore, that we elected officials of both parties are so narrowly self-interested that we are incapable of reforming the practices and institutions of our democracy to meet the challenges of our times. Public expectations for government seldom run higher than "Maybe they won't do too much harm."

I am a conservative. I believe it is a healthy thing for Americans to be skeptical about the purposes and practices of public officials and to refrain from expecting too much from their government. Self-reliance is the ethic that made America great. But when healthy public skepticism becomes widespread cynicism bordering on alienation, conservative no less than liberal officeholders should recognize that we share the primary responsibility for convincing Americans that our government still embodies our national ideals. When the people come to believe that their government is so dysfunctional or even corrupt that it no longer serves basic constitutional ends, our culture could fragment beyond recognition.

Many, if not most, Americans believe we in government conspire to hold on to every political advantage we have, lest we jeopardize our incumbency by a single lost vote. They believe we would pay any price, bear any burden, to ensure the success of our personal ambitions, no matter how injurious the effect on the national interest. And who can blame them, when the wealthiest Americans and richest organized interests can make huge donations to political parties and gain the special access to power such generosity confers on the donor.

Were Congress and the president to agree to ban soft money—the five- and six-figure checks that have effectively nullified all legal limits on campaign contributions—even while agreeing to reasonable increases in hard money limits imposed more than a quarter of a century ago, we would remove one of the most durable impediments to achieving bipartisan consensus on reforming entitlements, the tax code, government spending, HMOs, education and tort law.

Soft money's practical effect on the legislative process is to elevate both parties' allegiance to their chief donors above our ideological distinctions and our responsibility to address pressing national priorities. Indeed, partisan deference to core supporters of both parties is a less significant cause of legislative gridlock than is our gratitude to the chief underwriters of our campaigns in elections that are less a battle of ideas than a test of political treasuries.

Trial lawyers, as major donors to the Democratic Party, prevent any reform of HMOs that doesn't encourage explosive increases in costly litigation, while insurance companies, as major donors to the Republican Party, resist even basic fairness in empowering patients to make life-or-death decisions regarding their own health care. Surely, we can do better than this.

When the new Congress and the new president are sworn in, let us remove soft money's negative effect on bipartisan cooperation and on our public discourse. Let us take this sensible first step on the long road to convincing the American people that their representatives in Congress and their president are patriots first and partisans second.

In the early seventies, I proposed that free television be made available in TV spots and that privately paid-for TV spots be banned, but the FCC didn't even dignify my petition with a response. Far more modest proposals have been essentially laughed out of Congress. Why would a mafia in charge of the most powerful machine in the world willingly yield?

JERRY BROWN, "We the People" radio broadcast

In the 1990s, the terrorism that had afflicted much of the world for decades came to the United States, beginning with the bomb that was detonated in the basement garage of the World Trade Center in New York City on February 26, 1993, some of whose victims are being treated here. In March 1994 four Arab immigrants were convicted of the crime by a federal jury.

Foreign terrorists were again suspected when a truck bomb exploded outside the Alfred P. Murrah Federal Building in Oklahoma City, Oklahoma, on April 19, 1995, killing 168 and injuring some 500 others, but in this case the terrorist was an American, Timothy McVeigh, a Persian Gulf War veteran and right-wing extremist who, in 1997, was convicted of planning and implementing the attack. He was executed in June 2001.

TERRORISM

Flanked here by federal agents in Helena, Montana, following his arrest in April 1996, Ted Kaczynski, a former mathematics professor at the University of California, Berkeley, was discovered to be the "Unabomber," whose seventeen-year campaign of letter-bomb terror dating from 1978 was responsible for three deaths and twenty-three injuries.

Investigators inspect the scene at Olympic Centennial Park in Atlanta, Georgia, where a crude pipe bomb exploded on July 27, 1996, killing one, injuring 111 others, and disrupting one of the most security-conscious Summer Olympic Games ever staged.

On October 12, 2000, two suicide bombers, later believed to be members of the radical Islamic terrorist group al-Qaeda, pulled alongside the USS *Cole* in a small boat and blew a massive hole in the missile destroyer while it docked in Aden, Yemen, killing seventeen sailors and injuring thirty-nine others.

The second of two commercial jetliners hijacked by al-Qaeda terrorists and crashed into the World Trade Center on September 11, 2001, approaches its target while smoke billows from the crash of the first airliner.

102.

Naftali Bendavid and Bob Kemper: The Disputed Election of 2000

Unlike many presidential elections, the outcome of the contest in 2000 between Republican George W. Bush, Governor of Texas, and Democrat Al Gore, the Vice President, was uncertain to even the savviest prognosticator in the weeks preceding the vote. And unlike other elections, it continued to be uncertain in the weeks after the polls had closed. On the evening of the election, November 7, the broadcast and print media alternately declared Bush and Gore the winner, until it was realized that electoral victory in what proved to be the deciding state of Florida was "too close to call." The newspaper account reprinted below describes the range of emotions felt by the candidates and their supporters on election night as conflicting reports of victory and loss were communicated. In the hours after midnight Gore placed two separate phone calls to Bush, first to concede defeat then to retract his concession, after it became clear that the reported results were not final. Ballot counting and political campaigning continued, and when a statewide machine recount of the Florida gave Bush the victory by less than 1,000 votes, Gore requested a manual recount in several Florida counties where there had been ballot inconsistencies. When the Florida Supreme Court narrowly supported Gore (by a vote of 4 to 3) by calling for a manual statewide recount, Bush appealed to the U.S. Supreme Court, which narrowly ruled (by a vote of 5 to 4) to reverse the Florida court's request for a recount. Amid a storm of controversy, the 25 electoral votes in Florida were awarded to Bush, giving him the state-by-state electoral college victory (by a vote of 271 to 266) and thus the presidency. The final tally had Gore winning the nationwide popular vote by 500,000, marking the first time since 1888 that the candidate winning the popular vote lost the presidency.

Source: *Chicago Tribune*, November 9, 2000, "Frantic Moments, Rumors in the Rain and a Tense Call."

At 2 a.m. Wednesday, a crowd waited with glum defiance in a cold rain at Nashville's Legislative Plaza for Vice President Al Gore to concede to Texas Gov. George W. Bush.

Rumors swept the restless crowd: The key state of Florida, claimed by Bush, was in fact too close to call. Gore had called Bush to retract his concession. The election was not over after all. Bafflement prevailed.

At 3:04 a.m., Gore campaign chairman William Daley emerged and capped one of the most extraordinary hours in American politics by announcing there would be no concession. "We simply cannot be certain of the results of this national election," he announced, and the crowd erupted jubilantly.

What happened during the crucial hour between Gore's apparent defeat and the revival of his hopes is a story of wildly oscillating emotions, hastily called meetings, a sharp exchange between the candidates, and dreams dashed and revived. It was a chaotic end to a long, tense night.

At about 1:30 a.m., the telephone rang in the governor's mansion in Austin, Texas. Bush, on his way to the kitchen, picked it up.

On the other end was Gore, who had been watching the election in his suite at Loews Vanderbilt Plaza in Nashville. The vice president had decided his lifelong crusade was over and he called Bush, congratulated him and admitted he'd lost the election.

Bush graciously told Gore he was a good man and said he respected him. "I understand this is difficult for you and your family," Bush added. He asked Gore to give his best to Gore's wife, Tipper, and the four Gore children.

"It was a very cordial conversation," said one person who was able to hear the Bush side of the exchange.

A long night of waiting seemed to be over for both men. Bush and his family, after ending their dinner early, had been sequestered in the mansion's living quarters as the electoral map tilted first one way and then the other.

But when Bush hung up, emotions long held in check erupted in a cathartic rush of joy. Bush, his wife, Laura, and his parents, former President George Bush and former First Lady Barbara Bush, rushed into each other's arms.

"There was lots of hugging and kissing and tears in the eyes and back-slapping," said one person who was there.

A block away, at a stage constructed in front of the Texas Capitol, a campaign official announced Bush would arrive in 20 minutes to claim victory.

Only a few hundred people had remained in the damp, chilly night. But as word spread that Florida, and hence the election, had gone for Bush, people ran from all directions, shouting, cheering, applauding, trying to get back inside the barricades to await him.

But in making the concession call, Gore was relying on television coverage of the Florida contest, not his campaign's own field reports. The networks said Bush was winning Florida by 50,000 votes and they had anointed him as the next president.

At 1:45 a.m. in Nashville, Gore and his wife got into the vice presidential limousine, walking past downcast, red-eyed staffers. Gore's motorcade wound its way the few blocks from their hotel to Legislative Plaza, where hundreds of supporters were waiting.

As the motorcade was en route, Michael Whouley, Gore's director of field operations, decided to check the Web site of Florida's secretary of state, where vote tallies were being regularly updated.

Whouley was in the "boiler room" at Gore headquarters, the campaign nerve center, and what he saw shocked him: Only 6,000 votes separated Gore and Bush in Florida, not 50,000, and a significant number of votes had yet to be counted.

Whouley immediately paged Michael Feldman, Gore's traveling chief of staff, who was in the motorcade when he felt his beeper vibrate. Feldman in turn called Daley, who was in another van in the motorcade.

The caravan was just two blocks from the plaza where Gore was to speak. By the time it arrived, even more Florida votes had been counted and now just 600 votes separated the candidates.

Legislative Plaza was an emotional location for Gore. His parents had met there, and he had eulogized his father on the site. About 2 a.m., when Gore arrived, it was beautiful, with the state Capitol and the nearby war memorial ablaze in spotlights.

As the crowd waited in forlorn expectation, prominent Gore supporters began arriving sadly.

In a holding room at the War Memorial, where Gore had expected to steel himself for his concession speech, Daley took him aside and told him how thin the Florida margin was.

Gore, Daley and a small group of other aides discussed the situation. They hurriedly concluded that Gore could not concede with the difference so small, a margin that would trigger an automatic recount under Florida law.

At 2:15 a.m., with both the Nashville and Austin crowds puzzled and waiting, Daley called Bush campaign chairman Don Evans and told him Gore had changed his mind.

A little after 2:30 a.m., Gore called Bush and did something probably unprecedented in presidential history: He retracted his concession. Bush was stunned, and it is clear the conversation was testy.

"Let me make sure I understand," Bush told Gore. "You are calling me back to retract the concession?" When Gore assured him he was, Bush replied, "Mr. vice president, you have to do what you have to do."

Gore told Bush, "You don't have to get snippy about it."

After the call, the mood in the Texas governor's mansion turned abruptly from joy to "unbelieving," said one witness.

Gore hung up and got into his limousine to return to his hotel, leaving so quickly that part of his motorcade was left behind.

Oblivious to the drama unfolding so near them, thousands of people on the streets of Nashville and Austin waited to hear from candidates who would never appear. It fell to the campaign managers to break the news.

Evans took the stage in Texas to address Bush's bewildered supporters. "We hope and believe that we have elected the next president of the United States," Evans said. "They're still counting."

Daley walked to the front of a long stage designed for a presidential victory speech, with teleprompters on each side.

"I've been in politics a very long time but I don't think there's ever been a night like this one," Daley began. He reported that Gore would not yet concede.

"Our campaign continues," Daley added.

◆

What is politics but persuading the public to vote for this and support that and endure these for the promise of those?
GILBERT HIGHET, "The Art of Persuasion," *Vogue,* 1951

103.

Al Gore: Concession Speech

When, on the evening of December 12, the U.S. Supreme Court overruled an earlier decision by the Florida Supreme Court to allow a recount of the Presidential election in Florida, the election of 2000 finally came to a close, with Republican George W. Bush set to become the forty-third President of the United States. The election dispute, which preoccupied the country for more than a month, hinged on Democratic allegations of procedural errors in the counting of votes in several Florida counties. The standard used to judge what constituted a Bush vote and what constituted a vote for the Democratic candidate, Al Gore, posed the major stumbling block to resolving the matter. As discussions of the irregularities filled the media, Americans added a new word to their vocabularies, chad (the small section of paper punched out on a ballot when a vote is cast), some of which "hung," or remained stuck to, some ballots, thus making it difficult and in some cases impossible to determine the voters' intentions. Although recounts in four disputed counties had shown Bush maintaining a statewide lead of more than five hundred votes, the Gore campaign alleged that election officials had not counted several hundred pro-Gore ballots. As charges and countercharges filled the nation's airwaves, some observers feared that a winner would never be determined accurately. On December 13, the day after the U.S. Supreme Court finally ruled against further recounts, Gore gave the concession speech that is reprinted below.

Source: *Vital Speeches of the Day,* January 1, 2001.

GOOD EVENING. Just moments ago, I spoke with George W. Bush and congratulated him on becoming the 43rd president of the United States, and I promised him that I wouldn't call him back this time.

I offered to meet with him as soon as possible so that we can start to heal the divisions of the campaign and the contest through which we just passed.

Almost a century and a half ago, Senator Stephen Douglas told Abraham Lincoln, who had just defeated him for the presidency, "Partisan feeling must yield to patriotism. I'm with you, Mr. President, and God bless you."

Well, in that same spirit, I say to President-elect Bush that what remains of partisan rancor must now be put aside, and may God bless his stewardship of this country.

Neither he nor I anticipated this long and difficult road. Certainly neither of us wanted it to happen. Yet it came, and now it has ended, resolved, as it must be resolved, through the honored institutions of our democracy.

Over the library of one of our great law schools is inscribed the motto, "Not under man but under God and law." That's the ruling principle of American freedom, the source of our democratic liberties. I've tried to make it my guide throughout this contest as it has guided America's deliberations of all the complex issues of the past five weeks.

Now the U.S. Supreme Court has spoken. Let there be no doubt, while I strongly disagree with the court's decision, I accept it. I accept the finality of this outcome, which will be ratified next Monday in the Electoral College. And tonight, for the sake of our unity as a people and the strength of our democracy, I offer my concession.

I also accept my responsibility, which I will discharge unconditionally, to honor the new president-elect and do everything possible to help him bring Americans together in fulfillment of the great vision that our Declaration of Independence defines and that our Constitution affirms and defends.

Let me say how grateful I am to all those who supported me and supported the cause for which we have fought. Tipper and I feel a deep gratitude to Joe and Hadassah Lieberman who brought passion and high purpose to our partnership and opened new doors, not just for our campaign but for our country.

This has been an extraordinary election. But in one of God's unforeseen paths, this belatedly broken impasse can point us all to a new common ground, for its very closeness can serve to remind us that we are one people with a shared history and a shared destiny.

Indeed, that history gives us many examples of contests as hotly debated, as fiercely fought, with their own challenges to the popular will.

Other disputes have dragged on for weeks before reaching resolution. And each time, both the victor and the vanquished have accepted the result peacefully and in the spirit of reconciliation.

So let it be with us.

I know that many of my supporters are disappointed. I am, too. But our disappointment must be overcome by our love of country.

And I say to our fellow members of the world community, let no one see this contest as a sign of American weakness. The strength of American democracy is shown most clearly through the difficulties it can overcome.

Some have expressed concern that the unusual nature of this election might hamper the next president in the conduct of his office. I do not believe it need be so.

President-elect Bush inherits a nation whose citizens will be ready to assist him in the conduct of his large responsibilities.

I personally will be at his disposal, and I call on all Americans—I particularly urge all who stood with us to unite behind our next president. This is America. Just as we fight hard when the stakes are high, we close ranks and come together when the contest is done.

And while there will be time enough to debate our continuing differences, now is the time to recognize that that which unites us is greater than that which divides us.

While we yet hold and do not yield our opposing beliefs, there is a higher duty than the one we owe to political party. This is America and we put country before party. We will stand together behind our new president.

As for what I'll do next, I don't know the answer to that one yet. Like many of you, I'm looking forward to spending the holidays with family and old friends. I know I'll spend time in Tennessee and mend some fences, literally and figuratively.

Some have asked whether I have any regrets and I do have one regret: that I didn't get the chance to stay and fight for the American people over the next four years, especially for those who need burdens lifted and barriers removed, especially for those who feel their voices have not been heard. I heard you and I will not forget.

I've seen America in this campaign and I like what I see. It's worth fighting for and that's a fight I'll never stop.

As for the battle that ends tonight, I do believe as my father once said, that no matter how hard the loss, defeat might serve as well as victory to shape the soul and let the glory out.

So for me this campaign ends as it began: with love of Tipper and our family; with faith in God and in the country I have been so proud to serve, from Vietnam to the vice presidency; and with

gratitude to our truly tireless campaign staff and volunteers, including all those who worked so hard in Florida for the last 36 days.

Now the political struggle is over and we turn again to the unending struggle for the common good of all Americans and for those multitudes around the world who look to us for leadership in the cause of freedom.

In the words of our great hymn, "America, America": "Let us crown thy good with brotherhood, from sea to shining sea."

And now, my friends, in a phrase I once addressed to others, it's time for me to go.

Thank you and good night, and God bless America.

Vice President Gore and I put our hearts and hopes into our campaigns. We both gave it our all. We shared similar emotions, so I understand how difficult this moment must be for Vice President Gore and his family.

GEORGE W. BUSH, acceptance speech,
December 13, 2000

104.

Eric Schlosser: *Fast Food Nation*

The rise of the fast-food industry transformed American eating habits in the second half of the twentieth century. Inexpensive, convenient, and delicious, fast food became a staple of the American diet. Originally offering only hamburgers and french fries, the industry rapidly diversified, adding tacos, burritos, pizza, and other items to their menus. McDonald's, Burger King, Taco Bell, and numerous other companies spread across the United States and even the world, establishing restaurants virtually everywhere, from small towns in Montana to major European metropolises. In the process the "golden arches" of the McDonald's logo became an internationally recognized symbol of American culture. Although the fast-food industry continued to generate record profits, a growing chorus of critics arose in the late twentieth century. Some pointed out that the high fat and high calorie content of fast-food menus had contributed to a staggering increase in obesity rates in the United States, which in turn gave rise to serious health problems such as heart disease and diabetes. Critics also chastised the industry for its low wages, poor working conditions, food safety problems, and misuse of agricultural land and animals. Reprinted below are excerpts of an Atlantic Monthly Online *interview with Eric Schlosser, an award-winning investigative journalist and the author of* Fast Food Nation. *The interviewer was Julia Livshin.*

Source: *The Atlantic Monthly Online*, December 14, 2000, "Interview with Eric Schlosser, Author of *Fast Food Nation*."

You write that the market for fast food in the United States is becoming increasingly saturated. What sort of future do you see for the fast-food industry? Might it become obsolete?

That's a very good question. In a way, the future of the fast-food industry is tied to the future of this country. If we continue to allow the growth of a low-wage service economy, one in which unions are weak and workers have little say about their working conditions—well, then the fast-food chains will have a bright future. On the other hand, if we bring the minimum wage up to the level it was thirty years ago, in real terms, and we enforce the rules about overtime, and make it easier

to organize service workers, the fast-food chains will have to change their business model. Or go out of business. Access to cheap labor, and a lot of it, has been crucial to their success.

I also think that the desire for uniformity and cheapness and reassurance that the American people have had over the last two decades, which has really helped the fast-food chains, could wane. People may become more concerned about what they're eating and reject the idea that everything should be the same everywhere they go. The chains are in a vulnerable position right now, if only because they've expanded so far and wide across the country that they're already reaching the limits of demand for fast food. And if there's a different consciousness in this country, something less conformist, they may really be in trouble.

From an economic standpoint, are the fast-food chains providing something valuable?

Well, there's no question that they're providing jobs for millions of people. At the same time, how good is it ultimately for society to have jobs that are short-term and that essentially provide no training? You could argue that for some teenagers short-term jobs are a good thing as a source of extra income. But I would argue that there should be a major restructuring of the fast-food industry's employment practices so that these aren't just make-work jobs but jobs that actually provide a meaningful kind of training. For the poorest, most disadvantaged people in this society, simply having a job and having some kind of structure in their lives can be useful. But given the tremendous impact that these companies have on our workforce, they can and should provide more than just a place to show up every day. Another thing that's important to consider is the sort of work that these fast-food jobs have replaced. The old diners and hamburger stands relied on skilled short-order cooks. If you look at the restaurant industry as a whole, jobs at fast-food chains are the lowest paying and have the highest turnover rate. So to the degree that the fast-food companies have grown and thrived and replaced more traditional eating places, they have encouraged the rise of a workforce that is poor, transient, and unskilled.

Same question from the standpoint of food. Fast food is convenient and cheap. Is the fast-food industry providing a valuable service by catering to the consumer needs of a certain segment of society?

There's no question that fast food is inexpensive and easily accessible. For people who don't have time to prepare meals, for households in which both parents work, there's no question it provides a service. But again, at what cost? As I say in the book, the real cost never appears on the menu. The fast-food companies have directed a large amount of their marketing at low-income communities. They are serving extremely high-fat food to people who are at the greatest risk of the health consequences from obesity. They could be selling low cost food that doesn't have the same health consequences, especially for children. The fast-food chains, with their kids' meals and Happy Meals, are creating eating habits that will last a lifetime. And by heavily marketing unhealthy foods to low-income children they are encouraging health problems among the segment of the population that can least afford them.

If you see a change for the better taking place, do you envision these same companies changing their own policies about what they're going to be marketing and holding their suppliers to more stringent food production standards, or do you see a whole new industry taking over?

I think it'll be determined by how easily these companies can change. The McDonald's Corporation, at the moment, in many ways reminds me of the Soviet-era Kremlin. I was unable to get a single question answered after weeks of calling them, e-mailing them, and faxing them. It was what I imagine it must have been like dealing with the old Communist Party bureaucrats. Can the McDonald's Corporation remake itself into a company that behaves ethically, has a stronger social conscience, and changes its menu? That remains to be seen. It may be that new companies will emerge, embodying a different set of values, selling better and healthier food.

Both this book about fast food and your article about strawberry picking are concerned with the plight of workers in these industries. How did you get interested in labor issues?

There are strong connections between the strawberry article and this book. The workers that I met in the meatpacking plants in Colorado and Nebraska were the same kinds of people that I met in the strawberry fields of California. Many of the meatpacking workers that I met in Colorado and Nebraska had previously been farm workers in California. They'd come to the High Plains because there was a shortage of work in the fields in California and because the pay promised to be higher in Colorado and Nebraska. Although I was appalled at the lives of California's migrant farm workers and the injuries they suffer, what's happening in meatpacking plants in Colorado and Nebraska, in Kansas and Texas, is even worse. It's criminal. These are poor immigrants, few of them speak English, and a large proportion are illiterate. They are peasants, manual laborers from rural villages in Mexico and Guatemala. When they get badly hurt in these meatpacking plants, which happens all the time, they're unable to do manual labor the same way ever again. They are permanently prevented from earning an income the way that they have earned an income their whole lives.

Much of this book builds upon what I learned in California's strawberry fields. My interest in the subject of immigrant labor began in the mid 1990s when there was a growing anti-immigrant movement in California. Illegal immigrants were

being blamed for all of the state's economic problems. And I instinctively felt that couldn't be right, because it seemed to me that the largest industry in the state—agriculture—was benefiting enormously from illegal immigrants. Today there's a vast underclass of migrant workers in this country. We've had a migrant agricultural workforce for more than a century. But for the first time we're developing a migrant industrial workforce. This has ominous implications for workers in other industries. Until the late 1970s, meatpacking was one of the highest paid industrial jobs in the United States. And then the Reagan and Bush administrations stood aside and allowed the meatpacking industry to bust unions, to hire strikebreakers and scabs, to not only hire illegal immigrants for these jobs, but to transport them here from Mexico in company buses. Now meatpacking is one of the nation's lowest paying industrial jobs, as well as the most dangerous. I'm sure other companies, in other industries, are contemplating the same tactics. And it just can't be allowed. . . .

Writing in the September 1998 issue of The Atlantic *about mad-cow disease, Ellen Ruppel Shell noted, "[M]ost of the conditions thought to have led to the epidemic in Britain also existed here. Despite official protestations to the contrary, and despite regulatory changes recently implemented, some of them still do. Given current agricultural practices, avoiding an American outbreak of this disease may be only a matter of chance. The question is, how lucky do we feel?" Now, five years later, mad-cow disease has resurfaced in Europe, creating widespread panic. What are your thoughts about the probability of an American outbreak?*

Ellen Ruppel Shell's article was terrific. So how lucky should we feel, right now, in December of 2000? Extremely lucky.

But there are so many unknown factors about this disease, and how it's spread, and how long it incubates, that our luck may run out. Cattle in the United States are still being fed cattle blood, as well as rendered livestock wastes from hog slaughterhouses. They're still being fed dead horses. And poultry in the United States are routinely being fed the rendered waste from cattle slaughterhouses. The potential for this pathogen to jump from species to species exists. Somehow it might wind up infecting people. We've taken a big risk by turning ruminants into unwitting cannibals and carnivores. The European Union is now banning the use of all slaughterhouse wastes in animal feed. We should do the same thing, immediately.

Do you think there's a false sense of security, that people in this country assume that since there's a food safety system in place it must be effective?

With each new *E. coli* outbreak there is a greater anxiety about the food that we eat. But there's still an enormous lack of awareness about how our food-safety system works and how the meatpacking industry has been able to work it. The industry has for years spread large sums of money throughout the political process. And the USDA has always had close ties to the industry. If you look back at Teddy Roosevelt's campaign against the meatpacking industry, you'll find that the same battle has been fought now for almost a century. It's a battle to get this industry to assume responsibility for the meat that it sells. Automobile companies are held responsible for cars that are fundamentally defective, that explode on impact, etc. But the meatpacking industry has, with remarkable success, fought every attempt to make it liable for the sale of contaminated, potentially deadly, meat.

Very few people realize that the U.S. government does not have the power to order the recall of contaminated meat. The Clinton administration made a sincere effort to reform the nation's food-safety and inspection program, but the Republicans in Congress were determined to impede any major overhaul of the system. So what we wound up with is a watered-down food-safety system. One of the most remarkable things is that meatpacking companies today are routinely testing their meat for dangerous pathogens, but don't have to reveal the results of these tests to the government. A recent investigation by the Inspector General of the USDA suggested that companies are shipping meat that they've tested and that they *know* to be contaminated. By not revealing the test results to the USDA, they're able to ship this meat. It's incredible what is being sold in supermarkets throughout the country as we speak.

You warn that "Anyone who brings raw ground beef into his or her kitchen today must regard it as a potential biohazard, one that may carry an extremely dangerous microbe, infectious at an extremely low dose." And you say that the levels of poultry contamination are even higher. How would you respond to someone who has always eaten poultry and ground beef, has never been sick, and who might perceive this as alarmism?

I don't think that I'm being an alarmist. I'm just letting people know what's in their meat. There's no question that the level of contamination in poultry is much, much higher, and the level in ground turkey is highest of all. The pathogens most commonly found in poultry—*Salmonella* and *Campylobacter*—are not as deadly, relatively speaking, as the *E. coli* 0157:H7 that turns up in ground beef. Keep in mind, though, that every year about 30,000 Americans are hospitalized for *Salmonella* and *Campylobacter* infections they got from tainted food. And when the Centers for Disease Control says that there are about 76 million cases of food poisoning in the United States every year, that's not being alarmist. That's a fact.

As for people who think they've never been sickened by ground beef or poultry, my response would be: how do you know? The symptoms of food poisoning often don't appear for days after the contaminated meal was eaten. As a result, most cases of food poisoning are never properly diagnosed. There may be some people with cast-iron stomachs who never get sick, and good for them. But there are millions of people, especially children and the elderly, who are extremely vulnerable to foodborne pathogens.

By the way, I'm not a vegetarian. I have a lot of respect for people who are vegetarian for religious or ethical reasons. Despite everything I saw and learned while researching this book, I'm still a meat eater. But I don't eat ground beef anymore. I've seen where it comes from and how it's now being made. One of my favorite dishes in the world used to be steak tartare, which is raw ground beef seasoned and then served. I think you'd have to be a great thrill-seeker or out of your mind to eat steak tartare today. . . .

In the book you quote Upton Sinclair's famous statement about The Jungle*'s reception: "I aimed for the public's heart, and by accident I hit it in the stomach." While successful in igniting a public-health scandal, which led to the enactment of food-safety legislation, Sinclair's exposé did nothing to improve the plight of packinghouse workers. If you had to choose, which of the issues in* Fast Food Nation *do you personally feel most strongly about? Where, in your opinion, is the need for regulatory action most urgent?*

Well, ideally, you'd hit both. There is an immediate instinct in most people to worry first about themselves, and that's totally understandable and natural. A large part of the book pertains to food safety and what's in the meat and what we're eating and what the consequences are. It's much more of a challenge to try to get readers to care about other people, about poor and exploited people who are in need of help. I hope the section on meatpacking workers will bring some attention to and empathy for their plight. Of greatest immediate concern to me are the forty to fifty thousand meatpacking workers who are being injured every year and the roughly one hundred thousand Americans, mainly children and the elderly, who are being sickened by dangerous *E. coli* such as 0157:H7. There are some very simple steps that could be taken very quickly that would reduce the number of injuries in meatpacking and reduce the number of food poisoning cases in the United States. This isn't rocket science. It's technologies and procedures that could be implemented if not tomorrow then next month. The tragedy is they're not being implemented right now because of complacency and greed.

For example?

Well, to improve worker safety, there could be an immediate and tough crackdown on the meatpacking companies by OSHA (the Occupational Safety and Health Administration) and strict enforcement of the worker safety laws that we already have. The easiest step would be to slow down the production line. The big beef slaughterhouses in this country process between 300 and 375, sometimes up to 400 cattle an hour. In Western Europe slaughterhouses tend to slaughter 75 to 100 cattle an hour. In Australia it's about 115. The number of injuries at a plant is often directly related to the speed of the line, so the first thing would be to force these companies to slow down their production lines.

As for food safety, the meatpacking companies should be held strictly accountable for the products that they sell. Manufacturers of stuffed animals are held accountable. The government can force them to recall stuffed animals that are defective and that might choke children. In the same way, the meatpacking companies should be held accountable for the sale of contaminated meat. There should be legislation passed immediately that gives the federal government the power to recall tainted meat. It should not be up to the meatpacking companies to issue voluntarily recalls. The federal government should also be given the power to impose large civil fines on meatpacking companies that knowingly ship tainted meat. We should also reorganize the food-safety system in the United States so that there is a single food-safety agency, like there is in many Western European countries. About a dozen federal agencies have jurisdiction over food safety right now. The Department of Agriculture is in charge not only of inspecting our meat, but also of promoting its sale. There's an inherent conflict of interest. We need an independent food-safety agency whose first priority is public health.

In the epilogue you say that the likelihood of such regulatory legislation being passed is slim.

When I wrote the epilogue last spring, the odds were slim. Now they're just about down to none. The meatpacking and restaurant industries work closely with the right-wing Republicans in Congress. Nevertheless, at some point, if enough people demand change and enough pressure is applied, these things could happen. What I'm afraid of is that it might take another large outbreak and a lot of children getting sick for Congress to act.

In the epilogue of the book I also talk about the most immediate way to bring about change, which is through pressure put on the fast-food chains. At the moment the industry is remarkably responsive to consumer demand because the market for fast food is highly saturated and all of the chains are worried about holding on to their customers. The McDonald's Corporation is the world's largest purchaser of beef. I have no doubt that if McDonald's told its suppliers to change their labor practices or their food-safety practices, they would do so—without much delay. Earlier this year, in response to protests by PETA (People for the Ethical Treatment of Animals), McDonald's imposed new rules on its suppliers specifying how livestock should be raised and slaughtered, stressing the humane treatment of animals. The rules set forth how much living space hogs and chickens should be provided, that sort of thing. Well, I'd like McDonald's to take the same sort of interest in the ethical treatment of human beings—in the working conditions and the dangers faced by the people who make their Big Macs.

2001

105.

Myles Brand: Reforming College Athletics

American college sports became a big business in the late twentieth century. Although men's college football and basketball had long enjoyed a large fan base, these sports achieved unprecedented levels of popularity and prosperity in the 1980s and 1990s. Division I universities within the National Collegiate Athletic Association (NCAA) generated millions of dollars each year through the sale of tickets, apparel, merchandise, and television broadcast rights. Some university presidents, however, feared that the success of college athletics came at the expense of academic integrity. Scholarship athletes routinely entered college with lower grades and test scores than regular students, and the graduation rates for major-sport athletes at large schools stood far below those of non-athletes. The situation became so serious that in the 1990s some college basketball teams graduated fewer than 15 percent of their athletes (though the criteria for these statistics was controversial). A number of scandals further tarnished the academic integrity of athletic programs. In response to these problems, a handful of university presidents called for sweeping reforms. For example, Myles Brand, the president of Indiana University, warned that many athletic departments had become completely unaccountable to the academic mission of their universities and instead saw winning games and generating revenue as their top priority. In a speech before the National Press Club in January 2001, Brand outlined a series of reforms he believed would restore the original mission of college athletics. Several months prior to the speech, Brand had dismissed Bobby Knight, the temperamental but wildly successful coach of Indiana's basketball team. In 2002 Brand was named the president of NCAA. Excerpts of Brand's speech are reprinted below.

Source: *Vital Speeches of the Day*, April 1, 2001.

As I was preparing to talk to this distinguished group of journalists, I found myself thinking about the question What makes news? As a professional philosopher, I have a taste for this kind of abstract thought. I've recently received some answers to my question. They came in the form of an object lesson.

Last May, I took part in a news conference on Indiana University's Indianapolis Campus. I entered a large conference room overflowing with reporters and photographers who were waiting to learn the results of our investigation into allegations made against Coach Bob Knight. At that news conference, I announced a set of firm and clear guidelines that were to govern Knight's future behavior as IU's head basketball coach. The event was televised on state and national news programs. It received extensive coverage on the front pages, sports pages, and editorial pages of newspapers across the nation.

Of course, as you know, that's not the end of the story. This past September, we held another press conference. This time, I relieved Bob Knight of his coaching responsibilities. Again, the media coverage was voluminous.

But then I had a parallel experience. In November, we held another news conference in the same room. We announced that IU had received the largest private gift in its history—$105 million from the Lilly Endowment. The grant the foundation has given us—which is the largest single gift they have ever made—will fund the Indiana Genomics Initiative. As you know, scientists have recently completed a working draft of the human genome. Yet the 3 billion bits of information that make up the human genetic code are still, for all intents and purposes, alphabet soup. The task now is to translate those codes into words and sentences that tell us how to cure and prevent debilitating diseases such as Alzheimer's, diabetes, and cancer—diseases that are the source of so much suffering.

Our announcement of this remarkable grant received good notice locally, but it was treated as a one-day story. Conversely, the Bob Knight saga played out over weeks and months. While I received thousands and thousands of e-mails expressing various points of view on the Knight matter, the announcement of the genomics project drew only a handful of e-mails and letters, despite the fact that the genomics project will have dramatically greater significance in people's lives.

Clearly, there is a disconnect here. University presidents believe their real job is to preserve and create environments where new knowledge can be discovered, knowledge that makes life richer, more rewarding, and, as in the case of the genome project, more liveable. But often, the public at large sees the university differently. For them, the most visible and vital role played by institutions such as IU is as a sponsor of athletic teams.

Universities must accept a share of the responsibility for this disconnect. Division IA institutions—through their athletic departments—have been eager recipients of profitable television broadcast contracts. With more time to fill, networks demand more games, on more days, at a variety of times. Long before *Survivor* and *Temptation Island,* college sports provided the reality programming that has recently become so popular. Football and basketball games are relatively inexpensive content featuring real people and unpredictable outcomes. They present a cast of players that changes from season to season, with the coaches taking on star status. The often legendary stars of these dramas are glorified by announcers, many of whom are themselves former coaches.

In pursuit of even more entertainment dollars, many universities have launched an arms race in the building of new settings for these dramas. They replace adequate, if aging, sports facilities, with stadiums and arenas matching the best that pro franchises have to offer. Coaches' and athletic directors' salaries rise rapidly, with many exceeding seven figures. Little expense is spared in training aids, such as video equipment and workout rooms, and there are increased ancillary personnel, including media and marketing people. The number of Division IA athletic departments with expenditure budgets exceeding $50 million annually is increasing. Yet despite increased revenue, athletic departments tend to overreach; the vast majority of Division IA athletic programs cannot balance their budgets without university subventions. These subsidies are sometimes overt, but mostly they are buried in the operating budget, for example, in support for physical plant and debt service.

This enormous interest in college sports has led to the blending together of intercollegiate athletics with entertainment, which in turn has led to growing commercialization. . . .

All this increasingly jeopardizes the essential mission of our universities. In fact, I believe the situation has reached crisis proportions. It threatens to undermine the integrity of a system of higher education that has been widely acknowledged to be the best in the world. This problem will do serious damage if it is left unchecked. . . .

How are we to resolve these issues? How can we stabilize, or better, reverse these trends that have been present for some time, but have, in the past several years, accelerated? Two extreme solutions have emerged, each with its strong advocates. One seeks to radically downsize intercollegiate athletics, and the other would separate intercollegiate athletics from its university moorings by professionalizing it. Neither approach is tenable. . . .

Clearly, both of these extreme solutions have problems. Each is unrealistic.

The purported benefits each claims are unlikely to materialize. Any attempt to eliminate a major Division IA athletic program would create an irresistible outcry. Hastening the movement toward full commercialization of basketball and football would likewise be resisted, though probably not to the same degree. But here, too, the inertia and tradition of the current situation makes radical change implausible, at best.

More important, both of these extreme solutions suffer from a deeper problem. They both neglect the positive side of intercollegiate athletics. Intercollegiate athletics, when conducted well and with good common sense, increase pride in the institution. They strengthen the university's connections with alumni, students, faculty, and the broader community. Well-functioning Division IA football and basketball programs generate sufficient revenue to support a wide range of nonrevenue sports, including women's sports. As a result, all student-athletes, including low-income and minority students, have a genuine opportunity to receive an education and graduate.

Successful programs also provide significant economic benefits for their local communities. A football Saturday will generate several million dollars for local businesses. True, turning college teams into professional ones will also have economic impact—but likely not at the same level of many current successful programs. Universities, most especially public institutions, have an obligation to assist their local communities and state economically. Public universities receive tax relief and a portion of their budget from state sources, and they have a responsibility to give back.

Thus, the central issue, is not to find a way to dismantle intercollegiate athletics, but rather to effectively limit its excesses so that its positive features can flourish.

If we are to restore the proper role of intercollegiate athletics we must make an absolute commitment to the academic mission and integrity of the university. James Duderstadt takes this approach in his excellent recent book, *Intercollegiate Athletics and the American University; A President's Perspective* (University of Michigan Press, 2000). Duderstadt served as president of the University of Michigan from 1988 to 1996.

As I said earlier, universities exist to discover, apply, transmit and preserve knowledge. Any activity undertaken by a university must serve, at least indirectly, these purposes. This does not mean that universities are seminaries. They are, rather, part of the booming, buzzing confusion of the real world; they are social institutions of enormous complexity and of critical importance to the health and welfare of the country. But it does mean that when a university undertakes ancillary activities, including entertainment through theater or athletics, those activities must ultimately serve an academic purpose and, crucially, they must not interfere with the university's pursuit of its academic mission.

The two extreme positions, eliminating intercollegiate athletics and wholly professionalizing them, accept this principle of academic integrity. But these approaches reject the additional premise that Division IA athletics contributes to the fulfillment of this academic mission. We must justify that premise, and show that the excesses of intercollegiate athletics can be curtailed.

To accomplish this goal we must renew the reform movement. Call it Academics First. Academics First is a fundamental commitment to taking the steps necessary to elevate the academic mission and integrity of the university to absolute first priority. . . .

Athletic programs do a reasonably good job of providing academic tutorial services. My primary recommendation here is that these efforts should be integrated into university-wide academic services. Such oversight will provide safeguards against academic misconduct of the type that occurred at the University of Minnesota. Integrating the programs with those of the general student body will assist not only academically, but also will help reverse the social isolation of student athletes.

Action by university presidents can be effective, too, in decreasing commercialization of college athletics. Working together, especially through conferences, presidents can limit the times and days when basketball games are played, the number of breaks in games for commercials, the type and prevalence of advertising in the stadiums and arenas, and the logos worn by players and coaches, to name a few examples.

One consequence of limiting commercialization is a reduced revenue stream. That should lead to cost containment and some downsizing of the athletic enterprise, provided that presidents do not succumb to pressures to make up these losses with funds from elsewhere in the university. Is this a good thing? Yes, if the academic mission of the institution comes first. . . .

One especially challenging factor in these efforts is dealing with celebrity coaches. I have some firsthand experience in this area. Some coaches, through their successes or styles, attract a great deal of media attention. That is not necessarily bad; in fact, it can be good for the university and the athletic program. It all depends on whether the coach is committed to academics first and understands that the university is more important than any one individual, even a celebrity coach. Interestingly, Bob Knight is a staunch supporter of academics, and he had an understanding of the importance of institutional integrity.

In any case, the challenge increases when a coach develops a following independent of the university, when his popularity and style create a fan support system that can influence the institution's governing board and business and elected leadership. Successful coaches often establish decades-long tenure. Thus, a president can be faced with a strong, established support network in dealing with a celebrity coach. In the best case, there is harmony and common purpose—but not always. When that occurs, the president must, with the concurrence of the governing board, act in the best long-term interests of the university. Once again, the responsibility lies with the university president.

To sum up, intercollegiate athletes, mostly because of Division IA football and men's basketball, is at a crucial juncture. The value system of the entertainment industries and the resulting commercialization are distorting the role and purpose of intercollegiate athletics and negatively affecting universities. Extreme solutions, such as eliminating almost entirely intercollegiate athletics or acceding to the trend toward professionalization, lose the benefits of a well-functioning intercollegiate athletic program. I believe that these benefits can be preserved, provided that there is a revitalization of the reform movement. While we don't want to turn off the game, we can lower the volume.

To do so requires the leadership of university presidents. Of course, they will need help, help from their governing boards, athletic directors, and faculty committees, and help from each other, especially at the conference level. Presidents face pressure from athletic departments and boosters to try to gain an advantage through, for example, new facilities and higher salaries; they must deal sometimes with entrenched coaches whose actions are not always in the best interests of the university. But I have great confidence in my colleague presidents, and I firmly believe that they are best positioned to effectively lead a reform movement to take back intercollegiate athletics. That reform movement should fly the banner "Academics First."

———————◆———————

Son, looks to me like you're spending too much time on one subject.
SHELBY METCALF, basketball coach at Texas A&M University, recounting his response to the report card of a player who received four Fs and one D

Nobody in football should be called a genius. A genius is a guy like Norman Einstein.
JOE THEISMANN, sports announcer and former football player, 1996

106.

PAUL WELLSTONE: The Downside of Standardized Tests

One of the first efforts to create standardized intelligence tests came during World War I, when the U.S. Army required every recruit to take an IQ exam. In the years that followed, standardized tests became a mainstay of the American college admissions process. The best-known of these, the Scholastic Aptitude Test (SAT), remains widely used as part of college applications and is a critical factor in helping universities decide which high school students to admit. In the 1980s and 1990s, states across the country began to administer standardized tests at primary and secondary schools, as legislatures required students to pass exams before advancing to a higher grade. Advocates of testing argued that standardized tests provided an objective measure of how well schools educated their students and brought needed scrutiny to failing schools. Critics, in contrast, contended that schools spent too much time preparing their students for standardized exams, rather than providing them with a broad education. President George W. Bush made standardized testing a central feature of the education bill he submitted to Congress in 2001. In the following article for Roll Call *magazine, U.S. Senator Paul Wellstone of Minnesota warned of the dangers of placing undue emphasis on standardized tests. Wellstone was a professor of political science at Carleton College for twenty years before his election to the Senate, where he was an outspoken liberal defender of the disadvantaged until his death in a plane crash.*

Source: *Roll Call*, February 28, 2001, "High-Stakes Tests Pose High-Stakes Risks for Vulnerable Kids."

ACCOUNTABILITY is the buzz word in education reform today. Our system of education needs more accountability. But when "accountability" is used as a euphemism for high-stakes, standardized testing of students, it represents a hollow promise. Far from improving education, high-stakes testing marks a major retreat from accuracy, from quality and from equity.

When used correctly, standardized tests can be effective in diagnosing inequality and for identifying where we need improvement. They enable us to measure achievement across groups of students, helping to ensure that states and districts are held accountable for improving the achievement of all students regardless of race, income, gender, limited English proficiency or disability. However, they are not a panacea.

Widespread abuse of tests for high-stakes purposes has subverted the benefits tests can bring. Use of a single standardized test as the sole determinant for graduation, promotion, tracking, and ability grouping is not fair and has not fostered greater equality or opportunity for students. When we impose high-stakes tests on an educational system where there are gross inequalities in terms of resources, facilities, teacher quality and other factors, while doing nothing to address the underlying causes of those inequalities, we set up children to fail.

Many talk about using tests to motivate students to do well and to ensure that we close the achievement gap. This kind of talk is unfair because it only tells a small part of the story. We cannot close the achievement gap until we close the wide gaps in investment between poor and rich schools, no matter how "motivated" some students are. We know where these key investments should be: quality teaching, well-equipped schools, parental involvement, and early childhood education, to name just a few.

High-stakes testing holds children responsible for our inaction and unwillingness to live up to our promises and obligations to children. Instead of making sound investments and taking responsibility to improve students' lives, we place the responsibility squarely on children. Policy makers and educators cannot expect that the poorest children, who face every disadvantage, will be able to do as well on those tests as those who have every advantage. Taking seriously President Bush's admonishment to "leave no child behind" would mean making major and substantial investments in efforts to level the playing field for all children in this country. As Members of Congress, we can start by fully funding IDEA, Title I, and Head Start.

If one does not believe that failure on tests is often bound to a lack of opportunity, look at who is failing. In Minnesota, in the first round of testing, 79% of low income students failed the reading portion of the high school exit exam and 74% failed the math portion. These numbers have improved with repeated rounds of testing, but it is clear that those with the least opportunity arc losing out in public education. This pattern extends nationwide. In Massachusetts, African American and Latino students are failing tests at twice the rate of whites. In Texas, blacks and Latinos are failing at three times the rate of whites.

Even if all children had the opportunity to learn the material covered by such tests, we still cannot close our eyes to the hard evidence that the results of a single standardized test used alone are not a reliable or fair basis for making decisions about students' futures.

The 1999 National Research Council report, High Stakes, concludes that "no single test score can be considered a definitive measure of a student's knowledge," and that "an educational decision that will have a major impact on a test taker should not be made solely or automatically on the basis of a single test score."

The Standards for Educational and Psychological Testing, 1999 Edition, which has served as the standard for test developers and users for decades, asserts that: "In educational settings, a decision or a characterization that will have a major impact on a student should not be made on the basis of a single test score." Even test publishers, including Harcourt Brace, CTB McGraw Hill, Riverside and the Educational Testing Service, consistently warn against this practice.

Another often overlooked problem with standardized tests is that scoring is not always accurate. And when a test is a high-stakes test, the consequences of scoring mistakes can be devastating. Mistakes in grading standardized tests are far from hypothetical. In my own state of Minnesota last year, 50 students were mistakenly kept from graduating because of a scoring error on their high-stakes graduation exam. In 1999, 8,600 New York students were mistakenly held in summer school because their tests were graded incorrectly.

The effects of high-stakes testing go beyond their impact on individual students to greatly impact the educational process in general. They have had a deadening effect on learning. Studies indicate that public testing encourages teachers and administrators to focus instruction on test content, format and preparation, overemphasizing basic skills and underemphasizing problem-solving and critical thinking skills not well assessed through standardized tests. Further, they neglect content areas that are not covered such as science, social studies and the arts. A recent poll in Texas which showed that only twenty-seven percent of teachers in Texas believed that modestly increased test scores reflected increased learning and higher quality teaching. Eighty-five percent of teachers said that they neglected subjects not covered on the exam.

We must never stop demanding that children do their best. We must never stop holding schools accountable. Measures of student performance can include standardized tests, but only when coupled with other measures of achievement, more substantive education reforms, and a much fuller, sustained investment in schools.

As a United States Senator, I am absolutely committed to the fight to stop the abuse of high-stakes tests. I will also continue to take every opportunity, on the Senate floor and elsewhere, to fight to ensure that these high-stakes tests are not used unless children are given the tools to learn the material they are being asked to master.

The famous sociologist Gunnar Myrdal once said that ignorance is never random. If we were unaware of the negative impact of high-stakes tests, it might excuse our over-reliance on them. But the evidence now is clear and overwhelming: making high-stakes tests the sole determinant for students and their schools, imposing major penalties on those who fail, is counter-productive. Before we threaten to withhold billions from schools in the name of accountability, politicians and educators at all levels, from the White House on down, must first be held accountable to give children what they need to learn.

◆

Ultimately, the most radical idea of all is that given enough time, given dedicated, enthusiastic teachers, and given high ideals, everyone can be educated.

DIANE RAVITCH, historian, from the public television documentary *School: The Story of American Public Education*

107.

Club Drugs

Imported from Europe, raves swept across the United States in the early 1990s and remained a staple of American youth culture at the start of the next century. Hedonistic dance parties that some saw as expressions of community, raves typically featured electronic dance music known as techno; hundreds, even thousands, of high school- and college-age revelers; and lots of drugs. Raves became a testing ground for new party drugs that offered different kinds of hallucinatory experiences. Most of these new drugs, not surprisingly, came with dangerous side effects, and some were often used to incapacitate women, who were then raped. Date rape or acquaintance rape, so called because the rapist was known by the victim, became an increasing public concern at the turn of the twenty-first century, especially on college campuses. Pamphlets, such as the one excerpted below, warned about the dangers of using club drugs.

Source: Troy, Michigan, Performance Resource Press, Inc., 2001.

THE TERM "club drugs" refers to mostly illegal drugs that are popular among young people who frequent all-night dance parties or "raves." Included in the club drug category are the commonly called "date rape" drugs, which are primarily strong sedative drugs that put the user into a very deep sleep. As the following information shows, use of any of these drugs is very dangerous. The dangers increase with how and where the drug was made, how much of the drug is taken, and whether the user ingests alcohol or other drugs along with club drug.

METHYLENEDIOXYMETH-AMPHETAMINE (MDMA)

Other names: ecstasy, XTC, X, Adam, clarity, lover's speed
• MDMA was developed and patented in the early 1900s as an appetite suppressant, although it was never tested on people. MDMA is taken orally, usually in a tablet or capsule form.
• Because MDMA is similar to the stimulant amphetamine and the hallucinogen mescaline, it can produce both stimulant and psychedelic effects in users. MDMA's effects last approximately three to six hours. However, the confusion, depression, sleep problems and other associated effects can last weeks after the drug is taken.
• One's sense of touch and sexual pleasure is reportedly greatly intensified when under the influence of MDMA, hence the origin of one of its street names—ecstasy—and one of the reasons it is cited as a "date rape" drug.
• Chronic use of MDMA can produce long-lasting, perhaps permanent, brain damage and memory impairment.
• MDMA use may lead to heart attacks, strokes and seizures. In high doses, it can be extremely dangerous, even fatal.

• The stimulant effect of MDMA enables users to dance or perform other physical activity for extended periods. This may lead to dehydration, hypertension and heart or kidney failure.

GAMMA-HYDROXYBUTYRATE (GHB)

Other names: G, liquid ecstasy, grievous bodily harm, Georgia home boy

• GHB is often manufactured in homes from recipes and ingredients found and purchased on the Internet. It is manufactured as either a clear liquid or a white powder that can be made into a tablet or capsule.

• GHB is a central nervous system depressant. In low doses, it relaxes the body and relieves anxiety. As the dose increases, the sedative effect causes deep sleep, which is why GHB is grouped with the "date rape" drugs. Larger doses will result in dangerously slowed breathing and heart rates, as well as in coma and/or death. There is no way to tell how much GHB will cause adverse physical reactions that will lead to death—each person's tolerance is different.

• The drug is usually abused either for its intoxicating/sedative/euphoriant properties or for its growth hormone-releasing effects, which can build muscles.

• GHB's intoxicating effects begin 10 to 20 minutes after the drug is taken. The effects typically last up to four hours, depending on the dosage.

• GHB overdose can occur quickly and cause drowsiness, nausea, vomiting, headache, loss of consciousness, loss of reflexes, impaired breathing and death.

• GHB is cleared from the body relatively quickly, so it is sometimes difficult to detect in emergency rooms and other treatment facilities. . . .

ROHYPNOL

Other names: roofies, rophies, Roche, the forget-me pill

• Rohypnol® (flunitrazepam) belongs to the class of drugs known as benzodiazepines, which include Valium®, Halcion®, Xanax® and Versed®. It is not approved for prescription use in the US, although it is approved in Europe and is used in more than 60 countries as a treatment for insomnia, as a sedative and as an anesthetic.

• Rohypnol® is tasteless and odorless, and it dissolves easily in carbonated beverages. It's usually taken orally, although it can be ground up and snorted.

• The drug can cause amnesia. Individuals may not remember events they experienced while under the influence of the drug. This may be why one of the street names for Rohypnol® is "the forget-me pill"—the drug has been used in sexual assaults.

• A dose of Rohypnol® as small as 1 mg. can impair a user for 8 to 12 hours. The sedative and toxic effects are intensified if taken with alcohol.

• Other adverse effects associated with Rohypnol® include decreased blood pressure, drowsiness, visual disturbances, dizziness, confusion, gastrointestinal disturbances and urine retention.

108.

Approval of Stem Cell Research

Along with the mapping of the human genome, few areas of scientific inquiry provided more hope for medical breakthroughs than embryonic stem cell research, which offered the possibility that scientists could regenerate any tissue in the human body. Scientists believed that tissue regeneration would play a critical role in curing a vast array of medical conditions, from Parkinson's disease and diabetes to paralysis and heart failure. The potential benefits of stem cell research received widespread attention in the national media in 2001, particularly as the administration of George W. Bush weighed the question of whether it would provide it federal funding. Religious and scientific groups lobbied the administration as it pondered its choices. Most scientists called for full and unlimited support for stem cell research, whereas many religious leaders condemned stem cell research as immoral and harmful because it inherently involved the destruction of thousands of human embryos; the latter believed this violated the sanctity of human life. After several months of internal discussion and debate on the issue, the Bush Administration announced its position on embryonic stem cell research in August 2001. The official White House statement is reprinted below.

Source: "Embryonic Stem Cell Research," August 9, 2001, http://www.whitehouse.gov

"As a result of private research, more than 60 genetically diverse stem cell lines already exist." I have concluded that we should allow federal funds to be used for research on these existing stem cell lines "where the life and death decision has already been made." This allows us to explore the promise and potential of stem cell research "without crossing a fundamental moral line by providing taxpayer funding that would sanction or encourage further destruction of human embryos that have at least the potential for life."
—George W. Bush

Federal funding of research using existing embryonic stem cell lines is consistent with the President's belief in the fundamental value and sanctity of human life. The President's decision reflects his fundamental commitment to preserving the value and sanctity of human life and his desire to promote vital medical research. The President's decision will permit federal funding of research using the more than 60 existing stem cell lines that have already been derived, but will not sanction or encourage the destruction of additional human embryos. The embryos from which the existing stem cell lines were created have already been destroyed and no longer have the possibility of further development as human beings. Federal funding of medical research on these existing stem cell lines will promote the sanctity of life "without undermining it" and will allow scientists to explore the potential of this research to benefit the lives of millions of people who suffer from life destroying diseases.

Federal funds will only be used for research on existing stem cell lines that were derived: (1) with the informed consent of the donors; (2) from excess embryos created solely for reproductive purposes; and (3) without any financial inducements to the donors. In order to ensure that federal funds are used to support only stem cell research that is scientifically sound, legal, and ethical, the NIH will examine the derivation of all existing stem cell lines and create a registry of those lines that satisfy this criteria. More than 60 existing stem cell lines from genetically diverse populations around the world are expected to be available for federally-funded research.

No federal funds will be used for: (1) the derivation or use of stem cell lines derived from newly destroyed embryos; (2) the creation of any human embryos for research purposes; or (3) the cloning of human embryos for any purpose. Today's decision relates only to the use of federal funds for research on existing stem cell lines derived in accordance with the criteria set forth above.

The President will create a new President's Council of Bioethics, chaired by Dr. Leon Kass, an expert in biomedical ethics and a professor at the University of Chicago, to study the human and moral ramifications of developments in biomedical and behavioral science and technology. The Council will study such issues as embryo and stem cell research, assisted reproduction, cloning, genetic screening, gene therapy, euthanasia, psychoactive drugs, and brain implants.

BACKGROUND

Embryonic stem cells. Embryonic stem cells, which come from the inner cell mass of a human embryo, have the potential to develop into all or nearly all of the tissues in the body. The scientific term for this characteristic is "pluripotentiality."

Adult stem cells. Adult stem cells are unspecialized, can renew themselves, and can become specialized to yield all of the cell types of the tissue from which they originate. Although scientists believe that some adult stem cells from one tissue can develop into cells of another tissue, no adult stem cell has been shown in culture to be pluripotent.

The potential of embryonic stem cell research. Many scientists believe that embryonic stem cell research may eventually lead to therapies that could be used to treat diseases that afflict approximately 128 million Americans. Treatments may include replacing destroyed dopamine-secreting neurons in a Parkinson's patient's brain; transplanting insulin-producing pancreatic beta cells in diabetic patients; and infusing cardiac muscle cells in a heart damaged by myocardial infarction. Embryonic stem cells may also be used to understand basic biology and to evaluate the safety and efficacy of new medicines.

The creation of embryonic stem cells. To create embryonic stem cells for research, a "stem cell line" must be created from the inner cell mass of a week-old embryo. If they are cultured properly, embryonic stem cells can grow and divide indefinitely. A stem cell line is a mass of cells descended from the original, sharing its genetic characteristics. Batches of cells can then be separated from the cell line and distributed to researchers.

The origin of embryonic stem cells. Embryonic stem cells are derived from excess embryos created in the course of infertility treatment. As a result of standard in vitro fertilization practices, many excess human embryos are created. Participants in IVF treatment must ultimately decide the disposition of these excess embryos, and many individuals have donated their excess embryos for research purposes.

Existing stem cell lines. There are currently more than 60 existing different human embryonic stem cell lines that have been developed from excess embryos created for in vitro fertilization with the consent of the donors and without financial inducement. These existing lines are used in approximately one dozen laboratories around the world (in the United States, Australia, India, Israel, and Sweden).

Therapies from adult and embryonic stem cell research. To date, adult stem cell research, which is federally-funded, has resulted in the development of a variety of therapeutic treatments for diseases. Although embryonic stem cell research has not yet produced similar results, many scientists believe embryonic stem cell research holds promise over time because of the capacity of embryonic stem cells to develop into any tissue in the human body.

———————◆———————

As the discoveries of modern science create tremendous hope, they also lay vast ethical mine fields. As the genius of science extends the horizons of what we can do, we increasingly confront complex questions about what we should do.
GEORGE W. BUSH, address on stem cell research, August 9, 2001

109.

James L. Watson: Globalization and Culture

The ever-accelerating development of modern technology in the late twentieth century made it possible for people, products, images, and ideas to traverse the world with unprecedented speed. In the process, a global economy emerged that created growing networks of interdependence and influence, along with, some argued, a transnational cosmopolitan culture that encompassed how people dressed, what they ate, and how they worshiped and spent their free time. While many celebrated the benefits of the shrinking world and the expanding world market, others saw them as damaging to the environment, national traditions, and the quality of human life. These opposing worldviews came to a head at the end of November 1999, when protest demonstrations near the meeting of the World Trade Organization (WTO) in Seattle, Washington, erupted into riots. Ironically, the nongovernmental groups (NGOs), or activist organizations, behind these protests were themselves, in many ways, the product of the instantaneous, borderless communication made possible by the Internet. At the heart of these developments was the often evoked but elusive concept of "globalization." In the article excerpted below, which first appeared in the online version of Encyclopædia Britannica *in 2001, Harvard University professor James L. Watson, the editor of* Golden Arches East: McDonald's in East Asia, *defines globalization, discusses the influence of American culture, and provides examples of globalization's impact around the world.*

Source: http://www.britannica.com, 2001.

GLOBALIZATION IS the process by which the experience of everyday life, marked by the diffusion of commodities and ideas, is becoming standardized around the world. An extreme interpretation of this process, often referred to as globalism, sees advanced capitalism, boosted by wireless and Internet communications and electronic business transactions, destroying local traditions and regional distinctions, creating in their place a homogenized world culture. According to this view, human experience everywhere is in jeopardy of becoming essentially the same. This appears, however, to be an overstatement of the phenomenon. Although homogenizing influences do indeed exist, people are far from creating a single overarching world culture. The actual process of globalization has been fitful, chaotic, and slow. . . .

EXPERIENCING GLOBALIZATION

Research on globalization has shown that it is not an omnipotent, unidirectional force leveling everything in its path. Because a global culture does not exist, any search for it would be futile. It is more fruitful to instead focus on particular aspects of life that are indeed affected by the globalizing process.

The breakdown of time and space is best illustrated by the influential "global village" thesis posed by communications scholar Marshall McLuhan in Gutenberg Galaxy (1962). Instantaneous communication, predicted McLuhan, would soon destroy geographically based power imbalances and create a global village. Later, geographer David Harvey argued that the postmodern condition is characterized by a "time-space compression" that arises from inexpensive air travel and the ever-present use of telephones, fax, and, more recently, e-mail.

There can be little doubt that people perceive the world today as a smaller place than it appeared to their grandparents. In the 1960s and 70s immigrant workers in London relied on postal systems and personally delivered letters to send news back to their home villages in India, China, and elsewhere; it could take two months to receive a reply. The telephone was not an option, even in dire emergencies. By the late 1990s, the grandchildren of these first-generation migrants were carrying cellular phones that linked them to cousins in cities such as Calcutta (Kolkata), Singapore, or Shanghai. Awareness of time zones (when people will be awake; what time offices open) is now second nature to people whose work or family ties connect them to far-reaching parts of the world.

McLuhan's notion of the global village presupposed the worldwide spread of television, which brings distant events into the homes of viewers everywhere. Building on this concept, McLuhan claimed that accelerated communications produce an "implosion" of personal experience—that is, distant events are brought to the immediate attention of people halfway around the world.

The spectacular growth of Cable News Network (CNN) is a case in point. CNN became an icon of globalization by broadcasting its U.S.-style news programming around the world, 24 hours a day. Live coverage of the fall of the Berlin Wall in 1989, the Persian Gulf War in 1991, and extended coverage of events surrounding the terrorist attacks in New York City and Washington, D.C., on September 11, 2001, illustrated television's powerful global reach. Some governments have responded to such advances by attempting to restrict international broadcasting, but satellite communication makes these restrictions increasingly unenforceable. . . .

Entertainment

The power of media conglomerates and the ubiquity of entertainment programming has globalized television's impact and made it a logical target for accusations of cultural imperialism. Critics cite a 1999 anthropological study that linked the appearance of anorexia in Fiji to the popularity of American television programs, notably Melrose Place and Beverly Hills 90210. Both series featured slender young actresses who, it was claimed, led Fijian women (who are typically fuller-figured) to question indigenous notions of the ideal body.

Anti-globalism activists contend that American television shows have corrosive effects on local cultures by highlighting Western notions of beauty, individualism, and sexuality. Although many of the titles exported are considered second-tier shows in the United States, there is no dispute that these programs are part of the daily fare for viewers around the world. Television access is widespread, even if receivers are not present in every household. In the small towns of Guatemala, the villages of Jiangxi province in China, or the hill settlements of Borneo, for instance, one television set—often a satellite system powered by a gasoline generator—may serve two or three dozen viewers, each paying a small fee. Collective viewing in bars, restaurants, and teahouses was common during the early stages of television broadcasting in Indonesia, Japan, Kenya, and many other countries. By the 1980s video-viewing parlours had become ubiquitous in many regions of the globe.

Live sports programs continue to draw some of the largest global audiences. The 1998 World Cup men's football (soccer) final between Brazil and France was watched by an estimated two billion people. After the 1992 Olympic Games, when the American "Dream Team" of National Basketball Association (NBA) stars electrified viewers who had never seen the sport played to U.S. professional standards, NBA games were broadcast in Australia, Israel, Japan, China, Germany, and Britain. In the late 1990s Michael Jordan, renowned for leading the Chicago Bulls to six championships with his stunning basketball skills, became one of the world's most recognized personalities.

Hollywood movies have had a similar influence, much to the chagrin of some countries. In early 2000 Canadian government regulators ordered the Canadian Broadcasting Corporation (CBC) to reduce the showing of Hollywood films during prime time and to instead feature more Canadian-made programming. CBC executives protested that their viewers would stop watching Canadian television stations and turn to satellite reception for international entertainment.

Such objections were well grounded, given that, in 1998, 79 percent of English-speaking Canadians named a U.S. program when asked to identify their favourite television show.

Hollywood, however, does not hold a monopoly on entertainment programming. The world's most prolific film industry is in Bombay (Mumbai), India ("Bollywood"), where as many as 1,000 feature films are produced annually in all of India's major languages. Primarily love stories with heavy doses of singing and dancing, Bollywood movies are popular throughout Southeast Asia and the Middle East. State censors in Islamic countries often find the modest dress and subdued sexuality of Indian film stars acceptable for their audiences. Although the local appeal of Bollywood movies remains strong, exposure to Hollywood films such as Jurassic Park (1993) and Speed (1994) caused young Indian moviegoers to develop an appreciation for the special effects and computer graphics that had become the hallmarks of many American films. . . .

Food

The average daily diet has also undergone tremendous change, with all nations converging on a diet high in meat, dairy products, and processed sugars. Correlating closely to a worldwide rise in affluence, the new "global diet" is not necessarily a beneficial trend, as it can increase the risk of obesity and diabetes. Now viewed as a global health threat, obesity has been dubbed "globesity" by the World Health Organization. To many observers, the homogenization of human diet appears to be unstoppable. Vegetarians, environmental activists, and organic food enthusiasts have organized rearguard actions to reintroduce "traditional" and more wholesome dietary practices, but these efforts have been concentrated among educated elites in industrial nations.

Western food corporations are often blamed for these dietary trends. McDonald's, KFC (Kentucky Fried Chicken), and Coca-Cola are primary targets of anti-globalism demonstrators (who are themselves organized into global networks, via the Internet). McDonald's has become a symbol of globalism for obvious reasons: on an average day in 2001, the company served nearly 45 million customers at more than 25,000 restaurants in 120 countries. It succeeds in part by adjusting its menu to local needs. In India, for example, no beef products are sold.

McDonald's also succeeds in countries that might be expected to disdain fast food. In France, for example, food, especially haute cuisine, is commonly regarded as the core element of French culture. Nevertheless, McDonald's continues to expand in the very heartland of opposition: by the turn of the 21st century there were more than 850 McDonald's restaurants in France, employing over 30,000 people. Not surprisingly, many European protest movements have targeted McDonald's as an agent of cultural imperialism. French intellectuals may revile the Big Mac sandwich for all that it symbolizes, but the steady growth of fast-food chains demonstrates that anti-globalist attitudes do not always affect economic behaviour, even in societies (such as France) where these sentiments are nearly universal. Like their counterparts in the United States, French workers are increasingly pressed for time. The two-hour lunch is largely a thing of the past.

Food and beverage companies attract attention because they cater to the most elemental form of human consumption. We are what we eat, and when diet changes, notions of national and ethnic identity are affected. Critics claim that the spread of fast food undermines indigenous cuisines by forcing a homogenization of world dietary preferences, but anthropological research in Russia, Japan, and Hong Kong does not support this view.

Close study of cultural trends at the local level, however, shows that the globalization of fast food can influence public conduct. Fast-food chains have introduced practices that changed some consumer behaviours and preferences. For example, in Japan, where using one's hands to eat prepared foods was considered a gross breech of etiquette, the popularization of McDonald's hamburgers has had such a dramatic impact on popular etiquette that it is now common to see Tokyo commuters eating in public, without chopsticks or spoons.

In late-Soviet Russia, rudeness had become a high art form among service personnel. Today customers expect polite, friendly service when they visit Moscow restaurants—a social revolution initiated by McDonald's and its employee training programs. Since its opening in 1990, Moscow's Pushkin Square restaurant has been one of the busiest McDonald's in the world.

The social atmosphere in colonial Hong Kong of the 1960s was anything but genteel. Cashing a check, boarding a bus, or buying a train ticket required brute force. When McDonald's opened in 1975, customers crowded around the cash registers, shouting orders and waving money over the heads of people in front of them. McDonald's responded by introducing queue monitors—young women who channeled customers into orderly lines. Queuing subsequently became a hallmark of Hong Kong's cosmopolitan, middle-class culture. Older residents credit McDonald's for introducing the queue, a critical element in this social transition.

Yet another innovation, in some areas of Asia, Latin America, and Europe, was McDonald's provision of clean toilets and washrooms. In this way the company was instrumental in setting new cleanliness standards (and thereby raising consumer expectations) in cities that had never offered public facilities. Wherever McDonald's has set up business, it rapidly has become a haven for an emerging class of middle-income urbanites.

The introduction of fast food has been particularly influential on children, especially since so many advertisements are designed to appeal to them. Largely as a consequence of such advertising, American-style birthday parties have spread to many parts of the world where individual birth dates previously had never been celebrated. McDonald's and KFC have become the leading venues for birthday parties throughout East Asia, with special rooms and services provided for the events. These and other symbolic effects make fast food a powerful force for dietary and social change, because a meal at these restaurants will introduce practices that younger consumers may not experience at home—most notably, the chance to choose one's own food. The concept of personal choice is symbolic of Western consumer culture. Visits to McDonald's and KFC have become signal events for children who approach fast-food restaurants with a heady sense of empowerment. . . .

SUBJECTIVITY OF MEANING—THE CASE OF TITANIC

A cultural phenomenon does not convey the same meaning everywhere. In 1998, the drama and special effects of the American movie *Titanic* created a sensation among Chinese fans. Scores of middle-aged Chinese returned to the theatres over and over—crying their way through the film. Enterprising hawkers began selling packages of facial tissue outside Shanghai theatres. The theme song of *Titanic* became a best-selling CD in China, as did posters of the young film stars. Chinese consumers purchased more than 25 million pirated (and 300,000 legitimate) video copies of the film.

One might ask why middle-aged Chinese moviegoers became so emotionally involved with the story told in *Titanic*. Interviews among older residents of Shanghai revealed that many people had projected their own, long-suppressed experiences of lost youth onto the film. From 1966 to 1976 the Cultural Revolution convulsed China, destroying any possibility of educational or career advancement for millions of people. At that time, communist authorities had also discouraged romantic love and promoted politically correct marriages based on class background and revolutionary commitment. Improbable as it might seem to Western observers, the story of lost love on a sinking cruise ship hit a responsive chord among the veterans of the Cultural Revolution. Their passionate, emotional response had virtually nothing to do with the Western cultural system that framed the film. Instead, *Titanic* served as a socially acceptable vehicle for the public expression of regret by a generation of aging Chinese revolutionaries who had devoted their lives to building a form of socialism that had long since disappeared.

Chinese President Jiang Zemin invited the entire Politburo of the Chinese Communist Party to a private screening of *Titanic* so that they would understand the challenge. He cautioned that *Titanic* could be seen as a Trojan horse, carrying within it the seeds of American cultural imperialism.

Chinese authorities are not alone in their mistrust of Hollywood. There are those who suggest, as has China's Jiang, that exposure to films such as *Titanic* will cause people everywhere to become more like Americans. Yet anthropologists who study television and film are wary of such suggestions. They emphasize the need to study the particular ways in which consumers make use of popular entertainment. The process of globalization looks far from hegemonic when one focuses on ordinary viewers and their efforts to make sense of what they see. . . .

Another case in point is anthropologist Daniel Miller's study of television viewing in Trinidad, which demonstrated that viewers are not passive observers. In 1988, 70 percent of Trinidadians who had access to a television watched daily episodes of The Young and the Restless, a series that emphasized family problems, sexual intrigue, and gossip. Miller discovered that Trinidadians had no trouble relating to the personal dramas portrayed in American soap operas, even though the lifestyles and material circumstances differed radically from life in Trinidad. Local people actively reinterpreted the episodes to fit their own experience, seeing the televised dramas as commentaries on contemporary life in Trinidad. The portrayal of American material culture, notably women's fashions, was a secondary attraction. In other words, it is a mistake to treat television viewers as passive.

THE TIES THAT STILL BIND

Local culture remains a powerful influence in daily life. People are tied to places, and those places continue to shape particular norms and values. The fact that residents of Moscow, Beijing, and New Delhi occasionally eat at McDonald's, watch Hollywood films, and wear Nike athletic shoes (or copies thereof) does not make them "global." The appearance of homogeneity is the most salient, and ultimately the most deceptive, feature of globalization. Outward appearances do not reveal the internal meanings that people assign to a cultural innovation. True, the standardization of everyday life will likely accelerate as digital technology comes to approximate the toaster in "user-friendliness." But technological breakthroughs are not enough to create a world culture. People everywhere show a desire to partake of the fruits of globalization, but they just as earnestly want to celebrate the distinctiveness of their own cultures.

Today, electronics and automation make mandatory that everybody adjust to the vast global environment as if it were his little home town.
MARSHALL MCLUHAN, *War and Peace in the Global Village*, 1968

110.

GEORGE W. BUSH: Declaration of War on Terrorism

On the morning of September 11, 2001, nineteen Middle Eastern terrorists hijacked four American passenger jets and used the planes as guided missiles to attack symbolic targets on the eastern seaboard of the United States. Two planes slammed into the World Trade Center Towers in New York City, causing both towers to collapse. A third plane crashed into the Pentagon, near Washington, D.C., and a fourth went down in the Pennsylvania countryside when passengers resisted the hijackers. The devastating series of attacks killed more than 3,000 Americans, more than had died in the Japanese attack at Pearl Harbor, Hawaii, 60 years previously. In the hours and days following September 11, American and foreign intelligence services identified Osama bin Laden, a Saudi millionaire living in exile in Afghanistan, as the mastermind behind the attacks. On September 20, President George W. Bush spoke before a Joint Session of Congress and outlined America's response to the events of September 11. In the speech, televised live around the nation and the world and excerpted here, Bush announced that "Our war on terror begins with al-Qaeda (the terrorist network associated with bin Laden), but it does not end there. It will not end until every terrorist group of global reach has been found, stopped, and defeated." Less than three weeks after Bush's speech, American forces launched a military campaign in Afghanistan to capture bin Laden and overthrow Afghanistan's Taliban government, which had long aided and abetted bin Laden and other terrorists. Although bin Laden's whereabouts and fate were unknown at the end of 2001, the American campaign in Afghanistan succeeded in toppling the Taliban from power and inflicting major damage on bin Laden's terrorist network. With American support, a new pro-Western government was installed in Afghanistan in early 2002.

Source: "Address to a Joint Session of Congress and the American People," September 20, 2001, http://www.whitehouse.gov

MR. SPEAKER, Mr. President Pro Tempore, members of Congress, and fellow Americans: In the normal course of events, Presidents come to this chamber to report on the state of the Union. Tonight, no such report is needed. It has already been delivered by the American people.

We have seen it in the courage of passengers, who rushed terrorists to save others on the ground—passengers like an exceptional man named Todd Beamer. And would you please help me to welcome his wife, Lisa Beamer, here tonight. We have seen the state of our Union in the endurance of rescuers, working past exhaustion. We have seen the unfurling of flags, the lighting of candles, the giving of blood, the saying of prayers—in English, Hebrew, and Arabic. We have seen the decency of a loving and giving people who have made the grief of strangers their own. My fellow citizens, for the last nine days, the entire world has seen for itself the state of our Union—and it is strong. Tonight we are a country awakened to danger and called to defend freedom. Our grief has turned to anger, and anger to resolution. Whether we bring our enemies to justice, or bring justice to our enemies, justice will be done.

I thank the Congress for its leadership at such an important time. All of America was touched on the evening of the tragedy to see Republicans and Democrats joined together on the steps of this Capitol, singing "God Bless America." And you did more than sing; you acted, by delivering $40 billion to rebuild our communities and meet the needs of our military. Speaker Hastert, Minority Leader Gephardt, Majority Leader Daschle and Senator Lott, I thank you for your friendship, for your leadership and for your service to our country.

And on behalf of the American people, I thank the world for its outpouring of support. America will never forget the sounds of our National Anthem playing at Buckingham Palace, on the streets of Paris, and at Berlin's Brandenburg Gate. We will not forget South Korean children gathering to pray outside our embassy in Seoul, or the prayers of sympathy offered at a mosque in Cairo. We will not forget moments of silence and days of mourning in Australia and Africa and Latin America. Nor will we forget the citizens of 80 other nations who died with our own: dozens of Pakistanis; more than 130 Israelis; more than 250 citizens of India; men and women from El Salvador, Iran, Mexico and Japan; and hundreds of British citizens. America has no truer friend than Great Britain. Once again, we are joined together in a great cause— so honored the British Prime Minister has crossed an ocean to show his unity of purpose with America. Thank you for coming, friend.

On September the 11th, enemies of freedom committed an act of war against our country. Americans have known wars—but for the past 136 years, they have been wars on foreign soil, except for one Sunday in 1941. Americans have known the casualties of war—but not at the center of a great city on a peaceful morning. Americans have known surprise attacks—but never before on thousands of civilians. All of this was brought upon us in a single day—and night fell on a different world, a world where freedom itself is under attack.

Americans have many questions tonight. Americans are asking: Who attacked our country? The evidence we have gathered all points to a collection of loosely affiliated terrorist organizations known as al Qaeda. They are the same murderers indicted for bombing American embassies in Tanzania and Kenya, and responsible for bombing the USS Cole. Al Qaeda is to terror what the mafia is to crime. But its goal is not making money; its goal is remaking the world—and imposing its radical beliefs on people everywhere. The terrorists practice a fringe form of Islamic extremism that has been rejected by Muslim scholars and the vast majority of Muslim clerics—a fringe movement that perverts the peaceful teachings of Islam. The terrorists' directive commands them to kill Christians and Jews, to kill all Americans, and make no distinction among military and civilians, including women and children.

This group and its leader—a person named Osama bin Laden—are linked to many other organizations in different countries, including the Egyptian Islamic Jihad and the Islamic Movement of Uzbekistan. There are thousands of these terrorists in more than 60 countries. They are recruited from their own nations and neighborhoods and brought to camps in places like Afghanistan, where they are trained in the tactics of terror. They are sent back to their homes or sent to hide in countries around the world to plot evil and destruction. The leadership of al Qaeda has great influence in Afghanistan and supports the Taliban regime in controlling most of that country. In Afghanistan, we see al Qaeda's vision for the world.

Afghanistan's people have been brutalized—many are starving and many have fled. Women are not allowed to attend school. You can be jailed for owning a television. Religion can be practiced only as their leaders dictate. A man can be jailed in Afghanistan if his beard is not long enough. The United States respects the people of Afghanistan—after all, we are currently its largest source of humanitarian aid—but we condemn the Taliban regime. It is not only repressing its own people, it is threatening people everywhere by sponsoring and sheltering and supplying terrorists. By aiding and abetting murder, the Taliban regime is committing murder.

And tonight, the United States of America makes the following demands on the Taliban: Deliver to United States authorities all the leaders of al Qaeda who hide in your land. Release all foreign nationals, including American citizens, you have unjustly imprisoned. Protect foreign journalists, diplomats and aid workers in your country. Close immediately and permanently every terrorist training camp in Afghanistan, and hand over every terrorist, and every person in their support structure, to appropriate authorities. Give the United States full access to terrorist training camps, so we can make sure they are no longer operating. These demands are not open to negotiation or discussion. The Taliban must

act, and act immediately. They will hand over the terrorists, or they will share in their fate.

I also want to speak tonight directly to Muslims throughout the world. We respect your faith. It's practiced freely by many millions of Americans, and by millions more in countries that America counts as friends. Its teachings are good and peaceful, and those who commit evil in the name of Allah blaspheme the name of Allah. The terrorists are traitors to their own faith, trying, in effect, to hijack Islam itself. The enemy of America is not our many Muslim friends; it is not our many Arab friends. Our enemy is a radical network of terrorists, and every government that supports them. Our war on terror begins with al Qaeda, but it does not end there. It will not end until every terrorist group of global reach has been found, stopped and defeated.

Americans are asking, why do they hate us? They hate what we see right here in this chamber—a democratically elected government. Their leaders are self-appointed. They hate our freedoms—our freedom of religion, our freedom of speech, our freedom to vote and assemble and disagree with each other. They want to overthrow existing governments in many Muslim countries, such as Egypt, Saudi Arabia, and Jordan. They want to drive Israel out of the Middle East. They want to drive Christians and Jews out of vast regions of Asia and Africa. These terrorists kill not merely to end lives, but to disrupt and end a way of life. With every atrocity, they hope that America grows fearful, retreating from the world and forsaking our friends. They stand against us, because we stand in their way.

We are not deceived by their pretenses to piety. We have seen their kind before. They are the heirs of all the murderous ideologies of the 20th century. By sacrificing human life to serve their radical visions—by abandoning every value except the will to power—they follow in the path of fascism, and Nazism, and totalitarianism. And they will follow that path all the way, to where it ends: in history's unmarked grave of discarded lies.

Americans are asking: How will we fight and win this war? We will direct every resource at our command—every means of diplomacy, every tool of intelligence, every instrument of law enforcement, every financial influence, and every necessary weapon of war—to the disruption and to the defeat of the global terror network. . . . Our response involves far more than instant retaliation and isolated strikes. Americans should not expect one battle, but a lengthy campaign, unlike any other we have ever seen. It may include dramatic strikes, visible on TV, and covert operations, secret even in success. We will starve terrorists of funding, turn them one against another, drive them from place to place, until there is no refuge or no rest. And we will pursue nations that provide aid or safe haven to terrorism. Every nation, in every region, now has a decision to make. Either you are with us, or you are with the terrorists. From this day forward, any nation that continues to harbor or support terrorism will be regarded by the United States as a hostile regime.

Our nation has been put on notice: We are not immune from attack. We will take defensive measures against terrorism to protect Americans. Today, dozens of federal departments and agencies, as well as state and local governments, have responsibilities affecting homeland security. These efforts must be coordinated at the highest level. So tonight I announce the creation of a Cabinet-level position reporting directly to me—the Office of Homeland Security. And tonight I also announce a distinguished American to lead this effort, to strengthen American security: a military veteran, an effective governor, a true patriot, a trusted friend—Pennsylvania's Tom Ridge. He will lead, oversee and coordinate a comprehensive national strategy to safeguard our country against terrorism, and respond to any attacks that may come.

These measures are essential. But the only way to defeat terrorism as a threat to our way of life is to stop it, eliminate it, and destroy it where it grows. Many will be involved in this effort, from FBI agents to intelligence operatives to the reservists we have called to active duty. All deserve our thanks, and all have our prayers. And tonight, a few miles from the damaged Pentagon, I have a message for our military: Be ready. I've called the Armed Forces to alert, and there is a reason. The hour is coming when America will act, and you will make us proud.

This is not, however, just America's fight. And what is at stake is not just America's freedom. This is the world's fight. This is civilization's fight. This is the fight of all who believe in progress and pluralism, tolerance and freedom. We ask every nation to join us. We will ask, and we will need, the help of police forces, intelligence services, and banking systems around the world. The United States is grateful that many nations and many international organizations have already responded—with sympathy and with support. Nations from Latin America, to Asia, to Africa, to Europe, to the Islamic world. Perhaps the NATO Charter reflects best the attitude of the world: An attack on one is an attack on all. . . .

Americans are asking: What is expected of us? I ask you to live your lives, and hug your children. I know many citizens have fears tonight, and I ask you to be calm and resolute, even in the face of a continuing threat.

I ask you to uphold the values of America, and remember why so many have come here. We are in a fight for our principles, and our first responsibility is to live by them. No one should be singled out for unfair treatment or unkind words because of their ethnic background or religious faith. . . .

We will come together to give law enforcement the additional tools it needs to track down terror here at home. We will come together to strengthen our intelligence capabilities to know the plans of terrorists before they act, and find them before they strike. We will come together to take active steps that strengthen America's economy, and put our people back to work. Tonight we welcome two leaders who embody the extraordinary spirit of all New Yorkers: Governor George Pataki, and Mayor Rudolph Giuliani. As a symbol of America's resolve, my administration will work with Congress, and these two leaders, to show the world that we will rebuild New York City.

After all that has just passed—all the lives taken, and all the possibilities and hopes that died with them—it is natural to wonder if America's future is one of fear. Some speak of an age of terror. I know there are struggles ahead, and dangers to face. But this country will define our times, not be defined by them. As long as the United States of America is determined and strong, this will not be an age of terror; this will be an age of liberty, here and across the world.

Great harm has been done to us. We have suffered great loss. And in our grief and anger we have found our mission and our moment. Freedom and fear are at war. The advance of human freedom—the great achievement of our time, and the great hope of every time—now depends on us. Our nation—this generation—will lift a dark threat of violence from our people and our future. We will rally the world to this cause by our efforts, by our courage. We will not tire, we will not falter, and we will not fail.

It is my hope that in the months and years ahead, life will return almost to normal. We'll go back to our lives and routines, and that is good. Even grief recedes with time and grace. But our resolve must not pass. Each of us will remember what happened that day, and to whom it happened. We'll remember the moment the news came—where we were and what we were doing. Some will remember an image of a fire, or a story of rescue. Some will carry memories of a face and a voice gone forever.

And I will carry this: It is the police shield of a man named George Howard, who died at the World Trade Center trying to save others. It was given to me by his mom, Arlene, as a proud memorial to her son. This is my reminder of lives that ended, and a task that does not end.

I will not forget this wound to our country or those who inflicted it. I will not yield; I will not rest; I will not relent in waging this struggle for freedom and security for the American people. The course of this conflict is not known, yet its outcome is certain. Freedom and fear, justice and cruelty, have always been at war, and we know that God is not neutral between them.

Fellow citizens, we'll meet violence with patient justice—assured of the rightness of our cause, and confident of the victories to come. In all that lies before us, may God grant us wisdom, and may He watch over the United States of America.

111.

Lucas Miller, Kate Zernike, and Jere Longman: Air Travel After September 11

Because the weapons used in the terrorist attacks of September 11 were hijacked commercial airliners, it was no surprise that airport security received the closest scrutiny in the wake of the tragedy. The government's first response was its most sweeping. Hours after the attacks the Federal Aviation Administration brought civil aviation to a standstill, first by safely landing some 4,500 planes and next by grounding all commercial aircraft until new security measures could be installed. In the days following, even casual observers made note of the rare silence overhead as no civil plane took flight. On September 13 commercial airspace was reopened on a limited basis, and it was many days more before air traffic reached levels of normalcy. By that time National Guard troops were stationed at major airports, the Federal Air Marshal program was expanded, airplane cockpit doors were reinforced, and new procedures were instituted for flight crews, airport security, and aviation schools. With the resumption of regular service, airline passengers found themselves in a very altered environment. The three articles reprinted below were published shortly after the attacks. The first, from Slate.com, is a proposal to add in-flight security personnel to virtually every commercial flight. The next two, from The New York Times, *survey passenger fears and frustrations and the long waits incurred due to heightened security precautions.*

Sources: "Air Time: Let's Put a Cop on Every Flight," September 20, 2001, http://www.slate.msn.com

The New York Times, September 26, 2001.

The New York Times, September 29, 2001.

A. LUCAS MILLER
IN-FLIGHT SECURITY

Like everyone else, I have been trying to think of steps that could be taken to prevent future airliner hijackings. Here's an easy suggestion that lies within conventional law enforcement: Place an armed police officer on nearly every commercial airplane. The attorney general has already announced an increase in the assignment of sky marshals to flights. But with over 35,000 flights a day, the nation's 4,000 U.S. marshals will be able to man only a small portion of the planes in the air. Other federal agencies would lend a hand, but even the FBI has only 11,500 agents. In contrast, this country has 700,000 police officers.

This system would require training, clearance of a few legal hurdles, and a new coordination system, but those are relatively painless and inexpensive tasks. Other solutions proposed so far—replacing incompetent security guards, installing new passenger-identification technology—are expensive. Besides, most of these measures stop at the airport gate: If a terrorist slips past, the passengers and crew are completely exposed. This is why Israelis have, for years, placed an armed undercover agent on their flights.

Consider the approach taken by the Long Island Rail Road. In 1993, a passenger named Colin Ferguson shot 26 people, killing six of them, because of "black rage." Since then, police officers from New York have been able to take the train for free, identifying themselves to the conductors. There's already some precedent for a similar program on airlines: Right now, when a federal agent checks in for a commercial flight, he identifies himself and notifies the pilot that he is armed. With a little organization, we could build a system that would cover most major U.S. flights.

Cops are proficient in the use of firearms, which is what would be needed to face multiple hijackers armed with knives. It's harder to fight someone with a knife than you might think. I have been taught methods both in the police academy and in karate class: One can attack the knife-wielder when his arm is extended or use the meaty part of one's weaker forearm to absorb a strike—in other words, to get slashed—and then seize the weapon with the stronger arm. But both my academy and karate instructors ended such lessons with a warning: "Prepare to get cut."

The reaction of most police officers would be to shoot a knife-wielding attacker (the guidelines for the use of lethal force for every law-enforcement agency that I know of authorize such a reaction). Because of the dangerous nature of an airborne plane, I would venture to say that a cop could legally use deadly force in a greater range of incidents on-board. For instance, anyone physically attacking the pilot would be fair game.

Police officers involved in shootings hit their targets with roughly one out of three bullets fired. This sounds like we are lousy shots, but that is much, much better than the general public, criminals included. And presumably an officer on a plane would not be facing well-armed assailants. In the case of Tuesday's attack, even a bad marksman might have saved many lives.

Of course, bringing a gun onto a plane is dangerous, no matter who's carrying it. The on-board cops would need special ammunition, designed to avoid breaching the fuselage (a brand called Glaser Safety Slugs is supposedly lethal to humans but not airplanes). And cops are already well-trained to prevent attackers from taking their guns. In short, you must secure the weapon in its holster and deliver a strike, perhaps to the eyes, taking advantage of the position of the attacker's busy hands. If an officer feels that he is in danger of actually losing possession of the weapon, using it on the attacker is justified.

Of course, these techniques aren't foolproof. The officer would have to ride in the cockpit or immediately outside, and stay there except when necessary. Contact with passengers would have to be limited so as to protect the cop from ambush. Or cops could check in discreetly and remain unidentified to the passengers. This would increase the deterrent effect of the program, though the terrorists might be savvy enough about American police officers to "make" one anyway (the drug dealers I used to chase had little trouble recognizing me as I strolled on their block trying to look nonchalant).

Police officers registered in this program would devote a period of time to the airline—perhaps a 48-hour period each month. In return, they would receive travel vouchers good for free flying (additional payment would help encourage participation, too). The airlines would have to maintain a national database of qualified police officers, including photos and other identifying information. Each officer would have to attend training both in the proper procedures for taking law-enforcement action on an airplane as well as the more mundane procedures of the conventional crew of an airplane. Laws would have to be changed to give the police jurisdiction in the air above states other than their own.

Having cops on planes would not make America immune to the dangers of terrorism. But such a program might well have prevented last Tuesday's attacks. Some might think my proposal is self-serving, but I can assure them that I will not be participating in my program; I was already afraid of flying.

B. KATE ZERNIKE
FEAR OF FLYING

For air travelers and flight crews, there seems to be no such thing as an overreaction in the days since Sept. 11.

Since the nation's airports opened after the terrorist hijackings, passengers have been removed from planes, flights have been grounded or diverted and entire concourses at airports have been evacuated because of suspicious activity—even movements that might have gone unnoticed three weeks ago.

On Friday, a Virgin Atlantic Airways 747 flying from London to Los Angeles made an emergency landing in the Canadian prairie city of Edmonton, after a flight attendant noticed a cellphone that had slipped behind a seat. The 386 passengers and crew were unloaded to a bus while the Royal Canadian Mounted Police and a local police explosives disposal unit searched the plane, ultimately finding no threat.

An Amsterdam-bound Northwest Airlines flight from Dulles International Airport was delayed 23 hours on Sept. 18 after two pilots and a flight engineer escaped from their DC-10 on ropes from the cockpit window after being warned about a suspicious passenger.

A flight attendant had telephoned a friend about the passenger, the friend phoned the Federal Bureau of Investigation, which in turn called the airport, which dispatched agents and police cars to surround the plane.

The 215 passengers were escorted off one by one, and were put up in a hotel overnight. Kurt Ebenhoch, a spokesman for Northwest, said the pilots had to be examined for injuries by a doctor before being cleared to fly the next day.

Another plane was held on the tarmac at Dulles on Friday after a Saudi pilot asked to sit in the jump seat, a privilege customarily extended to other pilots before Sept. 11. The F.B.I. assured the crew that the man posed no danger, but the crew asked that he be transferred to another flight, and several passengers were so rattled that they decided not to fly.

And at Logan International Airport in Boston early last week, 500 people were evacuated from 11 flights in Terminal B—where the two hijacked planes that hit the World Trade Center originated—after a security person recalled seeing a knife in a bag as it passed through the X-ray machine, but forgot to stop the passenger to examine the bag by hand.

"Things that may be very innocent, all of a sudden you're doing double checks," said Sharon Williams, the manager of Terminal B at Logan. Phil Orlandella, the director for media relations at Logan, characterized the new attitude as "zero tolerance."

The airlines admit the reactions may seem extreme.

John Riordan, a spokesman for Virgin Atlantic, said: "Are we being triply cautious at the expense of incurring a delay? I think we are. It's almost a ridiculous comment to say safety is paramount. It is the only thing."

Other planes, including one bound for Mexico City from Los Angeles, have been turned around because of bomb threats. Crews are double-checking passengers' names on a list of suspects given to them by the F.B.I., several airlines said, which has resulted in several other delays. Passengers with Middle Eastern looks or names have sometimes been asked to leave the planes. Airlines say the crews have discretion to make these requests out of suspicion.

"Most of these cases are just fear related," said Herb Hunter, a spokesman for the pilots union at United. "Fear always has a way to overreact."

C. JERE LONGMAN
AIRPORT DELAYS

More rigorous screening procedures and an increase in business and leisure travelers have produced daunting lines at airports around the country in the past two days.

At Philadelphia International Airport today, a line almost a quarter of a mile long stretched to a hotel where clerks sold water, juice and coffee to passengers, some of whom arrived three or four hours before their scheduled flight departures.

At Terminal C in Newark today, ticket lines exceeded an hour.

"This is worse than Christmas," sighed Brook Midgley, 21, a nanny who was returning to Kansas.

Most passengers interviewed said they had anticipated delays, and had left enough time to get to their flights— sometimes three, four or even five hours. But some said the long lines would make them miss their scheduled departures.

Much of the delay was caused by a directive issued on Wednesday night by the Federal Aviation Administration ordering more thorough examination of laptop computers and other carry-on luggage. The directive requires that passengers who set off metal detectors must be examined with a security wand and patted down by hand. Operators of scanning machines must stop the machine to look at each image as carry-on luggage passes through.

The agency also asked the airlines to try to screen as much checked luggage as possible. At several airports, security officers occasionally hand-checked luggage at ticket counters. Scrutiny of passengers was often greater, too.

Security will soon become even greater under measures announced by President Bush on Thursday. A new federal agency will oversee all airport security and National Guard troops will be deployed at all commercial airports.

At La Guardia Airport in New York, Mahiuddin Ahmed, a researcher at Memorial Sloan-Kettering Cancer Center who waited in line at the US Airways terminal with about 300 other people today, found security quite tight. Mr. Ahmed said he was questioned by the police when he got to the counter.

Mr. Ahmed, a native of Bangladesh, said he was told that his name was close to that of a wanted person.

"They called my work and I was eventually cleared by the Port Authority," said Mr. Ahmed, who was traveling to Fort Lauderdale, Fla., to visit his parents. "I know it's necessary and I'm not angry, but if they're going to do it, they should warn you ahead of time. They said if I had brought my passport, it would have taken 20 minutes."

The tightened security has coincided with a steady increase in the number of air passengers in the last few days, industry analysts said. Today, about 120,000 travelers were expected through Pittsburgh International Airport on US Airways, said an airline spokesman, compared with 60,000 a week ago.

At various airports surveyed, most passengers accepted the inconvenience patiently, saying they preferred to be safe in the wake of the Sept. 11 terrorist attacks.

"The more they have to do to keep us safe, the better," said Jan Schoonmaker as she returned to Pittsburgh from Orange County, Calif.

Still, some passengers have begun to express irritation.

At the Pittsburgh airport, where there is a communal security checkpoint before passengers board a train to the terminals, the wait on Thursday was two hours or longer to pass through metal detectors.

Today, lines were shorter here, but some passengers reported waiting 45 minutes to an hour to check bags and another 20 to 25 minutes for a security check. The situation appears to be fluid, changing daily at many airports as officials try to strike the right balance between tight security and passenger convenience.

On Saturday, for instance, US Airways in Pittsburgh will begin allowing curbside check-in again, said Charles Piroli, a passenger service supervisor with the airline. Other airlines here, however, will not offer that amenity right away.

Meanwhile, airlines that specialize in short-haul flights, like US Airways, could be affected if travelers choose to drive three to five hours instead of waiting in long lines to fly, said David Stempler, president of the Air Travelers Association, a group based in Washington that represents passengers.

"I would drive next time, if it continues like this," said Tony Wesner, a paint company executive on his way back to Raleigh, N.C., from Baltimore-Washington International Airport. "Why would I spend three and four hours in an airport if it takes me four or five hours to drive?"

The current protracted check-in process also raises questions about what kind of lines can be expected when Americans return in full force to begin flying again.

"What no one has seen yet is the impact with normal travel volume," said Jim Lehman, the senior vice president of AAA in the Western Pennsylvania region. "It's going to be a challenge the F.A.A. is going to have to deal with, making sure security is as tight as it can be while not deterring people from traveling."

Los Angeles International Airport, which once handled 2,100 flights a day with relative efficiency, has become a complex ballet of improvised checkpoints and enormously long lines, but surprisingly little actual security checking. Only taxis, registered buses and chauffeur-driven cars are now allowed to pull up to the curbs at the terminals, but several drivers said they had only rarely been asked to show identification. But confusion reigned at a remote parking area five miles from the airport terminals, where people in regular cars were forced to drop off and pick up passengers.

Mr. Stempler of the Air Travelers Association said he had seen security guards performing checks that ranged from thorough to cursory within a few feet of each other on Wednesday at Dulles Airport outside Washington. He also said security appeared to be growing more lax at some airports as lines grow long and officials want to speed up the check-in process. "It's ridiculous how uneven it is," Mr. Stempler said.

At O'Hare Airport in Chicago, police officers patrolled drop-off and pick-up points today. Around noon, lines folded back on each other at the United terminal as people waited with photo ID's and tickets to enter the terminal. By 2 p.m., though, the lines began to dwindle. Passengers said cars were not searched as they dropped off passengers.

"If you pull up to drop somebody off in Seattle, they search your car," said Evan Kharasch, a professor at the University of Washington.

Harold Saulsby, a corporate training expert on his way to Tampa, Fla., said the multiple checks of laptop computers was a measure that had begun to grate on him because airports should have the technology to distinguish computers from bombs.

"There are freedoms that we take for granted," Mr. Saulsby said. "Maybe we can give some back and feel a lot safer. But there comes a point where you cross a line and begin obstructing freedom. I hope we don't get to that point."

———————◆———————

If planes don't fly, the whole economy shuts down.
JAY ROCKEFELLER, defending his support for passage of a
$15 billion bailout to the airline industry after the
September 11 Attacks, September 22, 2001

112.

EVAN THOMAS: The American Taliban

In the aftermath of the terrorist attacks of September 11, 2001, the United States launched a major military campaign against the al-Qaeda terrorist network and its Taliban supporters in Afghanistan. The Taliban, a group of Islamic extremists who had seized power in Afghanistan in 1996, allowed Saudi dissident Osama bin Laden to use Afghanistan as a base for his al-Qaeda terrorists in planning their attacks on the United States. When the Taliban refused to turn over bin Laden and his followers to the U.S. government, President George W. Bush ordered the U.S. military to dislodge the Taliban from power and to destroy al-Qaeda. The American military campaign proceeded with astounding success, and within two months it had toppled the Taliban from power and devastated al-Qaeda terrorist cells in Afghanistan. When American troops and their Afghan allies quelled an uprising of Taliban prisoners at Mazar-e Sharif, they were stunned to find an American citizen among them. John Walker Lindh, a twenty-year-old Californian, had joined the Taliban a year earlier after converting to Islam and traveling through the Middle East. During his stay in Afghanistan, Lindh met bin Laden and other top al-Qaeda leaders, and fought alongside Taliban soldiers. The U.S. government prosecuted Lindh for aiding the enemy in wartime. He agreed to a plea bargain, and a federal judge sentenced him to twenty years in prison. Reprinted below are excerpts from a Newsweek *article written after Lindh's capture.*

Source: *Newsweek*, December 17, 2001, "American Taliban."

THE STUDENT was old for the madrasa, the primitive Islamic fundamentalist school in a remote corner of Pakistan. Most of the students were children, boys who had yet to reach adolescence. But this tall, bearded youth was 19, almost a man. He was a "model student," says his teacher, Mufti Mohammad Iltimas. The American had no interest in girls or parties or world events. His only real interest was studying. He seemed fixated, determined to memorize every word of the Quran, all 6,666 sentences of the ancient holy book that dictates every aspect of a devout Muslim's life, behavior and being.

His only respite from studying, apart from the occasional foray to the cyber tea shop in Bannu to ship e-mails home, was books on Islam. He slept on a rope bed in his teacher's study, in a place with no hot water, and no electricity after 10 p.m. And he peppered the mufti with questions about the devout life: "Should I recite verses in a soft voice or a loud one? While I am worshiping, how should I hold my hands?"

Most teenagers, when they rebel, say they want more freedom. John Walker Lindh rebelled against freedom. He did not demand to express himself in differ-

John Walker Lindh (left) is led away by a Northern Alliance soldier on December 1, 2001, after his capture following the uprising of Taliban prisoners near Mazar-e Sharif, Afghanistan.

ent ways. Quite the opposite. He wanted to be told precisely how to dress, to eat, to think, to pray. He wanted a value system of absolutes, and he was willing to go to extreme lengths to find it. Lindh, who grew up surrounded by upper-middle-class affluence in California, was determined to fit in at the Islamic religious school, an austere one-story building in a tiny village outside the town of Bannu in the Northwest Frontier Province of Pakistan. Speaking with Mufti Iltimas, Lindh was critical of America as a land that exalted self above all else. Americans were so busy pursuing their personal goals, he said, that they had no time for their families or communities. In the Islamic world, by contrast, he felt cared for by others. "In the U.S. I feel alone," he said. "Here I feel comfortable and at home."

And yet the young American, who went by the name Suleyman al-Faris, did not seem to enjoy the company of others. As the local mufti, Iltimas was constantly being invited out for lunches and dinners, and he would ask his protégé to come along. Suleyman would always decline, saying that socializing was a "waste

of time." Suleyman was perhaps not as comfortable as he claimed to be. True, the villagers sent him food and did his laundry free of charge. But when the weather turned hot in April, he had trouble sleeping. He began to suffer from rashes and the incessant dust. He said he wanted to go into the cooler mountains. Then he vanished.

He did not surface for seven months. When he did, discovered by a NEWSWEEK reporter who first broke John Walker Lindh's story on our Web site and in last week's magazine, it was at a prison fortress in Afghanistan. Lindh's body was caked with dirt and soot, and his hair was matted with sweat and blood. Shot in the leg during a revolt by Taliban prisoners, he had been hiding in a basement from American bombs. John Walker, as he later referred to himself to CNN journalists, was roundly vilified as a traitor. Talk-show hosts and tabloid headline writers described him as "a rat" and widely suggested that he should be shot for helping instigate America's first combat death, that of CIA operative Johnny (Mike) Spann. President George W. Bush seemed more forgiving, calling Walker a "poor fellow" who had been "misled." Defense Secretary Donald Rumsfeld, on the other hand, coolly stated, "We found a person who says he's an American with an AK-47 in a prison with a bunch of Al Qaeda and Taliban fighters. He will have all the rights he is due." Walker's parents, San Francisco lawyer Frank Lindh and his legally estranged wife, Marilyn, were horrified. Their son was "sweet" and "shy," they said. How could he have ended up trapped in a siege with a gang of terrorists?

The story of John Phillip Walker Lindh, a.k.a. Suleyman al-Faris, a.k.a. Abdul Hamid (his Taliban nom de guerre), a.k.a. John Walker, is one of the truly perplexing and intriguing mysteries of the post-September 11 universe. He grew up in possibly the most liberal, tolerant place in America, yet he was drawn to the most illiberal, intolerant sect in Islam, the Taliban. He told his parents he was converting to Islam partly because it was a gentle, peace-loving religion, yet he became a self-described "jihadist," a holy warrior, and told our reporter that he "supported" the September 11 terrorist attacks. His parents say he's a "victim" who was "in the wrong place at the wrong time." But how, if he was really such a "good boy," did he get there?

John Walker, to use the name that has stuck, may remain a psychological puzzle. But he can be at least partly understood as a product of—or, more precisely, a reaction against—the culture and mores of a certain time and place. He was born in 1981, a year after the end of the so-called Me Decade that gave rise to a host of self-improvement and self-realization fads. His adolescent years were spent in Marin County, north of San Francisco. Marin County has been gently mocked by the cartoon strip "Doonesbury" as the epicenter of the self-esteem movement, a land of hot tubs, Rolfing and est, a bastion of moral relativism where divorces were for a time listed alongside marriages in the newspaper. Walker was named John after John Lennon, the Beatle. His father says he was not bothered when his two sons rejected the "strict Catholic manner" of his own upbringing. His mother was a child of the '60s who dabbled in Buddhism and home-schooled John for a time. He

was sent to an elite alternative high school where students were allowed to shape their own studies and had to check in with their teacher only once a week.

Walker discovered his passion for Islam online, after sampling other possibilities. . . . He began visiting Islamic Web sites, asking questions like "Is it all right to watch cartoons on TV or in the movies?" His family says the turning point may have come at the age of 16 when he read "The Autobiography of Malcolm X," which describes the conversion to Islam of the famous black militant. Some Internet postings examined by NEWSWEEK show that young Walker soon became pretty militant himself. In a 1997 message to a hip-hop site, he demanded to know why a rapper named Nas "is indeed a 'God'? If this is so," Walker indignantly asks, "then why does he smoke blunts, drink Moët, fornicate, and make dukey music? That's a rather pathetic 'god', if you ask me." He quizzes an online correspondent about the Five Percent Nation of Islam—a small North American sect—about its adherents' vision of bliss and how to pursue it. "I have never seen happiness myself," writes Walker. "Perhaps you can enlighten me . . . where I can go to sneak a peek at it." Selling off his hip-hop CD collection on a rap-music message board, he converted to Islam.

He began wearing Islamic dress, a long white robe and pillbox hat, and calling himself Suleyman. His flowing robes raised some eyebrows, even in Marin County, which is deeply tolerant of almost any form of self-expression. "It was like watching Jesus Christ walk down the street," says a former neighbor. "That's not your normal Marin attire, unless it's purple." Walker's parents balked at calling him "Suleyman" (he remained "John" to them), but they tried to be nonjudgmental, even supportive, about his conversion. They were "proud of John for pursuing an alternative course," says his father. They did not object when he dropped out and took the high-school-diploma equivalency exam.

At about this time, late 1998, Walker's parents were splitting up. Frank went to live with a friend, Bill Jones, and Marilyn moved to a nearby apartment with young daughter Naomi. Their teenage son became obsessed with memorizing the Quran and the Sharia, Islam's elaborate, fixed rules for living and worship. He became convinced that he needed to go to Yemen because Yemeni Arabic was the closest to the "pure" language of the Quran. His parents, though strapped for money because of their separation, agreed to pay for it. Frank later told NEWSWEEK that he wanted to support his son's "passion" and "commitment to learning."

Walker was troubled to discover that Islam was not quite as "pure" as he had hoped. He later complained to his mullah, Mufti Iltimas, that he was disappointed during his stay in Yemen to find Islam divided among the Sunni and Shiites and many other sects and factions. All Muslims should follow one code, one law—the absolute truth of every word of the Quran, he believed. Walker, who had been oblivious to politics in the United States, began to absorb some of the politics of radical Islam. In October 2000, when suicide bombers blew a hole in the side of the USS Cole as the American destroyer was refueling in the Yemeni harbor of Aden, Frank Lindh e-mailed his son to lament that some of the 17 young sailors killed in the blast were the same age as his son. Walker wrote back that bringing the U.S. destroyer into a Yemeni harbor was "an act of war" against Islam. His son's message "raised my concerns," Frank told NEWSWEEK, "but my days of molding him were over."

Frank disagreed with his son, but he didn't cut off the money. In late 1999 John Walker came home, mostly to see his mother, who had worried about him. John felt uncomfortable in America, however, and wanted to rejoin the Islamic world. In California he fell in with a large Islamic missionary group, the Tablighi Jamaat, which, according to intelligence sources, is sometimes used as a recruiting ground by extremist groups. Walker was taken under the wing of a Pakistani missionary named Khizar Hiyat, who had invited the impressionable Walker to join him on a drive to Nevada as he was spreading the word. After a brief return to Yemen, Walker traveled with Hiyat in Pakistan for a month before choosing the austere madrasa outside Bannu.

It is not clear how Walker wound up in Afghanistan. . . . "He was intrigued by Afghanistan," said [a] friend. "He said he was interested in getting a bird's-eye view of how Sharia was being applied. . . . In his search for purity, Walker gravitated to the most extreme expression of Islam, the Taliban.

It never occurred to Frank and Marilyn that their son would become a holy warrior. "He was the last person you would expect to go and fight," Frank told NEWSWEEK. Added Marilyn: "He would freeze. He's totally not streetwise." Yet somehow, in fairly short order, Walker was at a Qaeda training camp in Afghanistan, using the nom de guerre Abdul Hamid, learning to fire an AK-47 and crossing paths with none other than Osama bin Laden. According to his interview with CNN, Walker fought with Pakistanis in Kashmir in the summer of 2001. When the United States struck back after the September 11 attacks, Walker was sent to fight against the Northern Alliance in Konduz. Sold out by their leader, Walker and several hundred other Taliban marched 100 miles, surrendered and then were herded into container trucks and shipped to a fortress prison near Mazar-e Sharif. Walker's own story of what happened next, first told to NEWSWEEK reporter Colin Soloway as Walker lay wounded and stunned after the revolt and siege at Qala Jangi prison, is hair-raising:

The Taliban began revolting as soon as they arrived at the prison. Two of the mujahedin threw grenades, hidden in their robes, killing two Northern Alliance generals. "After that they put us in the basement and left us overnight," recalled Walker. "Early in the morning they began taking us out, slowly, one by one, into the compound . . . Our hands were tied, and they were kicking and beating some of us. Some of the mujahedin were scared, crying. They thought we were all going to be killed." Walker saw "two Americans . . . taking pictures with a digital camera and a video camera. They were there for interrogating us." The Americans were Mike Spann and another CIA operative later identified only as "Dave." A video taken by an Afghan cameraman shows Walker sitting cross-legged, slumped silently before the two CIA men. Spann squats down and starts asking questions: "Who brought you here? Wake up! Who brought you here to Afghanistan? How did you get here?" Then Spann and Dave conduct some theater, speaking loudly so Walker can hear. "The problem is," says Dave, "he needs to decide if he wants to live or die . . ." Spann tries to evoke some empathy from the prisoner. "There were several hundred Muslims killed in the bombing in New York City. Is that what the Quran teaches? I don't think so. Are you going to talk to us?" Walker makes no response.

Shortly after this footage was shot, "someone either pulled a knife or threw a grenade at the guards or got their guns, and started shooting," recalled Walker in his interview with NEWSWEEK. "As soon as I heard the shooting and screaming, I jumped up and ran about one or two meters, and was shot in the leg."

The CIA's Spann was beaten, shot and killed by the mob. Dave was believed to have been rescued by American Special Forces and British SAS troopers. The rebellious prisoners holed up in the basement, and American bombs began to fall. The Northern Alliance tried to burn them out by pouring in diesel fuel and lighting it, and then to drown them with thousands of gallons of water. Finally, after six days, Walker and 85 bedraggled others surrendered.

Walker's parents had not heard a word from their son after he left the madrasa at Bannu in May 2001. . . . After September 11, Frank and Marilyn were worried sick; Frank began visiting mosques in the San Francisco area, showing a photo of his son in full Islamic dress. Lindh says he dreaded the worst. "I would look at the moon and just wonder if John was somewhere seeing it, too," he says. "I didn't have the sense that he was."

When Frank Lindh at last saw the videotape of his wounded and battered son being loaded onto a hospital gurney, he sobbed uncontrollably. His friends had to hold him up. Marilyn also seemed to be in shock when NEWSWEEK interviewed her the next day. Her son, she said, had been "brainwashed." When the TV satellite trucks showed up outside and the death threats began, she fled with her daughter to an undisclosed location. Frank, meanwhile, embarked on the TV talk-show circuit. He steadfastly refused to be judgmental. "I don't think John was doing anything wrong," he told CBS's "The Early Show.". . . As for Walker's comment to NEWSWEEK that he "supported" the September 11 attacks, Lindh suggested that his son may have been in shock (he may have been otherwise addled; Walker said he had been a heavy hashish user, according to one Northern Alliance source). The family's latest defense is that their son did not have access to Western media, only the Taliban version of September 11, which may not have reported the atrocities and civilian death toll.

Just in case the U.S. government did not share this benign view of his son's activities, Frank Lindh went out and hired one of the best-known trial lawyers in America, James Brosnahan, a former federal prosecutor who worked on the Iran-Contra case. . . . One source said that Attorney General John Ashcroft and other top Justice Department officials were "disgusted" with Walker's actions and want to "make an example of him." Because he is a U.S. citizen, he is not a candidate for the military tribunals that will be set up to try Al Qaeda and other terrorists. He could possibly be tried for treason, but that crime is hard to prove—there must be two witnesses to convict. Walker's fellow Taliban may not be the most credible in court. In the NEWSWEEK Poll, 41 percent of Americans believe that Walker should be charged with treason and put on trial for fighting with the enemy; an additional 42 percent say he should be tried only if there is specific evidence of his fighting against Americans. Walker may have some useful intelligence to bargain with. Though he was but a lowly foot soldier, the CIA would like to learn more about Al Qaeda's recruiting. Sources say that Walker has proudly informed his interrogators that he was not merely Taliban but Al Qaeda. If Walker can inform on the terror network, he might be able to negotiate a plea bargain. Passions may cool, but facing an American jury in the present atmosphere could be one more unwise decision for a young man who has already made some seriously bad ones.

———————◆———————

If it be not treason, it grazes the edge of treason.
JOHN SHARP WILLIAMS, in debate in the U.S. Senate,
characterizing George W. Norris' opposition to
American involvement in World War I,
April 4, 1917

113.

ROBERT G. KAISER: America and the Aftermath of September 11

While most Americans were convulsed with grief and anger in response to the terrorist attacks of September 11, 2001, disbelief may have been an even more widespread experience. In the weeks and months following the event, as Americans asked themselves why the tragedy had occurred, many confronted for the first time the "New World Order" in which the United States was the sole remaining superpower. While many countries expressed an unprecedented solidarity with the United States, Americans noted with dismay the number of people around the world who actually welcomed the attacks. In his essay for the Encyclopædia Britannica 2001 Year in Review, *written only months after the fact, Robert Kaiser, an associate editor of the* The Washington Post, *attempts to provide a context for the horrific events of September 11.*

Source: *Encyclopædia Britannica 2001 Year in Review.*

FOR YEARS we said we lived in a global village. On Sept. 11, 2001, terrorists bent on wreaking havoc in New York City and Washington, D.C., proved that this was so. Never before had the world so intimately shared the same tragic disaster. Because the attacks occurred in the morning on the U.S. East Coast, perhaps 90% of the Earth's population was awake when two airplanes flew into the World Trade Center and another crashed into the Pentagon. Transported to New York by some of the most powerful images ever conveyed by television, billions of people vicariously experienced the horror.

Rare are the events that jolt the entire globe. In truth, there may never have been another that had the impact of September 11. The detonation of the first atomic bomb or the bringing down of the Berlin Wall may have been more important historical events, but neither had an audience as big or as raptly attentive as that on September 11. In part because nearly everyone was jolted, we will need a long time to grasp the true import of that date. It became a cliché almost immediately afterward that "everything has changed." Giving that phrase real content will take years.

Some of the things that changed were quickly obvious. The United States lost its innocence and its isolation, becoming in just a few days a different kind of global power. For 56 years after World War II, Americans had policed the globe as beneficent gendarmes, trying to keep the world safe for democracy and capitalism. Suddenly on September 11 the mission changed. The goal became to keep America itself safe.

For the first time, other nations rushed to America's side, offering condolences and active assistance. The North Atlantic Treaty Organization invoked Article 5 of its founding treaty, declaring that the terrorist actions constituted an attack against all NATO members, which would respond—as required by the treaty—as if they had been attacked themselves. Article 5 had never before been invoked. In Moscow the young president of Russia phoned the young U.S. president aboard Air Force One and pledged his country's cooperation for a war against terrorism. Vladimir Putin's call was the first the administration of George W. Bush received from a foreign leader. On September 19 the Organization of American States agreed by acclamation to invoke the Rio Treaty, a mutual defense pact. One after another the countries of the world lined up with the United States. Most did so without evident hesitation, a few because Bush made it so clear, in his speech to Congress on September 20, that the U.S. expected their support: "Every nation in every region now has a decision to make: Either you are with us or you are with the terrorists."

Ultimately, only Iraq offered sympathy to the terrorists; no other government would take their side. This was a huge change. The nations of the world had never before been so united on an important global issue. The collapse of international factions into a united front against terrorism signaled powerfully that, as U.S. Secretary of State Colin Powell put it in a speech in Shanghai on October 18, "not only is the Cold War over, the post-Cold War period is also over." Suddenly the world had a new cause and a new sense of shared challenge. Old alignments seemed to disappear.

But that near unanimity among political leaders was not so evident on the streets of the world's cities, towns, and villages. Within hours of the September 11 attacks, cameras caught Palestinians on the West Bank exulting over the terrorists' successes. Posters carrying the likeness of Osama bin Laden blossomed throughout the Muslim world. Public opinion polls and questioning reporters found that citizens of many lands felt sympathy for the terrorists and antipathy for the United States.

In China government officials had to censor Internet discussions, which included much cheering for a blow struck against American arrogance. A poll taken in Bolivia found that Bin Laden was the most admired man in that Andean nation. In Muslim countries certain myths took hold: that it was not the Arabs on board who hijacked the aircraft and flew them into the Pentagon and the WTC but, in fact, Israeli intelligence agents who were responsible for the attacks; that the Americans had no proof that Bin Laden was behind what had happened. One of the ugliest myths, written and repeated time and again in the Arab world, was that several thousand Jews who ordinarily worked in the World Trade Center did not show up for work on September 11—an implication that they had been warned of the attacks. In fact, many of the nearly 3,000 victims in the World Trade Center were Jewish.

These expressions of hostility toward the United States and sympathy for those who killed so many innocent people shocked and alarmed many Americans, who wondered how foreigners could wish them ill. Americans hold their country in a high regard, and many did not realize how ambivalent others could be in their attitudes toward the world's only superpower. Anti-Americanism was nothing new, of course, but this latest strain had special characteristics related to America's overwhelming power and the way it had been used and perceived through the 1990s.

Before September 11, Americans had clearly grown comfortable with their cushy position, above the world's frays. Americans liked being richer than the rest and well insulated from their tribulations. In 2001 the new U.S. administration was becoming famous for a go-it-alone approach to international affairs, infuriating allies and rivals by its unilateral policies and decisions and by its reluctance to join other nations in collective action. One example was the international effort to do something about global warming by controlling the emissions of "greenhouse gases," especially the carbon monoxide produced by the burning of fossil fuels. On September 11 the international community was preparing for a conference that would complete a final agreement on emissions controls, but the United States, the producer of one-fourth of the world's greenhouse gases, had opted not to participate.

On those occasions when the United States did play an active part in world affairs and did join other countries in some collaborative efforts, it was usually on its own terms. Many Americans considered this reasonable and appropriate. Why should they give others any influence over matters they wanted to, and could, control themselves?

September 11 created a new reality. Beginning with that communication from Russian Pres. Vladimir Putin, President Bush spent most of the first days after the attacks speaking and meeting with foreign leaders, building what he called a new global coalition against terrorism. "We will rally the world," Bush said, and he did just that. A president regarded warily by many world leaders as a unilateralist and a bit of a cowboy was suddenly courting support from every conceivable precinct. On September 24 the House of Representatives voted to release $582 million of the $819 million in back dues to the United Nations. Concerns that just before September 11 dominated American policy suddenly disappeared. So, for example, Uzbekistan, with its corrupt and authoritarian regime

that had been held at arm's length by the United States before September 11, became an important ally and a base for American military operations soon afterward.

"Working well with others" became a category on school report cards in the U.S. in the last generation, but globally, this had not been an American value. George Washington, the founding father, offered his countrymen the vision of a United States totally insulated from foreign entanglements in his famous Farewell Address 205 years before September 11, and that remained a tantalizing goal for many Americans. Washington, of course, could not have imagined the technological changes that would shrink the world in our time. Even Americans who experienced those changes remained reluctant to accept their true implications.

September 11 ended the dream of "fortress America." The 19 Arab terrorists who hijacked four airliners that day obviously were not restrained by any sense that the United States enjoyed special protection from hostile foreign forces. The shock that went through the American population after September 11, all but eliminating air travel and tourism for weeks, also marked a turning point for the American experiment, though it was impossible to explain just how. That might take years to clarify.

The horror planned for September 11 was supposed to be worse, and very nearly was. The fourth hijacked airplane was evidently aimed at the Capitol or the White House in Washington—we may never know its target for certain. A direct hit on either would have been symbolically devastating, adding enormously to the impact of the attacks. But a group of brave and resourceful passengers on United Airlines Flight 93 prevented its hijackers from fulfilling their mission, forcing the plane down in a Pennsylvania farm field, where the lives of everyone on board ended.

The fate of Flight 93 was a demonstration of how the modern global village can function. Passengers on board the flight, who thought they were flying from Newark, N.J., to San Francisco, made calls to relatives on the ground with cellular telephones and learned that a hijacked plane already had been flown into the World Trade Center in New York. One of them was Jeremy Glick, 31, sales manager for a technology firm, who told his wife to "have a good life" and promised to go down fighting against the terrorists. Glick and several other passengers, all apparently held in the galley at the rear of the Boeing 757, were plotting to rush the cockpit of the plane, 110 feet forward of the galley, to disrupt whatever plan their hijackers had in mind. One of the other plotters, Todd Beamer, told a telephone operator whom he had reached via an onboard "airfone" about this plan. The operator heard him shout to his comrades, "Are you guys ready? Let's roll!" The operator then heard screams and sounds of a scuffle before the line went dead. In the next few moments, the plane took a series of sharp turns and then plunged into the Pennsylvania countryside near the town of Shanksville, just south of Johnstown. Somehow, the passengers had disrupted the hijackers and forced the plane to Earth.

In that case the technological wizardry of the age contributed to heroism and a self-sacrifice that may have saved many lives in Washington. This was one example of how the events of September 11 were made possible by modern technology or modern styles of life. Other examples of the same phenomenon were not so uplifting.

Eerily, the terrorists, avowed enemies of secular modernity, were able to have the enormous impact they had by mastering skills and technologies that were part of what they claimed to detest. Their ability to move freely between their countries of origin, principally Saudi Arabia and Egypt, and the flying schools and Internet cafés of the United States they so ardently hated, and then into the cockpits of those four Boeing jetliners, was perhaps the most powerful symbol of what September 11 really represented— on one hand, angry young Arabs who belonged to a movement dedicated to anti-modernism and an anti-American crusade; on the other hand, a hypermodern America open to the world, open even to these fanatics who were determined to inflict great harm on the United States. In an age of irony, this ultimate irony: the terrorists could do the damage they did only by acquiring skills from American flying schools, exploiting America's porous airport-security arrangements, and mastering the arts of hiding in plain sight in a society they abhorred. In the real global village of 2001, we were all startled to discover, such trickery was amazingly simple. On September 10, it soon became clear, we had not understood the world we lived in; a month later we understood it a lot better, though far from thoroughly.

The easy, comforting notion of a global village implies that all the world's peoples are intimate neighbours, sharing more than they do not share. But this is not the global village that September 11 revealed so starkly.

In the real modern world, different peoples have taken what are sometimes radically different paths and reached very different destinations. In Europe and North America, where technology, education, and tradition produced the greatest wealth, the failure of the Muslim world to match this prosperity was just a fact of modern life, little remarked upon before September 11. Most Muslims lived in relative poverty; some were rich from oil; and almost none, rich or poor, occupied the most modern precincts of the global village. The most modern and successful nation in the Middle East, the centre of the Muslim world, was not Muslim at all: Israel. But Israel was a hated symbol to many of its Arab neighbours.

The gulf that divides Muslim, mostly Arab peoples from Europeans and Americans, and also Asians, may be the most significant dividing line in the 21st-century world. Put simply, the secular global economy created by the richer countries gave great benefit to many and was a model to be emulated for many more. South Koreans, Chinese, Cypriots, and Chileans all subscribed to the same broad propositions that animated Americans, Germans, and Japanese: technological progress is good; wealth earned from global trade is desirable; consumerism and the democratization of wealth are goals to be pursued. For most of the adherents of this loose creed, political democracy was also part of the formula—democratic governments, most agreed, were most likely to achieve the prosperity so many were seeking.

Many Muslims and Arabs embraced the rich world's ideals—this is evident from the fact that millions of them have found ways to establish residency in rich countries and pursue new lives in them. The governments and especially the religious establishments of the Arab world, however, were not part of the fledgling consensus joined by so many other nations. No Arab government was a democracy, and no Arab nation was a full participant in the technological revolution of the age. Only a few oil-rich autocracies even took a stab at participation.

The Muslim world has never experienced anything comparable to the enlightenment of the 17th and 18th centuries that prepared the Christian nations of Europe for the Industrial Revolution and modernity. For Muslim fundamentalists—for example, the Wahhabi sect that dominates the religious life of Saudi Arabia—nonparticipation in the modern world is seen as a good thing, a way to avoid pollution of Muslim values by infidels. But such fundamentalists are surrounded by the temptations of the wealthy world, and often by neighbours in their own countries who do not share their disdain for modernity. Tens of thousands of well-to-do Saudis, for example, own houses or apartments in Europe or the United States and happily partake of modern pleasures when visiting those places. Yet at home they support a system that denies such pleasures to most of their countrymen and provides few opportunities for citizens to express themselves or influence their government.

The Arab world differs from the modernized West and Asia in another important respect. When countries get rich, their birthrates decline. Birthrates are so low in the developed European nations that they are all facing shrinkage of their native populations. Japan is in a similar position. Conversely, the Arab countries are experiencing rapid population growth. Saudi Arabia is growing more than 3% a year; Egypt, about 2%. Burgeoning populations aggravate tensions in these societies, none of which is creating opportunities for young people sufficient to satisfy the growing number of working-age citizens.

All of these factors are related to the success Bin Laden and his allies have had in building the al-Qaeda terrorist movement that shook the world on September 11. Obviously, only a tiny fraction of the young men of the Arab and Muslim worlds joined al-Qaeda and other like-minded groups. Might there be many more in the future? The possibility could not be dismissed lightly after September 11.

Americans took comfort from their own response to September 11. The country found many heroes to thank, from those passengers on Flight 93 to the fire fighters and police officers of New York City, so many of whom gave their lives that day in service to their country and community. Americans poured hundreds of millions of dollars into charities to support the victims' families and stoically put up with the practical consequences of the attacks, which included a sharp economic downturn, closures and postponements of various meetings and events, and total disruption of domestic airline travel in the United States. Countless Americans remarked on a new mood in the country, a new spirit of coopera-

tion and sharing, and a new recognition, as many put it, of what "really matters" in their lives.

At year's end it was still too early to know the more profound impact of September 11 and its aftermath. Would Americans' lost innocence be translated into a real commitment to confronting the underlying problems confronting the global village? Or would a quick war on terrorism be followed by a relapse into American exceptionalism and another retreat from international engagement? The terrorists of September 11 challenged the United States to confront the fact that it overwhelms all other nations in its wealth, power, and influence and to accept the responsibilities that accompany such preponderance. The terrorists succeeded in making America the target. Americans would have to choose a response to that new status.

—◆—

Let those who say that we must understand the reasons for terrorism come with me to the thousands of funerals we are having in New York City and explain those insane, maniacal reasons to the children who will grow up without fathers and mothers, to the parents who have had their children ripped from them for no reason at all.

RUDOLPH GIULIANI, mayor of New York City, remarks to
the United Nations General Assembly,
October 1, 2001

INDEX

Note: An asterisk (*) following a proper name indicates that the person is the author of one or more selections in this volume. In the case of multiple references, the more important ones are listed first. Page numbers in *italics* refer to photographs.

Able v. *United States*, 415
Abortion, 77–82
"Academic Advocates" (Himmelfarb), 277
Academic freedom, postmodernism controversy, 277–282
Academics First, 478
ACLU, *see* American Civil Liberties Union
Acquired immunodeficiency syndrome, *see* AIDS
Action on Smoking & Health, 321
Addiction, tobacco, 319
"Advanced Notice of Proposed Rulemaking" (BIA), 398
Advertising, 223, 319
Affirmative action, 138, 186
Afghanistan, war on terrorism, 494, 496; also, 121, *148*, 508, 509
African Americans, national concerns and class division, 42–52; and the Democratic Party, 151–155; and basketball, 210–218; Simpson trial, 283, 289, 290; in sports, 421–423; also 149, 187, 202, 206, 425
Ageism, 392
Agostini v. *Felton*, 417
AIDS (acquired immunodeficiency syndrome), memoir, 59–60; also *195*, 295
"Air Time: Let's Put a Cop on Every Flight" (Miller), 499
Air travel, after September 11 attacks, 499–504
Akron v. *Akron Center for Reproductive Health, Inc.*, 78, 82
Al-Qaeda, *148*, *462*, 494–497, 505, 510, 515
Alaska, *Exxon Valdez* oil spill, 92–96; also 444
Alaska Oil Spill Commission, 92
Albright, Madeleine K.*, on the U.S. in the UN, 262–266
Alcohol use, 17, 443
Alfred P. Murrah Building, Okla. City, *461*
Alyeska Pipeline Service Company, 93, 96
American Civil Liberties Union (ACLU), 66
American Enterprise, 438
"American Gothic" (Oates), 273
American Indians, see Native Americans
"American Taliban, The" (Thomas), 505
Americans with Disabilities Act of 1990, 102–107
Ames, Aldrich, 235–248

Ames, Maria del Rosario Casas, 235, 243, 244
"Analyzing Dr. Laura" (Goldberg), 378
Anand, Viswanathan, 337–338
Angelou, Maya, 290
Anti-Americanism, 512
Antitrust laws, 138
Antz, 98
Architecture, 219–223
Armey, Dick*, on NEA funding, 110–113
Armstrong, Lance, *402*
Arrested Development*, 382–383
Art, government funding, 108–115; reading and life, 183–184; Brooklyn Museum, 412–418
"Art, Humanities, and Museums Amendments of 1990," 108
Artificial intelligence, and chess, 335–338
Assad, Hafez, 124
"Assessment of the Aldrich H. Ames Espionage Case and Its Implications for U.S. Intelligence, An," 235
Association of American Colleges, The, 57
AT&T, 304, 305
Atlantic Monthly, The, 165, 224
Atlantic Monthly Online, The, 469
Austin, Warren Robinson, 266
Autobiography of Malcolm X, The, 507
Automobiles, *see* Cars
Aviation, *see* Air travel

Baby Bells, *see* Regional Bell Operating Companies
Baby Boomers, 165–174; also 388, 430
Baby Busters, *see* Generation X
"Bad Plumbing" (Gitter), 324
Bailey, F. Lee, *250*
Baker, Dean, 431
Bakker, Jim, 12–14
Bakker, Tammy, 12–14
Baltimore, Md., 340–342
Baraka, Amiri, 288, 289, 290
Barber, James, 369
Barlow, John Perry*, on the Information Age and open societies, 89–92
Barnes, Julian, 282
Baseball, 438–440

Basketball, 210–218
Bassett, Beverly, 233
Baxter, Nathan, 368
Beamer, Todd, 514
Beck, Roy*, on impact of immigration, 224–231
Bedford Stuyvesant Restoration Corp., 114
Bendavid, Naftali*, on the 2000 election, 463–465
Bennett, William J.*, on immigration in California, 267–270
Benton, Robert, 296
Benton Foundation, 302
Bentsen, Lloyd, 63
Berlin Wall, Ger., 6–8
Beverly Enterprises, 233
Bible, Geoffrey*, on Big Tobacco 319–320
Bierce, Ambrose, 400
Bilingual education, 343–347; also 270
Bin Laden, Osama, 494–495, 505, 508, 512, 515
Black Americans, see African Americans
Blau, Andrew, 303
Bligh Reef, Alsk., 92–93, 95–96
Bloods (Piru gangs), 206–209
Bloom, Allan*, on education, 28–37
Blue collar, see Working class
Bobinger, Trey, 321
Boesky, Ivan, 317
Bollywood, 490
Bombay, India, and globalization, 490
Bongiorno, Lori*, on Liggett Group settlement, 320–321
Books, in an era of television, 181–185
Boomers, see Baby Boomers
Boorstin, Daniel, 185
Bork, Robert, 25, 26
Borneo, and globalization, 490
Borrowed Time: An AIDS Memoir (Monette), 59
Bosnia and Herzegovina, 148
Botstein, Leon, 182
Bowhead whales, 348
Bowling Alone: The Collapse and Revival of American Community (Putnam), 448
Bradley, Bill*, on the FTA, 144–146
Braidhill, Kathy, 209
Branch Davidians, 179, 180
Brand, David*, on televangelism, 12–14
Brand, Myles*, on college athletics, 475–479
Brandenburg Gate, Ger., 6
Brennan, William J., Jr.*, on Edwards v. Aguillard, 9–11; also 107
Briggs, Vernon, 230
Broadcast spectrum, 304, 306–308
Brooke Group, 321
Brookhiser, Richard*, on Whitewater, 231–234
Brooklyn Museum of Art, and the "Sensation" exhibit, 412–418; also 114
Brooklyn Museum v. City of New York and Rudolph Giuliani, 412–418; also 54
Brown, Jerry, 233, 460
Bryan, William Jennings, 11
Bryce, James, 205
Buchanan, Pat*, convention speech, 156–160
Buckley, William F., Jr.*, on politics and Supreme Court nominees, 25–26; also 442

Buffett, Warren, 386
Bunk, etymology, 55
Bureau of Alcohol, Tobacco, and Firearms (ATF), 179
Bureau of Indian Affairs (BIA), 394, 398
Bush, Barbara*, Wellesley College commencement speech, 99–101
Bush, George H. W.*, Robertson's convention speech, 64–68; inaugural address, 72–76; Operation Just Cause, 87–88; on Operation Desert Storm, 128–130; also 136, 146, 404
Bush, George W.*, disputed election of 2000, 463–465; declaration of war on terrorism, 494–498; also 405, 406, 468, 485, 487, 506, 512, 513
Business, women in corporate America, 21–24; and union policies, 38–41; also 317–318
Business Week, 320
Butcher, Kristin, 268
Byrd, James, Jr., 407

Cable News Network (CNN), 489
Cable television, 302, 305, 308
Cabrini-Green, Chicago, 51
Calculation, 335–337
California, street gangs, 206–209; immigration, 267–270; bilingual education, 343–345; also 149–150, 405
California Civil Rights Initiative, 270
California Department of Justice, 206
California v. Cabazon Band of Mission Indians, 393
Campaign finance reform, and soft money, 458–460; also 450
Canada, 490
Canadian Broadcasting Corporation (CBC), 490
Capitalism, 350, 354
Carbon dioxide emissions, 163
Cars, and road rage, 454–458; also 221
Carson, Johnny, 97
Carville, James, 178
Casey, William, 4, 5
Cats (Webber), 53
Cellular phones, 195
Censorship, 111
Center for Media Education, 307
"Central Command Briefing, Riyadh, Saudi Arabia" (Schwarzkopf), 131
Central Intelligence Agency, see CIA
Centrally planned economic system, 353, 354
Chandler, Raymond, 338
Chapin, Schulyer, 413–414
Cherokee Nation v. Georgia, 394
Chess, and computers, 335–338
"Chess Genius," 338
Chicago Tribune, 463
Child abuse, 308
Child molesters, see Pedophilia
Child Pornography Prevention Act of 1996, 322–324
Children, health care, 189; educational television, 307, 308, 309; pornography issues, 322–324; and drug use, 444; standardized testing, 481, 482

China, and globalization, 490–493; also 124
Chiptest, 336
Chuck D, 381–382; also *53*
Church-state separation, *Edwards* v. *Aguillard*,
   9–11; Clarence Thomas, 137–138
Churchill, Winston, 52, 125
Chuvakhin, Sergey Dmitriyevich, 238, 242
CIA, and the Ames case, 235–248
Cigarettes, 16, 17
Cinema, *see* Movies
Civics education, 449
Civil-rights movement, 42, 46, 407
Civil union act, *see* Vermont Civil Union Act of
   2000
Clark, Bill, 296
Cleaver, Kathleen, 289
Clinton, Bill*, inaugural address, 175–178; on
   urban renewal, 202–205; Whitewater
   Scandal, 231; State of the Union Address,
   258–261; on Oklahoma City bombing,
   271–272; Starr Report, 362–365; reaction of
   Lieberman, 366–371; also *53*, 339, 342, *356*,
   371, 404, 405, 408, 447, 452
Clinton, Hillary*, on health care reform,
   189–194; also 232, 234
Cloning, *196*
Closing of the American Mind, The (Bloom), 28
Cloud, John, 437
Club drugs, 483–484
CNN, *see* Cable News Network
Coale, John P., 320
Coalition Against Racism and Nazism, 143
Cocaine, 443, 444
Cochran, Johnnie, *250*, 286, 287, 288, 290
Code of Ethics for Government Service, 117
Colautti v. *Franklin*, 80
Cold War, 6–8, 119, 144, 314
Colleges, speech codes 186–188; cost, 327–330;
   reforming athletics, 475–479
Columbia Journalism Review, 161–162
Columbine High School murders, Colo.,
   250, 435–437
Commentary, 42, 277, 335
Committee for Economic Development, 52
Common Cause, 116–117
Commonweal, 327, 418
Communications Act of 1934, 302
Communications Decency Act of 1996 (CDA),
   308–309
Communism, 84–86, 119, 350
"Compassion on Campus" (Will), 186
Compton, Calif., 206
Computer imaging, and child pornography, 323
Computers, and chess, 335–338; also 375
Coney Island, N.Y., 211
"Conflagration," 179
Congress, and NEA funding, 108–115; Child
   Pornography Prevention Act, 322–324; and
   soft money, 459, 460
Congressional Quarterly Weekly Report, 136
Congressional Record, 108, 115
Constitution (U. S.), 80, 90–91, 136–139, 357–361
Containment policy, 85, 86

Contract with America, 251–253
Copyright, 372–377
Corlett, Candace*, on marketing to older women
   on the Internet, 388–392
Corporate welfare, 307
Corporations, and women, 21–24; also 220
Costas, Bob*, on baseball, 438–440
Counterintelligence Center, 246
Coupland, Doug, 166
Cousins, Gregory, 93–96
Cox, Archibald, 116–117
Crab Supernova, 183
Crack cocaine, 207–208
Cranston, Alan, 115–116
Creationism, 9–11
Creationism Act, 9–11
Crime, street gangs, 206–209; Ames case,
   235–248; hate crimes, 407–411; and drug
   legalization, 445–446; club drugs 483–484;
   also 202, 314; *see also* Terrorism
Crips, 206–209
Cuban Museum of Arts and Culture, Inc. v. *City of
   Miami*, 416
Cultural imperialism, 489
Cultural pluralism, and higher education, 57
Culture, Rapaille's insights into American
   character, 452; also *53–54*
Current, 267
Cyberspace, 89–92

Daley, William, 463–465
Date rape drugs, 483, 484
Davis, Angela, 286, 289
De Gaulle, Charles, 127
Death of Literature, The (Kernan), 181
Death penalty, 138
Declaration of War on Terrorism, 494–498
DeConcini, Dennis, 115–116, 237, 239
Deep Blue, 335–338
Deep Thought, 336
Defense, radio spectrum allotments, 304
Defense of Marriage Act, 432
Deford, Frank*, on Tiger Woods, 332–334
DeGeneres, Ellen, 330–331; also *97*
Democratic Party, Richards convention speech,
   60–63; Jackson convention speech, 151–155;
   Latino voters, 403–407; suburban politics,
   446–448; election dispute of 2000, 463; Gore
   concession speech, 466–468; also 460
Department of Agriculture, 474
Department of Education, 449
Deregulation, 115
Dern, Laura, *97*
Detroit News, The, 330
Development, and urban sprawl, 219
Diabetes, stem cell research, 486
"Dictatorships and Double Standards"
   (Kirkpatrick), 84
Diet, 490–492
Digital Millennium Copyright Act, 372–377
Digital technology, 91, 306, 307, 372–377
Dionne, E. J., Jr.*, on suburban politics, 446–448
Dirks v. *SEC*, 326

Disability, 102–107
Discrimination, 102–107
Dividends, 385, 430
DNA testing, 425–426
Dole, Bob*, acceptance speech, 310–316; also 256, 307
Dole, Elizabeth, 316
Domestic violence, 288, 289
Dominica, 143
Don Quixote (Cervantes), 183
"Don't Believe the Hype" (Public Enemy), 381–382
"Double Talk? The Debate over Bilingual Education," 343
Douglas, Michael, 27
Dove, Rita, 284
Dow Jones Industrial Index, 428
Dow 36,000: The New Strategy for Profiting from the Coming Rise in the Stock Market (Glassman and Hassett), 384
Dr. Laura, *see* Schlessinger, Laura
Driving, and road rage, 454–458
Driving While Black (D.W.B.), 286
"Drop the GATT" (Nader), 254
Drugs, and public health, 17; trafficking, 207–209; legalization, 441–446; club drugs, 483–484
Dukakis, Michael, 60–63; also 72
Duke, David, 140–144
Dunaway, John A.*, on the Columbine murders, 435–437
Durbin, Richard, 447

Earth in the Balance (Gore), 163
Ebony, 290
Economy, organized labor, 38–41; NAFTA, 144–146; GATT, 254–257; free markets, 350–354; stock market bubble, 427–431; globalization, 488–493; also 312, 427
Ecstasy, *see* Methylenedioxymethamphetamine
Educated classes, housing, 220
Education, creationism and evolution issue, 9–11; liberal education debate, 28–37; myth-making, 55–59; importance of reading, 181–185; speech codes, 186–188; pitfalls of postmodernism, 277–282; children's educational television, 302, 307; cost, 327–330; bilingual, 343–347; school vouchers, 357–361; standardized testing, 480–482; also 66–67, 114, 313, 449
Edwards, Edwin, 140, 141, 143
Edwards v. *Aguillard*, 9–11
Eitzen, Stanley*, on sport, 419–424
Elders, Joycelyn, 139
Elections, disputed election of 2000, 463–465; also 307, 459, 466–468
Electronic Frontier Foundation (EFF), 89–92
Elementary schools, and bilingual education, 344
"Ellen," 330–331
"Ellen DeGeneres Paved the Way for Other Gays to Tell the World the Truth" (Price), 330
Embryonic stem cells, 485, 486
"Embryonic Stem Cell Research," 485
Emergency services, 304

Emily's List, 162
Employment, 339–342, 470
Encyclopaedia Britannica, 511
English language, in bilingual education, 343–347
Entertainment industry, 367, 489–490, 492–493
Environment, Gore's proposals, 163–165; also 92
Equal Education Opportunity Act, 343
Equal Protection Clause, 138
"E.R.," 294, 295, 296, 298
Eskimos, 348–349
Espionage, 235–248
Ethnicity, 145
European Union, 428
"Everything Is Everything" (Hill), 382–383
Evolution, 9–11
Exxon Valdez oil spill, 92–96

Falwell, Jerry, 12–14
Families, and the economy, 39–40; also 312, 346
Family and Medical Leave Act, 40
Farrakhan, Louis, 283, 287, 290
Fast Food Nation (Schlosser), 469–474
Federal Aviation Administration (FAA), 502
Federal Bureau of Investigation (FBI), Waco Crisis, 179–181; and the Olympic bombing, 324; also 285
Federal Communications Commission (FCC), 303, 306, 307
Federal Deposit Insurance Corporation (FDIC), 234
Federal Home Loan Bank Board, 116
Feminism, 288
Ferguson, Colin, 500
Fiji, and globalization, 489
Films, *see* Movies
Financial capital, and the civic spirit, 450
Finn, Chester E., Jr., 56
First Amendment, 9–11, 137–138, 412–418
Fitzgerald, Peter, 447
Five Percent Nation of Islam, 507
Flavor Flav, *53*
Florida, and disputed election of 2000, 463
Folklore, see Urban legends
Football (soccer), *401*
Ford, Gerald, 261
Foreign aid, 126
Foreign policy, 452
Forget-me pill, *see* Rohypnol
Fortune Brands, 385
Foster, Jodie, *97*
Foster, Vince, 234
France, 454, 491
"Frantic Moment, Rumors in the Rain and a Tense Call" (Bendavid and Kemper), 463
Franz, Dennis, 297
Free speech, 89–92, 186–188, 412–418
Free trade, 144–146; also 254
Frey, Darcy*, on poverty and basketball, 210–218
Fukuyama, Francis, 270
Fulghum, Robert, 141
Furness, Betty, 389, 391
Furrow, Buford, Jr., 408, 409

Gambling, and Native Americans, 393–400
Gamma-hydroxybutyrate (GHB), 484
Gangs, *see* Street gangs
Gangs 2000: A Call to Action, 206
Gates, Bill, *318*
Gates, Henry Louis, Jr.*, on Simpson trial, 283–291
"GATT Hypocrisy" (Nader), 256
Gelernter, David, 335
General Agreement on Tariffs and Trade (GATT), 254–257
General Electric Co., 385
Generation gap, 165–174
Generation X, 165–174
Genetic code, 476
Geography of Nowhere, The (Kunstler), 219
George, Nelson, 218
George Bush Presidential Library and Museum, 87, 99
Gergen, David*, on the Los Angeles riots, 149–150; also 234
Gershon, Nina, 412–418
Getting It Gazette, The, 162
"Ghost of Tom Joad, The" (Springsteen), 300
GI Bill, 328
GI Generation, 167, 389
Gift, Roland, 289
Gingrich, Newt*, Contract with America, 251–253; also 256, 271, 310, *356*
Gitter, Max*, on the Olympic bombing and the media, 324–326
Giuliani, Rudolph, 408, 412–418, 516
Glaser Safety Slugs, 500
Glassman, James K.*, on stocks, 384–387
Glenn, John, 115–118
Glick, Jeremy, 514
"Global village" theory, 489, 514
Global warming, 163, 513
Globalization, 254–257, 488–493: also 185
"God and Money" (Brand), 12
Goldberg, Helene*, on talk radio, 378–380
"Golden Age of Higher Education—and Other Bunk, The" (Kincaid), 55
Goldman, Ronald, 287
Golf, 332–334
Gorbachev, Mikhail, 6–8, 120, 127
Gordon-Reed, Annette, 426
Gore, Al*, on the environment, 163–165; disputed election of 2000, 463–465; concession speech, 466–468
Government funding, and the NEA, 108–115; bilingual education, 343; stem cell research, 485, 486
Graff, Gerald, 282
Gray whales, 348
Great Books education, 34–35, 183
Greenspan, Alan*, on free markets, 350–354
Greising, David*, on Liggett Group settlement, 320–321
Griswold v. *Connecticut,* 81
Ground beef, 473
Growth funds, 430
Guatemala, and globalization, 490

Gulf War, *see* Persian Gulf War
Gulko, Boris*, on chess, 335–338
Gun violence, 208–209, 500

Hacker, Andrew, 150
Hackney, Sheldon, 186, 188
Hale, David, 233
Hanks, Tom, *98*
Hannegan v. *Esquire,* 416
Harding, Tonya, 424
Harper's Magazine, 197, 210
Harris, David, 212
Harris, Eric, 435–437
Harvard Cup, 336–337
Hassett, Kevin A.*, on stocks, 384–387
Hatch, Richard, *98*
Hate crimes, 407–411
"Hazards of Duke: Populism and Louisiana's Ghosts, The" (Maginnis), 140
Hazelwood, Joseph, 93–96
Health, public health issues, 15–20; health care reform, 41, 189–194; also, 59, 183
Heart disease, 486
Heflin, Howell*, on the Keating Five, 115–118
Helms, Jesse, 111
Hemings, Sally, 425–426
Hemp, 441
Henderson, Russell, 408
Hero worship, 289
Heroin, 443
Hess, Michael D., 414
Higginbotham, A. Leon, 284, 286, 287
High schools, and bilingual education, 344
"High-Stakes Tests Pose High-Stakes Risks for Vulnerable Kids" (Wellstone), 480
Higher education, and mythmaking, 55–59
Highet, Gilbert, 465
"Highway of Death" (Kuwait–Iraq), *147*
Hijackings, 499, 511
Hill, Anita, 136, 287, 288, 289
Hill, Lauren*, 383
"Hill Street Blues," 294, 295
Himelstein, Linda*, on Liggett Group settlement, 320–321
Himmelfarb, Gertrude*, on postmodernism, 277–282
Hip-hop, 381–383
Hirst, Damien, 413–414
Hispanic Americans (Latinos), and voting, 403–407
Hiyat, Khizar, 508
Hmong people, 225
Hollywood, Calif., 490
Holmes, Oliver Wendell, Jr., 188
"Holy Virgin Mary, The" (Ofili), 412–414
Homelessness, 341
"Homicide: Life on the Street," 299
Homosexuality, 330–331, 432–434
Hong Kong, and globalization, 491
Hooks, Bell, 287, 288
Hopkins, Sir Anthony, *97*
Horowitz, Roger, 59–60
Housing, 219–223

How Democracies Perish (Revel), 85
Howard, Arlene, 498
Howard, Edward Lee, 240
Howard, George, 498
Howe, Neil*, on the new generation gap, 165–174
Hu Yaobang, 120
Hubbell, Webb, 234
Hubl, Milan, 270
Hussein, Saddam, 124, 128, 129, 130, 135

IBM, 335
Illinois, and suburban voting trends, 447
Iltimas, Mohammad, 505, 506, 508
Immigrant labor, 471
Immigration, free-trade agreement, 145–146;
     into Wausau, 224–231; also 267, 268, 345
In vitro fertilization (IVF), stem cell research,
     486–487
*Inaugural Addresses of the Presidents of the United
     States: From George Washington 1789 to George
     Bush 1989*, 72
Independence Day (Ford), 296
Index funds, 430
Indian Gaming Regulatory Act (1998), 393,
     396–400
Industrial Revolution, 275
Information, importance of reading skills, 183
Information Age, and open societies, 89–92; and
     reading, 185; Telecommunications Act, 303
Insider trading, 325–326
Insurance, and health care reform, 189–194
"Integrity in the College Curriculum"
     (Association of American Colleges), 57
International Space Station (ISS), *196*
International trade, and FTA, 144–146; and
     GATT, 254–257
International Whaling Commission, 347–349
Internet, and open societies, 89–92; Telecommu-
     nications Act, 302, 308; marketing to older
     women 388–392; also 322, 376
"Interview with Eric Schlosser, Author of *Fast
     Food Nation*" (Livshin), 469
Iran-Contra Affair, 1–5
Iraq, Operation Desert Storm, 128–130; Persian
     Gulf War, 131–135; also 124
"Is Chess Finished?" (Gulko), 335
Islam, *see* Muslims
Isolationism, 262, 513
IVF, *see* In vitro fertilization

Jackson, Jesse L.*, convention speech, 151–155;
     also *355*
Jackson v. *Benson*, 358
Jacob, John E.*, on African Americans and
     poverty, 49–52
James, Leon*, on road rage, 454–458
Japan, and globalization, 491; also 123, 126, 429
Jefferson, Thomas, 425–426
Jefferson County Colorado Sheriff's Office
     Report, on Columbine murders, 435
Jeffries, Leonard, 277
Jewell, Richard, 324–326
Jiang Zemin, 492

Johnson, Corey, 212, 216, 217
Johnson, Louis, 217
Jolly Roger Press, 275
Jones, Paula Corbin, 363
Jones, Tarre, 382–383
Jordan, Daniel P.*, on Jefferson paternity debate,
     425–426
Jordan, Michael, *401*, 422, 490
Jordan, Vernon, 363
Joseph Burstyn, Inc. v. *Wilson*, 416
Joy Luck Club, The (Tan), 83–84
Jury system, 284

Kaczynski, David, 275
Kaczynski, Ted*, manifesto, 275–276; also *461*
Kafka, Franz, 182
Kaiser, Robert*, on aftermath of September 11
     attacks, 511–516
Kantor, Mickey, 257
Kapor, Mitchell*, on the Information Age and
     open societies, 89–92
Kasparov, Garry, 335–338
Kavanaugh, Brett, 365
Keating, Charles, 115–118
Keating Five, The, 115–118
Kemper, Bob*, on the 2000 election dispute,
     463–465
Kennan, George, 86
Kennedy, Edward M., 411
Kennedy, John F., Jr., *249*
Kernan, Alvin, 181
KGB, 236, 238–241
Kincaid, Jamaica, 284, 289
Kincaid, James R.*, on higher education, 55–59
"Kindly Inquisitors: The New Attacks on Free
     Thought" (Rauch), 187
King, John William, 407
King, Martin Luther, Jr., 285, 288
King, Rodney, 149, 288
Kinsley, Michael*, on the collapse of communism,
     84–86
Kirkpatrick, Jeanne, 84
Klebold, Dylan, 435–437
Knight, Bob, 476, 478
Koresh, David, 179–181
Krauthammer, Charles, 335, 337
Ku Klux Klan (KKK), 140, 230
Kunstler, James Howard*, on housing, 219–223
Kunstler, William, 295
Kuwait, 124, 128–130, 131–135

Labor, 38–41
Labor unions, favored legislation, 38–41
Lacayo, Richard, 174
Language, bilingual education, 343–347
Lapham, Lewis*, on Ross Perot, 197–201
Lasater, Dan, 234
"Last Shot, The" (Frey), 210
Latinos (people), see Hispanic Americans
"Law and Order," 294, 295
Law enforcement, and Waco, 179–181; and street
     gangs, 208–209; African Americans' distrust,
     285, 286, 288; air travel, 499–501; also 319

LeBow, Bennett S., 321
LeCain, Lloyd, 94
Lee, Spike, 283, 289
Legalization, of drugs, 441–446
Lehman, Arnold, 413–414
Lemon v. *Kurtzman*, 137, 417
Lesbianism, 330–331
Lewinsky, Monica, 231, *356*, 362, 363, 366
Lhota, Joseph, 414–415, 416–417
Liability, 308, 319, 375
Libraries, 309
Lieberman, Joe*, on the Clinton-Lewinsky affair, 366–371
Lifestyles, public health impact, 17; also 19, 20
Liggett Group, Inc., 320, 321
Lincoln, Abraham, 371
Lincoln Savings and Loan Association, 116
Lindh, Frank, 506, 508, 509, 510
Lindh, John Walker, *see* Walker Lindh, John
Lippman, Walter, 261
Lipsitz, George, 331
Liquid ecstasy, *see* Gamma-hydroxybutyrate
Literacy, 181–185, 344
Literature, 181–185; also 83
"Live with TAE: Interview" *(American Enterprise)*, 438
Livshin, Julia, 469–474
Local exchange carriers (LECs), 304
Local telephone service, 304–306
Lockport, N.Y., 273
Logan International Airport, 501
Loma Prieta earthquake, *249*
Long, Huey, 141
Long-distance carriers, 305
Long Island Rail Road, 500
Longman, Jere*, on air travel after September 11 attacks, 502–504
Los Angeles, Calif., riots, 149–150, 208–209, *249;* street gangs, 206–209
"Lost Generation, The" (Deford), 332
Louisiana, 140–144
Loury, Glenn, 290
Low Power Television (LPTV), 307
Lung cancer, 319
Lyons, James*, on bilingual education, 343–347

Machine intelligence, *see* Artificial intelligence
"MacNeil/Lehrer NewsHour," 343
Madison Guaranty, 232
Maginnis, John*, on David Duke, 140–144
Makah Indians, and whale hunting, 347–349
"Making Americans: Immigration and Tolerance" (Bennett), 267
Mall, Washington, D.C., *195*
Mapplethorpe, Robert, 108, 110
Marbury family, 212, 213, 215, 216
Marijuana, 441, 443, 444
Marin County, Calif., 507
Market capitalization, 429
Marotta, George*, on the stock market, 427–431
Marriage, and civil unions, 432–434
Marsalis, Wynton, *54*, 283, 286
Marshall, John, 394

Martin, Will, 348, 349
Marxism, 85
Mason, W. Dale, 400
Mass Immigration and the National Interest (Briggs), 230
Mass merchandising, 221
Massachusetts, standardized testing, 481
"Masterpiece Theatre," 293
Mazar-e Sharif, Afghanistan, 509
McCaffrey, Barry R.*, on legalization of drugs, 441–446
McCain, John*, and the Keating Five, 115–118; on soft money, 458–460; also 307
McCall, H. Carl, 321
McCollister, John, 380
McDonald, Erroll, 286, 287
McDonald's Corporation, and globalization, 491–492; also *317*, 470, 474
McDougal, James, 232
McDougal, Susan, 232, 233
McFarlane, Robert C., 3, 5
McGrath, Charles*, on television, 292–299
McGwire, Mark, *402*
McLuhan, Marshall, 489, 493
McVeigh, Timothy, 271, 273–274
Meatpacking, 471, 474
Media, racial divide in Simpson trial, 289; and Olympic bombing, 324–326
Media Access Project, 307
Medicine, stem cell research, 485; also *195–196*
Melville, Herman, 349
Menopause, 391
Mercantilist capitalism, 354
Metcalf, Shelby, 479
Methylenedioxymethamphetamine (MDMA), 483–484
Mexico, and FTA, 144–146
Meyerhoff, Harvey, *53*
Middle class, among African American population, 42–49
Middle East, 128, 131
Middlebury College, Vt., 327, 328
Midler, Bette, *97*
Milch, David, 298
Military, Operation Desert Storm, 128; Persian Gulf War, 131–135; also 314
Military Review, 131
Miller, Daniel, 493
Miller, Lucas*, on in-flight security, 499–501
Million Man March, *250*, 283, 287
Milwaukee Parental Choice Program, 357–361
Minimum wage, 40
Minnesota, standardized testing, 481
Minors, *see* children
Missouri, 77
Mobility, and housing, 223
Monette, Paul*, on living with AIDS, 59–60
Monopolies, 304, 307
Mortality, public health issues, 16–20
Mosley, Walter, 286
Movies, 27, *97–98*, 293, 294, 377, 490
Mujahedin, 509
Murdoch, Rupert, 420

Murray, David, 269
Music, 300–301, 381–383
Muskie, Edmund*, Tower Commission, 1–5
Muslims, 496, 505, 507
Mutual funds, 430
"My Negro Problem, and Ours" (Podhoretz), 285

NAACP, see National Association for the
    Advancement of Colored People
Nadelmann, Ethan, 442
Nader, Ralph*, on GATT and WTO, 254–257,
    389, 391
NAFTA, see North American Free Trade
    Agreement
Nahl, Diane*, on road rage, 454–458
NAMES Project, 195
Narcotics trafficking, see Drug trafficking
NASDAQ, 428
Nation, The, 254
National Association for the Advancement of
    Colored People (NAACP), 140
National Association of Bilingual Education, 343
National Basketball Association (NBA), 490
National Council on Disability, 102
National Endowment for the Arts (NEA),
    108–115
National Gambling Impact Study Commission Report,
    393
National Indian Gaming Commission, 397, 399
National Research Council, 481
National Review, 25, 179, 231
National Security Council (NSC), 1–5
National Transportation Safety Board (NTSB), 92
Native Americans, and whale hunting, 347–349;
    and gambling, 393–400
Natural law, 136–137
NBA, see National Basketball Association
NEA, see National Endowment for the Arts
"'Necessary' of Modern Life? A Very Expensive
    College Education, A" (O'Brien), 327
Neighborhoods, and community spirit, 448
Netherlands, The, 445
"New Generation Gap, The" (Howe and Strauss),
    165
New Republic, The, 84, 140, 324
New York, standardized testing, 481
New York City, Brooklyn Museum, 412–418;
    September 11 attacks, 511; also 411
New York Public School Athletic League, 214
New York Stock Exchange, 428
New York Times, The, 231, 499
New York Times Magazine, The, 292, 407
New Yorker, The, 273, 283
"News Hour with Jim Lehrer, The," 343
Newsweek, 186, 332, 335, 505
Newton, Johari, 383
"Nice Try" (Buckley), 25
Nicotine, 319
9/11 attacks, see September 11 attacks
1984 (Orwell), 85
Ninth Amendment, 137
Nixon, Richard*, on the post-Cold War world,
    119–127; also 63

Nobody's Fool (Benton), 296
Noriega, Manuel, 87
North, Oliver, 1, 4, 5, 355
North American Free Trade Agreement
    (NAFTA), 144–146; also 254–257
North Atlantic Treaty Organization (NATO), 511
Northern Alliance (Afg.), 509
"Notebook: Music Man" (Lapham), 197
Novels, and television, 296, 298
NPR, 452
NSC, see National Security Council
"N.Y.P.D. Blue," 294, 296–298

Oates, Joyce Carol*, on McVeigh, 273–274
O'Brien, Dennis*, on cost of higher education,
    327–330
Obscenity, Communications Decency Act of
    1996, 308
Obstruction of justice, 362, 365
Office of Homeland Security, 497
Office of National Drug Control Policy, 441
Office of the Independent Counsel (OIC), 362
Ofili, Chris, 412–414
Oil spills, 92–96
Oklahoma City bombing, 271–272, 273, 461
Olympic Games, bombing, 324, 462; also 317
"On Being Black and Middle Class" (Steele),
    42–49
Onassis, Jacqueline Kennedy, 249
Open video system (OVS), 308
Operation Desert Sabre, 131
Operation Desert Shield, 128
Operation Desert Storm, 128–130
Operation Just Cause, 87, 147
Opiates, 443
"Ordeal of Immigration in Wausau, The" (Beck),
    224
O'Reilly, Jane*, on the Year of the Woman,
    161–162
Organization of American States (OAS), 512
Organized labor, 38–41
O'Rourke, P. J., 130
Orwell, George, 85
Owens, Major R.*, on NEA funding, 113–115

Palm handheld computers, 195
Panama, 87
Parker, Dorothy, 223
Parker, Marcy, 348
Parkinson's disease, 486
Pataki, George, 498
Paternity testing, 425
Patriarchy, 287
"Peanuts," 183
Pedophilia, 322
Pentagon, 494, 511
Performance Resource Press, Inc., 483
Perjury, 362, 365
Perot, H. Ross, 197–201; also 355
Persian Gulf War, Operation Desert Storm,
    128–130; Schwarzkopf on operations,
    131–135; also, 124, 147, 351
Personal digital assistants (PDAs), 195

Personal Responsibility and Work Opportunity
    Reconciliation Act (1996), 339–342
Philip Morris Companies Inc., 319, 320, 385
Photography, and child pornography, 323
Piehl, Anne Morrison, 268
Piercy, Marge, 24
Piru gangs, *see* Bloods
Pluripotentiality, in stem cells, 486
Podhoretz, Norman, 285
Poindexter, John M., 3, 4, 5
Poiter, Sidney, 290
Police, *see* Law enforcement
Political fundraising, Whitewater Scandal, 232
Pollution, *Exxon Valdez* oil spill, 92–96; Gore's
    proposals, 163–165
Populism, 141
Pornography, 308, 322–324
Porter, John Edward, 447
Postmodernism, 277–282
Poverty, 49, 145
Powell, Colin, 135, 512
Praise the Lord ministry, *see* PTL ministry
Pregnancy, and abortion, 77
Presidency, Dukakis, 60–63; Dole, 310; election
    of 2000, 463; Gore, 466–468; *see also* Bush,
    George H. W.; Bush, George W.; Clinton,
    Bill; Reagan, Ronald
Presidential Character, The (Barber), 369
President's Council of Bioethics, 486
Price, Deb*, on Ellen DeGeneres, 330–331
Price to book ratio, 430
Price-to-earnings (P/E) ratio, 386, 429
Prince William Sound, Alsk., 92
Prohibition, 443
Proposition 187 (Calif.), 267, 404–406
Proposition 227 (Calif.), 343, 406
Psychiatry, 378–380
PT Cruiser, 453, *453*
PTL ministry (Praise the Lord ministry), 12–14
Public Enemy*, 381–382; also *53*
Public health, 15–20, 319, 471–474
Public interest, broadcasting, 307
Public Papers of the Presidents of the United States, 6,
    69, 128, 175, 202, 258, 271
Putin, Vladimir, 512, 513
Putnam, Robert D.*, on civic and community
    unity, 448–451

Qala Jangi prison (Afg.), 509
Quindlen, Anna, 160
Quran, 505, 508

Race and racism, African Americans, 42–52;
    David Duke, 140–144; Simpson trial, 283,
    286, 287; in sports, 419, 421–423; also, 44,
    149, 150, 187
Radio, 302, 378
Radio spectrum, *see* Broadcast spectrum
Raised ranches, advertising tactics, 220
Rap music, 381–383
Rapaille, Clotaire*, on how Americans think,
    452–454
Rape, 483, 484

Rauch, Jonathan, 186, 187
Ravitch, Diane, 56, 482
Reading, importance of, 181–185; also 293
Reagan, Ronald*, Tower Commission Report on
    Iran-Contra, 1–5; remarks at the
    Brandenburg Gate, 6–8; and organized labor,
    38–41; farewell address, 69–72; also 113
Reed, Ishmael, 287
*Regan v. Taxation Without Representation of
    Washington*, 416
Regional Bell Operating Companies (Baby
    Bells), 304, 305
Regionalism, and architecture, 220
Rehnquist, William*, on *Webster v. Reproductive
    Health Services*, 77–82
Religion, church–state separation, 9–11;
    televangelism, 12–14; exhibit controversy,
    412–418
Reno, Janet, Waco Crisis, 179–181; also 363, 437
Report of the President's Special Review Board (Tower
    Commission), 1
Reproductive rights, 77–82
Republican National Convention Address, 64
Republican Party, Robertson convention speech,
    64–68; Buchanan convention speech,
    156–160; Contract with America, 251–253;
    Dole acceptance speech, 310–316; Latino
    voters, 404–407; suburban politics, 446–448;
    also, 460, 463
Resolution Trust Corporation, 232
Reuther, Walter, 41
Revel, Jean-François, 85
Rice, Elmer, 294
Richards, Ann*, on Dukakis, 60–63
Riegle, Donald, 115–116
Right to privacy, 323
Rigolot, Carol*, on books and reading, 181–185
Riley, Pat, 421
Ripken, Cal, *401*
Rivers, Jerome K., 321
Road rage, 454–458
Road Rage and Aggressive Driving (James and
    Nahl), 454
Robertson, Pat*, on Bush, 64–68
Rockefeller, Jay, 504
Roe v. Wade, 77–82
Roemer, Buddy, 141
Rohrabacher, Dana*, on NEA funding, 108–109
Rohypnol (forget-me pill), 484
Roll Call magazine, 480
Roosevelt, Theodore, 369
Rose Law Firm, 233, 234
"Roseanne," 299
*Rosenberger v. Rectors and Visitors of the University of
    Virginia*, 417
Rossiter, Clinton, 367
Roszak, Theodore, 392
Royal Academy of Art, 412–413
Royce, Justice, 327
Rudolph, Eric Robert, 324
Rumsfeld, Donald, 506
Rural areas, 113, 220
Russia, and globalization, 491; also 235

Saatchi, Charles, 413
Sadler, Eric, 381–382
Saint John's College, 329
Sakharov, Andre, 122
Salisbury, Harrison, 185
San Francisco, Calif., *249*
Sanders, Sue, 387
Saudi Arabia, 128
Savings and loan scandal, and the Keating Five,
    115–118; also 114, 232
Schaffer, Beverly Bassett, *see* Bassett, Beverly
Schlesinger, Arthur, Jr., 150
Schlessinger, Laura, 378–380
Schlosser, Eric*, interview, 469–474
Schmoke, Kurt L.*, on welfare reform, 339–342
Schools, and vouchers, 357–361; Columbine
    murders report, 435–437; standardized
    testing, 480, 482; also 66, *250*, 309
Schorr, Lisbeth B., 150
Schwartz, Felice N.*, on women in corporate
    America, 21–24
Schwarzkopf, H. Norman*, on the Persian Gulf
    War, 131–135
Scowcroft, Brent*, Tower Commission report
    on Iran-Contra, 1–5
Seminole Tribe of Florida v. *Florida*, 397
Senate Ethics Committee, 115–118
Senate Select Committee on Intelligence, 236
Senior citizens, 389
"Sensation: Young British Artists from the Saatchi
    Collection" exhibit, 412–418; also *54*
September 11 attacks, Bush's declaration of war
    on terrorism, 494–498; and air travel,
    499–504; the American Taliban, 505, 509,
    510; aftermath, 511–516; also *148, 462*
Serrano, Andres, 108, 110, 112
Service Employees Union, 38
Sexual abuse, 322, 323
Sexual harassment, 136, 364
Sexual politics, 287
Shapiro, Robert, 287, 290
Sharia, 508
Shell, Ellen Ruppel, 471
Shepard, Matthew, 408
Shocklee, Hank, 381–382
Shultz, George, 3, 4
Silent Generation, 166
Simpson, Nicole Brown, 287, 289
Simpson, O. J., *250*, 283, 287, 288, 290, 291
"Simpsons, The," 299
Sinclair, Upton, 473
Sixties, influence on higher education, 56
Skateboarding, *54*
Skinner, B. F., 276
Sky marshals, 499
Slate.com, 499
Slaughterhouses, 473
"Smell of Blood, The" (Himelstein, Greising, and
    Bongiorno), 320
Smith, Anna Deavere, 288, 289
Smith, Benjamin, 408
Smith, Curtis*, interview with Costas, 438–440
Smoking, 16, 17, 319

Soccer, *see* Football
Social classes, and African Americans, 42
Social issues, reviving community spirit, 448–451;
    also 219, *249–250, 295*
Soft money, 458–460
Soloway, Colin, 509
Somalia, *147*
Soros, George, 442
Sosa, Sammy, *402*
Southeast Asia, 429
Soviet Union, 6, 7, 71, 75, 119, 235, 353
Spanish language, 343–347
Spann, Mike, 509
Special prosecutor, Whitewater scandal, 231
Speech codes, 186–188
Spielberg, Steven, *98*
Spill: The Wreck of the Exxon Valdez—Final
    Report, 92
Sports, escaping poverty with basketball,
    210–218, 422–423; and society, 419–424;
    baseball, 438–440; college athletics, 475–479;
    also 332, *401–402*, 490
Spousal abuse, 289
Springsteen, Bruce*, 300–301
Standardized testing, 480–482; also 57
Standards for Educational and Psychological
    Testing, 481
"Stare decisis" principle, 137
Starr, Kenneth*, and the Starr Report, 362–365;
    also 231, 370
"Starr Report, The" (Starr), 362–365
Statutory construction, 138
Steele, Shelby*, on class issues among African
    Americans, 42–49
Stein, Herb, 126
Steinmetz, Donald W., 357–361
Stem cell research, 485–487
Stempler, David, 503
Stern, Howard, 378
Stevens, Wallace, 288
Stock market, 384–387, 427–431
Stone, John P.*, on the Columbine murders,
    435–437
Stone, Oliver*, on greed, 27
Strauss, William*, on the new generation gap,
    165–174
Street gangs, in California, 206–209; also 225
"Street Scene" (Rice), 294
Stroud, Cleveland, 421
"Suburban Prize" (Dionne), 446
Suburbs, urban sprawl, 219; politics, 446–448;
    reviving community spirit, 448
Suleyman al-Faris, *see* Walker Lindh, John
Sullivan, Andrew*, on hate crimes, 407–411; also
    434
Super Bowl, 419
Supreme Court, church-state separation, 9–11;
    politics and nominees, 25–26; abortion
    ruling, 77–82; Clarence Thomas, 136–139;
    Native American tribal gambling, 393–395;
    disputed election of 2000, 463; also 365
Supreme Court of Florida, 463
Supreme Court of Wisconsin, 357

"Survivor," *98*
Swaggart, Jimmy, 12, 13
Sweeney, John J.*, on organized labor, 38–41

Tablighi Jamaat, 508
Taft, William Howard, 368
Taliban, war on terrorism, 494, 496; also, 505, 508, 509, 510
Tan, Amy*, 83–84
Taxation, 51, 398
Technology, 89, *195–196,* 275, 302, 335, 372
Telecommunications, 302, 351, 489
Telecommunications Act, 302
"Telecommunications Act of 1996 and the Changing Communications, Landscape, The" (Benton Foundation), 302
Telephones, 302, 303–306
Televangelism, 12–14
Television, dramas, 292–299; and globalization, 489–490, 493; also *97–98,* 181, 221, 306, 308, 309
Templeton, John, 431
"Tennessee" (Arrested Development), 382–383
Termination policy, 396
Terminator X, *53*
Terrorism, Oklahoma City bombing, 271–272; Timothy McVeigh, 273–274; Unabomber manifesto, 275–276; Olympic bombing, 324; Columbine High School murders, 435–437; Bush's declaration of war on terrorism, 494–498; September 11 attacks, 511–516; also *461–462*
Texas, 179–181, 481, 482
Texas v. *Johnson,* 416
Theismann, Joe, 479
"Thirteen Ways of Looking at a Black Man" (Gates), 283
"Thirteen Ways of Looking at a Blackbird" (Stevens), 288
Thirteeners, *see* Generation X
Thomas, Clarence*, Senate confirmation, 136–139; also 288, *317*
Thomas, Evan*, on John Walker Lindh, 505–510
Thomas, Russell, 210, 215, 216
Thomas, Todd, 382–383
Thomas Jefferson Foundation, 425
Tierney, James E., 321
Tikkun, 378
Till, Emmett, 47
Time magazine, 12
Time Warner Cable of New York City v. *Bloomberg L.P.,* 415
Tissue regeneration, and stem cells, 485
Titanic (Cameron), 492–493
Title IX, 423
Tobacco industry, the case against, 319–321; also *318*
Tomahawk cruise missiles, *148*
Totalitarianism, 84, 85
Tower, John*, report on Iran-Contra scandal, 1–5
Tower Commission Report, 1–5
Trade barriers, 352
Traffic separation scheme (TSS), 94

Treaty of Neah Bay, 347
Trinidad, 493
"Triumph of the Prime-Time Novel, The" (McGrath), 292
Turing test, 335, 338
Turner, Patricia A., 285
Turner, Ted, 420
Twain, Mark, 118, 377
Two Nations (Hacker), 150
"Two Nations of America, The" (Gergen), 149

Unabomber manifesto (Kaczynski), 275–276
Unions, *see* Labor unions
United Airlines Flight 93, 513–514
United Nations, and the U.S.A., 262–266; also 128
United Nations Peacekeeping Forces, 264–266
United States Copyright Office, 372–377
United States District Court, Eastern District of New York, 412–418
United Way of America, 339, 342
Universal service, 306, 309
Universities, *see* Colleges
University of Pennsylvania, 186
Unz, Ron*, on bilingual education, 343–346
Urban areas, 202–205, 206, 219
Urban League, 49
Urban legends, 285
U.S. News & World Report, 149
USS *Cole,* *462,* 508
Utility companies, 305
Uydess, Ian L., 321

V-chip, 309–310
Valenti, Jack, 309
Vargas, Arturo*, on Latino voters, 403–407
Vegetarianism, 490
Vermont Civil Union Act of 2000, 432–434
Viagra, *196*
Victimization, 48
Violence, 308, 309; *see also* Crime; Terrorism
Vital Speeches of the Day, 15, 21, 38, 42, 49, 55, 60, 119, 144, 151, 156, 181, 189, 262, 339, 350, 366, 388, 403, 419, 427, 466, 475
Volunteerism, 449
Voting, impact of Latino voters, 403–407; and effect of soft money, 459; election dispute 463–465
Vouchers, 357–361

Waco Crisis, 179–181
Walker, Marilyn, 506, 508, 509
Walker Lindh, John, the American Taliban, 505–510, *506*
Wall Street (Stone), 27
Wall Street Journal, The, 386
Wallace, Paul, 392
Wallace v. *Jaffree,* 418
Walt Disney Corporation, 420
War, *147–148; see also* Persian Gulf War, Terrorism
Warner, Margaret*, on bilingual education, 343–346; also 68

Warren, Earl, 291
Warren, Robert Penn, 298
Washington, and whale hunting, 347
Washington, D.C., *250*, 511
Washington, George, 513
Washington Post, The, 446, 458
Watson, James L.*, on globalization and culture, 488–493
Wausau, Wisc., 224–231
Webster v. *Reproductive Health Services,* 77–82
Webvan.com, *318*
Weinberger, Caspar, 4
Welfare reform, 339–342
Wellesley College, 99
Wellstone, Paul*, on standardized testing, 480–482; also 342
West, Cornel, 287
West Virginia State Bd. of Ed. v. *Barnette,* 415
Western culture, and higher education, 56
Whale hunting, 347–349
"Whaling Commission Approves Combined Russian-Makah Gray Whale Quota," 347
"What Do Our 17-Year-Olds Know?" (Finn and Ravitch), 56
"What's So Bad About Hate?" (Sullivan), 407
Whelan, Elizabeth M.*, on public health issues, 15–20
"Where Thomas Stands on Constitutional Questions" (Thomas), 136
White collar, *see* Educated classes
Whitewater Development Corporation, 231
"Whitewater Runs Deep" (Brookhiser), 231
Whitewater scandal, 231–234
"Who Killed Communism?" (Kinsley), 84
Wiesel, Elie, *53*
Will, George*, on campus speech codes, 186–188; also 52
Williams, John Sharp, 510

Williams, Patricia, 288, 290
Williams, Serena, *402*
Williams, Venus, *402*
Wilson, Pete, 405, 406
Wilson, William Julius, 283, 286, 290
Winnie the Pooh (Milne), 182
Wireless service, 304
Wisconsin, 224–231, 357–361
Wisdom, John, 283
Wish List, The, 162
Within Our Reach (Schorr), 150
Women, in business, 21–24; *Webster* v. *Reproductive Health Services,* 77–82; Year of the Woman, 161–162; Internet marketing, 388–392; female athletes, 423–424; also 287, 288, 405
"Women: The Year of" (O'Reilly), 161
Woods, Tiger, 332–334, *333*, 422
Woollcott, Alexander, 223
Woolsey, R. James, 245
Worcester v. *Georgia,* 394
Working class, portrayal in movies, 296
World Health Organization, 490
World Intellectual Property Organization, 372
World Trade Center, *461*, *462*, 494, 498, 511
World Trade Organization (WTO), 254–257; also 488
Wyeth Ayerst, 391

X, *see* Methylenedioxymethamphetamine
Xers, *see* Generation X

Yacktman, Donald A., 321
Yates, Sidney*, on NEA funding, 109–110
"Youngstown" (Springsteen), 300–301
Yuppies, 168

Zernike, Kate*, on air travel after September 11 attacks, 501–502

APPENDIX:

CONTENTS OF

THE ANNALS OF AMERICA

Volume 1
Discovering a
New World

1493

1. Christopher Columbus:
   Discovery of the New World, 1

1564–1565

2. John Sparke:
   The Attractions of Florida, 6

1602

3. John Brereton:
   An Account of New England, 11

1606

4. *First Charter of Virginia*, 15

5. *On the Value of Colonies to England*, 18

1607–1614

6. John Smith:
   Starving Time in Virginia, 21

1609

7. William Symonds:
   Britain's Claim to a New World Empire Justified, 32

1616

8. John Smith:
   Encouragement of Settlers in New England, 36

1619

9. John Pory:
   The Work of a Colonial Legislature, 40

1620

10. *The Apprenticeship of Orphans*, 59

11. John Robinson:
    Spiritual Advice to Pilgrim Planters, 61

12. *The Mayflower Compact*, 64

1620–1644

13. William Bradford:
    Of Plymouth Plantation, 65

1624–1656

14. *Toleration in the Early Colonies*, 87
    Regulations for Colonists in New Amsterdam
    New Netherland Freedoms and Privileges
    Maryland Toleration Act
    Maine Township Order on Religious Liberty
    New Netherland Restrictions on Religious Meetings

1628

15. Jonas Michaëlius:
    Attempts to Christianize the Indians, 92

1629

16. Francis Higginson:
    On the Riches of New England, 95

17. *First Charter of Massachusetts*, 100

18. *Rights and Privileges of Patroons,* 104

1630

19. John Cotton:
    The Divine Right to Occupy the Land,
    107

20. John Winthrop:
    A Model of Christian Charity, 109

21. *Two Songs of the Colonists,* 116
    "Forefathers' Song"
    "We Gather Together"

1631

22. Thomas Dudley:
    Hardships in Massachusetts Bay Colony,
    118

1632

23. Thomas Morton:
    On Puritan Intolerance, 125

1633

24. John Eliot:
    A College Proposed for Massachusetts Bay,
    130

1633–1639

25. John Winthrop:
    Life Among the Puritans, 132

1634

26. *The Oath of Freemen in Massachusetts,*
    148

1636

27. John Cotton:
    *Democracy as Detrimental to Church and
    State,* 149
    Proposals and Replies
    Letter to Lord Saye and Sele

1637

28. John Winthrop:
    The Exclusion of Heretics, 154

1639

29. *Fundamental Orders of Connecticut,* 157

1640

30. *Plan of Civil Government for Providence,*
    160

1641

31. *Massachusetts Body of Liberties,* 163

1642

32. John Winthrop:
    A Negative View of Democracy, 168

1642–1646

33. *On Parental Duty and the Apprenticeship
    of Children,* 170
    Massachusetts Bay School Law
    Virginia Act for Training of Poor Children

1643

34. *The New England Confederation,* 172

35. Anonymous:
    New England's First Fruits, 175

1646

36. John Eliot:
    Puritan Missions to the Indians, 180

1647

37. *Massachusetts School Law,* 184

38. Nathaniel Ward:
    The Simple Cobbler of Aggawam, 185

1648

39. *The Cambridge Platform,* 190

1650

40. *Charter of Harvard College,* 195

41. Anne Bradstreet:
    Two Poems, 197

"The Prologue"
"To My Dear and Loving Husband"

42. *Connecticut Blue Laws*, 199

43. Adriaen van der Donck *et al.*:
Criticisms of New Netherland, 204

1651

44. *Sumptuary Regulations in New England*, 210

45. Peter Bulkeley:
A City Set Upon a Hill, 211

1652

46. Roger Williams:
The Hireling Ministry—None of Christ's, 213

1654

47. Edward Johnson:
Sions Saviour in New England, 217

1655

48. *Exclusion of Jews from Military Service in New Amsterdam*, 221

49. Andrew Marvell:
"Bermudas," 222

1657

50. *Toleration for Quakers*, 223

1660–1669

51. *Virginia Slave Laws*, 225
On Running Away with Negroes
On the Nativity Conditions of Slavery
On Baptism and Bondage
On Corporal Punishment
On the Killing of Slaves

1661

52. Anonymous:
Incentives for Building Towns in Virginia, 227

53. *Constitutionalism in Massachusetts*, 231

1666

54. Anonymous:
Opportunities for Settlers in Carolina, 240

1674–1677

55. *Plymouth Colony School Laws*, 243
Fishery Profits for Schools
A School for Each Fifty Families

1675

56. Benjamin Tompson:
New England's Crisis, 245

1676

57. *Regulation of Wages and Prices in Connecticut*, 247

58. William Hubbard:
The Happiness of a People, 248

59. Anonymous:
On Bacon's Rebellion in Virginia, 255

1677

60. *Charter of West New Jersey*, 262

1682

61. William Penn:
First Frame of Government of Pennsylvania, 265

1684

62. Increase Mather:
An Arrow Against Profane and Promiscuous Dancing, 272

1688

63. *Against the Traffic of Mens-body*, 274

64. *New England ABC*, 276

1689

65. Anonymous:
On the Rebellion Against Governor Andros, 277

1691

66. *Right to the Land by Occupancy,* 282

1692

67. Thomas Brattle:
    Condemnation of Witchcraft Trials, 285

1693

68. Increase Mather:
    Insufficiency of Evidence Against Witches,
    293

69. Cotton Mather:
    Wonders of the Invisible World, 297

1696

70. William Penn:
    The People Called Quakers, 299

1697

71. William Penn:
    *Plan of Union for the English Colonies in
    America,* 308

1700

72. Francis D. Pastorius:
    German Settlers in Pennsylvania, 310

73. Samuel Sewall:
    On Accommodating the Indians, 315

74. Samuel Sewall:
    The Selling of Joseph, 316

1701

75. Cotton Mather:
    A Christian at His Calling, 319

1705

76. Robert Beverley:
    Low Character of Immigrants to Virginia,
    325

1710

77. Cotton Mather:
    Proposal for Discussion Groups, 327

1711

78. John Urmstone:
    Self-Reliance on the Frontier, 329

1717

79. John Wise:
    On Democracy in Church Government, 330

1718

80. *Indenture of Apprentices in New York,* 335

1721

81. Jeremiah Dummer:
    A Defense of the New England Charters, 336

82. Theodorus Frelinghuysen:
    A Revivalist Sermon, 344

1722

83. William Douglass:
    Against Inoculation for Smallpox, 348

1723

84. Samuel Shute:
    Self-Government in Massachusetts, 360

1725

85. *Pennsylvania Flour Inspection Law,* 364

86. "The Little Mohee," 367

1727

87. *Statutes of the College of William and
    Mary,* 369

1728

88. Benjamin Franklin:
    Credo, 373

89. William Byrd:
    Surveying the Frontier, 375

1729

90. William Douglass:
    Plan for a Map of North America, 385

1732

91. Jonathan Belcher:
    Power of the Purse—Legislative Revolt in Massachusetts, 387

1733

92. *Molasses Act,* 394

1735

93. James Alexander:
    The Trial of John Peter Zenger, 397

1740

94. *Civil Rights for Religious Minorities,* 418

95. *Royal Currency Order,* 421

1741

96. Jonathan Edwards:
    Sinners in the Hands of an Angry God, 423

1742

97. Charles Chauncy:
    Revivalism and True Religion, 434

98. Henry Melchior Mühlenberg:
    On the Right to Appoint Clergy, 440

99. Cadwallader Colden:
    Encroachment on Indian Lands, 443

1743

100. William Bollan:
     Smuggling in the Colonies, 454

101. Jonathan Edwards:
     On the Great Religious Revival, 458

1745

102. *Regulations at Yale College,* 464

1747

103. Benjamin Franklin:
     The Speech of Polly Baker, 468

1748

104. Peter Kalm:
     A Trip to America, 471

105. Benjamin Franklin:
     Advice to a Young Tradesman, 479

1750

106. Jonathan Mayhew:
     On Unlimited Submission to Rulers, 481

1751

107. Benjamin Franklin:
     On the Increase of Mankind, 489

108. Benjamin Franklin:
     Colonial Problems, 494

1753

109. Benjamin Franklin:
     The Challenges of Educating Native Americans, 497

110. *Royal Instructions Concerning Land Grants,* 499

1753–1754

111. *Dispute Over a Sectarian Control of Colleges,* 500
     William Livingston:
     Opposition to a Sectarian College
     James Alexander:
     A Protest Against a Sectarian College
     Thomas Clap:
     Defense of a Sectarian College

1754

112. Samuel Davies and Gilbert Tennent:
     Reasons for Founding Colleges in America, 518

113. Benjamin Franklin:
     Albany Plan of Union, 522

114. Benjamin Franklin:
     The Problems of Colonial Union, 525

Volume 2
Resistance and
Revolution

1755

1. George Washington:
   On Braddock's Defeat, 1

1756

2. Gottlieb Mittelberger:
   Journey to Pennsylvania, 3

1756–1758

3. John Woolman:
   Journal Entries on Slavery, Taxation, and the Military, 7

1757

4. Peter Fontaine:
   A Defense of Slavery in Virginia, 19

5. Joseph Noyes:
   Academic Freedom at Yale College, 21

1758

6. Samuel Davies:
   The Curse of Cowardice, 23

7. Nathaniel Ames:
   The Future State of North America, 28

8. Benjamin Franklin:
   The Way to Wealth, 30

1759

9. Richard Corbin:
   The Management of Plantations, 44

10. Francis Alison:
    A Plea for Uniform Education in the Colonies, 46

11. *Defense of the Virginia Paper Currency*, 48

1760

12. Benjamin Franklin:
    Great Britain's Interest in Her Colonies, 51

13. Joseph Galloway:
    Importance of an Independent Judiciary, 62

14. John Galt:
    An American Painter in Rome, 68

1761

15. James Otis:
    Against Writs of Assistance, 74

1763

16. John Woolman:
    A Plea for the Poor, 78

17. *Proclamation of 1763*, 84

1764

18. Thomas Fitch *et al.*:
    On the Right to Raise Revenue, 87

19. Thomas Pownall:
    The King and the Colonies, 98

20. James Otis:
    Rights of the British Colonies, 103

21. *Charter of Rhode Island College*, 115

22. *A Remonstrance of Distressed and Bleeding Frontier Inhabitants*, 118

23. Benjamin Franklin:
    Concerning a Massacre of Friendly Indians, 122

1765

24. George Croghan:
    Early Exploration of the Ohio Valley, 134

25. *The Stamp Act*, 143

26. *Virginia Stamp Act Resolutions*, 148

27. Francis Bernard:
    Boston Stamp Act Riots, 149

28. John Adams:
    A Burdensome and Unconstitutional Tax, 154

29. Daniel Dulany:
    On the Propriety of Imposing Taxes in the British Colonies, 156

30. *No Taxation Without Representation*, 158

31. Soame Jenyns:
    The Objections to the Taxation of Our American Colonies Considered, 160

1766

32. *London Merchants Against the Stamp Act*, 162

33. *Northampton County Resolutions on the Stamp Act*, 164

34. Francis Bernard:
    The Growing Opposition to England, 165

1766–1767

35. *The Artist in Colonial New England*, 174
    R. G. Bruce to John Singleton Copley
    Benjamin West to Copley
    Copley to West
    Copley to Bruce or West

1767

36. Henry Moore:
    On the Progress of Manufacturing, 179

37. *Act Suspending the New York Assembly*, 181

38. John Dickinson:
    On the Suspension of the New York Assembly, 182

39. Charles Woodmason:
    Lawlessness on the South Carolina Frontier, 185

1768

40. Benjamin Rush:
    On Medical Education in the Colonies, 196

41. Thomas Gage:
    On the Growing Economic Competition with England, 198

42. *A Circular Letter Against Taxation*, 199

43. *Boston Boycott Agreement*, 201

44. *Resolutions of a Boston Town Meeting Against the King*, 202

1770

45. Thomas Gage:
    Rioting in Boston, 205

46. Thomas Gage:
    On the Desirability of Closing the Frontier, 208

1772

47. Joseph Warren:
    Against a British Army in the Colonies, 211

48. Samuel Adams:
    The Rights of the Colonists, 217

1773

49. Benjamin Franklin:
    Rules by Which a Great Empire May Be Reduced to a Small One, 221

1773–1774

50. *Resistance to the Tax on Tea*, 240
    Resolutions of the New York Sons of Liberty
    Resolutions of the Citizens of Philadelphia

51. "Revolutionary Tea," 245

1774

52. *The Independence of the Massachusetts Legislature*, 246

53. Lord Dartmouth:
    On Securing the Submission of Massachusetts, 248

54. Gouverneur Morris:
    Against Revolutionary Enthusiasm, 251

55. *A Proposal for a Continental Congress*, 254

56. *The Quartering Act*, 255

57. *Resolutions Against Trade with England*, 256

58. Thomas Jefferson:
    A Summary View of the Rights of British America, 258

59. *Resistance and Reprisal*, 266

60. Joseph Galloway:
A Plan for the Union of Great Britain and the Colonies, 268

61. *Declaration and Resolves of the Continental Congress*, 270

62. *The Association of the Continental Congress*, 273

63. John Jay:
Address to the People of Great Britain, 277

64. *On the Depravity of Kings and Sovereignty of the People*, 283

65. *Proposals for Manufacturing*, 285

66. *Maryland Endorses Resistance*, 287

67. Samuel Seabury:
The Controversy Between Great Britain and Her Colonies, 289

68. John Trumbull:
"An Elegy on the Times," 296

1775

69. Daniel Leonard:
The Dangers of Rebellion, 304

70. John Adams:
The Rule of Law and the Rule of Men, 308

71. Edmund Burke:
On Conciliation with America, 312

72. Patrick Henry:
Give Me Liberty or Give Me Death, 321

73. *Preamble to the Massachusetts Articles of War*, 323

74. Joseph Warren:
The Battles of Lexington and Concord, 325

75. *An Appeal to Canada*, 327

76. John Adams:
The Formation of New State Governments, 329

77. Nathaniel Niles:
"The American Hero," 335

78. *The Necessity for Taking Up Arms*, 337

79. Horatio Gates:
On Recruiting an American Army, 342

80. Jonathan Boucher:
Civil Liberty and Nonresistance, 343

81. *Reconciliation Rejected*, 353

82. *The Authority of the People*, 356

83. Thomas Gage:
The Rebellion in America, 359

84. Lord Dunmore:
Martial Law in Virginia, 360

85. *Instructions to Vote Against Independence*, 361

86. Abigail Adams:
Doubts About Independence, 362

87. *Funds for Specific Research*, 363

88. Isaac Backus:
Civil Government and Religious Taxes, 366

89. John Adams:
The Virtues of New England, 367

90. Benjamin Franklin:
Autobiography, 368

1776

91. "Yankee Doodle," 380

92. *Massachusetts Suspends the Royal Authority*, 381

93. *Virginia Opposes the Arming of Slaves*, 383

94. Tom Paine:
Epistle to the Quakers, 385

95. Tom Paine:
Plain Arguments for Independence, 389

96. *Replies to Tom Paine*, 399
William Smith:
The Advantages of Union with England
Charles Inglis:
The True Interest of America

97. John Adams:
   The Foundation of Government, 410

98. James Wilson:
   The Legal Right to Form a Government,
   413

99. John Adams:
   On the Importance of Property for the Suffrage, 422

100. *The People as Constitution Makers,*
   424

101. *Instructions for a Declaration of Independence,* 428

102. *Boston's Instructions to Its Delegates to the Continental Congress,* 430

103. *Virginia Declaration of Rights,* 432

104. *The First Virginia Constitution,* 434

105. John Dickinson:
   Speech Against Independence, 438

106. Thomas Jefferson:
   Debate on Independence, 442

107. *The Declaration of Independence,* 447

108. Samuel Hopkins:
   The Inconsistency of Slavery, 450

109. *Declaration on the Free Exercise of Religion,* 453

110. *Concord's Call for a State Constitutional Convention,* 455

111. Tom Paine:
   The American Crisis, 456

112. Benjamin Rush:
   On the Progress of the War, 462

1777

113. *Black Voices Raised for Freedom,* 482

114. *The Constitution of Vermont,* 483

115. Nicholas Cresswell:
   On General Washington, 487

116. Benjamin Rush:
   On the Care of the Wounded, 490

117. "Johnny Has Gone for a Soldier," 492

1778

118. Benjamin Rush:
   On the Need for a General in the South,
   493

119. George Washington:
   On the Organization of the Army, 495

120. George Washington:
   Against the Appointment of Foreign Officers, 501

121. Thomas Jefferson:
   On the Superiority of Science to Politics,
   502

122. John Adams:
   On an Alliance with France, 503

123. Count d'Estaing:
   Appeal to French Canadians to Aid America, 504

124. George Washington:
   Against War with Canada, 506

125. Alexander Hamilton:
   War Profiteering, 509

126. George Washington:
   On the Lack of a National Spirit, 510

127. *Two Patriotic Songs,* 511
   Francis Hopkinson:
   "A Toast"
   William Billings:
   "Let Tyrants Shake" ("Chester")

1779

128. Alexander Hamilton:
   A Proposal to Arm and Then Free the Slaves, 530

1780

129. *Massachusetts Bill of Rights,* 532

130. *The Cumberland Compact,* 536

131. James Bowdoin:
   The Encouragement of Knowledge, 540

132. *On the Formation of New States,* 549

133. Thomas Pownall:
   The New Relation Between the Old and the New World, 550

1781

134. *The Articles of Confederation,* 555

135. Thomas Rodney:
     First Steps Toward Peace, 561

1781–1782

136. Thomas Jefferson:
     Notes on the State of Virginia, 563

1782

137. Robert Morris:
     The Incorporation of the Bank of North America, 574

138. Alexander Hamilton:
     Arguments for Increasing the Power of the Federal Government, 575

139. Hugh H. Brackenridge:
     A Negative View of Indian Rights, 580

140. Michel Guillaume Jean de Crève-coeur:
     What Is an American?, 583

1783

141. George Washington:
     Address to the Officers of the Army, 598

142. George Washington:
     On Disbanding the Army, 601

143. George Washington:
     Public Lands for Veterans, 608

144. *Virginia's Opposition to the Federal Congress,* 610

145. Alexander Hamilton:
     Arguments for a Strong Federal Government, 612

146. William Cushing:
     The Quock Walker Case—Slavery Unconstitutional in Massachusetts, 617

147. *Virginia's Cession of Western Lands,* 618

Volume 3
Organizing the New Nation

1784

1. *A Plan of Government for the Western Territory,* 1

2. John Filson:
   Daniel Boone in the Wilderness, 3

3. "The Wayfaring Stranger," 6

4. Alexander Hamilton:
   The Unjust Treatment of Loyalists, 7

1785

5. John Carroll:
   On the Selection of a Roman Catholic Bishop in America, 14

6. James Madison:
   Against Religious Assessments, 16

7. John Adams:
   Foreign Commerce and Federal Union, 21

8. Noah Webster:
   The Union of the American States, 24

9. *The Disposition of Lands in the Western Territory,* 36

10. *Apprehensions About the Dangers of Aristocracy,* 39

11. Thomas Jefferson:
    An American Education for American Youth, 41

1786

12. Thomas Jefferson:
    Virginia Statute of Religious Freedom, 53

13. Benjamin Rush:
    On the Need for General Education, 55

14. Benjamin Rush:
    A Plan for the Establishment of Public Schools, 57

15. Thomas Jefferson:
    On the Barbary Pirates, 59

16. *The Causes of Shays's Rebellion*, 61

17. Thomas Grover:
    Reasons for Rebellion, 62

18. *On the Inadequacies of the Central Government*, 63
    John Jay to George Washington
    Washington to Jay

19. Noah Webster:
    Diseases of the Body Politic, 65

20. *The Annapolis Convention*, 68

1787

21. Abigail Adams:
    On Suppressing Shays's Rebellion, 80

22. Thomas Jefferson:
    The Good Sense of the People, 82

23. Thomas Jefferson:
    On the Need for a Little Rebellion Now and Then, 83

24. Benjamin Rush:
    The Defects of the Confederation, 85

25. James Madison:
    On the Balance of National and Local Authority, 88

26. Joel Barlow:
    The Unfinished Revolution, 90

27. Thomas Jefferson:
    On the Necessity for a Separate Executive, 94

28. James Madison:
    The Federal Convention of 1787, 95

29. *The Constitution of the United States*, 122

30. Richard Henry Lee:
    On the Rights that Must Be Preserved in the New Constitution, 130

31. *Debate on the Ratification of the Constitution in New York*, 139
    George Clinton:
    Against the Adoption of the Constitution
    Alexander Hamilton:
    For the Adoption of the Constitution

32. James Madison:
    A Plurality of Interests and a Balance of Powers, 145

33. Anonymous:
    Anti-Federalist Arguments from Pennsylvania, 150
    On the Balance of Powers
    Against the Federal Commerce Power

34. James Wilson:
    A Defense of the Constitution, 157

35. Anonymous:
    The Constitution as an Instrument of Aristocracy, 164

36. Luther Martin:
    The People Versus the States, 166

37. Oliver Ellsworth:
    On a Religious Test for Holding Public Office, 169

38. *Reasons for Dissent by the Anti-Federalists of Pennsylvania*, 172

39. Thomas Jefferson:
    On the Omission of a Bill of Rights from the Constitution, 185

40. Anonymous:
    The Commerce Power Under the New Constitution, 186

41. Robert Yates and John Lansing:
    Arguments Against Consolidating the States into One Government, 189

42. *The Northwest Ordinance*, 191

43. Tench Coxe:
    Prospects for American Manufacturing, 196

44. *Judicial Review in a Southern Court*, 204

45. Philip Freneau:
    "The Indian Burying Ground," 206

46. Benjamin Rush:
    Thoughts on Female Education, 207

1787–1788

47. Alexander Hamilton and James Madison:
    Federalist Papers, 213

1788

48. James Iredell:
    Some Objections to the Constitution An-
    swered, 247

49. Reservations of the Massachusetts Ratifying
    Convention, 250

50. Melancton Smith:
    Changes Needed Before Ratifying the Con-
    stitution, 254

51. Anonymous:
    On the Power of the Judiciary, 261

52. Oliver Ellsworth:
    The Economic Advantages of a Federal
    Union, 264

53. Anonymous:
    Factions and Public Liberty, 266

54. John Jay:
    Arguments for Adopting the Proposed Fed-
    eral Constitution, 270

55. The Interest of the Few and the Rights of the
    Many, 276

56. Debates in the Virginia Ratifying Conven-
    tion, 278
    George Mason:
    Against Imposing Direct Taxes
    Patrick Henry:
    Against Ratification
    Edmund Pendleton:
    For Ratification

57. Virginia's Recommended Amendments to
    the Constitution, 290

58. Anonymous:
    The Constitution Attacked as Setting Up
    Government by the Few, 294

59. William Lenoir:
    The Interest of the Few and the Liberties of
    the People, 300

60. Consideration of a Bill of Rights, 304
    Thomas Jefferson to James Madi-
    son
    Madison to Jefferson

61. An Orderly Transition to a New Govern-
    ment, 308

62. Rufus Putnam:
    On a Treaty with the Indians, 309

63. Benjamin Rush:
    Plan of a Federal University, 312

64. Philip Freneau:
    "The Indian Student," 315

65. Benjamin Rush:
    Recommendations for Publishing a Newspa-
    per, 317

66. Philip Freneau:
    The Past and Future of America, 319

1789

67. David Ramsay:
    The Influence of the Revolution on the
    Minds and Morals of the Citizens,
    333

68. John Trumbull:
    Pictures of the Revolution, 339

69. Thomas Jefferson:
    On the New Constitution, 342

70. George Washington:
    First Inaugural Address, 344

71. William Maclay:
    Titles and Ceremonials, 347

72. James Madison:
    A Bill of Rights Proposed, 354

73. The Bill of Rights, 364

74. Benjamin Franklin:
    On the Press as an Unofficial Tribunal,
    365

75. The Judiciary Act of 1789, 368

76. Benjamin Franklin:
    Remarks on the Revision of the Pennsylva-
    nia Constitution, 372

77. Noah Webster:
    Toward a National Language, 375

78. James Wilson:
    The Study of Law in the United States,
    380

1789–1790

79. *That the Earth Belongs to the Living,* 389
    Thomas Jefferson to James Madison
    Madison to Jefferson

1790

80. William Selby:
    "Ode for the New Year," 395

81. Royall Tyler:
    Prologue to The Contrast, 405

82. Alexander Hamilton:
    First Report on the Public Credit, 407

83. Thomas Jefferson:
    The Hamiltonian System, 416

84. Benjamin Franklin:
    Against the Slave Trade, 421

85. Noah Webster:
    The Education of Youth in America, 424

86. *On the Blessings of Civil and Religious Liberty,* 433
    Moses Seixas to George Washington
    Washington to the Hebrew Congregation at Newport, R.I.

87. Patrick Henry:
    Resolution on the Assumption of State Debts, 435

1791

88. *Petition by Freedmen for Equality Under the Law,* 437

89. Robert Coram:
    The Origin and Rights of Property, 438

90. John Leland:
    The Rights of Conscience, 445

91. *Controversy Over the Constitutionality of a United States Bank,* 449
    Thomas Jefferson:
    Against the Bank
    Alexander Hamilton:
    For the Bank

92. Alexander Hamilton:
    Report on Manufactures, 459

93. James Madison:
    Concerning Public Opinion, 472

94. *Sea Chanteys,* 473
    "A-Roving"
    "Haul Away, Joe"

1792

95. James Madison:
    Freedom, Power, and the Stability of Governments, 489

96. James Madison:
    Political Parties, 490

97. John Laurance and James Madison:
    General Welfare and the Limits of Government Authority, 491

98. James Madison:
    The Mutability of Fashion, 496

99. James Madison:
    The Right to Property and Property in Rights, 497

100. Philip Freneau:
     Rules for Changing a Republic into a Monarchy, 499

101. Joel Barlow:
     Equality in America, 504

1792–1793

102. Hugh H. Brackenridge:
     A Satirical View of Senators and Philosophers, 513

1793

103. George Washington:
     Proclamation of Neutrality, 520

104. Thomas Jefferson:
     For Our Alliance with France, 531

105. James Monroe:
     On the Role of the Executive in Foreign Affairs, 535

106. Alexander Hamilton:
     Neutrality and the National Interest, 540
     Pacificus, No. III
     Pacificus, No. V

107. James Madison:
For Congressional Leadership in Foreign Affairs, 546

108. Eli Whitney:
The Invention of the Cotton Gin, 551

1794

109. Alexander Hamilton:
Against an Alliance with France, 553

110. George Washington:
Proclamation on the Whiskey Rebellion, 558

111. Alexander Hamilton:
Liberty and Anarchy, 561

112. *The Jay Treaty*, 564

113. Ann Julia Hatton:
"Alknomook," 570

114. Gustavus Vassa:
The Slave Ship, 571

1795

115. *The Naturalization of Immigrants*, 581

116. Timothy Pickering:
On Peace with the Indians, 583

117. *Debate on the Jay Treaty*, 587
Alexander Hamilton:
In Defense of the Treaty
Robert Livingston:
An Attack on the Treaty

1796

118. Samuel Harrison Smith:
The Objects Proper to Liberal Education, 597

119. George Washington:
A National University, 604

120. "The Right of Free Elections," 605

121. George Washington:
Farewell Address, 606

Volume 4
Domestic Expansion and Foreign Entanglements

1797

1. Moses Austin:
Exploring the Ohio Valley, 1

2. James Smith:
The Rich Land of the Frontier, 10

3. *An Act to Prevent the Spreading of Contagious Sickness*, 13

4. Albert Gallatin:
A Profit Sharing Agreement, 19

1798

5. Tadeusz Kosciuszko:
American Will and Testament, 21

6. Benjamin H. Latrobe:
Thoughts on Education, 22

7. Benjamin Rush:
Independence and Education, 28

8. Timothy Dwight:
On the Duty of Americans at the Present Crisis, 33

9. Charles Brockden Brown:
On the Essential Equality of the Sexes, 40

10. Edward Livingston:
Against the Alien Act, 49

11. *Debate on the Sedition Act*, 53
"Long John" Allen:
For the Sedition Act
Albert Gallatin:
Against the Sedition Act

12. *The Suppression of "Foreign" Opinion*, 59
The Alien Act
The Sedition Act

13. *The Kentucky and Virginia Resolutions of 1798*, 62
The Kentucky Resolutions
The Virginia Resolutions

14. Fisher Ames:
    Undeclared War and Self-Defense, 68

15. George Washington:
    On the Disloyalty of Army Officers, 71

16. *Opposition to a Standing Army*, 72

17. *Songs of Patriotism*, 73
    James Hewitt:
    "New Yankee Doodle"
    Robert Treat Paine:
    "Adams and Liberty"
    Joseph Hopkinson:
    "Hail, Columbia!"

18. William Manning:
    How the Few and Many Differ in Their Interests, 76

1799

19. Alexander Hamilton:
    The Beginnings of Expansion, 101

20. *Massachusetts' Reply to the Kentucky and Virginia Resolutions of 1798*, 102

21. *The Kentucky Resolutions of 1799*, 106

22. John Ward Fenno:
    Our Economic Interests in the Caribbean, 107

23. William Duane:
    The Army and a Free Press, 112

24. Thomas Jefferson:
    On Science and the Perfectibility of Man, 113

25. George Washington:
    Last Will and Testament, 115

26. Gouverneur Morris:
    Appeal to Washington to Return to Public Life, 119

1800

27. "Down in the Valley," 121

28. James Madison:
    The Freedom of the Press, 122

29. *Land Act of 1800*, 129

30. Tunis Wortman:
    Despotism and the Freedom of Political Discussion, 131

31. Benjamin Nones:
    The Right To Be Poor and Radical, 138

32. Thomas Jefferson:
    A Simple and Inexpensive Government, 140

1801

33. "Jefferson and Liberty," 142

34. Thomas Jefferson:
    First Inaugural Address, 143

35. *A Plan of Union for Protestant Churches*, 146

36. Thomas Jefferson:
    On Accommodating Slaves, 147

1802

37. Thomas Jefferson:
    The Threat of the French in Louisiana, 150

38. Gouverneur Morris:
    On the Union of Talents and Property, 153

39. François André Michaux:
    Frontier Kentucky, 154

1803

40. Thomas Jefferson:
    The Lewis and Clark Expedition, 158
    Confidential Message to Congress
    Instructions to Meriwether Lewis

41. John Marshall:
    Marbury v. Madison, 165

42. Thomas Jefferson:
    The Politics of the Louisiana Purchase, 171
    Letter to John Breckinridge, August 12
    Letter to Breckinridge, August 18
    Proposed Constitutional Amendment

43. Thomas Jefferson:
    On the Admission of New States, 173

44. Samuel White:
    Opposition to the Louisiana Purchase, 175

1804

45. Timothy Pickering:
    On Northern Secession, 189

46. Abigail Adams:
    On Presidential Appointments, 191

1805

47. Red Jacket:
    Against White Missions Among Native Americans, 194

48. John Adams:
    On a Natural History of the Country, 196

49. Benjamin Rush:
    On Political Parties and the Romance of History, 199

50. Fisher Ames:
    The Passions and Tyranny of the Many, 201

1806

51. Benjamin H. Latrobe:
    Gentlemen-Architects and Building-Mechanics, 204

52. Lorenzo Dow:
    The Jerks, 208

53. *The Trial of the Journeymen Boot- and Shoe-Makers,* 210

1807

54. *Act to Prohibit the Importation of Slaves,* 216

55. Thomas Jefferson:
    On Misreporting by the Press, 219

56. Fortescue Cuming:
    A Tour to the Western Country, 221

57. Joel Barlow:
    Preface and Postscript to The Columbiad, 227

58. *The Embargo Act,* 233

1808

59. Thomas Jefferson:
    On the Civil and Religious Powers of Government, 234

60. George Hay:
    Aaron Burr's Conspiracy, 235

1809

61. Jacob Henry:
    Private Belief and Public Office, 239

62. Thomas Campbell:
    Christian Union, 242

1810

63. John Randolph:
    Against Trade Restrictions, 248

64. Albert Gallatin:
    The State of Manufacturing, 259

65. Thomas Jefferson:
    On Authorities Beyond the Law, 268

66. Charles J. Ingersoll:
    The National Character of Americans, 270

67. Timothy Dwight:
    The Restless Frontiersman, 278

1811

68. *State Aid for Jewish Schools,* 282

69. Josiah Quincy:
    Against the Admission of New States, 283

70. James Madison:
    The Civil and Religious Functions of Government, 287

71. *On a Northern Confederation,* 288
    Benjamin Waterhouse to John Adams
    Adams to Waterhouse

72. *Debate Over War with England,* 291
    Felix Grundy:
    War as a Means of Continental Expansion
    Richard Johnson:
    For War with England
    John Randolph:
    Against War with England

1812

73. David Hosack:
    On the Progress of Medical Education, 307

74. John Adams:
    Thoughts on Current Politics, 311

75. James Madison:
    War Message, 314

76. Obadiah German:
    Unprepared for War with England, 319

77. John Adams:
    Party Divisions in America, 324

78. "Ye Parliament of England," 325

1813

79. Henry Clay:
    For a Vigorous Prosecution of the War, 327

80. *Opposed Views on Aristocracy,* 331
    John Adams to Thomas Jefferson, July
    9
    Adams to Jefferson, August
    Adams to Jefferson, September 2
    Jefferson to Adams, October 28
    Adams to Jefferson, November 15

81. Thomas Jefferson:
    Isolation and Independence, 340

1814

82. John Taylor:
    True and False Aristocracies, 342

83. Thomas Jefferson:
    On the Censorship of Religious Books,
    348

84. Thomas Jefferson:
    *Elementary, General, and Professional
    Schools,* 350

85. Francis Scott Key:
    "The Star-Spangled Banner," 353

86. Daniel Webster:
    Against Conscription, 355

1815

87. *New England and the Union,* 371

88. Noah Worcester:
    War and Popular Delusion, 375

89. Thomas Jefferson:
    The Sphere of Religion, 383

90. Richard Rush:
    Jurisprudence and the Common Law, 385

91. Thomas Jefferson:
    *On the Constitutional Powers of the
    Branches of Government,* 390

92. Thomas Jefferson:
    On the Balance of Power in Europe, 391

93. Robert Finley:
    *National Uniformity in Textbooks and
    Curricula,* 393

94. Hezekiah Niles:
    National Unity and Prosperity, 397

95. Hugh H. Brackenridge:
    Should Beasts Vote?, 400

96. "Hunters of Kentucky," 405

97. Alexander J. Dallas:
    Proposal for a National Bank, 406

1816

98. Thomas Jefferson:
    *On the Present Need to Promote Manufac-
    turing,* 412

99. Thomas Jefferson:
    The Rulers and the Ruled, 414

100. Thomas Jefferson:
    On Republican Government, 416

101. Thomas Jefferson:
    On Civil and Natural Rights, 419

102. William Plumer:
    State Control of Dartmouth College, 420

103. Thomas Jefferson:
    The Roots of Democracy, 422

104. John Randolph:
    Against a Protective Tariff, 427

105. *Hints to Emigrants from Europe,* 429

106. Jacob Bigelow:
    The Future of the Arts and Sciences, 449

107. *Displacement of Free African Americans,* 451

1817

108. John C. Calhoun:
Roadways and Waterways, 457

109. James Madison:
On the Commerce Clause, 462

110. John Quincy Adams:
On the Revolutions in Latin America, 464

1818

111. John Adams:
The Meaning of the American Revolution, 465

112. Elias Pym Fordham:
Opportunities in the West, 470

113. *Land Sale Advertisement,* 473

114. *An Irish Colony in Illinois,* 476

115. Daniel Webster:
Contracts and Corporate Charters, 477

116. Henry Clay:
Internal Improvements and the Powers of Congress, 482

117. Henry Clay:
Recognition for Latin American Governments, 488

118. Thomas Jefferson:
The Education of Women, 490

119. Baron de Montlezun:
American Women and American Character, 492

120. *French Emigrants to America,* 495

121. Robert Lee:
A Society for a National Literature, 497

122. Anonymous:
Opposition to Paper Money, 500

123. James Madison:
Agriculture and Conservation, 503

124. *A Christian Indictment of Slavery,* 507

125. *Report on the Proposed University of Virginia,* 510

126. *Public Works in the State of Virginia,* 515

1819

127. John Marshall:
Dartmouth College v. *Woodward,* 522

128. *Apprentice Labor Act,* 528

129. John Marshall:
M'Culloch v. *Maryland,* 530

130. Spencer Roane:
Defense of the Power of State Courts, 539

131. William Ellery Channing:
An Attack on Orthodox Calvinism, 544

132. Henry M. Brackenridge:
A Vindication of Civil Rights for Jews, 552

133. Giovanni Antonio Grassi:
Observations on the United States, 560

134. William Cobbett:
A Year in the United States, 567

135. Emma Hart Willard:
Education and the Weaker Sex, 574

136. Rufus King:
Against the Extension of Slavery to the New States, 579

137. Anonymous:
Against Restriction of Slavery to the Southern States, 587

1820

138. John Quincy Adams:
Slavery and the Constitution, 589

139. *Missouri Enabling Act,* 591

140. Thomas Jefferson:
A Firebell in the Night, 603

141. *Against a Protective Tariff,* 604
Fredericksburg Remonstrance
Salem Memorial

142. Henry Clay:
Manufacturing and a Protective Tariff, 612

143. Daniel Raymond:
     The Role of Labor in the National Wealth,
     623

144. James Flint:
     The Panic in Indiana, 632

145. Daniel Webster:
     Property and Political Power, 634

146. *For Wider Suffrage,* 640

147. John Quincy Adams:
     On America and European Alliances,
     642

148. Robert Mills:
     The Beginnings of American Architecture,
     645

149. James Kirke Paulding:
     *On the Scarcity of Romantic Fiction in
     America,* 648

150. Joseph Rodman Drake:
     "The American Flag," 650

Volume 5
Steps Toward
Equalitarianism

1821

 1. John Marshall:
    Cohens v. *Virginia,* 1

 2. *Debate on Property and Suffrage,* 4
    Speech by Nathan Sanford
    Reported Speech of Martin Van
       Buren
    Speech by James Kent
    Reported Speech of P. R. Livingston
    Speech by John Cramer
    Speech by David Buel, Jr.
    Speech by John Ross
    Speech by Peter Jay

 3. John Quincy Adams:
    *A Pessimistic View of Relations with Latin
    America,* 26

 4. Anonymous:
    *Motives for Stopping the Domestic Slave
    Trade,* 27

1822

 5. Thomas Jefferson:
    On Sectarian Rivalry, 30

 6. William Duane:
    Pennsylvania Common Schools, 32

 7. Zerah Hawley:
    Frontier Schools, 35

 8. Richard Furman:
    A Religious Defense of Slavery, 37

1823

 9. John Quincy Adams:
    The Caribbean and Our National Interest,
    57

10. John Quincy Adams:
    Russia and the Pacific Northwest, 61
       Memo of July 17
       Letter to Richard Rush

11. Richard Rush:
    *The Affinity of British and American Inter-
    ests,* 66

12. *America and Europe,* 68
       James Monroe to Thomas Jefferson
       Jefferson to Monroe

13. John Quincy Adams:
    On America and the Holy Alliance, 71

14. James Monroe:
    The Monroe Doctrine, 73

15. Anonymous:
    Fears About Prison Labor, 76

16. George Ticknor:
    Curriculum Reform at Harvard, 77

17. Anonymous:
    On the Louisiana Penal Code, 79

18. Felix Grundy:
    A Protest Against the Caucus System, 85

19. John Taylor:
    An Interpretation of the Constitution,
    88

20. Charles J. Ingersoll:
    The Influence of America on the Mind,
    95

21. John Howard Payne:
    "Home, Sweet Home," 103

22. Edward Everett:
    On Greek Independence, 104

1824

23. *Debate on the Greek Revolution,* 108
    Daniel Webster:
    For a Resolution of Sympathy
    John Randolph:
    Against Moral Crusading in Foreign
    Policy

24. Henry Clay:
    The Protective Tariff, 114

25. Edward Everett:
    *The Circumstances Favorable to the Progress
    of Literature in America,* 118

26. *Aldridge* v. *The Commonwealth of Virginia,*
    127

27. John Marshall:
    Gibbons v. *Ogden,* 128

28. *The Beginning of Reform Judaism,* 134

1825

29. John Quincy Adams:
    Inaugural Address, 138

30. *Child Labor in Massachusetts,* 155

31. Philip Lindsley:
    Education for Every Child of the Republic,
    157

32. *Strike of Boston Carpenters,* 161
    Resolutions of the Journeymen Car-
    penters
    Resolutions of the Master Carpenters
    Resolutions of the Builders

33. William Cullen Bryant:
    American Society as a Field for Fiction,
    164

34. *Songs of the Erie Canal,* 169
    "Low Bridge, Everybody Down"
    "E-RI-E"

35. Edward Livingston:
    On the Formation of New Laws, 171

36. John Bannister Gibson:
    Against Judicial Review, 174

37. *The Courts and Public Opinion,* 179

38. John Quincy Adams:
    A Policy for Internal Improvements,
    185

39. John Quincy Adams:
    *On Participating in a Congress of Ameri-
    can Nations,* 188

1826

40. *Report on Executive Patronage,* 203

41. Timothy Flint:
    Backwoodsmen, 205

42. Albert Gallatin:
    The Land West of the Rockies, 209

43. *Country Courting Songs,* 214
    "On Top of Old Smoky"
    "Paper of Pins"

1827

44. *First American High School Law,* 216

45. Lemuel Shaw:
    Law as a Restraint on Power, 217

46. Samuel Cornish and John Russwurm:
    The First African American Newspaper,
    222

47. Anonymous:
    On Educating African American Women,
    225

48. Anonymous:
    A Plea for Manufacturing in the South,
    226

49. *A Union of Trade Associations,* 227

1828

50. James Hall:
    Letters from the West, 231

51. Duke Bernhard:
    Observations by a German Visitor, 238

52. *The Nashoba Community,* 253

53. James Fenimore Cooper:
On Popular Elections and on the American Girl, 255
  The Merits and Demerits of Popular Elections
  The American Girl

54. Thomas Dartmouth Rice:
"Jump, Jim Crow," 265

55. Jeremiah Day and James Kingsley:
Curriculum Changes at Yale, 266

56. Hugh S. Legaré:
On Limiting the Power of the Supreme Court, 275

57. *A Petition for Free Use of Public Lands*, 279

58. Anonymous:
Abuses of the Apprentice Labor System, 280

59. *On the Unconstitutionality of the Protective Tariff*, 282

1829

60. Richard M. Johnson:
Sunday Observance and the Delivery of Mail, 284

61. Mrs. Samuel Harrison Smith:
The Inauguration of Andrew Jackson, 288

62. Frances Wright:
Of Existing Evils and Their Remedy, 290

63. *Demand for a Ten-Hour Day*, 297

64. Thomas Skidmore:
The Unequal Distribution of Property, 298

65. William Lloyd Garrison:
The Dangers of Slavery, 303

66. Catharine Beecher:
The Profession of a Woman, 308

67. Philip Lindsley:
The Dangers of a Sectarian College, 310

68. Josiah Holbrook:
Lyceums and Popular Education, 314

69. John Neal:
American Painters and Painting, 321

70. Edgar Allan Poe:
"To Science," 324

71. *A Plea for Manhood Suffrage*, 325

72. *On the Degradation Caused by Universal Suffrage*, 329

73. Andrew Jackson:
First Annual Message to Congress, 330

1830

74. Daniel Webster:
Liberty and Union, Now and Forever, One and Inseparable, 347

75. Zelotes Fuller:
The Tree of Liberty, 355

76. George McDuffie:
Defense of a Government Bank, 361

77. Anonymous:
Corporate Power, 369

78. Andrew Jackson:
Veto of Maysville Road Bill, 374

79. *Labor Parties in New York*, 378

80. George Bancroft:
The Importance of a University for New York City, 380

81. Anne Royall:
A Tennessee Revival, 383

82. *Public Schools for Philadelphia*, 385
  Equal Knowledge for Equal Liberty
  Against Equal Education

83. Henry Clay:
A System of Real Reciprocity, 392

84. James Madison:
Nullification and the Rule of Law, 398

85. William Ellery Channing:
Remarks on National Literature, 404

86. William Ellery Channing:
Association and Individual Action, 412

87. Andrew Jackson:
On Indian Removal, 418

88. "Shenandoah," 421

1831

89. William Lloyd Garrison:
    For Immediate Abolition, 422

90. *An African American View of Civil Rights,* 424

91. John Marshall:
    Cherokee Nation v. *State of Georgia,* 427

92. Thomas Hart Benton:
    The Mischiefs of a National Bank, 430

93. Francis Patrick Kenrick:
    Episcopal Rights and Parish Autonomy, 437

94. Emma Hart Willard:
    "Rocked in the Cradle of the Deep," 440

95. Frederick Robinson:
    A Brief Exposure of Bar Associations, 441

96. Timothy Walker:
    Defense of Mechanical Philosophy, 447

97. Stephen Simpson:
    Political Economy and the Producers of Wealth, 463

98. Nat Turner:
    Confession, 472

1831–1832

99. Alexis de Tocqueville:
    American Notes, 482

1832

100. Thomas R. Dew:
     Pro-Slavery Arguments, 506

101. David Moulton and Mordecai Myers:
     Against Appointing Chaplains to the Legislature, 511

102. William Cullen Bryant:
     Songs of the City, 519
     "Hymn of the City"
     "Spring in Town"

103. George Catlin:
     Letter from the Yellowstone River, 521

104. *For and Against the Bank Renewal Bill,* 524

Andrew Jackson:
Veto Message
Daniel Webster:
Reply to Jackson

105. Frances Trollope:
     The American Poor, 542

106. Calvin Colton:
     Manual for Emigrants to America, 546

107. Samuel Francis Smith:
     "America," 554

108. Joseph Caldwell:
     On the Need for Popular Education, 555

109. Thomas Cooper:
     A Defense of Intellectual Freedom, 561

110. *South Carolina Ordinance of Nullification,* 574

111. John C. Calhoun:
     States' Rights and Nullification, 576

112. *The Threat of Disunion,* 585
     Andrew Jackson:
     Proclamation to the People of South Carolina
     Reply to Jackson's Proclamation

Volume 6
The Challenge
of a Continent

1833

1. John Greenleaf Whittier:
   Man's Property in Man, 1

2. Lydia M. Child:
   Proposals for Equal Treatment of African Americans, 5

3. *Declaration of the American Anti-Slavery Society,* 12

4. *New York Carpenters' Strike,* 15

5. Ely Moore:
   Trade Unions and the "Mechanic" Arts, 17

6. Mathew Carey:
   The Poor in a Land of Milk and Honey, 23

7. Edward Everett:
   A Plea for Support of an Ohio College, 26

8. *Play-Party Songs*, 31
   "Jennie Jenkins"
   "Bowling Green"
   "Cindy"
   Daniel Decatur Emmett:
   "Old Dan Tucker"

9. William M. Gouge:
   Paper Money and Banking, 34

10. Charles A. Davis:
    A Humorist's View of the Bank Controversy,
    41
    Major J. Downing to Mr. Dwight, No-
    vember 12
    Downing to Dwight, December 14

11. Henry Clay:
    The Bank and the Power of the Executive,
    46

1834

12. Andrew Jackson:
    The Autonomy of the Executive, 58

13. James Madison:
    *On Presidential Appointments and the Bal-
    ance of Powers*, 63

14. *A Petition Against Usury Laws*, 66

15. Frederick Robinson:
    Labor as the Source of Reform, 69

16. William Leggett:
    *The Struggle for Power Between the Many
    and the Few*, 74

17. Theodore Dwight:
    The Arts in America, 76

18. Francis Lieber:
    Space and Time in America, 84

19. Davy Crockett:
    Frontier Politics, 87

20. "Zip Coon," 89

1835

21. Davy Crockett:
    A Tour of the Lowell Mills, 90

22. John James Audubon:
    Frontier Law and Mississippi Squatters,
    92

23. Joseph H. Ingraham:
    The Plantations of Mississippi, 97

24. Gjert Hovland:
    Opportunities for Land and for Work,
    115

25. Theophilus Fisk:
    The War of Capital Against Labor, 118

26. George S. White:
    The Moral Influence of Manufacturing,
    123

27. Anonymous:
    Land Speculation as a Cause of Strikes,
    127

28. George Bancroft:
    *"The Common Man in Art, Politics, and
    Religion"* 128

29. Thaddeus Stevens:
    Education as a Public Duty, 136

30. William H. Seward:
    Prosperity and Education, 140

31. Charles G. Finney:
    The Work of Man and the Work of God,
    145

32. Gustave De Beaumont:
    *Religious Sects and Religious Freedom in
    America*, 150

33. Samuel F. B. Morse:
    The Dangers of Foreign Immigration, 158

34. Andrew Jackson:
    *A Permanent Habitation for the American
    Indians*, 164

35. James Kirke Paulding:
    Uncle Sam, 166

36. John Savage:
    People v. Fisher, 172

37. Theodore Sedgwick:
    Corporations and Currency, 174

38. John Young:
    Property Under the Common Law, 181

39. John Vethake:
"Banks, Monopolies, and the Good of the Greatest Number" 185

40. Songs of the Sea, 189
"Leave Her, Johnny!"
"Blow Ye Winds"

41. George McDuffie:
The Natural Slavery of Blacks, 191

42. Resolutions on Abolitionist Propaganda, 197

43. Abolitionist Protest Against the President, 199

44. Alexis de Tocqueville:
About Democracy in America, 205
Letter to Eugene Stoffels
Author's Introduction

1835–1837

45. William Johnson:
Diary of a Free African American, 215

1836

46. Thomas Cole:
American Scenery, 231

47. Charles P. McIlvaine:
The Scourge of Intemperance, 240

48. Anonymous:
The Aims of the Philadelphia Trades' Union, 245

49. Employer Opposition to Trade Unions, 247

50. William Cullen Bryant:
On the Right to Strike, 248

51. Labor Unions and Conspiracy, 251

52. The Evils of Female Labor, 256

53. On the Ruinous Competition of Convict Labor, 261

54. Robert Rantoul, Jr.:
On the Barbarity of the Common Law, 262

55. Daniel Webster:
Technical Progress and Prosperity, 266

56. Franklin Pierce:
The Military Academy, 273

57. John Savage:
Slums as a Common Nuisance, 279

58. Abraham Lincoln:
A Candidate Shows His Hand, 281

59. William B. Travis:
Message from the Alamo, 282

60. Andrew Jackson:
The Independence of Texas, 293

1837

61. Guns and Ballots, 296

62. Andrew Jackson:
Farewell Address, 298

63. George Templeton Strong:
The Panic of 1837, 311

64. Martin Van Buren:
Against Government Aid for Business Losses, 314

65. David Henshaw:
The Rights and Powers of Corporations, 317

66. Roger B. Taney and Joseph Story:
Charles River Bridge v. Warren Bridge, 326

67. John L. O'Sullivan:
The Greatest Good of the Greatest Number, 333

68. William Harper:
The Inequality of Men, 340

69. John C. Calhoun:
The Danger of Abolitionist Petitions, 346

70. Aaron Clark:
Immigrants in a Crowded City, 351

71. Daniel D. Barnard:
The American Experiment in Government, 353

72. William Ellery Channing:
Against the Annexation of Texas, 357

73. Charles Hodge:
The Education of Ministers, 363

74. Ralph Waldo Emerson:
The American Scholar, 367

75. Harriet Martineau:
    Mechanics and Working Girls, 379

76. Francis J. Grund:
    Reflections on America, 384

77. Edward Beecher:
    The Riots at Alton, 391

78. Asa Green:
    Mob Violence, 399

1837–1838

79. John Greenleaf Whittier:
    "The Farewell," 413

1838

80. J. J. Flournoy:
    Black Workers and White Labor, 415

81. *Mass Appeal of African Americans, Threatened with Disfranchisement,* 416

82. William Ellery Channing and Ellis Gray Loring:
    Petition on Behalf of Abner Kneeland, 422

83. Abraham Lincoln:
    The Danger to Our Liberty, 424

84. William Lloyd Garrison:
    Declarations of a Peace Convention, 430

85. Joseph Smith:
    A Pillar of Light, 432

86. James Fenimore Cooper:
    The American Scene, 438

1839

87. Frances Anne Kemble:
    Life on a Georgia Plantation, 455

88. Theodore Weld:
    Slavery As It Is, 464

89. *A Protest Against Women Abolitionists,* 469

90. John Quincy Adams:
    The Declaration and the Constitution, 471

91. Hans Barlien:
    A People from All Nations of the World, 480

92. Michel Chevalier:
    Work, Speculation, and Democracy, 482

93. Frederick Marryat:
    The English Language in America, 495

94. John L. O'Sullivan:
    America and the Perfectibility of Man, 502
    The Course of Civilization
    The Great Nation of Futurity

95. "Life Is A Toil," 512

1840

96. Martin Van Buren:
    Executive Order for a Ten-Hour Day, 523

97. Richard Henry Dana:
    Despotism on the High Seas, 524

98. Orestes A. Brownson:
    Labor and Social Democracy, 534

99. Albert Brisbane:
    Social Waste and the Benefits of Association, 544

100. *A Catholic Petition for Common School Funds,* 548

101. Horace Mann:
    On the Art of Teaching, 554

102. Daniel Webster:
    For a Uniform Bankruptcy Law, 561

103. Henry Clay:
    Against the Growing Power of the Executive, 565

104. William Ladd:
    International Organizations to Keep the Peace, 573

105. Anonymous:
    Mike Fink and Davy Crockett, 574

Volume 7
Manifest
Destiny

1841

1. William H. Seward:
    Uprooting the Native Americans, 1

2. Hans Brandt:
   Poor Prospects for Immigrants to America, 3

3. *Public Lands and Squatters' Rights,* 6

4. Gustaf Unonius:
   Problems of Frontier Land Ownership, 8

5. Anonymous:
   Banking and the Merchant-Capitalist, 16

6. Gilbert Vale:
   Happiness for All Through the Diffusion of Wealth, 17

7. *Constitution of the Brook-Farm Association,* 26

8. Henry Wadsworth Longfellow:
   "The Village Blacksmith," 43

1842

9. Horace Mann:
   The Pecuniary Value of Education, 44

10. Francis Wayland:
    Our Present System of Colleges, 47

11. Philip Hone:
    Rebellion in Rhode Island, 52

12. Thomas Dorr:
    The People's Right to Remake Their Constitution, 56

13. Lemuel Shaw:
    Commonwealth of Massachusetts v. Hunt, 61

14. Lydia M. Child:
    Against Capital Punishment, 66

15. Isidore Löwenstern:
    The Philadelphia Penitentiary, 72

16. Charles Lenox Remond:
    An African American Protest Against Segregation in Travel, 74

1842–1843

17. *Pro-Slavery Churches,* 77
    James G. Birney:
    The Guilt of the Churches Supporting Slavery
    Stephen S. Foster:
    A Brotherhood of Thieves

1843

18. John C. Calhoun:
    On Territorial Expansion, 87

19. Jesse Applegate:
    A Day on the Oregon Trail, 89

20. Andrew Jackson:
    The Annexation of Texas as Essential to the United States, 95

21. Dorothea Dix:
    Plea for Humane Treatment of the Insane, 97

22. *The Sylvania Association,* 107

23. William Henry Channing:
    The Christian Destiny of America, 108

24. James Russell Lowell:
    Opposition to Nationalism in Literature, 110

25. Horatio Greenough:
    Remarks on the Training of American Artists, 113

26. John Neal:
    The Power of the Press, 118

27. John W. Pitts:
    Opposition to Fees for Lawyers, 124

28. Job Durfee:
    Science and Political Progress, 128

29. Henry David Thoreau:
    An Attack on Technology, 143

30. Daniel Webster:
    On Securing Trade with China, 157

31. John Greenleaf Whittier:
    "Massachusetts to Virginia," 159

1844

32. Anonymous:
    Criticism of the Nativist Party, 162

33. Nathan Appleton:
    Labor and Wealth in Europe and America, 163

34. Daniel Webster:
    For Reform of the Naturalization Laws, 168

35. Nathaniel Hawthorne:
    Earth's Holocaust, 170

36. Ralph Waldo Emerson:
    Young America, 182

37. John Tyler:
    Dorr's Rebellion, 188

38. *Texas Without War,* 192

39. Joshua Giddings:
    Texas and Slavery, 201

40. *African American Resolutions on Segregated Schools,* 202

41. *The Injustice of Tenant Farming,* 203

42. William Kirkland:
    The Paradise of the Poor, 205

43. George Henry Evans:
    A New Homestead Policy, 208

44. Timothy Walker:
    The Right of Eminent Domain, 210

45. John H. Griscom:
    Report on Sanitary Conditions in New York City, 213

46. Calvin Colton:
    The Relation Between Labor and Capital, 219

47. *A Dialogue on Female Labor,* 229

48. Robert Owen:
    Religion and Marriage, 231

49. J. W. C. Dietrichson:
    Organizing an Immigrant Church, 234

50. Rufus Choate:
    The State and Mental Culture, 235

51. Truman Marcellus Post:
    The Need for Colleges in the West, 242

52. Alexander H. Everett:
    Greenough's Statue of Washington, 246

1845

53. Wendell Phillips:
    Concerning the Impossibility of Union with Slaveholders, 261

54. *Resolutions of a New York Antirent Convention,* 264

55. *The Restless Pursuit of Wealth,* 266

56. Asa Whitney:
    A Railroad to the Pacific, 272

57. William Gregg:
    Southern Manufacturing, 276

58. *Songs of the Underground Railroad,* 282
    "Go Down, Moses"
    "Steal Away"
    "Follow the Drinking Gourd"

59. *The Natural Right to Property,* 283

60. James K. Polk:
    The Annexation of Texas and Oregon, 286

61. John L. O'Sullivan:
    Our Manifest Destiny, 288

62. Robert Owen:
    An Open Letter to Capitalists, 292

63. *Immigrant Labor and the War Against Capitalism,* 294

64. Margaret Fuller:
    On the Emancipation of Women, 296

65. *Strike of Pittsburgh Women,* 300

66. James K. Polk:
    Reaffirmation of the Monroe Doctrine, 301

67. Robert J. Walker:
    Tariffs and Revenue Laws, 303

68. Lewis C. Levin:
    Nativists and the Foreign-Born, 313

1846

60. Robert C. Winthrop:
    The Oregon Question, 317

70. Anonymous:
    California and the National Interest, 323

71. Abbott Lawrence:
    A New England View of Tariffs, 329

72. John C. Calhoun:
    Against General Resolutions on Foreign Affairs, 336

73. Anonymous:
   Vote Yourself a Farm, 338

74. Anonymous:
   Work, Wealth, and Free Land, 339

75. "Elanoy," 340

76. Walt Whitman:
   The Duty of a Government, 341

77. Samuel J. May:
   The Enfranchisement of Women, 342

78. James Russell Lowell:
   War and Slavery, 348

1847

79. Ralph Waldo Emerson:
   "Ode Inscribed to W. H. Channing,"
   359

80. Charles Sumner:
   A War to Strengthen the Slavery Interests,
   361

81. *Territorial Expansion and the Extension of
   Slavery,* 366

82. Albert Gallatin:
   The Unjust War with Mexico, 369

83. "Green Grow the Lilacs," 373

84. James K. Polk:
   California and Mexico, 374

85. George C. Beckwith:
   War and Its Remedies, 379

86. Anonymous:
   Hired Help on the Farm, 385

87. *The Ten-Hour Day,* 386

88. Daniel Webster:
   A Railroad in New Hampshire, 388

89. "Pat Works on the Railway," 391

90. Joseph Henry:
   *First Annual Report on the Smithsonian In-
   stitution,* 392

91. Ole M. Raeder:
   Norwegian Immigrants in America,
   398

1848

92. John Humphrey Noyes:
   The Oneida Community, 403

93. Benjamin Hallett:
   The Sovereignty of the People, 410

94. "No Irish Need Apply," 421

95. Frederick Douglass:
   *An African American View of the Mexican
   War,* 422

96. Roger S. Baldwin:
   *The Executive Prerogative in Foreign Pol-
   icy,* 423

97. *Debate on the Yucatán Bill,* 426
   John Niles:
   Against Intervention in the Internal
   Affairs of Other Nations
   John C. Calhoun:
   The Inapplicability of the Monroe
   Doctrine

98. *The Seneca Falls Declaration on Women's
   Rights,* 438

99. "Buffalo Gals," 441

100. A. J. Downing:
   In Praise of Farming, 442

101. *Factory Rules at Lowell, Massachusetts,*
   459

102. Horace Mann:
   Twelfth Annual Report, 460

103. *Pennsylvania Child Labor Law,* 474

104. James Russell Lowell:
   English Thought and American Writers,
   475

1849

105. Alexander Mackay:
   Apostles of the Democratic Creed, 477

106. Theodore Parker:
   A Critique of American Churches, 486

107. Anonymous:
   Letter from the Sierra Nevadas, 488

108. "Days of Forty-Nine," 491

109. Frank Soulé *et al.*:
San Francisco During and After the Gold Rush, 492

110. Edward Everett:
State Funds for Harvard, 502

111. Charles Sumner:
Segregation and the Common School, 507

112. Charles Lyell:
The Relative Merits of Black and White Labor, 516

113. *The Wisconsin Phalanx*, 517

114. Anonymous:
The Hardships of Farming, 522

115. "Sea Gulls and Crickets," 537

116. Anonymous:
Social Injustice and Civil Disorder, 538

117. Henry David Thoreau:
Resistance to Civil Government, 540

118. Charles Sumner:
War and the Common Law of Nations, 548

119. John C. Calhoun:
Constitutional Government, 552

120. Henry Wadsworth Longfellow:
"The Republic," 563

Volume 8
A House
Dividing

1850

1. Henry Clay:
Compromise Resolutions, 1

2. Horace Mann:
Slavery in the Territories, 7

3. John C. Calhoun:
Either Slavery or Disunion, 16

4. Daniel Webster:
A Plea for Harmony and Peace, 24

5. John Greenleaf Whittier:
"Ichabod," 28

6. William H. Seward:
A Higher Law than the Constitution, 29

7. Henry Clay:
Slavery and Expansion, 36
Proposals of the Committee of Thirteen
Defense of the Proposals

8. Anonymous:
A Defense of the President's Plan for Compromise, 43

9. *Resolutions of the Nashville Convention*, 49

10. *The Compromise of 1850*, 52

11. *Military Presidents*, 58

12. *Massachusetts Compulsory Schooling Law*, 63

13. Francis Wayland:
Schooling Adapted to all Classes in Society, 64

14. Anonymous:
Railroad Land Grants, 71

15. *Hillside Ditches and Circular Plowing*, 75

16. Lemuel Shattuck:
A Plan for the Promotion of Public Health, 76

17. Herman Melville:
Hawthorne, Shakespeare, and a Great American Literature, 83

18. A. J. Downing:
A Few Words on Rural Architecture, 90

19. Anonymous:
The Late Cuba Expedition, 93

20. Millard Fillmore:
A Golden Rule for Foreign Affairs, 109

21. Daniel Webster:
America's Interest in Foreign Democratic Institutions, 110

22. Theodore Parker:
The State of the Nation, 114

1851

23. A. J. Downing:
    Country Churches, 122

24. Henry David Thoreau:
    Walking Westward, 125

25. *Nostalgic Songs of the Westward Movement*,
    128
    "Sweet Betsy From Pike"
    "Joe Bowers"
    "Acres of Clams"

26. Adin Ballou:
    The Hopedale Community, 131

27. Levi Coffin:
    The Underground Railroad, 134

28. Anonymous:
    A Uniform System of Jurisprudence, 139

29. Jonathan Baldwin Turner:
    An Industrial University for Illinois,
    157

1852

30. *The Suitability of Moral Declarations in
    Foreign Policy*, 167
    Lewis Cass:
    In Defense of Such Declarations
    James C. Jones:
    In Opposition to Such Declarations

31. Charles Magill Conrad:
    Instructions for Commodore Perry, 174

32. *Economic Effect of Railroads*, 177

33. Josiah Sutherland:
    Free Land and the Supply of Labor, 180

34. Horace Greeley:
    Women's Rights, 184

35. Charles Sears:
    The North American Phalanx, 185

36. Anonymous:
    Arguments Against the Maine Liquor Law,
    191

37. *A Public Library for Boston*, 197

38. Harriet Beecher Stowe:
    Uncle Tom Defies Simon Legree, 200

39. *Songs of Slaves and Their Masters*, 203
    "Blue Tail Fly"
    "All the Pretty Little Horses"

1853

40. *Plan for an African American School*, 204

41. Charles Loring Brace:
    The Children's Aid Society, 208

42. *Appeal by the Women of Massachusetts for
    Civil Rights*, 210

43. Jesup W. Scott:
    The Promise of the Great Plains, 211

44. "Canaday-I-O," 214

45. Francis and Theresa Pulszky:
    Observations of Some Hungarian Visitors,
    215

46. Fredrika Bremer:
    The American Proclivity for Association,
    220

47. Wilbur F. Storey:
    *Against the Imitation of European Univer-
    sities*, 222

1854

48. Richard Baker:
    *The Crime of Mrs. Douglass in Teaching
    African American Children to Read*, 224

49. Frederick Law Olmsted:
    King Cotton and His Subjects, 237

50. George Fitzhugh:
    The Failure of Free Society, 243

51. *Opposition to the Kansas-Nebraska Bill*, 251

52. Stephen A. Douglas:
    Defense of the Kansas-Nebraska Bill, 254

53. John Greenleaf Whittier:
    "The Kansas Emigrants," 260

54. Ralph Waldo Emerson:
    On the Fugitive Slave Law, 261

55. "The Abolitionist Hymn," 265

56. William J. Grayson:
    The Hireling and the Slave, 266

57. Charlotte L. Forten:
The Difficulty of Being an African American Christian, 273

58. Abraham Lincoln:
Fragments on Government and Slavery, 275

59. Abraham Lincoln:
Against the Extension of Slavery, 276

60. William H. Seward:
Providing for the Indigent Insane, 283

61. *The Ostend Manifesto*, 289

62. James B. Finley:
Life in the Backwoods, 294

63. James G. Bell:
Riding Herd to California, 300

64. Henry David Thoreau:
Where I Lived, and What I Lived For, 308

1855

65. Philip Schaff:
The Emergence of an American Character, 329

66. David Christy:
The Kingdom of Cotton, 335

67. William S. Tyler:
The College and the Church, 340

68. *Massachusetts Personal Liberty Act*, 346

69. Frithjof Meidell:
The Birth and Growth of a Railroad Town, 349

70. *California African Americans Appeal for Legal Equality*, 352

71. *Arkansas Resolutions on the Kansas-Nebraska Act*, 354

1856

72. *An Appeal to Southerners to Settle Kansas*, 365

73. Charles Sumner:
The Crime Against Kansas, 367

74. Theodore Parker:
The Present Crisis in American Affairs, 372

75. *Settlers' Songs*, 376
"The Little Old Sod Shanty"
"Kansas Boys"

76. Christopher C. Andrews:
Economic Advantages of the Frontier, 378

77. *Constitution of the Vigilantes of San Francisco*, 383

78. W. H. Wallace *et al.*:
Martial Law in the Washington Territory, 385

79. Anonymous:
The Progress of the Americans in the Art of Writing, 392

80. Walt Whitman:
Letter to Emerson, 400

81. Walt Whitman:
Wicked Architecture, 407

82. George William Curtis:
The Duty of the American Scholar, 411

83. John A. Engelhard:
Southern Education for Southerners, 427

84. John P. Sanderson:
Adverse Views on Foreign Immigration, 429

85. Freeman Hunt:
Business Success, 435

1857

86. Roger B. Taney:
Dred Scott v. Sandford, 440

87. *African American Protest Over the Dred Scott Decision*, 450

88. *Ohio Resolution on the Dred Scott Decision*, 451

89. Robert J. Walker:
Address to the People of Kansas, 453

90. Abraham Lincoln:
The Dred Scott Decision and the Declaration of Independence, 459

91. Edmund Ruffin:
    Advantages of Independence for the Slave-holding States, 466

92. George Fitzhugh:
    Slaves Without Masters, 475

93. J. W. Fowler:
    Plantation Management, 478

94. Hinton R. Helper:
    Slavery and the Deficiency of Commerce in the South, 479

95. Henry J. Gardner:
    New England Nativism, 484

96. "Cape Cod Chantey," 487

97. *Rhode Island Child Labor Law,* 488

98. *Report on Higher Education in New York,* 489

99. *Slums and Tenant Housing in New York,* 491

100. Lewis Cass:
    Trade with China Under Suitable Guarantees, 497

101. Oliver Wendell Holmes:
    "Ode for a Social Meeting," 500

102. Count Gurowski:
    Virtues of the American Mind, 501

Volume 9
The Crisis of
the Union

1858

1. *The Union and Popular Sovereignty,* 1
   Abraham Lincoln:
   A House Divided
   Stephen A. Douglas:
   Reply to Lincoln

2. *The Lincoln-Douglas Debates,* 8
   Douglas' Speech at Ottawa, August 21
   Lincoln's Reply at Ottawa, August 21
   Lincoln's Speech at Freeport, August 27

   Douglas' Reply at Freeport, August 27
   Lincoln's Speech at Jonesboro, September 15
   Douglas' Reply at Jonesboro, September 15
   Lincoln's Speech at Charleston, September 18
   Douglas' Speech at Galesburg, October 7
   Lincoln's Reply at Galesburg, October 7
   Lincoln's Speech at Alton, October 15
   Douglas' Second Speech at Alton, October 15

3. William H. Seward:
   An Irrepressible Conflict, 32

4. *The Right of the United States to Rule Mexico,* 35

5. Anonymous:
   On the Need for Physical Fitness, 41

6. Oliver Wendell Holmes:
   On Old Age, 48

7. Rufus Choate:
   American Nationality, 54

8. Ellis Lewis:
   Mott v. Pennsylvania Railroad Company, 61

9. George Templeton Strong:
   The First Atlantic Cable, 65

10. *On Supporting the Local Economy,* 67

11. *Farmers' Platform,* 68

12. Ralph Waldo Emerson:
    Farming, 70

13. Anonymous:
    A Plea for Scientific Agriculture, 76

14. Henry P. Tappan:
    A Call for a Secularized University, 79

15. David Smith Terry and Stephen J. Field:
    On Sunday Closing Laws, 85

1859

16. Anonymous:
    The Influence Abroad of American Inventiveness, 95

17. Carl Schurz:
    True Americanism, 97

18. *Nullification in the North,* 107

19. Louis Antoine Godey:
    How To Be the Perfect Housewife, 108

20. Abraham Lincoln:
    Labor, Education, and the American Farmer, 121

21. Peter Cooper:
    The Cooper Union for the Advancement of Science and Art, 127

22. Horace Greeley:
    Interview with Brigham Young, 132

23. Henry David Thoreau:
    A Plea for Captain John Brown, 136

24. John Brown:
    Last Speech to the Court, 143

25. "John Brown's Body," 145

26. Daniel Decatur Emmett and Albert Pike:
    "Dixie," 146

1860

27. Oliver Wendell Holmes:
    The Brahmin Caste of New England, 148

28. Elizabeth Cady Stanton:
    The Natural Rights of Civilized Women, 151

29. Henry Wadsworth Longfellow:
    "The Children's Hour," 157

30. Abraham Lincoln:
    Address at Cooper Union, 158

31. Walt Whitman:
    "I Hear America Singing," 170

32. Henry Wheeler Shaw ("Josh Billings"):
    An Essa on the Muel, 171

33. *The Pony Express,* 172

34. *Defense of an African American Pioneer Land Claim,* 174
    Petition of Sylvester Gray
    Report of the Senate Committee on Public Lands

35. Herman Melville:
    "Misgivings," 187

36. *Party Platforms of 1860,* 188
    Constitutional Union Platform
    Republican Platform
    Democratic Platform (Douglas)
    Democratic Platform (Breckinridge)

37. *Georgia Debate on Secession,* 192
    Robert Toombs:
    For Secession
    Alexander H. Stephens:
    Against Secession

38. *Southern Secession,* 204
    Mississippi Resolutions
    South Carolina Declarations

39. James Buchanan:
    The Impending Disruption of the Union, 209

40. *War or Compromise,* 220
    Benjamin F. Wade:
    Opposition to Compromise
    John J. Crittenden:
    Compromise Resolutions

41. John Sherman:
    Secession Means War, 224

1861

42. James Russell Lowell:
    The Government's Right to Self-Defense, 230

43. Fernando Wood:
    Proposal for the Secession of New York City, 233

44. *Economic Reasons for Secession,* 236

45. Jefferson Davis:
    Inaugural Address, 238

46. Henry Timrod:
    "Ethnogenesis," 242

47. *Compromise Resolutions of the House of Representatives,* 244

48. John J. Crittenden:
    The Union at Any Price, 246

49. Abraham Lincoln:
    First Inaugural Address, 250

50. *A Plan to Avoid Civil War,* 256
    William H. Seward:
    Suggestions to the President on Domestic and Foreign Policy
    Abraham Lincoln:
    Reply to Seward

51. Robert E. Lee:
    Resignation from the United States Army,
    258
    Letter to General Scott
    Letter to Anne Marshall

52. Jefferson Davis:
    War Message, 259

53. Abraham Lincoln:
    A War to Preserve the Union, 268

54. Ethel Lynn Beers:
    "All Quiet Along the Potomac To-Night," 274

55. Benjamin F. Butler:
    African American Refugees in the Northern Army, 276

56. *An Alliance Between the Confederacy and Native Americans,* 278

57. "Song of the Mississippi Volunteers," 295

58. Abraham Lincoln:
    Military Proclamations and Civil Law, 296

59. *A Southern Christian View of Slavery,* 298

60. *Patriotic Songs of North and South,* 303
    George Frederick Root:
    "The Battle-Cry of Freedom"
    Harry McCarty:
    "The Bonnie Blue Flag"

61. *War, Industry, and Invention,* 305

1861–1864

62. Mary Boykin Chesnut:
    Diary of a Southern Belle, 307

1862

63. John S. Rock:
    African American Hopes for Emancipation,
    318

64. Julia Ward Howe:
    "The Battle Hymn of the Republic,"
    322

65. Charles Sumner:
    Resolutions on Secession and Reconstruction, 323

66. William H. Seward:
    American and European Interests in Mexico, 326

67. Abraham Lincoln:
    A Plea for Compensated Emancipation,
    328

68. Rose O'Neal Greenhow:
    Diary of a Confederate Spy, 329

69. David Ross Locke ("Petroleum V. Nasby"):
    Ameriky for White Men, 333

70. Thaddeus Stevens:
    Concerning Wartime Taxes in the North,
    335

71. *The Homestead Act,* 337

72. Public Lands for the Benefit of Agriculture and the Mechanic Arts, 339

73. "The Brass-Mounted Army," 341

74. George B. McClellan:
    Advice to the President on Conducting the War, 343

75. *Discussion of War Aims,* 345
    Horace Greeley:
    Freeing the Slaves
    Abraham Lincoln:
    Saving the Union

76. *African American Opposition to Lincoln's Offer of Colonization,* 363

77. Alexander Walker:
    Butler's Brutality in the South, 365

78. John Greenleaf Whittier:
    "Barbara Frietchie," 371

79. Anonymous:
Dilemma of a Norwegian Immigrant, 372

80. James Sloan Gibbons:
"Three Hundred Thousand More,"
374

81. Joseph Emerson Brown:
Opposition to Conscription in the Confederacy, 375

82. Anonymous:
Financial Resources of the North, 378

83. Anthony Trollope:
American and European Cities, 383

84. Israel Benjamin:
The Spirit of America, 386

85. Emily Dickinson:
Two Poems, 391
"I Cannot Live with You"
"I Like to See it Lap the Miles"

86. Orestes A. Brownson:
The Preservation of Catholic Orthodoxy in America, 392

87. Nathaniel Hawthorne:
Lincoln and the American Character, 395

1863

88. Abraham Lincoln:
Emancipation Proclamation, 398

89. *Songs About Freedom,* 400
"Many Thousand Gone"
Henry Clay Work:
"Kingdom Coming"

90. Abraham Lincoln:
Appointment of General Hooker, 401

91. John Lansing Burrows:
Opposition to the Theater in Time of War, 402

92. William Tecumseh Sherman:
The Press and Wartime Security, 405

93. *Resolutions Against Foreign Mediation,* 407

94. Clement L. Vallandigham:
A Plea to Stop the War, 409

95. *The Question of Continuing the War,* 416
New Jersey Peace Resolutions
Protest of the New Jersey Soldiers

96. *Government Seizure of Property in the Confederacy,* 419

97. William H. Seward:
Our Policy of Nonintervention, 422

98. Abraham Lincoln:
Habeas Corpus in Time of Rebellion, 424

99. George E. Pickett:
Reflections on the Charge at Gettysburg, 429

100. Braxton Bragg *et al.:*
Conscription Problems in the South, 430

101. William Tecumseh Sherman:
The Executive and the Caprice of the People, 432

102. Louis Agassiz:
The Future of Free African Americans, 434

103. Abraham Lincoln:
Emancipation as a Military Measure, 436

104. Anonymous:
Canals and Railroads, 439

105. *Manufacturers' Objection to an Income Tax,* 441

106. *Opposition to the Rise of Labor Unions,* 455

107. Abraham Lincoln:
The Beginning of Reconstruction, 458

108. James Henry Gooding:
A Soldier's Plea for Equal Pay, 459

109. Patrick S. Gilmore:
"When Johnny Comes Marching Home," 461

110. Abraham Lincoln:
The Gettysburg Address, 462

111. James Alexander Seddon:
Economic Problems of the Confederacy, 463

112. Thomas Buckner:
Race Rioting in Detroit, 467

113. Lindley Miller:
"Marching Song of the First
Arkansas," 472

114. Abraham Lincoln:
A Program for Reconstruction, 473
Proclamation of Amnesty
Annual Message to Congress

115. Edward Dicey:
Money and Manners in the North,
478

116. Henry Wadsworth Longfellow:
"Paul Revere's Ride," 483

1864

117. James Jackson Jarves:
The Conditions and Prospects for Art in
America, 485

118. Frank H. Alfriend:
A Southern National Literature, 491

119. Alexander H. Stephens:
Civil Rights in the Confederacy, 493

120. Henry Clay Work:
"Come Home, Father," 497

121. Frank Wilkeson:
How Americans Die in Battle, 498

122. Walter Kittredge:
"Tenting on the Old Camp Ground,"
502

123. John L. Ransom:
Andersonville Diary, 517

124. Henry Timrod:
"Charleston," 528

125. An Act to Encourage Immigration, 530

126. A Call for an International Trades' Assembly, 532

127. William H. Seward:
Trade with Japan, 533

128. Abraham Lincoln:
Opposition to the Congressional Plan for
Reconstruction, 534

129. George Perkins Marsh:
The Instability of American Life, 535

130. Thomas Low Nichols:
Work and Play in America, 537

1865

131. The First International to Abraham Lincoln, 543

132. James D. Burn:
American Laborers and Immigrants, 544

133. Advertisement to Supply Immigrant Contract Labor, 549

134. E. W. Wynkoop:
Army Atrocities Against Native Americans, 550

135. Henry Clay Work:
"Marching Through Georgia," 554

136. Abraham Lincoln:
Second Inaugural Address, 555

137. Jefferson Davis:
A Final Exhortation to the Confederate
People, 557

138. Walt Whitman:
"Come Up from the Fields Father," 559

139. George E. Pickett:
The Night Before Appomattox, 560

140. Horace Porter:
The Meeting at Appomattox Court House,
562

141. Robert E. Lee:
General Order Number Nine, 572

142. Abraham Lincoln:
Last Public Address, 573

143. Gideon Welles:
The Death of President Lincoln, 576

144. Andrew Johnson:
Proclamation of Amnesty and Pardon for
the Confederate States, 593

145. Andrew Johnson:
Provisional Government in North Carolina, 595

146. David Ross Locke ("Petroleum V.
Nasby"):
A Platform for Northern Democrats, 597

147. *Sheep in the Midst of Wolves,* 599

148. John H. Reagan:
An Open Letter to the People of Texas, 600

149. Charles H. Smith ("Bill Arp"):
Open Letter to Artemus Ward, 604

150. Robert E. Lee:
The Restoration of the Union, 607

151. Thaddeus Stevens:
The Rights of the Conqueror, 608

152. *Opposing Views on the Restoration of the Union,* 612
A Republican Editorial
A Democratic Editorial

153. Ira Steward:
Shorter Hours and Higher Wages, 615

154. John Sherman:
On Postwar Industrial Expansion, 622

155. Horace Greeley:
The First Fruits of Reconstruction, 623

156. Benjamin G. Humphreys:
Justice but Not Equality for African Americans, 626

157. *Mississippi Black Code,* 628
Apprentice Law
Vagrancy Law
Civil Rights of Freedmen
Penal Code

158. Ulysses S. Grant:
Report on Conditions in the South, 635

159. John Greenleaf Whittier:
"Laus Deo!," 638

Volume 10
Reconstruction
and Indus-
trialization

1866

1. William F. G. Shanks:
The American Soldier, 1

2. Andrew Johnson:
Veto of Freedmen's Bureau Bill, 3

3. Andrew Johnson:
Against the Radical Republicans, 8

4. *Debate on Civil and States' Rights,* 11
Andrew Johnson:
Veto of Civil Rights Bill
Lyman Trumbull:
Reply to Johnson

5. *Civil Rights Act,* 21

6. Alexander H. Stephens:
For Immediate Restoration of the State Governments, 23

7. *Report of the Joint Committee on Reconstruction,* 26

8. David Davis:
Ex Parte Milligan, 31

9. Innes Randolph:
"The Good Old Rebel," 37

10. Herman Melville:
Consideration for Our Late Enemies, 38

11. Walt Whitman:
"When Lilacs Last in the Dooryard Bloomed," 44

12. Amasa Walker:
Wealth and the Division of Labor, 66

13. *Efforts to Encourage Immigration to the South,* 73

14. George Nye Boardman:
Government Aid to the Poor, 74

15. *Religious Schooling for Wayward Youths,* 77

16. Anonymous:
A Norwegian in Minnesota, 78

17. Andrew Johnson:
Representation for All Southern States, 81

1867

18. Thomas J. Wood:
Difficulties of Law Enforcement in Mississippi, 86

19. Andrew Johnson:
Veto of Tenure of Office Act, 90

20. *Congressional Interference with the Command of the Army*, 92

21. *The Struggle Between Congress and the President Over Reconstruction*, 93
    First Reconstruction Act
    Andrew Johnson:
    First Reconstruction Veto
    Andrew Johnson:
    Second Reconstruction Veto

22. Ferdinand V. Hayden:
    Trees for the Arid West, 102

23. *Proposal for an Agricultural Society*, 104

24. Andrew C. Cameron:
    The Problems and Prospects of Labor, 105

25. *Child Labor and School Attendance*, 112

26. Walt Whitman:
    "One's-Self I Sing," 114

1868

27. *Illinois Proposal for a Compulsory School Law*, 115

28. *Knowledge, Mental Training, and Classical Study*, 117

29. Samuel J. Tilden:
    Arraignment of the Republican Party, 122

30. *The Impeachment of Andrew Johnson*, 126
    Charles Sumner:
    For Conviction
    James Grimes:
    For Acquittal

31. *Civil War Amendments to the Constitution*, 133

32. *The Ku Klux Klan*, 135

33. *The Knights of the White Camelia*, 137

34. *Spirituals*, 141
    "Didn't My Lord Deliver Daniel?"
    "Mary and Martha"
    "The Gospel Train"
    "Joshua Fit the Battle of Jericho"
    "Ezekiel Saw the Wheel"
    "My Lord, What a Mourning"

1869

35. *Congressional Debate on Haiti and Santo Domingo*, 143

36. Charles W. Eliot:
    The Training Proper in Scientific Schools, 156

37. Henry C. Wheeler:
    Call for a Farmers' Convention, 162

38. Charles Francis Adams, Jr.:
    The Struggle for Erie, 164

39. Henry Eno:
    Silver in Nevada, 191

40. William H. Seward:
    The Promise of Alaska, 193

41. Samuel L. Clemens ("Mark Twain"):
    Spirit of the Tennessee Press, 197

42. Charles W. Eliot:
    The Elective Curriculum, 201

43. Henry Adams:
    The Constitution and Civil Service Reform, 210

44. *Against Religious Exercises in Public Schools*, 214

45. Francis Parkman:
    The Diffusion of Education and the Degradation of Culture, 216

1870

46. *Negro National Labor Union Platform*, 221

47. Frederick Law Olmsted:
    The Unplanned Growth of Cities, 224

48. *Concerning the Annexation of the Dominican Republic*, 231
    Ulysses S. Grant:
    For Annexation
    Charles Sumner:
    Against Annexation

49. *Against the Importation of "Coolie" Labor*, 239

50. Bret Harte:
    "Plain Language from Truthful James," 241

51. Red Cloud:
    Native American Rights, 242

52. Samuel L. Clemens ("Mark Twain"):
    My Watch, 245

1871

53. *African American Appeal for Protection of Life and Property*, 247

54. *The Ku Klux Klan Act*, 249

55. *Federal Grand Jury Report on the Ku Klux Klan*, 252

56. Wendell Phillips:
    Resolutions Against the Profit System, 254

57. "The Schooner *E. A. Horton*," 255

58. P. S. Dorney:
    Anti-Chinese Rioting in Los Angeles, 256

59. Frederick Law Olmsted:
    The Chicago Fire, 273

60. Count von Hübner:
    Observations of an Austrian Diplomat, 279

1872

61. Charles Loring Brace:
    The Lost Children of New York, 289

62. Francis A. Walker:
    The Dilemma of Indian Policy, 292

1873

63. Francis Ellingwood Abbot:
    Nine Demands of Liberalism for Separation of Church and State, 299

64. "John Henry," 300

65. Samuel F. Miller and Stephen J. Field:
    Slaughter-House Cases, 302

66. *The Farmers' Declaration of Independence*, 309

1874

67. *Declaration of Purpose of the National Grange*, 312

68. Sidney Lanier:
    "Corn," 315

69. Samuel Ab Thomas:
    Wage Slaves in Pennsylvania Coal Mines, 320

70. James S. Pike:
    African American Legislators of South Carolina, 322

71. *Militant White Supremacy*, 325

72. *Revival Songs*, 327
    "Gimme That Old-Time Religion"
    "She'll Be Comin' 'Round the Mountain"

73. Charles W. Eliot:
    Concerning Property Exempt from Taxation, 328

1875

74. *Secret Labor Organizations*, 333

75. Edward King:
    Postwar Plantation Life, 334

76. William Tecumseh Sherman:
    Military Lessons of the War, 340

77. Thomas P. Westendorf:
    "I'll Take You Home Again, Kathleen," 345

78. Samuel L. Clemens ("Mark Twain"):
    The Curious Republic of Gondour, 346

1876

79. Blanche K. Bruce:
    African American Hopes for Assimilation, 350

80. *An Act to Keep Children off the Stage*, 353

81. Ulysses S. Grant:
    The Separation of Church and School, 365

82. Alexander Lyman Holley:
    Theory and Practice in Industrial Engineering, 366

83. *Work Songs*, 372
    "Buffalo Skinners"
    "Drill, Ye Tarriers, Drill!"
    "Factory Girl"

1877

84. *On Permitting Women to Preach,* 375

85. Morrison R. Waite and Stephen J. Field:
Munn v. Illinois, 377

86. Brigham Young:
Riches of the Desert, 383

87. Edwin R. Meade:
Chinese Immigration to the United States,
386

1878

88. *The Knights of Labor,* 391

89. William Gladstone:
*A Comparison of American and British
Institutions,* 393

90. "Here Rattler Here," 399

1879

91. Edwin L. Godkin:
Communism in California, 401

92. *McGuffey's Lessons,* 405

93. Henry James:
*Things Present and Absent in American
Life,* 416

94. Walt Whitman:
The Great American Landscape, 420

95. Robert Louis Stevenson:
Fellow Travelers, 438

96. Henry George:
Progress and Civilization, 443

97. Rutherford B. Hayes:
Veto of the Army Appropriation Act, 449

1880

98. William McElroy:
Advice to a Young Politician, 451

99. James Baird Weaver:
The Greenback Party, 455

100. David A. Wells:
*The Communism of a Discriminating In-
come Tax,* 459

101. Sidney Lanier:
*The Development of Small Farming in the
South,* 466

102. *Barbed Wire Fences,* 472

103. *Cowboy Songs,* 475
"The Dying Cowboy"
"Cowboy's Life"
"The Old Chisholm Trail"
"Good-Bye, Old Paint"

1881

104. George M. Beard:
*Modern Civilization and American Ner-
vousness,* 479

105. Wendell Phillips:
The Scholar in a Republic, 488

106. Carl Schurz:
*The Native American Dilemma—Civiliza-
tion or Extinction,* 495

107. Helen Hunt Jackson:
Indians and Whites, 504

108. James G. Blaine:
*A Congress of Nations of North and South
America,* 508

1882

109. *Standard Oil Trust Agreement,* 510

110. "Jesse James," 517

111. Samuel L. Clemens ("Mark Twain"):
Political Liberty in the South, 531

112. *Chinese Exclusion Act,* 534

113. "Charles Guiteau," 536

114. William Graham Sumner:
Inequality, Liberty, and Progress, 537

115. Carroll D. Wright:
The Factory System, 547

1883

116. Mary Baker Eddy:
Christian Science, 556

117. *Labor and Capital,* 561
Samuel Gompers:
Testimony of a Labor Leader
Thomas L. Livermore:
Testimony of a Factory Manager
Timothy D. Stow:
Testimony of a Physician

118. Joseph P. Bradley and John M. Harlan:
Civil Rights Cases, 577

119. Frederick Douglass:
The Color Line in America, 584

120. A. J. McWhirter:
An Appeal to European Immigrants To Come to the South, 587

121. William Graham Sumner:
What Social Classes Do Not Owe Each Other, 594

122. Henry George:
The Paradox of Poverty, 601

Volume 11
Agrarianism
and
Urbanization

1884

1. Laurence Gronlund:
Collective Control of the Instruments of Production, 1

2. Henry Demarest Lloyd:
Monopoly and Social Control, 7

3. T. Thomas Fortune:
The Common Cause of Black and White Labor, 12

4. Thomas T. Crittenden:
Trade and Commerce for the Southwestern States, 16

5. Preston M. Sutton:
The Liberal Arts in an Agricultural College, 18

6. George Ticknor Curtis:
Presidential Elections and the Spoils System, 22

7. "The Dodger," 29

8. Lester F. Ward:
Mind as a Social Factor, 30

1885

9. Mariana Griswold Van Rensselaer:
Church Architecture in America, 36

10. Louis Sullivan:
Characteristics and Tendencies of American Architecture, 40

11. George Washington Cable:
The Freedman in American Society, 44

12. John Fiske:
American Federalism and World Federation, 65

13. Josiah Strong:
The Superiority of the Anglo-Saxon Race, 71

14. Theodore Roosevelt:
Public Office and Private Gain, 76

15. *A Practical Program for Economists,* 81

16. Woodrow Wilson:
The Declining Prestige of the Presidential Office, 86

1886

17. Grover Cleveland:
A Skeptical View of Pension Legislation, 90

18. Andrew Carnegie:
The Picture Lover and the Picture Buyer, 92

19. John H. Vincent:
The Chautauqua Movement, 96

20. Charles Taze Russell:
What Jehovah's Witnesses Stand For, 103

21. Emma Lazarus:
"The New Colossus," 107

22. Henry Clews:
The Folly of Organized Labor, 108

23. Alexander Clark:
Socialism and African Americans, 111

24. A. S. Wheeler:
The Product of Labor, 113

25. August Spies:
Address at the Haymarket Trial, 117

26. "Eight Hour Day," 122

1886–1887

27. Rutherford B. Hayes:
Wealth in the Hands of the Few, 123

1887

28. *The Interstate Commerce Act*, 126

29. James Cardinal Gibbons:
A Defense of the Knights of Labor, 131

30. Walt Whitman:
On the Sources of His Style, 147

31. James Cardinal Gibbons:
The Progress of the Catholic Church in America, 148

32. *Colorado Child Labor Law*, 150

33. Henry James:
The Inequities of the American Copyright Law, 151

34. Grover Cleveland:
Surplus Revenues and the Tariff, 154

35. Edward Bellamy:
A Utopian Social Economy, 160

1888

36. Theodore Roosevelt:
The Issues of the Coming Election, 170

37. James Bryce:
Politics, Character, and Opinion in America, 172

38. Theodore Roosevelt:
The Americanization of Immigrants, 189

39. Seth Low:
American City Government, 190

40. Matthew Arnold:
Civilization in the United States, 194

41. *Machines and Apprentice Labor*, 197

42. Ira Aten:
The Fence-Cutters, 199

1889

43. Carl Schurz:
The Need for a Rational Forest Policy, 200

44. Hamilton S. Wicks:
The Oklahoma Land Rush, 203

45. Theodore Roosevelt:
False Sentimentality About Native Americans, 207

46. Lewis H. Blair:
Southern Treatment of African Americans, 210

47. John E. Bruce:
Plea for Organized Resistance to White Men, 214

48. William Brough:
"Let Us All Speak Our Minds," 216

49. Andrew Carnegie:
The Birth and Growth of Trusts in a Free Market, 217

50. Andrew Carnegie:
Private Fortunes for Public Benefit, 222

51. David A. Wells:
Machines and Economic Change, 227

52. Richard T. Ely:
The Needs of the City, 234

1889–1890

53. *African Americans in the Post-Reconstruction Era*, 240
Henry W. Grady:
The New South
Joshua A. Brockett:
Reply to Grady

1890

54. Robert G. Ingersoll:
The Absurdity of Religion, 267

55. Russell H. Conwell:
    Acres of Diamonds, 271

56. Ward McAllister:
    How "The Four Hundred" Lives, 279

57. Jacob Riis:
    Ethnic Groups Among the New York Tenements, 286

58. John Ireland:
    State Schools and Religious Instruction, 296

59. Calvin M. Woodward:
    The Educational Value of Manual Training, 302

60. Alfred Thayer Mahan:
    Sea Power and History, 307

61. Edward Everett Hale:
    A High Court for the Americas, 315

62. Hannis Taylor:
    The Growing Inefficiency of the House of Representatives, 318

63. *The Sherman Antitrust Act,* 323

64. Benjamin R. Tucker:
    The State and Anarchism, 325

65. Oliver Wendell Holmes:
    The American Appetite for Old World Titles, 330

66. John Wesley Powell:
    Institutions for the Arid Lands, 332

67. "The Farmer Is the Man," 355

68. Washington Gladden:
    The Embattled Farmers, 356

1891

69. William A. Peffer:
    The Rise of Farmer Organizations, 361

70. Grover Cleveland:
    Against a Free Silver Policy, 365

71. William Dean Howells:
    Democratic Art, 366

1892

72. Richard Olney:
    On the Interstate Commerce Commission, 368

73. James Baird Weaver:
    Wealth, Poverty, and Monopoly, 369

74. *Illinois Sweatshops,* 375

75. Howell Davies:
    Convict Labor for Strikebreaking, 382

76. Charles K. Harris:
    "After the Ball," 385

77. Walter B. Hill:
    A Nation of Presidents, 386

78. George Bird Grinnell:
    The Last of the Buffalo, 388

79. Joseph Mayer Rice:
    The Absurdity of Primary Education, 396

80. Charles W. Eliot:
    Failures of Popular Education, 404

1893

81. David J. Brewer:
    An Independent Judiciary as the Salvation of the Nation, 423

82. James B. Thayer:
    The American Doctrine of Judicial Review, 430

83. Edward C. Billings:
    Labor and the Antitrust Laws, 435

84. John Peter Altgeld:
    Reasons for Pardoning the Haymarket Rioters, 438

85. John Peter Altgeld:
    The Choice Before Labor—Organization or Annihilation, 445

86. Josiah Strong:
    The Discontent of the Working Classes, 450

87. Lester F. Ward:
    Competition and Society, 458

88. Frederick Jackson Turner:
    The Significance of the Frontier in American History, 462

89. *Controversy Over Hawaii,* 479
    Benjamin Harrison:
    For Annexation
    Grover Cleveland:
    Against Annexation

90. E. V. Smalley:
Life on the Prairie Farms, 482

1894

91. William Graham Sumner:
The Absurdity of Social Planning, 487

92. Carl Schurz:
Civil Service Reform, 493

93. Herbert Welsh:
Political Machines and City Government, 498

94. *Songs of New York,* 502
James Blake:
"Sidewalks of New York"
Charles H. Hoyt:
"The Bowery"

95. Jacob S. Coxey:
Business Depression and Public Works, 504

96. Rena M. Atchison:
The Perils of Unrestricted Immigration, 506

97. *The Pullman Strike and Boycott,* 509
Statement of the Strikers
Statement of the Company

98. *State Authority Versus Federal Supremacy in Law Enforcement,* 525
Governor Altgeld to President Cleveland, July 5
Cleveland to Altgeld, July 5
Altgeld to Cleveland, July 6
Cleveland to Altgeld, July 6

99. Samuel Gompers:
The Laborer's Right to Life, 530

100. Henry Demarest Lloyd:
The Business Corporation and the Community, 535

101. Uriel S. Hall:
Reasons in Favor of an Income Tax, 539

102. W. H. "Coin" Harvey:
For Bimetallism in Money Policy, 543

103. Hamlin Garland:
Provincialism and Individuality in American Literature, 547

104. *Songs of the Nineties,* 552
Felix McGlennon and Monroe H. Rosenfeld:
"Her Golden Hair Was Hanging Down Her Back"
William B. Gray:
"She Is More To Be Pitied Than Censured"

105. Caspar W. Whitney:
Evolution of the Country Club, 555

106. Paul Bourget:
The Unrestrained Nature of American Pleasures, 562

107. Henry Drummond:
A Portrait of Dwight Moody, 568

108. Francis W. Parker:
Democracy and the Common School, 575

Volume 12
Populism, Imperialism, and Reform

1895

1. Katharine Lee Bates:
"America the Beautiful," 1

2. Henry Cabot Lodge:
Overseas Expansion and the National Future, 2

3. Richard Olney:
On American Jurisdiction in the Western Hemisphere, 5

4. Booker T. Washington:
The Road to African American Progress, 9

5. John R. Williams:
Immigrant and African American Labor in the Coal Mines, 12

6. Frederick Taylor:
A Piece-Rate System of Wages, 16

7. David J. Brewer:
In Re Debs, 18

8. M. W. Fuller and J. M. Harlan:
United States v. E. C. Knight Company, 23

9. Lester F. Ward:
   Plutocracy or Paternalism, 29

10. Antonín Dvořák:
    Music in America, 33

11. Montgomery Schuyler:
    The Chicago Architects, 51

12. Henry J. Fletcher:
    Migration to the Cities, 56

13. F. J. Kingsbury:
    In Defense of the City, 61

14. Theodore Roosevelt:
    Police Reform in New York City, 67

15. Edward B. Whitney:
    Political Dangers of the Income Tax Decision, 71

16. James Laurence Laughlin:
    Against Free Coinage of Silver, 75

17. John L. Spalding:
    Religion as an Essential Part of Education, 78

1896

18. Theodore Roosevelt:
    The Monroe Doctrine and the National Honor, 83

19. Henry Cabot Lodge:
    For Intervention in Cuba, 85

20. Henry Cabot Lodge:
    For Immigration Restrictions, 88

21. Henry B. Brown and John M. Harlan:
    Plessy v. Ferguson, 92

22. William Jennings Bryan:
    The Cross of Gold, 100

23. Daniel De Leon:
    The Aims of Socialism, 106

24. William Allen White:
    What's the Matter with Kansas?, 112

25. George W. Steevens:
    The Materialistic Americans, 115

26. Grover Cleveland:
    American Interests in the Cuban Revolution, 119

1897

27. John Philip Sousa:
    "The Stars and Stripes Forever," 124

28. John Dewey:
    My Pedagogic Creed, 125

29. Jane Addams:
    Foreign-Born Children in the Primary Grades, 130

30. Rufus R. Wilson:
    The Growth of an American School of Sculpture, 135

31. Josiah Quincy:
    City Government in America, 138

32. Susan B. Anthony:
    The Status of Woman, Past, Present, and Future, 144

33. *Songs of Errant Ladies,* 148
    Arthur J. Lamb:
    "A Bird in a Gilded Cage"
    Paul Dresser:
    "Just Tell Them That You Saw Me"

34. Theodore Roosevelt:
    Obstacles to Immediate Expansion, 150

35. Philip G. Hubert:
    The Business of a Factory, 152

36. Thomas B. Reed:
    Empire Can Wait, 158

37. William McKinley:
    The Alternatives in Cuba, 161

1898

38. *American Ultimatum to Spain,* 167
    March 26
    March 27

39. Albert Shaw:
    The Blowing Up of the Maine, 168

40. William McKinley:
    War Message, 173

41. Henry Watterson:
    The Right of Our Might, 193

42. Walter Hines Page:
    The Significance of the War with Spain, 195

43. Albert J. Beveridge:
The Taste of Empire, 198

44. Henry Holcomb Bennett:
"The Flag Goes By," 203

45. Thomas Davidson:
Schooling for Breadwinners, 204

46. William T. Harris:
Educational Creed, 211

47. Francis W. Parker:
Salvation on Earth Through Education, 214

48. Harry McClintock:
"Hallelujah, I'm a Bum," 215

49. Josiah Strong:
A Nation of Cities, 216

50. *Boss Rule and Ward Politics,* 220

51. George D. Herron:
Christianity and the Use of Private Property, 226

52. Furnifold M. Simmons:
For the Restoration of White Supremacy in North Carolina, 229

53. William McKinley:
The Acquisition of the Philippines, 231

54. Charles Denby:
The Evident Fitness of Keeping the Philippines, 233

1899

55. Morrison I. Swift:
Imperialism and the Threat to Liberty, 236

56. Rudyard Kipling:
"The White Man's Burden," 246

57. George Hoar:
The Lust for Empire, 248

58. Edwin Markham:
"The Man with the Hoe," 253

59. John Dewey:
The School and Social Progress, 255

60. Henry A. Rowland:
An Appeal for Pure Scientific Research in America, 262

61. Edwin M. Royle:
The Vaudeville Theater, 266

62. Bret Harte:
The Short Story in America, 273

63. Paul Dresser and Theodore Dreiser:
"On the Banks of the Wabash, Far Away," 278

64. *The Trusts in America,* 279
Aaron Jones:
A Farmer's View
Benjamin R. Tucker:
An Editor's View
John W. Hayes:
A Union Leader's View
Laurence Gronlund:
A Socialist's View
Clement Studebaker:
A Manufacturer's View

65. Elbert Hubbard:
A Message to Garcia, 309

66. John D. Rockefeller:
On the Advantages of Trusts, 312

67. Samuel M. Jones:
A Golden-Rule Government for Cities, 316

68. *Open Letter to President McKinley from Massachusetts African Americans,* 321

69. John Hay:
The Open Door Policy, 327

70. Alfred Thayer Mahan:
Arbitration and the Moral Aspect of War, 329

71. Charles Eliot Norton:
The Desertion of Ideals, 335

1900

72. Albert J. Beveridge:
In Support of an American Empire, 336

73. William Jennings Bryan:
The Paralyzing Influence of Imperialism, 345

74. Finley Peter Dunne:
Observations on the Philippines, 352

75. William Vaughn Moody:
   "An Ode in Time of Hesitation," 355

76. Charles Sanders Peirce:
   The Function of a University, 357

77. *The Evils and Advantages of Industrial Combinations,* 359

78. George Ade:
   Two Fables for Moneymakers, 365

79. *Railroading Songs,* 369
   "Casey Jones"
   "Wabash Cannonball"

80. Louis Sullivan:
   The Young Architect, 385

81. Finley Peter Dunne:
   Troubles of a Candidate, 387

1901

82. *The Employment of Women,* 390
   Henry T. Finck:
   Employments Unsuitable for Women
   Ida Husted Harper:
   Women Ought to Work

83. John Bates Clark:
   The Demos of the Future, 399

84. Thomas Hardy:
   "On an Invitation to the United States," 402

85. *The Padrone System,* 403

86. Frank Lloyd Wright:
   Art and the Machine, 409

87. Alexander Dowling:
   The Constitutionality of a Compulsory School Law, 417

88. Ida B. Wells Barnett:
   Lynching and the Excuse for It, 420

89. Brooks Adams:
   War as an Extreme Phase of Economic Competition, 424

90. William McKinley:
   Reciprocal Trade Agreements, 428

91. *Charter of the United States Steel Corporation,* 430

92. Theodore Roosevelt:
   Controlling the Trusts, 433

1902

93. Jacob Riis:
   The Streets and Alleys of the Poor, 437

94. Lyman Abbott:
   The Cause and Cure of Anarchism, 441

95. Amos P. Wilder:
   Governor La Follette and What He Stands For, 444

96. Daniel Mason:
   American Composers, 448

97. William J. Ghent:
   The Coming Economic Feudalism, 450

98. George F. Baer:
   On the Divine Right to Property, 455

99. Frank Norris:
   A Deal in Wheat, 456

100. "The Boll Weevil," 475

101. George Kennan:
   The Vested Rights of Reservation Indians, 476

102. Lincoln Steffens and Claude H. Wetmore:
   Corruption and Reform in St. Louis, 483

103. Jane Addams:
   Industrial Amelioration and Social Ethics, 487

104. Charles H. Vail:
   Principles of Socialism, 493

105. William Rainey Harper:
   Academic Freedom, 498

106. Hughie Cannon:
   "Bill Bailey, Won't You Please Come Home?," 502

107. *Declaration of the National Woman's Christian Temperance Union,* 503

1903

108. William Graham Sumner:
   An Abomination in Statecraft, 504

109. *Treaty with Cuba*, 507

110. William James:
The Ph.D. Octopus, 508

111. David Parry:
Organized Labor as the "Great Muscle Trust," 513

112. W. E. Burghardt Du Bois:
What African Americans Want, 519
The Spiritual Strivings of Black Folk
On Mr. Booker T. Washington

113. Delos O. Kinsman:
State Income Taxes, 528

114. S. S. McClure:
The Challenge of the Muckrakers, 533

1904

115. Ida M. Tarbell:
The Growth of the Standard Oil Company, 535

116. Lincoln Steffens:
The Shame of Our Cities, 542

117. George Washington Plunkitt:
Practical Politics, 559

118. George M. Cohan:
Nostalgia for Broadway, 567
"The Yankee Doodle Boy"
"Give My Regards to Broadway"

119. Thorstein Veblen:
Business and the Community, 568

120. George F. Roesch:
The Constitutionality of a New York Child Labor Law, 571

121. John M. Harlan and Oliver Wendell Holmes, Jr.:
Northern Securities Company v. *United States*, 576

122. Mark Hanna:
Socialism and the Labor Unions, 583

123. Robert Hunter:
Ten Million in Poverty, 586

124. Hugo Münsterberg:
The American Passion for Money Explained, 591

125. Theodore Roosevelt:
No Empire Without a Navy, 596

126. Andrew B. Sterling:
"Meet Me in St. Louis, Louis," 598

Volume 13
The
Progressive
Era

1905

1. Theodore Roosevelt:
Corollary to the Monroe Doctrine, 1

2. David Wilcox:
Government Control of Railroad Rates, 4

3. R. W. Peckham, J. M. Harlan, and O. W. Holmes, Jr.:
Lochner v. *New York*, 8

4. *Manifesto of the Industrial Workers of the World*, 16

5. Daniel De Leon:
The Political Power of Labor, 19

6. Louis D. Brandeis:
The Law and the Laboring Classes, 23

7. *Songs of Parody and Protest*, 26
Joe Hill:
"The Preacher and the Slave"
"Hold the Fort"

8. *Principles of the Niagara Movement*, 27

9. Richard R. Wright, Jr.:
African Americans in the Labor Movement, 30

10. Félix Klein:
The American Philanthropist, 35

11. Jack London:
How I Became a Socialist, 36

12. Vincent Bryan:
"In My Merry Oldsmobile," 39

1906

13. William P. Hepburn:
Regulation of Railroad Rates, 40

14. Finley Peter Dunne:
Lithrachoor and Andhrew Carnaygie, 42

15. David Graham Phillips:
The Political Trust, 45

16. John Vaughn:
Thirty Years of the Telephone, 63

17. Upton Sinclair:
The Meat-Packers of Chicago, 67

18. John A. Ryan:
The Right to a Living Wage, 76

19. George M. Cohan:
"You're a Grand Old Flag," 84

20. Florence Kelley:
Obstacles to Enforcing Child Labor Laws,
85

1907

21. Walter Rauschenbusch:
A Christian Alliance with Labor, 90

1908

22. Samuel L. Clemens ("Mark Twain"):
A Visit to Heaven, 94

23. Charles Sprague Smith:
A Creedless Church for a Creedless People,
106

24. George E. Walsh:
Entertainment for the Millions, 109

25. Frederick Dwight:
A Dim View of the Automobile, 113

26. Octave Chanute:
The Wright Brothers' Flights, 118

27. Giuseppe Giacosa:
Impressions of America, 120

28. Count Vay de Vaya und zu Luskod:
The Land of Mammon and Moloch, 123

29. Charles V. Tevis:
Tobacco War in Kentucky, 129

30. Arthur Twining Hadley:
The Constitution and Private Property, 133

31. Eugene V. Debs:
Capitalism and Socialism, 137

32. *The Social Gospel of the Protestant
Churches,* 142
Social Creed of the Methodist Episco-
pal Church
The Church and Industry

33. *Gentlemen's Agreement About Japanese Immigration,* 145

34. David Starr Jordan:
The Moral Aspect of the Protective Tariff,
147

35. Hervey White:
Our Rural Slums, 150

36. James J. Hill:
*The Natural Wealth of the Land and Its
Conservation,* 153

1909

37. Theodore Roosevelt:
The Conservation of Public Lands, 161

38. *Report of the President's Commission on
Country Life,* 165

39. Theodore Roosevelt:
The Threat of Japan, 173

40. William Howard Taft:
Defense of a High Tariff, 176

41. Daniel H. Burnham and Edward H.
Bennett:
Plan of Chicago, 181

42. Ellwood P. Cubberley:
*Education and the Changing National
Life,* 201

43. John D. Rockefeller:
The Difficult Art of Giving, 207

44. Morris Hillquit:
*Socialism and Individualism in Industrial
Life,* 212

45. Herbert Croly:
The Land of Promise, 214

46. Ben B. Lindsey:
    The Origin of the Juvenile Court, 227

47. Anonymous:
    The Achievement of Thomas A. Edison,
    231

48. Harry McClintock:
    "Big Rock Candy Mountain," 235

1910

49. Abraham Flexner:
    Medical Education in the United States,
    237

50. William Allen White:
    The Growth of Democracy in America, 247

51. Theodore Roosevelt:
    The New Nationalism, 250

52. William James:
    The Moral Equivalent of War, 254

53. Robert Henri:
    *The New York Exhibition of Independent
    Artists,* 260

1911

54. Albert G. Spalding:
    Our National Game, 265

55. Woodrow Wilson:
    Commission City Government, 269

56. William Howard Taft:
    Veto of Arizona Enabling Act, 272

57. George Santayana:
    *The Genteel Tradition in American Philoso-
    phy,* 277

58. Franklin P. Adams:
    "The Rich Man," 288

59. *A Labor-Management Agreement,* 303

60. Clarence Darrow:
    The Closed Shop, 304

61. E. D. White and J. M. Harlan:
    *Standard Oil Company of New Jersey et al.
    v. United States,* 310

62. Theodore Roosevelt:
    A Square Deal for the Trusts, 319

1911–1912

63. *Senate Hearings on Interstate Commerce,*
    322
    J. R. Moorehead:
    The Plight of Small Business
    C. U. Carpenter:
    A Justification of Big Business
    T. J. Brooks:
    The Antitrust Laws as Applied to
    Farmers

1912

64. William Dean Howells:
    The Cinematographic Show, 333

65. "The Titanic," 338

66. Mary Antin:
    The Promise of Free Education, 339

67. Louis D. Brandeis:
    Business as a Profession, 342

68. Walter E. Weyl:
    The New Spirit of Socialism, 345

69. *The Progressive Party Platform,* 347

70. Woodrow Wilson:
    The Fear of Monopoly, 356

71. Victor L. Berger:
    Socialism and Economic Evolution,
    361

72. James Oppenheim:
    "Bread and Roses," 363

73. *Recommendations of the Aldrich Commis-
    sion,* 364

74. William Howard Taft:
    The Cabinet and the Congress, 366

75. Henry Cabot Lodge:
    Corollary to the Monroe Doctrine, 368

76. William Howard Taft:
    Dollar Diplomacy, 369

1912–1913

77. *The Armory Show,* 374
    Walt Kuhn:
    Letter to Walter Pach

Frederick Gregg:
Preface to the Catalogue for the International Exhibition of Modern Art
Theodore Roosevelt:
Modern Art

1913

78. Lewis Einstein:
America and Anglo-German Rivalry, 378

79. Charles Nagel:
Against a Literacy Test for Immigrants, 397

80. *The Concentration of Economic Power,* 400

81. Louis D. Brandeis:
The Money Trust, 405

82. Woodrow Wilson:
First Inaugural Address, 412

83. Woodrow Wilson:
Repudiation of "Dollar Diplomacy," 415

84. Woodrow Wilson:
Rebuke to the Tariff Lobby, 417

85. P. Harvey Middleton:
Movies Speed Up Labor, 418

86. George K. Turner:
The Puzzle of the Underworld, 420

87. Charles A. Beard:
The Constitution as a Product of Economic Interests, 429

88. Elihu Root:
The Proper Pace of Political Change, 436

1914

89. *The Profit-Sharing Plan of the Ford Motor Company,* 449

90. Vachel Lindsay:
"Abraham Lincoln Walks at Midnight," 453

91. Mary Antin:
In Defense of the Immigrant, 454

92. Robert Frost:
"Mending Wall," 463

93. George Harvey:
Diplomats of Democracy, 464

94. Woodrow Wilson:
The Tampico Affair, 468

95. Walter Lippmann:
The Trusts and Private Property, 470

96. *The Clayton Antitrust Act,* 487

97. Woodrow Wilson:
Appeal for Neutrality, 491

98. Theodore Roosevelt:
On Speaking Softly and Carrying a Big Stick, 492

99. Carl Sandburg:
"Chicago," 499

1915

100. *Congressional Commission on Industrial Relations,* 501
Louis D. Brandeis:
Industrial Absolutism
John Lawson:
Working Conditions at Colorado Fuel and Iron

101. Ralph Chaplin:
"Solidarity Forever," 515

102. W. A. Hamor:
The Role of Chemistry in Industry, 516

103. Graham R. Taylor:
Industrial Suburbs, 520

104. Walker D. Hines:
Our Irresponsible State Governments, 523

105. Elihu Root:
The Invisible Government, 528

106. Van Wyck Brooks:
Highbrow and Lowbrow, 532

107. Walter Prichard Eaton:
Class-Consciousness and the Movies, 535

108. Joseph H. Odell:
Billy Sunday, 540

109. Washington Gladden:
Religion and the Public Schools, 546

110. Randolph Bourne:
Who Owns the Universities?, 551

111. *Proposals for Academic Freedom*, 554

112. Rufus M. Jones:
The Incompatibility of War and Christianity, 555

113. William Jennings Bryan:
American Protest Over the Sinking of the Lusitania, 559

114. Thomas Hoier:
"Don't Bite The Hand That's Feeding You," 562

115. Robert Herrick:
Recantation of a Pacifist, 563

116. Leonard Wood:
Military Unpreparedness, 566

117. Henry L. Stimson:
American Military Needs, 569

118. Francis G. Wickware:
Suspicions of Sabotage, 573

119. Edgar Lee Masters:
Spoon River Epitaphs, 576
"Anne Rutledge"
"Knowlt Hoheimen"
"Editor Whedon"

Volume 14
World War and
Prosperity

1916

1. Carl Vrooman:
The Revolution in Agriculture, 1

2. Warren H. Wilson:
The Interaction of Country and City, 4

3. J. J. Carty:
Pure Science and Industrial Research, 9

4. Howard E. Coffin:
Industrial Organization for National Defense, 14

5. R. F. Pettigrew:
Public Utilities and the People's Property, 20

6. John D. Rockefeller, Jr.:
The Partnership of Labor and Capital, 23

7. D. W. Griffith:
The Rise and Fall of Free Speech in America, 28

8. *The "New Manner" in Poetry*, 34
Amy Lowell:
The New Manner in Modern Poetry
Walter Lippmann:
Miss Lowell and Things

9. Carl Sandburg:
Poems for the People, 38
"To a Contemporary Bunkshooter"
"I am the People, the Mob"

10. William Howard Taft:
Limited Presidential Power, 41

11. John M. Work:
The Gold Brick Twins, 45

12. Oswald Garrison Villard:
Preparedness Is Militarism, 48

13. Simeon Strunsky:
Armaments and Social Class, 53

14. Charles W. Eliot:
Shall We Adopt Universal Military Service?, 60

1917

15. Woodrow Wilson:
Peace Without Victory, 65

16. Elihu Root:
The European War and the Preservation of America's Ideals, 70

17. Franz Boas:
Patriotism, 74

18. Woodrow Wilson:
War Message, 77

19. *Opposition to Wilson's War Message*, 101
Speech by George W. Norris
Speech by Robert M. La Follette

20. Norman Thomas *et al.*:
Tolerance for the Conscientious Objector,
111

21. *The Press in Wartime,* 115

22. George M. Cohan:
"Over There," 117

23. H. L. Mencken:
Puritanism as a Literary Force, 118

24. Ezra Pound:
Two Poems from Exile, 126
"The Rest"
"Salutation"

25. Doris Stevens:
*Suffragettes—Criminals or Political Prison-
ers?,* 127

26. Theodore Roosevelt:
The Children of the Crucible, 129

27. Charles A. Beard:
*Reasons for His Resignation from Columbia
University,* 131

1918

28. Randolph Bourne:
War as the Health of the State, 135

29. *Songs of World War I,* 140
"Hinky Dinky Parlay-Voo"
Sidney D. Mitchell:
"Would You Rather Be A Colonel
With An Eagle On Your Shoulder,
Or A Private With A Chicken On
Your Knee?"
Geoffrey O'Hara:
"K-K-K-Katy"

30. James Thurber:
University Days and Draft Board Nights,
143

31. *Interpretation of President Wilson's Fourteen Points,* 151

32. *The Archangel Expedition,* 158

33. Lenin:
An Open Letter to American Workers,
161

34. Woodrow Wilson:
*Appeal to the Voters to Return a Democratic
Congress,* 166

35. John B. Densmore:
The Mooney-Billings Case, 168

36. Carl Sandburg:
"Memoir of a Proud Boy," 174

37. Thorstein Veblen:
Business and the Higher Learning, 176

1919

38. Woodrow Wilson:
The League of Nations, 180

39. *Peace At Any Price,* 183

40. Woodrow Wilson:
*Appeal for Support of the League of Na-
tions,* 187

41. *The Senate and the League of Nations,* 194
Henry Cabot Lodge:
Reservations
Senate Debate

42. *Program of Social Reconstruction,* 208

43. *Government Mills in North Dakota,* 215

44. Andrew W. Mellon:
Industrial Research, 217

45. *Principles of Progressive Education,* 235

46. Vachel Lindsay:
"Bryan, Bryan, Bryan, Bryan," 237

47. Oliver Wendell Holmes, Jr.:
Abrams et al. v. *United States,* 244

48. Robert Benchley:
The Making of a Red, 248

1920

49. A. Lawrence Lowell:
The Management of Universities, 251

50. John J. Mahoney:
The Schooling of Immigrants, 255

51. J. McKenna and W. R. Day:
United States v. *United States Steel Corporation et al.,* 258

52. Lothrop Stoddard:
    The Crisis of the Ages, 266

53. George Santayana:
    Materialism and Idealism in the American Character, 270

54. W. L. George:
    Random Impressions, 276

1921

55. Franz Boas:
    A Refutation of the Concept of Race in America, 282

56. William Allen White:
    Criticism of the Ku Klux Klan, 284

57. James Bryce:
    Public Opinion in America, 285

58. Warren G. Harding:
    The Return to Normalcy, 292

59. Edward E. Purinton:
    Business as the Savior of the Community, 298

1922

60. George Sylvester Counts:
    The Selective Character of American Secondary Education, 304

61. Kirby Page:
    Labor Policies of the United States Steel Corporation, 310

62. *Child Labor in the Anthracite Coal Mines,* 319

63. Harry Emerson Fosdick:
    The Fundamentalist Controversy, 325

64. D. H. Lawrence:
    Benjamin Franklin, 331

65. George Jean Nathan:
    The Native Theater, 338

66. Deems Taylor:
    Music in the United States, 345

67. Frank Moore Colby:
    Humor in America, 351

68. H. L. Mencken:
    On Being an American, 354

1923

69. Anonymous:
    Listening In, 373

70. William Carlos Williams:
    "The Crowd at the Ball Game," 375

71. Thorstein Veblen:
    The New Order of Business, 376

72. Frank H. Knight:
    The Ethics of Competition, 385

73. G. Sutherland, W. H. Taft, and O. W. Holmes, Jr.:
    Adkins v. *Children's Hospital,* 391

74. E. E. Cummings:
    "the Cambridge ladies," 399

75. Louis Sullivan:
    The Chicago Tribune *Competition,* 400

76. William E. Borah:
    The Release of Political Prisoners, 405

77. Calvin Coolidge:
    The Destiny of America, 409

78. Sinclair Lewis:
    The Norse State, 414

79. Robert Frost:
    "A Brook in the City," 421

1924

80. *Objections to the Child Labor Amendment,* 422

81. Louis Marshall:
    Against Immigration Restrictions Based on National Origins, 423

82. Herbert Hoover:
    Moral Standards in an Industrial Era, 428

83. Thomas J. Walsh:
    Teapot Dome, 431

84. Henri Hauser:
    Observations on American Farming, 438

85. Lewis Mumford:
    Mechanical Architecture, 441

86. Andrew W. Mellon:
    Fundamental Principles of Taxation,
    445

87. *Drinking Songs of Prohibition,* 449
    "Away With Rum"
    "Little Brown Jug"
    "No More Booze"
    "How Dry I Am"

88. Robert L. Duffus:
    The Age of Play, 465

1925

89. Will Rogers:
    The Normal Majority, 469

90. Frederic C. Howe:
    Wartime Hysteria, 472

91. E. T. Sanford and O. W. Holmes, Jr.:
    Gitlow v. *New York,* 476

92. Robinson Jeffers:
    Two Poems, 481
    "Science"
    "Shine, Perishing Republic"

93. William Mitchell:
    Military Aviation and National Defense,
    482

94. Frederick Jackson Turner:
    Sectionalism and National Unity, 493

95. Edwin Arlington Robinson:
    "New England," 500

1926

96. Hawthorne Daniel:
    Living and Dying on the Installment Plan,
    501

97. E. E. Cummings:
    "next to of course god," 505

98. Hiram W. Evans:
    The Klan's Fight for Americanism, 506

99. Henry Pratt Fairchild:
    American Nationality and the Melting Pot,
    511

100. H. L. Mencken:
    Ring Lardner, 516

1927

101. Calvin Coolidge:
    Intervention in Nicaragua, 519

102. Roy A. Haynes:
    The Success of Prohibition, 523

103. Bartolomeo Vanzetti:
    Last Statement in Court, 527

104. Heywood Broun:
    Plea for Sacco and Vanzetti, 530

105. Oliver Wendell Holmes, Jr.:
    Nixon v. *Herndon,* 534

106. Alfred E. Smith:
    Defense of Catholics in Public Office, 536

107. Charles A. Lindbergh:
    Alone Over the Atlantic, 557

108. Andrew Furuseth:
    Work Is Worship, 561

109. Will Rogers:
    America Only, 564

110. Stephen Vincent Benét:
    "American Names," 567

1928

111. Calvin Coolidge:
    Veto of the McNary-Haugen Bill, 568

112. *Protest Songs of the Farmers,* 573
    Bob Miller and Emma Dermer:
    "Eleven Cent Cotton"
    "Down on Penny's Farm"

113. Benton MacKaye:
    Indigenous America, 575

114. Stephen Ewing:
    The Mockery of American Divorce, 577

115. Felix von Luckner:
    Prohibition in America, 583

116. John R. Tunis:
    The Great God Football, 585

117. Henry Ford:
    Youth, Industry, and Progress, 590

118. Herbert Hoover:
     Rugged Individualism, 595

119. James R. Randolph:
     Rockets and World Politics, 600

120. Allen Tate:
     "Ode to the Confederate Dead,"
     603

121. James Weldon Johnson:
     Race Prejudice and the African American Artist, 605

122. Stephen Vincent Benét:
     To the American Muse, 612

Volume 15
The Great
Depression

1929

1. Richard Müller-Freienfels:
   The Mechanization of American Life, 1

2. Robert S. and Helen Merrell Lynd:
   The Automobile and Family Life, 6

3. Robert E. Sherwood:
   Renaissance in Hollywood, 10

4. William Henry Nugent:
   The Sports Section, 16

5. E. Boyd Barrett:
   The Catholic Church Faces America, 22

6. William E. Borah:
   Western Farming and the Tariff, 28

1929–1931

7. *The Stock Market Crash*, 32
   Black Thursday on Wall Street
   Frederick Lewis Allen:
   Fear, Panic, and Forced Selling

1930

8. Sherwood Anderson:
   Lift Up Thine Eyes, 40

9. "The Death of Mother Jones," 44

10. Ernst Toller:
    Aimee Semple McPherson and the Movies, 45

11. *Southern Agrarians Take Their Stand*, 51

12. Edwin L. James:
    America as a World Power, 56

13. Archibald MacLeish:
    "American Letter," 59

14. Sinclair Lewis:
    The American Fear of Literature, 62

15. Hart Crane:
    "To Brooklyn Bridge," 70

1931

16. Henry L. Stimson:
    The United States and the Caribbean, 72

17. E. E. Cummings:
    "i sing of Olaf," 78

18. Herbert Hoover:
    Veto of the Muscle Shoals Bill, 79

19. *State-Controlled Apprenticeship in Wisconsin*, 82

20. Charles A. Beard:
    The Myth of Rugged American Individualism, 83

21. Robert M. La Follette, Jr.:
    Hoover and Unemployment, 93

22. Lotus D. Coffman:
    Adult Education for the Unemployed, 98

23. *American Emigrants to the Soviet Union*, 101

24. Florence Reece:
    "Which Side Are You On?," 115

25. F. Scott Fitzgerald:
    Echoes of the Jazz Age, 116

26. Frederick Lewis Allen:
    Alcohol and Al Capone, 122

27. Constance Rourke:
    Humor and the American Character, 126

1932

28. Oscar Ameringer:
Overproduction and Underconsumption, 129

29. Florence Converse:
"Bread Line," 132

30. Social Creed of the Protestant Churches, 133

31. Songs of the Hungry, 134
Jim Garland:
"I Don't Want Your Millions, Mister"
"Beans, Bacon, and Gravy"

32. Adolf A. Berle and Gardiner C. Means:
The Corporation and Private Property, 136

33. George Sutherland and L. D. Brandeis:
New State Ice Company v. Liebmann, 140

34. Malcolm Cowley:
The Flight of the Bonus Army, 148

35. George Soule:
Are We Going To Have a Revolution?, 152

36. Franklin D. Roosevelt:
Commonwealth Club Address, 158

37. Unemployment as a National Problem, 167

38. Franklin D. Roosevelt:
Call for Federal Responsibility, 185

39. Herbert Hoover:
Against the Proposed New Deal, 188

40. Henry Ford:
Advice to the Unemployed, 192

41. Teachers in the Depression, 194

1933

42. Senate Hearings on Federal Aid for Unemployment Relief, 197
Sumner H. Slichter:
National Assistance and Decentralized Control
Donald R. Richberg:
The Need for a Planned Economy

43. Franklin D. Roosevelt:
First Inaugural Address, 205

44. Business Stability and Government Regulation, 208

45. Franklin D. Roosevelt:
Progress of the Recovery Program, 210

46. Nathaniel Peffer:
A Warning to America, 213

47. Franklin D. Roosevelt:
Recognition of Soviet Russia, 219
First Letter to Mr. Litvinov
Second Letter to Mr. Litvinov

48. Henry A. Wallace:
Declaration of Interdependence, 220

49. Chester C. Davis:
Planned Harvests, 224

50. Ralph Borsodi:
The Family as a Unit of Production, 229

51. Learned Hand:
The Judge's Freedom Before the Law, 233

52. John M. Woolsey:
U.S. v. One Book Called Ulysses, 236

53. E. B. White:
"I Paint What I See," 240

54. Robert Morss Lovett:
A Century of Progress?, 241

1934

55. Abrogation of the Platt Amendment, 244

56. Walter Lippmann:
The Limits of Self-Reliance, 245

57. Harry L. Hopkins:
18,000,000 on Relief, 261

58. Franklin D. Roosevelt:
Relief, Recovery, and Reform, 263

59. John Maynard Keynes:
Notes on the New Deal, 268

60. The Goals of National Planning, 272

61. Henry A. Wallace:
Old and New Frontiers, 275

62. Louis Adamic:
New Americans, 279

63. Anonymous:
   Hollywood Against Upton Sinclair, 284

1935

64. Gardiner C. Means:
   The Making of Industrial Policy, 286

65. Hugh S. Johnson:
   The New Deal Experiment, 293

66. Charles Evans Hughes:
   A. L. A. Schechter Poultry Corporation et al. v. United States, 301

67. Franklin D. Roosevelt:
   The Second New Deal, 309

68. Franklin D. Roosevelt:
   A Program for Social Security, 315

69. Huey Long:
   Sharing Our Wealth, 318

70. Lawrence Dennis:
   American Fascism, 333

71. Henry A. Wallace:
   Pigs and Pig Iron, 336

72. Kenneth Fearing:
   "Dirge," 339

73. H. Richard Niebuhr:
   The Captive Church, 340

74. Bennett Champ Clark:
   Detour Around War, 344

75. Robinson Jeffers:
   "Rearmament," 349

1936

76. Louis D. Brandeis:
   The Ashwander Rules, 350

77. Franklin D. Roosevelt:
   The Good Neighbor Policy, 352

78. Frances Perkins:
   A Policy for Labor, 353

79. Robert Frost:
   "Two Tramps in Mud Time," 355

80. Selig Perlman:
   Collective Bargaining, 357

81. Norman Thomas:
   American Socialism, 360

82. H. L. Mencken:
   American English, 366

83. Huddie Ledbetter and John Lomax:
   "Goodnight Irene," 371

84. Otis Ferguson:
   Listening to Benny Goodman, 372

85. Robert Robins:
   Television, 376

86. Franklin D. Roosevelt:
   What the New Deal Has Done for Business, 379

87. Herbert Hoover:
   The New Deal and European Collectivism, 384

88. Charles E. Coughlin:
   Money Changers in the Temple, 388

89. *1936* Literary Digest *Poll,* 391

90. "Franklin D. Roosevelt's Back Again," 394

91. Stuart Chase:
   The Depletion of Our National Resources, 395

92. Robert M. Hutchins:
   American Higher Learning, 400

93. Horace M. Kallen:
   Toward a Consumer Economy, 407

94. Carl Sandburg:
   The People, Yes, 414

1937

95. *Supreme Court Reform,* 431
   Franklin D. Roosevelt:
   Address to the People
   Report of the Senate

96. *The Future of the Great Plains,* 445

97. Woody Guthrie:
   "So Long (It's Been Good To Know Yuh)," 452

98. Odette Keun:
   TVA in Foreign Eyes, 453

99. Aloisius Muench:
    Rural Families and Welfare, 462

100. *Urban Problems*, 466

101. Mary Ross:
    Why Social Security?, 471

102. Joel Seidman:
    The Sit-Down Strike, 475

103. *Labor Racketeering*, 484

104. William Allen White:
    The Challenge to the Middle Class, 486

105. Ferdinand Lundberg:
    The American Plutocracy, 492

106. Ralph Adams Cram:
    What Is a Free Man?, 498

107. Franklin D. Roosevelt:
    Quarantine the Aggressors, 502

1938

108. Chester I. Barnard:
    An Incentive Economy, 506

109. John L. Lewis:
    Industrial Unions, 511

110. Alfred Hayes:
    "Joe Hill," 515

111. Henry A. Wallace:
    Agricultural Policies of the New Deal, 516

112. John Collier:
    A New Deal for Native Americans, 523

113. Irving Berlin:
    "God Bless America," 525

114. Raoul de Roussy de Sales:
    Love in America, 526

115. *A Christian Social Order*, 541

116. *Report on Conditions in the South*, 542

117. Jonathan Daniels:
    Can the South Rule Itself?, 549

118. Joseph C. Grew:
    Protest Against Japan's "New Order" in the Far East, 555

1939

119. E. B. White:
    The Townsend Plan, 560

120. Granville Hicks:
    On Leaving the Communist Party, 565

121. Harold J. Laski:
    Federalism and Giant Capitalism, 567

122. Robert A. Taft:
    New Problems of Government, 571

123. Grace Overmyer:
    Report on the WPA Four Arts Project, 575

124. John Crowe Ransom:
    "Address to the Scholars of New England," 581

125. André Maurois:
    Impressions of a Long Voyage, 583

126. Culbert L. Olson:
    Migratory Labor and Civil Liberties, 587

127. John Steinbeck:
    Okies, 592

128. Albert Einstein:
    Letter to President Roosevelt, 601

Volume 16
The Second
World War
and After

1940

1. Archibald MacLeish:
    The Irresponsibles, 1

2. *Stop Hitler Now!*, 6

3. Franklin D. Roosevelt:
    The Hand That Held the Dagger, 8

4. Stephen Vincent Benét:
    "Nightmare at Noon," 11

5. Philip Murray:
    Collective Bargaining and Industrial Democracy, 15

6. Woody Guthrie:
"Union Maid," 21

7. James Bryant Conant:
Education for a Classless Society, 22

8. Wendell L. Willkie:
Acceptance Speech, 27

9. Franklin D. Roosevelt:
The Destroyer Deal, 31

10. Franklin D. Roosevelt:
Martin, Barton, and Fish, 36

11. Franklin D. Roosevelt:
Proposal for Lend-Lease, 40

1941

12. Franklin D. Roosevelt:
The Four Freedoms, 42

13. Burton K. Wheeler:
The Menace of Lend-Lease, 46

14. Frank Knox:
Lend-Lease and National Defense, 48

15. Joseph C. O'Mahoney:
The Defense of Economic Freedom, 61

16. Robert M. Hutchins:
America and the War, 66

17. Charles A. Lindbergh:
America First, 72

18. Zechariah Chafee:
Free Speech in America, 76

19. Donald Benedict *et al.*:
Why We Refused to Register for the Draft, 80

20. Franklin D. Roosevelt:
Discrimination in Wartime Employment, 82

21. W. C. Handy:
How the Blues Came To Be, 83

22. *The Atlantic Charter,* 89

23. Franklin D. Roosevelt:
Total National Defense, 90

24. Robert A. Taft:
Opposition to the Roosevelt War Policies, 94

25. Franklin D. Roosevelt:
Request for a Declaration of War, 103
Message to Congress
Fireside Chat

1942

26. Robert Frost:
"The Gift Outright," 109

27. Beardsley Ruml:
The Pay-As-You-Go Income Tax Plan, 110

28. Harold J. Ockenga:
Evangelical Christianity, 115

29. David Low:
Leonardo Da Disney, 120

30. Karl Shapiro:
"University," 123

31. *African American March on Washington,* 124
A. Philip Randolph:
Why Should We March?
Program of the March on Washington Movement

32. *War Songs,* 127
"I Got My Questionnairy"
"Gee, But I Want To Go Home"
Lew Brown, Charlie Tobias, and Sam H. Stept:
"Don't Sit Under the Apple Tree (With Anyone Else But Me)"
Frank Loesser:
"Praise the Lord and Pass the Ammunition"

1943

33. Franklin D. Roosevelt:
The Casablanca Conference, 130

34. Frederick C. Crawford:
Jobs, Freedom, and Opportunity, 132

35. "Talking Union," 138

36. Michael Darrock:
What Happened to Price Control?, 140

37. R. H. Jackson, Hugo Black, W. O. Douglas, and Felix Frankfurter:
West Virginia Board of Education et al. v. *Barnette et al.*, 148

38. Bill Steele:
What Should You Bring Overseas?, 179

39. Ernie Pyle:
Americans at War, 181

40. William L. Shirer:
American Radio Traitors, 187

41. Walter Lippmann:
Foreign Policy and Vital Interests, 192

42. Wendell L. Willkie:
Toward One World, 198

1943–1944

43. *Modern Painting in America*, 206
Stuart Davis:
The Dynamic American Scene
Adolph Gottlieb and Mark Rothko:
Aesthetic Credo
Jackson Pollock:
Universal Art

1944

44. Franklin D. Roosevelt:
A New Bill of Rights, 211

45. Frank T. Hines:
The G.I. Bill of Rights, 215

46. John Desmond:
Entertainers at the Front, 220

47. William Benton:
What a Free-Enterprise System Is and Is Not, 225

48. David E. Lilienthal:
The Tennessee Valley Authority, 230

49. H. Black, F. Frankfurter, F. Murphy, and R. H. Jackson:
Korematsu v. *United States*, 234

50. Denis W. Brogan:
American Schooling, 242

51. Gunnar Myrdal:
African American Leadership in North and South, 247

52. Reinhold Niebuhr:
Democracy and the Children of Light, 254

53. E. E. Cummings:
Poetical Reflections on America, 259
"plato told"
"a salesman is an it that stinks Excuse"

54. E. B. White:
Christmas 1944, 261

1945

55. Robert A. Taft:
Should the Government Guarantee Employment?, 263

56. Henry A. Wallace:
An Economic Bill of Rights, 268

57. John Fischer:
The Defects of Civil Service, 275

58. *General and Special Education in a Free Society*, 280

59. Ralph B. Wagner:
Public Relations, 285

60. Frank Lloyd Wright:
Architecture of Democracy, 301

61. *The Yalta Agreement*, 304

62. *The Act of Chapultepec*, 310

63. Luis Muñoz-Marín:
The Future of Puerto Rico, 312

64. *Second Thoughts About Atomic Power*, 316

65. *Charter of the United Nations*, 321

66. Arthur H. Vandenberg:
Sovereignty and the United Nations, 331

67. Harry S. Truman:
Announcement of the Dropping of an Atomic Bomb on Hiroshima, 334

68. William L. Laurence:
Atomic Bomb on Nagasaki, 337

69. Douglas MacArthur:
Today the Guns Are Silent, 339

70. *The Control of Atomic Energy*, 341

71. Harry S. Truman:
    Postwar Foreign Policy, 343

72. Eugene V. Rostow:
    Our Worst Wartime Mistake, 344

73. Allan Nevins:
    The Pearl Harbor Controversy, 350

1946

74. Louis N. Ridenour:
    Pilot Lights of the Apocalypse, 355

75. Bernard M. Baruch:
    A Choice Between the Quick and the Dead, 360

76. Winston Churchill:
    The Iron Curtain, 365

77. Henry A. Wallace:
    The Price of Peace, 370

78. William J. Donovan:
    Call for a Central Intelligence Agency, 391

79. James T. Farrell:
    Themes in American Realism, 395

80. *Responsibilities of Broadcasting*, 401

81. Hugo Black:
    United States v. *Lovett, Watson, and Dodd*, 404

82. "Hallelujah I'm A-Travelin'," 409

1947

83. Walter B. Weisenburger:
    Objections to Industry-Wide Collective Bargaining, 410

84. Robert A. Taft:
    Analysis of the Taft-Hartley Act, 414

85. Richard A. Lester:
    The "Labor Monopoly" Issue, 425

86. Merle Travis:
    "Sixteen Tons," 433

87. Harry S. Truman:
    The Truman Doctrine, 434

88. George C. Marshall:
    The Marshall Plan, 438

89. George F. Kennan:
    Sources of Soviet Conduct, 440

90. Harry S. Truman:
    Loyalty Order, 446

91. J. Edgar Hoover:
    The Menace of the Communist Party, 451

92. Henry Steele Commager:
    Who Is Loyal to America?, 457

93. David E. Lilienthal:
    This I Deeply Believe, 464

94. *Racial Discrimination in Washington, D.C.*, 466

95. Thomas E. Dewey:
    Public Service, 471

96. *Paternalism in Government*, 487

97. Percival and Paul Goodman:
    Community, 488

98. Jean Paul Sartre:
    Americans and Their Myths, 494

1948

99. Dwight D. Eisenhower:
    On the Unsuitability of Military Men for Public Office, 497

100. Henry C. Simons:
     Liberalism and a Free Society, 499

101. Harry S. Truman:
     Civil Rights Message, 510

102. Harry S. Truman:
     Desegregation of the Armed Forces, 513

103. *Universal Declaration of Human Rights*, 514

104. Arthur H. Vandenberg:
     Collective Security Within the United Nations, 518

105. Albert Einstein:
     An Open Letter to Russian Colleagues, 519

106. *House Un-American Activities Committee Report on Communism,* 523

107. Lee Hays and Walter Lowenfels: "Wasn't That A Time!," 527

108. E. B. White: *Sound,* 529

109. John Kouwenhoven: *Vernacular Art,* 530

110. Simone de Beauvoir: *Goodbye to America,* 542

1949

111. Harry S. Truman: *Inaugural Address,* 561

112. Robert A. Taft: *The Republican Party,* 565

113. Adolf A. Berle: *The Emerging Common Law of Free Enterprise,* 573

114. Bernard Iddings Bell: *An Indictment of American Education,* 578

115. *Debate on the North Atlantic Treaty,* 587
   Dean Acheson:
   For the Treaty
   Robert A. Taft:
   Against the Treaty

116. Harry S. Truman: *The Point Four Program,* 595

117. Alexander Meiklejohn: *Professors on Probation,* 600

118. Alistair Cooke: *A Generation on Trial,* 605

119. Bernard De Voto: *Due Notice to the FBI,* 608

120. Eleanor Roosevelt: *The United Nations,* 613

121. E. B. White: *The Capital of the World,* 617

Volume 17
Cold War in
the Nuclear Age

1950

1. Harry S. Truman: *The Hydrogen Bomb Program,* 1

2. Henry Cabot Lodge: *For Abolishing the Electoral College,* 2

3. Henry Steele Commager: *The American Political Party,* 6

4. Wayne L. Morse: *The Need for a Bipartisan Foreign Policy,* 11

5. Joseph R. McCarthy: *Communists in the State Department,* 16

6. Herbert H. Lehman: *Freedom and Individual Security,* 21

7. Joe Glazer: "Too Old To Work," 24

8. Martha Wolfenstein and Nathan Leites: *American Film Plots,* 25

9. Gilbert Seldes: *Pandora's Box—Television,* 28

10. William Faulkner: *Nobel Prize Acceptance Speech,* 33

11. Harry S. Truman: *United Nations Police Action in Korea,* 34

12. Harry S. Truman: *Veto of the Internal Security Act,* 35

13. Dean Acheson: *The Strategy of Freedom,* 42

14. Herbert Hoover: *Military Policy for the Cold War,* 46

15. *The Issue of Limited War in Korea,* 50
   The Joint Chiefs of Staff to General MacArthur
   General MacArthur to the Joint Chiefs of Staff

16. William R. Tansill: *Civil Supremacy Over the Military,* 67

1951

17. Harry S. Truman:
    Message to Douglas MacArthur, 73

18. Harry S. Truman:
    Korea and the Policy of Containment, 75

19. Douglas MacArthur:
    Farewell Address to Congress, 79

20. *Senate Report on Organized Crime,* 85

21. Russell W. Davenport *et al.*:
    The Transformation of American Capitalism, 89

22. John Courtney Murray:
    The State Church and Democratic Society, 96

23. Paul Campbell (The Weavers):
    "Kisses Sweeter Than Wine," 100

24. Thomas Hart Benton:
    Regionalism, 101

25. Mark Van Doren:
    "No Word, No Wind," 106

26. William Benton:
    For the Expulsion of Senator McCarthy, 108

1952

27. William O. Douglas:
    The Black Silence of Fear, 114

28. Charles B. Marshall:
    The Limits of Power Politics, 119

29. John Foster Dulles:
    A Policy of Instant Retaliation, 123

30. Eleanor Roosevelt:
    Defense of American Territorial Policies, 128

31. Harry S. Truman:
    Veto of the McCarran-Walter Immigration Act, 131

32. Peter F. Drucker:
    Productivity Is an Attitude, 137

33. Clarence B. Randall:
    American Industry and Executive Recruitment, 142

34. John Kenneth Galbraith:
    Countervailing Power, 147

35. William J. Grede:
    America, A Frontier, 154

36. Florence R. Kluckhohn:
    American Women and American Values, 159

37. John Dewey:
    On Progressive Education, 181

38. Aaron Copland:
    The Composer in Industrial America, 184

39. Harold Rosenberg:
    Action Painting, 189

40. Adlai E. Stevenson:
    Acceptance Speech, 196

41. Dwight D. Eisenhower:
    I Shall Go to Korea, 199

1953

42. John Foster Dulles:
    Containment or Liberation?, 204

43. J. Robert Oppenheimer:
    Atomic Weapons and American Policy, 206

44. Dwight D. Eisenhower:
    Atoms for Peace, 211

45. George Gallup:
    Mass Information or Mass Entertainment, 215

46. Mike Mansfield:
    Tidelands Oil for Education, 220

47. Daniel Bell:
    Crime, Ethnic Groups, and Urban Politics, 223

48. Langston Hughes:
    Bop, 228

49. Dwight Macdonald:
    Mass Culture, 230

50. Dylan Thomas:
    Life Among the Culture Vultures, 239

51. Joe Glazer:
    "Automation," 242

52. *A Letter to Presbyterians,* 243

53. Harry S. Truman:
    Reply to a Congressional Subpoena, 248

1954

54. John Foster Dulles:
    The Strategy of Massive Retaliation,
    250

55. Earl Warren:
    *Brown et al. v. Board of Education of
    Topeka et al.,* 253

56. David M. Potter:
    Democracy and Abundance, 258

57. Adolf A. Berle:
    *The Capitalist Revolution and "The City of
    God,"* 263

58. Agnes de Mille:
    Dance in America, 285

59. *The Oppenheimer Case,* 289
    Opinion of the AEC
    Opinion of Henry D. Smyth

60. George F. Kennan:
    A Cultural Curtain, 295

61. *Resolution of Condemnation of Senator Mc-
    Carthy,* 298

1955

62. Luther Youngdahl:
    United States v. *Lattimore,* 300

63. William Faulkner:
    On Privacy, 304

64. James MacGregor Burns:
    Republicans, Democrats—Who's Who?,
    311

65. *Federalism Today—A Report to the Presi-
    dent,* 316

66. Clifton Fadiman:
    King of the Tame Frontier, 322

67. *Unilateral Disarmament,* 326

68. Dwight D. Eisenhower:
    Open Skies Proposal to Russia, 330

69. Arthur Miller:
    The American Theater, 332

70. W. H. Auden:
    The Anglo-American Difference, 344

71. *Organizing the Unorganized,* 365

1956

72. Dwight D. Eisenhower:
    Veto of Natural Gas Bill, 370

73. *Declaration of Southern Congressmen on
    Integration of Schools,* 371

74. Herbert Ravenel Sass:
    Mixed Schools and Mixed Blood, 373

75. Woody Guthrie:
    "This Land Is Your Land," 378

76. Harlow H. Curtice:
    Automotive Research at General Motors,
    379

77. Ezra Taft Benson:
    Price Supports and Farm Surpluses,
    383

78. Frederick W. Copeland:
    The Illusion of Owning a Business, 389

79. *Interview with Billy Graham,* 393

80. Fred Allen:
    The Life and Death of Vaudeville, 400

1957

81. Dwight D. Eisenhower:
    The Crisis in the Middle East, 411

82. Max Lerner:
    American Speech, 416

83. Arthur J. Brodbeck and David M.
    White:
    How to Read "Li'l Abner," 422

84. Harvey Swados:
    The Myth of the Happy Worker, 427

85. James H. Gray:
    A Canadian Looks at America, 445

86. Ernest Gruening:
    Alaska's Fight for Statehood, 451

87. Dwight D. Eisenhower:
The Little Rock School Crisis, 457

88. Walter Lippmann:
The Portent of the Moon, 460

89. "Oh Russia, Let That Moon Alone!,"
462

90. Eugene Kinkead:
"Brainwashing" in Korea, 463

1958

91. Lyndon B. Johnson:
Political Credo, 469

92. Norman Cousins:
Wanted—Two Billion Angry Men,
473

93. Hubert H. Humphrey:
First Step Toward Disarmament, 475

94. Edward Teller and Albert L. Latter:
For Continued Experimentation with Nuclear Weapons, 480

95. Earl Warren:
Federal Court Congestion, 487

96. *Proposal to Limit the Power of the Supreme Court,* 491
William E. Jenner:
For Limiting Appellate Power
Thomas C. Hennings, Jr.:
Against Limiting Appellate Power

97. Earl Warren:
Perez v. *Brownell,* 499

98. John D. Williams:
The Nonsense About Safe Driving,
511

99. *Health and Medical Care,* 516

100. Lawrence Gowing:
The White of American Painters, 518

1958–1959

101. *Statehood for Hawaii,* 522
George W. Malone:
Against Statehood
Fred A. Seaton:
For Statehood

1959

102. John Foster Dulles:
Peace Through Law, 528

103. Henry B. du Pont:
The Greatest Invention of Them All, 530

104. Hyman G. Rickover:
Education, Our First Line of Defense, 536

105. Robert H. Thayer:
America's Cultural Relations Abroad, 545

1960

106. Dwight D. Eisenhower:
The U-2 Incident, 550

107. *The Super-City,* 554

108. Kenneth Allsop:
Black, White, and the Blues, 562

109. William D. Workman, Jr.:
The Case Against Forced Integration, 567

110. Karl Shapiro:
What Is American Poetry?, 575

111. David Riesman:
The Uncommitted Generation, 582

112. John F. Kennedy:
Address to the Ministers of Houston, 589

Volume 18
The Burdens of
World Power

1961

1. Dwight D. Eisenhower:
Farewell Address, 1

2. John F. Kennedy:
Inaugural Address, 5

3. John F. Kennedy:
Federal Aid to Education, 8

4. Newton N. Minow:
The Vast Wasteland, 12

5. Dean Rusk:
Formulating Foreign Policy, 20

6. Adlai E. Stevenson:
The Bay of Pigs, 25

7. Louis Eisenstein:
Tax Ideologies, 32

8. Orlando W. Wilson:
Police Arrest Privileges in a Free Society,
36

9. Barry Goldwater:
Total Victory in the Cold War, 42

10. *The Crisis of World Capitalism—A Soviet View*, 46

11. Walter Millis:
The Peace Game, 48

12. John F. Kennedy:
A Long Twilight Struggle, 54

1962

13. Melvin J. Lasky:
America and Europe, 58

14. Edward T. Hall:
Why Are We "Ugly Americans"?, 63

15. W. H. Ferry:
Problems of Abundance, 83

16. Michael Harrington:
Poverty in an Affluent Society, 88

17. J. S. Dupré and W. E. Gustafson:
Defense Contracting and the Public Interest,
94

18. Rachel Carson:
The "Control" of Nature, 101

19. *Senate Report on Urban Mass Transportation*, 108

20. Clement Greenberg:
Action Painting—A Reprise, 114

21. *Principles of the John Birch Society*, 118

22. Archibald MacLeish and Mark Van Doren:
Dialogue on the American Dream, 122

23. William J. Brennan, Jr.:
Baker v. Carr, 130

24. *On the School Prayer Decision*, 136

25. Lloyd W. Lowrey:
For Strengthening the States in the Federal System, 138

26. John F. Kennedy:
Soviet Missiles in Cuba, 140

1963

27. Martin Luther King, Jr.:
Letter from Birmingham Jail, 143

28. James Baldwin:
My Dungeon Shook, 149

29. John F. Kennedy:
African Americans and the Promise of America, 152

30. Martin Luther King, Jr.:
I Have a Dream, 156

31. *Songs of the Civil Rights Movement*, 160
"Oh Freedom"
"Which Side Are You On?"
"We Shall Not Be Moved"
"Keep Your Eyes on the Prize"
"Woke Up This Morning With My Mind Stayed on Freedom"
"Ain't Gonna Let Nobody Turn Me Round"
"This Little Light of Mine"
"We Shall Overcome"

32. Howard Morgan:
On the Staffing of Regulatory Agencies, 165

33. R. Sargent Shriver:
Two Years of the Peace Corps, 179

34. Jerome B. Wiesner:
Science in the Affluent Society, 186

35. John F. Kennedy:
For the Nuclear Test-Ban Treaty, 192

36. John F. Kennedy:
Undelivered Dallas Speech, 197

37. Mike Mansfield:
Eulogy for John F. Kennedy, 202

38. Lyndon B. Johnson:
Let Us Continue, 203

39. J. William Fulbright:
Violence in the American Character, 206

1964

40. Lyndon B. Johnson:
    The War on Poverty, 212

41. Lyndon B. Johnson:
    The Great Society, 216

42. Herbert Harris:
    Why Labor Lost the Intellectuals, 219

43. J. William Fulbright:
    Old Myths and New Realities, 225

44. Louis Lasagna:
    Problems of Drug Development, 232

45. *The Integrity of Science*, 238

46. *Conclusion of the Warren Commission Report*, 246

1965

47. John R. Tunis:
    Laugh Off $11 Million?, 252

48. *Corporate Support for the Performing Arts*, 255

49. *Mississippi Accepts the Civil Rights Law*, 259

50. Nathan Glazer:
    The Peoples of the U.S.A., 261

51. James Ridgeway:
    More Lost American Indians, 268

52. Edmund K. Faltermayer:
    The Half-Finished Society, 273

53. Ben J. Wattenberg and Richard M. Scammon:
    A Prophecy, 280

54. Eric Larrabee:
    Automation, Jobs, and Leisure, 285

55. Ralph Nader:
    Unsafe Automotive Design, 291

56. *Baiting the Hook with Merchandise*, 311

57. Adlai E. Stevenson:
    The Meaning of the United Nations, 317

58. Robert F. Kennedy:
    Counterinsurgency, 323

59. W. Averell Harriman:
    The Challenges to Peace and Freedom, 328

60. *The Sonic Boom*, 331

1966

61. Harry M. Caudill:
    Paradise Is Stripped, 333

62. Frank L. Whitney:
    The Total Redevelopment of Cities, 338

63. Charles F. Powers and Andrew Robertson:
    The Aging Great Lakes, 343

64. Eleanor Garst:
    The A-Sexual Society, 348

65. W. J. Brennan, Jr., H. Black, and W. O. Douglas:
    Ginzburg et al. v. United States, 350

66. Robert S. McNamara:
    Military Hardware, Economic Assistance, and Civic Action, 356

67. J. William Fulbright:
    The Arrogance of Power, 362

68. Lyndon B. Johnson:
    The Obligation of Power, 368

69. Stokely Carmichael:
    Black Power, 373

70. Kirk Douglas:
    On Patriotism, 380

71. Walter Lippmann:
    The University, 382

72. James S. Coleman *et al.*:
    Equal Opportunity in Education, 388

73. Andrew Hacker:
    Corporate America, 396

74. Tom C. Clark:
    Sheppard v. Maxwell, Warden, 402

75. Earl Warren and Byron R. White:
    Miranda v. Arizona, 427

76. Arnold L. Fein:
    The Warren Report and Its Critics, 435

1967

77. *Crime in a Free Society*, 442

78. Gerald Stern:
    Public Drunkenness—Crime or Health Problem?, 448

79. Richard N. Goodwin:
    The Growth of Federal Power, 455

80. *The Clorox Case*, 461

81. Herbert A. Deane:
    On the New Student Nihilism, 467

82. Tom Hayden:
    The Occupation of Newark, 472

83. Daniel P. Moynihan:
    The Politics of Stability, 484

84. *An Interview with Gunnar Myrdal*, 490

85. J. Anthony Lukas:
    The Case of a Runaway Flower Girl, 497

86. David Sanford:
    The Seedier Media, 500

87. *The View from Iron Mountain*, 502

88. Robert S. McNamara:
    Nuclear Strategy, 527

89. Irving Kristol:
    American Intellectuals and Foreign Policy, 535

90. Richard H. Rovere:
    Reflections on Vietnam, 544

91. Robert McAfee Brown:
    The Draft and Civil Disobedience, 554

92. *An End to the Draft?*, 558

93. Paul H. Douglas:
    Tax Loopholes, 560

94. Daniel S. Greenberg:
    The Politics of Pure Science, 567

95. Virlis L. Fischer:
    Water and the Southwest, 573

1968

96. Eugene Rabinowitch:
    Turning the Clock Toward Midnight, 578

97. Daniel X. Freedman:
    The Use and Abuse of Psychedelic Drugs, 583

98. Richard S. Lewis:
    The Kennedy Effect, 590

99. *Constitutional Reform in Maryland*, 596
    Clinton I. Winslow:
    Description of the Proposed Constitution
    Richard Homan:
    Account of the Defeat

100. Robert F. Kennedy:
     Vietnam—Illusion and Reality, 599

101. Eugene V. Rostow:
     The Choice in Foreign Policy, 605

102. Lyndon B. Johnson:
     Withdrawal Speech, 613

103. Thomas A. Johnson:
     African Americans in Vietnam, 617

104. *The Dollar Crisis*, 621
     Richard A. Nenneman:
     On the President's Measures
     The Dollar Under Siege

105. John W. Gardner:
     Poverty, 639

106. *Hunger in the United States*, 640

107. Robert B. Rigg:
     Military Occupation of the Cities, 643

108. *Business and the Urban Crisis*, 647

109. *On Civil Disorders*, 651

110. Martin Luther King, Jr.:
     Showdown for Nonviolence, 663

111. Erwin N. Griswold:
     Dissent, Protest, and Disobedience, 670

112. *Student Revolt*, 674
     Statement of Columbia Student Strikers
     Maurice B. Mitchell:
     Statement of the Chancellor of the University of Denver

113. Irving Kristol:
The Strange Death of Liberal Education,
677

114. Scott Buchanan:
A Message to the Young, 680

Volume 19
Detente and
Domestic Crises

1969

1. *Epilogue:*
The Legacy of 1968, 1
The Walker Report
Richard M. Nixon:
Bring Us Together

2. Richard M. Nixon:
First Inaugural Address, 8

3. George Wald:
A Generation Unsure It Has a Future,
12

4. John N. Mitchell:
What Kind of World Do You Want?, 15

5. Jesse B. Ritter, Jr.:
A Breakdown of Law and Order, 20

6. Jane Goodsell:
"Psychodelerium Tremens," 25

7. Walter J. McNerney:
Improving Medical Care, 26

8. *Open Letter to the U.S. Voter on Oil Taxes,*
31

9. Earl Warren:
Interview on Justice in America, 35

10. Neil Armstrong, Edwin E. Aldrin, and
Michael Collins:
The Moon Landing, 44

11. *Proclamation of the Delano Grape Workers,* 47

12. Joseph L. Rauh, Jr.:
Fraud and Violence in a Union Election,
53

13. J. B. Colwell:
*A Vindication of the Military-Industrial
Complex,* 57

14. *Debate on the Safeguard Antiballistic Missile,* 61

15. *Firearms and Violence,* 66

16. *Exchange of Letters between Richard M.
Nixon and Ho Chi Minh,* 71

17. *Poverty and the Welfare System,* 73

18. Jesse Jackson:
Letter from Jail on Black Economic Opportunity, 80

19. Edward W. Brooke:
The Philadelphia Plan, 82

20. Frank H. Mentz:
Open Letter to Congress on Vietnam, 84

21. Richard M. Nixon:
The Pursuit of Peace in Vietnam, 86

22. William P. Rogers:
Strategic Arms Limitation Talks, 92

23. Spiro T. Agnew:
The Television News Medium, 95

1970

24. *Santa Barbara Declaration of Environmental Rights,* 100

25. Theodore H. White:
Direct Elections—An Invitation to National Chaos, 102

26. Richard J. Daley:
Urban Housing Needs, 104

27. *Memorandum on the Proposed Equal
Rights Amendment,* 109

28. Abraham A. Ribicoff:
School Segregation in the North, 114

29. Daniel P. Moynihan:
Benign Neglect, 116

30. *Resolution Against Busing to Achieve Integration,* 120

31. Francesco Cordasco:
Survival of the Urban Catholic School, 121

32. Mortimer M. Caplin *et al.:*
Privacy of Income Tax Returns, 125

33. Richard M. Nixon:
The Cambodia Invasion, 127

34. *Kent State—May 4, 1970,* 132

35. Ben East:
Is It Taps for Wild Alaska?, 139

36. Gladwyn Hill:
After Earth Day, 145

37. Robert A. Campbell:
Federal Funding of Medical Research,
148

38. Jean-Jacques Servan-Schreiber:
The Multinational Challenge of the Seventies, 155

39. J. William Fulbright:
Old Myths and New Realities in the Middle East, 159

40. Theodore M. Hesburgh:
Civil Rights Enforcement, 166

41. A. J. Cervantes:
Revenue Sharing in the Cities, 170

42. Royal Little:
Interview on the Conglomerates, 175

1970–1973

43. *An All-Volunteer Army,* 179
Gates Commission Report, 1970
Interview with Lt. Gen. Bernard W. Rogers

1971

44. Jerome Rosow:
Blue Collar Blues, 187

45. Warren E. Burger:
Court Reform, 192

46. *The Winter Soldier Investigation,* 201

47. *Trial of Lieutenant William Calley,* 206
Lt. Calley:
Last Statement to the Court
Capt. Daniel:
Letter to President Nixon

48. John V. Lindsay:
New National Cities, 211

49. George Sternlieb:
The City as Sandbox, 213

50. Art Linkletter:
Drug Abuse, 218

51. Richard M. Nixon:
Wage and Price Controls, 222

52. Daniel Ellsberg:
Interview on the Pentagon Papers, 226

53. *Attica, September 1971,* 237

54. *The Police Crisis,* 249

55. Anthony W. Smith:
The Corporation and the Profit Motive, 254

56. Frank Church:
Farewell to Foreign Aid, 259

1972

57. Peter Harnik:
Funmobile Folly, 264

58. *The Leisure Boom,* 269

59. Erwin Knoll:
The Education of Henry Durham, 273

60. *The ITT Affair,* 279

61. *The Shanghai Communique,* 283

62. Arthur H. Westing and E. W. Pfeiffer:
The Cratering of Indochina, 286

63. Richard M. Nixon:
The Moscow Summit, 291

64. George S. McGovern:
Where I Stand, 299

65. *The Press as Watchdog,* 304

1973

66. Henry Kissinger:
Vietnam Truce, 309

67. Lewis F. Powell:
San Antonio School District v. *Rodriguez,* 313

68. Marlon Brando:
Unfinished Oscar Speech, 321

69. Karl E. Meyer:
The Traffic in Art and Antiquities, 323

70. Henry Kissinger:
The Year of Europe, 328

71. Fred R. Harris:
Oil—Capitalism Betrayed in Its Own Camp, 332

72. Dewey F. Bartlett:
The Energy Crisis, 337

73. Warren E. Burger and William O. Douglas:
Miller v. California, 340

74. Terry Bledsoe:
Black Dominance of Professional Sports, 346

75. Leonid I. Brezhnev:
Television Address to the American People, 349

76. John W. Dean III:
Watergate Testimony, 354

77. Richard M. Nixon:
Press Conference on Watergate, 371

78. John J. Sirica:
The Scope of Executive Privilege, 380

79. Edwin J. Holman:
Self-Governing the Medical Profession, 385

80. Ralph Nader:
The New Violence, 387

81. *Resignation of Spiro T. Agnew*, 390

82. *The Biggest Business in America*, 395

83. *Nairobi Draft on Monetary Reform*, 398

84. Nicholas deB. Katzenbach:
Reworking Foreign Policy, 404

85. *Managing in a Shortage Economy*, 413

86. Barry Commoner:
Is the Fuel Crisis Real?, 419

87. *The Crisis of Public Confidence*, 422

Volume 20
The Challenge of Interdependence

1974

The Crisis of the Presidency: *A Special Section* xlii

1. *Listen, Mr. Nixon*, 1

2. Warren E. Burger:
The U.S. v. Richard M. Nixon, 4

3. *Articles of Impeachment*, 16

4. Richard M. Nixon:
Release of Additional Transcripts, 20

5. Richard M. Nixon:
Resignation from the Presidency, 22

6. *A New President Is Sworn In*, 30

7. Gerald R. Ford:
First Address to Congress and the Nation, 32

8. Gerald R. Ford:
The Pardon of Richard Nixon, 36

9. *World Energy Conference Communiqué*, 39

10. Henry Kissinger:
American Policy Toward Southeast Asia, 42

11. Henry Kissinger:
The Challenge of Interdependence, 46

12. Francis A. J. Ianni:
The Ethnic Succession in Organized Crime, 51

13. Warren Shore:
Social Security—A Great Ripoff?, 58

14. *The Foreign Grab for U.S. Land*, 60

15. *Egyptian-American Relations*, 66

16. Arthur A. Hartman:
U. S.–Soviet Detente, 68

17. Richard M. Nixon:
Address to the People of the Soviet Union, 74

18. Walter Mondale:
Beyond Detente, 77

19. Gerald R. Ford:
Amnesty Program for Military Deserters and Draft Evaders, 86

20. *Allocation of the World's Resources*
A. Gerald R. Ford, 87
B. Carlos Andres Pérez, 89

21. *The Ordination of Women*
A. An Open Letter from the Ordaining Bishops, 93
B. Remarks by Carter Heyward, 94
C. Open Letter from Bishop Paul Moore, Jr., 95

22. Herbert Schlosser:
Responsibility and Freedom in Television, 96

23. June K. Edwards:
The Textbook Controversy, 100

24. *Pop Art,* 103

25. *Culture in America,* 107

1975

26. Edward S. Herman:
The U.S. and the Third World Economies, 117

27. William I. Spencer:
Policies of the Multinational Corporations, 121

28. *The Sports Boom Is Going Bust,* 127

29. Ron Fimrite:
Baseball Is Bigger Than Ever, 132

30. Claude E. Welch:
Medical Malpractice, 135

31. *No Alternative to Nuclear Power,* 142

32. Robert H. Boyle:
The PCB Menace, 144

33. Kenneth D. Kaunda:
America's African Policy, 147

34. *Pros and Cons of the Equal Rights Amendment,* 150

35. Patricia Hutar:
International Women's Year, 159

36. Henry Kissinger:
The Evacuation of Vietnam, 164

37. Gerald R. Ford:
The Mayaguez Incident, 168

38. Ellsworth Bunker:
Panama and the U.S., 169

39. Aleksandr Solzhenitsyn:
America, You Must Think About the World, 173

40. Gerald R. Ford:
Address to the Helsinki Conference, 182

41. Norman Macrae:
Agenda for a World Leader, 186

42. *The U.S. Postal Service Crisis,* 191

43. Floyd Harrington:
CB Radios, 195

44. Eldridge Cleaver:
Why I Am Returning to the U.S., 199

45. Daniel P. Moynihan:
The United Nations Resolution on Zionism, 201

46. Konstantin Bushuyev:
A Soviet View of the Soyuz-Apollo Project, 207

47. *Rockefeller Panel Report on Illegal CIA Activities,* 210

48. *CIA Assassination Plots,* 217

49. *New York City's Fiscal Crisis,* 221

50. *African Americans and the National Economy,* 231

51. David M. Alpern:
Big Government, 235

52. *Objections to Astrology,* 239

1975–1976

53. *The Task of the Churches—Two Views,* 241

54. *The Right to Die,* 253

1976

55. *The Flow of Wealth and Population to the Sunbelt,* 262

56. Martin Kaplan:
    The Ideologies of Tough Times, 271

57. *Senate Committee Findings on Illegal Intelligence Activities,* 276

58. Daniel Schorr:
    Congress and Freedom of the Press, 285

59. Stephen A. Bennett:
    Fair Trial v. Free Press, 287

60. Neal R. Peirce:
    The "Sunset" Challenge to Bureaucratic Growth, 290

61. *What Future for the American Family?,* 292

62. *The Plight of American Education,* 295

63. John A. Coleman:
    The Crisis of American Catholicism, 299

64. *Immigrants in the Labor Market,* 307

65. Eli Ginzberg:
    The Pluralistic Economy of the U.S., 309

66. Anthony Sampson:
    The Lockheed Connection, 321

67. *Coping With Terrorism,* 325

68. Carl Sagan:
    The Viking Landing on Mars, 331

69. Thomas A. Vanderslice:
    Technology as Problem Solver, 336

70. R. Emmett Tyrrell:
    The American Novel in Decline, 342

71. Henry Fairlie:
    Eating in America, 344

72. Jimmy Carter:
    Acceptance Speech, 347

    The American Bicentennial:
    A *Special Report*

73. *The Bicentennial Celebration,* 352

74. Archibald MacLeish:
    Bicentennial of What?, 356

75. Ourselves as Others See Us:
    Foreign Press Commentary on the U.S. in the Bicentennial Year, 360

Volume 21
Opportunities and Problems at Home and Abroad

1977

1. Marlene W. Lehtinen and Gerald W. Smith:
   Debate on Capital Punishment
   A: Lehtinen:
      An Argument for the Death Penalty, 1
   B: Smith:
      Arguments Against the Death Penalty, 6

2. Gerald R. Ford:
   State of the Union Address, 11

3. Jimmy Carter:
   Inaugural Address, 14

4. Jimmy Carter:
   Letter to Andrei Sakharov, 17

5. George F. Kennan:
   "Democracy" as a World Cause, 18

6. Jimmy Carter:
   The Moral Equivalent of War, 22

7. Anita Bryant and Brian McNaught:
   Gay Rights
   A: Bryant:
      The Battle for Miami, 27
   B: McNaught:
      Why Bother with Gay Rights?, 31

8. Midge Decter:
   Looting and Liberal Racism, 36

9. Jimmy Carter:
   Amnesty for Illegal Aliens, 44

10. Herman Badillo, Hans F. Sennholz, Richard S. Schweiker, and Morgan F. Murphy:
    Controversy About Illegal Aliens, 46

11. Paul Simon and Jesse Helms:
The Panama Canal Treaties—Pro and Con, 53

12. Edward M. Kennedy:
The Case for Airline Deregulation, 56

13. Knut Hammarskjöld:
What to Do About Hijacking, 59

14. Marilyn French:
The National Women's Conference, 65

1978

15. *A Declaration for Older Persons,* 71

16. Cy Brickfield:
Our Aging Workforce, 73

17. *Proposition 13*
A: Jerry McCaffery and John H. Bowman:
Participatory Democracy—The Effects of Proposition 13, 78
B: William A. Norris:
The Constitutional Attack, 89

18. Arthur F. Burns and Jimmy Carter:
"Our Most Serious Domestic Problem," 91

19. *The Bakke Case*
A: Charles Lawrence III:
The Bakke Case—A Preview, 96
B: Editorial:
The Bakke Case in a Higher Court, 103

20. Andrew Young:
U.S. Political Prisoners, 105

21. Vine Deloria:
Civilization and Isolation—A Native American View, 106

22. *The Camp David Accords,* 114

23. David G. Winter, Abigail J. Stewart, and David C. McClelland:
Advantages of a Liberal Arts Education, 119

24. Fred Friendly:
The Public's Right to Know, 125

25. *The Jonestown Tragedy,* 129

1979

26. *The Reopened Door: Reestablishment of Relations with China*
A: George H. Dixon:
Speech, 135
B: Sen. John Heinz:
Statement Concerning Resolution to Approve Extension of U.S.-China Trade Agreement, 140

27. *Three Mile Island and the Future of Nuclear Energy*
A: Sen. James A. McClure:
Speech, 141
B: Ken Bossong:
Editorial, 144

28. John C. Sawhill:
The Collapse of Public Schools, 146

29. Lee Iacocca:
The Chrysler Bailout, 150

30. Cyrus Vance, Paul H. Nitze, and Henry Kissinger:
Views of SALT II, 154

31. *Visit to the United States of John Paul II,* 163

32. Orville Bach:
The Little Fish and the Big Dam, 166

33. Jimmy Carter:
A National Malaise, 170

1979–1981

34. *The Iranian Hostage Crisis, 1979–1981,* 173

1980

35. George McGovern:
The Soviet Grain Embargo of 1980, 201

36. *The Humanities in American Life,* 205

37. *The Gold Boom,* 209

38. James R. Arnold:
The Frontier in Space, 214

39. Irvin R. Nathan:
ABSCAM Ethics, 224

40. Malcolm E. Wheeler:
    The Pinto Case, 235

41. Walter Jacob:
    Refugees and Their Problems, 242

42. Lisa Birnbach:
    The Preppy Handbook, 247

43. Jesse Helms, Edward M. Kennedy, and Thomas Emerson:
    School Prayer, 248

44. Red Smith:
    On Playing in Ivan's Yard, 254

45. Ronald Reagan:
    Acceptance Speech, 256

46. Richard M. Scammon and Ben J. Wattenberg:
    Is It the End of an Era?, 259

1981

47. Clifford M. Hardin:
    Can a President Control His Own White House?, 267

48. Ronald Reagan:
    First Inaugural Address, 274

49. Ronald Reagan:
    Address to the Nation on the Economy, 279

50. George Gilder:
    Supply-Side Economics, 285

51. *Reagan Administration Review of the Iran Hostage Agreements,* 291

52. Russell Baker:
    Indians Did It in Smoke, 293

53. Ira Berkow:
    The Baseball Effect on America, 295

54. Ronald Reagan:
    Responses to an Assassination Attempt, 299

55. *Overselective Service,* 300

56. *The Strike of the Air Traffic Controllers,* 304

57. James G. Watt:
    Interview, 310

58. *The Environmental Super-Fund: Moynihan vs. Gorsuch,* 317

59. William Greider:
    The Education of David Stockman, 321

1982

60. Ronald Reagan:
    The State of the Union, 341

61. David Durenberger:
    The New Federalism, 345

62. John Kenneth Galbraith:
    Mr. Reagan's Deficit, 348

63. Ronald Reagan:
    Address on Tax and Budget Reconciliation, 355

64. Bruce J. Ennis:
    The Insanity Defense, 360

65. David C. Anderson:
    30 Million Handguns, 364

66. *The "Law of the Sea" Treaty*
    A: *Statement by the President,* 368
    B: Lee H. Hamilton:
       Speech to the House, 370

67. Louis Harris:
    Public Attitudes Toward the Threat of Nuclear War, 372

68. William J. Brennan, Jr., and Warren E. Burger:
    Educational Rights of Illegal Aliens, 376

69. William Safire:
    The Computer Tattoo, 380

70. John Egerton and John Holt:
    Can We Save the Schools?
    A: Egerton:
       Yes, But There Isn't Much Time, 382
    B: Holt:
       No, and They're Not Worth Saving, 386
    C: Egerton:
       But What Are the Alternatives?, 389

71. Mortimer J. Adler:
    The Paideia Proposal, 390

72. Geraldine A. Ferraro:
    Who Will Fight for the Worth of Women's Work?, 393

73. Ludmilla Thorne:
    The Littlest Defector, 399

74. *Prolonging Death Is No Triumph,* 405

75. Annie Dillard:
    Living Like Weasels, 406

1983

76. *A Nation at Risk,* 410

77. *Environmental Protection Reagan Style*
    A: *The President's Press Conference,* 413
    B: *The Filthiness Issue,* 414

78. *Who Will Stop the Acid Rain?,* 418

79. *The Challenge of Peace,* 422

80. Hugh Sidey:
    How to Do Nothing Well, 425

81. John Noble Wilford:
    Farewell to Pioneer, 427

82. *Overturn of the Legislative Veto,* 429

83. Larry Long and Diana DeAre:
    The Slowing of Urbanization, 432

84. Robert Heilbroner:
    Economic Prospects, 436

85. Barbara Honegger and Hans Küng:
    Women's Challenge
    A: *Honegger:*
        The ERA Alternative, 442
    B: *Küng:*
        Will the Pope Win Over Women?, 446

86. *Private Violence,* 448

87. *The Destruction of Korean Airlines Flight 007,* 453

88. Ronald Reagan:
    The Beirut Massacre, 455

89. *The Long Report*
    A: *The Commission's Report,* 459
    B: *Remarks by the President,* 462

90. John McClaughry:
    The Case Against Reverend Moon, 463

91. Chester E. Finn, Jr.:
    How to Lose the War of Ideas, 468

1984

92. Michael Harrington and W. Warren Wagar:
    Nineteen Eighty-Four
    A: Harrington:
        That Year Is Here, 473
    B: Wagar:
        The Year That Never Came, 476

93. Richard P. Turco, Owen B. Toon, Thomas P. Ackerman, James B. Pollack, and Carl Sagan:
    The Climatic Effects of Nuclear War, 478

94. *Politics and Bathhouses,* 489

95. Nancy Shulins:
    Not in My Backyard, 491

96. *Interviews with King Hussein and President Assad,* 497

97. *Beauty Pageants,* 504

98. Mark Helprin:
    Liberty Enlightening the World, 507

99. *Ads For Prescription Drugs,* 510

100. Mario Cuomo:
    Keynote Address, 514

101. Jesse Jackson:
    Campaign Speech, 521

102. *The 1984 Olympics,* 526

103. Lowell P. Weicker, Jr.:
    Religion in Politics, 531

104. *American Ignorance*
    A: Kalev Pehme:
        Who Reads Great Books?, 535
    B: Bill Granger:
        Ignorance—Our Cultural Blight, 536

105. Glenn Doman:
    Function Determines Structure, 538

106. Daniel J. Boorstin:
    Myths of a Scientific Society, 541

107. Gerald W. McEntree:
    Labor Strategy Next Time, 545

108. *Pastoral Letter on the U.S. Economy, 547*

1985

109. James Cook:
     Nuclear Follies, 550

110. Myra and David Sadker:
     Sexism in the Classroom, 561

111. *Visit to Bitburg, 566*

112. Ronald Reagan:
     A Tax System That Is Unwise, Unwanted, and Unfair, 569

113. Nancy Johnson and George Kittle:
     Aid to the Contras
     A: Representative Johnson:
        Aid to the Contras, 574
     B: Kittle:
        What the Contra Aid Vote Means, 575

114. *The Taking of TWA Flight 847*
     A: *The President's Press Conference, 579*
     B: Ze'ev Chafets:
        Why the U.S. Was a Target, 581
     C: Charles Krauthammer:
        Looking Evil Dead in the Eye, 582

115. Robert MacNeil:
     The Mass Media and Public Trust, 585

116. *What Will the Bank Dicks Do Now?, 593*

117. Phoebe Ellsworth:
     Juries on Trial, 598

118. *A World Without Insurance?, 602*

119. Stuart M. Butler:
     The Privatization of the Postal Service, 606

120. *The Hands of Anger, Frustration, Humiliation, 608*

1986

121. *For and Against a One-Term Presidency*
     A: Griffin R. Bell, Herbert Brownell, William E. Simon, and Cyrus Vance:
        For a Single Six-Year Presidential Term, 610

     B: Arthur Schlesinger, Jr., *For the Status Quo, 612*

122. *The End of* Challenger
     A: John Noble Wilford:
        News Article, 614
     B: *Rogers Commission Report, 617*
     C: Comment by *Scientific American, 620*

123. Oriana Fallaci:
     The Europeans' Qaddafi Cowardice, 623

124. John Halford:
     Cultural Terrorism, 626

125. Roger Morris:
     Reclaiming the Reclamation Beat, 629

126. Desmond M. Tutu:
     Sanctions vs. Apartheid, 634

127. Ben Sharp and Dan Sharp:
     What Soccer Means, 636

128. Byron R. White and Harry A. Blackmun:
     Crime in the Bedroom, 638

129. Theodore H. White:
     The American Idea, 645

130. Steven Greenhouse:
     The Average Guy Takes It on the Chin, 647

131. Alice Hughey:
     The Changing Face of Star Wars, 651

132. Stephen M. Walt:
     Reagan Has Fooled Us Again, 655

133. Don McLeod:
     Democrats on the Budget Bandwagon, 657

134. Adam Platt:
     The Japanese Look Is Here to Stay, 660

135. *Arms to Iran, Money to the Contras, 663*

SUMMARY INDEX OF
AUTHORS AND SOURCES IN
THE ANNALS OF AMERICA

Abbot, Francis Ellingwood
The Demands of Liberalism (editorial): The Index, Jan. 1, 1874, **10:**299–300

Abbott, Lyman
Anarchism: Its Cause and Cure, 1902, **12:**441–44

Acheson, Dean
Speech in Senate on the North Atlantic Treaty: Mar. 19, 1949, **16:**587–91
The Strategy of Freedom, Nov. 29, 1950, **17:**42–45

Ackerman, Thomas P. et al.
The Climatic Effects of Nuclear War: Scientific American, Aug. 1984, **21:**478

Adamic, Louis
Thirty Million New Americans: Harper's, Nov. 1934, **15:**279–84

Adams, Abigail
Letter to John Adams, Nov. 27, 1775, **2:**362–63
Letter to Thomas Jefferson, Jan. 2, 1787, **3:**80–81
Letter to Thomas Jefferson, July 1, 1804, **4:**191–93

Adams, Brooks
Reciprocity or the Alternative: Atlantic Monthly, Aug. 1901, **12:**424–27

Adams, Charles Francis, Jr.
A Chapter of Erie: North American Review, July 1869, **10:**164–78

Adams, Franklin Pierce
The Rich Man (poem), **13:**288

Adams, Henry (Brooks)
Civil-Service Reform: North American Review, Oct. 1869, **10:**210–14

Adams, John
Instructions of the Town of Braintree [Mass.] to Their Representatives (on the Stamp Act), Oct. 14, 1765, **2:**154–55
Novanglus, No. VII: Massachusetts Gazette, Feb. 6, 1775, **2:**308–12
Autobiography (on formation of new state governments), 1775, **2:**329–34
Letter to Abigail Adams, Oct. 29, 1775, **2:**367
Letter to George Wythe, Jan. 1776, **2:**410–12

Letter to James Sullivan, May 26, 1776, **2:**422–23
Letter to Samuel Adams, July 28, 1778, **2:**503–4
Letter to John Jay, May 8, 1785, **3:**21–23
Letter to Benjamin Waterhouse, Aug. 7, 1805, **4:**196–98
Letter to Benjamin Waterhouse, July 12, 1811, **4:**290
Letter to Benjamin Waterhouse, Mar. 11, 1812, **4:**311–13
Letter to William Keltelas, Nov. 25, 1812, **4:**324–25
Letters to Thomas Jefferson, July–Nov. 1813, **4:**331–39 *passim*
The "American Revolution": Niles' Weekly Register, Mar. 7, 1818, **4:**465–69

Adams, John Quincy
Letter to John Adams, Dec. 21, 1817, **4:**464
Memoirs (on the Missouri Compromise), Mar. 3, 1820, **4:**589–91
Letter to Henry Middleton, July 5, 1820, **4:**642–44
Memoirs (on the relations with Latin America), Mar. 9, 1821, **5:**26–27
Letter to Hugh Nelson, Apr. 28, 1823, **5:**57–61
Memo to Baron Tuyl (on hemispheric security), July 17, 1823, **5:**61–62
Letter to Richard Rush, July 22, 1823, **5:**62–65
Memoirs (on America and the Holy Alliance), Nov. 7, 1823, **5:**71–73
Inaugural Address, Mar. 4, 1825, **5:**138–42
First annual message to Congress, Dec. 6, 1825, **5:**185–88
Message to Congress on Panama Congress, Dec. 26, 1825, **5:**188–90
The Jubilee of the Constitution, A Discourse, Apr. 30, 1789, **6:**471–79

Adams, Samuel
Report of the Committee of Correspondence to the Boston Town Meeting, Nov. 20, 1772, **2:**217–20
Speech in Massachusetts Ratifying Convention,

Jan. 31, 1788, **3:**251–52

Addams, Jane
Foreign-Born Children in the Primary Grades, July 1897, **12:**130–35
Democracy and Social Ethics, 1902, **12:**487–93

Ade, George
More Fables, 1900, **12:**365–68

Adler, Mortimer J.
The Paideia Proposal, Chs. 1, 11, 1982, **21:**390

Agassiz, Louis
Letter to Samuel Howe, Aug. 9, 1863, **9:**434–36

Agnew, Spiro T.
Television News Coverage: An address to the Midwest Regional Republican Committee, Nov. 13, 1969, **19:**95
Letter to President Richard M. Nixon, Oct. 10, 1973, **19:**390
Statement in U.S. District Court at Baltimore, Oct. 10, 1973, **19:**390

Albright, Madeleine K.
Speech on American involvement in the United Nations, Jan. 1995, **22:**262

Aldrin, Edwin E.
Speech to a Joint Session of Congress, Sept. 16, 1969, **19:**44

Alexander, James
A Brief Narrative of the Case and Trial of John Peter Zenger, Printer of the New York Weekly Journal (Stanley N. Katz, ed.), 1963, **1:**397–417
The Querist: or, A Letter to a Member of the General Assembly of the Colony of New-York, May 30, 1754, **1:**503–5

Alfriend, Frank H.
Editorial on a Southern national literature: Southern Literary Messenger, May 1864, **9:**491–93

Alison, Francis
Letter to Ezra Stiles, May 27, 1759, **2:**46–47

Allen, Fred
Much Ado About Me, 1956, 17:400–10

Allen, Frederick Lewis
Only Yesterday, 1931, **15:**34–39; 122–25

Allen, John (Long John)
Speech in Congress on the Sedition Act, July 5, 1798, **4:**53–56

Allsop, Kenneth
Black, White, and the Blues (Letter from Chicago): Encounter, Apr. 1960, **17:**562–67

Alpern, David M.
Big Government: Newsweek, Dec. 15, 1975, **20:**235

Altgeld, John Peter
Reasons for Pardoning the Haymarket Rioters (Fielden, Neebe, and Schwab), 1893, **11:**438–44
Speech to the Laboring Men of Chicago, Sept. 8, 1893, **11:**445–50
Telegrams to Grover Cleveland, July 5–6, 1894, **11:**525–29

Alumnus, An (pseud.) *see* Engelhard, John A.

American, An (pseud.) *see* Morse, Samuel F. B.

Americanus (pseud.) *see* Hamilton, Alexander

Ameringer, Oscar
Testimony before House Subcommittee of the Committee on Labor, Feb. 1932, **15:**129–31

Ames, Fisher
Letter to Timothy Pickering, July 10, 1798, **4:**68–70
The Dangers of American Liberty, 1805, **4:**201–3

Ames, Nathaniel
A Thought Upon the Past, Present, and Future State of North America: Astronomical Diary and Almanack, 1758, **2:**28–29

Anderson, David C.
30 Million Handguns: Across the Board, Feb. 1982, **21:**364

Anderson, Sherwood
Lift Up Thine Eyes: Nation, May 28, 1930, **15:**40–43

Andrews, Christopher C.
Minnesota and Dacotah: In Letters Descriptive of a Tour Through the North-West, 1856, **8:**378–83

Anthony, Susan B.
The Status of Woman, Past, Present, and Future: Arena, May 1897, **12:**144–48

Antin, Mary
The Promised Land, 1912, **13:**339–42
They Who Knock at Our Gates, 1914, **13:**454–62

Applegate, Jesse
A Day with the Cow Column, 1843, **7:**89–95

Appleton, Nathan
Labor, Its Relations in Europe and the United States Compared, 1844, **7:**163–68

Armey, Dick
Congressional debate on the Arts, Humanities, and Museums Amendments, Oct. 11, 1990, **22:**108

Armstrong, Neil
Speech to a Joint Session of Congress, Sept. 16, 1969, **19:**44

Arnold, James R.

The Frontier in Space: American Scientist, May–June 1980, **21**:214

Arnold, Matthew
Civilization in the United States, 1888, **11**:194–97

Arp, Bill (pseud.) *see* Smith, Charles H.

Atchison, Rena M.
Un-American Immigration: Its Present Effects and Future Perils, 1894, **11**:506–8

Aten, Ira
Letter to L. P. Seiker, Aug. 31, 1888, **11**:199

Auden, W(ystan) H(ugh)
The Anglo-American Difference: The Anchor Review, 1955, **17**:344–50

Audubon, John James
Ornithological Biography (*Delineations of American Scenery and Character*), 1831–1839, **6**:92–97

Austin, Moses
Journal (on traveling across the Ohio Valley to the Mississippi River), Mar. 25, 1797, **4**:1–9

Babatunde, Jose, Jr.
Editorial on the Bicentennial: Sunday Tide (Port Harcourt), July 3, 1976, **20**:375

Bach, Orville
The Late Little T: A Lesson in Defeat, Outdoor Life, Oct. 1980, **21**:166

Backus, Isaac
Memorial to Massachusetts Assembly in behalf of the Warren Association, Sept. 1775, **2**:366

Badillo, Herman *et al.*
Testimony on illegal aliens: Congressional Digest, Oct. 1977, **21**:46

Baer, George Frederick
Letter to W. F. Clark, July 17, 1902, **12**:455

Baker, Richard
Opinion of the (*Norfolk, Va., Circuit*) *court in the trial of Mrs. Margaret Douglass,* 1854, **8**:224–26

Baker, Russell
Indians Did It in Smoke: The New York Times, Mar. 4, 1981, **21**:293

Baldwin, James
My Dungeon Shook: Letter to My Nephew (in *The Fire Next Time*), 1963, **18**:149–52

Baldwin, Roger S.
Speech in Senate on the executive prerogative in foreign policy, Mar. 31, 1848, **7**:423–25

Balk, Alfred *et al.*
A symposium on "Coping with Terrorism": Atlas World Press Review, Sept. 1976, **20**:325

Ballou, Adin
The Hopedale Community, 1851, **8**:131–34

Bancroft, George
Statement to New York Convention of Literary and Scientific Gentlemen on establishing a university for New York City, Oct. 1830, **5**:380–82
The Office of People in Art, Government, and Religion, Aug. 1835, **6**:128–36

Barber, Stephen
Editorial on the Bicentennial: The Australian (Canberra), Feb. 20, 1976, **20**:367

Barlien, Hans
Letter to Jens Rynning, Apr. 23, 1839, **6**:480–81

Barlow, Joel
An Oration Delivered . . . at Hartford, Conn., to the Society of the Cincinnati, July 4, 1787, **3**:90–93
Advice to the Privileged Orders in the Several States of Europe, 1792–1795, **3**:504–12
The Columbiad: Preface and Postscript, 1807, **4**:227–32

Barlow, John Perry
Statement by the Electronic Frontier Foundation, 1990, **22**:89

Barnard, Chester I.
The Functions of the Executive, 1938, **15**:506–11

Barnard, Daniel D.
An Address Delivered Before the Philoclean and Peithessophian Societies of Rutgers College, July 18, 1837, **6**:353–57

Barnett, Ida B. Wells
Lynching and the Excuse for It: Independent, May 16, 1901, **12**:420–23

Barrett, E. Boyd
The Catholic Church Faces America: American Mercury, Jan. 1929, **15**:22–27

Bartlett, Dewey F.
Speech in the U.S. Senate on the energy crisis: June 28, 1973, **19**:337

Baruch, Bernard Mannes
Report to the UN Atomic Energy Commission, June 14, 1946, **16**:360–65

Bates, Katharine Lee
America the Beautiful (song), **12**:1

Bauer, Gritta *et al.*
A symposium on "Coping with Terrorism": Atlas World Press Review, Sept. 1976, **20**:325

Beame, Abraham
Statement on the need for fiscal restraint in New York City, July 31, 1975, **20**:221

Beard, Charles Austin
An Economic Interpretation of the Constitution of the United States, 1913, **13**:429–36
A Statement (on resignation from Colum-

bia University): New Republic, Dec. 29, 1917, **14:**131–34

The Myth of Rugged American Individualism, 1932, **15:**83–93

Beard, Dita
Memorandum to W. R. Merriam, June 25, 1971, **19:**279

Beard, George Miller
American Nervousness, Its Causes and Consequences, 1881, **10:**479–88

Beaumont, Gustave de
Religious Movements in the United States, 1835, **6:**150–57

Beauvoir, Simone de
America Day by Day, 1948, **16:**542–46

Beck, Roy
The Ordeal of Immigration in Wausau: The Atlantic Monthly, Apr. 1, 1994, **22:**224

Beckwith, George C.
The Peace Manual: or, War and its Remedies, 1847, **7:**379–84

Beecher, Catharine Esther
Suggestions Respecting Improvements in Education, 1829, **5:**308–10

Beecher, Edward
Narrative of Riots at Alton: in Connection with the Death of Rev. Elijah P. Lovejoy, 1838, **6:**391–99

Beers, Ethel Lynn
All Quiet Along the Potomac To-Night (song), **9:**274–75

Begin, Menahem
Remarks on Camp David accords: Presidential documents, Sept. 17–18, 1978, **21:**114

Belcher, Jonathan
Letter to Lords of Trade, Dec. 23, 1732, **1:**387–88

Bell, Bernard Iddings
Crisis in Education, 1949, **16:**578–87

Bell, Daniel
Crime as an American Way of Life: Antioch Review, June 1953, **17:**223–28

Bell, Griffin *et al.*
Arguments for a one-term presidency: The New York Times, Dec. 31, 1985, **21:**610

Bell, James G.
A Log of the Texas-California Cattle Trail, 1854: Southwestern Historical Quarterly, Vol. XXXV, 1932, **8:**300–8

Bellamy, Edward
Looking Backward: 2000–1887, 1888, **11:**160–69

Benchley, Robert Charles
The Making of a Red: Nation, Mar. 15, 1919, **14:**248–50

Bendavid, Naftali
Frantic Moments, Rumors in the Rain and a Tense Call: Chicago Tribune, Nov. 9, 2000, **22:**463

Benedict, Donald *et al.*
Why We Refused to Register, 1941, **16:**80–81

Benét, Stephen Vincent
American Names (poem), **14:**567
John Brown's Body (poem), **14:**612–14
Nightmare at Noon (poem), **16:**11–14

Benjamin, Israel J.
Drei Jahre in Amerika, 1859–1862 [*Three Years in America, 1956*], 1862, **9:**386–90

Bennett, Edward H.
Plan of Chicago, 1909, **13:**181–86

Bennett, Henry Holcomb
The Flag Goes By (song), **12:**203

Bennett, Stephen A.
Fair Trial v. Free Press: Trial, Sept. 1976, **20:**287

Bennett, William J.
Making Americans: Immigration and Tolerance: Current, Feb. 1995, **22:**267

Benson, Ezra Taft
As Ye Sow So Shall Ye Reap, Aug. 25, 1956, **17:**383–89

Benton, Thomas Hart (1782–1858)
Speech in Senate on Second Bank of the U.S., Feb. 2, 1831, **5:**430–36

Benton, Thomas Hart (1889–1975)
An Artist in America, 1951, **17:**101–5

Benton, William
The Economics of a Free Society, 1944, **16:**225–30
Testimony before Senate Subcommittee on Privileges and Elections of the Committee of Rules, regarding the expulsion of Senator Joseph R. McCarthy, Sept. 28, 1951, **17:**108–13

Berger, Patrick F.
Death on Demand: Commonweal, Dec. 5, 1975, **20:**253

Berger, Victor L.
Socialism, the Logical Outcome of Progressivism: American Magazine, Nov. 1912, **13:**361–62

Berkow, Ira
The Baseball Effect on America: The New York Times, May 31, 1981, **21:**295

Berle, Adolf Augustus
The Modern Corporation and Private Property, 1932, **15:**136–39
The Emerging Common Law of Free Enterprise, Dec. 13, 1949, **16:**573–77
The 20th Century Capitalist Revolution, 1954, **17:**263–68

Berlin, Irving

God Bless America (song), **15:**525

Bernard, Sir Francis
Letter to Earl of Halifax, Aug. 31, 1765, **2:**149–53
Letter to Earl of Shelburne, Dec. 22, 1766, **2:**165–68

Bernhard, Karl, Duke of Saxe-Weimar Eisenach
Travels Through North America During the Years 1825 and 1826, 1828, **5:**238–42

Bethe, Hans, *et al.*
No alternative to nuclear power: Bulletin of the Atomic Scientists, March 1975, **20:**142

Beveridge, Albert Jeremiah
Campaign speech at Indianapolis, Sept. 16, 1898, **12:**198–202
Speech in Senate on an American Empire, Jan. 9, 1900, **12:**336–45

Beverley, Robert
The History and Present State of Virginia, In Four Parts, 1705, **1:**325–26

Bible, Geoffrey
Interoffice memo, Philip Morris Companies Inc., 1996, **22:**319

Bigelow, Jacob
Inaugural address (as Rumford professor at Harvard University), Dec. 11, 1816, **4:**449–51

Bill Arp (pseud.) *see* Smith, Charles H.

Billings, Edward C.
Opinion of the (Louisiana Federal Circuit) court in *U.S. v. Workingmen's Amalgamated Council of New Orleans et al.,* 1893, **11:**435–37

Billings, Josh (pseud.) *see* Shaw, Henry Wheeler

Billings, William
Let Tyrants Shake (Chester) (song), **2:**512

Bingham, John A.
Speech in House of Representatives on resolution, regarding Haiti and Santo Domingo, Jan. 13, 1869, **10:**152–54

Birnbach, Lisa
The Official Preppy Handbook: Ch. 1, 1980, **21:**247

Birney, James Gillespie
The American Churches, the Bulwarks of American Slavery, 1885, **7:**77–81

Black, Hugo Lafayette
Concurring Opinions in *West Virginia Board of Education et al. v. Barnette et al.,* 1943, **16:**153–54
Opinion of the Court in *Korematsu v. U.S.,* 1944, **16:**234–37
Opinion of the Court in *U.S. v. Lovett,*

Watson, and Dodd, 1946, **16:**404–8
Dissent in Ginzburg et al. v. U.S., 1966, **18:**353–54

Blackmun, Harry A.
Crime in the Bedroom (Bowers v. Hardwick): 86 U.S. 140, **21:**638

Blaine, James Gillespie
Letter to Thomas O. Osborn, Nov. 29, 1881, **10:**508–9

Blair, Lewis H.
The Prosperity of the South Dependent Upon the Elevation of the Negro, 1889, **11:**210–14

Blake, James
Sidewalks of New York (song), **11:**502–3

Bledsoe, Terry
Black Dominance of Sports: Strictly from Hunger: Progressive, June 1973, **19:**346

Bloom, Allan
The Closing of the American Mind, 1987, **22:**28

Boardman, George Nye
Political Economy and the Christian Ministry: The Bibliotheca Sacra, 1866, **10:**74–77

Boas, Franz
Preserving our Ideals, Mar. 7, 1917, **14:**74–76
The Problem of the American Negro: Yale Review, Jan. 1921, **14:**282–84

Bogdanov, Radomar
Editorial on the Bicentennial: Novosti (Soviet News Service, Moscow), **20:**374

Bok, Bart J.
Objections to Astrology: The Humanist, Nov.–Dec. 1975, **20:**239

Bollan, William
Letter to Lords of Trade, Feb. 26, 1743, **1:**454–57

Bongiorno, Lori
The Smell of Blood: Business Week, Apr. 1, 1996, **22:**320

Boorstin, Daniel J.
Myths of a Scientific Society: Science Digest, Dec. 1984, **21:**541

Borah, William Edgar
Political Prisoners, Mar. 11, 1923, **14:**405–8
Speech in special session of Congress on the Smoot-Hawley Tariff Bill, Sept. 26, 1929, **15:**28–31

Borsodi, Ralph
Flight from the City, 1933, **15:**229–32

Bossong, Ken
Guest editorial on Three Mile Island accident: Chemical & Engineering News, May 1979, **21:**144

Boucher, Jonathan
On Civil Liberty; Passive Obedience, and Non-Resistance (in *A View of the Causes and*

Consequences of the American Revolution), 1797, **2:**343–52

Bourget, Paul
Outre-Mer: Impressions of America, 1895, **11:**562–67

Bourne, Randolph Silliman
Who Owns the Universities? (editorial): New Republic, July 17, 1915, **13:**551–53
Unfinished Fragment on the State, 1918, **14:**135–40

Bowdoin, James
A Philosophical Discourse, Addressed to the American Academy of Arts and Sciences, Nov. 8, 1780, **2:**540–48

Bowman, John H.
Participatory Democracy: The Effects of Proposition 13: Public Administration Review, Nov.–Dec. 1978, **21:**78

Boyle, Robert H.
The PCB Menace: Sports Illustrated, Dec. 1, 1975, **20:**144

Brace, Charles Loring
First circular of the New York Children's Aid Society, Mar. 1853, **8:**208–9
The Dangerous Classes of New York, and Twenty Years' Work Among Them, 1872, **10:**289–91

Brackenridge, Henry Marie
Speech in Maryland House of Delegates on the "Jew Bill," 1818, **4:**552–60

Brackenridge, Hugh Henry
Letter to Mr. Baily (editor): Freeman's Journal or the North American Intelligencer, 1782, **2:**580–83
Modern Chivalry, 1792–1815, **3:**513–19; **4:**400–4

Bradford, William
Journal (1620–1644), in *Of Plymouth Plantation 1620–1647* (Samuel Eliot Morison, ed.), 1963, **1:**65–86

Bradley, Bill
Speech on the North American Free Trade Agreement, Apr. 1991, **22:**144

Bradley, Joseph P.
Opinion of the Court in the *Civil Rights Cases,* 1883, **10:**577–81

Bradstreet, Anne
The Prologue (poem), **1:**197–98
To My Dear and Loving Husband (poem), **1:**198

Bragg, Braxton, *et al.*
Message to Samuel Cooper, July 25, 1863, **9:**430–31

Brand, David
God and Money: Time, Aug. 3, 1987, **22:**12

Brand, Myles

Speech to the National Press Club on the reform of college athletics, Jan. 2001, **22:**475

Brandeis, Louis Dembitz
The Opportunity in the Law, May 4, 1905, **13:**23–25
Business—A Profession, 1912, **13:**342–44
Breaking the Money Trust: Harper's Weekly, Nov. 22, 1913, **13:**405–12
Testimony before U.S. Commission on Industrial Relations, Jan. 23, 1915, **13:**501–8
Dissent in *New State Ice Company* v. *Liebmann,* 1923, **15:**142–48
Opinion of the Court in *Ashwander* v. *TVA* (*Ashwander Rules*), 1936, **15:**350–51

Brando, Marlon
Unfinished Oscar Speech, Mar. 27, 1973: New York Times, Mar. 30, 1973, **19:**321

Brandt, Hans
Letter to friends in Norway, June 22, 1841, **7:**3–6

Brasher, Christopher
The Olympics Must Change: The Observer (London), May 13, 1984, **21:**526

Brattle, Thomas
Letter to an English clergyman, Oct. 8, 1692, **1:**285–92

Bremer, Fredrika
Hemmen i den nya Verlden [*Homes of the New World*], 1853, **8:**220–21

Brennan, William Joseph, Jr.
Opinion of the Court in *Baker* v. *Carr,* 1962, **18:**130–35
Opinion of the Court in *Ginzburg et al.* v. *U.S.,* 1966, **18:**350–52
Educational rights of illegal aliens: The New York Times, June 16, 1982, **21:**376
Opinion of the Court in *Edwards* v. *Aguillard,* 1987, **22:**9

Brereton, John
A Brief and True Relation of the Discovery of the North Part of Virginia, 1602, **1:**11–14

Brewer, David Josiah
The Nation's Safeguard, Jan. 1893, **11:**423–30
Opinion of the Court in *In Re Debs,* 1894, **12:**18–22

Brezhnev, Leonid I.
Address on radio and television to the American people, June 24, 1972, **19:**349

Brickfield, Cy
Our Aging Workforce: Enterprise, June 1978, **21:**73

Brisbane, Albert
Social Destiny of Man: or, Association and Reorganization of Industry, 1840, **6:**544–48

Brockett, Joshua A.

Reply to Henry W. Grady's *The Race Problem in the South,* Jan. 1890, **11:**250–52

Brodbeck, Arthur J.
How to Read "Li'l Abner" Intelligently, in *Mass Culture* (Bernard Rosenberg and David M. White, eds.), 1957, **17:**422–27

Brogan, Denis
The American Character, 1944, **16:**242–47

Brooke, Edward W.
Excerpts from testimony before the Senate Judiciary Committee in favor of the Philadelphia Plan, Oct. 27, 1969, **19:**82

Brookhiser, Richard
Whitewater Runs Deep: National Review, March 21, 1994, **22:**231

Brooks, T. J.
Testimony before Senate Committee on Interstate Commerce, 1912, **13:**331–32

Brooks, Van Wyck
America's Coming-of-Age, 1915, **13:**532–35

Brough, William
Let Us All Speak Our Minds (song), **11:**216

Broun, Matthew Heywood (Campbell)
It Seems to Me (columns on Sacco and Vanzetti): New York World, Aug. 5, 6, 1927, **14:**530–34

Brown, Charles Brockden
Alcuin, A Dialogue, 1798, **4:**40–48

Brown, Henry B.
Opinion of the Court in *Plessy* v. *Ferguson,* 1896, **12:**92–95

Brown, John
Final speech to the Virginia Court, Nov. 2, 1859, **9:**143–44

Brown, Joseph Emerson
Letter to Jefferson Davis, Apr. 22, 1862, **9:**375–78

Brown, Lew
Don't Sit Under the Apple Tree (With Anyone Else But Me) (song), **16:**128

Brown, Robert McAfee
Because of Vietnam . . . 'In Conscience I Must Break the Law': Look, Oct. 31, 1967, **18:**554–58

Brownell, Herbert et al.
Arguments for a one-term presidency: The New York Times, Dec. 31, 1985, **21:**610

Brownson, Orestes (Augustus)
The Laboring Classes (Review of Thomas Carlyle's *Chartism*): Boston Quarterly Review, July 1840, **6:**534–43
Catholic Schools and Education: Brownson's Quarterly Review, Jan. 1862, **9:**392–95

Bruce, Blanche K.
Speech in Senate on African American hopes for assimilation, Mar. 31, 1876, **10:**350–53

Bruce, John E.
Plea for Organized Resistance to White Men, Oct. 5, 1889, **11:**214–15

Bruce, R. G.
Letter to John Singleton Copley, Aug. 4, 1766, **2:**174–75

Bryan, Vincent
In My Merry Oldsmobile (song), **13:**39

Bryan, William Jennings
Speech at the Democratic National Convention, Chicago (Cross of Gold Speech), July 8, 1896, **12:**100–5
Acceptance speech at Military Park, Indianapolis, Aug. 8, 1900, **12:**345–52
Telegram to James Gerard (Lusitania Note), May 13, 1915, **13:**559–61

Bryant, Anita
The Battle for Miami: The Anita Bryant Story, Ch. 2, 1977, **21:**27

Bryant, William Cullen
Review of Catherine Sedgwick's *Redwood:* North American Review, Apr. 1825, **5:**164–69
Hymn of the City (song), **5:**519–20
Spring in Town (song), **5:**520
Editorial on the right to strike: New York Evening Post, June 13, 1836, **6:**248–51

Bryce, James Bryce, Viscount
The American Commonwealth, 1888, **11:**172–88
Modern Democracies, 1921, **14:**285–91

Buchanan, James
Last annual message to Congress, Dec. 3, 1860, **9:**209–20

Buchanan, Pat
Speech to the Republican National Convention, Aug. 1992, **22:**156

Buchanan, Scott
A Message to the Young: Center Magazine, Mar. 1968, **18:**680–81

Buckley, William F., Jr.
Nice Try: National Review, Oct. 23, 1987, **22:**25

Buckner, Thomas
A Thrilling Narrative from the Lips of the Sufferers of the Late Detroit Riot, 1863, **9:**467–71

Buel, David, Jr.
Speech in New York State constitutional convention, Sept. 1821, **5:**18–22

Bulkeley, Peter
The Gospel-Covenant; or The Covenant of Grace Opened, 1651, **1:**211–12

Bunker, Ellsworth
Speech to the Rainier Club in Seattle, Washington, May 22, 1975, **20:**169

Burger, Warren E.
Court Reform: An address to the National Con-
ference on the Judiciary, Mar. 12, 1971,
19:192
Miller v. *California,* June 21, 1973, **19**:340
United States v. *Richard M. Nixon,* July 24,
1974, **20**:4
Educational rights of illegal aliens: The New
York Times, June 16, 1982, **21**:376

Burke, Edmund
Speech Delivered in House of Commons, on
Moving his Resolution for Conciliation with
the American Colonies, Mar. 22, 1775,
2:312–20

Burn, James D.
Three Years Among the Working-Classes in the
United States During the War, 1865,
9:544–49

Burnham, Daniel Hudson
Plan of Chicago, 1909, **13**:181–86

Burns, Arthur F.
Burns's Parting Thoughts: Across the Board,
May 1978, **21**:91

Burns, James MacGregor
Republicans, Democrats: Who's Who?: New
York Times Magazine, Jan. 2, 1955,
17:311–15

Burrows, John Lansing
The New Richmond Theatre. A Discourse De-
livered . . . in the First Baptist Church, Rich-
mond, Va., Feb. 8, 1863, **9**:402–5

Bush, Barbara
Commencement Address at Wellesley College,
June 1, 1990, **22**:99

Bush, George
Inaugural Address, Jan. 20, 1989, **22**:72
Address to the nation following the invasion of
Panama, Dec. 1989, **22**:87
Speech announcing the start of Operation
Desert Storm, Jan. 16, 1991, **22**:128

Bush, George W.
Speech to Congress and the nation on American
response to September 11 terrorist attacks,
Sept. 20, 2001, **22**:494

Bushuyev, Konstantin
A Soviet view of the Soyuz–Apollo project:
Space World, Nov. 1975, **20**:207

Butler, Benjamin Franklin
Report to Simon Cameron on "Contraband,"
July 30, 1861, **9**:276–78
Speech in House of Representatives on resolu-
tion, regarding Haiti and Santo Domingo,
Jan. 13, 1869, **10**:143–45 *passim*

Butler, Stuart M.
The Privatization of the Postal Service: The
New York Times, Aug. 9, 1985, **21**:606

Byrd, William
History of the Dividing Line, c. 1728,
1:375–84

Cable, George Washington
The Silent South, 1885, **11**:44–50

Caesar (pseud.) *see* Hamilton, Alexander

Caldwell, Elias B.
Speech at organizational meeting of the Ameri-
can Colonization Society, Dec. 21, 1816,
4:452–55

Caldwell, Joseph
Letters on Popular Education, Addressed to the
People of North-Carolina, 1832, **5**:555–60

Calhoun, John Caldwell
Speech in House of Representatives on the
Bonus Bill, Feb. 4, 1817, **4**:457–61
Address to the People of the United States (on
the South Carolina Exposition), Nov.
1832, **5**:576–84
Speech in Senate on the danger of Abolitionist
petitions, Feb. 1837, **6**:346–50
Speech in Senate on the Oregon Bill, Jan. 24,
1843, **7**:87–88
Speech in Senate against general resolutions on
foreign affairs, Jan. 26, 1846, **7**:336–38
Speech in Senate on the Yucatán Bill, May 15,
1848, **7**:433–37
A Disquisition on Government (Richard K.
Cralle, ed.), 1854, **7**:552–62
Posthumous speech in Senate on Clay's Com-
promise of 1850 (Fourth of March
Speech), 1850, **8**:16–24

Calley, William L., Jr.
Statement to the court on the day of his sen-
tencing, Mar. 30, 1971, **19**:206

Cameron, Andrew Carr
The Address of the National Labor Congress to
the Workingmen of the United States, Aug.
1867, **10**:105–11

Camillus (pseud.) *see* Hamilton, Alexander

Campbell, Paul (pseud.) *see* Weavers, The

Campbell, Robert A.
Letter to Senator Mark O. Hatfield, June 23,
1970, **19**:148

Campbell, Thomas
Declaration and Address on the principles of
the Christian Association of Washington,
Sept. 7, 1809, **4**:242–47

Cannon, Hughie
Bill Bailey, Won't You Please Come Home?
(song), **12**:502

Caplin, Mortimer M., *et al.*
Letter to Lawrence F. O'Brien, Apr. 9, 1970,
19:125

Carey, Mathew
Appeal to the Wealthy of the Land, 1833,

6:23–26

Carmichael, Stokely
What We Want: New York Review of Books, Sept. 22, 1966, **18:**373–80

Carnegie, Andrew
Triumphant Democracy, 1886, **11:**92–96
The Bugaboo of Trusts: North American Review, Feb. 1889, **11:**217–21
Wealth (also known as *The Gospel of Wealth*): North American Review, June 1889, **11:**222–26

Carpenter, C. U.
Testimony before Senate Committee on Interstate Commerce, Dec. 9, 1911, **13:**327–30

Carroll, John
Letter to Cardinal Antonelli, Feb. 27, 1785, **3:**14–16

Carson, Rachel
Silent Spring, 1962, **18:**101–7

Carter, Jimmy
Speech accepting the nomination of the Democratic Party for the presidency of the U.S., July 15, 1976, **20:**347
Inaugural Address: Congressional Quarterly, Jan. 1977, **21:**14
Letter to Andrei Sakharov: National Archives, Feb. 5, 1977, **21:**17
Speech: The Moral Equivalent of War: Congressional Quarterly, April 1977, **21:**22
Message on amnesty for illegal aliens: Congressional Digest, Oct. 1977, **21:**44
Address on inflation: Presidential documents, Oct. 1978, **21:**93
Speech on a national malaise: Presidential documents, week ending July 20, 1979, **21:**170

Carty, J. J.
The Relation of Pure Science to Industrial Research: Science, Oct. 13, 1916, **14:**9–14

Cass, Lewis
Speech in Senate on the moral declarations in foreign policy, Feb. 10, 1852, **8:**167–70
Letter of Instruction to Envoy Reed on trade with China, May 10, 1857, **8:**497–99

Catlin, George
The Manners, Customs, and Condition of the North American Indians, 1841, **5:**521–23

Cato (pseud.) *see* Clinton, George; Livingston, Robert R.; Smith, William (1727–1803)

Caudill, Harry M.
Paradise Is Stripped: New York Times Magazine, Mar. 13, 1966, **18:**333–38

Cervantes, A. J.
Federal Revenue Sharing and the Cities: An address to the Federal Agency Review Work-

shop, Oct. 13, 1970, **19:**170

Chafee, Zechariah
Free Speech in the United States, 1941, **16:**76–79

Chafets, Ze'ev
Why the U.S. Was a Target (in TWA Fl. 847 hijacking): The New York Times, July 2, 1985, **21:**581

Chamberlain, Gary M.
How to Solve the Police Crisis: Interviews with three police chiefs: The American City, Sept.–Oct. 1971, **19:**249

Channing, William Ellery
Discourse at the Ordination of the Rev. Jared Sparks, May 5, 1819, **4:**544–51
Remarks on National Literature, 1830, **5:**404–11
Remarks on Associations, 1830, **5:**412–17
Note to letter to Henry Clay on annexation of Texas, Aug. 1837, **6:**357–62
Petition to Governor of the Commonwealth of Massachusetts on pardoning Abner Kneeland, 1838, **6:**422–23

Channing, William Henry
A Confession of Faith (creed): The Present, Sept. 1843, **7:**108–9

Chanute, Octave
The Wright Brothers' Flights: Independent, June 4, 1908, **13:**118–20

Chaplin, Ralph
Solidarity Forever (song), **13:**515

Chase, Stuart
Rich Land, Poor Land, 1936, **15:**395–400

Chauncy, Charles
Letter from a Gentleman in Boston to Mr. George Wishart, Aug. 4, 1742, **1:**434–39

Chesnut, Mary Boykin
A Diary From Dixie (Isabella O. Martin and Myrta L. Avary, eds.), 1905, **9:**307–17

Chevalier, Michel
Lettres sur l'Amerique du Nord [*Society, Manners, and Politics in the United States,* 1836], 1839, **6:**482–94

Child, Lydia Maria
An Appeal in Favor of That Class of Americans Called Africans, 1833, **6:**5–11
Letters from New-York, 1846, **7:**66–71

Choate, Rufus
The Power of a State Developed by Mental Culture, Nov. 18, 1844, **7:**235–42
American Nationality: July 4, 1858, **9:**54–61

Christy, David
Cotton Is King, 1855, **8:**335–40

Church, Frank
Farewell to Foreign Aid: Speech in the U.S. Senate, Oct. 29, 1971, **19:**259

Churchill, Sir Winston (Leonard Spencer)
Alliance of English-Speaking People, Mar. 5, 1946, **16:**365–69

Citizen of Boston, A (pseud.) *see* Henshaw, David

Citizen of Pennsylvania (pseud.) *see* Rush, Benjamin

Citizens' Advisory Council on the Status of Women
The Proposed Equal Rights Amendment to the Constitution—A Memorandum, Mar. 1970, **19:**109

Clap, Thomas
The Religious Constitution of Colleges, 1754, **1:**505–8

Clark, Aaron
Letter to the New York City Common Council, June 5, 1837, **6:**351–53

Clark, Alexander
Socialism: The A.M.E. Church Review, July 1886, **11:**111–12

Clark, Bennett Champ
Detour Around War: Harper's Monthly, Dec. 1935, **15:**344–48

Clark, John Bates
The Society of the Future: Independent, July 18, 1901, **12:**399–402

Clark, Thomas Campbell
Opinion of the Court in *Sheppard* v. *Maxwell, Warden*, 1966, **18:**402–6

Clay, Henry
Speech in the House of Representatives on additional military force, Jan. 1813, **4:**327–30
Speech at organizational meeting of the American Colonization Society, Dec. 21, 1816, **4:**451–52
Speech in House of Representatives on the "American System," Mar. 13, 1818, **4:**482–87
Speech in House of Representatives on Latin American governments, Mar. 25, 1818, **4:**488–89
Speech in House of Representatives on a protective tariff, Apr. 26, 1820, **4:**612–22
Speech in House of Representatives on the Protective Tariff of 1824, Mar. 31, 1824, **5:**114–18
Speech at Cincinnati, on exposition of the "American System," Aug. 3, 1830, **5:**392–97
Speech in Senate on resolutions of censure, Mar. 28, 1834, **6:**46–48
Campaign speech at Hanover County, Va., June 27, 1840, **6:**565–72
Proposed Resolutions on sectional conflict, including supporting speech in Senate, Jan.

29; Feb. 5, 6, 1850, **8:**1–7
Report to Senate by the Committee of Thirteen, May 8, 1850, **8:**36–37
Speech in Senate on Committee of Thirteen Report, May 13, 1850, **8:**37–43

Cleaver, Eldridge
Why I am returning to the U.S.: New York Times, Nov. 18, 1975, **20:**199

Clemens, Samuel Langhorne (Mark Twain)
Journalism in Tennessee, c. 1869, **10:**197–201
My Watch, 1870, **10:**245–46
The Curious Republic of Gondour: Atlantic Monthly, Oct. 1875, **10:**346–49
The Suppressed Chapter of *Life on the Mississippi*, n.d., **10:**531–34
Extract from Captain Stormfield's Visit to Heaven: Harper's Monthly, Jan. 1908, **13:**94–106

Clement, Alain
Editorial on the Bicentennial: Le Monde (Paris), May 11, 1976, **20:**363

Cleveland, Grover
Veto message to Senate on an act granting a pension to Elizabeth S. De Krafft, June 21, 1886, **11:**90–91
Third annual message to Congress, Dec. 6, 1887, **11:**154–59
Letter to E. Ellery Anderson, Feb. 10, 1891, **11:**365–66
Special message to Senate on treaty for annexation of Hawaii, Dec. 18, 1893, **11:**480–82
Telegrams to John Altgeld, July, 5, 6, 1894, **11:**528–29 *passim*
Final message to Congress, Dec. 7, 1896, **12:**119–23

Clews, Henry
The Labor Crisis: North American Review, June 1886, **11:**108–11

Clinton, Bill
First Inaugural Address, Jan. 20, 1993, **22:**175
Speech to an African American congregation in Memphis, Tenn., on urban renewal, 1993, **22:**202
State of the Union Address, Jan. 24, 1995, **22:**258
Speech at the memorial service for the victims of the Oklahoma City bombing, Apr. 23, 1995, **22:**271

Clinton, George
Letter to Citizens of the State of New York (by Cato): New-York Journal, Oct. 11, 1787, **3:**139–42

Clinton, Hillary
Speech to American Medical Association on health care reform, June 1993, **22:**189

Cobbett, William

A Year's Residence in the United States of America (by Peter Porcupine), 1820, **4**:567–73

Coffin, Howard E.
Organizing Industry for National Defense: World's Work, May 1916, **14**:14–20

Coffin, Levi
Reminiscences (of the Underground Railroad), 1880, **8**:134–38

Coffman, Lotus D.
Adult Education, Feb. 25, 1931, **15**:98–101

Cohan, George M.
The Yankee Doodle Boy (song), **12**:567
Give My Regards to Broadway (song), **12**:568
You're a Grand Old Flag (song), **13**:84–85
Over There (song), **14**:117–18

Colby, Frank Moore
Humor, in *Civilization in the United States* (Harold E. Stearns, ed.), 1922, **14**:351–53

Colden, Cadwallader
The History of the Five Indian Nations of Canada, 1755, **1**:443–46

Cole, Thomas
Essay on American Scenery: American Monthly Magazine, Jan. 1836, **6**:231–39

Coleman, James S., *et al.*
Equality of Educational Opportunity, 1966, **18**:388–96

Coleman, John A.
American Bicentennial—Catholic Crisis: America, June 26, 1976, **20**:299

Collier, John
Annual Report of the Secretary of the Interior for the Fiscal Year Ended June 30, 1938, 1938, **15**:523–25

Collins, Michael
Speech to a Joint Session of Congress, Sept. 16, 1969, **19**:44

Colson, Charles
Memorandum for H. R. Haldeman, Mar. 30, 1972, **19**:281

Colton, Calvin
Manual for Emigrants to America, 1832, **5**:546–54
Junius Tracts, No. VII, Mar. 1844, **7**:219–28

Columbus, Christopher
Letter to Lord Sanchez, Mar. 14, 1493, **1**:1–5

Colwell, J. B.
Industry and Defense: A Timely Vindication of the U.S. Military-Industrial Complex: Ordnance, July–Aug. 1969, **19**:57

Commager, Henry Steele
Who Is Loyal to America? Harper's, Sept. 1947, **16**:457–64
The American Political Party: American Scholar, Summer 1950, **17**:6–11

Commoner, Barry
An interview on the fuel crisis: Chicago Tribune, Nov. 19, 1973, **19**:419

Conant, James Bryant
Education for a Classless Society, Mar. 28, 1940, **16**:22–27

Conrad, Charles Magill
Instructions to John P. Kennedy (on relations with Japan), Nov. 5, 1852, **8**:174–77

Continentalist (pseud.) *see* Hamilton, Alexander

Converse, Florence
Bread Line (poem), **15**:132–33

Conwell, Russell Herman
Acres of Diamonds, 1905, **11**:271–79

Cook, James
Nuclear Follies: Forbes, Feb. 11, 1985, **21**:550

Cooke, Alistair
A Generation on Trial: New Republic, July 4, 1949, **16**:605–7

Coolidge, Calvin
The Destiny of America, May 30, 1923, **14**:409–14
Message to Congress on intervention in Nicaragua, Jan. 10, 1927, **14**:519–23
Veto message to Senate on the McNary-Haugen Bill, May 1928, **14**:568–73

Cooper, James Fenimore
Notions of the Americans: Picked Up by a Traveling Bachelor, 1828, 1836, **5**:255–64
The American Democrat, 1838, **6**:438–44

Cooper, Peter
Letter to Trustees of the Cooper Union for Advancement of Science and Art, accompanying the Trust-Deed, 1859, **9**:127–31

Cooper, Thomas
Defense of intellectual freedom before the Board of Trustees at South Carolina College, 1832, **5**:561–73

Copeland, Frederick W.
The Illusion of Owning a Business: Atlantic Monthly, Sept. 1956, **17**:389–93

Copland, Aaron
Music and Imagination, 1952, **17**:184–89

Copley, John Singleton
Letter to Benjamin West, Nov. 12, 1766, **2**:176–77
Letter to R. G. Bruce or Benjamin West, 1767, **2**:177–78

Coram, Robert
Political Inquiries: To Which Is Added, a Plan for the General Establishment of Schools Throughout the United States, 1791, **3**:438–44

Corbin, Richard
Letter to Overseer of Virginia plantation, Jan. 1, 1759, **2:**44–45

Cordasco, Francesco
The Catholic Urban School: The Patterns of Survival: An address to the National Catholic Education Association Convention, Apr. 1970, **19:**121

Corlett, Candace
Speech on marketing to female Internet users over age 50, May 1999, **22:**388

Cornish, Samuel
To Our Patrons (salutatory): Freedom's Journal, Mar. 16, 1827, **5:**222–24

Costas, Bob
Live with TAE: Interview: American Enterprise, June 2000, **22:**438

Cotton, John
God's Promise to His Plantation, 1630, **1:**107–9

Certain Proposals made by Lord Saye, Lord Brooke, and Other Persons of Quality as Conditions of Their Removing to New-England, with the Answers Thereto, 1636, **1:**149–52

Letter to Lord Saye and Sele, 1636, **1:**152–53

Coughlin, Charles E.
A Third Party (radio address), June 19, 1936, **15:**388–91

Counts, George Sylvester
The Selective Character of American Secondary Education, 1922, **14:**304–10

Cousins, Norman
Wanted: Two Billion Angry Men (editorial): Saturday Review, Feb. 1, 1958, **17:**473–75

Cowley, Malcolm
The Flight of the Bonus Army: New Republic, Aug. 17, 1932, **15:**148–52

Coxe, Tench
An Address to an Assembly of the Friends of American Manufacturers, Convened for the Purpose of Establishing a Society for the Encouragement of Manufactures and the Useful Arts, Aug. 9, 1787, **3:**196–203

Coxey, Jacob Sechler
Business Depression and Public Works ("Bills"), 1894, **11:**504–5

Cram, Ralph Adams
What Is a Free Man?: Catholic Rural Life Objectives, 1937, **15:**498–502

Cramer, John
Speech in New York State constitutional convention, Sept. 1821, **5:**15–18

Crane, (Harold) Hart
To Brooklyn Bridge (poem), **15:**70–71

Crawford, Frederick C.
Jobs, Freedom, Opportunity, Apr. 13, 1943, **16:**132–37

Cresswell, Nicholas
Journal (on General Washington), July 13, 1777, **2:**487–90

Crèvecoeur, Michel Guillaume Jean de
Letters from an American Farmer (by J. Hector St. John), 1782, **2:**583–92

Crittenden, John Jordan
Compromise Resolutions, Dec. 18, 1860, **9:**221–24

Speech in Senate on saving the Union, Mar. 2, 1861, **9:**246–49

Crittenden, Thomas Theodore
Speech to the Southern Immigration Association of America on trade and commerce for Southwestern states, Mar. 1884, **11:**16–18

Crockett, David (Davy)
A Narrative of the Life of David Crockett, of the State of Tennessee, 1834, **6:**87–89

An Account of Col. Crockett's Tour to the North and Down East, 1835, **6:**90–92

Croghan, George
Diary (on exploration of the Ohio Valley), 1765, **2:**134–43

Croly, Herbert
The Promise of American Life, 1909, **13:**214–27

Cubberley, Ellwood Patterson
Changing Conceptions of Education, 1909, **13:**201–6

Cuming, Fortescue
Sketches of a Tour to the Western Country, 1810, **4:**221–27

Cummings, E(dward) E(stlin)
the Cambridge ladies (poem), **14:**399

next to of course god (poem), **14:**505

i sing of Olaf (poem), **15:**78–79

plato told (poem), **16:**259–60

a salesman is an it that stinks Excuse (poem), **16:**260

Cuomo, Mario
Keynote Address: Vital Speeches of the Day, Aug. 15, 1984, **21:**514

Curtice, Harlow H.
Accelerating the Pace of Technological Progress, May 16, 1956, **17:**379–83

Curtis, George Ticknor
How Shall We Elect Our Presidents?: Century Illustrated Monthly Magazine, Nov. 1884, **11:**22–28

Curtis, George William
The Duty of the American Scholar to Politics and the Times, Aug. 5, 1856, **8:**411–14

Cushing, William

Opinion of the (Massachusetts Superior) court in the *Quock Walker Case,* 1874, **2:**617

Daley, Richard J.
Remarks before the Committee on Banking and Currency, Feb. 4, 1970, **19:**104

Dallas, Alexander James
Letter to Congress on establishing a National Bank, Dec. 24, 1815, **4:**406–11

Dana, Richard Henry
Two Years Before the Mast, 1840, **6:**524–34

Daniel III, Aubrey
Letter to President Nixon, Apr. 3, 1971, **19:**207

Daniel, Hawthorne
Living and Dying on Installments: World's Work, Jan. 1926, **14:**501–5

Daniels, Jonathan Worth
A Southerner Discovers the South, 1938, **15:**549–55

Darrock, Michael (pseud.)
see Nielsen, Waldemar A.

Darrow, Clarence Seward
Why Men Fight for the Closed Shop: American Magazine, Sept. 1911, **13:**304–9

Dartmouth, William Legge, 2d Earl of
Letter to Thomas Gage, Apr. 9, 1774, **2:**248–51

Davenport, Russell W., *et al.*
U.S.A. The Permanent Revolution, 1951, **17:**89–95

Davidson, Thomas
Educational Problems Which the Nineteenth Century Hands Over to the Twentieth, 1898, **12:**204–10

Davies, Howell
Letter from a Welsh immigrant, Jellico, Tenn., Jan. 11, 1892, **11:**382–84

Davies, Samuel
A General Account of the Rise and State of the College, Lately Established in the Province of New-Jersey, 1754, **1:**518–21
The Curse of Cowardice: A Sermon Preached to the Militia of Hanover County, in Virginia, May 8, 1758, **2:**23–28

Davis, Charles A.
Letters of J. Downing, Major . . . to Mr. Dwight, 1834, **6:**41–46

Davis, Chester C.
Toward Planned Harvests: Review of Reviews and World's Work, Dec. 1933, **15:**224–28

Davis, David
Opinion of the Court in *Ex Parte Milligan,* 1866, **10:**31–36

Davis, Jefferson

Inaugural Address, Feb. 18, 1861, **9:**238–41
War message in special session of the Confederate Congress, Apr. 29, 1861, **9:**259–68
Final address to the People of the Confederate States of America, Apr. 4, 1865, **9:**557–58

Davis, Stuart
The Cube Root: Art News, Feb. 1–14, 1943, **16:**206–9

Day, Jeremiah
Original Papers in Relation to a Course of Liberal Education (Yale Report of 1828): American Journal of Science and Arts, Jan. 1829, **5:**266–75

Day, William Rufus
Dissent in *U.S. v. United States Steel Corporation et al.,* 1920, **14:**263–65

Dean III, John W.
Testimony before the Select Committee on Presidential Campaign Activities of the U.S. Senate, June 25 and 26, 1973, **19:**354

Deane, Herbert A.
On the New Student Nihilism: Graduate Faculties Newsletter (Columbia University), June 1967, **18:**467–72

DeAre, Diana
The Slowing of Urbanization: Scientific American, July 1983, **21:**432

Debs, Eugene Victor
Impromptu speech at Girard, Kan., on aims for the Social Democratic Party, May 23, 1908, **13:**137–42

Decter, Midge
Looting and Liberal Racism: Commentary, Sept. 1977, **21:**36

Deford, Frank
The Lost Generation: Newsweek, June 2, 1997, **22:**332

De Leon, Daniel
Reform or Revolution, Jan. 26, 1896, **12:**106–12
The Preamble of I.W.W. (also known as *Socialist Reconstruction of Society*), July 10, 1905, **13:**19–22

Dell, Nat
Toward a Professional Army: An interview with Lt. General Bernard W. Rogers: Soldiers, Aug. 1973, **19:**181

Deloria, Vine
Civilization and Isolation: an Indian View: North American Review, 1978, **21:**106

De Mille, Agnes
The Dance in America, in *Profile of America* (Emily Davie, ed.), 1954, **17:**285–89

Denby, Charles
Shall We Keep the Philippines?: Forum, Nov. 1898, **12:**233–35

Dennis, Lawrence
A Portrait of American Fascism: American Mercury, Dec. 1935, **15:**333–35

Densmore, John B.
A Report Addressed to the Secretary of Labor [*Wilson*] (on the Mooney-Billings Case), Nov. 1, 1918, **14:**168–73

Dermer, Emma
Eleven-Cent Cotton (song), **14:**573–74

Desmond, John
The Troupers Go to the Troops: New York Times Magazine, Apr. 2, 1944, **16:**220–24

De Voto, Bernard Augustine
Due Notice to the FBI: Harper's, Oct. 1949, **16:**608–12

Dew, Thomas R.
The Pro-Slavery Argument, 1832, **5:**506–11

Dewey, John
My Pedagogic Creed, Jan. 16, 1897, **12:**125–30
The School and Society, 1900, **12:**255–62
Introduction to Elsie R. Clapp's *The Use of Resources in Education,* 1952, **17:**181–84

Dewey, Thomas E(dmund)
Government, the Nation's Biggest Industry, June 5, 1947, **16:**471–74

Dicey, Edward
Six Months in the Federal States, 1863, **9:**478–82

Dickinson, Emily
I Cannot Live With You (poem), **9:**391–92
I Like to See It Lap the Miles (poem), **9:**392

Dickinson, John
Letters from a Farmer in Pennsylvania to the Inhabitants of the British Colonies, 1768, **2:**182–84
Speech . . . Favoring a Condition of Union with England, July 1, 1776, **2:**438–42

Dietrichson, J. W. C.
Letter from Muskego, Wis., settlement, Sept. 25, 1844, **7:**234–35

Dillard, Annie
Living Like Weasels: Teaching a Stone to Talk, 1982, **21:**406

Dionne, E. J., Jr.
Suburban Prize: Washington Post, Sept. 29, 2000, **22:**446

Dix, Dorothea Lynde
Memorial to the Legislature of Massachusetts on humane treatment of the insane, 1843, **7:**97–106

Dixon, George H.
Speech on trade with China: Vital Speeches of the Day, Nov. 15, 1979, **21:**135

Dole, Robert J.

Acceptance speech as presidential nominee at the Republican National Convention,* Aug. 15, 1996, **22:310

Doman, Glenn
Function Determines Structure: IAHP In-port, Oct.–Dec. 1984, **21:**538

Donck, Adriaen van der, *et al.*
The Representation of New Netherland, 1650, **1:**204–9

Donovan, William Joseph (Wild Bill)
A Central Intelligence Agency: Apr. 13, 1946, **16:**391–94

Dorney, P. S.
A Prophecy Partly Verified: Overland Monthly, Mar. 1886, **10:**256–60

Dorr, Thomas Wilson
Speech in Rhode Island Constitutional (Dorrite) Assembly on people's right to remake their Constitution, May 3, 1842, **7:**56–60

Douglas, Kirk
That Kind of Corn: Center Diary: 14, Sept.–Oct. 1966, **18:**380–81

Douglas, Paul H.
The Problem of Tax Loopholes: American Scholar, Winter 1967–68, **18:**560–66

Douglas, Stephen Arnold
Speech in Senate on the Kansas-Nebraska Bill, Jan. 30, 1854, **8:**254–60
Campaign speech at Chicago, July 9, 1858, **9:**4–7
The Lincoln-Douglas Debates, 1858, **9:**8–32

Douglas, William O(rville)
Concurring Opinions in *West Virginia Board of Education et al. v. Barnette et al.,* 1943, **16:**153–54
The Black Silence of Fear: New York Times Magazine, Jan. 13, 1952, **17:**114–18
Dissent in *Ginzburg et al. v. U.S.,* 1966, **18:**354–56
Miller v. California, June 21, 1974, **19:**340

Douglass, Frederick
Peace! Peace! Peace! (editorial): North Star (Rochester, N.Y.), Mar. 17, 1848, **7:**422
Address to the people of the United States at the Convention of Colored Men, Louisville, Ky., Sept. 24, 1883, **10:**584–86

Douglass, William
Letter to Cadwallader Colden, May 1, 1722, **1:**348–50
Letter to Cadwallader Colden, Sept. 1729, **1:**385–86

Dow, Lorenzo
Travels, 1806, **4:**208–10

Dowling, Alexander
Opinion of the (Indiana Supreme) court in *The State v. Bailey,* 1901, **12:**417–19

Downing, Andrew Jackson
Rural Essays, 1853, **7:**442–44
Rural Essays, 1853, **8:**90–92
Rural Essays, 1853, **8:**122–25
Downing, Major Jack (pseud.) *see* Davis, Charles A.
Drake, Joseph Rodman
The American Flag (poem), **4:**650–51
Dreiser, Theodore
On the Banks of the Wabash, Far Away (song), **12:**278
Dresser, Paul
Just Tell Them That You Saw Me (song), **12:**149–50
On the Banks of the Wabash, Far Away (song), **12:**278
Drucker, Peter F.
Productivity Is An Attitude: Nation's Business, Apr. 1952, **17:**137–41
Drummond, Henry
Mr. Moody: Some Impressions and Facts.: McClure's, Dec. 1894, **11:**568–74
Duane, William
More of Good Order and Regular Government! (editorial): Philadelphia Aurora, May 16, 1799, **4:**112–13
Letter to Senate of the Commonwealth of Kentucky on Pennsylvania common schools, July 12, 1822, **5:**32–35
Du Bois, William Edward Burghardt
The Souls of Black Folk, 1903, **12:**519–27
Dudley, Thomas
Letter to Bridget, Countess of Lincoln, Mar. 1631, **1:**118–24
Duffus, Robert L.
The Age of Play: Independent, Dec. 20, 1924, **14:**465–68
Dulany, Daniel
Considerations on the Propriety of Imposing Taxes in the British Colonies, for the Purpose of Raising a Revenue, by Act of Parliament, 1766, **2:**156–58
Dulles, John Foster
A Policy of Boldness: Life, May 19, 1952, **17:**123–28
Testimony before Senate Committee on Foreign Relations, Jan. 15, 1953, **17:**204–5
Speech to Council on Foreign Relations, New York City, on strategy of massive retaliation, Jan. 12, 1954, **17:**250–52
Peace Through Law, Jan. 31, 1959, **17:**528–30
Dummer, Jeremiah
A Defense of the New-England Charters, 1721, **1:**336–43
Dunaway, John A.

Jefferson County, Colorado, Sheriff's Office Report on the Columbine High School murders, May 15, 2000, **22:**435
Dunmore, John Murray, 4th Earl of
Proclamation . . . Offering Freedom to the Slaves Belonging to the Rebels in Virginia, Nov. 7, 1775, **2:**360–61
Dunne, Finley Peter
The Phillippine Peace (by Mr. Dooley), 1900, **12:**352–54
Mr. Dooley's Philosophy, 1900, **12:**387–89
The Carnegie Libraries (by Mr. Dooley), 1906, **13:**42–45
Du Pont, Henry B.
The Greatest Invention of Them All, Apr. 15, 1959, **17:**530–35
Dupré, J. Stefan
Contracting for Defense: Private Firms and the Public Interest: Political Science Quarterly, June 1962, **18:**94–101
Durenberger, David
Speech on the New Federalism: Vital Speeches of the Day, Jan. 1, 1982, **21:**345
Durfee, Job
The Influence of Scientific Discovery and Invention on Social and Political Progress, Sept. 6, 1843, **7:**128–32
Dvořák, Antonín
Music in America: Harper's New Monthly, Feb. 1895, **12:**33–36
Dwight, Frederick
Automobiles: The Other Side of the Shield: Independent, Dec. 3, 1908, **13:**113–17
Dwight, Theodore
Things As They Are: or, Notes of a Traveller Through Some of the Middle and Northern States, (reissued as *Summer Tours,* 1847), 1834, **6:**76–83
Dwight, Timothy
The Duty of Americans, at the Present Crisis, Illustrated in a Discourse, July 4, 1798, **4:**33–39
Travels in New-England and New-York (on Vermont), 1823, **4:**278–81
East, Ben
Is It Taps for Wild Alaska?: Outdoor Life, May 1970, **19:**139
Eaton, Walter Prichard
Class-Consciousness and the 'Movies': Atlantic Monthly, Jan. 1915, **13:**535–40
Eddy, Mary Baker
Christian Science, c. 1883, **10:**556–60
Edwards, Jonathan
Sinners in the Hands of an Angry God, July 8, 1741, **1:**423–33
Letter to Thomas Prince, Dec. 12, 1743,

1:458–63

Edwards, June K.
The textbook controversy: Christian Century, Nov. 13, 1974, **20:**100

Egerton, John
Can We Save the Schools? The Progressive, Mar. 1982, **21:**382

Einstein, Albert
Letter to Franklin D. Roosevelt, Aug. 2, 1939, **15:**601–2
Open letter to Russian Colleagues, Feb. 1948, **16:**519–23

Einstein, Lewis
The United States and Anglo-German Rivalry: National Review (London), Jan. 1913, **13:**378–82

Eisenhower, Dwight David
Letter to Leonard V. Finder, publisher of the Manchester (N.H.) Evening Leader, Jan. 22, 1948, **16:**497–98
Campaign Speech at Detroit, Oct. 24, 1952, **17:**199–203
Speech to UN General Assembly on atoms for peace, Dec. 8, 1953, **17:**211–14
"Open Skies" proposal at Geneva, Switz., July 21, 1955, **17:**330–32
Veto message to House of Representatives on the Natural Gas Bill, Feb. 17, 1956, **17:**370–71
Radio and television address on the Middle East crisis, Feb. 20, 1957, **17:**411–15
Radio and television address on the Little Rock, Ark., school crisis, Sept. 24, 1957, **17:**457–60
Radio and television address on the U-2 Incident, May 25, 1960, **17:**550–54
Farewell Address, Jan. 17, 1961, **18:**1–5

Eisenstein, Louis
The Ideologies of Taxation, 1961, **18:**32–36

Eitzen, D. Stanley
Speech on sports and American society, Fort Collins, Colo., Nov. 1998, **22:**419

El-Din, Ahmad Baha
Editorial on the Bicentennial: al-Arabi (Kuwait), July 1976, **20:**375

Eliot, Charles William
The New Education: Its Organization: Atlantic Monthly, Feb., Mar. 1869, **10:**156–61
Inaugural address (as president of Harvard University), Oct. 19, 1869, **10:**201–9
The Exemption From Taxation, Dec. 12, 1874, **10:**328–32
Wherein Popular Education Has Failed: Forum, Dec. 1892, **11:**404–8
Shall We Adopt Universal Military Service?:

World's Work, Nov. 1916, **14:**60–64

Eliot, John
Letter to Simonds D'Ewes, 1633, **1:**130–31
The Day-Breaking, if not the Sun-Rising of the Gospell with the Indians in New England (by John Wilson), 1646, **1:**180–83

Ellsberg, Daniel
Ellsberg Talks: An interview by J. Robert Moskin: Look, Oct. 5, 1971, **19:**226

Ellsworth, Oliver
Letter to a Landholder, Dec. 17, 1787, **3:**169–72
Open letter to citizens of New Hampshire, Mar. 10, 1788, **3:**264–66

Ellsworth, Phoebe
Juries on Trial: Psychology Today, July 1985, **21:**598

Ely, Richard Theodore
Report of the Organization of the American Economic Association, 1886, **11:**81–86
The Needs of the City, Dec. 1889, **11:**234–39

Emerson, Ralph Waldo
The American Scholar, Aug. 31, 1837, **6:**367–78
The Young American, Feb. 7, 1844, **7:**182–88
Ode Inscribed to W. H. Channing (poem), **7:**359–60
Speech at New York on the Fugitive Slave Law, Mar. 4, 1854, **8:**261–65
The Man With the Hoe (also known as *Farming,* 1870), 1858, **9:**70–75

Emerson, Thomas
Statements on School Prayer: Congressional Digest, Dec. 1980, **21:**248

Emmett, Daniel Decatur
Old Dan Tucker (song), **6:**33
Dixie (song), **9:**146–47

Engelhard, John A.
Fremont in the South (letter to editors by An Alumnus): North Carolina Standard, Sept. 27, 1856, **8:**427–29

Ennis, Bruce J.
The Insanity Defense: The Nation, July 24–31, 1982, **21:**360

Eno, Henry
Letter to William Eno, Aug. 21, 1869, **10:**191–92

Estaing, Charles Hector, Comte d'
A Declaration Addressed in the Name of the King of France, to All the Ancient French in North America, Oct. 28, 1778, **2:**504–5

Evans, George Henry
Memorial to Congress by Citizens of New York: Working Man's Advocate, Nov. 30, 1844, **7:**208–9

Evans, Hiram Wesley

The Klan's Fight for Americanism: North American Review, Mar.–Apr.–May 1926, **14:**506–11

Everett, Alexander H.
Greenough's Statue of Washington: United States Magazine and Democratic Review, June 1844, **7:**246–50

Everett, Edward
Affairs of Greece: North American Review, Oct. 1823, **5:**104–7
The Circumstances Favorable to the Progress of Literature in America, Aug. 26, 1824, **5:**118–27
Speech at St. Paul's Church, Boston, on behalf of Kenyon College, Ohio, May 21, 1833, **6:**26–30
Second speech in Massachusetts legislature on aid to colleges, 1849, **7:**502–6

Ewing, Stephen
The Mockery of American Divorce: Harper's Monthly, July 1928, **14:**577–83

Fadiman, Clifton
Party of One (Review of A. C. Spectorsky's *The Exurbanites*): Holiday, Nov. 1955, **17:**322–25

Fairchild, Henry Pratt
The Melting-Pot Mistake, 1926, **14:**511–16

Fairlie, Henry
An American Ordeal—the Barbecue: Manchester Guardian Weekly, Aug. 1, 1976, **20:**344

Fallaci, Oriana
I and Qaddafi, You and Qaddafi: Washington Post, Apr. 20, 1986, **21:**623

Faltermayer, Edmund K.
The Half-Finished Society: Fortune, Mar. 1965, **18:**273–80

Farmer, James
Which Side Are You On? (song), **18:**161

Farrell, James T(homas)
Social Themes in American Realism, c. 1946, **16:**395–400

Faulkner, William
Acceptance speech for Nobel Prize for Literature, 1949, Dec. 10, 1950, **17:**33–34
On Privacy, The American Dream: What Happened to It?: Harper's, July 1955, **17:**304–10

Fearing, Kenneth
Dirge (poem), **15:**339–40

Fein, Arnold L.
JFK in Dallas: The Warren Report and Its Critics: Saturday Review, Oct. 22, 1966, **18:**435–41

Fenno, John Ward
Editorial on economic interests in the

Caribbean: Gazette of the United States, Mar. 4, 1799, **4:**107–11

Ferguson, Otis
The Spirit of Jazz: New Republic, Dec. 30, 1936, **15:**372–76

Ferraro, Geraldine A.
Who Will Fight for the Worth of Women's Work?: Vital Speeches of the Day, Nov. 15, 1982, **21:**393

Ferry, W. H.
Caught on the Horn of Plenty: Bulletin of the Center for the Study of Democratic Institutions, Jan. 1962, **18:**83–88

Field, Stephen Johnson
Dissent of the (California Supreme) court in *Ex Parte Newman,* 1858, **9:**90–94
Dissent in *Slaughter-House Cases,* 1873, **10:**306–8
Dissent in *Munn* v. *Illinois,* 1877, **10:**379–83

Fillmore, Millard
First annual message to Congress, Dec. 2, 1850, **8:**109–10

Filson, John
The Discovery, Settlement, and Present State of Kentucky (Appendix: *The Adventures of Colonel Daniel Boon[e]*), 1793, **3:**3–6

Fimrite, Ron
It's a Grand New Game: Sports Illustrated, Aug. 11, 1975, **20:**132

Finley, James Bradley
Autobiography (on life in the backwoods), 1854, **8:**294–99

Finley, Robert
Memoirs (on national uniformity of textbooks and curricula), c. 1815, **4:**393–97

Finn, Chester E., Jr.
How to Lose the War of Ideas: Commentary, Aug. 1983, **21:**468

Finney, Charles Grandison
What A Revival of Religion Is, c. 1835, **6:**145–50

Fischer, John
Let's Go Back to the Spoils System: Harper's, Oct. 1945, **16:**275–80

Fischer, Virlis L.
Water and the Southwest: American Forest, Nov. 1967, **18:**573–77

Fisk, Theophilus
Capital Against Labor, May 20, 1835, **6:**118–23

Fiske, John
Manifest Destiny: Harper's New Monthly, Mar. 1885, **11:**65–71

Fitch, Thomas, *et al.*
Reasons Why the British Colonies, in America

Should Not be Charged with Internal Taxes,
1764, **2:**87–98
Fitzgerald, F(rancis) Scott (Key)
Echoes of the Jazz Age: Scribner's, Nov. 1931,
15:116–21
Fitzhugh, George
*Sociology for the South, or the Failure of Free
Society,* 1854, **8:**243–50
Cannibals All! or, Slaves Without Masters,
1857, **8:**475–78
Fletcher, Henry J.
The Drift of Population to Cities: Remedies:
Forum, Aug. 1895, **12:**56–60
Flexner, Abraham
*Medical Education in the United States and
Canada: A Report to the Carnegie Founda-
tion for the Advancement of Teaching,* 1910,
13:237–47
Flint, James
Letter from Jefferson, Ind., May 4, 1820,
4:632–34
Flint, Timothy
Recollections of the Last Ten Years, 1826,
5:205–9
Flournoy, J. J.
*Open letter to contractors for mason's and car-
penter's work of Athens, Ga.:* Southern
Banner, Jan. 13, 1838, **6:**415–16
Fontaine, Peter
Letter to Moses Fontaine, Mar. 30, 1757,
2:19–21
Ford, Gerald R.
Remarks following the swearing-in ceremony,
Aug. 9, 1974, **20:**30
Oath of office taken by the President, Aug. 9,
1974, **20:**30
Address to a joint session of Congress, Aug. 12,
1974, **20:**32
The pardon of Richard M. Nixon, Aug. 9,
1974, **20:**36
*Amnesty program for military deserters and
draft evaders,* Sept. 16, 1974, **20:**86
*Address to the United Nations General Assem-
bly,* Sept. 18, 1974, **20:**87
Letter to Congress on the Mayaguez incident,
May 15, 1975, **20:**168
*Address to the Helsinki conference on security
and cooperation in Europe,* Aug. 1, 1975,
20:182
Address to the National Press Club, Oct. 29,
1975, **20:**226
State of the Union Address: Congressional
Quarterly, Jan. 1977, **21:**11
Ford, Henry
Success: Forum, Oct. 1928, **14:**590–94
On Unemployment: Literary Digest, June 11,

1932, **15:**192–94
Fordham, Elias Pym
*Personal Narrative of Travels in Virginia,
Maryland, Pennsylvania, Ohio, Indiana,
Kentucky; and of a Residence in the Illinois
Territory: 1817–1818* (Frederic A. Ogg,
ed.), 1906, **4:**470–73
Forten, Charlotte L.
Journal (on being an African American
Christian, 1854), 1953, **8:**273–75
Fortune, T. Thomas
*Black and White: Land, Labor, and Politics in
the South,* 1884, **11:**12–15
Fosdick, Harry Emerson
Shall the Fundamentalists Win?: The Chris-
tian Work, CII, June 10, 1922, **14:**325–30
Foster, Stephen Symonds
*The Brotherhood of Thieves; or A True Picture
of the American Church and Clergy,* 1843,
7:81–86
Fowler, J. W.
*Instructions to Overseers of Mississippi planta-
tion,* 1857, **8:**478–79
Frankfurter, Felix
Dissent in *West Virginia Board of Education
et al.* v. *Barnette et al.,* 1943, **16:**154–58
Concurring opinion in *Korematsu* v. *U.S.,*
1944, **16:**237–38
Franklin, Benjamin
Articles of Belief and Acts of Religion, Nov. 20,
1728, **1:**373–74
The Speech of Polly Baker, 1747, **1:**468–70
Advice to a Young Tradesman, 1748,
1:479–80
*Observations Concerning the Increase of
Mankind, Peopling of Countries,* 1751,
1:489–93
Letter to James Parker (Appendix: *The Impor-
tance of Gaining and Preserving the Friend-
ship of the Indians to the British Interest
Considered,* by Parker), 1751, **1:**494–96
Letter to Peter Collinson, May 9, 1753,
1:497–98
Albany Plan of Union, 1754, **1:**522–24
Letter to William Shirley, Dec. 1754,
1:525–26
The Way to Wealth, 1758, **2:**30–34
*The Interest of Great Britain Considered, with
Regard to her Colonies,* 1760, **2:**51–61
*A Narrative of the Late Massacres, in Lan-
caster County,* 1764, **2:**122–28
*Rules by Which a Great Empire May Be Re-
duced to a Small One:* London Public Ad-
vertiser, 1773, **2:**221–26
Autobiography, c. 1775, **2:**368–79
An Account of the Supremest Court of Judica-

ture in Pennsylvania, viz., The Court of the Press: Federal Gazette, Sept. 12, 1789, **3:**365–68

Queries and Remarks Respecting Alterations in the Constitution of Pennsylvania, 1789, **3:**372–75

Editorial on the slave trade (by Historicus): Federal Gazette, Mar. 25, 1790, **3:**421–23

Freedman, Daniel X.
The Use and Abuse of Psychedelic Drugs: Bulletin of the Atomic Scientists, Apr. 1968, **18:**583–90

Frelinghuysen, Theodorus
The Acceptable Communicant, c. 1721, **1:**344–47

French, Marilyn
The National Women's Conference: Horizon, Jan. 1978, **21:**65

Freneau, Philip
The Indian Burying Ground (poem), **3:**206
The Indian Student (poem), **3:**315–16
The Philosopher of the Forest, Number X, 1788, **3:**319–22
Rules of Changing a Limited Republican Government into an Unlimited Hereditary One (editorial): National Gazette, 1792, **3:**499–504

Frey, Darcy
The Last Shot: Harper's, Apr. 1993, **22:**210

Friendly, Fred
The Public's Right to Know: The Wall Street Journal, Oct. 5, 1978, **21:**125

Frost, David, *et al.*
Transcript of the telecast of the David Frost Show of July 15, 1969, on WNEW-TV, New York, **19:**61

Frost, Robert (Lee)
Mending Wall (poem), **13:**463–64
A Brook in the City (poem), **14:**421
Two Tramps in Mud Time (poem), **15:**355–56
The Gift Outright (poem), **16:**109

Fulbright, J(ames) William
Rockefeller Public Service Award Address, Washington, D.C., Dec. 5, 1963, **18:**206–11
Speech in Senate on the American myth, Mar. 25, 1964, **18:**225–31
The Fatal Arrogance of Power, Apr. 21, 1966, **18:**362–67
Old Myths and New Realities—II: The Middle East: A speech in the U.S. Senate, Aug. 24, 1970, **19:**159

Fuller, Margaret
Woman in the Nineteenth Century, 1845,
7:296–99

Fuller, Melville Weston
Opinion of the Court in U.S. v. E. C. Knight Company, 1895, **12:**23–24

Fuller, Zelotes
The Tree of Liberty, Feb. 28, 1830, **5:**355–61

Furman, Richard
Exposition of the Views of the Baptists, Relative to the Coloured Population of the United States, in a Communication to the Governor of South-Carolina, 1822, **5:**37–40

Furuseth, Andrew
Work Is Worship, Sept. 1927, **14:**561–64

Gage, Thomas
Letter to Earl of Shelburne, Jan. 23, 1768, **2:**198
Letter to Earl of Hillsborough, Apr. 10, 1770, **2:**205–8
Letter to Earl of Hillsborough, Nov. 10, 1770, **2:**208–10
Letter to Lord Dartmouth, Oct. 15, 1775, **2:**359–60

Galbraith, John Kenneth
American Capitalism: The Concept of Countervailing Power, 1952, **17:**147–54
Mr. Reagan's Deficit: What to Do About It: Current, May 1982, **21:**348

Gallatin, Albert
Profit Sharing Agreement, 1797, **4:**19–20
Speeches in Congress on the Sedition Act, July 5, 10, 1798, **4:**56–58
Report in House of Representatives on the state of manufacturing, Apr. 19, 1810, **4:**259–67
American Counter-statement (annexed to the Protocol of the Seventh Conference of the American and British Plenipotentiaries), Dec. 19, 1826, **5:**209–14
Peace with Mexico, 1847, **7:**369–73

Galloway, Joseph
A Letter to the People of Pennsylvania, 1760, **2:**62–68
A Plan for a Proposed Union between Great Britain and the Colonies, Sept. 1774, **2:**268–69

Gallup, George Horace
Mass Information or Mass Entertainment, Apr. 14, 1953, **17:**215–20

Galt, John
The Life and Studies of Benjamin West, 1816, **2:**68–73

Gardner, Henry J.
Inaugural address (as governor of Massachusetts), Jan. 9, 1857, **8:**484–87

Gardner, John W(illiam)
Poverty (in *The Cycle of Despair: the Negro*

and the City): Life, Mar. 8, 1968, **18:**639–40

Garland, Hamlin
Provincialism, 1894, **11:**547–52

Garland, Jim
I Don't Want Your Millions, Mister (song), **15:**134–35

Garrison, William Lloyd
The Dangers of the Nation, July 4, 1829, **5:**303–7
To the Public (salutatory): Liberator, Jan. 1, 1831, **5:**422–23
Declaration of Sentiments of the New-England Non-Resistance Society Convention, 1838, **6:**430–32
Notes on women abolitionists at the American Anti-Slavery Society meeting: Liberator, May 31, 1839, **6:**470

Garst, Eleanor
The A-Sexual Society: Center Diary: 15, Nov.–Dec. 1966, **18:**348–49

Gates, Henry Louis, Jr.
Thirteen Ways of Looking at a Black Man, The New Yorker, Oct. 23, 1995, **22:**283

Gates, Horatio
Instruction . . . For Recruiting Troops, Massachusetts Bay, July 10, 1775, **2:**342

George, Henry
Progress and Poverty, 1879, **10:**443–48
Social Problems, 1883, **10:**601–6

George, Walter Lionel
Hail, Columbia!, 1923, **14:**276–81

Georgia Jaycees
Resolution: Proper Perspective on Schools, Feb. 22, 1970, **19:**120

Gergen, David
The Two Nations of America: U.S. News & World Report, May 11, 1992, **22:**149

German, Obadiah
Speech in Senate on war with England, June 13, 1812, **4:**319–24

Ghent, William J.
The Next Step: A Benevolent Feudalism: Independent, Apr. 3, 1902, **12:**450–55

Giacosa, Giuseppe
Impressioni d'America [*Impressions of America*], 1908, **13:**120–23

Gibbons, James, Cardinal
Memorial to His Eminence Cardinal Simeoni, Feb. 20, 1887, **11:**131–36
Installation address (as titular head of the Church of Santa Maria, Trastevere, Italy), Mar. 25, 1887, **11:**148–50

Gibbons, James Sloan
We Are Coming, Father Abraham, Three Hundred Thousand More (poem), **9:**374–75

Gibson, John Bannister
Dissent of the (Pennsylvania Supreme) court in Eakin v. Raub, 1825, **5:**174–78

Giddings, Joshua
Speech in House of Representatives on the annexation of Texas, May 21, 1844, **7:**201

Gilder, George
Supply-Side Economics: Nation's Business, April 1981, **21:**285

Gilmore, Patrick Sarsfield
When Johnny Comes Marching Home (song), **9:**461

Ginsberg, Eli
The Pluralistic Economy of the U.S.: Scientific American, Dec. 1976, **20:**309

Gitter, Max
Bad Plumbing: The New Republic, Nov. 25, 1996, **22:**324

Gladden, Washington
The Embattled Farmers: Forum, Nov. 1890, **11:**356–60
Religion and the Schools: Atlantic Monthly, Jan. 1915, **13:**546–51

Gladstone, William Ewart
Kin Beyond Sea: North American Review, Sept.–Oct. 1878, **10:**393–99

Glassman, James K.
Dow 36,000: The New Strategy for Profiting from the Coming Rise in the Stock Market, 1999, **22:**384

Glazer, Joe
Too Old To Work (song), **17:**24
Automation (song), **17:**242–43

Glazer, Nathan
The Peoples of America: Nation, Sept. 20, 1965, **18:**261–67

Godey, Louis Antoine
How To Be the Perfect Housewife: Godey's Lady's Book and Magazine, Mar. 1859, **9:**108–10

Godkin, Edwin Lawrence
A New Kind of State Constitution (editorial): Nation, Apr. 3, 1879, **10:**401–4

Goldberg, Helene
Analyzing Dr. Laura: Tikkun, Nov.–Dec. 1998, **22:**378

Goldwater, Barry M(orris)
Speech in Senate on total victory in the Cold War, July 14, 1961, **18:**42–45

Gompers, Samuel
Testimony before Senate Committee on Education and Labor, 1883, **10:**561–67
Letter to Peter Grosscup, Aug. 14, 1894, **11:**530–35

Gooding, James Henry
Letter to Abraham Lincoln, Sept. 28, 1863,

9:459–60

Goodman, Paul
Communitas: Means of Livelihood and Ways of Life, 1947, **16:**488–94

Goodman, Percival
Communitas: Means of Livelihood and Ways of Life, 1947, **16:**488–94

Goodsell, Jane
Psychodelerium Tremens (poem): Congressional Record for Apr. 18, 1969, **19:**25

Goodwin, Richard N.
The Shape of American Politics: Commentary, June 1967, **18:**455–61

Gordon, Elaine
Arguments in favor of the Equal Rights Amendment: State Government, Spring 1975, **20:**150

Gore, Al
Earth in the Balance, 1992, **22:**163
Presidential election concession speech, Dec. 13, 2000, **22:**466

Gottlieb, Adolph
Preamble of the Federation of Modern Painters and Sculptors, 1943, **16:**209

Gouge, William M.
A Short History of Paper Money and Banking in the United States, 1833, **6:**34–40

Gowing, Lawrence
Paint in America: New Statesman, May 24, 1958, **17:**518–21

Grady, Henry Woodfin
The Race Problem in the South, Dec. 13, 1889, **11:**240–50

Graham, Billy
Interviewed by editors of Look *Magazine,* Feb. 7, 1956, **17:**393–99

Granger, Bill
Ignorance—our cultural blight: Chicago Tribune, Nov. 14, 1984, **21:**536

Grant, Ulysses Simpson
Report to Andrew Johnson, Dec. 18, 1865, **9:**635–37
Message to Senate on annexation of the Dominican Republic, May 31, 1870, **10:**231–33
Speech at Des Moines, on separation of church and school, 1876, **10:**365

Grassi, Giovanni Antonio
Notizie varie sullo stato presente della repubblica degli Stati Uniti dell'America settentrionale scritte al principio del 1818 [*Commentaries on the Present Condition on the Republic of the United States of North America Written Principally in 1818*], 1819, **4:**560–67

Gray, Daniel

Address to the people of Hampshire County, Mass., regarding the causes of Shays's Rebellion, **3:**61

Gray, James H.
A Canadian Looks Us Over: Atlantic Monthly, Mar. 1957, **17:**445–50

Gray, Sylvester
Petition to Congress on a Negro pioneer land claim, Mar. 23, 1860, **9:**174–75

Gray, William B.
She Is More To Be Pitied Than Censured (song), **11:**553–54

Grayson, William J.
The Hireling and the Slave (poem), **8:**266–72

Grede, William J.
America, A Frontier, Oct. 10, 1952, **17:**154–59

Greeley, Horace
Letter to Paulina W. Davis, Sept. 1, 1852, **8:**184–85
Two Hours with Brigham Young, July 13, 1859, **9:**132–35
The Prayer of Twenty Millions (editorial): New-York Daily Tribune, Aug. 19, 1862, **9:**345–48
First Fruits of Reconstruction (editorial): New-York Daily Tribune, Nov. 15, 1865, **9:**623–25

Green, Asa
A Glance At New York, 1837, **6:**399–402

Greenberg, Clement
How Art Writing Earns Its Bad Name: Encounter, Dec. 1962, **18:**114–18

Greenberg, Daniel S.
The Politics of Pure Science: Saturday Review, Nov. 4, 1967, **18:**567–73

Greenhouse, Steven
The Average Guy Takes It on the Chin: The New York Times, July 13, 1986, **21:**647

Greenhow, Rose O'Neal
My Imprisonment, 1863, **9:**329–33

Greenough, Horatio
American Art, 1843, **7:**113–17

Greenspan, Alan
Speech on the growth of market capitalism, 1998, **22:**350

Greer, Colin
Paving Streets with his Life: New York Times, Nov. 6, 1976, **20:**307

Gregg, Frederick
Preface to the Catalogue for the International Exhibition of Modern Art, 1913, **13:**375–76

Gregg, William
Essays on Domestic Industry, Or An Inquiry Into the Expediency, of Establishing Cotton Manufactures in South Carolina (by South

Carolina), 1845, **7:**276–81

Greider, William
The Education of David Stockman: The Atlantic, Dec. 1981, **21:**321

Greising, David
The Smell of Blood: Business Week, Apr. 1, 1996, **22:**320

Grew, Joseph Clark
Note to Hachiro Arita, Japanese Minister for Foreign Affairs, Dec. 30, 1938, **15:**555–59

Griffith, David Wark
The Rise and Fall of Free Speech in America, 1916, **14:**28–33

Grimes, James
Opinion in Senate on the impeachment of Andrew Johnson, Mar. 1868, **10:**130–33

Grinnell, George Bird
The Last of the Buffalo: Scribner's, Sept. 1892, **11:**388–95

Griscom, John H.
The Sanitary Condition of the Laboring Population of New York, A Discourse Delivered . . . at the Repository of the American Institute, Dec. 30, 1844, **7:**213–18

Griswold, Erwin N.
Dissent—1968 Style, Apr. 16, 1968, **18:**670–73

Gronlund, Laurence
The Coöperative Commonwealth, 1884, **11:**1–7
Testimony before Chicago Conference on Trusts, Sept. 1899, **12:**293–97

Grossman, Edward, et al.
Symposium on "Culture and the Present Moment": Commentary, Dec. 1974, **20:**107

Grover, Thomas
To the Printer (letter): Hampshire (Mass.) Herald, Dec. 1786, **3:**62

Gruening, Ernest
Alaska Fights for Statehood: Atlantic Monthly, Jan. 1957, **17:**451–56

Grund, Francis J.
The Americans, in Their Moral, Social, and Political Relations, 1837, **6:**384–91

Grundy, Felix
Speech in House of Representatives on war with England, Dec. 1811, **4:**291–92
Resolutions in Tennessee legislature on the caucus system, 1823, **5:**85–87

Guard, Theodore de la (pseud.) *see* Ward, Nathaniel

Gulko, Boris
Is Chess Finished?: Commentary, July 1997, **22:**335

Gurowski, Adam G. de, Count
America and Europe, 1857, **8:**501–5

Gustafson, W. Eric
Contracting for Defense: Private Firms and the Public Interest: Political Science Quarterly, June 1962, **18:**94–101

Guthrie, Woodrow Wilson (Woody)
So Long (It's Been Good To Know Yuh) (song), **15:**452–53
Union Maid (song), **16:**21
This Land Is Your Land (song), **17:**378–79

Hacker, Andrew
A Country Called Corporate America: New York Times Magazine, July 3, 1966, **18:**396–401

Hadley, Arthur Twining
The Constitutional Position of Property in America: Independent, Apr. 16, 1908, **13:**133–37

Hale, Edward Everett
The High Court of America, Dec. 1890, **11:**315–17

Halford, John
Cultural Terrorism: The Plain Truth, Feb. 1986, **21:**626

Hall, Edward T.
Our Silent Language: Science Digest, Aug. 1962, **18:**63–66

Hall, James
Letters from the West, 1828, **5:**231–38

Hall, Uriel S.
An Income Tax: Reasons in Its Favor: Forum, Mar. 1894, **11:**539–42

Hallett, Benjamin
Mr. Hallett's Argument in the Rhode Island Causes, before the Supreme Court of the United States, Jan. 1848, **7:**410–20

Hamilton, Alexander
To the Printer (letter by Publius): New-York Journal, Oct. 19, 1778, **2:**509
Letter to John Jay, Mar. 14, 1779, **2:**530–31
The Continentalist, No. VI, July 4, 1782, **2:**575–79
Resolutions for a General Convention, June 30, 1783, **2:**612–16
Letter to Citizens of New York (by Phocion), 1784, **3:**7–13
Letter to Francis Childs (by Caesar); New York Daily Advertiser, Oct. 17, 1787, **3:**142–45
The Federalist (Nos. 1, 78, 84), 1787–1788, **3:**213–15; 228–38
Report in House of Representatives on public credit, Jan. 14, 1790, **3:**407–15
Opinion to George Washington on the proposed First Bank of the U.S., Feb. 23, 1791, **3:**452–59
Report on Manufactures, Dec. 5, 1791,

3:459–72

Pacificus, Nos. III, V: Gazette of the United States, July 6, 13, 1793, **3**:540–45

Americanus, No. II, Feb. 8, 1794, **3**:553–57

Tully, III, Aug. 28, 1794, **3**:561–63

Camillus, No. 1, July 22, 1795, **3**:587–89

Letter to Harrison Gray Otis, Jan. 26, 1799, **4**:101–2

Hamilton, Lee H.

Speech on the "Law of the Sea" Treaty: Congressional Digest, Jan. 1983, **21**:370

Hammarskjöld, Knut

Hijacking as an International Crime: International Review of Criminal Policy, No. 32, 1976, **21**:59

Hamor, W. A.

The Value of Industrial Research: Scientific Monthly, Oct. 1915, **13**:516–19

Hampden (pseud.) *see* Roane, Spencer

Hancock, John

Speech in Massachusetts Ratifying Convention, Jan. 31, 1788, **3**:250–51

Hand, (Billings) Learned

How Far Is a Judge Free in Rendering a Decision?, May 14, 1933, **15**:233–36

Handy, W(illiam) C(hristopher)

Father of the Blues: An Autobiography (Arna Bontemps, ed.), 1941, **16**:83–89

Hanna, Marcus Alonzo (Mark)

Mark Hanna: His Book, 1904, **12**:583–85

Hardin, Clifford M.

Can a President Control His Own White House? Vital Speeches of the Day, Jan. 1981, **21**:267

Harding, Warren Gamaliel

Speech to special session of Congress on return to normalcy, Apr. 12, 1921, **14**:292–98

Hardy, Thomas

On an Invitation to the United States (poem), **12**:402

Harlan, John Marshall

Dissent in *Civil Rights Cases,* 1883, **10**:581–83

Dissent in *U.S. v. E. C. Knight Company,* 1895, **12**:24–28

Dissent in *Plessy v. Ferguson,* 1896, **12**:95–100

Opinion of the Court in *Northern Securities Company v. U.S.,* 1904, **12**:576–80

Dissent in *Lochner v. New York,* 1905, **13**:11–14

Standard Oil Company of New Jersey et al. v. United States: United States Reports [Supreme Court], Vol. 221, pp. 1ff, **13**:310–18

Harnik, Peter

Funmobile Folly: National Parks and Conservation Magazine, Jan. 1972, **19**:264

Harper, Ida Husted

Women Ought to Work: Independent, May 16, 1901, **12**:394–98

Harper, William

Memoir on Slavery, 1837, **6**:340–46

Harper, William Rainey

The President's Report to the Board of Trustees at the University of Chicago, 1902, **12**:498–501

Harriman, W(illiam) Averell

Speech at the Sunday Evening Forum, Tucson, Ariz., on American relations with the Far East, Oct. 31, 1965, **18**:328–31

Harrington, Floyd

Citizen's Band Radios: Soldiers, Oct. 1975, **20**:195

Harrington, Michael

The Other America, 1962, **18**:88–94

That Year [1984] Is Here: Maclean's, Jan. 9, 1984, **21**:474

Harris, Charles K.

After the Ball (song), **11**:385–86

Harris, Fred R.

Oil: Capitalism Betrayed in Its Own Camp: Progressive, Apr. 1973, **19**:332

Harris, Herbert

Why Labor Lost the Intellectuals: Harper's, June 1964, **18**:219–24

Harris, Louis

A Talk with Louis Harris (interview): Bulletin of the Atomic Scientists, Aug.–Sept. 1982, **21**:372

Harris, William Torrey

The Pedagogical Creed, 1898, **12**:211–14

Harrison, Benjamin

Message to Senate on treaty for annexation of Hawaii, Feb. 15, 1893, **11**:479–80

Harte, Bret

Plain Language from Truthful James (poem), **10**:241–42

The Rise of the 'Short Story': Cornhill Magazine, July 1899, **12**:273–77

Hartman, Arthur A.

Testimony before the House Committee on Foreign Affairs, May 15, 1974, **20**:68

Harvey, George Brinton McClellan

The Diplomats of Democracy (editorial): North American Review, Feb. 1914, **13**:464–67

Harvey, W. Hope (Coin)

Coin's Financial School, 1894, **11**:543–47

Hassett, Kevin A.

Dow 36,000: The New Strategy for Profiting from the Coming Rise in the Stock Market,

1999, **22:**384

Hatton, Ann Julia
Alknomook (song), **3:**570

Hauser, Henri
L'Amérique vivante [*Living America*], 1924,
14:438–41

Havemann, Joel *et al.*
*Federal Spending—The North's Loss Is the
Sunbelt's Gain:* National Journal, June
26, 1976, **20:**262

Hawley, Zerah
*A Journal of a Tour Through Connecticut,
Massachusetts, New-York, the North Part of
Pennsylvania and Ohio,* 1822, **5:**35–37

Hawthorne, Nathaniel
Earth's Holocaust: Graham's Magazine, May
1844, **7:**170–81
Sketch of Abraham Lincoln, 1883, **9:**395–97

Hay, George
*Speech for the prosecution in the trial of Aaron
Burr,* 1808, **4:**235–38

Hay, John
*Circular letter to Germany, Russia, and En-
gland* (on Open Door Policy), Sept. 6,
1899, **12:**327–28

Hayden, Ferdinand Vandiveer
*Letter to commissioner of the General Land Of-
fice,* July 1, 1867, **10:**102–3

Hayden, Tom
The Occupation of Newark: New York Review
of Books, Aug. 24, 1967, **18:**472–83

Hayes, Alfred
Joe Hill (song), **15:**515–16

Hayes, John W.
Testimony before Chicago Conference on Trusts,
Sept. 1899, **12:**287–93

Hayes, Rutherford Birchard
*Veto message to House of Representatives on the
Army Appropriation Act,* Apr. 29, 1879,
10:449–50
Diary (on concentrated wealth),
1886–1887, **11:**123–25

Haynes, Roy A.
*Speech at national meeting of the Woman's
Christian Temperance Union,* Jan. 26,
1927, **14:**523–26

Hays, Lee
Wasn't That A Time! (song), **16:**527–28

Heflin, Howell
*Statement to the Congressional Ethics Commit-
tee investigating the Keating Five,* Oct. 22,
1990, **22:**115

Heilbroner, Robert
Reflections: Economic Prospects: The New
Yorker, Aug. 29, 1983, **21:**436

Heinz, John

Testimony on trade with China: Senate Committee on Finance, Nov. 15, 1979,
21:140

Helms, Jesse
The Panama Canal Treaties—Pro and Con:
American Legion Magazine, Jan. 1978,
21:53
Statements on School Prayer: Congressional
Digest, Dec. 1980, **21:**248

Helper, Hinton Rowan
*The Impending Crisis of the South: How to
Meet It,* 1857, **8:**479–84

Helprin, Mark
Liberty Enlightening the World: Art & An-
tiques, June 1984, **21:**507

Helvidius (pseud.) *see* Madison, James

Hennings, Thomas C., Jr.
*Testimony before Senate Subcommittee on Inter-
nal Security of the Committee on the Judiciary, regarding appellate jurisdiction of the
U.S. Supreme Court,* Mar. 4, 1958,
17:495–99

Henri, Robert
*The New York Exhibition of Independent
Artists:* The Craftsman, May 1910,
13:260–64

Henry, Jacob
*Speech in North Carolina House of Commons
on holding public office,* 1809, **4:**239–41

Henry, Joseph
*First annual report of the Board of Regents of
the Smithsonian Institution,* Dec. 8, 1847,
7:392–98

Henry, Patrick
Give Me Liberty or Give Me Death, Mar. 23,
1775, **2:**321–23
Speech in Virginia Ratifying Convention, June
1788, **3:**280–86
*Speech in Virginia Assembly on the assumption
of state debts,* Dec. 23, 1790, **3:**435–36

Henshaw, David
*Remarks Upon the Rights and Powers of Corpo-
rations, and the Rights, Powers, and Duties
of the Legislature Toward Them* (by a Citizen of Boston), 1837, **6:**317–25

Hepburn, William Peters
*Speech in House of Representatives on the regu-
lation of railroad rates,* Feb. 7, 1906,
13:40–42

Hermann, Edward S.
The Income Counter-Revolution: Commonweal, Jan. 3, 1975, **20:**117

Herrick, Robert
Recantation of a Pacifist: New Republic,
Oct. 30, 1915, **13:**563–65

Herron, George Davis

Between Caesar and Jesus, 1899, **12:**226–28

Hesburgh, Theodore M.
Statement made on the occasion of releasing a report on civil rights enforcement, Oct. 12, 1970, **19:**166

Hewitt, James
New Yankee Doodle (song), **4:**73–74

Heyward, Carter
Remarks on the ordination of women: Christianity and Crisis, Sept. 16, 1974, **20:**94

Hicks, Granville
On Leaving the Communist Party: New Republic, Oct. 4, 1939, **15:**565–67

Higginson, Francis
New England's Plantation or A Short and True Description of the Commodities of that Country, 1629, **1:**95–99

Hill, Gladwyn
After Earth Day: National Wildlife, Aug.–Sept. 1970, **19:**145

Hill, James Jerome
The Natural Wealth of the Land and Its Conservation, May 14, 1908, **13:**153–60

Hill, Joe
The Preacher and the Slave (song), **13:**26–27

Hill, Lauryn
Everything Is Everything (song), 1999, **22:**383

Hill, Walter B.
The Great American Safety-Value: Century Magazine, July 1892, **11:**386–88

Hillquit, Morris
Socialism in Theory and Practice, 1909, **13:**212–13

Himelstein, Linda
The Smell of Blood: Business Week, Apr. 1, 1996, **22:**320

Himmelfarb, Gertrude
Academic Advocates, Commentary, Sept. 1995, **22:**277

Hines, Frank T.
G.I. Bill of Rights, Sept. 19, 1944, **16:**215–20

Hines, Walker Downer
Our Irresponsible State Governments: Atlantic Monthly, May 1915, **13:**523–28

Historicus (pseud.) *see* Franklin, Benjamin

Hoar, George Frisbie
Speech in Senate on acquisition of Puerto Rico, Cuba, and Philippine Islands, Jan. 9, 1899, **12:**248–53

Ho Chih Minh
An Exchange of Letters: White House press release, Nov. 3, 1969, **19:**71

Hodge, Charles
Review of Nathaniel Taylor's *A Plea for Voluntary Societies and a Defence of the Decisions of the General Assembly of 1836:* Biblical Repertory and Princeton Review (Philadelphia), Jan. 1837, **6:**363–66

Hoffman, Walter E.
Statement in U.S. District Court at Baltimore pronouncing sentence on Spiro T. Agnew, Oct. 10, 1973, **19:**390

Hoier, Thomas
Don't Bite The Hand That's Feeding You (song), **13:**562

Holbrook, Josiah
The American Lyceum, 1829, **5:**314–20

Holley, Alexander Lyman
The Inadequate Union of Engineering Science and Art, Feb. 22, 1876, **10:**366–72

Holman, Edwin J.
Hard Cases Make Bad Law: Journal of the American Medical Association, Oct. 29, 1973, **19:**385

Holmes, Oliver Wendell (1809–1894)
Ode for a Social Meeting (poem), **8:**500
The Last Blossom (The Autocrat of the Breakfast-Table): Atlantic Monthly, May 1858, **9:**48–53
Elsie Venner (The Professor's Story): Atlantic Monthly, Jan. 1860, **9:**148–50
Over the Teacups, 1890, **11:**330–32

Holmes, Oliver Wendell (1841–1935)
Dissent in *Northern Securities Company* v. *U.S.,* 1904, **12:**580–83
Dissent in *Lochner* v. *New York,* 1905, **13:**14–15
Dissent in *Abrams et al.* v. *U.S.,* 1919, **14:**244–47
Dissent in *Adkins* v. *Children's Hospital,* 1923, **14:**397–99
Dissent in *Gitlow* v. *New York,* 1925, **14:**480
Opinion of the Court in *Nixon* v. *Herndon,* 1927, **14:**534–35

Holt, John
Can We Save the Schools? The Progressive, Mar. 1982, **21:**382

Homan, Richard
Maryland Voters Reject Proposed New Constitution: Chicago Sun-Times, May 16, 1968, **18:**598–99

Hone, Philip
Diary (on the Dorr Rebellion), Apr.–May 1842, **7:**52–55

Honegger, Barbara
The ERA Alternative: Chicago Sun-Times, July 1983, **21:**442

Hoover, Herbert Clark
Speech at Cleveland, Ohio, on moral standards in an Industrial Era, May 7, 1924, **14:**428–30

*Campaign speech at Madison Square Garden,
New York City,* Oct. 22, 1928, **14:**595–600

*Veto message to Senate on the Muscle Shoals
Bill,* Mar. 3, 1931, **15:**79–82

*Campaign speech at Madison Square Garden,
New York City,* Oct. 31, 1932, **15:**188–91

*Speech at Republican National Convention,
Cleveland,* June 10, 1936, **15:**384–88

Our National Policies in This Crisis (radio
address), Dec. 20, 1950, **17:**46–49

Hoover, J(ohn) Edgar
*Testimony before House Un-American Activities
Committee,* Mar. 26, 1947, **16:**451–57

Hopkins, Harry Lloyd
Federal Emergency Relief (radio address),
Dec. 1934, **15:**261–63

Hopkins, Samuel
*A Dialogue Concerning the Slavery of the
Africans,* 1776, **2:**450–52

Hopkinson, Francis
A Toast (song), **2:**511–12

Hopkinson, Joseph
Hail, Columbia! (song), **4:**75

Hosack, David
*Sketch of the Origin and Progress of the Med-
ical Schools of New York and Philadelphia:*
The American Medical and Philosophical Register, July 1812, **4:**307–11

Hovland, Gjert
Letter to Torjuls Maeland, Apr. 22, 1835,
6:115–17

Howe, Frederic C.
The Confessions of a Reformer, 1925,
14:472–76

Howe, Julia Ward
The Battle Hymn of the Republic (song),
9:322–23

Howe, Neil
The New Generation Gap: The Atlantic
Monthly, Dec. 1992, **22:**165

Howells, William Dean
Criticism and Fiction, 1891, **11:**366–67
Editorial on "cinematographic show" (Editor's
Easy Chair): Harper's Monthly, Sept.
1912, **13:**333–37

Hoyt, Charles H.
The Bowery (song), **11:**503

Hubbard, Elbert Green
A Message to García, 1899, **12:**309–11

Hubbard, William
*The Happiness of a People in the Wisdom of
their Rulers Directing and in Obedience of
their Brethren Attending Unto What Israel
Ought To Do,* May 3, 1676, **1:**248–54

Hubert, Philip G.
The Business of a Factory (The Conduct of

Great Businesses Series): Scribner's,
Mar. 1897, **12:**152–57

Hübner, Joseph Alexander, Graf von
Promenade autour du monde [*Trip Around the
World in 1871*], 1873, **10:**279–88

Hughes, Charles Evans
Opinion of the Court in A.L.A. Schechter
Poultry Corporation et al. v. U.S., 1935,
15:301–9

Hughes, Langston
Bop, 1953, **17:**228–29

Hughey, Alice
The Changing Face of Star Wars: The National Voter, Sept.–Oct. 1986, **21:**651

Humphrey, Hubert Horatio, Jr.
First Step Toward Disarmament: Nation, May
24, 1958, **17:**475–79

Humphreys, Benjamin G.
*Message to Mississippi legislature on freedmen
of Mississippi,* Nov. 20, 1865, **9:**626–28

Hunt, Freeman
*Worth and Wealth: A Collection of Maxims,
Morals and Miscellanies for Merchants and
Men of Business,* 1856, **8:**435–39

Hunter, Robert
Poverty, 1904, **12:**586–90

Hutar, Patricia
*Address to the International Women's Confer-
ence in Mexico City,* June 20, 1975, **20:**159

Hutchins, Robert Maynard
The Higher Learning in America, 1936,
15:400–7
America and the War (radio address), Jan.
23, 1941, **16:**66–72

Hutchinson, Bruce
Editorial on the Bicentennial: Globe and
Mail (Toronto), Nov. 28, 1975, **20:**369

Iacocca, Lee
The Chrysler Bailout: Iacocca: An Autobiography, Chs. xviii–xix, 1984, **21:**150

Ianni, Francis A. J.
*New Mafia—Black, Hispanic and Italian
Styles:* Society, Mar.–Apr. 1974, **20:**51

Ingersoll, Charles Jared
Inchiquin, the Jesuits Letter (by Some Unknown Author), 1810, **4:**270–78
*A Discourse Concerning the Influence of Amer-
ica on the Mind,* Oct. 18, 1823, **5:**95–103

Ingersoll, Robert Green
Why Am I an Agnostic?, 1890, **11:**267–71

Inglis, Charles
*The True Interest of America Impartially
Stated, in Certain Strictures on a Pamphlet
Intitled Common Sense,* 1776, **2:**403–9

Ingraham, Joseph Holt
The South-West (by A Yankee), 1835,

6:97–104

International Monetary Fund

First Outline of Reform of the International Monetary System and Related Issues, Sept. 24, 1973, **19:**398

Iredell, James

Answers to Mr. [George] Mason's Objections to the New Constitution (by Marcus), Jan. 1788, **3:**247–50

Ireland, John

State Schools and Parish Schools, 1890, **11:**296–302

Jackson, Andrew

First annual message to Congress, Dec. 8, 1829, **5:**330–36

Veto message to the House of Representatives on the Maysville Road Bill, May 27, 1830, **5:**374–78

Second annual message to Congress, Dec. 6, 1830, **5:**418–21

Veto message to Senate on the Second Bank Renewal Bill, July 10, 1832, **5:**524–35

Proclamation to the People of South Carolina, Dec. 10, 1832, **5:**585–93

Message to Senate on resolution of censure, Apr. 15, 1834, **6:**58–62

Seventh annual message to Congress, Dec. 7, 1835, **6:**164–66

Eight annual message to Congress, Dec. 21, 1836, **6:**293–95

Farewell Address, Mar. 4, 1837, **6:**298–310

Letter to Aaron V. Brown, Feb. 12, 1843, **7:**95–97

Jackson, Helen Hunt

A Century of Dishonor, 1881, **10:**504–7

Jackson, Jesse, Jr.

Why We're in Jail: Chicago Sun-Times, Sept. 11, 1969, **19:**80

Campaign Speech: The New York Times, Feb. 27, 1984, **21:**521

Speech to the Democratic National Convention, July 1992, **22:**151

Jackson, Robert H(oughwout)

Opinion of the Court in West Virginia Board of Education et al. v. Barnette et al., 1943, **16:**148–53

Dissent in Korematsu v. U.S., 1944, **16:**240–41

Jacob, John E.

Speech to members of Congress on the state of black America, March 1988, **22:**49

Jacobs, Walter

Refugees and Their Problems: National Journal, July 26, 1980, **21:**242

Jain, Girilal

Editorial on the Bicentennial: Times of India (Bombay and New Delhi), July 7, 1976, **20:**376

James, Edwin L.

Our World Power and Moral Influence: International Digest, Oct. 1930, **15:**56–58

James, Henry

Hawthorne, 1879, **10:**416–19

Letter to the American Publishers' Copyright League, Nov. 15, 1887, **11:**151–54

James, Leon

Road Rage and Aggressive Driving, 2000, **22:**454

James, William

The Ph.D. Octopus: Harvard Monthly, Mar. 1903, **12:**508–13

The Moral Equivalent of War: McClure's, Aug. 1910, **13:**254–60

Jarves, James Jackson

The Art Idea, 1864, **9:**485–91

Jay, John

Address to the People of Great Britain (on the rights of the colonists), Sept. 5, 1774, **2:**277–82

Letter to George Washington, June 27, 1786, **3:**63–64

An Address to the People of the State of New-York on the Subject of the Constitution, Agreed upon at Philadelphia, Sept. 17, 1787, **3:**270–75

Jay, Peter Augustus

Speech in New York State constitutional convention, Sept. 1821, **5:**23–25

Jeffers, Robinson

Science (poem), **14:**481

Shine, Perishing Republic (poem), **14:**481–82

Rearmament (poem), **15:**349

Jefferson, Thomas

A Summary View of the Rights of British America, July 1774, **2:**258–65

Autobiography (on proceedings of the Continental Congress), June 7, 8, 1776, **2:**442–46

Letter to David Rittenhouse, July 19, 1778, **2:**502

Notes on the State of Virginia, 1781–82, **2:**563–73

Letter to John Banister, Oct. 15, 1785, **3:**41–42

Virginia Statute of Religious Freedom, 1779, **3:**53–54

Letter to John Adams, July 11, 1786, **3:**59–61

Letter to Edward Carrington, Jan. 16, 1787, **3:**82–83

Letter to James Madison, Jan. 30, 1787, **3:**83–84

Letter to Edward Carrington, Aug. 4, 1787, **3:**94

Letter to James Madison, Dec. 20, 1787, **3:**185–86

Letter to James Madison, July 31, 1788, **3:**304–5

Letter to Francis Hopkinson, Mar. 13, 1789, **3:**342–43

Letter to James Madison, Sept. 6, 1789, **3:**389–92

The Anas (on the Hamiltonian System), 1790, **3:**416–21

Opinion to George Washington on the proposed First Bank of the U.S., Feb. 15, 1791, **3:**449–52

Letter to Alexander Hamilton, Apr. 28, 1793, **3:**531–35

Letter to William Mumford, June 18, 1799, **4:**113–15

Letter to Gideon Granger, Aug. 13, 1800, **4:**140–41

First Inaugural Address, Mar. 4, 1801, **4:**143–46

Letter to James Monroe, Nov. 24, 1801, **4:**147–49

Letter to Robert Livingston, Apr. 18, 1802, **4:**150–52

Confidential message to Congress on the Lewis and Clark Expedition, Jan. 18, 1803, **4:**158–60

Instructions to Meriwether Lewis, June 20, 1803, **4:**160–64

Letters to John Breckinridge, Aug. 12, 18, 1803, **4:**171–73

Proposed Constitutional Amendment on the Louisiana Purchase, 1803, **4:**173

Letter to Wilson C. Nicholas, Sept. 7, 1803, **4:**173–74

Letter to John Norvell, June 14, 1807, **4:**219–20

Letter to Samuel Miller, Jan. 23, 1808, **4:**234–35

Letter to J. B. Colvin, Sept. 20, 1810, **4:**268–70

Letter to John Adams, Oct. 28, 1813, **4:**333–36

Letter to Baron von Humboldt, Dec. 6, 1813, **4:**340–41

Letter to N. G. Dufief, Apr. 19, 1814, **4:**348–49

Letter to Peter Carr, Sept. 7, 1814, **4:**350–53

Letter to P. H. Wendover, Mar. 13, 1815, **4:**383–85

Letter to W. H. Torrance, June 11, 1815, **4:**390–91

Letter to Thomas Leiper, June 12, 1815, **4:**391–92

Letter to Benjamin Austin, Jan. 9, 1816, **4:**412–13

Letter to Pierre S. du Pont de Nemours, Apr. 24, 1816, **4:**414–15

Letter to John Taylor of Caroline, May 28, 1816, **4:**416–18

Letter to Francis Gilmer, June 7, 1816, **4:**419–20

Letter to Samuel Kercheval, July 12, 1816, **4:**422–26

Letter to Nathaniel Burwell, Mar. 14, 1818, **4:**490–91

Letter to John Holmes, Apr. 22, 1820, **4:**603–4

Letter to Thomas Cooper, Nov. 2, 1822, **5:**30–31

Letter to John Monroe, Oct. 24, 1823, **5:**69–70

Jenner, William E.

Speech in Senate, July 26, 1957, *and Testimonies before the Senate Subcommittee on Internal Security of the Committee on the Judiciary,* Feb. 19, Mar. 5, 1958, **17:**491–95

Jenyns, Soame

The Objections to the Taxation of Our American Colonies, by the Legislature of Great Britain, Briefly Consider'd, 1765, **2:**160–61

Jerome, Lawrence E.

Objections to Astrology: The Humanist, Nov.–Dec. 1975, **20:**239

J. Hector St. John (pseud.) *see* Crèvecoeur, Michel Guillaume Jean de

John Paul II

Remarks on the Pope's visit: Presidential documents, Oct. 6, 1979, **21:**163

Johnson, Andrew

Proclamation of Amnesty and Pardon for the Confederate States, May 29, 1865, **9:**593–94

Proclamation on a Provisional Government for North Carolina, May 29, 1865, **9:**595–96

Veto message to Senate on the Freedmen's Bureau Bill, Feb. 19, 1866, **10:**3–7

Impromptu speech at the White House, Feb. 22, 1866, **10:**8–11

Veto message to Senate on the Civil Rights Bill, Mar. 27, 1866, **10:**11–18

Second annual message to Congress, Dec. 3, 1866, **10:**81–85

Veto message to Senate on the Tenure of Office Act, Mar. 2, 1867, **10:**90–92

Veto message to House of Representatives on the First Reconstruction Act, Mar. 2, 1867, **10:**95–98

Veto message to House of Representatives on the

Second Reconstruction Act, Mar. 23, 1867, **10:**98–102

Johnson, Edward
Wonder-Working Providence of Sions Saviour in New England, 1654, **1:**217–20

Johnson, Hugh Samuel
The Blue Eagle from Egg to Earth, 1935, **15:**293–300

Johnson, James Weldon
Race Prejudice and the Negro Artist: Harper's, Nov. 1928, **14:**605–12

Johnson, Lyndon Baines
My Political Philosophy: Texas Quarterly, Winter 1958, **17:**469–73
Speech to joint session of Congress, including Supreme Court members and Cabinet, Nov. 27, 1963, **18:**203–6
Message to Congress on the war on poverty, Mar. 16, 1964, **18:**212–16
Speech at University of Michigan on the Great Society, May 22, 1964, **18:**216–18
The Need for Scholars, May 11, 1966, **18:**368–72
Foreign policy speech, announcing withdrawal from politics, Mar. 31, 1968, **18:**613–16

Johnson, Nancy
Aid to the Contras: Lakeville (Connecticut) Journal, June 20, 1985, **21:**574

Johnson, Richard Mentor
Speech in House of Representatives on war with England, Dec. 1811, **4:**292–94
Report of Senate Committee on Post Offices and Postal Roads, Jan. 19, 1829, **5:**284–88

Johnson, Thomas A.
The U.S. Negro in Vietnam (series): New York Times, Apr. 29, May 1, 1968, **18:**617–21

Johnson, William
William Johnson's Natchez: The Ante-Bellum Diary of a Free Negro (William R. Hogan and Edwin A. Davis, eds.), 1951, **6:**215–20

Jones, Aaron
Testimony before Chicago Conference on Trusts, Sept. 1899, **12:**279–81

Jones, James C.
Speech in Senate on the moral declarations in foreign policy, Mar. 18, 1852, **8:**170–73

Jones, Rufus Matthew
The Quaker Peace Position: The Survey, Apr. 3, 1915, **13:**555–58

Jones, Samuel Milton
The New Patriotism: A Golden-Rule Government for Cities: Municipal Affairs, Sept. 1899, **12:**316–21

Jordan, Daniel P.

Statement on the TJMF Research Committee Report on Thomas Jefferson and Sally Hemings: Thomas Jefferson Foundation, Jan. 26, 2000, **22:**425

Jordan, David Starr
The Moral Aspect of the Protective Tariff, Aug. 1908, **13:**147–49

Josh Billings (pseud.) *see* Shaw, Henry Wheeler

Judd, Norman B.
Speech in House of Representatives on resolution, regarding Haiti and Santo Domingo, Jan. 13, 1869, **10:**149–50

Junius (pseud.) *see* Colton, Calvin

Kaczynski, Ted
A Manifesto: Industrial Society and the Future, 1995, **22:**275

Kaiser, Robert G.
9-11: Encyclopædia Britannica 2001 Year in Review, **22:**511

Kallen, Horace M.
The Decline and Rise of the Consumer, 1936, **15:**407–13

Kalm, Peter
Travels into North America, 1770, **1:**471–79

Kaplan, Martin
The Ideologies of Tough Times: Change, Aug. 1976, **20:**271

Kapor, Mitchell
Statement by the Electronic Frontier Foundation, 1990, **22:**89

Kato, Tsugio
Unattributed remarks on the Bicentennial: Shukan Asahi (Tokyo), Jan. 16, **20:**265

Katzenbach, Nicholas deB.
Foreign Policy, Public Opinion, and Secrecy: Foreign Affairs, Oct. 1973, **19:**404

Kaunda, Kenneth D.
Speech at a White House reception, Apr. 1975, **20:**147

Kelley, Florence
Obstacles to the Enforcement of Child Labor Legislation, Dec. 1906, **13:**85–89

Kemble, Frances Anne (Fanny)
Journal of a Residence on a Georgian Plantation in 1838–1839, 1863, **6:**455–63

Kemper, Bob
Frantic Moments, Rumors in the Rain and a Tense Call: Chicago Tribune, Nov. 9, 2000, **22:**463

Kennan, George
Have Reservation Indians Any Vested Rights?: Outlook, Mar. 29, 1902, **12:**476–82

Kennan, George Frost
The Sources of Soviet Conduct: Foreign Affairs, July 1947, **16:**440–46

Seek the Finer Flavor, 1954, **17:**295–98

"Democracy" as a World Cause: The Cloud of Danger, II:5, 1977, **21:**18

Kennedy, Edward M.

The Case for Airline Deregulation: Enterprise, Nov. 1977, **21:**56

Statements on School Prayer: Congressional Digest, Dec. 1980, **21:**248

Kennedy, John F(itzgerald)

Speech to the Greater Houston Ministerial Association on the "religion issue," Sept. 12, 1960, **17:**589–91

Inaugural Address, Jan. 20, 1961, **18:**5–7

Message to Congress on federal aid to education, Feb. 20, 1961, **18:**8–11

Speech at University of Washington on foreign policy, Nov. 16, 1961, **18:**54–57

Radio and television address on the Soviet missiles in Cuba, Oct. 22, 1962, **18:**140–42

Radio and television address on African Americans and the American promise, June 11, 1963, **18:**152–55

Radio and television address on the Nuclear Test-Ban Treaty, July 26, 1963, **18:**192–97

Undelivered Dallas speech, Nov. 22, 1963, **18:**197–201

Kennedy, Robert F(rancis)

Counterinsurgency, July 9, 1965, **18:**323–27

Speech at Chicago, on Vietnam, Feb. 8, 1968, **18:**599–605

Kenrick, Francis Patrick

Pastoral address to the Roman Catholic Congregation of St. Mary's, Philadelphia, Apr. 22, 1831, **5:**437–39

Kent, James

Speech in New York State constitutional convention, Sept. 1821, **5:**9–13

Keun, Odette

A Foreigner Looks at the TVA, 1937, **15:**453–61

Key, Francis Scott

The Star-Spangled Banner (song), **4:**353–54

Keynes, John Maynard, Baron

Sees Need for $400,000 Monthly to Speed Recovery: New York Times, June 10, 1934, **15:**268–71

Kincaid, James R.

Address to University of Southern California Academic Honors Convocation on curricula, March 1988, **22:**55

King, Edward

The Great South, 1875, **10:**334–39

King, Martin Luther, Jr.

Letter from Birmingham Jail, Apr. 16, 1963, **18:**143–49

I Have a Dream, Aug. 28, 1963, **18:**156–59

Showdown for Nonviolence: Look, Apr. 16, 1968, **18:**663–69

King, Rufus

Speeches in Senate on the Missouri Bill, 1819, **4:**579–86

Kingsbury, F. J.

The Tendency of Men to Live in Cities, Sept. 2, 1895, **12:**61–66

Kingsley, James L.

Original Papers in Relation to a Course of Liberal Education (Yale Report of 1828): American Journal of Science and Arts, Jan. 1829, **5:**266–75

Kinkead, Eugene

A Reporter at Large: The Study of Something New in History: The New Yorker, Oct. 26, 1957, **17:**463–68

Kinsley, Michael

Who Killed Communism?: The New Republic, Dec. 4, 1989, **22:**84

Kinsman, Delos O.

The Income Tax in the Commonwealths of the United States, Nov. 1903, **12:**528–33

Kipling, Rudyard

The White Man's Burden (poem), **12:**246–47

Kirkland, William

The West, The Paradise of the Poor: United States Magazine and Democratic Review, Aug. 1844, **7:**205–8

Kissinger, Henry

News Conference on the signing of the Vietnam truce, Jan. 24, 1973, **19:**309

The Year of Europe: An address to the annual meeting of the Associated Press Editors, Apr. 23, 1973, **19:**328

Letter to Senator Edward Kennedy on American policy in Southeast Asia, Mar. 25, 1974, **20:**42

The Challenge of Interdependence, a speech to the United Nations General Assembly, Apr. 15, 1974, **20:**46

News conference on the evacuation of Vietnam, Apr. 29, 1975, **20:**164

Kittle, George

What the Contra Aid Vote Means: Lakeville (Connecticut) Journal, June 27, 1985, **21:**575

Kittredge, Walter

Tenting on the Old Camp Ground (song), **9:**502

Klein, Félix

In the Land of the Strenuous Life, 1905, **13:**35–36

Kluckhohn, Florence R.

American Women and American Values, 1952,

17:159–62

Knight, Frank H.
The Ethics of Competition: Quarterly Journal of Economics, Aug. 1923, **14**:385–91

Knoll, Erwin
The Education of Henry Durham: Progressive, Jan. 1972, **19**:273

Knox, Frank
Statement before Senate Committee on Foreign Relations on the Lend-Lease Bill, 1941, **16**:48–50

Kosciuszko, Tadeusz
American will and testament, c. Apr. 20, 1798, **4**:21

Kouwenhoven, John
Made in America, 1948, **16**:530–42

Kramer, Hilton, *et al.*
Symposium on "Culture and the Present Moment": Commentary, Dec. 1974, **20**:107

Krauthammer, Charles
Looking Evil Dead in the Eye: Time, July 5, 1985, **21**:582

Kristol, Irving
American Intellectuals and Foreign Policy: Foreign Affairs, July 1967, **18**:535–43
The Strange Death of Liberal Education: Fortune, May 1968, **18**:677–79

Kuhn, Walt
Letter to Walter Pach, Dec. 12, 1912, **13**:374–75

Küng, Hans
Will the Pope Win Over Women? The New York Times, Nov. 16, 1983, **21**:446

Kunstler, James Howard
The Geography of Nowhere, 1993, **22**:219

Kurtz, Paul
Objections to Astrology: The Humanist, Nov.–Dec. 1975, **20**:239

Ladd, William
Essay on a Congress of Nations, 1840, **6**:573–74

La Follette, Robert Marion (1855–1925)
Speech in Senate on Wilson's war message, Apr. 4, 1917, **14**:104–11

La Follette, Robert Marion (1895–1953)
The President and Unemployment: Nation, July 15, 1931, **15**:93–98

Lamb, Arthur J.
A Bird in a Gilded Cage (song), **12**:148–49

Landsburg, Morrie
A Conversation with Chief Justice Earl Warren, May 1969: McClatchey Broadcasting, Sacramento, Calif., **19**:35

Lanier, Sidney
Corn (poem), **10**:315–19
The New South, 1880, **10**:466–71

Lansing, John
Letter . . . to the Governor of New York; Containing Their Reasons for not Subscribing to the Federal Constitution, 1787, **3**:189–91

Lapham, Lewis H.
Notebook: Music Man: Harper's, July 1993, **22**:197

Larrabee, Eric
Time to Kill: Automation, Leisure and Jobs: Nation, Sept. 20, 1965, **18**:285–91

Lasagna, Louis
Problems of Drug Development: Science, July 24, 1964, **18**:232–38

Laski, Harold Joseph
The Obsolescence of Federalism: New Republic, May 3, 1939, **15**:567–71

Lasky, Melvin J.
America and Europe: Encounter, Jan. 1962, **18**:58–63

Latrobe, Benjamin Henry
Letter to Ferdinand Fairfax of Shenandoah, May 28, 1798, **4**:22–28
Letter to Robert Mills, July 12, 1806, **4**:204–7

Latter, Arthur L.
Our Nuclear Future, 1958, **17**:480–86

Laughlin, James Laurence
Facts About Money, 1895, **12**:75–78

Laurance, John
Speech in House of Representatives on the "general welfare" clause of the Constitution, Feb. 1792, **3**:491–95

Laurence, William L.
Atomic Bomb on Nagasaki: New York Times, Sept. 9, 1945, **16**:337–39

Lawrence, Abbott
Letter to William C. Rives, Jan. 16, 1846, **7**:329–36

Lawrence III, Charles
The Bakke Case: A Preview: Saturday Review, Oct. 15, 1977, **21**:96

Lawrence, D(avid) H(erbert)
Studies in Classic American Literature, 1924, **14**:331–38

Lawson, John
Testimony before U.S. Commission on Industrial Relations, Jan. 29, 1915, **13**:508–15

Lazarus, Emma
The New Colossus (poem), **11**:107

Ledbetter, Huddie
Goodnight Irene (song), **15**:371
Kisses Sweeter Than Wine (song), **17**:100–1

Lee, Richard Henry
Letters from the Federal Farmer to the Republican, Oct. 8–15, 1787, **3**:130–38

Lee, Robert
National Literature (letter to editor): Niles'

Weekly Register, May 16, 1818, **4:**497–99

Lee, Robert E(dward)
Letter to Winfield Scott, Apr. 20, 1861, **9:**258
Letter to Anne Marshall, Apr. 20, 1861, **9:**258–59
Farewell address to his army, Apr. 10, 1865, **9:**572
Letter to Josiah Tattnall, Sept. 7, 1865, **9:**607–8

Legaré, Hugh Swinton
Review of James Kent's *Commentaries on American Law:* Southern Review, Aug. 1828, **5:**275–78

Leggett, William
The Division of Parties (editorial): New York Evening Post, Nov. 4, 1834, **6:**74–76

Lehman, Herbert H(enry)
Freedom and the General Welfare, Apr. 1950, **17:**21–23

Lehtinen, Marlene W.
Debate on Capital Punishment: Crime and Delinquency, July 1977, **21:**1

Leites, Nathan
Movies: A Psychological Study, 1950, **17:**25–27

Leland, John
The Rights of Conscience Inalienable, and Therefore Religious Opinions not Cognizable by Law: or, The High-flying Church-man Spirit of his Legal Robe, 1791, **3:**445–49

Lenin, Nikolai
Open letter to American workers, Aug. 20, 1918, **14:**161–66

Lenoir, William
Speech in North Carolina Ratifying Convention, 1788, **3:**300–3

Leonard, Daniel
Letter to the Inhabitants of the Province of Massachusetts-Bay (by Massachusettensis), Jan. 9, 1775, **2:**304–7

Lerner, Max
America as a Civilization, 1957, **17:**416–21

Lester, Richard A.
Reflections on the 'Labor Monopoly' Issue: Journal of Political Economy, Dec. 1947, **16:**425–32

Levin, Lewis C.
Speech in House of Representatives on the naturalization laws, Dec. 18, 1845, **7:**313–16

Lewis, Ellis
Opinion of the (Pennsylvania Supreme) court in *Mott* v. *Pennsylvania Railroad Company,* 1858, **9:**61–64

Lewis, John L(lewellyn)
Address to the First Constitutional Convention of the Congress of Industrial Organizations,

1938, **15:**511–15

Lewis, Richard S.
The Kennedy Effect: Bulletin of the Atomic Scientists, Mar. 1968, **18:**590–95

Lewis, Sinclair
Minnesota: The Norse State: Nation, May 30, 1923, **14:**414–20
Acceptance speech for Nobel Prize for Literature, Dec. 12, 1930, **15:**62–70

Lieber, Francis
Letters to a Gentleman in Germany Being Written After a Trip from Philadelphia to Niagara (also known as *The Stranger in America; or, Letters to a Gentleman in Germany, 1835*), 1834, **6:**84–86

Lieberman, Joe
Speech in the Senate on the Bill Clinton-Monica Lewinsky affair, Sept. 1998, **22:**366

Liedtke, Klaus
Editorial on the Bicentennial: Stern (Hamburg), April 8, 1976, **20:**360

Lilienthal, David Eli
TVA: Democracy on the March, 1944, **16:**230–34
Testimony, reported by Alfred Friendly, before Joint Congressional Committee on Atomic Energy, Feb. 4, 1947, **16:**464–66

Lincoln, Abraham
Letter to the editor: Sangamo Journal, June 18, 1836, **6:**281
The Perpetuation of Our Political Institutions, Jan. 27, 1838, **6:**424–29
Fragments on Government and Slavery, c. July 1, 1854, **8:**275–76
Speech at Peoria, Ill., on the Kansas-Nebraska Act, Oct. 16, 1854, **8:**276–82
Speech at Republican Convention, Springfield, Ill., June 26, 1857, **8:**459–66
Speech at Republican Convention, Springfield, Ill. (House Divided Speech), June 16, 1858, **9:**1–4
The Lincoln-Douglas Debates, 1858, **9:**8–32
Annual Address Before the Wisconsin State Agricultural Society, Milwaukee, Sept. 30, 1859, **9:**121–26
Speech at Cooper Union, New York City, Feb. 27, 1860, **9:**158–69
First Inaugural Address, Mar. 4, 1861, **9:**250–55
Letter to William Seward, Apr. 1, 1861, **9:**257
Speech to special session of Congress on a war to preserve the Union, July 4, 1861, **9:**268–74
Letter to Orville Browning, Sept. 22, 1861, **9:**296–97
Special message to Congress on a joint resolu-

tion for compensated emancipation, Mar. 6, 1862, **9:**328–29

Letter to Horace Greeley, Aug. 22, 1862, **9:**348

Emancipation Proclamation, Jan. 1, 1863, **9:**398–99

Letter to "Fighting Joe" Hooker, Jan. 26, 1863, **9:**401–2

Letter to Erastus Corning, June 12, 1863, **9:**424–28

Letter to James C. Conkling, Aug. 26, 1863, **9:**436–39

Letter to Andrew Jackson, Sept. 11, 1863, **9:**458

Gettysburg Address, Nov. 19, 1863, **9:**462–63

Proclamation of Amnesty, Dec. 7, 1863, **9:**473–75

Third annual message to Congress, Dec. 8, 1863, **9:**475–78

Pocket-veto statement to Congress on the Wade-Davis Bill, July 8, 1864, **9:**534–35

Second Inaugural Address, Mar. 4, 1865, **9:**555–56

Last public address, Apr. 11, 1865, **9:**573–76

Lindbergh, Charles Augustus

Lindbergh's Own Story of Epochal Flight (interview): New York Times, May 23, 1927, **14:**557–61

Speech at New York, on America's participation in World War II, Apr. 23, 1941, **16:**72–76

Lindsay, John V.

For New National Cities: Proposal at a conference on cities of NATO countries, May 26, 1971: New York Times, June 9, 1971, **19:**211

Lindsay, (Nicholas) Vachel

Abraham Lincoln Walks at Midnight (poem), **13:**453–54

Bryan, Bryan, Bryan, Bryan (poem), **14:**237–43

Lindsey, Benjamin Barr

The Beast and the Jungle: Everybody's Magazine, Dec. 1909, **13:**227–31

Lindsley, Philip

An Address, Delivered in Nashville . . . at the Inauguration of the President of Cumberland College, Jan. 12, 1825, **5:**157–61

Baccalaureate address at Cumberland College, 1829, **5:**310–14

Linkletter, Art

Drug Abuse: An address to a special United Nations Audience, Sept. 14, 1971, **19:**218

Lippmann, Walter

Drift and Mastery, 1914, **13:**470–74

Miss [Amy] Lowell and Things: New Republic, Mar. 18, 1916, **14:**37–38

The Drouth: On Self-Reliance in This Age:

Today and Tomorrow, June 5, 1934, **15:**245–46

U.S. Foreign Policy: Shield of the Republic, 1943, **16:**192–98

The Portent of the Moon: Today and Tomorrow, Oct. 10, 1957, **17:**460–61

The University: New Republic, May 28, 1966, **18:**382–87

Little, Royal

As They See It: An interview by James Cook: Forbes, Dec. 15, 1970, **19:**175

Livermore, Thomas L.

Testimony before the Senate Committee on Education and Labor, 1883, **10:**567–72

Livingston, Edward

Speech in House of Representatives on the Alien Act, June 21, 1798, **4:**49–52

A System of Penal Law, for the State of Louisiana, 1833, **5:**171–73

Livingston, Peter R.

Speech in New York constitutional convention, Sept. 1821, **5:**13–15

Livingston, Robert R.

Examination of the Treaty of Amity, Commerce, and Navigation, Between the United States and Great Britain, in Several Numbers (by Cato), 1795, **3:**589–92

Livingston, William

Editorial on sectarian control of colleges: Independent Reflector, Mar. 22, 29, 1753, **1:**500–3

Lloyd, Henry Demarest

Lords of Industry: North American Review, June 1884, **11:**7–12

Wealth Against Commonwealth, 1894, **11:**535–38

Locke, David Ross (Petroleum V. Nasby)

Negro Emigration (letter), Apr. 2, 1862, **9:**333–34

Lays Down a Platform for the Coming Campaign (letter), June 23, 1865, **9:**597–98

Lodge, Henry Cabot

Our Blundering Foreign Policy: Forum, Mar. 1895, **12:**2–4

Speech in Senate on intervention in Cuba, Feb. 20, 1896, **12:**85–87

Speech in Senate on immigration restrictions, Mar. 16, 1896, **12:**88–92

Corollary to the Monroe Doctrine, July 31, 1912, **13:**368–69

Reservations with regard to the Versailles Treaty, Nov. 6, 1919, **14:**194–96

Lodge, Henry Cabot, Jr.

Speech in Senate on a resolution to abolish the electoral college, Jan. 25, 1950, **17:**2–5

Loesser, Frank

Praise the Lord and Pass the Ammunition (song), **16:**129

Lomax, John
Goodnight Irene (song), **15:**371

London, Jack
War of the Classes, 1905, **13:**36–39

Long, Huey Pierce
Radio address on the "Share-the-Wealth" program, Jan. 1935, **15:**318–20

Long, Larry
The Slowing of Urbanization: Scientific American, July 1983, **21:**432

Longfellow, Henry Wadsworth
The Village Blacksmith (poem), **7:**43
The Republic (poem), **7:**563
The Children's Hour (poem), **9:**157
Paul Revere's Ride (poem), **9:**483–84

Longman, Jere
Airport Delays: The New York Times, Sept. 26, 2001, **22:**502

Loring, Ellis Gray
Petition to governor of the Commonwealth of Massachusetts on pardoning Abner Kneeland, 1838, **6:**422–23

Lovett, Robert Morss
Progress—Chicago Style: Current History, Jan. 1934, **15:**241–43

Low, Sir David
Leonardo Da Disney: New Republic, Jan. 5, 1942, **16:**120–22

Low, Seth
An American View of Municipal Government in the United States, in James Bryce's *The American Commonwealth,* 1888, **11:**190–94

Lowell, Abbott Lawrence
The Relation Between Faculties and Governing Boards: Annual Report of Harvard University, 1919–1920, **14:**251–54

Lowell, Amy
The New Manner in Modern Poetry: New Republic, Mar. 4, 1916, **14:**34–37

Lowell, James Russell
Introduction (salutatory): The Pioneer, Jan. 1843, **7:**110–13
The Biglow Papers, 1848, **7:**348–50
A Fable for Critics, 1848, **7:**475–76
E Pluribus Unum: Atlantic Monthly, Feb. 1861, **9:**230–33

Lowenfels, Walter
Wasn't That A Time! (song), **16:**527–28

Löwenstern, Isidore
Les Etats-Unis et la Havane souvenirs d'un voyage [*Memoir of a Trip to the United States and Havana*], 1842, **7:**72–73

Lowrey, Lloyd W.

Amending the Constitution to Strengthen the States in the Federal System (Statement of Principles): State Government, Winter 1963, **18:**138–39

Luckner, Felix, Graf von
Seeteufel erobert Amerika [*Sea Devil Conquers America*], 1928, **14:**583–84

Lukas, J. Anthony
The Case of a Runaway Flower Girl: New York Times, Oct. 19, 1967, **18:**497–99

Lundberg, Ferdinand
America's 60 Families, 1937, **15:**492–98

Lyell, Sir Charles
A Second Visit to the United States of North America, 1849, **7:**516–17

Lynd, Helen Merrell
Middletown: A Study in Contemporary American Culture, 1929, **15:**6–10

Lynd, Robert S.
Middletown: A Study in Contemporary American Culture, 1929, 15:6–10

Lyons, James
Double Talk? The Debate over Bilingual Education: The NewsHour with Jim Lehrer, Sept. 21, 1997, **22:**343

McAllister, Ward
Society As I Have Found It, 1890, **11:**279–86

MacArthur, Douglas
Address aboard the U.S.S. Missouri, on the surrender of Japan, Sept. 2, 1945, **16:**339–40
Message to Joint Chiefs of Staff on Chinese intervention in the Korean War, Dec. 29, 1950, **17:**51–52
Farewell address to special session of Congress, Apr. 19, 1951, **17:**79–84

McCaffery, Jerry
Participatory Democracy: The Effects of Proposition 13: Public Administration, Nov.–Dec. 1978, **21:**78

McCaffrey, Barry R.
Testimony before U.S. House of Representatives, Subcommittee on Criminal Justice, Drug Policy, and Human Resources, June 16, 1999, **22:**441

McCain, John
Ban the Soft Money: Washington Post, Nov. 19, 2000, **22:**458

McCarthy, Joseph R(aymond)
Speech at Wheeling, W. Va., on Communists in the State Department, Feb. 9, 1950, **17:**16–21

McCarty, Harry
The Bonnie Blue Flag (song), **9:**304–5

McClaughry, John
The Case Against Reverend Moon: National Review, Dec. 23, 1983, **21:**463

McClellan, George Brinton
Letter to Abraham Lincoln, July 7, 1862, **9:**343–44

McClelland, David C.
Advantages of a Liberal Arts Education: Psychology Today, Sept. 1978, **21:**119

McClintock, Harry
Hallelujah, I'm a Bum (song), **12:**215–16
Big Rock Candy Mountain (song), **13:**235–36

McClure, James A.
Speech on Nuclear Power: Vital Speeches of the Day, Mar. 1, 1979, **21:**141

McClure, Samuel Sidney
Concerning Three Articles in this Number of McClure's, and a Coincidence that May Set Us Thinking (editorial): McClure's, Jan. 1903, **12:**533–34

McCurdy, Jack
U. S. Education on the Skids: Chicago Sun-Times, Sept. 5, 1976, **20:**295

Macdonald, Dwight
A Theory of Mass Culture: Diogenes, Summer 1953, **17:**230–38

McDuffie, George
Report to House of Representatives by the Committee of Ways and Means on defense of a government bank, Apr. 13, 1830, **5:**361–69
Message to South Carolina legislature on natural slavery of Blacks, 1835, **6:**191–97

McElroy, William
An Old War Horse to a Young Politician (letter): Atlantic Monthly, June 1880, **10:**451–55

McEntree, Gerald W.
Labor Strategy Next Time: The New York Times, Nov. 30, 1984, **21:**545

McGlennon, Felix
Her Golden Hair Was Hanging Down Her Back (song), **11:**552–53

McGovern, George
Where I Stand: Progressive, July 1972, **19:**299
Testimony on the Russian Grain Embargo: Hearings, Subcommittee on International Finance, U.S. Senate, Jan. 22, 1980, **21:**201

McGrath, Charles
The Triumph of the Prime-Time Novel, The New York Times Magazine, Oct. 22, 1995, **22:**292

McIlvaine, Charles P.
Address to the Young Men of the United States on Temperance, c. 1830, **6:**240–44

Mackay, Alexander
The Western World; or, Travels in the United States in 1846–47, 1849, **7:**477–85

MacKaye, Benton
The New Exploration, a Philosophy of Regional Planning, 1928, **14:**575–77

McKenna, Joseph
Opinion of the Court in *U.S. v. United States Steel Corporation et al.,* 1920, **14:**258–63

McKinley, William
First annual message to Congress, Dec. 6, 1897, **12:**161–66
War message to Congress, Apr. 11, 1898, **12:**173–78
Instructions to peace commissioners in Europe on acquisition of the Philippines, Sept. 16, 1898, **12:**231–33
Speech to people of Buffalo, N.Y., on reciprocal trade agreements, Sept. 5, 1901, **12:**428–29

Maclay, William
Journal (on controversy between aristocrats and democrats), Apr.–May 1789, **3:**347–54

MacLeish, Archibald
American Letter (for Gerald Murphy) (poem), **15:**59–61
The Irresponsibles, 1940, **16:**1–5
Dialogue on the American Dream, 1962, **18:**122–29
An Address to the American Philosophical Association, **20:**356

McLeod, Don
Democrats on the Budget Bandwagon: Insight, Nov. 10, 1986, **21:**657

McNamara, Robert S(trange)
Voluntary Service for All Youth, May 1966, **18:**356–61
Speech to editors of the United Press International, San Francisco, on nuclear strategy: Sept. 18, 1967, **18:**527–35

McNaught, Brian
Why Bother with Gay Rights? The Humanist, Oct. 1977, **21:**31

MacNeill, Robert
The Mass Media and the Public Trust: Columbia Magazine, June 1985, **21:**585

McNerney, Walter J.
How to Improve Medical Care: An interview: U.S. News & World Report, Mar. 24, 1969, **19:**26

Macrae, Norman
America's Third Century: The Economist, Oct. 25, 1975, **20:**186

McWhirter, A. J.
Speech at Vicksburg, Miss., on Southern immigration, Nov. 21, 1883, **10:**587–94

Madison, James

A Memorial and Remonstrance (to the General Assembly of the Commonwealth of Virginia on religious assessments), 1785, **3:**16–20

Letter to Edmund Randolph, Apr. 8, 1787, **3:**88–90

The Federal Convention of 1787, 1840, **3:**95–121

Letter to Thomas Jefferson, Oct. 24, 1787, **3:**145–49

The Federalist (Nos. 10, 14, 39, 49), 1787–1788, **3:**216–28

Letter to Thomas Jefferson, Oct. 17, 1788, **3:**305–8

Comments and proposed Bill of Rights to House of Representatives, June 8, 1789, **3:**354–63

Letter to Thomas Jefferson, Feb. 4, 1790, **3:**393–94

Public Opinion: National Gazette, Dec. 19, 1791, **3:**472–73

Charters: National Gazette, Jan. 19, 1792, **3:**489–90

Parties: National Gazette, Jan. 23, 1792, **3:**490–91

Speech in House of Representatives on the "general welfare" clause of the Constitution, Feb. 1792, **3:**491–95

Fashion: National Gazette, Mar. 20, 1792, **3:**496–97

Property: National Gazette, Mar. 27, 1792, **3:**497–99

Helvidius, No. V: Gazette of the United States, *c.* Sept. 1793, **3:**546–51

Report for Virginia House of Delegates on the Virginia Resolutions of 1798, Dec. 1799, **4:**122–28

Veto message to House of Representatives on the chartering of an Episcopal church, Alexandria, Va., Feb. 21, 1811, **4:**287

War message to Congress, June 1, 1812, **4:**314–18

Veto message to House of Representatives on the Bonus Bill, Mar. 3, 1817, **4:**462–63

Speech to the Albemarle (Va.) Agricultural Society, May 12, 1818, **4:**503–7

Letter to Edward Everett, Aug. 1830, **5:**398–404

Letter to Edward Coles, Oct. 15, 1834, **6:**63–66

Maginnis, John
The Hazards of Duke: Populism and Louisiana's Ghosts: The New Republic, Nov. 25, 1991, **22:**140

Mahan, Alfred Thayer
The Influence of Sea Power Upon History, 1660–1783, 1890, **11:**307–15

The Peace Conference and the Moral Aspect of War: North American Review, Oct. 1899, **12:**329–34

Mahoney, John J.
Training Teachers for Americanization, 1920, **14:**255–58

Major Jack Downing (pseud.) *see* Davis, Charles A.

Malone, George W.
Minority Views of Senate Committee on Interior and Insular Affairs, regarding statehood for Alaska and Hawaii, Mar. 1958, **17:**522–24

Mann, Horace
Fourth Annual Report of the Massachusetts Board of Education, 1840, **6:**554–60

Fifth Annual Report, Jan. 1, 1842, **7:**44–46

Twelfth Annual Report, 1848, **7:**460–74

Speech in House of Representatives on slavery in the territories, Feb. 15, 1850, **8:**7–16

Manning, William
The Key of Libberty, 1798, **4:**76–86

Mansfield, Michael Joseph
Statement in Senate on tidelands oil for education, May 4, 1953, **17:**220–22

Eulogy for John F. Kennedy, Nov. 25, 1963, **18:**202–3

Marcus (pseud.) *see* Iredell, James

Markham, Edwin
The Man with the Hoe (poem), **12:**253–54

Marotta, George
Speech on the stock market expansion of the 1990s, March 2000, **22:**427

Marryat, Frederick
A Diary in America (on language), 1839, **6:**495–501

Marsh, George Perkins
Man and Nature (reissued as *The Earth as Modified by Human Action, 1874*), 1864, **9:**535–36

Marshall, Charles Burton
The Nature of Foreign Policy, Mar. 1952, **17:**119–23

Marshall, George Catlett
Commencement address at Harvard University on the Marshall Plan, June 5, 1947, **16:**438–40

Marshall, John
Opinion of the Court in Marbury v. Madison, 1803, **4:**165–70

Opinion of the Court in Dartmouth College v. Woodward, 1819, **4:**522–28

Opinion of the Court in M'Culloch v. Maryland, 1819, **4:**530–39

Opinion of the Court in Cohens v. Virginia, 1821, **5:**1–3

Opinion of the Court in *Gibbons v. Ogden*, 1824, **5:**128–33

Opinion of the Court in *Cherokee Nation v. State of Georgia*, 1831, **5:**427–30

Marshall, Louis

Letter to Calvin Coolidge, May 22, 1924, **14:**423–27

Martin, Luther

Genuine Information, Delivered to the Legislature of the State of Maryland, Relative to the Proceedings of the General Convention, Nov. 29, 1787, **3:**166–69

Martineau, Harriet

Society in America, 1837, **6:**379–84

Marvell, Andrew

Bermudas (poem), **1:**222

Mason, Daniel Gregory

Some American Composers: Outlook, Mar. 15, 1902, **12:**448–50

Mason, George

Speech in Virginia Ratifying Convention, June 1788, **3:**278–80

Massachusettensis (pseud.) *see* Leonard, Daniel

Masters, Edgar Lee

Anne Rutledge (poem), **13:**576–77

Knowlt Hoheimer (poem), **13:**577

Editor Whedon (poem), **13:**577

Mather, Cotton

The Wonders of the Invisible World, 1693, **1:**297–98

A Christian at His Calling: Two Brief Discourses, One Directing a Christian in his General Calling; Another Directing Him in his Personal, 1701, **1:**319–24

Essays To Do Good; Addressed to all Christians, whether in Public or Private Capacities, 1710 , **1:**327–28

Mather, Increase

An Arrow Against Profane and Promiscuous Dancing Drawn out of the Quiver of the Scriptures, 1684, **1:**272–73

Cases of Conscience Concerning Evil Spirits Personating Men, 1693, **1:**293–96

Matsuyama, Yukio

Unattributed remarks on the Bicentennial: Shukan Asahi (Tokyo), Jan. 16, 1976, **20:**365

Matteucci, Nicola

Editorial on the Bicentennial: Il Giornale (Milan), July 4, 1976, **20:**372

Maurois, André

Etats-Unis 39: Journal d'un voyage en Amérique [Journal of a Trip to America in 1939], 1939, **15:**583–86

May, Samuel Joseph

The Rights and Condition of Women, Nov. 8, 1846, **7:**342–47

Mayhew, Jonathan

A Discourse Concerning Unlimited Submission and Non-Resistance to the Higher Powers, Jan. 30, 1750, **1:**481–88

Maynard, Horace

Speech in House of Representatives on resolution, regarding Haiti and Santo Domingo, Jan. 13, 1869, **10:**154

Meade, Edwin R.

Speech to the Social Science Association of America, Saratoga, N.Y., on Chinese immigration, Sept. 7, 1877, **10:**386–90

Means, Gardiner C.

The Modern Corporation and Private Property, 1932, **15:**136–39

Industrial Prices and Their Relative Inflexibility, Jan. 17, 1935, **15:**286–92

Meidell, Frithjof

Letter to family, Springfield, Ill., Aug. 7, 1855, **8:**349–52

Meiklejohn, Alexander

Should Communists Be Allowed To Teach?: New York Times Magazine, Mar. 27, 1949, **16:**600–5

Melbourne, Anders

Editorial on the Bicentennial: Dagens Nyheter (Stockholm), July 4, 1976, **20:**375

Mellon, Andrew William

The Value of Industrial Research: Bulletin of the National Research Council, Oct. 1919, **14:**217–18

Taxation: the People's Business, 1924, **14:**445–49

Melville, Herman

Hawthorne and His Mosses: Literary World, Aug. 17, 1850, **8:**83–89

Misgivings (poem), **9:**187

Battle-Pieces and Aspects of the War: Supplement, 1866, **10:**38–43

Mencken, H(enry) L(ouis)

A Book of Prefaces, 1917, **14:**118–26

Prejudices: Third Series, 1922, **14:**354–62

Prejudices: Fifth Series, 1926, **14:**516–18

The American Language, 1936, **15:**366–70

Mentz, Frank H.

An Open Letter to the Congress of the United States, Sept. 26, 1969, **19:**84

Mettler, Eric

Editorial on the Bicentennial: Neue Zürcher Zeitung (Zurich), July 4–5, 1976, **20:**373

Meyer, Karl E.

International Art and Antiquities Traffic: New Yorker, Mar. 24 and 31, 1973, **19:**323

Michael Darrock (pseud.) *see* Nielsen, Waldemar A.

Michaëlius, Jonas
Letter to Adrian Smoutius, Aug. 11, 1628, **1:**92–94

Michaux, François André
Travels to the West of the Alleghanies, c. 1804, **4:**154–57

Middleton, P. Harvey
"Movies" Speed Up Labor: Technical World, Apr. 1913, **13:**418–20

Miller, Arthur
The American Theater: Holiday, Jan. 1955, **17:**332–43

Miller, Bob
Eleven-Cent Cotton (song), **14:**573–74

Miller, Lindley
Marching Song of the First Arkansas (song), **9:**472–73

Miller, Lucas
Air Time: Let's Put a Cop on Every Flight, Slate.com, Sept. 20, 2001, **22:**499

Miller, Samuel Freeman
Opinion of the Court in *Slaughter-House Cases,* 1873, **10:**302–6

Millis, Walter
A World Without War, 1961, **18:**48–54

Mills, Robert
Introduction to *Architectural Works* (projected work), c. 1820, **4:**645–47

Minow, Newton N(orman)
Speech to the 39th Annual Convention of the National Association of Broadcasters, Washington, D.C., on the vast wasteland, May 9, 1961, **18:**12–20

Mitchell, John N.
Address to the annual Law Day dinner of the Detroit Bar Association, May 1, 1969, **19:**15

Mitchell, Maurice B.
Letter to Friend of the University of Denver, Apr. 30, 1968, **18:**675–76

Mitchell, Sidney D.
Would You Rather Be a Colonel with an Eagle on Your Shoulder (song), **14:**141–42

Mitchell, William Lendrum (Billy)
Col. Mitchell's Statements on Government Aviation: Aviation, Sept. 14, 1925, **14:**482–92

Mittelberger, Gottlieb
Journey to Pennsylvania in the Year 1750 and Return to Germany in the Year 1754, 1756, **2:**3–6

Mondale, Walter
Beyond Detente: Foreign Affairs, Oct. 1974, **20:**77

Monette, Paul
Borrowed Time: An AIDS Memoir, 1988, **22:**59

Monroe, James
Letters to Thomas Jefferson, May 28, June 27, 1793, **3:**535–39
Letter to Thomas Jefferson, Oct. 17, 1823, **5:**68–69
Annual message to Congress, Dec. 2, 1823, **5:**73–75

Montaner, Carlos Alberto
Editorial on the Bicentennial: El Nacional (Caracas), April 23, 1976, **20:**366

Montlezun, Louis-Elizabeth, Baron de
Voyage fait dans les années 1816 et 1817, de New-Yorck à la Nouvelle-Orléans [*A Trip Made in the Years 1816 and 1817, from New York to New Orleans*], 1818, **4:**492–94

Moody, William Vaughn
An Ode in Time of Hesitation (poem), **12:**355–56

Moore, Ely
Address Delivered Before the General Trades' Union of the City of New-York, Dec. 2, 1833, **6:**17–22

Moore, Sir Henry
Letter to Lords of Trade, Jan. 12, 1767, **2:**179–80

Moore, Paul, Jr.
Open letter on the ordination of women: New York Times, Nov. 23, 1974, **20:**95

Moorehead, J. R.
Testimony before Senate Committee on Interstate Commerce, Dec. 9, 1911, **13:**322–27

Morgan, Howard
Letter to John F. Kennedy, 1963, **18:**165–66

Morris, Gouverneur
Letter to [John] Penn, May 20, 1774, **2:**251–53
Letter to Thomas Jefferson, Dec. 9, 1799, **4:**119–20
Letter to Robert Livingston, Oct. 10, 1802, **4:**153–54

Morris, Robert
Circular letter to governors of the states, Jan. 8, 1782, **2:**574–75

Morris, Roger
Reclaiming the Reclamation Beat: Columbia Journalism Review, Mar.–Apr. 1986, **21:**629

Morse, Samuel Finley Breese
Imminent Dangers to the Free Institutions of the United States Through Foreign Immigration, and the Present State of the Naturalization Laws (by An American), 1835, **6:**158–63

Morse, Wayne Lyman

The Rise or Sunset of Peace, Feb. 26, 1950, **17**:11–16

Morton, Thomas
New English Canaan; or, New Canaan, Containing An Abstract of New England, 1632, **1**:125–29

Moskin, J. Robert
Ellsberg Talks: An interview with Daniel Ellsberg: Look, Oct. 5, 1971, **19**:226

Moulton, David
Report of the select committee, on the several memorials against appointing chaplains to the [New York] Legislature, Apr. 16, 1832, **5**:511–18

Moynihan, Daniel Patrick
The Politics of Stability: New Leader, Oct. 9, 1967, **18**:484–90
Memorandum to President Nixon on the Status of the Negroes, Mar. 1, 1970, **19**:116
Address to the U.N. General Assembly on the resolution on Zionism, Nov. 10, 1975, **20**:201

Muench, Aloisius Joseph, Cardinal
Catholic Rural Life Objectives, 1937, **15**:462–65

Mühlenberg, Henry Melchior
Journal (on a meeting with Count Zinzendorf), Dec. 29–30, 1742, **1**:440–43

Müller-Freienfels, Richard
The Mysteries of the Soul, 1929, **15**:1–6

Mullins, James
Speech in House of Representatives on resolution, regarding Haiti and Santo Domingo, Jan. 13, 1869, **10**:148–49

Mumford, Lewis
Sticks and Stones, 1924, **14**:441–45

Muñoz-Marín, Luis
The Future of Puerto Rico (radio address), May 26, 1945, **16**:312–15

Münsterberg, Hugo
The Americans, 1904, **12**:591–96

Murakami, Yoshio
Unattributed remarks on the Bicentennial: Shukan Asahi (Tokyo), Jan. 16, 1976, **20**:365

Murphy, Frank
Dissent in Korematsu v. U.S., 1944, **16**:238–40

Murphy, Morgan F.
Testimony on illegal aliens: Congressional Digest, Oct. 1977, **21**:51

Murray, John Courtney
The Problem of State Religion: Theological Studies, June 1951, **17**:96–100

Murray, Philip
Testimony before Senate Committee on Educa-

tion and Labor, Feb. 6, 1940, **16**:15–20

Myers, Mordecai
Report of the select committee, on the several memorials against appointing chaplains to the [New York] Legislature, Apr. 16, 1832, **5**:511–18

Myers, Robert J.
The case for federal subsidy of the postal system: Los Angeles Times, Aug. 3, 1975, **20**:191

Myrdal, Gunnar
An American Dilemma: The Negro Problem and Modern Democracy, 1944, **16**:247–53
Interviewed by Donald McDonald on The American Dilemma—1967: Center Magazine, Oct.–Nov. 1967, **18**:490–96

Nader, Ralph
Unsafe at Any Speed, 1965, **18**:291–98
Profiled by Thomas Whiteside: The New Yorker, Oct. 15, 1973, **19**:387–89
Drop the GATT: The Nation, Oct. 10, 1994, **22**:254
GATT Hypocrisy: The Nation, Dec. 5, 1994, **22**:256

Nagel, Charles
Letter to William Howard Taft, Feb. 12, 1913, **13**:397–99

Nahl, Diane
Road Rage and Aggressive Driving, 2000, **22**:454

Nasby, Petroleum V. (pseud.) *see* Locke, David Ross

Nathan, George Jean
The Theatre, in *Civilization in the United States* (Harold E. Stearns, ed.), 1922, **14**:338–44

Nathan, Irvin
ABSCAM Ethics: Moral Issues and Deception in Law Enforcement, 1983, **21**:224

Neal, John
American Painters and Painting (editorial): The Yankee; and Boston Literary Gazette, July 1829, **5**:321–24
Newspapers: The Pioneer, Feb. 1843, **7**:118–23

Nenneman, Richard A.
What About This Dollar Mess?: The Christian Science Monitor, Jan. 18, 1968, **18**:621–25

Nevins, Allan
A Challenge to Historic Truth: New York Times Magazine, Dec. 16, 1945, **16**:350–54

Newton, Johari
Everything Is Everything (song), 1999, **22**:383

Nichols, Thomas Low
Forty Years of American Life, 1864, **9:**537–42

Niebuhr, Helmut Richard
Toward the Independence of the Church, 1935, **15:**340–44

Niebuhr, Reinhold
The Children of Light and the Children of Darkness, 1944, **16:**254–59

Niles, Hezekiah
The Prospect Before Us (editorial): Niles' Weekly Register, Sept. 2, 1815, **4:**397–99

Niles, John
Speech in Senate on the Yucatán Bill, May 9, 1848, **7:**426–32

Niles, Nathaniel
The American Hero (poem), **2:**335–36

Nitze, Paul H.
Testimony on SALT II: Congressional Digest, Aug.–Sept. 1979, **21:**154

Nixon, Richard M.
Victory Speech on winning the 1968 election, as recorded by the New York Times, Nov. 7, 1968, **19:**6
Inaugural Address, Jan. 20, 1969, **19:**8
An Exchange of Letters: White House press release, Nov. 3, 1969, **19:**71
The Pursuit of Peace in Vietnam: A television address, Nov. 3, 1969, **19:**86
The Cambodia Strike: Defense Action for Peace: A television address, Apr. 30, 1970, **19:**127
Television address on wage and price controls, Aug. 15, 1971, **19:**222
Address to a Joint Session of Congress on the Moscow Summit Meeting, June 1, 1972, **19:**291
News Conference at San Clemente, Calif., Aug. 22, 1973, **19:**371
Letter to Spiro T. Agnew, Oct. 10, 1973, **19:**390
Announcement of the release of additional transcripts, Aug. 5, 1974, **20:**20
Television address to the nation announcing the intention to resign, Aug. 8, 1974, **20:**22
Farewell to the White House staff, Aug. 9, 1974, **20:**25
Letter of resignation, Aug. 9, 1974, **20:**27
Principles of relation and cooperation between Egypt and the U.S., June 14, 1974, **20:**66
Address to the people of the Soviet Union, July 2, 1974, **20:**74
Speech to the Republican Congressional Committee on the post-Cold War World, Dec. 7, 1990, **22:**119

Nones, Benjamin
Letter to Caleb F. Wayne (editor): Gazette of the United States, Aug. 5, 1800, **4:**138–40

Norris, Frank (Benjamin Franklin Norris)
A Deal in Wheat, 1902, **12:**456–62

Norris, William A.
Proposition 13: The Center Magazine, Nov.–Dec. 1978, **21:**89

Norton, Charles Eliot
Letter to Charles Waldstein, Nov. 18, 1899, **12:**335

Novak, Michael
Symposium on "Culture and the Present Moment": Commentary, Dec. 1974, **20:**107
Jonestown: Socialism at Work: American Enterprise Institute, Reprint No. 94, Mar. 1979, **21:**131

Novanglus (pseud.) *see* Adams, John

Noyes, John Humphrey
History of American Socialisms, 1870, **5:**253–55
Bible Communism, 1848, **7:**403–9

Noyes, Joseph
Letter to corporation of Yale College, Sept. 14, 1757, **2:**21–22

Nugent, William Henry
The Sports Section: American Mercury, Mar. 1929, **15:**16–21

Oates, Joyce Carol
American Gothic: The New Yorker, May 8, 1995, **22:**273

O'Brien, Dennis
Necessary of Modern Life?: Commonweal, Mar. 28, 1997, **22:**327

Ockenga, Harold J.
The Unvoiced Multitudes, Apr. 7, 1942, **16:**115–20

Odell, Joseph H.
The Mechanics of Revivalism: Atlantic Monthly, May 1915, **13:**540–45

O'Hara, Geoffrey
K-K-K-Katy (song), **14:**142

Olmsted, Frederick Law
Slavery in its Effects on Character, and the Social Relations of the Master Class: New-York Daily Times, Jan. 12, 1854, **8:**237–42
Public Parks and the Enlargement of Towns, Feb. 25, 1870, **10:**224–31
Chicago in Distress: Nation, Nov. 9, 1871, **10:**273–79

Olney, Richard
Letter to Charles Perkins, Dec. 28, 1892, **11:**368–69
Note to Thomas F. Bayard, July 20, 1895, **12:**5–8

Olson, Culbert L.
Testimony before Senate Subcommittee of the Committee on Education and Labor, Dec.

1939, **15**:587–91

O'Mahoney, Joseph C.
Final Report and Recommendations of the Temporary National Economic Committee, Mar. 11, 1941, **16**:61–65

Oppenheim, James
Bread and Roses (song), **13**:363

Oppenheimer, J. Robert
Atomic Weapons and American Policy: Foreign Affairs, July 1953, **17**:206–10

O'Reilly, Jane
Women: The Year of: Columbia Journalism Review, Nov./Dec. 1992, **22**:161

O'Sullivan, John L.
The Democratic Principle (salutatory): United States Magazine and Democratic Review, Oct. 1837, **6**:333–40
The Course of Civilization (editorial): *ibid.,* Sept. 1839, **6**:502–9
The Great Nation of Futurity (editorial): *ibid.,* Nov. 1839, **6**:509–11
Annexation (editorial): *ibid.,* July 1845, **7**:288–92

Otis, James
Speech in Massachusetts Superior Court on the Writs of Assistance, Feb. 24, 1761, **2**:74–77
The Rights of the British Colonies Asserted and Proved, 1764, **2**:103–15

Overmyer, Grace
Our Little Renaissance: The Four Arts Project, 1939, **15**:575–81

Owen, Robert
Address . . . To the People of the United States: New-York Daily Tribune, Sept. 24, 1844, **7**:231–33
To the Capitalists and the Men of Extensive Practical Experience in New York (open letter): New-York Daily Tribune, Apr. 2, 1845, **7**:292–93

Owens, Major R.
Congressional debate on the Arts, Humanities, and Museums Amendments, Oct. 11, 1990, **22**:108

Ozick, Cynthia *et al.*
Symposium on "Culture and the Present Moment": Commentary, Dec. 1974, **20**:107

Pacificus (pseud.) *see* Hamilton, Alexander

Page, Kirby
The United States Steel Corporation: Atlantic Monthly, May 1922, **14**:310–18

Page, Walter Hines
The War with Spain, and After (editorial): Atlantic Monthly, June 1898, **12**:195–97

Paine, Robert Treat
Adams and Liberty (song), **4**:74–75

Paine, Thomas
Epistle to Quakers: 1776, **2**:385–88
Common Sense, 1776, **2**:389–98
The Crisis (No. 1): Pennsylvania Journal, Dec. 19, 1776, **2**:456–61

Parker, Francis Wayland
Talks on Pedagogics, 1894, **11**:575–84
The Pedagogical Creed, 1898, **12**:214–15

Parker, Theodore
An Oration Delivered Before the Onondaga Teachers' Institute at Syracuse, N.Y., Oct. 4, 1849, **7**:486–88
The State of the Nation: Nov. 28, 1850, **8**:114–21
The Present Crisis in American Affairs: The Slave-Holders' Attempt to Wrench the Territories from the Working People, and to Spread Bondage Over all the Land, May 7, 1856, **8**:372–75

Parkman, Francis
The Tale of the 'Ripe Scholar': Nation, Dec. 23, 1869, **10**:216–20

Parry, David
Annual Report of the President to Executive Committee and Members of the National Association of Manufacturers, 1903, **12**:513–18

Pastorius, Francis D.
A Particular Geographical Description of the Lately Discovered Province of Pennsylvania, Situated on the Frontiers of this Western World, America, 1700, **1**:310–14

Paul Campbell (pseud.) *see* Weavers, The

Paulding, James Kirke
National Literature: Salmagundi Magazine, 2nd series, Vol. II, 1835, **4**:648–50
The Diverting History of John Bull and Brother Jonathan (Supplement: *The History of Uncle Sam and His Boys*), 1835, **6**:166–72

Payne, John Howard
Home, Sweet Home (song), **5**:103

Peckham, Rufus W.
Opinion of the Court in Lochner v. New York, 1905, **13**:8–11

Peffer, Nathaniel
Manchuria: A Warning to America: Harper's, Feb. 1933, **15**:213–18

Peffer, William A.
The Farmer's Side, 1891, **11**:361–65

Pehme, Kalev
Who Reads Great Books? Publishers Weekly, Sept. 21, 1984, **21**:535

Peirce, Charles Sanders
Review of Clark University, 1889–1899. Decennial Celebration: Science, Apr. 20, 1900, **12**:357–59

Peirce, Neal R.
The "Sunset" Challenge to Bureaucratic Growth: Washington Post, Mar. 16, 1976, **20:**290

Peirce, Neal R. *et al.*
Federal Spending—The North's Loss Is the Sunbelt's Gain: National Journal, June 26, 1976, **20:**262

Pendleton, Edmund
Speech in Virginia Ratifying Convention: June 1788, **3:**286–90

Penn, William
Frame of Government of Pennsylvania, Apr. 25, 1682, **1:**265–71
Primitive Christianity Revived, in the Faith and Practice of the People Called Quakers, 1696, **1:**299–300
Plan for a Union for the [English] Colonies in America, 1697, **1:**308–9

Pérez, Carlos Andres
Open letter to the President of the United States: International Herald Tribune, Sept. 27, 1974, **20:**89

Perkins, Frances
A National Labor Policy: Annals of the American Academy of Political and Social Science, Mar. 1936, **15:**353–55

Perlman, Selig
The Principle of Collective Bargaining: Annals of the American Academy of Political and Social Science, Mar. 1936, **15:**357–59

Peter Porcupine (pseud.) *see* Cobbett, William

Petroleum V. Nasby (pseud.) *see* Locke, David Ross

Pettigrew, R. F.
Congress Should Stop Giving Away the People's Property, The Public, Dec. 8, 1916, **14:**20–22

Pfeiffer, E. W.
The Cratering of Indochina: Scientific American, May 1972, **19:**286

Phillips, David Graham
The Treason of the Senate: Cosmopolitan, Apr. 1906, **13:**45–52

Phillips, Wendell
Introduction to *Can Abolitionists Vote or Take Office Under the United States Constitution?,* 1845, **7:**261–64
Labor Reform Party Platform, Sept. 4, 1871, **10:**254–55
The Scholar in a Republic, June 30, 1881, **10:**488–94

Phocion (pseud.) *see* Hamilton, Alexander

Pickering, Timothy
Letter to Anthony Wayne, Apr. 8, 1795, **3:**583–87
Letter to Rufus King, Mar. 4, 1804, **4:**189–91

Pickett, George Edward
Letter to La Salle Corbell, July 6, 1863, **9:**429–30
Letter to La Salle Corbell Pickett, Apr. 8/9, 1865, **9:**560–61

Pierce, Franklin
Speech in House of Representatives on U.S. Military Academy, West Point, N.Y., 1836, **6:**273–78

Pike, Albert
Dixie (song), **9:**147

Pike, James S.
The Prostrate State: South Carolina Under Negro Government, 1874, **10:**322–25

Pitts, John W.
Eleven Numbers Against Lawyer Legislation and Fees at the Bar, Written and Printed Expressly for the Benefit of the People, 1843, **7:**124–27

Platt, Adam
The Japanese Look Is Here to Stay: Insight, Nov. 3, 1986, **21:**660

Plebeian, A. (pseud.) *see* Smith, Melancton

Plumer, William
Message to New Hampshire legislature on state control of Dartmouth College, June 5, 1816, **4:**420–21

Plunkitt, George Washington
Plunkitt of Tammany Hall (William L. Riordon, ed.), 1905, **12:**559–67

Podhoretz, Norman *et al.*
Symposium on "Culture and the Present Moment": Commentary, Dec. 1974, **20:**107

Poe, Edgar Allan
To Science (poem), **5:**324

Polk, James Knox
Inaugural Address, Mar. 4, 1845, **7:**286–88
Message to Congress on the Monroe Doctrine, Dec. 2, 1845, **7:**301–3
Third annual message to Congress, Dec. 7, 1847, **7:**374–78

Pollack, James B. *et al.*
The Climatic Effects of Nuclear War: Scientific American, Aug. 1984, **21:**478

Pollock, Jackson
Interview on universal art: Arts and Architecture, Feb. 1944, **16:**210

Porcupine, Peter (pseud.) Cobbett, William

Porter, Horace
The Surrender at Appomattox Court House, 1865, **9:**562–71

Pory, John

Proceedings of the First Assembly of Virginia, 1619, **1:**40–46

Post, Truman Marcellus
Plea for Western Colleges, No. IV: (Appended to first report of the Society for the Promotion of Collegiate and Theological Education at the West), 1844, **7:**242–45

Potter, David M.
People of Plenty, 1954, **17:**258–62

Pound, Ezra
The Rest (poem), **14:**126
Salutation (poem), **14:**127

Powell, John Wesley
Institutions for the Arid Lands: Century Magazine, May 1890, **11:**332–40

Powell, Lewis F.
San Antonio Independent School District et al. v. Rodriguez et al., Mar. 21, 1973, **19:**313

Powers, Charles F.
The Aging Great Lakes: Scientific American, Nov. 1966, **18:**343–47

Pownall, Thomas
The Administration of the Colonies, 1764, **2:**98–103
A Memorial Most Humbly Addressed to the Sovereigns of Europe on the Present State of Affairs, Between the Old and the New World, July 1780, **2:**550–54

Price, Deb
Ellen DeGeneres Paved the Way for Other Gays to Tell the World the Truth: The Detroit News, May 16, 1997, **22:**330

Publius (pseud.) *see* Hamilton, Alexander

Pulszky, Francis
White, Red, Black: Sketches of American Society in the United States, 1853, **8:**215–20

Pulszky, Theresa
White, Red, Black: Sketches of American Society in the United States, 1853, **8:**215–20

Purinton, Edward E.
Big Ideas from Big Business: Independent, Apr. 16, 1921, **14:**298–303

Putnam, Robert D.
Bowling Alone: The Collapse and Revival of American Community, 2000, **22:**448

Putnam, Rufus
Letter to Manasseh Cutler, May 16, 1788, **3:**309–11

Pyle, Ernie
Here Is Your War, 1943, **16:**181–86

Quincy, Josiah (1772–1864)
Speech in House of Representatives on a bill for admission of new states, Jan. 14, 1811, **4:**283–86

Quincy, Josiah (1859–1919)

The Development of American Cities: Arena, Mar. 1897, **12:**138–43

Rabinowitch, Eugene
New Year's Thoughts, 1968 (editorial): Bulletin of the Atomic Scientists, Jan. 1968, **18:**578–82

Raeder, Ole M.
America in the Forties: The Letters of Ole Munch Raeder (Gunnar J. Malmin, trans. and ed.) 1929, **7:**398–402

Ramsay, David
The History of the American Revolution, 1789, **3:**333–39

Randall, Clarence B.
A Creed for Free Enterprise, 1952, **17:**142–46

Randolph, A(sa) Philip
Why Should We March?: Survey Graphic, Nov. 1942, **16:**124–26

Randolph, Innes
The Good Old Rebel (song), **10:**37

Randolph, James R.
Can We Go to Mars?: Scientific American, Aug. 1928, **14:**600–2

Randolph, John, "of Roanoke"
Speeches in House of Representatives on the Nonintercourse Act of 1809, Mar., Apr. 1810, **4:**248–50
Speech in House of Representatives on war with England, Dec. 1811, **4:**294–98
Speech in House of Representatives on the Tariff Act of 1816, Jan. 1816, **4:**427–29
Speech at organizational meeting of the American Colonization Society, Dec. 21, 1816, **4:**455–56
Speech in House of Representatives on the Greek Revolution, Jan. 20, 1823, **5:**111–13

Ransom, John Crowe
Address to the Scholars of New England (poem), June 23, 1939, **15:**581–83

Ransom, John L.
Andersonville Diary (July–Sept., 1865), 1881, **9:**517–28

Rantoul, Robert, Jr.
Oration at Scituate, Mass., on barbarity of the common law, July 4, 1836, **6:**262–66

Rapaille, Clotaire
Interview by National Public Radio, 2000, **22:**452

Raspberry, William
. . . And What Government Can't Do: The Washington Post, Dec. 21, 1978, **21:**133

Rauh, Joseph L., Jr.
Letter to George P. Schultz, Secretary of Labor, July 9, 1969, **19:**53

Rauschenbusch, Walter
Christianity and the Social Crisis, 1907,

13:90–93

Raymond, Daniel
Thoughts on Political Economy, 1820, **4:**623–31

Reagan, John Henninger
Open letter to people of Texas, Aug. 11, 1865, **9:**600–4

Reagan, Ronald
Acceptance Speech: Vital Speeches of the Day, Aug. 15, 1980, **21:**256
First Inaugural Address: Presidential papers, Jan. 20, 1981, **21:**274
Address to the nation on the economy: Presidential papers, Feb. 5, 1981, **21:**279
Responses to an assassination attempt: Presidential documents, week ending June 22, 1981, **21:**299
State of the Union Address: Presidential documents, week ending Jan. 29, 1982, **21:**341
Address on tax and budget reconciliation: Presidential documents, week ending Aug. 26, 1982, **21:**355
Statement on the "Law of the Sea" Treaty: Presidential documents, week ending July 9, 1982, **21:**368
Press conference on Anne M. Burford's resignation from E.P.A.: Presidential documents, week ending Mar. 11, 1983, **21:**413
Speech on the Beirut Massacre: Vital Speeches of the Day, Nov. 15, 1983, **21:**455
Press conference on the Long Report: Presidential documents, week ending Dec. 31, 1983, **21:**462
Speech on U.S. tax system: Presidential documents, week ending May 28, 1985, **21:**569
Press conference on TWA Fl. 847 hijacking: Presidential documents, week ending June 21, 1985, **21:**579
Press conference on Iran arms sales: Presidential documents, week ending Nov. 29, 1986, **21:**664
Speech in West Berlin, Ger., calling for Berlin Wall to be torn down, June 12, 1987, **22:**6
Farewell Address to the Nation, Jan. 11, 1989, **22:**69

Red Cloud
Speech at Cooper Union, New York City, on Native American rights, July 16, 1870, **10:**242–44

Red Jacket
Speech at Buffalo Creek (New York) on white missions among Native Americans, 1805, **4:**194–96

Reece, Florence
Which Side Are You On? (song), **15:**115; **18:**161

Reed, Thomas Brackett
Empire Can Wait: Illustrated American, Dec. 4, 1897, **12:**158–61

Rehnquist, William
Opinion of the U.S. Supreme Court in *Webster* v. *Reproductive Health Services,* 1989, **22:**77

Remond, Charles Lenox
Speech to Legislative Committee of the Massachusetts House of Representatives on segregation in travel, Feb. 1842, **7:**74–76
Spirited Meeting of the Colored Citizens of Philadelphia (Resolutions): The Liberator, Apr. 10, 1857, **8:**451

Reuss, Henry
Milwaukee State of the Union Hearings: Poverty and the Welfare System, Aug. 14, 1969, **19:**73

Ribicoff, Abraham A.
Excerpts from a speech in a Senate debate over amendments to an aid-to-education bill, Feb. 9, 1970, **19:**114

Rice, Joseph Mayer
The Public-School System of the United States, 1893, **11:**396–403

Rice, Thomas Dartmouth (Daddy)
Jump, Jim Crow (poem), **5:**265

Richards, Ann
Keynote Address to the Democratic National Convention, July 1988, **22:**60

Richardson, Elliott
Statement in the U.S. District Court at Baltimore on the sentencing of Spiro T. Agnew, Oct. 10, 1973, **19:**390

Richardson, Jack *et al.*
Symposium on "Culture and the Present Moment": Commentary, Dec. 1974, **20:**107

Richberg, Donald Randall
Testimony before Senate Subcommittee of the Committee on Manufactures regarding federal aid for unemployment relief, Jan. 1933, **15:**200–4

Rickover, Hyman George
Education and Freedom, 1959, **17:**536–45

Ridenhour, Carlton
Don't Believe the Hype (song), recorded by Public Enemy, 1988, **22:**381

Ridenour, Louis N.
Pilot Lights of the Apocalypse (play): Fortune, Jan. 1946, **16:**355–59

Ridgeway, James
More Lost Indians: A Trip to the Sioux Country: New Republic, Dec. 11, 1965,

18:268–73

Riesman, David
The Uncommitted Generation: Encounter, Nov. 1960, **17:**582–88

Rigg, Robert B.
Made in USA: Army, Jan. 1968, **18:**643–47

Rigolot, Carol
Speech to gifted high school students on the importance of reading, Apr. 1993, **22:**181

Riis, Jacob August
How the Other Half Lives, 1890, **11:**286–95
The Battle With the Slum, 1902, **12:**437–41

Ritter, Jesse P., Jr.
Nightmare for the Innocent in a California Jail: Life, Aug. 15, 1969, **19:**20

Roane, Spencer
Letters to editor (by Hampden): Richmond Enquirer, June 11, 15, 1819, **4:**539–43

Robertson, Andrew
The Aging Great Lakes: Scientific American, Nov. 1966, **18:**343–47

Robertson, Pat
Speech to the Republican National Convention, Aug. 16, 1988, **22:**64

Robins, Robert
Testimony before Federal Communications Commission on television, June 25, 1936, **15:**376–78

Robinson, Edwin Arlington
New England (poem), **14:**500

Robinson, Frederick
A Letter to the Hon. Rufus Choate, Containing a Brief Exposure of Law Craft, and Some of the Encroachments of the Bar Upon the Rights and Liberties of the People, June 25, 1831, **5:**441–47
An Oration Delivered Before the Trades Union of Boston, July 4, 1834, **6:**69–74

Robinson, John
Letter of Instruction to the Plymouth Pilgrims, 1620, **1:**61–63

Robinson, William E.
Speech in House of Representatives on resolution, regarding Haiti and Santo Domingo, Jan. 13, 1869, **10:**150–52

Rock, John S.
Speech to Massachusetts Anti-Slavery Society on African American hopes for emancipation, Jan. 23, 1862, **9:**318–22

Rockefeller, John Davidson
Testimony before U.S. Industrial Commission on the advantages of trusts, Dec. 1899, **12:**312–16
Random Reminiscences of Men and Events, 1909, **13:**207–11

Rockefeller, John Davidson, Jr.

Labor and Capital—Partners: Atlantic Monthly, Jan. 1916, **14:**23–28

Rodney, Thomas
Letter to Caesar Rodney, June 14, 1781, **2:**561–62

Roesch, George F.
Opinion of the (New York Municipal) court in *City of New York* v. *Chelsea Jute Mills,* 1904, **12:**571–75

Rogers, Bernard W.
Toward a Professional Army: An interview by Nat Dell: Soldiers, Aug. 1973, **19:**179

Rogers, Will
Column on the normal majority: New York Times, Feb. 22, 1925, **14:**469–71
Column on William Thompson and the America First Foundation: New York Times, Nov. 13, 1927, **14:**564–66

Rogers, William P.
Strategic Arms Limitation Talks: An address to Diplomatic and Consular Officers Retired, Nov. 13, 1969, **19:**92

Rohrabacher, Dana
Congressional debate on the Arts, Humanities, and Museums Amendments, Oct. 11, 1990, **22:**108

Roosevelt, Eleanor
What I Think of the United Nations: United Nations World, Aug. 1949, **16:**613–17
Statement to Committee III (Social, Humanitarian, and Cultural) of the UN General Assembly on defense of American territorial policies, Nov. 24, 1952, **17:**128–30

Roosevelt, Franklin Delano
Campaign speech at the Commonwealth Club of San Francisco, Sept. 23, 1932, **15:**158–66
Campaign speech at Albany, N.Y., Oct. 13, 1932, **15:**185–87
First Inaugural Address, Mar. 4, 1933, **15:**205–8
Fireside Chat, July 24, 1933, **15:**210–13
Letters to Maxim Litvinov, Nov. 16, 1933, **15:**219–20
Fireside Chat, June 28, 1934, **15:**263–67
Annual message to Congress, Jan. 4, 1935, **15:**309–15
Message to Congress, Jan. 17, 1935, **15:**315–17
Speech at Chautauqua, N.Y., on the Good Neighbor Policy, Aug. 14, 1936, **15:**352–53
Campaign speech at Chicago, Oct. 14, 1936, **15:**379–83
Address to the People on a judiciary reform bill, Mar. 9, 1937, **15:**431–37
"Quarantine" address at Chicago, Oct. 5,

1937, **15:**502–5

Speech at the University of Virginia, June 10, 1940, **16:**8–10

Press Conference on the destroyer-bases deal, Sept. 3, 1940, **16:**31–35

Campaign speech at Madison Square Garden, New York City, Oct. 28, 1940, **16:**36–39

Press Conference on the Lend-Lease program, Dec. 17, 1940, **16:**40–41

Annual message to Congress, Jan. 6, 1941, **16:**42–45

Executive Order No. 8802 (on establishing the Committee on Fair Employment Practices), June 25, 1941, **16:**82–83

Navy Day Address, Oct. 27, 1941, **16:**90–94

Message to Congress on declaration of war with Japan, Dec. 8, 1941, **16:**103–5

Fireside Chat, Dec. 9, 1941, **16:**105–8

Speech at White House Correspondents' Association Dinner on the Casablanca Conference, Feb. 12, 1943, **16:**130–32

Annual message to Congress, Jan. 11, 1944, **16:**211–14

Roosevelt, Theodore

American Ideals, 1910, **11:**76–81

Speech to Union League Club, Washington, D.C., on the 1888 election, Jan. 1888, **11:**170–72

Letter to James Bryce, Jan. 6, 1888, **11:**189–90

The Winning of the West, 1910, **11:**207–10

The Enforcement of Law: Forum, Sept. 1895, **12:**67–70

Letter to the editors: Harvard Crimson, Jan. 2, 1896, **12:**83–84

Letter to Alfred Thayer Mahan, May 3, 1897, **12:**150–51

First annual message to Congress, Dec. 3, 1901, **12:**433–36

Letter to Theodore Burton, Feb. 23, 1904, **12:**596–98

Fifth annual message to Congress, Dec. 5, 1905, **13:**1–3

Special message to Congress, Jan. 22, 1909, **13:**161–64

Letter to Philander Knox, Feb. 8, 1909, **13:**173–76

Speech at Osawatomie, Kan., on the "new nationalism," Aug. 31, 1910, **13:**250–54

The Trusts, the People, and the Square Deal: Outlook, Nov. 18, 1911, **13:**319–21

A Layman's View of an Art Exhibition: Outlook, Mar. 29, 1913, **13:**376–77

The World War: Its Tragedies and Its Lessons: Outlook, Sept. 23, 1914, **13:**492–99

The Children of the Crucible, Sept. 11, 1917, **14:**129–31

Root, Elihu

Experiments in Government, Apr. 1913, **13:**436–38

Speech in New York constitutional convention on the Short Ballot Amendment, Aug. 30, 1915, **13:**528–31

America's Present Needs, Jan. 25, 1917, **14:**70–74

Root, George Frederick

The Battle-Cry of Freedom (song), **9:**303–4

Rosenberg, Harold

The American Action Painters: Art News, Dec. 1952, **17:**189–96

Rosenfeld, Monroe H.

Her Golden Hair Was Hanging Down Her Back (song), **11:**552–53

Rosenquist, James

An interview on Pop art: Art News, May 1974, **20:**105

Rosow, Jerome

Productivity: The Blue Collar Blues: An address to the American Management Association annual conference, Feb. 9, 1971, **19:**187

Ross, John

Speech in New York State constitutional convention, Sept. 1821, **5:**22–23

Ross, Mary

Why Social Security?, 1936, **15:**471–74

Rostow, Eugene V.

Our Worst Wartime Mistake: Harper's, Sept. 1945, **16:**344–49

Security or Retreat, Feb. 20, 1968, **18:**605–13

Rothko, Mark

Preamble of the Federation of Modern Painters and Sculptors, 1943, **16:**209

Rourke, Constance Mayfield

American Humor: A Study of the National Character, 1931, **15:**126–28

Roussy de Sales, Raoul de

Love in America: Atlantic Monthly, May 1938, **15:**526–30

Rovere, Richard H.

Half Out of Our Tree: New Yorker, Oct. 28, 1967, **18:**544–54

Rowland, Henry Augustus

The Highest Aim of the Physicist, Oct. 28, 1899, **12:**262–66

Royall, Anne

Letters from Alabama, 1830, **5:**383–85

Royle, Edwin M.

The Vaudeville Theatre: Scribner's, Oct. 1899, **12:**266–72

Ruffin, Edmund

Consequences of Abolition Agitation: De Bow's

Review, June, Sept., Oct., Nov., Dec. 1857, **8:**466–75

Ruml, Beardsley
Pay-As-You-Go Taxation—The Dangers in Income-Tax Debt and What We Can Do To Get Free of It, Oct. 15, 1942, **16:**110–15

Rush, Benjamin
Letter to John Morgan, Jan. 20, 1768, **2:**196–97
Letter to Richard Henry Lee, Dec. 30, 1776, **2:**462
Letter to George Washington, Dec. 26, 1777, **2:**490–92
Letter to Patrick Henry, Jan. 12, 1778, **2:**493–94
Letter to Richard Price, May 25, 1786, **3:**55–56
A Plan for Establishing Public Schools in Pennsylvania, and for Establishing Conducting Education Agreeably to a Republican Form: Addressed to the legislature and citizens of Pennsylvania, 1786, **3:**57–59
Address to the People on the defects of the Confederation, 1787, **3:**85–88
Thoughts upon Female Education, July 28, 1787, **3:**207–12
Plan of a Federal University (by Citizen of Pennsylvania): American Museum, Oct. 1788, **3:**312–14
Letter to Andrew Brown (editor): Federal Gazette, Oct. 1, 1788, **3:**317–18
Of the Mode of Education Proper in a Republic, 1798, **4:**28–32
Letter to John Adams, Aug. 14, 1805, **4:**199–201

Rush, Richard
American Jurisprudence, 1815, **4:**385–89
Letter to John Quincy Adams, Aug. 19, 1823, **5:**66–68

Rusk, Dean
Informal remarks to State Department aides on formulating foreign policy, Feb. 20, 1961, **18:**20–24

Russell, Charles Taze
Food for Thinking Christians (reissued as *Millennial Dawn,* 1886), 1881, **11:**103–6

Russwurm, John
To Our Patrons (salutatory): Freedom's Journal, Mar. 16, 1827, **5:**222–24

Ryan, John Augustine
A Living Wage, 1906, **13:**76–84

St. John, J. Hector (pseud.)
see Crévecoeur, Michel Guillaume Jean de

Sadat, Anwar El
Principles of relation and cooperation between Egypt and the U.S., June 14, 1974, **20:**66

Remarks on Camp David accords: Presidential documents, Sept. 17–18, 1978, **21:**114

Sadker, David
Sexism in the Classroom: Psychology Today, Mar. 1985, **21:**561

Sadker, Myra
Sexism in the Classroom: Psychology Today, Mar. 1985, **21:**561

Sadler, Eric
Don't Believe the Hype (song), recorded by Public Enemy, 1988, **22:**381

Safire, William
The Computer Tattoo: The New York Times, Sept. 9, 1982, **21:**380

Sagan, Carl
The Viking landing on Mars: NASA News Release 76–74, as reprinted in Space World, Oct. 1976, **20:**331

Sagan, Carl et al.
The Climatic Effects of Nuclear War: Scientific American, Aug. 1984, **21:**478

Sampson, Anthony
The Lockheed Connection: Atlas World Press Review, May 1976, **20:**321

Sandburg, Carl
Chicago (poem), **13:**499–500
To a Contemporary Bunkshooter (poem), **14:**38–40
I Am the People, the Mob (poem), **14:**40
Memoir of a Proud Boy (poem), **14:**174–75
The People, Yes (poem), **15:**414–20

Sanders, Marion K. et al.
Symposium on "Coping with Terrorism": Atlas World Review, Sept. 1976, **20:**325

Sanderson, John P.
Republican Landmarks: The Views and Opinions of American Statesmen on Foreign Immigration, 1856, **8:**429–35

Sanford, David
The Seedier Media: New Republic, Dec. 2, 1967, **18:**500–2

Sanford, Edward T.
Opinion of the Court in *Gitlow* v. *New York,* 1925, **14:**476–80

Sanford, Nathan
Speech in New York State constitutional convention, Sept. 1821, **5:**4–6

Santayana, George
The Genteel Tradition in American Philosophy, Aug. 25, 1911, **13:**277–88
Character and Opinion in the United States, 1920, **14:**270–75

Sartre, Jean Paul
Americans and Their Myths: Nation, Oct. 18, 1947, **16:**494–96

Sass, Herbert Ravenel
Mixed Schools and Mixed Blood: Atlantic
   Monthly, Nov. 1956, **17:**373–78
Savage, John
Opinion of the (New York Supreme)
   court in *People* v. *Fisher,* 1835, **6:**172–74
Opinion of the (New York Supreme)
   court in *Meeker* v. *Van Rensselaer,* 1836,
   6:279–81
Sawhill, John C.
The Collapse of Public Schools: Saturday Re-
   view, Aug. 1979, **21:**146
Saxton, Bruce *et al.*
Symposium on "Coping with Terrorism": Atlas
   World Press Review, Sept. 1976, **20:**325
Scammon, Richard M.
This U.S.A., 1965, **18:**280–85
Is It the End of an Era?: Public Opinion,
   Oct.–Nov. 1980, **21:**259
Schaff, Philip
*America, A Sketch of the Political, Social, and
   Religious Character of the United States of
   North America,* 1855, **8:**329–34
Schlesinger, Arthur, Jr.
Arguments against a one-term presidency: The
   New York Times, Jan. 10, 1986, **21:**612
Schlosser, Eric
*Interview with Eric Schlosser, Author of Fast
   Food Nation:* The Atlantic Monthly On-
   line, Dec. 14, 2000, **22:**469
Schlosser, Herbert
*Address to the Association of National Adver-
   tisers,* Oct. 29, 1974, **20:**96
Schmoke, Kurt L.
*Speech to United Way of America's National
   Conference on Welfare Reform,* Sept. 1997,
   22:339
Schorr, Daniel
*Testimony before the Committee on Standards of
   Official Conduct,* House of Representa-
   tives, 94 Congress, 2 Session, Sept. 15,
   1976, **20:**285
Schurz, Carl
True Americanism, Apr. 18, 1859, **9:**97–106
Present Aspects of the Indian Problem: North
   American Review, July 1881, **10:**495–504
The Need for a Rational Forest Policy, Oct. 15,
   1889, **11:**200–3
*The Necessity and Progress of Civil Service Re-
   form,* Dec. 12, 1894, **11:**493–97
Schuyler, Montgomery
Architecture in Chicago (Great American Ar-
   chitects Series): Architectural Record,
   Dec. 1895, **12:**51–55
Schwartz, Felice N.
Speech to the Wharton School, University of

*Pennsylvania, on women in corporate Amer-
   ica,* Oct. 1987, **22:**21
Schwarzkopf, H. Norman
*Central Command Briefing, Riyadh, Saudi
   Arabia:* Military Review, Feb. 27, 1991,
   22:131
Schweiker, Richard S.
Testimony on illegal aliens: Congressional
   Digest, Oct. 1977, **21:**50
Scott, Jesup W.
The Great West: De Bow's Review, July 1853,
   8:211–13
Seabury, Samuel
*A View of the Controversy Between Great-
   Britain and Her Colonies* (letter by A
   Westchester Farmer), 1775, **2:**289–95
Sears, Charles
*Report on the first nine years of the North
   American Phalanx,* Dec. 1852, **8:**185–90
Seaton, Frederick Andrew
*Statement before the Senate Subcommittee on
   Territories and Insular Possessions of the
   Committee of Interior and Insular Affairs,
   regarding statehood for Hawaii,* Feb. 25,
   1959, **17:**524–27
Seddon, James Alexander
Letter to Jefferson Davis, Nov. 26, 1863,
   9:463–67
Sedgwick, Theodore
What Is A Monopoly?, 1835, **6:**174–80
Segal, George
An interview on Pop art: Art News, May
   1974, **20:**103
Seidman, Joel
Sit-Down: New Frontiers, Jan. 1937,
   15:475–83
Seixas, Moses
Letter to George Washington, Aug. 17, 1790,
   3:433–34
Selby, William
Ode for the New Year (poem), **3:**395–96
Seldes, Gilbert
The Great Audience, 1950, **17:**28–33
Sennholz, Hans F.
Testimony on illegal aliens: Congressional
   Digest, Oct. 1977, **21:**48
Servan-Schreiber, Jean-Jacques
*The Multinational Challenge of the Seventies:
   Reform Without Revolution: Remarks before
   the Joint Economic Committee subcommittee
   on Foreign Economic Policy,* Congress of
   the U.S., July 1970, **19:**155
Sewall, Samuel
Letter to William Ashurst, May 3, 1700, **1:**315
The Selling of Joseph: A Memorial, 1700,
   1:316–18

Seward, William Henry
Oration at laying of corner-stone of works on Owasco River, Auburn, N.Y., Oct. 14, 1835, **6:**140–44
Letter on treaty with the Seneca Indians, June 15, 1841, **7:**1–3
Speech in Senate on slavery, Mar. 11, 1850, **8:**29–35
Speech in Senate on treatment for the indigent insane, June 19, 1854, **8:**283–89
Speech at Rochester, N.Y., on slavery, Oct. 25, 1858, **9:**32–35
Memo to Lincoln on domestic and foreign policy, Apr. 1, 1861, **9:**256–57
Dispatch to Charles F. Adams on American and European interests in Mexico, Mar. 3, 1862, **9:**326–27
Letter to William Dayton, May 11, 1863, **9:**422–23
Instructions to Robert H. Pruyn on trade with Japan, Aug. 20, 1864, **9:**533–34
Speech to Citizens of Alaska, Aug. 12, 1869, **10:**193–97

Shanks, William F. G.
Personal Recollections of Distinguished Generals, 1866, **10:**1–3

Shapiro, Karl (Jay)
University (poem), **16:**123–24
What Is American Poetry? (Introduction to *American Poetry*), 1960, **17:**575–82

Sharp, Ben
What Soccer Means: The New York Times, June 29, 1986, **21:**636

Sharp, Dan
What Soccer Means: The New York Times, June 29, 1986, **21:**636

Shattuck, Lemuel
Report of a General Plan for the Promotion of Public and Personal Health, 1850, **8:**76–83

Shaw, Albert
The Progress of the World (editorial): American Monthly Review of Reviews, Apr. 1898, **12:**168–73

Shaw, Henry Wheeler (Josh Billings)
An Essa on the Muel, 1860, **9:**171–72

Shaw, Lemuel
Profession of Law in the United States, May 1827, **5:**217–21
Opinion of the (Massachusetts Supreme) court in *Commonwealth* v. *Hunt,* 1842, **7:**61–65

Shellabarger, Samuel
Speech in House of Representatives on resolution, regarding Haiti and Santo Domingo, Jan. 13, 1869, **10:**146–48

Sherman, John

Letter to a group of Philadelphians, Dec. 22, 1860, **9:**224–29
Letter to William Tecumseh Sherman, Nov. 10, 1865, **9:**622–23

Sherman, William Tecumseh
Letter to John Sherman, Feb. 18, 1863, **9:**405–6
Letter to John Sherman, Aug. 3, 1863, **9:**432–33
Memoirs (on military lessons of the war), 1875, **10:**340–45

Sherwood, Robert E(mmet)
Renaissance in Hollywood: American Mercury, Apr. 1929, **15:**10–16

Shirer, William L(awrence)
The American Radio Traitors: Harper's, Oct. 1943, **16:**187–92

Shocklee, Hank
Don't Believe the Hype (song), recorded by Public Enemy, 1988, **22:**381

Shore, Warren
Social Security—A Great Ripoff?: Chicago Today, Apr. 29, 1974, **20:**58

Shriver, R(obert) Sargent, Jr.
Two Years of the Peace Corps: Foreign Affairs, July 1963, **18:**179–86

Shulins, Nancy
Not in My Backyard: Chicago Tribune, Feb. 12, 1984, **21:**491

Shute, Samuel
Memorial to Massachusetts Privy Council, Aug. 1723, **1:**360–63

Sidey, Hugh
How to Do Nothing Well: Time, Aug. 22, 1983, **21:**425

Siminov, Vladimir
Remarks on the 1984 Olympic Games: Soviet News Agency, July 1984, **21:**526

Simmons, Furnifold M.
To the Voters of North Carolina: Raleigh News and Observer, Nov. 3, 1898, **12:**229–31

Simon, Paul
The Panama Canal Treaties—Pro and Con: American Legion Magazine, Jan. 1978, **21:**53

Simon, William E. *et al.*
Arguments for a one-term presidency: The New York Times, Dec. 31, 1985, **21:**610

Simons, Henry C.
A Political Credo (Introduction to *Economic Policy for a Free Society*), 1948, **16:**499–510

Simpson, Stephen
The Working Man's Manual: A New Theory of Political Economy, on the Principle of Production the Source of Wealth, 1831, **5:**463–71

Sinclair, Upton (Beall)
The Jungle, 1906, **13:**67–75
Sirica, John J.
In Re Subpoena to Nixon, Aug. 29, 1973, **19:**380
Skidmore, Thomas
The Rights of Man to Property!, 1829, **5:**298–302
Slichter, Sumner H.
Testimony before Senate subcommittee of the Committee on Manufactures regarding federal aid for unemployment relief, Jan. 1933, **15:**197–200
Smalley, E. V.
The Isolation of Life on Prairie Farms: Atlantic Monthly, Sept. 1893, **11:**482–86
Smith, Alfred E(manuel)
Catholic and Patriot: Governor Smith Replies [*to Charles C. Marshall*]: Atlantic Monthly, May 1927, **14:**536–42
Smith, Anthony W.
The Profit Motive and the Environment: An address to the Conservation Committee of the Garden Club of America, Oct. 12, 1971: National Parks and Conservation Magazine, Jan. 1972, **19:**254
Smith, Charles H. (Bill Arp)
Bill Arp, So Called. A Side Show of the Southern Side of the War, 1866, **9:**604–6
Smith, Charles Sprague
A Creedless Church for a Creedless People: Independent, Jan. 2, 1908, **13:**106–9
Smith, Gerald W.
Debate on Capital Punishment: Crime and Delinquency, July 1977, **21:**1
Smith, James
Tours into Kentucky and the Northwest Territory (1795, 1797): Ohio Archaeological and Historical Publications, 1907, **4:**10–12
Smith, John
Generall Historie of Virginia, New England and the Summer Isles, 1624, **1:**21–31
A Description of New England, 1616, **1:**36–39
Smith, Joseph
The Pearl of Great Price, c. 1838, **6:**432–37
Smith, Melancton
An Address to the People of the State of New-York Showing the Necessity of Making Amendments to the Constitution, Proposed for the United States Previous to its Adoption (by A Plebeian), 1788, **3:**254–60
Smith, Red
On Playing in Ivan's Yard: The Red Smith Reader, 1982, **21:**254
Smith, Samuel Francis

America (song), **5:**554
Smith, Samuel Harrison
Remarks on Education; Illustrating the Close Connection Between Virtue and Wisdom, To Which Is Annexed a System of Liberal Education, 1796, **3:**597–603
Smith, Mrs. Samuel Harrison (Margaret Bayard)
Letter to Mrs. Kirkpatrick, Mar. 11, 1829, **5:**288–90
Smith, William (1697–1769)
The Querist: or, A Letter to a Member of the General Assembly of the Colony of New-York, May 30, 1754, **1:**503–5
Smith, William (1727–1803)
Letters to the People of Pennsylvania (by Cato), Mar. 1776, **2:**399–403
Smyth, Henry De Wolf
Dissent from the decision of the Atomic Energy Commission in the matter of J. Robert Oppenheimer, 1954, **17:**292–94
Solzhenitsyn, Aleksandr
Speech in Washington, D.C., June 30, 1975: Society, Dec. 1975, **20:**173
Soulé, Frank, et al.
The Annals of San Francisco, 1855, **7:**492–502
Soule, George
Are We Going To Have a Revolution?: Harper's, Aug. 1932, **15:**152–58
Sousa, John Philip
The Stars and Stripes Forever (song), **12:**124–25
South Carolina (pseud.) *see* Gregg, William
Spalding, Albert G.
America's National Game, 1911, **13:**265–69
Spalding, John Lancaster
Means and Ends of Education, 1895, **12:**78–82
Spalding, Rufus P.
Speech in House of Representatives on resolution, regarding Haiti and Santo Domingo, Jan. 13, 1869, **10:**143–46 *passim*
Sparke, John
Principal Navigations, 1589, **1:**6–10
Speech (Todd Thomas)
Tennessee (song), recorded by Arrested Development, 1992, **22:**382
Speich, Don
U.S. Education on the Skids: Chicago Sun-Times, Sept. 5, 1976, **20:**295
Spencer, William I.
An Interview, "Who Controls MNCs?": Harvard Business Review, Nov.–Dec. 1975, **20:**121
Spies, August

Statement to the Cook County Criminal Court, Chicago, on the Haymarket Trial, Oct. 7, 1886, **11**:117–21

Springsteen, Bruce
Youngstown (song), 1995, **22**:300

Stanfield, Rochelle L. *et al.*
Federal Spending—The North's Loss Is the Sunbelt's Gain: National Journal, June 26, 1976, **20**:262

Stanton, Elizabeth Cady
Speech to New York legislature on a bill for woman suffrage, Feb. 18, 1860, **9**:151–56

Starr, Kenneth W.
The Starr Report, 1998, **22**:362

Steele, Bill
What Should You Bring Overseas?: Yank, Mar. 26, 1943, **16**:179–80

Steele, Shelby
On Being Black and Middle Class: Commentary, Jan. 1988, **22**:42

Steevens, George W.
The Land of the Dollar, 1897, **12**:115–18

Steffens, Lincoln
Tweed Days in St. Louis: McClure's, Oct. 1902, **12**:483–87
The Shame of the Cities: Introduction; and Some Conclusions, 1904, **12**:542–46

Steinbeck, John
The Grapes of Wrath, 1939, **15**:592–600

Stephens, Alexander Hamilton
Speech in Georgia legislature on secession, Nov. 14, 1860, **9**:199–203
Speech in Georgia legislature on civil rights in the Confederacy, Mar. 16, 1864, **9**:493–96
Testimony before Joint Congressional Committee on Reconstruction, Apr. 11, 1866, **10**:23–26

Stept, Sam H.
Don't Sit Under the Apple Tree (With Anyone Else But Me) (song), **16**:128

Sterling, Andrew B.
Meet Me in St. Louis, Louis (song), **12**:598–99

Stern, Gerald
Public Drunkenness: Crime or Health Problem?: Annals of the American Academy of Political and Social Science, Nov. 1967, **18**:448–55

Sternlieb, George
The City as Sandbox: Public Interest, Fall 1971, **19**:213

Stevens, Doris
Jailed for Freedom, 1920, **14**:127–28

Stevens, Thaddeus
Speech in Pennsylvania legislature on repeal of the public school law, Apr. 1835, **6**:136–40

Speech in House of Representatives on an internal revenue bill, Apr. 8, 1862, **9**:335–37
Speech at Lancaster, Pa., on the Reconstruction program, Sept. 6, 1865, **9**:608–12

Stevenson, Adlai E(wing)
Acceptance speech at the Democratic Convention, Chicago, July 26, 1952, **17**:196–99
Statements in UN General Assembly on the Bay of Pigs, Apr. 17, 18, 20, 1961, **18**:25–31
The Fundamental Meaning of the United Nations, June 23, 1965, **18**:317–22

Stevenson, Robert Louis
Across the Plains (in *From Scotland to Silverado,* James D. Hart, ed., 1966), 1892, **10**:438–42

Steward, Ira
A Reduction of Hours an Increase of Wages, 1865, **9**:615–21

Stewart, Abigail J.
Advantages of a Liberal Arts Education: Psychology Today, Sept. 1978, **21**:119

Stille, Ugo
Editorial on the Bicentennial: Corriere della Sera (Milan), July 4, 1976, **20**:373

Stimson, Henry Lewis
Military Needs of the United States, 1915, **13**:569–72
The United States and the Other Republics, Feb. 6, 1931, **15**:72–78

Stoddard, Lothrop
The Rising Tide of Color Against White World-Supremacy, 1920, **14**:266–70

Stone, John P.
Jefferson County, Colorado, Sheriff's Office Report on the Columbine High School murders, May 15, 2000, **22**:435

Stone, Oliver
Wall Street (movie), 1987, **22**:27

Storey, Wilbur F.
Editorial on H.P. Tappan, president of University of Michigan: Detroit Free Press, Dec. 28, 1853, **8**:222–23

Story, Joseph
Dissent in Charles River Bridge v. *Warren Bridge,* 1837, **6**:331–32

Stow, Timothy D.
Testimony before Senate Committee on Education and Labor, 1883, **10**:572–77

Stowe, Harriet Beecher
Uncle Tom's Cabin; or, Life Among the Lowly, 1851–1852, **8**:200–2

Strauss, William
The New Generation Gap: The Atlantic Monthly, Dec. 1992, **22**:165

Strong, George Templeton
Diary (on the Panic of 1837), Apr.–May

1837, **6:**311–14

Diary (on the first transatlantic cable), July 1–Sept. 29, 1858, **9:**65–67

Strong, Josiah

Our Country: Its Possible Future and Its Present Crisis, 1885, **11:**71–76

The New Era, or The Coming Kingdom, 1893, **11:**450–57

The Twentieth Century City, 1898, **12:**216–20

Strunsky, Simeon

Armaments and Caste: Annals of the American Academy of Political and Social Science, July 1916, **14:**53–59

Sullivan, Andrew

What's So Bad About Hate?: The New York Times Magazine, Sept. 26, 1999, **22:**407

Sullivan, Louis Henry

Characteristics and Tendencies of American Architecture, Nov. 18, 1885, **11:**40–44

The Young Man in Architecture, June 1900, **12:**385–87

The Chicago Tribune *Competition:* Architectural Record, Feb. 1923, **14:**400–5

Sumner, Charles

Report on the War with Mexico, 1847, **7:**361–65

Argument before the Supreme Court of Massachusetts, in the case of *Sarah C. Roberts* v. *The City of Boston*, Dec. 4, 1849, **7:**507–16

War System of the Commonwealth of Nations, May 28, 1849, **7:**548–51

Speech to the Senate on the Kansas-Nebraska Act (The Crime Against Kansas), May 19–20, 1856, **8:**367–71

Resolutions to Senate on secession and reconstruction: Feb. 11, 1862, **9:**323–25

Opinion in Senate on the impeachment of Andrew Johnson, Mar. 1868, **10:**126–30

Speech in Senate on the annexation of the Dominican Republic: (Naboth's Vineyard Speech), Dec. 21, 1870, **10:**233–39

Sumner, William Graham

The Challenge of Facts, 1914, **10:**537–47

What Social Classes Owe to Each Other, 1883, **10:**594–601

The Absurd Effort to Make the World Over: Forum, Mar. 1894, **11:**487–93

War, 1903, **12:**504–6

Surkin, Marvin

Paving Streets With His Life: The New York Times, Nov. 6, 1976, **20:**307

Sutherland, George

Opinion of the Court in *Adkins* v. *Children's Hospital*, 1923, **14:**391–96

Opinion of the Court in *New State Ice Company* v. *Liebmann*, 1923, **15:**140–42

Sutherland, Josiah

Speech in House of Representatives on the Homestead Bill, Apr. 22, 1852, **8:**180–83

Sutton, Preston M.

Speech in Iowa General Assembly on liberal arts bill of 1873, 1884, **11:**18–22

Swados, Harvey

The Myth of the Happy Worker: Nation, Aug. 17, 1957, **17:**427–32

Sweeney, John J.

Speech to City Club of Cleveland, Ohio, on the future of labor, Jan. 1988, **22:**38

Swift, Morrison I.

Imperialism and Liberty, 1899, **12:**236–46

Symonds, William

Virginia, A Sermon Preached at White-Chappel, Apr. 25, 1609, **1:**32–35

Taft, Robert A(lphonso)

New Problems of Government, July 14, 1939, **15:**571–74

Speech in Senate on the Roosevelt war policies: Oct. 28, 1941, **16:**94–103

Speech before the National Industrial Conference Board of New York, Jan. 18, 1945, **16:**263–67

Speech in Senate on the Taft-Hartley Act, Apr. 23, 1947, **16:**414–24

The Republican Party: Fortune, Apr. 1949, **16:**565–72

Speech in Senate on the North Atlantic Treaty, July 11, 1949, **16:**591–95

Taft, William Howard

Speech at Winona, Minn., on the Payne-Aldrich Tariff, Sept. 17, 1909, **13:**176–80

Veto message to House of Representatives on the Arizona Enabling Act, Aug. 15, 1911, **13:**272–77

Message to Congress on the Cabinet and the Congress, Dec. 19, 1912, **13:**366–67

Last annual message to Congress, Dec. 3, 1912, **13:**369–73

Our Chief Magistrate and His Powers, 1916, **14:**41–44

Dissent in *Adkins* v. *Children's Hospital*, 1923, **14:**396–97

Tan, Amy

The Joy Luck Club, 1989, **22:**83

Taney, Roger Brooke

Opinion of the Court in *Charles River Bridge* v. *Warren Bridge*, 1837, **6:**326–31

Opinion of the Court in *Dred Scott* v. *Sandford*, 1857, **8:**440–49

Tansill, William R.

The Concept of Civil Supremacy Over the Military in the United States, 1951, **17:**67–72

Tappan, Henry Philip
The University: Its Constitution, and Its Relation, Political and Religious: A Discourse, June 22, 1858, **9:**79–84

Tarbell, Ida Minerva
The History of the Standard Oil Company, 1904, **12:**535–41

Tate, Allen
Ode to the Confederate Dead (poem), **14:**602–4

Taylor, Deems
Music, in *Civilization in the United States* (Harold E. Stearns, ed.), 1922, **14:**345–51

Taylor, Frederick Winslow
A Piece-Rate System, June 1895, **12:**16–17

Taylor, Graham R.
Satellite Cities: A Study of Industrial Suburbs, 1915, **13:**520–23

Taylor, Hannis
The National House of Representatives: Its Growing Inefficiency as a Legislative Body: Atlantic Monthly, June 1890, **11:**318–23

Taylor, John
An Inquiry into the Principles and Policy of the Government of the United States, 1814, **4:**342–48
New Views of the Constitution of the United States, 1823, **5:**88–94

Teller, Edward
Our Nuclear Future, 1958, **17:**480–86

Tennent, Gilbert
A General Account of the Rise and State of the College, Lately Established in the Province of New-Jersey, 1754, **1:**518–21

Terry, David Smith
Opinion of the (California Supreme) court in Ex Parte Newman, 1858, **9:**85–90

Tevis, Charles V.
A Ku-Klux Klan of To-day: The Red Record of Kentucky's "Night Riders": Harper's Monthly, Feb. 8, 1908, **13:**129–32

Thayer, James B.
The Origin and Scope of the American Doctrine of Constitutional Law: Harvard Law Review, Oct. 25, 1893, **11:**430–35

Thayer, Robert H.
Speech to the Virginia Women's Forum, Richmond, on cultural relations abroad, Nov. 5, 1959, **17:**545–49

Theodore de la Guard (pseud.) *see* Ward, Nathaniel

Thomas, Clarence
Where Thomas Stands (testimony before the Judiciary Committee): Congressional Quarterly, Sept. 21, 1991, **22:**136

Thomas, Dylan
A Visit to America (recorded radio address), Mar. 30, 1954, **17:**239–41

Thomas, Evan
American Taliban: Newsweek, Dec. 17, 2001, **22:**505

Thomas, Norman (Matoon)
After the New Deal, What?, 1936, **15:**360–65

Thomas, Norman (Matoon) *et al.*
The Religion of Free Men (letter): New Republic, May 26, 1917, **14:**111–14

Thomas, Samuel Ab
Letter from Arnot, Tioga County, Pa., 1874, **10:**320–21

Thoreau, Henry David
Paradise (To Be) Regained, 1843, **7:**143–56
Civil Disobedience: Dial, 1849, **7:**540–48
Walking, May 31, 1851, **8:**125–28
Walden; or, Life in the Woods, 1854, **8:**308–16
A Plea for Captain John Brown: Read to Citizens of Concord, Mass., Oct. 30, 1859, **9:**136–43

Thorne, Ludmilla
The Littlest Defector: National Review, Mar. 1983, **21:**399

Thurber, James (Grover)
My Life and Hard Times, 1933, **14:**143–50

Ticknor, George
Efforts for Reform in Harvard College, July 23, 1823, **5:**77–79

Tilden, Samuel J.
Speech at New York State Democratic Convention, Albany, on arraignment of the Republican Party, Mar. 11, 1868, **10:**122–26

Timrod, Henry
Ethnogenesis (poem), **9:**242–43
Charleston (poem), **9:**528–29

Tobias, Charlie
Don't Sit Under the Apple Tree (With Anyone Else But Me) (song), **16:**128

Tocqueville, Alexis de
Journey to America (George Lawrence, trans.; J.P. Mayer, ed.), 1962, **5:**482–505
Letter to Eugene Stoffels, Feb. 21, 1835, **6:**205–6
Democracy in America: Introduction (Henry Reeve[s], trans.), 1856, **6:**206–14

Toller, Ernst
Quer Durch Reisebilder und Reden [*Travel Sketches and Discourses*], 1930, **15:**45–50

Tompson, Benjamin
New-England's Crisis (poem), **1:**245–46

Toombs, Robert
Speech in Georgia legislature on secession, Nov. 1860, **9:**192–99

Toon, Owen B. *et al.*
The Climatic Effects of Nuclear War: Scientific American, Aug. 1984, **21:**478
Travis, Merle
Sixteen Tons (song), **16:**433
Travis, William B.
Message from the Alamo, Feb. 24, 1836, **6:**282
Trilling, Lionel *et al.*
Symposium on "Culture and the Present Moment": Commentary, Dec. 1974, **20:**107
Trollope, Anthony
North America, 1862, **9:**383–85
Trollope, Frances
Domestic Manners of the Americans, 1832, **5:**542–45
Truman, Harry S.
Address to nation on the dropping of an Atomic Bomb on Hiroshima, Aug. 6, 1945, **16:**334–36
The Fundamentals of U.S. Foreign Policy, Oct. 27, 1945, **16:**343–44
Speech to joint session of Congress on the Truman Doctrine, Mar. 12, 1947, **16:**434–37
Executive Order 9835 (Loyalty Order), Mar. 21, 1947, **16:**446–51
Speech to House of Representatives on the civil rights program, Feb. 2, 1948, **16:**510–12
Executive Order 9981 (establishment of President's Committee on Equality in Armed Services), July 26, 1948, **16:**513–14
Inaugural Address, Jan. 20, 1949, **16:**561–65
Special message to Congress on the Point Four Program, June 24, 1949, **16:**595–99
White House Press Release on the Hydrogen Bomb Program, Jan. 31, 1950, **17:**1
White House Press Release on UN police action in Korea: June 27, 1950, **17:**34–35
Veto message to House of Representatives on the Internal Security Act, Sept. 22, 1950, **17:**35–42
Message to Douglas MacArthur, Jan. 13, 1951, **17:**73–75
Message to nation on Korea and the Policy of Containment, Apr. 11, 1951, **17:**75–79
Veto message to House of Representatives on the McCarran-Walter Immigration Act, June 25, 1952, **17:**131–36
Letter to Mr. Verde, chairman of House Committee on Un-American Activities, Nov. 13, 1953, **17:**248–49
Trumbull, John (1750–1831)
An Elegy on the Times (poem), **2:**296–303
Trumbull, John (1756–1843)
Letter to Thomas Jefferson, June 11, 1789,

3:339–41
Trumbull, Lyman
Speech in Senate on Johnson's veto of the Civil Rights Bill, Apr. 4, 1856, **10:**18–21
Tsuchida, Jutaro
Unattributed remarks on the Bicentennial: Shukan Asahi (Tokyo), Jan. 16, 1976, **20:**365
Tuchman, Phyllis
Interviews with George Segal and James Rosenquist on Pop art: Art News, May 1974, **20:**103
Tucker, Benjamin R.
Relation of the State to the Individual, Oct. 14, 1890, **11:**325–29
Testimony before Chicago Conference on Trusts, Sept. 1899, **12:**282–87
Tully (pseud.) *see* Hamilton, Alexander
Tunis, John Roberts
The Great God Football: Harper's Monthly, Nov. 1928, **14:**585–89
Laugh Off $11 Million?: New Republic, Jan. 2, 1965, **18:**252–54
Turco, Richard B. *et al.*
The Climatic Effects of Nuclear War: Scientific American, Aug. 1984, **21:**478
Turner, Frederick Jackson
The Significance of the Frontier in American History, July 12, 1893, **11:**462–78
The Significance of the Section in American History, 1925, **14:**493–500
Turner, George K.
The Puzzle of the Underworld: McClure's, July 1913, **13:**420–29
Turner, Jonathan Baldwin
A Plan for an Industrial University for the State of Illinois, Nov. 18, 1851, **8:**157–66
Turner, Nat
Confession (given to Thomas R. Gray), Nov. 1, 1831, **5:**472–81
Tutu, Desmond M.
Sanctions v. *Apartheid:* The New York Times, June 16, 1986, **21:**634
Twain, Mark (pseud.) *see* Clemens, Samuel Langhorne
Tyler, John
Message to House of Representatives on the Dorr Rebellion, Apr. 9, 1844, **7:**188–91
Tyler, Royall
The Contrast: Prologue, 1790, **3:**405–6
Tyler, William S.
Prayer for Colleges, 1855, **8:**340–46
Tyrrell, R. Emmett
Kiss Me, She Cried: The New York Times, Mar. 5, 1976, **20:**342
Ujiie, Hisashi

Unattributed remarks on the Bicentennial: Shukan Asahi (Tokyo), Jan. 16, 1976, **20:**365

Unonius, Gustaf
A Pioneer in Northwest America 1841–1858, The Memoirs of Gustaf Unonius (Jonas O. Backlund, trans.; Nils W. Olsson, ed.), 1950, **7:**8–16

Unz, Ron
Double Talk? The Debate over Bilingual Education: The NewsHour with Jim Lehrer, Sept. 21, 1997, **22:**343

Urmstone, John
Letter to the secretary of the Society for Propagating the Gospel, July 7, 1711, **1:**329

Vail, Charles H.
The Socialist Movement, 1902, **12:**493–98

Vale, Gilbert
Political Economy: The Diamond, Supplement to the 2nd Series, Apr., Aug. 1841, **7:**17–26

Vallandigham, Clement Laird
Peace—Liberty—The Constitution, Mar. 7, 1863, **9:**409–15

Van Buren, Martin
Speech in New York State constitutional convention, Sept. 1821, **5:**6–9
Message to special session of Congress on government aid for business losses, Sept. 4, 1837, **6:**314–16
Executive Order for a Ten-Hour Day, Mar. 31, 1840, **6:**523

Vance, Cyrus R.
Testimony on SALT II: Congressional Digest, Aug.–Sept. 1979, **21:**154

Vance, Cyrus R. et al.
Arguments for a one-term presidency: The New York Times, Dec. 31, 1985, **21:**610

Vandenberg, Arthur Hendrick
Speech in Senate on the Charter of the United Nations, July 23, 1945, **16:**331–33
Vandenberg Resolution, May 19, 1948, **16:**518–19

Vanderslice, Thomas A.
Address to the Executives' Club of Chicago, Nov. 1976, **20:**336

Van Doren, Mark
No Word, No Wind (poem), **17:**106–7
Dialogue on the American Dream, 1962, **18:**122–29

Van Rensselaer, Mariana Griswold
Church Architecture in America: Century Magazine, Jan. 1885, **11:**36–39

Vanzetti, Bartolomeo
Last statement before the (Massachusetts Superior Criminal) court in *Common-*

wealth v. *Sacco and Vanzetti,* Apr. 9, 1927, **14:**527–29

Vargas, Arturo
Speech on the impact of Latino voters, Sept. 1999, **22:**403

Vassa, Gustavus
The Life of Olaudah Equiano or Gustavus Vassa, The African, 1837, **3:**571–80

Vaughn, John
The Thirtieth Anniversary of a Great Invention: Scribner's, Sept. 1906, **13:**63–67

Vay de Vaya und zu Luskod, Count
Inner Life of the United States, 1908, **13:**123–28

Veblen, Thorstein Bunde
The Theory of Business Enterprise, 1904, **12:**568–70
The Higher Learning in America, 1918, **14:**176–79
Absentee Ownership and Business Enterprise in Recent Times, 1923, **14:**376–85

Vethake, John
The Doctrine of Anti-Monopoly: New York Evening Post, Oct. 21, 1835, **6:**185–89

Vietnam Veterans Against the War
The Winter Soldier Investigation: An Inquiry into American War Crimes, Jan. 31–Feb. 2, 1971, **19:**201

Villard, Oswald Garrison
Preparedness Is Militarism: Annals of the American Academy of Political and Social Science, July 1916, **14:**48–53

Vincent, John Heyl
The Chautauqua Movement, 1886, **11:**96–102

Vrooman, Carl
The Agricultural Revolution: Century Illustrated Monthly Magazine, Nov. 1916, **14:**1–4

Wade, Benjamin Franklin
Speech in Senate on war or compromise, Dec. 17, 1860, **9:**220–21

Wagar, W. Warren
The Year [1984] *That Never Came:* The Futurist, Dec. 1983, **21:**476

Wagner, Ralph B.
Don't Neglect Your Relations!, Nov. 20, 1945, **16:**285–88

Waite, Morrison Remick
Opinion of the Court in *Munn* v. *Illinois,* 1877, **10:**377–79

Wald, George
Speech delivered at Kresge Auditorium of the Massachusetts Institute of Technology, Mar. 4, 1969, **19:**12

Walker, Alexander
Letter to Jefferson Davis, Sept. 13, 1862,

9:365–70

Walker, Amasa
The Science of Wealth: A Manual of Political Economy, 1866, **10:**66–73

Walker, Francis Amasa
Report of the Commissioner of Indian Affairs, Nov. 1, 1872, **10:**292–98

Walker, Robert John
Report to Congress on tariffs and revenue laws, Dec. 3, 1845, **7:**303–12
Inaugural Address (as governor of Kansas), May 27, 1857, **8:**453–59

Walker, Timothy
Defense of Mechanical Philosophy: North American Review, July 1831, **5:**447–52
Constitutional Power of the State Legislatures to take Private Property for Public Uses: Western Law Journal, May 1844, **7:**210–13

Wallace, Henry A(gard)
Radio address on a declaration of interdependence, May 13, 1933, **15:**220–24
New Frontiers, 1934, **15:**275–79
Radio address on pigs and pig iron, Nov. 12, 1935, **15:**336–39
Report of the Secretary of Agriculture, 1938, **15:**516–23
Testimony before Senate Committee of Commerce on Franklin D. Roosevelt's "Economic Bill of Rights," Jan. 25, 1945, **16:**268–75
The Fight for Peace, Oct. 1946, **16:**370–74

Wallace, William H., *et al.*
A Brief Notice of the Recent Outrages Committed by Isaac I. Stevens, Governor of Washington Territory, May 17, 1856, **8:**385–92

Walsh, George E.
Moving Picture Drama for the Multitude: Independent, Feb. 6, 1908, **13:**109–13

Walsh, Thomas James
The True History of Teapot Dome: Forum, July 1924, **14:**431–37

Walt, Stephen M.
Reagan Has Fooled Us Again: Chicago Tribune, Oct. 23, 1986, **21:**655

Ward, Lester Frank
Mind as a Social Factor: Mind, Oct. 1884, **11:**30–35
The Psychic Factors of Civilization, 1893, **11:**458–62
Plutocracy and Paternalism: Forum, Nov. 1895, **12:**29–32

Ward, Nathaniel
The Simple Cobler of Aggawam in America (by Theodore de la Guard), 1647, **1:**185–89

Warner, Margaret
Double Talk? The Debate over Bilingual Education: The NewsHour with Jim Lehrer,

Sept. 21, 1997, **22:**343

Warren, Earl
Opinion of the Court in Brown et al. v. Board of Education of Topeka et al., 1954, **17:**253–58
Speech at annual meeting of the American Law Institute on Federal Court congestion, May 21, 1958, **17:**487–91
Dissent in Perez v. Brownell, 1967, **17:**499–500
Opinion of the Court in Miranda v. Arizona, 1966, **18:**427–31

Warren, Joseph
Oration Delivered at Boston (on a British Army), Mar. 5, 1772, **2:**211–16
Address of Provincial Congress of Massachusetts, to the Inhabitants of Great Britain (on the Battles of Lexington and Concord), Apr. 26, 1775, **2:**325–26

Washington, Booker T(aliaferro)
Speech at Cotton States and International Exposition, Atlanta, Ga., Sept. 18, 1895, **12:**9–11

Washington, George
Letter to Mary Ball Washington, July 18, 1755, **2:**1–2
Reorganization of the Army, Jan. 28, 1778, **2:**495–500
Letter to Gouverneur Morris, July 24, 1778, **2:**501
Letter to Henry Laurens, Nov. 14, 1778, **2:**506–8
Letter to Benjamin Harrison, Dec. 30, 1778, **2:**510–11
Address to the officers of the Army on John Armstrong's "Newburgh Address," Mar. 15, 1783, **2:**598–601
Circular letter to the state governors, June 8, 1783, **2:**601–7
Letter to Congress, June 17, 1783, **2:**608–9
Letter to John Jay, Aug. 1, 1786, **3:**64–65
First Inaugural Address, Apr. 30, 1789, **3:**344–46
Letter to Hebrew Congregation, Newport, R.I., Aug. 1790, **3:**434
A Proclamation (on neutrality), Apr. 22, 1793, **3:**520
Proclamation Warning the Insurgents in the Western Parts of Pennsylvania to Desist from Their Opposition to the Laws, Aug. 7, 1794, **3:**558–60
Message to Congress on a national university, Dec. 7, 1796, **3:**604–5
Farewell Address: American Daily Advertiser, Sept. 19, 1796, **3:**606–15
Letter to James McHenry, Sept. 30, 1798,

4:71–72

Last will and testament, July 9, 1799, **4**:115–19

Waterhouse, Benjamin

Letter to John Adams, July 8, 1811, **4**:288–90

Watson, James L.

Globalization and Culture: Britannica.com, 2001, **22**:488

Watt, James G.

Interview: Nation's Business, Sept. 1981, **21**:310

Wattenberg, Ben J.

This U.S.A., 1965, **18**:280–85

Is It the End of an Era?: Public Opinion, Oct.–Nov. 1980, **21**:259

Watterson, Henry

In Hoc Signo (editorial): Louisville Courier-Journal, Apr. 20, 1898, **12**:193–94

Wayland, Francis

Thoughts on the Present Collegiate System in the United States, 1842, **7**:47–51

Report to the Corporation of Brown University, on Changes in the System of Collegiate Education, Mar. 28, 1850, **8**:64–70

Weaver, James Baird

Letter of acceptance (as presidential nomination for the National Greenback Labor Party), July 3, 1880, **10**:455–58

A Call to Action, 1892, **11**:369–74

Weavers, The (singing group)

Kisses Sweeter Than Wine, **17**:100–1

Webster, Daniel

Speech in House of Representatives on the Conscription Bill, Dec. 9, 1814, **4**:355–58

Brief in U.S. Supreme Court in *Dartmouth College v. Woodward,* 1818, **4**:477–82

Speech in Massachusetts constitutional convention on property and political power, Dec. 15, 1820, **4**:634–39

Resolution to House of Representatives on the Greek Revolution, Dec. 8, 1823, **5**:108–11

Speech in Senate on Samuel Foote's resolution, Jan. 26–27, 1830, **5**:347–55

Speech in Senate on Jackson's veto message on the Second Bank Renewal Bill, July 11, 1832, **5**:535–41

Speech to the Society for the Diffusion of Useful Knowledge, Boston, Nov. 11, 1836, **6**:266–73

Speech in Senate on James Wall's amendment to the Bankruptcy Bill, May 18, 1840, **6**:561–65

Instructions to Caleb Cushing on securing trade with China, May 8, 1843, **7**:157–58

Speech to Boston Whigs on reform of the naturalization laws, Nov. 1844, **7**:168–69

Extemporaneous speech at the opening of the Northern Railroad from Franklin to Grafton, N.H., Aug. 28, 1847, **7**:388–90

Speech in Senate on Clay's Compromise of 1850 (Seventh of March Speech), 1850, **8**:24–27

Letter to J. G. Hülsemann, Dec. 21, 1850, **8**:110–13

Webster, Noah

Sketches of American Policy, 1785, **3**:24–35

The Devil is in You, 1786, **3**:65–68

An Essay on the Necessity, Advantages and Practicability of Reforming the Mode of Spelling, 1789, **3**:375–79

On the Education of Youth in America, 1790, **3**:424–32

Weicker, Lowell P., Jr.

Religion in Politics, 1984, **21**:531

Weisenburger, Walter B.

Should Industry-Wide Bargaining Be Abolished?: The Sign, Feb. 1947, **16**:410–14

Weisinger, Mort

$10 Billion a Year Employment Thievery in Big Business: Parade, Dec. 9, 1973, **19**:395

Welch, Claude E.

Medical Malpractice: New England Journal of Medicine, June 26, 1975, **20**:135

Weld, Theodore Dwight

American Slavery As It is: Testimony of a Thousand Witnesses, 1839, **6**:464–68

Welles II, Edward R.

Open letter on the ordination of women: Christianity and Crisis, Sept. 16, 1974, **20**:93

Welles, Gideon

Diary (on assassination of Abraham Lincoln), Apr. 15–May 12, 1865, **9**:576–82

Wells, David Ames

The Communism of a Discriminating Income-Tax: North American Review, Mar. 1880, **10**:459–65

Recent Economic Changes, 1889, **11**:227–33

Wellstone, Paul

High-Stakes Tests Pose High-Stakes Risks for Vulnerable Kids: Roll Call, Feb. 28, 2001, **22**:480

Welsh, Herbert

A Definite Step Toward Municipal Reform: Forum, Apr. 1894, **11**:498–502

West, Benjamin

Letter to John Singleton Copley, Aug. 4, 1766, **2**:175–76

Westchester Farmer, A (pseud.) *see* Seabury, Samuel

Westendorf, Thomas P.

I'll Take You Home Again, Kathleen (song), **10**:345–46

Westing, Arthur H.
The Cratering of Indochina: Scientific American, May 1972, **19:**286

Wetmore, Claude H.
Tweed Days in St. Louis: McClure's, Oct. 1902, **12:**483–87

Weyl, Walter E.
The New Democracy, 1912, **13:**345–46

Wheeler, A. S.
Speech to Commercial Club of Boston on the labor question, Oct. 16, 1886, **11:**113–17

Wheeler, Burton K.
Speech in Congress on the Lend-Lease Act, Jan. 12, 1941, **16:**46–47

Wheeler, Henry C.
Letter to farmers of the Northwest, Mar. 1869, **10:**162–63

Wheeler, Malcolm E.
The Pinto Case: The Forum, Fall 1981, **21:**235

Whelan, Elizabeth M.
Speech to the New York Academy of the Sciences on public health risks, Sept. 1987, **22:**15

White, Byron R.
Dissent in Miranda v. Arizona, 1966, **18:**431–34
Crime in the Bedroom (Bowers v. Hardwick), 86 U.S. 140, **21:**638

White, David M.
How to Read "Li'l Abner" Intelligently, in *Mass Culture* (Bernard Rosenberg and David M. White, eds.), 1957, **17:**422–27

White, E(lwyn) B(rooks)
I Paint What I See (poem), **15:**240–41
One Man's Meat (column on the Townsend Plan): Harper's, Oct. 1939, **15:**560–64
The Talk of the Town (column on Christmas 1944): The New Yorker, Dec. 23, 1944, **16:**261–62
The Second Tree from the Corner, 1953, **16:**529–30
Here Is New York, 1949, **16:**617–20

White, Edward Douglass
Opinion of the Court in *Standard Oil Company of New Jersey et al. v. U.S.,* 1911, **13:**310–16

White, George S.
Memoir of Samuel Slater . . . with Remarks on the Moral Influence of Manufactories in the United States, 1835, **6:**123–27

White, Hervey
Our Rural Slums: Independent, Oct. 8, 1908, **13:**150–53

White, Samuel
Speech in Senate on the Louisiana Purchase, Nov. 2, 1803, **4:**175–76

White, Theodore H.
Direct Elections: An Invitation to National Chaos: Life, Jan. 20, 1970, **19:**102
The American Idea: The New York Times Magazine, July 6, 1986, **21:**645

White, William Allen
What's the Matter with Kansas? (editorial): Emporia Weekly Gazette, Oct. 1, 1896, **12:**112–14
The Old Order Changeth, 1910, **13:**247–50
Letter to Herbert Bayard Swope, Sept. 17, 1921, **14:**284–85
The Challenge to the Middle Class: Atlantic Monthly, Aug. 1937, **15:**486–92

Whiteside, Thomas
Profiles (Ralph Nader—II): New Yorker, Oct. 15, 1973, **19:**387

Whitman, Walt
Duties of Government (editorial): Brooklyn Eagle, Apr. 4, 1846, **7:**341–42
Leaves of Grass (Appendix: *Letter to Ralph Waldo Emerson*), 1856, **8:**400–6
Wicked Architecture: Life Illustrated, July 19, 1856, **8:**407–10
I Hear America Singing (poem), **9:**170
Come Up From the Fields Father (poem), **9:**559–60
When Lilacs Last in the Dooryard Bloomed (poem), **10:**44–50
One's-Self I Sing (poem), **10:**114
Specimen Days and Collect, 1898, **10:**420–22
Letter to W. S. Kennedy, Feb. 25, 1887, **11:**147–48

Whitney, Asa
Memorial to Congress on a railroad to the Pacific, Jan. 28, 1845, **7:**272–75

Whitney, Caspar W.
Evolution of the Country Club: Harper's New Monthly, Dec. 1894, **11:**555–62

Whitney, Edward B.
Political Dangers of the Income-Tax Decision: Forum, Aug. 1895, **12:**71–74

Whitney, Eli
Letter to Eli Whitney, Sr., Sept. 11, 1793, **3:**551–52

Whitney, Frank L.
The Impact of the Total Redevelopment of Cities, Mar. 21, 1966, **18:**338–42

Whittier, John Greenleaf
Justice and Expediency, May 1833, **6:**1–5
The Farewell (poem), **6:**413–14
Massachusetts to Virginia (poem), **7:**159–61
Ichabod (poem), **8:**28
The Kansas Emigrants (poem), **8:**260–61
Barbara Frietchie (poem), **9:**371–72
Laus Deo! (poem), **9:**638–39

Wicks, Hamilton S.
The Opening of Oklahoma: Cosmopolitan, Sept. 1889, **11**:203–6

Wickware, Francis G.
Neutrality: The American Year Book . . . 1915, 1916, **13**:573–76

Wiesner, Jerome B.
Science in the Affluent Society, Oct. 23, 1963, **18**:186–91

Wilcox, David
Testimony before House Committee on Interstate and Foreign Commerce, Jan. 21, 1905, **13**:4–7

Wilder, Amos P.
Governor [Robert M.] La Follette and What He Stands For: Outlook, Mar. 8, 1902, **12**:444–48

Wilford, John Noble
Farewell to Pioneer: The New York Times, June 14, 1983, **21**:427

Wilkeson, Frank
Recollections of a Private Soldier in the Army of the Potomac, 1887, **9**:498–501

Will, George F.
Compassion on Campus: Newsweek, May 31, 1993, **22**:186

Willard, Emma Hart
A Plan for Improving Female Education, 1819, **4**:574–78
Rocked in the Cradle of the Deep (poem), **5**:440

Williams, John D.
The Nonsense About Safe Driving: Fortune, Sept. 1958, **17**:511–15

Williams, John R.
Letter to William Thomas, Nov. 10, 1895, **12**:12–15

Williams, Roger
The Hireling Ministry None of Christs, 1652, **1**:213–16

Williams, William Carlos
The Crowd at the Ball Game (poem), **14**:375

Willkie, Wendell Lewis
Acceptance speech at Elwood, Ind., Aug. 17, 1940, **16**:27–31
One World, 1943, **16**:198–205

Wilson, Irvin A.
Testimony before Senate Subcommittee of the Committee on Manufactures, regarding Chicago teachers in the Depression, May 9, 1932, **15**:194–96

Wilson, James
An Address to the Inhabitants of the Colonies of New Hampshire, Feb. 13, 1776, **2**:413–21
Speech in Pennsylvania Ratifying Convention, 1787, **3**:157–63

Inaugural address (as professor of the College of Philadelphia law school), Dec. 15, 1789, **3**:380–88

Wilson, Orlando W.
Police Arrest Privileges in a Free Society: A Plea for Modernization, 1960, **18**:36–42

Wilson, Rufus R.
The Growth of an American School of Sculpture: Illustrated American, Aug. 21, 1897, **12**:135–37

Wilson, Warren H.
Country Versus City, Dec. 1916, **14**:4–9

Wilson, Woodrow
Congressional Government: A Study of American Politics: Introduction, 1885, **11**:86–89
Speech at Seattle, on commission city government, May 20, 1911, **13**:269–72
Campaign speech at Lincoln, Nebr., Oct. 5, 1912, **13**:356–60
First Inaugural Address, Mar. 4, 1913, **13**:412–15
Statement to American bankers in the Four Power Consortium on Taft's "Dollar Diplomacy," Mar. 1913, **13**:415–16
Statement to Press on the tariff lobby, Mar. 26, 1913, **13**:417
Speech to Congress on the Tampico affair, Apr. 20, 1914, **13**:468–70
Speech to Senate on neutrality, Aug. 19, 1914, **13**:491–92
Speech to Senate on a league for peace, Jan. 22, 1917, **14**:65–69
War message to Congress, Apr. 2, 1917, **14**:77–82
Appeal to the Voters to Return a Democratic Congress, Oct. 25, 1918, **14**:166–67
Speech to Senate on the Covenant of the League of Nations, Feb. 14, 1919, **14**:180–83
Speech at Omaha, on the League of Nations, Sept. 8, 1919, **14**:187–93

Winslow, Clinton I.
Local Government and the Courts: Baltimore Sun, Jan. 10, 1968, **18**:596–98

Winter, David G.
Advantages of a Liberal Arts Education: Psychology Today, Sept. 1978, **21**:119

Winter, Thomas
The case for competition in the postal system: Los Angeles Times, Aug. 3, 1975, **20**:193

Winthrop, John
A Modell of Christian Charity, 1630, **1**:109–15
Journal (on life among the puritans), 1633–1639, **1**:132–38
A Declaration of the Intent and Equity of the Order Made at the Last Court, to This Effect, That None Should Be Received to In-

habit Within This Jurisdiction but Such as Should Be Allowed by Some of the Magistrates, May 1637, **1:**154–56

A Reply to the Answer: Made to the Discourse About the Negative Vote, 1642, **1:**168–69

Winthrop, Robert Charles
Speech in House of Representatives on the Oregon question, Jan. 3, 1846, **7:**317–23

Wise, John
A Vindication of the Government of New-England Churches, 1717, **1:**330–34

Wolfenstein, Martha
Movies: A Psychological Study, 1950, **17:**25–27

Wolff, George
Symposium on "Coping with Terrorism": Atlas World Press Review, Sept. 1976, **20:**325

Wood, Fernando
Message to New York City Common Council on a proposal for secession of New York City, Jan. 6, 1861, **9:**233–35

Wood, Leonard
The Military Obligation of Citizenship, 1915, **13:**566–69

Wood, Thomas J.
Testimony before House of Representatives Committee on Mississippi law enforcement, Jan. 28, 1867, **10:**86–89

Woodmason, Charles
Petition to South Carolina legislature on local governmental agencies, Nov. 7, 1767, **2:**185–95

Woodward, Calvin Milton
Manual Training in Education, 1890, **11:**302–7

Woodward, George W.
Speech in House of Representatives on resolution, regarding Haiti and Santo Domingo, Jan. 13, 1869, **10:**154–55

Woolman, John
Journal (on slavery, taxation, and the military), 1756–1758, **2:**7–18
A Plea for the Poor, 1763, **2:**78–83

Woolsey, John M.
Opinion (U.S. District Court, New York) in *U.S. v. One Book Called* Ulysses, Dec. 6, 1933, **15:**236–39

Worcester, Noah
A Solemn Review of the Custom of War; Showing that War Is the Effect of Popular Delusion, and Proposing a Remedy, 1815, **4:**375–82

Work, Henry Clay
Kingdom Coming (song), **9:**400–1
Come Home, Father (song), **9:**497
Marching Through Georgia (song), **9:**554

Work, John M.
The Gold Brick Twins, 1916, **14:**45–48

Workman, William D., Jr.
The Case of the South, 1960, **17:**567–75

Wortman, Tunis
A Treatise, Concerning Political Enquiry, and the Liberty of the Press, 1800, **4:**131–37

Wright, Carroll Davidson
The Factory System as an Element in Civilization, Sept. 8, 1882, **10:**547–55

Wright, Frances
On Existing Evils, and Their Remedy, June 2, 1829, **5:**290–97

Wright, Frank Lloyd
The Art and Craft of the Machine, 1901, **12:**409–16
When Democracy Builds, 1945, **16:**301–4

Wright, Richard R., Jr.
The Negro in Times of Industrial Unrest: Charities, Oct. 7, 1905, **13:**30–34

Wright, Robert
Speech at organizational meeting of the American Colonization Society, Dec. 21, 1816, **4:**456

Wynkoop, E. W.
Testimony sent to Senate Committee on the Sand Creek, Colo., incident, Jan. 16, 1865, **9:**550–53

Yankee, A (pseud.) *see* Ingraham, Joseph Holt

Yates, Robert
Letter . . . to the Governor of New York; Containing Their Reasons for not Subscribing to the Federal Constitution, 1787, **3:**189–91

Yates, Sidney R.
Congressional debate on the Arts, Humanities, and Museums Amendments, Oct. 11, 1990, **22:**108

Young, Andrew
Interview on U.S. political prisoners: The New York Times, July 14, 1978, **21:**105

Young, Brigham
Interviewed by Horace Greeley on the Mormon Church, July 13, 1859, **9:**132–35
Discourses (on settlement in the West), *c.* 1877, **10:**383–85

Young, John
Opinion (New York State Court for the Correction of Errors) in *Coster v. Lorillard,* 1835, **6:**181–84

Youngdahl, Luther
Opinion of the Court in *U.S. v. Lattimore,* 1955, **17:**300–4

Zernike, Kate
Fear of Flying: The New York Times, Sept. 29, 2001, **22:**501